THE METHODIST EXPERIENCE IN AMERICA

A History
Volume I

Russell E. Richey,
Kenneth E. Rowe,
and
Jean Miller Schmidt

ABINGDON PRESS
NASHVILLE

THE METHODIST EXPERIENCE IN AMERICA
VOLUME 1
A HISTORY

Library of Congress Cataloging-in-Publication Data

Richey, Russell E.
  Methodist experience in America / Russell E. Richey, Kenneth E. Rowe, and Jean Miller Schmidt.
    p. cm.
ISBN 978-0-687-24672-4 (miscellaneous/miscellaneous—printed 6x9 : alk. paper)   1. United Methodist Church (U.S.)—History.   2. Methodist Church—United States—History.   3. United States—Church history.   I. Rowe, Kenneth E.   II. Schmidt, Jean Miller.   III.Title.
  BX8235.R534   2010
  287.0973—dc22

                                                                                                      2010023441

"Journal of Thomas Rankin, 1773–1778" is from the United Methodist Archives and History Center, Drew University, Madison, New Jersey.

Excerpts from the James Meacham Journals, 1788–1797, located in the Rare Book, Manuscript, and Special Collection Library, Duke University.

"Target: Denver," text by Paige Carlin, pictures by George P. Miller, *Together* (March 1969): 18-24. Used by permission of The United Methodist Publishing House.

"Letters of Francis Asbury to Freeborn Garrettson, Sept. 2, 1785, Sept. 1786," are from Wesleyan University Library, Special Collections & Archives.

10 11 12 13 14 15 16 17 18 19—10 9 8 7 6 5 4 3 2 1
MANUFACTURED IN THE UNITED STATES OF AMERICA

With gratitude to
Merle
James
Steve

CONTENTS

Snapshot II. Methodism in 1884: Wilkes-Barre, Pennsylvania

Chapter XI. Reshaping the Church for Mission: 1884–1939

PREFACE

This volume is a companion to our *Methodist Experience in America: A Sourcebook*, already published (as MEA II). We crafted MEA I and II together, selecting our documents first, endeavoring to encompass as much of the American Methodist experience as possible, and now writing this narrative over against the documents. The overall structure of this volume, MEA I, follows the sixfold periodization and organization of documents in MEA II. At three of the important transition years, 1816, 1884, and 1968, we take "snapshots" of Methodism in community. The locale for 1816 is Baltimore; for 1884 is Wilkes-Barre, Pennsylvania; and for 1968 is Denver. In the snapshots we provide the rationale for these three exhibitions of local Methodism.

A Quick Overview

Our three snapshots at 1816, 1884, and 1968 capture important transitional points in the Methodist movement. They also invite glimpses into three distinct Methodist phases that this volume depicts: a Pietist, a nurturing, and an advocating. Methodism features/featured all three—piety, nurture, and advocacy—in every period but, we think, has tended to accent one.

We depict early Methodism in both its United Brethren and its Wesleyan expressions as mediating distinctive practices of the international Pietist movement. Featuring itinerant evangelizing, revivalistic preaching, dramatic conversions, and lively testimony, early Methodism vocalized its religious seriousness, its piety. To be sure, it made provision for nurture in classes, and it showed unusual courage in antislavery advocacy, but grounded both in its convictions about the universality of grace and the imperative to save all from the wrath to come. Iconic for this phase of Methodism were emotional love feasts, revivalistic quarterly conferences, and promoted camp meetings.

A century later, Methodism was consumed by various nurturing tasks. In age-graded Sunday schools, through its widely read *Advocates*, Berean lessons, magazines, and books, in its numerous colleges, on the mission field, and in Freedmen's Aid, post–Civil War Methodism (particularly northern Methodism) cared for the enculturation of Christians, the cultivation of family religion, and the suffusing of society with Christian values. In the interest of home and family protection, Methodism advocated temperance, Sabbath observance, and increasingly a host of other social reforms. It presumed that society could be Christianized and that culture could accommodate Methodist piety and practice. Iconic for this phase of Methodism were the international lesson, the Akron Plan Sunday school facility, station churches, and religious life centered on the Sabbath.

By its third century, Methodism put a premium on advocacy. Its icons were the caucus, convention-center annual conferences, and eventually digital and Web exhibition of commitment, cause, and concern. The church gathered but also fragmented by ethnic identity, sexual orientation, and ideological concern. Conceiving of itself as global, United Methodism launched short-term missions in every direction. Northerners went south, southerners went north; U.S. groups went to Latin America, local churches worked near and far on Habitat houses. Piety and nurture could be had in retreats, modules, or packages, DISCIPLE Bible studies, and Walks to Emmaus.

Methodism defined its mission in these three epochs in interesting fashion. In its first *Discipline*, The Methodist Episcopal Church (MEC) Americanized the answer to Wesley's query, "What may we reasonably believe to be God's Design in raising up the Preachers called Methodists?" to read: "To reform the Continent, and to spread scriptural Holiness over these Lands" (Sources 1785a). Looking back from the vantage of the 1866 Centenary, distinguished editor and historian Abel Stevens nicely captured the import of the 1785 ambitions to evangelize and reform the entire continent. He said,

> Though American Methodism was many years without a distinct missionary organization, it was owing to the fact that its whole organization was essentially a missionary scheme. It was, in fine, the great Home Mission enterprise of the north American continent, and its domestic work demanded all its resources of men and money.[1]

By the 1880s, Methodism in its various denominational expressions reshaped mission into connectionally ordered, well-led, and amply financed foreign and home missionary societies. And Methodist women mounted, staffed, and resourced their own. If mission had been initially what Methodism *was*, by the late nineteenth century, mission was what Methodism *did*, and did robustly and organizationally. By the end of the twentieth century, many United Methodists collapsed mission to the first statement made in the *Discipline* under Part V, Organization and Administration, "The mission of the Church is to make disciples of Jesus Christ. Local churches provide the most significant arena through which disciple-making occurs."[2] Mission, initially Methodism's very being, became its order and eventually a point of *advocacy*.

Piety, nurture, and advocacy belong together, and the three Methodist moments put the emphasis differently. Early Methodism, a preaching movement, preached its nurture and preached its commitments. Late–nineteenth-century Methodism, a teaching church, taught its piety and its social concerns. Late–twentieth-century Methodism, increasingly a worshiping or sacramental church, ritualized and packaged spirituality and formation. The challenge for the church, in any period, we suppose, is to hold the three together effectively. Piety, nurture, and advocacy; word, order, and sacrament; the prophetic, royal, and priestly offices—they do belong together.

Their belonging together and mutually reinforcing one another are treated in the numbered chapters. We begin with the several independent, relatively spontaneous implantings of Pietist practices. We trace the reinforcing of and unfolding of this missionary enterprise, note how the American Revolution permitted its rapid indigenization, and then follow American Methodism's efforts to be a church in and for the new nation.

Dynamics in Methodist Evolution

The peculiarities of Methodism's entry into and spread across American society have produced tensions and paradoxes that it has held together and/or lived between. The following narrative exhibits those tensions at various points, and we assume that one or more may well structure the courses or lectures of faculty using our volumes.[3] The tensions, some characterizing the movement as a whole, others marking life on an individual or grassroots level, include

- a vital piety confident of God's providential and governing care and of grace-enabled free will and moral agency (Arminianism),
- law, discipline, human responsibility, and self-control and also self-direction and liberty, through prevenient and free grace in conversion and in living the Christian life,
- the letter (rules, works, fruits) and the Spirit (testimony),
- authority vested in bishop, presiding elder, and preacher-in-charge and lay empowerment and lay offices (formal and informal),
- centralized decision making in conference and license to improvise, experiment, and appoint on the circuit, in missions, and on frontiers,
- an ordered, even communal Christian life (class) and openness to emotional expression and innovations in praxis (love feast),
- community (conference) and individual expression (free will),
- love of God and love of neighbor, individual and social holiness,
- expectations of holiness and perfection that pressed toward spiritual elitism and preaching of a universal atonement that embraced the human family,
- white male domination of office and decision making and a gospel of universalism that transcended lines drawn by race, language, gender, culture, and ethnicity,
- the war against sin within and against the world and Calvinism without,
- rules and practices against worldliness and a transformative impulse,
- a commitment to conform (to "Large Minutes," Wesleyanism, the *Discipline*) and an independent, Americanizing streak, a license to poach and borrow,

- an evangelical catholic spirit and a highly competitive denominational Methodist triumphalism.

The Narrative Line

In charting the explosive growth and multiple divisions that Methodism experienced in living out these tensions, this volume follows central developments in the Methodist Episcopal, Methodist, and United Methodist experience. We attend as appropriate to the UBC, EA and EC, MPC, and MECS; to movements now distinct denominations— AMEC, AMEZC, CMEC, and the several holiness churches—and to missions and other aspects of the larger Wesleyan story. We have endeavored to incorporate women's and minority, especially African American, experience as much as possible into the narrative rather than separate such into subplots. This has proved tricky, especially when we reach the complexities of the twentieth century, and we need to concede here that we do not have a single conceptual maneuver in terms of which to achieve integration and inclusion. We have endeavored, nevertheless, to tell a Methodist story, recognizing its complexities, conflicts, richness, and texture.

Readers in the several Methodist and Wesleyan denominations and in United Methodism *outside the U.S.* should be alerted that the MEA set focuses on the U.S.— "America" in popular parlance. We made the decision to delimit our attention and selections in this manner with a view to primary users and the assumption that Methodists in other contexts need materials in their own linguistic-cultural tongue. We believe that U.S. United Methodists need as full a view of their story as possible, including attention to predecessor denominations, the experience of women, the church at the local level, Methodism's ethnic and racial diversity, our theological and ideological conflicts, and the sagas of unity. We allude, therefore, to missions and the increasing global reach of United Methodism but stay with the American story. We also share the conviction argued persuasively in *An Introduction to World Methodism* by Kenneth Cracknell and Susan J. White that, despite Wesleyanism's global fragmentation, Methodism divides into two broad streams and the Methodist experience in British and American contexts establishes "two quite distinct traditions."[4] In MEA we treat the spring of that latter stream.

Using This Narrative with the *Sourcebook*

We have developed the two-volume MEA set—and it is a set—as texts for the United Methodist history course, the course required for U.S. United Methodist candidates for ministry. We reference selections from MEA II, the *Sourcebook,* throughout this narrative as (Sources) with a date or date with letter. The date or date-with-letter guides the reader to the appropriate selection. In the allusions here to MEA II, this volume provides some comment, contextualizing, interpretation, and explanation for individual documents as is appropriate to the flow of the narration.

The periodization approximates that which we selected for the *Sourcebook*. In addition we indicate in the table of contents and in each chapter title the period covered. Honoring the indicated periodization means that we return again and again to certain topics, for instance, organizational developments, pressures for democratization, women's roles, and race relations. However, certain themes or topics that extend through the time frames covered by several chapters seemed to us to be better treated in a single discussion rather than chopped up into several chapters. We call attention therefore to the subheadings that, in several instances, target a discussion that extends beyond the time frame of the chapter. Note, for instance, the discussion of education (Sunday schools and colleges) in chapter 6, of missions in 7, of orphanages and homes in 9, of hospitals and deaconesses in 11, of worship, ecumenism, autonomous churches, and the Judicial Council in 13, and of divorce in 14. In these sections, we provide background to an important development and/or trace it beyond the indicated temporal boundaries of the chapter.

This narrative and MEA II, the *Sourcebook*, may serve those teaching and studying evangelism, mission, polity, and theology and provide background material for our denominational kindred in African American, Holiness, and Pentecostal churches. For users beyond the UMC and beyond the UMC history courses, we call special attention in MEA II to the MEA document index, which guides readers to documents by nineteen major categories, including "African American," "Episcopacy," "Missions," "Polity," and "Women."

As another special feature of this volume, we include historical prefaces from the first *Disciplines* of the United Brethren, Methodist Episcopal, Evangelical Association, Methodist Protestant, and Methodist Episcopal, South, denominations. Each preface sets forth formally and concisely the new movement's originating impulse and self-understanding. At an early stage in our planning we hoped to include the prefaces as well from some of the churches (African American, Holiness, Pentecostal), now independent, that share early chapters of our common history. Space considerations oblige us to limit ourselves here to prefaces from United Methodist predecessor denominations. We can make those others available in digital format and may explore doing so in an MEA folder on the websites of the UMC General Commission on Archives and History (GCAH) and/or our schools. The availability on the GCAH site of a two-hundred-page online version of the Kenneth E. Rowe and now Christopher J. Anderson *United Methodist Studies: Basic Bibliographies* makes the inclusion of such here unnecessary.[5]

We should acknowledge that the MEA *Narrative* and *Sourcebook* presume the availability and use of other Methodist resources and have been shaped calculating the respective place that our volumes will occupy in the overall scheme of denominational formation. In particular, we have assumed prior treatment of the Wesleys and early British Methodism in Richard P. Heitzenrater, *Wesley and the People Called Methodists*. The MEA set has been shaped also with the presumption that readers will have in hand the standards for other United Methodist required courses—the current edition of Thomas Edward Frank, *Polity, Practice, and the Mission of The United Methodist Church*; Rex Matthews, *Timetables of History for Students of Methodism*; Theodore Runyon, *The New Creation: John Wesley's Theology Today*; and the two volumes of Thomas A. Langford, *Practical Divinity*, the second volume providing the rich theological fare that we have consequently omitted. We presume as well ready access to other standard Methodist studies items: Scott J. Jones, *United Methodist Doctrine: The Extreme Center*; Ted A. Campbell, *Methodist Doctrine: The Essentials*; Walter Klaiber and Manfred Marquardt, *Living Grace: An Outline of United Methodist Theology*; Karen B. Westerfield Tucker, *American Methodist Worship*; W. Harrison Daniel, *Historical Atlas of the Methodist Movement*; and our own *Perspectives on American Methodism*.[6]

The authors express appreciation to The United Methodist Publishing House for its patience with us in the slow production of this set and thank the UMPH, Abingdon Press, and Kingswood Books for permission to reproduce ideas, notes, phrasing, and occasionally more extended discussion from and to draw upon our previous individual or collaborative UMPH publications:

> *Grace Sufficient: A History of Women in American Methodism, 1760–1939*
> *United Methodism in America: A Compact History*
> *United Methodism at Forty: Looking Back, Looking Forward*
> *Marks of Methodism: Theology in Ecclesial Practice*
> *The Methodist Conference in America: A History*
> *Questions for the Twenty-first Century Church*
> *Episcopacy in the Methodist Tradition: Perspectives and Proposals*
> *Doctrine in Experience: A Methodist Theology of Church and Ministry*

We also appreciate the support of our several institutions, their deans, and their libraries and their librarians.

Jean Miller Schmidt, Iliff School of Theology
Kenneth E. Rowe, The Theological School, Drew University
Russell E. Richey, Candler School of Theology, Emory University

CHAPTER I

LAUNCHING THE METHODIST MOVEMENTS: 1760–68

Where does one start the story of United Methodism? With the formative experiences in the Susanna and Samuel Wesley home? Or with John and Charles Wesley in Georgia in the 1730s? Or with John's Aldersgate experience? Or with George Whitefield's American tours and the First Great Awakening? Or with competitive "spontaneous" beginnings in the 1760s through Robert Strawbridge in Maryland, through William Otterbein and Martin Boehm in the middle colonies, and through Barbara Heck, Philip Embury, and Thomas Webb in New York? Or with the roots of the several evangelical movements in Pietism?

Pietism

The story of United Methodism requires a wide perspective. Pietism, because it underlay or affected the several Methodist movements, provides such a canvas, and William Otterbein (1726–1813)[1] will first claim our attention, as he does in MEA I (Sources 1760). Pietism was a transatlantic, transconfessional, diffuse religious reform impulse that sought to sustain the authentic witness of the faith but that in so doing defined itself initially over against orthodoxy and later over against aspects of the Enlightenment. The faith so "preserved" differed. Pietist or Pietist-like assumptions, beliefs, mores, and communal structures typified the patterns of life and thought espoused by its Lutheran pioneers, Philipp Jakob Spener (1635–1705) and August Hermann Francke (1663–1727); by the Moravians; by Roman Catholic Jansenists; by the Hasidic Jews; by late Puritanism; by British evangelicalism (Anglican and Presbyterian); and by the panoply of colonial revivalism.[2] Diversely expressed, the movement named itself diversely. In the North American context it bore the identity of evangelicalism or revivalism.

Pietist and Pietist-like movements characteristically emphasized

1

- experimental religion, locating the religious impulse in the heart (will and affections);
- both consciousness and expression of the heart's commitments (conversion and testimony);
- an obedient life, strict moral codes, and corporate discipline as appropriate expressions thereof;
- the accessibility of the biblical word and rule to the awakened lay spirit;
- growth in the faith through active devotions but also through education, educational programs, and literature, all adjusted to suit age, culture, and circumstance;
- the importance of a witness communally shared through prayer, Bible reading, hymns, and preaching;
- everyday life as a sacrament to be shaped and enlivened by a vibrant faith and expressed in holy living; and
- biblical doctrine or doctrines as the light by which all this activism stays on course.

(For expressions of such experimental religion in early Methodist movements, see Sources 1760, 1773, 1775a, 1780b, 1785a, 1785b, 1785c, 1787, 1789a, 1791b, 1791c, 1798 on class meetings, and 1800b.)

Pietist emphasis on doctrine proved insufficient, careless, or imprecise to the "scholastics" who were typically in positions of authority and viewed themselves as consolidators of the sixteenth-century reformations. Those in power complained as well that Pietists did not measure up to what tradition had expected in zeal for the ritual or sacramental life. Opponents, therefore, found the movement's slights as objectionable as its emphases.

Protestant Pietism shaped experimental religion around the conversion experience, understood not simply as a forensic alteration in one's status with God but as a discernible inner change. In this transformation one became a reborn Nicodemus, a re-creation in Christ, whose character and life manifested a new identity in fruits of the Spirit. Pietism resourced those reborn and those seeking rebirth in small groups that encouraged members to make the Scripture normative for everyday life, that sheltered individuals and families from "the world," and that empowered them to counter its claims and demands. In and through such conventicles, little churches within the church, *collegia pietatis*, laity (male and female) gained voice and exercised leadership, a challenge and threat to public and religious conventions. Pietism drew such leadership into active missionary endeavor at home and abroad. It extended the gospel and invitation into Christian community to populations previously ignored or over previously insurmountable confessional barriers. And wherever it prospered, it challenged those who had settled for formal, notional, legal, or outward religiosity and repudiated the easy compromise that religion had made with status, wealth, power, display, and prerogative.

Against such worldliness, Pietists invoked the witness of the prophets and the teaching of Jesus. In such worldliness, Pietism discerned the sin or sins that separated individuals from God. In particular, Pietism offered a prophetic critique of established, more priestly, and unregenerate forms of Christianity and leaders so characterized. Though it sought reform, it eschewed polemics and sought the widest possible unity among likeminded persons. The several resources that Pietism offered—new identity, community voluntarily created, a competitive missionary spirit, courage to persist despite society's disdain, willingness to forge new alliances—proved highly functional in the new American environment.

Pietism provided a new way of life for its adherents and motivation to tackle society's ills. It spoke of corruption, of power, of authority, of legitimacy. By identifying the corrupt—the luxury of gentility or laxness of clergy—it broke social conventions of deference and passive obedience. It did not, however, weave these elements of social critique into a program for systemic reform or a theory of new world order or a vision of the godly state or even of the church as an anticipation thereof. Such a civil or societal theology, as offered by Puritans and other Calvinists, had brought chaos to Europe. Pietists, though highly communal on a local level and creatively productive of new ecclesial institutions, would work their transformations from the bottom up rather than the top down. Renewal would start with the conversion experience rather than parliamentary act, with a conventicle rather than a reform program, with missionary outreach rather than armed insurrection.

That beginning point for change has earned for Pietism labels of individualistic, moralistic, and otherworldly. And certainly by contrast to Puritanism, Pietism offered a social ethic unwedded to a theory of the state and strategies for reform. Yet some who felt Pietism's denunciation of worldliness found it radically transformative. Others experienced it as socially revolutionary. Many denounced it as tasteless. Where it prevailed, Pietism had the capacity to shape society and culture. The transmission of this culture then became a communal and preeminently a family project, permitting and requiring vital roles for women as well as men. In the eighteenth and particularly in the nineteenth century, women involved themselves on behalf of revival—within families, nurturing the piety of spouse, children, and servants; in congregations, through prayer groups and Sunday schools; and outward into community, nation, and world through mission, benevolent, and reform societies. Pietism lowered the gateway into ministry and raised the expectations of laity, thereby drawing women as well as men, blacks as well as whites into public witness, lay preaching, and eventually formal ministry.

Pietism made religion a communal endeavor. And when it wedded itself to republicanism—which offered a rather more civil and systemic theory of corruption, of power, of authority, of legitimacy—Pietism readily took up the agenda of Puritanism. It would

3

Christianize America and the world, albeit with the procedure of conversion and revival. But this wedding, achieved during the Second Great Awakening and through the emergence of popular denominations, and the ambivalences and tensions it produced lie ahead. At this point, we look at the entry of Methodist forms of Pietism into the New World.

Colonial Inroads

Pietism came into American life through many channels. One collective identification of these diverse channels was subsequently termed the *First Great Awakening,* a several-decade effervescence of heart religion, revived discipline, revivalistic preaching, and mass conversions, successively disturbing the religious status quo in the middle, New England, and southern colonies. Though such activity brought ministers from various confessions or denominations into local or regional prominence, the actors who achieved transcolony reputations were Jonathan Edwards (1703–58) and George Whitefield (1714–70).[3] The latter, by his six evangelistic tours, 1738–70, gave the seaboard colonies a good exposure to Calvinistic Pietism and Calvinistic Methodism. He popularized and legitimated patterns of extemporaneous, expressive, open-air preaching. He showed the power of itinerant evangelists to stir conversions among diverse peoples and across confessional lines. He made theatrical revivalism the prototypical American religious style. He pioneered in promotion, self-promotion, and use of the press, all for evangelistic purpose. And Whitefield gave Methodism its first American hearing (Sources 1768). Many who found their way into the Wesleyan orbit had been affected by Whitefield's preaching. Some of his converts provided key leadership to early classes and societies, notably Edward Evans and James Emerson in Philadelphia. And Whitefield issued an early call to John Wesley to send itinerants.

Whitefield's role and salience as Methodism's colonial herald contrast with those of the Wesleys, John and Charles, whose efforts in Georgia (1736–37) left little in the way of continuing Methodist influence and some considerable embarrassment. The Georgia episode evidenced more of the Wesleys' Anglo-Catholic piety than of their Pietism. Only after his return from Georgia, it should be noted, did John become involved with the Moravian-led Fetter Lane Society, undergo his Aldersgate experience, and make his visit to the Moravian headquarters at Herrnhut. The Georgia mission left its enduring and important effect in John Wesley's own development. It established for Wesley and within Methodism concern for the well-being and evangelization of Native Americans and African Americans. And it came to belong to the longer story of American Methodism through its literary placement in the Wesley saga as "the second rise of Methodism."[4] By other routes the leaven of Pietism and the Methodist versions thereof came to the colonies.

Otterbein and Boehm

William Otterbein belonged to a family of pastor-theologians steeped in the German Reformed tradition and the Pietism of their native Herborn. Confessional, churchly, apologetic, orthodox, covenantal, and christocentric, Herborn Pietists grounded the religious life in doctrine and Scripture as read through the Heidelberg Catechism. This sixteenth-century ecumenical, pastoral, personal compilation guided Herborn Pietists to a life lived in the Spirit. It mapped the spiritual life as a pathway, ladder, or series of steps toward salvation and as followed under and directed by covenant. Herborn kept its counsel understandable, attainable, and practical, and accented the Christian's ability to live a holy life.[5]

Like his five brothers and father, William studied at the Reformed university at Herborn, a nursery of Pietism, where recognition of his abilities earned him a teaching role as tutor. He passed ordination examinations, subscribed to the Reformed confessions, and was ordained (1749). He served for three years in Germany, demonstrating early his ability as a teacher, preacher, and pastor. His organizing of Bible and prayer groups earned Otterbein a formal reprimand from authorities for holding such "divisive" conventicles. He then responded to the plea for ministers made by Michael Schlatter (1716–90), leader of the Pennsylvania (Reformed) Coetus (synod or conference) and on a recruitment mission for pastors. In 1752, Otterbein aligned with Coetus and became pastor in the important Reformed community of Lancaster, Pennsylvania. There he found himself amidst the religious ferment through which churchly and Pietist groups emerged to give stability and direction to the Dutch and German settlements in the middle colonies. Otterbein served in Lancaster (1752–58) and Tulpehocken, Pennsylvania (1758–60); Frederick, Maryland (1760–65); York, Pennsylvania (1765–74); and Baltimore, Maryland (1774–1813), but consistently itinerated to preach to German communities in southeastern Pennsylvania and northern Maryland, while continuing to play leadership roles within the Coetus (which was related to the Amsterdam Classis). Otterbein exercised "episcopal-like" leadership among the Pietist Germans comparable, argues J. Steven O'Malley, to that provided by Theodorus Frelinghuysen for the Dutch—that of identifying, nurturing, ordering, and deploying like-minded preachers.[6]

In 1755 Otterbein experienced "a more perfect consciousness of salvation in Christ" (conversion experience) and redoubled his efforts to hold himself and his congregants to a covenanted and disciplined life through prayer and Bible groups. Otterbein's evangelical Pietist convictions radiate through the little gospel he preached in 1760 in Germantown before the Coetus (Sources 1760). In it, Otterbein detailed the human plight of sin and death, the good news of Christ's victory through the cross, the imperative of human response to God's gracious atoning act and of inner struggling to permit the

Spirit to destroy the Satan within, the possibility of reaching assurance of one's new standing, and the life of holiness that Christ-in-us thereby makes possible and necessary. His call for repentance and summing up of the Christian way as one of "denial, inward renewal, and holiness" made clear to hearers and readers that Otterbein taught Reformed doctrine that eschewed hyper-Calvinist notions of predestination and made a significant place for human volition and responsibility. The same effort and discipline, insisted Otterbein, should inform the corporate life of the Christian community, much needed amidst the moral confusion characteristic of new communities. He therefore made provision in the churches with which he worked for small prayer, for Bible study groups, for the *collegia pietatis*, for the catechizing and schooling of children, and for a covenant to order the entire community. An example of the latter is "The Constitution and Ordinances of The Evangelical Reformed Church of Baltimore" (Sources 1785b).[7]

During Otterbein's ministry in York and on one of his itinerations, he attended a "great meeting" near Neffsville in Lancaster County.[8] The event, perhaps in 1767, a several-day ingathering, anticipatory of the later camp meetings, had been common in the colonial German community since the early 1720s (the site was Long's Barn, a UMC Heritage Landmark).[9] The leader at this event was Martin Boehm (1725–1812), a Mennonite preacher whose evangelistic style, personal religious experience, and insistence on assurance resembled those of Otterbein. After hearing Boehm, Otterbein embraced him, announcing, "Wir sind Bruder!" Thus began an association that would eventuate in the United Brethren in Christ.

Boehm, a Swiss-German Mennonite, had been selected by lot as preacher in the late 1750s and made bishop in 1761 by his Lancaster County congregation. A farmer, Boehm received his training, not in the university like Otterbein, but through the traditioning of the Mennonite community. Believer's baptism, opposition to oaths and violence, a life lived out of the New Testament, and personal assurance through the Spirit defined Boehm. Like Otterbein, he itinerated, responding to pleas from Mennonite communities in Pennsylvania and Virginia. His evangelistic efforts yielded "revival" among the Mennonites but also controversy. Sometime in the late 1770s a Mennonite conference excommunicated him. Among its findings were "sins" of association and of insufficient stress on the sacraments. Boehm had wandered into patterns of expansive revivalism unsettling to more traditional Mennonites. Boehm's example and influence drew colleagues as well as adherents, and the movement gravitated into increasing contact with those of Otterbein and of early Methodism.

The further association of the communities around Otterbein and Boehm into proto-denominational and denominational organization we will cover in chapter 4, but here we exhibit through the following historical statement from its *Discipline* the United Brethren's understanding of its beginnings.

Of the Origin of the United Brethren in Christ

In the century last past it pleased the Lord our God, to awaken persons in different parts of the world, who should raise up the Christian religion from its fallen state, and preach the gospel of Christ crucified in its purity.

At this time the Lord in mercy remembered the Germans in America, who, living scattered in this extensive country, had but seldom an opportunity to hear the gospel of a crucified Saviour preached to them in their native language.

Amongst others he raised up an *Otterbein*, a *Bœhm*, and a *Guething*, armed them with spirit, grace and strength, to labour in his neglected vineyard, and call, also, amongst the Germans in America, sinners to repentance. These men obeyed the call of their Lord and Master; their labours were blessed; they established in many places excellent societies, and led many a precious soul to Jesus Christ. Their sphere of action spread itself more and more, so that they found it necessary to look about for more fellow labourers in the vineyard; for the harvest was great, and the labourers but few. The Lord called others, who also were willing to devote their strength to his service; such, then, were accepted by one or other of the preachers, as fellow labourers.

The number of members of the society, in the different parts of the country, continued from time to time to increase, and the gracious work spread itself through the states of Pennsylvania, Maryland, and Virginia. Great meetings were appointed and held annually several times; when, on such occasions, Otterbein would hold particular conversations with the preachers then present; represent to them the importance of the ministry, and the necessity of their utmost endeavours to save souls. At one of these conversations, it was resolved to hold a conference of all the preachers, in order to take into consideration, how, and in what manner they might be most useful.

The first conference was accordingly held in Baltimore, in the year 1789. There were present:

William Otterbein,	Adam Lehman,
Martin Bœhm,	John Ernst,
George Adam Guething,	Henry Weidener.
Christian Newcomer,	

The second conference was held in York county, in Paradise township, at the house of brother Spangler, in the year 1791, where there were present the following persons, viz.

William Otterbein,	John Ernst,
Martin Bœhm,	John G. Pfrimmer,
George Adam Guething,	John Neidig,
Christian Newcomer,	Benedict Sander.
Adam Lehman,	

And after mature deliberation, how they might labour most usefully in the vineyard of the Lord, they again appointed such as fellow labourers, of whom they had cause to believe that they had experienced true religion in their own souls.

In the mean time the number of members continued to increase more and more; the preachers therefore were obliged to appoint an annual conference, in order to unite themselves more closely, and labour most usefully to one common end; for some were Presbyterians, or church Reformed, some were Lutherans, others Mennonites, and yet others were Methodists. They, therefore, appointed a conference to be held the 25th of September 1800, in Frederick County, Maryland, at the house of brother Frederick Kemp. There were present as follows:

William Otterbein,	Christian Krum,
Martin Bœhm,	Henry Krum,
George Adam Guething,	John Hershey,
Christian Newcomer,	Jacob Geisinger,
Adam Lehman,	Henry Bœhm,
Abraham Dracksel,	Dietrick Aurauf.
John George Pfrimmer,	

They united themselves into a society, which bears the name of "*The United Brethren in Christ;*" and elected William Otterbein and Martin Bœhm, as superintendents or bishops, and agreed that each of them should be at liberty to baptise in such manner, as should best accord with his conviction.

From this time forth the society increased still more; preachers were appointed, who travelled continually (because the number of preaching places could in no other wise be attended), and the work spread itself into the states of Ohio and Kentucky. It became necessary therefore to appoint a conference in the state of Ohio, because it was conceived too laborious for the preachers, who labored in those states, to travel such a distance annually to the conference.

In the mean time brothers Bœhm and Guething died, and brother Otterbein desired, that another bishop should be elected (because infirmity and age would not permit him to superintend any longer), who should take charge of the society, and preserve discipline and order; for at a conference formerly held, it was resolved, that whenever one of the bishops die, another should be elected in his place. Therefore brother Christian Newcomer was then elected as bishop, to take charge of the superintendence of the society.

The want of a discipline in the society has long since been deeply felt; and partial attempts thereto having at different times been made, it was at length resolved at the conference in the state of Ohio, that a general conference should be held, who should take upon themselves to complete the same, so as to accord with the word of God. The members of this conference were to be elected from amongst the preachers in the different parts of the country, by a majority of the votes of the members of the society; and there were present at the conference, that were duly elected, the following preachers, namely: Christian Newcomer, Abraham Hiestand, Andrew Zeller, Daniel Treyer, George Benedum, Abraham Tracksel, Christian Berger, Abraham Meyer, John Schneider, Henry Kumler, Henry Spade, Isaac Nighswander, Christian Krum, and Jacob Baulus.

These met on the sixth of June, 1815, near Mountpleasant, Westmoreland county, Penn. where they, after mature deliberation, found it to be necessary, good and beneficial to deliver the following Doctrines and Rules of discipline to the society in love and humility, with the sincere desire, that these doctrines and rules together with the Word of God might be attended to and strictly observed. For God is a God of order, and where there is no order and discipline, there all love and communion will be lost. Therefore, let us attend to the counsel of our Lord, who taught us: That in lowliness of mind, we should esteem each other better than ourselves. Seek to be minded as Jesus Christ also was! Who took upon him the form of a servant, and became obedient even unto death of the cross, to obtain for us grace and strength, that we, from motives of love and humility, might submit one to the other. He who cannot submit himself, the same lacketh grace, love and humility; hence Jesus saith: Whoso amongst you shall desire to be the greatest, shall be the other's servant. If then we are to be the servants of each other, we must love one another. Jesus saith: Thus shall all men know that ye are my true disciples, if ye have love to one another: and whoso hath not love, the same continueth in death. Then let us practise love, that we may enjoy the glory and felicity, which Jesus obtained by prayer for his disciples, of his heavenly father, that we may be *one* even as he and the father are one. Therefore, beloved brethren, let us strive to be likeminded, unanimous and concordant; and no one speak or think evil of the other: but implore the Lord, that he would graciously grant us his spirit and an earnest desire to lead a truly Christian life, to the honour and glory of his holy name, and to our own eternal welfare. Amen.[10]

Methodist Beginnings in America

Similar "spontaneous" initiatives established small communities that identified themselves with the Wesleyan movement. To term them *spontaneous* is to locate them alongside other evangelical impulses within the English-speaking orbit and with the Great Awakening generally. It is also to indicate that these beginnings occurred through what Dee Andrews calls "Wesleyan migration to the greater middle Atlantic"[11] rather than through Wesley's design or appointment. And it is to recognize these as lay endeavors, created out of the religious experience of Methodism's folk and out of their need for the identity- and community-forming resources of Pietism.[12] The absence of an official commissioning makes the actual beginnings of Methodism tricky to specify, one reason for a long-standing and ongoing bragging-rights-contest between New York and Baltimore Methodists concerning priority. As early as 1787, the *Discipline* found a way of finessing the question of priority and adopted the phrase "About the same Time" to date the beginnings of Methodism around Barbara Heck and Philip Embury in New York City and Robert and Elizabeth Strawbridge in Frederick County, Maryland.

Of the Rise of Methodism (so called) in Europe and America

Quest. 1. What was the Rise of Methodism, so called, in Europe?

Answ. In 1729, two young Men, reading the Bible, saw they could not be saved without Holiness, followed after it, and incited others so to do. In 1737, they saw likewise, that Men are justified before they are sanctified: but still Holiness was their Object. God then thrust them out, to raise an holy People.

Quest. 2. What was the Rise of Methodism, so called, in America?

Answ. During the Space of thirty Years past, certain Persons, Members of the Society, emigrated from England and Ireland, and settled in various Parts of this Country. About twenty Years ago, Philip Embury, a local Preacher from Ireland, began to preach in the City of New-York, and formed a Society of his own Countrymen and the Citizens. About the same Time, Robert Strawbridge, a local Preacher from Ireland, settled in Frederick County, in the State of Maryland, and preaching there formed some Societies. In 1769, Richard Boardman and Joseph Pilmoor, came to New-York; who were the first regular Methodist Preachers on the Continent. In the latter End of the Year 1771, Francis Asbury and Richard Wright, of the same Order, came over.

Quest. 3. What may we reasonably believe to be God's Design, in raising up the Preachers called Methodists?

Answ. To reform the Continent, and spread scripture Holiness over these Lands. As a Proof hereof, we have seen in the Course of fifteen Years a great and glorious Work of God, from New-York through the Jersies, Pennsylvania, Maryland, Virginia, North and South Carolina, even to Georgia.[13]

Both the New York and the Maryland ventures date to the mid-1760s, both involved important female as well as male initiatives,[14] both drew in black as well as white converts, both expressed the aspiration of immigrants for the order and community construction that Pietism provided, and both involved Irish immigrants. In the former case, the community twice exiled itself, from the Palatinate (Germany) and then from Ireland. Here, as for the Reformed and Mennonites, religious community solidified around and gave expression to ethnic identity (Irish and Irish-Palatine).

Early Leaders

Strawbridge (ca. 1732–81), a local preacher before emigrating, began preaching and established, with the help of his wife, Elizabeth, a Methodist class in their home in Sam's Creek and subsequently erected there a log meeting house.[15] Elizabeth gained the first convert, John Evans, who became the class leader. Robert Strawbridge itinerated in Maryland, both Eastern and Western Shores, in Virginia, and into Pennsylvania. He established classes that became the nucleus of later societies in Baltimore, Georgetown,

Washington, D.C., and Leesburg. Preachers converted by him included Black Americans, like Jacob Toogood; notable white leaders of the Methodist movement William Watters and Freeborn Garrettson; and many of the early local preachers, including Richard Owens, Hezekiah Bonham, Sater Stevenson, and Richard Webster.

Pietist and revivalistic movements contain both a self-authorizing principle—the conversion-produced confidence in the leading of the Spirit—and a prophetic edge—the courage to repudiate authority not similarly led. Lacking constraints on his exercise of the religious office, Strawbridge, though not ordained, began to baptize as early as 1762/63 and eventually to offer the Lord's Supper, both sacraments undertaken out of a sense of mission to his new flock and to their needs. No plea apparently issued from the Strawbridge connection for Wesley to send over preachers, to provide for ordinations, or to spread his wing over their efforts. Indeed, initially cooperative with Wesley's early missionaries, Strawbridge resisted their efforts to bring him and his circles into conformity, thus showing something of the Irish spirit that he and others built into the foundations of Methodism.

New York Methodism took another course and issued a plea for Wesley's ordering of and provisioning for its life (Sources 1768). Thomas Taylor, who wrote John Wesley, sought legal guidance on how to establish societies in accordance with the Wesleyan scheme, monetary assistance, and "an able, experienced preacher—one who has both gifts and graces necessary for the work." Of great importance also was his immediate and firsthand description of New York Methodism. As for Sam's Creek, some developments in the spontaneous, lay-led beginnings of what would be John Street Church come down to us via later accounts and legends. Several families of Palatine immigrants, including some who had associated with the Methodists in Ireland, settled in among the New York Lutheran community, associated with Trinity Lutheran, and offered their children for baptism. Barbara Ruckle Heck enjoys credit for initiating New York Methodism. She found members of her family trivializing the time by playing cards, swept the cards into the fire, and implored her cousin Philip Embury, who had been a class leader and local preacher in Ireland: "Philip, you must preach to us, or shall we all go to hell together, and God will require our blood at your hands!" He complied in his own room with five auditors, including two servants, one a Black woman named Betty. A class was formed, and with continued preaching the members outgrew Embury's room and moved to a rigging loft.

Onto this small Methodist community in 1767 stumbled Captain Thomas Webb, whose impact—preaching in his scarlet regimentals with green patch over an eye—and whose doctrine Thomas Taylor detailed in the importuning letter of 1768 to John Wesley (Sources 1768). Webb (1725–96) saw military service in the colonies in the Seven Years' War (French and Indian War), lost an eye, married, became barrack master at Albany, returned to England to sell his commission, underwent conversion, gravitated

11

into the Methodist orbit, did some preaching, returned to Albany, and there began preaching and conducting meetings. In 1766 he relocated with his wife to Jamaica, New York, and began preaching there, elsewhere on Long Island, and in the city. His efforts at home converted two dozen, over half of them African Americans. Where he met success, he established classes in true Wesleyan fashion.

After associating with Embury, he encouraged the New Yorkers in plans to buy land and build a preaching house, providing the largest donation himself (thirty pounds) and raising a comparable amount. They purchased a lot on John Street, thus beginning Methodism's presence in that now historic site, and Embury preached in the building on October 30, 1786, "declaring that the best dedication of the church a minister could make was to preach in it a faithful sermon." One trip by Webb for funds took him to Philadelphia, where he encountered another small group, a legacy of Whitefield's efforts, and organized and developed what would become St. George's. Two years later, the first two of Wesley's appointees, Richard Boardman and Joseph Pilmore, were able to encourage the hundred or so Methodists into acquiring an unfinished German Reformed property. On November 26, 1769, Webb preached the inaugural Sunday sermon.

Like Otterbein, Boehm, and Strawbridge, Webb itinerated widely to preach and to organize. Frank Baker calls him a "consolidator," a term that nicely captures the initiatives he undertook and the fact that he made contact with religious communities already in the process of formation. His efforts, nevertheless, have seemed key to Methodist beginnings at Albany and Schenectady, on Long Island, in the Philadelphia area (Chester and Bristol), in New Jersey (Trenton, Burlington, and New Mills), and in Delaware (Wilmington and New Castle). Everywhere he convinced "his fellow sinners of sin," offered "free and universal grace," taught the divinity and coeternity of Son and Spirit with the Father, grounded hope on Christ's tasting death for everyone, insisted that sinners were justified by faith alone, but that grace could be resisted or lost, and pointed believers toward the holiness that the Spirit made possible.[16]

Another individual operating on his own initiative and authority was Robert Williams (ca. 1745–75), a Welsh local preacher who had preached effectively in northern Ireland. He offered himself for the colonies after Taylor's appeal for assistance (Sources 1768) and when Wesley had begun to seek volunteers for America. Wesley allowed him to come at his own expense and with the understanding that he would be accountable to Wesley's officially commissioned missionaries. Williams apparently intended, from the start, to publish and sell Methodist materials, an enterprise already underway when Wesley's appointees, Boardman and Pilmore, arrived. Williams had also taken charge in New York and itinerated as far south as Virginia.

Letters like Taylor's requesting help and efforts like Webb's and Williams's connecting existing small beginnings began the process by which spontaneous efforts "found" the authority of Wesley and the British movement. And much of the subsequent story readily and naturally navigates onto national, formal, organizational, and leadership levels and easily comes to focus around Francis Asbury and colleagues. However, we should not lose sight of the spontaneity—the initiatives of the Methodist folk, female and male, black and white, English- and German-speaking, who in new community after new community would lay the foundations on which the record-keeping preachers would build. The Emburys and Hecks did so more than once. They soon moved on into upper New York and thence into what is now Ontario, there to participate in the constituting of Canadian Methodism.[17] Such "spontaneous" beginnings exhibited, as Andrews notes, "the imperatives of Wesleyan Methodism—missionary drive, cross-denominational appeal, enthusiastic preaching, and household recruitment of followers."[18]

Pietist Communities

These imperatives, actually Pietist imperatives generally, brought individuals into face-to-face, family-like communities, but families without established "heads," without formal structure, with little literature other than the Bible, with little purpose beyond themselves, connected to no larger ecclesial authorities, lacking clarity about norms, ritual, belief, and practices. These families, in short, lacked legitimacy. Such communities might cry out for a leader "of wisdom, of sound faith, and a good disciplinarian" only to find themselves yielding grudgingly the family-like atmosphere that informality had afforded. Ordering of spontaneous Pietist communities would not be conflict free.

CHAPTER II

STRUCTURING THE IMMIGRANT INITIATIVES: 1769–78

"When I came to Philadelphia I found a little Society, and preached to a great number of people" (Sources 1769). So reported Richard Boardman, who, with Joseph Pilmore, composed the first of four pairs of preachers sent by John Wesley to the colonies. Francis Asbury and Richard Wright followed in 1771, Thomas Rankin and George Shadford in 1773, and James Dempster and Martin Rodda in 1774. Several preachers came to the colonies on their own, including John King, Joseph Yearbry, and William Glendenning. Wesley's itinerants came to bring order to Pietist ferment.

Occupying Canaan under Wesleyan Order

Joseph Pilmore (1739–1825), who had been educated at Wesley's Kingswood School near Bristol, followed Wesley's precept and example by keeping a journal, as also would Francis Asbury, Thomas Rankin, Thomas Coke, and many other itinerants. On landing, October 22, 1769, Pilmore noted that they encountered Captain Webb, "a real Methodist," and discovered the Philadelphia society. Boardman preached, the next day, "on the call of Abraham to go forth into the Land of Canaan." Boardman, the senior of the two and Wesley's assistant for America, proclaimed what would be, and truth be told continues to this day to be, the wandering Arminian's as it was the wandering Aramean's presumption. Methodists should claim, occupy, and if necessary, conquer this new Canaan, this land of heathens. "O may he now give his Son the heathen for his inheritance," writes Boardman. However, as his sketchy report to Wesley indicated, Boardman found chosen people (Methodists) already in Canaan and receptive to the Methodist message—eager hearers, both black and white, civilian and military (Sources 1769). Methodist itinerants functioned with biblical self-images of themselves as Abrahams or Pauls and so crafted their journals. A more accurate biblical type might have been Ezra or Nehemiah. Itinerants did more rebuilding walls, restoring temples, renewing covenant, and less occupying new ground or opening the gospel than they thought. Pilmore wrote Wesley and expressed surprise "to find Captain Webb in town, and a society of about one hundred members, who desire to be in close connection with you."[1]

So thinking themselves Abrahams or Pauls, Pilmore and Boardman went about the work of Ezra and Nehemiah. That meant rebuilding on the Wesleyan system—preaching in the open air, itinerating on a planned basis, making and meeting appointments, inviting into connection all of any confession who would "flee the wrath to come," admitting the same as probationers, organizing classes, holding love feasts, maintaining the society's boundaries, establishing circuits, and cultivating good relations with the churches and their clergy. Implementing the Wesleyan system meant also discerning those who could serve in key leadership posts—steward, class leader, exhorter, local preacher—and appointing them to these key local posts.[2]

Two weeks after arriving, Pilmore "read and explained the Rules of the Society to a vast multitude of serious people." In late November, he cooperated with Webb in acquiring a shell of a building from the "Dutch Presbyterians" (German Reformed), St. George's, since 1968 an officially designated Heritage Landmark of United Methodism. Ten days later, Pilmore laid out the "Wesleyan" order to the Philadelphia society, distilling the General Rules into an eight-point program:

1. That the Methodist Society was never designed to make a Separation from the Church of England or be looked upon as a Church.
2. That it was at first and is still intended for the benefit of all those of every Denomination who being truly convinced of sin, and the danger they are exposed to, earnestly desire to flee from the wrath to come.
3. That any person who is so convinced, and desires admittance into the Society, will readily be received as a probationer.
4. That those who walk according to the Oracles of God, and thereby give proof [of] their sincerity, will readily be admitted into full connexion with the Methodists.
5. That if any person or persons in the Society, walk disorderly, and transgress the holy Laws of God, we will admonish him of his error—we will strive to restore him in the spirit of meekness—we will bear with him for a time, but if he remain incorrigible and impenitent, we must then of necessity inform him, he is no longer a member of the Society.
6. That the Church now purchased, is for the use of this Society, for the Public Worship of Almighty God.
7. That a subscription will immediately be set on foot to defray the Debt upon the said Church—and an exact acct. kept of all the Benefactions given for that purpose.
8. That the Deeds of settlement shall be made as soon as convenient, exactly according to the Plan of the settlement of all the Methodist Chapels in England, Scotland, and Ireland.

In enumerating these Methodist commitments and referencing deeds and plan of settlement, Pilmore declared colonial uniformity with Methodist standards, connection to Wesley, and submission to his ordering. The references (Society, Deeds, Plan) and their import—colonial compliance with organizational protocols determined at the 1763 Leeds conference—doubtless mystified some auditors. What Pilmore specified was that American Methodism would run according to the "Large Minutes," the compilation Wesley had made of his conversations with his preachers in conference over matters of doctrine and discipline, copies of which each preacher in full connection with Wesley carried as an operational manual. The "Large Minutes" of 1763 included a "Model Deed," which specified a pattern of ownership for Methodist properties obliging trustees to allow Wesley "and such other persons as he shall from time to time appoint, and at all times, during his natural life, and no other persons, to have and enjoy the free use and benefit of the said premises." It provided further "that the said persons preach no other doctrine than is contained in Mr. Wesley's *Notes Upon the New Testament*, and four volumes of *Sermons*."[3]

It would be Pilmore and Boardman's endeavor and that of their missionary successors to make good on these commitments and bring colonial Methodists into connection and order. They discovered, for instance, that the John Street property had been legally secured "essentially wrong," not on the plan of the "Model Deed," the trustees enjoying "absolute power" without "being accountable to any one . . . contrary to the whole occonemy [economy] of the Methodists [and] . . . likely to prove hurtful to the Work of God." They succeeded in persuading the trustees to "fix" the deed. On one Wesleyan imperative, itinerancy, Boardman led. He insisted that he should exchange with Pilmore every few months so that one or the other was in Philadelphia or New York. Pilmore was reluctant but acquiesced. Boardman was, however, less forceful and able than Pilmore. The work in New York suffered because of the movement of Embury and the Palatines out of the city and upstate. Boardman did not try to follow them. He was willing to preach in new areas, visiting New England in March 1772, reaching Boston, making him the first to introduce Methodism into New England. Though he succeeded in forming a society in Boston, it was short-lived. Boardman returned to England in July 1773.

Frontier Challenges

These efforts of Wesley's appointees, from the start, marked three larger challenges or opportunities or defining frontiers, each of which Pilmore encountered repeatedly, remarking upon them first November 5–6. The first, an ecclesiastical marker, was how to stay within the Church of England and, in general, how to sustain the Methodist commitment, as Pilmore explained it, not "to make divisions . . . or promote a Schism but to gather together in one the people of God that are scattered abroad, and revive *spiritual religion*." The second, a theological marker, was how to make clear the Methodist doctrines, particularly those of free grace and free will in a context where "rigid predestinarians" took pains to keep their families and servants from hearing the Methodist gospel. The third, a social marker, was how to negotiate the social and class structure of American society and especially to make space among the Methodists and in a slaveholding context for the many "poor Affricans" who proved "obedient to the faith."[4] Pilmore's struggles on all three fronts set the pattern for the first generation of Methodist leadership. They would sustain Wesley's commitment to remain within the church. They would do battle with the Calvinists. They would build a biracial fellowship (Sources 1769, 1771).

The next of Wesley's appointees, Francis Asbury and Richard Wright, arrived in late 1771. Asbury had explored his intentions on shipboard: "Whither am I going? To the New World. What to do? To gain honour? No, if I know my own heart. To get money? No: I am going to live to God, and to bring others so to do. In America there has been a work of God."

On October 27 when he landed in Philadelphia, went to St. George's, and heard Pilmore preach, he concluded, "I feel that God is here." Asbury functioned with a subtle and effective variant of the invasion/conquest motivation. He did not need to bring God and God's order to America; he needed only to evoke the order God intended. With a mandate from God, not just Wesley, Asbury felt singled out to lead and direct, notwithstanding whoever else might be humanly so delegated. Though not officially in charge, Asbury judged defective the order that Boardman and Pilmore had achieved. The societies in New York and Philadelphia did not sufficiently heed Methodist discipline, and Boardman and Pilmore did not sufficiently heed the Methodist preacher's self-discipline—itinerancy. They were content "to be shut up in the cities." He exclaimed, "I have not yet the thing which I seek—a circulation of preachers, to avoid partiality and popularity." He added,

> However, I am fixed on the Methodist plan, and do what I do faithfully as to God. I expect trouble is at hand. This I expected when I left England, and I am willing to suffer, yea, to die, sooner than betray so good a cause by any means. It will be a hard matter to stand against all opposition, as an iron pillar strong, and steadfast as a wall of brass: but through Christ strengthening me I can do all things.[5]

Continuing to complain about his colleagues' urban captivity, Asbury itinerated around New York—Westchester, Long Island, and Staten Island. By March 1772 Asbury was "much comforted" and "well pleased" when the preachers gathered in Philadelphia and Boardman appointed himself to Boston, Pilmore to Virginia, Wright to New York, and Asbury to Philadelphia. Pilmore itinerated as far south as Savannah, traveling with Robert Williams, encountering Methodist preachers John King and Robert Strawbridge, and preaching to communities already taking Methodist shape. Williams, Jesse Lee reported, would attend Anglican service, then "standing on a stump, block, or log" begin "to sing, pray, and then preach to hundreds of people." Their collective efforts "awakened" many souls and gathered the converts to the Methodist cause, according to Lee.[6] With the ordering of the appointments in conference, itineration on a continental scale, and connecting of the several spontaneous initiatives, the preachers had the blueprints for American Methodism.

Pilmore's southern tour added to those blueprints another distinctively American feature. Most notable were his recurrent settings for preaching—"under a fine Shady Tree"; "under a shady tree"; in Baltimore Forest with "about five hundred people assembled in the Wood"; "in the Wood" outside the new chapel, Deer-Creek; "in the Wood" at the Forks of the Gunpowder; "under a fine shady tree" in Portsmouth; and with "a large congregation under the shady trees" outside Portsmouth.[7] Camp meetings would be several decades ahead, but already preachers took to the woods to accommodate heat, crowds, the mixing of two races, and the peculiar southern pattern of event-based community. And already one can feel, through Pilmore's experience, the beginnings of Methodist engagement with the forest, with the land, with the American landscape. Methodism would come to understand its mission in continental terms, a purpose constructed by the daily building on the American soil.

On his tour, Pilmore labored for a biracial fellowship and continued to honor the Wesleyan commitments to remain within the church and do battle with the Calvinists. Each posed a struggle, particularly the former, as Pilmore worked south and dealt more extensively with the gentility and slave owners. Pilmore proved effective in starting societies. His heart lay there and not in constant itineration: "Frequent changes amongst gospel preachers, may keep up the spirits of some kinds of people, but is never likely to promote the spirit of the Gospel nor increase true religion."[8]

Order and Freedom

Asbury, on the other hand, incarnated the itinerancy and modeled what would be an effective continental strategy. He exhibited also, from the start, patterns of rhetoric and of self-understanding peculiarly apt for the colonial setting and the Revolutionary epoch. Two terms, *power* and *liberty*, terms with multiple signification, recur through his journal to describe the preaching event.[9] Both, particularly the former, specified the divine agency at work. Both captured the feeling with which Asbury preached. Both described the effect of the preaching. Both pointed to the apparent experience of the hearers. Both recur through the journals of Asbury's compatriots in itinerancy. Both counterpoised a peculiar Methodist, religious, and bottoms-up revolution to that being plotted in colonial assembly.

By *liberty* or *freedom*, its frequent substitute, and by *power*, Asbury described a new order of reality, a new dominion, a new civitas. What that would look like, how

American Methodism would manifest itself, where it would differ from Old World ec-clesia, and how it would engage the emerging American political order were yet to be determined. Freedom or liberty on Methodist lips did not then carry Commonwealth or Lockean import or connect political to religious tyranny or call for political action and organization or conflate colonial agenda and Methodist effort. Liberty had more to do with Arminian freedom, with prevenient grace, with universal atonement, with offers to flee the wrath to come. But it also had something to do with slavery and with the standing of all persons before God and with the quality of human community. Asbury grasped at this new reality while taking Communion, praying:

> Lord, prepare my heart. My bleeding Lord! let my soul feel thy melting love. Lord, make all thy people glad together in thee, that thou mayest be glorified in and by us both now and ever. At the table I was greatly affected with the sight of the poor Negroes, seeing their sable faces at the table of the Lord. In the evening I had a full house and much Di-vine assistance.

The next day, he noted: "I had *liberty* and *love* in preaching at five, and this day felt *power* to live to God." At its heart, this new order would be a community of love.

Clearly, however, freedom, order, and community or liberty, power, and love belonged together. In September 1772 Asbury carried the New York society through a series of queries and answers—not unlike those of Wesley's conferences—designed to offer the Methodist freedom through preaching but to safeguard the society's experience of God's power and its own efforts to live in love through the Wesleyan rules barring the un-qualified and unruly. And so, when Asbury received a letter from Mr. Wesley, it required first "a strict attention to discipline," then appointing him "to act as assistant." Wesley also directed that Asbury rein in Robert Williams and enjoin him not to print more books without consent. At the same time Asbury received word of his appointment (from Boardman) to Maryland for the winter. The next day, Sunday, he noted, "Preached with *power* in the morning, and spoke *freely* to a large congregation in the evening. My soul is blest with peace and *love* to God."[10] Freedom, order, and love indeed belonged to-gether. And when they cohered, Methodism offered the colonies a taste of the king-dom. So in slaveholding Maryland at the Methodist Henry Watterses, Asbury reported:

> Lord's day, 8. We had a very melting time indeed, while I preached to about two hun-dred souls, from Rom. vi, 17, 18. We had also many people at Richard Webster's while I preached, with liberty in my soul, from 1 Cor. iv, 20: "The kingdom of God is not in word, but in power." This day I have been free from evil, happy, and joyful in my God. At the widow Bonds' there were many people, both black and white, rich and poor, who were all exhorted to seek the Lord while he may be found. Some of the young women of this family are serious and thoughtful.[11]

In this one entry Asbury captured much of early Methodism—
a biracial (Sources 1769, 1771),
highly emotional, affective, and expressive (Sources 1780b),
family-based community (Sources 1775a),
sensitive to the religious sensibilities of women (Sources 1775a, 1785c, 1787),
empowering as leaders young men, like William Watters, then itinerating with Robert
    Williams and widows like Bond, who would be termed mothers in Israel,
knit together through class and society structure into a tribe,
which would travel together toward the kingdom.

A community of love and affect (melting, happy, joyful), with liberty in the soul and
its own sense of power, Methodism would claim the Canaan of this new world.

Conquest by Conferencing

In his role as assistant, Asbury convened a quarterly meeting, the body in the Wesleyan system charged with oversight of a circuit. This late December 1772 conference
was the first quarterly meeting for which records remain. Meeting at Joseph Presbury's,
Gunpowder Neck, on the western shore of Maryland, it defined business with six questions. After standard queries such as "What are our collections?" and "How are the
preachers stationed?" the conference asked, "Will the people be contented without our
administering the sacrament?" The question posed issues of unity and authority for the
little movement and specifically whether the inertias of Methodism's spontaneous beginnings or the imperatives of Wesleyan order would prevail. Should the Robert Strawbridge cohort, the planters of American Methodism, set policy, ordain themselves, and
connive sacramental authority? Or should the Wesleyan principle of not separating, so
zealously preached by Pilmore, Williams, and others, prevail? Pilmore and Williams were
even then deeper in Anglican territory, farther south, reassuring churchpeople of their
commitments, cultivating clerical support. Williams, for instance, solicited alliance with
the evangelical Anglican priest Devereux Jarratt, whose influence radiated out from his
Bath, Virginia, parish promising:

> That the Methodists were true members of the church of England—that their design
> was to build up, and not to divide the church—that the preachers did not assume the
> office of priests—administered neither the ordinance of *baptism*, nor the *Lord's Supper*,
> but looked to the parish ministers in all places for *these*—that they travelled to call sin-
> ners to repentance—to join proper subjects in society for mutual edification, and to do
> all they could for the spiritual improvement of those societies.

Jarratt, recalling the promise long after the fact, concluded from Williams and
Methodist literature that *"he that left the church, left the Methodists."* Pilmore, who

frequently preached this adage, believed it so deeply that after leaving the colonies, he eventually took orders and returned to be an Episcopal priest. Jarratt was but one of several Anglican priests who would interest themselves in and support the Methodist effort. Writing a decade later to George Shadford, Asbury identified three others as especially friendly and helpful: Charles Pettigrew of North Carolina, later bishop of that diocese; Samuel Magaw of Dover and then Philadelphia; and "Mogden," apparently Uzal Ogden of New Jersey.[12] All attended Methodist quarterly meetings and welcomed Methodists to the sacrament.

Under the question about the sacraments then lay a complex of other issues having to do with the nature and structure of the movement, its relation to the Church of England, the authority of Wesley, the duty of the preachers, and the meaning of connection. Asbury's answer (recorded in the minutes) indicated a divided house and divergent policy: "I told them I would not agree to it at that time, and insisted on our abiding by our rules. But Mr. Boardman had given them their way at the quarterly meeting held here before, and I was obliged to connive at some things for the sake of peace."[13]

For the quarterly conference to take up and treat the sacraments question and for it to be resolved in this fashion was, in a sense, presumptuous. It presumed that it had the authority to legislate. Thus began the process by which the conference achieved supremacy in Methodist polity and Methodist polity itself emerged. The conniving at authority by the American quarterly conference was, doubtless like the very Strawbridge initiatives it critiqued, a fall-back and spontaneous gesture. Yet it paralleled more intentional organizational ordering. Wesley was during this time gravitating toward recognizing the British conference as the decision-making body for the movement; his successor in authority, rights, prerogative, and power; and the community that would hold together the Methodist connection. The American movement would gradually appropriate to itself what Wesley designed to center the whole, namely, an ordering of itself in and through conference.

This early quarterly meeting exhibited two other important features. Asbury reported, "Many people attended, and several friends came many miles." Quarterly conferences would quickly become a great spiritual festival, the center really of Methodism's liturgical life (including eventually its sacramental life), the gathering that most clearly and fully exhibited Methodist community to a wider public. Already as Jesse Lee reported, the Anglican priest and Methodist sympathizer Jarratt "would frequently preach, meet the classes, hold love-feasts, and administer the Lord's supper among them."

The second development is indicated in Asbury's concluding judgment: "Great love subsisted among us in this meeting, and we parted in peace." Similarly for the next quarterly meeting (conference), in late March, Asbury reported that Strawbridge preached, "All was settled in the most amicable manner," and "The whole ended in great peace." The temper and quality of the preachers' life together in conference became increasingly important. In conferences, the Methodist people and especially the Methodist preachers would establish the bonds of their unity.[14]

Discipline: Rankin and Asbury

Asbury functioned as assistant only half a year to be displaced by Thomas Rankin, who arrived in June 1773 with the new title "general assistant." Asbury greeted Rankin's appearance with the notation, "To my great comfort arrived Mr. Rankin," a generous judgment, given the later tension between the two men. More to the point Asbury observed, "He will not be admired as a preacher. But as a disciplinarian, he will fill his place."[15] Asbury did much to undermine Rankin's administration, behaving in a fashion that he (Asbury) would not have suffered. And Asbury's subverting judgments about Rankin have generally prevailed. But Asbury had it right in regard to order. Rankin came with the confidence of Wesley and a mandate. He had had prior experience in the colonies, had a decade of experience as itinerant, had been made assistant and superintendent successively of four circuits, and had served as a riding companion to Wesley. Lest his oral instructions to Rankin be unclear, Wesley followed them with a letter in late 1773 full of admonition and heady counsel:

> If you suffer any one to remain a leader who does not stay at the Society, that will be *your* fault. Improper leaders are not to be suffered upon any account whatever. You must likewise deal honest with the Societies, whether they will hear or whether they will forbear....
>
> ...You have hurt yourself by giving way to reasoning, and if you don't take care you will hurt others. There has been good, much good done in America, and would have been abundantly more had Brother Boardman and Pilmoor continued genuine Methodists both in doctrine and discipline. It is *your* part to supply what was wanting in them. Therefore are you sent. Let Brother Shadford, Asbury, and you go on hand in hand, and who can stand against you? Why, you are enough, trusting in Him that loves you, to overturn America.[16]

Wesley's command with respect to a "leader" pointed to the regimens of conferencing—Christian conversation—at the grassroots level, namely, in class meetings. These small groups, a signature of Wesleyanism, quite literally constituted the people called Methodist. To be a Methodist meant to be a member of a class, so specified the "Large Minutes." So Pilmore specified in Philadelphia (points 2–5 above). So eventually the Methodist *Discipline* would specify (Sources 1785a; 1798: Section II). In early American Methodism as in the British movement, particularly in areas of some population density, classes divided by race and gender and guided, often for years, by a single leader (typically a white male) did the pastoring, nurturing piety and sustaining discipline and self-discipline. Into the class converts came as probationers.

Under the leader's guidance and oversight, probationers moved into membership and a members' class.

The weekly class meetings provided the regular pastoring, discipline, guidance, nurture, instruction, mentoring, and encouragement that the system afforded. Within their bonds of accountability and love (stratified by gender, by race, and increasingly in North America by marital status) community and fellowship developed. From them and from their leadership came exhorters, local preachers, and traveling preachers. Little bands of pilgrims toward holiness, the classes embodied and sustained the order and the goals of Wesleyanism.[17] Creating classes, staffing them with capable leaders, and sustaining their good order were arguably a preacher's highest priorities. And getting the system of them in order in colonial America, Rankin's charge.

Rankin indeed sought order. And he enjoyed the distinction of establishing as well the third element in the Wesleyan conferencing order—the annual conference. Classes of a dozen or so provided spirituality and order for members; quarterly meetings for all the local circuit leaders (stewards, class leaders, exhorters, local preachers); annual conferences for traveling preachers. Rankin convened the first annual conference—still deemed the basic body of Methodism—in July 1773 in Philadelphia (Sources 1773). He judged some of those deemed members to be "not closely united to us" and "our discipline . . . not properly attended to, except at Philadelphia and New York; and even in those places it was on the decline."[18] Though the secretary structured the *Minutes* in the Wesleyan question-and-answer format, the queries that Rankin put rather more resembled vows or imperatives than points for discussion. Rankin followed orders. He demanded and got acceptance of Wesley's authority, adherence to his doctrines and discipline, suspension of sacraments, conformity with the church, guarding of love feasts, honoring of rules about publishing, and disfellowshiping of deviants. The *Minutes* show Strawbridge as appointed, as they did also in 1775, but then for the last time. He would not abide the new discipline. William Watters, another colonist, received an appointment.

The *Minutes* posed and answered a query that would thereafter provide an annual checkup for the movement, a gauge of its spiritual temperature, a reading of its revivalistic pulse: "What numbers are there in the society?" The answers also indicated what would be a growing pattern. Methodism centered itself in the upper South or Chesapeake region, with almost half of the 1,160 members in Maryland (500). Four of the ten appointments went to Baltimore. That area also saw the most aggressive establishment of preaching houses—Strawbridge, on Sam's Creek (1764), Leesburg (1766–68), Bush, near Aberdeen (1769), Evans (1770), Watters (1772), Fork (1773), and Gunpowder (1773).[19] All in actual attendance, the ten and Thomas Webb, were British born. They had come to bring Wesleyan and British order just at the time that the colonies were deciding to throw off such order.

Tensions and Controversies as Revolution Looms

Rankin itinerated through the Methodist communities, presided over innumerable quarterly conferences, and welcomed in African Americans, perhaps more than the *Minutes* actually suggest. His itinerations put him in contact with various kindred spirits, including Otterbein: "I have met with a friendly and loving spirited man in this place, a Mr. Utterbine, Minister of the Dutch Presbyterian congregation. He seems to be a man of an excellent spirit and wishes us good luck in the name of the Lord."[20]

Otterbein had only recently (May 1774) relocated to Baltimore to become pastor of its German Reformed Church (the Heritage Landmark Old Otterbein). Rankin well should have found him a congenial and companion spirit. Otterbein had continued his established pattern of itinerating, organizing and nurturing outlying communities, and raising up leaders. Not long after arriving in Baltimore, Otterbein gathered those preachers into conference, six including himself attending what have been known as the Pipe Creek meetings. The first of these semiannual affairs met May 29, 1774. It specified a class structure for communities in Baltimore, Pipe Creek, Sam's Creek, Fredericktown, and Antietam. The *Minutes*, extant for 1774–76, show the conference to have concerned itself with discipline in the classes and with expansion into new communities (Sources 1785b). The resemblance to Wesleyan organization (itineration, classes, discipline, conference) was more than superficial. Asbury had encountered Otterbein in early May: "Had a friendly intercourse with Mr. Otterbein and Mr. Swope, the German ministers, respecting the plan of Church discipline on which they intended to proceed. They agreed to imitate our methods as nearly as possible."[21] Thus began the long and complex relationship of mutual influence between the German- and English-speaking Pietist impulses. Both movements continued association with their respective "mother" churches. Both movements experienced disruptions during the Revolution. For the Wesleyans it proved severe and of their own making.

Rankin's efforts yielded unity, but ironically also discord, a consequence of putting British-born leaders into a colonial society riven with crisis over that exact point— British control. Rankin's penchant for and opinions on Methodist and British order created tensions. "I was not long in America," he wrote, before he told some of his friends, that "if God had any love for the people in this country, he would punish them by some vast affliction, for their great pride and luxury."[22] In October 1774, Rankin noted in his journal, "From the first of my coming here, it has always been impressed on my mind, that God has a controversy with the inhabitants of the British colonies; and so I said to some in my first visit to New York." In late 1774, Rankin mused about and spoke with equal candor to the political and military crisis then engulfing the colonies:

> The British Colonies in America have been highly favoured of God. The people have lived at the full, but like Jeshurun, they have waxed fat, and forgot the rock from whence

they were hewen, and the hole of the pit from whence they were digged. May the Lover of Souls turn them to Himself, as the rivers in the South.

And again, in 1776:

I had frequent opportunities from the first general congress that was held in Philadelphia, till now; to converse with several of its members; and also with many members of the Provincial Congress, where I travelled. I found liberty to speak my mind with freedom and so far as I could see they were not offended. I could not help telling many of them, what a farce it was for them to contend for liberty, when they themselves, kept some hundreds of thousands of poor blacks in most cruel bondage? Many confessed it was true, but it was not now the time to set them at liberty.[23]

Wesley's words on behalf of liberty for the slaves had appeared in an American imprint not long before, in 1774:

It cannot be that either war, or contract, can give any man such a property in another as he has in his sheep and oxen. Much less is it possible that any child of man should ever be *born a slave*. Liberty is the right of every human creature as soon as he breathes the vital air. And no human law can deprive him of that right, which he derives from the law of nature.

If therefore you have any regard to justice, (to say nothing of mercy, nor of the revealed law of God) render unto all their due. Give liberty to whom liberty is due, that is to every child of man, to every partaker of human nature.[24]

Liberty for the slave became a characteristic, if not necessarily a uniform or even majority, Methodist concern for the next decade at least. However, American colonists generally did not share the priority and passion, and many of them had a different sort of liberty in mind and were willing to live with the inconsistency that Rankin, Wesley, and others detected. Some colonists found these and other Methodist actions and words to be rather more treasonous than prophetic and the little movement potentially subversive of "American" liberties. Methodism suffered politically because of its status as part of Anglicanism and as a reform run by a High Church Tory (even as it profited evangelistically from the same umbrella). Was Methodism part of the feared Anglican plot to impose an episcopate on the colonies? Was it a friend or foe to the colonial cause and American liberties?

Wesley and Revolution

The crisis of the Revolution, because it disrupted control mechanisms from Wesley and the English Conference, gave the American movement an extremely short period of being ordered from abroad, of having expatriate leadership, and of being treated as a mission or colony. In short, American Methodism indigenized unusually rapidly. The second annual conference admitted five preachers, four of them colonists, and seven on trial, all colonists. Future leaders among this number were William Watters and Philip Gatch. Joseph Pilmore and Richard Boardman had earlier returned to England. Well over half the appointments went to colonists.

In early 1775, John and Charles Wesley wrote separately to Rankin counseling neutrality, sending along as well a short letter "to all the preachers":

> My Dear Brethren,—You were never in your lives in so critical a situation as you are at this time. It is your part to be peace-makers, to be loving and tender to all, but to addict yourself to no party. In spite of all solicitations, of rough or smooth words, say not one word against one or the other side. Keep yourselves pure....
>
> See that you act in full union with each other.[25]

The third annual conference heeded Wesley's advice. It met in May 1775 in Philadelphia, the very time and place of the Second Continental Congress. Rankin noted their consciousness of Wesley's prudent counsel and their efforts to draw further wisdom locally from William Stringer, the evangelical Anglican:

> We conversed together, and concluded our business in love. Mr. Stringer spent some time with us. We wanted all the advice and light we could obtain respecting our conduct in the present critical situation of affairs. We all came unanimously to this conclusion, to follow the advice that Mr. Wesley and his brother had given us, and leave the event to God. We had abundant reason to bless God for the increase of His work last year. We had above a thousand added to the different societies, and they had increased to ten Circuits. Our joy in God would have been abundantly more, had it not been for the preparations for war that now rung throughout this city (Philadelphia).[26]

The conference declared a "general fast for the prosperity of the work, and for the peace of America, on Tuesday the 18th of July."[27]

Unfortunately Wesley did not heed his own counsel. He issued in 1775 the first of several publications on the American situation, *A Calm Address to Our American Colonies* (Sources 1775b), a Tory tract largely extracted from Samuel Johnson's *Taxation No Tyranny*. It sold forty thousand copies in less than a month.[28] This publication, related public statements by both Wesleys, and intemperate loyalist actions by several preachers in America imaged Methodism publicly as a Tory movement.

Despite that public impression, Methodists could be found along the complete spectrum on the war. A few Methodists became active collaborators with the British army, others sympathized with the loyalist cause, a number were principled loyalists who returned to Britain or after the war sought refuge in Canada, a few were neutralists or pacifists, many were supporters of the Revolution, and a few, including preachers, were active participants in the Revolutionary cause. Methodists ranged between the Thomases, from Webb to Ware, from the Tory collaborator to the American soldier.

Collaborators, Loyalists, Pacifists, Persecuted, Patriots

Webb, the soldier, took advantage of itinerancy to move around the middle colonies for surveillance purposes. He crossed military lines. He fed information to the British command. He defied colonial authorities. He kept up epistolary contact with Lord Dartmouth and passed along military advice. He was arrested and tried by the Continental Congress, and though not convicted, he was held as a prisoner of war.[29] Also arrested for military action, threatened with execution, and equally indiscreet in his loyalism was one of the last pair of preachers sent by Wesley, Martin Rodda, who arrived in 1774. Rodda's indiscretion? Allegedly taking leadership in the gathering of a loyalist force on the Eastern Shore of Maryland in 1777. "Mr. Rodda's conduct," Lee observed, "brought many sufferings, and much trouble, on the Methodist preachers and people."

Several preachers, including Thomas Rankin and George Shadford, joined Webb in writing Lord Dartmouth with information about and advice on the American crisis. Loyalism to both Wesley and the British constitution informed the 1776 efforts by George Shadford in Virginia to defend the Anglican establishment during debates to abolish the same. Shadford spoke for "the whole Body of the people Commonly called Methodists in Virginia" who were "not Dessenters, but a Religious Society in Communion with the Church of England," and he insisted that "very bad Consequences would arise from the abolishment of the establishment." He prayed for the king and was threatened with imprisonment. Later, while in Maryland, he twice refused to take a test oath and was denied the pass that guaranteed safe travel. As Lee indicated, the Methodist cause was decidedly injured because "our head preachers were all from Europe, and some of them were imprudent in speaking too freely against the proceedings of the Americans."[30]

Further along the spectrum would be the principled loyalists. Especially noteworthy are those who moved to Canada and replayed their founding roles. Especially important in subsequent development of Canadian Methodism were the Methodists among the approximately 7,500 United Empire Loyalists who settled in Upper Canada, among them the Hecks and Emburys.[31]

Toward the center would be persons like Mary Evans Thorn (Parker), appointed by Pilmore a class leader, whose important memories of Philadelphia Methodism and her own spiritual pilgrimage during that period included roles of nursing and spiritual counseling for the sick and dying "whether by wounds or the plague" (Sources 1775a). So she met her later husband, Captain Samuel Parker, a ship owner, exiting to England with him in 1778 (or late 1777). In the same exodus, she claimed, were the "principled" Wesley appointees, including Thomas Rankin and perhaps Rodda. Leaving only Asbury of those Wesley had deputized for colonial service, Shadford followed, gaining a pass to travel through battle lines with the declaration that he was an Englishman and a Methodist preacher, a subject of Great Britain and unwilling to take a test oath.[32]

The Maryland test law sharply exposed Asbury's several scruples. It required an individual to disavow obedience to the king, to pledge allegiance to "the State of Maryland," and to "defend" its freedom and independence. Those refusing to swear were subjected to a variety of penalties, and they were prohibited from teaching, preaching, or traveling. Faced by the Maryland test laws, Asbury, the consummate centrist, in March 1778 went into hiding at Thomas White's in Delaware, "shut up in a friend's house," according to Lee. Asbury experienced the confinement as oppressive and depressing: "Three thousand miles from home—my friends have left me—I am considered by some as an enemy of the country—every day liable to be seized by violence and abused."[33]

The Tory image of Methodism, exaggerated by the demands of the Maryland test law, indeed brought hardship, suffering, beatings, and imprisonment on the many, including especially leaders, whose loyalties belonged either to the patriot cause or to kingdoms quite beyond this world. Philip Gatch was tarred and threatened with whipping. Caleb Pedicord bore whipping scars to his grave. Samuel Spragg escaped a mob. Some thirty-five Methodists were indicted for preaching in a six-month period on the Western Shore. Joseph Hartley, a Virginian, was arrested for preaching on the Eastern Shore in Maryland, posted bond, kept preaching, and was jailed. Also jailed were William Wrenn, Jonathan Forrest, and Freeborn Garrettson. Among the persecuted, Freeborn Garrettson (1752–1827) has left the fullest and most graphic account of sufferings.[34]

Garrettson witnessed against war, against slavery, against the genteel life, against patriarchy, against convention and reason, against all these forces of Satan and did so as one recently freed from all these bondages. He had, as he indicated, set free his own slaves as the first act after conversion. The violence of the attacks (and his *Experience and Travels of Mr. Freeborn Garrettson*, one of the first publications by and about American Methodism, reads like Saint Paul's account of his vicissitudes) owed much to Garrettson's status as and rejection of gentility.[35]

To patriarch and patriot, Garrettson appeared a turncoat, a counterinsurgent, or even worse, a radical. Would he, as a Methodist, extend the principles of the Revolution to every aspect of social existence? Was this a revolution on behalf of emotion and against reason (deism)? On behalf of the young and against order? On behalf of women and children and against patriarchy? On behalf of the outcast and against slavery? On behalf of peace and against war? On behalf of Christ's kingdom and against all earthly dominion? Transformed by conversion, Garrettson experienced, witnessed for, and preached a liberty that went beyond but stood in judgment over liberty that might be bought by guns and assured politically. Proclaiming "Lord, the oppressed shall go free" proved indeed a "divine kindling" with power to scorch not just hearts but the very fabric of society. With Garrettson, Asbury's language of power and liberty gathered in the nuances of the "Republican" or "Whiggish" social analysis and critique. He began the wedding of republican and Pietist accounts of human corruption, of the abuse of power, of the true authority over this world, of its legitimate representatives, and of real liberty. And Garrettson experienced and denounced the enemy of emotion, youth, women and children, the outcast, peace, and Christ—Satan. In Garrettson, Pietism took on American import.[36]

Others less eloquent about the union of Pietist and republican power and liberty simply signed on to the Revolutionary cause. Occupying the other extreme from Webb was Thomas Ware (1758–1842). Though his family loyalties were divided, Thomas Ware volunteered on the Revolutionary side. Not then a preacher but already under Methodist influence, he was immediately afterward put by Asbury on the Dover Circuit.[37] William Duke, William Watters, and Nelson Reed took the Maryland oath, thereby committing themselves to the Revolutionary cause. Also in the Revolutionary cause but not then under Methodist influence or in a leadership role was the future leader of The Evangelical Association, Jacob Albright (1759–1808). He served in a local militia.[38]

Jesse Lee (1758–1816), on the other hand, was drafted soon after beginning traveling. As "a Christian and as a preacher of the gospel," he recalled, "I could not fight. I could not reconcile it to myself to bear arms, or to kill one of my fellow creatures; however I determined to go, and to trust the Lord." He refused a gun, was put under guard, and was interrogated for his refusal to bear arms. He responded, "I could not kill a man with a good conscience, but I was a friend to our country, and was willing to do any thing that I could, while I continued in the army, except that of fighting." He served then as a noncombatant and played, in effect, chaplain roles.[39]

American Methodism

Methodists went into the American Revolution emblemed as British, Tory, and Anglican. They exited with rather more complex image problems but internally purged, transformed, and focused. While still confined in Delaware (and he, in fact, moved around considerably during his confinement), Asbury resolved:

> Tuesday, February 23, 1779: . . . My soul was not tormented by satan, as it has sometimes been, but was kept in sweet peace. I have yet been impressed with a deep concern, for bringing about the freedom of slaves in America, and feel resolved to do what I can to promote it. If God in His providence hath detained me in this country, to be instrumental in so merciful and great an undertaking, I hope He will give me wisdom and courage sufficient, and enable me to give Him all the glory. I am strongly persuaded that

if the Methodists will not yield on this point and emancipate their slaves, God will depart from them.[40]

Asbury published this witness against slavery in the earliest version of his journal but suppressed it later, a suppression that belonged to a general retreat, compromise, and forgetting. Later American Methodism would indeed want to forget the freedom and liberty it had preached and the social revolution it had announced. In fact, it had been good news to many, and colonists had readily embraced it. Notwithstanding the movement's image problems and all the suppression, Methodism had prospered during the Revolution and precisely in patriot rather than British-held areas. The overall membership numbers and the absence of report from New York and Philadelphia tell the tale. "What numbers are there in society":[41]

Year	New York	Philadelphia	Total
1773	180	180	1,160
1774	222	204	2,073
1775	200	190	3,148
1776	132	137	4,921
1777	96	96	6,968
1778	?	?	7,011
1779	?	89	8,577
1780	?	90	8,504
1781	?	271 (Pa. state)	10,539
1782	?	291 (Pa. state)	11,785
1783	?	119	13,740
1784	60	470	14,988

Wesley had sent over his missionaries to bring a Wesleyan order to the Pietist awakenings. By 1773 they had secured the movement with six circuits and anchored it in New York, Philadelphia, and Baltimore. Ten years later the American preachers they had raised up spread across the eastern seaboard onto thirty-eight circuits, overwhelmingly south of the recently drawn Mason-Dixon Line. The missionaries came to connect, control, and order. A strange set of providences interposed a Revolution, put the Wesleyan order to new purposes, chased away the British leadership, and left the American Methodists wandering toward a strange new freedom.

CHAPTER III

MAKING CHURCH: 1777–84

By 1777, the little American Methodist movement witnessed colonial Anglicanism collapsing, saw its British leadership departed or departing, pondered a future without guidance from Wesley or his general assistant, and worried about sacraments for the Methodist faithful. In May, a week prior to annual conference, several preachers gathered at Henry Gough's Perry Hall, near Baltimore, Asbury among them. The presession debated "whether we could give our consent that Mr. Rankin should baptize, as there appeared to be a present necessity," "drew a rough draught for stationing the preachers the ensuing year," and decided on "a committee . . . to superintend the whole."[1] Would American Methodism declare its independence, undertake ecclesial revolution, and establish itself as church sui generis?

Declarations of Independence

Indecision reigned as the several versions of the minutes of the annual conference that met at Deer Creek (Harford County, Maryland) on May 20 indicate. The official, later-published version, the one that Asbury would have sanctioned, queried, "As the present distress is such, are the preachers resolved to take no step to detach themselves from the work of God for the ensuing year?" It answered, "We purpose, by the grace of God, not to take any step that may separate us from the brethren, or from the blessed work in which we are engaged." The Leesburg and Philip Gatch versions of the minutes disclose continued debate on the sacraments and groundwork for authority exercised through committee in presbyterian fashion:

> Q. 11 Can any thing be done in order to lay a foundation for a future union, supposing the old preachers should be, by the times, constrained to return to Great Britain? Would it not be well for all who are willing, to sign some articles of agreement, and strictly adhere to the same, till other preachers are sent by Mr. Wesley, and the brethren in conference?
> A. We will do it.

Accordingly, the following paper was written and signed, "We, whose names are underwritten, being thoroughly convinced of the necessity of a close union between those whom God hath need as instruments in his glorious work, in order to preserve this union, are resolved, God being our helper, . . .

> 1. To devote ourselves to God. . . . 2. To preach the old Methodist doctrine, and no other, as contained in the Minutes. 3. To observe and enforce the whole Methodist Discipline, as laid down in the said Minutes. 4. To choose a committee of assistants to transact the business that is now done by the general assistants, and the old preachers who came from Britain. . . ."

Among the twenty-five signers were Wesley's British preachers, Francis Asbury, William Glendenning, Thomas Rankin, George Shadford, and Martin Rodda. The subsequent query established the committee to superintend the whole.

> Q. 12 Who shall act as a committee of assistants agreeably to the preceding plan?
> A. Daniel Ruff, William Watters, Philip Gatch, Edward Drumgoole, William Glendenning.[2]

Francis Asbury was neither included in the committee nor given an appointment. He doubtless already intended to go into hiding. American Methodism had connived some independence, put a committee at its helm, and established the senior American, Watters, as its chair.

Over the next conference, in 1778, the chair of this new committee, William Watters, presided, Asbury having gone into semi-hiding at Judge Thomas White's in Delaware. The (later) published Minutes suggest a stable, holding operation and the recognition of Asbury to have succeeded to leadership as second in rank to the departed Rankin, as appointed by Wesley, and as former "assistant," a stature seemingly indicated by Asbury's placement on the list of "assistants"—first.[3] The two manuscript minutes for this conference neither accord Asbury that placement nor suggest stability. Both put Freeborn Garrettson first among the assistants. Both indicated that the matter of the sacraments again surfaced and was again deferred. Both appointed the next conference for Broken Back Church in Fluvanna County, Virginia, an item of business curiously omitted from the (later) published Minutes.[4]

Fluvanna Schism

Two conferences occurred in 1779, the first at Kent County, Delaware, ostensibly as the Minutes indicated, "For the convenience of the preachers in the northern stations, that we all might have an opportunity of meeting in conference: it being unadvisable for brother Asbury and brother Ruff, with some others, to attend in Virginia." The reasoning continued, "[I]t is considered also as preparatory to the conference in Virginia:—Our sentiments to be given in by brother Waters." "Sentiments" rather dramatically understates the import of actions taken by those gathered around Asbury. First, they recognized him "as General Assistant in America," according to manuscript minutes, "because Originally Appointed by Mr. Wesley to Act Jointly therein with Mr. Rankin & Mr. Shadford." Asbury's authority refined itself by the time the *Minutes* were published. He ought to act as general assistant "1st on account of his age; 2d, because originally appointed by Mr. Wesley; 3d, being joined with Messrs. Rankin and Shadford, by express order from Mr. Wesley." Second, they vested quite considerable power in Asbury, comparable to that enjoyed by Wesley, as both published and manuscript minutes indicate. The latter put it:

> How far shall this Power Extend
> A. To the Hearing Each Preacher in Conference for or Against any Matter—to offer his Reasons—& then the Right of Determination to Lay in his breast—to Act According to the Printed Minutes of Conference & in his Absence the Committee to Act in Like Manner.[5]

Third, their reference here to "Printed Minutes" meant Wesley's "Large Minutes." Its specification, superfluous if the body thought itself firmly under Wesley's authority, like the appointment of Asbury to office, further established the American conference's legislative competence, an irony given its manifest intent not to separate.

A fourth sentiment to be conveyed was to "guard against a separation from the church, directly or indirectly" by all means. This Asburian gathering undertook all the actions to forestall what they clearly anticipated, namely, a further declaration of independence at Fluvanna. Asbury so noted in his journal, "As we had great reason to fear that our brethren to the southward were in danger of separating from us, we wrote them a soft, healing epistle." The following week Asbury also wrote personally to John Dickins, Philip Gatch, Edward Dromgoole, and William Glendenning urging that "the preachers in the south" not separate.[6]

Asbury's fears draw our attention to the overt schism that unfolded, notwithstanding efforts to prevent it. We easily overlook the schismatic effect of actions taken by the conference around Asbury. They, too, made schism. They did so by convening illegally, by acting in the name of the conference, by appointing a president without regard to the existence of one, and by two further actions that their (later) published *Minutes* just somehow omitted: making provision for successors "in case of Br. Asburys Death or absence" and providing for their own subsequent meeting: "14th When and where Shall our next conference be held Ans. Whereas it is thought that without some Extraordinary change in affairs it will not be possible for all the Preachers to attend in Virginia let it be in the Baltimore Circuit the last Tuesday in April."[7]

The regularly called conference met as called at Fluvanna (Sources 1779), undeterred by the Asburian cabal and its actions. It suffered no unclarity about the Delaware conference's acts or intent. William Watters attended both. He apparently did not preside over the latter. Philip Gatch led, a position indicated by his standing first in several key listings. The Fluvanna conference carried on the business of the movement, examined its members, collected and disbursed collections, stationed the preachers, and attended to discipline. Then it recognized the Episcopal Establishment as dissolved, resolved, in effect, to become "dissenters," and ratified procedures by which a new church would be brought into being. The signatories to this act did not include Watters, whose sympathies lay, and subsequent allegiance would fall, with the group around Asbury.

The church Fluvanna established combined features of Wesleyanism, Presbyterianism, and Anglicanism. They added a dose of American freedom. A committee, created through election by the preachers, took the authority that had been vested in Wesley or his general assistant—legislative and administrative authority—including presumably Wesley's power to appoint. A presbytery, similarly constituted and composed of the same four individuals, enjoyed the right to administer the sacraments, the prerogative to ordain, and apparently the obligation to determine who else received sacramental ability. The preachers undertook these acts so as to provide for the sacraments of baptism and the Lord's Supper, a gesture constituting the new entity as dissenting from the Church of England. However, the rites themselves apparently would have had an Anglican feel, "after the Church order," but shortened, made extempore, and honoring individual conscience at key points (mode of baptism, kneeling in supper). The democratic character of this scheme, limited within the conference and to the preachers, consisted in the power to elect and the right of review—to judge whether, and obligation to follow if, "the said committee shall adhere to the Scriptures" (Sources 1779). Wesleyan, Presbyterian, Anglican, democratic, the Fluvanna conference opened a route that American Methodism would follow, albeit very slowly.

Moses and Aaron

The two conferences created, in effect, a northern party and a southern party, one still Anglican and seemingly awaiting Wesley's directions, the other refining its goals. Each claimed the promises. Each regarded itself as the sole holder of the covenant. Each operated on an illegal, irregular, or theologically suspect pretext. The Fluvanna conference, regularly appointed, convened, and conducted, had defied Wesleyan precept and its own commitments, had broken with the church, had ordained its members, and had rendered itself theologically problematic and ecclesiologically schismatic. It had made no effort to include any in the laying on of hands who might represent the wider church, longer tradition, apostolic witness, ecclesial succession, or Wesley personally. It accorded no place in its record for Asbury or any around him. The Delaware gathering (and it might be noted that both conferences occurred below the Mason-Dixon Line) honored Wesleyan precept and remained within the church but did so by usurpation. Who separated?

Winners write the history. Asbury and company did so later, claiming the Mosaic mantle, letting the fact of the 1779 Fluvanna conference stand in the *Minutes* but reducing its actions from thirty-one to eight and excising those that evidenced the independence. The next time around, the Asburian cabal played for keeps, reserving all legitimacy to itself. Its 1780 conference, in Baltimore at the new Lovely Lane Chapel, represented the "southern" conference only by a disciplinary action: "Quest. 20. Does this whole conference disapprove the step our brethren have taken in Virginia? Answ. Yes." And then, "Quest. 21. Do we look upon them no longer as Methodists in connection with Mr. Wesley and us till they come back? Answ. Agreed." Philip Gatch, the leader of the Fluvanna conference, along with Reuben Ellis, was present to hear the conditions, along with a more humbling set proposed by Asbury. However, the conference preferred to appoint its own deputation and agreed to send Asbury, Garrettson, and Watters to convey this action and the conditions of reinstatement—suspension of the sacraments and meeting together in Baltimore the following year. En route, Asbury continued to lobby those aligned with the other conferences whom he encountered, as he had done over the course of the year.[8]

Watters, one of the emissaries and the one with standing in both conferences, has left a poignant account of their mediation (Sources 1780a). They found "the Virginia Dissenters," as the "Leesburg Minutes" called them, or the "southern dissenting brethren," as Garrettson termed them, resolute in their course and willing to defend their ecclesial irregularities with classic Wesleyan reasoning—God blessed their sacramental celebrations. Providential argumentation did not sway Asbury. He pulled no punches: "I read Mr. Wesley's thoughts against a separation: showed my private letters of instructions from Mr. Wesley; set before them the sentiments of the Delaware and Baltimore conferences; read our epistles, and read my letter to brother Gatch, and Dickins's letter in answer." All accounts of the proceedings attested the pain and emotion that both the emissaries and the southerners felt over the separation(s) but also the intransigence of the latter. Eventually while Asbury, Garrettson, and Watters prayed and prepared to depart, the southerners capitulated, agreeing to reunite, suspend the sacraments, accept Asbury's itinerating general superintendency, and write Wesley "a circumstantial letter," as Garrettson termed it. Asbury curiously omitted reference to this latter critical condition.[9]

Wandering toward Prerogative?

Received opinion has it that the children of Israel waited for the commandments from Wesley, being, as Garrettson put it, "only a society...mostly united...to the

Church of England," wandered collectively until 1784, and then crossed the Jordan together, this time with Moses and Joshua, into the promised land of ecclesial self-sufficiency and independence. An alternative reading might be that colonial Methodists had been, Judges-like, drifting into independence from the very start and continued in such settling in the promised land through and beyond 1784.[10]

Such conniving at independence can be well illustrated, ironically, in the 1780 Asburian or northern conference. Its resolutions to "sit on the original plan" and its disfellowshiping of the separating "southern" brethren rightly stand out. However, that body took a number of legislative initiatives, some highly important, registering by its presumption of prerogative, a high measure of independence notwithstanding its effort to remain loyal to Wesley and the church.

Several of its actions proved too presumptuous to be (later) published. Question 2, for instance, reaffirmed Asbury as general assistant and asserted explicitly his possession of comparable power. "Does this conference," it asked, "acknowledge Francess Asbury as Mr. Wesley's representative to exercise the same pour [power] and travel in the same manner when circumstances will admit[?] Ansr yes." A later query indicated that Asbury had come forth with a plan for a Kingswood school. The conference specified plans for chapels, namely, on the octagon form, with separate seating for men and women and no tub pulpit "but a square projection and a long seat behind." It also affirmed Wesleyan and Pietist expectations that preachers model Christian practice—"preachers frain the use of Snuff, Drams, Chewing & Smoakg. Tobacco." Thus the American conference acted to provide for itself what the "Large Minutes" claimed for Wesley or the British conference.

It also legislated independently. Of particular note were its actions on slavery and African American membership, actions of such prophetic courage that when the church published the *Minutes* in 1794, it suppressed certain of the statements. The conference required "those travelling Preachers who hold slaves to give promises, to set them free." (And the Leesburg manuscript minutes continued with a condition obviously too embarrassing to later print—"*on pain of future exclusion.*") The 1780 conference further mandated that the preachers witness to the evils of slavery and hold the people accountable to free their slaves. A query, later suppressed, asked, "Who of our friends have freed their slaves?" and provided that "the Conference keep a register yearly of the names of the masters, slaves, and age." The conference specified the witness and its reasoning as follows:

> Does this conference acknowledge that slave-keeping is contrary to the laws of God, man, and nature, and hurtful to society; contrary to the dictates of conscience and pure religion, and doing that which we would not others should do to us and ours?—Do we pass our disapprobation on all our friends who keep slaves, and advise their freedom?
> Answ. Yes.

The manuscript minutes used the word *insist* rather than *advise* and concluded that question "Shall we read the minutes in every Society? and the thoughts of slave keeping, which was approved last Conference & tell the people, they must have but one year more, before we exclude them? Agreed." Lee later commented that the preachers "went too far in their censures" and their actions incited rather than convinced. He did not note the obvious, namely, these actions were taken by one side of the split movement and not the Virginia side.[11]

The conference balanced this remarkable commitment to antislavery with troubling concessions to racism. It specified that gatherings of African Americans should be presided over by a "helper" or "proper white person" and that "the Negroes" not be permitted "to stay late or meet by themselves." The preachers obviously did not foresee or desire the emergence of Black leadership beyond limited levels or imagine themselves and the laity trusting it. Methodists would live in this ambiguity. Asbury, for instance, reported the next year traveling with Harry Hosier (1750?–1806) but complained when Hosier refused to accompany him to Virginia and worried that Hosier might be "ruined" by the adulation of mixed congregations. Much appreciated by the preachers, Hosier became the most widely known Black lay preacher in the founding era. Born a slave in North Carolina, later sold to a Maryland farmer, gaining freedom after the Revolution, Hosier experienced a religious conversion and joined the Methodists, becoming one of the movement's first Black preachers. His sermon "The Barren Fig Tree," preached in Adam's Chapel, Fairfax County, Virginia, in May 1781, is one of the first recorded Methodist sermons preached by an African American. With Bishops Coke and Asbury and other preachers, "Black Harry," as he was called, traveled up and down the eastern seaboard (Sources 1784c). Known to his colleagues for his intelligence, remarkable recall, and most important, his inspired preaching, Hosier frequently accompanied the bishops on preaching tours in order to draw larger crowds.

White Methodists recognized that slavery was wrong but had great difficulty in seeing the way through to genuine equality and to the importance of permitting Black leadership to develop. Black Methodists would embrace and treasure the affirmation Methodists extended and the denunciation of slavery they offered but quickly found their growth in the faith and in the movement stymied, rebuffed, held back.[12]

Revival through Quarterly Meetings

Two other 1780 actions, foreshadowing other aspects of Methodist practice, deserve remark. One concerned family religion, specifying that the preachers, "if possible ... speak to every person one by one in the family where they lodge, before prayer, if time will permit; or give a family exhortation after reading a chapter [of the Bible]." This action encouraged the preachers to take advantage of the situation they and successors would face on the ever moving American frontier, namely, of bedding down for the night with people not initially in the Methodist fold. It also pointed ahead to close relations that would develop between preachers and those with whom they would stay regularly as circuits stabilized. It could not foresee the reciprocity in such relations, the caring for preachers by the Methodist faithful, including especially the older women, the "mothers in Israel," some of them widows, who mothered the young men in Methodist ministry.

A second action with half a century's worth of influence regulated the middle unit in Methodist organization, the quarterly conference or meeting, the terms being interchangeable.

> Quest. 18. Shall we recommend our quarterly meetings to be held on Saturdays and Sundays when convenient? Answ. Agreed.
> Quest. 19. Shall not the Friday following every quarter day, be appointed as a day of fasting? Answ. Agreed.

Already the Americans were making this business meeting of the circuit into festival. Its character and existence the Leesburg version of the minutes indicated, "May it not be recommended for to begin Quarterly meeting on Saturdays 12 oclock preaching, Exhortation, Prayer. Sunday Preaching, Exhortation. Mon. Lovefeast 9, Preaching & exhortation 11. Temporal Business to be done Saturday evening & Monday morning. Ansr. Agreed." Later in 1780, Thomas Ware described one such New Jersey event, noting its public character, the crowds, the number of preachers, the deep affections, the appeal to diverse peoples, and its ceremony, specifically, the centerpiece of this event, the love feast (Sources 1780b). Freeborn Garrettson reported another on the Delmarva Peninsula, also for late 1780, where he saw "the power of God in a wonderful manner" during "breaking bread" and crowds of 1,500 one day and "near 4000" the next for preaching. Asbury recorded one, at Barratt's Chapel, Delaware, the prior week, with a crowd of "between one and two thousand people." Prior to the emergence of camp meetings, the quarterly meeting served as Methodism's public event, sometimes attracted thousands, ingathered the Methodist tribe and its leadership, sequenced the movement's sacred ceremonies, and produced conversions.[13]

Indeed, despite disruption caused by the war, continued persecution, and the after-effects of internal discord, Jesse Lee reported "a gracious revival of religion in many places" for 1780, especially on the Eastern Shore of Maryland. Again, in 1781, he noted revival there and a "blessed revival of religion" in Virginia and parts of North Carolina. The engines of revival were the quarterly meetings, classes, family religion, and personal discipline of Methodism. And the results showed, despite the war turmoil, in the growth of the small movement: 1777—6,968; 1778—6,095 (partial count); 1779—8,577; 1780—8,504 (numbers affected by the schism); 1781—10,539; 1782—11,785; 1783—13,740.[14]

Crossing Jordan: Covenant and Connectionalism

Just before his 1780 conference, Asbury became a citizen of Delaware. Although no more invested in things political, he had committed himself to the American preachers and they to him. The next year the conference met at Choptank in Delaware on April 16 and "adjourned to Baltimore the 24th of said month." The two sessions were "considered but one conference," as Lee put it. For precedent the *Minutes* cited Wesley's holding of an Irish conference. Thus began the "Baltimore system" of governance, multiple conference sessions whose final legislative word came from its Baltimore meeting, represented by a single set of *Minutes*. This strange pattern continued until 1787. It reflected some appreciation for the convenience of multiple conferences experienced during the division, the necessity within a far-flung movement of providing both access and unity, and the clear prominence of Baltimore as Methodism's capital. It unified the movement and unified legislation and decision making in conference.[15]

The arrangement of multiple conferences acting in concert anticipated the creation of the annual conference as the basic body of American Methodism but actually pointed to an underlying and even more fundamental reality. Conferences served the convenience of an undivided connection of preachers.

> To this day, according to the language of the *Discipline*, a preacher was "admitted on trial," not into a particular annual conference, but "into the traveling connection." The annual conferences arose from subdivisions of the church, its territory, and its one body of ministers, who formed one connection. The church did not arise from the amalgamation of annual conferences. The annual conference is thus a unit of administration, created first by the superintendents for their convenience and that of the preachers, and later by the authority of the General Conference. This unit of administration is territorial, for, within its prescribed boundaries, every annual conference, great or small, exercises precisely the same powers, under the same rules and regulations.[16]

The connection, never adequately defined or explained, became for Americans as for the British the fundamental ecclesial reality, awkwardly attested by this Baltimore system of governance. American Methodism came into being very unlike the emerging political entity and unlike some of its denominational competitors. It emerged not from the compact of competent parts—congregations or other local entities—but from the missional actions of "the Preachers in Connection."[17]

Appropriately the first action in 1781 reuniting the movement also established the disciplinary and doctrinal standards of an emerging American connection as those of Wesleyanism: "How many of our preachers are now determined after mature consideration, close observation and earnest prayer to preach the old Methodist doctrine, and strictly enforce the discipline, as contained in the notes, sermons, and minutes published by Mr. Wesley?"

The "Leesburg Minutes" made the stipulations clearer: "as contained in the notes of New Testament, and four Volumes of Sermons, and . . . Set forth in the Original minutes of conference." Thirty-nine names follow in the published *Minutes*, an additional five in the Leesburg version, neither, ominously, including that of James O'Kelly, who was apparently not present. Others present, Lee implied, refused to disavow the separation or the authority under which subscription occurred or the suspension of the sacraments. Rather more of the spirit and style of Fluvanna carried over than authorities surmised. Later in the year Asbury encountered holdouts, particularly among Virginia local preachers who remained eager for the ordinances. Searching for resources to deal with the "spreading fire of division," Asbury began reading and marking Richard Baxter's *Cure for Church Divisions* for possible abridgement. The 1781 conference also established a three-month probation period for members and two-year probation for preachers. It specified a program of study for preachers, namely, Wesley's "Rules," "Character of a Methodist," and "Plain Account of Christian Perfection," anticipating the Course of Study established in 1816.[18]

Tensions in Canaan

By prescribing the Wesleyan standards, by pledging to "preach the old Methodist doctrine, and strictly enforce the discipline," American Methodism thus charted its way toward independence establishing by its own acts the authority of Wesleyan practice. Included within that practice was respect for ordination and the Anglican sacramental system, respect represented by their pledge not to separate. How, though, if they rejected the radical autonomy of Fluvanna, would they assure ordination and have access to sacraments? Would they continue as a reform under some Americanized Anglicanism? The Americans gestured toward continuing relations in a remarkable 1782 minuted tribute to Devereux Jarratt:

> The Conference acknowledge their obligations to the Rev. Mr. Jarratt, for his kind and friendly services to the preachers and people, from our first entrance into Virginia, and more particularly for attending our conference in Sussex, in public and private; and advise the Preachers in the South to consult him and take his advice in the absence of brother Asbury.[19]

But they could count on two hands the other priests whose support made continuing relations thinkable: Samuel Magaw (Philadelphia), Charles Pettigrew (North Carolina), Samuel Auchmuty and John Ogilvie (both New York), and Uzal Ogden (New Jersey). By explicit request as well as by precipitative action and restiveness, Wesley's correspondents made him aware of their desire for a better solution. Asbury wrote Wesley repeatedly in the 1780s with updates on events and pleas for some plan for or some conveyance of ordination.[20]

Meanwhile, the Americans moved ahead, defining their future, continuing the curious combination of loyalty to Wesleyan substance but independence of Wesley's control. This tightrope they walked skillfully with legislation at the 1783 conference, specifying "How shall we behave toward European preachers—should any come?" And the answer: "if they are recommended by Mr. Wesley will be subject to the American Conference and keep the circuit they are appointed to and follow the directions of the London and American minutes we will receve them ether as assistants or helpers."

Certification by Wesley but adherence to American authority, allegiance to *both* minutes—that formula proved skillfully drawn. Wesley wrote Jesse Lee and the conference later that year directing similarly that the Americans not receive any preachers "who will not be subject to the American Conference, and cheerfully conform to the Minutes both of the English and American Conferences" and "who make any difficulty of receiving Francis Asbury as the General Assistant." Asbury read and transformed Wesley's nuanced statement about subjection to conference and recognition of his (Asbury's) authority into a warrant for authoritarianism: "I received a letter from Mr. Wesley, in which he directs me to act as general assistant; and to receive no preachers from Europe that are not recommended by him, nor any in America, who will not submit to me, and to the minutes of the conference." Asbury's attitude doubtless had something to do with an attempted coup against him, led by his British compatriot, William Glendenning, "who had been devising a plan," said Asbury, "to lay me aside, or at least to abridge my powers." Wesley's letter, Asbury continued, "settled the point." Americanization, if that be the appropriate term to describe the localization of Methodism, would inspire quite different impulses—some toward wider and wider franchise, others toward great concentration of power.[21]

Driving the indigenization were remarkable successes and growth, 13,740 in the society and thirty-five circuits by 1783, requiring, decreed conference, *two* days of Thanksgiving "for our public peace, temporal and spiritual prosperity, and for the glorious work of God." Peace, prosperity, and providence made it possible for Methodists to provide better for the Methodist family and to hold themselves to higher standards. The *Minutes* draw attention to Methodist women, specifically to the spouses of itinerants, naming eleven individually, who were to be provided for annually with twenty pounds, the monies *apportioned* to fifteen districts, apparently according to resources and numbers. Baltimore would deliver as much as Pennsylvania and the Jerseys, thirty pounds, with lesser amounts expected elsewhere. Apportionment had detractors at its inception. Lee noted that the innovation was opposed by "some of the leading men in particular circuits." He defended it with a connectional insight: "[T]he Methodist cause is but one in every place." This conference also legislated against "spirituous liquors," obliging preachers to teach against imbibing "by precept and example." It dealt again with the matter of slavery and with legislation, indicating that precept and example were required there as well: "What shall be done with our local Preachers who hold slaves.... We will try them another year." Would the Methodists stand by their convictions on race? Could Methodists convert both slaves and slaveholders into shared understandings and expectations about liberty? Could revival and race be held together? Would Methodists indigenize without accommodating? What complexion would an American Methodism assume?[22]

Transferring the Mantle (Ordinations and Order)?

As American political independence from Britain loomed, John Wesley busied himself working for some solution to the oft-repeated American Methodist requests. The signing of the Peace of Paris and recognition of the United States prompted action. Wesley's gradual appreciation of his stature as a scriptural bishop, of his right to ordain, and of the precedents and exigencies under which elders might exercise such powers belongs to other accounts, including his own (Sources 1784a). He had exhausted the obvious—Robert Lowth, bishop of London, who had responsibility for the religious order of the colonies, rebuffed requests for regular ordinations. He had been given detailed, thoughtful plans for a reformed church by trusted lieutenants, notably Joseph Benson and John Fletcher. He had seen Lady Huntingdon's connection take ordinations into their own hands. He had long been aware of authorities, including Lord Peter King, Bishop Edward Stillingfleet, dissenter Edmund Calamy, and Bishop Benjamin Hoadly, who cited instances of ordination by presbyters (elders) and argued that presbyters and bishops belonged to the same order. Wesley put to work on the case his new assistant and troubleshooter, Thomas Coke (1747–1814), who had earned a law degree and taken orders in the Church of England before affiliating with the Methodists.[23]

Coke and Wesley carried on an extended discussion of how to effect ordinations for America, some of it by letter. In April 1784, Coke volunteered to serve as a deputy, outlining three reasons: to gather for Wesley "fuller Information concerning the State of the Country," to ensure "a Cement of Union remaining after yr. [your] Death between the Societies of Preachers in the two Countries," and to equip himself for appropriate oversight following Wesley's death. By August having gained two compatriots for America, Richard Whatcoat (1736–1806) and Thomas Vasey (c. 1746–1826), Coke understood that the deputation included his own ordination, that it involved some continued oversight of the American movement, and that others than he and Wesley were worrying over the appropriate way of transmitting ordination and authority across the Atlantic:

> Honoured and dear Sir,
>
> The more maturely I consider the subject, the more expedient it seems to me that the power of ordaining others should be received by me from you, by the imposition of your hands; and that you should lay hands on Brother Whatcoat and Brother Vasey, for the following reasons:—1. It seems to me the most scriptural way, and most agreeable to the

practice of the primitive churches. 2. I may want all the influence in America which you can throw into my scale. Mr. Brackenbury informed me at Leeds that he saw a letter in London from Mr. Asbury, in which he observed "that he should not receive any person deputed by you to take any part of the superintendency of the work invested in him," —or words that implied so much.[24]

On September 1 and 2, despite opposition from virtually all others in his inner circle of counselors and without his brother's knowledge, Wesley, with the assistance of James Creighton, a clerical associate from Ireland, ordained Whatcoat and Vasey as deacons, the following day as elders, and Coke as a "Superintendent."

In solving one problem, Wesley had created others, innocently enumerating them in Coke's "Certificate of Ordination." The first, long agonized over but to continue to haunt American Methodists to the present, was his (Wesley's) authority to ordain and the legitimacy therefore of all subsequent ordinations. Wesley addressed that by speaking of being "providentially called at this time to set apart some persons for the work of the ministry in America." A second, also embedded in this rationale, inhered as well in the commendation of Coke "as a fit person to preside over the Flock of Christ." What was to be the relation of these newly ordained Britishers to the newly independent Americans and specifically of Coke to Asbury? The third and fourth problems nestled in Wesley's statement of the case:

> Whereas many of the People in the Southern Provinces of North America who desire to continue under my care, and still adhere to the Doctrines and Discipline of the Church of England, are greatly distressed for want of Ministers to administer the Sacraments of Baptism and the Lord's Supper according to the usage of the same Church...

Third, did the Americans indeed desire to continue under his care? What would be the continuing relation between the American and the British conferences and between the Americans and Wesley? Fourth, what kind of church did Wesley intend for the Americans? What did he mean by adhering "to the Doctrines and Discipline of the Church of England"? Was he recognizing, as it were, an American "Church of England"? And what should be its relation to other efforts to reconstitute Anglicanism for America?[25] Fifth, why the curious term "superintendent," why not "bishop," and why if merely "superintendent" the necessity of "ordination"? Finally, did the use of "ordination," consistently employed, square with Wesley's and Coke's notion that superintendents remained elders, that superintendency was an office, not an order?

At Full Liberty to Follow the Scriptures and the Primitive Church

The same issues can be discerned in Wesley's letter to "Our Brethren in North-America" (Sources 1784a), the second starkly in Wesley's identification of "Dr. Coke and Mr. Francis Asbury, to be joint *Superintendents* over our Brethren in North-America" and the others notwithstanding Wesley's exhortation to be "at full liberty, simply to follow the Scriptures and the Primitive Church." Wesley did not intend by "full liberty" to remove himself from the determination of how and under whose local leadership Americans might "follow the Scriptures and the Primitive Church." Nor did Wesley resolve the matter of the identity and relations of the proposed religious establishment by his provision of a "little Sketch" for a reformed church (Sources 1784a), including a revised Book of Common Prayer (BCP) titled *The Sunday Service for the Methodists in North America*, a reduced version of the Thirty-nine Articles of Religion (to twenty-four by Wesley), and a hymnbook, *A Collection of Psalms and Hymns for the Lord's Day*. Revision to the BCP had been something of a post-Restoration Anglican pastime and alterations to the Articles very much in keeping with the church's latitudinarian temper. Even the continuation of the Methodist theological norms of Wesley's *Sermons* and *Notes* belongs, as Richard Heitzenrater has observed, to the boundary-setting tradition of the Anglican Book of Homilies. What have been read as provisions for radical independence might well be seen as appropriate intra-Anglican adjustments for the new political realities of the American scene. Indeed, as Heitzenrater notes, Wesley had provided and refined the resources that defined the Church of England—BCP (*Sunday Service* and hymnbook), Articles, and Homilies (*Sermons* and *Notes*).[26]

Preparing himself to address these issues or problems, Coke read and reflected further while on shipboard (Sources 1784b). He could scarcely have imagined the practical, rough-and-ready, colonial resolutions that Asbury had concocted and would concoct. They met in mid-November at a quarterly meeting at Barratt's Chapel, Delaware, since 1968 a UMC Heritage Landmark and center. Their encounter began a long-term struggle for control of the American movement, a personal struggle but also a corporate struggle over the issues inherited from Wesley—the nature of the American connection, its ecclesial self-understanding, the character and powers of episcopacy, the sources of legitimacy, relations with Wesley, and the appropriate posture toward the emerging Episcopal Church. Intensifying its personal and ecclesial tensions, the Asbury-Coke relation reverberated with the inchoate impulses now termed *postcolonial*. However, unlike many later colonized situations, including many, if not most, Methodist missions, the Americans had embraced and been embraced by a missionary turned native. Under Asbury, the Americans achieved rapid indigenization—a very short, minimally intrusive, postcolonial direction from abroad.

The scenario for Methodist postcolonial politics unfolded at Barratt's Chapel (Sources 1784b). Coke had Anglican orders and was well educated. He enjoyed standing as confidant to Wesley. He had been personally ordained by Wesley. He possessed the design and documents for an American church. He doubtless expected, as indicated in comments to John Dickins, in his initial take-charge behavior at Barratt's Chapel, and in his private disclosure of plans to Asbury, simply to announce the new order and ordain Asbury into it.[27] At most, Asbury would respectfully "be consulted in respect to every part of the execution of it" (Sources 1784b, p. 75). Asbury countered with precedent-setting gestures. First, he transformed a quarterly meeting into a deliberative council or conference, fifteen sitting "in Conference," according to Garrettson. Second, to this body he referred Coke's disclosure, effectively transforming pronouncements into proposals. Third, he engineered the decision to convene a conference of all the traveling preachers, appointing Garrettson to travel to issue the call. Fourth, he conveyed to the gathering of preachers the selection of the superintendents, indicating his willingness to serve "if the preachers unanimously choose me." He continued, "I shall not act in the capacity I have hitherto done by Mr. Wesley's appointment." One of the remarkable letters by Adam Fonerden, a Baltimore layperson, described the whole plan, including the service of the three Wesley ordinands, as "left to our choice,"[28] implicitly making the selection of Coke as well as Asbury up to the impending conference.

These maneuvers have sometimes been read as Asbury's commitment to American, republican, or democratic principles. To be sure, they logically followed from the five war years' practice of making policy in conference and by consensus. They had several times been anticipated by conference's recognition of Asbury's presidency. And they paralleled constitutional developments simultaneously unfolding in Britain. However, they probably had as much or more to do with the hand that Coke held and what would be required to beat it. Asbury trumped Coke by empowering conference, surrendering some of what had been Wesley's prerogative—and might have been his as superintendent—to the plenary of preachers.

The first *Discipline* by its title pointed back to Wesley's power to convene whom he would, to pose the questions, to answer them, to keep the record, and to structure it into constitution-like form (the "Large Minutes"): *Minutes of Several Conversations between The Rev. Thomas Coke, LL.D. The Rev. Francis Asbury and Others . . . Composing a Form of Discipline* (Sources 1785a). That first Discipline quaintly recalled Wesley's authority. It was the last to do so. Barratt's Chapel pointed ahead to more modest episcopal roles in conference. Barratt's Chapel also determined who would retain the lion's share of what remained of Wesley's authority. That determination was symbolized in a fifth of Asbury's gestures—one more expressive of his style and self-understanding. Asbury presumed, notwithstanding Coke's credentials and sole title then as superintendent, on his right to appoint Coke to ride and sent Coke on a circuit of eight hundred or one thousand miles. For a companion on that trip Asbury sent—and the qualifiers Coke employed disclose much about the limits of Methodist egalitarianism—"his black (Harry [Hosier] by name)" (Sources 1784c).[29]

Preparations for a Christmas Conference

Coke indicated (Sources 1784b) that he and Asbury agreed to establish a school modeled after Wesley's Kingswood academy. To scout a possible site, Coke met Asbury on

December 14 at Abingdon, Maryland (the future site of Cokesbury College and an official UMC Heritage Landmark). From there they traveled to Perry Hall, the residence
of Harry Dorsey Gough, an important way station then and thereafter for Methodist
preachers and another historic site. At Perry Hall, the three ordained Britishers, their
former compatriot, Asbury, and *no* native-born Americans completed the transformation of Wesley's pronouncements into proposals. Preparing the agenda for the Christmas
Conference, they worked especially on altering the "Large Minutes." Richard, later
bishop, Whatcoat reported:

> December 19th, I preached in Hunt's chapel and rode to Mr. Henry Gough's; spent the
> evening with Dr. Coke, Mr. Asbury, and brother Vasey, in great peace. Twentieth, my
> rheumatism returned; we began to prepare for our conference, and to consider some of
> our rules and minutes, as necessary to the helping forward the Lord's work in our con-
> nection, with great deliberation and impartiality, in the fear of God, may we hope to the
> end—21st, we went through some more of our minutes—22d and 23d, we continued in
> the same exercise—24th, we rode to Baltimore.[30]

They rode carrying British designs for an American church—Wesley's "Letter," their
recension of his "Large Minutes," the revised Articles, the *Sunday Service,* the hymnbook, their ordination certificates, and doubtless also Wesley's *Sermons* and *Notes.*

Advantage Coke? Had Perry Hall assured the Americans of a neocolonial rather than
a postcolonial (Barratt's Chapel) future? Had Perry Hall nullified Asbury's cleverness at
Barratt's Chapel? Did the British-dominated ride from Perry Hall to Baltimore undo the
long ride from Barratt's Chapel upon which Asbury had sent Coke? To Asbury, outnumbered three to one on that ride to Baltimore, it may have so seemed. And the
Christmas Conference, though it shifted the odds in Asbury's favor, would not fully decide the contest. Longer term, Barratt's Chapel determined the church that the Americans would build. The designs that Coke brought from Wesley and polished at Perry
Hall proved indispensable. However, the foundations had been well laid by Asbury and
the colonists. Only what those colonial Pietist foundations undergirded would stand.
After these first encounters of Coke and Asbury, the latter had the winning hand. Coke
might have the blueprints, but Asbury had the foremen and workers. The church they
made would be his.

CHAPTER IV

CONSTITUTING METHODISMS: 1784–92

Beginning with the Christmas Conference of 1784 and for the next decade, the Methodist Pietist movements wrestled with the ambiguities inherited from Wesley, with others of their own making, with implications of American independence, with their relations to one another, and with problems of growth. Their resolutions, often hurried, tentative, and partial, produced formal, denominationally constitutive documents, most notably for The Methodist Episcopal Church (Sources 1785a). The denomination-in-formation, the United Brethren (Sources 1785b and sidebar in chapter 1), came to key preparatory formulations. The African Methodist Episcopal Church (Sources 1794) and The Evangelical Association (Sources 1791b) point back into this revolutionary decade to dramatic defining experiences. Methodist preaching of liberty yielded minimal gains for women, but they did succeed in solidifying important nonpublic roles (Sources 1785c, 1787).

Constitution making sharpened identities, forced choices, demanded compromises. Methodist (MEC) decisions on matters of race, ethnicity, language, prerogative, and franchise influenced, if they did not cause, the emergence of the other Pietist denominations—UB, AME, EA. The MEC also came, albeit strangely and awkwardly, to clarify its relation with the emerging Episcopal Church (Sources 1791a). And the MEC suffered a major denominational schism, that with the Republican Methodists (Sources 1792a). The latter came as a cost of the MEC's solution of acute governance problems, achieved through experimentation with a council and the eventual establishment of a General Conference.

1784 and All That

We then rode to Baltimore, where we met a few preachers: it was agreed to form ourselves into an Episcopal Church, and to have superintendents, elders, and deacons. When the conference was seated, Dr. Coke and myself were unanimously elected to the superintendency of the Church, and my ordination followed, after being previously ordained deacon and elder.[1]

Asbury's breathless account of the Christmas Conference, which met at Lovely Lane Chapel and Otterbein's new brick church,[2] Baltimore, and similarly terse ones from other participants (see Coke's in Sources 1784b) provide us what little we know of the actual event. It left the record of its labors in the first *Discipline* (Sources 1785a and sidebar in chapter 1) and 1785 *Minutes*. Key details—for instance, Asbury's insistence that both he and Coke be elected; the exact membership, including whether African Americans, Harry Hosier (Sources 1784c) and Richard Allen, were present; the origin of the church's new name, reportedly suggested by John Dickins; how business was done—emerge from the informal accounts.[3]

Jesse Lee termed the gathering a general conference, yet numbered it among the succession of annual conferences as thirteenth, neither designation being appropriate. It was not the year's conference or the antecedent to the first General Conference of 1792. Rather it functioned as a constitutional convention, irregularly called by the Barratt's Chapel quarterly conference, a clever maneuver on Asbury's part. By his insistence on the calling of a conference and on its consent by election of both superintendents, Asbury balanced the willed consent of the collectivity of American preachers against Wesley's provision for ecclesial order, his selection of the two superintendents, and his close connection to and actual hands on Coke. Strangely, the Christmas Conference did not capitalize on the precedent by treating its own sitting, or for that matter the right of any conference to sit, or the provision for decision making by debate and majority rule. Strictly speaking, conference was not provided for in the *Discipline*. Its existence was assumed, implicit in the delineation of its annual tasks and rights of election. Conference's nature and authority neither Asbury nor Coke nor the assembled preachers thought it appropriate or necessary to specify by statute. Modest little details, constitutional niceties, with respect to conference—composition, call, powers, presidency—the Christmas Conference did not treat.[4]

Or perhaps we should say that its one clear action with respect to such issues, among its first and most disastrous, seemingly undid Asbury's cleverness, the prior decade's precedent of American conference autonomy, and the premise of its own assembling. It conceded final authority to Wesley: "During the life of Rev. Mr. Wesley, we acknowledge ourselves his Sons in the Gospel, ready in Matters belonging to Church-Government, to obey his Commands" (Sources 1785a). This rubric, soon to be struck, accorded with Wesley's clear anticipation that independence did not mean independence but some real and continuing control on his part, including the right to call conference, to designate superintendents, and to make other key appointments.[5]

The most obvious reason for the Christmas Conference's strange concessions and constitutional oversights derived from its procedure. Setting a precedent that extends to the present, it worked by revising its minutes, in this instance, the 1780 recension of Wesley's "Large Minutes," composing in so doing what it initially subtitled and eventually termed "A Form of Discipline." The procedure and product preserved the ambiguous relation to Wesley. The "Large Minutes" were, after all, his, and he may well have made many of the modest additions and somewhat more extensive omissions. The conference preserved Wesley's question/answer format, precise wording of all but a few of those formulations, and their seemingly haphazard ordering. On the other hand, it presumed on its right to approve, to alter, to add to, and to subtract from what had been Wesley's document and what had been revised at Perry Hall. The conference presumed also to add a rubric on United States political autonomy to the Articles and to remove the descent into hell from the Creed. Asbury noted that the conference determined "all things by a majority of votes." Some have wondered and still wonder whether Methodism does its best thinking by ballot and under time pressure. Asbury's explanation doubtless still stands: "We were in great haste, and did much business in a little time."[6]

Its business (Sources 1784b, 1784c, 1785a) included

- transformation of the "Large Minutes" of Wesley's gatherings into a constitution-like *Discipline* for a denomination;
- proclamation that the church would be episcopal and naming of it as Methodist Episcopal;
- acceptance of the threefold ministry of superintendents (bishops), elders, and deacons;
- provisions for election of superintendents by and for their accountability to conference;
- selection of elders (thirteen or so) and effective creation of an office with sacramental and supervisory roles, the presiding elder (today's district superintendent);
- acceptance of Wesley's plan for the church, in principle if not in every detail, including his prepared liturgy, hymnbook, and revised Articles of Religion;
- acceptance of Wesley's disciplinary expectations, guidelines for admission into society, and rules for the exercise of ministries;
- prohibition of "Ministers or Travelling-Preachers" drinking "spirituous Liquors";
- courageous and extensive legislation against slavery, including the mandate that all Methodists, laity as well as preachers, emancipate their slaves (Sources 1785a, Q. 42–43);
- provision for white oversight of African American gatherings;
- acceptance of the proposal of a college and its naming for the two superintendents;
- rules for the administration of the sacraments but none for confirmation;[7]
- setting of a common salary for elders, deacons, and helpers of twenty-four pounds (Pennsylvania currency);
- rules concerning marriage outside the faith and for conflict resolution for both people and preachers;

- appointment of missionaries for Nova Scotia (Freeborn Garrettson and James O. Cromwell);
- and conversion of Wesley's connectional purpose from ecclesial into spatial, that is, continental terms (Sources 1785a, Q. 4).[8]

By these several accomplishments, American Methodism appropriated the distinctives of the Wesleyan reform and linked itself with the core beliefs and polity of the church catholic, Wesley's *Sermons* lurking in the background as both the statement of its own convictions and a Wesleyan interpretation of "catholic" standards.

Coke preached ordination sermons and ordained Asbury on successive days deacon, elder, and superintendent (and all references employed "ordain" for the latter office). Preaching at Asbury's ordination as superintendent, Coke made the historic case for the legitimacy of the act and an explicit case for the episcopal character of the office by delineating ten "grand characteristics of a Christian bishop." At Asbury's request, William Otterbein participated in the laying on of hands for the episcopal ordination, a fact noted by Coke (Sources 1784b) but curiously omitted from Asbury's ordination certificate, which read:

> I, Thomas Coke, Doctor of Civil Law; late of Jesus College, in the University of Oxford, Presbyter of the Church of England, and Superintendent of the Methodist Episcopal Church in America ... by the imposition of my hands, and prayer, (being assisted by two ordained elders).

Equally curious, Coke warranted the ordination on his Anglican credentials, omitting explicit reference to Wesley. What relation Methodism would strike with the other remnant of Anglicanism in the United States and what it meant by its middle name remained unclear.[9]

Otterbein: Baltimore and Environs

Equally unclear was the relation between William Otterbein's Evangelical Reformed Church of Baltimore (Sources 1785b) and the German Reformed Pennsylvania Coetus (synod or conference). Both the church and its pastor enjoyed some affiliation with the Coetus. Otterbein rejected the Baltimore church's first call in deference to the Coetus, which did not view his going there as the most appropriate resolution of conflict within the congregation. Otterbein changed his mind, partially influenced by encouragement from Asbury, with whom he had become acquainted the prior year, and settled in Baltimore in May 1774. A year later, his ministry, based there and lasting for thirty-nine years until his death in November 1813, was blessed by the Coetus. Neither pastor nor congregation, however, viewed the German Reformed relation as one of ownership or control. And Otterbein continued in Baltimore the wider itinerations, care for outlying German communities, and nurture of persons into ministry that made him as much a competitor to as agent of the Coetus. One vehicle for his oversight was a semiannual gathering of preachers that met initially at Pipe Creek, Maryland. These conferences, begun the same month Otterbein settled in Baltimore, in May 1774, and providing mutual counsel for the various classes ministered to by the six attending preachers and some eighteen class leaders, continued at least through 1777. Acting as first host and as secretary of this body that called itself the "United Ministers" was Benjamin Schwope, Otterbein's predecessor in Baltimore, advocate of his coming there and co-laborer in later revival and organization. At the October 1777 and perhaps last conference, Asbury and Shadford spoke.[10] This same year, the Mennonites expelled Martin Boehm for preaching false doctrine, engaging in irregular practices, and fraternizing with other religious communities—including Methodists! Increasingly, Boehm partnered with Otterbein in leading the new evangelical party developing among German pastors and people.

The Baltimore church prospered under Otterbein's leadership, growing steadily in membership. To accommodate such growth, it erected in 1785 a brick and stone building, now the oldest in Baltimore, a UMC Heritage Landmark known as Old Otterbein. On the first of the same year, congregation and pastor signed a denomination-creating covenant: the Constitution and Ordinances of the Evangelical Reformed Church of Baltimore (Sources 1785b). What made the constitution "denomination-creating," Otterbein the effective leader of a movement, and this congregation its center? The congregation made provision in articles 12–16 for "fraternal unity" among preachers and "churches in Pennsylvania, Maryland, and Virginia," which recognized "the superintendence of William Otterbein" and accepted this congregation's rules, practices, doctrine, and order. And they differentiated this movement from the German Reformed as a whole by explicit repudiation of the hallmark Reformed doctrines of predestination and irresistible grace (article 13). The constitution stipulated that congregations be divided, by gender, into class meetings or "special meetings," the *collegia pietatis*, which would maintain order, exercise oversight, discipline members, encourage growth in the faith, and in which members would pray and sing together. Their mandated character and agenda—"to flee the wrath to come"—suggests some Wesleyan influence, as does the rule for ecumenically open Communion. The strongly Reformed tenor remains, however, reflected in the Calvinist ministerial order, government by vestry, doctrine of scriptural authority, and covenantal theology—including the act of covenanting to constitute the church and produce a constitution.

A church order created by covenanting differs from one generated by appointing. It differs in its adhesive principle and typically, therefore, in the power lodged at the center and the control the center can have over the parts. Not surprisingly, the movement around Otterbein and that around Asbury stumbled in several efforts at unity, largely over differences in discipline (and language), despite close relations between the two leaders, Otterbein and Asbury. Also not surprisingly, the covenantal basis for unity made it possible for the Otterbein movement to find common ground with Pietists from quite different confessional backgrounds. Just such a confessionally diverse group Otterbein succeeded in convening in 1789 at Baltimore. That gathering and another at York in 1791 figure in United Brethren memory as preparatory events (sidebar in chapter 1). Later recollections placed in these conferences ten preachers of the Reformed tradition, six from the Mennonites, one from the Moravians, and one from the Amish, three of the group ordained. The official narrative also claimed Lutheran adherents. The listing of names, placing first William Otterbein and Martin Boehm, indicated leadership and its nature. The two were first among equals, a fraternal rather than hierarchical basis for unity. Four others are named who would be prominent as their successors in the move-ment—George Adam Guething, John Neidig, Christian Newcomer, and John G. Pfrim-mer. Theirs would be a fellowship of revivalists, a covenant grounded in a shared piety, whose unity would have to be hammered out theologically and structurally (Sources 1785b and sidebar in chapter 1).[11] At this stage, the "United Ministers" agreed to rec-ognize each other's ordinations, to preach in homes or barns in their neighborhoods in addition to their resident pastorates, to hold quarterly meetings in regions, and to gather at an annual conference for mutual support, theological education, and missional strategizing.

Praying in the New Order: Gender and Gentility

The power of piety and of American practice to shape community became obvious in reaction to one of the MEC Christmas Conference's commitments. Lee conceded with respect to Wesley's liturgy that initially societies in "the large towns, and in some coun-try places" read the Sunday service and morning prayers (Sources 1784b for January 22–February 6). However, he continued, after "a few years the prayer book was laid aside, and has never been used since in public worship." The preachers, he explained, were "fully satisfied that they could pray better, and with more devotion with their eyes shut, than they could with their eyes open."[12] Unfortunately, when the Lees shut their eyes, they rather lost sight of much of what was happening in Methodism, including partic-ularly what the women did through prayer, even in sensitive areas like family and race relations.

The power of prayer and its governing role in the overall Methodist impulse emerge in the diary of Elizabeth McKean of St. George's, Philadelphia (Sources 1785c), and also that of Jacob Albright (Sources 1791b). McKean moved upward in cycles from the joys of private prayer, through the scrutiny of class and recognition of her sinfulness, to the provisioning in sacrament, and by preaching, to intercessory roles on behalf of her sisters and mother, only to begin again, calendaring her spiritual progress and evangelistic outreach by Methodist rhythms and through lavish use of the Wesleyan means of grace. She and countless "sisters" bore along the gracious Methodist impulse on the class and society level in efforts uncaptured by the recollections of a Lee or the year-end summations for conference. Women held the office of class leader only briefly and sporadically, but they used the class relations, family networks, and the home contexts for evangelization and nurture. Such efforts yielded converts particularly within their own families and homes. One such came through a servant of her socially prominent mistress, Catherine Livingston, of that New York politically and socially elite family. Livingston compounded the disgrace to her family of conversion and association with the Methodists by later showing the singularly poor taste of falling in love with and marrying a Methodist itinerant, Freeborn Garrettson. She described her conversion (Sources 1787) and religious pilgrimage in the Pietist pattern, a pattern made prototypical for Methodists with the frequent publication of the Wesley convert's narrative, *Account of the Experience of Mrs. Hester Ann Rogers*, printed in England in 1796 and reprinted "by John C. Totten for the Methodist Episcopal Church, and sold by Ezekiel Cooper" in 1804.[13]

McKean, Livingston, and Rogers employed Pietist language to map their inner state, the spiritual highs and lows through which they moved to conversion (and eventually to sanctification). They measured progress in Pietist terms by their ability to discipline the outer by the inner, by their daily walk, by their fashion. And Pietists generally and Wesley in particular imaged the holy path by tracing with some vividness the alternative, worldly path to destruction. The latter path the McKeans, Livingstons, and Rogerses described vividly—trifling, lukewarm, dull, frivolous—and knew well—balls, cards, polluted enjoyments, public amusements, "hurry, fashion and company." The worldly foil for true religion these women knew because they lived it prior to their conversion—gentility, the genteel life, the code of honor. Against gentility and its practices Methodists preached. And the *Discipline*, following Wesley, explicitly proscribed gentility by identifying its behavior and dress (Q. 18 in Sources 1785a but also Q.s 15, 24, 51, 61, 66). To renounce it when all things were "become new," as did Livingston (Sources 1787), was an act of social and familial defiance. It meant disavowing family, friends, culture, practices, and lifestyle and in turn being renounced by all that she knew and all whom she knew.[14]

Liberty

For the social elite, particularly women, who turned to Methodism, conversion proved personally transformative and socially revolutionary. They made sense of their dislocation with the "liberty" language of the new republic. The language of liberty and the repudiation of gentility had quite as revolutionary import at the other end of the social spectrum. Slaves, free Black Americans, and poor whites heard the demonization of gentility as promising release from precisely the class who oppressed and exploited them. Slaves and free Black Americans responded to Methodism's inversion of the world's values, with the full range of emotions, as early itinerants like Philip Bruce reported (Sources 1788). Black Americans heard and accepted the liberating word often in mixed contexts, prompting interesting reactions by whites, as William Colbert recorded in 1790 "at friend Scrivinors" on the Calvert Circuit: "the blacks behind began to shout aloud jump and fall—the whites to look wild and go off." He expressed sorrow "that prejudice moved so many to day. A young woman among them that went off said that she would come no more, and that she believed I should kill myself."[15]

Many whites, like this young woman, reacted angrily, sometimes violently to the Colberts and Garrettsons who embraced Black Americans and preached against slavery.[16] Others, those of the middling sort, embraced Methodism's transvaluation of values, for instance, a woman who lectured the preachers at another Christmas conference, in 1791 at Lane's Chapel, Virginia, where both Asbury and James O'Kelly preached powerful sermons. She interrupted Communion, reported James Meacham, with fifty preachers surrounding the Lord's Table:

> In this time a precious dear woman, sister Whitehead, rose up and begged the preachers to excuse her, she was weak and a poor woman, but she was awfully impressed with grief and that was almost more than she could bear up under. She said when she turned her eyes upon the young sisters and saw them catching after the modes of fashions of the wicked world that ought to be examples of the flock. Numbers looking at them and justifying themselves by such and such preachers and something else with. They would stand in the pulpit and explode the cursed practice of slavery, and then they themselves would marry a young woman who held slaves and keep them fast in bloody slavery. Members who have been professors of the religion of Jesus Christ for ten or twelve years would come to me and apparently be happy as saints in Heaven, and follow them home and you will see their slaves in the field and kitchens cruelly oppressed, half starved, and nearly naked. O! my Lord, is this the religion of my adorable master Jesus? How can I keep grieving over these cruel oppressions who are in error. And I fear they will be slaves to the devil in Hell forever. So the dear woman swooned away being greatly exhausted.

"I hope," continued Meacham, every bit as vocal an enemy to slavery and gentility, "this lecture may never be forgotten."[17]

And the Colberts and Meachams, in turn, found inspiration and power in the religious community of Black Americans. Ten days prior to his encounter with the angry white woman, Colbert had reported meeting at night with a Black class "in a place calld the Swamp" and "had sweet communion with this dear family." In late August, at a quarterly meeting, he noted that "the black people gave in wonderful experiences." In mid-August 1789 after holding a class meeting, having family prayers, and retiring for the evening, Meacham awoke "in raptures of Heaven by the sweet Echo Singing in the Kitchen among the dear Black people (who my Soul loves)." He continued:

> I scarcely ever heard anything to equal it upon earth. I rose up and strove to join them—ah—I felt the miserable weight of oppression intolerable upon my heart—while the proud whites can live in luxury and abomination making a mock of God and his word, the African upholds him by his Swet and labour of his willing hands—and if they serve the Lord God it must be in the dead of the night when they ought to be taking rest to their bodys, O blood, blood how aweful it Cryes up before God, against my poor unjust professing Bro—well I must have patience—hope God will work for his own Glory.[18]

In February 1794, on the Montgomery Circuit, Colbert reported meeting "a black Class which I believe have vital religion." Later that year, traveling with Richard Whatcoat, Colbert "preached at Americus Scarboroughs...and administerd the sacrament.... At night I preached again (to the black people)...and a great shout we had with them." Throughout his labors among blacks and whites, Colbert praised Black Methodists in glowing terms, only rarely discerning white fervor or finding personal sustenance therein. Two years later, while on Delmarva Peninsula, Colbert would be criticized "for calling the Black people *Brethren*, and *sisters*."[19] Similarly, William Spencer on the Surry Circuit in Virginia spoke of meeting "dear black people, that I really believed loved Jesus." He continued:

> The Lord gave me Liberty in speaking to them, and I hope good was done. I think in general, the dear black people, that profess Religion, are much more engaged than the whites. God bless the dear Creatures, my Soul loves them, and I humbly hope and trust that my dear Lord Jesus will bless my Labours among them.[20]

Such advocacy on the part of preachers and their preaching of liberty, testimony against slavery, and repudiation of gentility produced intense reactions among some whites. Others, when converted, nevertheless charted their journey in Pietist and anti-genteel terms. The Virginian Stith Mead, later to compose one of American Methodism's early ventures in hymnody, *Hymns and Spiritual Songs* (1805), recalled the intrafamily discord that Methodism's strictures against genteel practices produced:

> Jan. 1790—Mr. Samuel Mead, a brother next youngest to me, who appears to be a sincere penitent for his sins, and myself travelled to the State of Georgia, to see our relations, whose god is in this world, with the rich and fashionable gay.[21] I strove to encourage my brother, as I was a believer unto salvation, and he was only a seeker of religion. In Feb. we arrived in Georgia, and was received with much persecution from many of our relations, who soon raised a dancing party, when my brother was caught in the snare of Satan—I was much persuaded to stay and partake with them, but refused; having several miles to ride to Col. A. Gordon's, a brother-in-law, where I lived. My

sisters often danced before me, others suggested I was deranged, and soon would be raving mad—but blessed be God, in the midst of all my temptations and trials, I find him to be a "friend that sticketh by me, nigher than a brother." I often took up my cross with a trembling hand, to pray in my father's family.[22]

The reactions in this southern family, like those in the Livingstons in New York, should indicate that elites took Methodist strictures against dancing, gambling, finery, racing, and cards not as petty moralism but as attacks on their authority, values, and way of life. Nor does the later notion of separate male (public) and female (domestic) spheres do justice to Methodist denunciation of "worldly" social practices, though it would indeed be one way the concern with gentility would cash itself out several decades later. Moralism and separate spheres compartmentalize these ethical concerns into individualism or the home, the former interiorizing ethics, the latter distinguishing it from political and economic spheres. Eventually, to reiterate, Methodists with other Protestants did compartmentalize and domesticate codes on finery, cards, and dancing, as nineteenth-century middle-class society separated family and home from the market and public square and individualized practices into private morality. But in the 1780s and 1790s, those lines were not yet cleanly drawn, and perhaps more important, Methodists did not heed them. Instead, they called women and the lowly to defy family, to repudiate social convention, and to join in overthrowing the economic system of slavery. Methodists even braved into the political sphere to petition legislatures, as did the 1785 conference meeting at Green Hill's seeking rights of manumission in North Carolina, and to meet with the new president, as did Coke and Asbury in 1785 and again after Washington's inauguration, and later to overture him (Sources 1789b). To many, Methodism represented a reckless assault on the entire socioeconomic-political structure, a perception reached particularly in the South where genteel ideals predominated and where Methodism enjoyed its initial successes. So noted Asbury while in Charleston, looking back from 1795:

> I was deeply dejected. I have been lately subject to melancholy than for many years past; and how can I help it: the white and worldly people are intolerably ignorant of God; playing, dancing, swearing, racing; these are their common practices and pursuits. Our few male members do not attend preaching; and I fear there is hardly one who walks with God; the women and Africans attend our meetings, and some few strangers also. Perhaps it may be necessary for me to know how wicked the world is, in order that I may do more as a president minister.[23]

Biracial but Segregated

The antislavery preaching of the Cokes, Meachams, Colberts, Garrettsons, and Asburys as well as their successes in bringing African Americans into Methodist fellowship, it should be noted, took place primarily in slaveholding areas. No small part of Methodism's appeal to slaves and freed persons derived from this double witness to liberty—freedom from slavery to cosmic powers of sin and death and freedom from its collusive force, human enslavement of fellow human beings. And Methodism's willingness to confront the slave owner directly *and* to embrace African Americans in "society" gave its witness a decided edge over the Quakers, who preached antislavery but showed little eagerness to include African Americans in their own fellowship. Both communities, as well as antislavery Presbyterians and Baptists, to be sure, contributed to the significant numbers of manumissions below the Mason-Dixon Line, particularly just below it in Delaware, Maryland, and Virginia.[24]

Such advocacy never proved popular. So discovered Bishop Coke on his 1785 tour south, where his antislavery statements and reputation earned him the threat of flogging by a mob, disputes with Jesse Lee and the North Carolina Methodist slaveholder, Green Hill, estrangement from Devereux Jarratt, and strained relations in conferences. And taking on slavery in its own lair and inviting all persons into community subjected Methodism to just the corrosive pressures denounced by Sister Whitehead, the prophesying woman heard by Meacham and his fifty preachers. Over the same dynamic, Asbury worried in a letter in 1785 to Freeborn Garrettson: "With respect to slavery, I am clear, and always was, that if every Preacher would do his duty we should not need to make any Minutes, use no force, but only loving and argumentative persuasion." Writing to Garrettson in September 1786, he recognized a more subtle force that implicated the laity equally. Noting that "Harry the wonderful Black has been my faithful companion this [summer]," and continued with him, he counseled Garrettson "not to be so anxious about Building Houses." "You will," he predicted,

> find it easier to get into debt than to pay and you will make rich men necessary and they will rule you and impede your discipline if you are not well aware. We groan under a heavy debt in [New] York, Philadelphia, and Baltimore and it weakens the hands of the poor among us and strengthens the hands of the few Rich to oppose our strictness of discipline.[25]

In 1786, Methodism began to break its membership out by race, then claiming 18,791 whites and 1,890 blacks.

The power of American society to compromise Methodism's antislavery stand became obvious almost immediately in reactions to the Christmas Conference's legislation. With respect to the slavery strictures (Sources 1785a), Lee observed:

> These rules were short lived, and were offensive to most of our southern friends; and were so much opposed by many of our private members, local preachers, and some of the travelling preachers, that the execution of them was suspended at the conference held in June following…and they were never afterwards carried into full force.[26]

Even the antislavery zealots, like Garrettson, played their part in the qualification of Methodism's tentative egalitarianism. Garrettson, while in mission in Nova Scotia in 1785, initiated the segregation of Black persons into their own "little house" where he "preached to them separately, in order to have more room for the whites." Five years later, he traveled with Harry Hosier (Sources 1784c) throughout the summer, a fact he repeatedly detailed in his manuscript journal but obliterated from the published version. Methodists had a hard time "recognizing" Black leadership, in the sense of writing it out of the record and of refusing to legitimate Black leaders on the record with formal credentials. It would be another decade, not till 1800, that the MEC would permit African Americans even the status of local deacon.[27]

So Methodists strove internally and against one another to hold together ethic and evangelism, human liberty and cosmic liberty. Increasingly, they yielded on the former or spiritualized the former into the latter. So in 1787 conference decreed:

> *Quest. 17. What directions shall we give for the promotion of the spiritual welfare of the negroes?*
>
> *Answ.* We conjure all our Ministers and Preachers, by the love of God, and the salvation of souls, and do require them, by all the authority that is invested in us, to leave nothing undone for the spiritual benefit and salvation of the negroes, within their respective circuits or districts; and for this purpose to embrace every opportunity of inquiring into the states of their souls, and to unite in society those who appear to have a real desire of fleeing from the wrath to come, to meet such in class, and to exercise the whole methodist discipline among them.[28]

African Methodists look back on the same year as the beginning of their migration toward independence. Historians disagree about whether the exact incident to which Richard Allen pointed can be credibly dated to 1787, but there can be no doubt that the racist and segregating spirit of which he complained was then quite alive and well.[29] Still, as the official account makes clear, independence derived from self-affirmation as well as white racism, from the empowering message of Methodism as well as from its failure to live that witness.[30]

Itinerating into Order and Disorder

African Methodism represented but one of several fronts on which Methodism would gradually draw a boundary. Another front seemingly secured by the Christmas Conference, that with Anglicanism, would actually prove troublesome for years to come. In retrospect, it may appear that Methodists in 1784 anticipated the American religious future—embracing disestablishment, offering a denominational ordering of religion, achieving autonomy from European headquarters, institutionalizing voluntarism. In fact, American Methodists would only slowly understand their prescience and accept their self-definition. And key players, most notably Coke and Wesley, had less insular notions about the American Methodist future.

Indeed, immediately before or during the Christmas Conference, Coke and Asbury had met with two Maryland Anglicans, John Andrews and William West, at the latter's request, in the hope of heading off the independence promised in Wesley's letter and arranging some continuing unity on the basis of a scheme for American Episcopal governance outlined two years earlier by William White. In 1787, in England to be ordained bishop, White sought but failed to meet with John Wesley, another effort toward reconciliation missed. And in 1789 a general convention met in Philadelphia to organize the Protestant Episcopal Church.

In 1791, without Asbury's knowledge (Sources 1791a), Coke overtured Bishop White about union of the two churches, outlining advantages to Episcopalians, Methodist conditions, and probable roadblocks (among them, Asbury). White acknowledged the difficulties but responded favorably. Coke then met three times with White and Dr. Samuel Magaw, long a friend to Methodists and then vice president of the University of Pennsylvania, in Philadelphia. They worked out a scheme that predicated union on some relaxation of Episcopal ministerial standards, reordinations of Methodist preachers, and re-consecration of the two bishops and that permitted some continuing oversight of specifically Methodist work by the two Methodist bishops. Coke also wrote the High Church Episcopal bishop of Connecticut, Samuel Seabury, summarizing the plans.[31]

The overtures came to naught. Seabury never responded. Coke returned to England (at news of Wesley's death). Asbury discovered the scheme, responded negatively, and resisted submission of the plan to the 1792 General Conference. Two churches came into being. The Methodist Episcopal Church and the Protestant Episcopal Church shared the same middle name, a common history, essentially the same liturgy, governance, and orders derived from Anglicanism, some common practices, considerable knowledge of each other, initial strength in the same areas of the upper South, and an interest in the same constituencies. Their rivalry would take various forms. In letters, subsequently published, Jarratt expressed his assessment of Methodist leaders and his disappointment in Methodist failure to honor the commitment not to separate. Methodists found disappointment in their leaders who remained loyal to the church and sought orders—Joseph Pilmore, Thomas Vasey, and William Duke. They more than retaliated for those modest losses in beating the Episcopal Church to the scattered peoples, particularly the lower and middling sort, nominally or formerly adherent to the Church of England. Episcopal efforts to hold their own, Methodists simply outflanked and bested with their evangelistically more effective connectionalism, itinerancy, empowerment of laity, class system, discipline, Arminian gospel, and encouragement to holiness. Episcopalians would eventually respond by impugning Methodist orders. And then they would find resources and amusement at Methodist expense in exposing the secret explorations that Bishop Coke made in 1791 with Bishop William White concerning Methodist return to the Anglican fold (Sources 1791a).[32]

Coke's misadventure belongs in the larger story of his efforts to sustain Wesley's vision of a global connection, of his (Coke's) central role therein, of his deteriorating relation with Asbury, and of the American Methodist search for workable government. By prior understanding, Coke returned to Britain after the three 1785 American conferences (and consolidating of plans for the Cokesbury academy). He would be back in the U.S. in 1787, 1789, and 1791, punctuating his American visits with presiding or oversight roles in Ireland, the West Indies, and British North America. In Britain, he also embroiled himself in complicated politics over the future of Methodism after Wesley, over relations with the established churches, and with Charles and John Wesley. Coke returned to the U.S. in 1787 with explicit, written directions from Wesley to "appoint a General Conference of all our preachers in the United States, to meet at Baltimore on 1st May 1787" and further that "Mr. Richard Whatcoat may be appointed Superintendent with Asbury." Wesley had proposed, in addition, that Freeborn Garrettson be superintendent for British North America. Such directives accorded with the "binding minute" to obey Wesley's commands and with Wesley's vision of a global connection. They hardly accorded with American sensitivities.[33]

Nor did they accord with the relative power and authority of the two superintendents in the American context. While Coke had been struggling with Wesley's mantle and authority, Asbury had been consolidating influence with and power over the American itinerants. He did so, as he would continue to do (Source 1789a), by riding with them through their circuits, preaching and praying, by making the quarterly meetings and presiding in conference, by meeting classes and staying in Methodist homes, by hearing their efforts to preach and counseling with them, by filling the appointments with insight about both preachers and circuits—in short by traveling the entire connection. So Asbury exhibited, daily and constantly, privately and publicly, the office of itinerating general superintendent. So he understood himself as the exemplum traveling preacher (Sources 1798). Coke might write letters of counsel and direction. Coke's name might go first on *Minutes* and *Discipline*. In conference, Coke might preach and preside. And when the two superintendents traveled together, Coke might claim the pulpit. However, Asbury ran the show. Coke performed; Asbury governed.[34]

Of Wesley's several directives through Coke, the Americans honored only the most inconsequential. They met May 1 in Baltimore rather than as they had appointed at Abingdon, Maryland, on July 24. They also rescheduled the two other conferences for Charleston in late March and Virginia in late April, gathering for the latter as many as three thousand at Rough Creek, Virginia, where O'Kelly and Lee led the opposition to Coke, to Wesley's exercise of authority, and to the nomination of Whatcoat. Of the May 1 meeting, Asbury noted, "We had some warm and close debates in conference; but all ended in love and peace." Thomas Ware reported, more candidly, that many preachers took great offense at the presumption of resetting the conference date, at the implicit conferring of decision making to the superintendents, at the appointment rather than election of superintendents, and at the fear that Whatcoat's elevation might produce the recall of Asbury. The fear doomed Whatcoat's episcopal chances at that juncture. The conference responded more formally by qualifying Coke's authority, stipulating in the *Annual Minutes* to the first question—who are the superintendents—the answer: "Thomas Coke, (when present in the States), and Francis Asbury." Confirming that on his part, Coke gave the conference a certificate promising not to exercise superintending authority when absent and limiting it when present to ordaining, presiding, and traveling. They also rescinded the binding minute of loyalty to Wesley from the *Discipline* (Sources 1785a, Q. 2), sometimes described as dropping Wesley's name from the *Minutes*.[35]

Garrettson, already serving in Nova Scotia, expected to be appointed superintendent of missions in British North America and the Caribbean, and his manuscript journal shows him actually elected (he used but crossed out the word *bishop*) but declining. Instead, he was appointed to preside in the Peninsula, occupying an office effectively recognized in the *Minutes* the prior year, that of presiding elder. Another change in nomenclature occurred sometime after the 1787 conferences, namely, of Coke and Asbury's substitution of the word *bishop* for *superintendent*, an alteration ratified in the 1788 conferences and *Discipline*. The "bishops" also took it upon themselves to alter the Wesley "minute" ordering of the *Discipline*, arranging it instead as its new subtitle indicated, "under proper heads, and methodized in a more acceptable and easy manner," prefacing it with a historical account "Of the Rise of Methodism (so called) in Europe and America."[36]

After the 1787 conference, Lee noted, Lee and others wrote "a long and loving letter to Mr. Wesley" requesting him "to come over to America and visit his spiritual children." Wesley was not mollified by the letter or indifferent to the multiple affronts or amused by Coke and Asbury's assumption of the episcopal title. He wrote Asbury the next year, comparing himself, as "father of the whole family," to Coke and Asbury, calling the latter "the elder brother of the American Methodists." He continued,

> But in one point, my dear brother, I am a little afraid both the Doctor and you differ from me. I study to be little: you study to be great. I creep; you strut along. I found a school: you a college! nay, and call it after your own names! O beware, do not seek to be something! Let me be nothing, and "Christ be all in all!"[37]

In 1789, still smarting, John wrote Charles, noting the independent strain in Asbury and recalling words the latter had reportedly said, "Mr Wesley and I are like Caesar and Pompey—He will bear no equal and I will bear no superior." John then concluded, "Does not this satisfy every man who reads it, that the charge of seceded from Mr. Wesley, is well founded; and that these men made a rent in the connection."[38]

Asbury's authority also loomed larger as an issue in the U.S. It loomed larger, quite apart from Asbury's personality and even apart from the incredible appointive power lodged in the episcopal office. It loomed larger because the countervailing authority, that of conference, fragmented as Methodism continued to expand. Lee termed the years of 1787 and 1788 the greatest revival for southern Virginia ever known, particularly in the Sussex, Brunswick, and Amelia circuits, where he claimed 4,200 converted for 1787 and comparable intensive growth in areas of Maryland and North Carolina for 1788. In 1788 Methodism added 11,481 members and nineteen circuits, extending its penetration beyond the upper South or Chesapeake, creating new circuits in South Carolina, western Pennsylvania, Kentucky, (West) Virginia, Ohio, New York, and Georgia, and establishing significant toeholds beyond the Appalachians and Alleghenies. The circuits numbered eighty-five. The number of conferences also expanded. Six were appointed for 1788, but seven held according to Lee, the last of which was in Philadelphia, not Baltimore. And for 1789, eleven conferences met, Baltimore falling near the middle of the schedule. The Baltimore system of governance by which the legislative acts of all the conferences were finalized at Baltimore, no longer workable, was among the early casualties of Methodist growth. And with Methodist work so extended and conference government so fragmented, would Methodism's one voice be that of Asbury?[39]

The Council

The eleven conferences of 1789—through all of which legislation had to pass—established the unwieldiness of Methodism's political apparatus and prompted a short-lived and unpopular solution, a council. Laid before the 1789 conferences by the bishops who "had made it a matter of prayer" and presented it as "the best that they could think of," the council was, according to the enabling legislation, to "be formed of chosen men out of the several districts as representatives of the whole connection." The representatives designated by the following rubric were "our bishops and presiding elders." Lee, who reproduced the entirety of this legislation, complained that the council was new, dangerous, unworkable, and not genuinely representative:

> This plan for having a council, was entirely new, and exceedingly dangerous. A majority of the preachers voted in favour of it, but they were soon sensible, that the plan would not answer the purpose for which it was intended. The council was to be composed of the bishops, and the presiding elders: the presiding elders were appointed, changed, and put out of office by the bishop, and just when he pleased; of course, the whole of the council were to consist of the bishops, and a few other men of their own choice or appointing.[40]

The council possessed two other features well devised to doom it. One was the provision that its enactments required unanimity, in effect allowing Asbury veto power. Another feature, that legislation would be binding only in concurring conferences, Lee thought also a "dangerous clause," prone to divide the connection.[41]

In its first meeting, the council adopted a constitution that remedied these three glaring defects. It provided for election of "the most experienced elders in the connection... by ballot in every conference," a two-thirds majority rather than unanimity as requisite for legislation (plus, however, "the consent of the bishop"), and only the concurrence of "a majority of the several conferences." Even in this revised form, many experienced the council as what Thomas Neely termed "a dangerous centralization of power."[42]

Outspoken on the issue of centralized power and leading the charge against the council was Irish-born James O'Kelly.[43] Asbury reported, "I received a letter from the presiding elder of this district [South Virginia], James O'Kelly; he makes heavy complaints of my power, and bids me stop for one year, or he must use his influence against me. Power! Power!"[44]

Others shared O'Kelly's concern. The conference at Charleston sought to constrict the council's power to "advice only" and to make the "consent of the conference decisive." At Petersburg, Asbury reported, "Our conference began; all was peace until the council was mentioned. The young men appeared to be entirely under the influence of the elders, and turned it out of doors." James Meacham, a young preacher at that conference, noted in his journal for September 1, 1790, the opposition to the council in southern Virginia, an opposition that he thought would lead either to expulsions or to separation. Four days later he reported receiving "4 Letters from the Travelling Preachers, they are much oppos'd to the Council." William McKendree, later to be Asbury's colleague as bishop, then possessed great confidence in O'Kelly, whose word "was next to gospel with me." Asbury is reported to have said, "Ye have all spoken out of one mouth. Henceforth you are all out of the union." Following the Leesburg conference where similar agitation prevailed, Asbury backed down and made yet another concession:

> To conciliate the minds of our brethren in the south district of Virginia, who are restless about the council, I wrote their leader a letter, informing him, "that I would take my seat in council as another member"; and, in that point, at least, waive the claims of episcopacy.

Not satisfied, the southern Virginia preachers met under O'Kelly's leadership at Mecklenburg and resolved "to send no member to Council."[45]

The second meeting of the council did not stem the tide of opposition. O'Kelly had, in fact, rallied Coke to that side. Lee also played an important oppositional role.

Nevertheless as its *Minutes* attest, the council did show a capacity to act, to initiate, to address itself to the connection's needs, a political capacity that had been missing. Its first apparent action showed sensitivity to the widespread concern about the limits of the council's power but nevertheless carved out clear areas for connectional authority and initiative:

> Q. What power do this council consider themselves *invested* with by their electors?
> A. First, they *unanimously* consider themselves invested with *full* power to act *decisively* in all temporal matters. And secondly, that of *recommending* to the several conferences any new canons [rules], or alterations to be made in any old ones.[46]

It proceeded in traditional Wesleyan fashion through thirty-one policy queries and action answers. It dealt extensively with publishing—calling for book stewards in every district, identifying books to be published (including the four volumes of Wesley's *Sermons*), and providing counsel on American Methodism's first periodical, the *Arminian Magazine*, which lived only the two years that the council existed, 1789 and 1790. Notwithstanding the magazine's failure, these publishing initiatives and the 1789 settling of John Dickins and the publishing agency in Philadelphia—"the first publishing house in America to initiate the systematic printing and distribution of evangelical books"—constituted Methodism as a textually defined as well as an oral community, a development to which we return in chapter 6.[47]

The council made financial provision and further rules of conduct for Cokesbury College and authorized similar schools in any districts where resources availed. It faced a variety of money and cash flow problems. It authorized Native American missions, empowering the "bishop"—note the singular—to expend one salary (twenty-four pounds) for "a Teacher, or Preacher, among any of the *Indian Nations*." And it treated what had been a major concern of the 1789 council, namely, worship, stipulating divisions within buildings and separate doors so "that men and women should sit a-part in public congregations," as "we think it primitive, prudent, and *decent*." The 1789 council had insisted that further preaching houses be built only with conference and presiding elder support and direction, had called for worship at 10:00 or 11:00 on Sundays "where we have Societies and regular Preaching," and had given directions for such worship—"Singing, Prayer and reading the Holy Scriptures, with Exhortation or Reading a Sermon, in the Absence of a Preacher; and the officiating Person shall be appointed by the Elder, Deacon, or travelling Preacher, for the Time being." That first council had also provided for a three-year probation for deacons.[48]

Methodism had, in the immediately prior years, wanted for connectional administrative and legislative authority, for a body to frame policy. The council demonstrated that some central authority, countervailing that of the bishop(s), could work. Was it not needed? Without some collective voice for the preachers, was it not appropriate for the bishops to speak on behalf of Methodism to President George Washington, assuring him of Methodist support and soliciting his commitment to religious liberty (Sources 1789b)? And was it surprising that four months after the second council, Bishop Coke would take it upon himself to engage in secret overtures to the Episcopalians (Sources 1791a)?

General Conference

On Coke's return to the U.S. in early 1791, Asbury discovered "the Doctor's sentiments, with regard to the council, quite changed." Sizing up the situation, Asbury continued, "James O'Kelly's letters had reached London. I felt perfectly calm, and acceded to a general conference, for the sake of peace." So at the Petersburg conference of that year, as Asbury reported, "The affair of the council was suspended until a general conference." At about that point, news of John Wesley's death (March 2) reached Asbury and Coke. Coke preached a memorial sermon in Baltimore and Philadelphia in early May, on 2 Kings 2:12, on the departure of Elijah in the whirlwind, leaving Elisha crying, "My father, my father!" Was he (Coke) Elisha? Did Elijah's mantle fall on single shoulders? Did Wesley's death not end but intensify the special relation that Coke had enjoyed with the prophet? Was the monarchical principle to continue in Methodism? Methodists on both sides of the Atlantic sought to counter Coke's pretensions by consolidating the authority of conference.[49]

A general conference had been proposed by both Lee and O'Kelly but dismissed, when the plan for a council was initially introduced. Lee reiterated that proposal on July 7, 1791, submitting the matter in writing, as also may have Coke in May, just prior to his return to England. "This day," recorded Asbury, "brother Lee put a paper into my hand, proposing the election of not less than two, nor more than four preachers from each conference, to form a general conference in Baltimore, in December, 1792, to be continued annually." Lee's conception of delegation or representation would have to wait its time, and his notion of an annual meeting did not prevail. But he, O'Kelly, and Coke had their way. The first General Conference met in Baltimore, November 1–15, 1792. When it gathered, the council proposal was given a very unceremonious burial. "For soon after we met together," Lee reported, "the *bishops* and the preachers in general, shewed a disposition to drop the *council*, and all things belonging there. And the bishops requested that the name of the *council* might not be mentioned in the conference again."[50]

No minutes of this first General Conference survive. It left its record in the *Discipline*, which it revised. Perhaps most important, it decided to give itself the legislative power for the church, to establish itself as a permanent body, and to convene again in four years in a conference "to which, all the preachers in full connection were at liberty to come." That plenary definition of itself, its claim to a future, and its assumption of the authority to legislate for the church, specifically to revise the *Discipline*—two-thirds majority being required for new actions or total rescission of existing legislation but only a majority to amend—provided what Asbury had sought through the council, namely, a politically competent and sovereign center to the movement. Thus, said Tigert, "this body became the permanent organ of connectional government in American Methodism." Given its connectional supremacy, General Conference also claimed the right and responsibility to elect and try bishops.[51]

The 1792 General Conference gave further impetus toward what would in the future be termed *annual conferences* by authorizing the uniting of two or more of the districts (the purview of the presiding elders) and between three and twelve circuits (the assignment of the traveling preachers) into district (annual) conferences. It defined conferences, both general and annual, by their membership—the traveling preachers in full connection.[52]

The *Discipline* distinguished the presiding elder (today's district superintendent) from the eldership in general, formally recognizing what had emerged as the key conference leadership, administrative, disciplinary, and appointing office (Sources 1798, section V). Given supervisory responsibility for a district of circuits and the various levels of preachers attached to them, the presiding elder would enjoy the authority of the bishop in the bishop's absence and the power of advisory and supportive roles in the bishop's presence, notably responsibilities to preside when Methodists convened (conferenced) and to appoint, to receive, and to change Methodist leaders. The *Discipline* matched, or perhaps mismatched, these quasi-episcopal duties with the normal elder's standing as an appointive position and assented to the bishop's authority to select, station, and change the presiding elder. By making the office appointive rather than elective, the church built into every conference and into the fabric of conference life the council principle that Lee and O'Kelly thought so flawed. Ironically, the General Conference buried the council as a device for connectional governance but buried it, in effect, on the conference level. That perception lay ahead, after annual conferences had formally emerged as geographically defined entities and the presiding eldership assumed aristocratic "ownership" of a fixed population of preachers. However, the 1792 General Conference clearly worried some over the power it was lodging in the presiding eldership, for it limited the term of presiding elders in one place to four years.[53]

Schism

Perhaps motivating the limits put on the presiding eldership and its accountability to the bishops were the independence, high-handed criticisms of the bishops, and political machinations of the presiding elder from the Virginia–North Carolina border, James O'Kelly. The second day of General Conference, O'Kelly placed a motion giving preachers who thought themselves "injured" by the bishop's appointment the "liberty to appeal to the conference" and the right, if the appeal was sustained, to another appointment. Unfortunately, the following "long" debate was not minuted. Lee indicated that "the arguments for and against the proposal were weighty, and handled in a masterly manner." He continued, "There never had been a subject before us that so fully called forth all the strength of the preachers. A large majority of them appeared at first to be in favour of the motion."[54]

The motion, and doubtless much of the affirmative argument, self-servingly enunciated in O'Kelly's account of the event (Sources 1792a), made appeal to what we would now term the language or ideology of republicanism—the rhetoric of the Revolution and the early American republic. Republicanism held, and O'Kelly preached a radical Whiggery that bifurcated social reality into a people with real but fragile rights and hostile, "kingly" authority whose natural tendency was to tyranny and usurpation of rights. The liberties of the people, if they were to be preserved, demanded collective resolve on the part of the people, a unity founded in virtue, watchful monitoring of authority, forceful response against authority's inducements, and resistance to luxury. Liberty and virtue were easily corrupted and the people's resolve dissipated; authority was ever encroaching; freedom's hope demanded vigilance; unless liberty were defended, the people would be reduced to slavery. So taught the history of republics, and so O'Kelly discovered in the tyrannical behavior of Asbury and Coke.

This republican imagery made considerable sense to some Methodist preachers. Should not an American church conduct itself along American principles? Had they not been injured by appointments? Did not Coke and Asbury connive to increase their power? Had not the preachers been obliged to check episcopal tyranny already? Was not the preachers' liberty in danger? Would it not be better safeguarded in conference rather than episcopal hands?[55] The rhetoric had appeal. Thomas Ware concurred in Lee's judgment that the motion initially seemed destined for passage but for the spirit with which the campaign was led and the radical character of the argument:

> Some of them said that it was a shame for a man to *accept* of such a lordship, much more to *claim* it; and that they who would submit to this absolute dominion must forfeit all claims to freedom, and ought to have their ears bored through with an awl, and to be fastened to their master's door and become slaves for life. One said that to be denied such an appeal was an insult to his understanding, and a species of tyranny.[56]

Critical to the change in sentiment was an adroitly crafted letter that Asbury, sick in bed, sent to the conference:

> Let my absence give you no pain—Dr. Coke presides. I am happily excused from assisting to make laws by which myself am to be governed: I have only to obey and execute. I am happy in the consideration that I never stationed a preacher through enmity, or as

a punishment. I have acted for the glory of God, the good of the people, and to promote the usefulness of the preachers.

Asbury invoked a more benign view of Methodist political authority and of his exercise of the episcopal office, one contrary to the republican charge of tyranny, one that presumed a connectional, even providential, good achieved through the appointment process. The motion failed.[57]

O'Kelly walked out with a party of supporters to form a rival movement that took the republican banner into its name. James Meacham made this entry in his journal:

[H]e has taken his fare well of conference. I think my poor heart scarcely ever felt the like before, I could not refrain from weeping deeply I hope God will still direct aright, & give us our dear old bro. & yokefellow back again—if he comes not back, I fear bad consequences will accrue.[58]

As Meacham's affection and fear suggest, the Republican Methodists had considerable appeal, some of it based on O'Kelly himself, some on what would be the movement's efforts to create a polity protective of liberty, grounded in Scripture alone, and explicitly antislavery. Enunciating such principles as he preached and in his apologetic writings (Sources 1792a), O'Kelly initially garnered considerable support, particularly in lower Virginia and upper North Carolina.

Asbury labored diligently to contain the threat primarily on an interpersonal or relation level but also intellectually. He responded, implicitly, by editing and publishing, in Wesley-like fashion, *The Causes, Evils, and Cures of Heart and Church Divisions; Extracted from the Works of Mr. Richard Baxter and Mr. Jeremiah Burroughs*. Explicitly, at the 1796 General Conference's direction, he and Coke answered O'Kelly by carefully annotating the *Discipline* (Sources 1798), defending Methodist episcopacy as essential to bedrock Methodist principles of itinerancy and connectionalism, arguing for presiding elders as providentially given extensions of these principles, and in short, defending the entire Methodist Episcopal system. Asbury also commissioned Nicholas Snethen, his "silver trumpet," to refute O'Kelly, which Snethen did with several tracts, including *A Reply to an Apology for Protesting against the Methodist Episcopal Government*. Snethen established the historiographical tradition on the Republicans as schismatic, heretical (particularly on the doctrine of the Trinity), driven by O'Kelly's megalomania, excessive in its portrayal of Asbury.[59] Thereafter, Methodists have sought to minimize the effect of the Republican departure and discount its size and importance.

O'Kelly's was not the only fracturing of Methodism then occurring. In 1792, William Hammett was in the process of drawing off Charleston Methodists into a church committed to following Wesley's primitive Methodism and taking that as its name. Hammett, along with William Warrener, had been ordained by Wesley in 1786 for service in British America, had accompanied Coke on the latter's second voyage over, and had served effectively in the West Indies until, suffering ill health, brought to Charleston in 1791 by Coke. An effective preacher, Hammett almost immediately built a loyal following who petitioned Asbury informally and then both bishops in writing to appoint him. Although apparently vacillating when Hammett himself brought the petition to the May 1791 conference in Philadelphia, Asbury ultimately refused. Hammett then formed Trinity Church in Charleston, eventually formed a second Charleston church, St. James, developed some following among local preachers in the area, and established beachheads in Savannah, Georgetown (South Carolina), and Wilmington (North Carolina), the latter an African American congregation. He attacked Coke and Asbury and set forth the Primitive Methodist cause in a series of pamphlets, gathered in 1792 as *A Rejoindre: Being a Defence of the Truths Contained in an Appeal to Truth and Circumstances; in Seven Letters Addressed to the Reverend Mr. Morrell.* Like O'Kelly, he attacked episcopal tyranny and argued for a right of appeal to conference of an appointment thought injurious. He criticized Asbury for duplicity and Coke for complicity in slaveholding (a complicity thereafter for Hammett himself). He died in 1803, and his movement succumbed soon thereafter.[60]

In the same time frame, Black Methodists under Richard Allen took important steps along the way toward independence, walking out of St. George's and establishing Bethel Church as an African congregation (Sources 1792b).[61] (Not all Black Methodists in Philadelphia followed Allen into Mother Bethel Church. A small group decided to give mother Methodism a little more time to treat them with dignity and respect. The new church organized in 1794 as African Zoar Church, "Mother Zoar Church," and met in an abandoned butcher shop. Two years later (1796) the congregation purchased land and erected their first building.[62] Freedom from control by St. George's Church, however, took time, being achieved only in 1835 when the first Black local preacher, Perry Tilghman, was appointed preacher-in-charge.) Despite the continued loyalty to the MEC of some African Americans, the separations would prove to be the most tragic and significant. Both the Allen movement and the Republican Methodists, later to take the name Christians, held up Methodism's antislavery banner, championed liberty, and called for a more democratic church. These issues would not go away, and the schisms cost the MEC some of its most fervent opponents of slavery, most articulate exponents of liberty, most egalitarian spirits. William Warren Sweet estimates that the overall losses suffered in the 1790s by the MEC to the Republicans, to William Hammett, and to other causes amounted to some 10,000.[63]

Constituting

Typically we have viewed the constitution-making decade as producing the establishment and consolidation of an independent denomination (the MEC). In fact, the decade witnessed the beginnings of multiple separations: of the Methodist Episcopals from the Church of England; of the American Methodists from Wesley; within the U.S., of the Methodists from the Episcopalians; within the Methodist camp, of black from white; of German- and English-speaking Pietists from one another; and of democratic Methodists from the church they experienced as tyrannically ruled by bishops. The decade saw also the constituting of gender and class patterns within the churches. Liberty had many meanings.

CHAPTER V

SPREADING SCRIPTURAL HOLINESS: 1792–1816

Successive MEC General Conferences from 1792 to 1816 confronted issues of the new constitutional order: a quadrennial General Conference with plenary authority but fluid membership, increasingly unavailable or incapacitated bishops charged with itinerating across the connection to preside and appoint, conferences composed only of traveling preachers called together annually, presiding elders with powers derived from the bishops, an array of other officers authorized to voice concerns only within quarterly conferences, and an active people (especially women) whose piety and practice energized the whole and whose prayer and praise composed their most effective mode of communicating.

Explosive growth for Methodism lay ahead. Owed it more to polity or practice, to effective itinerancy or lay witness, to connectional muscularity or community piety? What weaned America from its predominantly Calvinist colonial nursing? What transformed denominations from ethnically closed to evangelistically open systems? What altered revivalism from expectant waiting to active invitation? What gave the Wesleyan voice and its metaphors such appeal?[1] What brought the numbers into the Methodist family (from 15,000 in 1784 to more than ten times that in 1810 to close to 500,000 in 1830)?

By 1810 Methodists constituted 7.4 percent of the population in Maryland and 8.4 percent in Delaware. The great bulk of Methodists then, as previously, lived between South Carolina and New York, 125,540 of the 171,751 total. And Methodist growth looked westward from those middle Atlantic or Chesapeake states.[2] What occurred during, what explained, Methodism's explosive period? At the very least, Americans accepted or found their appropriate denominational/confessional counterpart to Wesley's Arminian doctrine. So Methodist or Methodist-type revivalistic evangelism shaped American society and American religion, ordering individual and corporate life around offering and responding to prevenient grace.[3]

Spirituality and Order: United Brethren, Evangelical Association, Methodist Episcopal

Controverted and ambiguous national or connectional matters commanded attention and loom large in Methodism's early histories and most subsequent narratives. However, Methodism prospered as much from the bottom up as the top down. So recognized Bishops Coke and Asbury in their commentary on the *Discipline* (Sources 1798). Of necessity they explained and defended the authority granted bishops and presiding elders. But they made clear that "Christian experience" and particularly its regular, weekly, corporate expression in class meetings constituted "the pillars of our work." The rhythms of these basic, membership aspects of Methodist life can be well seen in the schematization of class meeting times, composition, and leadership for John Street Church, New York City (Sources 1802).[4]

The "constituting," bedrock character of piety, indeed of Pietism, can be readily seen throughout the Methodist movements, perhaps nowhere more graphically than in the extant accounts of early conferences of the United Brethren (UBC) (Sources 1800b) and The Evangelical Association (EA) (Sources 1807 and UB Sidebar in Chapter 1 and EA below). As with the MEC, the UBC and EA conferences addressed opportunity and problem legislatively, exercised discipline over their membership, authorized evangelistic itineration, and resolved questions of power and authority. Religious practice undergirded this evolution of polity. At each UBC conference, the preachers received the Lord's Supper, spoke their experience (witnessed) in gathering, prayed and sang hymns, heard the Scriptures read and preached, tested their own and candidates' spirituality, connected themselves and their people as a community of love, and identified leaders to accompany Martin Boehm and William Otterbein (formally elected bishops in 1800).[5] Increasingly George Adam Geeting (1741–1812) and Christian Newcomer (1749–1830), and later Andrew Zeller (1755–1839), assumed the mantle of leadership, the latter two to be elected bishops, Geeting to be a longtime secretary. He minuted the conferences from 1800 on as the UBC formalized itself as a church. It was a gradual process, not a one-time, 1784-like event. Lacking the Wesleyan movement's crisis over orders and sacraments and not requiring a transatlantic transfer of authority, the UBC had evolved more gradually out of Reformed and Mennonite contexts and continued that evolution slowly. Not until 1813, for instance, were preachers ordained, when Otterbein, after Boehm's death and anticipating his own, consecrated William Newcomer and two others, with the assistance of a Methodist elder, William Ryland.[6]

The emergence of the United Brethren as a distinct movement involved disengagement from the German Reformed. The first stage might be seen in the 1800 gathering of the "United Ministers" on Peter Kemp's farm near Frederick, Maryland (Sources 1800b). The conferees agreed to meet annually; adopted a new name, *Vereinigten Bruderschaft zu Christo* (United Brethren in Christ); approved believer's as well as infant baptism; selected their two founders, Otterbein and Boehm, as *Eltesten* (bishops); and empowered them to appoint preachers to circuits *upon consultation with pastors and circuits.* They clustered circuits around three centers, later conferences, southeastern Pennsylvania, Maryland and northern Virginia, and the Miami River valley in Ohio.

The UBC took care to designate itself as *unparteiische* (interdenominational) and to emphasize that it was only a "society." Under these arrangements, Otterbein had no objection to being asked, along with Boehm, to give leadership to the group popularly known as the "New Reformed" or "United Brotherhood," just as he had offered to do in 1789. With his classical theological education, profound faith, and great preaching prowess, Otterbein emerged as senior leader. The gentle and humble Boehm gladly deferred to him. Despite the more prominent leadership role, Otterbein continued to be a member in good standing in the German Reformed Coetus (conference), attending regularly as health permitted. By 1804, however, the Coetus began expulsion of others, first of whom was George Geeting, whom Otterbein had brought into the Reformed ministry and who had identified himself with the United Ministers. The synod did not mention Geeting's Pietism but instead cited his "disorderly conduct," a veiled reference to *unrestrained emotional worship* at meetings he led in and about his Antietam, Maryland, church. Epithets such as *strabbler* (struggler, or foot stamper), *knierutscher* (knee slider), and *springbungen* (holy rollers, literally jumpers) mocked revivalists. Such hyperspirited worship drove a wedge of separation between the New Reformed and the Old Reformed.

Newcomer, as second-generation leader, played a particularly important stabilizing role within the UBC and also in unity explorations with both the MEC and the EA, as his journal indicates (Sources 1813c). Newcomer related warmly to Bishops Francis Asbury and William McKendree, much as had Otterbein and Boehm earlier. His journal also attests the vibrant spirituality, much of it eucharistic, in and through which Newcomer exercised leadership. That spiritual grounding can be seen in the Rules adopted by the UBC in 1813 (Sources 1813a), which expected from preachers a renewed heart and the pursuit of holiness as preconditions for membership. In turn, the preachers built the new church "by doctrine and life, by prayer and a godly walk." The UBC set forth similar expectations for society leaders, heads of families, and members. The UBC kept protocols for discipline simple and scriptural, a source of continuing concern and critique from Asbury and the Methodists, who implored the UBC to adapt the MEC *Discipline* for UBC usage. With Asbury's encouragement, the MEC Philadelphia Conference had translated the MEC *Discipline* into German in 1807–8, but the UBC paid it little heed, leaving it to the EA to make such a formal adoption. UBC inaction on discipline finally stopped a series of negotiations with the MEC, carried on by the Baltimore Conference and formalized in letters between the two denominations from 1809 to 1814. Of concern to Methodists as well were UBC patterns of term episcopacy and less resolute itinerancy. By 1815 when the UBC gathered for its first General Conference, unity with the MEC was off the table (Sources 1800b, 1813c).[7] If the UBC adjusted its discipline less than did the MEC, it had given more attention to doctrinal formulation than its Wesleyan colleagues and continued to do so with further confessional refinements in 1815 and 1819 (Sources, pp. 38–40; compare 1785b). The denomination continued to reflect practices as well as doctrine out of its Mennonite and Reformed past. It elected bishops for term; kept centralized power lean; selected the presiding elders (district superintendents) through ballot and appointed pastors through a stationing committee, neither by episcopal appointment; structured class meetings loosely and as voluntary; maintained a single ordination to elder; and effectively located ministerial identity in the congregation, not conference.

Like the UBC, the Evangelical Association (EA) developed gradually with no one transition crisis. Competing for German-speaking members with the UBC in Pennsylvania, Maryland, and Virginia, the EA, like its leader and first bishop, Jacob Albright (1759–1808), emerged out of and remained in close association with the Methodists. Though catechized Lutheran, Albright found a spiritual home after his conversion experience with the Methodists and in the early 1790s professed commitment to the discipline, order, practices, and doctrine of the Methodists (Sources 1791b, p. 108). Licensed as an exhorter by the Methodists, Albright began preaching in 1796, itinerating through German-speaking communities. Insisting that salvation came through a renewed heart, not traditions, liturgies, and catechisms, he received ridicule from the Lutherans, Reformed, and Mennonites, and in 1797 expulsion by the Lutherans. Like his Methodist compatriots, he gathered converts into classes, held camp meetings, and raised up others to preach. Albright brought together class leaders in 1803 in the EA's first formal translocal assembly. That organizing conference recognized Albright as leader, ordained him, commissioned two other preachers as associates, and constituted itself as a society. The EA met in its first regular annual conference in 1807 at the farm of Samuel Becker, near Kleinfeltersville, Pennsylvania (Sources 1807), a gathering of five itinerant preachers, three local preachers, and twenty class leaders. The society adopted the name *Neuformirten Methodisten Conferenz* (Newly Formed Methodist Conference). It elected and ordained Albright as bishop and asked him to prepare a German translation of the MEC *Discipline,* "for the instruction and edification of the societies" (Sources 1807), and to appoint the preachers to their circuits. Albright licensed several preachers, selected George Miller (1774–1816) to be his chief assistant, presided at the first Communion service, and began to baptize. Although he was determined to travel widely, Albright's health failed and he died the next year (1808). A log chapel was opened in Kleinfeltersville, Pennsylvania, the first EA church building.[8] John Dreisbach preached the dedicatory sermon, taking his text from Psalm 27:4.

From the start the EA entertained hopes for unity either with the UBC or with the

MEC. Such explorations, including the possibility of becoming the German conference of the MEC, went nowhere with Asbury over the EA's persistent use of the German language and despite affinities. For instance, using the Methodist liturgy, George Miller ordained John Dreisbach and John Walter as elders and two lay preachers as deacons. The EA followed the Methodist signature in holding regular camp meetings. In 1814, George Miller, aging heir-apparent to Albright, retired. John Dreisbach was elected presiding elder and given oversight over the whole association (twelve preachers in the one conference in eastern Pennsylvania). In 1816 Dreisbach convened the organizing General Conference (near Lewisburg along the upper Susquehanna River), which sustained the commitment to a German-only ministry, approved expansion into Ohio and upstate New York, authorized negotiations with the UBC, rearranged and improved the *Discipline*, and authorized a new hymnal, *Das Geistliche Saitenspiel* (Sources 1807, p. 154).[9] The General Conference also embraced a new name, *Evangelische Gemeinschaft* (Evangelical Association), the first American church body to adopt the term *Evangelical* in its name. The following preface to the 1832 *Discipline* sets forth the EA's understanding of its history.

Introduction and Preamble: To the Gentle Reader [Evangelical Association]

THIS Doctrine of Faith and Church Discipline of our Evangelical Association, was originally composed and published by several *farmers* and *mechanics*, (a class of people, from among whom our Lord selected his Ministers, and blessed their labour in promulgating his word, in the primitive days of true Christianity,) namely by converted preachers: to whom our Conference committed the charge: for the first time by George Miller, A.D. 1809; and the second time, improved, by John Dreisbach and Henry Niebel, A.D. 1816; and the third time completed, by the General Conference, held in Hains township, Centre county, Pa., A.D. 1830. Being principally a collection from other Christian Rituals, briefly and plainly compiled, according to the word of God, the Holy Scriptures; to the edification of our Association, and all who desire to be edified thereby. And whoever will take the pains of perusing this little volume, may readily conceive the clear and simple way or method this Evangelical Association, as a plain people, (who have not acquired their qualification for Divine duty in Universities and Colleges, but from God himself), have chosen to pursue, in order to live a godly life according to his word; endeavoring together to serve the Almighty, in observing these lawful instructions, by the grace which the Lord imparted unto us.

Though this Evangelical Association, since their union with God and among themselves, has been exposed to much derision, scorn and oppression, and the slanderous invective of those who esteem themselves wise, yet it suffered itself not to be deterred or confounded in the progress of working out their souls salvation; being mindful, that all this cannot destroy the character of man in the sight of God, or take away that filial confidence of Him and his grace, from those who, in faith, wait upon His goodness.

Howbeit this body of the Church has not inherited or received her church government or ordination from others, but (as God has commanded the believers to build up his Church in union and love,) through the grace of God given unto them, they established it according to the regulations of the primitive Christians, in order to administer among themselves the blessed and necessary ordinances. Yet we are neither afraid or ashamed to acknowledge, that we have imitated, in part, our plan of government from other well ordered Rituals. The Episcopal form of government especially was introduced into this Association. And we hope no true Christian will therefore take offence or umbrage at this our regulation in the Lord, agreeable to his word: since he has nowhere prohibited that a religious community has not a perfect right, duly to use every sanctified means of grace, ordained of God, to their souls salvation. For we strive through grace to follow that which is good; and such undertakings God has blessed in all our transactions which we have hitherto attempted. And we pray and wait upon the Almighty, by humbly submitting under his holy will, for his grace, that He might bless this small essay (which we have accomplished with many sighings and tears,) to the souls of many, and thereby water the plants of His hands and give a happy increase to this branch of His Church among the German people of America, Amen! He that loves God and the souls of men, let him say: Amen! Success to the undertaking! Success to the edification of all! Amen!

We are indeed not going to build a house for the LORD, for the Heaven of Heavens cannot contain Him—and who are we, that we should prepare any thing for God?—but we desire to worship Him in the house of God, (his Church, which He hath redeemed by Christ,) under a becoming discipline and regulation, in proportion to each ones talent, according to the custom of the Apostles and the primitive Christians, and thus to glorify God in obedience of the truth.

MAY the God of love add his blessing with power to the edification of the Christian world, and especially to the melioration of the hearts of those who read or hear this small volume read.

Chapter I.
Section I.
Of the Origin of this Evangelical Association.

By the convincing instruction and advice of that devout minister of the gospel, *Jacob Albright,* several individuals united in the year 1800, to pray with and for each other, in order to flee the wrath to come, and to be redeemed from sin, inasmuch as they were deeply convinced of their sinful condition and sighed earnestly for deliverance.

In order properly to commence and accomplish this important work, they set apart each Sabbathday and each Wednesday evening for meeting together in prayer and devotional exercises: seeking diligently to avoid everything evil and sinful, and to do all manner of good, so far as God gave them power and ability. The number of those who were disposed to attend such meetings increased daily.

This was the origin of this Evangelical Association, which first took its rise in Pennsylvania; and on account of their distinguished zeal and worshipping God from other Christian denominations, they were called "*The Albrights*," probably because Jacob Albright was the instrumental cause of their solemnity uniting together to serve God.

Consequently this Association, primarily, was nothing else than a friendly adhering together of such persons who possessed a form of godliness, but desired to be made partakers of the power also. Thus the whole intent and motive of their uniting together was, to pray with and for each other; to admonish one another, and to be admonished; to watch one over the other in love, and assist each other in working out their souls' salvation.[10]

Although the book of discipline declared the new church to be an *episcopal* church, the General Conference did not elect a bishop. For the next twenty years the Evangelical Association was led by two presiding elders, Dreisbach and Henry Niebel, who were elected for two-year terms. A publishing house for the new church opened in New Berlin, Pennsylvania, in 1817.[11] Sunday schools for children were introduced in 1832, a denominational newspaper, *Der Christliche Botschäfter*, began publication in 1834, and a missionary society formed in 1838. Not until 1839 was the church's second bishop, John Seybert (1791–1860), elected and consecrated, a bachelor known for frugality and simplicity and a former Lutheran. The new bishop began an aggressive plan of church expansion westward to Ohio and Indiana, Michigan and Illinois, even Canada. In contrast to United Brethren, Evangelicals clung firmly to the German language.[12]

Methodists: Conferencing the Continent

Like the UBC and the EA, Methodists developed further their structures for spirituality and order in the period leading up to Asbury's death in 1816. Two salient expressions of these developments—camp meeting and General Conference—often dominate two distinct and largely unrelated narratives. They should not. Camp meetings and General Conferences belong to the one story of Methodism's conferencing the continent, indeed the globe.[13]

In the new church (MEC), the bishops called or appointed conferences with traveling difficulties and the appointment process in mind. The number of such ill-defined annual conferences in the still small movement swelled to seventeen in 1792 and nineteen in 1793. The 1796 General Conference addressed that chaos by specifying and establishing geographical boundaries for six annual conferences. So ordered and defined, General Conference reasoned, annual conferences would each have a share of the seasoned itinerants, would be large enough to possess the dignity needed by "every religious synod," and would facilitate more effective deployment of the itinerants. In particular, it would permit the bishops to appoint married preachers more locally and the unmarried across the continent.[14]

The reordered conference structure responded to the ongoing expansion of Methodism westward. Patterns evident from the beginning continued. The Methodist people moved west—adherents, members, "mothers in Israel," class leaders, exhorters, local preachers. Often these lay Methodists found one another in a new settlement and began the organizing process. Such spontaneous starts nevertheless ran by the book, the *Discipline*, under the guidance of class leader and the nearest local preacher. Other class-forming patterns began as a traveling preacher heard of settlements beyond his present itinerant rounds and appointed preaching for himself and his junior "yokefellow" wherever he could find a willing household. Thus the line of Methodism moved with western settlements and often as the very first phase of sociopolitical community formation. New classes and preaching places stressing a circuit's capacity demanded additional preachers and circuits and eventually new conferences.

Anticipating that challenge, General Conference in 1796, even as it delineated annual conference boundaries, appended the following proviso to its demarcation of the Western Conference: "*Provided,* That the bishops shall have authority to appoint other yearly conferences in the interval of the General Conference, if a sufficiency of new circuits be anywhere formed for that purpose."[15] General Conference reiterated that proviso up to 1832.[16] Annual conferences marched westward with overall American settlement. So after reducing the number of conferences in the interest of communication, efficiency, and fraternal authority, the preachers in General Conference authorized their increase as the church exploded west, north, and south. Six in 1796, seven in 1800, nine in 1812, eleven in 1816, twelve in 1820 along with three provisos, seventeen in 1824, twenty-two in 1832, and twenty-nine in 1836.[17]

Conferences Politicized: Toward a Delegated General Conference

The 1796 General Conference had also determined "Who shall attend the yearly conferences?": "Those who are in full connexion, and who are to be received into full connexion." It explained: "This regulation is made that our societies and congregations may be supplied with preaching during the conferences."[18] By 1804, having drawn these geographical and demographic boundaries, the MEC had come to understand that a preacher actually belonged to a specific conference.[19] Individual conferences, once convened primarily as instruments of mission and ministry, thereafter became social and political units, within which preachers increasingly either lived out their itinerant careers or located to farm and to raise a family.

The establishment of conferences as sociopolitical units made their representation in General Conference critical. That perception dawned slowly as annual conferences stabilized, preachers began to identify themselves with a specific conference, and General Conference sat repeatedly in one locale. By convening regularly in Baltimore, welcoming first all conference members, then those in full connection, and (after 1800) those who had traveled four years, General Conferences came to be numerically overwhelmed and dominated by the two nearby annual conferences, Baltimore and Philadelphia, from which preachers could more conveniently attend. The numbers for 1804 and 1808 indicate the concern:

	1804	1808
Philadelphia	41	32
Baltimore	29	31
Virginia	17	18
New York	12	19
South Carolina	5	11
New England	4	7
Western	4[20]	11[21]

To remedy the imbalance and overrepresentation of Baltimore and Philadelphia Conferences, Jesse Lee proposed in 1804 a principle of delegation. His motion did not pass then. However, between 1804 and 1808, concern about some measure for conference equity spread. A memorial for equal conference representation made the rounds of the annual conferences and was endorsed by the four more distant (the last four conferences listed above). Philadelphia, Baltimore, and Virginia did not concur.

The 1808 General Conference could not avoid the issue of annual conference representation. Bishop Asbury guided the body toward eventual compromise by establishing a committee of two persons from each conference.[22] Out of this group, Joshua Soule, Ezekiel Cooper, and Philip Bruce were commissioned to draft plans for a delegated General Conference. Soule and Cooper produced different visions. Cooper advocated a decentralized conference order, essentially that which pertains today, with a bishop for each conference, or failing that, the election of presiding elders. Soule proposed a delegated conference and explicitly limited General Conference's legislative power in several crucial areas, among them any alteration of the plan of an "itinerant general superintendency" or modification of "our present existing and established standards of doctrine." Soule's draft, with this set of "Restrictive Rules" at its heart, came eventually to be regarded as the constitution of the church (Sources 1808), but it passed only after considerable debate and testing of alternatives. Cooper pressed for the election of presiding elders, an effective delimitation of the power and authority of bishops and an issue that would not go away. Lee sought delegation through seniority rather than election, a proposal brought into compromise legislation.

The Teaching Office

From their introduction the Restrictive Rules were recognized as a critical turn in the denomination's history. Soule's effort at precision left several matters ambiguous.

What were the standards of doctrine? Were the Articles of Religion the intended reference as the manuscript minutes of General Conference seem to indicate or the fuller array of Wesleyan transmissions (*Sermons* and *Notes* in particular)?[23] Who would judge the constitutionality of General Conference actions? Was it the arbiter of its own decisions? Did plenary authority lodge now in General Conference in its "full powers to make rules and regulations" or remain in the whole body of preachers? And by making bishops presiding officers and no longer members of General Conference, had the church subjected the former to the latter? Where, in short, was Methodism's teaching office?[24]

Bishop Asbury, until he died in 1816, continued to operate as though the teaching office were his. He had been as much member, mover, and voice as chair and presider in annual conferences and General Conferences. Even more his teaching, direction, and tutelage had occurred and continued in utterances, prayers, sermons, counsel, and directives offered in conference and on the road, over meals, and in homes. That teaching-on-the-road occurred because when Asbury traveled, he would be joined by preachers over whose circuit the bishop traversed or to whose quarterly meeting Asbury was headed. For instance, William Colbert, then a young preacher, spent eight days in the 1790s with Bishop Asbury in Pennsylvania. Colbert constantly attended to Asbury, heard the bishop preach each day, and under the bishop's watchful supervision, prayed, preached, and exhorted.[25]

Asbury exercised the teaching office in formal ways as well. The presumption and concern of his teaching inform a series of valedictories, albeit apologetic, patronizing, even jeremiadic, in tone (Sources 1813b). Asbury had achieved preeminence by deferring publicly to but isolating the seldom present Coke and treating as "junior bishops," his other compatriots, Richard Whatcoat (1736–1806), elected in a close election in 1800 over Lee, and William McKendree (1757–1835), elected in 1808 following a spirited sermon to General Conference.[26] McKendree, the first American-born to be elected, found new ways to exercise the episcopal teaching and leadership role through committees, with cabinets of presiding elders, and by setting conference agendas. Dramatically in the 1812 General Conference and apparently without advance notice to Asbury, McKendree delivered an agenda-outlining address, setting the precedent for the Episcopal Address that thereafter began the serious work of the conference (Sources 1812a). Asbury responded in astonishment, as McKendree's biographer reported:

> His address was read in Conference; but as it was a new thing, the aged Bishop [Asbury] rose to his feet immediately after the paper was read, and addressed the junior Bishop to the following effect: "I have something to say to you before the Conference." The junior also rose to his feet, and they stood face to face. Bishop Asbury went on to say, "This is a new thing. I never did business in this way, and why is this new thing introduced?" The junior Bishop promptly replied, "You are our *father*, we are your sons; you never have had need of it. I am only a *brother*, and have need of it." Bishop Asbury said no more, but sat down with a smile on his face.[27]

Unlike Whatcoat, who had been willing to function in a secondary part, McKendree sought collegiality and parity, expecting to have a say on appointments and initiating a genuine sharing of presidential roles by dividing the conferences.

Camp and Quarterly Meetings

The conference order and protocol for which McKendree stood seemed to contrast with the disorder, noise, emotion, energy, conflict, and raw religiosity of the camp meeting. Conference and camp meeting, however, constituted two sides of Methodism's practice of spiritual assembly, sides the church succeeded in holding together in practice and policy but not in concept or polity. The origins and authorship of camp meetings have been and will remain contested, definition itself providing no small part of the unclarity. Multiday preaching and sacramental gatherings had long been practiced in Western Christianity and by various denominations in newly or sparsely settled areas of colonial America, notably by the Pennsylvania Germans. Definition emerged with the well-reported Presbyterian-initiated, multidenominational encampments in the summers of 1800 and 1801 at Cane Ridge, Kentucky. McKendree, then presiding elder of the Kentucky district, recognized immediately the value of the camp meeting. So did Bishop Asbury, who, along with a number of Methodist leaders, communicated the revivalistic import of camp meetings to Bishop Coke and through the (British) *Methodist Magazine*[28] to the Methodist world.

"There is," wrote Ezekiel Cooper to Coke, "a great and glorious Revival in Tennessee and Kentuckey, among both Presbyterians and Methodists, who join in Christian fellowship, and help each other in the blessed work." He continued,

> Some of our Ministers, and some of the Presbyterian Clergy, join as a band of brothers to make war against the kingdom of the Devil; and the fruit of their joint labours is wonderful. Their meetings continue for days together; the people come from far in their waggons, &c. to their great meetings: They bring provisions with them, pitch their tents in the woods, and there continue for days, worshipping the Lord together.[29]

By late 1802, Asbury had turned from observer and reporter to promoter. He directed Methodist leaders to establish camp meetings in connection with annual conferences. He wrote George Roberts of the Baltimore Conference:

> The campmeetings have been blessed in North and South Carolina, and Georgia. Hundreds have fallen and have felt the power of God. I wish most sincerely that we could have a campmeeting at Duck Creek out in the plain south of the town, and let the people come with their tents, wagons, provision and so on. Let them keep at it night and day, during the conference; that ought to sit in the meeting.

Zachary Myles of Baltimore informed Coke, "Mr. Asbury wrote word to our preachers, to make preparation for the erection of a Camp within two miles of this City, at our next Conference in April."[30]

More typically, Methodists structured camp meetings in relation not to annual conference but to the staple of local Methodist religious life, quarterly meetings. They had become, as we have noted already, two-day, multifunction, highly liturgical, often crowd-gathering events. The quarterly meetings were camp meetings without the tents or brush arbors. Once the camp meeting emerged and had the church's blessing, routinely and for several decades, quarterly conferences across the whole church voted to hold one of their warm-weather sessions as a camp meeting, as did Smithfield (Sources 1811b).[31] Exploding across the North American landscape, camp meetings became a hugely successful engine of Methodist growth and a highly familiar signature of its organizational life.

Preachers spent a considerable portion of their time, particularly in the summer, in going to or conducting camp meetings. Jacob Lanius, for instance, attended successive camp meetings (in different places) from late July through mid-September, breaking then "in order to get to conference in time," only to attend two more thereafter.[32] Peter Cartwright narrated his life story, *Autobiography of Peter Cartwright* and *Fifty Years as a Presiding Elder*, as one camp meeting after another, indicating that he spent his summers in camp meetings, befitting the office he held, which obliged him to preside at the quarterly meetings/camp meetings.[33] Cartwright's colorful stories of faith and fisticuffs have imaged the camp meeting as a western affair. However, camp meetings blossomed as much in the East where they put increasingly urbanized Methodism in touch with its fervid past as in the frontier where they served well to command the attention and to create the community around the Methodist message and program requisite for individual transformation and corporate formation.

Jesse Lee, the first historian of American Methodism, who had traced revivals in relation to conference and quarterly conference meetings, after 1802 narrated the Methodist story as a series of camp meetings. And as he concluded his history in 1809, he did so in a short overview of the camp meeting, its staging, rules, layout, and rhythms, noting that this signature practice had "never been authorized by the Methodists, either at their general or annual conferences."[34] Camp meetings could be celebrated for their redemptive love and experienced assurance, as did Fanny Lewis for one near Baltimore in 1803 (Sources 1803). But others reacted negatively to their emotionalism and display (crying, shouting, jerking, falling) and to the crowds of disorderly or disruptive persons who congregated around or outside.[35] Methodists found it necessary to order them carefully and also to defend them against critics within and without, as did John Totten in some fifty pages of closely set type (Sources 1810b).

Rhythms of Methodist Spirituality

Methodist preachers ran conferences and camp meetings, but Methodism as a whole ran predominantly as a movement of and for women, whose spiritual agency was pervasive, if not always prominent.[36] Indeed, as American Methodism grew in numbers and stabilized itself, as early as the 1790s in New York, a decade later elsewhere, women lost places in the offices of the church, offices to which Wesley had admitted them, most notably as class leaders. He had appointed women to head all-women classes, sometimes those mixed male-female. In celebrating and publicizing as saints and heroes of the movement, Hester Ann Rogers, Elizabeth Ritchie Mortimer, and Grace Murray, women who held that office, Wesley established expectations and precedents that would continually stimulate women to honor calls to public witness and leadership they experienced and to test boundaries and limits imposed by the (male) preachers. A few who felt the call to preach found occasion to exercise that gift and, perhaps more important, to convey to contemporaries and later generations the spiritual agonies that impressed them into service. So, for instance, Fanny Newell (1793–1824) at a camp meeting held in connection with the New England Conference of 1809 and then under preaching of the circuit preacher Ebenezer F. Newell underwent spiritual duress culminating in a subsequent dream as a call to preach (Sources 1809). Marrying Newell, experiencing near death in childbirth, and suffering frail health, she nevertheless lived out the dream-call by itinerating with her husband in the years after 1818 on the Maine frontiers of Methodism, indeed sometimes taking his place and/or standing in for him. Her memoirs, first published in 1824 soon after her death from tuberculosis and in several editions thereafter, modeled the faithful and holy life, the precedent of preaching, and the important role of public office as spouse-to-itinerant.[37] Jarena Lee (1783–1850?), converted under Richard Allen and married in 1811 to a preacher, Joseph Lee, experienced a call to preach that Allen initially discounted but eventually, as bishop of the African Methodist Episcopal Church (AME), embraced (Sources 1811a). Her journal, published in 1836 and in augmented form in 1849, one of the earliest spiritual witnesses of African American women, like that of Newell assumed great importance in the long contest by women for ordination in the Methodist family of denominations.

The major legislative battles for women's official leadership lay decades ahead (see chapter 7). In early nineteenth-century Methodism, the primary modality of Methodist witness, overall and for women, was through lives that testified to gospel order and to steady progress toward loving, compassionate holiness. Here polity, power, and privilege constituted no advantage, indeed, a probable disadvantage. In addition, Methodism functioned day to day, in women's sphere, in homes, on a domestic level. Classes met in homes and shops, even in New York, Baltimore, and Philadelphia, where Methodism boasted church buildings that accommodated some of the meetings (Sources 1802).[38] Outside these cities, Methodist buildings and preaching places were the houses of their adherents and friends. And membership effectively also had a domestic character in that members belonged through their classes. Their good standing, still registered by ticket from the class leader, opened up participation on larger levels. Even the preachers were, in a sense, domesticated. As they traveled around the circuit, they stayed with families or widows, such preacher homes a centerpiece of the itinerant plan in established circuits and a project to be worked on in frontier areas.

Within a Methodism so constituted day to day on a domestic level, women exercised a variety of roles, despite, perhaps because of, the constraints on their access to office.[39] Authorizing the informal roles were spirituality, Christlike love, and the blessing of holiness. And American Methodists, like their British counterparts, warranted and celebrated this authorization from above by publishing women's diaries, pious lives, conversion and sanctification accounts, and funeral sermons. The first of these to appear from the American Methodist press was Elizabeth Singer Rowe's *Devout Exercises of the Heart* (Sources 1791c).[40] The classic, Wesley-endorsed modeling of Hester Ann Rogers was published often and widely sold. Their authority secured by the Holy Spirit, women found ample places to exhibit and vocalize their grasp of the Christian and Methodist message. In class meetings, in love feasts, with preachers around the table, with their husbands and children, on camp meeting occasions, women interceded in prayer and praise and hymn and testimony for the movement, its members, and its leaders. Methodists claimed the importance and recognized the great variety of these informal roles with an authorizing, frequently used, biblical title, "mother in Israel." So Bishop Asbury wrote Mrs. Ann Willis implicitly acknowledging her influence with him, presuming that she would continue to make her home a place of religious transformation and therefore exhorting her to be a "mother in Israel" (Sources 1812b). On the bedrock of spiritual influence Methodists would create significant structures of nurture, mission, social transformation, and care.

Racializing the Church

By 1810, Black Methodists constituted roughly half the membership in South Carolina, more than 40 percent in Maryland, and close to 40 percent in Delaware. In the latter two states those numbers included both free and slave, and the church had played no small part in the fight against slavery, as we will note below in a closer look at Baltimore.[41]

Methodism began constitutionally, legislatively, and programmatically committed to antislavery. Methodists conveyed their resolve in the day to day of preaching and circuit life, as we have noted. They also took public stands. Ezekiel Cooper, one of early Methodism's most effective and articulate leaders, later to be book agent and, in effect, the church's official spokesperson, carried on a newspaper campaign for manumission in the *Maryland Gazette*, the *Maryland Journal*, and the *Virginia Gazette* in the early 1790s.

We have noted that O'Kelly witnessed against slavery in publication and through his movement. His stance and his schism drained antislavery numbers and resolve from the movement as a whole. More clearly, Methodism found itself facing greater resistance and opposition to its commitment from within and beyond its own ranks, the consequence of its growth and evangelistic outreach in slaveholding areas and of the waning of the societal antislavery sentiments bred during the Revolutionary epoch.

Even where the antislavery commitment remained strong, Methodists found it extraordinarily difficult to translate idealism into practice, preachment into inclusive fellowship, and antislavery into interracial community. So segregated classes, virtually from the start, continued to evolve toward segregated ecclesial structure, sometimes with white leadership support, often in the face of white efforts at control, as AME narratives indicate (Sources 1816), Richard Allen's biography charts (Sources 1792b), and letters to Bishop Asbury attest. In 1794 Bethel Church, Philadelphia, issued a "Public Statement" of some 2,200 words explaining why its members needed separate accommodations:

> Whereas from time to time many inconveniences have arisen from white people and people of color mixing together in public assemblys, more particularly in places of public worship, we have thought it necessary to provide for ourselves a convenient house to assemble in separate from our white brethren.
>
> 1st. To obviate any offence our mixing with our white brethren might give them.[42]

Within Black Methodism, spirituality and order interplayed, African American commitment to stay Methodist being one indicator thereof. More programmatically, Black Methodists continued authorizing their own music, message, and leadership and creating systems of nurture, formation, outreach, and social service. Richard Allen, for instance, produced the first hymnal under Black auspices in 1801. Recognizing the emerging African American leadership (and the emerging segregated system), the General Conference of 1800 empowered bishops to ordain Black local deacons, though, as Jesse Lee indicated, deciding not to include that provision in the *Discipline*.[43] Richard Allen (Philadelphia) and Daniel Coker (Baltimore) were among those first ordained. Functioning restively under white elders, the African American leaders and congregations pressed for the prerogatives that would give them ecclesial legitimacy and standing (full ordination as elders and conference membership).[44] They also spoke out publicly against slavery, as did Daniel Coker (Sources 1810a), and informally to bishops and conference on their decidedly second-class treatment by fellow Methodists.

The MEC under Asbury's leadership, though continuing to voice opposition to slavery, gradually retreated, searching for enforceable standards as southern commitment to the slave system strengthened and southern legislatures voted to prohibit manumission. The 1800 General Conference, for instance, sustained the Wesleyan witness in its pastoral letter by imploring a state-by-state antislavery petition to legislatures (Sources 1800a), an item publicly burned in Charleston.[45] Drafted by three clergy (Ezekiel Cooper, William McKendree, and Jesse Lee), "agreed to" by the conference, and signed by the three bishops—Asbury, Coke, and Whatcoat—the address was published in broadside format and widely distributed.[46] Asbury had second thoughts about the wisdom of such tough talk. Six months after it was issued, he wrote in his journal: "Nothing could so effectually alarm and arm the criticism of South Carolina against the Methodists as the *Address of the General Conference*."[47] The 1804 General Conference, conceding that the church's official stance caused offense in the South, published a version of the *Discipline* without the section on slavery. It made that self-censorship a policy in 1808. That General Conference also authorized "each annual conference to form their own regulations relative to buying and selling slaves."[48] By 1816, in response to the report of the Committee on Slavery that "under the present existing circumstances in relation to slavery, little can be done to abolish a practice so contrary to the principles of moral justice. They are sorry to say that the evil appears to be past remedy," General Conference resolved to adjust *Discipline*-limiting prohibition against slaveholders' holding office to states permitting emancipation.[49] By that time, some Black Methodists decided that the MEC would simply not accommodate their needs and gathered to form the AME (Sources 1816), a narrative that we resume in the next chapter and in the Baltimore "Snapshot."

Transitions

Asbury died en route to the 1816 General Conference, Coke a year earlier on board a ship in the Indian Ocean, and Lee in a camp meeting in Maryland. In their different ways they had modeled and enforced an itinerant, missional form of ministry that they insisted was the primitive, apostolic, New Testament form. So Asbury reiterated in his several valedictories.[50] In identifying Methodism's three orders and ordinations in 1816, Asbury elevated his own, the itinerant general superintendency, yet one last time and one rung higher. Wesley had called Coke and Asbury "superintendents." They converted that to the more conventional but honorific "bishops." In his last formal utterance, read posthumously at General Conference, Asbury claimed the title "Apostle" (Sources 1813b). The claim confirmed his critics' charges. His episcopal compatriots (Whatcoat and Coke), now deceased, would doubtless have appreciated such candor earlier. His more numerous supporters and mourners, especially those gathered for the 1816 General Conference, including Bishop McKendree, knew that Methodism's apostolic age had passed and they were now on their own.[51]

While sitting, General Conference had Asbury's remains brought to Baltimore and interred with sermonic and ceremonial honor in the new Eutaw Street Church where it was meeting. General Conference elected Enoch George and Robert Richford Roberts to the episcopacy, entertained again the question of electing presiding elders, raised preachers' salaries to one hundred dollars, condemned pew rental as a funding device, and worried over other Methodist slippage on discipline, dress, sacramental practice, and doctrine. Electing Joshua Soule as book editor, General Conference authorized, as had the 1812 Conference, the publication of a magazine. It appeared two years later. Variously titled, the *Methodist Magazine* was to live on for almost two centuries. Among its early important communications was notice of the April 1819 formation of the Methodist Missionary Society, with the Women's Auxiliary to be constituted three months later. Another institution also continuing to the present, the Course of Study, the conference established with the directive to the bishops to prescribe a reading regimen for candidates for the ministry. Its episcopal leadership now all American-born and with new institutions in formation, the MEC looked forward to a new day.

METHODISM IN 1816: BALTIMORE

In 1816 Baltimore was the heart and soul of Methodism, its center, its capital city, its place of greatest strength, its site of holiest memories, its Jerusalem.[1] There, perhaps, Methodism had made its greatest impact. There it had already become the dominant Protestant denomination.[2] There also Methodism's contradictions and tensions came to focus.[3] There it had the numbers, the leadership, and increasingly the resources to affect social policy and the social order. There its commitments to holiness and reform came early to clash. For there, in Baltimore and environs, Methodism was black and white, rich and poor, professional and artisan, German- and English-speaking, young and old, urban and rural. As such, it participated actively in the contradictions and tensions that were Maryland, "a middle temperament" or "the middle ground" of American society.[4]

That middle temperament was especially affected by and expressed in the politics of slavery and freedom. By 1816 boasting the largest population of free Black Americans in the country, Maryland was nevertheless a slave state. But solely a southern plantation economy Maryland was not.[5] Led by Baltimore, Maryland in 1816 experienced a mercantile and building boom and competed for the nation's business, in part fueled by the euphoria and public spirit born of the War of 1812. Maryland had taken the brunt of the war, had seen the bombs bursting in air, and had come through with a vital sense of its place in national affairs.[6] The new public spirit palpably bubbled in politics, business, church life, society, and culture. It expressed itself in a literary and cultural effervescence—newspapers and magazines; writers, poets, and painters; a literary journal; a club for conversation; "the country's first planned museum," Rembrandt Peale's Baltimore Museum and Gallery; and a university featuring degrees for the professions, medicine, law, and divinity.

In 1816 critics spoke of Baltimore as "the Athens of America."[7] They referred as much to its appearance as to its culture and art. New buildings abounded, many Greek Revival—major monuments to George Washington, row houses, and especially the

Merchant's Exchange Building housing city and federal offices, trading facilities, professional offices, and a fireproof vault. From the latter merchants traded with the nation and the world, now easily reached over the national road and soon via Chesapeake steamships. Churches also invested in Baltimore, hiring the best European and American architects—Benjamin Henry Latrobe, Robert Mills, Maximilien Godefroy, and Robert Cary Long Sr—for Greco-Roman, Gothic, and neoclassical statements of Episcopal, Roman Catholic, Baptist, and Unitarian purpose.[8] Methodism built on a more modest scale. Its contribution to the look of Baltimore lay elsewhere.

Methodism in Black and White

The strong religious communities, and especially the Quakers and Methodists, contributed to building in Baltimore, by shaping the moral climate of Maryland and, in particular, an ethic of liberty and antislavery. Members responded and manumitted their slaves. In consequence, the population of freed African Americans was significant and growing, and the slave population shrinking, absolutely and relatively, from manumissions and migration or sale west.[9] Free and slave labor and free and slave persons and black and white interacted in complex ways, making Maryland quite unlike slave states farther south. The presence of free African Americans affected the character of Maryland slavery; conversely, the presence of slaves qualified the quite imperfect freedom accorded African Americans. Slave and free worked, prayed, lived side by side. Both could be found within the covenants that defined society—labor contracts, church covenants, marriages. Such covenants reverberated and proved vulnerable to the changing fate of both freedom and slavery in Maryland and the nation at large. In the prior decade, for instance, African Americans had seen their prerogatives reduced. Both state and church moved to strip them of the franchise and limit the offices they could hold.[10] Methodists did permit African Americans to hold office as local preachers, exhorters, trustees, and class leaders. And Baltimore Methodism employed African Americans in all these positions, though honoring local law and custom that a white be present at Black gatherings and sometimes charging that person with leadership.[11] Baltimore African Americans found that dependency on whites for pastoral services distasteful and inadequate and had expressed their discontent a year prior in a formal accord with the elder in charge.[12] And in 1816 Baltimore witnessed firsthand General Conference's perplexity over slavery and willingness to concede further to the states' authority. General Conference, as we noted, had deemed "the evil" "to be past remedy" and limited the *Discipline*'s prohibition against slaveholders' holding office to states permitting emancipation.[13]

For Baltimore Methodists, the years 1815 and 1816 registered the ambiguities and imperfections in the moral climate and in race relations. For those years the "Colored" class rolls attest that many African Americans, some one-seventh thereof, had their fill of white domination.[14] Beside name after name is an X followed by the explanation "gone with Coker."[15] These members had cast their lot with Daniel Coker, whose name, first on the list of local preachers, was also stricken through and who had led Baltimore African Americans into a declaration of independence, the acquisition of separate property, and affiliation with Richard Allen in organizing in 1916 a new denomination, the African Methodist Episcopal Church.[16] Preaching at that organizing conference in Baltimore, Coker compared the African American plight to that of the Jews in Babylon and listed the leadership of the Philadelphia and Baltimore Black Methodist communities (Sources 1816). The new church elected Coker bishop, turning to Allen only when Coker demurred. In a later commentary on the prospects for Africans in the U.S., as well as prospects for Methodism in Africa, Coker undertook a mission to Africa, in ambiguous relation to the colonization efforts in which white Methodists, from Baltimore and elsewhere, would invest heavily.[17] Allen, by contrast, spoke out early and often against colonization.

With the loss to the AME, Baltimore Methodism reported 1,430 Black members in 1816, down from 1,552 the preceding year and with another 100-member loss to follow. The white membership for 1816 was 1,954, up from 1,667 the previous year. Despite the losses, the proportions of 1,954 white to 1,430 Black were comparable to those of the preceding years when Baltimore consistently reported just under 40 percent African American membership.[18] African Americans had responded to the Methodist gospel, as had poor people generally. In Baltimore, Methodism's appeal reached beyond the lower classes. Some 20 percent of Methodists were artisans. However, about 30 percent of the membership was white collar; and Methodists constituted the largest population among the city's wealthiest. This spread across classes contrasted with the sharper class profile of other denominations—concentrations of the poor within Roman Catholic ranks and of the social elites within Presbyterian and Episcopal denominations.[19] Class diversity gave Baltimore its strength, but also its vulnerabilities and divisions.

Divided by Languages

In 1816 Baltimore Methodists spoke two languages, English and German. William Otterbein, the dominant figure among United Brethren, had died in 1813. Also dead by 1816 were efforts to unite Methodists and Brethren. Negotiations between the two denominations had been Baltimore-based, between the Baltimore Conference and the "Original," later Eastern, Conference of the UBC, and carried on from 1809 through 1814 by the exchange of letters and delegates.[20] Here, too, control proved a decisive issue, the Methodists, as we have noted, insisting on adherence to Methodist standards of discipline, licensing, itinerancy, record keeping, and membership. In 1814, the Methodists had concluded the relations, terming it "unnecessary to continue the ceremony of annual letters, etc." but leaving "the door of friendly intercourse open."[21] The intercourse did continue, at both informal and formal levels. Informally, German dialects (as well as African and Irish versions of English) would be heard in the recounting of religious experience in love feasts and in the cries at camp meetings.[22] More formally, Bishop Christian Newcomer of the UBC recorded, in 1816, visiting his counterpart, William McKendree (soon after Asbury's death), attending the General Conference of the MEC, visiting Methodist camp meetings, and preaching in English and German. Newcomer also attended the conference of "the Albright Brethren" (Sources 1813c).[23] Such intercourse notwithstanding, the tendency was toward separate denominations (or structures within denominations) to accommodate linguistic and racial differences.

Defined by Calendar

For all three groups and the AME as well, conference defined calendar, program, discipline, governance, legislation, and jurisprudence. Methodism ran on conference time—not on a liturgical year; not on the Christian rhythms of Advent, Christmas, Epiphany, Lent, Easter, Pentecost; not on Julian or Gregorian time; not on American civil time, with special attention to the Fourth of July; not even on the Christian week. Time ran by conference calendar—the weekly meeting of the class; the quarterly gathering of the circuit; the annual meeting of the preachers; and the quadrennial convening of leadership in General Conference.

Annual conferences established the mean time, the church year, the sacred calendar. Each conference had its own unique church year, an artifact of the episcopal tour, of the migration of Bishops Asbury and McKendree around the connection, of the time appointed for their sitting. Baltimore's time ran from March to March, from the sitting of one Baltimore Conference to the next. The church year 1816 began then on March 8, 1816, when the preachers gathered in Georgetown with McKendree presiding. This particular conference did not meet in Baltimore—did not meet in the "preachers' room" in Light Street Church, an architectural statement of Baltimore's centrality—but many did, including those of 1815 and 1817, making hospitality and housing the responsibility of the membership and deploying the preachers *each day* into the city and countryside for services whenever conference was not actually in session. Appointing a committee to arrange such preaching constituted one of the first and most important acts in the organization of conference. For 1816: "Bro's. George, Roszel, & Hemphill were appointed to Superinted [sic] the Congregations & make arrangements for preaching to them during the sitting of the Conference."[24]

From such preaching, by the conference's best, the region might experience rejuvenation, and revivals flowed often from annual conference sessions. Not, however, from this one, which doubtless worried about the connection, its concern prompted by the ill health of Bishop McKendree and especially the absence of Bishop Asbury, halted en route at what would prove to be his final stop, having missed only one other session of the Baltimore Conference, that during the Revolution.[25]

Conference was very much the people's affair, a revivifying experience for the connection, even though only the itinerants were members and the conference might, on occasion, meet with closed doors. It was, after all, the annual event that renewed the leadership for every circuit and station. Baltimore was favored by some continuity; assigned to the Baltimore City Station in 1815 were Alfred Griffith, Thomas Burch, Frederick Stier, and Lewis R. Fechtige; when appointments were read, Fechtige was reappointed and was joined by Stephen G. Roszel, Andrew Hemphill, and Richard Hunt; of that group, only Roszel continued in 1817.[26] They were assisted by the local preachers, individuals like James Armstrong, James R. Williams, and Joseph Shane—the unpaid pastoral continuity in Baltimore staying in place for years, while itinerants changed yearly, and the evangelistic outreach of the Baltimore ministerium, preaching regularly two or three times each Sunday and ranging out of Baltimore to a distance of twenty miles.[27] Especially notable was Shane, born in Baltimore in 1780, admitted to the traveling connection in 1800, located 1804, and then a merchant and justice of the peace:

> He was almost the apostle, on the old "Severn circuit," adjacent to Baltimore: preached more frequently: attended more funerals: baptised more children: solemnized more marriages: than any one man of his times. His services throughout Baltimore City, in the various churches, were frequent and useful. Some of the best judges of preaching did not hesitate to pronounce him a superior preacher for plainness and directness.[28]

During this conference away from Baltimore (in George Town), local preachers, like Shane, and their counterparts across the entire connection would take responsibility for the circuits, hold the services, preach the sermons, and carry on the pastoral care until the newly stationed preachers arrived.

If Baltimore depended on the conference, the conference also depended on Baltimore, especially financially. Of the $3,363.49 collected from the circuits by the end of the year, Baltimore City had contributed $885.37, Fells Point $62.83, and Baltimore Circuit $90.13. That ingathering, almost one-third of the total, made it possible for the conference to meet, not the $90 that each preacher was due, but at least the $85 salary that conference set. Baltimore preachers shared in that largess, getting exactly the common fare, no more. And it was one of the Baltimore preachers of that year, namely, Roszel, who had moved to interpolate the General Conference legislation to fit the conference year, set the *common* salary, and stipulate "that if any of the Preachers of this Conference have received more than ninety dollars as their Annual allowance, it shall be refunded to the Conference Stewards" (of which he was chief).[29]

General Conferences also commanded Baltimore interest. In 1816 General Conference again met in Baltimore, which meant that for the entire month of May the members stayed with Baltimore families and Baltimore Methodists enjoyed meals, conversation, debates, politicking, and worship with the church's leadership. Detailed records of planning and preparation do not seem to survive, but one senses that the Baltimore Conference endeavored to draw all its people, not just those of Baltimore, into engagement with the General Conference. In its last action before setting its next meeting in Baltimore it resolved "that the last friday in April, or the friday before the General Conference, be observed a day of solemn fasting and prayer, before Almighty God, for his blessing on the General Conference, and the Connection at large."[30] Baltimore experienced this high point in the Methodist calendar through the presence of conference and was atypical in having both annual conferences and General Conferences with such frequency. Less central places in the Methodist world experienced conference as a period of absence, particularly the absence of their leaders. Peter Cartwright, who attended the 1816 General Conference, reported being away almost three months.[31]

Baltimore Methodists were especially active around the 1816 General Conference owing, in part, to the recent death of Francis Asbury. The conference gathered at Light Street Church. In its first action of business, after the election of a secretary, the General Conference (MEC) of 1816 received a petition "from the male members of the Methodist Episcopal Church in the city of Baltimore" to remove Asbury's remains there. The body was brought to Light Street and then, after funeral services, taken by the conference, "several ministers of other denominations and a vast throng of citizens" in solemn procession to Eutaw Street to be buried. McKendree preached there; other churches, including Otterbein's, also joined in memorials; several preachers delivered orations in conference.[32] The funeral and burial in the city again registered the preeminently "connectional" character of Baltimore Methodism.

A Quarterly "Church"

Baltimore was, indeed, unique in experiencing firsthand the defining moments in the Methodist sacred year, both annual conferences and General Conferences. Other Methodists participated only through reports or minutes. Baltimore did share with other stations and circuits the quarterly rhythms of the Methodist year, the appointment by Nelson Reed, its presiding elder, of quarterly conferences. These events—not Christmas or Easter, not New Year's Eve watch night or Good Friday, not Thanksgiving or the Fourth of July—were the high points on the calendar. Then the people gathered, as well as their officers, stewards, class leaders, exhorters, local preachers, and traveling preachers. On these two days, still typically Saturday and Sunday, the circuit or station did its business.[33] It received and disbursed "quarterage" for the preachers, presiding elder, and bishops from the stewards; issued licenses or made recommendations, as appropriate; heard appeals from disciplinary actions on a class level; received complaints against ex-

horters or preachers; and conducted trials. The essential business accomplished in an afternoon session, the quarterly conference spent Saturday evening and all day Sunday in
religious festival—prayer meetings, preaching, love feast, the sacrament.[34] One of the
warm weather quarterly meetings would often be appointed as a camp meeting, thus extending the fare of the meeting into a full Methodist liturgical feast, evangelical and revivalistic to be sure, but nevertheless highly stylized and zealously defined by its quarterly
rites—love feast, preaching in abundance, and Communion. Love feasts were especially
powerful scenes in the quarterly drama—held behind closed doors; members admitted
by quarterly ticket from preacher or class leaders; nonmembers limited to one or two visits; involving Scripture, singing, prayer, and the sharing of bread and water; and drawing their nurturing energy, bonding quality, and revivifying power from the relating of
religious experience.[35] One contemporary looking back from a couple of decades later
remarked,

> The old quarterly meeting conferences and love-feasts! what was more characteristic of
> practical Methodism than they? The horses and carriages, and groups of men, women,
> and children plodding the highways on foot, for twenty miles or more, as on a holy pil
> grimage; the assemblage of preachers, traveling and local, from all the neighboring ap
> pointments; the two days of preaching and exhorting, praying and praising; the powerful
> convictions, and more powerful conversions; and especially the Sunday morning love-
> feast, with its stirring testimonies and kindling songs; its tears and shoutings—how pre
> cious their reminiscences! Alas, for the changes which are coming over us![36]

The stylized, quarterly liturgical weekend was an American original. In quarterly
meetings, Methodism was most fully church; there members heard the word truly
preached, received the sacraments duly administered, and experienced the blessings of
love feast; there the preachers and leaders met with all the classes who supported them
and were in turn supported; there the larger world heard the evangelical call through
preaching and exhortation; and primarily there the conversions would occur. And when,
as in 1814, the Baltimore Conference took alarm at the flagging of the Methodist spirit,
its first word of admonition, in a formal, printed address to the "brethren," was "to take
into consideration, the expediency & necessity of regularly attending, as far as practicable, the quar(r)terly meetings of your circuits."[37] Baltimore heeded such injunctions
and did experience revival, not in 1816, but in 1817 and the year thereafter.[38]

The Weekly Calendar

As far as the weekly calendar was concerned, Baltimore City Station was a trendsetter in having preaching houses—Light Street (1786, rebuilt 1797), Old Town (1798),
Sharp Street (the African Church, 1802), and Eutaw Street (1808)—and therefore a
regular pattern of Sabbath preaching. A preaching plan was worked out for the entire

year and deployed the four preachers in rotation among the churches and over Sunday services at 10:00, 3:00, and night and in weeknight services (Sources, p. 24). Each traveling preacher typically preached in all four churches each week. Local preachers were also worked into the rotation.[39] Members, at least white members, did not "belong" to one of the preaching houses. They held membership in a class and through the class in the four churches in Baltimore City Station. Members attended preaching according to choice (again excepting the African Americans) and might follow a favorite preacher around from appointment to appointment.[40] Baltimore Methodists, preachers and people alike, all had appointments beyond the local church; no one belonged to a congregation.

The meeting houses honored Methodist precept by seating men and women separately and made that statement to the world by providing two doors for entry. Racial divisions the meeting houses expressed inside with an "African" gallery and, by 1816, also outside with the separate African churches. The buildings themselves were modest, houselike in appearance, on a scale with the homes and shops around and scarcely distinguishable as "religious" (Sources, p. 22). Even Eutaw, grand by Methodist standards, was a modest two-story structure, without cross or steeple to state its purpose.[41] Otterbein's church, on the other hand, was a large brick church in high Georgian (neoclassical) style with a tall, elegant clock tower.

Interiors were whitewashed and the furnishings spare. Pews and pew rentals, already a concern at the 1816 General Conference, had not apparently troubled Baltimore, and the 1817 conference heard and transcribed the General Conference letter of concern into its own minutes, without remarking this issue.[42] Congregational singing was unaccompanied by organ or choir. Hymnals of the day did not include tunes. By common practice, the preacher or song leader sang or read one or two lines and, when the congregation had sung them, lined out more.

Baltimore's weekly "Sabbath" rhythm increasingly set the pattern for urban Methodism but remained atypical. Outside of town, on the Baltimore Circuit, Methodists would gather at a home or a meeting house for weekday preaching once a fortnight. So Henry Smith described the Baltimore Circuit, a stable set of appointments for a senior and junior preacher for two weeks. The preachers moved yearly; the appointments remained. Such a pattern pertained on the Baltimore Circuit, for instance, with the Joseph Taylors:

> Brother Taylor and his wife both embraced religion under the first Methodist preachers, when they were quite young. These two good people were the main stay of the society in that neighborhood for many years. At first they had preaching in their house, and afterward they built a small frame meeting-house near their dwelling, where there has been week-day preaching ever since. Thursday is their day, and eleven o-clock is their hour. It has been so, perhaps, for fifty years, and they never were clamorous about

having Sunday preaching. It has become quite a habit with them to go to preaching once in two weeks.[43]

Compared with this weekday preaching pattern, the Sunday rhythm for Baltimore City Station, then, differed from most of Methodism, but even there the preaching houses were just that, houses for preaching. Other services—baptisms, marriages, funerals—and class meetings took place in other houses, the people's homes.[44]

Here, too, the African American pattern diverges. Many of the Black classes met in a preaching house or at a school.[45] And many, though not all of them, had white leadership (white male leadership).[46] Men also served as leaders of many of the women's classes. Class life and worship life segregated itself, then, by sex and race (and of course, by language, the German Methodists continuing as separate denominations). (Baltimore City Station had already given up separate classes for probationers.) Class leaders did not, in Baltimore, function as surrogates for pastors as they did in the larger four-week circuits. The four itinerants moved effectively through the life of Baltimore Methodism. But the class leaders were at least *sub-pastors* who stayed year after year; who oversaw the intense, probing, enabling sessions of prayer, testimony, and discipline that nurtured individuals in the faith; who inquired into each individual's spiritual estate; and who led in the disciplining of those whose talk veered from orthodoxy or whose walk veered from the path toward perfection into uncharitableness, worldliness, profanity, mistreatment of servants or spouses, and other infractions of Wesley's code of ethics.[47] Ironically, stable classes and stable class leadership had a way of undoing the supervisory design by growing too large to sustain the intimacy. Black and white Baltimore classes, for instance, ranged from twenty-five to sixty persons, hardly the ideal dozen or fifteen that early Methodism had advised.

Institutions

Baltimore laity formed a variety of new institutions to further the interests of Methodism. Again in 1816 they attempted to start a college. Calling it Asbury College, they organized it as a stock company with Samuel K. Jennings, a doctor and local preacher, as head. The institution did not open until later and then only briefly.[48] More successful than secondary education had been efforts at literacy, notably the Male Free School, begun in 1801, operated (apparently daily) out of a room in the old parsonage for Light Street and in 1812 moved into its own building on Courtland Street. Key to this, as well as to the college, was another doctor, George Roberts.

The year 1816 saw the founding of a successor institution, male and female Sunday schools, the Asbury Sunday School Society and the McKendrean Sunday School Society.[49] The former was organized in a meeting chaired by Stephen Roszel, operated initially in rented quarters, held classes Saturday evening and Sunday, outgrew its quarters, and moved the next year into the Male Free School. The young scholars from this institution marched on Sundays to one of the Baltimore preaching houses. In the latter, organized at Eutaw Street Church, women took the instructional responsibilities and held the major offices—Sarah Hammond, president; Sarah McConnell, vice president; Elizabeth Morsell, treasurer; and Caroline Hammond, secretary.[50]

First president of the Asbury Sunday School Society was John Kingston, proprietor of another important Baltimore Methodist institution, the bookstore. His store and those of John Hagerty, a superannuated preacher, of Abner Neal, a local preacher, and of John Jully Harrod and James Turner specialized in the sale and publication of Bibles and books that constituted the primary business of Methodism. With book receipts often rivaling monies taken in collections and preachers therefore dependent upon a lively trade in saleable items, the bookstore was a popular gathering place for Methodist preachers.[51] Laity also congregated there, and these institutions functioned for Methodists like London coffeehouses and rural country stores. There, to "the headquarters of the church in Baltimore," one went for connectional and Baltimore news and gossip.[52] At a later point, Lewis G. Wells, an African American and a local preacher, operated a bookstore and published a competitive hymnbook that led to some controversy.[53] The bookstores were doubtless not hurt by two actions of General Conference that year. One was a directive to the book agents to "publish more small books and fewer large ones."[54] The other request was for a "Course of Study," an order to which the Baltimore Conference responded the next year with its list of required reading.[55]

Baltimore Methodists, notably John Hagerty, John Kelso, and Adam Fonerden, played key roles also in the establishment of the Maryland Bible Society in 1810.[56] Methodists later (1817) supported the formation of the American Colonization Society and local auxiliaries thereof.

Another "institution" less important perhaps in Baltimore City than on the Baltimore Circuit was the preacher's house, a pre-parsonage Methodist arrangement in which hostess and/or host welcomed, fed, accommodated, clothed, and counseled the itinerants. These were far more vital to and more typical of the connection than the sometimes bizarre, occasional accommodations that enliven the retrospective itinerants' accounts. Notable, for instance, in Baltimore was the home of John Kelso:

> John Kelso, a prince in Israel, was one of the class leaders in those early days. Wealthy, industrious, and universally respected, with a magnificent home at least for those times, which was always open to the preachers of the gospel, when his good wife freely dispensed the best things they had in their well supplied larder.[57]

By 1816, Baltimore had made housing provision for both its married and its unmarried ministers. The more prevalent hosting arrangement obtained on the Baltimore Circuit. The home of Samuel Merryman had heard the first Methodist sermon for that community, one by Robert Strawbridge, and that family continued the hospitality, the son Caleb taking over the responsibility.[58] The next stop on the circuit was the home of Phineas Hunt. "His house," said Henry Smith, "had been a preachers' home from the time the Methodist preachers first visited that neighborhood, and continued so till after his death, when sister Hunt broke up house-keeping." The laity doubtless gained much from this arrangement; they also gave much—counseling, instructing, encouraging, witnessing to the young itinerants. Smith observed of Hunt: "I never knew a man that loved to talk about experimental religion more than father Hunt. What preacher or private member was ever in his company long but heard him tell 'how the Lord had brought him?' "[59]

Similar roles were performed by the women in the Martin Tschudy household, Mrs. Tschudy and her daughter Barbara; the one was called "the preachers' mother" and the latter "the preachers' nurse."[60] Among other homes for preachers on the Baltimore Circuit also notable was that of Robert North Carnan.

Through the institution of the preacher's home, as well as in the official roles scripted by the *Discipline*—class leader, steward, exhorter, local preacher—the laity on such a stable circuit sustained the Methodist connection. Women especially could exercise the unofficial roles according to their gifts and without the gender constraints that Methodists were imposing on official positions. Such men and women had authority based on competence, wealth, position, and tenure, for they were, as Smith noted, "many of the first converts to Methodism."[61]

Coda

By winning and holding converts among the prominent and the poor, Methodism "established" itself in Baltimore and in Maryland. Methodism took the middle place on this middle ground that was Maryland. It was ground that proved difficult to hold, a battlefield for freedom and slavery, a middle that was already giving way. The Baltimore notations of 1816, "gone with Coker," would be repeated: gone with the "Reformers" in the 1820s, gone to the MECS in the 1840s.

CHAPTER VI

BUILDING FOR MINISTRY AND NURTURE: 1816–50s

Successive historians of American Methodism—Jesse Lee, Nathan Bangs, Abel Stevens, Matthew Simpson, James Buckley, and Holland McTyeire—helped shape the church that they then interpreted historically. No mere participant observers, these nineteenth-century figures held important offices, played central roles, and sought to make and/or remake the church. In rendering historical accounts, they wrote autobiography, apologia, directive, doctrine, and exhortation. They did not typically feature their own agency, activities, or accomplishments. With literary modesty, they simply narrated Methodism as their life's mission writ large. Not surprisingly, they have left us histories important on a variety of primary and interpretive levels.

Interring Asbury: Establishing a New Order

Methodism's second major historian, Nathan Bangs (1778–1862), certainly can be seen as shaper of the story he then narrated. "No name is more fully identified with the history of American Methodism, for the last sixty years, than that of Nathan Bangs." So affirmed one younger prominent contemporary and close observer of Methodist affairs, who continued, "His biography, when it comes to be fitly written, will be, to a large extent, a history of the Church."[1]

In treating the momentous year 1816 in his history, Bangs devoted almost thirty pages to an Asbury eulogy. Bangs covered the bishop's last days, noted that he had died en route to General Conference, recalled his being disinterred for ceremonial reburial during General Conference, and celebrated the distinguishing marks of his leadership and piety. After long, detailed encomium, Bangs dared to note that even "the sun has its spots" and ventured "with great deference" two errors in the bishop's administration,[2] two infrastructural matters on which Asbury failed to encourage Methodist development or ensure its prosperity. The first had to do with "learning and a learned ministry," education and educational institutions, Methodism's intellectual self-promotion, and the church's place in and place for culture, science, knowledge, and literature. The second had to do with support for ministry, ministers and ministerial families, and implicitly the great Asburian taboo, married itinerants. In the judgment of Bangs, Asbury mistakenly had kept Methodism "aloof from the world," discouraging education so as to protect piety and discouraging property (churches and parsonages) so as to safeguard itinerancy. Such concerns recur through Bangs's narrative and constituted his life's work.[3]

His counsel and leadership—the topics for this chapter—guided the church, in the eyes of some contemporaries and some recent interpreters, toward a softening of discipline, an embrace of the world, a compromise of fundamental Wesleyan practices and precepts, an abandonment of the evangelistic mission to society's marginalized, and a loss of Methodism's prophetic nerve. Such reactions and convictions yielded the several important pre–Civil War divisions (AMEZ, MPC, WMC, MEC-MECS, FMC), prompted various related reform efforts, and produced enduring ethical quandaries over status, authority, class, gender, race, and above all, slavery. The reformers appealed to the social holiness and innovating Wesley of field preaching and itinerancy, of General Rules, of social criticism, of antislavery. The next chapter, which covers the same period as this one, explores these political and polity developments, the reforming impulses, Methodism's countercultural edge, its appeals to revivalistic piety, its internal divisions and ensuing conflict, and its experience of radical change and discontinuity.

This chapter charts Methodism's attention to nurture, to order in congregational worship and church life, to tradition, to institutions—in short, to recovery of the churchly Wesley—the Wesley of Oxford, of Kingswood, of the *Arminian Magazine*, of the *Christian Library*, of the sacraments, and of conference. These Bangs-supported initiatives reflected Methodist aspirations for respectability, progress, recognition, and refinement. Led by upwardly mobile preachers and laity in Methodism's station churches (towns and cities, South and North),[4] the quest for order effected the denomination's evolution from side street to Main Street (Sources, pp. 22–23) and toward inclusion in the Protestant establishment. The stories of both chapters—of growing societal leadership and of prophetic witness—need sympathetic portrayal. The dialectic between the impulses described in these two chapters continued and continues to shape American Methodism. Institutionalization, prophetic critique thereof, and the interaction in American Methodist life of the churchly and the revivalistic Wesley subtly modulated—for all parties—the movement's dynamic Pietism into various scripted practices.

Nathan Bangs: Transitioning the Teaching Office

Connecticut-born, educated in village schools, a teacher before his conversion and call, Bangs saw that Methodism faced competition on a flank that Asbury had not adequately protected.[5] Methodism's imperatives for Bangs? Hold on to those convicted of sin in class meeting, camp meeting, or revival! Nurture after converting! Bring up the children baptized in the faith! Sustain itself in the East even as it itinerated west! Create media, church structures, and institutions for formation, education, advocacy, and transmission!

Methodism should look to its self-preservation and therefore establish practices, policies, resources, buildings, and connectional systems that would hold members in the church as frontier gave way to farming community, crossroads to villages and towns, struggling circuits to robust congregations. Bangs knew whereof he spoke. Having settled in Canada to teach in 1799, Bangs began itinerating in 1801 and was admitted on trial with a typically terse notation: "Recommended from Niagara Circuit 2 Years in Experience, pious travelled 9 Months approved, useful, clear—received."[6] He served successive frontier appointments in upper Canada and Quebec, then districts of the New York Conference, before being sent to the Albany District in 1808.

Bangs then held successive term appointments as presiding elder, as preacher in New York, and again as presiding elder before being elected book agent in 1820. (For a glimpse of the primary role of the presiding elder, that of holding quarterly conferences, see Sources 1811b, noting attention to discipline, granting and renewal of licenses, trials, and relation of quarterly meeting to camp meeting. For a presiding elder's role in a more difficult trial, see Sources 1830.) The New York Conference elected him secretary in 1811, sent him repeatedly to General Conference beginning with the first delegated General Conference (Sources 1812a), and thereafter called on him for or appointed him to almost every task that required study or statement.[7]

From such conference leadership posts and comparably responsible ones on a national level, Bangs participated actively in building and promoting Methodism's sociocultural-missional infrastucture. He was perhaps Methodism's most visible figure between the death of Bishop Francis Asbury and the Civil War leader Bishop Matthew Simpson. Elected to the office of book agent, he assumed responsibility for the publishing enterprise of the church, undertook the editing of the newly established *Methodist Magazine*, exercised the leading role creating the weekly *Christian Advocate*, championed important causes like missions and education, indeed crafted their warranting, authorizing, and constituting documents, and assumed authority to interpret signal Methodist events and developments.

His editor's posts gave Bangs a connection-wide and unequaled voice. The entire church read his word and later that of other *Advocate* and magazine editors—most prominently, John McClintock, Thomas E. Bond, Matthew Simpson, Daniel Curry, William Nast, J. B. McFerrin, Daniel B. Whedon, Thomas O. Summers, Abel Stevens, J. J. Tigert, J. M. Buckley, J. R. Joy, and Nolan B. Harmon.[8] The editor's voice proved more available, regularized, permanent, uniform, and influential than anyone else's in the church, including that of the itinerating bishops (McKendree, George, Roberts, and successors). (As an indication of the importance of Methodist media, note the medium of the following documents [Sources 1815, 1821b, 1827a, 1829, 1830b, 1834, 1841a, 1841b, 1842a].)

The voice of Methodist publishing was heard, indeed, had already succeeded in creating a textually defined national Wesleyan community, putting into hands and homes the Methodist witness in verse, in narrative, in doctrine, in discipline. Texts transmitted, texts inculcated, texts converted, texts sustained, texts modeled, texts bonded, texts ritualized, texts disciplined, and texts set boundaries. Methodism had been the first to establish a publishing house and center its evangelical and evangelistic mission by marketing Wesleyan materials. Gradually what began as a business to reprint the received Wesleyan (British) message and to transmit official American (MEC) actions began to shape the witness and thereby an increasingly connection-wide textual community.[9]

Bangs contributed actively to this subtle transfer of connectional intellectual leadership and community. Bangs's effectiveness as official spokesperson earned him other teaching office responsibilities in successive General Conferences, as head of Methodist missions, as president of Wesleyan University, as denominational apologist and historian, as presiding elder, and as episcopal candidate.[10]

An American Methodist Voice and Identity

Bangs established himself as Methodist spokesperson with apologetic works that appeared in 1815, 1816, 1817, and 1820: *The Errors of Hopkinsianism Detected and Refuted*, *The Reformer Reformed*, *An Examination of the Doctrine of Predestination*, and *A Vindication of Methodist Episcopacy*.[11] These books, along with others, like Asa Shinn's *An Essay on the Plan of Salvation* of 1813, defended Wesleyan theology and Methodist ministry, orders, and episcopacy against the church's most powerful critics. In the first three, Bangs responded to Calvinists who derided its thought and in the last to Episcopalians who questioned its ecclesial legitimacy.[12]

Neither the challenges to Wesleyan Arminian theology and Methodist orders nor Methodist responses were new. Encounters and exchanges, particularly with Calvinists (Congregationalists and Presbyterians), recur through the journals of itinerants. However, for formal apologetics American Methodism had depended upon and would continue to privilege the British defense of the faith, preeminently, of course, Wesley's writings, the *Sermons* and *Notes*, which constituted official standards, and the *Works* more generally, which were sold by Methodist preachers both as imported items and under American imprint. American Methodists continued in provincial dependence upon British theology throughout the nineteenth century. That dependence was both popular and official.

British works constituted the theological fare in the Course of Study, recommended by Bangs on behalf of a committee, authorized by the 1816 General Conference, and detailed in conference journals (the Baltimore Conference did so at its next meeting).[13] This first venture in more formalized preparation for ministry, a prescribed reading list, included Wesley's *Sermons* and *Notes*, John Fletcher's four volumes of *Checks to Antinomianism*, Joseph Benson's *Sermons on Various Occasions*, and Thomas Coke's six-volume *Commentary on the Holy Bible*.[14] The Course of Study, with its standardized theological fare and occasional updates, would shape Methodist belief and practice for more than a century.

In confronting the Calvinists, Bangs picked up where Fletcher left off. With his anti-Calvinist works, particularly *The Errors of Hopkinsianism Detected and Refuted* and *The Reformer Reformed*, Bangs made the case for hallmark Methodist doctrines of prevenient grace, human responsibility and freedom, holiness, and moral agency against Samuel Hopkins and other consistent Calvinists who represented the premier American theological legacy, that of Jonathan Edwards. He produced these two works with the formal approval of the New York Conference.[15] His theological statements and the normative works on the Course of Study thereafter obligatory for those entering ministry addressed the concerns raised by the Committee of Safety at the 1816 General Conference: "[T]hat, in some parts of the connexion, doctrines contrary to our established articles of faith, and of dangerous tendency, have made their appearance among us, especially the ancient doctrines of *Arianism, Socinianism* and *Pelagianism*."[16] Later apologists would defend the denomination against critics of its polity as well as detractors of its doctrine (Episcopalians and Baptists as well as Presbyterians and Congregationalists).

The Book Concern

Bangs assumed the role of book agent in 1820, accountable to General Conference, which had authorized new publications, to the New York Conference, and to a local oversight committee. Connectional oversight of the Book Concern had presented a challenge to Methodism from the start.[17] The very first conference, that of 1773, had upbraided Robert Williams for printing Wesley's books on his own and stipulated conference and Wesley's approval for publishing (Sources 1773). The council (under Asbury) had claimed oversight of publishing and was small enough to act effectively.

Before and after the two years of the council, a committee advised John Dickins, the church's first book agent, Asbury always playing an active advising role. But conference and then General Conference reserved to itself the right to determine what would be published in the church's name. In 1796, General Conference delegated some oversight to Philadelphia, then the site of Dickins's work. Ezekiel Cooper became book agent in 1798 when Dickins died. By 1809, the *Minutes* listed John Wilson and Daniel Hitt as book agents first under "New York Conference."[18]

Under Bangs's predecessors, the Methodist Book Concern had attempted to be an

American voice. Agents printed the *Minutes* and *Disciplines*, put out official American *Hymnbooks* (Sources, p. 29), which sold some ten thousand annually, issued the few apologetic works, and twice ventured a magazine, the *Arminian Magazine* (1789–90) and the *Methodist Magazine* (1797–98). However, for much of the magazines' content and for much of their fairly considerable publication lists, agents reprinted British works. The authoritative works (Wesley, Coke, Fletcher, Benson, Clarke), inspirational life stories (Rogers, Rowe, Sources 1791c), tracts, and other cheap items remained overwhelmingly British.[19]

The sales system (also on the British model) effectively distributed Methodist literature throughout the connection, capable of radiating an American voice, could it be sounded. The system, simple but elegant, made every preacher a traveling salesman, put inventory in the itinerants' saddlebags, and gave these underpaid circuit riders high incentive (namely, commissions) to push the products. General Conference authorized the practice in 1800, permitting 18 to 25 percent to be divided between regional distributor (presiding elder) and traveling salesman (preacher). In 1812 General Conference regularized preachers' take as 18 percent. Book money augmented, sometimes rivaled, the meager salaries (quarterage) paid the preachers.[20] The historian William Warren Sweet estimated that preachers might well make more by sales than they would receive in quarterage, officially established but dependent upon actual contributions. The 1812 General Conference and that of 1816 directed that the book agents recommence a magazine.[21]

Magazine, Papers, Tracts, Sunday School Literature

In 1818 at General Conference's behest, Joshua Soule launched the *Methodist Magazine*, authorized as the *Methodist Missionary Magazine* and variously titled thereafter (*Methodist Magazine and Quarterly Review*, *Methodist Quarterly Review*, *Methodist Review*, *Religion in Life*, *Quarterly Review*, now again *Methodist Review*), a venture that the church sustained for almost two centuries as a print serial and now continues electronically. Soule's successor, Bangs, gave American Methodism its national voice (his voice).

Bangs transformed what had been essentially a distributing operation for British reprints and official denominational publications (*Minutes*, *Disciplines*, *Hymnbooks*) into a full-fledged publishing house capable of its own printing and binding. He expanded the serious and popular adult fare, entered the tract market, established Sunday school literature, added serials for children and youth to a diet previously limited to Wesley's *Catechism*, and effectively Americanized the Book Concern. He built, of course, on the work of his predecessors and contended from the start with regional competition that shared the innovative and Americanizing task. The greatest achievement of the Bangs years, for instance, the launching of what would be the newspaper with the widest national readership, the *Christian Advocate*, capitalized on earlier efforts, *New England Mis-*

sionary Magazine, 1815, edited by Martin Ruter (New Hampshire); *Western Christian Monitor*, 1816, edited by William Beauchamp (Ohio); *Zion's Herald*, 1823 (Boston); and *Wesleyan Journal*, 1825 (Charleston). Initially the several regional efforts converged, the *Wesleyan Journal* and *Zion's Herald* merging with the *Christian Advocate* (*Zion's Herald* was relaunced in 1833 as the New England paper and continued in various formats with that name until 2006, when it became *The Progressive Christian*).

The immediate and national success of the *Christian Advocate*, 5,000 copies of the first issue, 25,000 subscribers in two years, made it a vital authoritative Methodist voice and the most widely distributed periodical in the world.[22] Its importance ironically derived in part from continuing competition with regional and reforming impulses. Even as, indeed even before, the *MQR* and *Advocate* claimed connectional prerogatives, resistance to centralized power and authority took literary and serial form. The story of reform, democratization, antislavery, division, and Civil War constitutes the next two chapters' charge. Here we would note that the 1820s and 1830s saw Methodism's perennial struggles over concentrated power, particularly that exercised by bishop and conference, take critical expression in reforming papers. Specifically, the *Wesleyan Repository*, begun in 1821 in Philadelphia and moved to Baltimore, renamed *Mutual Rights*, edited by William S. Stockton, later Dennis B. Dorsey, championed various democratic reforms: conference rights for lay members, representation for local pastors, and election of presiding elders (Sources 1821b). The *Christian Advocate* gained importance as it tilted against the reformers, coordinating on a weekly basis the denomination's response to criticism and dissent.

Within only a couple of years of the founding of the *Advocate*, annual conferences pressed for their own papers. General Conference responded by growing a branch of the Book Concern in Cincinnati, established as a distributing center, into a parallel operation and authorized the *Western Christian Advocate*, begun in 1834. It quickly outstripped "every religious and secular paper in the region by garnering 14,000 subscribers by 1840 and twice that number by 1860."[23] By 1840 the number of officially recognized *Advocates* had grown to six, seven if the count includes the reformers' paper, now that of a distinct denomination, the Methodist Protestant Church, *Mutual Rights and Methodist Protestant*. MEC-sanctioned papers by then appeared from New York, Cincinnati, Nashville, Pittsburgh, Richmond, and Charleston. And *Zion's Herald* had reappeared under the aegis of the New England Conference alone. Methodist papers competed with one another, with Baptist and other denominational voices, and with the secular press. They covered national and world events, scientific developments, medical nostrums, farming information, obituaries, and everything Wesleyan, in short, anything and everything that would appeal to Methodists as citizens and saints and thereby sustaining a connection-wide textual community.[24]

The *Advocates* constituted but one aspect of the Book Concern's advance into popular literature. It became as well the engine for the church's evangelistic and missionary enterprise and for its dramatic expansion into popular nurture and family care. Methodism started with the adults, producing cheap tracts for the Methodist Tract Society, formed in 1817. In 1823, Bangs launched the *Youth's Instructor and Guardian*, a monthly aimed at youth and families and featuring woodcut illustrations. And in 1827, when Methodists disengaged from the American Sunday School Union to constitute their own agency, Bangs established the *Child's Magazine* and increased the overall production of Sabbath instruction materials (explored in a later section on the Sunday school).

With religious literature for all ages and with the creation of a Methodist Bible Society in the mid-1820s, the church disengaged itself from the Calvinist-dominated Protestant establishment or "Evangelical United Front," the interlocking directorate of supposedly interdenominational missionary, tract, Bible, and reform societies. For the next four decades, essentially until the crisis of civil war stimulated Protestant cooperation in separate northern and southern societies, Methodists would build a Christian America in parallel with but independent of other denominations. In that missionary campaign, Methodist literature figured prominently.[25]

The Book Concern (New York) burned in 1836, consuming critical records and important manuscripts, including the journal of Francis Asbury. That was not the only fire that this literary-cultural advance faced. By that point, a few "croakers" complained of the passing of Methodism's fervid, wild-eyed, loud-voiced, slain-in-the-spirit Asburian age.[26] Sometimes they did so on the pulpit, through conference "semi-centennial sermons." Sometimes they "croaked" through the pages of magazines or *Advocates*. Sometimes, as in the cases of Peter Cartwright and James B. Finley, they made a vocation, in the press, on the stump, in tall tales, in furthering their denominational political careers, of championing frontier and camp meeting against city and college (Sources 1822). They touted nature, "the brush college" ministry, countering the Nathan Bangses in the East and the Martin Ruters in the West who had raised the banner of nurture. Nature would continue to receive its due. No camp meeting or revival would, it seems, go unnoticed by the *Advocates*. However, by 1840, the West itself would lead the denomination in cultural, educational, missional, and theological experiments. The Cincinnati Book Concern launched two important new serials for the church, a monthly *Ladies' Repository* (Sources 1841b, 1842a, 1872b), the first Methodist paper to be entirely reproduced on the Web, and *Der Christliche Apologete* edited by William Nast. The one recognized the serious religious, educational, and cultural interests and capacities of Methodist women. The other translated Methodist idiom into German and, perhaps as important, mediated German theological advances into Methodist conversations.

Paralleling the MEC's German publication efforts were those of the UBC and EA, their printing ventures helping the churches negotiate into an English-language society. As with the MEC, the UBC began simply, publishing hymnbooks (in 1808) and printing the *Disciplines* (in 1815), putting the latter into English as early as 1817. Its first periodical, the *Union Messenger,* appeared through the initiative in 1834 of an individual, William Rhinehart (1800–1861) of Virginia, stimulating his appointment that same year to head a publishing house. He immediately launched the UBC's paper, an English-language biweekly, the *Religious Telescope,* which continued until merged with the *Evangelical Messenger* in 1946. Other publications, including a history of the denomination (Henry Spayth's *History of the Church of the United Brethren in Christ,* 1850), followed. For the Evangelical Association, John Dreisbach (1789–1871), effective successor to the denomination's founder, played the key publishing role. With Albright's death in 1808 and the ill health of other key leaders, Dreisbach was made an elder, became conference secretary, was elected the church's first presiding elder (1814), and presided over annual conferences and the 1816 General Conference (Sources 1807). Bilingual and the object of several overtures from Asbury and the MEC, Dreisbach published a catechism in 1809, several German hymnbooks, and in 1815 a corrected and enlarged *Discipline.* A successor as head of publications, W. W. Orwig (1810–89), edited the EA's paper, *Der Christliche Botschäfter,* from 1837 to 1843. He also published the church's first history and was elected its third bishop.[27] As with Bangs, these editors exercised the teaching office. The same can be said of leadership through publishing for the Methodist Protestants, the Wesleyans, the MECS, and the Free Methodists, to which we turn in the next chapter. Methodism's print revolution was in full swing. Bangs, his counterparts, and his successors had created media for nurture on a geographic and demographic scale that the world had never known.

With its age-, purpose-, and taste-differentiated literary fare, with regionally based production and strategy centers, and with its incredible, nationally deployed energetic and motivated workforce of itinerant preachers and colporteurs (book peddlers), Methodism (in competition with other denominations that aspired to similar effectiveness) constituted itself a great national school and committed itself to bringing literacy to the masses. Before the era of the public school, preachers and Sunday school teachers "shouldered the principle burden of schooling." Especially in the South and West, "churches were schools and church people were schoolmasters and mistresses for a long stretch of the nineteenth century."[28] And Sunday school libraries were the first public libraries.

Parsonages and Home Altars vs. Classes and Circuits

Another cause championed by Nathan Bangs was housing—housing for worship and housing for preachers. Houses of worship and parsonages he thought key to an effective Methodist ministry on a local level and to the retention within the traveling order of the best and brightest. Bangs advocated and celebrated a ministry of pastoral presence. He thought it imperative that Methodists occupy cities, towns, and villages and provide there their full missional repertoire—prayer meetings, classes, mission and tract societies, Sunday schools, literature, regular Sabbath worship, and sacraments. "It had been long evident to many of our ministers and people," he insisted, "that for the want of having a preacher stationed in all important places, we had lost much of the fruits of our labor."[29] Methodist itinerants, Bangs believed, converted in revival or camp meeting only to lose the converts to denominations with a settled ministry and adequate houses for worship.

Because of inadequate houses, Methodism lost its ministry as well. The "numerous locations," of which Asbury complained, owed to "the want of parsonages for the accommodation of preachers' families." Bangs entered the diagnosis and complaint as he looked back to the 1810s and exulted in the progress as he wrote of the 1830s.[30] Even frontier conferences, like Mississippi, joined Bangs in advocating parsonages "on all the circuits and stations" (Sources 1827a). An 1840s "Committee on Parsonages" of the North Carolina Conference echoed the appeal. Acknowledging there were "6 Districts, 49 Circuits & Stations, 60 members of Conference," of whom forty-six were married, they complained that married preachers remained unpopular and that there "are at present but two parsonages in the whole Conference." The conference (preachers) went on to insist that "the want of parsonages and ample support for the ministers, is an evil of no ordinary magnitude," as it divided preachers' interest and effort between their farm and family in one place and pastoral charge in another location and eventuated in locations. They then passed a series of resolutions calling for at least two parsonages in each district, preferably in villages rather than the country, and urging presiding elders and preachers to press this cause.[31] The hardships of married ministries wanting parsonages Mary Orne Tucker, "A Pioneer Preacher's Wife," made a central motif of her autobiography (Sources 1838).[32]

Progress, people, and parsonages moved slowly, but they moved. The 1856 General Conference (MEC) directed conferences to report on the number and value of church buildings and parsonages. An analysis in 1858 revealed that the northern church boasted 2,174 parsonages for the then 5,365 traveling preachers. Perhaps surprisingly, the progress had been slower in some of the larger, older, wealthier conferences, like Baltimore (one-third) and Philadelphia (one-fourth), than for Vermont (one for every preacher and a half) and a group of conferences affording one for every two (North Indiana, New York East, Maine, Oneida, East Maine, Troy, Genessee, Ohio, Rock River, Detroit, South Eastern Indiana, Indiana, and New Hampshire).[33]

More adequate buildings and a more stable and settled ministry gradually came to deliver the pastoring and nurturing that Bangs advocated, but a pastoral-style ministry posed other issues for the system. One that had been and would be perennially raised had to do with the nature and requirements of itinerancy. In 1832 General Conference determined that ministry could be too "present" and stable, complaining of the "evil of no small magnitude" of "the same preachers to be continued from year to year in town and city stations."[34] The bishops returned to another dimension of that theme twelve years later in their address to the 1844 General Conference, laying blame on preachers as well as congregations and complaining of "locality in our traveling ministry," of preachers "with local views, and habits, and interests," and of the "itinerant system" as reduced to "the removal of the preachers once in two years from one station to another."[35]

Stationed pastors—appointed to a charge with a single congregation or society and therefore present in a community 24/7, not simply stopping by every two, four, or six weeks—took on more and more of the nurturing, "local" functions once the prerogative of the class leader. Stations emerged gradually and naturally in small towns and villages as individual societies grew large enough to support a preacher's salary. The urban circuits (Sources, p. 24) in locales where Methodism had prospered and acquired multiple church buildings (Baltimore, New York, Philadelphia, Cincinnati) required more of a deliberate break in policy, as occurred in 1838 when, in New York City, John Street, Bedford Street, Duane Street, and Green Street separated.[36] Stationed preachers and stationed preachers' wives reflexively usurped roles ascribed by *Discipline* to the class leaders. And while class leaders struggled to find time for their duties, preachers and wives dedicated their entire lives to the cause.

Preachers' wives (preachers marrying), discouraged by precept and practice in the early nineteenth century, became in the decades before the Civil War regular, indeed esteemed, resource persons for local church leadership (Sources 1838). This vocation emerged most fully when preachers were stationed and the preachers' families became part of the congregation they served. By contrast, the preacher still on circuit left behind a wife who was frequently quite isolated—from her husband's circuit, from the local community, from Methodist ministries, and from leadership, indeed, from participation roles altogether.[37] However, in a station, the preacher's wife evolved into a vital helpmeet in ministry and increasingly an essential congregational leader. Many had their own "call" to what became an informal but nevertheless prescribed office. They undertook responsibilities and assumed roles that communities came to expect, especially among other women and with the children—in teaching, in visiting, in comforting the ill and bereaved, in witnessing, in heading missionary societies, in modeling family piety, in interpreting her husband (to women and other preachers), in supporting the ministry, in negotiating the frequent moves, in short, in functioning as a subminister.[38]

In such station churches in small towns and cities, the class meeting's function in discipline, spiritual formation, and nurture increasingly devolved onto preacher and preacher's wife and onto the lay leadership of the missionary and tract societies and the Sunday school. Educational buildings lay ahead, but already in the 1830s and 1840s Methodists began building larger, Main Street buildings, structures with two rooms and eventually two stories, plants suitable for meeting and teaching (Sources, p. 23).

Reflexively Methodists meeting for the missionary cause or as Sabbath school teachers conducted their gathering with prayers, hymns, testimony, and exhortation—offering an alternative small-group experience in the style of the class meeting. And while a missionary society (treated below) lacked the explicit disciplining oversight and the disciplinary charge of the class, it compensated with far more energizing responsibilities. It had a purpose, a cause, an explicit mandate from Jesus himself, and a role in bringing in his millennial reign. Its purposes, global, even transcendent, looked beyond the group to the children, the unconverted, and the heathen. And particularly for the women, they gathered and organized for missions, for the tract society, or for the Sunday school with a panoply of new leadership roles open to women as well as men. These roles had a great cause; their own heroines, the Mary Masons in home missions and the Ann Wilkinses in foreign (Sources 1842c); reasons to network, to write, and to speak; and media with which to broadcast their efforts, the *Advocates* and, after 1841, the *Ladies' Repository* (Sources 1841b). It must have been quite a relief to be able to meet without a male class leader, perhaps less spiritually adept than themselves, intruding into their privacy with one-hundred-year-old questions.

Methodists have spilled much ink, from the late 1820s to the present, over the "decline" of the class meeting (Sources 1827a, 1841a).[39] Many contemporary "croakers" seem not to have noticed that they "declined," in no small measure, because other structures and instrumentalities replaced their essential functions. Others who noticed differed in opinion over whether Sunday schools, missionary societies, and settled preachers and ministers' wives could deliver the kind of discipline that Wesley had envisioned and over whether the appointment of preachers to stations robbed circuits and rural society of ministry, a point eloquently made by editor Thomas Bond (Sources 1841a).

Worship and Formality

The hymnal, along with the Bible and the *Discipline*, were said to be the circuit rider's library, and the hymnbook, the guide to a member's spiritual pilgrimage. Both laity and preachers read more widely than those images suggest. Indeed, it was the preacher's responsibility to keep his circuit well supplied with books. Nevertheless hymnbooks, along with catechisms and spiritual guides like the *Experience of Hester Ann Rogers,* were among the best sellers that the preachers peddled, as their financial records show.[40] The Methodist movements kept hymnbooks in print, the MEC's *Pocket Hymn Book* undergoing several editions from its first appearance in 1785, including a supplement issued under Asbury's direction in 1808. That same year, the UBC published a second German-language hymnbook. And in 1810 the EA published the first of its several in German, its first in English appearing in 1835 some ten years later than a comparable effort by the UBC (Sources, pp. 29–30).[41] These several early nineteenth-century hymnbooks augmented the by then Pietist standards (English and German) with lusty, sometimes crude verse born out of the camp meetings.[42]

The hymnbooks guided individual devotion and public worship, the Methodists having laid aside Wesley's effort at a Book of Common Prayer, the *Sunday Service*, and retained little in the way of worship-leadership guidance to its preachers and members. The church was clear that singing came first. In their modest directions, the early *Disciplines* (Sources, p. 35) encouraged Methodists to several services of worship, wherever practicable "on the sabbath day":

> Let the morning-service consist of singing, prayer, the reading of a chapter out of the Old Testament, and another out of the New, and preaching.
>
> Let the afternoon-service consist of singing, prayer, the reading of one chapter out of the Bible, and preaching.
>
> Let the evening-service consist of singing, prayer, and preaching.
>
> But on the days of administering the Lord's supper, the two chapters in the morning-service may be omitted.

These simple directives sufficed for movements whose religiosity, sustained by the bi-weekly visits of the circuit rider, came to fulfillment in camp meetings and conversion, in which the class meeting provided a new family, and for which *Disciplines* guided commitment to lives of self-denial, avoidance of finery, and repudiation of the world's sinful ways. Increasingly, however, small-town and urban Methodism found that sisters who had bonded in class to pray for conversion of sons and husbands succeeded, thereby creating the new opportunity and challenge of a Christian family. To be sure, *Disciplines* had always provided guidance on marriage, instruction of children in the faith, and family prayer, the latter indeed included under Wesley's first "Instituted" means of grace: "Prayer, private, family, public." And that disciplinary and Wesleyan rubric included the mandate to preachers to ask everywhere, "Have you family prayer?" However, in early American society, Methodism had led with countercultural expectations and style that had in many instances produced family tensions, controversy, conflict, and divisions, particularly for the more genteel. Increasingly in the nineteenth century, the church found itself uniting rather than dividing families and responding by making greater provision for accenting the family over the class meeting, encouraging the creation of a family altar, intensifying the pastoral roles of the preachers, and softening its strictures against the world—in a word, domesticating itself.[43]

Family worship and weekly Sunday worship needed better resources, among them hymnals. Asbury's 1808 supplement had brought back Wesley texts neglected earlier. But as Bangs complained, "[U]nhappily, those who made this selection had taken the liberty to alter many of the hymns, by leaving out parts of stanzas, altering words, shortening or lengthening hymns, without much judgment or taste. By this injudicious method the poetry was often marred, and the sentiment changed much for the worse." That judg-ment, expressed in somewhat more muted terms, prefaced the 1821 *Collection of Hymns*.[44] Along with this edition, the 1820 General Conference authorized the publi-cation of a tune book. The committee charged with this task drew upon the "best Eu-ropean authors" as well as tune book efforts that individual North American Methodists had made with an eye to creating a resource "for worshiping congregations."[45] That same General Conference offered directives as well on another of Bangs's pet passions, better church facilities, nevertheless legislating against the renting or selling of pews and ask-ing congregations that had resorted to the mechanism "as far as possible, to make those free which have already been built with pews." This set of protocols, a clear indication of Methodist movement toward Main Street presence, also guided presiding elders and preachers to resist building until three-fourths of necessary funds were in hand.[46]

The next General Conference, that of 1824, attended to the paucity of directives for worship. Its Committee on the Itinerancy complained that

> in regard to public worship and the administration of the ordinances [sacraments], it ap-pears there is a great want of uniformity. The reading of the Scriptures, the Lord's prayer, and the apostolic benediction are frequently omitted; and in the administration of the ordinances some use the form in the Discipline, some mutilate it, and others wholly neglect it.

At the following General Conference, the committee noted "an evident improve-ment the last four years." The greater liturgical sensitivity was doubtless motivated by the strictures made in 1824 to the *Discipline,* which specified, "In administering the or-dinances [sacraments] and in the burial of the dead, let the form of discipline invariably be used. Let the Lord's prayer also be used on all occasions of public worship in con-cluding the first prayer and the apostolic benediction in dismissing the congregation."[47]

The 1836 *Collection of Hymns* and companion *Methodist Harmonist* continued Methodism's gravitation toward more formality in worship. This hymnal referenced the tune name and page number. The bishops in their prefatory communiqué reiterated a refrain that leaders from Wesley on had sung, that members purchase and use only hymnbooks "published by our own agents, and signed with the names of your bishops." They so insisted, confident "that we are putting into your hands one of the choicest se-lections of evangelical hymns, suitable for private devotion, as well as for family, social and public worship."[48] Methodist Protestants and the MECS sought worshiping unifor-mity by issuing new hymnals soon after organization as separate churches (Sources, p. 29). The MECS, under longtime and influential editor Thomas O. Summers, found a formula for countering the competitive, nonofficial hymnals that had haunted Method-ism since Wesley's day by issuing *Songs of Zion* in 1851, a practice that southern Method-ism would contribute later to the whole church.[49]

Sacramental practice tracked both aspirations for recovery and claiming of more churchly patterns and continued appreciation of Methodism's Pietist/conversionist revivalism. In towns and cities where liturgical life increasingly centered on Sundays, baptism and Holy Communion could be regularized and both celebrated monthly, as the 1834 Cincinnati appointment/circuit plan illustrates (Sources, p. 24). More frequent Communion was a recovery of Wesleyan principle. On baptismal practice, Methodists had more consistently defended the mode of sprinkling and baptism of infants against all critics, especially the testy Baptists. Peter Cartwright, for example, recalled for circa 1814 that the Baptists "made so much ado about baptism by immersion that the uninformed would suppose that heaven was an island, and there was no way to get there but by *diving* and *swimming*."[50]

Still, what mattered most was not whether or how one was baptized but whether one was "converted."[51] And the power of the conversion experience drove requests for rebaptism, a matter on which Methodists remained inconsistent. The United Brethren were even more so. With a loosely defined polity, minimal disciplinary regulations, need to accommodate Mennonite as well as magisterial (Lutheran and Reformed) sentiments, and commitment to an "unpartisan" unity in Christ, the UBC affirmed infant dedication and deferred baptism to a time when the rite would be more "spiritually meaningful." As late as 1889, the revision of the UBC's "Confession of Faith" announced, "The baptism of children shall be left to the judgment of believing parents."[52] Also, the UBC traditionally did not oppose rebaptism.

None of the churches in this period—UBC, EA, which tracked the Methodists, and the several flavors of the latter—deepened their understanding of the sacraments even as they selectively experimented with more formal practice. Here American Methodists followed the lead of the British and specifically the counsel of Richard Watson, who, between 1821 and 1826, in his *Theological Institutes* produced one of the first Methodist systematic theologies.[53] The fourth part included treatment of the sacraments of baptism and the Lord's Supper but showed little of Wesley's concern about the sacramental character of the rite or grasp of its regenerative power. So in the "first American complete and standard" edition of Wesley's works published by the MEC beginning in 1831, editor John Emory (elected bishop the following year) wrote the following disclaimer about Wesley's commitment to Anglican baptismal (sacramental) regeneration:

> That Mr. Wesley, as a clergyman of the Church of England, was originally a *high-churchman*, in the fullest sense, is well known. When he wrote this treatise ["On Baptism"] in the year 1756, he seems still to have used some expressions, in relation to the doctrine of baptismal regeneration, which we at this day should not prefer. Some such, in the judgment of the reader, may perhaps be found under this second head. This last sentence, however—"if we repent, believe, and obey the Gospel: supposing this, as it admits us into the Church here, so into glory thereafter"—contains a guarded corrective.

It explains also the sense in which we believe Mr. W. intended much of what goes before to be understood.[54]

Methodism's ecclesiology and ecclesiological practice remained as underdeveloped as its sacramental theology. It was not until 1836 that any recognizable concept of church membership was put into the *Discipline*, not until 1856 that the relation of baptized children to the church was spelled out in the *Discipline*, and not until 1864 that a form for receiving members into the church was added to the Ritual. By then Wesley's Arminianism was being replaced by theologian Daniel Whedon's "freedomism." What in Wesley had been "*gracious* [God-given] ability" became simply "*human* ability."

Regular Sunday worship, stationed preachers, and proper church buildings slowly changed the very nature of Methodism. Early Methodism had once been truly "church," with its panoply of services and the proper administering of the Communion, at quarterly conferences. By 1832 John P. Durbin was urging Methodists to follow the lead of Fifth Street, Philadelphia, and Green Street, New York City, and build with both heritage and opportunity in view. He counseled a two-story facility of seventy by eighty feet with basement, vestibule, and side and back galleries. The basement should "contain a large lecture room for the services on week-day evenings, for conferences, &c. It should also contain a large room, or rooms for prayer meetings, and for Sabbath schools; and smaller rooms for class meetings." He presumed that women and men would sit separately, as they had from the beginning and by disciplinary command,[55] and counseled that the "seats on the *left* of every aisle *be made a little larger* than those on the right as there are generally more ladies in attendance at church than gentlemen." However, seeing no reason for separate doors for men and women, he proposed a single central aisle so that couples could meet in the aisle rather than congregate at the doors. Seats should be free with kneeling boards attached to the back. In the interest of comfort, the altar should be cushioned and the aisles carpeted to reduce noise and commotion. "We hope," he concluded, "the cushions and carpets will offend none until they have tried them, and found how much they contribute to the convenience and comfort of all concerned. They do not spring from *pride*, but from a desire to have the house of God present an air of neatness, comfort, and respectability, corresponding with the purity and elevation of its design."[56] The first Communion table with a marble top in any Methodist church was seen at the dedication of the new church in Green Street in New York City. It was a gift, but was "a stone of stumbling and rock of offense to some."[57] Such facilities lent themselves to more formal patterns of worship (or at least regularized revivalism within congregational life in protracted meetings) and less reliance on quarterly meetings and camp meetings. (For the judgment by Free Methodist founder B. T. Roberts that this formality compromised Methodism's "gospel for all," see chapter 8 and Sources 1860.) By 1839 as world Methodism celebrated a centennial, George Cookman could exult on the progress made (Sources 1839), confident that "Good old Methodism" was quite capable of improvements, despite opinions to the contrary of "a certain class of deplorable croakers."

In 1844, the bishops, not above a certain degree of croaking, complained in their Episcopal Address that the emergence of the station and erosion of the circuit gave quarterly meeting conferences "scarcely... an existence except in name." They continued, "Members of the Church, as in former days of Methodism, would come together from the different appointments to improve their spiritual state, and strengthen their Christian fellowship, by mutual attendance on the means of grace, and by religious intercourse in conversation and prayer."[58] The bishops counseled a revivification of the quarterly conference. There was, however, no returning to that simpler Methodism. Greater formality and organization became increasingly the order of the day.

The Sunday School: Background

In the 1820s, the Sunday school movement underwent a revolution, substantively and programmatically, fueled in the latter regard in no small part by Methodism's new media.[59] The substantive changes, from basic education with the poor to nurture of members' piety, proved dramatic. Begun in the 1780s in England and endorsed by John Wesley, the Sunday school initially provided rudimentary religious instruction and Bible knowledge to poor working children on their one day off. American Methodists followed Wesley's example but slowly. Francis Asbury taught children when opportunity presented itself and in 1783 founded a Sunday school for African American children in the home of Thomas Crenshaw in Hanover County, Virginia.[60] In 1785, William Elliott, a Methodist in Accomack County, Virginia, taught white children (including his own) and slaves and servants on Sundays, albeit at different hours.[61]

American Methodism carried Wesley's rules for the instruction of children into the *Discipline*[62] but took its first official action with respect to Sunday schools in 1790. The Charleston conference, the first of the fourteen that year, queried, "What can be done for the instruction of poor children (whites and blacks) to read?"

> Answ. Let us labour, as the heart and soul of one man, to establish Sunday schools, in, or near the places of public worship. Let persons be appointed by the bishops, elders, deacons or preachers to teach (gratis) all that will attend, and have a capacity to learn; from six o'clock in the morning till ten; and from two o'clock in the afternoon till six, where it does not interfere with public worship.[63]

Carrying forth this mandate, Bishop Asbury issued a pastoral letter the next year and republished it in the 1792 *Minutes* instructing laity and preachers to cooperate in founding "in, or near every place of worship" separate Sunday schools for boys and girls. "We have but small hope of coming properly at the lambs of the flock," he wrote, "till you have schools of your own founding, and under your direction."[64] In their 1798 annotated *Discipline*, Bishops Asbury and Coke appealed to both Old and New Testaments in reinforcing "Of the Instruction of Children," noting that half the human race was under sixteen and encouraging particularly the scripture catechism with children (not indicating whether Wesley's or John Dickins's).[65]

These exhortations yielded meager results. In a few places successful Sunday schools did take hold. Mary Mason led New York Methodists in founding Sunday schools (1812).[66] Philadelphia (1814)[67] and Baltimore (1816), as already noted, also saw strong institutions.[68] They remained dedicated to rudimentary education, fittingly undertook instruction not in a church building but in separate facilities, and drew support from citywide Sunday school societies. These urban Sunday schools proved the exceptions. Presiding elder, southern *Advocate* editor, and historian John B. McFerrin observed that before 1818 "no moves have been made in the [Tennessee] Conference for the organization of Sunday-schools," or for that matter "West or south of Pittsburgh."[69]

Sunday Schools and Catechisms

In the 1820s, Sunday schools changed substantively. Increasingly they ceded to the public schools the basic responsibilities to educate the citizenry. Limiting their focus to nurturing the faith, they expanded their clientele to include the middle class as well as the poor and the children of the church and the church's adherents. They welcomed the talent of the women of the church, profiting from their gifts in teaching, formation, and nurture. And they reclaimed the Wesleys' dual emphasis on knowledge and piety, honored expectations about education as formative of the new republic, drew on Romantic theories about human nature and early development, brought such into conformity with Methodist theological understandings, thus harmonizing educational and soteriological dynamics, and so fit together the Sunday school with revivalistic conversion. The Sunday school would be the church's nursery of piety. Sequenced curricula, improved materials, planning and organization, and clear formational goals would elicit knowledge, understanding, and appropriation of biblical truths, impression of such spiritual and moral lessons on the heart, the transformation of the soul, and experience of the forgiveness and grace by which conversion occurred. God's freely offered grace would make use of loving teachers. Receptive young minds would respond to caring instruction. Little souls would be drawn away from sin by loving tutelage. The theory worked. Conversions occurred. Children grew up to be regenerate adults and church members.[70]

With its now-muscular media, Methodism capitalized readily and programmatically on the new theological, pedagogical, and psychological theory. In April 1827, deciding not to subsume its work in the Calvinist-dominated American Sunday School Union, the MEC founded the Sunday School Union of The Methodist Episcopal Church

(SSU). It was based in New York City with Nathan Bangs, head of the Methodist Book Concern, as corresponding secretary.[71] The next year, General Conference endorsed the SSU, and the *Discipline* specifically commended Sunday schools in every pastoral appointment.[72] The mandate seemed hardly necessary. A year's time had produced 251 auxiliary societies, 1,025 Sunday schools, 2,048 Sunday school superintendents, 10,290 teachers, and 63,240 students.[73]

Bangs and successors turned the Book Concern into an engine for the Sunday School Union, putting into children's hands in its founding year the *Child's Magazine* and a Sunday school hymnal, *Selection of Hymns for the Sunday-School Union of The Methodist Episcopal Church*. The Book Concern also published a new set of graded catechisms, replacing the older catechisms of Wesley and John Dickins and reflecting the intellectualist moral psychology then current. Drafted by the eminent British Methodist theologian Richard Watson as companion to his systematic theology, *Theological Institutes* (1823–29), also to be normative in America, these catechisms started even the youngest children (under age seven) with the Wesleyan basic doctrines of sin and salvation, provided age-adapted prayers, and taught the Lord's Prayer. Also in 1827, John P. Durbin, one of a succession of editors committed specifically to caring for Sunday school needs and one of the church's great educators, gave Methodist children (and their eager but untrained teachers) the Bible in easy format. Durbin prepared the first of what would be a series of Scripture lesson books, *Scripture Questions on the Evangelists and Acts*, counseling teachers on how to address queries also put in the *Child's Magazine*. *Scripture Questions* coached Methodist laity on a new, direct approach to Bible study.[74]

Aided by these manuals, teachers invited children to their own careful reading and thorough examination of the Scriptures on matters of ultimate concern for their little souls. For July 1829, across the church, children were asked, "How do you prove that the saving grace of God is free in all?"[75] For answers to such queries students and teacher had biblical texts to probe and to memorize. Though still pointed to conversion, the system of nurture provided "means" for redemption through early, weekly engagement with Scripture, aided by question books serving up Methodism's evangelical doctrines of sin, grace, forgiveness, repentance, and regeneration as the Bible illustrated them.

Sunday school cheap books, tracts, Bibles, lesson books, and teachers' manuals poured forth. At the end of just the first year, the annual report could boast

> that 773,000 books have been printed for the use of our sabbath schools since our organization, besides 154,000 numbers of the *Child's Magazine*, and several hundred thousand tickets for rewards.... Upwards of 60 depositories have been established in various parts of the country for supplying the schools with greater convenience.[76]

The church's response calmed the fears of Bangs and company that Methodist children would be tainted by the covert Calvinism of the rival American Sunday School

Union.[77] (See Sources 1827a for the encouragement that the Mississippi Conference offered in its "Address . . . to the members within its bounds.") Nevertheless Bangs explained the cause, promoted the Sunday school, and provided teacher-training counsel in a new regular feature of the ever more widely circulated weekly, the *Christian Advocate*.

Successive editors, heads of the Sunday school enterprise, bishops, and General Conferences increased the incentives for, created new resources for, and added age levels to the Sunday school. The 1840 General Conference, for instance, extended the age level to young people; required circuits and stations to establish Sunday schools; made them accountable to the official governance body on the local level, the quarterly conference; mandated preachers to exercise oversight on, visit, report about, and preach on the Sunday school; urged the appointment of Sunday school agents to travel across the connection as Sunday school promoters; and authorized a new serial.[78] Begun in 1841, the *Sunday School Advocate* succeeded famously, its subscriptions soon surpassing the *Advocate*, itself a trendsetter in circulation (secular and religious).[79] Daniel Kidder, who assumed responsibility for the Sunday School Union and the editorship of the *Sunday School Advocate* in the mid-1840s, boosted circulation to 200,000 subscribers. To encourage Sunday school libraries, Kidder published ten- to twenty-five-cent cloth-bound books (and even cheaper paper "Juvenile books" sold from eight to seventy-seven cents a dozen)[80] and negotiated listing of Religious Tract Society of London items, some eight hundred Sunday school books.[81] (For a glimpse of how all this counsel and these resources functioned, see the depiction of an 1850s Sunday school, Sources 1858b.)

Kidder also undertook, at the behest of the 1848 General Conference (MEC), to prepare a new general catechism "on Christian doctrine, ordinances, and duties, to be accompanied with Scripture proofs" and a companion elementary catechism "in shorter and plainer words, adapted to the capacities of young children."[82] Kidder subsequently crafted a third, a study version for older youth and adults.[83]

The catechisms built in graded fashion on one another so as to carry the child into maturity as a believer growing into greater appreciation of Wesleyan understandings of God, creation, salvation, the means of grace, death, and judgment. The beginner's equipped children to participate in worship, instructing them in the Lord's Prayer, the Ten Commandments, the Apostles' Creed, the Beatitudes, and "the Baptismal Covenant." It included "Prayers for the Young"; the most familiar prayer ("Now I lay me down to sleep") and Wesley's table grace ("Be present at our table, Lord") remain staples of Methodist instruction.[84] Kidder designed the church's new catechisms "not only to exercise the memory, but to discipline the mind, to enlighten the understanding, and to improve the heart."[85] However, as contrasted with the older class meeting scheme of membership, which had focused primarily on the heart, catechisms along with the entire system of the Sunday school sought the shaping of Christian character through instruction, formal doctrines, and apologetics. Dissemination of this popular literature occurred through the post, via preachers and colporteurs, and through six regional Book Concern outlets.[86] A particularly fine catechism for German Methodists appeared in the 1860s, the work of the editor-educator William Nast (1807–99), leader of MEC missions to German Americans. And in 1858 and 1860 the book editor for the MECS, Thomas O. Summers (1812–82), produced first a two-part *Scripture Catechism* and then a collection of catechisms for the southern church. There was, however, a more notorious catechism for the MEC and MECS, one designed for slaves, which we treat in the next chapter.

The Missionary Impulse

The plantation mission led by William Capers and launched by the South Carolina Conference in 1829, to which we return in the following chapter, may have been the most significant (if problematic) of Methodism's missionary endeavors. It was not the first such effort. Indeed, Capers, then presiding elder (PE) of the Charleston District, had learned his craft as missionary among the Creek. And work among Native Americans is often credited with being the beginning of Methodist missions. In a sense, however, Methodism had been from the start a missionary movement, as contemporaries themselves recognized:

> Though American Methodism was many years without a distinct missionary organization, it was owing to the fact that its whole organization was essentially a missionary scheme. It was, in fine, the great Home Mission enterprise of the north American continent, and its domestic work demanded all its resources of men and money.[87]

So pronounced Abel Stevens, one of Bangs's successors as official spokesperson, historian, apologist, and editor. The author of several multivolume Methodist histories and the first history of Methodist women,[88] Stevens, like Bangs, held, by General Conference election, critically important editorships: *Zion's Herald*, the *National Magazine*, and finally the *Christian Advocate*. A close student of the system, Stevens recognized Methodism's intrinsic missionary style: the empowerment of all to testify, its aggressive appointment process, the elasticity of circuits, the prerogative of preachers to expand on their own authority, the eager recruitment (primarily of white males) into leadership roles, and decentralized training through apprenticeship. Methodism's intrinsic missionary style and the incredible, explosive exfoliation of the church west by expansion of circuits and conferences for the period leading up to the Civil War will be the subject of the next chapter (also the conflicts and schisms experienced).

As early as the Christmas Conference, however, the new church determined to set apart individuals for extension efforts in Nova Scotia and Antigua (Freeborn Garrettson among them). And Methodism did from an early period use the term *missionary* to refer to appointments into frontier areas. The formalization and organization of Methodist missions really began, according to the first historian of the impulse, not with these official acts but with the spontaneous efforts by the convert John Stewart, part African American, part Native American, to evangelize among the Wyandotte in Ohio (Sources 1815).[89] From 1815 until his death in 1823 and working initially through another African American as interpreter, Jonathan Pointer, Stewart converted a number of Wyandottes, including several chiefs.[90] Thus began what would be early efforts at outreach toward Cherokee, Choctaw, Creek, Potawatomi, Oneida, Menomini, Chippewa, Kaw, Shawnee, Kansas, Chickasaw, Quapaw, and Flathead peoples (see discussion in the next chapter).[91]

Stewart's example and the difficulty of reinforcing his work came to the attention of Bangs and others. Motivated as well by the organization of interdenominational and denominational missionary efforts on both sides of the Atlantic and by the passage in Congress of a "Civilization Fund Act" encouraging educational endeavor among Native Americans, Methodists came to recognize that

- in other cross-cultural, multilingual, distant, or international evangelistic contexts as well, Methodism's operative missionary scheme—conference expansion through enlarged circuits and revolving itinerants—would not work (foreign missions were already entertained);
- some Christianizing efforts demanded longer appointments, language skills, and other specializations;
- such missionary deployments necessitated the church's invention of new organizational and financial schemes, capable of drawing together and focusing the resources of the entire connection rather than leaving all initiatives to conferences and circuits.[92]

So in 1819, under Bangs's leadership, the church established a Missionary Society to provide "pecuniary aid . . . to enable the Conferences to carry on their missionary labours on a more extended plan" and "to extend the influence of divine truth, by means of those missionaries which may, from time to time, be approved and employed by the Bishops and Conferences for that purpose."[93]

The new society, essentially a mechanism to champion and fund-raise for bishop-appointed and conference-initiated efforts,[94] called for a network of auxiliaries. Later that same year Mary Morgan Mason (1791–1868) persuaded a group of women to help her found an auxiliary society to the denominational Missionary Society. Bangs termed this the first.[95] The organizers of this Female Missionary Society affirmed their conviction that "we are not called to the more arduous employments of active life; we are exempted from the toils and cares of official stations in the Church; but God has, nevertheless, required of *us* that our all should be devoted to his service."[96] Auxiliaries to the denominational (male) and female societies followed at conference and local levels.[97]

Thus began an organizational networking across the church that would be immensely important, especially in the provision of a space for women's initiatives and for development of female leadership. The career of Irish-born Mary Morgan (Mason) illustrates the importance of the voluntary society as a context for women's religiosity. Not nurtured in the faith by her parents, who had immigrated to Philadelphia, Mary Morgan experienced conversion at age seventeen under the influence of her uncle John Morgan, a local Methodist preacher. Despite her parents' objections, who burned her spiritual journal and discouraged attendance at class meetings, but with her uncle's support, she resolved to adhere to strict Methodist discipline, giving up "gay clothing" and "vain amusements."

Relocating in 1810 to live with her uncle and family and to teach in a Quaker school for poor girls, she joined the John Street Methodist Episcopal Church and intensified her spiritual pursuits. By "the instructions of a mother in Israel," she prayed for "a perfect submission to his will, a perfect confidence in his power, perfect faith, and perfect love, which casteth out all fear that hath torment." In August she attended a camp meeting up the East River. Sustained by friends praying there for sanctification, she began to seek the blessing for herself: "While I was thus praising God for what I had already received, he imparted faith to believe on him for the blessing I so much desired. In a moment, O glory! . . . my idols were taken away . . . and my whole soul was sweetly lost in wonder, love, and praise." The next day she felt a steady peace and a more constant communion with God, and she returned to the city, she tells us, with deep regret.[98]

Strengthened in the faith, Mary Morgan began to exercise significant leadership in New York Methodism. In 1812, about a year after her arrival in New York City, Mary Morgan had established a Sunday morning Bible class. From those foundations emerged the New York Sunday School Union (1816). On November 8, 1813, she was instrumental in the formation of the New York Female Assistance Society, "for the relief of the sick poor of their sex." Also in 1816 she helped to form the Asbury Female Mite Society for the relief of the wives, widows, and children of retired Methodist itinerant preachers.[99] Within a period of six years she was primarily responsible for founding four religious voluntary associations, the Sunday school and missionary societies having tremendous long-lasting consequences.

Married in 1817 to Thomas Mason, a preacher from the South Carolina Conference, then assisting Joshua Soule in managing the New York City–based Methodist Book Room, later pastor of Allen Street Church and then Troy District presiding elder, she bore ten children but found time to sustain the voluntary organizations that she had birthed and to create more. She was one of the founders, in 1822, of the Asylum for Lying-in-Women and remained one of its managers for more than thirty years. In 1833, she became female superintendent of the Greene Street Sunday school and, in 1838, directress of the Female Benevolent Society for the relief of poor women. Mason made perhaps her greatest contribution, however, in leading the New York Female Missionary Society for more than forty years, which tellingly succumbed with her death in 1868 (at age seventy-six).[100]

From 1837 to 1857, the major commitment of the Female Missionary Society was to support Mrs. Ann Wilkins, a thirty-year-old widow at the time she volunteered for missionary service in Liberia (Sources 1842c). Through correspondence between Mason and Wilkins, the members of the Female Missionary Society invested themselves in the Liberian witness. In one letter, Mason promised Wilkins, "You may always look to our Female Missionary Board as to a family of sisters, who are ever ready to sympathize with you in all your afflictions and, as far as in their power, to lighten your burdens and to assist you in your labor of love."[101] And missionary Wilkins anchored the sisterhood bond on her end within her school (in her own home) by conferring on her girl students the names of Methodist women. Thus there was a "little Mary Mason," and Wilkins never tired of sharing the young girl's progress in both knowledge and piety with the American woman for whom she was named. According to the missionary, Mary was "an extraordinary child for any country or color." When Wilkins was ill, the little girl cared for her, "ready to hear the lowest whisper, and attend with cheerfulness to my requests."[102]

Such poignant connections encouraged women to join an auxiliary, their annual or life memberships supporting the missionaries in the field. The denominational societies functioned the same way, the monies raised through two-dollar annual or twenty-dollar life contributions making one a member. The missionary societies did not, at this point, appoint or deploy the missionaries. That remained the prerogative of the bishops—whether among the Wyandotte, for the French in Louisiana, among the slaves, in the territories, including those on the West Coast, abroad in Liberia, or elsewhere in the world. The missionary societies promoted and financed. The bishops drew on the funds raised to support missionaries whom they appointed, as they appointed others within conferences.[103]

The MEC established a Sunday School Union in 1827, as already noted, with similar expectations about connection-wide formation of auxiliaries and other voluntary societies that would follow on the same formula. So in its first, organizing conference, that of 1832, the Indiana Conference instructed each preacher "to form the Quarterly Conference of his Circuit or Station into a Bible Sunday School and Tract Society, auxiliary to these several societies of the Methodist Episcopal Church, and also to form as many subordinate or branch societies in his Circuit as in his power."[104]

By the 1840s, the church began to experiment with other schemes of finance. One such was the practice of setting of "Times of Collections," as the New England Conference did beginning in 1845 and the Philadelphia Conference in 1848:

Bible 2nd S. Aug.; Sabbath School Union (MEC) Sept.; Biblical Institute 2nd. S. Oct.; Preachers' Aid 2nd. in Dec.; Missionary cause last S. Feb.; Wesleyan Education Society 1st S. April

1. The Bible collection in June: 2. the Sunday School Union in July, August or September; 3. The Education in October; 4. The Missionary in November or December; 5. The Philadelphia Conference in February and March; 6. The ten cent collection during the year at the discretion of each preacher.[105]

Pew rents, another scheme for finance on the local level, would bring issues of class to the fore and produce a major schism, as we will see in chapter 8.

Circuits, stations, and conferences functioned with templates for organization and operation that made Methodism a highly organized but locally and regionally staffed, directed, and energized machine. A study in simplicity, this voluntary—not bureaucratic—system, like its interdenominational and denominational competition, operated with a single executive secretary, an annual reporting meeting, and quadrennial General Conference endorsement of design and staffing. Of necessity it depended upon and welcomed the creativity, experimentation, and innovation on the local level.

Individual chapters of missionary and Sunday societies, particularly in Methodism's growing urban areas (New York, Baltimore, Boston, Philadelphia, and Chicago), did more than raise money to support distant ventures. Women's societies in particular showed what direct, hands-on missionary initiatives could accomplish in slum areas and among society's marginalized persons. One of the first such church-related attempts attracted national interest and long served as a model for churches working slum areas. It was called Five Points Mission, and it came about through the sustained efforts of the Ladies' Home Missionary Society and Methodist women who refused to accept the city as irremediable. Beginning in 1843, the society began working among New York's slum dwellers. They besieged incoming immigrants' ships with tracts and Bibles, founded chapels along the docks, and established Sunday schools and Bible classes in poor neighborhoods, but with only limited success. At the persistent urging of new member Phoebe Palmer (see below on her holiness leadership), the society in 1848 turned to the needs of Five Points, the city's worst slum. The notoriety of Five Points spread so far that Charles Dickens, when he came to New York in 1842, insisted on visiting the site.[106]

The work commenced modestly. The society rented a room for religious services and announced a meeting. The turnout, which filled the room, was a spectacle. Children encased in filth and rags poured from garrets, alleys, and cellars of the neighborhood. A Sunday school with an initial enrollment of seventy was organized. Encouraged, the women decided after a few months to open a day school—children who spent six days of the week congregating in street gangs, sweeping street corners for pennies, or begging meals could not be expected to reform their ways after once weekly Sunday lessons. By the winter of 1850–51 one hundred children were in daily attendance, and two full-time teachers were employed. The rented room was crowded and in steady use. The women persuaded the mission's advisory committee of Methodist businessmen to purchase a site for a suitable mission building. A gaunt building known as the Old Brewery stood on the chosen site, abandoned as a business for twenty years, and had become what the women called a pest-house of sin. Into its hundred tiny rooms crowded up to a thousand persons. Irish immigrants occupied the upper floors, African Americans, the basement rooms. By year's end wreckers' balls swung into action and leveled the spot. A new brick building rose in its place, five stories high, with an apartment for the minister and a chapel that seated five hundred persons. The two upper floors contained twenty three-room apartments opened to poor families for five dollars a month, while the ground floor was given over to offices and schoolrooms. The project caught the public imagination, especially after five Broadway hotels provided Thanksgiving dinner for five hundred persons that fall.[107]

Additions ensued, both in premises and in program. Lewis M. Pease, the New York Conference preacher appointed to the mission, expanded the day school and offered hot lunches and free clothing to the children. From 772 children enrolled in 1853, attendance rose to 1,200 in 1856 and 2,500 in 1860. The goal was not simply to shelter and educate the children until they were old enough to enter the city's job market. The hope, whenever possible, was to remove them from the city completely, to find them homes with rural Protestant families. Each issue of the mission's monthly magazine featured stories, written with elaborate pathos, of orphans and beggars desperately in need of a loving home. The managers blanketed the neighboring communities in Westchester County, New Jersey, and Long Island with circulars describing the sufferings of the poor in New York, pleading with all who could to hire some of the city's unemployed, or at least offer room and board in return for farm or domestic labor.

Despite the emphasis on work with children, the superintendent could not limit the mission's scope. As the teachers visited the tenements of the Five Points to gather their charges for school, they encountered families without food or fuel, parents without jobs, mothers sick and without medicines, houses filthy and poorly ventilated. When possible, they offered immediate assistance—loaves of bread, tea, medicines. By the 1860s the mission was providing four thousand hot meals a week to adult residents and was operating a medical dispensary. Since few tenements had the luxury of running water, the mission enlarged its bathing facilities and opened them to the community.

As the first year drew to a close, Pease became increasingly convinced that exhortation and prayer meetings had little effect upon the filth and wasted lives at the Five Points. Visits with the poor and conversations with the parents of schoolchildren showed him that drunkenness, crime, and prostitution were not simply willed acts of immorality but response to the despair of slum life. The poor needed regular jobs before they could be expected to profit from lectures on morality.

Pease persuaded a local shirt manufacturer to provide him with piecework for the neighborhood women, and he converted his evening prayer room into a sewing shop by day. Within a week forty women were busily engaged at the mission. Pease sought not only to provide charity in return for a job done, and thus to lift the morale of the poor and test their good intentions, but also to teach the adults of the neighborhood useful trades to prepare them for outside jobs. By February 1851, he could report that sixty adults had obtained regular employment in the garment industry, while another forty were still at his mission learning such simple trades as sewing, baking, and cobbling.[108]

The officers of the society believed that their constitution prohibited them from supporting the new initiatives and asked the bishop to remove Pease. He resigned and rented two dwellings adjacent to the mission, conveniently emptied when a friendly judge arranged a police raid. There Pease opened the Five Points House of Industry in May 1851. By the end of the first year, his organization had provided shelter and work for three hundred persons.[109]

Both institutions continued thereafter side by side. The Methodist women soon decided that placement of indigent children in the country, job training, and the distribution of food and clothing were within their province. More schoolrooms were added at the rear of the building, and school attendance rose to six hundred pupils. The society also built a four-story addition at the side of the mission, greatly increasing its street frontage. The addition housed an office for the superintendent and a room for the managers, as well as rooms for making, storing, and distributing clothing. The mission also established a library and reported that eighty to one hundred young men used it every evening.

By the 1860s the expanded Five Points Mission and House of Industry were established in the life of the city, affording visitors from far and wide a demonstration center where they could see how urban mission could be done. The mission became a regular stop for visitors interested in the wonders of New York piety. The reputation of the mission became so well known that Abraham Lincoln paid a visit on February 24, 1860.[110] When Methodist women in Chicago organized to support a rescue mission modeled after the Five Points Mission, the editor of the *Northwestern Christian Advocate* prophesied that the cause of city missions was "destined to actuate the heart of the church with a power little dreamed of."[111]

Phoebe Worrall Palmer and Tuesday Meetings

Another women's initiative with enduring, transformative, and institution-creating effect was the Tuesday Meeting for the Promotion of Holiness established by two Worrall sisters, Sarah Lankford and Phoebe Palmer. It would revive American Methodism's perfectionist emphasis, create space for women to speak publicly, blossom in the holiness camp meetings of the 1850s and 1860s (Sources 1867b), stimulate the revival of 1857–58, and result in the formation of a number of holiness denominations (Sources

1843). Raised in a large, devout family associated with the Duane Street Methodist Episcopal Church in New York City, the sisters and their spouses established in the mid-1830s a home together on New York's Lower East Side. On May 21, 1835, Sarah Lankford received the blessing of entire sanctification while reading *An Account of the Experience of Hester Ann Rogers.* She had come to the words, " 'Reckon thyself dead unto sin'; and thou art alive unto God from this hour!" Following these instructions, she fell on her knees and cried, "Yea, Lord from this hour...I dare reckon myself dead, indeed unto sin." From that moment she trusted that God had made her holy, although it was a week later before she felt the witness of the Spirit. Immediately she began to pray that her sister might also experience the blessing of holiness and urged her to seek it.[112] Sarah had been leading women's prayer meetings at both the Allen Street and the Mulberry Street Methodist Episcopal Churches but decided to combine these two meetings into one, to be held at their home on Tuesday afternoons. This gathering became known as the Tuesday Meeting for the Promotion of Holiness. It would continue for nearly sixty years under the leadership of one or the other of these two sisters.

Phoebe (1807–74), who from her conversion at eighteen had longed "for the full assurance of faith," who had been gravely ill, and who had already experienced the deaths of two infants, lost a third, a daughter Eliza at eleven months, in a tragic nursery fire in August 1836.[113] After her daughter's death, Phoebe Palmer intensified the quest for the deeper spiritual experience. She began to teach the Young Ladies' Bible Class in the Allen Street Sunday School in April 1837 and to study the New Testament for a deeper understanding of sanctification. In July she asked the members of the Tuesday Meeting to pray that she might receive full salvation. On July 26, 1837, a date she would always refer to as her "day of days," Phoebe Palmer made "an entire surrender" to God of everything in her life, her "body, soul, and spirit; time, talents and influence," as well as "the dearest ties of nature, [her] beloved husband and child." Receiving the assurance that her consecration was accepted by God, Palmer knew this was the experience of sanctification she had been seeking.[114]

Although Palmer had shied away from public speaking, the experience increasingly evoked inner promptings to witness to the blessing of full salvation. In 1840 Phoebe Palmer assumed the leadership of the Tuesday Meeting when her sister and brother-in-law moved away from New York City. The meeting began to include men as well as women, after Professor Thomas C. Upham of Bowdoin College, a Congregational minister whose wife was a member, asked if he might also attend. He subsequently experienced entire sanctification under Phoebe Palmer's guidance. Many prominent Methodist figures became regular attenders of the Tuesday Meeting, including Nathan Bangs, Bishops Edmund S. Janes and Leonidas Hamline, and educators Stephen Olin and John Dempster. By the 1850s the meeting had become broadly evangelical, drawing ministers and laypeople from almost every Protestant denomination.

The practices of the Tuesday Meeting established a new template for the religious life, one that stimulated an entire holiness movement.[115] Palmer explained:

> After the opening exercises, any one is at liberty to speak, sing, or propose united prayer.... Testimony follows testimony in quick succession, interspersed with occasional singing and prayer, as the circumstances may seem to demand.... In these meetings the utmost freedom prevails. The ministry does not wait for the laity, neither does the laity wait for the ministry.... How small do all merely earthly distinctions appear, when brought under the equalizing influences of pure, perfect love! And it is this equalizing process, that, to our mind, forms one of the most important characteristics of this meeting.[116]

Laywomen and laymen, equally recipients of the gifts of the Holy Spirit, were expected to testify, even publicly, to their faith. Palmer elaborated a theology that explained that mandate, grounding it in a new understanding of human religious development (see below). Both the Tuesday Meeting template and its theology spread. Home meetings patterned after the Tuesday Meeting began to be organized in various parts of the Northeast and, later, throughout the country. By 1886 some two hundred such meetings were operating in the United States and abroad.

During the 1840s, Phoebe Palmer began what would be a public speaking and writing vocation. Invitations came quickly. In the summer of 1840 she made her first evangelistic trip outside the city, visiting Rye, Williamsburg, and Caldwell's Landing, New York (the new home of Sarah and Thomas Lankford). Eventually her speaking itinerations would be national, indeed, transatlantic. Reinforcing the Tuesday Meeting movement and her evangelistic efforts, Phoebe Palmer began to promote holiness through a vigorous publishing program. She became a regular contributor to the *Guide to Christian Perfection*, begun in Boston in 1839 and edited by the Reverend Timothy Merritt. This magazine, eager for responses from those who had experienced "the grace of sanctification," had opened itself from the start to "the female members of the church." The magazine urged that, since "many of you have experienced the grace of sanctification, should you not then, as a thank-offering to God, give an account of his gracious dealing with your souls, that others may be partakers of this grace also?"[117] Women did respond to the editor's request, establishing through their writing important connections with other women. Phoebe Palmer's first contribution was a description of her spiritual journey toward holiness. It appeared serially in three parts, each titled "Letter from a Lady to Her Friend" and signed simply "P.P.," in December 1839 and January and March 1840. Through this medium, Palmer advised other women that God's will was to make them "happy and useful," and therefore that they, too, should seek holiness. Summing up its importance in her experience, Palmer wrote, "So conscious am I that all my sufficiency is of God, that for worlds I would not be left one hour without the *witness* that I have returned all my redeemed powers to Him, who has purchased them unto himself."[118] The July 1841 issue of the *Guide* contained the holiness experience of Sarah Lankford, including her account of how the *Life* of Hester Ann Rogers had guided her to the experience. Other women wrote that they had found "H. A. Rogers' Life" helpful in seeking sanctification.[119]

During the 1840s, Phoebe Palmer also published several books, including *The Way of Holiness* (1843), *Entire Devotion to God* (1845), and *Faith and Its Effects* (1848). In her first and probably most influential book, *The Way of Holiness*, Palmer described her experience of sanctification. Addressing the question "Is there not a shorter way?" she outlined the holiness theology that would become so widely characteristic of the holiness movement as a whole (Sources 1843). In Palmer's view, entire sanctification was presently available to all regenerate Christians who were ready to meet the scriptural requirements of consecrating all to God and believing God's promises. Employing what would be called her "altar terminology," Palmer explained that Christ was the altar that sanctified, or made acceptable, the Christian's total consecration of self. Once this consecration was complete, the seeker should exercise faith and lay claim to the scriptural promise of entire sanctification, with or without an accompanying emotional experience. That was what Phoebe Palmer meant by a "shorter way." And public testimony to the experience of holiness was essential to its retention. These emphases gradually came to distinguish the holiness movement that ensued.

Through the Tuesday Meetings, her writings, the speaking engagements, and letter writing, Phoebe Palmer became a spiritual guide for many Methodist women and a significant denominational voice. Among her closest friends were kindred spirits like Melinda Hamline, wife of Methodist Bishop Leonidas L. Hamline, and Mary D. Yard James, a Methodist woman exemplary for her piety and well known in Methodist circles in New York and New Jersey. Palmer also threw herself into leadership on a local level. In 1848 the Palmers transferred their membership from the Allen Street ME Church to a small, struggling mission congregation and as we noted above, succeeded in persuading the Ladies' Home Missionary Society to begin the Five Points mission.[120]

From 1850 on, Phoebe Palmer entered into the most active years of her public career. As new dimensions of her ministry unfolded, Walter Palmer began to travel with his wife and take an active part in her evangelistic meetings. By 1857–58, Phoebe and Walter found themselves at the center of a remarkable evangelical revival that was interdenominational, largely urban, and primarily led by laypeople.[121] Following the successes of these years, the Palmers accepted an invitation in 1859 to visit the British Isles. Walter gave up his medical practice altogether and never returned to it; he became a full partner with his wife in the vocation of holiness evangelism.

In her public ministry as a holiness evangelist, Phoebe Palmer had encountered some resistance; other women told her stories of their being forbidden to speak in public. As a justification for herself and them, Palmer wrote *Promise of the Father* (1859), a defense of women's right to preach on the basis of the gift of the Spirit to both women and men at Pentecost (Sources 1859b). Claiming that the model of Pentecost should be normative in the church, Palmer presented some four hundred pages of well-reasoned argumentation: from exegesis of scriptural passages, especially the Pauline passages usually used to silence women; from historical precedent, beginning with the ministry of women in the early Christian church and culminating with women's leadership and even preaching in the eighteenth-century Wesleyan movement; from the inconsistent practice in so many churches of welcoming women's voices in some areas but silencing them in others; from the authority of various church leaders and scholars; and from the pragmatic needs of the church for women's gifts. Although Phoebe Palmer did not press for ordination of women, she insisted that women be permitted to pray and testify in the church and even to preach Christ for the conversion of sinners. A shorter version of the argument appeared ten years later, titled *Tongue of Fire on the Daughters of the Lord* (1869). In 1872, Phoebe Palmer became ill with kidney disease and died two years later. Sixteen months later her widowed sister, Sarah, became the second Mrs. Walter Palmer. She continued the work of the Tuesday Meeting and the *Guide to Holiness* until her own death in 1896, at the age of ninety.

Class Meetings and New Denominational Order

Tuesday Meetings, missionary societies, Sunday schools, preachers' wives, and stationed preachers affected the place of Wesley's class (Sources 1798, p. 132) as the institutional foundation of religious life and of discipline. Essential on the circuit, the disciplinary function of class meetings and the once-vital leadership roles of the class leader declined or, as we have seen, were transferred and transmuted into the weekly rhythms of Sunday-oriented congregations. Pronouncements of declension, rendered with prophetic image and force, come easily to Protestants generally and to Methodists particularly. The decline of the class meeting became, therefore, a convenient jeremiadic metaphor (along with itinerancy, holiness, and camp meetings). After all, mandated by Wesley and the *Discipline*, the class proved a highly usable and everywhere-visible symbol of change and, for many Methodists, of declension.

The erosion of the class, though occurring at different paces in different locales, evidenced itself in various ways.[122] As late as 1851, the MEC theologian John Miley published a guide for effective classes and class leadership, *Treatise on Class Meetings*. By then, class attendance had become more sporadic, members finding the probing questions unhelpful and the meetings too long and boring. Leaders became harder to recruit, and those willing and capable increasingly took on oversight of multiple classes. In places classes swelled to inordinate size, both a reflection and a cause of their changing character. As early as 1817, the flagship St. George's, Philadelphia, minuted the "flagrant violation of the nature and design of class meeting":

The evil to which they allude, is the unreasonable number of fifty, sixty or seventy members in one class. Such classes might properly be termed congregations. We say of a truth there is not a leader in this city, who can inquire how the soul of each member in such a class prospers, and give such advice, exhortation and reproof as occasion may require.[123]

Exercises of class discipline, including trials of members for wayward behavior, continued—for failing to attend, being immoral or intemperate, marrying outside the faith, and preaching while female (Sources 1824, 1830a). However, by the mid-1820s, as statistics from New York indicate, classes over fifty were not unusual, and more than half the classes exceeded thirty persons.[124] Leaders with large and/or multiple classes found it difficult to exercise the oversight, provide the personal guidance, sustain the disciplines, and undertake the visitation theoretically required.

The impossibility of genuine pastoring within the class structure and the changes in delivery of pastoral services went hand in hand. So also the definition of membership and changing conceptions of Christian maturation evolved together. Both forms of immediacy, whether of camp-meeting conversion or Tuesday Meeting holiness, and of gradual nurture through the Sunday school displaced the reporting systems of the probationary class and indeed of much of the disciplinary processes of the class system as a whole. Gradually, Methodists came to view their membership as lodged not in a class but in a congregation—whether that was part of a circuit or a station in its own right. And below the congregational level were the Christian home and the ever-increasing system of purposive meetings (prayer, missionary, tract, reform) and of the Sunday school.

MECS Bishop James O. Andrew captured the enormity of the structural change as he noted how it affected the exercise of the episcopal office (Sources 1859a). To guide leaders in running the organization, Abel Stevens produced in 1847 *An Essay on Church Polity*, and MEC Bishop Osmon C. Baker issued in 1855 what would be a standard, *A Guide Book in the Administration of the* Discipline *of The Methodist Episcopal Church.* Robert Emory, son of another bishop and president of Dickinson College, published a *History of the* Discipline *of The Methodist Episcopal Church* in the 1840s, which went through several editions in Emory's life and several more in a version revised and updated in the 1850s by W. P. Strickland. By the 1850s and 1860s, such manuals guided best practices, even for institutions undergoing transformation like class meetings (Miley, *Treatise on Class Meetings*) and camp meetings (B. W. Gorham, *Camp Meeting Manual: A Practical Book for the Camp Ground in Two Parts*).[125] Abel Stevens, then at the helm of the *Christian Advocate*, offered comparable counsel on preaching, worship, and congregational singing.[126] Methodist Almanacs exhibited the structural, missional, and programmatic complexity of the church. The *Ladies' Repository* (1841–76) covered items of interest to the women of the church, and a *National Magazine* (1852–58), edited by Abel Stevens, attended to "literature, art and religion." Stevens, like Bangs, attended in various ways to the distinguishing marks of Methodism, launching, for instance, several important history series.

Conferences began to publish their journals or minutes so that Methodist faithful could see the church at work closer to home. These journals well exhibited the new complexity that made class meetings obsolete. By the 1850s, the New England Conference organized itself into various committees to do its work while sitting and elected officers for ongoing leadership to the following conference societies: the Missionary Society, the Domestic Missionary Society, the Sabbath School Society, the Committee on Church Building, the Visitors to the Biblical Institute, the Visitors to the Wesleyan University, and the Visitors to the Wesleyan Academy. In 1849, the conference reported its financial statistics on a fold-out page (two pages), by district and charge. The first page summarized preachers' finances by columns—quarterage, house rent, traveling expenses, fuel, table expenses, total receipts, and deficiencies. The second page also by columns summarized collections for Sabbath School Union, American Bible Society, Chapel Fund, Preachers' Aid Society, Missionary Society, Biblical Institute, and Wesleyan Education Society. In 1850, the conference replaced the fold-out chart with a five-page table.

The next year, presuming perhaps that laity across the conference would take intense interest in its proceedings, the New England Conference published its proceedings in eight chapters, beginning with an initial one analytical of the several-day gathering. It began with an address: "Will the readers of these 'Minutes' permit us to introduce them to the New England Conference, and its attendant religious exercises." No other conference quite rivaled New England in exhibiting itself (and New England even outdid itself in 1864 with a highly detailed, nine-page "daguerreotype" of its daily proceedings). However, on conference as well as national and local levels, Methodism had become an institution-creating church. Perhaps nothing exhibited its organizational creativity and energy more than collegiate education.

Experiments: Liberal and Ministerial Education

Methodism's very earliest experiment with higher education, an ill-fated venture titled Cokesbury, launched after the church's organization in 1784, slavishly followed Wesleyan formulae. American Methodists would have their own Kingswood, thought Coke and Asbury, immodestly naming it for themselves.[127] Cokesbury was intended to serve preachers' sons, orphans, and competent friends. It functioned at a general, modest, lower educational level as well—basic education and secondary education.

The bishops had high hopes for this endeavor, never mind that the infant denomination lacked the resources, the trained leadership, the support, and the constituency for educational institutions. Nor did higher education suit the operative patterns of ministerial recruitment and training. Itinerancy increased its ranks by recruiting new riders,

135

coupled them with experienced horsemen, trained those "yokefellows" on trial through observation and apprenticeship, and obliged the new recruits to a program of individualized reading. Several years of stasis in an institution would do the prospect and the itinerancy no good. Not when riders were needed! So thought many. Cokesbury was an English institution for which American Methodists were not prepared. Repeated (and suspicious) fires "providentially" made that clear.

Absent formal academic institutions, Methodism pursued several formational, educational, vocational purposes instead through its publishing efforts. Indeed, as we have seen, with every preacher a colporteur, with every circuit a sales district, with products priced for the market, with monetary incentives for energetic promotion, and with clarity that the Word speaks through the written word, the gospel through texts, Methodism carried on its educational endeavor despite Cokesbury's demise. *Cokesbury* appropriately later became southern Methodism's name for its publishing enterprise and even later Abingdon's marketing and bookstore designation. And Methodist publishing, a published normative four-year reading list for ministry, the connectional Course of Study, and effective distribution to all probationary (on trial) preachers of the required books constituted Methodist theological education well into the twentieth century. However, with Asbury dead and no longer able to voice Providence's cautions about colleges, Methodism reclaimed the Cokesbury agenda.

Colleges: The Founding Era

Three decades later, Methodism started over. It established academies in 1817 in Newmarket, New Hampshire, and two years later in New York City. The next General Conference took up the matter and did so with a new sense of education's importance to denominational well-being. The 1820 report of "The committee appointed to take into consideration the propriety of recommending to the annual conferences the establishment of seminaries of learning" spoke with paranoid urgency. Almost all institutions of higher education, it insisted,

> are under the control of Calvinistic or of Hopkinsian principles, or otherwise are managed by men denying the fundamental doctrines of the gospel. If any of our people, therefore, wish to give their sons or daughters a finished education, they are under the necessity of resigning them to the management of those institutions which are more or less hostile to our views of the grand doctrines of Christianity.
>
> Another capital defect in most seminaries of learning... is, that experimental and practical godliness is considered only of secondary importance.... Religion and learning should mutually assist each other, and thus connect the happiness of both worlds together.[128]

Approving the report, the first point of which was verifiable, General Conference recommended that all the annual conferences "establish, as soon as practicable, literary institutions under their control."[129] Assigning responsibility for college development to conferences was a default move for General Conference. Annual conferences constituted the primary agency for the church's work on the ground. So empowering the conferences meant that the educational idea and imperative quickly became a national Methodist passion. Annual conferences responded, sometimes collaboratively, in a spate of foundings, some two hundred by the Civil War, thirty or so of which survived and flourished. Among the early conference efforts were Augusta in Kentucky (1822), McKendree in Illinois (1828), Randolph-Macon in Virginia (1830), Wesleyan University in Connecticut (1831), Dickinson and Allegheny transferred to the Methodists in the 1830s, and in the same decade, Emory in Georgia, Emory and Henry in Virginia, Indiana Asbury University, and two women's colleges, Wesleyan in Georgia and Greensboro in North Carolina.

Methodist motives might seem sectarian. In actuality, the founders of Methodist colleges intended to counter sectarianism and provide an antidote to Presbyterian and Episcopal domination of existing institutions, including the supposedly public universities. Methodist schools would free, not bind, minds (of all who enrolled), recognize the imperative of educated leadership, both lay and ministerial, serve the community at large, command support from civic and state authorities, and of course, therefore admit young people from various religious communities. Denominational control would serve intellectually liberating, not constraining, purposes.[130]

Still, countering Calvinist education hegemony, holding on to one's own youth, and nurturing their leadership talent were no passing fevers of the 1820 General Conference. These purposes continued to be central to the church's educational rationale and agenda. Stephen Olin, the third president of Wesleyan, spelled out in 1844 the Methodist plight in a talk devoted to Christian education. Without our own colleges, he insisted, "few of our sons are likely to be educated, and . . . only a small portion of that few are likely to be retained in our communion." He estimated three-quarters of this talent had been lost: "Many of them have gone to other denominations, many more have gone to the world. All were the legitimate children of the Church. They were her hope, and they should have become the crown of her rejoicing."[131]

Unusual perhaps for its day, Methodism invested in collegiate education for women from essentially the same point that it did for men, in the 1830s. Both Greensboro College in North Carolina and Wesleyan College in Georgia claim priority.[132] Something of the importance of such institutions in encouraging women's leadership and development can be seen in the commencement address of one of Wesleyan's early graduates, Alice Culler Cobb (Sources 1858a).

In founding schools and colleges, Methodists had several purposes in view: moral/Christian formation, the advancement of knowledge, and the training of leaders.

Indeed, they were—the men's colleges, that is—the primary formal training alternative to the Course of Study for education of preachers. The colleges—Wesleyan, Dickinson, Randolph-Macon, and Emory—constituted the seminaries of their day. Wesleyan, for instance, graduated 919 over its first forty years. Of these, a third entered the Methodist ministry. That college alone produced three-quarters of the northern preachers (MEC) who earned college degrees.[133] Northern Methodists by the 1870s and 1880s could call Wesleyan "the mother of our denominational institutions" and "the crown and glory of our Church" and "mother of us all."

While the numbers and percentage of college-educated preachers remained small and the Course of Study the normal pathway to ordination and conference membership, the Wesleyan ideal of a scholar pastor became the hope for station churches and the aspiring preacher. Methodism's collegiate venture reflected and contributed to the church's commitment to literacy, nurture, and culture. Increasingly, the first career of those called to ministry was teaching, not farming. An American Methodism committed to education-through-religion and religion-through-education re-created the Protestant clerical paradigm, that of the Annesleys and Wesleys, that was possible with married preachers. Sons would also hear God's call, a dramatic change to the profile of its ministry. By the Civil War, roughly half of those entering the Virginia Methodist and Baptist ministry were sons of pastors.[134]

Staffing the colleges also had its effect on ministry, as they drew on conference members for presidents and faculty, expanding greatly the numbers of what would now be termed *extension* ministers. By the 1850s, the collegiate drain on the itinerancy prompted expressions of concern. In 1860, the bishops put it explicitly: "To us it seems inharmonious with the itinerant character of our ministry, and incompatible with the designs of our Conference associations, for men, who never intend to enter the pastoral work, but to make teaching a profession for life, to be admitted to membership in the Conferences."

General Conference responded by reaffirming the appropriateness of full connection for those appointed to the colleges. Its Committee on Education deemed it "highly desirable" that ministerial teachers "should constitute a large proportion in, at least, all our collegiate faculties." They continued, "[M]inisterial agency is preferable where the adult mind is to be educated. The moral influence investing his character, and the social powers of his spiritual tendencies are protectives and reformatory to youth." And from this would follow conversions.[135]

If Asbury-the-bishop incarnated Methodist connectionalism and exercised the teaching office in the early years and Bangs and the editors did so in the early nineteenth century, the college presidents constituted the key leadership and incarnated connectionalism for the pre–Civil War and Civil War decades. To that end, Methodism placed within the colleges its very best talent. The conferences appointed the brightest stars to presidencies and to faculty. From the colleges came much of the church's literary production. And if faculty members or a president left, they often went from there to a national teaching office, as editor of an *Advocate* or as bishop. The Ignatius Fews, Augustus Longstreets, John Durbins, Wilbur Fisks, Stephen Olins, and Martin Ruters knit the church together on education's behalf.[136]

Through the colleges, the church would carry on its larger mission of reforming the nation, joining with other denominations in common endeavor to instill Protestant commitment, republican ideals, and civic virtue in the nation's rising leaders. As with missions, Methodism did its fund-raising for these colleges with the highly decentralized conference system. Conferences made the colleges a primary benevolence, legislating approval, appointing agents to solicit funds, and raising modest funds. The college served a vital function within this decentralized system. The conferences pressed for educational institutions out of their sense of Methodism's capacity to take its part in the larger Christian endeavor to shape a Protestant America.

Theological Education, Croakers, and Semi-Centennial Sermons

On the eve of the Civil War, Methodism began to think seriously about formalizing its program for ministerial education through the establishment of theological seminaries. Efforts had already been made by New England Methodists with the creation of the Wesleyan Theological Institute in Newbury, Vermont, out of which later emerged Boston University School of Theology (1867). Garrett-Evangelical traces its history to the 1855 founding of Garrett Biblical Institute. However, James Strong gained notoriety in 1853 with a forthright case for post-baccalaureate theological education comparable to that offered at Princeton and Andover (Sources 1853c). Later a faculty member at the institution created in response to his plea, Drew Theological Seminary, and also advocate of lay membership in General Conference (Sources 1864a), Strong published a dozen volumes in biblical studies, including the *Exhaustive Concordance of the Bible*, and was co-editor with Drew president John McClintock of the ten-volume *Cyclopaedia of Biblical, Theological, and Ecclesiastical Literature*. Strong represented and advocated a church and a ministry for an upwardly modern denomination.

Not everyone favored that initiative or embraced the vision of the church that an educated ministry would create. Indeed, Strong's advocacy elicited another round of "croaking" by those, like Peter Cartwright (1785–1872), who thought the "brush college" superior in forming effective preachers to either colleges or theological schools. In his *Autobiography* and *Fifty Years as a Presiding Elder*, Cartwright drew together several genres—the Wesleyan journal, the western tall tale, the Hebraic jeremiad, the conference semi-centennial sermon—into a highly readable account of "his" camp-meeting, brush-college Methodism. The careful reader should have been alerted by Cartwright's prefatory admissions that "my memory is greatly at fault" and that he had long ago thrown his "manuscript journals to the moles and bats." Repeatedly, in various ways, Cartwright asked, "What has a learned ministry done for the world . . . ?" Not much. By contrast, his Methodism, graphically and colorfully described in his books—that of class, circuit, camp meeting, apprenticed brush college, and Course of Study—had wrought wonders. It had "prospered in these United States without parallel in the history of the Church of Jesus Christ, since the apostolic age." He added,

> [I]n about sixty years, more than a million of members had been raised up and united in Church fellowship in the Methodist Episcopal Church; and this, too, by a body of un-educated ministers. . . . [N]ot one of them was ever trained in a theological school or Biblical institute, and yet hundreds of them preached the Gospel with more success and had more seals to their ministry than all the sapient, downy D.D.'s in modern times, who, instead of entering the great and wide-spread harvest-field of souls, sickle in hand, are seeking presidencies or professorships in colleges, editorships or any agencies that have a fat salary, and are trying to create newfangled institutions where good livings can be monopolized, while missions of poor, dying sinners are thronging the way to hell without God, without Gospel; and the Church putting up the piteous wail about the scarcity of preachers.[137]

Cartwright and John Durbin, contemporaries, products of Kentucky Methodism, and important players in the life of the church, represented different trajectories: Durbin (editor, college president, agency head), that outlined by Nathan Bangs, but Cartwright certainly not. Cartwright's rustic image, carefully cultivated, had nevertheless permit-ted him to hold the presiding elder's office for half a century, to be elected to thirteen General Conferences, to lead the church in founding educational institutions, to take stands against slavery, and even to run for Congress against Abraham Lincoln. Ordained deacon by Asbury and elder by McKendree, Cartwright gloried in the Methodism they embodied. Others did as well. Indeed, the semi-centennial sermon, preached by order of conferences by those who, like Cartwright, had weathered a half century of itinerancy, became a nineteenth-century Methodist preaching genre. Such efforts yielded nostal-gia, the jeremiad, croaking, reforming primitivism.[138] They also pointed toward a dif-ferent form of institutionalization than that advanced by Durbin (and Bangs), namely, toward a highly routinized revivalism, a highly scripted Pietism. The differences repre-sented by Durbin and Cartwright figured in Methodist divisions to which we now turn.

CHAPTER VII

DIVIDING BY MISSION, ETHNICITY, GENDER, AND VISION: 1816–50S

Two proposals surfaced at the 1816 MEC General Conference that would constitute for quadrennia thereafter key items in a democratizing agenda. One motion provided for election of presiding elders, offered interestingly by Nathan Bangs, a later critic of this and related reforms.[1] Not a new idea, it had been proposed previously by Methodist leaders, for instance, by Ezekiel Cooper and Jesse Lee in 1808, and Lee and Nicholas Snethen in 1812, each of whom, like Bangs, had exercised the office of presiding elder. General Conference also entertained a petition from local preachers for representation, a role in the administration of discipline, and opportunities for salary.[2] With the spirit of the recently deceased Asbury hovering to sustain his principles, the 1816 Conference defeated both democratizing proposals. But issues of participation and prerogative had already embroiled, even divided, the young denomination, and more controversy, conflict, and schism lay ahead. Increasingly, the dynamic tensions within the Methodist movement posed themselves as choices—indigenization or order; liberty or uniformity; antislavery or evangelization; popularizing or connection; discipline or influence; spontaneity or formation; democracy or adherence to authority.

Division: Ordering and Disordering

Particularly stressed would be the connectional structure—Methodism's governing system, its connective tissue, its legitimizing authority. The conference system had proved remarkably elastic and open—welcoming, indeed virtually "impressing," young, white, English-speaking males into trial and full connection, sometimes indiscriminately. As Methodism spread and successively evangelized across the expanding American society, it became more diverse economically, racially, linguistically, and culturally. Would those diversities—and that of gender—be reflected in the conferences? Would Methodism's ministry and governance—focused in the conferences—embrace the church's pluralism? The 1816 General Conference altered the *Discipline* to replace the dynamic Wesleyan terms *society* and *connection* with the more traditional term *church*. Led by its "committee of safety," it worried about order, orthodoxy, rules on "dress, family worship, love-feasts, class and society meetings," and the better education of preachers (Course of Study). To some, the stress on order and authority compromised the Wesleyan genius. The contests between reform and order led to division again and again and again.

Division was a key ingredient in Methodism's explosive growth. One year's success on a circuit led to its division into two. The same pertained on a conference level, the bishops from 1796 onward being empowered with the "authority to appoint other yearly conferences in the interval of the General Conference, if a sufficiency of new circuits be anywhere formed for that purpose,"[3] a proviso reiterated up to 1832.[4] By that point the pattern had been established. Conferences would march west with overall American settlement. Distinct religious territories would emerge on the landscape much as political ones did, indeed in advance of the latter. And this was all accomplished by division. The South Carolina Conference, which at one time or another embraced Georgia and Florida and parts of North Carolina, yielded multiple conferences by division. So also the Western Conference, which covered Kentucky, Tennessee, western Virginia, and Ohio. By 1817, Missouri, Ohio, Tennessee, Genesee, and Mississippi were reporting; by 1827, Pittsburgh, Kentucky, Illinois, Holston, Maine, and Canada. By 1857, the MEC boasted forty-seven conferences, despite having "lost" those that exited to constitute the MECS.[5] Ordered division, then, expressed the Methodist connectional and appointive genius. However, even such planned divisions had their "connectional" cost. Each created a separation. Each divided the "fraternity" of the traveling preachers who constituted a conference. Each set off some members into a new conference entity from those with whom they felt deep bonds of brotherhood.

Authority: Local vs. Connectional

Three divisions of the very late eighteenth and early nineteenth century, with mainly regional or local effect, raised issues of local prerogative versus connectional order and challenged the bishops and episcopal order. William Hammett, ordained by Wesley for missionary service, served in the West Indies but later, with Coke's assistance, settled in Charleston, as already noted. He built a strong following there, resisted the authority of Asbury and Coke over his congregation, and led in a 1792 schism. Taking the name of Primitive Methodists and gaining adherents in Charleston and elsewhere in the Carolinas, the movement largely dissipated after Hammett's death in 1803. At the northern reaches of the denomination, a group of "Reformed Methodists," led by Pliny Brett, who had itinerated from 1805 to 1812, sought church government and local authority more akin to those appreciated in New England Congregationalism. They protested episcopacy, emphasized the attainability of entire sanctification, and repudiated war and slavery. Formally organized in 1814 at a convention in Vermont, they drew several thousand adherents across New England, New York, and Canada. By the Civil War, most of the Reformed movement had affiliated with the Methodist Protestants. Another separate Methodist body, also with the name Primitive Methodists, developed around the eccentric figure of Lorenzo Dow, the export of American-style camp meeting revivalism to Britain after 1805, and import-of-the-export as a distinct denomination, beginning in 1829. The Primitives, also a critic of established MEC order, developed strength in Pennsylvania and especially in Canada.[6]

Race and Antislavery

Other divisions tested the terms and boundaries of brotherhood and ethical commitments. Contests to Methodist connectionalism and authority came repeatedly, out of local, racial, language, ethnic, gender, and theological interest and as a natural extension of the unarticulated but vital principle that communities respond best when they effect, indeed lead, their own evangelization. The AMEs, as we have seen, most dramatically posed that very question for the young denomination. Would it permit African Americans to be the agents of their own evangelization (Sources 1792b)? Hence the importance of the AMEs tracing their founding to Richard Allen's walkouts from St. George's in 1787 and 1792. Full separation in 1816 followed requests from Allen and the Bethel Church for the prerogatives that would have accorded their ministries and that congregation fuller standing within the Methodist connection, despite its segregated status and in recognition of its financial assessments. These included ordination, representation, some say in appointments, property ownership, and the ability to exercise discipline. Much of the jostling occurred between the Black congregations in Philadelphia and Baltimore with the white elders appointed to be in charge and the presiding elders. At points, the entire Methodist system became involved. For instance, Asbury ordained Allen a "local deacon," an action that the 1800 General Conference accepted but refused to recognize by inclusion in the *Discipline*. Daniel Coker, whose role in Baltimore and in the formation of the AMEs we examined in the 1816 "Snapshot," had been ordained a local deacon in 1808, also by Asbury as he notes (Sources 1816). A similar set of provocations to those in Philadelphia and Baltimore produced a Wilmington-based coalition, that of the African Union Church, organized in 1813. These schisms cost the MEC Black membership and, more significantly, Black leadership.[7] Losing that voice, articulate in sustaining the Wesleyan commitment to antislavery and unqualified affirmation that Black Americans were fully children of God (created *imago dei*), the MEC found itself ever more sensitive to the concerns and counsel of its slaveholding membership. Another drain on its antislavery witness came from the earlier division, already discussed, largely among whites, that in 1792 involving Virginia and North Carolina followers of the "Republican Methodist" James O'Kelly

(Sources 1792a). This schism, as much as any, made denominational leaders wary of democratizing slogans and proposals.[8]

The organization of the African Methodist Episcopal Zion Church in 1820 was closely related to a reformist separation among white Methodists also in New York led by Samuel Stilwell, a trustee at the flagship John Street Church and sometime leader of a Black class (Sources 1802), and his nephew, William Stilwell, a preacher then in charge of two of the African American congregations. The background and evolution of the AMEZs resembled the pattern of segregation and frustrated requests experienced by the AMEs.

At roughly the same time Allen gathered Black Americans in Philadelphia into the Methodist fold, James Varick (1750–1827) led Black Methodists in New York from deference to dignity. Varick was born into slavery about 1750 in Orange County, New York, near Newburgh, and his mother and father earned freedom from the Van Varcks, a Dutch Reformed Church family. The young family migrated to New York City and joined Wesley Chapel (later John Street Church). James attended the city's first school for Black children. Apprenticed to a shoemaker, Varick opened his own shoemaking business by 1783, in 1790 married Aurelia Jones, and with her had seven children, four of whom lived to adulthood.

By 1793 Wesley Chapel had six Black classes with membership of 143. As Black membership grew, the church introduced segregation. By 1786 Varick was numbered among Black class leaders. In 1796 (at age forty-six), he was granted permission to hold separate prayer and preaching services under supervision of a white pastor. He ran a school in his home, later in his church. In 1799 the new society selected Black trustees (including Peter Williams Sr., long-standing sexton at John Street Church) and announced a public fund drive to build an African *Methodist* church in the city. In 1800 the new congregation purchased a lot on the corner of Church and Leonard Streets and began building a church. The following year Varick opened Zion African ME Church (Mother Zion). Bishop Asbury blessed the church, and the first separate Communions and baptisms led by white elders began. A year later, the new church negotiated articles of agreement with New York Conference limiting the power of trustees to maintain property for MEC but making no provision for authority in matters of church policy and program.

Black deacons were ordained—James Varick, Abraham Thompson, and June Scott in 1806, and William Miller and Daniel Coker (who thereafter went to Baltimore) in 1808. This cadre's influence extended beyond Black Methodists, for instance, leading New York and New York African Americans in successive New Year's Day antislavery, antislave-trade celebrations. They also pressed for control over their facilities of the two congregations, Zion and Asbury (founded in 1814), and for elder's ordination, strategic issues after 1818 when they started a new building and found themselves competing with the AMEs who had begun to work the New York area. Alliance with the AMEs had some attraction for New York Black Methodists, as did alignment with the Episcopal Church. However, Zion eventually sought a middle way between full break with the MEC and continued subservient status.

Gathering twenty-two preachers in a conference (1821), they proposed to the Philadelphia and New York Annual Conferences that they set apart "a Conference for African Methodist preachers, *under the patronage of the white Methodist Bishops and Conference*" (Sources 1821a).[9] The Philadelphia Conference largely assented to the memorial. However, the New York Conference, though finding it expedient to appoint "coloured preachers" who would "labour among them and take the pastoral charge of them until the next General Conference," effectively parried the request for orders and noted that setting off an annual conference was the prerogative of General Conference.[10] Stilwell, the elder in charge of the two African churches, had already advocated independence, and a committee had been working on *The Doctrines and Discipline of the African Methodist Episcopal Church in America*. Proceeding to organize on this platform and on the basis of Philadelphia's more generous posture, the New York Black Methodists met in their first conference on June 21, 1821, with two white elders, William Phoebus, as president, and Joshua Soule, as secretary. No bishop being available for that conference, elders were not ordained. The following year, however, Stilwell and two other renegade Methodist elders ordained a number of elders, among them James Varick and Christopher Rush, Zion's first two bishops. When the 1824 MEC General Conference failed to embrace this new conference, its distinct denominational identity was secured. Varick convened the first General Conference of the AMEZ Church in 1826, which reelected him to the episcopacy. Varick died the next year, just days after New York's deadline for freeing all slaves. Rush succeeded Varick as superintendent, leading the AMEZs until his health failed in 1852.

Despite the organization of the several African Methodisms, numbers of free Black Americans and slaves remained in the MEC, continuing efforts to achieve fuller agency and incorporation into the life of the church. Illustrative was the plea in 1832 by Philadelphia African Americans for what AME and AMEZ had sought and what the petitioners argued would staunch further loss to those denominations, namely, Black preachers (Sources 1832a). Not until 1864, amidst civil war, would the Philadelphia Conference plead for and General Conference (MEC) authorize Black structures—circuits and conferences—"furnishing them with ministerial service by [fully ordained] preachers of their own color."[11] Later that year, Black congregations and leaders from Philadelphia and Baltimore Conferences transferred into the new all-Black Delaware and Washington Conferences, respectively, an empowering but segregating accommodation. We return below to other dimensions of Methodism's unhappy efforts to work across racial lines before the Civil War.

The same New York Conference session that dealt with the Zion overture received word from the presiding elder that William M. Stilwell had withdrawn with a group of white Methodists.[12] Stilwell and his uncle voiced concerns about how New York Methodists were using their money. In particular, they questioned what they deemed an expensive, lavish, high-handed, and therefore inappropriate renovation of the John Street Church, in so doing resisting the authority of other local leaders, the bishops, conference, and the *Discipline* and appealing for their independent stance to the original charter granted to John Street. The Stilwellites enunciated democratic and primitivist principles, making the Bible alone their rule and permitting women the suffrage in matters of church governance. The movement prospered in the 1820s in the New York area, losing much of its strength to the Methodist Protestants and disappearing completely with the younger Stilwell's death in 1851.

Language Lines

Not all the cleavages within the Methodist family can be traced to a decisive moment and a legislative contest or produced such serious trauma. The separate organization of the German movements, the United Brethren and the Evangelical Association, as we have noted, reflected their distinct origins in the broader evangelical movement and the specific leaven of Reformed, Lutheran, and Mennonite Pietism. Still the first conference of the former in 1789 and its formal organization in 1800 and the first conference of the latter in 1803 and its formal organization in 1807 represented failures (on both sides) to carry through on the looser comity they had enjoyed with the Methodists (Sources 1800b). On all sides efforts were made, from time to time, to bring the movements closer.

Christian Newcomer, who assumed leadership from Otterbein and Boehm of the UBC, indicated as early as 1803 eagerness for closer ties with the Methodists (Sources 1813a, 1813c). The Baltimore Methodist Conference reciprocated, conveying through him a proposal for closer union and pressing for adoption of a *Discipline* to make that possible. Fourteen letters exploring that possibility went between Baltimore (and Philadelphia) Conferences and the United Brethren. Methodists insisted on a *Discipline* as the basis for unity. Newcomer drafted one and had it printed in 1813, ironically just as the Methodists were giving up on negotiations. In his eagerness, Newcomer and the Eastern Annual Conference over which he presided had apparently not achieved assent to the new *Discipline* by the Miami (Ohio) Annual Conference.[13] The latter's opposition resulted in the calling of the first General Conference, thus giving this branch of the German Pietists a "Methodist-like" conference structure. However, as it settled its polity, the UBC developed a profoundly different ecclesiology than the MEC (and EA): term episcopacy, elective presiding elders (district superintendents [DSs]), single ordination, appointment of preachers by committee (not by bishop), a congregational locus for ministerial identity, loosely structured and voluntary class meetings, and a general wariness about hierarchy and centralization.

Similarly, as *Die sogenannten Albrechtsleute*, "Those Designated as Albright's People"[14] (Sources 1807), organized themselves and adopted a Discipline (1809), the EA received overtures from both Methodists and the UBC for unity. Each wanted accord on its own terms. For instance, in 1810 John Dreisbach encountered Asbury and Martin Boehm's son Henry. Asbury entreated him to withdraw from Albright, "go with them to Baltimore to attend their Conference; there to join them, and to travel a year with Jacob Gruber, who was then presiding elder, for the purpose of better acquainting myself with the English language... that I might be able to preach,... both in German and English." Dreisbach counteroffered denominational unity:

> "If you will give us German circuits, districts and conferences, we are willing to make your Church *ours*, be *one* people with you, and have one and the same Church government." "That cannot be—it would be inexpedient," was the bishop's reply.[15]

Reinforcing this hesitance, especially Asbury's hesitance, was the language itself and Asbury's conviction that continuing to function in German represented a denominational dead end, a sentiment that he registered with Dreisbach.[16]

In 1813, the two German groups explored unity but disagreed, as had the UBC and the MEC, on ecclesiology, episcopacy, and standards for conference membership.[17] Again, in 1816, when the EA convened in General Conference and selected its name The Evangelical Association, the EA received another overture from the UBC about unity. Delegations from the two denominations met the following year but failed on the same issues. Gestures toward unity would be made over the years, but the conference fraternities proved difficult to unite. Early Methodism experimented with intercultural, bilingual community but found differences along language and polity lines difficult to bridge.

Women in Ministry

Gender, like race, language, caste, and culture, scripted religious roles and particularly leadership roles.[18] In the exercising and/or testing of these scripts, Methodists experienced divisions on the most intimate levels. From Methodist beginnings in the 1760s, as we have noted, women, who constituted the majority, played incredibly important parts—often informally, through relationships and within families—in making Methodist disciples (both evangelizing and forming). They modeled the Christian life, converted family and friends, provided money, hosted and mentored preachers, prayed and testified in love feasts, led classes, and exhorted. They gradually lost public voice, however, including that most important local disciplinary office, class leader. The denomination's retreat did not proceed evenly, however, and a few women in the early nineteenth century claimed and exercised calls to preach. By the 1830s, particularly in the MEC, the quest for respectability and order (chapter 6) led to suppression of such "public" forms, providing "domestic" alternatives instead in (1) the "office" of preacher's wife; (2) intracongregational organizations for gendered participation and leadership— Sunday schools, missionary and other societies; and (3) a media attentive to gender roles. The latter, in particular—the *Advocates*, Sunday school and missionary materials, published letters, notices and obituaries, and serials devoted particularly to women, *Ladies' Repository* (MEC, 1841–76) and *Southern Lady's Companion* (MECS, 1848–54)— exhibited women's religious experience (Sources 1841b), championed the new religious leadership roles, including that of the preacher's wife, and defined women's religious sphere.

As Methodism grew, so also grew the number of married preachers and the number of stations, the appointments to a single church about which *Advocate* editor Thomas Bond complained (Sources 1841a). Small-town and urban "station" congregations, as we noted in the last chapter, erected substantial buildings and increasingly provided parsonages. Such congregations came to expect preachers to have wives and came to expect the preacher's wife to invest time and talent domestically, within Sunday school, mite society, and missionary endeavor. By the 1850s, the wife had ample models and some guidebooks for these "parishlike" roles, the advice tendered by both preachers and spouses. *The Itinerant's Wife* by the Reverend Herrick M. Eaton, published in 1851, recognizing that the vocation of preacher's wife was beginning to resemble a career, spelled out appropriate demeanor, educational requirements, appropriate reading, and more specialized skills.[19] Along with such counsel came words of encouragement for women charting new ground in a denomination and in communities not used to preachers' wives, indeed, in some instances opposed to them in principle: learn to be a gypsy; be prepared for quite indifferent housing; expect profound loneliness through separation from spouse, family, and friends; steel yourself for continual partings; balance service with duties as wife and mother; in short, "love the itinerancy."[20] Such encouragement was much needed, as the diary of Mary Orne Tucker indicates (Sources 1838).

The vocation of preacher's wife may well have permitted many women who had heard a call to ministry to exercise that within accepted bounds. Some women, whether traveling with itinerant husbands or within stations, effectively honored such a call, in leading, teaching, exhorting, and preaching alongside their spouses. In a number of instances before the Civil War, both within and beyond Methodism, women experienced and publicly affirmed a call to preach. Although never ordained or embraced with conference membership, these few found support for their ministries from eager hearers and encouragement from other ministers. Sometimes, a woman's preaching ministry succeeded too much or in some other way exposed her to those intent on holding to the *Discipline*.

Such occurred for Sally Thompson (Sources 1830a), who enjoyed remarkable support and requests to preach from quite a number of preachers and at least one presiding elder before being tried and excommunicated. Her expulsion came after successful preaching in New England and New York State for more than ten years. By her own published account,[21] Thompson (1798–185-?) had been "encouraged in her ministerial labors" by many ministers in Boston since she preached at a revival in that city in 1820. But when Thompson moved to Herkimer County in upstate New York in the late 1820s, she was greeted with resentment and hostility. At first the local circuit preacher allowed her to hold meetings, but then changed his mind. Thompson tried to reassure the preachers that she had no intention of undermining their authority. She rarely traveled to a church without an invitation, or spoke until the presiding ministers had opened the meeting. Nevertheless, an 1830 quarterly meeting resolved that none of the brethren should convey her to or from a meeting; no collection or subscription should be taken up for her; and no preaching appointments should be made for her.

Certain of her call, however, she continued to accept invitations to preach and was ordered to appear in front of a committee to face disciplinary action. She was accused of evil speaking, immorality, and insubordination to the church (Sources 1830a). In the trial, Thompson was forbidden to testify. The two dozen who testified, class leaders and local preachers, though disagreeing about details, portrayed her as a sincere, faithful preacher who had been "the instrument of great good." The trial committee accordingly pronounced her "not guilty." Before Thompson could savor her victory the presiding elder (DS), Ephraim Hall, immediately appealed the case to the next level, a quarterly conference of the Westford Circuit, and as her account indicates, two months later she received written notice of expulsion.[22] No matter that individual preachers affirmed her and Methodist people responded to her message, female preaching was disorderly, insubordinate, unacceptable under any circumstances. Thompson managed to cobble together enough support to continue preaching for another three years, but after repeatedly refusing to submit to the hierarchy's "limits and rules," she was finally forced out of the church. Thompson could have tried to appeal the ruling, but instead, she decided to join a church more tolerant of female preaching. Six years after her excommunication, she became a member of the Christian Church, traveling as an itinerant for at least another dozen years.[23] Thompson's trial was a harbinger of the sweeping backlash against female preaching that took place during the 1830s and 1840s. Other women also left the Methodists because they felt frustrated by the growing restrictions on female speech.

Others flew more successfully under the radar. Among those in the MEC was Fanny Butterfield Newell (1793–1824). Born in 1793 in Maine and converted at age fifteen, she heard a call to preach in 1809 (Sources 1809), through a messenger in a dream who instructed her to take on the mantle of the preacher under whom she had been converted, Brother Henry Martin (who had recently died).[24] Marrying the Reverend Ebenezer F. Newell, the following year, she traveled with him around circuits in Vermont and Maine. Her call to preach was reaffirmed in 1811 by another powerful near-death religious experience, not long after the birth of her first child. Taken up into heaven, she met Christ, who greeted her with the words, "Fanny, you must not come yet; thou shalt not die, but live, and declare the works of the Lord to the children of men."[25] After one of her preaching dreams, Fanny Newell wrote in her diary,

> Could I preach as well awake as when asleep, I should think "wo[e] is me, if I preach not the Gospel";—and even now, if I were a man I should be willing to go and preach Jesus.... My mind is led to view Jesus as the only Savior, and he is every way sufficient to save a helpless soul who trusts in him for grace, and receives power daily to conquer every foe.[26]

Though of frail health and despite misgivings, she did indeed leave children behind some years later to undertake a frontier preaching mission with her husband in St. Croix, at the eastern edge of Maine, near the New Brunswick border. Although this experience lasted just a year and she died young, of tuberculosis, her witness lived on in her memoirs, which went through four editions by 1848.

Like Newell, the African American Jarena Lee (1783–1850?) published an account of her call and ministry, *The Life and Religious Experience of Jarena Lee*, in 1836 and in a revised version in 1849 (Sources 1811a).[27] The autobiography, particularly in this 1849 version, vividly depicts the challenges facing a woman, and especially an African American woman, in preaching.[28] Born in Cape May, New Jersey, in 1783, to free parents, Jarena was converted at age twenty-one under the preaching of Richard Allen. Experiencing a call to preach around 1811, she sought Allen's counsel. He encouraged her to limit her ministry to roles that Methodists permitted women, including holding prayer meetings and exhorting (delivering the sermon-like message following the sermon). That same year, she married Joseph Lee, pastor of a Black church in Snow Hill, New Jersey, just outside Philadelphia. Within six years, death took five members of her family, including her husband, leaving her with two infant children. She moved to Philadelphia and to Bethel Church, by then the flagship congregation of the African Methodist Episcopal (AME) Church. There she exercised the roles in leading prayer meetings and exhorting that Allen had sanctioned. In one exhortation, heard by Allen, she compared herself to Jonah fleeing a call. Whereupon Allen publicly recalled that earlier confession and pronounced her as called as any other preacher present.

Thereafter Jarena Lee began a career of itinerant preaching, first in the Philadelphia area; later from upper New York State to Maryland and as far west as Ohio. In one year in the 1820s, she claimed to have traveled more than two thousand miles and preached more than one hundred seventy-five sermons. She often traveled on foot, spoke to large congregations, both black and white, and depended upon the hospitality of those among whom she preached. When possible, she traveled with "a Sister," that is, another woman evangelist, among them Sister Zilpha Elaw, another African American preacher who published an account of her call and ministry.[29] Though experiencing much opposition to women preaching, she prospered with the support of Allen, with whom she left a son when traveling. Allen permitted her to preach at Bethel and took her to the 1823 AME General Conference. He died in 1831. When she sought support of the AME Book Committee for her autobiography, she heard a "No," five years later. By the end of her career, a number of Black women were actively preaching, but none were officially recognized by the AME male hierarchy. Troubled by these growing restrictions, the newly formed AME women's missionary society (Daughters of Zion) twice petitioned the denomination's General Conference to authorize licensing women to preach, but was defeated each time (1848 and 1852). The women went on preaching wherever they found support, and many gained renown as charismatic religious leaders.

A comparable figure among the Methodist Protestants, to whom we return below, was Hannah Pearce Reeves (1800–1868). Born in England, converted at age eighteen, and a charter member of the Bible Christians, a small Methodist denomination, she was convinced by her conversion that she was called to preach. She itinerated for the Bible Christians some nine years, eventually meeting a Wesleyan Methodist lay preacher by the name of William Reeves who was much impressed with her extemporaneous delivery. Reeves immigrated to the United States, where he became an itinerant preacher of the newly organized Methodist Protestant Church in 1830. Reeves corresponded with Hannah Pearce for a year before persuading her to come to America and marry him. Convinced that it was God's will, she sailed to America in April 1831. They were married in Zanesville, Ohio, in July, and from the day of their marriage "labored together in the gospel ministry" until her death in 1868.[30] She was an effective preacher, as an auditor reported to an Ohio newspaper and the denominational serial, the *Methodist Protestant*: "During my journeyings, I have witnessed many displays of talent and eloquence in the pulpit, but never heard a sermon which left such an impression on my mind as that delivered by Mrs. Reeves."[31] That same month, October, she preached by invitation to the Ohio Annual Conference of the MPC. A committee of key leaders of that denomination (including founders Nicholas Snethen and Asa Shinn) visited her to ascertain her wishes about accepting her own circuit appointment. She responded that all she wanted was the conference's concurrence in her labors with her husband.[32] From then on the couple traveled his circuit with the blessing of the church, Hannah sometimes taking separate appointments. When he was ill, especially for an extended period during 1832, she took his appointments; she was even invited to preach in meetings of the MEC and the AME Church.

In the UBC, several women were recommended or licensed to preach in the 1840s and 1850s, among them Lydia Sexton (1799–1894). Converted as a mature, twice-widowed woman of thirty-four, with a child from each former marriage, she and her sister-in-law became members of the first United Brethren class meeting in Dayton.[33] Soon the other members of the family were converted and joined the church as well, and Lydia and her third husband, Joseph Sexton, set up an altar for family devotions. Though initially afraid to speak in prayer meeting or class and reproved by the presiding elder for never having "a word to say for Jesus," she came to the conviction that she was called to preach.[34] The family moved west, to Indiana and later to Missouri. When a son became seriously ill, Lydia covenanted with God that if his life were spared, "the remainder of my days should be devoted to his [God's] service, whatever might be the inconvenience or consequences." Within a week she agreed to preach, and an appointment was "given out" for her to preach in her own home. Her husband, then class leader, voiced misgivings at first, but consented when she told him there was no peace for her otherwise. After about a year of preaching, Lydia Sexton applied for a preacher's license, was examined by the presiding elder, and was granted a preacher's license by the Iroquois Illinois Quarterly Conference (in 1851).[35] The license was renewed annually, even after 1857, when the UBC General Conference legislated against women preaching. She itinerated until 1871, the last year holding the post of chaplain to the Kansas State Penitentiary. Sometimes accompanied by her husband, Lydia did the preaching, since unlike the husband in other itinerating couples, he was not ordained.

The few women who preached or exhorted, the considerable number of preachers' wives charting new forms of ministry, and the Methodist majority (women) creating and leading the various Sunday school, Tuesday Meeting, and missionary efforts all evidenced Methodism's continuing but evolving dependence on its women but its difficulty in affirming that dependence formally in the *Discipline* and recognizing their callings and even calls. Roles and opportunities that the Civil War brought would occasion the further testing of restraints and constraints.

Native American Missions

The church experienced a similar difficulty—as did other denominations—when it took the gospel across cultural lines. With Native Americans, as with African Americans, Methodism struggled to make them full partners in their own evangelization.[36] Under such an indigenizing practice, American Methodism had prospered and grown rapidly, drawing its leadership out of the ranks of those being evangelized—an early type of postcolonial, William Taylor–like, self-supporting or three-self missions (self-propagating, self-supporting, self-governing).[37] This being-itself-a-missionary-movement had been something of a happy accident. An ocean separated colonial Methodism from Wesleyan authority. The flight of his British deputies during the Revolutionary period left the Americans and an Americanized Asbury in charge. Coke was never allowed to exercise significant authority. But Methodism never recognized or enunciated this indigenizing principle and evangelizing commitment. And when confronted with persons and communities very unlike themselves, like African Americans and Native Americans, white Methodists found great difficulty in bringing them into full agency of their own evangelization. In its missions, domestic and foreign, Methodism retreated from its postcolonial genius into colonial paternalism.

The Wyandotte experience, the motivation as we have noted for the development of the "sending" missionary structure, illustrates the challenges that led to that "retreat." James B. Finley (1781–1857), presiding elder over the Wyandotte area in northern Ohio, reinforced the efforts of John Stewart for several years by appointing itinerants as missionaries. By 1821, he had recognized that effective evangelization required more stable, full-time leadership than passing itinerants could provide and that both a school and a mission farm would serve the effort among the Wyandotte, and he selected a site in Upper Sandusky. For these projects, he sought and gained the endorsement of Wyandotte leadership, seven chiefs assenting in a formal response witnessed by a U.S. government agent. Finley was thereafter appointed to the Wyandotte Mission and established a school with Harriet Stubbs as "matron and instructor." He organized a church, eliciting as members four of the chiefs, Between-the-Logs, Mononcue, John Hicks, and Peacock, who with Squire Gray Eyes became an oversight committee for the school.[38] In the next couple of years, Charles Elliott, William Walker Jr., and Lydia Barstow came as additional teachers, and Finley served as superintendent of the mission. In 1823, Bishop William McKendree and John Johnston, an agent for Indian Affairs, separately visited and praised the mission. The same year, Finley along with several Wyandotte extended the mission among tribe members in Canada and in Michigan (the Huron Mission), forming classes in both places. Finley and successors brought Native Americans into limited levels of leadership. Chiefs Between-the-Logs and Mononcue, for instance, were early licensed to preach and in 1826 visited New York, Philadelphia, and Baltimore, along with Finley on a preaching tour. Several other Wyandotte were licensed to preach and included in the preaching schedules. And as of 1826 fifteen functioned as class leaders. The stability and doubtless leadership development that Finley offered ended with his appointment in 1827–28 to be presiding elder again. Thereafter the Wyandotte Mission experienced successive appointments of missionaries who did not speak their language, reincorporation into a circuit, white incursions on their land, gradual migration of tribe members west, and eventually in 1842 a formal treaty relinquishing their Ohio property.[39] Methodism neither crossed the language and culture barrier nor raised Wyandotte leaders to conference membership.

Methodism launched missions among the Creek in 1821, the Cherokee in 1822, the Choctaw in 1824, and the Chickasaw in 1835, southeastern tribes with well-developed institutions of self-government, inhabiting adjoining areas of the Carolinas, Tennessee, Georgia, and Alabama. The effort among the Cherokee, promising given significant intermarriage, cultural exchange, and earlier Protestant missions, came at the behest of

Richard Riley, himself part Cherokee, who invited a Methodist preacher from the Tennessee Conference, Richard Neely, to preach at his house. A Methodist society was formed, and Riley appointed class leader. By the end of 1822 a school had been established and a meeting house built by the Cherokee. In the summer, a well-attended camp meeting was held at Riley's. (A later one, for 1829, was well described by missionary, later longtime editor of the *Nashville Christian Advocate*, and even later head of MECS missions, John B. McFerrin, in Sources 1829.) Many Cherokee were converted, including John Ross, chief of the nation for many years.[40] Evangelization and indigenization surpassed what had been achieved among the Wyandotte. By 1827, mission superintendent William McMahon claimed 675 members organized in three circuits, four schools, several licensed exhorters and local preachers, and one preacher, Turtle Fields, "eminently distinguished for his deep piety and devotion to the interests of the mission." And by 1830, the mission boasted 1,028 members and eight circuits or stations.[41]

In 1828, the discovery of gold in Georgia Cherokee territory brought invasive and predatory actions by white settlers and a series of confiscatory laws from the Georgia legislature, in effect repudiating a Revolutionary-era treaty and Cherokee status as a sovereign nation. The legislature's declaration of Cherokee laws null and void occasioned an unsuccessful appeal to the U.S. Supreme Court. A later Supreme Court ruling reversed this decision, only to be ignored by Georgia leaders, President Andrew Jackson, and Congress. The latter contributed to the extrusion cause by passing the Removal Bill of 1830. The Georgia governor notified missionaries to depart or face arrest. A number, including two Methodists, James J. Trott and Dickson C. McLeod, superintendent of the mission, were marched over twenty miles in chains to jail. The Cherokee resisted valiantly, and many missionaries protested against removal as well. On September 25, eight Methodist missionaries, including Trott, McLeod, and McFerrin, met to draw up resolutions asking their denomination to support the Cherokee Nation. Declaring their "unanimous opinion" that removal would be "ruinous" to the Cherokee, they called upon American Christians to express their sympathy for the "aggrieved condition of the Cherokees" and oppose these policies of Georgia and the federal government. The resolutions were printed in October in the New York *Christian Advocate* (Sources 1830b) and the *Cherokee Phoenix*. Cherokee Elias Boudinot added an editorial to the latter, praising Methodists for being the first missionaries to speak out for his people's rights, a sentiment shared across the nation.[42] Unfortunately the Methodist missionaries found little support from their own conference, the Tennessee, which refused to interfere with "political affairs." Under such pressures and not surprisingly, the mission, which might well have yielded full conference status without the oppression, deteriorated, the membership report for 1835 half of what it had been. By that point, the mission had two traveling preachers, Turtle Fields and John F. Boot, among the first Native Americans ordained. By the expiration date for removal in 1838, fewer than two thousand Cherokee had emigrated. Suddenly more than fourteen thousand Cherokee men, women, and children were forcibly herded into concentration camps and shamefully removed to Indian Territory west of the Mississippi on the Trail of Tears.[43] The deportation included three Cherokee preachers, Boot, A. Campbell, and Weelooker, who transferred to the Arkansas Conference. By the 1840s an Upper and Lower Cherokee Mission could report significant leadership below annual conference level, sixteen local preachers, and sixteen exhorters plus a number of class leaders.

In 1821 William Capers of the South Carolina Conference, whom we noticed in the last chapter and revisit below for his role in establishing the mission to the slaves, was appointed missionary to the Creek Nation of Georgia and Alabama by Bishop McKendree. Although not yet open to having Christian preaching in their nation, the Creek chiefs assented to the establishment of an Asbury Manual Labor School.[44] Among its students were James McHenry, Samuel Checote, and George W. Steadham, all of whom later became prominent Methodists as well as leaders of the Creek Nation. The Creek, too, were forced to move to Indian Territory in 1836.[45] A mission to the Choctaw people of Mississippi prospered under the efforts of the Reverend Alexander Talley, M.D., appointed by the Mississippi Conference in 1827. Preaching successfully from village to village, Talley, aided by two other missionaries, three interpreters, and four teachers, claimed some four thousand members by 1830. Apparently rationalizing removal as the best way to protect Native Americans from exploitation, Talley accompanied a band of Choctaw to Indian Territory during the winter of 1830–31.[46] West of the Mississippi the Cherokee, Choctaw, and Creek, as also the Chickasaw and Seminole, struggled to reconstruct their national lives. Although removal brought bitterness and distrust of whites and their religion, the Mississippi, Tennessee, and Missouri Conferences continued to send missionaries into Oklahoma and environs.[47]

In the 1820s and 1830s a number of annual conferences began work with peoples of the Great Lakes region. With the help of Mohawk evangelist Daniel Adams, John Clark of the New York Conference started a mission among the Oneida in Green Bay, Wisconsin, in 1832. Soon a Methodist class was formed, a mission house was built and dedicated, and a school was organized. Electa Quinney, a young Housatannuck (Stockbridge) woman, was hired as the first teacher. She and Daniel Adams married and, in 1837, went to the Seneca Mission in Indian Territory. After her husband's death, Mrs. Adams "continued in service, highly esteemed for her intelligence and good work."[48] Work among the Chippewa began as part of the Genesee Conference's mission to the Mohawk. In 1822, Peter Jones, a Chippewa living among the Mohawk, met Methodist preacher Seth Crawford. The following year Jones and his sister Mary were converted at a Methodist camp meeting. He became a Methodist preacher and was one of the founders of Methodism among the Chippewa at Sault Sainte Marie.[49] Other Native Americans were instrumental in the work among tribes in the Great Lakes region.

Three young Ojibwa men—John Johnson, George Copway, and Peter Marksman— had been sent to Ebenezer Manual Labor School in Illinois with three non–Native American youth who were committed to missionary service. All of them became prominent church leaders. Peter Marksman was called by one historian "the outstanding Michigan Methodist Indian preacher of the nineteenth century,"[50] a ministry described in his conversion and call to the ministry (Sources 1842a).

By the early 1830s, the MEC began entertaining the idea of a mission to the numerous tribes in the Pacific Northwest (including the Chinook, Salish, and Nez Percé peoples). The "moving spirit" in the founding of the Oregon Mission was Wilbur Fisk, president of Wesleyan University (Connecticut), who proposed to the Missionary Society (MEC) in 1833 that the Reverend Jason Lee be appointed "missionary to the Flathead Indians." Fisk's original vision became formative for Lee upon his acceptance of the appointment: "Live with them—learn their language—preach Christ to them—and, as the way opens, introduce schools, agriculture, and the arts of civilized life."[51] Jason Lee, his nephew, the Reverend Daniel Lee, and Cyrus Shepard, a schoolteacher, established the mission on the Willamette River, a location where a school could be supported by farming grain and vegetables.[52] From the beginning, Jason Lee struggled with the Native Americans' opposition to their children attending school, the deaths of several Native American children from "imported" diseases, and the ill health of Daniel Lee and Cyrus Shepard. In 1837 a sizable group of reinforcements arrived at the mission, having traveled by sea from Boston, around Cape Horn, and through the Hawaiian Islands. They included a medical doctor and his family and several white women, one of whom, Anna Maria Pittman, would become Jason Lee's wife. After 1837, the history of the Oregon Methodist Mission became inseparable from the settlement of Oregon Territory and its annexation to the United States. Homer Noley referred to this as "Lee's *other* mission."[53]

At its 1844 General Conference The Methodist Episcopal Church created an Indian Mission Conference that, as the church divided over slavery, became part of The Methodist Episcopal Church, South (see below on this division). Convened by Bishop Thomas A. Morris (Sources 1844d) on October 23, 1844, at Riley's Chapel, two miles east of Tahlequah in Indian Territory (Oklahoma), the conference functioned in English, Choctaw, and Cherokee and included among its twenty-seven members: William McIntosh (Cherokee), John F. Boot (Cherokee), and William Okchiah (Choctaw). As Homer Noley suggests, the statistics for that conference "represented twelve years of reconstruction by Native American Christians since being exiled from their native homes": 27 local preachers, 85 white members, 133 Black members, and 2,992 Native American members.[54] Methodist missions in Kansas became part of the Kansas District of the Indian Mission Conference. The Shawnee Mission Manual Labor School opened in October 1839, with four teachers and seventy-two students from a number of tribes (especially Shawnee and Delaware). In Arkansas two schools were established in the early 1840s: Fort Coffee Academy for the education of Choctaw boys and a school for girls at nearby New Hope. The MECS organized its own Committee on Missions, chaired by Capers, which established Jerome Berryman (Sources 1844d) as mission superintendent, locating him at the Shawnee Mission, overseeing two other districts (the Cherokee and Choctaw) in addition to the Kansas. The MECS Indian Mission struggled with relocation problems, drought, pre–Civil War border turmoil (Kansas and Missouri especially), as well as a variety of language and culture tensions that derived from the missionary endeavor to Christianize by civilizing.[55] Especially telling was the church's tardiness in translating the Bible and essential Wesleyan resources (*Discipline*, catechisms, Sunday school materials), a point made eloquently by Cherokee preacher Walter Duncan (Sources 1853b).

Methodist inability to translate its message fully was but one in a series of problems that haunted the missions to Native Americans. However well intentioned, Methodist overtures functioned within the interactions of white settlers and traders with Native Americans, often highly predatory, aggrandizing, and exploitive. Prejudices, stereotypes, and mistrust haunted both sides of missionary relations. Further, missions typically worked in some partnership with federal and state policies regarding Native Americans, another taint on its integrity. When missions succeeded and individuals or groups converted, they often found themselves alienated from their own people and not incorporated into the Methodist community. The itinerant system, which revolved white preachers in and out of missionary settings, provided little occasion for cultural understanding, skill development, strategic wisdom, and pastoral experience, much less real fluency in Native American languages. The mission schools, even granting the appropriateness of their civilizing agenda, suffered for lack of policy, supervision, and resources. Yet despite such severe problems and despite opposition among Native Americans themselves, some significant Christianization occurred, often as we have noted through the efforts of Native American preachers.[56]

One such preacher proved also to be one of the early and forceful critics of Christianization through acculturation. William Apess, a Pequot born in Massachusetts and a Methodist Protestant–ordained preacher, spoke fully in his own words about the appalling racism of the early republic. Apess fought for the U.S. in the War of 1812 and then focused the nation's attention on the plight of Native peoples. His autobiography, *A Son of the Forest*, was first published in New York in 1829. Four years later (1833) Apess initiated and led the only successful Native American revolt in New England before 1850. In his 1835 publication, *Indian Nullification of the Unconstitutional Laws of Massachusetts*, Apess detailed the story. Although arrested, jailed for thirty days, and forced to pay a stiff fine, he succeeded. The Mashpee of Cape Cod won the right to elect their own local political representatives. In his writings, Apess viewed Euro-Americans as hypocritical in their actions and their rhetoric regarding Native Americans. Damning the pretension of Christians and Christian missionaries, he saw "instructing" as but a veil for "destroying." Apess repeated that equivalence with frequent play on "conversion" not in the sense of helping Native Americans toward the Christian faith but in the sense of stealing their land. Apess's militant consciousness anticipated pan-Indian rhetoric and politics of the 1980s.[57]

Mission to the Slaves

A plantation mission or mission to the slaves, an effort to control as much as to convey the gospel to African Americans,[58] began before the church divided North and South (the topic of the next chapter). After 1844, it functioned, more happily, under MECS auspices. This mission inverted what had been the enabling, indigenizing, self-actualizing genius of Methodist evangelism. And, of course, plantation or slave missions cohered with what had been a steady erosion of Methodism's constitutive commitment to antislavery. The accommodation to southern sentiments and its slaveholding members had been gradual, as we have noted, the 1816 General Conference conceding that "the evil appears to be past remedy."[59] In its own Missouri Compromise, also in 1820, the MEC effectively ended the prohibition against preachers and circuit or station leaders holding slaves. In 1824, the MEC embraced as an antislavery cause the American Colonization Society and the Liberian Mission, which dealt with slavery by exporting freedmen to evangelize Africa. Church leaders, notably Wilbur Fisk, president of Wesleyan University, and Bangs, secretary of the Missionary Society and MEC spokesperson through the *Christian Advocate*, threw their support to colonization. Other editors, save that of *Zion's Herald*, followed suit. Henry Bascom, several-time college president, later editor, still later bishop, served for two years as an agent for the American Colonization Society and set forth its aims in a repeatedly delivered speech (Sources 1832b). By the 1840s annual conferences, except in the South, had endorsed the colonization cause, the bishops lined up in its favor, and much of its intelligentsia signed on as well. Donald Mathews concluded, "[T]here was no religious denomination more closely connected with colonization than the Methodist Episcopal Church."[60] We will return to the contest within the church over slavery and its growing sectionalism. Here we note that the retreat from antislavery and the mission to the slave developed together.

Despite the losses to the AMEs and AMEZs, the MEC retained a significant African American membership, including sizable numbers in slave states and within conferences where both slaves and free Black Americans would belong. By 1828, the year before the "Mission" really began, the MEC claimed 59,056 "Coloured" among its 421,156 members, primarily in four conferences: South Carolina, 18,460; Virginia, 9,090; Baltimore, 10,402; and Philadelphia, 8,352, for the first three of these constituting roughly a third of its membership.[61] Among those worrying in the 1820s about the church's care of its Black membership were William Capers, superintendent of the Creek mission and a slave owner, and his friend James O. Andrew, presiding elder, not a slave owner but later a bishop and *the* slaveholder-by-marriage bishop over whom the church divided. Under their leadership and with the conviction that conversion made for a better and certainly less revolt-prone slave, first South Carolina and later other southern conferences sent missionaries, primarily at the request of planters, to preach, establish Sunday schools, catechize, and otherwise care for plantation slaves.[62] They enjoyed the endorsement of the MEC Missionary Society and of the several *Advocates*, including that established in 1836, the *Southern Christian Advocate*, which Capers then edited. On its organization, the MECS committed itself to "Missions Among the People of Color," "furnishing the entire colored population of the South and South-west with the preaching of the gospel, the administration of the ordinances, and the moral discipline of the Christian church," which, it claimed, despite post–Nat Turner fears of slave revolts or perhaps because of fears of slave revolts, enjoyed societal affirmation. "Let it ever be the *glory* of the Methodist E. Church, South," it continued, "that she has genuine pity for the slave, effective benevolence, exulting charity, energetic, *practical zeal*, commensurate with the utmost spiritual wants of this portion of our population." The MECS expressed its commitment by deploying 127 missionaries serving 120 missions but only 17 churches and 6 Sunday schools.[63]

The MECS carried on its plantation or slave mission until the Civil War, its way of nurturing the slave while ever increasing its commitment to the institution of slavery. However, as narratives by ex-slaves and interviews of ex-slaves have shown, slaves frequently found white southern efforts transparent and looked elsewhere for gospel solace, nurture, insight, and proclamation. Many experienced greater comfort from Christianized slave preachers who drew together African practices and a prophetic reading of Scripture into a highly expressive style of song and rhetoric offered during the slaves' precious time and space, from sundown to sunup and in the hush arbors. Thus emerged the "invisible institution" described by Albert Raboteau and others.[64] After freedom, its dynamisms would animate the several Black Methodisms: AME, AMEZ, CME, and MEC.

Slave Catechisms

The plantation or slave mission aimed to regain some of the evangelistic momentum that Methodism had enjoyed among African Americans when it preached an egalitarian and antislavery gospel. The mission was not an inconsequential effort. By 1843, the plantation missions had seventeen missionaries working, claimed 6,556 slave members, and provided instruction to 25,025 slave children.[65] One missionary laboring in Georgia on the Savannah River Mission reported in 1835 itinerating weekly to nine plantations, catechizing orally 165 children, praying "with the old and sick in their houses or hospitals," and lecturing or preaching "every night, and three or four times each Sabbath, beginning at sunrise."[66]

To guide the plantation mission, especially after the 1831 Nat Turner slave revolt, Capers needed an instructional resource that could be kept in white hands (preachers, planters, and spouses) but used with slaves. He created and published in 1833 *A Catechism for Little Children (and for use on) the Missions to the Slaves in South-Carolina.*[67] Capers took this catechism (Sources 1833) through several editions, expanding it for use with adult slaves and constituting it an official publication of the MECS, which kept it in print even after the Civil War.[68] Its patronizing character and tone, Capers explained in his report for the 1836 South Carolina Conference Missionary Society:

> Our missionaries inculcate the duties of servants to their masters, as we find those duties stated in the Scriptures. They inculcate the performance of them as indispensably important. We hold that a Christian slave must be submissive, faithful, and obedient, for reasons of the same authority with those which oblige husbands, wives, fathers, mothers, brothers, sisters, to fulfill the duties of these relations. We would employ no one in the work who might hesitate to teach thus; nor can such a one be found in the whole number of the preachers of this Conference.[69]

The little catechisms, which guided and enjoyed considerable success across slaveholding areas, cohered with a pro-slavery sentiment then increasingly part of the southern "gospel," a sentiment that enjoined Christian masters to a genuine patriarchy. Methodist leaders who enunciated such exhortations included Holland N. McTyeire, in *Duties of Christian Masters* (1859), James O. Andrew, in "Four Letters on the Religious Instruction of Negroes," which appeared in the *New Orleans Christian Advocate* (1856), William A. Smith, in *Lectures on the Philosophy and Practice of Slavery* (1856; Sources 1856), and Richard H. Rivers, in *Elements of Moral Philosophy* (1859).[70] Capers contributed to that pro-slavery ethos and ethic after being elected bishop with the "third edition" of his catechism (1847).

The first *Catechism for Little Children* combined salvation and duty reinforced with the Lord's Prayer and hymns in four lessons. When expanded for adults, the catechism grew to twelve lessons, buttressed by scriptural passages on duty to God and master. Obedience and servitude were deemed religious duties (Eph. 5:22–6:4; 1 Tim. 6:1-2) and sins specified to which slaves were believed tempted: sexual immorality (Matt. 5:27-28), lying and false witness (Zech. 5:3; James 5:12), Sabbath breaking (Num. 15:32-36; Neh. 13:17-18), and drunkenness and stealing (1 Cor. 5:9-11; Rev. 21:7-8). The Ten Commandments and twenty hymns with similar themes taught a strange Methodism of law and obedience, not grace and love.[71] Thus did the southern church's leadership build a scheme for a certain kind of nurture and mission into the slave system.

Missions across Boundaries: Domestic and Foreign

The MEC made several efforts before the Civil War to evangelize among French speakers with only limited results.[72] Other missions, including those to "Destitute Portions of the Regular Work" and across some language or culture lines, succeeded and succeeded better than those to the Native Americans and African Americans in empowering communities to resource themselves. With Germans and despite the competition of the UBC and the EA, the MEC enjoyed remarkable success, due in no small measure to William (Wilhelm) Nast (1807–99). Born in Stuttgart, Germany, he trained for the Lutheran ministry at the Blaubeuren seminary and the University of Tübingen. Exposure there to the great rationalist philosophers F. C. Baur and D. F. Strauss deterred him from ministry, and he eventually came to the U.S. to teach. First as a tutor in a Harrisburg, Pennsylvania, Methodist family and then as a German instructor in a Methodist chapel close to West Point, Nast began to regain his faith, aided by study of English and German Evangelicals and Pietists, among them Jeremy Taylor, William Law, Richard Baxter, and F. A. G. Tholuck. Appointed to Kenyon College to teach Greek and Hebrew, Nast experienced spiritual renewal at a Methodist camp meeting and sought admission to the Ohio Conference. In 1835 he became that conference's missionary to the growing German population. Door-to-door and street evangelism initially yielded little. The next year he created a five-week circuit of three hundred miles and twenty-two preaching places. By 1838 under MEC auspices and with his leadership emerged a congregation and Sunday school; by 1839 *Der Christliche Apologete* (a German advocate); by 1844 German districts within three annual conferences; and by 1864 four separate German conferences and a college (Baldwin-Wallace). He traveled as missionary across the U.S. and trained others as missionaries, within ten years deploying thirty-two. From his editor's post, which he held for more than half a century, Nast produced a stream of materials for German Methodists, including catechisms, as we have noted, but also hymnals, prayer books, a translation of Wesley's standard sermons, a biography of Wesley, and biblical commentaries. By his efforts and those of his "apostles," Methodism was then exported back to Germany, capitalizing on transatlantic networks and connections.[73]

Missions among Hispanic or Latino peoples began after the annexation of Texas, the Mexican-American War of 1846–48, and the Treaty of Guadalupe Hidalgo.[74] By those events, the U.S. Protestants acquired a new project for missions among that conquered minority of the Southwest, previously by Mexican law all considered Roman Catholic. The significant efforts by Methodists among Mexican Americans and beyond them with Spanish-speaking peoples of the Americas followed the Civil War. Foundations were laid by the conversion of Benigno Cárdenas, a Mexican priest in Santa Fe, New Mexico, and Alejo Hernández, a seminary student in Mexico. By annexation, Cárdenas's diocese came under the supervision of a French-born bishop. Cárdenas traveled to Rome to protest against this bishop, stopping in London on his return trip. There Methodist missionary William Rule encouraged Cárdenas to affiliate with the Methodists and work as a missionary among the Spanish-speaking population of New Mexico. Cárdenas agreed, joining the Reverend Enoch Nicholson, who was being sent to New Mexico by the Methodist Missionary Society. On November 20, 1853, on the plaza in Santa Fe in front of the governor's palace, Cárdenas preached "the first sermon in Spanish by a Methodist in the Southwest" (Sources 1853a).[75] Although this incident is often portrayed as a Methodist success story, the sober reality of the missionary report is that Methodism did not do well in Catholic and non-English-speaking regions. With Walter Hansen, a Swedish minister from Wisconsin who spoke Spanish, Cárdenas began ministry to Mexican Americans. Hansen quit in less than a year, and Cárdenas asked New York for help, but received none. The mission board failed to commission Cárdenas as superintendent, and the ministry itself failed after 1855. In the following years lay missionary Ambrosio Gonzales sustained the mission without clergy or mission board help, but only briefly.

In 1862 Alejo Hernández was in seminary in Mexico studying for the priesthood when he joined Benito Juárez's army of resistance against the French invaders. While on military duty Hernández happened to read an anti-Catholic tract, *Nights with the Romanists*, left by another soldier during the Mexican-American War. Intrigued by the many references to Scripture in that book, he is said to have made his way to Brownsville, Texas, "in search of the Bible." In a small English-speaking church there he had a conversion experience. He later described that experience in a letter to a friend, "I felt that God's spirit was there; although I could not understand a word that was being said, I felt my heart strangely warmed.... I went away weeping with joy." Hernández went back to Mexico, but suffered persecution there for witnessing to his newfound faith and returned to the United States. There he met Methodists (MECS) in Corpus Christi, Texas, and in 1871 and 1874 was ordained deacon and elder, becoming the first Mexican ordained to the Methodist ministry. He served only four years, in Corpus Christi and in Mexico City, before he died of a stroke at age thirty-three.[76]

The establishment of the Rio Grande Mission Conference by the MECS in 1858 gave structure for such mission. The following year, George F. Pierce, elected bishop in 1854 after serving as president of Emory College, toured the mission area, attended the conference, and outlined plans for a substantial missionary enterprise across the Southwest and into Mexico. He left enabling appointments "to be supplied," and the Civil War would lead the whole endeavor to be supplied, a narrative we will resume in the next section.[77]

While home missions pushed toward the Pacific, a sense of missionary obligation for lands beyond the seas gained expression in the church. Stephen Olin, president of Wesleyan University, in an 1851 address voiced the growing concern. Multitudes of members of the church, he argued, "burn with a desire to have some part in overturning the idol temples of India and China; but not one ... can consecrate himself or his property to the enterprise through any channel provided by his own denomination." The responsibility for inaction, Olin felt, lay with the Missionary Society, whose constitution expressed an "inherent partiality for home missions." The time had come, he declared, when "the church must act" to develop a program of overseas missions worthy of its heritage.[78] "The line between domestic missions and foreign missions," observer and missions head John M. Reid later noted, "is not clearly defined."[79] Missions increasingly became a rubric covering a range of ministries lacking the means of self-support. Included were conference appointments to "Destitute Portions of the Regular Work"; city missions that included efforts with seamen, smaller ethnic or language groups, and the unchurched and destitute; missions in the new states; and foreign missions.[80] Missionary experience, practice, and theory in the several fields interplayed, as we have already seen in the relation of Native American and slave missions.

William Taylor (1821–1902) exemplified the mutual interaction of mission, domestic and international. After serving circuits in the Baltimore Conference and stations in Georgetown and North Baltimore, Taylor transferred to the California mission in 1849. Strategies and experience there informed evangelistic tours (1857–62) back east in the U.S. and Canada and then forty years of worldwide mission initiatives and advocacy of the "Pauline Method" of self-supporting missions.

The relation of the several missions owed, as well, to the extensive attention that missions garnered in the *Advocates*, later in serials like the *Missionary Advocate* (1845) and the *Heathen Woman's Friend* (1869) and through the mission societies, permitting North American Methodist women, men, and children to invest imaginatively and vicariously in conversion of various "heathen." In the 1840s and 1850s through the narratives of Melville Cox[81] and Ann Wilkins in Liberia, Robert and Henrietta Maclay in China (and later Japan and Korea), and William and Clementina Butler in India, Methodists became emotionally involved in various missions beyond the Americas. The Lambuths, James William and Mary (McCellen), who gave "five dollars and myself for work in China," held similar fascination for the MECS.[82] Another wrinkle in the domestic-foreign missionary story was what would now be termed *reverse missions*, namely, Methodist evangelism in Christian Europe: Ludwig S. Jacoby to Germany in 1849, Ole P. Petersen to Norway in 1853, John P. Larsson to Sweden in 1854, and Christian B. Willerup to Denmark in 1858.

As evangelism across language, cultural, racial, and oceanic lines progressed, Methodist missionary leadership gathered coworkers into conferences. A Liberian Annual Conference emerged in 1834 and, as we have seen, an Indian (Native American) Mission Conference in 1844. The latter received immediate episcopacy oversight. The former requested such to successive General Conferences, beginning in 1836. Eventually Bishop Levi Scott itinerated to Liberia and in 1853 held the first annual conference, ordaining Africans (for the first time) as deacons (eleven) and elders (eight). Scott returned to endorse a proposal for missionary bishops. The 1856 MEC General Conference favored that over other options that would have recognized the Liberian Conference as a distinct and independent church. This innovation required amendment of the Third Restrictive Rule, so judged both the 1852 and the 1856 General Conferences. The latter passed, and annual conferences ratified the rule to read:

> They shall not change or alter any part or rule of our government, so as to do away Episcopacy, or destroy the plan of our itinerant General Superintendency but may appoint a Missionary Bishop or Superintendent for any of our foreign missions, limiting his jurisdiction to the same respectively.[83]

The Liberian Conference elected an African American, Francis Burns (1809–63). A local preacher in New York State, he had been sent to Liberia by the Missionary Society. He returned to the U.S. in 1844 for ordination, taught in the Monrovia Seminary, edited *Africa's Luminary,* and served for a decade as presiding elder, for six of those years also as president of the Liberian Conference. Burns was consecrated by Bishops Edmund Janes and Osmon Baker at the Genesee Conference in 1858, the first African American bishop. As missionary bishop, Burns was neither a general nor an itinerant superintendent, his episcopal authority limited to his assigned field. The MEC, James Kirby concludes, "not only created a new form of episcopacy, but opened a Pandora's box of questions about the nature of the episcopal office itself." Thus missions drew lines between cultures and languages. Politics drew another set of lines.[84]

Contest over Presiding Elders

The democratizing impulses associated with several of the prior schisms, discussed earlier in this chapter, came to focus in the reform efforts of the 1820s—to permit conference election of the episcopal lieutenants or surrogates known as presiding elders (district superintendents), to allow some conference role and representation to the two-thirds of the Methodist ministry functioning as local rather than itinerant preachers, and to permit laity a say in the governing annual conferences and General Conferences. Here, as with the Republican Methodists, a set of legislative proposals gave focus to concerns, practices, and styles that went far deeper and presented the church again with the question about whether and to what extent its internal life would draw on the best aspects of American democracy.

In the 1820s, controversy over these three matters and particularly over the election of presiding elders (PEs) divided the church. The office, perhaps as Tigert argued, "coeval with the Church itself," took on an ever more aristocratic aspect as the context for its exercise contracted. Lee had observed for 1785:

The form of the minutes of conference was changed this year, and all the *Elders*, who were directed to take the oversight of several circuits, were set to the right hand of a bracket, which inclosed all the circuits and preachers of which he was to take charge.

This may be considered as the beginning of the presiding elder's office; although it was not known by that name at that time; yet, in the absence of a *Superintendent*, this *Elder* had the directing of all the preachers that were inclosed in the bracket against which his name was set.

The 1786 *Discipline* specified superintending duties for the elder, including "To exercise within his own district, during the absence of the superintendents, all the powers invested in them for the government of our church."[85] From this legislation, which applied generically to elders, the church gradually elaborated two distinct offices, the traveling elder and the presiding elder, the latter first formally defined by rubric in the *Discipline*, in 1792, permitted a term limit of four years in a given district, and the manner of selection specified:[86]

Quest. 1. By whom are the presiding elders to be chosen?
Ans. By the bishop.[87]

Asbury and Coke defended the office and particularly the bishops' selection of its holders in one of their longer apologetic expositions in their annotated *Discipline* (Sources 1798).

If the preachers had issues about the nature and episcopal authority of the office from the start, they developed more specific grievances as the years passed. Initially in Asburian Methodism, the PE was not a fixture in a defined social system but connectionally itinerant like Asbury himself. Moving across the whole church, he deployed leading preachers like Ezekiel Cooper and Jesse Lee similarly on a connection-wide scale, as Edwin Schell has shown. Similarly with other PEs, Asbury moved them around the connection. Moreover, the districts themselves changed year to year, due to the church's rapid expansion, the fluidity of district and conference boundaries, and the appointive instincts of Asbury. Some of the movement, that west, would not be surprising. McKendree, for instance, served as PE for eleven years, successively in Virginia, on the Kentucky District, and on the Cumberland District (Tennessee, Illinois, and Missouri). However, William Colbert itinerated as PE in the East, appointed for the Albany, Chesapeake, and Genesee Districts. Freeborn Garrettson served as PE several times, in both New York and Philadelphia Conferences, and Enoch George in South Carolina, Holston, and Baltimore.

While such wide deployments continued as the church marched west, they decreased dramatically in the eastern conferences (Baltimore, Philadelphia, Virginia, and New York), which had more stable boundaries, even before Asbury's death and certainly afterward. Increasingly after conference boundaries were drawn in 1796, preachers came to be members of a continuing and well-defined body. And PEs were increasingly chosen from and deployed within that specific conference. The slow evolution of conference as a membership entity and of the PE as an office within it and the church's very modest ability to explain its polity to itself made the office into an explosive symbol. With bishops itinerating connectionally, not necessarily presiding at a given conference in successive years, the PEs exercised considerable intraconference authority and served as lightning rods for congregational and ministerial concerns over power.

Conferences did have one way, then as now, to comment on the PEs, their effectiveness, and the appropriateness of the bishops' selections. Every four years, conferences determined how they would be represented at General Conference. Baltimore sent all of the PEs from 1811 and 1812 as part of its fourteen-preacher delegation. Four years later, the conference left out of its fourteen two of the six 1815 PEs (five preachers named PE in 1816 were not part of the 1816 delegation). To the 1820 General Conference, Baltimore sent nine delegates, including only half of its six PEs.

In the Episcopal Address to the 1820 General Conference, McKendree deemed 1808 to have settled governmental and constitutional issues. "It is presumed," he asserted, "that no radical change can be made for the better at present."[88] Undeterred by this admonition, Timothy Merritt of New England and Beverly Waugh of Maryland put the issue of an elective presiding eldership again before General Conference.[89] The proposal divided the bishops (William McKendree, ill but staying nearby the conference, Enoch George, and Robert R. Roberts) as well as the body. George may have authored the proposal, as also a measure to reach compromise, a committee of six, three from each side of the issue.[90] While the committee conferred, General Conference elected Joshua Soule to the episcopacy. John Emory drafted a consensus document for the committee providing for episcopal nomination and conference election of PEs. General Conference passed the compromise (61 to 25). Soule, elected but not yet consecrated as bishop and the author of the 1808 "constitution," then tendered his resignation in a stinging challenge to the constitutionality of the measure just passed. The letter, read by McKendree, stated,

> I was elected under the constitution and government of the Methodist Episcopal Church UNIMPAIRED. . . .
>
> I solemnly declare, and could appeal to the Searcher of hearts for the sincerity of my intention, that I cannot act as Superintendent under the rules this day made and established by the General Conference.[91]

McKendree submitted a letter of his own also pronouncing the legislation unconstitutional and himself "under no obligation to enforce or to enjoin it on others to do so."[92] These dramatic acts won the day, and the conference subsequently accepted Soule's resignation and suspended the legislation until the next General Conference.

Broadening the Agenda

To the subsequent round of annual conferences, McKendree submitted a letter setting forth his position on the unconstitutionality of elective presiding elders and asking that the annual conferences concur in that judgment. McKendree reiterated points that Coke and Asbury had advanced (Sources 1798), among them that an effective general superintendency, supported by an appointive presiding eldership, protected "our itinerant plan of preaching the gospel," which "by removing preachers from District to District, and from Conference to Conference, (which no Annual Conference nor Presiding Elder can do,) perpetuate and extend missionary labors for the benefit of increasing thousands, who look unto us as teachers sent of God."[93] Seven conferences complied, but the older five northern and eastern conferences did not.[94] The preachers were not alone in appealing to the democratic impulses of the Jacksonian era and worrying over actual and potential abuse of power and authority by bishops and presiding elders. Among the laity taking a public stand was William Stockton, a New Jersey, later Philadelphia printer. He founded what would become an important medium in a broadening reform cause, the *Wesleyan Repository and Religious Intelligencer* (Sources 1821b). Appearing first in April 1821 as a semimonthly and succeeded in 1824 by the Baltimore periodical *The Mutual Rights of Ministers and Members of The Methodist Episcopal Church*,[95] the paper permitted Stockton, other laity, and ministers to advocate election of presiding elders, but also lay representation and a constellation of reform measures: rights of local preachers, procedures in church trials, checks on episcopal tyranny—in short, the reform of the church. Such advocacy involved risk, particularly for preachers under appointment. In consequence, many wrote under pseudonyms.

Among those taking that risk was Nicholas Snethen (1769–1845), former traveling companion of Asbury, secretary of the 1800 General Conference, antislavery advocate, chaplain to the House of Representatives, and unsuccessful candidate for Congress. Snethen framed the reform cause in republican (American democratic) terms. "[T]he love of power is so general among men," he asserted, "that in any order of society, civil or religious, those who yield the principle of liberty will never want a master." He continued, "[T]he spirit of infallibility, is not given to church rulers; the passions of men in official stations do not become docile and inoffensive, in proportion, as legal checks and restrains are removed; ... there is infinite danger in trusting unlimited power in the hands of any man, or sets of men."[96] In an essay titled "On Church Freedom," he argued that the "very essence of church freedom, consists in having a voice personally, or by our representatives, in and over the laws by which we are to be governed, and in being judged by our peers."[97] So Snethen defended the liberties of the fraternity of preachers against encroachments by episcopacy, encroachments most effectively made through appointment of presiding elders.

Snethen spoke not only on behalf of the traveling preachers (the ordained, full members of conference) but also for preachers outside that fraternity, the local preachers of which he had been one. Local preachers constituted a diverse but large population. Outnumbering the traveling preachers three to one, they, with class leaders, constituted at this period the mainstay of Methodist congregational or local ministry. The office itself derived from Wesley. It was exercised under the authority of the traveling preacher and quarterly conference. By 1796 the *Discipline* devoted a distinct paragraph to it. Ordination to deacon's orders had been legislated in 1789 and to elder's orders in 1812.[98] The office served as the entry into itinerancy for some, a permanent status for others, and the station to which traveling preachers resorted for family, health, or financial reasons. The *Minutes* annually asked, "Who have located this year?" and then identified by name those who had left the "traveling" fraternity. Lee and Bangs cited the number each year, again sounding a somber note.[99] The General Conference Committee of Ways and Means reported in 1816 on loss to church through locations of its experienced, trained, and pious "ornaments."[100] Included among the ranks of this population, quite literally left out of the fraternity, were some of its brightest stars, persons who had exercised conference and national leadership. Many continued active ministries but were excluded from the associations, activities, and authority of annual conference.

What was the church, what was the conference, to do with local preachers, particularly with the gifted persons who remained in ministry, but had "located" from the traveling ranks? The 1820 General Conference made a stab at the problem, providing the district conference for local preachers, transferring to it licensing and trial authority previously vested in the quarterly conference, and giving it some of the character of an annual conference.[101] Separate and very unequal, this experiment was doomed, though lasting as disciplinary provision until 1836, when its functions and authority were restored to quarterly conference.

The democratic political principles that pointed toward election of PEs and rights for local preachers could be invoked on behalf of the laity. Ought they also to be included in annual conference? General Conference? Ought they to be involved in the body or bodies that acted legislatively on, for, and over them? Snethen thought so, deeming the MEC nearly as autocratic and popish as the Roman Catholic Church. The reformers looked back on 1808 as a missed opportunity to make the Methodist system accord with democratic and biblical practice: "[W]hat scripture authority can you produce to authorise you to govern Americans otherwise than as free men?"[102] They spoke of rights and liberties, invoking Whiggish, country, or republican principles on behalf of a decentralized political structure in which power devolved from below, including that of the "fraternity" of annual conference. The opposition, the *constitutionalists* as they were termed, functioned with a different set of political principles, more federalist or centrist in character, arguing on behalf of connection and episcopacy.[103] Bangs grasped the difference as "two opposite views" of "the doctrine of responsibility":

> The former traced responsibility from the General Conference, who made the regulations and judged of episcopal acts, to the episcopacy, and thence down through the several grades of Church officers: the latter traced it up through the societies, to quarterly and annual conferences, to the General Conference.[104]

The issues were joined, and a decade of intense politicking followed. The General Conference of 1824, which met in Baltimore, evidenced its bitterness. The heatedness showed particularly over the suspended legislation. A decisive resolution interpreted the votes taken in the conferences:

> Whereas a majority of the Annual Conferences have judged the resolutions making presiding elders elective, and which were passed and then suspended at the last General Conference, unconstitutional; therefore
> *Resolved,* That the said resolutions are not of authority and shall not be carried into effect.[105]

The measure passed sixty-three to sixty-one. Similar split votes came on elections to the episcopacy, the constitutionalists putting in Soule and the reformers putting in Elijah Hedding. General Conference also rejected petitions for representation of laity and local preachers, authorizing a circular to be conveyed by PEs to members, explaining why no change in "the present order of our Church Government" was needed or wanted.[106] While General Conference met, a number of reformers who thought differently, including seventeen members of General Conference, convened to constitute the Baltimore Union Society.[107] The new society embraced the periodical *The Mutual Rights of Ministers and Members of The Methodist Episcopal Church,* employing it to encourage the formation of other such societies "whose duty it shall be to disseminate the principles of a well balanced church government, and to correspond with each other."

The contagion spread its convictions, publications, and organization, gaining adherents south in Virginia and North Carolina and west into Ohio and Pennsylvania. The reform particularly rocked Methodism's center, the Baltimore Conference. Other union societies emerged, and the Maryland and D.C. reformers met in a convention in November 1826, Nicholas Snethen in the chair, and issued a call for a General Convention of Reformers the next year.

The Baltimore Annual Conference, rent with the controversy, sought to suppress the movement. In 1827, under the presidency of Bishops McKendree, George, Soule, and Roberts, it denied appointment to Dennis B. Dorsey (by vote of conference and in review of his character) for dissemination of and refusal to address questions about his advocacy of *Mutual Rights*. Broadcasting that gesture, it then passed a motion deeming it "highly censurable in any member of Conference, to circulate, or in any way, or manner, to support any works defamatory of our Christian, and ministerial character, or in opposition to our Discipline and Church Government."[108] Laity and preachers lined up on one side or the other. The controversy continued in exchanges in pamphlets and between *Mutual Rights* and the newly created *Christian Advocate* (New York) and the *Methodist Magazine* (MQR). Expulsions and trials occurred, as the Methodist Protestant "Brief Historical Preface" indicates (see below).

An important stage in the emerging division occurred with the publication by Alexander McCaine (1768?–1856) of *History and Mystery of Methodist Episcopacy*. Irish born, trained for the Anglican priesthood, converted under the schismatic William Hammett in Charleston, McCaine had emerged as a significant MEC leader, serving as presiding elder and elected as secretary of the 1820 General Conference though not a member. His book charged conspiracy, arguing that the present monarchical form of government was surreptitiously introduced, not intended by Wesley, and was imposed upon the societies, "under the sanction of Mr. Wesley's name."[109] Immediate responses came from John Emory, *Defence of "Our Fathers"* and Thomas Bond, "An Appeal to the Methodists, in Opposition to the Changes Proposed in Their Church Government."[110] Bond insisted that the proposed reforms—election of presiding elders, inclusion in conference of local preachers and laity—struck the very genius of Methodism, itinerancy itself, the principle of sacrifice inherent in it, and "the MISSIONARY character of our ministry."[111]

Bond appealed to and defended a national itinerancy—"the different conferences contribute to the supply of each other's necessities"[112]—an ideal even then suffering erosion through the politicizing of conference, the church's growth, and yawning sectionalism. The parties indeed functioned with very different ecclesiologies.

Recriminations against Reformers intensified. Presiding elders in the Baltimore Conference levied charges and initiated trial proceedings against twenty-five laity and eleven local preachers, expelling the former and suspending the latter, Alexander McCaine included. The charges were "1st. Becoming a member of the Union Society. 2d. Directly or indirectly supporting the *Mutual Rights*...3d. Approving the 'History and Mystery' written by Alexander McCaine."[113]

In that climate, the union societies, now some twenty-four in number, met in a general convention in November 1827.[114] The convention elected officers, established a committee of vigilance and correspondence, and drafted a memorial to General Conference, again setting forth the democratic case in church government (Sources 1827b). Early the next year, a quarterly conference confirmed the expulsions and suspensions. The Baltimore Conference followed suit, expelling two elders, Dennis Dorsey and William C. Poole, and reproving James Sewell. The excommunication procedures were initiated as the character of each came up for review and juridical procedures intended to test spiritual fitness and gift for ministry were turned to political use.

Methodist Protestants

The MEC General Conference of 1828 was in no mood for democratic reform. It declared the (suspended) presiding elder legislation void, dismissed the memorials from the Reformers' convention (rejecting lay representation), confirmed the suspensions, and offered relief from these decisions only if the union societies were dissolved and *Mutual Rights* suspended (Sources 1828).[115] Having faced this challenge to its polity and constitution, the conference also initiated the first amendment of the constitution, refining procedure for amendment of the Restrictive Rules. The original version (Sources 1808) required concurrence "of all the annual conferences," the dissent of a single conference functioning as a veto. The amendment substituted a majority of three-fourths of the members of annual conferences and excepted the first doctrinal restrictive rule. To the entire connection, and not to the several annual conferences as constituted bodies, would future constitutional appeals be made. By the action, Tigert noted, "The Annual Conference rightfully ceased to be in any sense a constitutional unit."[116]

With expulsions continuing and new congregations forming, the second General Convention of Methodist Reformers met in Baltimore and laid plans for another conference and the formation of a new denomination. Articles of Association were adopted (to be worked into a *Discipline* two years later), which provided for equal lay and clergy representation in annual conferences and General Conferences and an elective presidency, but retained the "Articles of Religion, General Rules, Means of Grace, Moral Discipline, and Rites and Ceremonies in the main of the Methodist Episcopal Church."[117] The convention deputized agents, including Nicholas Snethen and Alexander McCaine, to travel on behalf of the cause. By the time the 1830 General Convention met, the Reformers had organized twelve annual conferences. That convention, also in Baltimore, where the movement had its greatest strength,[118] ratified the new *Constitution and Discipline*,[119] elected as president Francis Waters (ordained but functioning as an educator), at his prompting chose the name The Methodist Protestant Church, appointed a book committee, and authorized the transformation of *Mutual Rights* into an official church weekly.[120] The new entity accomplished two of the three major Reformers' aims, an elective superintendency and lay representation; local preachers were not granted conference membership. The president would station preachers, though subject to revision by an annual conference committee. Its disciplinary preface traced the Reform cause back to Wesley and scriptural holiness:

Methodist Protestant "Brief Historical Preface"[121]

"In the year 1729, two young men in England, reading the Bible, saw they could not be saved without holiness; followed after it, and incited others so to do. In 1737, they saw likewise, that men are justified before they are sanctified; but still holiness was their object. God then thrust them out to raise a holy people." These were John and Charles Wesley.

"In the latter end of the year, 1739, eight or ten persons came to Mr. Wesley, in London, who appeared to be deeply convinced of sin, and earnestly groaning for redemption. They desired (as did two or three more the next day) that he would spend some time with them in prayer, and advise them how to flee from the wrath to come, which they saw continually hanging over their heads. That he might have more time for this great work, he appointed a day when they might all come together, which from thence forward they did every week. To these and as many more as desired to join with them (for their number increased daily) he gave those advices, from time to time, which he judged most needful for them; and they always concluded their meeting with prayer, suited to their several necessities." This was the rise of the United Society in Europe. Such a society is no other than, "a company of men having the form and seeking the power of godliness, united in order to pray together, to receive the word of exhortation, and to watch over one another in love, that they may help each other to work out their salvation."

Philip Embury, a preacher from Ireland, began to preach in the city of New York, some time in the year 1766, and formed a society of his own countrymen and a few of the citizens. In the same year Captain Thomas Webb, preached in a hired room, near the barracks. About the same time Robert Strawbridge, settled in Frederic county, state of Maryland, and formed some societies. Richard Boardman, and Joseph Pilmoor, came over from England, in 1769, to New York, in the character of missionaries; and toward the close of the year 1771, Francis Asbury and Richard Wright, came over also by the direction of Mr. Wesley, to assist the American Methodist preachers and societies.

At the close of the year 1784, the Methodist societies, in these United States, were organized by a conference of preachers exclusively, into what is called the Methodist Episcopal Church, and made independent of Mr. Wesley. The government was so framed by the conference, as to secure to the itinerant ministers, the unlimited exercise of the legislative, executive, and judicial powers of the church, to the entire exclusion of all other classes of ministers, and all the people. Subsequent general conferences exhibited marked dissatisfaction at the leading features of the government, and a very respectable minority struggled hard to effect some salutary improvements, but without producing any important changes. The opposition of the minority continued with unabating ardour, until the membership became more fully acquainted with the genius of the government, under which their spiritual guides had placed them, without their knowledge or consent. In 1820, a periodical was instituted, entitled the Wesleyan Repository, and was continued up to the sitting of the general conference of 1824. Numerous petitions were presented to that body, praying for a representation of ministers and laymen in the rule making department; but no change, either in the principle or in the practical operations of the government, could be obtained.

Immediately after the rise of the general conference of 1824, a meeting, composed of some distinguished members of the conference, and of reformers from different parts of the United States, was held in this city, at which it was determined, to publish a periodical pamphlet entitled; "The Mutual Rights of the ministers and members of the Methodist Episcopal Church," "for the purpose of giving the Methodist community a suitable opportunity to enter upon a calm and dispassionate discussion of the subjects in dispute." The meeting also determined to resolve itself into a Union Society; and recommended that similar societies be raised in all parts of the United States, "in order to ascertain the number of persons in the Methodist E. Church, friendly to a change in her government." This measure was followed by much persecution of reformers. In Tennessee, fourteen official members were expelled for attempting to form a Union Society.

Some time during the spring of the year 1826, the Baltimore Union Society, recommended state conventions to be held in the several states, for the exclusive purpose of making inquiry into the propriety of preparing *one united* petition to the approaching general conference of 1828, praying for REPRESENTATION; and to elect delegates to meet in a general convention for the purpose. Conventions were accordingly held, and delegates elected; in consequence of which, reformers, in different parts of the country, were made to feel the displeasure of men in power. In North Carolina, several members of the Granville Union Society, were expelled for being members thereof. In the fall of 1827, eleven ministers were suspended, and finally expelled from the Methodist E. Church in this city, and twenty-two laymen, for being members of the union society, and supporters of the mutual rights. About fifty of the female friends of the suspended and expelled brethren immediately withdrew from the church, after addressing a letter to the preacher in charge, in which they say; "to find our dear companions, fathers, brothers, children and friends, treated as criminals and enemies, persecuted, suspended, and expelled; denounced as backsliders and disturbers of the peace, and ourselves treated coldly and distantly by our former friends, and by our pastors; and *all for a mere difference of opinion about church government,* is more than we feel bound in Christian charity longer to endure; and, therefore, we feel it our duty, in the fear of God, to *withdraw* from the church." The expelled brethren and their friends immediately organized under Mr. Wesleys' [sic] general rules, taking the title of, the Associated Methodist Reformers.

November, 1827, the general convention assembled in this city, composed of ministers and lay delegates, elected by the state conventions and union societies. This convention prepared a memorial to the general conference of May 1828, praying that the government of the church might be made representative, and more in accordance with the mutual rights of the ministers and people. To this memorial, the general conference replied, in a circular, by claiming for the itinerant ministers of their church, an exclusive divine right to the same unlimited and unamenable power which they had exercised over the whole church, from the establishment of their government in 1784. Soon after the rise of the general conference several reformers in Cincinnati, Lynchburg, and other places, were expelled for being members of union societies, and supporters of the mutual rights.

The reformers now perceiving, that all hope of obtaining a change in the government of the church had vanished, withdrew in considerable numbers, in different parts of the United States, and called another general convention, to assemble in this city, November 12, 1828. This convention drew up seventeen *"Articles of Association,"* to serve as a provisional government for the Associated Methodist Churches, until a Constitution and book of Discipline could be prepared by a subsequent convention, to be held in November 1830.

Agreeably to appointment, the Convention assembled, in the city of Baltimore, in St. John's Church, Liberty street, on the 2nd day of November, 1830, and continued its session to the 23rd inclusive. During which period it formed, and adopted the following Constitution and Discipline, for the government of the Methodist Protestant Church.

The Rev. Francis Waters, D.D. of Baltimore, was elected President; Mr. Wm. C. Lipscomb, of Georgetown, D. C. was chosen Secretary, and Mr. William S. Stockton, of Philadelphia, assistant Secretary...

Not an End but a New Beginning to Division

Over the next decades, Methodist Protestants competed with Methodist Episcopals even as new churches emerged, in each of which divisions race figured (Wesleyans, MECS, Free Methodists, CMEs). On that form of "liberty" The Methodist Protestant Church took a pass. The reforming denomination denied its "colored members" the vote and membership in General Conference and permitted each annual conference to form its own rules "for the admission and government of coloured members within its district; and to make for them such terms of suffrage as the conferences respectively may deem proper."[122] The church expressed its ambivalence in its constitution with this qualification:

> But neither the General Conference nor any Annual Conference shall assume powers to interfere with the constitutional powers of the civil government or with the operations of the civil laws; yet nothing herein contained shall be so construed as to authorize or sanction anything inconsistent with the morality of the holy scriptures.[123]

Methodist ambivalence on slavery betokened its growing "respectability," the adherence to it in North and South of the propertied (and slaveholding) class, the church's coming to terms with culture, its concern for and investment in the social order.[124] Methodist Protestants, strong in what would become border states, evidenced the doubleness of Methodist acculturation. They embraced societal values of democracy but also of ambivalence on slavery. Yet they sought to transform society by bringing in converts, instilling values, and providing uplift (Sunday schools, missions, colonization, educational endeavor [founding of colleges particularly]).[125] In reforming the continent and spreading Scripture holiness over these lands, Methodism found itself both a change agent and a changed entity.

CHAPTER VIII

DIVIDING OVER SLAVERY, REGION, AUTHORITY, AND RACE: 1830–60s

By the 1830s Methodists (the MEC) in a variety of ways had qualified and compromised their constitutive commitments to antislavery and to African Americans as fully and equally children of God. In the North, they segregated early, circumscribed the authority of Black congregations, and denied African Americans full ministerial rights. So the MEC lost Black leadership and commitments through the AME and AMEZ exits. Republican and Stilwellite schisms also drained antislavery resolve. In the South, facing the moral dilemma of choosing between testifying against slavery or testifying to the slave, they elected the latter. To "save" the slave, they evangelized on the slaveholder's terms. General Conference after General Conference hedged the disciplinary provisions against slaveholding, subordinating them ever more firmly to state slave statutes.[1] Winking at what little remained of disciplinary resolve, the MEC welcomed slaveholders to membership, indeed to congregational leadership and into the ministry. They embraced the American Colonization Society (Sources 1832b), with its ideal of evangelizing Africa while ridding America of free Black persons whose activity and commitments might endanger slavery—abolition by extrusion. Under southern auspices, slaveholder conditions, and truly patronizing protocols, the MEC launched the mission to the slave (Sources 1833, 1836). And it put into leadership—into the episcopacy, at the helm of *Advocates*, and in the colleges—individuals willing to compromise, if necessary, to safeguard the unity of the church and its key institutions.

A Sectional Church

In the 1830s, however, a new antislavery movement emerged, represented in the East by the immediatist William Lloyd Garrison, who connected abolition with an array of radical reforms, and in the Midwest and among Methodists by Christian abolitionists who knit antislavery together with perfectionist evangelicalism. Abolition in both its variants pronounced slaveholding a sin and slavery evil, called Christians to repent therefrom, embraced slaves freed from and slaveholders converted from this evil, supported the Underground Railroad, and attacked the institution and any and all of its alliances, North and South. This aggressive, denunciatory critique enraged the South and induced southerners, Methodists included, to defend slavery, an apology that grew more explicit and vehement over the next several decades, leading Methodists to articulate a "doctrine" that the church as spiritual stood above and apart from politics. Eventually some southern Methodists joined other Protestants in issuing outright biblical and theological justifications of slavery (Sources 1856).[2] Slave disquiet, slave conspiracies, and slave insurrections, most notably those of Methodist Denmark Vesey in Charleston in 1822 and of millenarian Nat Turner in Virginia in 1831, reinforced slaveholder and southern support for its peculiar institution. Defensive apologetics read the Bible for its literal sense, noted slavery's place in Old Testament and New, and drew upon Scripture for a slaveholder's ethic.

The revived antislavery of the 1830s exposed and widened a sectionally divided Methodism. Several regionalizing changes in Methodism made the church (its conferences and laity) particularly receptive or hostile to the antislavery gospel. Of great importance were the media then available, newspapers and magazines, which we have already seen proved important in the spread of the Protestant Methodist cause. In the MEC, one national paper, *Christian Advocate and Journal* (New York), and one connectional review, the *Methodist Magazine* (MQR), competed for Methodist Episcopal attention with regional papers, the *Western Christian Advocate* (Cincinnati), *Zion's Herald* (Boston), the *Pittsburgh Christian Advocate*, and three southern papers—the *Southwestern Christian Advocate* (Nashville), the *Richmond Christian Advocate*, and the *Southern Christian Advocate* (Charleston).[3] Second, preachers, particularly those in the eastern conferences, increasingly lived out their careers in a single conference and came to view their membership as conference based. The *Minutes* reflected that regional orientation. Beginning in 1824, they were structured on a conference-by-conference rather than unified, question-by-question basis. Reinforcing that conference orientation, the reward structure—including election to General Conference and appointment to the presiding eldership—presupposed close annual conference ties and collegial support. And General Conference came to structure itself in accordance with such conference membership patterns. It routinely established important committees, "one from each annual conference," and did so even as the number of conferences expanded. By 1836, General Conference made the politically representative intent crystal clear: "that the said committee consists of one member from each annual conference, to be selected by the delegates from each conference."[4] As the church gave itself more sophisticated structure, it did so honoring region and representation, a formula for political activism. That would be ominously indicated in the provision in

1840 for ten standing committees, four to be representative: episcopacy, boundaries, itinerancy, and *slavery*.[5]

Ominously, the bishops elected in the politicized atmosphere of the Methodist Reform movement, none from the South, acquired regional commitments. Robert Richford Roberts (Philadelphia) and Enoch George (Baltimore), elected in 1816; Joshua Soule (Maine), elected but demurring in 1820 and reelected in 1824; and Elijah Hedding (New England), elected in 1824, with the aged and ill William McKendree constituted the church's episcopal leadership. Between 1824 and division in 1844, Hedding made one tour south, and Soule one north. George and Hedding worked Philadelphia and north. Roberts and Soule, Baltimore and south. "The bishops were localized," affirmed Tigert. Kirby concurs, "McKendree was American Methodism's last real itinerant general superintendent."[6]

Sectional media, sectional ministry, and sectional episcopacy reinforced the powerful sectional currents in the society as a whole, especially those that divided North and South. The MEC increasingly divided along regional lines, in various ways, on various issues, including (already) the knotty constitutional problems posed by the Reformers. Energizing intradenominational sectionalism were societal developments that would not stay out of the sanctuary—a revived abolitionism in the North; a southern economy tied ever more securely to the institution of slavery; fierce, sometimes violent competition between pro-slavery and Free-Soilers in the expansion west; and a Congress and court system embroiled over slavery and its "protection." The sectionalizing forces indeed infected the whole social order, a point eloquently made by the abolitionists as they traced out the dependency on slavery that ran through northern society. Sectional division of the churches produced intense moral warfare and principled posturing, undergirded by fears and hopes about slavery. Several popular, evangelical denominations with national constituencies divided North and South, the Presbyterians in the late 1830s, the Baptists and Methodists in the mid-1840s. The church splits elicited prophecy from prescient editors and agonized statespersons, including John C. Calhoun and Henry Clay, who wondered whether a nation could hold together if Christians could not.

Schisms anticipated, set precedent for, and established a moral and religious warrant for, and aggravated, if they did not "cause," the growing division of the nation.[7] The MEC/MECS schism will be our focus, but four divisions can be traced directly to the sectional/slavery crisis—those represented by the Wesleyan Methodist Church, The Methodist Episcopal Church, South, the Free Methodist Church, and the Colored Methodist Episcopal Church. (To some extent later holiness movements also trace their concerns with the church back to this politicizing of it.) The United Brethren Church and The Evangelical Association saw abolitionist activity but, as predominantly northern bodies, escaped some of the intensity of the struggle and did not suffer rupture.[8] To reiterate, the church divisions prefigured, if they did not directly effect, the division of the nation.[9]

A Divided Church Divides the Nation

The Methodist division of 1844 as also that of 1830 and the comparable schisms within Presbyterian and Baptist communions turned, at least in part, on differing ecclesiologies. Subsequent historiography has divided, essentially along sectional lines, about whether the issues that divided the church were at bottom constitutional, ecclesial, and theological or political, sectional, and ethical (over slavery and race).[10] Was the schism over the relation of church to the civil order and the limits of moral witness, the power and authority of General Conference vis-à-vis those of the bishops, whether Scripture was to be read by its ethical tendency or literally by what it said or did not say? Or was it fundamentally about slavery? In our judgment, race and slavery underlie the controversy and divisions, as well as the subsequent polemics and historiography. However, those who framed fundamental issues with constitutional, ecclesial, and theological rhetoric believed what they said. And since those who spoke with such language sought thereafter to live within the ideational world they had built, we cannot afford simply to dismiss that rhetoric. The church divided over slavery. But in dividing and once divided, the church(es) lived out, in the several parts, the polemical positions taken. Ideology became important, even if, in the first instance, it masked racism and social self-interest.

The contest embroiled the *Advocates* and the conferences. In the New England Conference (MEC), converts to the abolitionist cause, notably La Roy Sunderland (1804–85) and Orange Scott (1800–1847), used existing structures—camp meetings, quarterly conferences, rallies, letters, petitions, and elections—to attack colonization (Sources 1832b), the church's acquiescence in slavery, and editors' suppression of antislavery.[11] A particular target was Nathan Bangs, editor of the *Christian Advocate* (New York) after 1834, who denied abolitionists access but in articles and editorials defended the status quo. In late 1834 Orange Scott, Shipley Willson, and others circulated "An Appeal on the Subject of Slavery Addressed to the Members of the New England and New Hampshire Conferences" (Sources 1834). The "Appeal" charged that Bangs did "apologize for the crimes of the enslavers of the human species and attempt to justify the system"; positively it set forth the Methodist case against slavery, including a reprinting of Wesley's condemnation.[12] Orange Scott followed up the attack of the "Appeal" with a weekly column "Slavery" that ran from January to April. Responses, criticisms, and a counter-column prompted Scott et al. to publish the "Appeal" along with a "Defense of the 'Appeal'" as a *Zion's Herald . . . Extra*.[13] In May, abolitionists established a New England Wesleyan Anti-Slavery Society. In June, abolitionists gained six of the seven delegates to the following General Conference. They failed to pass antislavery resolutions, the questions not being put by the presiding bishop, Elijah Hedding, but did beat back motions of censure on their activities.

Bishop Hedding had a hand in a "Counter-Appeal" signed also by key members of the church's intelligentsia, including D. D. Whedon (1808–85), theology and Bible professor; Wilbur Fisk (1792–1839), president of Wesleyan University; and Abel Stevens (1815–97), later to edit *Zion's Herald* and the *Christian Advocate*. Hedding joined with Bishop John Emory in a pastoral letter to that conference (and also New Hampshire), published in the *Christian Advocate*, further reprimanding the abolitionists.[14] Other conferences adhered more to the bishops' position, and the subsequent General Conference acted to muffle the antislavery cause.[15] Indeed, General Conference censured two delegates for abolitionist activity. It issued a "Pastoral Address," which dealt with "abolitionism" at some length and exhorted the members and friends of the church "to abstain from all abolition movements and associations, and to refrain from patronizing any of their publications." The address expressed "the solemn conviction, that the only safe, Scriptural, and prudent way for us, both as ministers and as people, to take, is wholly to refrain from this agitating subject, which is now convulsing the country, and consequently the Church."[16]

The bishops endeavored to see that the following annual conferences take this "safe, Scriptural, and prudent way." They suppressed abolition. The New York Conference welcomed this posture and condemned *Zion's Watchman*, launched the prior year by La Roy Sunderland, to "defend the discipline of the Methodist Episcopal Church against the SIN OF HOLDING AND TREATING THE HUMAN SPECIES AS PROPERTY."[17] The 1836 New England Conference followed suit, at least to the extent of charging Sunderland with slandering Nathan Bangs. However, it also created a committee on slavery and abolition. Hedding, who presided using tactics of delay, "failed" to bring that committee's report up for action. He penalized Orange Scott by stripping him of his presiding eldership. In the next conference session, Hedding brought charges against both Sunderland and Scott. The bishop also denied that abolitionists had the right to introduce memorials or the committee to publish its report. Analogous to the suppression of petition and debate in the Congress, this episcopal stance gave to abolition a second cause, "conference rights." Thereafter Scott and another reformer, George Storrs, went from conference to conference (in the North) preaching abolition and raising the conference rights banner.[18] The bishops attempted to inhibit this abolitionizing and employed the annual review of the character of the preachers to press charges against those who "agitated" the issue.

The church's papers generally followed the bishops' practice of muzzling the controversy, led in that cause by Nathan Bangs and the New York–based *Christian Advocate*. Abolitionist ferment, however, drew active response in southern papers and conferences, where tacit acceptance of slavery turned into articulation of the doctrine that the church as spiritual should not indulge itself in politics and even an explicit proslavery rationale.[19] In his prospectus (1837) for the *Southern Christian Advocate*, William Capers, the editor, noted that service to Methodists and Methodist adherents alone would be sufficient rationale, but viewed it as justified, indeed necessitated, because of the feelings "on the subject of our domestic institutions."[20]

Southern conferences issued resolutions condemning abolition, denying that slavery was sin, and insisting that the institution ought, as a civil matter, to be beyond the church's attention, for instance: "It is the sense of the Georgia Annual Conference that slavery, as it exists in the United States, *is not a moral evil*."[21] The South Carolina Conference resolved to similar effect. Much of the church, including some of its strongest conferences, like Baltimore, found itself torn between the two poles, fighting both explicit pro-slavery sentiment and abolitionism.[22]

Bishops presiding over the southern conferences did not muzzle these defenses of slavery and attacks on abolition as their episcopal counterparts had the abolitionists. The problem, as they saw it, was not slavery but abolition. In their address to the next (1840) General Conference, the bishops called to mind the "Pastoral Address" of 1836 and its counsel "to abstain from all abolition movements," but regretted "that we are compelled to say, that in some of the northern and eastern conferences, in contravention of your Christian and pastoral counsel, and of your best efforts to carry it into effect, the subject has been agitated in such forms, and in such a spirit as to disturb the peace of the Church."[23] That finding would hold for the next thirty years (at least), and for South as well as North, during which Methodist media and Methodist conferences found themselves politically agitated by the moral crisis of slavery.

The sectional crisis swept the church itself into political activity, turned internal church structures and processes to partisan use, and developed the political dimensions of annual conferences and General Conferences. Indeed, memorials, resolutions, and legislation on slavery, elections of "slates" to General Conference, trials, and other "political" use of the annual reviews made conferences into political forums, and political forums seemingly persuaded and possessed of their own sovereignty. The crisis also and obviously tuned the church into the political affairs of American society. This acculturation made less obvious and persuasive the bishops' plea that church government was "peculiarly constructed" and "widely different from our civil organization."[24] Each of the parties contributed to this embrace of society and culture. Methodist abolitionists adopted antislavery tactics and gospel. Conservatives, including the bishops, employed the "proved" congressional strategy of compromise and concession to the South and suppression of northern activism. Southerners proposed exceptions to church precept against slavery, thus permitting slaveholders to be ordained. They also offered legislation to prevent Black Americans from testifying in church trials where civil law proscribed manumission and "colored" testimony. Proposed by Emory President Ignatius A. Few, the Few Resolution added yet one more symbolic concession to slaveholders: "*Resolved,* That it is inexpedient and unjustifiable for any preacher among us to permit colored persons to give testimony against white persons, in any state where they are denied that privilege in trials at law." The proposal had a complicated fate at the conference and even a more important symbolic one thereafter.[25] In a richly symbolic gesture, the bishops refused to bring into General Conference a petition by Baltimore African American Methodists protesting this latter action.[26] The church thus made its concession to culture, specifically the slave culture.

A Wesleyan Methodist Connection

In the 1840 General Conference, southerners won the key battles. Conservative hands were placed at the helm of the northern papers, Thomas Bond over the *Christian Advocate*, Abel Stevens over *Zion's Herald*, and Charles Elliott over the *Western Christian Advocate*.[27] Conceding defeat, Orange Scott, La Roy Sunderland, and Jotham Horton withdrew, the first stage in the formation of yet another Methodist body, the Wesleyan Methodist Connection (Sources 1842b). The Wesleyans condemned first the MEC's compromise with slavery: "The M.E. Church, is not only a slaveholding, but a slavery defending, Church." They withdrew, second, claiming that the church had abandoned true Wesleyanism: "The government of the M.E. Church contains principles not laid down in the Scriptures, nor recognized in the usages of the primitive Church—principles which are subversive of the rights both of ministers and laymen."[28] Thus the movement presented itself as it titled its paper *True Wesleyan*. It pledged itself in its organizing convention at Utica in 1843 to Wesleyan principles on slavery, to "the cause of the bleeding slave," to temperance, "which has already done so much for the restoration of the degraded," to "every branch of moral reform," and to be "co-workers, even in the front rank, battling side by side with those who contend with the Lord's enemies." Insisting that it "retained all that is essential to the identity, life, body and soul of Wesleyan Methodism" and only separated "from some of its objectionable features, which have been engrafted upon it in this country," the Wesleyans exhorted followers "to make holiness your motto."[29]

These "come-outers" appealed to and recruited among northern Methodists with sympathies for the slave, some 6,000 adhering initially, 15,000 by their first General Conference convened in 1844. Ironically, the Wesleyan Methodist solicitations had more transforming effect on the Methodist Episcopal conferences from outside than they had had earlier as an inside reforming impulse. Northern conferences increasingly reclaimed their antislavery heritage, passing resolutions to that effect in preparation for the 1844 General Conference. "Whole conferences," reported Abel Stevens, "which once rejected antislavery resolutions now sustain them with scarce a dissent, and it cannot be doubted that soon, very soon, all our northern conferences will be of one mind on the subject."[30] Southern conferences and papers intensified their defenses, proclaimed slavery to be no moral evil, insisted that the institution itself lay beyond the church's purview, proposed the election of a slaveholding bishop, and prepared for division, should that be necessary.[31]

General Conference of 1844

The General Conference of 1844, meeting just a year after the Wesleyans organized, would war over the incredibly troubling issues posed by slavery: the nature of sin, the relation of the church to the social and political orders, the "real" meaning of church membership, constraints to be placed on office holding for classes of people (African Americans),[32] the nature and unity of the ministerial fraternity, the relation of episcopacy and conference, the location of sovereignty, the exercise of authority, and of course, preeminently slavery itself. The MEC put the questions to itself, in memorials and petitions that poured in to General Conference from annual conferences and quarterly meetings:

> [May 4, New Hampshire] C. D. Cahoon presented . . . memorials, on the subject of slavery, from Claremont and Athens, which were referred to the Committee on Slavery. Also a memorial of the New Hampshire Conference on slavery, which document he asked to have read. A. B. Longstreet moved to dispense with the reading. This motion was lost; and the document was then read, and referred to the Committee on Slavery. Also certain resolutions of the New-Hampshire Conference, on the appointment of slaveholders to the office of Missionary Secretary, or missionaries, under the direction of the Parent Board, which were read and referred to the Committee on Slavery. Also resolutions on the subject of coloured testimony: read and referred to the same committee.[33]

Particularly striking were the concurrences in resolutions that had gone annual conference to annual conference, testing for common conference resolve. Faced with the steady torrent of memorials, the conference on its thirteenth day resolved to receive no petitions or memorials after that week and required that "every member, when his Conference is called for memorials or Conference resolutions, shall present at once all such documents as he may have in his possession, or under his control."[34]

The 1840 General Conference, on a motion by Nathan Bangs, had authorized the full reporting of its proceedings in the *Christian Advocate,* and that precedent, followed thereafter, has left us with a full account of the month-long drama of 1844.[35] At this General Conference, the conservative middle and particularly the Baltimore Conference, not the abolitionists and New Englanders, would tackle slavery, the result apparently of a deal struck between the parties just prior to conference.[36] The first slavery resolution prompted a motion to establish a committee "to be constituted by one member from each Annual Conference," a proposal that Capers and the South met by attempting "to lay this on the table," hoping that "the motion would not be entertained." Capers "hoped to hear no more of a Committee on Slavery. It never did and never could do any Good. It had done much evil and always would do."[37] The South suffered the first of a series of defeats.[38] Another came over an appeal from the Baltimore Conference by Francis A. Harding, who "had been suspended from his ministerial standing for refusing to manumit certain slaves which came into his possession by his marriage." Baltimore had judged him, as a slaveholder, acceptable only to the slaveholding region of the conference and therefore unfit to travel.[39] General Conference's concurrence foreshadowed the decision that would be made in the case of Bishop James O. Andrew, whom the conference knew to be in the same situation and whose entanglement in slavery compromised the church's symbol of itself, its principles, and its unity—a superintendency, genuinely itinerant, really general. In their opening address, the bishops had been insistent on this very point:

> [T]he superintendency... is *general, embracing the whole work in connectional order, and not diocesan, or sectional.* Consequently any division of the work into districts, or otherwise, so as to create a particular charge, with any other view, or in any order, than as a prudential measure to secure to all the Conferences the annual visits of the Superintendents, would be an innovation on the system.
> ... *[O]ur superintendency must be itinerant, and not local.* It was wisely provided in the system of Methodism, from its very foundation, that it should be the duty of the Superintendent "to travel through the connection at large."[40]

Both South and North looked forward, some with dread, to the test: a bishop elected when not entangled with slavery, now by marriage and bequest a slaveholder, and prohibited by Georgia law from manumission, a situation that Andrew himself explained in some detail (Sources 1844b). To forestall impending division, Capers moved and Stephen Olin (1797–1851), newly elected president of Wesleyan University, seconded the establishment of a committee to draft a plan "for the permanent pacification of the church." Olin, a centrist who had served and enjoyed a following in both South and North, urged unity and conciliation. He asked the conference to suspend "our duties for one day, and devote it to fasting and prayer, that God might help us if he would, that if we have not union we might have peace."[41] With others, he wanted to preserve unity and was later reported to have whispered: "Brother A., I would gladly lay my head upon the block this very day to save the union of the Methodist Episcopal Church."[42] Olin represented a dying species, a member of the fraternity of preachers who had itinerated nationally (that is, in North and South). The question at hand was, Could Andrew as well? Would he be accepted in northern conferences? Neither pacification nor prayers proved able to stave off the problems posed by a slaveholding bishop.

Andrew had come to General Conference prepared to resign, had so indicated to southern delegates, but had been formally overtured to desist.[43] The Committee on Episcopacy, to which the matter had been referred, reported the facts of the situation, prompting a motion requesting his resignation.[44] After heated exchanges, Ohio delegates proposed a substitute that recognized his slaveholding status, deemed that to "greatly embarrass the exercise of the office as an itinerant General Superintendent, if not in some places entirely prevent it," and called for him to "desist from the exercise of this office so long as this impediment remains" (Sources 1844a).[45] This framing of the issue permitted constitutional questions to subsume moral and political ones. James Finley, earlier head of the Wyandotte Mission, then presiding elder from Ohio and one of the movers, put the constitutional question baldly:

> [T]his General Conference is restricted against doing anything which will destroy our itinerant general superintendency. This principle must be conceded. That Bishop Andrew has become connected with the great evil of slavery, he himself has declared on this floor.... [T]his connection with slavery has drawn after it circumstances that will embarrass his exercising the office of an itinerant general superintendent, if not in some places entirely prevent it.... Hence, the question follows, Will this General Conference permit one of its vital and constitutional principles to be broken down and trampled under foot, because one of her general officers has seen fit to involve himself in circumstances which will trammel that office in more than half of all the field of his labour?[46]

Bishop Andrew claimed the floor to speak on his own behalf. He explained his "embarrassment," the impossibility of his freeing his slaves under Georgia law, his love for "the coloured people," and his sense that he functioned properly under the *Discipline* (Sources 1844b).

The constitutional issues broadened and sharpened as the debate proceeded to include the relative powers of the episcopacy and General Conference. "There ought," argued L. L. Hamline (1797–1865), editor of the *Ladies' Repository*, "to be two questions before us. First. *Has the General Conference constitutional authority to pass this resolution?* Second. *Is it proper or fitting that we should do it?*" Addressing himself to the first, Hamline insisted that conference indeed possessed the authority to remove a bishop "for anything unfitting that office, or that renders its exercise unwholesome to the Church." Indeed, enunciating what would be the MEC constitutional principle, he affirmed, "This conference, adjunct (but rarely) with the annual conferences, is supreme. Its supremacy is universal." Methodist government, he explained, differs from civil, with its separation and distribution of powers. General Conference itself possesses all three: "It has legislative, judicial, and executive supremacy." General Conference grants the bishops certain executive authority, to be sure, but does so by statute. Any powers delegated to and exercised by the bishops that are not explicitly conveyed by the Restrictive Rules can be rescinded and reclaimed by General Conference. The speech, which elected him to the episcopacy, concluded with an arresting image:

> This conference is the sun in our orderly and beautiful system. Look into the Discipline. First you have our "articles of religion," in which God appears. What is next in order? The General Conference, which, like the orb of day, rises to shed light on the surrounding scene. It is first shaped or fashioned, and then, like Adam by his Maker, is en-

dowed with dominion, and made imperial in its relations; and saving the slight reservations of the constitution, is all-controlling in its influence. Let it never be lost sight of, that the General Conference is "the *sun of our system*."[47]

Against this judgment, southerners enunciated what would be the constitutional principle of the MECS. Voicing their disagreement with Hamline and a very different reading of the *Discipline*, William Winans argued,

> Properly speaking, the General Conference, as such, possesses not a particle of original administrative power. All the administrative power it does possess is conferred upon it by its own action in another capacity. It is purely a creature having delegated attributes, and none others. What are these delegated powers? They are few, and exceedingly simple. Where are they found? Where every Methodist ought to look, in the book of Discipline.... God forbid that the majority of this conference should be invested with plenary power to be used at will! [Amen, Amen.][48]

Concurring and as himself drafter of the Restrictive Rules that were being debated, Bishop Soule rejected the notion that bishops were but officers of General Conference and focused the constitutional issue on his office and his person:

> I desire to understand my landmarks as a bishop of the Methodist Episcopal Church—not the bishop of the General Conference, not the bishop of any annual conference. I thought that the constitution of the Church—I thought that its laws and regulations—I thought that the many solemn vows of ordination—the parchment which I hold under the signatures of the departed dead—I thought that these had defined my landmarks—I thought that these had prescribed my duties—I thought that these had marked out my course.[49]

John Price Durbin (1800–1876), earlier an editor of the *Christian Advocate*, then president of Dickinson College, responded directly to the conception of episcopacy presented by Winans and Soule (Sources 1844b). He seconded Hamline's and the northern notion of General Conference's plenary authority and of the episcopacy's derived power (Sources 1844b, p. 275). Durbin then reviewed the history of the relation of conference and superintendency and the constitutional appropriateness of the resolution.[50] The constitutional framing of the issue would prove to have long-term significance in both regions (churches), serving to resolve into political philosophy the host of issues posed by racism and slavery.

Division

After more than a week of intense debate, the other four bishops submitted a letter proposing that the matter concerning Bishop Andrew be held over until the next General Conference, arguing that a decision whether affirmatively or negatively, will most extensively disturb the peace and harmony of that widely-extended brotherhood which has so effectively operated for good in the United States of America and elsewhere during the last sixty years, in the development of a system of active energy, of which union has always been a main element.[51]

The New Englanders thought harmony need no longer be bought at the price of slavery. Delegates of those conferences caucused and agreed to "secede in a body, and invite Bishop Hedding to preside over them."[52] Hedding then withdrew his signature from the bishops' initiative, announcing that what he thought would be a peace measure would not be.[53] That effectively collapsed what Tigert concluded was the only "hope of harmonizing the difficulties of the Conference."[54] The motion for Andrew "to desist" then passed.

On the next business day Capers offered resolutions to divide the church,[55] which were referred to a committee of nine. The southerners proposed an amicable division of the church through a constitutional amendment providing for two General Conferences, a northern and a southern, and

> That each of the two General Conferences thus constituted shall have full powers, under the limitations and restrictions which are now of force and binding on the General Conference, to make rules and regulations for the church, within their territorial limits respectively, and to elect Bishops for the same.

Two days later, the South offered an interpretive resolution:

> [T]hat the continued agitation on the subject of slavery and abolition in a portion of the church; the frequent action on that subject in the General Conference; and especially the extra-judicial proceedings against Bishop Andrew, which resulted, on Saturday last, in the virtual suspension of him from his office as Superintendent must produce a state of things in the South which renders a continuance of the jurisdiction of this General Conference over these Conferences inconsistent with the success of the ministry in the slaveholding states.[56]

That was followed by the submission of a carefully worded "Protest" that reiterated and refined the position that the southern delegates had moved toward in the resolution and in their side of the debate.[57] It set forth understandings of the impending division, of the nature of the church, of slavery, of episcopacy, and of conference that would define and characterize the southern church (MECS). Among those points was the insistence that "the episcopacy is a co-ordinate branch, the executive department proper of the church" and "not a mere creature" of General Conference.[58]

As if timed so as to accent the emerging northern understanding of General Conference supremacy, the following day, the Committee on Slavery reported resolutions rescinding the proscription in church trials of testimony by "persons of colour," stipulating that no slaveholding bishop be elected, urging that conference take measures "entirely to separate slavery from the church," but proposing no change in the General Rules on slavery.[59] The fuller and also carefully honed northern understanding of conference and episcopacy came in "The Reply to the Protest." The "Reply" insisted that the action in the case of Bishop Andrew followed the recurring and basic principle of itinerancy—the examination of character—a principle exercised in annual conference over traveling preachers and in General Conference over bishops. It rejected "episcopacy supremacy" as "at variance with the genius of Methodism," "the express language of the Discipline," and "the exposition of it by all our standard writers."[60]

The Committee of Nine on the Division of the Church followed the design outlined by Capers and reported plans for an amicable division of the church. It provided for measures to assure peaceful delineation of a boundary between the churches and to divide property. A key provision, an enabling constitutional revision of one of the restrictive articles, required three-fourths majorities in annual conferences—and assured that the debates and acrimony of General Conference would become those of the following annual conferences (Sources 1844c). Peter Cartwright, who spoke immediately on the introduction of these resolutions, "thought the proposed arrangements would create war and strife in the border conferences."[61] Concurring, *Christian Advocate* editor Thomas Bond wondered if the intent of the committee had been "to provide for peace, and love, and harmony still to be perpetuated in the great Methodist family.... Why then ... if the object is to procure peace and to prevent conflicts—why, then, does it provide for a border warfare from Delaware to the Ohio River?"[62] The resolutions nevertheless passed.

Legislative Posturing

After adjournment, the delegates from the slaveholding states met,[63] called a convention to be held in Louisville, May 1, 1845, for the annual conferences "within the slaveholding States," and issued an explanatory address "To the Ministers and Members of the Methodist Episcopal Church, in the Slaveholding States and Territories."[64] It deferred discussion of the "equivocal suspension of Bishop Andrew" for later communications, stated the call in terms of slavery, and set forth a southern ecclesiology of the division:

> The separation proposed is *not* schism, it is *not* secession. It is a State or family, separating into two different States of families, by mutual consent. As the "Methodist Episcopal Church" will be found North of the dividing line, so the "Methodist Episcopal Church" will be found South of the same line.[65]

Such mutuality did not last. Annual conferences, North and South, obliged to deal with the matter, confirmed the predictions of Bond and Cartwright. The initial volleys in what would be a war—section against section, conference against conference, church against church—expressed sentiment about the prior General Conference. The Kentucky Conference, the first in the South to meet after separation, set the pattern by establishing a committee of division, condemning the actions of General Conference,[66] and approving the holding of the Louisville Convention. North Carolina, meeting with Bishop Soule as president, took action to make itself politically expressive. It amended the rules so that "any members of the church who may be invited by the members shall be permitted to be present as spectators during our sessions" and then drafted a pastoral address, which it adopted, ordered published in the *Richmond Christian Advocate*; and required to be read by the pastors "at every appointment."[67] Other conferences in the slaveholding states followed suit with formal expressions of disapproval over the 1844 General Conference, the establishment of committees on separation or division, approval of the convention, passage of the amendment to the sixth Restrictive Rule that would permit the division of property (particularly the Book Concern, now UMPH; and pension resources, the Chartered Fund, now General Board of Pension and Health Benefits [GBPHB]) and provision for dissemination of actions. Such initiatives were taken without dissent, according to Bishop Soule.[68] Dissent nevertheless flowed from their actions.

In resolutions, in pastoral letters, and especially in a torrent of editorial remarks, the southern conferences expressed their resentments against the 1844 General Conference portraying the (northern) majority as repressive, acting illegally, motivated by abolitionism.[69] The editors of the northern papers (*Zion's Herald*, the [New York] *Christian Advocate and Journal*, the *Western Christian Advocate*, the *Pittsburgh Christian Advocate*, and the *Northern Advocate*) entered countercriticisms.[70] The first MEC conferences to meet voted before this *Advocate* warfare was felt and acted favorably on the key constitutional issue in the division of the church, the amendment of the sixth Restrictive Rule, so as to permit proportional division of the Book Concern and the Chartered Fund. New York, which met June 12, passed the constitutional amendment 143 to 38. Providence, which met next in early July, did so unanimously.

By August when North Ohio met, MEC resentment was building, and that conference defeated the amendment, as did most of the following conferences. Ohio voted 132 to 1 against the change. These conferences also put their judgments before the public.

Illinois resolved:

> (1) That we do not concur in the resolution of the late General conference to alter the sixth Restrictive Rule....

(2) That we do not concur in, but strongly deprecate and oppose, any sectional division of, or separation from, the Methodist Episcopal Church, . . .

(4) That a copy of these resolutions be forwarded to the Western Christian Advocate, by the secretary, for publication, with a request that all the General conference papers copy.

(5) That each of the bishops be furnished with a copy of the foregoing resolutions, and be requested to lay them before the several annual conferences at their next sessions.[71]

Ohio expressed pain over "the *politico-religious* aspect which the question of division has assumed at the south."[72] In truth, MEC (northern) conferences assumed an equal, if not more intense, politico-religious aspect. Ohio, in fact, found itself initially chaired by Bishop Joshua Soule, on an invitation tendered by Bishop L. L. Hamline to the very Soule who, with James O. Andrew, had already pledged allegiance to the southern conferences. Ohio voted such presidency "inexpedient and highly improper"[73] and forced Soule from the chair.

Conferences, North and South, roiled with politics. And each controversial act seemed to stimulate others. The property issue alone, defeated by the votes of the northern conferences, festered for years, drawing attention from conferences as well as *Advocates*. Even its resolution ten years later, by the U.S. Supreme Court, did not end the comments. Nor did the formal organization of the southern church halt the acrimony. The 1845 Louisville Convention had proceeded with calm deliberation to carry out the will of the several southern conferences, voting "That it is right, expedient, and necessary to erect the Annual Conferences represented in this Convention, into a distinct ecclesiastical connexion, separate from the jurisdiction of the General Conference of the Methodist Episcopal Church, as at present constituted."[74]

The convention in turn called the first General Conference for the MECS, which met in Petersburg in 1846, as the new church's *Discipline* adopted then explains, narrating its history as that of American Methodism:

Of the Organization of The Methodist Episcopal Church, South
TO THE MEMBERS of the METHODIST EPISCOPAL CHURCH, SOUTH

Dearly Beloved Brethren,

We think it expedient to give you a brief account of the rise of Methodism, both in Europe and America. "In 1729, two young men, in England, reading the Bible, saw they could not be saved without holiness; followed after it, and incited others so to do. In 1737, they saw, likewise, that men are justified before they are sanctified: but still holiness was their object. God then thrust them out to raise a holy people."[75]

In the year 1766, Philip Embury, a local preacher of our society, from Ireland, began to preach in the city of New-York, and formed a society of his own countrymen and the citizens; and the same year, Thomas Webb preached in a hired room near the barracks. About the same time, Robert Strawbridge, a local preacher from Ireland, settled in Frederick county, in the state of Maryland, and preaching there, formed some societies. The first Methodist church was built in New-York in 1768 or 1769; and in 1769 Richard Boardman and Joseph Pilmoor came to New-York, who were the first regular Methodist preachers on the continent. In the latter end of the year 1771, Francis Asbury and Richard Wright of the same order, came over.

We believe that God's design in raising up the preachers called Methodists in America, was to reform the continent, and spread Scripture holiness over these lands. As a proof hereof, we have seen, since that time, a great and glorious work of God, from New-York, through the Jersey, Pennsylvania, Delaware, Maryland, Virginia, North and South Carolina, and Georgia; as also, of late, to the extremities of the western and eastern states.

We esteem it our duty, and privilege most earnestly to recommend to you, as members of our Church, our FORM OF DISCIPLINE, which has been founded on the experience of a long series of years; as also on the observations and remarks we have made on ancient and modern Churches.

We wish to see this little publication in the house of every Methodist; and the more so, as it contains the articles of religion maintained more or less, in part or in whole, by every reformed Church in the world.

Far from wishing you to be ignorant of any of our doctrines, or any part of our discipline, we desire you to read, mark, learn, and inwardly digest the whole. You ought, next to the word of God, to procure the articles and Canons of the Church to which you belong. This present edition is small and cheap, and we can assure you that the profits of the sale of it shall be applied to charitable and religious purposes.

We remain your very affectionate brethren and pastors, who labor night and day, both in public and in private, for your good.

JOSHUA SOULE, JAMES O. ANDREW, WILLIAM CAPERS, ROBERT PAINE.

Chapter I.
Section I.

Of the Origin of the Methodist Episcopal Church, and of the Methodist Episcopal Church, South.

The preachers and members of our society in general, being convinced that there was a great deficiency of vital religion in the Church of England in America, and being in many places destitute of the Christian sacraments, as several of the clergy had forsaken their churches, requested the late Rev. *John Wesley* to take such measures, in his wisdom and prudence, as would afford them suitable relief in their distress.

In consequence of this, our venerable friend, who, under God, had been the father of the great revival of religion now extending over the earth, by the means of the

Methodists, determined to ordain ministers for America; and for this purpose, in the year 1784, sent over three regularly ordained clergy: but preferring the episcopal mode of Church government to any other, he solemnly set apart, by the imposition of his hands and prayer, one of them, viz., *Thomas Coke*, Doctor of Civil Law, late of Jesus College, in the University of Oxford, and a presbyter of the Church of England, for the episcopal office; and having delivered to him letters of episcopal orders, commissioned and directed him to set apart *Francis Asbury*, then general assistant of the Methodist Society in America, for the same episcopal office; he, the said *Francis Asbury* was solemnly set apart for the said episcopal office by prayer, and the imposition of the hands of the said *Thomas Coke*, other regularly-ordained ministers assisting in the sacred ceremony. At which time the General Conference, held at Baltimore, did unanimously receive the said *Thomas Coke* and *Francis Asbury* as their bishops, being fully satisfied of the validity of their episcopal ordination.

Section II.

Of the Organization of the Methodist Episcopal Church, South.

In the judgment of the delegates of the several annual conferences in the slaveholding states, the continued agitation of the subject of slavery and abolition in a portion of the Church, the frequent action on that subject in the General Conference, and especially the proceedings of the General Conference of the Methodist Episcopal Church of 1844, in the case of the Rev. James O. Andrew, D.D., one of the bishops, who has become connected with slavery by marriage, produced a state of things in the south, which rendered a continuance of the jurisdiction of that General Conference over the conferences aforesaid inconsistent with the success of the ministry in their proper calling. This conviction they declared in solemn form to the General Conference, accompanied with a protest against the action referred to, assured that public opinion in the slaveholding states would demand, and that a due regard to the vital interests of Christ's kingdom would justify, a separate and independent organization. The developments of a few months vindicated their anticipations. The Church in the south and south-west, in her primary assemblies, her quarterly and annual conferences, with a unanimity unparalleled in ecclesiastical history, approved the course of their delegates, and declared her conviction that a separate jurisdiction was necessary to her existence and prosperity. The General Conference of 1844, having adopted a "Plan of Separation," provided for the erection of the annual conferences in the slaveholding states into a separate ecclesiastical connection, under the jurisdiction of a southern General Conference; the delegates of the aforementioned conferences, in a published address, recommended that a convention of delegates from the said conferences, duly instructed as to the wishes of the ministry and laity, should assemble at Louisville, Ky., on the first day of May, 1845.

The convention met, delegates having been formally appointed in pursuance of this recommendation; and after a full and minute representation of all the facts in the premises, acting under the provisional "Plan of Separation," declared, by solemn resolution, the jurisdiction hitherto exercised by the General Conference of the Methodist Episcopal Church over the conferences in the slaveholding states *entirely dissolved*, and erected the said annual conferences into a separate ecclesiastical connection, under the style and title of *The Methodist Episcopal Church, South*; the first General Conference of which was held in the town of Petersburg, Virginia, on the first day of May, 1846.[76]

Border Warfare

The organization of the new church did not halt the acrimony; indeed it stimulated border warfare. The 1845 convention, in implementing the Plan of Separation, took action calculated to ensure further politicization, authorizing the bishops to incorporate into its conferences "any societies or stations adjoining the line of division, provided such societies or stations, by a majority of the members, according to the provisions of separation adopted by the late General Conference, request such an arrangement."[77] Existing conference boundaries and the line drawn thereby between the MEC and the MECS did not circumscribe loyalties or sentiments about slavery. Conference boundaries crossed state lines. The northern conferences encompassed slaveholding areas. Some antislavery or more often antislaveholder sentiment existed in southern conferences, notably in Kentucky. Itinerants and presiding elders enjoyed close relations with circuits and congregations cut off by the new lines.

Furthermore, the above provision for changing church loyalty created a new set of problems. Who counted and who got counted when elections were held? If no vote had been taken in a boundary setting, to which church could adherence be presumed? How long did such voting go on? Could small segments of a circuit go their own way? And did the boundary remain the line as originally established or the line as redrawn by subsequent acts of realignment?[78] Conference lines that had been drawn and redrawn many times for convenience in itineration and appointment making now took on great political significance. Border conferences developed a territorial imperative. And for land, conferences squared off against one another. Especially affected were the Delmarva Peninsula, western Virginia, Kentucky, Ohio, and Missouri.

In the ensuing border skirmishes, each side attempted to claim and consolidate within its borders the congregations and circuits that, in its judgment, it should have by right, by prior possession, by family relation, by convictions. Each side saw the other's comparable actions as illicit. Each side accused the other of deceit, intrigue, and misconduct. Philadelphia (MEC) believed itself not a border conference. It thought having land (the Baltimore Conference, MEC) and water (the Chesapeake) between it and the MECS would save it from incursions, but found boundaries with the MECS on the Delmarva Peninsula difficult to hold. On the peninsula, Virginia (MECS) preachers excited congregations with the information that the MEC members were abolitionists and thus gained adherents. In response, the Philadelphia Conference devoted much effort and a "Pastoral Address...to the Societies...of the Northampton and Accomac Circuits."[79] The Baltimore Conference viewed Virginia (MECS) efforts in Westmoreland, King George, Lancaster, and Warrenton in similar fashion.[80] Ohio thought illegal the MECS efforts in Cincinnati and especially on the Kanawha District, actually in Virginia, but some seventy-five miles from the border and separated by five circuits from the MECS territory.[81] A few areas in Kentucky toyed with adherence to the MEC but stayed with the MECS. Intense conflict ensued in Missouri.[82] Such warfare turned conference membership—for ministers and people—from fraternal and missional into political and "military" purposes. The border contests ironically also induced the MEC to tone down its antislavery rhetoric, indeed to quiet it, a strategy designed to hold slaveholding congregations, circuits, and districts within the northern church. Nevertheless, the border contests intensified animosities throughout the two churches.

Symbolizing this spirit, the 1848 MEC General Conference, after having received fraternal delegations from the British and Canadian Methodists and returned their fraternal expressions, pointedly rebuffed a similar expression from the MECS. Lovick Pierce had presented its "Christian salutations," seeking "warm, confiding, and brotherly, fraternal relation" and expecting acceptance "in the same spirit of brotherly love and kindness." Instead, the MEC, noting the "serious questions and difficulties existing between the two bodies," did not "consider it proper, at present, to enter into fraternal relations with the Methodist Episcopal Church, South." Pierce responded that his communication was "final on the part of the M.E. Church, South." He said, "She can never renew the offer of fraternal relations between the two great bodies of Wesleyan Methodists in the United States. But the proposition can be renewed at any time, either now or hereafter by the M.E. Church."[83]

The 1848 MEC General Conference also undid the work of 1844. It declared that the constitutional amendment had failed. Under the guidance of a Committee on the State of the Church, the conference repudiated, declared "null and void," the Plan of Separation, judging that the 1844 General Conference could not legally divide the church.[84] And MEC General Conference authorized the formation of a Western Virginia Conference, a stake on territory also claimed by the MECS. In response, the southern church also organized a West Virginia Conference.

In their address to the 1850 MECS General Conference, the southern bishops summarized the points of political contention:

But your Messenger (fraternal delegate Lovick Pierce) was rejected, and your offers of peace were met with contempt. Your Commissioners, charged with the management of the interests of the Southern Church in relation to the Book Concern and Chartered Fund, were treated with like discourtesy. Your claims were disposed of in a summary manner. The Plan of Separation was repudiated; the Southern claim to any portion of the Book Concern was denied; and the very men who, from sheer hatred to slavery, drove the South into separation, proved their sincerity and consistency by not only retaining all the slave-holding members already under their charge, but in making arrangements to gather as many more into the fold as practicable. The Plan of Separation was repudiated with the avowed purpose of invading Southern territory; and as an earnest of their intentions in this respect, a new Conference was organized, entirely within the limits of the Southern Church.[85]

New Antislavery Churches

In the late 1850s conference politicization around slavery and antislavery intensified in both the MPC and the MEC, stimulated in no small part by northern outrage over the Fugitive Slave Law of 1850,[86] challenging the churches' quiescence on slavery and producing new antislavery denominations. A two-decade division within the MPC occurred and an anti-slavery Methodist Church emerged when the 1858 Methodist Protestant General Conference turned down petitions to strengthen its antislavery commitments. For the MEC, the new antislavery front opened in the Genesee Conference (New York), which found itself embroiled in controversy over slavery, holiness, choirs, pew rent, secret societies—all touchstones for accommodation to the social order.[87] The conference divided itself politically between "Nazarites" who called for return to the fraternal, revivalistic old standards, including unqualified commitment to antislavery, and those they characterized as "New School Methodists" or the "Buffalo Regency" (Sources 1860).

The leader of this primitivist reform impulse was B. T. Roberts. A product of small-town "western" New York Methodism, Roberts had gone east to college, to Wesleyan University, and grew close to its centrist-holiness commitments and its president, Stephen F. Olin. There Roberts met and married Ellen Stowe, who frequented the Wesleyan campus visiting relative faculty member Harvey Lane, and who otherwise lived in New York with relatives George and Lydia Lane, the former then head of the MEC Book Concern, arguably the most powerful and well-connected position in the entire church. The Lanes were connected to Phoebe and Walter Palmer, the latter the Lanes' physician. Ellen and later B. T. came under the magnetic influence of Phoebe and her brand of Wesleyan holiness. By 1848 when Roberts returned to his home conference (Genesee) to begin ministry, the holiness-centrism represented by the New York–Middletown axis had failed, proving unable to hold together a church troubled by slavery. Roberts's mentor, Stephen Olin, in declining health, died soon thereafter (1851). At the 1852 General Conference, Ellen's uncle, George Lane, was replaced as head of the Book Concern by Thomas Carlton, a member of the Genesee Conference and closely tied to its power structure. Also in 1852 the bishop sent the Robertses from small-town appointments to the city, specifically to Niagara Street, once Buffalo's largest but in decline, though boasting a big facility and burdened with a huge debt. A significant part of the decline (the loss of 158 members) had occurred during Thomas Carlton's ministry there.

Roberts undertook at Niagara Street a style of revival and reform that called Methodism back to what he took to be its core values, practices, and commitments—outreach to poor persons, a disciplined life, the quest for holiness, camp meetings, and antislavery. He and a camp-meeting network of like-minded reformers also issued from the pulpit and in the press a withering critique of practices they deemed to stand in the way of revival, practices that introduced and/or symbolized emerging class distinctions within the church—pew rental, then the key device for funding ever more lavish churches, and secret societies, especially the Masons, the purported context within which the Genesee elite (Carlton and company) ran the conference. Through trials, harassment, and expulsions, Roberts and colleagues were forced from church editorships and from pulpits. The reformers founded their own paper, the *Northern Independent*, held laymen's conventions, garnered support for ousted ministers, and in 1860 founded the Free Methodist Church.[88]

To stem defections to the Free Methodists, the MEC General Conference passed in 1860 a "new chapter" on slavery explicitly declaring that "the buying, selling, or holding of human beings, to be used as chattels, is contrary to the laws of God and nature, inconsistent with the Golden Rule, and with that rule in our Discipline ... to 'do no harm and to avoid evil of every kind.' "[89] Border conferences meeting thereafter were deluged with petitions and resolutions calling for its repeal. Some, such as East Baltimore and Philadelphia, acted to demand repeal, and the latter then directed "the printing in tract form of 5,000 copies of the report of its Committee on the State of the Church; also, its publication in the *Christian Advocate and Journal*, *Methodist*, and *Baltimore Christian Advocate*."[90]

The Lay Voice (Again)

Laity had things to say about the fundamental social issues on which the church was then speaking. Within the MEC and the MECS, quarterly conferences did permit laity a voice. Increasingly, the laity felt restive at having their opinions and influence confined to quarterly conference as conferences embroiled themselves politically and spoke on national questions. So in episcopal Methodism the issue that Methodist Protestants championed—lay representation—resurfaced. A politicized episcopal Methodism faced but defeated resolutions for lay representation, the MEC in 1852 and the MECS in 1854. The issue would return, necessitated by the locality of quarterly conference and the divisive issues before the church (Sources 1864a). The controversy in the Genesee Conference had widened to division through the holding of a succession of Laymen's Conventions, the first in 1858, the second in 1859, the third in 1860, each of them functioning politically. They issued resolutions, circulated petitions, gathered money, and organized "Bands." In 1859 a Ministers' and Laymen's Union was formed within the New York Conference, a body dedicated to preserving the status quo on the slavery issue within the MEC. In response, a rival antislavery society of the New York East Conference, also ministers and laity, pressed for change.

In 1860, Baltimore Conference laity at a camp meeting at Loudoun took matters into their own hands.[91] They called a laymen's conference for December. Other lay or public meetings followed, each expressing itself, often with resolutions on the sectional crisis and recent (MEC) General Conference actions. An important laymen's convention sat concurrently with the annual conference of 1861 at Staunton and nudged it into an act of secession. The first item of business for this annual conference was the memorial from the "Convention of Laymen which assembled in Baltimore in December last, relating to the action on Slavery by the General Conference . . . 1861." Conference also took up memorials from Light Street, Alexandria, and Frankford Circuit. On the tenth day, after testy sessions with presiding Bishop Levi Scott, the conference put and passed a motion protesting an 1860 General Conference action on slavery (the New Chapter) (1) as unconstitutional, (2) as breaking the organic law of the Constitution of the church, (3) as destroying the unity of the church, (4) as false, heterodox, and unscriptural, (5) as misinterpreting the existing rules on slavery, and (6) as a bar to reception of members, ordination of deacons, and ordination of bishops. The conference then acted to break with the MEC:

> 1st. Be it resolved by the Baltimore Annual Conference, in Conference assembled, That we hereby declare that the General Conference . . . by its unconstitutional action has sundered the ecclesiastical relation which has hitherto bound us together as one Church, so far as any act of theirs could do so. That we will not longer submit to the jurisdiction of said General Conference but hereby declare ourselves separate and independent of it, still claiming to be, notwithstanding, an integral part of the Methodist Episcopal Church.

The next (1862) Baltimore Annual Conference met in Baltimore rather than in Virginia, that is, outside the Confederacy, and recognized the actions of the previous conference as an act of severance and those not present as withdrawing.

This annual conference entertained but voted down lay delegation, 34 against 22.[92] It had seen the power of lay initiative, and so had the southerners who took an earlier liking to the idea. The MECS approved lay representation in 1866. Laity, they recognized, belonged in politicized and business-like conferences that legislated on social issues and stated the church's position and set policy for the whole. And with the collapse of quarterly meeting into station or small circuit, laity demanded a role on more effective conference levels, that is, annual and general. The MEC heard from its laity on the matter in 1864 (Sources 1864a), finally conceding to the proposal in 1872 but only on the General Conference level. Women's rights to representation and ordination lay ahead. Politics hovered over conference activities, and conferences ordered themselves (or disordered themselves) for politics.[93]

CHAPTER IX

Embracing the War Cause(s): 1860–65

By 1860, membership in the Methodist denominations (UBC, EA, MPC, MEC, MECS) had reached 1,800,000 (Sources, p. 22), 5.7 percent of the total U.S. population. Then Methodist adherents—those attending and supporting the church—far exceeded actual membership, and the number of adherents was closer to 3,800,000, making the Methodist family the largest U.S. communion, surpassing both Catholics and Baptists.[1] Dispersing itself across the expanding nation and evangelizing its many peoples—the MEC had already established California and Oregon Conferences, the MECS had formed the Pacific Conference, UBC missionary efforts on the West Coast were under way, and the EA was soon to follow—Methodism embraced and reflected the nation in its many hues. With its numbers, its spread, its internal diversity, its growing prosperity, its connectional apparatus, its effective media, and its presence in city as well as town and countryside, Methodism felt itself entitled to a place in civic and religious leadership, a role in making America a Protestant nation.

That sense of civil religious entitlement would bring Methodists to the fore on both sides of the Civil War. President Lincoln's blessing on Methodists for support of the war cause (Sources 1864b) could equally have been uttered by his Confederate counterpart. At the same time Methodists, North and South, betrayed the various, complex, and changing attitudes toward the two governments and the war. At one extreme were Unionist sympathizers in border and Appalachian regions of the Confederacy and Copperheads (southern sympathizers) in Ohio and elsewhere in the lower Midwest. At the other were Methodists who emerged as public theologians, spokespersons for war, on patriotism, and on slavery. In sermons, letters, diaries, and resolutions, Methodists participated actively in giving meaning(s) to the bloody sacrifices, including that of the president. And for decades thereafter the war experience indelibly stamped Methodism, North and South, its leaders-to-be, its institutions, its practices, and its self-understanding.[2]

Patriotism, Confederate Style

As state after state seceded, the Confederate States of America formed, and war began, southern Methodists (MECS and MPC)—some of whom opposed, some of whom championed secession—came first cautiously, then increasingly to speak and preach about the new nation and the war. Despite several decades of commitment to spirituality and neutrality, despite explicit counsel from the southern bishops to stay above the fray, and deploring "the too extensive influence of the war spirit among our preachers," some editors, conferences, and individual ministers began to preach patriotism as a religious duty, the Confederate cause as one ordained by God, and the war one for independence.[3] Such sermonic and editorial endorsements—the MECS General Conference did not meet during the war and therefore offered no official church position—helped the South garner popular support and recruit Methodists into the Confederate army. Methodist preachers acted as well as voiced support, volunteering as regular soldiers, noncombatants, and chaplains, some seventy-two of the ordained being appointed as officers or serving in the enlisted ranks in 1861 alone.[4]

Endorsements came also on official levels. Annual conferences did convene until occupation or war conditions prohibited. Conferences voted approval of secession, the Georgia Annual Conference acting a month before the state by its commitment. The 1861 Tennessee Conference requested Bishop Joshua Soule to "appoint as many preachers of this conference as he may deem proper to the chaplaincy of our army." Appoint he and the other bishops did. Methodists came to constitute almost half of the Confederate chaplaincy (47 percent of the 938 of the total 1,308 chaplains whose denominational identity can be established).[5] The southern Missionary Society also met, received what would be meager contributions for missions, but constituted the southern army as itself a mission. The MECS bishops convened concurrently with the Missionary Society and by 1863 recognized Bishop Robert Paine as Methodist superintendent of the army and W. W. Bennett, president of Randolph-Macon, as the man in charge of publication for the army. Also in 1863, the Missionary Society drafted a nine-point enabling "Army Mission" program. Union occupation of Nashville in 1862 dispersed leadership from MECS headquarters, putting the Missionary Society into its own itineration and shutting down the Methodist Publishing House and the *Nashville Christian Advocate*. Book editor Thomas O. Summers and book agent John B. McFerrin fled. Another editor, Edmund Sehon, stayed but only to be imprisoned. Other *Advocates* took up some of the communication and publication slack, all succumbing, however, by war's end.

Chaplains and Army Missionaries

Methodist army missionaries, chaplains, and local and traveling preachers pastoring though under arms worked the camps, distributing Bibles and tracts, conducting services, holding revivals, organizing army churches, writing letters for soldiers or teaching them to read and write, nursing the wounded, praying with the maimed, burying the dead, and consoling those to be executed.[6] Often chaplains and army missionaries accompanied regiments from their own town or region. The latter were cared for financially by the MECS and sometimes split time between home pulpit and the troops. The former, poorly paid and meagerly provisioned, something of an afterthought within the Confederate army, worked under often indifferent, sometimes hostile, only occasionally supportive commanding officers.[7] The lack of consistent support from officers, symbols of the elite, the genteel and planter class, would color ministerial class attitudes thereafter, encouraging greater dependence on and attention to professionals and merchants. Army service also permitted Methodist preachers to attend to their own image and self-image. Functioning as chaplains or missionaries gave preachers opportunity to demonstrate and exhibit the interconnection of piety, patriotism, and manliness, and some debated even a further symbolization of male honor—whether chaplains should bear arms.[8]

Points of southern Methodist pride and self-congratulation long after the war was over were the revivals and conversions within the Confederate army, celebrated in the 1877 volume *A Narrative of the Great Revival in the Southern Armies During the Late Civil War between the States of the Federal Union*.[9] Mission was the Methodist business, so chaplains evangelized from the start. Pastoral care and the distribution of Bibles effectively served that purpose for individual soldiers suffering the tedium of long encampments.[10] Chaplains also conducted revivalistic campaigns, especially in the fall of 1862 and thereafter as the carnage and casualties mounted. Revivals were also stimulated by the initiative of General "Stonewall" Jackson to solicit from denominational leaders and from the chaplains themselves a more regularized ministry—the appointment of more chaplains, their itineration to cover unstaffed regiments, services at headquarters, associations of chaplains for more cooperative endeavor, and better supplies. Jackson's counsel and particularly the formation of Chaplains Associations spread throughout the Confederate army. By associating, working together, and offering morning, noon, or tattoo (evening) services, chaplains (Protestants) could sustain significant revival campaigns of a week's duration and even longer—revivals occurring of twenty-one days, of thirty days, and the record in a Georgia regiment, of four months and five days. The first two of these produced 100 and 140 conversions, respectively.[11] More generalized revivals occurred in the Army of Tennessee and the Army of Northern Virginia. The former produced 321 conversions and 728 church memberships in one month and overall bringing 13 percent of the army into Christian commitment.[12]

Preachers who stayed with or returned to their congregations supported families of the soldiers, visited hospitalized men, and conducted funerals and memorials for those killed. Congregations, always dominated by women, became even more so. And for southern women, the war called forth new roles and duties, as for all those who stayed behind. Largely uninvolved in the early phases of the women's rights efforts, southern women found themselves obliged to take over and take on responsibilities abandoned as their men exited into the army. They managed the farms and plantations, oversaw the slaves, presided within the family, kept congregations going, supported the war effort with home manufactures, took over whatever schooling continued, and served as nurses. The war encouraged southern women to have stronger interest in politics, in society, in national affairs. And it further stimulated female networking and formation of women's voluntary associations.[13] The home front saw no revivals comparable to those among the troops, and women's "religious work," which had typically reinforced the evangelization of "their" men, turned to pondering the ways of providence, to writing letters of nurturing encouragement or condolence, to making sense of the carnage and impending defeat, and to sustaining the society's grief work. As the war progressed and casualties mounted, women took on the church's rituals for burial and the burden of mourning those killed.[14] The new roles, enforced self-reliance, increased networking, and the defeat of a South committed to patriarchy opened new possibilities for southern women.

Overall the war wrought devastation on southern Methodism as on southern religion generally. Attendance dropped; contributions shrank; ministerial salaries went unpaid; congregations lost their leaders; churches were destroyed, damaged, or commandeered as Union armies advanced. The war effort, calling for sacrifice on all fronts, obliged the churches to invest in what would be a lost cause. Methodists placed college endowments in Confederate bonds, melted church bells, and sold property.[15] Most tragically, the South as well as the North lost the members and leaders who gave their lives for the cause.

Reaffirming an MECS Identity

The trauma of the war, Lincoln's Emancipation Proclamation, and the continued critique of the South by the northern church prompted an "Address to Christians throughout the World by the Clergy of The Confederate States of America." This statement was signed by the religious leaders of the South—Baptists, Disciples, Episcopalians, Lutherans, Presbyterians, and Methodists. The latter included the presidents of two MPC districts and of the MPC Lynchburg College and a who's who of the MECS—four editors; presidents of Wofford, Randolph-Macon, and Trinity; prominent preachers; and three bishops, James O. Andrew, John Early, and G. F. Pierce. These Christians declared that *"the war against the Confederate States has achieved no good result."*[16] They indicated that their commitment to the Confederacy and that of southerners generally remained firm, indeed changed "from all lingering attachment to the former Union, to a more sacred and reliable devotion to the Confederate Government." These leaders pled that the *"moral and religious interests of the South ought to be appreciated by Christians of all nations"* and went on to reiterate, in the face of Lincoln's Emancipation Proclamation, their support for the system of slavery:

> Most of us have grown up from childhood among slaves; all of us have preached to and taught them the word of life; have administered to them the ordinances of the Christian Church; sincerely love them as souls for whom Christ died; we go among them freely, and know them in health and sickness, in labor and rest, from infancy to old age. We are familiar with their physical and moral condition, and alive to all their interests; and we testify in the sight of God, that the relation of master and slave among us, however we may deplore abuses in this, as in other relations of mankind, is not incompatible with our holy Christianity, and that the presence of the Africans in our land is an occasion of gratitude on their behalf before God; seeing that thereby Divine Providence has brought them where missionaries of the Cross may freely proclaim to them the word of salvation, and the work is not interrupted by agitating fanaticism. The South has done more than any people on earth for the Christianization of the African race.

Southern conferences were animated as well by northern religious intrusion, the MEC's especially, particularly after Bishop Edward Ames secured from Secretary of War Stanton an 1863 directive ordering officers to turn over to the MEC, churches belonging to the MECS "in which a loyal minister, who has been appointed by a loyal Bishop of said Church does not officiate."[17] In some instances the recipients of the property transfers were northerners. In other instances, members of the MECS who had opposed secession assisted in that project. Though few, some southern Methodists, particularly in western Virginia and eastern Tennessee, favored the Union and opposed secession and the Confederacy. The most prominent dissenter and critic, William G. "Parson" Brownlow (1805–77), a member of the Holston Conference, located and become editor successively of several Tennessee papers, the most important being the *Knoxville Whig*. Though a defender of slavery, he employed his editorials to support the Union, that is, until he was arrested and his paper was suppressed in 1861. Brownlow aided Bishop Matthew Simpson in the organization of an MEC Holston Conference. Forty preachers from Tennessee and six from elsewhere constituted that new entity in 1865, which began with one hundred churches and six thousand members. A year later it claimed another fifty churches and three times that membership. Brownlow went further in such collaboration, being elected governor that same year and U.S. senator in 1869. His last senatorial act was the introduction of a bill for land acquisition for Fisk University.[18]

With such takeovers occurring at various places under Union army control, with portions of the church within the Union throughout the war (Kentucky, Louisville, Missouri, and western Virginia Conferences) and their continuing commitment uncertain, and with Confederate defeat looming, northerners advocated that and southerners wondered whether the MECS should simply cave in, dissolve. The MECS decided not.

Ministers and laity in the Missouri Conference gathered in 1865 and issued a declaration of independence (Sources 1865a): "*Resolved,* That we consider the maintenance of our separate and distinct ecclesiastical organization as of paramount importance and our imperative duty." This Palmyra Manifesto, whose commitment and sentiments were embraced across the church, grounded continuation of the MECS on "our Church doctrines and discipline" and on opposition to the MEC's "prostitution of the pulpit to political purposes." So the war and reconstruction experiences solidified a Methodist version of a doctrine widely shared across southern Protestantism, that of the spirituality of the church, the legacy of its "official" policy of neutrality toward slavery.[19] Its antipolitical political creed posited southern purity and orthodoxy in contrast to northern prostitution and heresy. One southern apologist illustrated (and critiqued) the latter with resolutions of the wartime MEC conferences, documenting some thirty-two "teachings," a few of which illustrate what the South would increasingly construe as the character and commitments of northern Methodism:[20]

1. That the Church is the guardian of the nation....

3. That she has the right to dictate the duty and polity of the Government....

6. That the General Government is under obligations to the M.E. Church.

7. That it is to the interest of the Government that the M.E. Church be established throughout the South....

10. That there be perfect political, social and ecclesiastical equality of the races.

11. That the right of the negroes to all the privileges of citizenship is a *divine right*....

13. That the supremacy of negroes over white people in the South is to the interest of the Government....

17. That God is a partisan in the war and that it is just and holy on the part of the North....

32. That we rejoice in the triumph of our principles by means of fire and sword.

By contrast, as the Mississippi Conference resolved, the southern church was/is to "Preach Christ and him crucified. Do not preach politics. You have no commission to preach politics."[21] The politically fervid atmosphere of southern conferences continued into Reconstruction sustaining (or criticizing) MEC efforts on behalf of the freed slaves and worrying as well over efforts by the AME and AMEZ. Early in the war, some Methodists believed independence would give the South, under religious leadership, the opportunity to carry through on the Christianization of the peculiar institution, as Capers and company had hoped.[22] Defeat dissolved the necessity of championing or redeeming slavery. Survival was challenge enough: "And Are We Yet Alive." Fittingly, the MECS had moved that hymn, when publishing its hymnal in 1847, from its prior location under "Christian Fellowship" and placed it first (#272) among seven conference hymns and among three for "Opening Conference."[23] The MECS sang that hymn at its next General Conference (1850). It would be that church's theme song for the next decade as it construed what had been the war and slavery experiences into a civil religion of the lost cause.

Northern War Fervor

If surrender and emancipation ended the MECS's burden of slavery and burdened it with the "lost cause," secession and war ended the necessity for the MEC to temper critique of slavery so as to hold onto its southern borders. And the war furthered northern Methodism's (UBC, EA, MPC, MEC) embrace of the Protestant crusade to Christianize America. Indeed, if one date and one action might be taken to symbolize Methodism's inclusion within the Protestant establishment, it might well be Lincoln's response and General Conference's (MEC's) 1864 formal declaration to Lincoln of its patriotism, support for the war, and endorsement of the Emancipation Proclamation (Sources 1864b). General Conference took that action under the "Stars and Stripes," which it decreed by unanimous and rising vote would fly over its entire session. Northern conferences of the UBC were no less resolute in their commitment to the cause of liberty and those fighting on its behalf (Sources 1864c). Indeed, from the outbreak of the war, northern conferences brought the flag into their sessions, encouraged the war effort and Methodist participation therein, supported chaplains, demanded stronger national action on slavery, and denounced the secessionists.[24] To sustain the Methodist peoples in the Union cause, preachers, editors, and bishops articulated a theology of the nation, views of providence, and a social ethic that reworked the Wesleyan doctrines and discipline into a civil religion.

In the North as in the South, Methodists experienced opposition or indifference to the "righteous" patriotic banner, especially in the border conferences. As we noted in the last chapter, several had responded vehemently to the 1860 new disciplinary chapter on slavery, Philadelphia demanding repeal, Baltimore dividing. Kentucky and Missouri, with a small MEC and a large MECS population, proved a religious as well as military battleground. In Kentucky, the MECS conference tilted toward the Union cause, and some eighteen preachers eventually withdrew and joined the MEC. Southern Methodists in Missouri tilted toward the Confederacy and harassed preachers of the MEC until northern troops secured the state within the Union and northern Methodists could return the favor. There, too, members and preachers switched into the MEC.[25] In Ohio, opponents of the war, southern sympathizers, supporters of the peace Democrats (specifically the gubernatorial efforts of former congressman Clement L. Vallandigham), and resisters to the abolitionist cause coalesced into a Copperhead church. Calling itself the Christian Union, it survived the war as a holiness denomination, the Churches of Christ in Christian Union. However, it showed its true colors in the 1864 call for its organizing convention, which pledged "the pure and peaceable Gospel of Christ can be preached, unmixed with politics, fanaticism, or other foreign matter." Centered in Ohio but drawing some adherence also in southern Illinois, the Christian Union claimed 180 congregations by 1865, much of its membership and leadership drawn out of the MEC.[26]

The outbreak of war, however, brought much of the MEC, MPC, EA, and UBC around to support of the Union, rallied by antislavery editors placed at the helm of the *Christian Advocate* (Edward Thompson) and the *Central Christian Advocate* (Charles Elliott) by the 1860 General Conference. Gilbert Haven (1821–80) assumed the editorship of *Zion's Herald* only after the war but throughout contributed to it, to the New York paper, and to the widely read *Independent* columns, essays, and sermons championing the war as God's cause, indeed as a millennial mandate, to cleanse nation (and church) of the sin of slavery (see his appeal in his very first issue, to which we return in the next chapter, Sources 1867a). Bishop Matthew Simpson, a friend and confidant of Lincoln and eulogist at his Springfield funeral, spoke frequently and eloquently on behalf of the nation and national unity, against slavery, for the war as divinely commissioned, and in the effort to raise money for the Union cause (Sources 1864e). In sermons and exhortations, waving a "battle-torn flag," he evangelized for patriotism, turned revivalism political, elicited camp-meeting fervor, and brought convictions and conversions.[27] Many northern Methodists swung during the war into crusade mentality. Conferences passed patriotic resolutions, administered oaths to themselves and their probationers, and called for days of national fasting and prayer. The Philadelphia Conference virtually reversed its actions of the prior year, made loyalty a disciplinary imperative, and required an affirmative to an additional ordination question: "Are you in favor of sustaining the Union, the Government and the Constitution of the United States against the present rebellion?" Then it adopted the "Report of the Committee on the State of the Country," which denounced the "unjust and wicked rebellion" and extended a similar oath of loyalty to all conference members.[28]

Two years later, the Philadelphia Conference instructed "the Presiding Elders . . . not to employ as supplies, any person who is either disloyal or pro-slavery." It reaffirmed previous stands of loyalty, supported the war effort, declared its loyalty to the government and the Constitution, urged it as "a religious duty not to speak evil of ministers and magistrates," and denounced slavery as against the law of God and the principles of the Revolution. Philadelphia then endorsed emancipation and rescinded its action of 1861 calling for repeal of the "New Chapter."[29] The 1863 Newark Conference featured a flag-raising service among its six enumerated public services, heard R. B. Yard, chaplain of the First New Jersey Regiment, declare, "Our soldiers are grieved at every evidence of disloyalty at home," and closed one session singing "My Country, 'tis of Thee." It also passed a resolution requiring the presiding elders, when presenting "candidates for admission on trial, to state whether or not these candidates are loyal to the government of this country." It affirmed the "Report of the Committee on the State of the Country," with a page and a half of whereases, the first of which declared, "That unconditional and uncompromising loyalty to the principles and constituted forms of our republican government, is the duty of all Christian people."[30] The 1863 meeting of the National Association of Local Preachers of The Methodist Episcopal Church passed declarations of loyalty "to the Discipline and Government of the Methodist Episcopal Church," to the "Constitution and laws of the United States," and to "the recognized rulers of our nation and the perpetuity of our National Union."[31]

The 1864 General Conference (MEC) heard Bishop Thomas A. Morris preach on the spirit of Methodism. Beginning ten affirmations with "The Spirit of Methodism is … ," Morris characterized Methodism as a church committed to American society, capitalism, progress, and the Union. Methodism's spirit? The spirit of truth, the spirit of revival, the spirit of enterprise, the spirit of sacrifice, the spirit of progress, the spirit of improvement, the spirit of loyalty to the civil government, the spirit of patriotism, the spirit of liberty, and the spirit of liberality.[32] Under just such commitments, General Conference (MEC) joined other Protestant denominations in petitioning Congress to amend the preamble of the Constitution to affirm God's governance of the country:

> We, the people of the United States, humbly acknowledging Almighty God as the source of all authority and power in civil government, the Lord Jesus Christ as the Ruler among the nations, his revealed will as the supreme law of the land, in order to constitute a Christian government, and in order to form a more perfect union. . . .

General Conference's action, in response to its Committee on the State of the Country, issued a series of resolutions calling for recognition of God in the Constitution and amendment of the Constitution to end slavery. It also began, belatedly, the process of revising the General Rules so that holding, buying, or selling slaves would be a bar to church membership.[33]

Northern conferences of the UBC, for instance, that of Miami (Ohio), passed similar statements calling for the nation to carry through on the war effort, end the rebellion, and complete the overthrow of slavery with constitutional guarantees of freedom (Sources 1864c).[34] Similarly, having lost much of its southern and slavery-oriented territory just prior to the Civil War, as we noted in the last chapter, Methodist Protestantism expressed its support in its 1862 General Conference for the Emancipation Proclamation and its repudiation of disloyalty to the Union cause.[35]

Methodist laity responded to such challenges and volunteered in record numbers, perhaps some 125,000 all told.[36] So did the preachers, both as chaplains and as soldiers. One regiment, the Seventy-third Illinois, even earned the designation "the preacher regiment" because of the number therein, the result of the mobilizing efforts of one minister, James Jaquess.[37] An Ohio minister, Charles C. McCabe (1836–1906), recruited thousands, his sermons producing the 122nd Ohio Regiment, for which he then served as chaplain. Known as the "singing chaplain," he was captured, incarcerated in the Libby Prison in Richmond, and freed in a prisoner exchange but not before teaching other prisoners "The Battle Hymn of the Republic." Another recruiter-minister from Ohio, Granville Moody, accepted command of the 74th Ohio Regiment, preaching as well as leading and becoming known as the "gallant fighting preacher."[38]

Union Chaplains: Ordained and Lay

Methodists constituted the largest chaplains' cohort within the Union armies, as on the Confederate side. Of the 2,154 regimental chaplains, 38 percent were Methodist. The next largest confessional contribution came from Presbyterians at 17 percent.[39] The role was not much better initially envisioned on the Union side; both armies gave way to desultory customs, not statutes, concerning chaplains. However, President Lincoln was clearer than Jefferson Davis on their necessity, writing seven Washington ministers as war loomed and asking that they serve as military hospital chaplains. And Congress and the War Department followed through with acts and directives establishing the office. Among the requisites were ordination and testimonials of "present good standing with a recommendation for his appointment as an army Chaplain from some authorized ecclesiastical body, or not less than five accredited ministers belonging to said denomination."[40]

Union chaplains worked every bit as ecumenically as their southern counterparts, partly aided by, partly competing with the U.S. Christian Commission. Founded in 1861 by the Young Men's Christian Association (YMCA) as a religious counterpart to another relief organization, the U.S. Sanitary Commission, and endorsed by a YMCA-called convention of chaplains, the interdenominational Christian Commission intended to extend the revivalistic triumphs of the 1857–58 "businessmen's awakening" into the northern armies. With strong lay leadership, aggressive fund-raising, business-like revivalistic method, and rhetoric of masculine Christianity, the Christian Commission rallied northern laymen through its network of YMCA chapters to the cause of evangelizing the troops. The Christian Commission, effectively organized on both its recruitment and its deployment ends, placed its lay volunteers in the camps, in hospitals, and toward the front, each equipped with a handbook of duties and regulations and wearing a badge to signify his commission. Ministering to spirit and body and serving six-week stints, the lay volunteers circulated tracts, Bibles, and Scripture cards; cared for the dying, wounded, and lonely men; distributed stamps, envelopes, and stationery; wrote letters for soldiers; and led prayer meetings in "chapel tents" and YMCA rooms. By war's end the Christian Commission had deployed some 5,000 volunteers, handed out 2.5 million publications, preached about 50,000 sermons, and conducted 75,000 prayer meetings. The Christian Commission enjoyed the support of President Lincoln and General Grant, and the soldiers in diaries and letters appreciatively noted its ministrations. And with such endorsement, particularly that of Grant, the commission played important roles in a revival that broke out in the Union armies in late 1863 and continued to 1865, a revival that followed very bloody battles.[41]

The number and percentage of Methodists working within the Christian Commission and instrumental in these revivals are hard to calculate. Its volunteers included 458 MEC ministers, and the *Advocates* reported on its work. It enjoyed the backing of key Methodists, among them especially Bishop Edmund S. Janes (1807–76). Elected to the episcopacy in 1844, Janes served as one of the twelve-member commission and one of four clergy on it. Along with two other commissioners, he issued the first Circular (November 16, 1861) and as a member of the executive committee of five published the Plan of Operations. The commission sent him to Washington to negotiate with the government on its behalf, and he received from Edwin M. Stanton, secretary of war, a handwritten authorization of access for the Christian Commission "for the performance of their religious and benevolent purposes in the armies of the United States, and in the forts, garrisons, and camps, and military posts." Bishop Matthew Simpson (1811–84) also became part of the commission, delivering one of the plenary addresses at its 1863 meeting, participating with four other trustees in closing down its work, and summarizing its accomplishments before the House of Representatives.[42] Simpson also figured in another negotiation with Edwin Stanton, namely, that with Bishop E. R. Ames, which empowered the MEC to take over confiscated MECS churches. Charles McCabe, after release from prison, labored for the commission in fund-raising, established a personal goal of $250,000, and perfected patterns of promotion that would later transform denominational practice. Methodist laity, however, along with laity from other Protestant denominations in the Christian Commission, led the revivals in the northern armies, converting between 100,000 and 200,000 men. Impressive revivals, a veritable "pentecostal season," broke out in 1864 and continued till war's end in the Union armies in Virginia and Tennessee and within the army marching south with Sherman. Sherman's troops took Charleston "singing Methodist hymns."[43]

Northern Methodist Women and the War

Although it celebrated male religiosity, the Christian Commission and its relief effort rival, the U.S. Sanitary Commission (USSC), depended on the involvement of women, sometimes in volunteer roles, sometimes in paid capacity, sometimes in auxiliaries, sometimes in leadership posts within, always for their labor and resources. Black women, excluded from these organizations, formed their own, a Colored Women's Sanitary Commission (Philadelphia). Soldiers' Aid societies emerged spontaneously to gather supplies, roll bandages, collect foodstuff, prepare soldiers' wardrobes, visit the wounded, and conduct fairs and teas as fund-raisers. With thousands of such emerging, a number of prominent New York women established in 1861 a coordinating agency, the Woman's

Central Relief Association (WCRA), which was absorbed by and worked in tension with and in collaboration with the USSC. Male-female and local-national tensions surfaced also as the War Department pressed for efficiency, coordination, and uniformity. Local ladies' aid societies often preferred to direct their efforts and provisions toward their own military spouses, sons, and neighbors and to avoid the growing bureaucracy, increased profiteering, and outright corruption. Suspicions of the USSC led some ladies' aid societies to align with the Christian Commission.

Fund-raising teas and fairs, which raised $100,000 in Chicago, $146,000 in Boston, $280,000 in Cincinnati, $320,000 in Pittsburgh, and $2 million in New York City, elicited and displayed northern patriotism at a point when self-doubt about and outright opposition to the war had emerged. They required considerable planning, organization, publicity, and follow-through—savvy that would thereafter be put to good use within northern Methodism. They constituted a public realm within which women held sway and dramatized their civic and patriotic commitments. And the fairs functioned to bring together women across class and religious lines. Women claimed and men could but observe "mothering" responsibilities and duties quite beyond the domestic sphere.[44]

Even more civic "mothering" responsibilities were exercised within the male realm of the military by women who volunteered as nurses, cooks, or laundresses. Some nine thousand earned the status and pension of "nurse," a role and title reserved for upper-class white women and for men. Lower-class and Black women, including Methodists whose names and efforts often went undocumented, worked in hospitals and camps without such recognition. Recruiting nurses, some paid, many volunteer, were the noted reformer Dorothea Dix and the WCRA, headed by Dr. Elizabeth Blackwell, the first U.S. woman to hold a medical degree. Whether paid or volunteer, in nursing or other roles, women confronting the horrors, the carnage, and the suffering and participating in the very masculine endeavor of war found it prudent to accent their responsibilities as familial and mothering, as self-sacrificial and morally pure, and as appropriately domestic and respectable. They cared for the "boys," their boys. This empowerment by enlarging the domestic sphere had its limits. Women in all capacities worked within hierarchical military and hospital command structures. Authority and privilege adhered strictly to rules of race and gender, with Black women at the bottom.[45] Such racist attitudes help explain why African Americans had sought and continued to seek separate religious institutions.

Homes for Children and the Aged: A Wesleyan Recovery

The Civil War created other urgent demands for care and opportunities for caring than those expended on the military. Children were orphaned or left homeless by the war's mass killings and also by more routine loss of parents through abandonment, illness, and death. Older adults, too, as we note below, lost or outlived the family safety-net support system. President Abraham Lincoln summoned Americans in his second inaugural address "to care for him who shall have born the battle, for his widow and his orphan." In response, Methodists established, immediately and over several decades, Wesley-like institutions capable of sustained care. (This section, in tracing these war-stimulated initiatives, ranges beyond the temporal boundaries of the chapter.)

Orphanages

German Americans rapidly filling up the Midwest reacted first to the command and the crisis. Churches in the mother country had been building and supporting orphanages for more than a century. Since the early 1850s, Pastor William Ahrens had been urging German Methodists in America to open a *Waisenhaus* (orphanage) as the Methodist Conference in Germany had already done. Ahrens's appeals in the German Methodist newspaper, *Christliche Apologete*, bore fruit in 1864 when two German conferences opened orphanages, one on a farm near Berea, Ohio, and another in Warrenton, Missouri, to shelter Civil War and other orphans. These homes were taken into the hearts of German Methodists, who supported them well.[46] Similarly, the Evangelical Association responded to the wartime challenge and established an orphans' asylum. An offer of one hundred acres of Ohio land added to the enthusiasm for the project, and Ebenezer Orphan Home opened in Flat Rock, Ohio, in 1866.[47]

Also in 1866 a Home for Colored Orphans was founded in New Orleans by the two-year-old Black MEC Mississippi Mission Conference (see next section on Black conferences). The white superintendent, John P. Newman, sent to oversee northern Methodism's ministry among ex-slaves in Mississippi, Louisiana, and Texas, energetically supported the project. A house was rented in the city of New Orleans and opened to needy Black children in a few months. Support for a permanent home came from a wealthy Methodist, William Gilbert, owner of the Gilbert Clock Company of Winsted, Connecticut, who gave the Freedmen's Aid Society of the MEC forty thousand dollars to establish a home and school for children of Black soldiers who fought for the Union. This lead gift, supplemented by grants from the federal Freedmen's Bureau, the state of Louisiana, and other private donors recruited by Newman, enabled the managers in 1869 to purchase a 1,700-acre sugar plantation at Baldwin, Louisiana, hoping to make the home self-supporting. Ten acres surrounding the large brick mansion were reserved for the use of the hundred or so children and their matron. A schoolhouse was erected on the premises by the Freedmen's Bureau, and teachers for the home's more than one hundred "clean, obedient, cheerful and happy" children were supplied by the church's Freedmen's Aid Society.[48] Daily chapel services, weekly prayer meetings, and a Sunday school provided religious nurture.[49]

Soon after the Civil War, southern Methodists also formed institutions for children orphaned by the war and by poverty. In 1869 a Georgia pastor, Jesse Boring, began a churchwide campaign to build Methodist orphanages across the South.[50] The 1870 General Conference of the MECS endorsed Boring's plan and recommended each annual conference move as quickly as possible to establish an orphanage.[51] Orphanages were established almost immediately by the North and South Georgia and Kentucky Conferences in the early 1870s; other conferences followed their lead in the 1880s. The largest growth in orphanage building by southern Methodists came after Boring's death in 1890. By 1900 every MECS conference had established at least one orphanage, fourteen in all, a fitting tribute to Boring's vision.[52]

Methodist women in San Francisco opened a home for Chinese children (Gum Moon Home) in 1870. The Woman's Missionary Society of the Pacific Coast, later the national Woman's Home Missionary Society, provided help and support for the work with finances and with volunteer workers. Shelter was provided for thirty to forty girls ranging in age from two to eighteen. A day school program for more than a hundred children was begun. Once each month mothers met at the home, thus providing important contact for children, placed in the home by impoverished families, with their parents.[53]

In these caring initiatives, Methodists responded to crises. In so doing, they reclaimed an important aspect of the Wesleyan heritage, engaged denominational and women's organizations, created institutions that in many cases continue to the present, and laid foundations for an expanded social welfare role for the church. First in orphanages, then in homes for the aged, and eventually in hospitals, Methodists would show the concern for persons in extreme need after the fashion of John Wesley. Prison ministry, after all, lay at the very foundations of the Wesleyan movement, and over his career, Wesley found ways to dispense medicines and medical advice and to care for poor, needy, and aged persons. His popular *Primitive Physic*, a family medical manual, expressed and conveyed his concern for health and health care.[54]

Both the Civil War and the extraordinary societal changes that followed—with the nation's dramatic urban expansion, unregulated factories, massive immigration from abroad, extraordinary exodus of African Americans from south to north, and growing slums—produced great vulnerabilities for families and children and little in the way of safety nets. For children after a parent's death or during a serious illness, church-related orphanages appeared to be the answer, as state and local governments were slow to develop caring agencies. Methodists, on the other hand, viewed orphanages as a matter of Christian duty, a calling over which to take religious pride, and a ministry of organization and order for which they were well prepared by wartime benevolent activities.

The denominational initiative by the MECS we have already noted. In the urban East Methodist women assumed much of the responsibility in the formation of children's homes.[55] When a delegation of them visited a Philadelphia jail to distribute religious tracts in 1873, they were shocked to find dozens of young children behind bars, awaiting trial in grim cells because they had no bail money or because their parents could not be located. These women reacted in customary Methodist fashion. They formed a committee to correct this injustice and garnered a lead gift of ten thousand dollars in 1874. Ellen Simpson, wife of the church's most visible and powerful bishop and Lincoln confidant, helped mobilize the energy to build the best known of the nineteenth-century Methodist homes for children, The Methodist Episcopal Orphanage in Philadelphia.[56]

The women had a clearly defined, if not easily attained, mission in mind: to open a home

> where orphan children may be received and provided with wholesome nourishment, may be comfortably clad, attended in sickness, taught the rudiments of an English education, may have their moral character carefully developed and habits of regularity and industry established, so that they may become useful members of society.

They vowed to raise the necessary funds and to manage the home not only from their parlors, but to do much of the work involved in its day-to-day operation. Managers were expected to visit the home several times a week to instruct the children, to take them on trips, to sew clothing, and to assist the house parents.[57]

The orphanage opened in 1879 with six "fatherless boys." Three years later the children and staff moved into a renovated mansion on a twenty-acre suburban site donated by a prominent Methodist Civil War hero, Colonel Joseph M. Bennett. A new $90,000 stone building with accommodations for two hundred children was completed and dedicated debt-free in 1889. Churches in the Philadelphia area formed Orphanage Guilds, and Sunday schools took a special offering at Christmas to lend continuing support. When Mrs. Simpson died in 1897, she left a well-established orphanage with state-of-the-art buildings, a $100,000 endowment, and more than one hundred children in residence.[58]

On similar interventions, Methodists founded homes for wayward children in Baltimore (1873), in New York (1885), in Chicago (1889), in Seward, Alaska (1890), in Oakland, California (1892), in Fall River, Massachusetts (1893), in San Francisco (1897), and in Washington, D.C. (1898). After its founding in 1882, the Woman's Home Missionary Society (WHMS; treated in chapter 11) also began building a network of child care facilities. The gift of 160 acres of land in rural York, Nebraska, along with a pledge of $10,000 from town citizens in 1890, led to one of the earliest—Mothers' Jewels Home for Children. Believing a farming community was the right environment for needy and homeless children, the WHMS accepted the gift and went to work. Within a few months the farm housed forty children, and the staff began to place additional children in foster homes nearby.[59] Mothers' Jewels Home became an important project for the WHMS and helped to create interest in homes for children across the church. By 1916 the WHMS supervised a dozen such homes.

Methodist women in the North were alerted in the early 1870s to the plight of southern Black children by Jennie Culver Hartzell, wife of Joseph C. Hartzell, later a bishop but then pastor of the largest white congregation in New Orleans. She led the Woman's Home Missionary Society of the MEC to organize, support, and manage six residential homes for Black children in the South in the years following its organization in 1882.[60] A few Methodist institutions crossed the color line in the name of charity at a time when most American orphanages were rigidly segregated. Child savers responded with a mixture of Christian concern and racial prejudice. The New England Home for Little Wanderers was one of the first private charities to admit Black children on a more or less equal basis with whites. Though the New England Home was founded for Civil War and immigrant orphans, "little contrabands" from the South were also welcomed.[61]

Early in the new century southern Methodist women undertook extensive efforts on behalf of children. They started local groups for children of all ages. They designated officers to direct the work, encouraged children to collect funds for both home and foreign missions, and prepared special literature for their use. The women themselves undertook special studies on children. In 1912, more than 100,000 pieces of written material went to the local auxiliaries on child welfare, including such topics as education, child labor, recreation, health, and other social issues affecting the children and their families, the study subject for the year.[62] Their special concern for children had led them to institute orphanages, kindergartens, schools, and settlement houses and inclined them to support unpopular causes such as child labor laws. In 1896 the society established a home for orphaned children in Greeneville, Tennessee. A year later, Mrs. E. E. Wiley, the vice president for the WHMS, reported that the institution housed twenty children, ranging in age from eighteen months to nine years. In addition to being provided with housing, "the girls are taught to sew, cook, and keep house generally... the boys do all the outside work and the inside too when needed." By 1909 the home, then called Holston Industrial School, had ninety residents.[63]

The United Brethren's first orphanage opened in 1903 on a farm near Quincy, Pennsylvania. Methodist Protestant women opened a home for children in an abandoned school building in Denton, North Carolina, in 1910. Donation of a large property in nearby High Point and an offer to pay half the cost of a new building led the women to move their home to High Point, North Carolina, three years later and to rename it Methodist Protestant Children's Home.[64]

Orphanages typically limited admissions to children whose problem was poverty and who did not have serious behavioral or disability problems.[65] Many were "half orphans," children who had one living parent unable to provide for them and who otherwise would have entered the workhouse or become "little wanderers" on their own. Managers viewed their institutions as homes and stressed the "homelike" quality of their institutions in their reports. While most orphanage managers hoped to remove poor children permanently from their homes, other managers tried to serve as temporary caretakers of children until they could be restored to their families. This latter view triumphed in the twentieth century.

Though men were recruited as donors and trustees, women managed the daily operations and usually had some say in making major policy decisions. Since an entire staff might consist of a matron or superintendent and just one or two other workers, institutions depended on volunteer women board members, who spent large amounts of time in their orphanages caring for the children. Managers were also constantly active raising funds. Poorer orphanages had to find money just to feed their children, while better-funded systems tried to raise money for long-term endowments and larger and better buildings. Donations from churches were the single most important sources of income. Concerts, auctions, and fairs that gave their profits to orphanages were also common fund-raisers by the 1870s. Other sources of funding—such as dues, gifts, and bequests from individuals, and in some cases board money from parents—were crucial. Since a majority of orphans had at least one living parent, many orphanages urged surviving parents to pay a small amount toward their children's board. Managers saw even partial board payments made by parents as more than mere financial help for the orphanages. Such payments also strengthened bonds between children and their families. Donors also gave goods such as food, clothing, furniture, coal, books, and toys.

These children's homes enjoyed great support across the several Methodist denominations. As the turn of the twentieth century approached, dozens of new orphanages opened almost every year, and existing orphanages upgraded their dormitories and expanded educational and recreational facilities. But Methodism's passion for building orphanages cooled after 1910, and from 1920 to 1940 there was an actual decrease in numbers as some institutions closed their doors or modified their mission.

Homes for the Aged

The churches' program for elder care also blossomed in the years following the Civil War. Methodist women in Philadelphia, led by Jane Henry and Ellen Simpson (noted above for her initiative in the orphanage cause), had united to aid sick and wounded soldiers during the Civil War. At war's end the women pledged to continue their work in a new way by establishing a home for the aged. In 1867 the women purchased a large townhouse and selected a dozen needy women and men, including one couple, to make it their home. In the preindustrial age, such a venture would not have been needed as older adults were too few in number, too powerful, and too immersed in family support to require substantial public or private support systems. As the nineteenth century progressed, the status of older adults radically altered. Changes in family structure, religious belief, labor force participation, occupational opportunities, as well as advances in medicine and technology separated older adults from their traditional sphere and accepted patterns of life. Methodist thinking about older adults gradually appreciated this transformation and grasped the imperative of providing something other than the disdained poorhouse for elder care.[66]

By 1870, the Philadelphia women oversaw a new three-story brownstone with accommodations for one hundred guests, an infirmary, and a chapel "with stained glass windows and upholstered seats," the largest facility for the aged in the city of Philadelphia at the time. The next year the editor of *Ladies' Repository* published a feature article on the home, complete with an engraving of the handsome building, "hoping that in many other cities, the women of our Church will catch the inspiration to go and do likewise."[67] Managers and supporters of the Philadelphia home understood the importance of their benevolent institution. Mrs. H. H. Hubbert, corresponding secretary, stated in her 1891 annual report: "Not only do we in Philadelphia appreciate this resting-place for the aged, but constantly we have visitors from distant cities who have read of it, or heard from others, and come to see for themselves, in order that they may learn the better to plan for like work in their own localities."[68] Outgrowing its facilities, Simpson House, as the home came to be called, moved to a new suburban campus overlooking Philadelphia's Fairmount Park in 1898, and a state-of-the-art building with accommodations for 150, featuring central heating, electric lights, and an elevator, was completed two years later.[69]

Homes for the aged sprang up in other cities as MEC women followed the editor's advice—in Baltimore (1868), New Haven (1874), Washington, D.C. (1889), and Chicago (1890). The Woman's Home Missionary Society began building a network of homes for retired missionaries and deaconesses. Best known and earliest was the Bancroft-Taylor Rest Home in Ocean Grove, New Jersey, which opened in 1896. MPC women organized a home for the aged in Westminster, Maryland, in 1895.

A different, although equally significant, pattern occurred in the antebellum South, where few private homes for the aged were established, the poorhouse continued to be the primary shelter for impoverished older adults, and only whites were accommodated. Older slaves remained the responsibility of their owners. And the South had few immigrants, a population housed in northern poorhouses. After the Civil War, though, existing poorhouses filled with ex-slaves. Southern counties and cities moved quickly to establish two separate—and totally segregated—poorhouses. This dual system of poorhouses, along with homes for Confederate veterans and their spouses, may have alleviated the need for an extensive system of private, often church-related, homes for the aged. The southern poorhouse for Black citizens was equivalent to the northern poorhouse, especially after the development of private homes for the aged in the cities of the Northeast. With its high death rates, limited budget, and meager provisions, it was intended to shelter the South's most despised and impoverished citizens—and to warn away others who were considering applying for such assistance. In contrast poorhouses for white citizens were portrayed as suitable residences for upstanding, although penniless, people.[70]

In time, African American communities, rejected by the charitable institutions formed by white elites, organized their own institutions to care for needy older adults. As early as 1845, Stephen Smith, a local preacher and philanthropist in the AME Church, founded a Home for Aged and Infirm Colored People in Philadelphia.[71] Methodists in two of the new all-Black MEC annual conferences (see next section on their organization, after 1864) founded homes for the aged. The first residential care program for aged racial minority persons in the Methodist tradition had its beginning when the pastor of Sharp Street MEC, Baltimore, Nathaniel M. Carroll, conceived the idea that there should be a home to care for indigent Black persons in his city. When Mrs. Matilda Wilson, a member of his congregation, offered her home in 1868, Pastor Carroll's dream became a reality. Two years later the Washington Conference purchased larger quarters for their new home, adopted a constitution in 1886, and secured the first charter in 1893 when eighteen guests received care.[72] The Black conference in Louisiana opened a home for the aged in New Orleans in 1878. As the home expanded, new facilities were needed, and in 1887 Mr. Lafon gave twelve lots in the city for a new home.[73]

Women of several EA churches in Philadelphia met jointly to plan for a home for the aged in the spring of 1888. In August the German Home Society for Members of the Evangelical Association of North America in the City of Philadelphia was founded, incorporated, and trustees elected. In the spring of 1889 the first two *insassen* (inmates) arrived; the home flourished, and by the end of the first year of operation, the "inmate" population had grown to twelve and a large mansion in a fashionable neighborhood had been purchased and renovated. Though the Evangelical General Conference in 1903 resolved to establish additional homes for the aged, the offer of the Pfeiffer family to bequeath their family home in Cedar Falls, Iowa, and the promise of a generous cash gift led to the establishment of the denomination's second elder care facility, Western Old People's Home in 1911. In 1910 the Central Pennsylvania Conference of the United Evangelical Church (UEC) took steps toward the founding of a home for older people. Five years later property was acquired in Lewisburg, and the first building was dedicated in 1916.

The UBC began elder care institutions in 1893 when a retired minister, Z. A. Colestock, offered his home in Mechanicsburg, Pennsylvania, for use as a home for the aged. In 1913 the home moved to a farm near Quincy, Pennsylvania, to join the denomination's orphanage, which had opened in 1903. It was in 1913 also that UBC leaders contracted with the leaders of a dwindling Shaker settlement in southwestern (near Lebanon) Ohio to purchase four thousand acres of land. On a part of this property the Otterbein Home was built.

Annual reports depicted the new church homes as far more than poorhouses. They had become havens that any older Methodist could call "home." To rescue older adults from poverty was not sufficient if the church's new institutions then allowed them to suffer the burden of age. Instead, they had to prove they could provide a healthy, happier atmosphere for their charges. Churchwomen boasted that they provided warm rooms to sit in, comfortable beds to sleep in, wholesome food to eat, a chapel to go to, and plenty of devotional papers, magazines, and books to read. Managers claimed their homes supplied the warmth and companionship of the missing family. "It is, in its every appointment, A Home," said the superintendent of the Philadelphia home proudly in her 1891 report. The homes also stressed the value of a religious atmosphere. Daily Bible readings, weekly preaching services, monthly Communion services, and consultations with a pastor linked residents to their former church life.[74]

The homes accommodated men as well as women (unlike antebellum institutions) and married couples, too, but with rigorous admissions standards. In 1891 the Philadelphia Home admitted only fifteen of twenty-three applicants, and in 1892 only twelve of twenty-two. The homes required applicants to be church members in good standing, and religious leaders of the community, along with other "respectable persons," had to approve of their character. In some instances, this was further verified by a visiting committee that investigated the candidate.[75] Only later did Methodists view their homes for the aged as expressions of a sense of responsibility for the larger community.

Along with certificates attesting to their character, applicants had to be unable to support themselves, sometimes pay an admission fee, sign all property over to the institution, agree to obey all rules set by the matron, and be free from any incurable physical or mental disease. These institutions were not to be hospitals. In most cases, a doctor's examination was required before admittance to ensure that the applicant had no incurable disease. If residents became senile, they were often removed to the almshouse or hospital so that they would not disturb the tranquility of the "family." The managers wanted their institutions to be homes, not shelters for mentally ill or dying persons.

The location of the homes added to this rejuvenating process. During the last quarter of the nineteenth century, many urban institutions moved to less populated suburban sections of the cities. These new locations allowed the older adults to escape the noise and tensions of the city as well as to breathe the country's fresher air. The new, healthier environment was not directed at poverty-stricken people alone. If persons, through age, became old and therefore sick, they too needed the institutionalized care that the homes provided. The Methodist Home for the Aged in Philadelphia added a boarding house to the establishment in 1876, what we would call a nursing home.[76]

Most older Methodists, by reason of age alone and not wealth, became candidates for the care provided by these homes. Once "over the hill," they automatically became sickly and dependent. In response to this public conception of older adults, homes for the aged expanded their goals as well as their appeal. No longer alternatives to the almshouse, they had developed into substitutes for the family, church, and hospital. Based on the definition of old age as a disease, they then carefully quarantined their guests to preserve their dissipating strength and to guard them against the harmful effects of youthful society. By the beginning of the twentieth century, they would present themselves to the public not as mere residences for older folks, but as modern medical establishments especially equipped to deal with "the problem of old age."

The long shadow of the poorhouse was instrumental in the establishment of numerous homes for the aged. For urban elites who founded these homes and devised their rules and regulations, the poorhouse seemed an unjust end for hardworking, although impoverished elders. In committing both their finances and their time, the founders of homes for the aged expressed the belief that the poorhouse posed a real threat to dignified older age. The "guests" in the church homes, however, were limited to "worthy" Methodists who possessed the same ethnic background as the founders. By requiring high entrance fees and certificates of correct moral standing, the developers of church homes intentionally excluded the "less deserving" of needy older people. For those most likely to be impoverished, therefore, these homes had little meaning. For single and widowed women without children, immigrants who had arrived in the U.S. since the Civil War, and impoverished African Americans who gained no property as slaves and little as sharecroppers, the poorhouse remained a harsh reality.

Black Annual Conferences and the MEC's Southern Mission

With the end of the Civil War and the abolition of slavery in sight, the MEC acted to segment African Americans into separate conferences but *to grant them full clergy rights*. Baltimore African Americans had petitioned General Conference for such in 1848 and 1856 and reiterated the request in 1864. Although in one sense an empowering move, the legislation effectively made segregation denominational policy and did so in the face of eloquent challenges by Christian abolitionists like Gilbert Haven that the church model inclusivism, equality, and freedom in its organization, life, and work. Tellingly the new policy came with the endorsement of border conferences.[77] The 1864 Philadelphia Conference passed a supporting resolution calling for the bishops and presiding elders to organize "our colored people into district Circuits . . . with a view of furnishing them with ministerial service by preachers of their own color." So did the other conference with a substantial Black membership, Baltimore. In response, General Conference authorized the bishops "to organize among our colored ministers, for the benefit of our colored members and population, Mission Conferences."[78] The 1864 authorization, though conferring ordination and conference membership, limited the prerogatives for the new conferences, conferring on them "all the powers of other annual conferences, except a representation in the General Conference, a division of the proceeds of the Book Concern, and voting upon any constitutional question."[79]

Delaware and Washington Conferences were the first to be established. Bishop Edmund Janes, who presided over the former's organizing session, wrote of a "very pleasant" meeting with "my colored brothers—some thirty of them" and termed it "a grand beginning of good things to the poor colored people."[80] The Washington Conference, convened by Bishop Levi Scott, included Sharp Street (1802) and eight other station churches and circuits of the Baltimore area, organized into the Chesapeake District. Its second district, Potomac, gathered together twelve circuits and stations in the D.C., northern Virginia, and outer Maryland areas. Conscious of its mandate to care for the interests of Black Methodism, it published its *Minutes* from the start, began church extension efforts (doubling in three years, more than tripling in ten), and assumed responsibility for the various institutions and benevolent causes, including that of education. It made an early commitment to the Centenary Biblical Institute (later Morgan College and eventually Morgan State), founded in 1867, which enjoyed as well the support of the Baltimore Conference and whose purposes included education of ministers and teachers.[81]

In adopting the plan for African American "mission" conferences, MEC General Conference had looked beyond its own Black membership to that of the MECS. Already cooperating with other Protestants in missionary and relief organizations in the South and mindful of the challenges in educating and equipping freed slaves for citizenship and economic self-sufficiency, the MEC envisioned southern African Americans as a new field for evangelism and Black conferences as the harvest instrument. Responding to the challenge, as we shall see in the next chapter, Methodist women went south to teach, missionary preachers worked among both Blacks and whites, new Black leaders emerged, and committed abolitionists like chaplain-then-editor-then-bishop Gilbert Haven sought to build a genuinely interracial church (Sources 1867a).[82] In a gesture in that direction, the 1868 General Conference removed the restrictions on the rights and privileges of the Black and biracial conferences (Washington and Delaware but also those established by the MEC in the South—Alabama, Georgia, Holston, Mississippi, South Carolina, Tennessee, Texas, Virginia, and North Carolina) and voted to seat delegations that had been sent as provisional.[83]

Cross and Flag

Charles Darwin published *On the Origin of Species* in 1859, but Methodists, like Americans generally, had too much else on their minds to take much notice. The bloody sacrifices of the war culminated, at least for northern Protestants, in the assassination of Lincoln. At Lincoln's Springfield burial, Bishop Simpson delivered the eulogy.[84] He called Lincoln "our fallen chieftain," a "deliverer," "no ordinary man," "statesman," "an honest, temperate, forgiving man; a just man; a man of noble heart in every way." Simpson compared Lincoln to Jacob and Moses. But even those biblical types paled. Deliverance through Lincoln demanded explicit evocation of his and Christ's death on Good Friday. Fittingly, Simpson concluded with images of crucifixion and resurrection and hints of Christ as antitype for Lincoln: "We crown thee as our martyr, and Humanity enthrones thee as her triumphant son. Hero, martyr, friend, *farewell*." The King James Version did not, however, contain the exhortation that Simpson addressed, in good Methodist fashion, to America:

> Standing, as we do to-day, by his coffin, let us resolve to carry forward the policy so nobly begun. Let us do right to all men.... Let us vow, before Heaven, to eradicate every vestige of human slavery, to give every human being his true position before God and man, to crush every form of rebellion, and to stand by the flag which God has given us.[85]

Across northern Methodism as across northern Protestantism generally, sermons read Lincoln's death in biblical terms; drew on doctrines of God, Providence, and atonement; envisioned the war as ordained in God's redemptive and emancipative plans; saw America, now saved from the sin of slavery and disunion and cleansed by the spilling of blood, as God's new Israel; spun out millennial visions of the nation's future; and prophesied triumph for American values in the South and among the freed slaves.[86] Southern Methodists wanted no part of this conflation of church and nation, of Christianity and nation, of Christ and culture, indeed imagined themselves as always having been believers in the spirituality of the church. Southern Methodist embrace of flag and culture would have to wait a war or two. Nor were there unanimity and uniformity among the people and preachers of the northern Methodist churches. However, the war had brought much of northern Methodism into mainstream Protestantism and a sense of place in American society. Civil religion and American culture became theirs as well. Indeed, as Methodism looked ahead to a centennial, it did so believing itself "the leading Church of the country," bearing "before God and man, the chief responsibility of the moral welfare of the nation" (Sources 1865c). So posited editor-historian Abel Stevens affirming Methodism's connectional spirit, boosting a Centenary development fund, and demanding that the church build temples expressive of "national culture" and "advanced civilization" (Sources 1865b).

Buildings for National Churches

In the Civil War era, Methodists made extraordinary efforts to build monumental churches in Washington, D.C., the nation's capital city, and did so decades before the Episcopal Church began to build a National Cathedral.[87] The Methodist Episcopal Church ambition to build a national church of its own for official Washington began at the 1852 General Conference. A group of Washington Methodists presented a memorial to the Boston gathering asking the denomination as a whole to build a major Methodist church in the nation's capital city "of convenient and prominent location, combining commodiousness in its size and attractiveness in its interior and exterior style of architecture." Regarding the success of the plan of such "high importance to the interest of the Methodism throughout the country," bishops and conference delegates pledged to promote the project in all the conferences. In March 1853 the church's seven bishops issued a pastoral letter supporting the project.

Following two years of fund-raising, a lot near the capitol building was purchased, and a prominent architect was engaged to plan a large church in Gothic style. The foundation stone was laid with great fanfare in October 1854 by Bishop Matthew Simpson, who energetically supported the project. Fund-raising continued with a lead gift of $100 by President Franklin Pierce. By 1860 the foundation for the great church had been completed, but the outbreak of the Civil War brought fund-raising and construction to a halt. Only the foundation walls had been completed. At war's end, in 1866, the bishops appointed a prominent New York clergyman to act full time as fund-raiser for the project. Construction resumed, and three years later (1869) the Metropolitan Memorial ME Church was completed at a cost of $225,000.[88]

Dedication February 28, 1869, of what the press called "the Westminster Abbey of American Methodism," was timed to coincide with the inauguration of Methodist President Ulysses S. Grant when Washington was filled with dignitaries from across the land. Four days before the inauguration, two thousand people crowded into the sanctuary with a seating capacity of twelve hundred. A third of the pews were reserved for dignitaries, including President-elect and Mrs. Grant, Vice President-elect and Mrs. Colfax, Chief Justice Chase, and a large number of senators, representatives, and other leaders in state and church. Bishop Simpson read the opening prayers from the denomination's new (1864) liturgy for dedication of churches and preached the sermon. Descriptions of the event hit the headlines in newspapers across the country, including the *New York Times*. A lead story in *Harper's Weekly* called the new church "by far the handsomest and the most elaborate of the many fine churches in Washington" and included an engraving for the whole country to see:

> Its design is pure Gothic. It is built of brown stone, rough hewed. The building fronts 75 feet on C. Street and 115 feet on [John Marshall Place]. It is about fifty feet in height. At the northeast corner of the structure is to be constructed a tower and a spire, the utmost point of which will be 240 feet from the pavement.

To lend legitimacy, the keystone in the arch above the pulpit was carved out of debris from Solomon's Temple, the olive wood of the pulpit and altar rail was from the Garden of Gethsemane, and ivy from the grave of John Wesley was planted to cover its walls. Sixteen large stained glass windows commemorated founding fathers and mothers of the denomination. Because it was meant to be the national church, one pew was set aside for each state and territory in the Union and one for the president, vice president, chief justice, and cabinet officers. President Grant occupied the President's Pew for eight years (1869–77); President McKinley sat in the same pew regularly during his term of office (1897–1901). President Hayes (1877–80) and his wife, Lucy, as did President and Mrs. Clinton (1992–2000), chose to attend Washington's oldest Methodist Episcopal Church, Foundry Church, instead of Metropolitan Memorial Church. Foundry Church had built a large new church in Romanesque style at Fourteenth and G Streets in 1866.

The first chairman of the board of trustees was familiar with administrative duties. He was President Grant. Other trustees of the first board carved their place in the nation's history: Salmon P. Chase, chief justice of the Supreme Court; and Matthew G. Emery, the mayor of the city of Washington. At its inception, Metropolitan Memorial Church boasted only one hundred members, but it continued to flourish at its downtown location until the 1920s, when the expansion of government buildings necessitated the acquisition of the property by the District government for the completion of Judiciary Square in 1930. The congregation relocated and built an even grander Gothic church on a new site near American University; it was dedicated in 1932.[89]

Southern Methodists also early planned a visible presence in the nation's capital. The Washington, D.C., congregation of the Virginia Conference petitioned the 1858 General Conference for assistance in building a church that would worthily represent the Methodist Episcopal Church, South. The denomination's first congregation in Washington had been organized and its first modest building was erected in 1850 and rebuilt in 1869. The General Conference agreed that "Southerners who annually congregate in the metropolis of the Union" should be represented there by "a Church worthy of the noble body of Christians whose great purpose it is to spread Scriptural holiness over these lands without turning aside to make war upon the rights which we enjoy under the Constitution of a great and free people." The lengthy resolution, dripping with venom aimed at northern Methodists, concluded: "Every member of this body must feel that so great and influential a denomination as the Methodist Episcopal Church, South, should be represented by a large and flourishing society at the seat of the Central Government."[90] The impending Civil War brought the plan to naught. Not till 1906 did a campaign get under way for a major Methodist Episcopal Church, South, in the nation's capital. The Board of Church Extension was given the responsibility for planning a "representative" church building to cost not less than $275,000. The next year a choice lot was purchased at the junction of K Street, Massachusetts Avenue, and Ninth Street. But another war (World War I) interfered with the speedy completion of fund-raising and construction. Mount Vernon Methodist Episcopal Church, South, a monumental, white-marbled, Greek Revival–style church, which cost more than $500,000, was not completed until 1919 and came to full power under the pastorate of Clovis G. Chappell.[91]

The movement to establish a UBC presence in Washington began in the early 1890s when the denomination's Church Erection Society began a churchwide campaign to raise funds for a national church. Three years later Memorial United Brethren Church was completed on a "high and commanding" lot one mile north of the capitol building. Modest by Methodist standards, the small brick church of Romanesque design costing $17,000 was dedicated debt-free by Bishop Jonathan Weaver in January 1893.[92] When it was rebuilt in 1905, the UBC could boast, "The Church is one of the finest in our denomination. Our people may well rejoice in having had a part in the building of this metropolitan church in the great city of Washington."[93] The building of a substantial United Brethren church at the nation's capital was achieved through many obstacles and at great expense, but "the end justified the means," wrote the editor of the *Religious Telescope*. "All United Brethren take an honorable pride in having so fine and prosperous a church at the Nation's capital."[94]

Albright Memorial Evangelical Church in Washington was first proposed at a general missionary convention in Baltimore in 1923. Two years later the project got under way when the church's Board of Missions approved the plan, appointed a pastor as "missionary to Washington," and began a churchwide drive to raise funds. By the summer of 1926 the pastor had purchased a lot, pitched a tent for services, and recruited twenty-six charter members. That fall the General Conference of the church added its approval. The Woman's Missionary Society devoted its 1927 Day of Prayer Offering for this project. With gifts totaling almost $100,000, the first unit of a substantial church complex in Gothic style, the Sunday school, was completed in November 1927.[95] The large sanctuary was not completed until 1954.

CHAPTER X

RECONSTRUCTING METHODISM(S): 1866–84

The northern church celebrated Methodist beginnings in an 1866 centenary, and both episcopal Methodisms, an 1884 centennial of American Methodist organization. They structured the year-long and longer events as occasions for taking stock, celebrating accomplishments, projecting needs, and promoting development. Abel Stevens outlined the first cause in *The Centenary of American Methodism: A Sketch of Its History, Theology, Practical System, and Success* (Sources 1865c), and W. H. De Puy, the second in *The Methodist Centennial Year-Book for 1884: The One Hundredth Year of the Separate Organization of American Methodism*.[1] Between the two centennials occurred a reconciliation gesture between the two churches, the birth of the Colored Methodist Episcopal Church, the founding of the Woman's Foreign Missionary Society (WFMS) and Woman's Christian Temperance Union (WCTU), substantial home missionary and educational efforts by northern Methodism among the freed slaves, the beginning of (post-baccalaureate) theological education, the inclusion of laity in governance in episcopal Methodism, testing of lay rights and ordination barriers by women, changes in membership expectations and ritual, a Methodist world ecumenical conference, exploration of unity among Methodist bodies, the reunion among Methodist Protestants, and a veritable organizational revolution from top to bottom. Symbolized by the latter and its most visible and enduring creations—the centralized board and bureaucratic denominational structures—the centennial decades, in a very real sense, closed a chapter on one Methodist century and opened one for the next.

Some Methodists preferred to stay with the last chapter, thinking Methodism needed recommitment to holiness, revivalism, a rural style, and a gospel for the poor, not improvements expressive of bourgeoisification that catered to the church's social elite and its locally and nationally powerful. They experienced denominational centralization, development, the urban tilt, formalization, culture, and progress as pushing Methodism beyond the limits of genuine Wesleyanism and as abandoning the church's old landmarks. Such sentiments, voiced by the recently constituted and growing Free

Methodists, came also to expression in yet another holiness movement, organized through the National Camp Meeting Association for the Promotion of Holiness (Sources 1867b). Although holiness remained a defining Methodist commitment (Sources 1876a) and Phoebe Palmer's campaigns and networks enjoyed the backing of key leadership (Sources 1868), freelancing holiness evangelism as well as the plethora of new organizations raised significant issues of authority and control. More division—another holiness church and the emergence of pentecostalism—lay ahead.[2] The MEC especially, but other Methodist branches as well, provided holiness critics of grandeur and progress much to ponder.

The Centenary Jubilee

The 1860 and 1864 General Conferences (MEC) created committees to begin planning for an 1866 centennial of American Methodist beginnings, a commemoration perhaps postponed by the war. The 1864 body decided on twin goals, the spiritual renewal of the church in recognition of what God had accomplished through the Methodist connection and a financial campaign to underwrite the instrumentalities (institutions) of further progress. The bishops were asked to designate twelve ministers and twelve "laymen" to plan the fund-raising and decide on allocation of proceeds. They aspired to raise $2 million, identifying ten giving projects, some specific, some for general purposes (a Connectional Fund for the various church institutions). Primary beneficiaries were to be existing and proposed educational institutions in the U.S., Germany, and Ireland but also Sunday schools and missions. Profiting from the war experience in organization and mobilization, the committee divided the church into campaign districts, held subscription events in cities and large towns, sponsored centenary sermons in annual conferences, and set the first Sunday of January 1866 as a connection-wide occasion for remembrance and commitment. The *Advocates* promoted the cause and acknowledged gifts and pledges. By the time General Conference convened two years later (in 1868), $8,709,498 had been raised with more to come. Included in that effort were a $500,000 commitment by the trustees to Garrett Biblical Institute and $600,000 from robber baron Daniel Drew to establish Drew Theological Seminary. Other more local causes bear or bore their origins in this campaign in their name—countless Centenary churches; Centenary Collegiate Institute, Hackettstown; and Centenary Biblical Institute, Baltimore. Calculating where God had brought the church in a century, Bishop Matthew Simpson counted churches valued at $29.5 million, parsonages at $4.4 million, and educational institutions at close to $7.9 million. The MEC boasted two publishing houses and seven book depositories; sixteen official and six unofficial papers; two theological seminaries; and a hundred colleges and seminaries (pre-collegiate schools). Nine bishops, sixty-four annual conferences, and 7,576 itinerant and 8,602 local preachers served a little more than a million members. Outside the MEC, Simpson counted close to another million Methodists.[3]

The muscularity of Methodism owed in no small part to the growing well-being and even wealth of its members. Their philanthropy enriched Methodist benevolent institutions. Their rising confidence and consequent influence with ministers produced in time a new kind of partnership with clergy. Matthew Simpson, senior bishop of the MEC by the Civil War years, was notably sensitive to the fact that Methodists were becoming wealthier. He was also singularly adroit in garnering their support for the newly ascendant church's causes. Simpson documented the great social change affecting American Methodists in the Victorian era—the move from outsiders to insiders socially, from side street to Main Street architecturally, from marginality to predominance denominationally—in his centennial-era (1876) Cyclopaedia of Methodism. Its subtitle, Embracing Sketches of Its Rise, Progress, and Present Condition, with Biographical Notices and Numerous Illustrations, conveyed Simpson's celebrative tone, the thousand-plus pages provided textual evidence, and the myriad statistics established the factual proof. Simpson imaged the dramatic change of Methodism's social location with the large number (close to four hundred) of engravings, many to be sure of ministers living and dead, but some of rich Methodists, imposing collegiate halls, and cathedral churches. To Simpson, the Lord was rewarding the Methodists—his favored common people—for their diligence, and they were sharing their success with their church. They were also sharing it with ministers, especially bishops like Simpson. Their hospitality, lecture fees, and business advice gave him firsthand knowledge of how much better it was to be rich than poor. Living in a mansion in Philadelphia, where he rubbed elbows with the rich and famous, and tripping frequently to Washington, where he became friend and confidant of President Lincoln and the wartime Washington elite, Simpson "itinerated" in markedly different fashion than he had in the wilderness of western Pennsylvania where he began his ministry. Under the leadership of Simpson and company, the MEC had a jubilant centenary and focused the jubilee—freeing slaves, canceling debts, transferring property—on the South.

Lay Representation: A New Partnership

In earlier Methodism, laity (laymen primarily) had exercised on circuit levels important "ministerial" roles as local preachers, exhorters, class leaders, and stewards—functions significantly altered as upscale town and city congregations focused leadership on pastor, pastor's wife, and the Sunday school. The erosion or sidelining of lay "ministries" led to local preacher assemblies, organizations, and protests and to heightened sensitivity in episcopal Methodism to the several issues that had animated Methodist Protestantism. Methodist laity who participated actively in the commercial, political, and social life of their communities, states, and countries chafed at their exclusion from church governance, particularly as conferences made financial decisions for which lay purses would care or addressed themselves to matters of war and policy about which laity had keen concern, points noted in chapter 8 and eloquently voiced in 1864 by lay biblical scholar James Strong (Sources 1864a). Speaking to the General Conference (MEC) on behalf of a concurrently assembled Laymen's Convention, Strong envisioned a new lay-ministerial partnership, the next stage in Methodism's providentially guided transformation of "the moral culture of the American people." A twenty-first-century spokesperson might have invoked Methodism's mission statement—to reform the continent and spread scriptural holiness over the land. Strong looked not to the past but to the future, to growth and education, to the trajectory of Protestantism generally, to the witness of British Methodism. He was heard but not heeded, at least not then.

Partnership came more quickly in the southern church, within which lay conventions had spoken on matters of church and state in the run-up to Civil War and for whose postwar future a conference of laity and ministers had issued the Palmyra Manifesto (Sources 1865a). The MECS had, in 1850, recognized the importance of lay concurrence in financial and secular matters. On such "interests" and on a voluntary basis it permitted annual conferences to give voice and vote to one lay steward from each district.[4] In 1866, meeting for the first time since 1858, General Conference (MECS) approved a sense of the house resolution calling for lay representation in annual conferences and General Conferences. Offering the motion was Holland McTyeire (1824–89), then pastor in Alabama, having fled there after serving as firebrand editor of the *Nashville Christian Advocate*. His leadership on that and other initiatives earned him election to the episcopacy at that General Conference. When subsequently ratified, the MECS's policy provided for equal lay representation in General Conference and for four laity from each presiding elder's district in annual conferences. Laity would choose their own representation. Provision was made for separate lay and clerical ballots. And only preachers would vote on matters pertaining to ministerial relations.[5] Southern laity (laymen) took their seats in 1870.

Lay representation in the northern church required more of a campaign and found a campaign manager in George Crooks (1822–97), who for more than twenty years nurtured the reform movement, in the Philadelphia area in the 1850s and in New York after 1857. Beginning his ministry in Illinois, Crooks returned to his alma mater, Dickinson College (Carlisle, Pennsylvania), where he authored two textbooks, one on Latin and the other on Greek. In the fall of 1851, Crooks became pastor of fashionable Trinity Church in his native Philadelphia. Detecting among the laity a desire for increased participation in the life of their church, Crooks invited a group to meet in his church to discuss the matter. Soon the layfolk, joined by other ministers, began to map strategy. Believing that "lay representation in the church's conferences would more certainly secure a division of responsibilities between the ministry and the laity, and thereby arouse to a greater activity and usefulness the church, greatly increase its future prosperity, and secure the honor and glory of God," the rally resolved to call a general convention to be held in the same city on the third day of March 1852

> to consist of delegates from the various stations and circuits within the bounds of our church, to take into consideration the propriety of petitioning the General Conference to be held in Boston in May next for such action in their body assembled as will secure the introduction of Lay Delegation into our conferences.[6]

The convention appointed twenty influential laymen as a planning committee, with Crooks as one of their advisors, and requested the editors of the Methodist press to publish an account of the proceedings and the call to the proposed convention. Few Methodist papers heeded the plea. George Peck, editor of the *Christian Advocate* (New York), refused to print the address, petitions, and resolutions of the lay convention, to accept as paid advertisement the call for the spring convention, and to "lend the *Advocate*" to "revolutionizing the government of the Church."[7]

Three months of preparatory efforts brought 170 laymen representing thirty-three churches from several annual conferences to Philadelphia in March 1852. Electing the president of Girard College, William Allen, as chair, the convention adopted two strongly worded resolutions to the forthcoming General Conference. The convention called for equal lay representation in annual conferences and General Conferences and offered a detailed plan for implementation. "An Address to the People," probably crafted by Crooks, circulated in pamphlet form and in the press. Affirming themselves to be "very peaceable members of the church [who] would as soon harm their mothers as her," the reformers argued their case on the ground of expediency, not rights. Lay representation, they argued, would make Methodism work better and grow bigger. History proved it was dangerous, the petitioners asserted, for one group (in this case, clergy) to draw up rules for another. Above all, the reformers argued, lay representation "is in harmony with the spirit of Christianity, with the progressive movements of the age, and especially with the ideas of the American people."

To this convention, editor Peck opened the columns of the *Christian Advocate*, providing a full account of the convention and its address. Perhaps his advocacy figured in General Conference's failure to reelect him editor. At any rate, General Conference (MEC) replaced Peck with his predecessor, Dr. Thomas E. Bond (1782–1856), who demonstrated his suppressive mettle earlier, denying abolitionists access to the *Advocate*, and was known to be an able and uncompromising opponent of lay representation. Indeed, Bond had just presided at, delivered the keynote address to, and helped draft a petition on behalf of a counter convention of laity "in favor of sustaining the Church *as it is*." Called by another March 1852 gathering, which met at St. George's Church in Philadelphia, it drew 165 to a counter convention on the eve of the General Conference. Bond put it bluntly for General Conference:

> Having inherited the church from our ancestors in its purity and efficiency, and having enjoyed its unalloyed advantages ourselves, it is our duty and privilege to transmit it, in its beauty and strength, to those who shall come after us. . . . We must guard it with the utmost carefulness if we would not be recreant to God, and traitors to the world![8]

General Conference (MEC) established a Committee on Lay Delegation to deal with the numerous petitions for and against the reform. The committee concluded that such change would not be in the best interests of the church, that laity had already ample opportunities to serve their church, and that most of them opposed the change. The committee's report was overwhelmingly adopted by a vote of 171 to 3, which left no doubt where the preachers stood in 1852. The lay rights petitions went also to the next General Conference (1856), but the debate on slavery crowded out the issue.

By the next General Conference (1860), recognizing changes in the climate of opinion in the church, the bishops openly addressed the issue in their Episcopal Address. "We are of the opinion," they declared, "that Lay Delegation might be introduced into the General Conference with safety, and perhaps advantage."[9] Heeding the bishops' plea and the growing sentiment among the laity, General Conference passed a resolution expressing willingness to approve lay delegation "when the church desires it." It referred the question to a churchwide vote by "orders"—laymen over twenty-one voting in specially called meetings on a charge level and preachers in the 1862 annual conferences. By that point, George Crooks had moved to New York. Supported by laity dedicated to the cause, he founded and edited a vigorous independent Methodist newspaper (*The Methodist*) to champion lay rights, to address the issue of slavery, and to rival the crosstown, official *Christian Advocate*, which muted attention to the sensitive topics. Crooks made his editorial office in Wall Street the command post for the movement and devoted a number of issues to the cause beginning in the fall of 1861. By the time the votes were taken, secession and war concerns loomed large, and both ministry and laity voted down the proposed plan, the ministers voting 3 to 1 against and the laymen roughly 2 to 1 against.

A lay rights convention held concurrently with the next General Conference two years later (1864) maintained that the referendum was in no way decisive. The vote had been "very imperfectly and in some churches irregularly taken," and preoccupation with the war had interfered with proper consideration of the question, the laymen charged. The convention demanded action by the General Conference irrespective of the vote, commissioning Professor James Strong to make the case (Sources 1864a). They supplemented their declaration with various strong, pertinent arguments. But the conference was unmoved. It reaffirmed its previous willingness to approve lay representation when assured "that the church desires it" but discerned "no such declaration of the popular will as to justify. . . taking action."

By the time the 1868 General Conference gathered in Chicago, the demand of laity for representation had become so strong as to be irresistible. The conference not only called for another referendum on the question but also submitted a definite plan to "the godly consideration of . . . ministers and people," this time including laywomen as well as men (Sources 1870a). Women organized and issued an open letter to their sisters about the importance of voting in favor of lay representation.

The plan was approved by a decisive vote, laywomen and men voting 2 to 1 for representation and the clergy in the annual conferences voting by more than three-fourths majority to change the constitution. The General Conference completed the action by voting to concur. The great revolution—at least the first stage—was achieved. Crooks could only regret that the plan did not allow lay members in the annual conference and that women were not included. Crooks commented later, "In the [general] conference of 1872 the lay delegates quietly took their seats beside their clerical brethren; the wounded itinerancy uttered no groans, and the heavens did not fall!" Who, after all, could protest the inclusion of governors, senators, cabinet members, and leading industrialists (Sources, p. 31)?

The UBC introduced lay representation into its conference that same year—but into its annual conferences and not into its General Conference. Lay representation in UBC General Conferences was not added until a new constitution was adopted in 1889. The Evangelicals adopted lay representation into their conferences in 1903 at the General Conference level and 1907 at the annual conference level. So the witness of the Methodist Protestants finally prevailed.

The Organizational Revolution

In Brooklyn at the General Conference of 1872, the first to seat lay delegates, Judge William Lawrence, a distinguished representative from the Central Ohio Conference, veteran of the Ohio legislature as well as the U.S. Congress, presented the report of the "Special Committee on the Relationship of the Benevolent Institutions to the General Conference" (Sources 1872a).[10] The report called for putting the benevolent institutions of the denomination "under the full control of the General Conference by stipulating that boards of managers of the various agencies were to be elected by the General Conference itself" and reincorporating agencies as necessary to achieve this accountability. The enabling legislation, paralleled soon in the other Methodist churches, transformed what had been voluntary societies—the typical, widespread, parachurch organizations of the day—into truly denominational structures. Various motivations prompted the revolutionary change. An 1870 scandal, involving alleged mismanagement of funds by clergy executives in the MEC publishing house, helped further the cause of providing better oversight and opening the agencies to lay professionals. More positively, Methodist laity and ministers had participated actively in, indeed led, the Civil War relief efforts that had perfected centralized direction of locally energized and funded organizations. And they had but to read the papers to recognize the rapid incorporation of America—bringing consolidation, order, integration, efficiency, bureaucratization, and professionalization to business. Laity especially wanted similar accountability in governance and in finance in church (and state).

Furthermore, Methodism had recently birthed additional denominational societies adding to the issues of control, though one of these, the Board of Education, modeled the accountability being proposed. The Church Extension Society, founded in 1865, had been incorporated in Philadelphia and had begun its work with considerable fanfare and hope and would soon begin building a new church every day under the boosterism of Charles C. McCabe.[11] The Freedmen's Aid Society, also beginning what would be comparably impressive institution building throughout the South and discussed below, had been incorporated in Ohio in 1866, "not in any respect under the jurisdiction or control of the General Conference" (Sources 1872a). Only the Board of Education established in 1868 by General Conference to invest in higher education its portion of the $8 million raised during the Centenary was secured to the church by election of its board (six "laymen," six ministers).

These new societies—as for the most part they were—along with those created earlier, the Missionary Society (1819), the Sunday School Union (1827), and the Tract Society (1852) in the MEC and the Missionary Society (1845), Sunday-School Society (1854), and Tract Society (1854) of the MECS, were tied to the denominations by General Conference's election of their executives (corresponding secretaries). To be sure, the 1844 MEC General Conference had provided for a general mission committee to provide oversight for that agency and had authorized a full-time executive for the Sunday School Union. Still these missional, purposive, flexible, adaptive, expansive, pluraform, and decentralized societies, their executives, and hence their programs reported to a locally organized or conference-designated board of directors whose annual meeting in the headquarters city limited legal oversight to that one occasion and that city's clergy and lay leadership. Delegates to the General Conference of 1872 were disturbed to learn that "as our benevolent societies are now constituted and governed, they are practically controlled in their election of boards of managers by a few of the members who live near the places of meetings and they are really irresponsible to the church through any of its authorities."[12]

To be sure these New York and Philadelphia societies enjoyed mostly harmonious but dependent relations with the network of local and conference auxiliaries, male and female, whose voluntary fund-raising prowess, organizational effectiveness, promotional efforts, and product placement (Sunday school literature, tracts, missionary materials) made the enterprises function. The *Discipline* and annual conferences exhorted preachers to support the cause by forming local societies and making collections. Circuits, stations, and annual conferences, also under disciplinary guidance, kept records of the amount raised for each benevolent purpose. Still, not organized as agencies of the General Conference, the societies, whose membership derived from individual annual or lifetime financial commitment, were purely voluntary and auxiliary institutions functioning "to call forth the liberality of the church."

Much of the impetus for the 1872 revolution came from within the agencies whose leadership touted denominational control and centralization as imperative for program effectiveness. And they had struggled toward that end. For instance, John Price Durbin, head of the Missionary Society from 1850 to 1872, worked tirelessly to make missions a connectional enterprise. Previously presiding elder, president of Dickinson College, editor of the *Christian Advocate*, chaplain in the U.S. Senate, teacher, and minister, he understood the church top to bottom.[13] Durbin realized that he had to work persuasively through the conferences and presiding elders to get to the circuits and stations. The 1850 Troy Conference, an early responder to his initiatives, called for missionary organizations at every level—annual missionary meetings, collectors in "every class or neighborhood," reports and publication of the amounts collected—to be muscled by the presiding elders who were to meet with the preachers and preach on missions.[14] Other conferences passed very similar sets of programs for missions, often with some such introduction as "The Committee to whom was referred the papers from Dr. Durbin, Corresponding Secretary of the Missionary Society of the M.E. Church, presented their report, which was adopted."[15] Each conference, however, configured the program to suit its own taste.

A new constitution for the Missionary Society, approved by the 1852 General Conference, permitted each annual conference a "vice-president from its own body." Durbin also recognized the strategic value of moving its annual meetings out of New York and around the connection, Philadelphia already having been the first of the alternative anniversary meeting sites, followed by Boston and Buffalo.[16] To ensure carry through for missions and give the missionary society prominence and authority on a conference level, the presiding elders were appointed as members.[17] For added motivation, the General Conference of 1876, on motion of A. J. Kynett, directed that the boards of education, missions, church extension, Freedmen's Aid Society, and Book Concern together with the Sunday School Union and Tract Society should unite in the publication of a program journal to be sent free to all preachers of the church.[18] At the same time conferences began to display (to publish) their concerns and revenues with elaborate statistical tables. "Missionary Statistics" and eventually an appended "Missionary Report" showed just how each charge had performed. By 1872 such reports reached fifty pages in length.

Another corresponding (general) secretary, Alpha J. Kynett (1829–99), head of the Church Extension Society for thirty-two years, was most responsible for the 1872 General Conference report on benevolent institutions. Kynett knew exactly what the report signified. It meant that the General Conference would now command, as he put it, "[A]ll its great interest for the diffusion of Christian civilization...and having a controlling power in all the missionary operations carried on in the name of and on behalf of the church."[19]

Kynett acknowledged that the decision also altered the operations of the benevolent institutions. The General Conference would convert the major benevolent enterprises from society-type to board-type agencies. According to Kynett, the "carefully matured plan" of 1872 explicitly intended that the society structure "should be superseded by a Board, to be elected by the General Conference, and to be placed under its immediate control."[20] The bishops in their 1876 Episcopal Address reveled in the thought that now "under the government and direction of the general conference as her supreme authority" and by means of "the great agencies of the church," Methodism had become a mighty army "having unity of purpose and action." The centralization of denominational power in the hands of the General Conference had been accomplished. Southern Methodists, Evangelicals, and United Brethren took steps in the same direction in the same period, the MECS just two years later.

An important disciplinary change at the denominational level moved accountability in the opposite direction, providing some check on the authority of General Conference. This was the provision for judicial review. Here the southern church took the initiative. In 1854 it had empowered the bishops, acting collectively and in writing, with the prerogative of challenging a rule or regulation and thereby obliging General Conference to muster a two-thirds majority on the question. This action, consonant with its understanding of conference and episcopacy, the MECS confirmed and clarified in 1874.[21]

Consonant with its understanding of episcopacy, the northern church proceeded in a different fashion, generating from out of General Conference itself procedure and a body with judicial authority. General Conference had served as the supreme court to which appeal was made from annual conference judicial decisions and rulings on the law by presiding bishops. From 1860 to 1872 the General Conference had established a Committee of Appeals and referred such matters to it. In 1876, the MEC established a Judiciary Committee, a body of twelve ("one from each General Conference District") "to consider and report their decision on all questions of law coming up to us from Judicial Conferences."[22] And in 1884, the body's authority was extended to include "all records of Judicial Conference, appeals on points of law, and all proposed changes in the Ecclesiastical Code." The MEC body, however, did not have the power of judicial review that the southern bishops possessed, the ability to "arrest" or challenge legislation as unconstitutional.[23]

Both this committee and the southern College of Bishops would thereafter render "court" decisions, thereby leaving a body of *national* law. The MECS actually proceeded in formal fashion to direct its compilation, voting in its 1866 General Conference to request the bishops "to prepare for publication a Commentary on the Discipline, embracing Episcopal decisions, with a view to produce a harmonious administration thereof."[24] That produced Holland N. McTyeire's *A Manual of the Discipline of The Methodist Episcopal Church, South, including the Decisions of the College of Bishops,* a volume regularly updated.[25] The northern church proceeded somewhat later and in less formal fashion to compile a comparable manual.[26] In these efforts to establish judicial procedure as with the program boards, legitimate concern for order, coherence, consistency, and regularity in its body of law led Methodism, North and South, to consolidation at a national level.

The impetus for order and organization affected every level of the church, including the most basic, where new official boards brought to the local church comparable efficiency and accountability (see "Conclusion and Transition" of this chapter and the 1884 "Snapshot"). Similarly on regional levels, local church organization and the new centralized, accountable institutions allowed the churches to focus resources on new projects deemed beneficial to the general good, for instance, the hospitals that editor James M. Buckley advocated (Sources 1881a) and that we treat in chapter 11.

To finance an increasingly programmed Methodism, special Sundays *with special offerings* reached a scale that made them necessities for boards and agencies, but also serious rivals to ancient Christian festivals. The first was Children's Day, set for the second Sunday in June, six months removed from Christmas and at a period of the year when without some such stimulus Sunday school interest was in danger of flagging before the heat of summer. Begun as part of the Centenary program in 1866, Children's Day *with offering* for a Children's Educational Fund provided scholarships for higher education to "meritorious and needy Sunday School scholars of either sex, who, without such aid, be unable to obtain a complete education." Two years later, 1868, the General Conference made the day and the fund permanent with an asking of five cents for each child enrolled. Oversight of the MEC fund was committed to the newly organized Board of Education.[27] By 1884 the MEC General Conference ordered seven Sundays with special collections—for missions, church extension, tract distribution, Sunday school, Freedmen's Aid, higher education, and Bible distribution!

As the twentieth century dawned, fickle freewill special offerings, which frustrated agency budgeting and planning, were on their way out; financial planning was on its way into the church. The 1912 MEC General Conference approved the formation of a central treasury with power to set budgets and determine "fair-share" askings called *apportionments* (Sources 1912b). (That was one year before the U.S. Congress mandated the income tax.) The 1924 General Conference strengthened the plan to unify benevolence collections, forming a World Service Commission to set goals, review budgets, and make four-year plans (it has been the General Council on Finance and

Administration, GCFA, since 1972). Stewardship Sunday, pledge cards, and duplex offering envelopes followed shortly thereafter. The Every-Member Canvass to raise church budgets emerged in stewardship education materials in the 1930s. "God loves a cheerful giver" (2 Cor. 9:7).[28]

Women's Work in the Church[29]

The 1872 General Conference (MEC) established a special Committee on Woman's Work in the Church to deal with numerous resolutions and petitions pertaining to women's issues, submissions that outlined the church's agenda for the next half century and more. To this committee went evidence that Methodist women were effecting their own organizational revolution, capitalizing on the networking, enlarged vision, administrative skills, and organizational experience of Civil War relief work (Sources 1870a).[30] Petitioners, noting that recent developments were "a revival of the true spirit of Methodism," advocated the "licensing and ordaining of women as preachers," "The Ladies' and Pastors' Christian Union," "The Woman's Foreign Missionary Society," and the "enlargement of [women's] Christian and benevolent activity." Additional resolutions, referred elsewhere, asked about the propriety of striking male language and inserting the word *persons* in the *Discipline* so that women could be elected stewards, Sunday school superintendents, and members of the quarterly conferences. The same year Mrs. Susanna M. D. Fry alerted the church through articles in the *Ladies' Repository* to "ancient and modern deaconesses" and "ancient and modern (Catholic) sisterhoods," and urged Methodists to consider the establishment of a deaconess order that would further the work already begun by the Ladies' and Pastors' Christian Union (Sources 1872b).[31] Women and supportive church leaders had begun again the press for the pulpit (Sources 1869b), indeed, for full participation in the array of leadership roles and responsibilities (Sources 1870a).

General Conference had little difficulty with the first of these initiatives, the Ladies' and Pastors' Christian Union (LPCU). Organized in Philadelphia in March 1868, the LPCU sought to employ the church's women in a systematic program of home evangelistic work among poor and neglected persons, under the supervision of the ordained clergy. Supported by Bishop Matthew Simpson, the resident bishop of Philadelphia, it drew its vision and energy from its first corresponding secretary (chief executive), Mrs. Annie Wittenmyer (1827–1900), who had honed management skills in Civil War relief work, especially in supervision of army hospital kitchens under the auspices of the U.S. Christian Commission. Recognizing that "the entire system of religious activity in the church is undergoing a change," the LPCU sought an auxiliary society in each church, with the pastor as president. Churches should subdivide the work into small districts and appoint two or more women to visit house-to-house among the unconverted, to invite unchurched persons to worship, to assist sick and poor people, and to bring children into the Sunday school. The idea caught the church's imagination. Within a year, some fifty churches in ten states had established LPCU chapters. Methodist women had already reached out to some 23,000 families, appealed to nearly 11,000 "unconverted persons," visited 1,000 sick persons, helped 325 poor families, brought 419 children into the Sunday school, held meetings in 233 homes, and distributed some 100,000 pages of tracts.[32]

Ministers speaking at the first anniversary meeting of the LPCU indicated its appeal to the church's male leadership. The Reverend C. P. Masden of the Illinois Conference embraced the new society as providentially devised to fit the character of the times (now that Methodism had become predominantly middle class). He celebrated its fourfold aim: (1) to do a needed work that the pastor did not have time to do, (2) to give laypeople a religious activity beyond attending church and listening to sermons, (3) to evangelize the masses—now that "the log cabin" had given place to "the Gothic chapel"—and (4) to develop the individuality and spirituality of the women of the church who composed "three-fourths of our members."[33] With more candor, Bishop Simpson proclaimed, "The object of this association is not that woman shall take the pulpit, or engage in any work that may be questionable, but simply to go forward in the discharge of those duties that woman has ever performed, *though not systematically and regularly.*"[34]

Executive Annie Wittenmyer proved adroitly effective and skilled in working within the limited imagination of bishops and pastors. In *Women's Work for Jesus*, Wittenmyer argued that evangelizing the unchurched masses required home visitation. Women, whose sphere was the home, were uniquely qualified to go into people's homes and "talk of Jesus, and duty and heaven." They would be welcomed where men would not. And this work could best be done by "*the systematic, voluntary labors of Christian Women, under the direction of the regular pastorate.*"[35] Wittenmyer focused on Methodist women (and church women more generally) who enjoyed sufficient leisure time to devote two or three hours a week to visitation. This great undeveloped power "might become a mighty enginery for good if properly combined and directed."[36]

New Jersey preacher (later bishop) Isaac W. Wiley, a member of the General Conference Committee on Woman's Work in the Church and editor of the *Ladies' Repository*, used issues of that important serial to affirm with Wittenmyer that women's nature made them well adapted to this work and that home visitation was appropriate work for the "true woman."[37] General Conference (1872) concurred. It recognized the LPCU as a "regularly constituted society" of the church, approved its constitution, recognized its Board of Managers, and instructed pastors of all the churches to cooperate with the new society in its important work.[38]

Although its evangelistic focus, tethering to pastoral guidance, and self-imaging within "women's sphere" limited the scope of LPCU activities, leaders and members found their interests and imagination enlarged by the new organization. Annie Wittenmyer and board colleague Susanna Fry, encouraged by Bishop Simpson, who had become acquainted with and an advocate for Protestant deaconess work from his trip to Germany in the 1860s, traveled together in this country to urge the founding of benevolent institutions, including deaconess homes. In the fall of 1872 Wittenmyer herself visited the Lutheran deaconess centers at Kaiserswerth, Germany, with the thought that the LPCU might introduce deaconess work into American Methodism. However, her own energies soon became absorbed by the "Woman's Crusade" against alcohol and eventually the Woman's Christian Temperance Union, which she helped to found in 1874, becoming its first national president. A similar trajectory can be seen in the brief life of Mrs. Mary L. Griffith, wife of a Philadelphia Conference pastor, who at twenty-three succeeded in 1877 to the office of corresponding secretary (chief executive). Her *Women's Christian Work*, evoking images of women's work within women's sphere, called on Christian women "to be saved from a spirit of pride and exclusiveness, and to be possessed of a burning love for souls, just because they are *souls*," to offer themselves utterly to God and go out into "the waste places of the earth with light and comfort." Recognizing the revivals already attributed to the work of the LPCU, she urged her dear sisters to "come to this sweet work."[39] In 1880, however, Mary Griffith would address an eloquent appeal to the MEC General Conference (Sources 1880b) for granting women's rights as laity, for licensing and ordaining those called, and for expunging the word *male* from the *Discipline*. She died in 1884 at the age of twenty-nine.

The 1872 Committee on Woman's Work in the Church endorsed the LPCU and recommended the adoption of its constitution. It exhorted the women to "still greater zeal" in Sunday school, class meetings, prayer meetings, and love feasts. "In regard to woman's preaching," it discerned, "we must wait for further developments of Providence. We rejoice in the indications that women are called to be teachers of the Word of Life, and yet the instances are not sufficiently numerous to justify any new legislation in the Church on this subject." The committee did find women to be providentially called to missions, and General Conference recognized the Woman's Foreign Missionary Society (WFMS).[40]

Women's Missionary Societies

Women organized foreign missionary societies in the MEC in 1869, in the UBC in 1875, in the MECs in 1878, in the MPC in 1879, and in the EA in 1883. Separate women's home missionary societies followed in 1880, MEC; 1886, MECS (expanded in 1890); and 1893, MPC. The (UBC) Woman's Missionary Association extended its work to both foreign and home missions. All missionary work in the MECS was reorganized in 1910 into one Board of Missions, with the woman's work directed by the Woman's Missionary Council. (Women's home missionary organizations and deaconesses will be treated in the following chapters.)

Methodist women organized the Woman's Foreign Missionary Society (MEC) in Boston in March 1869 in response to pleas by Mrs. Clementina Butler and Mrs. Lois Parker, wives of Methodist missionaries to India. They urged that the gospel could be taken to the women of India only by women and that a sending agency, a woman's foreign missionary society, was therefore imperative. The small assemblage of women adopted a constitution and elected "national" officers. Setting an access-to-power pattern that would be strategically typical in the women's missionary societies, the WFMS selected Mrs. Osmon C. Baker (wife of Bishop Baker) as the first president and made the wives of the other bishops vice presidents. (When in 1880, MEC women organized the Woman's Home Missionary Society, they elected Mrs. Lucy Webb Hayes, the U.S. president's spouse, as president, an office she held till death in 1889.) The WFMS chose Mrs.[41] Harriet M. Warren, Mrs. Lois Parker, and Mrs. Jennie Fowler Willing as corresponding secretaries. At the urging of Clementina Butler, the WFMS fixed a membership fee at "two cents a week and a prayer" so that no woman should have to say that she could not afford to join.[42]

A monthly magazine for the organization, initially titled *The Heathen Woman's Friend* and edited for twenty-five years by Mrs. Harriet M. Warren, appeared almost immediately, in June of 1869.[43] WFMS set its annual subscription at a modest thirty cents. The first issue summoned Methodist women to the cause of carrying the knowledge of Christ and the blessings of Christian civilization to sisters across the world (and especially in India) and set forth the urgency of establishing local affiliates (Sources 1869a). The magazine with its stories, pictures, and communiqués gave Methodist women the world. Through it, they engaged and were engaged by their own public, a gendered universe. The magazine sustained the WFMS's generating interest in India and allowed readers to follow the careers and signal accomplishments in education and medicine of its first two missionaries, Isabella Thoburn (1840–1901) and Dr. Clara Swain (1834–1910), sent out together in 1869 and path makers in their respective fields. The magazine and such high-profile single women made the case for "Woman's Work for Woman" and for unmarried women missionaries—essentially a new ministerial career for educated women.[44]

The WFMS experienced friction with the Methodist Missionary Society (often referred to as the parent board) from the start. Its secretary, Dr. John P. Durbin, wrote approving their aim but advising them to "leave the administration of the work to the Board at home and the missions on the field." The leaders of the parent board who feared interference with regular collections for missions proposed that the women forward money raised to them. Having as leaders the wives of bishops and other Methodist heavyweights served the WFMS well. The women insisted that they had organized an independent society and they would raise and disburse their own funds for the work they had undertaken. They agreed, however, that they would "take no collections or subscriptions in any promiscuous [mixed] assembly" but would raise their funds in ways that would not interfere with the parent board and its work.[45] By the end of its first year, the WFMS had established regional branches—Philadelphia, New York, New England, Northwestern, Western, and Cincinnati—and dispatched its own missionary to India, Fannie J. Sparks.

The branch executive secretaries traveled, spoke, corresponded, promoted, and wrote for the magazine and, through all such activities, organized auxiliaries, creating a highly decentralized organization that elicited high levels of participation and ownership. Notably effective in such organizational evangelism and auxiliary formation were Clementina Butler, head of the New York Branch, Jennie Fowler Willing, head of the Northwestern Branch, and Mary Clarke Nind, head of the Western Branch. Butler, whose plea for a women's organization had created the WFMS, spoke from her firsthand missionary experience and enjoyed prestige as well from the distinguished missionary roles accorded her husband, William Butler. She made splashes on WFMS's behalf in the summer camp meetings. Willing also enjoyed important connections, her husband a preacher and presiding elder, her brother previously a prominent Chicago pastor, by 1872 president of Northwestern University, later to be an *Advocate* editor and bishop. Licensed to preach in Illinois and for a while professor of English at Illinois Wesleyan, Willing took charge of the American heartland, initially from Ohio to the West Coast, proving an able advocate for women's roles in missions and church leadership generally (Sources 1870a). Later Nind assumed responsibility for organizing Great Plains auxiliaries, her itinerations earning her respectful accolades as "Our Little Bishop" or "Mother Nind." She was one of the five women elected to but not seated by the 1888 General Conference and represented the church and WFMS in later ecumenical gatherings. Their efforts, supported by Methodist women leaders at all levels, built the largest U.S. women's missionary endeavor, measured by membership and contributions at home and teachers, schools, and colleges abroad.[46]

Women's missionary societies emerged in the other Methodist bodies soon after that in the MEC. In the southern church, the witness of missionary women, specifically Mary McClellan Lambuth in China, elicited interest on the part of those at home. Small groups in Nashville and Baltimore began efforts to support Bible women (missionaries) for China and to correspond with each other. Mrs. Willie Harding McGavock (1832–95) of the McKendree Church in Nashville, a leader in the local effort, met women of the WFMS and captained the effort to create a counterpart in the MECS. The "pulse of the whole machine," according to her biographer, she petitioned the 1874 General Conference to establish a women's missionary society. Unheeded the first time around, she began a campaign through correspondence and with a letter to the *Nashville Christian Advocate* encouraging formation of local societies and support for a denominational organization. Prominent Methodist women gathered at the site of the 1878 General Conference to give the men the word, and the MECS approved the establishment of a

Woman's Missionary Society as auxiliary to its Board of Missions and "subject to its advice and approval." The bishops, charged by the enabling legislation to appoint leadership, named Mrs. Juliana Hayes, leader of the Baltimore movement, as president, McGavock as corresponding secretary, and Mrs. James Whitworth, also of Nashville, as treasurer. McGavock and Hayes died in 1895 but until then worked tirelessly, traveling, organizing, encouraging, speaking, raising money, and furthering the missionary cause. They did so "strictly within the bounds of ideal womanliness." However, as in the case of the new women's organizations generally, their roles, experience, example, relations, and voice effectively transformed women's sphere of hearth, home, and family into its own public realm, albeit one gender defined. In building the auxiliary network and opening such gendered public roles to women across the South, southern women communicated with one another after 1880 through the *Woman's Missionary Advocate*. China missions and the figures of Mary Lambuth and later Laura Haygood focused and energized the ambitions and idealism of southern Methodist women.[47]

Organization of UBC women occurred a year after that in the MECS, in 1875, with a Woman's Missionary Association. Three years earlier, Lizzie Hoffman, a schoolteacher in Dayton, Ohio, spirited this development by creating the Woman's Missionary Association of the Miami Conference. Similar local efforts in the Ohio German and California Conferences led to support by a denominational organization, the Home, Frontier and Foreign Missionary Society, and a mostly cordial, autonomous-but-supervised working relation.

The UBC women focused initially on Sierra Leone and girls' schools there. They began in 1882 the *Woman's Evangel*, which epitomized their intentions within a much enlarged women's sphere. Women missionaries would not preach but write, work, and talk "for the salvation of their sisters who are in heathen blackness and darkness."

In the EA missionary efforts focused on the German homeland and later on Japan. By contrast with the supportive relationship between women organized for mission and the United Brethren denomination, when Emma Yost and others petitioned the EA in 1878, they were refused permission to organize. Two years later, Minerva Strawman (later Spreng) raised the issue again. The General Conference of the Evangelical Association in 1883 authorized a Woman's Missionary Society, but stipulated that women's groups could exist only on the local level and then under the supervision of the preacher. Apparently a woman's missionary society was regarded by "the German element" of the denomination as "usurping too much authority." In order to publish a periodical and support a special field of work, the women had to petition the Board of Missions. Both steps were finally approved in 1899, beyond the period this chapter covers.[48]

Organization of MPC women followed the pattern. An 1879 Pittsburgh gathering heard Lizzie M. Guthrie, a missionary to Japan, and voted on the spot to organize the Woman's Foreign Missionary Society of the MPC. They corresponded and mobilized the organization of conference branches and local auxiliaries, capitalizing on connections to prominent men in the denomination. The MPC General Conference of 1880 approved the organization, and the MPC women began their own missionary efforts in Japan, albeit initially tethered to and overseen by the parent denominational board. By 1888 the organization boasted three hundred auxiliary societies in seventeen conferences, a paper, the *Woman's Missionary Record,* with seventeen hundred subscribers, and the energy to raise and disburse funds, employ missionaries, and conduct their own business. Those prerogatives were granted, but the relationship between the society and the parent board continued to be an issue. When Methodist Protestants voted to seat four women as delegates in General Conference, all had been deeply involved in the Woman's Foreign Missionary Society.[49]

The Woman's Christian Temperance Union (WCTU)

The organization that most successfully expanded women's sphere, home, and mothering into a public realm and provided a context within which women could and would exercise the full array of leadership and political skills was the WCTU. Under the leadership of Frances E. Willard (1839–98), Methodist women who constituted the backbone of the organization and provided its leadership lived into the WCTU motto: "Woman will bless and brighten every place she enters, and she will enter every place." Generated from an 1873–74 crusade against saloons that spread out nationally from spontaneous beginnings in Ohio and predicated upon a social analysis that saw drunkenness, alcoholism, saloons, and the liquor industry as the determinate factors in crime, abuse, poverty, unemployment, and corruption, the WCTU capitalized on longstanding Methodist commitments to temperance and enjoyed strong support from prominent clergy in the Methodist churches, including Bishops Matthew Simpson and Randolph S. Foster of the MEC.[50]

The WCTU formally organized in the summer of 1874 and held its first national meeting that November, electing Annie Wittenmyer as president and Willard as corresponding (executive) secretary. Willard had only recently joined the crusade, visiting leaders and meetings, participating in a saloon pray-in, and accepting leadership of the Chicago branch. The prior three years she had served as president of the Evanston College for Ladies, overseeing its merger with Northwestern University but resigning in a dispute with the central administration. Earlier she held teaching positions in New York, Pennsylvania, and Illinois. By her own schooling in and long association with Evanston, she connected with the leadership and dynamic enterprises of midwestern Methodism and especially Evanston's, then becoming something of a Methodist mecca with Northwestern University, Garrett Biblical Institute, the Evanston Methodist Church, and her own school, Northwestern Female College—"my own Methodist hive," she called it.[51]

Through tireless travel, networking, speaking, and writing, Willard led the WCTU in establishing chapters across the country, becoming the nation's largest women's organization. In 1879, the WCTU elected her president, an office she held till her death in 1898. From that platform Willard enunciated a vision of a transformed society, transforming the church as well. Willard proposed that America deal systemically with the systemic evil (abusive, drunken husbands/saloons/liquor industry/corrupted politicians). Adroitly employing language of Sabbath, motherhood, and home and focusing on "home protection" and legislation to achieve temperance controls, Willard articulated an increasingly grand and complex set of reforms that required the ballots of those most affected—women. Suffrage, in Willard's advocacy, became key to treating causes and symptoms, in effect the full array of what would be social gospel interventions (Sources 1883b). Enunciating a "Do Everything Policy," she sent thousands of Victorian "ladies" out of the sanctuary and their homes into active participation in a wide range of issues, including woman suffrage; social (sexual) purity; concerns of labor, peace, and arbitration; welfare work; temperance; and health. Eventually and beyond the purview of this chapter, Willard schematized the WCTU's agenda under five major headings, "preventive, educational, evangelistic, social and legal, [and] organization," and structured the WCTU into fifty departments, each under the care of a superintendent. Ideally that structure functioned as template at every level from the local to the national, every level connected organizationally to the next. All "carefully mustered, officered, and drilled," the WCTU functioned as "womanhood's Grand Army of the Home," a "grand" exhibit as well of the organizational revolution. Through the WCTU, women gained invaluable training, achieved a sense of their own power, and moved through the church into social reform.[52]

Woman in the Pulpit[53]

In 1889 Frances E. Willard turned her advocacy toward the church with *Woman in the Pulpit*. She was blunt and exasperated:

> We stand once more at the parting of the roads; shall the bold resolute men among our clergy win the day and give ordination to women, or shall women take this matter into their own hands? Fondly do women hope, and earnestly do they pray, that the churches they love may not drive them to this extremity. But if her conservative sons do not yield to the leadings of Providence and the importunities of their more progressive brothers they may be well assured that deliverance shall arise from another place, for the women of this age are surely coming to their kingdom, and humanity is to be comforted out of Zion as one whom his mother comforteth.

The prior year she and four other women had been refused seating as official, elected lay delegates to the 1888 MEC General Conference (see chapter 11). Willard now suggested that if men continued to refuse to share power with the women, perhaps women should "take this matter into their own hands" and form a new church in which they could receive full clergy and laity rights. Neither advocacy by Jennie Fowler Willing and others for expanded leadership roles (Sources 1870a) nor two decades of pressure from below—of women's demonstrated experience in Civil War relief, of their assumption of various leadership posts, of women missionaries, of new women's organizations, of experiments with women in preaching roles—sufficed to make the case.

Among those, perhaps as many as seventy, whose call the MEC could not finally embrace was that of New Yorker Maggie Newton Van Cott (1830–1914).[54] Raised Episcopalian, married into the Dutch Reformed Church, Van Cott underwent a powerful conversion experience in the late 1850s and began attending Methodist prayer meetings at Duane Street. In a dream she experienced a call, ascended to the pulpit, and was endorsed by a "dear old gentleman" auditor, John Wesley. After her husband's death in 1866, she joined the MEC and sustained her husband's business, but began to teach Sunday school and to work at the Five Points Mission, a project of New York Methodism's Ladies' Home Missionary Society, led and backed by Phoebe Palmer, among others. Her effectiveness earned her invitations to speak as evangelist, and in 1868 she abandoned her husband's business to devote herself full time to evangelistic speaking. An invitation to preach by appreciative laity, grudgingly accepted by a dubious pastor, resulted in his support and his persuasive case to the presiding elder for an exhorter's license. That action by the Windham Circuit of the New York Conference in September 1868[55] was followed six months later by her successful appearance before a quarterly conference on a different circuit, which granted her a local preacher's license. The 1869 New York Conference entertained but defeated motions of censure against the presiding elder and of disapproval of licensing women as preachers.[56] More invitations to preach followed, including several in the Boston area, appreciatively treated, described, and endorsed by Gilbert Haven, the influential editor of the equally influential New England Methodist paper, Zion's Herald (Sources 1869b). The paper continued to cover her work as she supplied the pulpit of Trinity MEC, Springfield, the following spring. Springfield coincidentally hosted the New England Conference that spring, permitting some of its members to hear her preach. Trinity Church, "the leading Methodist Church in Western Massachusetts," according to Zion's Herald, renewed her license, an action that editor Haven celebrated.[57] The editor of the New York Christian Advocate, Daniel Curry (1809–87), weighed in negatively on this "disturbing element in the Conference" and on Haven's "characteristic zeal," expressing relief that the New England Conference had not seen fit to move toward admitting her.[58] Support for her ordination came later from Joseph Crane Hartzell (1842–1928), an MEC pastor, Freedmen's Aid executive, and editor (Southwestern Christian Advocate), who invited her to New Orleans. The San Francisco District Conference, where she preached in 1874, formalized that in a recommendation. Bishop Stephen M. Merrill, presiding over the California Conference, rejected the recommendation, ruling that lower judicatories had no right to grant women licenses to preach. His action was appealed to the 1876 General Conference (MEC), and California also submitted a petition favoring local preacher's licenses for women, neither of which was accepted.

That same year, the Jamaica Plain Quarterly Conference (Boston) granted Anna Oliver (1840–92) a local preacher's license, and she subsequently assumed interim pastoral duties in First Methodist (MEC) Passaic, New Jersey, not far from her birthplace, New Brunswick, where she had also taken BA and MA degrees (Rutgers Female College). Post-Rutgers, Oliver had spent a year teaching African American children in Georgia with the American Missionary Association, quitting over wage gender discrimination. She moved to Ohio, where she studied art at the McMicken School of Drawing and Design (University of Cincinnati), became engaged in the temperance cause, experienced a call to the ministry, and entered Oberlin's theological school (wellspring of a stream of perfectionism developed by its leaders Charles Grandison Finney and Asa Mahan). Finding that not to be fully affirming of women (in ministry), she transferred to the Boston University School of Theology, lecturing and preaching to pay her way, including a six-week summer stint in Brooklyn. She graduated with a BD in 1876, honored to deliver one of the commencement addresses.[59]

Assisted by the African American pastor-evangelist Amanda Smith, Oliver had the reorganized but struggling Passaic church "buzzing," as the local newspaper reported. During a year there, she increased membership 500 percent, lectured at New Jersey Methodism's Centenary College for Women, and pressed for social reforms in Passaic (care for homeless children, vocational training in the public schools, and curbs on the liquor trade). Not affirmation but reversals followed. The cabinet and bishop of the Newark Conference did not continue her in ministry, she experienced severe ill health, and her invitation to preach at the weekly meeting of the New York Methodist preachers was rescinded—the latter at the urging of then pastor, later editor, and historian James M. Buckley. In 1879 members of a heavily mortgaged Brooklyn church acquired the property at auction. They organized as an MEC church, took the precaution of obtaining a new deed without the obligatory "trust clause," and invited Oliver to become pastor. Some of the members withdrew. Those remaining committed the congregation to a five-point program—holiness teaching and preaching, trust in God in matters financial and spiritual, a full-orbed educational program, temperance, and gender inclusiveness in church life and governance.[60] The renamed Willoughby Avenue Methodist Episcopal Church prospered under Oliver's leadership, growing from thirteen to seventy members by summer and to more than a hundred by year's end. The Sunday school averaged two hundred attendees. (For a Sunday school at that period see the following 1884 "Snapshot" and Sources 1875.)[61]

It was not the New York East but the New England Conference that took the next step, namely, examining her for ordination and conference membership. It did so on the recommendation of the Jamaica Plain Quarterly Conference. The bishop presiding at the 1880 conference, Edward G. Andrews, however, refused to present her as a candidate for ordination. The Boston presiding elder, Lorenzo R. Thayer, indicated that he would appeal the ruling. The conference allowed her to speak, which she did for half an hour, making an eloquent case for pastoral work as uniquely "adapted to women," a case then subsequently published (Sources 1880a). Persuaded, the conference then voted instruction to its delegates to General Conference to use their influence "to remove all distinctions of sex in the office and ordination of our ministry."[62]

The 1880 bishop's, presiding elder's, and New England Conference's actions pertained as well to another female candidate for ordination, an 1878 graduate of Boston University School of Theology, Anna Howard Shaw (1847–1919). English-born, Shaw grew up in a family devoted to reform causes, living first in Massachusetts, then Michigan. She developed aspirations toward the ministry early and joined the Methodists in her twenties. Shaw experienced strong women mentors—Universalist minister Marianna Thompson, temperance advocate Mary Livermore, and high school principal and Methodist Lucy Foot. The latter encouraged her to attend Methodist Albion College, a coeducational institution with several women faculty, handsomely depicted by Simpson in his *Cyclopaedia of Methodism*. In Michigan, she had also been licensed as a local preacher. After two years at Albion, she entered Boston University School of Theology. Following graduation, she pastored two small Cape Cod churches (Wesleyan and Congregationalist) for six years before applying to the New England Conference for ordination. Believing her aspirations would be supported, she performed well in the ordination examination and was duly recommended by the conference, as her narrative indicates (Sources 1880c).[63]

In response to ruling against their ordinations, Shaw and Oliver elected different paths, Shaw to seek ordination elsewhere, Oliver to contest the decision. To the 1880 General Conference in Cincinnati went Thayer's appeal of the bishop's ruling, a petition from Brooklyn's Willoughby Avenue Church asking that the *Discipline* be revised so as permit the ordination of its pastor (Sources: front cover), and Anna Oliver in person with a printed case including her New England speech (Sources 1880a). General Conference was in no mood to change the *Discipline* "as it regards the status of women in our church."[64] Indeed, if anything, it took a big step backward, declaring local preachers' licenses granted to women rescinded. It would be forty years before the MEC revisited that action. Oliver continued her ministry, sustaining Willoughby's broad-gauged social witness. However, the church's finances suffered, and it folded three years later. Her health suffered as well, and she died in 1892.

Shaw also returned to her ministry with the Cape Cod congregations and indeed pursued ordination elsewhere, namely, with the Methodist Protestants. The MPC's New

York Conference meeting in Tarrytown accepted her candidacy and ordained her October 12, 1880, albeit with some stumbling along the way, as she indicates (Sources 1880c). After several more years in ministry, she took an MD degree (conferred in 1886) so as to address Boston slum conditions. Eventually she came to see alleviation of various social ills as requiring women's participation in the political process and became involved in the suffrage campaign first of the WCTU and then of the Woman Suffrage Association, serving the latter as vice president for twelve years and as president for eleven.

The MPC did not immediately turn its New York Conference's actions into policy. Indeed, its 1884 General Conference ruled her ordination out of order. The annual conference continued, however, its recognition, and five years later another MEC woman, Eugenia St. John, sought and received MPC orders from the Kansas Conference. The 1892 MPC General Conference seated women as lay delegates and authorized annual conferences to decide for themselves whether to ordain women. The UBC General Conference in 1889 voted in favor of women's ordination, and Ella Niswonger, the church's first seminary graduate, was ordained that year.

Theological Education

Methodism's entry into postbaccalaureate theological education had not come without a fight. Croakers like Peter Cartwright continued to champion the "brush college" and the Course of Study as the best formation for real ministry. But urban, more affluent, and better educated congregations aspired to leadership less manured and more mannered. Sounding just such a note of crisis was lay educator James Strong, whose *Christian Advocate* article (Sources 1853c) warned the church that its people "are hungry for a higher style of sermonizing, and they will have it, or leave our communion." Strong went on to outline the limitations in the Course of Study, to acknowledge the contributions that the colleges were making through biblical or theological departments, to argue that permitting the aspiring to further their education in seminaries of other denominations put the church at risk of losing them or their losing their theological bearings, and to make the case for a central theological school. The clergy editor, Thomas Bond, replied in the very next issue officiously opposing the idea and arguing that the church could stand on the success record of Methodist preaching. But Strong found his defenders. A layman from Connecticut, E. E. Griswold, supported Strong's contention of the ineffectiveness of Methodist preachers in the cultural climes of the growing urban centers by citing statistics showing that while the population of New York, Philadelphia, and Baltimore had increased in the previous decade, the numbers of Methodists in the same cities declined.[65]

The Civil War delayed that project, but soon thereafter, in 1867 to be exact, The Methodist Episcopal Church acted on Strong's recommendation. It opened its first postbaccalaureate theological seminary in Madison, New Jersey, and installed by then Dr. Strong as Drew Theological Seminary's first professor of exegetical theology, a fitting reward for his role in the battle. Strong had graduated valedictorian at Wesleyan University in 1844, taught languages at Troy Academy, at the age of thirty organized and built the Flushing Railroad, linking his Long Island hometown with Manhattan, of which he became president, and been elected mayor of Flushing. In 1856 Wesleyan granted him an STD, and in 1858 he went on the faculty of short-lived Troy University, serving as its acting president until 1861. Meanwhile Strong amassed a sizable personal library and spent his leisure devouring the classics of Bible, church history, and theology. From that research and his teaching came important theological writings, notably his twelve-volume *Cyclopaedia of Biblical, Theological, and Ecclesiastical Literature*, and especially his *Exhaustive Concordance of the Bible*. Strong, with four other faculty—Henry A. Buttz, John Miley, George R. Crooks, and Samuel F. Upham—the "big five," together gave a quarter century of teaching to Drew Theological Seminary students. Their program, shaped in the by then classic fourfold manner, featured four years of exegetical, historical, systematic, and practical theology. The "junior year" started off with Hebrew grammar and Greek Gospels. Systematics covered mental philosophy, methods of theological science, doctrinal theology, moral science and Christian ethics, apologetics, polemics, and comparison of heathen and Christian religion. Practical theology began with exercises in writing and speaking and concluded in the third year with homiletics, pastoral care, church polity and *Discipline*, Sunday schools, missions, and worship.[66]

By that point, both Boston "Theological School," moved to the University in 1867, and Garrett, also founded earlier, which had begun as biblical institutes so as to avoid denominational aversion to theological education, had metamorphosed into BD-granting programs (the degree nomenclature changed to MDiv in the 1970s).[67] The UBC followed suit and founded United Theological Seminary in Dayton, Ohio, in 1871. The MECS founded Vanderbilt University in 1872 in Nashville to train its ministers; the EA established a seminary at Naperville, Illinois, in 1873; and the MPC founded Westminster, now Wesley Theological Seminary, in 1884 in conjunction with Western Maryland College. Though the graduates from these newly founded seminaries constituted a small minority of Methodism's ministry, they raised the standard, modeled pastoral roles, and created aspirations among the various lay ministries of the church for comparable professional standing and respect. The pressures for professionalization and posturing between and among Methodism's distinct ministries lay ahead in the next century—indeed would constitute an important dynamic in denominational life.

Camp Meeting and Classroom Accountability

Also ahead lay new issues in doctrinal accountability inherent in the "schooling" of theology, the establishment of contexts for theologians to labor full time at their task, and their removal from the rigors of regularized accountability (once weekly, one might suggest, for *Advocate* heads and quadrennially for all editors). To this point and even beyond, Methodism had looked to its quadrennially *elected* editors—of *Methodist Quarterly Reviews*, of *Advocates*, of Sunday school publications—for its doctrinal guidance, for the monitoring of important European intellectual developments, for defense of the faith against the Calvinism dominant in American evangelicalism, and for translation of its own and British doctrine into popular belief and practice. Editors, like Albert T. Bledsoe (1809–77) in the South, who transferred from the Baptists, and Daniel D. Whedon (1808–85) in the North, reoriented Methodist theology, subtly countering Calvinism generally and the long-dead Jonathan Edwards particularly with defenses of human agency, responsibility, and free will. Thus the defense of the Arminian faith foregrounded the human will rather than divine grace. Similarly, early efforts to develop an American Methodist systematic as a "rational orthodoxy," relying on Scottish commonsense philosophy, accented the capacities of the human mind to know God and God's ways. Making important efforts at a Methodist systematic were Henry B. Bascom (1796–1850), Thomas Ralston (1806–91), and Thomas O. Summers (1812–82) in the South and Miner Raymond (1811–97), William F. Warren (1833–1929), and John Miley (1813–95) in the North. As teacher-theologians, Summers at Vanderbilt, Raymond at Garrett, Warren at Boston, and Miley at Drew represented a new day for Methodism, the professionalizing of its theology and its capacity to engage world intellectual currents on a more sustained basis.[68] At this point, no gap existed between seminary classroom and Sunday school assembly. However, the foundations for the professionalizing of theology had been laid.

In 1867, the year that Drew opened in Madison, New Jersey, A. E. Ballard, George C. M. Roberts, Alfred Cookman, and John Inskip called a National Camp Meeting for the Promotion of Holiness for Vineland (New Jersey).[69] Once an evangelistic extension of the quarterly meeting but not tethered legally by the "trust clause," camp meetings had increasingly taken a life of their own. Less tightly controlled by bishops and presiding elders, camp meetings had furthered the antislavery cause into Free Methodism and rallied defenders of slavery as well. Several, notably Martha's Vineyard (Massachusetts), Round Lake (New York), Ocean Grove (New Jersey), and Pacific Grove (California), metamorphosed into popular summer vacation retreats, an important trajectory.[70] The success of the 1867 event led organizers to establish a National Camp Meeting Association for the Promotion of Holiness and to call a second national "conference" for Manheim, Pennsylvania, the next year, a gathering that produced an attendance of some 25,000, including 300 preachers, and that featured preaching by Bishop Matthew Simpson. Early support from Methodism's leadership moderated as this venture generated other associations; spawned, encouraged, and sanctioned a new style of supraconference holiness itineration; and reinvigorated specifically holiness camp meetings across the country—camp meetings that functioned as both a preservation of earlier patterns and a prophetic judgment against a Methodism deemed to have abandoned its covenant. The issues in accountability that the camp meeting movement would pose lay ahead. In the 1860s and early 1870s the new movement gave energy to northern Methodism's holiness witness. Eventually the tension between these new associations and the church's leadership led to explicit breaks and the founding of new holiness denominations, among them, the Church of the Nazarene.

Palmer's altar theology and the renewed holiness impulse had found little resonance in southern Methodism until after Reconstruction. Then with the initial acquiescence of the MECS bishops and emerging leaders like Warren Candler and with the encouragement of the National Association, Georgia Methodists led in the rapid generation of holiness camp meetings and associations. However, early censorious missteps alienated Candler and confirmed the enmity of Emory's President Atticus Haygood. Candler and Haygood raised their voices (Candler as editor of the *Nashville Christian Advocate*; both eventually as bishops) to portray holiness associations, papers, camp meetings, and freewheeling itinerants as divisive, clannish, intemperate, and judgmental; second blessing theology as unfaithful to Methodist doctrine; and holiness cultivation of women's leadership as unbiblical. By the mid-1880s the MECS bishops began suppression of the still nascent southern holiness using punitive appointments and the threat thereof to whip the preachers into line, efforts that continued into the 1890s. The southern holiness effort and the reactions to it exposed and furthered party alignments within southern Methodism, a differentiation unthinkable during slavery. Gradually a small progressive group eager to modernize the church and the South emerged around Haygood. Institution builders but in a neoconservative mode found a champion in Candler. And several styles of traditionalists held up the old landmarks—the holiness folk through their camp meetings; revivalists under the leadership of itinerating, "professional" evangelists like Sam Jones; and small-town and rural "Old Methodists" who in Georgia found leadership from politician Rebecca Latimer Felton.[71]

Like the theology in the new seminaries, Phoebe Palmer's and the holiness movement's "altar theology" and shorter way put a premium on acts of the human will. The two theological trajectories reworked Wesleyan doctrine for the new day. The one sought to sustain the doctrine of perfection in a revivalistic context with a second conversion and a second blessing, claimed by an act of will, the shorter way. The other envisioned Methodist piety better enlivened by progress (toward reason and human ability) that remembered Wesley's emphasis on education and expectations for sacramental frequency and envisioned growth through nurture.

Nurturing Members

Stationed college- and/or seminary-trained ministers and the vibrant Sunday schools, Bible classes, and missionary societies had, we have noted, increasingly crowded the class meeting, absorbing some of the latter's formation and nurturing functions but not its probationary and disciplining responsibilities. The old lay offices—class leaders, stewards, and local preachers—suffered similarly, remaining official roles but seeing the local church's imagination and energy captured by Sunday school superintendents, trustees, and missionary secretaries. And Sunday school began its own evolution away from drilled memorization via the catechism toward instruction predicated upon new assumptions about how individuals grow into becoming Christian. Alternative practices of formation—the probationer's class and graded uniform lesson Sunday school—led to new rituals for membership and to accommodating church architecture, particularly the Akron Plan Sunday school facility. These changes both reflected and further altered understandings of church, ministry, Holy Spirit, vocation, Christian perfection, and lay leadership.[72]

The lay-led class meeting, through which one came to membership and whose tickets admitted one to Communion, remained in the *Disciplines* through most of the century,[73] exhortations to employ it and arguments for its importance continuing. However, the MECS in 1866 recognized its decline, making it permissive, "whenever it is practicable," and retitling that section "The Social Church meetings." The MECS also conceded that two or more classes might meet jointly.[74] That same year, the MECS introduced a ritual for "joining the church" and four years later located it with other rites. The MEC introduced its version two years earlier, in 1864.[75] Eventually churches held the reception rites on Communion Sundays, which the MECS encouraged pastors to offer monthly, permitting new members to take their first Communion.[76] The rites invited the prospective member to affirm baptismal vows, renounce sin, and commit to the church's rules, doctrines, sacraments, and institutions. The pastor then extended the right hand of fellowship.

To equip adults for the membership rite, probationer's classes came to replace the class meeting, an educational or formational process in lieu of disciplined probation. Garrett and later Drew Seminary Professor Daniel Kidder (1815–91) in his influential 1871 book, *The Christian Pastorate*, urged young preachers to establish classes to school probationers in the doctrines of the church and the duties of church membership.[77] To resource such probationer's classes, the MEC in 1872 published extracts from the *Discipline* in booklet form, including the historical statement, Articles of Religion, General Rules, and Ritual.[78] To guide probationers in digesting these standards, the MEC's publishers put out in 1875 an eighty-page *Probationer's Manual*.[79] Three years later James Porter, the retired book editor, published *Helps to Official Members of The Methodist Episcopal Church* in 1878.[80] The most widely and longest used guide appeared first in 1883, Stephen Olin Garrison's *Probationer's Hand-Book*. The Philadelphia pastor's effort, which endured for thirty years and sold more than half a million copies,[81] extracted and commented upon the doctrinal, liturgical, and ethical matter in the *Discipline*. Other resources included Jonathan T. Crane's *First Words for a Probationer*,[82] produced by the Tract Department of the Methodist Book Concern; Sunday School head (later bishop) John Vincent's call for serious instruction, reading, and discussion in probationer's classes in his 1882 *The Revival and After the Revival*;[83] and his tracts "Our Own Church Series," a series that began in 1884.[84]

Pastor, then general secretary John Vincent, his MECS counterparts, Thomas O. Summers (1812–82) and Atticus Green Haygood (1839–96), and Minnesota practitioners like Sara Jane Timanus Crafts (1845–1930) led Methodism to see the Sunday school as the great engine of formation, absorbing that dimension of and replacing the class meeting, effecting the conversion or transformation for which Methodists had looked to revivals, and eventually displacing the probationer's class as well. They capitalized on new theories of learning and of childhood, represented in the U.S. by Horace Bushnell, emphasizing growth, development, and nurture, and drew on educational experiments elsewhere to bring system, training, resources, and technique into religious education. And they developed a system that increasingly included adults as well as children.[85]

As pastor in Chicago in the 1860s, Vincent spoke to Sunday school assemblies, produced model lesson plans, and organized teacher-training events, earning a national reputation that landed him as corresponding (general) secretary of the Sunday School Union in 1868.[86] Under Vincent's leadership, Methodism developed the uniform lesson plan (the Berean), promoted national training conventions, expanded a Sunday school teacher's journal, established a system of "normal schools" to convey best practices and theory, founded Chautauqua as a Sunday school teachers' assembly (1874), and took that nationally in 1878 as the Chautauqua Literary and Scientific Circle. The uniform lesson plan, with its age-graded leaflets, golden texts (daily or weekly key texts for devotion or memorization), pictures, teachers' materials, home readings, questions, and hymns, did for the laity what the Course of Study achieved for the ministry, that is, put the entire denomination and all age groups on the same page scripturally and theologically. The uniformity and integration that this common lectionary achieved every Sunday depended on a cadre of teachers for each age group (women and men), functioning under the guidance and direction of a Sunday school superintendent, effectively the principal of a school system. And he—it was often "he" at this period—dramatized his high calling by leading the opening and closing assemblies. When operating in its ideal form, as carefully described by Pamela Goodwin (Sources 1875), the highly regimented Sunday school system required a very special building, and Goodwin's superintendent designed what would be the prototype.

Inventor and manufacturer of farm machinery Lewis Miller served as Akron (Ohio) Sunday school superintendent for more than thirty-five years.[87] The inspiration for a building that would achieve Vincent's design[88] and Miller's aspirations for separate instructional and proximate assembly and worship spaces came, tradition holds, at a Sunday school picnic in a natural amphitheater or geological punch bowl.[89] The children, Miller noted, grouped themselves but naturally faced the center. He sketched a building that would achieve the same plan and persuaded an architect and fellow church member, Jacob Snyder, to design a new complex to include a Sunday school building adjoining the older sanctuary. By 1870 the Akron Plan Sunday school was completed. Two stories high and capped by a dome, the building arrayed two tiers of classrooms opening into a large semicircular room. The desks in each class faced forward so that when its windowed door opened, the students need not move to heed or hear the superintendent.[90] With chalkboards, piano, Scripture mottos, stained glass, and carpet, the building achieved architecturally for the whole and its parts what the uniform lesson did instructionally—common progress.

Akron quickly became a Methodist pilgrimage site and the Akron Plan a distinctive American contribution to the grammar of architecture. Vincent used the *Sunday School Journal* and his 1887 book, *The Modern Sunday-School*, to promote the model.[91] And when his church in Plainfield, New Jersey, was built in the late 1880s, Vincent had it follow the Akron Plan paired with an auditorium-style sanctuary.[92] The combination became a standard in church building and architectural catalogs, often adapted, sometimes copied, championed, and idealized by the distinguished architect George Kramer (Sources 1897) and, along with Gothic or Romanesque exteriors, announced Methodism's Main Street status.

Methodism: Intercultural, Fraternal, Ecumenical

The Sunday school and educational activities generally became centerpieces of Methodism's missions and its work across ethnic and language lines at home as well as abroad (see treatment in chapter 7). In the 1830s American Methodists began missions in cities of several Latin American countries; however, these missions were to the English-speaking community, not to Spanish- or Portuguese-speaking European immigrants or Native peoples. Most English-language missions closed in the early 1850s due to lack of interest and funds. South American missions were reopened in 1865 by southerners who fled after the Civil War; but they were English-only missions as before, until 1867 when John F. Thomson preached his first sermon *in Spanish* in Buenos Aires, Argentina, marking the beginning of MEC missions to Native peoples in Latin America (Sources 1867c).[93] As in Latin America, Methodists in this period built further on earlier foundations for Spanish-language ministry in the Southwest U.S. (see chapter 7). By 1874, Alejo Hernández (ordained deacon in 1871), the father of border Methodism, had died, but southern Methodists had established a Mexican district, and by 1881, Santiago Tafolla had become its first Hispanic presiding elder. The same year the Woman's Missionary Society (MECS) sent two missionaries, Rebecca Toland and Annie

Williams, to launch a day school, the Laredo Seminary. Nannie Holding joined them in 1883 as principal, an office that she held for close to thirty years and for which service the school was renamed in her honor. By 1885, the church constituted the Mexican Border Mission Conference, Bishop Holland McTyeire presiding at the organizing session.[94] The MEC began work among Chinese Americans in this period, initiated in 1866 by three women from the Sixth Street Church, Sacramento, and specifically with a Sunday school to help the Chinese in their city learn English and study the Bible. The following year the California Conference launched a mission to the Chinese, sending Dr. and Mrs. Otis Gibson, former missionaries to China, to begin work in San Francisco. Gibson took the Chinese Sunday school in Sacramento as a model for efforts elsewhere (Sources 1870b), believing, as the report indicates and as he indicates later, that these schools would be the means of leading the Chinese to "adopt our higher form of civilization and our purer faith."[95] (Note that the school design shared features with the Akron Plan.) Within ten years, the Gibsons, who superintended the work for seventeen years, established similar schools in principal cities in California, Oregon, and Washington, benefiting in that endeavor from active support of the national and Pacific Coast Women's Mission Society. With the women's assistance they moved into social ministries, particularly the rescue and support of Chinese women prostitutes. And the Gibsons encouraged a Chinese and later a Japanese convert to become licensed as local preachers and begin the indigenization of leaders (Sources 1886).[96]

The Civil War brought confusion to Methodist ministries among Native Americans, especially within the diverse Oklahoma Indian Missionary Conference. At war's end, the conference was reorganized. At that point, Samuel Checote, under whose earlier leadership the Creeks rescinded laws forbidding the teaching of Christian religion, a Creek district was formed, the Bible and hymnal translated into Creek, and Native preachers trained, became the first Native American presiding elder (DS). Having twice seen division between races and regions destroy his native land, first in the disastrous removal of Native Americans from the Southeast and again in the Civil War, Checote looked for ways to bridge racial and cultural differences. As superintendent, he raised money for homes, schools, clinics, and churches for his people and vigorously defended the rights of the Creek Nation in petitions to Congress (Sources 1883a).[97] Native American women played an important role in linking home and church. Mrs. Samuel Checote made her home a center of Methodist life for both Native Americans and missionaries.

Although new missions were established in Indian Territory (Oklahoma) in the West, removal, continued white incursions seeking land or gold, armed conflict, and increased governmental control had a devastating effect on the church's missionary enterprise. In 1869 Methodist President Grant created a Board of Indian Commissioners to root out corruption in the government's procurement system, reorganized the appointment of missionaries to reservations, and enlisted church workers as Indian Agents, but placed them under federal control. In 1870 the Supreme Court denied citizenship to Native Americans, and the next year Congress ended treaty making with Native American tribes. At the same time the wholesale slaughter of buffalo began.

Missionaries went onto the federal payroll and served the government's purposes. Grant's "Peace Policy," endorsed by Methodist editor Daniel Curry, allowed clergy of only one denomination on designated reservations. Missionaries whose church had enjoyed long contact with particular tribes—Roman Catholics, for example—were summarily dismissed, and representatives of other churches—notably Methodists—were arbitrarily put in their place. Catholics received assignments on only seven reservations. Methodists, who had little success or experience in Native evangelism, were given 20 percent of the reservations! Southern Methodists, who had more experience than their northern counterparts, were also slighted in assignments. They received none! Dislocation, confusion, and denominational rivalry caused unmeasured damage. Religious divisions and growing government disenchantment brought a gradual end to the policy in 1882.

Ironically, during the period in which Grant's policy was in effect, northern Methodists lost interest in Native American mission work, given the opportunity made little effort, and spent little money to implement or extend their ministries. They permitted governmental subsidies to determine the extent of missions. In another irony, during part of this period, from 1881 to 1890, the president of the Board of Indian Commissioners was Clinton B. Fisk, a devoted Methodist and Drew Theological School trustee from 1876 to 1891.

Tragically, Methodists were implicated in the late nineteenth-century wars, when Native Americans resisted the duplicitous treatment and were met with military force. In particular, in the mid-1860s disputes on the southern plains culminated in the Sand Creek, Colorado, massacre. John Chivington, an MEC pastor-colonel, led Union troops to slaughter two hundred Cheyenne and Arapaho, who had recently signed a peace treaty with the U.S. Chivington received commendation from the army and was honored by Coloradans and Methodists at his death in 1894. The massacre, plus a military parade through Denver with mutilated bodies, ignited thirty years of war. The Plains tribes—Arapaho, Comanche, Kiowa, and Sioux—went on the warpath through 1879. During the gold rush in the Black Hills of western South Dakota, Methodists felt their sting. "Wild Bill" Hickok, celebrated western lawman and Methodist attendee, died from a Sioux gunshot in 1876. Lying in the Deadwood Methodist cemetery near Wild Bill were two others known in Deadwood Methodist lore: "Calamity Jane" and "Preacher Smith," Henry Weston Smith, Deadwood's newly appointed pastor who came to preach, killed by Sioux that same year.[98] Apache wars in Arizona and New Mexico flared continually from 1872 to 1889. Initial military failures against a loose confederation of Native Americans, forged by leaders including Crazy Horse and Sitting Bull, culminated in the Sioux annihilation of George Custer's cavalry at the Battle of the Little Big Horn in Montana. Methodist editor Charles Fowler agonized over Custer's defeat (Sources 1876c). Another MEC editor, Joseph Hartzell, actually called for all-out war "to exterminate the savages!"

In 1890, the U.S. military retaliated at Wounded Knee, South Dakota. The massacre left 350 Sioux men, women, and children dead, among them Chief Sitting Bull. The Methodist response was subdued; there was little outrage. The MEC newspaper advocating the cause of Native Americans, *Our Brother in Red,* did not even notice! Editor David Moore's commentary in the *Western Christian Advocate* was the exception.[99] Wounded Knee was the last military encounter between Native Americans and whites. Gradually Christian attitudes shifted. The pressure for reform in Native American policy was triggered in 1884 by Helen Hunt Jackson's *Century of Dishonor,* which detailed the unjust treatment that Native Americans received at the hands of the federal government. An Indian Rights Association was created. And in 1888, the MEC Woman's Home Mission Society offered an apology to Native Americans and pledged to work for reforms. The 1996 UMC General Conference adopted a formal apology for the church's implication in Chivington's massacre.[100]

Methodism devoted considerable missionary effort to the Reconstruction of the South, as we will note below. And as the southern church restabilized, it reasserted itself in the altar-against-altar competition that increasingly extended west as the American population moved into new territories.[101] In less intense ways, the MPC, EA, and UBC competed as they also moved west. But in the post–Civil War period, the churches took steps away from competition and toward unity.

The exchange of fraternal delegates or delegations from within and beyond the Methodist family had become commonplace on General Conference as well as annual conference levels. The MEC routinely received and sent formal expressions of fraternity—with Canadian, Irish, and British Methodists, with the separate German American denominations, with the African Methodists, and with other American communions. These ritualized gestures took enough General Conference time to warrant an inquiry into their importance and the appointment of a Committee on Fraternal Relations. The committee noted

> that the growing catholicity of the age is ever enlarging our circle of fraternal correspondence and increasing the number of delegations bringing fraternal greetings; that there is reasonable expectation that we shall soon be exchanging periodical salutations with Lutherans, Baptists, Episcopalians, and all other members of the Church Catholic, as well as Methodists and Presbyterians.

It therefore recommended as a measure to both respect and limit the fraternal greetings "that Wednesday, May 10th, 1876 be the day ordered for the reception of fraternal delegations," with the inevitable accompanying speeches and sermons confined to evenings as needed.[102] Was it not anomalous, given such fraternal excess, that the two bodies that claimed to be The Methodist Episcopal Church did not enjoy fraternal relations? That MEC General Conference (1872) undertook to remedy this state of war, authorizing exploration of formal fraternity and appointing a fraternal delegation to the General Conference of the MECS.[103]

In response, the 1874 MECS General Conference empowered a fraternal delegation to carry the proposal of a joint commission to "adjust all existing difficulties" standing in the way of fraternal relations.[104] The MEC reciprocated, and a Joint Commission on Fraternal Relations of three clergy and two laypersons from each church met at Cape May, New Jersey, in August 1876 (Sources 1876d). The first southern demand and the first action recalled the overture made by Lovick Pierce in 1848 and a staple in MECS self-understanding, that 1844 had not been a schism, namely, "there is but one Episcopal Methodism . . . our two General Conference jurisdictions being each rightfully and historically integral parts of the original Methodist Episcopal Church constituted in 1784." And further that each of "said Churches is a legitimate Branch of Episcopal Methodism in the United States, having a common origin in the Methodist Episcopal Church organized in 1784 . . . one Methodist family, though in distinct ecclesiastical connections."[105]

The southern commissioners convened separately and kept their own record. They noted that "the form of statement in a certain connection would exclude several colored organizations from the classification of Episcopal Methodisms of this country" and concluded that "the omission of reference to them could not be properly construed as an oversight."[106] The larger Methodist fraternity would be bracketed out by careful attention to constitutional, jurisdictional, and connectional concerns.[107] A formula for fraternity had been defined that would privilege the relation between the MEC and the MECS and keep relations with African American Methodists at very formal levels, the mere exchange of fraternal regards. The Joint Commissioners then went on to deal with the contests over property and territory between the two churches, setting out rules and procedures for adjudication of disputes.[108]

Further gestures of fraternity followed in what would be more than a half-century effort at reunion.[109] Both churches thereafter appointed fraternal delegations. Both participated in the first international Methodist Ecumenical Conference of 1881 at which Bishop Simpson celebrated the emerging Pan-Methodism and the family ties binding some thirty churches in twenty nations (Sources 1881b).[110] And both cooperated in the planning and mounting of the 1884 centennial of American Methodism.[111] The latter, a major production and gala affair at Baltimore, had been proposed by the MECS in 1878, was restarted by the delegations at the Ecumenical Conference, and was effectively planned by joint committees from the two churches, with other Methodist bodies invited only by letter. In the preliminary meetings, the record indicated "the utmost harmony prevailed." So also, the "same feeling of brotherly love characterized the Conference." The bonds of brotherhood took expression in a Communion service, a love feast, and a public celebration involving fifty-six Sunday schools, with some 25,000 children. Especially important were social events, including one at the home of the Reverend John F. Goucher:

> Representative brethren of the Methodist Episcopal Church, and of the Methodist Episcopal Church, South, were brought into closer acquaintance at Mr. Goucher's, and the bonds of fraternity were strengthened by the free and cordial expressions with which brother greeted brother.

Not participating in this greeting of brother and brother were the AME, AMEZ, and CME, all of which had sizable delegations present at the conference.[112] Bonds of fraternity could separate as well as unite.

The smaller Methodist bodies participated actively in this chapter in the long road to unification. Methodist Protestants had experienced schism on the eve of the Civil War, devastation during it, and loss of some congregations and preachers to the MECS thereafter. (Northern and western conferences revised the *Discipline* to include an antislavery plank.) It took until 1877 for the two wings to come together. In the interim the southern MPC received an overture concerning unity from the MECS, the latter's 1866 admission of laity into its governance having removed one of the significant divisive issues. The northern MPC Convention went even further in explorations with the Wesleyans, publishing a joint hymnal and drawing up proposals for a new "Methodist Church" to include the nonepiscopal (MP, Free, Wesleyan, Primitive) Methodist churches. The union was not consummated, but the northern MPC conferences employed the new name until reuniting with the southern conferences in 1877. Methodist Protestants were well represented at the 1881 Methodist Ecumenical Conference.

The UBC, which had escaped formal cleavage during the Civil War, had been party to explorations of unity in the 1850s, first with the Wesleyan Methodists and then among additional smaller churches—Free Presbyterians, Free Will Baptists, Congregational, and Evangelical Association. Members of these bodies met in an Unofficial Union Convention in 1855. The UBC also responded to an invitation to the Pan-Protestant American Evangelical Alliance, sending a large delegation to its 1873 meeting. On the eve of and immediately after the Civil War, William Nast, leader of German Methodism within the MEC, made an overture to the EA about closer relations. The EA sent a delegate to the 1868 MEC General Conference. Out of these exchanges came proposals for organic unity or for transferring language conferences (MEC German ones to the EA and EA English ones to the MEC). In the 1870s and 1880s the EA and UBC again extended overtures for unity. Neither prospect worked out. Both denominations, however, participated in the 1881 Methodist Ecumenical Conference and those that followed, eventually renamed World Methodist Conferences.[113]

Competing Black Methodisms

The MEC had, as we have noted, made provision in 1864 for Black annual conferences, gained access to some MECS church facilities where Union troops prevailed, and begun missionary efforts among southern African Americans and whites. In 1866 the MEC, unwilling to continue to channel its efforts through the Unitarian-led Freedmen's Aid Bureau, created its own Freedmen's Aid Society to elicit support for and coordinate efforts in evangelization, education, and institution building. The AME and AMEZ, effectively excluded from the South before the war, also entered the southern harvest with great energy and effectiveness, as did their Black Baptist counterparts.[114] Thus began a missionary contest for the hearts and commitment of African Americans who, as subsequent statements and interviews indicate, saw through the patronizing hypocrisy of their "inclusion" in the slaveholders' churches and moved their allegiance elsewhere. By war's end an MECS Black membership of more than 200,000 had dropped by two-thirds and by 1869 by nine-tenths (to less than 20,000).

The 1866 MECS General Conference, faced with the alienation of its Black membership and the emergence of African American communions highly critical of southern folkways, received a report from its Committee on the Religious Interests of the Colored People that outlined steps for amicable separations and continued relationship—full ordination, separate quarterly annual conferences and General Conferences, and Black presiding elders. The exact status vis-à-vis the MECS of such separate entities was ambiguous and the report itself variously understood.[115] Over the next quadrennium the separations continued apace. In 1870, facing the fact of "an African American Exodus," the MECS General Conference made provision for recognition, transfer of property, organization, and ordinations. The new Colored Methodist Episcopal Church (CME) met the same year, under the presidency of MECS Bishops Robert Paine and Holland N. McTyeire, created nine annual conferences, established a publishing house, and launched a journal, *The Christian Index*, with Samuel Watson as editor. The CME elected and Paine and McTyeire consecrated William H. Miles and Richard H. Vanderhorst as bishops. By 1874, the CME had added 2 bishops, ordained 607 traveling preachers, deployed 518 local preachers, established 535 Sunday schools, and garnered close to 75,000 members. However, the CME was castigated by its competitors with charges of being an "Old Slavery" or "rebel" church, and its recruitment efforts substantially trailed those of the MEC and the two African American churches. It did enjoy some level of support from the MECS. And the MECS heard guidance from Sunday school head, editor, later Bishop, then Emory president Atticus Haygood (1839–96), who urged southern Methodists to view the end of slavery as opening a new and better day and one that permitted race relations on a new plane (Sources 1880d). This counsel, spelled out in more detail in his 1881 *Our Brother in Black: His Freedom and His Future*, was much needed as Methodist President Rutherford Hayes had withdrawn federal troops (1876), Reconstruction had ended, and the era of Jim Crow, the Ku Klux Klan, and lynching had begun.

Through Reconstruction and beyond, the CME, MEC, and AME and AMEZ worked with differing dominant ecclesial strategies and three distinct notions of freedom, civic roles, and race relations.[116] The two Black denominations (AME and AMEZ) enjoyed significant leadership from northern African Americans and from southern African Americans involved in the Civil War and influenced thereby. Aspiring to regenerate the South, they invested heavily in education and uplift, aiming to equip members to exercise leadership in southern society, economy, and politics. Typified by Henry McNeal Turner (1834–1915), southern but born free, Union chaplain, politician, church organizer, presiding elder, editor, and bishop, the AME (and AMEZ) preached a "gospel of freedom," taught racial pride, sought full participation of African Americans in American society, continued the campaign that those churches had led in the prewar North, and aimed at nothing less than the empowerment of a people. A comparable exemplar of the CME, Lucius H. Holsey, pastor, bishop, founder of Paine College, and editor of *Hymnal, Discipline*, and *Manual of Discipline*, had been a house slave of a University of Georgia professor and married into the slave household of Bishop George F. Pierce, who performed the ceremony. Considering Pierce his mentor, willing to work cooperatively but deferentially with the MECS, and skilled in the subtleties of race diplomacy, Holsey with fellow bishop Isaac Lane led the CME in seeking a supportive relation with whites and especially with southern white Methodism. Preeminently realists, CME "Black traditionalists" preferred negotiation, counseled patience, made concessions to southern values, eschewed politics, did not violate racial barriers or challenge white supremacy, and rather sought white coinvestment in education.

Symbolizing and articulating the ideals in the MEC southern efforts were Gilbert Haven (1821–80) and James Lynch (1839–72). The former as columnist, then *Zion's Herald* editor, then bishop harassed a highly segregated northern Methodism and demanded that the MEC sanctify the bloody war sacrifices and live into the example of Christ and the teachings of Paul, North and South. His millennial vision of a church without caste (Sources 1867a) racially integrated at all levels and in every leadership sector captured the imagination of AME editor James Lynch, who transferred his considerable talents to the MEC. Lynch went south for the MEC, organizing its Mississippi Conference, establishing educational institutions through the Freedmen's Bureau, representing the state at Republican National Conventions and the conference at General Conferences, serving as secretary of state and presiding elder until dying of pneumonia in 1872. (Among the ironies of the day, the General Conference [MEC] that year debated whether it should follow Haven's counsel and elect "colored" bishops but elected him instead.)[117]

In places in the South, the anticaste Christian radicalism of Haven and Lynch held brief sway, and MEC women and men missionaries created interracial institutions, particularly at the conference level, as Black deacons and elders took their place within existing MEC conferences (Kentucky, Missouri) or were part of newly constituted southern MEC ventures. But even this modicum of egalitarianism proved too idealistic for white Methodists (MEC) in both the North and the South, and the small pockets of white Methodists in the South pressed for the segregation that their northern counterparts had earlier embraced. At the 1868 General Conference, Kentucky Methodists sought division into white and Black conferences; the African American Lexington Conference was created the next year, and more such segregating requests followed. So after an agonizing disquisition on the "caste spirit," and despite eloquent testimony from African American pastor, former senator, Union chaplain, and convert from the AME, Hiram Revels, on the evangelistic value of the interracial witness (Sources 1876b), the 1876 MEC General Conference opted for the official policy of local choice:

> *Resolved*, 1. That where it is the general desire of the members of an Annual Conference that there should be no division of such Conference into two or more Conferences in the same territory…, it is the opinion of this General Conference that such division should not be made.
>
> *Resolved*, 2. That whenever it shall be requested by a majority of the white members, and also a majority of the colored members of any Annual Conference that it be divided, then it is the opinion of this General Conference that such division should be made, and in that case the Bishop presiding is hereby authorized to organize the new Conference or Conferences.[118]

MEC segregation proceeded apace, but the MEC southern mission continued as well, much of it focused on building a network of Black educational institutions at all levels, from basic literacy to the formation of Black ministerial leadership and the training of a cadre of Black teachers. Working collaboratively in these efforts were the Freedmen's Aid and Southern Education Society (founded in 1866), the Board of Education, and the Woman's Home Missionary Society. By the end of its first year, this southern MEC mission had established fifty-nine schools with some five thousand students.

By 1892, after twenty-five years of operation, the Freedmen's Society boasted a "thoroughly unified system of schools," which was "so graded and located, and related in courses of study, as to form a federation of institutions, including professional, classical, academic, and industrial schools."[119] This "federated" system functioned under centralized national management, a Board of Managers elected by General Conference, which reported to a General Committee in the interim between General Conferences. Its corresponding (general) secretary ran a highly centralized operation, taking "personal direction" and responsibility for "the buying of lands, the erection of buildings, the employment of teachers, and the superintendence of institutions of learning of various grades." Southern white Methodists (MECS) sized up this highly coordinated enterprise differently, Bishop Warren A. Candler voicing their hysteria in *Dangerous Donations and Degrading Doles; or a Vast Scheme for Capturing and Controlling the Colleges and Universities of the Country.*[120]

The Freedmen's Aid and Southern Education Society had spent, by 1892, close to $3 million, $1 million of that ($1,010,980.25 to be exact) in the prior quadrennium. Real estate it valued at $1,808,800. In the prior fiscal year, the society had disbursed monies to the following collegiate or higher level institutions: Bennett College, Central Tennessee College, Claflin University, Clark University, Gammon Theological Seminary, George R. Smith College, Little Rock University, Morgan College, New Orleans University, Philander Smith College, Rust University, Samuel Huston College, U. S. Grant University, and Wiley University. For that year, 1892, the Freedmen's Aid and Southern Education Society claimed a total of 447 teachers and 9,310 students, though only 172 students in college. It boasted 326 persons preparing for the ministry and, over the prior quadrennium, "twelve hundred and fifty conversions . . . among the students." The society assured General Conference of the following results:

1. The property is absolutely safe to the Church.

2. Schools of similar grade have substantially the same courses of study.

3. Local responsibility and cooperation are being developed as rapidly as the financial ability of the people will justify.

4. College degrees, in course or honorary, are only conferred by institutions of collegiate grade, and then, as a rule, only in consultation with the authorities of the Society.

5. No new schools will be founded in the South, among our people, either white or colored, without the consent and cooperation of the central office.

6. No teachers can be employed not in thorough accord with the doctrines and usages of the Church.

7. The English Bible is introduced as a text-book in all grades of every school, whether theological, collegiate, or academic.

8. To a very great extent the same text-books are used in all schools of the same grade, making it possible to contract for them at the lowest rates, as well as to insure the use of the best books.[121]

Here, then, was one important result of the organizational revolution, a system that produced both teachers and conversions, both new citizens for the South and new ministers for the denomination. It was the national system as the church wanted it—written post–Civil War on a blank slate, as it were, without the distraction of preexisting institutions and their support systems and with nothing to stand in the way of national control, standardization, efficiency, and purpose.

Conclusion and Transition

By 1884, the American family of Methodist churches had developed a growing cluster of program boards and support services. Their administrative offices moved out of downtown church basements and into newly erected skyscrapers. Ambitious clergy traded desks for pulpits. Such Victorian high-tech inventions as typewriters, filing cabinets, and that pearl of great price for ministers, the mimeograph machine, became constant companions. Methodist Vatican cites were in the making—New York, Philadelphia, Washington, and Chicago for northern Methodists; Nashville and Atlanta for southern Methodists; Baltimore and Pittsburgh for Methodist Protestants; Harrisburg for Evangelicals; and Dayton for the United Brethren.

The challenges at a connectional level to which these boards responded—problems in accountability, common purpose, governance, and cohesion—were mirrored on the local level by the array of missionary, prayer, purposive, and reform societies. These men's and women's organizations and especially the Sunday schools posed afresh the query, Who's in charge? With such institutions and their leaders, as with the classes and class leaders, the settled pastor and the stable congregation experienced weekly issues, sometimes problems—of communication, initiative, accountability, control, and authority.

The problems and issues derived from the fact that the new dynamic entities did not mesh with or report to the existing authority structure, namely, the quarterly conference. And a Leaders' and Stewards' Meeting that, in some places, met monthly, still functioned with the focused spiritual and fiscal agenda outlined by Wesley. Osmon C. Baker, commentator on the *Discipline*, noted its promise: "No duties are so specifically assigned to the leaders' meeting as to require their being held in all our circuits and stations; yet when they are held monthly, they are found to be eminently adapted to promote the interests of the Church."[122] No script, however, outlined governance responsibilities. In 1852 the MEC dealt with part of the problem by providing a seat for "male superintendents of our Sunday schools . . . in the Quarterly Conferences . . . with the right to speak and vote on questions relating to Sunday schools, and on such questions only."[123] In 1864, the northern church made the superintendent a full member and granted the quarterly conference "supervision of all the Sunday-schools and Sunday-school societies within its bounds."[124]

In 1884, the General Conferences (MEC) effected the comparable revolution at the local level to that achieved in 1872 at the general. It authorized quarterly conferences to "organize, and continue during its pleasure, an Official Board, to be composed of all the members of the Quarterly Conference," to be "presided over by the preacher in charge," to discharge many of the duties of the Leaders' and Stewards' Meeting, and to "keep a record of its proceedings."[125] The creation of the official board brought to the local church what incorporation, consolidation, efficiency, bureaucratization, and professionalization brought to the church as a whole and, indeed, to American society, that is, corporate principles of finance, procedure, order, integration, governance, and cohesion. The change was dramatic as Presiding Elder Morris Crawford explained, his role having been transformed as well (Sources 1884). Bureaucratization at the top and corporate-like business efficiency in the local church went increasingly together.

METHODISM IN 1884:
WILKES-BARRE, PENNSYLVANIA

In 1884, Methodism's centennial year, First Methodist Episcopal Church in Wilkes-Barre, Pennsylvania, represented Methodism's strength and status in small industrial cities across the nation. At 432 members it had become the third largest congregation in the Wyoming Conference in northeastern Pennsylvania and was completing an ambitious building program. By the time the Wyoming Conference first met in the new building two years later (1886), the congregation's membership of 496 made it the second largest in the conference. The new church and Sunday school buildings spurred remarkable growth. Over the next three decades the membership quadrupled, reaching a peak it maintained until the mid-twentieth century and becoming the largest church in the conference. With strong programs, facilities designed by an architect with a national reputation, and ushers in swallow-tailed coats, its pew renters included the elite of Wilkes-Barre, and it enjoyed appointment of clergy rated among the top in the conference, indeed, in the denomination.

The City

First settled in the 1760s, Wilkes-Barre had become northeastern Pennsylvania's leading industrial center and one of the nation's fifty largest cities by the 1860s. The area's first settlers in 1769 came from New England to farm the Wyoming Valley on the upper Susquehanna River in northeastern Pennsylvania. However, the valley's underground wealth of anthracite coal gave it the potential to play a major role in industrial America. By 1869 the area had become the supplier of 80 percent of the nation's coal.[1] During that time, Wilkes-Barre grew into a major industrial center where mining, iron and steel, rails, textiles, and manufacturing combined in an interrelated system. While the collieries covered the entire region, the financial and administrative ends of the business were located in Wilkes-Barre. The city had become the headquarters for most major coal companies in the region. This created an intense demand for unskilled laborers and entrepreneurial talent and capital, both from within the region and from the outside. By 1884 Wilkes-Barre was a model industrial metropolis with a population in excess of 30,000.[2] Its pioneering electric streetcar system connected its ethnically diversified neighborhoods with the city center; its rail system linked its people and products to the principal cities of the East Coast and the Midwest.[3]

The Methodists

Methodist itinerants on the Newburgh, New York, Circuit first preached in the small village along the Susquehanna River in 1789. A Wilkes-Barre Circuit was formed in 1791. Two years later Bishop Asbury visited and preached in the courthouse. Church services remained infrequent, especially during the winter months, and dependent upon a preacher showing up. By the early 1810s, preachers came more frequently, and lay preachers held services on Sundays unscheduled for a circuit preacher. The growing congregation left the circuit in 1830 to become a station appointment with its own pastor. They shared Old Ship Zion Church on Public Square with Congregationalists, Presbyterians, and Episcopalians from 1811 to 1831, when they became sole owners of an aging church building. Both survival and denominational pride required a building of their own. Public preaching and the Sunday school, however, continued in the old one-room church on Public Square until 1849, when a more spacious church in Greek Revival style was built on nearby Franklin Street. This two-story church, with Sunday school, prayer meeting, and class meeting rooms below and sanctuary above, served the needs of the growing congregation until the 1880s.[4]

Methodism expanded dramatically in response to the rapid growth of Wilkes-Barre's economy and population in the middle years of the nineteenth century. The creation of new companies, the incorporation of more banks, and the increase in political offices in this seat of county government enlarged both workforces and their managers. By 1886 the city had nine Methodist churches—three MEC including First, two African American Methodist (one AME and one AMEZ), one Free Methodist, two Primitive Methodist, and one Evangelical Association, the latter reflecting miners from Wales and Germany, respectively, who flocked to the region at midcentury.[5]

In the twenty years from 1864 to 1884 membership of First Church grew by a third and the Sunday school tripled in size.[6] First Church's success in recruiting Wilkes-Barre's upper classes can be seen in the large number of community leaders in its ranks. By the 1880s 14 percent of Wilkes-Barre's upper class were Methodists, most of them in First Church.[7] Five of the nine trustees of First Church belonged to the city's first families or married into them, were members of the leading social clubs, and served as officers and directors of several major companies and charities—L. D. Shoemaker (lawyer), George Bennett and H. H. Derr (bankers), John Phillips (coal baron), and L. H. Taylor (medical doctor). But First Church reached only a small portion of the immigrant working population that was streaming into the city. Wilkes-Barre's two major urban groups—the one native-born, Protestant, and comparatively well-to-do; the other foreign-born, often Catholic or Jewish, and poor—took on the characteristics of two cities. The most striking fact about the complex class, religious, and ethnic alignments in places like Wilkes-Barre, writes Rowland Berthoff, was not that they were openly hostile, but "so equivocally related as to be mutually unintelligible and quite heedless of each other."[8] Social distance was increasing not only between the middle class and the poor, but between the middle class and the urban elite as well, and thus further complicated First Church's response to its city. Although some of the newly rich capitalists of the Gilded Age emulated their antebellum counterparts in supporting urban religious effort, many others remained aloof—some because they were committed to other reform approaches, others simply because they were preoccupied with their own economic or social advancement.

In earlier days, the newly urban—from the wealthiest to the poorest—were bonded by the experiences, perspectives, and practices shared across small-town and rural Methodism. Antebellum church leaders had invoked these loyalties both in appealing to the wealthy for support and in calling wanderers back to the fold. The evaporation in the late nineteenth century of confidence in such a shared value system underlay what would be uncertain and sometimes panicky efforts to develop new strategies in these years.

New Church Buildings, 1877, 1885

The energy that mined anthracite, built rail lines, and powered industry led Wilkes-Barre's Methodists to build a trendsetting new church in the decades following the Civil War to house their growing congregation and expanding program. Significant new buildings attested the congregation's self-confidence, its denominational pride, and its civic leadership role. A large gift from Priscilla Lee Bennett, wife of a prominent Wilkes-Barre banker and church trustee, daughter of coal baron Washington Lee, launched the building campaign in 1874. She offered to fully fund the building of a state-of-the-art Sunday school building if the trustees would raise additional money to build a new church. When additional lots in a fashionable residential neighborhood (Franklin Street near Market Square) were given in 1875, the trustees employed a prominent New York architect, Bruce Price, a hire that itself symbolized and furthered the church's growing prominence.[9]

Bruce Price (1845–1903), a nationally renowned architect of the late nineteenth century, was born in Baltimore. Too young to serve in the Civil War, he apprenticed with the Austrian-born Rudolph Niernsee, the most important Baltimore architect of the time. He spent a year in Paris broadening the scope of his studies with French teachers.

Upon his return, Price established an office in Baltimore for joint practice with Ephraim Baldwin. Although their association was brief, the partners received a number of commissions to design churches in the city, one of which was St. Paul's, built about 1870. In 1873 Price married the daughter of one of Wilkes-Barre's coal barons, Washington Lee, and moved his practice to Wilkes-Barre. (That made Price brother-in-law to First Church patroness Priscilla Lee Bennett, whose home he also designed.)

Price planned a two-phase building program: first, erect a new building to house the expanding Sunday school, and second, demolish the old church and rebuild on the same site. Price's design for First ME Church featured both a new exterior style (Gothic) and a new interior plan (auditorium-style sanctuary with Akron Plan Sunday school; see discussion in prior chapter). Plans for Price's church were featured in *American Architect and Building News* for September 1876.[10] The presiding elder reporting on progress in 1884 affirmed that when completed, it "will be the most elaborate and imposing church edifice within the bounds of our conference."[11]

First to be built was the Sunday school, delivered from the basement where it had been in the old Franklin Street church and given as much attention as the new sanctuary. In the semicircular apse, where medieval churches placed the high altar and lady chapels, Price located the Sunday school superintendent's platform. He—and it typically was he—was thus surrounded by his children and teachers. Patterned after the highly acclaimed building of First MEC, Akron, Ohio, the Sunday school featured two curving tiers of classrooms facing a large central auditorium. The plan efficiently gathered a large number of classes close to and in full view of the superintendent, who led the school in opening and closing exercises from a platform at its center, after which doors closed to allow individual class sessions.

The dedication in 1877 drew John Vincent, architect of the uniform lesson plan, founder of Chautauqua, systematizer of Methodist education, then general (corresponding) secretary of the denomination's Sunday School Union, his significance to carry him to the episcopacy in 1888. Vincent pronounced the three-story semicircular building to be the most complete Sunday school facility in the nation. The Sunday school's proud superintendent, George S. Bennett, described the building in a paper delivered before the Pennsylvania State Sabbath School Association in 1889:

> The first or ground floor contains a prayer room, church parlors, class-rooms, and the library. The second or principal floor is arranged especially for Sunday School uses. This is a vaulted room with a gallery running entirely around it. Beneath the gallery and facing the Superintendent, are placed the Primary and Intermediate Departments: their seats are on raised platforms. Large folding doors with glass panels and illuminated Scripture texts shut off these rooms from the Junior Department. The gallery over these rooms contains five large Senior Class rooms. The floors are a series of wide platforms and chairs are used for seats. Lifting glazed doors, beautifully ornamented with appro-

priate Scripture texts, shut off these rooms from the auditorium. The main floor is occupied by pupils of the Junior Department, who sit on chairs grouped around their class tables. The Normal Class [for teachers in training] sits at one side, and the Reserve Corps [of newly trained teachers] at the other side behind the Junior Classes. The Superintendent, from his platform, commands a view of the entire school. He can see every one, and every one can see him and the blackboard behind him. The rooms are so arranged that at the opening and closing exercises the school rooms can be made one audience room. The visitor's gallery is behind and over the head of the Superintendent, facing the school.[12]

Phase two of the building campaign began in September 1883 when the 1849 building was torn down and the cornerstone for the new church was laid. Over the next two years a massive three-towered stone-front building in Gothic style rose on North Franklin Street. Inside a broad worship space, inspired by the arrangement of the secular theater, welcomed worshipers. Galleries surrounded the central pulpit platform on three sides so that every hearer was as close as possible to the preacher. Behind the pulpit sat choir members, who reinforced the appeal of the preacher with their devotional singing, and behind the choir rose the pipes of an impressive organ. Built by the Hook & Hastings Company of Boston and costing $4,800, it was the gift of Mrs. Bennett.[13] Curved pews seating thirteen hundred circled the dominating pulpit, lush carpet covered the sloping floors, and stained glass windows by day and electric lights mounted in two enormous brass chandeliers by night flooded the interior with delicate hues. Steam heat from two basement coal-fired furnaces kept the large building cozy in winter.

Reasons for the overwhelming, but brief, popularity of auditorium–Akron Plan churches are varied, but much of the appeal lay in the connections to secular performance spaces. As worship services increasingly paralleled secular performances, architects naturally borrowed the setting of music halls and theaters for use in churches.[14] Correspondences between secular performance and sacred worship created a new relationship between the churchgoer and the service. Congregations increasingly became nonparticipating viewers, judging the service by secular standards.

Completed at a cost of $75,000, the new church was dedicated debt-free by Bishop Randolph Foster on October 4, 1885.[15] On the day after the church's dedication, the editor of the city's evening newspaper signaled the city's gratitude for the Methodist achievement:

> The new building which [the Methodists] have erected, and which was so successfully dedicated yesterday, is an ornament to this city, and should be a matter of pride to every citizen, whether an attendant there or not. It is assuredly one of the handsomest as well as one of the most complete church structures in this section of the state, and for the money expended in its erection, is not surpassed in elegance and good taste by any in the country. In short, it is a model edifice, and the people concerned in its

construction...have a title to congratulation in the fact that their magnificent building was so nearly paid for when dedicated to the praise of the Almighty.[16]

First Church remained Wilkes-Barre's largest concert space for the next thirty years and was regularly used for civic concerts and lectures as well as church services of the congregation and the denomination's Wyoming Conference.

The exterior as well as the interior decor and functionality exhibited the master vision of architect Bruce Price and proclaimed First Church's sense of place. With its neo-Gothic towers, stained glass, and wood and stone carvings, the church presided over Wilkes-Barre's city center. It was a Methodist cathedral, imaging without qualification what members and leaders valued, quietly but dramatically proclaiming the congregation's self-understanding, community status, and sense of refinement.[17]

Pastoral Leadership

A cathedral church, centrally located in a vibrant city and possessing a strong and growing congregation, deserved pastors equal to its leadership opportunities, and First Church came to expect its appointments to be just such. Pastors of leading churches enjoyed prominence as public figures, leaders in the city as well as the church, exercising ministries with broad public implications. To signal its expectation to the bishop that he should send preachers capable of playing leadership roles that accorded with its place in the city, First Church set the pastoral salary well above conference norms, indeed nudging it to $2,500 in 1884 to equal the top in the conference, that of First Church, Scranton.[18] And the congregation was not above aggressively seeking exceptional pastoral leadership on its own and doing so despite a rule in the 1884 *Discipline* terming negotiation between pastors and churches in advance of episcopal appointment making "contrary to the spirit of our itinerant ministry and subversive of our ecclesiastical polity." First Church acquired its new pastor in 1886, A. H. Tuttle, from outside the conference, from prestigious First MEC in Plainfield, New Jersey, setting a pattern. Wilkes-Barre effectively opted out of the regular appointment system of the Wyoming Conference for several generations.[19] The result? First Church enjoyed college- and seminary-trained pastors, tried and proved as ministers of leading churches in other cities, several with honorary doctorates.[20] Wilkes-Barre and the Wyoming Conference profited from proximity to the denomination's venture in postcollegiate theological education, Drew Theological Seminary. An increasingly educated congregation would understand why a pastor needed a shelf-lined library.

Ministers with such a profile who led a station church and its community deserved the title *pastor*, a designation that crept into Methodist parlance. The organization founded in 1868, the Ladies' and Pastors' Christian Union, signaled the shift in nomenclature. Shift it was. Methodist ministers had been called "to preach"; they called themselves and were called *preachers*; they distinguished sharply and safeguarded the office of preaching. Women could exhort and evangelize but not take a text and preach. The line between the two rhetorical exercises was fine and not clear to auditors and even to speakers. But now Methodists could call their minister *pastor*. The terminological change, to be sure a gradual one, indicated that Methodist ministry was becoming a profession as well as a calling. Wilkes-Barre expected pastoring, not just preaching, but presence, full-orbed leadership of the congregation, attention to the Sunday school and missionary societies, and above all, pastoral calls. Important in Victorian America, prominent pastors devoted as many hours to parish visiting as they could. And increasingly, the pastor as professional would surround himself with other professionals or professionals-to-be: organist, choirmaster, bandmaster, Christian educators, and even caterer.

Calendar, Program, and Order: The Social Congregation

The 432-member congregation understood that good stewardship on their big investments in real estate warranted use of their facilities for the benefit of the people more than once or twice a week. The church buildings increasingly became a "social home" for members. The church parlor was the chief symbol of the change.[21] Other homelike space accommodated the various activities of the church family. First Church, Wilkes-Barre, modeled the new congregational form. Like thousands of congregations, it transformed itself into a center not only for worship and Sunday school, but also for concerts, church socials, breakfasts and dinners, women's meetings, men's clubs, youth groups, girls' guilds, sewing circles, benevolent societies, and nameless other activities. Proponents of the change argued that the new congregational activities could overcome the impersonality of large churches, provide wholesome amusement for young people, and draw men more actively into membership and congregational work. By the 1880s Sunday church services were held at 10:30 a.m. and 7:30 p.m. with the 872-member Sunday school meeting at 1:45 p.m. Young People's Meeting (later Epworth League) met on Sunday at 6:30 p.m. Prayer meetings were held on Thursday evenings. A catechism class for young people on Fridays at 4:15 was added in 1892. For old-timers four large class meetings continued to be held in the church parlors, two on Sunday afternoons and two on Wednesday evenings. The sanctuary experienced change as well. As one strategy to address the chronic gender imbalance and to encourage membership, congregations abandoned separate seating for men and women, arguing that families should worship together and that separate seating diminished women. Organizational growth was as rapid as membership growth.

New-style social congregations employed a rhetoric of equality, friendliness, and democracy. And they were busy. They nurtured a sense of social responsibility among their members and extended their activities to meet the needs of their neighborhoods and regions. Their space and human resources supported kindergartens, employment bureaus, visiting nurses, circulating libraries, and dozens of clubs and classes for youth in the surrounding neighborhoods. Strict attention to personal discipline was beginning to fade, indeed really ceased as a congregational endeavor, but the desire for influence remained. Instead of disciplining a member for illicit forms of recreation, Methodists influenced recreational choices positively by providing their own picnics and parties, even dances. And prayer meetings and class meetings, where they persisted, continued to enable adults to grow in grace, the one through prayer, the other through rigorous self-examination as well.

Monitoring the members' morals remained the theoretical disciplinary expectation of the few remaining class leaders, but the congregational-level counterpart, the old Leaders' and Stewards' Meeting, no longer existed. The real energy of the church lay elsewhere. Indeed the new look of congregational organization was represented in the transformation of the old engine of discipline and church trials, the Leaders' and Stewards' Meeting, into an Official Board. The Official Board both accommodated and contained lay initiatives and energies, bringing the diverse organizations now honeycombing the church under a single (male) board but one chaired and appointed by the pastor. First Church implemented this disciplinary change immediately. Beginning in 1883–84, the church gave oversight to its life, programs, and outreach through an Official Board of nine male members, which met four times per year, and two sets of committees. The one, congregational, dealt with budget, finance, records, parsonage, music, Sunday school, and care of poor persons. The second, connectional, oversaw missions, temperance, tracts, higher education, church extension, and clergy pensions. A committee on pew rents was added in 1885 and one in support of the Freedmen's Aid Society in 1888. For women of the parish two groups vied for attention, the Ladies' Aid Society and the Woman's Foreign Missionary Society. A third, the Woman's Home Missionary Society, was added in 1886. A chapter of the Epworth League for young people was chartered in 1890 and a Men's Brotherhood in 1905.[22] Top executives of almost every church agency—Hunt of the Book Concern, Vincent of Sunday Schools, Kidder of Higher Education, McCabe of Church Extension, Hartzell of Freedmen's Aid Society, and Mrs. William Warren representing the Woman's Foreign Mission Society—visited the church in the centennial year. Reflecting its investment in these new organizations, First Church gave increasing amounts of money for purposes other than its own maintenance.

Public Worship

Public worship continued to remain focused on the sermon, but vied with organ voluntaries and choir anthems as organist and choirs now joined the preacher on an expanded platform up front in the new sanctuary. By the 1880s Methodists added more congregational singing, responsive readings, and public repetition of the Lord's Prayer along with the traditional hymns, lessons, collection, and sermon. Communion was offered monthly, and baptisms were routinely and regularly included in Sunday services rather than held privately after the service or in the parsonage. First Church made sure that copies of the denomination's hymnal, now with full ritual and musical settings, were in the pew racks on opening day.[23] Watchnight services became a regular feature on New Year's Eve.[24]

Auditorium sanctuaries like that First Church was building certainly would feature virtuoso preachers. They also made space for organs and vested choirs and music that was performed as well as participatory. A congregation that handed over the performance of its music to talented and well-known musicians was considered as prestigious as one that had a renowned preacher. Josiah G. Holland, editor of *Scribner's Monthly*, pointed out in 1875, "The churches are full, as a rule, where the music is excellent. This fact may not be very flattering to preachers, but it is a fact."[25] Fine music and good preaching in a comfortable environment drew the affluent and those who so aspired. The congregations, like an audience, gazed on the performers, listening intently and judging what they experienced. The theater format tempted members toward passivity, toward becoming religious consumers.

For all its investment in what would be Methodism's liturgical future, First Church retained commitments to Methodism's past. That duality shaped its weekly and annual means of grace. The weekly cycle now revolved around the Lord's Day (not the class meeting). The annual season featured the special days dedicated to the benevolent enterprises and collections on their behalf (see below). It included as well the revival in winter and camp meeting in summer, both major structures of congregational and individual piety. Both took advantage of a time of the year that offered opportunity for sustained religious activity. The revival began in January when business and domestic pressures eased following the holiday season. The camp meeting was held in the country in July or August. With the vacation now an established practice, the summer made not only nature but also time available to the church. Both were periods of intensified spiritual labor. The revival and camp meeting offered daily services structured around the sermon. Prayer, Scripture, and song complemented fervent preaching that reached out to the unrepentant soul and the once zealous heart now grown cold. Both were related to prevention. During these two seasons of leisure when work consumed less time and energy, they aimed to counter temptation and restrain self-indulgence.

To escape the city heat, many First Church families rented cottages or tents at the nearby district camp meeting during the course of the summer. Ten years earlier (1874) the Wilkes-Barre District of the Wyoming Conference purchased a permanent camp site on the western slope of the Susquehanna mountains five miles from the Wyoming depot. By the 1880s eighty cottages, a large dormitory, a catering cottage, and a large tabernacle had been built on the wooded grounds. But attendance had peaked in the previous decade. An attempt to revive the camp meeting by adding children's, women's, and youth assemblies in the 1890s did little to prevent the slipping attendance. Regular camp meetings were discontinued in 1908.[26]

Stewardship: Financial and Personal

When the old church was pulled down in the spring of 1883, the Official Board adopted a pledge-and-envelope system to raise money for current expenses and conference apportionments, replacing the pew rentals.[27] When pews became available again in 1885, pew rents were reinstated and soon became again the major source of income. Receipts for the following year illustrate First Church's giving pattern:[28]

Balance on hand April 1886	444.44
Envelope subscriptions	76.58
Special subscriptions	34.50
Home for Friendless	51.04
Wyoming Camp Ground	13.00
Pew Rents	4,936.70
Dime Collections	979.82
Missions, Church	611.62
Missions, Sunday school	888.38
Pensions, Sunday school	222.10
Special Collections	147.15
Total	8,405.33

The Wyoming Conference ordered nine collections to be taken up in each church during the conference year: education, missions, church extension, Episcopal Fund, Tract Society, superannuated (retired) preachers, Sunday School Union, Freedmen's Aid Society, and the American Bible Society.[29] In 1884 First Church, Wilkes-Barre, ranked first among the churches in the conference in benevolent giving.[30] The women of First Church raised a good deal of money on their own for their causes.[31] The ubiquitous concert, lecture, and chicken supper and ice cream social bespoke a people who labored continuously to raise money to meet building-related expenses and to reduce building-related debt. The Ladies' Aid Society held an average of four major fundraising events each year to help maintain and improve the church building and parsonage. First Church was a strong institution financially, a result of its size and the affluence of many of its members. Expenses were high, but First Church tended to have adequate resources to meet its budget. The church frequently was a major source of revenue for denominational mission programs. Wilkes-Barre Methodists proudly supported the three educational institutions in their area—Wyoming Seminary, a coeducational boarding school founded by Wyoming Valley Methodists in 1844, Drew Theological Seminary (Madison, New Jersey), founded in 1867, and Syracuse University, founded in 1870. To these schools Wilkes-Barre Methodists sent their children and their charitable gifts; several pastors and lay members of First Church served as trustees of all three institutions.

Old First's stewardship can be described by the terms *quality, prestige,* and *leadership.*

Quality was found in its worship services, church program, and facilities. Prestige came from being associated with a large, strong institution. Its members held important leadership positions in the community and the region. Attracting a disproportionately large number of the more affluent, the congregation also drew citywide, from a variety of peoples and from many neighborhoods. Possessing a large constituency, the church had the leadership and the financial resources needed to carry on a program that could not be equaled by smaller neighborhood congregations. Such an institution was looked to for leadership in both denominational and civic affairs. In one aspect of its leadership, First Church combined denominational and civic interests, namely, in starting new churches to accommodate the city's growth. First provided money and a nucleus of members to help start a new congregation, and its contributions to the Board of Church Extension helped finance other new churches.

Coda

For seventy years, until the decline of King Coal eroded its energy and membership, First Church modeled downtown Methodism. Noted for the excellence of its worship services and the prowess of its preaching, the congregation provided clerical and lay leadership to Wilkes-Barre. Its pastor, well known in the city and the denomination, participated actively in Methodist and civic affairs. The vibrancy of the central business district and the location of the church therein made the pastor's participation in civic functions effortless and just as readily featured him as an opinion maker to be consulted by community leaders.

The music program was the best in the city. A full-time professional choir director supervised the children's, youth, and adult choirs. A church orchestra played regularly at Sunday evening services. The church school was an institution of considerable strength. It offered classes for all age groups and a number of classes for adults, each having a different style and emphasis. Some of the adult Bible classes had membership of more than one hundred, providing opportunities for personal relationships and more intimate fellowship within a congregation that had more than a thousand members.

The downtown church provided not only a ministry to its members but also a voice for Methodism and Methodist commitments in the city. The building was large enough to accommodate denominational meetings. Its downtown location made it accessible to hotels in which out-of-town guests stayed. To its sanctuary, the bishop or other visiting dignitary came to preach. First Church was also used for community concerts because it had the only auditorium large enough to hold them.

To a later period belong the congregation's struggles to sustain its urban witness through deindustrialization, white flight, neighborhood transformation, urban renewal, social-cultural pluralization, divorces, smaller families, youth culture, and the media and digital revolutions. In addressing such challenges, Wilkes-Barre First United Methodist made good use of the remarkable foundations laid in the 1880s.

Figure 1

Membership, First UMC, Wilkes-Barre, Pennsylvania
1864–2004

Year	Church	Sunday School
1864	300	340
1874	336	840
1884	432	872
1894	751	804
1904	830	1,038
1914	1,627	1,164
1924	1,621	1,000
1934	1,645	833
1944	1,546	402
1954	1,609	342
1964	885	222
1974	649	116
1984	514	50
1994	286	70
2004	222	0*

* The Sunday school is now closed.

CHAPTER XI

RESHAPING THE CHURCH FOR MISSION:
1884–1939

In an address to the Methodists in North America, the 1884 Centennial Conference exhorted members to faithfulness in doctrinal orthodoxy, to continuing emphasis on the Wesleyan doctrines that relate to salvation, to the movement's mission "to promote holiness," and to the ongoing campaigns of morality and reform (especially temperance and Sabbath protection). Evoking the image of Israel poised to enter the promised land, the MEC/MECS delegates concluded:

> Before you is an ever-widening horizon. The world lies at your feet. The nations await your coming. Will you respond to the call? The grand march for the conquest of all lands for Christ has begun. The voice of the Lord bids us go forward. We dare not accept a secondary place. With our schools and colleges, with our wealth and culture, with our social power and our vast numbers, we must have a large share in the world's evangelization. We hold our place and our power for God and humanity. "None of us liveth to himself." [Rom. 14:7.] We inherit our privileges that we may make the most of them. Shall we prove worthy of our heritage? Will our Sunday-schools be lifted to the greatness of their calling? Will our missions be pushed to the limits of their opportunities? Will our Church literature receive the patronage it deserves? Will our educational work receive the touch of a new inspiration? In a word, shall the throbbings of new life be felt in all the departments of our connectional agencies? Surely not, unless we are ready to lay our wealth, our learning, our social power, and all our influence, and all our sympathy and zeal in humble consecration before the Lord. We pray you, brethren, be in earnest. Think on these things. "And the God of all grace, who hath called us into his eternal glory by Christ Jesus, after that ye have suffered awhile, make you perfect, stablish [sic], strengthen, settle you. To him be glory and dominion forever and ever. Amen." [1 Peter 5:10–11.]

Standing in the way of Methodism's entry into its divinely given commission and deplored by the Centennial Conference was "the spirit of strife and division," which, they noted, "is not yet wholly eradicated from our Zion." They went on to say, "We are happy to believe that the period of dissensions is well-nigh over."[1]

The Centennial Conference certainly caught important prospects for Methodism's second century: its valuation of education (and modernity), its evangelistic signature, its reform spirit, its institutional strength, its global missionary reach. Evangelization of the world and reforming societal practices that stood in the way of the gospel would indeed become consuming passions of the several Methodist churches.[2] That very year Robert Maclay negotiated to open Korea for Methodist missions. And the 1884 MEC General Conference had elected William Taylor missionary bishop for Africa, thus elevating Taylor's global evangelistic tours and his launching of self-supporting missions onto an episcopal plane. Eight "foreign" annual conferences sent delegates to that General Conference (Foochow, Germany-Switzerland, Italy, Liberia, North India, Norway, South India, and Sweden), and the 1884 *Discipline* authorized representation additionally for Japan and Mexico.[3] That General Conference also created the category of central conference and organized Norwegian, Danish, and Indian Mission conferences in the U.S.

But the prospects for holiness, evangelism, and unity within episcopal Methodism dimmed as holiness advocacy took more absolutist form. Its more strident, less compromising adherents then went out and were pushed out. An 1885 gathering that called itself "the First General Holiness Assembly" enunciated such "come-outer" sentiments in these terms:

> Every saved individual should be connected with the organic Church. Holiness is not a disintegrating but a conserving force; it is not intended to tear down but to build up; hence, professors of holiness should not voluntarily surrender their Church privileges for trivial causes. But if an oppressive hand be laid upon them in any case by Church authority, *solely* for professing holiness, or for being identified with the cause of Holiness, depriving them of the privileges of Christian communion, they should then adjust themselves to circumstances as may be required, in order to have the continued enjoyment of the ordinances of our holy religion.[4]

The adjustment of circumstances would launch new holiness and pentecostal denominations, several of them peopled by former Methodists (MECS and MEC), leaving behind a reduced but nevertheless principled Methodism's evangelical cohort.

Methodism would stretch as well on its modernistic or progressive wing, the churches developing or embracing new instruments for, convictions about, and theories of social betterment. Both the holiness folk and the social gospelers championed poor, marginal, and powerless persons. They differed on how and with what message to intervene. And their separate advocacies and campaigns pushed out the boundaries of the orthodoxy and Wesleyanism to which the Centennial Conference appealed. Both holiness and modernism extended Methodism's theological/programmatic contours. Over the long term this stretching, paralleled in other denominations and in the society generally, weakened the center and yielded Protestantism's two-party system and the culture wars of the late twentieth century.[5] In the short term, the holiness exits probably made it easier for Methodism to embrace progressive projects and ideals.

Laity Rights for Women

As we noted in chapters 9 and 10, the Civil War provided women the experience and training needed to stretch beyond the sharply defined role expectations of previous years and beyond limitations prescribed by notions of a woman's sphere. They had utilized and demonstrated organizational and managerial skills on an individual level as well as a national level, as they assumed various wartime duties. Middle-class women, especially in the North, also enjoyed increased leisure due to invention of labor-saving devices and products—canned foods, store-bought clothes, washing machines. Free to pursue activities outside their homes, denied space in American politics, and marginally involved in new corporate structures, many Methodist women invested their war energies and experience in their churches. Building the missionary societies, the WCTU, and the Ladies' and Pastors' Christian Union (and counterparts) into significant local and national organizations, they saw no reason why such proved abilities and talent should not be recognized and applied in denominational affairs as a whole.

Jennie Fowler Willing (1834–1916) had made such a case in 1870, linking women's future liberation with that of their recently freed African American sisters and brothers, referencing women's churchly accomplishments, and appealing to their responsible voting participation in the denomination's 1869 referendum on lay delegation (Sources 1870a). Her career demonstrated—had already shown and would continue to illustrate—what the church stood to gain by granting women full laity rights. Married to MEC pastor William Willing and without children, she was encouraged by William to pursue her interests and to receive a local preacher's license (1877). A popular evangelistic speaker and a prolific writer, she taught English at Illinois Wesleyan University in Bloomington, was a leading suffragist in Illinois, and was a founder of the WCTU. She organized the Northwestern Branch of the WFMS in 1870 and in the 1880s used her organizational energies in the newly formed Woman's Home Missionary Society. The Willings moved to New York City in 1889, and her concern turned to immigrant girls. After her husband died in 1894, she remained in New York and founded the New York Evangelistic Training School in 1895 for home missionaries.

One strategy for inclusion and participation, pursued by women as early as the 1870s, was to lobby for gender-neutral language in the *Book of Discipline*. Such changes or even inclusive construal of terms like *layman* and *laymen* would make women eligible for all lay offices in the church—stewards, Sunday school superintendents, trustees, and quarterly conference members. Some proposed to add exhorters and local preachers, first steps toward ordained ministry. Such legislation was proposed to the 1872 and 1876 General Conferences, but was unsuccessful. Another strategy was that of the test case. As we have noted already, by attending seminary and offering themselves for ordination, women tested male-limited ministry and conference membership.

A particularly dramatic test occurred in 1880 over the question about whether a woman might be invited to *address* a General Conference, and not just any woman but the denomination's most prominent, WCTU President Frances Willard, Methodist born and bred. She sought to bring the greetings of the Union to the all-male MEC General Conference, then meeting in Cincinnati. By her greetings, Willard would advertise the cause so dear to Methodists and promote the temperance efforts of the WCTU. A delegate and friend offered a resolution asking permission for ten minutes of conference time. Hardly had the resolution been put when another delegate, James M. Buckley, editor of the New York *Christian Advocate*, rose to speak in opposition. His remarks touched off a noisy debate that lasted two hours. Two-thirds of the delegates voted to hear Willard, but the implacable Buckley announced that, in spite of the vote, he would exhaust all parliamentary resources to prevent a woman's speaking before the conference. Buckley's statement and the tone of the opposition in the debate were so inhospitable that friends advised Willard to withdraw her request for an audience. She did, sending a note to her "Honored Brethren," thanking them for the final vote, but explaining that she had not been at a General Conference before and had no idea of the strong objection that would be raised. She concluded her note by saying, "I decline to use the hard-earned ten minutes allotted me," and signed her missive "Your sister in Christian work." (See her statement, Sources 1883b, for the role of the denomination in the temperance cause and in extending "Christ into all departments of life.")[6]

The 1880 MEC General Conference did rule that women who held local church offices could be members of a quarterly conference (the governing body of the local church) and, therefore, could vote for delegates from a local church to the lay electoral conference. The latter in turn chose delegates to General Conference, which meant that women might be elected as lay delegates to General Conference. Would General Conference seat them? In 1888 the issue of women's laity rights in the MEC was "put to the test" when five annual conferences elected women as lay delegates to General Conference, all from conferences in the Midwest—Rock River (northern Illinois/Chicago area), Kansas, Pittsburgh, Nebraska, and Minnesota Conferences—plus seventeen *reserve* delegates, most of them leaders in the women's missionary societies or the WCTU at either national or regional levels (see pictures, Sources, p. 32). Frances Willard represented the Rock River Annual Conference[7] and was overjoyed by the changed atmosphere that had yielded the elections. Her life partner, Anna Gordon, recorded that Willard was so moved that she could hardly speak for tears.

For months before the 1888 General Conference convened at the New York City Metropolitan Opera House, Methodists debated women's laity rights and attempted to influence General Conference delegates, a controversy significant enough to be covered by the secular press. Willard reached New York several days before the General Conference sessions were scheduled to begin. Willard was informed soon after her arrival that the bishops were revising their address to take note of the elections and that Buckley had been busy as a mole, undermining the roots of courtesy. There would be a floor fight over eligibility. Conservatives like Buckley claimed the second Restrictive Rule to the church's constitution implied that lay delegates must be *male* members. Progressives argued that *laymen* meant both women and men.

In their Episcopal Address and before the roll call and formal seating of delegates, the bishops declared that the five women could not be seated because their eligibility as delegates had not been properly determined according to the constitution of the MEC:

> For the first time in our history several "elect ladies" appear, regularly certified from Electoral Conferences, as lay delegates to this body.... If women were included in the original constitutional provision for lay delegates they are here by constitutional right. If they were not so included it is beyond the power of this body to give them membership lawfully except by the formal amendment of the Constitution, which cannot be effected without the consent of the Annual Conferences.[8]

The Metropolitan Opera House was packed, not a vacant seat in the boxes or balconies. Women occupied most of the balconies, including Willard and her four sister lay-delegates-in-waiting, watching the more or less dignified antics of the lay delegates below. The report on eligibility set off a noisy controversy. The Met reverberated with arias pro and con for almost a week. The libretto considered one simple question: Were women laymen? The delegates debated this tremendous technicality as if there were no other subject before the human mind. There was no frontal attention on the question of whether women should be accepted as delegates. Buckley, in supporting the stand of the committee on credentials, spoke learnedly and lengthily against what he called "the monstrous regiment" of liberated women. He could only rest his case on rhetoric, choosing words as weapons. Laymen meant men! One delegate, George Hughey, took him on his own terms and cited instances from the Bible, such as "except a man be born again.... Did this mean only lay men and not women?" Hughey noted that the *Discipline* used masculine personal pronouns throughout in referring to members and asked if this meant that women could not be disciplined under the rules of the church.

Many delegates spoke eloquently on such a broad interpretation of the word *laymen* so that it could mean, as one wag put it, "man embracing woman." It was the score that counted, however, and when the vote came, the report of the credentials committee was accepted by a margin of 39 votes. The majority ruled that the word *laymen* in church law did not include women. The chief opponents were clergy (who voted 154 to 122 against) and not laity (78 of whom were for the measure to 76 against). The women could go back to their homes, where they belonged. With a sheepish mien and a meticulous sense of detail, the delegates voted to pay their travel expenses. Mary Nind and Frances Willard, in their journals, spoke for the Cincinnati five about their election and dismissal (Sources 1888).

Willard wrote further about her lover's quarrel with her church in a letter to a friend:

> I love my mother church so well and recognize so thoroughly that the base and body of the great pyramid she forms are broader than its apex, that I would fain give her a little time in which to deal justly by the great household of her loving, loyal, and devoted daughters. I would wait four years longer, in fervent hope and prayer that the great body of her ministers and of her membership may make it manifest to all the world that the Church of Susanna Wesley, Lady Huntingdon, Barbara Heck, and Phoebe Palmer, does not hesitate to march with the progressive age it has done so much to educate, nor to fear to carry their logical sequence in its lifelong teachings as to woman's equality within the house of God.

She nevertheless admitted that she was "often urged and not a little tempted, and sometimes quite determined to take a new departure." Her remarks concluded with a challenge and a lightly disguised threat:

> The time will come, however, and not many years from now, when, if representation is still denied us, it will be our solemn duty to raise once more the cry "Here I stand, I can do no other," and step out into the larger liberty of a religious movement where majorities and not minorities shall determine the fitness of women as delegates, and where the laying on of hands in consecration [that is, ordination], as was undoubtedly done in the early church, shall be decreed on a basis of "gifts, graces and usefulness," irrespective of sex.[9]

After ruling the women ineligible to be seated under the constitution,[10] General Conference in a close vote referred the matter to the annual conferences by proposing a change to the Restrictive Rule applying to lay delegation—"and the said delegates may be men or women."[11] In annual conference balloting, both laity and clergy voted majorities in favor, but the latter not with the three-quarters required. In response in 1892, the Judiciary Committee ruled, unanimously, that women were ineligible, but on an amendment another construction of the Restrictive Rule was proposed—"and said delegates must be male members." The strategy was for this to fail in the annual conference votes, thus entailing the opposite reading of *laymen*. The proposal failed decisively but in a quite partial vote, the consequence of some conferences simply not balloting the question, not an outcome that gave conclusive force to the alternative reading.

Over several years Buckley addressed himself in the *Christian Advocate* to lay rights and other matters pertaining to women (Sources 1890). In 1891, opponents of women's laity rights collected and distributed his editorials in pamphlet form. Women's laity rights supporters countered with a booklet by George W. Hughey, refuting Buckley's arguments point by point. (Hughey's pamphlet was published by the Woman's Temperance Publishing Association, the publishing arm of the WCTU.)[12]

Buckley argued legislative intent, that *laymen* never would have been admitted to the General Conference in 1872 if the church had understood the term to include women. He argued abstract natural rights, that women had the right to "an influence equal to that of man," but not that this influence "should take the form of representation by delegates of her own sex and membership in the General Conference, and of ordination to the ministry, either or both." Buckley cited statistics revealing fears that representation, whether lay or clergy, would eventually be based entirely on proportional representation. As Carolyn Gifford suggested, "Taken to its logical conclusion, he reckoned that this would mean that women would take control of the General Conference because they vastly outnumbered men in the denomination.... For Buckley and other conservatives within the MEC the specter of a GC ruled by women was even more horrifying than one ruled by the laity."[13] Buckley appealed to Scripture. Responding in part to Frances Willard's *Woman in the Pulpit* (1889), Buckley criticized "female suffragists" for "making void the law of God" by ignoring the "plain sense" of Scripture in encouraging women to transgress their appropriate sphere. According to both nature and divine revelation, he believed, man was to rule (at home, in the church, and in the nation). Thus it was fundamentally unscriptural to admit women to the General Conference as delegates because it would make them rulers. He argued politics, attacking the WCTU and Frances Willard for interfering in the affairs of The Methodist Episcopal Church and advocating lay representation for women, their admission to the ordained ministry, and woman suffrage. Buckley charged schism, noting in the *Union Signal*, the "*official* organ" of the WCTU, efforts to connect the deaconess movement with the ordination of women and the threat that the WCTU might "organize a church" if representation continued to be denied to women. Finally, Buckley summed up: "All objections to the admission of women into the General Conference come at last to this—that they are *women* [emphasis in the original] and not men" (Sources 1890, 436). Women should not be given legislative functions, according to Buckley, because they were already preoccupied with work of equal importance that, when they confined themselves to it, exerted a greater influence for good.

Other Methodist churches were not burdened with Buckley or deterred by the controversy in the MEC. The MPC and UBC led the way, granting women full laity rights in 1892 and 1893, respectively. When the former divided just prior to the Civil War, one branch committed itself to a constitutional provision allowing annual conferences to determine who could vote and hold office. When the two Methodist Protestant churches reunited in 1877, the constitution of the new church gave to the annual conferences the power to decide on matters of suffrage and eligibility to hold office. Over the next several quadrennia, Methodist Protestants vacillated, empowering female members through recognition of the Woman's Foreign Missionary Society, but then reducing it to auxiliary status, and then finally by 1888 restoring its independence. As the women's abilities were "increasingly recognized and appreciated by the men of the denomination," local churches began to elect women as lay delegates to annual conferences. The Methodist Protestants not only seated three laywomen delegates in 1892 but also elected Eugenia St. John as a *clergy* delegate to General Conference.

In 1893, the General Conference of the UBC included lay delegates for the first time. At its previous General Conference (1889) the UBC had approved the licensing and ordination of women.[14] Clearly aware of the significance of their actions, the UBC bishops in their quadrennial address to the General Conference affirmed:

> Several conferences have chosen to send as delegates esteemed women from among them. These Christian women are here to-day accorded this highest representative trust in the Church, and are welcomed unchallenged to sit with us in the highest council of the denomination.... What a gathering is this to-day! It marks an epoch in our history. Fathers, young men of the shepherds of Israel; laymen, from all callings, who honor God with their substance; sisters, who represent the loving company at the early dawn of the resurrection morning, meeting first their risen Lord! May Jesus stand in our midst and breathe upon us these holy words, "Peace be unto you."[15]

Mattie Brewer and Mrs. S. J. Staves took their places alongside the men at the 1893 UBC Conference.[16]

In 1896 at both the MEC and the MPC General Conferences, women appeared as elected delegates. The Methodist Protestants seated those sent. In the MEC, the debate that ensued over the four women's right to be seated was so intense and prolonged that by the time a compromise was reached, the four women had left in disgust. Only in 1900 would women be extended equal laity rights in the northern church through the adoption of a new constitution. That meant the first MEC women lay delegates took their seats at the 1904 General Conference in Los Angeles. Twenty-four women were seated as elected delegates and thirty as lay reserves.

The MECS lagged, as did the EA. Not until 1922 did Methodist women in the South gain conference rights. That year eighteen women were seated. Championing this cause was Belle Harris Bennett, whose leadership roles will be noted as we treat the several progressive causes of Methodism's second century (Bennett's heading the southern church's women's home missionary organization, establishing the Scarritt Bible and Training School, opening settlement houses to care for urban poor people, and persuading the church to recognize deaconesses). When the MECS unified its missionary endeavor and subjected the women's foreign and home missionary efforts to denominational control, Bennett acquiesced in the takeover and agreed to head the Woman's Missionary Council within the male-dominated missionary board.

The loss of autonomy and of editorial freedom in its publications led Bennett and others to become ecclesial suffragists.[17] On Bennett's recommendation and among the last acts of the soon-to-be-merged-out-of-independence Woman's Home Mission Society (WHMS), its board prepared a petition to the 1910 General Conference. In addition to this WHMS request for full laity rights for women, the 1910 MECS General Conference received 148 memorials, 637 petitions, and hundreds of telegrams in support of women's laity rights in the church. Belle Harris Bennett was invited to address the General Conference on behalf of the WHMS memorial, the first time a woman's voice had been heard in a General Conference of her church (Sources 1910). In a brilliant speech by an astute veteran, she told delegates that "the great Church" they represented needed "the womanhood of the Church" in its councils and that "not a few" now believed that "the fulness of time" had come:

> My brethren, this is not a matter of reason with you, [but] a matter of prejudice.... Put this act on its passage, and it will come back to another General Conference to be ratified, and [by then] a great many of us will be gone home to God.... After twenty centuries we stand knocking at the door of the Church of God, saying yet, "My brothers, brothers, won't you take us in?"

Despite her eloquent appeal, the memorial lost by a vote of 74 to 188. Good to her word, Bennett led southern women in an even better-organized campaign for the 1914 General Conference, couching the appeal in less radical terms. The bishops opposed the measure, and again it failed. The 1918 General Conference, half of its delegates there for the first time, had a lot on its mind as we will note elsewhere—world war, possible unification with the northern church, race relations, temperance, adoption of the Social Creed, even modifying the Apostles' Creed.[18] General Conference passed legislation granting women lay rights, the bishops declared the change a constitutional issue, and therefore to the annual conferences the matter went. All but four concurred, and women were elected and seated in 1922. Bennett, though elected, was too ill to attend and died of cancer that summer.

The Evangelical Church never granted women conference rights, and former Evangelical women gained that prerogative only with the 1946 merger with the UBC. But even after the legal barriers fell in all of the churches, gender injustice remained. For example, the MEC Newark (New Jersey) Conference did not elect a woman delegate until 1924, and the Philadelphia Conference, not until 1936!

New Ministries for Men and Youth

New ministries for men were in the making as well. Although men were outnumbered by women two to one in most parishes, and perhaps because of it, organizations for men also became a fixture of late Victorian Methodist, Evangelical, and United Brethren church life. Precise origins of what came to be called the Brotherhood Movement remain elusive. At least a dozen brotherhoods sprang up among the Methodists during their centennial decade (1884–94) and the years immediately following. The Wesley Brotherhood appears to be the oldest, having been founded in Philadelphia in the early 1880s by a pastor, later bishop, Thomas B. Neely. It was an idea he perfected in the several fashionable Methodist parishes he served in his native city. The Mizpah Brotherhood was founded in Calvary ME Church, East Orange, New Jersey, by Pastor Amos Kendig in 1892 and spread rapidly throughout the Northeast. Methodist chapters of the interdenominational Brotherhood of Andrew and Philip were formed beginning in 1895, led by Methodist S. Parkes Cadman, pastor of New York's mighty Metropolitan Temple.[19]

As the decade wore on, the Methodist field became more crowded when the Oxford Brotherhood, the Charles Wesley Brotherhood, the St. James Brotherhood, the Methodist Club, the Methodist Men's Meeting, and the Methodist Men's Mutual Aid Society vied for the attention of the church's men. Largest of all by the turn of the century was the Brotherhood of St. Paul, founded in Little Falls, New York, by Methodist pastor, later bishop, Frederick Deland Leete, an idea he perfected during his previous four years as YMCA secretary in Utica, New York. A cross between the Catholic Knights of Columbus and a Methodist men's Bible class, each brotherhood tried to outdo the other with snazzy regalia, colorful badges and sashes, inspiring ritual, and snappy mottoes. The Wesley Brotherhood gets the prize for the snappiest motto: "Methodist men making the mind of the Master their main motive and mission." Competition must have been keen because each brotherhood published handbooks and newsletters proclaiming itself to be the oldest, the biggest, the best, and the most Methodist, announcing national and state conventions, and pushing local chapters.

At the turn of the century the competing brotherhoods increasingly felt the need to form one churchwide brotherhood. A uniting convention to bury the hatchet met appropriately enough in Philadelphia, the City of Brotherly Love, in 1898. Representatives from the several brotherhoods formed a single brotherhood of The Methodist Episcopal Church and elected Philadelphia's resident bishop, Thomas B. Neely, an old friend of the movement, as honorary president.[20] Proposals to the General Conference to adopt the organization and incorporate it into the church's official structure were not successful until 1908. By that time the church realized that it had a movement on its hands it needed to control, and the proposal was adopted. At the urging of the bishops in their Episcopal Address, the General Conference meeting in Buffalo, New York, that year

(1908) made the thousand-chapter Methodist Brotherhood official, and a paragraph was added to the *Book of Discipline* that authorized the formation of a chapter in each local church.

An Otterbein Brotherhood was organized for United Brethren men the next year (1909). The Evangelical Church delayed organizing its Albright Brotherhood until 1930.[21] Methodist laymen in pre–Civil War days may have become class leaders or local preachers, as well as trustees and church treasurers. Increasingly after the Civil War, they donned the badge and took the oath of allegiance to "the Brotherhood."

By January 1884 an Oxford League for young people may have been organized in the typical Victorian-era MEC. In that year Bishop Vincent organized a national youth organization called the Oxford League "modeled" on Wesley's Holy Club at Oxford a century and a half earlier. The goals of Vincent's Oxford League were to promote biblical and literary studies, to build religious piety and moral character, and to train middle-class teenagers in the works of "mercy and help." In 1889 in Cleveland, Ohio, the Oxford League merged with several other competing Methodist youth organizations to form the Epworth League of the MEC. A year later the southern church organized its own Epworth League along similar lines. By 1896 more than 20,000 local chapters had been established in local churches, North and South. The EA formed a Young People's Alliance in 1891, and the UBC formed a Young People's Union two years later.[22]

Each of these youth organizations served an important function in the ministry of the local church by building denominational loyalty. An early pamphlet of the Epworth League explained that one of the league's specific goals was to generate a sense of denominational loyalty among Methodist youth by having them read distinctively Methodist literature and by reinforcing commitments to the work of the local congregation. Early league handbooks were quite explicit in stating that denominational loyalty would be reinforced through the training of Methodist youth "in Church life and teaching; their employment in works of charity and social service, the inculcation of missionary ideals . . . and [their] direction to lives of service at home and abroad."[23] Under the auspices of the Department of Mercy and Help, terminology that Vincent made current, Epworth Leaguers were expected to participate in the social service work of the local congregation and to assist the local pastor. It was assumed that this training would produce a lifelong commitment to Christian service, lay and clergy ministries, and denominational objectives as well as personal growth (Sources 1893a).

Although each of these new organizations for women, for men, and for youth had its own set of objectives, all shared a general aim: to build a new partnership in ministry with the professional clergy. No longer needed to fill in during the pastor's absence, laywomen and youth as well as men were increasingly organized into distinctive ministries of their own aimed at supplementing the work of the pastor.

Central Conferences and the Ordering of Missions

By the 1880s Methodist ministries outside the U.S. labored under overlapping, often competing authorities. Missionaries deployed under male (mission board) or female (women's missionary society) authority. Male missionaries, if ordained, remained accountable also to their American annual conferences. Missionaries established, participated in, gave leadership to, but also served within and under local ministry structures. The MEC authorized organization of mission annual conferences abroad for Liberia in 1848 and for India in 1860 (within the U.S., the MEC in 1848 elevated Oregon and California missions into a mission conference). In 1864, the MEC advised the bishops, whose international itinerations and occasional presidency in mission conferences constituted yet another authority system, to organize mission conferences when and where their condition "shall render such organization proper."[24]

The 1868 General Conference granted mission conferences representation and recognized Liberia, Germany-Switzerland, and India to be "Annual Conferences endowed with all the rights, privileges, and immunities" of those in the U.S.[25] This action raised to a disciplinary level the fundamental question that lay at the heart of the Methodist missionary enterprise, remains unresolved two centuries later, and indeed was latent as a policy question when John Wesley sent Thomas Coke to be joint superintendent with Francis Asbury "over our Brethren in North America" (Sources 1784a). Should Methodism be one, accountable to father Wesley and/or successor authority, and ordered from a single country (England)? Or should the trajectory of the American movement toward indigenization, self-support, and full independence prevail? Which? Catholic uniformity and universalism, or Eastern Orthodox autocephalous churches? Reacting to the legislation, Daniel Wise, head of the Sunday School Union and former editor of *Zion's Herald,* and Daniel Curry, editor of the *Christian Advocate* (New York), went on record in articles opposing the notion that mature Methodist movements abroad should "remain ecclesiastically united to the parent Church, be governed by one discipline, superintended by our Bishops, and represented in our General Conference." An "ecumenical Methodism," they thought a bad idea.[26]

Methodist missions, like those of other churches, had nevertheless from the very start functioned as though Methodism were indeed "one" and replicated American offices, practices, polity, and institutions. And even as schools and colleges, modeled after their American counterparts, produced pastors and other leaders, U.S. missionaries tended to run the annual conferences, constituted an informal, if not organized leadership elite, represented in their collaboration yet another authority structure, and were typically returned to the U.S. as General Conference delegates.

In 1884, the MEC took two actions that gestured toward indigenization—authorization for central conferences and election of William Taylor (1821–1902) as missionary bishop for Africa. The latter responded to a memorial from the Liberian Conference requesting a bishop resident in Africa, but both actions might be seen as generated by India.[27] James Thoburn, later to be elected missionary bishop, had invited Taylor to India in 1870 to pursue the evangelistic efforts that had proved highly successful in South Africa, England, the West Indies, and Ceylon. Ignoring the boundaries to which comity agreements limited MEC missions, Taylor conducted campaigns in cities across India, organized classes, and oriented them toward congregational status and self-support.[28] His signature "Pauline Method of Missions" prospered, leading to the development of the Bombay and Bengal Mission, to Taylor's appointment as superintendent thereof, and to the mission's maturation into the South India Conference. Seeking his independence from the mission board, Taylor "located." Subsequently, he left India in 1875, effectively construed his "location" as the world, and undertook self-supporting Pauline evangelistic tours in South America (Peru, Chile, and Brazil). The South India Conference elected him, still technically "located," as a lay delegate to the 1884 General Conference. In electing Taylor as missionary bishop, General Conference gave the Pauline method a very high platform.

The proposal that yielded the central conference derived from the successful Thoburn-Taylor cooperation, the emergence of North and South India Conferences, and an initiative by the two conferences to provide for a delegated body to coordinate Methodist work across India. The two conferences met in adjacent cities in 1880, drafted protocols for membership and operation of a "Delegated Conference of the Methodist Church in India," and sent a memorial to the 1880 MEC General Conference requesting that disciplinary provision be made for such cooperative endeavor.[29] The 1880 overture never surfaced from committee, but the 1884 General Conference authorized the uniting of annual conferences or of "more than one form of Methodism" into central conferences. General Conference debated and passed this provision for an entity abroad with structure not unlike itself as a "central conference." When Bishop William Harris edited the 1884 *Discipline*, he termed the new entities "Central Mission Conferences," the title with which they would be referenced and operated for four decades.[30] The 1884 legislation allowed for creation of a central conference either by General Conference or by "a majority vote of all the Conferences or Missions wishing to unite." In 1892 the General Conference rescinded the latter measure of self-determination, and the powers of the central conferences were limited from the start to administration and coordination.[31] The authority to adjust the *Discipline* and to legislate for local circumstance would have to wait for a later day.

Women's Home Missionary Societies

In the 1884 *Discipline* immediately before the paragraph authorizing central conferences was one recognizing the ministry of and formally establishing the Woman's Home Missionary Society.[32] Women's home missions, particularly in the MEC and MECS, would take on monumental challenges and, in places, move in radically transformative directions.[33] Their social gospel potential was there from the beginning. In the late 1870s, the head of the Freedmen's Aid Society, Dr. Richard S. Rust, and his wife, Elizabeth Lownes Rust, visited Mrs. Jennie Hartzell and Dr. Joseph Hartzell. The latter, then New Orleans presiding elder and (founding) editor of the *Southwestern Christian Advocate*, would later be elected missionary bishop for Africa, succeeding Taylor.[34] Jennie Hartzell had begun to minister to the needs of freedwomen in New Orleans. Observing this initiative, the Rusts became convinced of the need for an organization that could work on behalf of "the poor black women and children of the Southland." At a meeting in Cincinnati on June 8, 1880, shortly after the close of the General Conference, about fifty MEC women resolved to form a Woman's Home Missionary Society (WHMS) "to enlist and organize the women of Methodism in behalf of the needy and destitute of all races and nationalities in this country," and with recommendation for special attention to "the Southern field."[35] They selected Elizabeth Rust as corresponding secretary and as president, Mrs. Lucy Webb Hayes, loyal Methodist and spouse of the U.S. president. Hayes served as national president of the society until her death in 1889, presiding at its annual meetings and presenting annual reports stressing the importance of the work.[36] Within a few years, WHMS had enlarged its mission, establishing bureaus, each headed by a secretary, to organize work with Native Americans, Mormons, African Americans and "illiterate whites" in the South, Chinese immigrants, and peoples in the regions of "New Mexico and Arizona" and the "Western and North-western Frontiers." By the end of the first decade there were some seventy corresponding secretaries at the annual conference level, and there were reported to be "over 55,000 members in more than 1900 adult and juvenile societies. *Woman's Home Missions* had reached a circulation of 15,500."[37]

In 1886, southern Methodist women established a Woman's Department of the Board of Church Extension, subsequently the Woman's Parsonage and Home Mission Society (still later the Woman's Home Mission Society).[38] Its authorization came as a result of the faith, vision, and genius for leadership of a frail woman from Kentucky, Lucinda B. Helm. She formulated the plan for a Woman's Department of Church Extension for Parsonage Building and gained its approval from the General Conference in 1886. As general secretary, she conducted all the correspondence of the department, provided the whole church with information about the new work through reports, leaflets, and articles for church papers, and communicated with the annual conference societies, visiting many of them. Within four years the work was represented in thirty-six conferences of the MECS and involved more than seven thousand women working together to establish parsonages for the itinerant ministry in the South and the West. Helm's vision always was "nothing less than the fullest and completest organized effort for *home missions*." In 1890 the General Conference recognized the Woman's Parsonage and Home

Mission Society as an official organization of the MECS. Lucinda Helm served as its general secretary until forced to retire in 1893 due to ill health and continued to edit the society's journal, *Our Homes,* until her death in 1897.[39]

Helm's work was carried on by another young woman from a prominent Kentucky family, Belle Harris Bennett (1852–1922). In 1884 Bennett was inspired by a summer conference at Lake Chautauqua, New York, to give her life wholly to God. Experiencing "the presence and power of God" and the "assurance of God-given leadership," she embarked on a life of remarkable significance for women in the MECS. She served for more than twenty-five years as president of the WHMS (1896–1910) and its successor, the Woman's Missionary Council (1910–22). Through her efforts, the Scarritt Bible and Training School was established in Kansas City in 1892, the Sue Bennett School was opened for poor children in the mountains of Kentucky in 1897, the first church settlement house (judiciously called a Wesley Community House) was begun in Nashville in 1901, and the General Conference of her church was persuaded to authorize deaconesses in 1902. Bennett played a central role, as we noted above, in the struggle for full laity rights for women in the MECS (Sources 1910).[40]

The motivations for, theories concerning, organizational style of, and operating procedures of foreign and home missionary societies mutually reinforced one another. Indeed, United Brethren and Evangelicals operated with a single structure for denominational missions, and women did as well. And the Methodist Protestants established their Woman's Home Missionary Society in 1893 at the end of a session of its Woman's Foreign Missionary Society and at the latter's initiative.[41] Women in all three of these churches, consistently or sporadically, found their organization and activities subjected to denominational (that is, male) control and supervision. That prospect, recurrently advanced in the interests of efficiency and coordination, required vigilance on the part of women across Methodism, indeed across Christian communities.

Wesleyan Service Guild

The Wesleyan Service Guild (WSG) was established in 1921 as auxiliary to both the WHMS and the WFMS (a "Business Women's Unit," to meet the needs of and focus the energies of a growing cadre of business and professional MEC women). Begun the prior year as an initiative of the Northwestern Branch of the Woman's Foreign Missionary Society, by May 1923 the WFMS and WHMS had elaborated protocols for the WSG as their joint auxiliary, but with its own Central Committee, constitution for local units, and monthly newsletter called *World Service Greetings.* Founder Marion Lela Norris served as its national secretary from its beginning to 1928 and also chaired its Central Committee.[42]

By its constitution, the Wesleyan Service Guild offered working women a fourfold program: (1) development of spiritual life, (2) opportunities for world service,

(3) promotion of Christian citizenship and personal service, and (4) provision for social and recreational activities. The spiritual part of the program was viewed as primary; "unlike so many organizational options available to women in the 1920s, [the WSG] was first and foremost a religious group," and its other purposes were understood to flow from this. Devotional guides were developed and distributed to the Spiritual Department chairs of the local units. By the end of the 1920s the Wesleyan Service Guild had an official hymn and a Ceremony of Lights for its basic worship ritual.

Guild members pledged their financial support to mission projects, among them work with young businesswomen in Japan and with immigrant children at Campbell Settlement in Gary, Indiana. The members met regularly, over an evening meal, to study and discuss foreign and home missionary work. During the Depression years, WSG leaders admirably attempted to function as a support system for women facing unemployment or salary reductions and to keep them involved in guild units regardless of their financial status. Though the WSG experienced some tension with the wives and mothers of the older societies over women's appropriate roles, all shared "the religious commitment to Christian service."[43] On Methodist merger in 1939, the WSG became the only women's missionary organization to continue as such into the new church and as a unit within the Woman's Division of Christian Service.

Missions to Korea

The Student Volunteer Movement (SVM) came into being in 1888 in a meeting under the auspices of the YWCA and YMCA and as an organization to channel into actual service the energy for and commitment to world missions excited by those two youth organizations. One of the five organizers, John R. Mott (1865–1955), would chair SVM for thirty-two years, head various other missionary and ecumenical endeavors, and become Methodism's most important figure in Christianity's ecumenical world mission and Christendom's twilight.[44] SVM's watchword, "the evangelization of the world in this generation," could have served Methodism's churches as well, as the scope of their late nineteenth- and early twentieth-century missions indicate.[45] Among auspicious Methodist missionary initiatives was that to Korea.

In 1885 the first Presbyterian and Methodist missionaries arrived in Korea (Sources 1885). A treaty with the U.S., signed in 1882, promised amity and commerce and perhaps some countervailing influence against long-standing (and continuing) domination by Japan, China, Russia, or all three. Roman Catholicism had established a Christian beachhead in the eighteenth century, but by the late nineteenth century Christianity was banned. An appeal for missionaries from several Korean Christians the next year caught the attention of the American churches and particularly of editor James Buckley, who ran a series of articles in the *Christian Advocate* introducing MEC readers to "Corea" and urging them to establish a mission. In 1884, Robert Maclay, missionary to

China and founder of the mission to Japan, visited Korea and gained permission from the royal family to begin educational and medical work in the country. Within a year the Woman's Foreign Missionary Society and the denomination's board of missions secured funds and recruited an impressive missionary team—a clergyman, the Reverend Henry G. Appenzeller,[46] he a recent graduate from Drew Theological School; his wife, Ella Dodge Appenzeller; a medical doctor, William Scranton; and an educator, Mary Scranton.[47]

In their first year, the Appenzellers opened a school for boys, which the Korean king named PaiChai HakDang (School to Nurture the Talent, now PaiChai University), at Chungdong, and Mary Scranton established a school for girls, Ewha HakDang (Pear Blossom School, now Ewha University). By the following year, Dr. Scranton offered Koreans a Western-style clinic that became Shibyungwon Hospital. An expanded hospital, consisting of five wards, opened the next year. The Korean king gave it the name Si Pyung Won, meaning "universal relief hospital." Western medicine proved an effective way to build relationships with the Korean people. During the first year, Scranton treated more than two thousand patients in the small hospital. Scranton firmly believed that the success of the hospital ministry was a key element of the Methodist mission—evangelizing people through medicine—though he soon found out that Korean women did not want to see male doctors. He therefore requested that the Woman's Foreign Missionary Society send female doctors and nurses to Korea. In 1887 the WFMS sent Meta Howard, MD, to Korea. Under Dr. Howard's direction, the first woman's hospital in Korea was established in Seoul. King Kojong appreciated the opening of the hospital for women and named it Po Kyu Nyo Koan Hospital, meaning "house for many sick women." A second hospital for women, the Lillian Harris Hospital, opened in another area of the city in 1893. Scranton's Si Pyung Won Hospital closed in 1900, but the Harris Hospital for Women and Children prospered and laid the groundwork for the Hospital and Medical School for Women of Ewha University founded in 1928, now a leading training institute for health-care professionals in Korea.[48]

Government leaders, impressed by the earnestness and goodness of their Western guests, lifted the ban on evangelism in 1887, after which Appenzeller preached his first public sermon in Korean, baptized his first converts, and began celebrating Holy Communion. Early missionary strategy in the several provinces stressed elementary education and promoted indigenous evangelical work, with medical work usually opening the way. The mission prospered among lower-class Koreans, and by 1895, ten years after the mission began, Appenzeller reported 817 members in a dozen locations in and near Seoul.

In 1890 Appenzeller began the Trilingual Press at PaiChai School, serving two purposes—disseminating the Christian message in print and providing work scholarships for students. This Korean, Chinese, and English press (later Methodist Publishing House, Seoul) published Bibles, hymnals, and Sunday school curricula. It became the home as well for several newspapers, including the *Korean Christian Advocate*, the first Korean-language Christian newspaper, and *Dongip* (the *Independence Daily*), which became the focus of PaiChai's commitment to the Korean independence movement. Appenzeller's other principal activity was participation in the translation of the Bible into Korean. He was a member of the Board of Bible Translators from 1886, a work he shared with several of the early Methodist and Presbyterian missionaries and a number of Korean translators. Appenzeller opened a bookstore in 1894, edited the *Korean Repository* and *Korea Review* to introduce Korea abroad, and was active in the scholarly Korean Asiatic Society.

A building program, underwritten by gifts and grants from home, permitted the completion in 1897 of the first Methodist church building in Seoul—Chung Dong MEC. (Appenzeller, like many missionaries, favored Western designs for churches and schools. Their brick walls, rectangular design, and sash windows stood out among Korean buildings with their thatched or tile roofs, sliding paper doors, and central courtyards.) Appenzeller's life was cut short in 1902, at the height of his career at the age of forty-four, by a collision of small coastal steamers as he traveled to attend a Bible translation meeting. The mission granted licenses to preach to the first Korean national in 1888. In 1901, the first deacons were ordained. With the ordination of elders in 1908, the MEC General Conference authorized the formation of a Korea Annual Conference.

Ten years after the northern church began its mission (1895), two experienced *southern* Methodist missionaries from China, Bishop Eugene R. Hendrix and Clarence F. Reid, arrived. The following year Reid established residence in Seoul, surveyed the Korean field, and began work in both Songdo and Seoul. In 1897 Reid was made superintendent of the newly established Korea Mission by the Board of Missions of the MECS. The two Methodist churches, frustrated by slow growth in the politically charged country, soon began to work together on evangelistic strategy, including a common Korean-language hymnal and catechism, joint support for schools, and by 1910 a central theological seminary in Seoul. Both churches prospered as a result of the dramatic revivals in Wonsan in 1903 and in Pyongyang in 1907.

Over the first decades of Methodist missions, Korea remained politically volatile. In 1884 a failed coup by Japanese-connected Koreans strengthened China's control of the country. During the 1904 war between Japan and Russia, Japan invaded Korea and within weeks forced King Kojong to sign a treaty entitling the Japanese to use Korea as a military base and to place powerful advisors in various branches of the government. By the Portsmouth Treaty, which ended the war in 1905, Russia recognized Japan's paramount position in Korea. King Kojong was removed, and the U.S. diplomatic mission closed. In 1910 Japan annexed Korea, appointed a Japanese military governor, began to integrate Korea fully into a Japanese orbit, made Japanese the official language of the country, and began repressive policies toward Korean religion and culture.

The client character of Korean politics affected Christianizing efforts there in several ways. American missionaries did not gain the privileges in Korea enjoyed in lands under Western colonial control. Nor were the social and political elites, who lived amidst and were attentive to the political struggles and Chinese-Japanese intrigues, inclined to accept a Western religion and alien ways of life that would subject them to persecution. Hence the relatively greater success of missionary efforts among poor people and in the countryside. Concern about Korean independence developed early, and from 1905 on, the commitment of many missionaries to Korean independence came into the open. Through this darkest period of Korean history, Christian leaders who grew up under the tutelage of missionaries became the backbone of the unceasing struggle to gain freedom, independence, and dignity from Japan's cruel exploitation and domination. And commitment to the cause of Korean self-rule made Christianity seem less alien, indeed empowering and indigenizing. Such sentiments could also generate attitudes toward missionaries. Even during Appenzeller's years of service, conflicts emerged regarding support of the early independence movement, questions about a more positive relationship between Korean religious and cultural traditions and the Christian gospel, and resentment over the missionaries' retention of administrative and financial power in the emerging Korean churches. Korean Methodism would early (1930) establish its own autonomy (Sources 1931). Conversely, the sensitive political climate may have reinforced the evangelicalism and individualism that predominate among Korean (and Korean American) Presbyterians and Methodists. Certainly from the start such notes were struck. Appenzeller put a premium on evangelism, individual conversion, conservative biblical hermeneutics, strict morals, and the social implications of Christian faith—all of which he learned at Drew. Missions abroad and missions within the U.S. went hand in hand.

Asian American Methodists[49]

Methodist ministries among Chinese Americans and Japanese Americans began in the 1870s, as we noted in chapter 10.[50] By the 1880s, efforts among the 100,000 Chinese Americans in California featured educational efforts for girls, care for abandoned girls and babies, and efforts to rescue women from prostitution, all by the Woman's Missionary Society of the Pacific Coast.[51] The home, later named Gum Moon (Golden Door), continues its ministry among San Francisco's Asian women and children. Less caring, indeed extremely hostile reactions to the growth of the Chinese American population—competition for jobs, ethnic antagonism, racism, acts of "ethnic cleansing" across the American West, anti-Chinese hysteria—led Congress to pass the infamous Chinese Exclusion Act in 1882 to protect America's racial purity.[52]

A few white Methodists championed the Chinese in their assertion of rights. Increasingly aware that many of his flock were forced to become "strangers" by economic interests as well as by ideology defining America as a homogenous white society, Methodist Otis Gibson filed lawsuits and wrote protests on behalf of the dispossessed. He lashed out at the developing racism and unfair treatment in his 1877 book, *The Chinese in America*, and in 1880 in the *Christian Advocate* (New York).[53] Referencing harassment that "our brother, Rev. Otis Gibson" had encountered for his advocacy, the 1880 MEC General Conference urged the federal government to enforce "all rights guaranteed by treaty to Chinese upon our shores and to afford them the protection which is accorded our citizens [including missionaries!] now residing within the bounds of the Chinese Empire." It exhorted the Methodist papers to similar editorializing and the Methodist people to stand up against racist hostility.[54] Two years later Methodist President Hayes vetoed the 1882 Chinese Exclusion Act as contrary to treaty with China, but soon bowed to pressure.

In 1893, Chinese American churches in several communities were linked into a separate district. A decade later, in 1904, Bishop Luther Wilson presided over the formation of the Pacific Chinese (later California-Oriental) Mission Conference. Its territory extended as far east as Texas. From 1882 to 1906 a school for Chinese was conducted by the UBC in Portland, Oregon. After the church's mission homes for men and women in San Francisco's Chinatown were destroyed by the earthquake in 1906, new mission homes were erected over the next several years. Although most Chinese remained on the West Coast, a growing number migrated to the urban centers of the East. By 1879 a Cantonese ministerial student, Chu Bok, aided by the pastor of Five Points Mission in New York's Chinatown, opened a school and held services in Chinese. Four years later a permanent Methodist mission in New York's Chinatown was established (now the Church of All Nations). By 1900, the EA had established a Chinese Sunday school in Chicago.

In 1877, when only a few Japanese had come to San Francisco, one of them, Kanichi Miyama (1847–1936), enrolled in an English class taught by Otis Gibson at the Methodist Mission in Chinatown. Baptized by Gibson, he organized a Japanese Gospel Society from which grew in 1879 the first Japanese Methodist Church in America, now known as Pine Street UMC. In 1881 Miyama abandoned plans for a career in business and prepared himself for the ministry. Admitted "on trial" in California Conference in 1884, Miyama was appointed to work with Gibson in expanding the mission's ministry to San Francisco's Japanese American community. On this foundation, Superintendent Frederick Masters envisioned a ministry expanded to Japanese Americans on the Pacific Coast from Los Angeles to Seattle (Sources 1886). Ordained elder in the California Conference in 1887, Miyama was assigned to work with the new Asian mission superintendent, M. C. Harris, a founding member of the missionary team that organized the MEC's first mission in Japan in 1873. Catering especially to university students, they first rented space in Central MEC and by 1894 built, occupied, and dedicated a two-story church building on Pine Street, complete with dormitory and schoolrooms. With more than five hundred members and probationers, the church had become the second largest church in the conference! When Japanese American youth were banned from the city's high schools, Harris opened one of the first private high schools for Japanese Americans in 1898. Miyama and Harris expanded Methodism's outreach to Japanese up and down the West Coast, and eventually to Canada and Hawaii. Miyama returned to Japan in 1890 and founded Ginza Church in Tokyo and churches in Nagoya and Kamakura.

Harris had a special talent for recruiting Japanese preachers. A second, Terujiro Hasegawa, was ordained in 1889, and six others followed in the early 1890s. In 1893 nine Japanese American churches were linked on a separate district in the California Conference, and by 1900 they sought and received permission from the General Conference to organize themselves into the Pacific Japanese Mission Conference with churches in sixteen cities from San Diego to Vancouver and out to Hawaii. The MECS established Japanese missions in California in 1897 in Alameda and Sonoma counties. As Japanese communities developed in other cities, evangelists from the Pacific Coast were sent to start missions, beginning in New York City in 1894. In its 1905 annual report, the Pacific Japanese Mission could report that the "present field includes the states of California, Oregon, and Washington, but loud calls are coming from Idaho, Montana and Nebraska."

Large-scale migration of Koreans to America and its territories began in 1903, initiated by American sugar planters recruiting workers for their plantations in Hawaii (annexed by the U.S. in 1898). Methodists among these immigrants established in Honolulu in 1904 the first Korean Methodist congregation on American soil. A year later, under the leadership of Pastor Hong Seung-Ha, the congregation dedicated a new building (the congregation now known as Christ UMC of Honolulu). By 1916 there were 31 Korean Methodist churches in Hawaii and 35 mission stations with total membership of 2,000. A wave of Koreans emigrated from Hawaii to California in 1903. Within a year Herbert Johnson, superintendentof the Japanese Methodist Mission in San Francisco, reached out to the Korean newcomers and organized prayer meetings in residential homes. After 1906, the year the great earthquake and fire devastated much of the city, several missions groups divided the West Coast Asian work among them. By this comity agreement, the MECS fell heir to missions among Korean immigrants in central and northern California. San Francisco's tiny Korean American community raised funds to build the first Korean Methodist Church on the mainland (now San Francisco Korean United Methodist Church) under the leadership of Ju Sam Ryang, one of the first native Korean preachers ordained by southern Methodists. Ryang opened the upper floor of the new church as a dormitory for Korean immigrants and taught them English at night. Ryang also began a Korean-language Methodist paper *Daedo* (the *Great Way*). In 1930 Ryang became the first bishop of the newly formed autonomous Korean Methodist Church.

Evangelists followed Korean laborers as they scattered to Montana, Idaho, Wyoming, Utah, and Nebraska. With the assistance of the Woman's Missionary Council of the MECS, a retired missionary from Korea, Frances Sherman, opened a mission school for Koreans in Los Angeles about the same time. Her primary purpose was to teach the Bible and English to Korean immigrants. Later known as Robertson Korean UMC, the church became the flagship Korean church on the West Coast. Korean churches soon followed in Oakland and other West Coast communities. Evangelistic Korean American Methodists planted churches in other cities across the country—beginning in New York (1921) and in Chicago (1928).[55] These congregations provided the core of the Korean American community and, much like other Asian American churches, gave meaning to and helped members cope with often harsh lives, taught basic educational skills, delivered social services, and provided ethnic solidarity—all within the context of the faith. The MECS included both Korean American and Japanese when it organized the California Oriental Mission in 1928.

Ministries to Filipinos began with the occupation of the islands after the Spanish-American War (see discussion in chapter 12). George Stull, a Methodist army chaplain with U.S. forces, held the first documented *Protestant* worship service on August 28, 1898, and American Methodists were the first denomination to organize a mission. In 1899, Bishop James Thoburn (MEC) preached the first Protestant sermon in the Catholic Philippines, and an all-Filipino congregation was organized by Nicholas Zamora, a lay mission worker, and a U.S. Methodist local preacher, Arthur W. Prautch. Despite a brief war and then ongoing struggle between American forces and an independence movement, Methodists succeeded by 1900 in building schools and churches in Manila, staffing them with American female and male missionaries, and recruiting local converts as preachers. The first district conference, staffed with one ordained preacher and six assistants, featured seven preaching places and 220 members on three circuits: Pandacan, Santa Cruz, and Tondo. Tondo became the early center of the ministry to Filipinos, while Central Methodist Episcopal Church in Manila became the center for ministry to native U.S. Methodists. Led by local preacher Felipe Marquez, the Tondo group met each week for Bible study, prayer, and services at the home of another local preacher, Pedro Castro. From there, they divided into smaller groups to hold services in homes of converts elsewhere in Tondo. Homer Stuntz arrived in 1901 as superintendent of the emerging mission, and a Methodist Publishing House opened in Manila, producing the first native (Tagalog) hymnal in 1902. Translations of the ritual and *Discipline* followed in 1903. Nicolas Zamora, ordained deacon in 1900, became the first native elder in 1903. The same year a training school for deaconesses opened. With matching grants from the WFMS and a Chicago Methodist, N. W. Harris, the school added other units and evolved into an accredited college, the Harris Memorial College. By comity arrangement with other American denominations, Methodists assumed responsibility for the area in Luzon north of Manila.

Aggressive evangelism and a responsive people produced converts—6,800 in the first three years—outpacing growth in every other mission of the MEC.[56]

Country	Members	Mission Begun
Philippine Islands	6,842	1900
Japan	6,561	1873
Korea	5,855	1885
Mexico	5,592	1873
All South America	5,863	1836
All Africa	3,632	1833

Rapid growth and expansion of circuits led to the formation of the Philippine Islands Mission Conference in 1905. The following year it became a full annual conference. Disappointed at lack of progress in giving leadership to the growing number of Filipino converts and ordinands, Zamora led a large group of Filipino preachers and layfolk out of the MEC in 1908 and formed an independent Evangelical Methodist Church, self-governing and self-supporting. Other preachers and laity, loyal to MEC, led by Felipe Marquez, continued to evangelize and organize new circuits, but leadership continued in the hands of American missionaries. A measure of independence from North American church governance came in 1944 when the Philippine Central Conference was authorized and the first native Filipino bishop, Dionisio Alejandro, elected.

By 1906 Filipinos were migrating to Hawaii, seeking jobs in sugar and pineapple farms. A Filipino mission was soon established, and Benito Ilustre became the first licensed minister. By 1921, eleven preachers, four nurses, and two women evangelists ministered in eighteen churches. Filipino immigrants arrived in California in 1920, and Methodist churches were formed in Los Angeles and San Francisco. In the 1930s, Filipino churches were established on the East Coast and in New York City and Washington, D.C.

Rethinking Missions

By the 1930s, American Protestants had begun to question what had been most probably their highest commitment, their most heroic enterprise, their energizing cause—missions. The factors producing these misgivings were diverse and included various impulses and movements covered in this section, in this chapter as a whole, and in the next chapter. The maturing of "mission" churches and leadership and the building of institutions and infrastructure produced aspirations for self-government, and with them the presumption that not everything good had to come from white Europeans and Americans. Nationalist and anticolonial sentiments would further link political domination, economic exploitation, and Christian missions. At home, the social gospel and other strains of liberalism, to which we turn below, in identifying systemic problems in

American society, laid groundwork for a significant and pervasive critique of Western civilization and culture.[57] The mutual recriminations of fundamentalists and modernists added to the rhetoric of denunciation. Further criticism of an acculturated Christianity, of missions and evangelism as an Anglo-Saxon–civilizing enterprise, and of Protestantism wedded to Western culture increased in the wake of World War I in various forms of Western self-assessment, particularly the theological movement known as neo-orthodoxy. The ecumenical movement, though developing out of the missionary movement, as it brought together persons from across the globe gradually came to question the competitive confessionalism that packaged and sold the gospel in one brand or another of denominationalized Western culture. Women's groups read study books that challenged the notion that individuals and societies had to accept Western dress, names, worship practices, and architecture to be saved.[58]

The event that gave traction to critique of missions from one angle or another was the publication in 1932 of a report of the interdenominational Laymen's Foreign Missionary Inquiry titled *Re-thinking Missions*.[59] The study of the missionary movement, its practices, and its effects, headed by Professor William Ernest Hocking of Harvard, was inspired by articles that R. C. Hutchison had published in the *Atlantic Monthly*. The articles questioned why Christian missionary efforts failed in Muslim territories. Hutchison's answer to his question generated the laymen's investigation funded mainly by John D. Rockefeller. Hutchison wasn't the only writer challenging Christian missions in secular magazines, but his answer was the bluntest: Muslims see Christianity as a religion whose adherents do not practice what they preach. The laymen's report held that good missionary work was accomplished by living with people and setting an example of the Christian ethic. Conversion by revival meetings and other somewhat manipulative techniques were not favored, although they were widely practiced then (and now).[60] Arlo Ayres Brown, president of Drew University since 1929, participated in preparing the report, was a member of the Appraisal Committee, and helped publicize its findings, as in his 1932 article in the MEC *Christian Advocate* (Sources 1932b). Missionaries, who assumed they were under an obligation to save and renovate the world, balked. Even today its conclusions are unpopular. The ensuing discussion in church conferences and papers in the 1930s exposed internal struggles in the mission boards and in the fields.

A similar rethinking went on with regard to home missions. Native Americans were finally granted U.S. citizenship in 1924. A mood of cultural pluralism and a belief that Native Americans possessed valuable cultures caused the nation and the churches to rethink their Native American policy. In 1934 President Roosevelt's new commissioner of Indian Affairs, John Collier, proposed a "New Deal" for America's Native people. The Allotment Act of 1887 was repealed, the Indian Reorganization Act (IRA) dropped an assimilationist mode, recognized tribes as "sovereign" nations, reintroduced tribal government, and gave permission to practice Native American culture, including religion, on reservations. Collier forced Methodists to decide what they believed to be essential to religious belief and practice and what could be adjusted in good conscience. That same year MEC mission executive Mark Dawber followed Collier's lead and proposed a controversial new Native American mission policy of inculturation and affirmation of "Indian" life and culture, a new direction that many veteran missionaries thought wrongheaded and dangerous (Sources 1934a).

Social Holiness to Social Gospel

Methodists are not generally credited with crafting the social gospel.[61] However, when they (northern Methodists particularly and quite early) grasped its import, they embraced, institutionalized, and internalized it much as they had the camp meeting a century earlier. Others, most notably Congregationalist pastor-editor Washington Gladden, Episcopalian economics professor Richard Ely, Christian socialist and politician George Herron, Congregationalist pastor-novelist Charles Sheldon, and eventually Baptist pastor-turned-seminary professor Walter Rauschenbusch, promoted the constellation of themes, concerns, and commitments to which we apply the term *social gospel*. Addressing social dislocations created by or in America's rapid industrialization, unfettered capitalism, crowded slum and tenement conditions, new immigration patterns, and exploitation of labor, these social prophets drew diversely on Romantic theological currents mediated by Horace Bushnell, Theodore Munger, the transcendentalists, and others. Their social critique also capitalized on the century of higher biblical criticism and on German philosophical and theological currents, especially as synthesized by Albrecht Ritschl. Few embraced Karl Marx, but the social gospelers found instructive the socialist translation and social experiments of the English Christian socialism of Frederick Denison Maurice and Charles Kingsley and especially of English Methodists Hugh Price Hughes, Samuel Keeble, and J. Scott Lidgett (see Sources 1891).[62] Reinforcing ethical convictions that the social gospelers found in the Old Testament prophets and the teachings of Jesus were indictments of American capitalism and of urban governance rendered by political reformers, first Populists and then Progressives, and by journalists and reporters, sometimes labeled muckrakers. The latter—Ida Tarbell (a Methodist),[63] Lincoln Steffens, Ray Stannard Baker, and Upton Sinclair—showed what lay underneath in the Gilded Age was not shiny at all, indeed was ugly and sordid.

The social gospelers were not alone in their concern for workers, immigrants, slum dwellers, and poor persons. The urban revivalism typified by Dwight L. Moody offered one version of "rescue." Moody, John R. Mott, and others labored on behalf of the YMCA, which after the Civil War focused on the city and its youth and by the 1890s included in its practical work physical, educational, social, and religious programming. The Salvation Army and the Christian and Missionary Alliance ministered hands-on in America's slums and across racial lines. Pentecostalism, too, preached an inclusive gospel in center cities, across Appalachia, and to marginalized people from coast to coast.[64] Black Baptists and Methodists went south with Reconstruction but then followed their members to northern cities in that great migration. Roman Catholics, whose numbers exploded with the waves of immigration from Central Europe and whose members labored on the factory floor, began engagement with organizing and organized labor before most Protestants even recognized that there were labor-management issues. And with Pope Leo XIII's *Rerum Novarum* ("Of New Things," popularly known as *The Rights and Duties of Capital and Labor*), an 1891 papal encyclical, Roman Catholic bishops and faithful had explicit guidance on how the church should deal with labor and labor unions. Laying the groundwork for the modern welfare state and concerned that workers were entitled to just reward for their labor, Leo addressed issues associated with the Industrial Revolution: the migration from fields to factories, the exploitation of workers, and the spread of communism.

American Methodists were slow to embrace liberal theology and the social gospel institutionally and formally. However, to allege that Methodists ignored America's social problems, lacked machinery for dealing with them, and wanted for theory with which to energize intervention and reform is neither accurate nor fair. Indeed as we have seen, through urban chapters of denominational and women's missionary societies, Methodists well before the Civil War had shown concern for workers, for children, for older persons, for immigrants, for temperance, and for political reform. Further, in the aftermath of the Civil War, northern Methodism had invested money and human resources in gearing up for and addressing the educational, infrastructural, and religious needs of the "freedmen."[65] The church's idealism also informed new missionary ventures at home and abroad. And in missions theory, but especially in temperance rhetoric, Methodism had its own sociological theory and version of a social gospel. Not everyone embraced Willard's radical "do everything" agenda, but Methodists North and South generally shared her and the WCTU's conviction that at the heart of America's problems— poverty, crime, abuse of spouses and children, urban decay, political corruption—lay drink and the liquor cabal. And further, as we will note below, Methodist deaconesses were actually providing the urban presence, strategies for intervention, and person-to-person attention about which the social gospelers wrote.

By the turn of the twentieth century, northern Methodism gained an intellectual resource, which for a half century would ground its social Christianity. Known as personal idealism, personalism, or transcendental empiricism, this philosophy was to have a major influence on Methodism nationally through the teaching of Boston University's Borden Parker Bowne and three generations of his successors: first, Albert C. Knudson, Edgar S. Brightman, Francis J. McConnell, and George Albert Coe; second, Walter G. Muelder, Georgia Harkness, L. Harold DeWolf, Paul Deats, S. Paul Schilling, and Peter Bertocci; and third, numerous people including Martin Luther King Jr. Bowne

(1847–1910) studied for several years in Europe (at Halle, Göttingen, and Paris) and soon after returning to the U.S. was called to a chair in philosophy at Boston University, a post he would hold for thirty-five years, the last twenty-two of them also as dean of the Graduate School. Bowne wove strands of idealism, neo-Kantianism, biblical criticism, romanticism, and rationalism together with those from his heritage (Methodism's moralism, high valuation of freedom, insistence on individual responsibility, optimism of grace, hope for perfection) into a distinctive modernist Methodist metaphysic. This tradition places at the center of theology the sacred personality of each human being in relation to the loving Personality of God. So accenting God's working through human history, the theology opened the door for countless leaders to understand their own vocation in terms of the social betterment of human life. A significant contribution to American philosophy, the personalist tradition, though focused at Boston University (BU), influenced northern Methodist theology and theological education generally, especially through required reading assignments in the Course of Study.[66]

This mainstreaming of liberalism elicited conservative consternation in Bowne's lifetime and later during Methodism's dalliance with fundamentalism (see further discussion below). Methodist theology generally had evolved over the course of the nineteenth century in interaction with the intellectual currents of the day, shifts so gradual as to escape much reaction from pulpit or pew.[67] Bowne's personalism, however, stood out. Critics viewed his teaching and many books as not enhancing Wesleyanism but undercutting it, indeed, as "contrary to our present existing and established standards of doctrine." Both Bowne and his colleague in Old Testament, Hinckley G. Mitchell, were subjected to heresy charges. Complaints against Mitchell, who had received a PhD from Leipzig—brought initially by a student at Boston, then levied in his annual conference, put then in the lap of the bishops, and eventually appealed to General Conference—focused on his teaching of the documentary hypothesis (of non-Mosaic and multiple biblical authorship) but also alleged that he did not believe in the Trinity, the divinity of Christ, or the Atonement. Similar fundamental charges against Bowne, then at the summit of a high-profile career as chair of BU's philosophy department and well along in an authorship that would produce seventeen books, resulted in his trial in the New York East Conference (Sources 1904). Bowne was further charged with aberrant teachings on sin, salvation, repentance, justification, regeneration, and assurance. Both men were acquitted eventually, *Advocate* editor Buckley assisting in the defense of Bowne.[68] The decisions marked a watershed, the vindication of progressive theology that opened the way to Methodist appropriation of social gospel thought and practice.

The intellectual lenses represented theologically by the social gospel and philosophically by personalism, when adopted and used, helped Methodists see America's problems in biblical and ethical terms. Other seminaries would play a similar role to Boston in mediating strains of theologically progressive or modernist views, if not specifically those of Bowne. In the South, for instance, Vanderbilt provided a learning context in which students encountered the views of John R. Mott and Washington Gladden, as the experience there in the 1910s of (later bishop) A. Frank Smith indicates: "I certainly was a social gospeler to the point that I felt we ought to integrate the Christian spirit into everything that was done. I was a great admirer of that man Rauschenbusch."[69] More decisive in Methodist appropriation of the social gospel and in the development of one of its crowning achievements, the 1908 Social Creed, were the leadership and advocacy of individual Methodists who got their hands dirty in the Gilded Age. We treat below such individual initiative among women and their instantiation of the social gospel through the deaconess movement and institutions for their training. In the 1880s the bishops and General Conferences abandoned their practice of issuing "pastoral letters" on social problems. The MEC's declaration on social policy would be issued in 1908 not in a pastoral letter penned by bishops but in a social creed hammered out by lay and clergy delegates in General Conference.[70] Individual prophetic actions, then, stimulated the engagement, should we say "recovery," of the church's broader and deeper social passion. Here we take note of Frank Mason North, William Carwardine, Mary McDowell, S. Parkes Cadman, Charles A. Tindley, Edgar J. Helms, and William Bell.

In 1891 North, then pastor in Middletown (Connecticut) and serving the community around Wesleyan University, from which he received four degrees, wrote a series of four articles on the topic of socialism and Christianity in *Zion's Herald*, New England's Methodist newspaper (Sources 1891).[71] Through this popular medium, Methodism engaged the social gospel. Socialism, North insisted, devoid of its atheism and materialism, could be Christianized. Further, the "city will test the church and decide its competence," and the "problem of poverty lies very close to the problem of sin." The church recognized a prophet in its midst, as do standard histories of the social gospel. The following year, 1892, North was appointed the head (corresponding secretary) of the New York City Mission and Church Extension Society. The same year, the New York East Conference, through a committee headed by North, broke new ground by framing a memorial to that year's General Conference urging a declaration of Christian duties on social concerns. General Conference took no action, but the prophetic act marks the beginning of the struggle to get the church to commit itself to a vigorous ministry of social justice on behalf of poor persons. That General Conference did authorize the City Evangelization Union, and North headed it from 1896 to 1912. For two decades in the New York City post, North engaged in building institutions; establishing the Church of All Nations; supporting mission initiatives among German, Italian, Polish, Russian, Chinese, and Japanese immigrants; working across racial lines; exhorting urban parishes to undertake ministries dealing with poverty, crime, and vice; championing urban causes through *The Christian City*; and encouraging the denomination in various ways to take on the challenges of an increasingly urban America. He put those convictions into verse in the 1903 hymn "Where Cross the Crowded Ways of Life."[72]

For decades, North led in Methodism's important social gospel initiatives and in Protestantism's institutionalization of the social gospel. Typically working collaboratively, he had a hand in the establishment of the Open and Institutional Church League (1894), the founding of the Methodist Federation for Social Service (1907), the formulation of the Social Creed (adopted in 1908), and the creation of the Federal Council of Churches (1908) and its adoption of North's expanded version of the Social Creed. In 1912, the MEC elected him one of the corresponding secretaries of the Board of Foreign Missions, a position he retained until 1924. From 1912 until 1916 he chaired the executive committee of the Federal Council of Churches, serving as the council's president (1916–20). North took an interest as well in world Methodist conferences and in efforts to reunite American Methodism. Understanding the problems of Black Americans were not only those of rural dwellers in the Jim Crow South, but also those of the waves of new Black city dwellers, North was one of the few leading MEC figures openly to support the National Association for the Advancement of Colored People (NAACP) from its foundation in 1909.

William Carwardine was a young pastor, leading a newly formed Chicago congregation, when Pullman workers struck (in 1894). The church, situated in a Pullman-built company town, rented makeshift worship space from the Pullman Palace Car company, catered to workers, and competed with a more upscale Presbyterian congregation for which George Pullman had built a handsome facility and whose minister he paid. Labor-management struggles in the U.S. had frequently turned violent and in Chicago particularly so—the 1886 bitter strike against the McCormick Reaper Works leading to the infamous Haymarket Riot, the dispersing of protesters, a bombing, indiscriminate firing by police, the wounding of some sixty police officers, along with an unknown number of civilians, and the deaths of seven policemen and at least four workers. The Pullman strike, begun in May 1894, went on for seven weeks until federal troops were called in "to protect the mail." Striking workers, housed in a company town, suffered multiple jeopardies—loss of income and/or job, blacklisting, potential loss of housing, harassment, and denunciation by the pastor of the company Presbyterian church. Carwardine, however, did not sanction Pullman's tactics or concur in his preacher's sermonizing.[73] From his own pulpit in Pullman, Carwardine declared the Sunday after the strike began: "I make no apology as a clergyman for discussing this theme. As ministers of the gospel we have a right to occasionally turn from the beaten path of biblical truth and consider these great questions of social, moral, and economic interest.... 'Never did men have a cause more just.'" Reports of the sermon hit the headlines of Chicago's newspapers. Later that year Carwardine published an account of the whole affair in a little book, *The Pullman Strike*. Carwardine combined intervention with prophecy, opening his home as a storehouse for relief supplies, gaining new jobs for blacklisted strikers, and testifying before a Strike Commission. His book narrated the drama and set forth the case for the church's engagement on labor's behalf (Sources 1894).[74]

Prophetic acts earn a prophet's reward. The membership in his congregation dropped from three hundred to one hundred. And from conference leaders came a reprimand and punitive transfer to a minor church near the Chicago stockyards.[75] Leaving Pullman did not stop the bold young pastor. He lectured in sixty-four cities, ran unsuccessfully for political office, and in 1905 became one of the first religious commentators for a major newspaper—the Chicago *Herald and Examiner*. Through the years, Carwardine continued to hammer away on two major themes: "the rights of property are at war with the rights of [persons]," and "If there is one law for the rich and another for the poor, there is no justice."

A devout Methodist, Mary McDowell worked with the WCTU in the 1880s, organizing youth groups and kindergartens. Later that decade she became a kindergarten teacher at Jane Addams's Hull House and founder of the settlement Woman's Club. Beginning in 1894, she developed a social services program for immigrant families living in the vicinity of Chicago's meatpacking houses and became known as the "Angel of the Stockyards" for her work there. McDowell gave staunch support to striking packinghouse workers in 1904 and 1921, cofounded the National Women's Trade Union League, pressured the federal government to investigate the conditions in which women and children worked and to establish the Women's Bureau of the Department of Labor, agitated for liberalized birth control laws, and marched for women's suffrage. McDowell was the only woman invited to the 1907 organizing meeting of the Methodist Federation for Social Service (MFSS). Unable to attend the historic meeting in Washington, McDowell joined MFSS's executive committee the following year, chairing the committee on settlement houses until 1923. She died in 1936 at the age of eighty-one.[76]

Yet another venture in urban ministry, functioning alongside settlement houses, city evangelization or missionary societies, deaconesses and deaconess houses, was the "open" or "institutional" church. Though often seen as an American original, the institutional church belongs in a set of transatlantic and especially British-to-American transfers of ministry strategies (including the social gospel as a whole). First in England and then in America, reformers sought to add to or reconfigure church buildings to make them social service centers (called central halls in Britain, institutional churches in America), to launch financial campaigns at the denominational level to raise funds to underwrite the new urban mission initiatives, and to establish social service unions and federations (Wesleyan Union for Social Service in Britain, Methodist Federation for Social Service in America) to initiate, oversee, and champion reform causes.[77] The open or institutional church movement became then another turn-of-the-century effort by American social gospel leaders in mainline denominations to regain ground the church had lost in the city, particularly among the working poor.[78]

An open or institutional church featured, in addition to the sanctuary, an array of other rooms or an additional building that, during the week, opened the church to the community and provided for training programs, child care, and other social services. Facilities permitted lectures, concerts, debates, clubs, and various social gatherings. In addition to flexible space, some institutional churches featured gymnasiums, swimming pools, and other recreational rooms. The church program as a whole was subdivided into special departments managed by committees. The movement consolidated in 1894 with the establishment of the Open and Institutional Church League to coordinate various programs and to pursue interdenominational cooperation.[79]

One of the first Methodist institutional churches was organized in New York City in 1895 by S. Parkes Cadman and his ministerial and lay associates. Cadman (1864–1936) was born in Shropshire, England, son of a miner and Wesleyan lay preacher. Young Cadman prepared for the Wesleyan Methodist ministry at Richmond Theological College, near London, and became acquainted with English home mission initiatives. While at Richmond, Cadman met a visiting American Methodist bishop, John Fletcher Hurst, who was so impressed with his ability that he invited him to America. Cadman arrived in America in 1890, joined the New York Conference, and began holding evangelistic campaigns in parishes in New York.[80] His extraordinary pastoral and homiletical skills and evangelistic successes led to his appointment in 1895 to Central ME Church (later called Metropolitan Temple) on Seventh Avenue near Fourteenth Street. Central Church's membership, once including distinguished New York families (among its illustrious members had been President Ulysses S. Grant and family), had drifted away. The neighborhood was populous, but few of the people were found in the church.

Cadman began by remodeling the premises, installing electric lights, eliminating pew rents,[81] and offering the use of old Central's plant all week long. By the late 1890s Cadman added "Pleasant Sunday Afternoon Services" to more formal morning and evening services and excused persons from wearing "Sunday" clothes. His church's program included five choirs and an orchestra, a kindergarten, youth club, gymnasium, game room, reading room, a loan fund and employment service, a soup kitchen, a food and clothing dispensary, cooking and sewing classes, a deaconess home, and a medical clinic.[82] In her 1904 book *The Burden of the City*, Isabelle Horton made a persuasive case for the crucial role of the deaconess in urban home mission work.[83]

Other Methodist institutional churches followed in Cincinnati in connection with Wesley Chapel; in Chicago, Halstead Street Mission; and in Boston, Morgan Memorial Church. The movement was promoted by the denomination's National City Evangelization Union, headed by North. From 1889 to 1916 the Union published its own newsletter, *Aggressive Methodism*, later called *The Christian City*, to promote expanded city missions and institutional churches.[84]

Urban African American churches, like that of Tindley Temple in Philadelphia, though not formally aligned with the institutional church movement or theologically identified with the social gospel, developed similar outreach programs, relation to the surrounding community, and missional self-understanding. With the mass exodus of African Americans from the South gradually filling new city slums, Charles Albert Tindley (1851–1933) conducted a street ministry, found jobs, distributed free meals to the poor, and gained a national reputation as a spirited evangelist. In the Great Depression of the 1930s as the community's plight worsened, the congregation started a soup kitchen to feed the hungry, a program that continues to this day. Tindley told his suffering congregation: "God is not the author and maker of this furnace" (Sources 1932a).

When he assumed the pastorate of the church that now bears his name in 1902 and after serving as presiding elder in the (all–African American) Delaware Conference, Tindley served a membership of 130. By the 1930s, the congregation swelled to more than 12,000, making it then the largest Methodist church worldwide. Tindley is now widely known for his hymnody, particularly "I'll Overcome Some Day," from which came the civil rights anthem.[85] Many of his hymns appeared in *New Songs of Paradise,* first published in 1934 by a firm that Tindley helped found.[86] And Tindley played an important creative role in what would become the enterprise of gospel music. One of his hymns appeared in *The Methodist Hymnal* of 1964; six plus an arrangement of one of his father's hymns appeared in *The United Methodist Hymnal* of 1989. More can be found in *Songs of Zion,* one of the UMC's supplemental worship resources.[87] "We'll Understand It Better By and By" (#515) and "Stand by Me" (#512) are among the best known and loved. His blueslike hymns reflect a theology of hope in their quest for the glorious hereafter that lies beyond the present travail.[88]

Edgar J. Helms, while serving an institutional church in Boston, founded Goodwill Ministries in 1902.[89] The son of poor Iowa farmers, Helms (1863–1942) knew from an early age what it was like to be poor, hungry, and out of work. In 1889 Helms enrolled at Boston University School of Theology. After graduation and ordination, he was appointed to Morgan Chapel, now Church of All Nations in Boston's South End. By 1902 the country was in a severe economic depression, and Boston's South End—a "world parish" with 50,000 immigrants speaking thirty-nine languages, many suffering discrimination and poverty—had become one of the city's most impoverished slum areas. As Helms led his church in outreach, he realized that in addition to a massive program of education and relief, people needed job experience and skills. Hence he began a workshop program, which he gradually expanded to train persons with disabilities. Participants in the workshop program gained employable skills, the ability to provide for themselves, and a sense of dignity and self-worth. And when World War I produced its share of persons with amputated limbs or paralysis, Goodwill's role expanded to become a leader in the field of rehabilitation.[90]

As word got around that Helms had great success in his efforts, other cities asked his help in emulating the Goodwill venture. The concept caught on, and the programs took the name Goodwill Industries. In 1916 the MEC General Conference allocated $1 million through its Methodist Centenary Fund to establish Goodwill stores in New York, San Francisco, Los Angeles, St. Louis, and other cities. The Centenary campaign envisioned the expansion of this ministry so that by 1924 there were thirty-one. Subsequently, under the direction of Helms, the Bureau of Goodwill Industries of the MEC's Board of Missions' Department of City Work developed more than one hundred Goodwill organizations across the country. The Home Missions Department of the MECS adopted the idea and began similar programs in the South under the leadership of G. E. Holley. By 1929 there were Goodwill plants throughout the South, with notable facilities in Louisville, Memphis, Nashville, Chattanooga, Dallas, Atlanta, and Columbia. The program won wide recognition for its work in the relief of those caught in the throes of the Great Depression of the 1930s.

By the 1940s Goodwill's expanding program needed support from other religious and community resources, and the movement gradually separated itself from the Methodist church (by 1946).[91] By 2000, Goodwill Ministries, the seventh largest nonprofit organization in the U.S., carried on Helms's mission by providing work and job training to disabled people, people making the transition from welfare work, and others, operating ministries in two thousand communities in twenty-six nations. Goodwill celebrated its one hundredth anniversary in 2002.

William Bell (1860–1933) promoted the social gospel among United Brethren and did so especially after election to the episcopacy. A native of Indiana and successful pastor there, Bell was selected to head the State Sunday School Association. In 1893, the denomination called him to the position of executive secretary of the Home, Frontier, and Foreign Missionary Society. Twelve years later, the UBC elected him to the episcopacy and assigned him to the Pacific coast area. The denomination called on Bell to represent its interests on several important national and ecumenical bodies, including the Federal Council of Churches. An effective preacher and speaker—William Jennings Bryan once proclaimed him without peer—Bell was a popularizer in print as well. He wrote several best sellers, the most notable of which was *The Social Message of Our Lord* (1909). Bell termed the social crisis the most important issue facing the church of his day. He called for a "correction of all false and malignant individualism" that would "guarantee a new sense of social responsibility." Bell openly favored a radical revision of the economic order. "God never intended," he wrote, "the oppressive ownership of wealth by the few." In fact, "Christ made it very clear that riches were not only undesirable, but the positive occasion of guilt." Bell believed that it was the state's duty to "assert the right to limit the individual fortune and compel the vast individual wealth of the world to yield in a sane way to such methods as will insure a more equitable distribution." He concluded that there was nothing inherently anti-God about socialism.[92]

Bishop Bell was responsible for the triumph of the social gospel at the 1909 UBC General Conference. Far more than any preceding or succeeding UBC General Conference, the 1909 one was intensely aware of the social crisis. The Episcopal Address recognized "the social crisis of this age" and included a firm recommendation that the church adopt the Federal Council of Churches' Social Creed of the Churches. Bishop Bell, speaking for his colleagues on the episcopal bench, insisted that "the church should not be behind the state in condemning and seeking to remedy all monopolies as contrary to social welfare." When he concluded the address urging the church to "seek to correct all unfairness and injustice in the making or using of wealth and seek to establish the Golden Rule as the rule of social life," the conference delegates broke into applause.[93] To top it all off, Bishop Bell invited his close personal friend, William Jennings Bryan, then at the height of his popularity, to give a keynote address to the conference, an address entirely devoted to social issues. The UBC formally adopted the FCC's Social Creed of the Churches in 1916 and formed a Social Service Commission in 1933.

The Evangelical Church was relatively slow to respond to the challenge of the social gospel and far longer retained the individual-oriented moral stance. Not until 1934 did the EC adopt a social creed, not until 1938 did it establish a denominational Board of Christian Social Action, but it did lead in the deaconess movement.

Deaconesses

On June 15, 1885, a young woman named Lucy Rider Meyer (1849–1922) addressed the Chicago Methodist Episcopal Preachers' Meeting on the training of Christian workers. She described the crying need for a training school to prepare women for religious leadership (Sources 1889, 1893b). Her case made, the ministers gave her project their blessing, but insisted she would have to find the money on her own. Against great financial odds, she opened the Chicago Training School for City, Home, and Foreign Missions that October and the Chicago Deaconess Home two years later.[94] And in 1888, the MEC General Conference, which had declined to seat the five women elected as delegates (Sources 1888, 1890), entertained two petitions asking that deaconess work be recognized as an official ministry of the MEC. One came from the Rock River Conference, the other from the Bengal Conference in India. The latter cited the need for deaconesses with authority to administer the sacraments to the secluded zenana women of India. These petitions for the approval of the deaconess office were referred to the Committee on Missions, chaired by James Thoburn, brother of Isabella and elected missionary bishop by that General Conference. With his strong advocacy, the committee reported in favor of establishing a deaconess order. When the recommendation reached the conference floor, delegates listened to an appeal from Lucy Rider Meyer delivered by the influential Thoburn.[95] General Conference established the office of deaconess and provided a plan for organizing deaconess work in the MEC, declining however to give deaconesses sacramental authority for the mission field in India or elsewhere.

The action, unthinkable without the advocacy of Rider Meyer and other strong women, also benefited from interest in deaconesses that had built for some time. Lutherans in Germany and Anglicans in England had restored the ancient order in the 1830s and 1840s.[96] In 1864, Methodist pastors in several German cities introduced *parish* deaconesses for the care of the sick. Ten years later (1874), the MEC's conference in Germany established a deaconess order under the name *Bethanienverein* (Bethany Society). By 1884, the society had established Bethany deaconess homes and hospitals in three cities—Berlin, Frankfurt, and Hamburg—and had recruited and trained more than sixty deaconesses.[97] Also in 1874, the Evangelical Association's conference in Germany authorized the formation of its own independent Bethany Deaconess Society in Germany. The new society opened its first hospital in 1885 in Frankfurt. In 1890, Evangelical deaconesses were sent to Lausanne, Switzerland, and in 1897, to Strasbourg and Vienna. Trained nurses, they also engaged in outreach work and conducted nurseries for children of working mothers. In 1889, the Martha and Mary Society of the German Synod of the Methodist Church in England became the third member of the Methodist family of churches to establish deaconess work in Germany.

In England, Methodist pastor Thomas B. Stephenson, who, following the Anglican lead, recognized that an order of dedicated women had a valuable part to play in the life of the church, founded an Order of Sisters for work in Methodism's National Children's Home for orphaned girls and boys as early as 1878. A visit to a Lutheran deaconess center in Kaiserswerth, Germany, in 1871 encouraged Stephenson to develop opportunities for women to serve in the church. In 1887 Hugh Price Hughes, one of the most prominent Methodist preachers in Britain at the time, and his wife, Katherine, recruited "Sisters of the Poor" for work in their West London Mission. Three years later, in 1890, Stephenson published the book *Concerning Sisterhoods* and founded a Wesley Deaconess Order with approval from the Wesleyan Methodist Church in England. The order's first residential house was in London; others were opened in several British cities shortly thereafter. Stephenson was warden of the order as well as principal of the National Children's Home until 1900. Deaconesses were also employed in overseas mission work from 1894. The Primitive Methodist and United Methodist Free churches established similar orders by the end of the nineteenth century.[98]

In the 1870s, American Methodists touted the European experiments. The aforementioned James Thoburn, then a well-known missionary leader, did so early, appreciating the potential value of "unemployed Phoebes" for ministry in India, an appreciation enhanced when in the 1880s he and sister Isabella visited a deaconess home in England

and then Rider Meyer's training school.[99] Others promoting deaconesses in print included Bishop Matthew Simpson,[100] Drew Theological Seminary professor John F. Hurst,[101] and pastor, later Northwestern president, editor, and bishop Charles H. Fowler.[102] Two women were especially forceful and effective in publicized advocacy: Annie Wittenmyer, head of the Ladies' and Pastors' Christian Union (LPCU), who had played deaconess-like roles during the Civil War, and another leader of the LPCU, Susanna Fry, an Ohio schoolteacher who encountered Protestant deaconess work on a trip to Germany. In a pair of articles published in *Ladies' Repository* in 1872—"Ancient and Modern Deaconesses" and "Ancient and Modern Sisterhoods"—Fry urged Methodists to consider establishing a Methodist deaconess order that would further the work already begun by the LPCU[103] (Sources 1872b, 1870a). Wittenmyer also wrote several articles after a visit to Lutheran deaconess homes in Germany. Both traveled as well across the country pleading for the expression of Christian benevolence in the founding of deaconess hospitals, orphanages, homes for the aged, and visitation and relief of the poor.[104]

For such a mandate, Lucy Rider unknowingly had equipped herself, preparing for a career as a medical missionary and then assuming family breadwinner responsibilities on the death of her father. Her unusual educational-experiential pedigree included an Oberlin BA in 1872, two years at Woman's Medical School in Philadelphia,[105] the position of "Lady Principal" of Troy Conference Academy in Poultney, Vermont, more study (of science at Boston School of Technology and teaching methods at Cook County Normal School), a year teaching chemistry at McKendree College, and then a four-year stint as field secretary of the Illinois State Sunday School Association.[106] During service with the Sunday School Association, Rider met many young women whose lack of training kept them from lives of usefulness. The idea of a "school for the purpose of training young women for leadership in Christian work" gradually became the "dominant note" in her thinking.[107] In the winter of 1884–85, Rider taught Bible in Dwight L. Moody's School for Girls in Northfield, Massachusetts, and endeavored to interest him in the idea of a Bible training school. He perhaps already had ideas for such a school (Moody Bible Institute, founded in Chicago in 1886). Before success with the Chicago preachers, Rider tried the idea with New York Methodist women, who thought that Methodist ministers there would not support it.

Marriage in May 1885 to Josiah Shelly Meyer, a secretary for the Chicago YMCA, enabled her to think seriously about becoming principal of a training school without compensation. Adding support of both the Woman's Foreign and the Woman's Home Missionary Societies (MEC) to that of Chicago preachers, the Meyers moved into and began converting a West Park Avenue brownstone into a school—the Chicago Training School for City, Home, and Foreign Missions (CTS). J. Shelly Meyer became the business agent for the school while continuing in his job for the YMCA. Methodist women donated money and furnishings and soon launched a systematic "Nickel Fund" campaign to support the school. The Meyers publicized school and cause in *The Message*, which began publication in January 1886. Eventually Methodist women of wealth and Chicago businessmen became major donors to the school, permitting the purchase of land and construction of a facility designed for the purpose.[108]

The school opened in October 1885 with only five pupils, increased to eleven by early November, and graduated fifteen in its first commencement in 1887. Rider Meyer served as principal and regularly taught courses on the Bible. The resident teachers were few in the beginning, but ministers, teachers, and physicians from the Chicago area regularly donated their time to give lectures. The course of study was comprehensive, including Bible classes, but also studies in "hygiene, in citizenship, in social and family relationships, in everything that could help or hinder in the establishment of the Kingdom of Heaven on earth." Since most of the students came from rural areas or small towns, an important aspect of the program from the beginning was the provision for fieldwork in the city (including house-to-house visitation).[109]

In 1887, Rider Meyer deployed trainees in a program of visiting and assisting the immigrant poor and needy in Chicago and announced this as deaconess work in the June *Message*. Several students in a rented apartment became the nucleus of a deaconess home, soon joined by Isabella Thoburn, principal of Lucknow Woman's College in India, then home on furlough. The October issue of *The Message* announced the joyful news of the establishment of this first deaconess home in American Methodism.[110] By March 1888, a dozen deaconesses occupied the home. A generous gift from an Oak Park Methodist woman enabled Rider Meyer to purchase a building adjacent to the school and join the two facilities.

The enabling legislation by the 1888 General Conference outlined the duties of deaconesses. It regulated deaconess work, charging each annual conference to establish a nine-member Conference Board of Deaconesses, at least three of whom must be women. These boards licensed qualified candidates twenty-five years of age or older who had served a probationary period of at least two years and were recommended by a quarterly conference. Unsalaried and living communally (Sources 1889, 1893b, 1902), deaconesses were also costumed, uniformly wearing a simple long black dress and a bonnet with white ties at the neck. They wore it for the sake of economy, to eliminate the need for an expensive wardrobe, and for instant recognition and protection as they worked in dangerous urban neighborhoods. It also gave them greater accessibility to poor people and a sense of "sisterly union." Although receiving no salary, the single women in this sisterhood of service were provided board, their uniform, and a monthly allowance.[111]

Two types of deaconess work developed, both designed to meet the needs of those in the slum neighborhoods of Chicago: nurse deaconesses and missionary deaconesses (also referred to as visitors or evangelists). To prepare students for the more technical service of the former, Rider Meyer included the basics of nursing in the course of study at CTS and called on Chicago physicians to teach them. Dr. Isaac Danforth, an early trustee of the school, helped Rider Meyer to establish a medical clinic at CTS for the dual purpose of offering better nursing training for the students and free medical care to Chicago's poor. Danforth himself was identified with "the cause of the urban poor and of women," being a pathologist at Rush College and Chicago Medical College, a staff physician at Saint Luke's Hospital, and dean of Woman's Medical College. He taught the CTS students the course on human anatomy, and Dr. Eliza H. Root taught them hygiene and obstetrics. The direct successor to this medical clinic was Wesley Hospital, established with the guidance of Danforth in 1901, a substantial six-story facility with a modern operating room and 145 beds. Although Rider Meyer never taught nursing at CTS, she completed her own medical training at Woman's Medical College of Northwestern University in 1887; she was listed in the CTS catalog as Lucy Rider Meyer, MD. The two-year training required for deaconesses was tailored to the needs of each type, nurses receiving both theoretical and practical preparation comparable to that of nursing schools, and all students being required to take courses in Bible, the *Discipline* of the MEC, historical and doctrinal studies, and methods of social service.[112] Eight women, four of them trained nurses, were in the second class of CTS deaconesses, consecrated and licensed in June 1890. In his graduation address, Bishop William Xavier Ninde, former president of Garrett Biblical Institute, summed up the significance of the occasion: "A sphere has been opened to consecrated womanhood, worthy of her unshrinking devotion and tireless energies. To these wider and more absorbing activities the Church she loves so well calls and welcomes her. She has found her place. She takes it with every divine and human sanction."[113]

Rider Meyer interpreted the work of these vocationally single deaconesses as that of "the Mother in the Church," as part of the "characteristic ministry of women" to care for children and heal the sick. For her, the real origin of deaconess work in America lay in "the mother instinct of woman herself, and in that wider conception of woman's 'family duties' that compels her to include in her loving care the great needy world-family as well as the blessed little domestic circle."[114]

Rider Meyer's deaconess model was not to be Methodism's only option. Left ambiguous in the empowering legislation of 1888 was whether the annual conferences or the Woman's Home Missionary Society could best protect deaconesses' goals and status within the church. Disagreeing with Lucy Rider Meyer on these matters was the other principal contender for the leadership of the deaconess movement, Jane Marie Bancroft Robinson (1847–1932). Born in Massachusetts, the daughter of an MEC pastor, Jane Bancroft earned a PhD from Syracuse University. From 1877 to 1885 she served as dean of the Woman's College and a professor of French at Northwestern University in

Evanston, Illinois. When Bryn Mawr College opened in 1885, she was awarded its first history fellowship and spent the next two years in Europe studying at the universities of Zurich and Paris. Becoming interested in the Methodist deaconesses and their work, she undertook with WHMS encouragement a thorough study of the deaconess movement in Europe, presented it to the WHMS on her return, and published it in 1889 as *Deaconesses in Europe and Their Lessons for America.*[115]

Speaking at the annual meeting of the WHMS in Boston shortly after her return to the United States in the fall of 1888, Bancroft inspired the women to inaugurate deaconess work. Bancroft chaired an implementing committee and became general secretary of the resultant Bureau for Deaconess Work. The WHMS resolved the ambiguity of deaconess governance in its own favor: "That the Woman's Home Missionary Society hereby expresses its willingness to assume the care of Deaconess Homes wherever such homes shall be entrusted to it, subject to the limitations of the *Discipline,* insofar and as rapidly as financial consideration will permit."[116] Bancroft began traveling across the country speaking about deaconess work and founding deaconess homes. In Cincinnati in the spring of 1891, Jane Bancroft married George O. Robinson, a Detroit lawyer and widower with four children. Robinson was an active MEC layman and founder of the Michigan *Christian Advocate.* He encouraged his new wife to continue her work with the Deaconess Bureau, which she did until 1904. She was elected president of the WHMS in 1908.[117]

These two gifted, extraordinarily well-educated, and dedicated Methodist women, Lucy Rider Meyer and Jane Bancroft Robinson, vied with each other for the leadership of the deaconess movement in the MEC for nearly twenty-five years. Rider Meyer wanted the church to accept responsibility for the welfare of the deaconesses during their active careers and in retirement. She saw the order as a lifetime commitment, a religious vocation that set women apart and freed them as far as possible from the usual female commitments, marriage and family. Rider Meyer wanted deaconess work to be directly under the supervision of the church through the annual conferences, to ensure that deaconesses would have the same status as male officers of the church. Her model was referred to as the "Church Plan." Bancroft Robinson deemed Rider Meyer's nunlike lifelong vocation neither viable nor desirable. Bancroft Robinson believed that the order should be open to women who wanted to undertake social service work for a short time before they made permanent decisions about what to do with their lives. She espoused a European model of deaconess work where the deaconesses worked under the supervision of a female superior within the motherhouse. She believed that the Woman's Home Missionary Society, a separate women's organization in the MEC, ought to supervise deaconess work in order to protect its autonomy.[118] The two sides took their case and arguments about the "original intention" of the 1888 legislation to successive General Conferences. The 1908 General Conference created a General Deaconess Board to guide all three forms of deaconess work: "the 'Church Plan,' the German Methodist, and the WHMS deaconesses." The new plan was recommended to all deaconesses in the opening Episcopal Address.[119] The solution, however, proved "illusory," both Rider Meyer and Bancroft Robinson being appointed to the newly organized board and continuing to maintain their own views.[120]

Despite, perhaps because of, the competition, the deaconess cause initially prospered. By 1910 more than a thousand MEC deaconesses had been consecrated for service in some ninety institutions. Between 1880 and 1915, nearly sixty religious training schools opened in the United States, "primarily for lay people and most of them for women." In addition to the Chicago Training School and among MEC institutions were the New England Deaconess Home and Training School in Boston; the Lucy Webb Hayes National Training School in Washington, D.C.; the National Training School in Kansas City, Kansas; and the National Training School in San Francisco. These functioned under the authority of the Bureau of Training Schools of the WHMS (MEC). A Training School for Colored Deaconesses was founded in Cincinnati in 1900. Other denominations in the Methodist family had also become part of the movement: the UBC beginning deaconess work in 1897, the EA in 1903, the MPC in 1908, and the MECS in 1902. The latter's Scarritt Bible and Training School, established in 1892 in Kansas City, Missouri, relocated to Nashville in 1924.[121]

Impetus for Scarritt's 1892 founding came from a Chicago visit in 1887 by Belle Harris Bennett to confer with Lucy Rider Meyer. Bennett had become convinced that southern women "longed to work in the Lord's vineyard," but did not "because they did not know how to work." Later presenting her idea to the Woman's Board of Foreign Missions in 1889, Bennett was promptly appointed "agent" of the board to raise funds and promote a training school.[122] Scarritt served initially to train women for missions, first for the Woman's Foreign Missionary Society, later for home missions work as well.

In 1902, Bennett petitioned the MECS General Conference to create an office of deaconess for the southern church. She and Mary Helm had already spent two years laying the groundwork for its acceptance. Approval came but not without "long and bitter debate" about whether such official recognition of women in the church would lead them to aspire to the ordained ministry or to compete with the work of the ordained minister. In granting the memorial, however, the General Conference made the Woman's Board of Home Missions entirely responsible for deaconess work.[123] Mary Helm tried to allay suspicions regarding the deaconess movement in an article in *Our Homes,* "What a Deaconess Is, and What She Is Not." As in the MEC, Helm explained, deaconesses in the MECS were consecrated, trained, uniformed, lived in a Deaconess Home, and received no salary. A deaconess was *not* a preacher, ordained, or a "Protestant nun."[124] In 1903 Bishop Eugene Hendrix consecrated the first deaconesses of the MECS. The early deaconesses in the MECS were said to be happy in their own work, "consummate homemakers," who had a sense of humor, exhibited patience in facing difficulties, worked beyond the call of duty, and were resourceful, adaptable, generous, persistent, and courageous.[125]

Getting the churches to accord the office the dignity and recognition its service warranted took patience. As early as 1896 the MEC General Conference requested that the bishops prepare a liturgy for consecration of deaconesses, but not until 1908 was such a liturgy added to the church's official ritual. The liturgy included the following elements: (1) presentation of the candidates, (2) a scripture reading, Matthew 25:31-40 ("...as you did it to one of the least of these who are members of my family, you did it to me"), (3) an address to the candidates that defined their serving ministry, and (4) vows assumed by the candidates. The early liturgies suggested singing the famous social gospel hymn "Where Cross the Crowded Ways of Life" at the opening of the service and the hymn "Take My Life, and Let It Be" immediately before the consecrating prayer. The central action of the service consisted of the vows and consecrating prayer in use from 1908 until 1992:

> O eternal God, the father of our Lord Jesus Christ, who didst call Phoebe and Dorcas into the service of thy Church: look upon these thy servants, who are now to be set apart to the Office of Deaconess. Give to them, we pray thee, such understanding of thy holy Gospel, such firmness of Christian purpose, such diligence in service, and such beauty of life in Christ, that they may be to all whom they teach or serve a worthy revelation of the meaning and power of the Christian life.

Deaconess candidates had the option of pursuing an independent "course of study" prescribed at the outset by annual conference deaconess boards. Not until 1920, however, was a unified, churchwide "Course of Study for Deaconesses" adopted.[126] In contrast to earlier curricula, the new course was weighted in the direction of the social sciences, social ethics, and social work theory and method. Over the years, texts covered such subjects as Bible, church history and theology (including works by such prominent social gospel authors as Walter Rauschenbusch, Richard Ely, Francis Peabody, and Harry Ward),[127] social work, nursing, and Christian education. The General Deaconess Board also produced a companion to the course of study to guide students through their reading, papers, and examination.[128]

Deaconesses were deployed according to their skills but also in accord with societal codes, including segregation by race. Two of the pioneering Black deaconesses, Anna Hall and Martha Drummer, graduated from the New England Deaconess Training School in Boston. By 1900 the northern church's WHMS established its first separate Deaconess Home and Training School for Colored People in Cincinnati. The WHMS also set up a separate bureau for the supervision of "colored" deaconesses. Mrs. M. C. B. Mason, wife of the first Black executive of the denomination's Freedmen's Aid Society, became the first supervisor. The racial contours of Black deaconess work can be seen in Anna Hall's report of her ministry (Sources 1902) and in her later career. A Georgia native, Hall attended Clark College in Atlanta. After deaconess training, she was, at age thirty-six, consecrated a deaconess. Following a short ministry in Atlanta, she devoted the next twenty-five years of her life to the education and spiritual development of the people of Liberia, where she served as a school principal. For her devotion to his country and its people, Liberia's president William Tubman appointed "Mama Hall," as she had come to be known, a Knight Commander of the Liberian Humane Order.

The deaconess movement seemed to be at its height in 1910, when 256 women came to study at the Chicago Training School. In actuality, by 1910 the movement had crested. Changing attitudes toward social Christianity, new, secular career opportunities for women, and a growing conservatism in the churches affected women's training schools and, with them, the deaconess movement. By 1914 Lucy Rider Meyer was alerting readers of the *Deaconess Advocate* to "our present crisis."[129] The crisis, a decline in professions that would continue, also had something to do with other religious vocational opportunities for women and other church doors that opened.

Methodist Hospitals

The Methodist Episcopal Hospital, Brooklyn, since 1972 a UMC Heritage Landmark, opened in December 1887 with a ceremony of speeches, prayers, and hymns. The event represented yet another "recovery" of the Wesleyan and early American Methodist healing ministry, a significant context within which the deaconess movement would labor, a Methodist-medical-science counterpart to contemporary healing claims and advocacy among proto-Pentecostals, and one more highly capitalized Methodist venture into care for the distressed.[130]

An important role in stimulating this founding and, in a sense, the Methodist hospital movement might be credited to James M. Buckley, powerful editor of the *Christian Advocate* (New York), whose resistance to women's rights we treated earlier. Motivated by the death of a friend whose life, he thought, might have been spared had he had medical care in Brooklyn and by the efforts that Catholic, Episcopal, and Jewish groups had made in founding hospitals, Buckley penned an editorial in the *Advocate* (Sources 1881a), affirming: "The Methodist Episcopal Church is today, so far as we can learn, without a hospital.... We are losing power while we fail to attend to these good works." Bishop Matthew Simpson echoed Buckley's plea later that year in one of his addresses to the first gathering of the world Methodist family in London (see Sources 1881b for another of Simpson's contributions to the event).[131]

A prosperous Methodist banker, George I. Seney, responded to Buckley with a gift of $400,000 and sixteen lots in hospital-poor Brooklyn. With considerable fanfare Methodists laid a cornerstone that same year but saw the completion delayed by the economic depression of the early 1880s. During the first year of operation, the hospital added an outpatient clinic, a children's ward, and a training school for nurses. Most patients coming to the hospital were unable to pay for medical treatment. Methodists therefore launched a coast-to-coast campaign to encourage churches and individuals to endow beds "in perpetuity" for $5,000 or for one year at $365. By the end of the first year, thirteen beds had been so endowed. Methodist women in New York–area churches organized Florence Nightingale Societies and immediately began to give generous support to the hospital. Conferences within the region devoted one Communion offering per year. It took ten years before all of the planned buildings were completed and equipped.[132]

Methodists in other cities followed New York's lead. Chicago Methodists opened theirs in 1888; Cincinnati in 1889; Omaha in 1891; Kansas City, Minneapolis, and Philadelphia in 1892; Washington, D.C., in 1894; Louisville in 1895; Boston in 1896; Spokane in 1898; and Indianapolis in 1899. Southern Methodists began founding a family of hospitals early in the twentieth century: in Atlanta (Emory University Hospital), 1905; in St. Louis, 1914; in Memphis, 1921; in Durham (Duke University Hospital), 1930; in Houston, 1922; and in Dallas, 1927. The Evangelicals founded five small hospitals by 1920, but the United Brethren had none.

These healing ventures represented a recovery. Wesley's medical manual, as we noted earlier, had been among the earliest publications of the Methodists in North America. Revised at Bishop Asbury's request to suit American physicians and climate by a noted Philadelphia doctor, Henry Wilkins, in 1792, it was kept in print by the church through the 1820s and issued in pirated editions by other publishers through the 1880s. Like Wesley, Asbury and numerous other circuit riders viewed it their duty to prescribe medical remedies for sick persons. *Christian Advocates* carried Wesley-like workable remedies in regular "Health and Disease" columns. By 1830, this minister-physician tradition was ending. In 1817 a circuit rider was found guilty of practicing medicine against the counsel of his presiding elder. After 1820, ministers generally decided either to preach or to practice medicine, not to do both.[133] By the 1860s clear lines of demarcation existed between these once united professions, and Methodist publications routinely praised the medical establishment and enthusiastically reported new medical developments available to doctors, such as articles on anesthesia, blood transfusions, and vaccinations.[134]

The quality of medical care improved rapidly after the Civil War with the passing of physician licensure laws (after 1873), the widespread use of anesthesia combined with antisepsis (1880s), in the 1890s the opening of a model medical school at Johns Hopkins University, Baltimore, the beginning of clinical and laboratory research, and the development and use of vaccines, antitoxins, and X-rays. Accompanying these developments, hundreds of hospitals were being built to serve as the infrastructure for scientific practice and healing power. America's churches, including the Methodists, participated in these changes by assuming they could contribute to human well-being and progress by building and sponsoring hospitals, making scientific medicine more available to their constituents and members, especially to the growing number of the nation's poor persons.[135]

The new deaconess orders at low cost staffed several of the earliest Methodist hospitals. Deaconess societies also founded hospitals of their own. The "mother" deaconess hospital, Christ Hospital in Cincinnati, Ohio, opened its doors and its beds in 1889. The hospital expanded the mission of the one-year-old Elizabeth Gamble Deaconess Home and Training School founded in that city the previous year. The institution took its name from Elizabeth Gamble, the wife of James Gamble, the ingenious chemist who invented and marketed Ivory soap and who assisted William Nast in founding Methodism's mission to America's growing German American community in America's heartland. Gamble persuaded Isabella Thoburn, then superintendent of the Chicago Deaconess Home, to establish deaconess work in Cincinnati, by offering a free residence and operating funds.

Immediately the small family of Cincinnati deaconesses discovered an overwhelming demand for nursing services. At first the city's sick were treated in the deaconess home. When the community pled for a separate hospital facility, James Gamble obliged with an eleven-room, three-story house a few doors from the deaconess home. Christ Hospital continued to be Gamble's favorite charity until his death in 1891. The deaconess home and hospital quickly outgrew their cramped city quarters and sought a new location. Taking up his deceased father's role as hospital benefactor, James Gamble Jr. purchased a large property located in a Cincinnati suburb. In July 1892 the deaconess newsletter, The Message, carried news that the new site on Wesley Avenue would accommodate up to one hundred deaconesses and as many hospital patients. The depression of 1893 delayed construction of a new deaconess home, training school, and hospital, however. The move to the institution's new campus was completed in 1898. A School of Nursing attached to the hospital opened in 1902. The school soon ranked as one of the best in the nation and was fully accredited. In 1911 an adjacent property was purchased and became the children's hospital. The sixty-bed hospital grew to four hundred beds when the more modern structure was occupied in 1931. In 1957 construction was begun on a new wing to house two hundred and fifty additional beds.[136]

Other deaconess hospitals followed, notably in Boston, Chicago, and Washington, D.C. In 1924 The Methodist Episcopal Church consolidated the denomination's General Deaconess Board and Board of Hospitals and Homes. By that year more than two hundred deaconesses were reported to be active in the health-care work of the church. The boards worked as one until the time of reunion in 1939 when deaconess work was placed under the supervision of the Woman's Division of the Board of Missions. Evangelical Deaconess Home and Hospital opened in Chicago in 1905 with a free dispensary, a laboratory, and a thirty-five-bed ward, the first hospital related to the Evangelical Association.

German American Methodists, strong in their piety and effective in their expression of faith in health and welfare ministries, founded and supported a considerable network of deaconess hospitals of their own across the country to help provide health care to the nation's burgeoning German American community. At the 1892 MEC General Conference, the German delegates resolved to establish a German motherhouse in Chicago as soon as $25,000 could be raised. When fund-raising fell short of the goal, German delegates at the 1896 General Conference turned to Cincinnati for a mother-house there if the required conditions could be met. They were, thanks to a gift from Mrs. Fannie Nast Gamble, daughter of William Nast, leader of Methodism's German American movement. The MEC's Central Deaconess Board authorized the Reverend Christian Golder, with his deaconess sister, Louise, to rent a house in Cincinnati to found a German Methodist deaconess hospital. The order released six German nurses from Christ Hospital to assist the Golders, who purchased a well-appointed private hospital, which they reopened as Bethesda Hospital in 1898.[137] In 1900 the plant was expanded with the purchase of a large home nearby for use as a deaconess home. In 1904 a maternity department was opened with eighty beds. A much larger, state-of-the-art maternity hospital opened in 1913, followed by a School of Nursing in 1914, absorption of the Ohio Hospital for Women and Children in 1915, and the opening of Bethesda Home for the Aged that same year.

Out of this beginning of hospital and society grew the Bethesda Institutions, a family of German American Methodist-sponsored hospitals, homes, and training schools in Brooklyn, New York; Akron, Ohio; Chicago; Milwaukee; Kansas City; Louisville; Detroit; Terre Haute, Indiana; and Los Angeles. The order launched a denomination-wide Bethesda Society in 1897. Directed by Ida Golder, wife of Christian, the society offered memberships for a dollar, using its funds for the care of the needy sick. The denomination's Central Deaconess Board considered the Cincinnati Bethesda home and hospital as the motherhouse of German Methodism and required that future homes and hospitals, as far as possible, be affiliated with it as branch houses and hospitals, having the same relation to the board as the motherhouse itself.[138]

A signal contribution to health care among African Americans occurred with the opening in 1876 of Meharry Medical College. The renowned Nashville institution was a venture undertaken by the MEC Freedmen's Aid Society and backed financially by five Methodist Meharry brothers (from Indiana). Founded during the era when the segregated policy of "separate but equal" became national policy and dictated every aspect of society, including medical care, Meharry Medical College provided one of the few contexts within which to train Black medical professionals.[139] A teaching hospital, Hubbard

Hospital, was added in 1910. Over the years Meharry expanded in depth and diversity, and with generous aid from the Carnegie and Rockefeller foundations and the Methodist Board of Education, by the 1960s had become the largest private, historically Black institution exclusively dedicated to educating health-care professionals and biomedical scientists in the U.S. A major resource for educating health-care professionals, Meharry has graduated nearly 15 percent of all African American physicians and dentists practicing in the U.S. Since 1970 Meharry has awarded more than 10 percent of the PhD's in biomedical sciences received by African Americans. The majority of Meharry's graduates practice in medically underserved rural and inner-city areas.[140]

In 1901 a devastating fire swept through Jacksonville, Florida, destroying 466 acres, killing seven citizens, and injuring and rendering homeless nine thousand. There seemed to be nowhere to turn for help. The utter destruction moved the local Methodist women to realize the need to establish a shelter and medical treatment facility for the Black citizens of the area. A one-room medical clinic was opened in 1901, from which quickly grew Brewster Hospital and Nurses' Training School.[141]

By the 1920s, seventy-five hospitals and clinics related to the MEC had opened to persons of any faith, many included dispensaries where medicines and supplies could be purchased under cost, and all were overseen by a standing Board of Hospitals and Homes. By 1960, some seventy-six general hospitals were being operated under Methodist auspices—a number second only to Lutherans among Protestants.[142] Methodism's late–nineteenth-century rush into the health-care field brought problems early in the twentieth century. Medical services and nursing education programs lacked standardization and accreditation.[143] Many of the hospitals were chronically underfunded, poorly housed, and loosely connected to a large number of church agencies—General Deaconess Board, Woman's Home Missionary Society, Board of Home Missions, and Board of Negro Education in the case of MEC hospitals.[144] Hospital and home administrators took the first step toward addressing these problems by forming a National Methodist Hospital and Home Association (NMHHA).[145] By the 1920s church leaders established Boards of Hospitals and Homes to enforce standards—medical, curricular, architectural, and financial.[146] At the same time the balance of power shifted from hospital trustees (heavily clergy) to medical decision makers. During the first two years of the MEC board, eighteen of its hospitals reached the standards adopted by the Board of Hospitals and Homes and the American College of Surgeons.[147]

To strengthen denominational ties and broaden financial support for the expanding family of hospitals, Methodists founded national organizations patterned after the Red Cross: the White Cross Society in the MEC in 1917 and the Golden Cross Society in the MECS in 1922. At the same time the UBC began a "little red Christmas stocking" program to raise money for the denomination's social welfare ministries. A red cardboard coin holder in the shape of a stocking was distributed to churches in the supporting area to be filled by children and adults with pennies, later dimes, and returned to the agency.[148]

By the early decades of the twentieth century, hospital trustees and administrators were deliberately seeking *paying* patients.[149] Trustees converted what were called free wards into paying wards, added private rooms, provided the option of private-duty nurses for those who could pay, introduced better food, and hired nurses and orderlies to do the maintenance chores previously done by patients. To alter the public image of the charity hospital as a place of death and suffering for indigent or working-class people, trustees began to advertise the hospital's medical prowess and the hotel-like accommodations. Income from paying patients represented three-quarters of the budgets of "ecclesiastical" hospitals, reported a U.S. government survey of the nation's hospitals in 1904. By 1920 the sixty-one hospitals of the MEC reported serving more than 100,000 patients; 50,000 of them received free or part-pay service, reducing charity care to less than 50 percent.[150]

Ironically just as America's cities were emerging as working-class centers and the church was focusing its attention on poor persons, immigrants, laborers, and children (as this chapter, including the next section, has documented), Methodist hospitals began to turn away from poor persons and to remodel their services around the needs of wealthier clients. The financial crisis of many Methodist hospitals caused trustees in these institutions to deny service to the poorest and neediest and to shunt the traditional "charity" cases off to the public institutions, changes that had dire long-term consequences for the delivery of health services to the cities' poor and working-class groups. The church's hospitals became increasingly dependent upon the services of private physicians, who provided them with needed private and paying patients.

Yet hospital spokespersons had no difficulty in describing Methodist hospitals as monuments of charitable purpose and action because they represented an immense investment of capital and goodwill, confident that hospitals supported by voluntary contributions confer as much benefit upon those who contribute the funds as upon those who are treated in them. Service as a donor, trustee, or volunteer was a symbolic announcement—"We care." It was in the vein of charity as the act of giving rather than the act of receiving.

Institutionalizing Social Christianity: MFSS and the Social Creed

The Methodist Federation for Social Service (MFSS; after 1948 the Methodist Federation for Social *Action* [MFSA]) did not spring full grown out of the consciousness of a little band of American Methodist clergy as some accounts of its founding imply.[151] Indeed, in the keynote address delivered in November 1908 to the federation's first national convocation in St. Louis, Herbert Welch, first president of the federation and later bishop, recognized the larger social movement that produced the federation and other social service organizations. He singled out as a model the Wesleyan Methodist

Union for Social Service (WMUSS or Wesleyan Union) in England formed three years earlier. Welch charged the organization "to put American Methodism where English Methodism has come to be, distinctly on the side of Christ's 'little ones'; not to appear as the advocate of any class, be it rich or poor, but as the friend of all . . . because they are [all children of God]; to be once again and more fully than ever 'the Church of the people.' "[152]

Two years earlier, in the winter of 1906, Welch, then president of Ohio Wesleyan University, had met Elbert Zaring,[153] editor of the Cincinnati-based *Western Christian Advocate*, and Worth Tippy,[154] pastor of Cleveland's Epworth Memorial Methodist Episcopal Church, later to serve the Federal Council of Churches for twenty years as its social service executive. The three began thinking about formation of an organization for the MEC similar to that of the WMUSS in England. Welch indicated that their concern for more effective urban witness, social reform, and analysis of societal problems was shared by Frank Mason North, then influential executive of the New York City Church Extension and Missionary Society, and other New York pastors, his colleagues from days in that conference.[155] They put organization on hold until one of their number could go to England, meet the leaders of the Wesleyan Union, and visit as many of the city missions as possible. Welch knew such fact finding would be instructive; he had spent a sabbatical year at Oxford University in 1902 and had some familiarity with the work of Hugh Price Hughes and English social programs.[156] The scouting trip became viable and enticing when a wealthy parishioner offered to pay Tippy's expenses for a three-month trip to England and his congregation granted him a leave for the summer.

Tippy set out to learn all he could about the work of the WMUSS and the work of the church's major missions in London, Manchester, and Leeds.[157] Since 1905 Tippy had been conducting experiments of his own in urban ministry in his Cleveland parish, turning laypeople into social workers, organizing a Charities Council, cooperating with city officials, and opening the church seven days a week as a neighborhood center. His savvy as participant-observer was later evident in his description of awakening Epworth Church, Cleveland, to its social ministry in a study book, *The Church, a Community Force*, for the Missionary Education Movement of the United States and Canada, an ecumenical educational and publication program sponsored by mainline denominations.[158] From June through July of 1907 Tippy traveled about England studying the Wesleyan movement at firsthand and particularly the young Wesleyan Methodist Union for Social Service, which he and colleagues viewed as a potential model for a similar agency in the U.S.

The Wesleyan Union had been founded in 1905 largely through the leadership of Samuel E. Keeble, the Union's first president.[159] It sought to widen the church's concentration on a few social problems by "the collection and study of social facts, the pursuit of social service, and the discussion of social problems and theories from the

Christian standpoint, with the view to educate public opinion and secure improvement in the conditions of life."[160] For five years, Keeble had publicly pled for a social union.[161] During his Manchester ministry, Keeble set up a society in his circuit to consider housing, education, health, and sanitation. This ambitious program received favorable comment in the denomination's newspaper, *Methodist Recorder*,[162] and other districts began to set up their own societies. During the Wesleyan Conference of 1905, a small group of young socially minded clergy under the inspiration of Keeble officially started the Union with its watchword "See and Serve." By the end of 1905 Keeble was able to announce that local branches had been established in every large city in Britain. Through these local branches, its magazine, *See and Serve*[163] (the Union's motto), and its tracts and publications, the Union influenced the thinking of younger church members and was one of the forces that led to the creation of a Social Welfare Department for the church in 1918. Methodists were urged by Keeble to "tactfully practise social permeation" of (that is, infiltrate) the various church organizations and meetings and to be ready for "a great work of social propagandism" when numbers were sufficient.[164]

Although sometimes worried by "socialism" within Methodist ranks, the Wesleyan press gave the new Union a cautious welcome. The new Union recruited able leadership and made effective use of the press, especially with a penny pamphlet series, "Social Tracts for the Times." Keeble wrote the first number, *Christianity and Socialism*. Through its newsletter, *See and Serve*, a series of scholarly conferences, and their published proceedings, the Union sought to address gaps in official Wesleyan social thinking: *The Citizen of Tomorrow* (1906), *Social Science and Service* (1909), and most important of all, *The Social Teaching of the Bible* (1909).

Fresh from his scouting tour, Tippy stopped in New York to consult with Frank Mason North. Tippy learned that North had been discussing the need for a social service caucus with Harry F. Ward, pastor of Union Avenue Methodist Episcopal Church in the stockyards district of Chicago, a settlement project aided by Northwestern University in Evanston. Shortly after Tippy returned to Cleveland, he invited four interested colleagues—North from New York, Ward from Chicago, and Welch and Zaring from Ohio—to meet in Cleveland to take the next step. Only three of the five were able to be present: Welch, North, and Tippy. After exchanging ideas on the nature of the proposed denomination-wide association of lay and clergy leaders concerned about issues of social justice, the group decided to proceed with the organization and called a conference for Washington, D.C., on December 3, 1907, to launch it. Invitations signed by all five were sent to prominent clergy working in the fields of church extension, religious journalism, education, and the parish ministry and to interested lay leaders, social workers, businesspeople, and public officials:[165]

> The Committee has in mind the formation of a society to stimulate wide study of social questions by the church, side by side with practical social service, and to bring the

church into touch with neglected social groups. It is an effort to apply the sane and fervent spirit of Methodism to the social needs of the time.[166]

Twenty-five lay and clergy leaders—including the five conspirers, North, Welch, Ward,[167] Zaring, and Tippy—attended the unofficial meeting in Washington. North moved the establishment of a Methodist Federation for Social Service, and the motion carried. A brief mission statement for the new voluntary organization set forth its aims: "to deepen within the church the sense of social obligation, to study social problems from a Christian point of view, and to promote social service in the Spirit of Christ." Welch was elected convener. Later that week the band of Methodist reformers breakfasted with progressive President Theodore Roosevelt in the White House. Moving quickly into action, the fledgling organization drafted the first Social Creed for presentation to the 1908 MEC General Conference slated to return where had it all begun, Baltimore.

Several important circumstances set the stage for adoption of the church's first statement of social principles by the 1908 General Conference. Six hundred of the eight hundred elected delegates were newcomers, many imbued with the spirit of social activism by their popular President Theodore Roosevelt, whom they invited to address a conference session (Sources 1908). The MFSS did its part to stimulate the progressive mood. It rented the Lyric Theater, where General Conference met in the daytime, for an evening rally at which more than one thousand persons heard the Methodist governor of Kansas, Edward Hoch, Ohio Wesleyan College president and new MFSS head Herbert Welch, and Chicago-area Methodist Bishop William Fraser McDowell urge the church to press for social justice rather than harp on the evils of drinking, dancing, theatergoing, and card playing. MFSS leaders had used their influence to insert into the Episcopal Address an affirmation of the rights of labor quite advanced in its time, stating that "we hold the right of those workingmen who desire to do so, to form labor unions for the advancement of their interest." The conference received a flood of petitions from members and local churches calling for the church to take action on the growing economic crisis, especially the growing rift between management and labor, and to champion the right of labor to organize.

That subject and particularly the right of workers to organize at the MEC's Book Concern tested the progressive resolve early in General Conference proceedings (we turn in chapter 12 to that conflict and the longer story of Methodism and labor). The progressive mood held, however, and General Conference debated and adopted the first Social Creed of Methodism:

The Methodist Episcopal Church stands—
For equal rights and complete justice for all men in all stations of life.
For the principle of conciliation and arbitration in industrial dissensions.

For the protection of the workers from dangerous machinery, occupational diseases, injuries and mortality.

For the abolition of child labor.

For such regulation of the conditions of labor for women as shall safeguard the physical and moral health of the community.

For the suppression of the "sweating system."[168]

For the gradual and reasonable reduction of the hours of labor to the lowest practical point, with work for all; and for that degree of leisure for all which is the condition of the highest human life.

For a release from employment one day in seven.

For a living wage in every industry.

For the highest wages that each industry can afford, and for the most equitable division of the products of industry that can ultimately be devised.

For the recognition of the Golden Rule and the mind of Christ as the supreme law of society and the sure remedy for all social ills.[169]

The creed's principal author was Harry Ward, who penned the statement on telegraph blanks borrowed from the backroom of the Western Union headquarters where the General Conference legislative committee on the Church and Social Problems was meeting with the federation's executive committee. Ward replaced a lengthy and ponderous subcommittee draft with a concise, hard-hitting eleven-point statement of what Methodists stood for. A single-issue creed, proclaiming just how pressing the matter of economic reform had become in the first decade of the new century, it was also prophetic—advocating much of the social legislation passed twenty-five years later by President Franklin Roosevelt's New Deal. The Social Creed also became Methodism's first major gift to the emerging ecumenical movement and perhaps the preeminent summation of the social gospel.

During the fall of 1908, Frank Mason North, an MFSS founder, active ecumenist, and social justice advocate, labored to create a second version of the creed. North added four affirmations concerning rights to a job, unemployment compensation, aid to dependent children, and old age disability insurance (the latter, of course, later enacted in the national Social Security program). North presented the "creed" to the Federal Council of Churches (FCC), representing most of America's Protestant churches, meeting in the fall of 1908. The FCC endorsed it wholeheartedly. The expanded statement known as "The Social Creed of the Churches" was gradually taken up by one denomination after another. Within the Methodist family, the Social Creed in either Methodist or ecumenical form was adopted by the UBC in 1912, by the MECS in 1914, and by the MPC in 1916; the EC lagged until 1934. Despite efforts to develop a common text, the social creeds of the several churches were continually modified. In 1932 North played a central role again in updating the text when the FCC creed adopted an extensive revision called "Social Ideals."

General Conference in 1908 recognized the MFSS as the denomination's "executive agency to rally the forces of the church in support of social reform." This affirmation was reaffirmed by the 1912 and 1916 General Conferences, but with the stipulation that three bishops be designated each quadrennium to sit on the federation's governing board. MFSS/MFSA's place within the denomination would change dramatically as the federation lived into its calling.

Methodism and American society sometimes heeded the church's social gospel prophets—such as Bishop Francis J. McConnell, Harry F. Ward, and Winifred Chappell—and at other times gave them the prophets' due. The 1932 MEC General Conference declared "the present industrial order is unchristian, unethical and anti-social," a victory for MFSS. But "Red-baiting" resumed. The Hearst newspaper chain launched reactionary attacks on MFSS, partly a reaction to Ward's "fact-finding" 1929 trip to Russia. In 1934–35, Hearst ran a series of syndicated articles calling upon the MEC to rid itself of the "red incubus." In 1934, denominational conservatives vilified Chappell for spending six weeks in the coal fields of West Virginia organizing miners (see next chapter). The following year, 1935, a Conference of Methodist Laymen, conservatives all, organized in Chicago to prepare for a showdown at the 1936 General Conference. Kindred groups formed in southern California and southern New Jersey. Stalwart fundamentalists Harold Paul Sloan of the Methodist League for Faith and Life (founded in 1925) and a pastor in Haddonfield, New Jersey, and Clarence True Wilson of the Board of Temperance, Prohibition and Public Morals threw their support. The 1936 MEC General Conference saw intense lobbying and debate by both left and right. The right won. And Methodism reached a low point in social advocacy, actually removing the Social Creed from the *Discipline*! In its place, the church added a statement on "the Spiritual life of the Church" drafted by the evangelical caucus.[170] However, when the three branches of Methodism united in 1939, the Uniting Conference harmonized the separate social statements and restored the consensus creed. In addition, General Conference added several new concerns, including respect for conscientious objection to war and the recommendation that the Social Creed be presented to each congregation at least once a year.[171]

CHAPTER XII

TAKING ON THE WORLD? 1884–1939

The previous chapter treated growing Methodist commitments to and institutions for social betterment—description of new developments being one task of the historian—and might leave the impression that the people in the Methodist churches moved in a progressive direction en masse. In fact, the real prophets were few, and as this chapter will attempt to show, Methodists could be found across the full spectrum from radicalism on the one end to archconservatism (including membership in the Ku Klux Klan) on the other. Much of Methodism remained centrist on theological, social, and political measures, as indeed it would for the duration of the twentieth century. Now solidly in the Protestant mainstream, perhaps even prototypically Protestant, Methodists experienced the quandaries and felt the tensions with which Protestants generally and American society struggled—on war and peace, on labor and industry, on theological and biblical matters, on ordination of women, and on race. So they wrestled with, even fought over, such issues, race proving to be especially vexing since racism and racial divisions were as much their own as society's problems. If more troubled by race than other mainstream Protestants, Methodists were less divided by the fundamentalist controversies. To some extent, the exit of a very considerable holiness population reduced the number and clout of those who could object to various forms of modernism, but such voices remained. We will treat below both the holiness exodus and the forces of antimodernism that continued to make their case within Methodism. Nor was the progressive wing of a piece. One interpreter proposes that advocates for social change could be found along a spectrum from social evangelism (changing attitudes) to social engineering (social work) to social reconstruction (radical transformation).[1]

Conflicts: Social, Economic, Racial, Theological

Methodist convictions might also be graphed as a matrix in relation to two axes, which over time did tend to collapse into one and which historians too readily have read as always a single line. One axis, let's say the horizontal one, might be termed concern for poor, homeless, outcast, exploited, and otherwise marginalized persons; it extends from interest in rectifying to indifference about such plights; and it measures social concern. Then the vertical axis would measure ideological, theological, and philosophical views from modernism at one end to antimodernism at the other (reader's choice as to which end goes up—more heavenly?). The two axes permit depiction of the reality that modernism and social concern did not always coincide, nor did antimodernism and indifference to marginalized persons. Modernist ideas, for instance, those of Boston personalism, could and did get appropriated by the social prophets. But modernist views (epistemologies privileging reason, science, the social sciences, and experimentation as the ways to truth; evolutionary, monistic, and naturalistic views of the universe; a humanism or individualism putting high estimations on human ability; commitments to tolerance, free inquiry, and liberty; optimism about what democracy, science, and culture might yield; willingness to apply historical and social scientific methods to Scripture) also could be and did get embraced by social conservatives, for instance, the gospel of wealth folk and social Darwinians. And movements and individuals much concerned about the infection of the church by modernist views, among them holiness advocates, worried about modernism because they were concerned about the poor, indeed oriented their ministries toward people on the lower social rungs. Over time, in what David Moberg and Timothy Smith have treated as a great reversal, evangelicals became socially as well as theologically conservative.[2] And social reform came to coincide with liberalism.

Labor, Round One

Modernism and social reform did not neatly or fully coincide at the 1908 MEC General Conference, notable as we have just seen for its overall progressive spirit and for adoption of the Social Creed. What could be more a citadel of Methodism's modernism than its intellectual headquarters, the Methodist Book Concern (now The United Methodist Publishing House or Abingdon Press)? And what motif ran through each commitment in the Social Creed but the rights of labor? Methodism's modernist leaders at the Book Concern, the executives overseeing the agency with the largest workforce, had turned their backs on the church's own employees, in the judgment of some reformers. That social justice indictment came to General Conference in Methodist petitions on behalf of the International Typographical Union (ITU) and in ITU overtures to Methodists ("Macedonian Appeal," Sources 1906). The ITU had inaugurated an eight-hour day for its members in all future contracts. The Book Concern as a contractor within a printers' association opposed the move, allied itself with an opposition movement, and fired every union member at each of its several printing plants across the country. The ITU appealed to Methodist clergy on behalf of employees ("Petition," Sources 1906). Months later the Book Concern gave in and implemented an eight-hour workday but refused to recognize the union or rehire striking union members. Supportive clergy and union members sought signatures for printed petitions favoring unions to be sent to the 1908 General Conference. For the first time the conference had passed a resolution affirming the "fundamental purposes of the labor movement" to be "essentially ethical" and therefore rightfully commanding the church's support.[3] But then it failed to order the publishing house to rehire striking workers and honor the union.

Neither union nor sympathetic Methodists gave up, and the MFSS began what would be a quarter-century effort to mediate the dispute. As a result of this effort after 1908, the 1912 MEC General Conference passed an MFSS recommendation for "the immediate application in every industry of the principle of collective bargaining" and recognized the federation as the executive agency to rally the forces of the church in support of this policy. But again efforts failed to unionize the publishing house. Over the next quadrennium, the federation and the union leaders prepared legislation to order the several units of the publishing house to negotiate a contract with the union. Again General Conference refused to order the publishing house to unionize, as did the following three General Conferences (1920, 1924, and 1928). Not until November 1931, just prior to the 1932 General conference, did the publishing house executive staff finally recognize the International Typographical Union. The Publishing House of the MECS continued to be a nonunion shop through merger with the northern church in 1939.[4]

Holiness Exodus

We return below to discuss other MFSS causes but here take note of comparable concern for the well-being of society's marginalized by persons in what might be termed the antimodernist camp. In 1894 Phineas Bresee launched a ministry to poor persons of Los Angeles in newly constructed Peniel Hall. He explained its humanitarian purpose in the first number of a monthly paper, the *Peniel Herald*:

> Our first work is to try to reach the unchurched. The people from the homes and the street where the light from the churches does not reach, or penetrates but little. Especially to gather the poor to the cross, by bringing to bear upon them Christian sympathy and helpfulness....
>
> It is also our work to preach and teach the gospel of full salvation; to show forth the blessed privilege of believers in Jesus Christ, to be made holy and thus perfect in love.[5]

Bresee had served pastorates in Iowa, been presiding elder there and an Iowa delegate to General Conference (1872), before moving to southern California. He served several large Methodist churches in the LA area, as vice chair and then chair of the board of the University of Southern California, and for a year as presiding elder of the LA district. He led the Southern California Conference delegation to the 1892 General Conference. That fall, Bishop John Vincent, presiding over conference and no friend of effusive, contentious revivalism, removed him from the district. And the presiding bishop in 1894, John Fitzgerald, refused Bresee's request for appointment to the independent Peniel city mission. Determined to pursue that course, Bresee located and within a year had generated out of the mission what was first a congregation and later a denomination, the Church of the Nazarene.[6] So Bresee joined the host of come-outers, creating a new home for hordes of such, many of them former Methodists.

Others sympathetic to Bresee's cause sought to hunker down and to remain within. One such was Kentucky evangelist Henry Clay Morrison, founding editor of the *Pentecostal Herald*, later president of Asbury College and founder of Asbury Seminary. Two years after being tried (and acquitted) by the Kentucky Conference for "contumacious conduct" (disobedience), he wrote of Bresee:

> Without doubt the times are ripe in all of our large cities for just such churches as the Nazarene in Los Angeles. There is a stiffness and coldness in our city churches that freezes out the common people, and, worst of all shuts out the Christ of the common people. The pastors of our city churches are not soul winners. There may be exceptions, but they are very rare. So far as the Holy Ghost is concerned, in most all of the great city churches, it is well understood that if He cannot come in without sanctifying the people from all sin, and putting in their mouths a testimony to the fact, He can, and shall stay out.[7]

Under Morrison, Asbury—College and Seminary—would become the nerve center for Methodism's holiness and conservative causes. There critique of Methodist authorities would prosper. There the question of staying in or coming out would remain live. There mainline Methodism would carry on conversations with its Wesleyan offspring.

Episcopal Methodism had experienced holiness-motivated criticism and holiness departures before. Both the Wesleyans and the Free Methodists, as we have seen, listed holiness concerns in their briefs against the MEC and, by the late nineteenth century, brought holiness critiques to the fore in their competition with the MEC. Notwithstanding the schismatic appropriation of the holiness banner, much of the intellectual and episcopal leadership of northern Methodism had emphasized and promoted the doctrine, featured it in new systematic theologies,[8] and frequented, supported, and/or celebrated its mainspring, Palmer's enterprise—Tuesday Meetings, publications, speaking tours, and correspondence. The institutionalization of holiness (post–Civil War) in the National Camp Meeting movement initially had enjoyed episcopal blessing. By the end of the nineteenth century, however, several developments loosened Methodism's hold on holiness teaching, put distance between holiness advocates and the regular ministry, and provided alternative promotion, assembly, communication, and support systems for freelance itinerating holiness revivalists.

Non-Methodist versions of holiness emerged: Oberlin perfectionism taught by Asa

Mahan and Charles Grandison Finney; "higher Christian life" views enunciated by Presbyterian minister William E. Boardman; *Principles of the Interior or Hidden Life* elaborated by Congregationalist Thomas C. Upham; and Keswick versions named by their association with a convention in that English town but popularized by Quakers Hannah Whitall Smith and Robert Pearsall Smith and Anglican H. W. Webb-Peploe and others. Such holiness views were popularized on transatlantic speaking and preaching tours, at Bible and prophecy conventions, in new publications, and especially by Dwight L. Moody's Northfield conferences, urban revivals, and Moody Bible Institute. These occasions, contexts, and institutions also mixed holiness doctrines with faith healing and premillennial teachings. Out of the interplay of such intellectual constellations, along with Princeton orthodoxy and Baconian epistemology, came not just holiness movements, but also pentecostalism and fundamentalism.[9]

The National Camp Meeting Association for the Promotion of Holiness, which began regular meetings in the 1870s with the support and encouragement of northern Methodism, stimulated the creation of more independent state and regional associations. These developed throughout rural and small-town America, especially in the South, Southwest, and Midwest. These quasi-ecclesial entities generated vocations for full-time evangelism, sometimes recognized and authorized by Methodist conferences and presiding elders, often functioning without such permission and without formal ordination. By the late 1880s, some two hundred such self-directed full-time preachers itinerated through camp meeting and other settings not subject to the authority of bishop, presiding elder, and preacher in charge. By the 1890s, the number swelled to three hundred. Increasingly, they shrank the Christian faith and the Wesleyan message to one note and made holiness—as sanctification, as instantaneous, as a second and separate work of grace, as a second blessing—not just the main thing but the only thing. Insisting that the second blessing was the only measure of true Christian faith, they denounced more conventional, staid station-and-circuit religious practices and leadership. They zeroed in on Methodism's middle-class character, educational investments, upscale buildings, and social activities—the religiosity typified by the Wilkes-Barre church (1884 "Snapshot").

By the 1880s, then, some leaders, for instance, John P. Brooks, active in the Western and then the Illinois Holiness Association and editor of the *Banner of Holiness*, bid Methodists to come out of the compromised denomination as an act of faith. His 1887 *The Divine Church* served, according to holiness historian Timothy Smith, as the "textbook of 'come-outism.'"[10] Across the country, holiness associations functioning already as quasi-churches wrestled with the question of whether to stay within or leave. Pastors whose membership and presiding elders whose preachers participated in what increasingly became Methodist-unfriendly associations sometimes acted hostilely and punitively.

The issue drove the southern bishops in their address to the 1894 General Conference to devote considerable attention to holiness. Reaffirming the Methodist teaching of "entire sanctification or perfect love" and celebrating witnesses to this experience in the life of the church, they complained of "a party with holiness as a watchword," who had "holiness associations, holiness meetings, holiness preachers, holiness evangelists, and holiness property" and who collapsed religious experience into "only two steps, the first step out of condemnation into peace, and the next step into Christian perfection." They went on to "deplore their teaching and methods in so far as they claim a monopoly of the experience, practice, and advocacy of holiness, and separate themselves from the body of ministers and disciples." The bishops warned against "mistaking excited moods and loud professions for pure and undefiled religion" and complained especially of intrusion of freelancing holiness evangelists into circuits and stations without invitation or permission of the preacher in charge.[11]

By the 1890s, both push and pull factors produced widespread defections and created new holiness entities large and small. Northern and southern Methodism, the United Brethren, and the Evangelical Association all lost heavily, but were not the only denominations so abandoned. In the 1890s, and in addition to the Church of the Nazarene, the following "came out" of Methodist denominations: the New Testament Church of Christ, the Burning Bush movement, the Association of Pentecostal Churches of America, the Apostolic Holiness Union, the Missionary Church Association, the Pentecostal Alliance, the Pentecost Bands of the World, and the Independent Holiness Church.[12] In some instances, smaller holiness bodies merged, as did the northeastern Association of Pentecostal Churches of America, the southern Holiness Church of Christ, and the West Coast Church of the Nazarene around the turn of the century (a union augmented in 1915 by the accession of the Pentecostal Mission, another southern movement). In the twentieth century, the holiness denominations, some with Wesleyan origins, collectively found one another as they faced their own defections into pentecostalism and settled into an uneasy membership in the Calvinist-dominated National Association of Evangelicals. By the 1900s, this larger holiness family included, in addition to the Nazarenes, the Salvation Army, the Christian and Missionary Alliance, the Church of God (Anderson), the Holiness Methodist Church, and the Pilgrim Holiness Church. In such consolidation and institutionalization endeavors, the holiness denominations tended to dampen their more radical testimony, to reduce the wingspan they had allowed women, to experience their membership's own entry into the middle class, and therefore to modulate the more radical social witness with which they began.

Toward a "Socialized Church"?

An ever more radical social witness occurred within the MEC as its new social service federation immediately launched a drive to encourage churches to actively engage the social order. Following the pattern of its British social mentors, the MFSS organized the first national conference of Methodist social workers in November 1908. Attendees at the St. Louis meeting heard stirring addresses: "The Socialized Church" by Frank Mason North, "The Church and the Social Need" by its president Herbert Welch, "What Workingmen Might Reasonably Expect from the Church" by Drew professor Edwin Earp, "The Value of a Social Settlement in an Industrial Neighborhood" by Chicago reformer Mary McDowell,[13] "The Deaconess in Social Settlement Work" by Isabelle Horton, and "The Deaconess as the Pastor's Social Assistant" by Bertha Fowler, the latter two deaconess leaders.[14]

To reach the church with its message, the MFSS resorted immediately to publications—leaflets, prophetic pamphlets and monographs, and studies of social problems. An early and popular item was the 1909 pamphlet, *The Methodist Church in Organized Charity*, by J. W. Magruder, a member of its executive committee and general secretary of Federated Charities in Baltimore.[15] In that compact but comprehensive study, Magruder characterized MFSS's social service approach during this period. Scientific social work demanded "order, economy, and an avoidance of the very appearance of the evil of paupering." Instead, organized charity, he insisted, involved a threefold process of emergency relief, adequate relief, and radical relief. The first, a temporary expedient, "first aid to the injured," extended adequate relief, which required time, thought, and skills, and aimed at "the physical, moral, intellectual, and spiritual redemption of any individual or family in distress." Radical relief, Magruder indicated, addressed root causes of distress, such as lawlessness, disease, unemployment, poor housing, child labor, in short, any evil that attacks the life, health, and character of the community. In treating the underlying pathology, radical relief would remove the need for either emergency relief or adequate relief. Magruder's optimism and confidence that social ills could be cured characterized MFSS's spirit during its early years. It worked, taught, investigated, and advocated with the deep conviction that the social movement led to the kingdom of God on earth.[16]

Despite its issues with the Methodist Book Concern, the MFSS succeeded in using that critical agency to publicize the "social crisis." Full texts of papers from its several national conferences (1908, 1922, and 1926) appeared there, as well as *The Abingdon War-Food Book*, with a foreword by Herbert Hoover, John Wesley's 1773 classic "Thoughts on the Present Scarcity of Provisions," along with up-to-date wartime recipes and menus provided by the federation.

In 1911, the MFSS launched an even more important means of communication, the still-running *Social Service Bulletin* (renamed *Social Questions Bulletin* in 1933). First edited by Harry Ward, the *Bulletin* provided timely analysis of political and social matters, kept church leaders aware of churchly and secular issues, brought members directly in touch with the MFSS leaders, and encouraged affiliates to propagate its social service ideas and undertake local initiatives. Similar extension of the MFSS witness came as other members of the Methodist family of churches established "social justice" caucuses, boards, agencies, or commissions—the MPC in 1916, the MECS in 1926, the EC in 1930, and the UBC in 1933. The social gospel found a curricular and institutional home as the several denominations' theological schools introduced a new field, "Christian sociology." The year after adoption of the Social Creed, 1909, Drew Theological Seminary established one of the first professorships of Christian sociology in an American theological school and hired a European university–trained professor, Edwin L. Earp, to be its first incumbent. As already noted, Earp spoke at the first MFSS conference, and he penned seven books before ending a thirty-year teaching career at Drew in 1938.

In 1911, Harry Ward began the first of thirty-four years as unpaid MFSS executive, an office he held while teaching Christian ethics first at Boston University School of Theology (1913–17) and then at Union Theological Seminary in New York (1918–41). No small measure of MFSS's commitment to the cause of working people and organized labor derived from Ward's experiences with the working poor in Chicago. Director of a Chicago settlement house, he became friends with pioneer social workers Jane Addams and Mary McDowell. Later, while pastor in Chicago's meatpacking district, he conducted funerals for packinghouse workers killed in frequent factory accidents. Moved by their oppression, Ward strongly supported the workers' drive to form a union in order to improve their conditions. During and between major U.S. labor disputes, he built labor and religious coalitions that transcended race, class, party, and faith in pursuit of social equality (Sources 1919a).

In 1912, Ward acquired a colleague who would serve a comparably long term (thirty-two years), Francis J. McConnell, elected president by the MFSS and elected bishop by the MEC the same year. Already well known across the church for his brilliance in defense of academic freedom and civil liberties, McConnell gained firsthand experience with social problems through MFSS and gave MFSS high connectional and national advocacy. In particular, McConnell helped Methodists grasp insights also advanced by political Progressives, namely, that some social problems needed more curative resources than individuals, churches, and agencies could muster and required state or federal attention. And since governments, particularly at the city level, might be corrupt and as much a problem as heartless corporations or exploitive slumlords, McConnell insisted that religious conviction should not stop with itself or with the church. Christians had an obligation to "protest against political and industrial evils" in order to "guard the intellectual and moral interest of the people." Given the scale of the problems, the church could not act effectively and redemptively on its own. In a 1922 book, *Christian Citizenship*, designed as a course of study for young people, he argued that the "distinction between secular and sacred" had caused "much harm." While wishing to avoid a "fusion" of church and state, McConnell insisted that the two were interdependent. "What we seek today," he said, "is not formal and official connection between the larger social groups and Christianity but the sanctification of all these groups by the Christian spirit." The "Christian ideal" for the state, he argued, was "the welfare of the people." The Christian citizen thus had an obligation to participate in the political process to make the state aware of one's Christian aims. In effect, McConnell elevated citizenship to moral duty. His Jesus would be a lobbyist of the people in an expanding regulatory state. Not surprisingly in the 1930s the bishop vigorously promoted President Franklin Roosevelt's government-sponsored Social Security program for older and needy persons.[17] Though these ideas were generally favorable in principle, Methodists found themselves in an embarrassing position. Objection by some church leaders to inclusion under the law impressed many people as inconsistent with the often expressed concern of the church for Social Security as a national policy. Churches continued to make their employees dependent upon old-age assistance and public charity if they could not save enough on relatively small earnings to ensure their own future. Not until the early 1950s did annual conferences declare clergy and lay employees of churches eligible for Social Security.[18]

Under the leadership of people such as Ward and McConnell, the social gospel itself was transformed from an individual or congregational endeavor into the coordinated programs of national Protestant organizations. Among key leaders in effecting this policy transformation and framing the MFSS program were a number of Methodist deaconesses,[19] two of whom, Grace Scribner and Winifred Chappell, served as co-executives of the federation and co-editors of the *Social Questions Bulletin*. Beginning in 1911, they were the MFSS's primary writers. Growing up in the poverty of Michigan's Upper Peninsula and then training as a deaconess, Grace Scribner served effectively in communication capacities with MFSS for twelve years until killed tragically by an automobile in 1923 while she was crossing Broadway in front of Union Theological Seminary in New York. Her friend Winifred Chappell, a native of Iowa and an instructor in the deaconess training school in Chicago, came to New York to replace her. Consecrated a deaconess in 1908, Chappell was elected to the federation's executive committee in 1914 and shared the federation's leadership with Ward and Bishop McConnell. She carved out a special place for herself through her editing, writing, speaking, and teaching. She edited the *Social Questions Bulletin* from 1922 through 1947. Few church leaders were more perceptive in discerning or more courageous in exposing the demonic side of unrestrained capitalism. She was a socialist to the core. She supported women's suffrage, labor unions, working men, and especially working women, but her heart was primarily aligned with poor and exploited persons. Her defense of working women of Passaic, New Jersey, in a 1926 strike against mill owners is vintage Chappell (Sources 1926). Between her and Harry Ward, Chappell may have been the more radical of the two. Of her it was said, "Everyone on the left knows her." The minds and energies of these four leaders—Ward, McConnell, Scribner, and Chappell—dominated the drive and direction of the federation for several decades. They served as the social gadflies of Methodism. Under their joint leadership, MFSS convened two national conferences on Christianity and the economic order in 1922 and 1926 that exposed the demonic side of capitalism.

Temperance and Prohibition

The intervention in the political sphere that McConnell and company advocated had been earlier and forcefully advanced by Frances Willard and her WCTU colleagues. How else to contend with pervasive corruption of the civic, economic, transportation, and familial realms allegedly to be traced to a single source, demon rum? Indeed, though industrial concerns recurred through the Social Creed, the church put its most public focus in the early twentieth century not on the economy or the plight of workers, but on the evils of alcohol. Temperance, solely interpreted as abstinence, had long been recommended in all congregations and Sunday schools. Temperance united progressives and conservatives, southerners and northerners, women and men, and did so across the family of Methodist denominations. Temperance Sunday with its pledge card became an annual event. Grape juice had been ordered for Communion services since the 1880s. Temperance literature of all kinds was penned, published, and promoted.

By the turn of the century, the WCTU had an ally in the temperance crusade and in moving the church beyond temperance conversions and pledges, namely, the Anti-Saloon League (established in 1895). A lobby, working across and beyond the churches and dedicated to its one cause, the league tracked politics and politicians, monitored and reported voting behavior, and urged its adherents to ballot their own prohibition convictions. Between 1909 and 1923, it circulated some two million books and five million pamphlets and even greater numbers of temperance ephemera.[20] Temperance offered, perhaps more compellingly than did the social gospel and certainly more persuasively to Methodist conservatives, the case for an active evangelicalism that emphasized practical, everyday application of the gospel and political involvement for the cause of "righteousness." So the MEC General Conferences of 1904 and 1908 saw it and summoned the church to achieve moral reform through the agency of the state.

Other Methodist bodies dedicated themselves equally to the cause, indeed had done so for years. The UBC, for instance, established a Temperance Commission in 1905, adopted the Social Creed in 1909, and threw its energies behind the social reform of prohibition.[21] By 1912, the MEC had established its own lobby and placed it in Washington, D.C.[22] The name given the political action group, the Board of Temperance, Prohibition and Public Morals (now General Board of Church and Society), promised Methodist commitment to a vigorous prohibition campaign (Sources 1916). Prohibition represents, in our judgment, the high-water mark of Methodist national influence. Methodism led that legislative campaign and effectively, if temporarily, imposed a distinctively Methodist moral absolute on the entire nation.

The church's societal and political ambitions were well symbolized in the Methodist building in the nation's capital. Neoclassical, befitting its prominent place on Capitol Hill—to the left is the Supreme Court, across the street looms the U.S. Capitol—the new Board of Temperance's building was completed in 1924 at a cost of $650,000. Famed orator and former presidential candidate William Jennings Bryan and reform-minded Pennsylvania governor Gifford Pinchot spoke at the dedication. Its adjacent apartment complex, constructed in 1931, has been home to scores of congressional representatives, Methodist bishops, and Supreme Court justices, men and women in leadership roles who have shaped the fabric of American society.

For the MEC, the prohibition cause had agency leadership. In the South and increasingly across the nation, the champion of prohibition was James Cannon Jr. (1864–1944).[23] Editor of the *Richmond and Baltimore Christian Advocate* from 1904 until election to the episcopacy in 1918, member of the Anti-Saloon League from 1900 until he died, and five times delegate to MECS General Conferences, Cannon used the press and the platform to campaign for legislated prohibition. He began with Virginia, succeeding with his first legislative initiative in 1903. By 1916, when full prohibition came before the Virginia legislature, Cannon had a seat on the senate floor next to an Anti-Saloon senator and "sat enthroned as the supreme ruler of Capitol Hill . . . at the very zenith of his power over the Virginia legislature." "When the time came to appoint the committees," claims his biographer critic, "it was found that the appointments to a number of them had to be submitted to Cannon for approval."[24] By that year, twenty-three states had gone dry, and Cannon and Anti-Saloon colleagues from across the country turned their attention to the national campaign. Cannon's nationwide speaking in and the successful conclusion of the prohibition campaign earned him the episcopacy. And he would continue to fight the cause on that platform, including advocacy abroad and opposition to wets at home, most notably presidential candidate Alfred E. Smith. Cannon opposed Smith's nomination at the 1928 Democratic Convention and then led an anti-Smith campaign. His biographer states, "Cannon took entire charge and opened headquarters in Richmond, whence he directed the movement in the fourteen Southern and border states. . . . He not only gave virtually his entire time to the campaign, but also made liberal personal loans to the anti-Smith war chest."[25] H. L. Mencken, acerbic journalist of American life and culture in the early twentieth century, declared war on the Methodist-led crusade. Between the *Baltimore Sun* and the *American Mercury*, Mencken had a national audience for his attacks on teetotaling Methodists who, he said, harbored "the haunting fear that somebody, somewhere, may be happy" and were determined to "turn the nation into a desert."[26]

After passage of the 18th Amendment and of the National Prohibition Enforcement Act (Volstead Act) when Prohibition became law of the land (in 1920), the MEC Board led by Clarence True Wilson turned to education and enforcement. During the period between the enactment of Prohibition in 1920 and its repeal in 1933, Methodism's primary social interest was to defend Prohibition. In 1922 Wilson toured the country in a "prohibition water-wagon," a specially fitted Ford Model T. When repeal came, Wilson undertook an every-state campaign to warn of the consequences. Prohibition—Methodism's moral absolutism—spawned outlandish bootlegging, proved vulnerable to organized crime, and made lawbreaking fashionable. The Depression, which followed, put joblessness and poverty, instead of temperance, on the church's social agenda. Other ideals, like peace and unification, claimed Methodist attention as well. Methodists would then gear up for another world war without perhaps ever coming fully to terms with this last great episode of Christendom. In consequence, some later Methodists would continue to yearn and campaign for a Christian America, having not lived through or adequately analyzed Prohibition's problematic premises.

Radicalism and Reaction: The "Red Scare" of the 1920s and 1930s

During World War I, the MFSS vigorously defended the rights of conscientious objectors and political dissenters. After the war, its continued commitment to civil liberties, opposition to political oppression, and defense of labor took the MFSS increasingly into combat with the power structures of American society and earned it the enmity of the country's elites. Bishop Francis J. McConnell, MFSS president, for instance, weighed in when the nation's steelworkers went on strike in 1919 against the deplorable conditions in the mills and for an eight-hour day and a livable wage. McConnell, then bishop in the Pittsburgh area, became the leader and spokesperson for an ecumenical commission investigating the crisis. Their report mobilized public sympathy for the workers and against the prevailing sixty-eight-hour workweek in steel. McConnell became the target of criticism for the commission's report. McConnell's other and later roles would make him equally suspect (presidency of the socially progressive Federal Council of Churches [1928–32], endowed professorships at Vanderbilt and Yale, and activity in the American Civil Liberties Union).

MFSS executive Harry Ward became another perennial target of an emerging religious and secular right. Ward pressed the church to engage the social order and especially to take the side of the working poor instead of management in labor relations (Sources 1919a). Under his leadership in 1922, 1926, and 1930, the MFSS sponsored national conferences on Christianity and the economic order. As early as 1919, Ward gave cautious support to the Russian Revolution, in the *Social Service Bulletin,* causing a stir. The FBI began keeping files on Ward, and a New York State investigating committee accused him of "teaching Bolshevism." At the same time his MFSS colleague Grace Scribner's weekly column on the social application of the gospel was dropped from the Methodist *Sunday School Journal.* In 1920, Ward joined other activists in founding the American Civil Liberties Union (ACLU), whose board he chaired into the 1950s. In

1929, Ward made a fact-finding trip to Russia. Thereafter "Red-baiting," reactionary attacks on the MFSS increased, came from various quarters, and became a Hearst press feature. In 1934–35, Hearst newspapers ran a series of syndicated articles calling on The Methodist Episcopal Church to rid itself of the "red incubus" of that "McConnell-Ward-Chappell radical aggregation." Church critics suggested that the MFSS change its name to the Marxist Federation for Social Strife! In the 1930s, Ward was summoned to appear before the House of Representatives' Dies Committee (forerunner of the House Un-American Activities Committee).[27]

The MFSS's social analysis gained pertinence and critics after the stock market crash and during the Depression. Its masthead proclaimed its commitment "to abolish the profit system in order to develop a classless society based upon the obligation of mutual service."[28] To the MFSS, the Depression revealed that capitalism had failed. The 1932 MEC General Conference concurred, declaring "the present industrial order is unchristian, unethical and anti-social because it is largely based on the profit motive, which is a direct appeal to selfishness," a victory for the MFSS.[29] To instruct the church on how to move the society from a capitalist to a socialist order, the MFSS issued eighteen "Crisis Leaflets" over the next quadrennium. And in 1934, *Social Questions Bulletin* editor Chappell undertook another of her hands-on efforts at social reconstruction, spending six weeks in the coal fields of West Virginia organizing miners (see her earlier similar effort in Passaic, Sources 1926).

To counter such prophetic actions, a Conference of Methodist Laymen, conservatives all, gathered in Chicago in early 1935 to organize for a showdown at the 1936 General Conference. In February, the Methodist Laymen issued a pamphlet titled *Which Way America?* The sole business of the church was regeneration of individual hearts and no other contribution to the construction of the social order. The Laymen discounted inequalities of wealth and income, rejected any "right of every man to a job," and credited laissez-faire capitalism with having "done an amazingly creditable job of maintaining employment even in the face of disturbing influences which have originated outside of its control." The New Deal's "social security" by government action, they thought, was wrong in principle and practice.

The MFSS responded in the March 1935 issue of its *Bulletin*. Profit seeking is not only selfish but also sinful. The capitalist system, which depends on it, must be supplanted with a more Christian motive, and the church acts within proper bounds when it urges dramatic social change. The federation urged the church to endorse "a planned economy," which continuously adjusts economic efforts to measure needs. "The motive of service is required and generated, just as the motive of service is required and generated by the profit-seeking economy." The result envisaged was a society without class distinction or privilege, and the democratic ownership and control of the national wealth.

Intense lobbying on both sides continued up to and into the 1936 General

Conference, which met in Columbus, Ohio.[30] Progressive causes of unification and peace loomed large, but conservatives had their day on the MFSS. General Conference reminded the church (and the MFSS) that it was not an official agency of the church, and it removed the Social Creed from the *Discipline*. In its place, the MEC added a statement on "the Spiritual life of the Church" drafted by the now powerful evangelical caucus.[31]

Methodist Fundamentalism

By 1936 a theologically conservative movement had largely petered out in northern Methodism and made little contribution to the socially conservative attacks on the MFSS. This earlier drama of Methodist antimodernism, echoing the larger fundamentalist movement, featured something of an intra-Drew central act. New Jersey pastor Harold Paul Sloan attacked his Drew student colleague and by then professor, Edwin Lewis, for the latter's article "The Problem of the Person of Christ," which appeared in 1922 in the *Methodist Review*. Aiding and abetting Sloan was Lewis's older Drew colleague and fellow theologian, John A. Faulkner.[32] Sloan encouraged the Methodist Episcopal Preachers' Meeting of Philadelphia to protest the publication of such a heretical article in a Methodist serial. It implored the Drew administration to ensure that "the objectionable teaching...not be repeated in the classroom as...instruction given to our theological students" and conveyed its denunciation to the Methodist people in the *Christian Advocate* (New York).[33] Sloan added to the indictment when Lewis's *Jesus Christ and the Human Quest* appeared in 1924. Lewis, he asserted, denies "the incarnation in any real sense," "reduces Jesus to an extraordinary human being," and rejects his "personal pre-existence."[34]

By that point, Sloan had launched a paper, *The Call to the Colors*, later renamed *The Essentialist*, to broaden the critique and fight the liberal corruption across northern Methodist theological education. Through this publication, independent preachers' meetings, petitions to General Conference, and appeals to the bishops, Sloan led a campaign, begun actually for the 1920 conference and continued through the 1920s, to purge both seminaries and the required Course of Study of liberalism. To coordinate the efforts, Sloan helped found the Methodist League for Faith and Life in 1925. Liberals generally and personalists particularly came in for rebuke, but Harris Franklin Rall of Garrett and Lewis became favorite targets. In 1927, the league formally called on the bishops to rectify the situation at Drew, terming Lewis's teaching in "defiance of the law and order of the Church" and as "contravening both the second and twentieth of our Articles."[35] Sloan took a petition to the 1928 General Conference that charged "flagrant disloyalty to Methodist doctrinal standards in seminaries, pulpits and Sunday-school literature"; it contained some ten thousand signatures from churches in forty-one states.[36] The MEC bishops responded tersely to the charges laid in their laps and opened the 1928 General Conference opposing heresy hunting. Sloan moved on to a more broadly gauged conservative campaign, not especially targeted at Methodists. When Lewis underwent a turn to neo-orthodoxy, offered a critique of liberalism, called Protestants to "re-enthrone Christ, the divine Christ" (Sources 1933), and produced a *Christian Manifesto* (in 1934), Sloan wrote a congratulating and conciliatory letter.[37] Sloan then published a review that began, "Here is a significant book indeed."[38] The 1936 MEC General Conference, a conservative affair on several measures as we have seen, Sloan's fifth, elected him editor of the *Christian Advocate* (New York). In the June issue he declared, "I am a conservative in theology, a progressive in social and economic questions, a radical in nothing, and a liberal in all things." His quadrennium of editing Methodism's mouthpiece represented a temporary setback for modernism, but perhaps even more the mellowing and mainstreaming of the church's champions of orthodoxy.[39]

In southern Methodism, antimodernism took more diffuse forms. It had its own antimodernist paper, the independent *Southern Methodist*, founded in 1921 and edited by Robert A. Meek, previously editor with the *New Orleans Christian Advocate*.[40] Southern conferences established affiliate branches of Sloan's League for Faith and Life and Bishops Collins Denny and Horace M. DuBose became members. In the twelve-pamphlet *Aftermath Series* (1923–24), southern Methodism had its counterpart to *The Fundamentals*, attacking higher criticism and suspect faculty and missionaries and defending blood atonement, the resurrection, pentateuchal dating, and ascribed biblical authorship. For straying from such standards, John A. Rice of Southern Methodist University was forced to resign because of his 1920 book, *The Old Testament in the Life of Today*. Such antimodernist actions and such fundamentalist beliefs, however, Bishop Edwin Mouzon called un-Methodist and Calvinist. Claiming their term for his title, Mouzon in his 1923 *Fundamentals of Methodism* insisted that grace and grace-produced Christian ethic, not dogma, lay at the heart of Methodism.

The modest dimensions of southern Methodist fundamentalism had less to do with episcopal scholarship than with other media or movements that channeled but also diffused its rather considerable antimodernist convictions. The exodus of holiness folk took out of southern Methodism, as we have already suggested, leaders, members, and whole congregations who, had they remained, would have added to the theological chatter. Foreign missions, as well, recruited and deployed many of an evangelical and conservative bent. Three other causes functioned on antimodernist platforms and did so more effectively in the South than theological fundamentalism—temperance, unification, and the Klan. Temperance could appeal, as noted, to progressive aspirations. It also could appeal to fears of immigrants, of cities, of Catholics, of Germans, and of German theology. Especially during and in the wake of WWI, conservatives noted that from the enemy came beer and the various theological and biblical heresies. Similarly, just such aberrant views had found a home in the northern church, and as we will note below, southern conservatives mounted a vigorous antimodernist-themed campaign against unification. In consequence, the prospect of unification divided the southern church throughout the 1920s and early 1930s. Led by a League for the Preservation of Southern Methodism, by several of the *Advocates*, and by a number of bishops, most prominently Collins Denny and William Ainsworth, the campaign against unification appealed to regionalism, racism, and fears of modernism.

So also did the Ku Klux Klan, revived in 1915 by ex-Methodist minister William J. Simmons. The Klan, argued W. J. Cash, "summed up within itself, with precise completeness and exactness, the whole body of the fears and hates of the time.... It was ... at once anti-Negro, anti-Alien, anti-Red, anti-Catholic, anti-Jew, anti-Darwin, anti-Modern, anti-Liberal, Fundamentalist, vastly Moral, militantly Protestant." It understood itself to be a religious organization and attracted individuals whose religiosity needed a host of negative referents:

> The Klan enabled churchmen to express their moral convictions in action, while ostensibly keeping the Christian church itself out of the political arena. Like the Anti-saloon League in the prohibition fight, like anti-evolution organizations in the fundamentalist controversy, the Klan provided a vehicle for enforcing the prevailing attitudes of the Southern churches upon the whole population, while not involving the churches officially.

Cash further asserted,

> Except in North Carolina and Virginia, the rural clergy belonged to it or had traffic with it almost en masse, and even in those two states the same thing was true in many districts. It was true, too, in many towns throughout the South, and everywhere the great body of the ministers either smiled benignly on it or carefully kept their mouths shut about it.[41]

In the definitive study of twentieth-century southern Methodism, Robert Sledge concurs, noting the Klan's moral agency role in supporting temperance and the prohibition effort, disciplining individuals who strayed from canons of community expectation (spousal abuse or infidelity), and monitoring and guarding racial and religious divisions and barriers.

Whether Klan penetration of Methodism and/or Methodist participation in the Klan reached the proportions that Cash alleges or that correspondence with Bishop Mouzon implies (Sources 1922) is open to question. But connections there were. A. Frank Smith, new to his appointment in San Antonio, was pressured to join, was told that "many leading preachers were early members of the Klan," and learned that the Klan, fifty strong and robed and hooded, had come to the West Texas Conference with a donation. He received his own counsel from Bishop Mouzon, who wrote, "I have been greatly distressed over the growth of the Ku Klux Klan in Texas and Oklahoma and nothing has distressed me so much as the fact that so many of our preachers have been misguided and have gone into this organization." Bishop Ainsworth wrote to the *Dallas Morning News*, "We have indeed fallen upon days of degeneracy if the Christian ministry has allied itself with the Ku Klux Klan and debased the pulpit by defense of its methods."[42] Moved later to First Church, Houston, Smith discovered the Klan to be in city government and in his own church. Klan endorsement had been, according to Smith, "the deciding factor in most of the city and county elections just as I got to Houston." And the "chief of police and most of the Houston police were members of the Klan. Without interference, Klansmen engaged in such extralegal practices as tapping telephones over the city, intercepting messages at the telegraph offices, and maintaining spies in the city post offices." Klan members in First Church included one of its officers, the Kleagle. Racism, then, served the antimodernist cause as it would later the anti-Communist. And vice versa! Underneath anticommunism, states' rights, and law and order lurked racism.

Southern Methodist Women and Racial Reform

By the 1920s MECS women through the Woman's Missionary Council had initiated two forms of outreach to the African American community. It collaborated with women of the CME in supporting a women's program (since 1906) at Paine College in Augusta, Georgia, an institution launched cooperatively in 1883. And beginning in 1912, it established a number of social settlements called Bethlehem Centers, the first adjacent to the Paine College campus. A second Bethlehem Center was begun the following year in Nashville, near Fisk University.[43]

The witness of these Bethlehem Centers helped shape an effort by southern Methodists to seek better relations between the races and to counter the spate of lynchings, race riots, and Klan activity that followed the First World War. In 1920 a young Methodist minister named Will Alexander led in the founding of the Commission on Interracial Cooperation (CIC), soon the major interracial reform organization in the South. Alexander credited the southern Methodist women involved with Bethlehem House in Nashville (on whose board he had served while a student at Vanderbilt) with teaching him to treat Black people as human beings. "The women had that attitude," he said, "and I learned something from them. These women were in a sort of anteroom of the church, with freedom and liberty to think and act."[44]

At its annual meeting in Kansas City in 1920, the Woman's Missionary Council approved the establishment of a Commission on Race Relations with special concern for the needs of African American women and children. The unanimous choice of a woman to chair this new commission was Carrie Parks (Mrs. Luke) Johnson from Georgia, long active in women's home mission work and the daughter and wife of southern Methodist clergy. On advice from Alexander, the commission accepted an invitation to send delegates to the forthcoming meeting of the National Association of Colored Women in Tuskegee. Johnson and Sara Estelle Haskin were chosen to go. During the meeting, they were simply given seats in the rear of the hall and invited to listen. At the conclusion of the sessions a gathering was arranged in the home of Margaret Murray Washington, widow of Booker T. Washington and organizer and president of the Tuskegee Women's Club, between the two white women and ten of the leading African American women in the South. The meeting began in an atmosphere of uncertainty and mistrust, the Black women suspecting that the white women might be there to learn how to "better" their domestic help. Carrie Parks Johnson later reported, "I wanted to speak to them, but I didn't know how. I wanted to invite their frankness and confidence. Only after an hour spent in the reading of God's word and in prayer [was it possible to have] a discussion of those things which make for righteousness and for more Christian relations." Led by Lugenia Burns Hope, wife of John Hope (president of Morehouse College in Atlanta) and founder and, for almost thirty years, head of the Atlanta Neighborhood Union, the Black women spoke of their hopes and fears for their families and their race. Mrs. Hope concluded this eventful gathering by saying, "Women, we can achieve nothing today unless you ... who have met us are willing to help us find a place in American life where we can be unashamed and unafraid." The impact on the two white women was considerable; as Carrie Johnson put it, "My heart broke, and I have been trying [ever since] to pass the story on to the women of my race."[45]

With the support of the CIC, Johnson organized a conference of about one hundred white women leaders from various groups in the South, which convened in the YWCA in Memphis, Tennessee, on October 6–7, 1920. Carrie Parks Johnson and Estelle Haskin relayed their experience at Tuskegee and the African American women's challenge. In an afternoon session, four distinguished African American women guests—Margaret Washington, Elizabeth Ross Haynes, Jennie B. Moton, and Charlotte Hawkins Brown— entered the room. With no prompting every white woman in the room rose to her feet. Spontaneously Belle Harris Bennett (Sources 1910) began to sing "Blest Be the Tie That Binds," and the women, black and white, joined in, many of them crying openly.

Carrie Johnson encouraged candor from the African American women. "We're here for some frank talk," she said. "In your own way tell us your story and try to enlighten us. You probably think we're pretty ignorant, and we are, but we're willing to learn."[46] Each of the four women spoke, Charlotte Hawkins Brown not until the second day. Born in the South, she had been educated in New England and had recently returned to North Carolina to open a preparatory school for African Americans. She began her speech by sharing an emotional account of having been forcibly removed by a group of white men from her berth in the Pullman car on her way to the Memphis meeting. "Friends," she said, "I came here with a feeling of humiliation, and I was glad that Mrs. Johnson didn't call on me yesterday. Last night I prayed, and I want to tell you it was a struggle. The thing that I have been praying for is that I may not lose hope in *you*." In a strong speech, Brown spoke about lynching, saying that Black women were convinced that white women could control their men. "So far as lynching is concerned, if the white women would take hold of the situation, lynching would be stopped." She talked about the oppressiveness of the myth of the promiscuous Black woman. She concluded, "I know that if you are Christian women, that in the final analysis you are going to have to reach out for the same hand that I am reaching out for but I know that the dear Lord will not receive it if you are crushing me beneath your feet."[47] By the afternoon of the second day the white women said, "This has been a great experience. We are humiliated. We are ashamed. But we are determined that this is not the end."[48]

A recent interpreter termed the meeting a "conversion experience" for the women present. Charlotte Brown later said that the conference was "the greatest step forward since emancipation." Will Alexander claimed that after the Memphis meeting, southern white women were the most effective force in changing southern racial patterns. The Federal Council of Churches called it "the strongest force yet organized in the nation in behalf of the colored race."[49] An emotional high does not automatically build an interracial women's movement based in mutuality and shared power. In preparation for the conference the Black women had hastily drafted a position paper dealing with their most pressing issues. Without even consulting them, however, Carrie Parks Johnson made significant alterations in their statement before reading it to the conference. She softened their condemnation of lynching, omitted a resolution on suffrage, and left out a preamble that demanded for Black women "all the privileges and rights granted to American womanhood." The Black women refused to allow the publication of this altered statement. After months of difficult negotiations, a compromise statement was worked out, but it was never published.[50]

Johnson died in 1929. Although she never openly questioned segregation, she had sought to educate white women about the inferior status imposed on their Black sisters. Other southern Methodist women carried on the leadership role in improving race relations in the South. Bertha Newell succeeded Johnson in 1928 as superintendent of the Bureau of Social Service of the Woman's Missionary Council and of the Bureau of Christian Social Relations in the 1930 reorganized WMC structure. Newell pressed the affiliate woman's missionary societies "to engage in more local interaction between white women and African American women." Summer Christian Leadership Schools for members of the woman's missionary societies of the CME became one forum for this increased interaction. Taught by leaders of the WMC, these events provided the opportunity for white and African American women to live and study together for a week. Follow-up interracial contacts proved significant, as sponsoring local white women's societies heard the reports afterward of African American women delegates who had attended from their communities, and women of both races frequently continued to work together on local projects. Through the 1930s, these summer leadership schools provided a crucial opportunity for African American and white Methodist women to experience enhanced mutual understanding and help.[51]

The most dramatic and heroic effort toward improved race relations was that made by Jessie Daniel Ames, a Methodist woman from Palestine, Texas (Sources 1934b). She led one of the most important women's crusades in American history, the Association of Southern Women for the Prevention of Lynching (ASWPL), founded in 1930. Considering lynching a woman's issue, she called on women to repudiate the claim that lynching protected southern womanhood. By 1942 more than forty-three thousand southern women, many of them Methodists, had signed the antilynching pledge, which read, "Lynching is an indefensible crime destructive of all principles of government, hostile to every ideal of religion and humanity, debasing and degrading to every person involved. We pledge ourselves to create a new public opinion in the South which will not condone for any reason whatever acts of mobs or lynchers."[52]

Women opposed to lynching created an extremely effective network: they secured pledges from law enforcement officers not to tolerate lynchings in their counties, they thwarted potential lynchings by immediate visits to officers demanding protection for the possible victims, and when a lynching was reported, the women in that vicinity who had signed the pledge investigated the crime and filed a report. In 1949 Dorothy Rogers Tilly, a soft-spoken Methodist woman from Atlanta, helped found the Fellowship of the Concerned, a successor to the ASWPL. The presence of its members at the trials of African Americans brought about significant changes in courtroom justice. As lynchings declined, the fellowship became, in the 1950s, an advocate for desegregation of schools and public facilities. For her active role in this organization, Dorothy Tilly was shunned by former church friends, harassed by the Klan, accused of being a Communist, and subjected to threatening phone calls, but she was never dissuaded from her conviction that the church must promote racial justice.

Renewed Efforts on Behalf of Ordination of Women

In 1920 the MEC restored to women the authorization to be licensed as local preachers, taken away by the General Conference of 1880. Benefiting from the suffrage campaign and the societal climate for women's rights, Methodist women relaunched the effort to attain ordination. Among the leaders this time around was Madeline Southard (1877–1967). Southard earned a master's degree from Garrett Biblical Institute in 1919 and published her thesis, "The Attitude of Jesus toward Women," in 1928. She taught at Methodist-related Taylor University and published a book, *The White Slave Traffic versus the American Home*. Southard worked as a lay evangelist in the United States and as a missionary in the Philippines and India.

In the compelling article "Woman and the Ministry" in the *Methodist Review*

(November-December 1919 and also printed separately), Southard identified and refuted the arguments that had been used to keep women out of the ministry. Noting that it had been forty years since the MEC refused ordination to Anna Howard Shaw, Southard rejected "time-worn" woman's sphere premises for exclusion. "Shall the Church cling to this argument," she asked, "when in all other fields it has been cast aside as obsolete?" Almost simultaneously, she founded the International Association of Women Preachers (IAWP), serving as president of this ecumenical organization (1919–39) and editor of its newsletter, the *Woman's Pulpit*. Elected to the 1920 General Conference by the Southwest Kansas Conference, she pursued the campaign with a memorial (petition) and letter to "fellow" delegates seeking for women the authorization to preach and "that equality of opportunity in the church that is rapidly coming to her in other fields" (Sources 1920).[53] Echoing her request were similar memorials, asking that women be licensed to preach, from a number of annual conferences, district superintendents, and deans and presidents of colleges, universities, and seminaries (including Garrett, Drew, and Boston). Conferences sent forty-one women as lay delegates, five of whom were African American.

Madeline Southard introduced a resolution calling for "ecclesiastical equality for women" with all appropriate changes to be made to the *Discipline*. The Committee on Itinerancy (Ordained Ministry), to whom the petition was referred, recommended that women be licensed as local preachers and that the issue of women's ordination be referred to a commission to report to the next General Conference. The report was adopted, efforts made from the floor to broaden the authorization to ordination as well as licensing of women, however, failing.[54] On the day the legislation passed, May 27, local churches in Denver and Wenatchee, Washington, licensed as local preachers Winifred Willard (Trinity Church, Denver) and Witlia D. Caffray (First MEC of Wenatchee). Symbolically Dr. James M. Buckley, long an opponent of women's laity and clergy rights in the church, had died earlier that year.

Just prior to the 1924 General Conference, Dr. Georgia Harkness, then associate professor of religious education at Elmira College, made a powerful case for the ministry as a vocation for women (Sources 1924b).[55] Referring to the church as "probably our most conservative institution," its "wall of prejudice" a "relic of medievalism," she urged a remolded public sentiment supportive of women's leadership, ordination serving to symbolize the stamp of the church's approval upon the admission of women to its ministry. "Ordination" she affirmed as "a step in this direction, but it is a step—not the final goal." The goal of attitudinal transformation sought by Harkness lay beyond the distance that the 1924 General Conference was willing to go. Its Commission on the Licensing and Ordaining of Women affirmed "the validity of a woman's call to preach" and recommended to the General Conference "the ordination of women as local preachers" in order to give women sacramental authority in the local situation to which they had been appointed. The commission explained that it could not recommend full clergy rights for women because, in Methodism's connectional polity, admitting women to the annual conference would introduce the "peculiar and embarrassing difficulties" of having to guarantee "to every effective minister a church and to every self-supporting church a minister." The legislation, passed after heated debate and defeat of a motion for clergy rights granted to men, gave women partial ministerial status. They could be ordained but not made members of the annual conference, be guaranteed appointment and minimum salary, or enjoy pension benefits. By the spring of 1927, eighty-one women had been ordained local deacons, and sixteen of them had gone on after two years to be ordained local elder.[56] Few women deacons experienced recommendation to elders' orders in such swift succession. Madeline Southard did not receive her elders' orders until 1922, and Georgia Harkness not until 1939. Full clergy rights for women in the MEC would be delayed until 1956, and Georgia Harkness's "welcome in the ministry" remained for most women only a fond hope. Nor did many women join Harkness on seminary faculties. One of the few was Mildred Moody Eakin (MA from New York University), who served as assistant professor of Christian education at Drew over a long teaching career (1932–54).

Southard's International Association of Women Preachers, later renamed the International Association of Women Ministers (IAWM), would over time gain membership from twenty-four countries and from thirty-five Christian denominations, including Roman Catholics. IAWM continues to publish a journal, the *Woman's Pulpit*, and conducts annual assemblies in various cities in the U.S., Canada, and other countries. It is and has always been a small organization. It has not been very visible in recent decades in the various denominational struggles for gender equality, and its earlier position as the professional association for women ministers has been largely eclipsed by the modern groups for female clergy, for instance, the UMC's women's caucus and the General Commission on the Status and Role of Women (COSROW).

However, from the 1920s through the 1950s, IAWM's annual assemblies provided social support, affirmation, and sustenance that, before the emergence of women's ministerial groups within denominations, was perhaps the only such support for otherwise relatively isolated women ministers. In addition, since its launch in 1922, the *Woman's Pulpit* constituted, until the mid-1970s, the most comprehensive repository of information about the status of gender equality in religious denominations around the world. Throughout its existence, the IAWM has lived its stated purpose—to develop the spirit of fellowship among women ministers. In 1923 Southard reported, "Another purpose that developed as we planned and prayed was to secure equal opportunity for women in the ecclesiastical world. Our association can honestly claim the obtaining of the license for women to preach in the Methodist Episcopal Church as a direct result of its work." Furthermore, the association was "to encourage young women whom God has called to preach."[57]

From Spontaneity to Formalism in Public Worship

Worship vitality needed order, and tradition needed progress, so some Victorian-era Methodists believed. Others, like southern Methodist preacher Oscar P. Fitzgerald, lamented, "The day of elegant written pulpit essays, quartette choirs, and *frigid gentility* had come."[58]

Newly affluent congregations took congregational literacy for granted and increasingly read their acts of worship from a printed page. By the 1860s, editor Daniel Curry celebrated the MEC's provision for written as well as extemporaneous prayers, espoused a "Ritual for the Pews," and insisted that Methodism alone could embrace the two distinct liturgical patterns, "the extemporaneous and the ritualistic."[59] Increasingly pastors fleshed out the basic pattern of worship—hymn, prayer, Scripture, collection, sermon—with more sophisticated hymns and anthems, soloists and quartets, sung responses such as the Gloria Patri, responsive readings of Psalms, and recitation of the Apostles' Creed, and paid more attention to the Christian Year. The "amens" and other spontaneous responses that had been commonplace in earlier days were frowned upon, and in more and more congregations they entirely disappeared. Orders of worship, at first only printed in the *Disciplines*, began to show up in the new hymnals as they came along. Late in the nineteenth century, a few churches contracted with printers for service bulletins on special occasions or even every Sunday.[60]

The MECS was first to include the general services of the church—Holy Communion, baptism, marriage, and burial—in its new hymnal of 1847. Northern Methodists followed their southern cousins in their new hymnal in 1878. *The Methodist Hymnal* (1905), a joint effort of Methodists North and South, was the first to include a full Order of Public Worship for non-Communion Sundays, a single page order placed up front facing the title page (Sources, pp. 35, 33). "Innovations" included unison reciting of the Apostles' Creed, responsive reading of a psalm, and singing of the Gloria Patri. Progressives desired to please conservatives who objected to "high church" pretensions by indicating with brackets that these three "innovations" might be omitted.

This 1905 order of worship is especially significant because it was generally used by the next generation and is used with minor variations in many congregations to this day. The order reflected the continuing diminishment of Scripture. Preaching during this period had come commonly to be based on a text consisting of a single verse or even part of a verse of Scripture. Indeed, the text was sometimes a pretext for a sermon that did not interpret the meaning of the text at all but used a key word, phrase, or image to launch into an unrelated topic that appealed to the preacher. While the recovery of the Psalter (familiarly known as the Responsive Reading) was a gain, the permission to substitute a psalm for the Old Testament lesson had the effect that many congregations rarely heard readings from the thirty-eight other books of the Old Testament. The insertion of announcements, collection, offertory music, and a hymn between Scripture reading and sermon both reflected and encouraged the increasing likelihood that the preaching would not be closely related to the Scripture lesson.

Communions became more frequent in this period as ordained clergy could be counted on for most churches on a regular basis. Southern Methodists led the way by mandating monthly Communion in their *Disciplines* beginning in 1870. Northern Methodists never had such a directive, but Matthew Simpson, in his celebratory *Cyclopaedia of Methodism* (1876), reported: "In cites and large towns this sacrament is usually celebrated monthly, but in country places it is seldom administered more than quarterly."[61] Communion wine became grape juice beginning in the 1880s after an enterprising New Jersey Methodist layman named Thomas Welch invented the process of canning (pasteurizing) grape juice and then proceeded to make a fortune marketing it to temperance-minded Methodists and other evangelical Protestants who thought Jesus drank grape juice![62] At the same time common cups (chalices) were gradually replaced by tiny individual glasses with pressure from sanitation-minded Methodists, but not without a protracted church fight. Experimentation with individual Communion cups began in the early 1890s and in the early decades of the twentieth century.[63] Opponents of the "great communion innovation" *prevailed* in preventing legislative approval but *failed* when it came to actual practice. Their use in congregations grew, assisted greatly by the influenza epidemic of 1918–19. By the 1920s, individual cups filled with grape juice had become almost universal in the Methodist family of churches.[64]

Choirs, organs, trained musicians, and even paid soloists raised standards for Methodist church music. Choirs began to appear in Methodist churches in eastern seaboard cities and country towns as early as the 1810s. By the 1840s and 1850s, choirs had become fixtures in numerous Methodist churches. Pianos and organs followed in their wake, but not without considerable turmoil. By 1864 a national organization of Associated Choirs pressed for the innovations. Meeting with the MEC General Conference's blessing in a ten-day choir convention, this organization sought both to safeguard the Wesleyan practice of congregational singing and to improve musical literature and leadership.[65] The 1878 MEC *Hymnal* gave official endorsement. The preface suggested that "there should be a choir and an organ, if possible, to lead the people," and that these supports to congregational song were best situated "in front of the congregation." Organs and choir galleries in previous decades were usually at the rear of the church. Four years later the MECS publisher and theologian Thomas O. Summers defended both organs and choirs and even composed the hymn "Praise Him with Organs" for the dedication of a new organ at McKendree Church in Nashville.[66]

While the avowed purpose of choir and organ was to improve congregational singing, they did not always have that effect; nevertheless, in many places the choirs and organs kept the spirit of Methodism alive within the context of choral music. In addition to leading hymn singing, the choirs often sang anthems and set pieces at the beginning of the service and during the offering.[67]

Worship wars then as now often focused on congregational song. Folk and formal styles clashed. Beginning with *The Methodist Hymnal* (MEC, 1878), there were fewer Wesley and revival hymns and more formal psalms, chorales, and hymns mostly of British-Anglican origin, such as "Holy, Holy, Holy." However, unofficial "Methodist" songbooks capitalized on the use of informal songs, spirituals, and other American folk hymns, like Joseph Hillman's *The Revivalist*. First published in 1868, Hillman's songbook became popular for use in Sunday schools and midweek prayer meetings. Many Methodists thought the Sunday schools and prayer meetings had all the "good" songs.

Hymn texts were now tied to tunes. In an earlier era congregations sang all of their hymns to a few well-known tunes. By midcentury, Methodists longed for a hymnal with tunes. The Associated Choirs of the MEC memorialized the 1864 General Conference desiring the appointment of a committee to prepare a collection of tunes that might become a denominational standard (Sources 1864d). Three years later (1867) such a collection of hymns and tunes was published: *The Centenary Singer*.[68] The 1878 MEC *Hymnal* was the first to offer printings with tunes interlined with texts, just in time for the growing presence of choirs and organs to help Methodists sing God's praises in four-part harmony. The MECS and the UBC added tunes to their official hymnals in 1874. The EA followed in 1877.

Hymnbooks relocated from pockets and purses to pews. Methodists, Evangelicals, and United Brethren of the previous generation were expected to buy their own hymnbooks and bring them to church on Sunday, so tiny, pocket-sized hymnbooks were the order of the day. After the Civil War, hymnals came out of pockets and purses. Congregants found hymnals waiting for them in neat racks attached to the back of each pew. The 1878 MEC *Hymnal*, issued only in large size, was the first to find its way into the new pew racks. The downside to the above two innovations was that hymnbooks were no longer available in Methodist homes where they long served as a handy treasury of doctrinal teaching and devotional reading.

Numerous congregations continued in the old ways or adapted their services in different ways, such as opting for a revivalist pattern where the sermon was preceded by a song service, featuring gospel songs and praise choruses based on popular musical styles. Many congregations blended the two worship styles, offering formal services upstairs in the sanctuary and informal services downstairs in the Sunday school, at Sunday evening and midweek prayer services, and at the almost mandatory twice yearly revival meetings—one in the winter in the church with a hired evangelist and the other in the summer at a camp meeting by the sea or around a lake. And as noted earlier, "promiscuous" seating (women and men side by side, families together), increasingly became the norm, as in other mainline churches of the era.

Environments for Worship, Education, and Fellowship

Methodism's centennial era in America (1866–84) coincided with its transformation into a solidly middle-class church. Nothing symbolized Methodism's new status and social location better than the network of impressive, even monumental, regional Methodist churches that came to dominate the urban landscape during the last quarter of the nineteenth century. An earlier generation of Methodists considered elegant churches to be detrimental to spiritual worship. The *Discipline* might continue the Wesley adage, "Let all our churches be built plain and decent,"[69] but with the rise of middle-class respectability, fine church buildings were seen to demonstrate the authority and influence of the Methodists, as well as the wealth and status of the membership. Midcentury church leaders like Abel Stevens assumed that Methodism's "permanent hold upon its congregations, especially in the larger communities, will depend much upon the convenience and even the elegance of its churches."[70] Within this context, prospective members were seen as audiences to be wooed rather than souls to be saved. The new churches also reflected the hierarchy developing in connectional Methodism, with its accompanying centralization of power. The new generation of upscale churches were important regional centers of Methodist strength and missionary outreach. In every major city and town Methodists built large and refined architectural monuments to their spirituality. In smaller cities and prosperous rural districts Methodists built more limited versions of the same churches.

Whether large or small, the new churches differed significantly from their predecessors in many ways. In the construction of its new churches, Methodism shunned classical (Greek Revival or American Colonial) architecture, whose imitation of pagan temples seemed an inappropriate way to express Christian faith. Gothic and Romanesque Revival styles, to even the most casual observer, marked both the spiritual and the temporal prosperity of the church. The plans, which were often supplied by leading architects and circulated through denominational departments of architecture, not only spread style but also marked the elaboration of functions in the modern church. The buildings were adapted to the broader social concerns that were becoming fundamental aspects of church life. Space was set aside for an office for the minister and for meetings of the trustees and official boards, as well as for the growing number of auxiliary organizations associated with the late Victorian congregation—Sunday schools, lending libraries, women's missionary societies, men's brotherhoods, and youth fellowships. Often the congregation built an adjoining hall for social and recreational gatherings and for social outreach ministries.

When Methodism's flagship church in Pittsburgh, Christ MEC, was gutted by fire in 1891, the congregation set out to build a trendsetting church for the city and for the denomination. The sale of the center-city site plus a sizable insurance settlement enabled the congregation to hire the nation's leading ecclesiastical architect, George Washington Kramer.[71] Construction began in May 1893, and a year and a half later, January 13, 1895, the monumental new church was dedicated by Bishop Charles H. Fowler. Celebrating rituals for such dedications, which began to appear in service books of the MEC in 1864 and MECS in 1870, became a proud chore for bishops.

Kramer's plan for the new Christ Church featured a new exterior style (Romanesque) and a new interior plan (auditorium-style sanctuary and Akron Plan Sunday school, discussed in chapter 10), promoted as the "Ideal Church" in his 1897 book, *The What, How and Why of Church Building* (Sources 1897). The massive church built around a large central tower, surrounded by broad transepts with curving, arcaded porticoes, was modeled after H. H. Richardson's monumental Trinity Episcopal Church, Boston, erected in 1877 for one of the era's pulpit princes, Phillips Brooks. The rough stone-faced exterior with deep-set, intricately carved openings made a powerful statement. Inside, a broad worship space inspired by the arrangement of the secular theater replaced the narrow Gothic sanctuary of old Christ Church. Kramer aimed to outdo his mentor Richardson. The steel-reinforced one-hundred-foot-wide transept arches supported a dome span of fifty feet, exceeding Trinity Church's dome by four feet. Galleries surrounded the central pulpit platform on three sides so that every hearer was as close as possible to the preacher. On the fourth side and behind the pulpit area, the space was filled with the ranks of the choir that reinforced the appeal of the preacher with its devotional singing, and on either side of the choir rose the gilded pipes of the organ. Curved pews surrounded the dominating pulpit, lush carpet covered the sloping floors and radiating aisles, plaster moldings on walls and ceiling echoed exterior Romanesque carvings, and large Tiffany stained glass windows flooded the interior with delicate hues. Olive and gold predominated in the color scheme. The auditorium plan's wide, open central space was more easily expressed in the curving wall or tall central lantern of the Romanesque. The chief alternative, Gothic, was less accommodating because the required narrow nave and deep chancel were less flexible. As a building, it was wonderfully elegant and highly efficient for its purpose in the days when large crowds regularly hung upon the words of the preacher, for which the nineteenth century was notable.

The emphasis on the word at the expense of the sacrament, and all that this implied for public worship and church architecture, was well advanced in the Methodist world when Christ Church, Pittsburgh, was rebuilt in 1895. Their token Communion tables looked inconspicuous beneath a pulpit that dominated the building. The conversion of the individual remained still the major Methodist concern, and the gifted evangelical preacher, the chief instrument. The result was a new conception of the church building as a place where large numbers of people could feel as much at home as in any secular meeting hall and could be brought into the closest possible encounter with the message and personality of the preacher. Turn-of-the-century Methodist preachers yearned to preach in a building where the physical arrangement of pews, gallery, and platform combined to concentrate and emphasize the power and centrality of their sermon.

Kramer brought the Sunday school out of the basement where it had been crammed in old Christ Church and gave it as much attention and space as the new sanctuary. Patterned after what came to be known as the Akron Plan, the Sunday school featured two curving tiers of classrooms facing a large central auditorium. The plan efficiently gathered a large number of classes close to and in full view of the superintendent, who led the school in opening and closing worship from a platform at its center, after which doors slid closed to allow individual class sessions. The new Christ Church, built at a cost of $275,000 and dedicated debt-free, modeled the dramatic changes being made in the primary spatial components of Methodist churches between 1875 and 1925.

Auditorium-style sanctuaries with Akron Plan Sunday schools were built by the thousands across the country.[72] Methodists were deeply involved in the spread of both plans by their newly formed denominational departments of architecture. The MEC formed a department of architecture in its Board of Church Extension as early as 1875. Within a decade the MECS and the UBC had formed similar offices in their church extension agencies. A Methodism growing into new urban responsibilities and building new facilities in expanding cities and country towns needed architectural guidance on a new scale. Denominational agencies began to make available church plan catalogs. The MEC board issued an annual catalog of plans prepared by Philadelphia architect Benjamin D. Price beginning in 1877.[73] Within a few years the MECS and the UBC issued a version of the same catalog, which was expanded and modified each year by Price through 1889 at least. His early designs consisted of simple wide rectangles that featured straight pews angled forward on each side to keep the cost down. Plan number 38 in the 1885 catalog, an exception, included fully curving pews and matching Communion rail.[74] By 1889 Price added three plans (numbers 54, 55, and 56) for churches with a full complement of theater-style features, including sloping floors, radiating aisles, curved pews, and circling Communion rail, ranging in price from $3,000 to $20,000.[75] From 1883 to 1887, 1,725 church and parsonage plans were sold.[76] With such guidance and under energetic promotion by church extension and Sunday school boards, the Methodist family of denominations opened its second century by building worship-education-fellowship complexes.

Christ Church, Methodist, in Pittsburgh was only one of the impressive new Romanesque Methodist churches. Baltimore's First Methodist Episcopal Church (1884–87) by celebrated architect Stanford White is Romanesque in style with Etruscan detailing, its massive granite walls enclosed by a conical tile roof and topped by a 225-foot tower with a huge weather vane. Stained glass windows by Louis Tiffany in shades of Pompeian red cast a rosy glow throughout the massive oval sanctuary. Inspired by the starry mosaics of Ravenna, the great vaulted ceiling over the 1,000 seats was painted to show the heavens as they appeared at 3:00 a.m. the day of the church's dedication, with all major stars and planets in their proper positions.[77] Another early notable Romanesque Methodist design was Weary and Kramer's First Methodist Episcopal Church, South, Birmingham, Alabama (1891).[78] The 1,400-seat sanctuary occupied the main body of the building with a gallery extending around three sides, which joined with the choir gallery above the pulpit, creating a continuous seating space circling the pulpit—the auditorium plan drawn out to its logical conclusion. Intricate fresco work and a magnificent chandelier graced the high domed ceiling. Handsome pews, lush carpet, and 142 stained glass windows complemented the interior.[79]

The affinity of the Romanesque Revival with the plan and function of the theater and multiroom Sunday school assured the connection of style and plan for many years after the 1890s when Romanesque style was out of fashion for other public buildings. Auditorium and Akron Plan Methodist churches dressed in Romanesque costume continued to be built, especially in the North and Midwest, until the 1920s. Much maligned and misunderstood by later generations, they represent what may be the most common type of Methodist church building still in use today. But by the 1920s, Methodists were among the first to actively and officially repudiate the Akron Plan as a new breed of religious educators promoted instead a multiroom, public school–like Sunday school. Dramatizing the change, First MEC, Akron, tore down its famous Sunday school building in 1914 and replaced it with a freestanding public school–like educational building. At the same time, Methodists began what would be a slow-paced recovery of Wesley's sacramental sensibilities and developed architectural ambitions that permitted a balance of Word and Table. In this recovery, Methodism tracked cultural and larger Christian trends. This dependence is monumentally illustrated in its embrace of the "aesthetic" or Gothic architecture. The leading proponent of this second Gothic Revival was the architect and medievalist Ralph Adams Cram (1863–1942) of Boston. Cram developed a theory that Gothic style had not exhausted itself, but had been prematurely cut off by the Renaissance and the Protestant Reformation in the sixteenth century and its cultural potential recovered in the nineteenth century. Inspired by the originality of the English Gothicists of the early nineteenth century, Cram felt that with creative scholarship, the Gothic style could be adapted to the needs of a modern age. Cram had made that case in his many books but especially in his designs and buildings. He proved highly successful in this endeavor, producing vast numbers of churches across the country, collegiate campuses (including Princeton University and the U.S. Military Academy at West Point), and even commercial buildings. Methodists followed the style in new educational buildings as well as in churches. Drew University erected Gothic Bowne Hall in 1912, and Duke, an entire campus in the early 1920s.[80]

Building on this legacy, many mainline Protestants offered their own interpretations of Gothic architecture. Chief among the interpreters was Elbert M. Conover, a New Jersey clergyman and 1913 graduate of Drew Theological Seminary. Several Methodist denominations established upgraded departments or bureaus of church architecture after World War I to improve the quality of church design and convey best practices as their congregations built or rebuilt. The first to do so, in 1917, was the MEC. Conover became its director in 1924. He recruited a staff of professional planners who advised building committees and local architects through printed material and slide projector lectures. The need for such guidance was great. Two years after he accepted the job, Conover noted that a lack of professional guidance

> resulted in the construction of many "horrible examples" from the standpoint either of the needs for worship, religious instruction or of architectural treatment. The increased wealth of the country made possible turrets, domes and contraptions often fearfully and wonderfully made with little reference to the wealth of precedent in church architecture in Europe.[81]

In 1934 Conover became director of a newly formed Interdenominational Architecture Bureau (later a department of the National Council of Churches). He held that position until his death in 1952. From both his MEC and interdenominational posts, Conover led first Methodists and then mainline Protestants in a full-scale assault on auditorium and Akron Plan churches (Sources 1928).

In his illustrated lectures to church building committees and in his books Conover insisted that church architecture itself was a form of evangelism. And the best form of evangelism was a building that was distinctively a church, not a structure that could be confused with any secular building. This, for Conover, had clear implications. In the churches illustrated in his widely circulated books—*Building the House of God* (1928), the *Church Building Guide* (1946), and *The Church Builder* (1948)—there is no mistaking either interiors or exteriors with anything but a place for Christian worship. They do not look like banks on the outside or theaters on the inside. The interiors have a divided chancel with choir stalls facing each other across the chancel. The altar stands at the remote end, and a pulpit and lectern at the nave end. He preferred that to the theater plan with pulpit, choir, and organ front and center (or in a corner), with sloping floors, curved pews, and radiating aisles that were still prevalent in many churches built earlier in the century. Outside, Conover's churches had a tower crowned by a cross. Like Cram (at least in his later years), Conover did not dogmatically insist upon the recreation of a particular Gothic style. He did believe, however, that modern church builders should be guided by the same "mystic" spirit that guided the church builders of the thirteenth and fourteenth centuries.[82] Most of the plans he promoted were neo-Gothic. Essentially they were lower-budget Ralph Adams Cram buildings for non-Episcopalians. Richey's home church in Durham, Trinity United Methodist, its substantial downtown facility destroyed by fire in January 1923, was rebuilt with a Gothic design from the Cram and Ferguson firm.[83] Other notable Gothic Revival churches were built in the same decade: African American St. Mark's MEC, New York City (1920); Trinity MEC, Springfield, Massachusetts (1929); First MEC, Germantown, Philadelphia (1898/1931); Chicago Temple MEC (1924), a skyscraper church with floors of offices and a cross-crowned Gothic spire that towered above every other building in the city; Highland Park MECS, Dallas (1927);

and First MEC, Pasadena, California (1924). Denver's Warren MEC, built in 1909, was a modest precursor (1968 "Snapshot").

Well-designed church buildings, Conover insisted, in their exterior and interior, above all should be beautiful because "ugliness, even if consecrated, will not be forgiven."[84] Only thus will the environment evoke and instill faith and reverence and inspire and promote worship. Enhancing religious practice aesthetically included attending to the centrality of the sacraments. Conover counseled, "Give to the table of the Lord the position of honor due it, with nothing but the communion rail between it and the people." It should not be overshadowed by the pulpit or crammed into a narrow passage.[85] Similarly in 1926, Edward G. Schutz, a Chicago district superintendent, counseled readers of the *Northwestern Christian Advocate* on the advantages of divided chancels, giving prominence of height to lectern and pulpit and a "place of honor" to the Communion table, "the focal center of the church, eloquent in its symbolism of the atonement of Christ, and of our Christian fellowship." Fred Winslow Adams, a Springfield, Massachusetts, pastor, writing in the *Methodist Review,* exhorted Methodists to join in "the revival of public worship," to recover the balance between pulpit and table, to remember that table, not rail, constituted the Christian altar, and to restore it visually and architecturally to centrality.[86]

Methodism's second Gothic Revival came to a halt as the economic depression deepened in the 1930s and World War II raged through the early 1940s. The well-designed and expertly built structures of the previous decades stand on their own as masterpieces of the adaptation of Gothic forms and principles to the needs of American and Methodist institutions. But in the same period a few church architects, trying to be "modern," rejected the depressing, dark, cluttered environment of newer Gothic Revival and older Romanesque Revival churches and turned to less ornamented circular and rectilinear forms. Formulas by architectural superstars of the era, Louis Sullivan (form follows function) and Mies van der Rohe (less is more), shaped their work. They incorporated new building materials and methods but without any consideration of new developments in the celebration of the liturgy. This approach alone simply reproduced older, neo-medieval interior plans. It was a case of putting old wine in new wineskins.

In 1914 Sullivan designed St. Paul's MEC in Cedar Rapids, Iowa, and it featured a semicircular worship space with a rectangular wing for classrooms and a high tower encased in modern brick form. One critic called Sullivan's church "an abstracted Roman theater." Another example was Boston Avenue Methodist Church, Tulsa, Oklahoma. Rich with oil money, the congregation instructed a team of talented young designers, architect Bruce Goff of Tulsa and Adah Robinson, chair of the art department in the University of Tulsa, to design a bigger, better, and taller building than the glitzy modernist Catholic church down the street. Twenty-two-year-old Goff, self-taught and an ardent admirer of Louis Sullivan and Frank Lloyd Wright, used a floor plan from Sullivan's design for the Cedar Rapids MEC to develop the church completed in 1929. It was composed of a half-circular auditorium-style sanctuary on the west and a rectangular four-story Christian education wing on the east. Connected by an illuminated bell tower rising 280 feet above the doorways and topped with 30-foot-high copper and glass fins, the church took the form of a skyscraper in the emerging Art Deco style. Robinson designed the interior, a pulpit-centered auditorium accommodating 1,800 in individual theater seats. While hailed by architectural critics around the nation, the high-style church broke no new ground liturgically.

Missions in War and Peace

Having endorsed their respective sides in the Civil War, Methodists readily rallied to the cause of the Spanish-American War (1898). It did not hurt that President William McKinley, publisher William Randolph Hearst, and the media generally construed as an act of war the explosion that destroyed the warship USS *Maine* while docked in Havana, killing 266 crew members. Nor did it hurt to have a Methodist in the White House. Nor were President McKinley's occupation of Roman Catholic Cuba and acquisition of Catholic Puerto Rico and the Philippines unwelcome. Expansionist politics and Christian evangelism could work hand in hand. Methodists applauded the president's "splendid little war" designed to uplift, civilize, and evangelize brown people. Mission executives jubilantly construed victory and evangelistic opportunity in providential terms. So pronounced Adna B. Leonard, head of the MEC Missionary Society and Board of Foreign Missions (1888–1912), eight times a delegate to General Conference, and an 1885 candidate for governor of Ohio (Sources 1898). And if religious leaders could speak like imperialists, politicians could preach like evangelists. So sounded Methodist Senator Albert Beveridge in 1900 in support of a joint resolution declaring American intent to hold the Philippines as a trusteeship under God for civilization, progress, and decency. "Almighty God," he asserted, "has marked us as His *chosen people*, henceforth to lead in the regeneration of the world." Repeating those words later in his remarks, he added, "This is the divine mission of America. . . . We are trustees of the world's progress, guardians of its righteous peace."[87]

Echoing Beveridge's sentiments, MEC Bishop James Thoburn reminded a U.S. Senate Committee on the Philippines in 1902 that "God put us in the Philippines." Following such a divine mandate, Methodists had by late 1900 set about building schools and churches in Manila and recruiting native converts as preachers. Homer Stuntz arrived to take superintendency of the emerging mission in 1901. Nicolas Zamora, the first native to be ordained (deacon in 1900), became the first native elder in 1903. A comity arrangement with other American denominations assigned Methodists to an area in Luzon north of Manila. Aggressive evangelism produced converts—6,800 in the first three years—outpacing growth in every other mission of the MEC.[88]

Southern Methodists beat the northern church to Cuba in this advance against Catholic and Spanish dominion. The WFMS of the MECS established three schools for girls in Cuba beginning in 1901. Under a comity agreement, Protestant mission leaders divided Puerto Rico into four regions, one of which was assigned to the UBC and another to the MEC. UBC pastor E. L. Ortt and his wife began Sunday school work in Ponce in 1899. The Ortts knew no Spanish and decided early to open a school to teach Puerto Rican children the *Protestant* language. In a 1901 letter to the mission board Ortt wrote, "The very language of Spain breathes Roman Catholicism, and, in order to teach these children a new gospel, a new life, it is necessary that we teach it to them in a new language, free from the accent of the language of oppression."[89] The UBC continued its Puerto Rico mission until 1931, when the United Evangelical Church in Puerto Rico was formed by a merger of three denominations: United Brethren, Disciples of Christ, and Congregational churches.

Charles Drees, a veteran MEC missionary from Peru and fluent in Spanish, went to San Juan in 1900 as mission superintendent, assisted by a native pastor, Manuel Andujar, and two Anglo deaconesses. Within two years the mission reported 5 churches with 640 members, 7 Sunday schools, a "McKinley" day school, and an orphanage. The expanding mission was organized as "Porto Rico Mission Conference" in 1913 with 35 churches and 18 ministers. From the earliest days of the mission, women were active in visitation and served as assistant pastors and as Christian educators.

Although some Methodists embraced the peace activism that followed in the first decade of the new century, joined peace societies, and supported the call for arbitration as a means of dealing with international disputes, most reverted to the crusade spirit as the United States edged toward participation in World War I (1914–18).[90] The MEC, the EA, and the UBC at their General Conferences between 1912 and 1916 supported the ideal of arbitration. However, three years into the bloody European war (1917), when German submarines sank three U.S. merchant ships and offered to help Mexico regain U.S. lands, American public opinion generally and Methodist attitudes shifted. Wilsonian-inspired idealism, crass nationalism, and anti-German sentiment produced a crusade mentality, support for democracy abroad, and undemocratic constraints on speech and action at home. Methodists endorsed President Woodrow Wilson's war to "make the world safe for democracy" and the prospect of the U.S. as a great Christianizing power with Methodism at its center.

When the U.S. entered the war in Europe, MEC publications on this theme multiplied. A good example is the pamphlet *Methodism and the Flag*, published by the New York Conference, which included an essay expressing enthusiastic support for the U.S. declaration of war as well as derisive condemnation of Christian pacifists—and a much-publicized and often-reprinted poem by Bishop Luther B. Wilson titled "Wave, Flag of Freedom, Wave."[91] The MECS and the MPC created War-Work Commissions. The

MEC established a National War Council with headquarters at Metropolitan Church in Washington, D.C. A flyer for the organization depicted marching troops in front of a horseback-riding Francis Asbury, around whose shoulders appeared the headings: "Methodism Cooperates with Government" and "Follows Her Sons to the Trenches." Evangelicals celebrated their founder, Jacob Albright, as a Revolutionary War hero and urged his latter-day flock to follow his example.

The ostensibly progressive Wilson administration put aside the Constitution, jailing thousands of dissidents and suppressing the antiwar movement. The military draft was reinstated, this time with clergy exemption and the limitation of conscientious objection to members of *pacifist* denominations (draft boards recognized only three—Friends [Quakers], Mennonites, and Church of the Brethren). The Methodist press openly attacked Quakers and other pacifists. Churches also tried to silence their pacifist members. A prominent district superintendent in the California Conference, E. P. Ryland, was dismissed for refusing to participate with his bishop and cabinet in a church-sponsored war bond rally in 1917.[92] Evangelicals, United Brethren, and German Methodists found the cornerstones of their churches painted yellow, their pastors threatened, and members insulted as un-American and un-Methodist. Postal authorities required the editor of the German-language Methodist newspaper, *Der Christliche Apologete*, to file English translations of all major articles with their office. And the church's chief editors, deeming the paper "not in full harmony with the spirit of the Church and the country" and insufficiently supportive of the Allied cause for "freedom, democracy, and humanity," required the paper's editors to sign a loyalty oath (Sources 1918b).

The UBC General Conference of 1917, on the other hand, noting that "a vein of pure German blood runs through our whole church from Otterbein to the present," passed a resolution requesting "our people everywhere to refrain from any unkind criticism of their German brethren in this country." And the independent Methodist Federation for Social Service and at least one annual conference went on record opposing patriotic excesses.

The incredible mobilization—millions under arms—elicited from the churches an equally monumental effort to support their men, physically, mentally, emotionally, and spiritually. Providing an adequate supply of chaplains, for instance, required its own mobilization. The 1918 MECS General Conference, realizing that it lacked sufficient numbers of the ordained who could be deployed as chaplains, authorized bishops to take emergency measures. Nolan Harmon (later a bishop), who expressed willingness to serve, received this telegram from Dr. E. O. Watson of the South Carolina Conference: "GO TO THE NEAREST METHODIST BISHOP AND BE ORDAINED DEACON AND ELDER STOP LET THIS TELEGRAM BE YOUR WARRANT AND THEN PROCEED TO THE SCHOOL FOR CHAPLAINS AT CAMP TAYLOR LOUISVILLE KENTUCKY OCTOBER 4 STOP." Harmon complied, found retired

Bishop Henry Clay Morrison, and was ordained successively deacon and elder in the bishop's chambers.[93]

Methodists channeled much of such support through national interdenominational agencies. For instance, Methodists sent some 325 chaplains, working collaboratively with the Federal Council's General Wartime Commission, established in 1917. (After World War I, this commission continued to be the primary liaison between the Protestant churches and the government and to be involved in selection and endorsement.) Methodists also channeled funds for and support of troops through an array of international interdenominational organizations, their apparatus, and worldwide connections, among them, the Student Christian Movement, World's Student Christian Federation, and the YMCA. The latter with its own National War Work Council proved especially vital, creating dispensary "huts" at army encampments, working with prisoners of war as well as Allied troops, and raising vast sums of money. Some five hundred Methodists worked in YMCA ministries. And one Methodist, John R. Mott, effectively led and coordinated the work of the several international agencies. Layman Mott, arguably Methodism's greatest ecumenical figure, moved relentlessly back and forth between the U.S. and Europe, working with counterpart ecumenists and political leaders. Mott was a forceful advocate for the creation of the World Council of Churches and was the preacher at the opening service of the WCC's inaugural assembly in Amsterdam in 1948. He continued such monumental efforts when the churches turned toward relief and the rebuilding of a devastated Europe. Mott shared the Nobel Peace Prize in 1946 for his work in establishing and strengthening international Christian student organizations that worked to promote peace.[94]

At war's end, when President Woodrow Wilson brought the Treaty of Versailles to the U.S. Congress for ratification, the EA, the MEC, and the MECS fought for its ratification. The treaty, ratified in 1919, included the Covenant of the League of Nations. The 1916 MEC General Conference had encouraged the nation to take the lead in an international league or federation. The same year, that church's bishops took a stand for world peace. Pastors and laity joined advocacy groups for the League of Nations and created and signed petitions urging the U.S. to join. The Woman's Missionary Council of the MECS in 1919 passed a resolution supporting the league, which it sent to public officials. Evelyn Riley Nicholson, president of the Woman's Foreign Missionary Society of the MEC from 1920 to 1940, played a major role in shaping the churches' thinking on peace. She was a member of the General Conference Committee on International Justice and Goodwill, which worked with the Federal Council of Churches to produce a pamphlet titled *What Pastors and Laymen Can Do in the Crusade for a Warless World.* She wrote the book *Way to a Warless World* (1924), which became an important voice for peace. Fittingly, a copy was placed in the cornerstone of the Methodist Church Center for the United Nations, which opened in 1962.

A dramatic shift in Methodist attitudes toward war—from crusade to pacifism—came as America debated signing the Treaty of Versailles and entering the League of Nations. Revulsion toward war derived as well from the grasp of WWI's incredible cost in lives, property, money, and social order and from media- and congressional-driven paranoiac notions that munitions makers had seduced the nations into the convulsive debacle. A series of international peace efforts followed that focused on disarmament, a ban on the use of chemical and biological weapons (gas especially), and the creation of an international judiciary capable of resolving disputes between nations. Methodist attitudes both tracked and led those of the nation generally. By 1924, the MEC General Conference established a churchwide Commission on World Peace and adopted the "Springfield Declaration on World Peace," calling for a crusade for peace, support of the League of Nations, and U.S. entry into the Permanent Court of International Justice (Sources 1924a). Pacifist sentiment would reign, particularly in northern Methodism, until the nation found itself again in world war. But by 1920, Methodist leaders championed warfare on other fronts, not just warfare against war, but against the beer trade internationally and against other perverse interests that sullied America and threatened clean American homes—gambling, prizefighting, prostitution, smoking, and desecrating the Sabbath. And for good measure to make learning to speak English compulsory in public schools and English the only language for newspapers. So Clarence True Wilson instructed the 1920 MEC General Conference. No Methodist timidity from the head of the Board of Temperance, Prohibition and Public Morals (predecessor to the General Board of Church and Society)![95] Having dried up America, Wilson wanted Methodism to purge Europe of what had led astray the very nation that had given the world Reformation—beer drinking. In response, General Conference passed a long resolution, "Temperance and Prohibition," giving thanks "to Almighty God" for the passage of national Prohibition (which took effect January 16, 1920), congratulating the WCTU, the Anti-Saloon League, and its own Board of Temperance for their effective advocacy, and pledging the church to carry on the fight. So "as a world church" and without Clarence True Wilson's virulent anti-Germanism, the MEC endorsed and committed itself to the World League against Alcoholism.[96]

At the end of World War I, Methodists became involved in Korean efforts to throw off Japanese hegemony. U.S. President Wilson's declaration of the right of self-determination of peoples inspired Korean nationalists to action. In 1919, thirty-six Korean leaders (sixteen of them Christian, nine Methodist) signed a declaration of independence. Methodist Syngman Rhee was elected president of a Korean provisional government. Half a million Koreans took part in unarmed demonstrations that occurred wherever the declaration was read. Japan reacted swiftly to crush the Independence Movement (called in Korean the Sam-il Movement for its date, March 1) by imprisoning leaders, including many pastors, and destroying 740 buildings, including 47 churches.

Of 19,525 persons arrested, 3,371 were Protestants—more than 17 percent of those arrested—an impressive figure considering that by 1919, the Protestants comprised only about 1 percent of the total population. Of the 471 women arrested, Protestants accounted for more than 65 percent (309), attesting to the empowering effect of religion on Korean women.

Methodists become linked with two of the most important symbols of the Korean Independence Movement: the martyrdom of Yu Kwan-sun and the massacre at Cheamni. Yu, a seventeen-year-old student at Ewha HakDang, a Methodist mission school, was arrested and imprisoned for taking a leading role in demonstrations. Yu refused to renounce her passion for independence and with others took part in demonstration while imprisoned. Brutally beaten and tortured, she died in prison in 1920. In the Methodist chapel in the village of Cheamni, on April 15, 1919, Japanese soldiers locked up protesters (mostly Methodists) for demonstrating on previous days. They then set the church on fire. Some Koreans tried to claw their way out, only to be cut down by awaiting bullets and bayonets. In the end, twenty-nine villagers were massacred and the whole village burned. In May of that year Western journalist Nathaniel Peffer delineated the role of the thirty-plus Methodist pastors active in the Independence Movement (Sources 1919b). In June the Board of Bishops of the MEC publicly protested Japanese brutality.[97]

President Rhee and his provisional government fled to exile in China. The Independence Movement, nevertheless, was not in vain. Galvanizing and uniting Koreans, it obliged the Japanese (for a time) to a more tolerant policy. Methodists—missionaries and converts alike—defiantly favored independence, a stance that would affect growth in the decades ahead.

Race and Reunion

The MEC and the MECS began formal conversations, as we noted, at a conference in Cape May, New Jersey, during the summer of 1876. Each church pledged to honor the other as a legitimate heir of the Christmas Conference and to send "fraternal delegates" to each other's future General Conferences (Sources 1876d). The two episcopal churches joined in celebrations of the common Wesleyan heritage at the First Ecumenical (now World) Methodist Conference in London, 1881 (Sources 1881b), and at a Centennial Methodist Conference in Baltimore, 1884. In 1894, the MECS General Conference proposed the exploration of closer relations between the two churches and authorized the establishment of a Commission on Federation of Methodism (delegations of nine, three bishops, ministers, and laity). In 1896, the MEC concurred, and a Joint Commission on Federation met in January 1898. It recommended adjusting rivalries in overseas mission fields and crafting a common catechism, hymnbook, and order of public worship. These appeared in 1905 (Sources, pp. 29–30, 33–36), the hymnal including a common order of worship.[98] The two churches agreed to share publication facilities in Asia, both participated in emerging national and world ecumenical ventures (as we note elsewhere in this chapter), and both would continue joint celebrations of the Methodist heritage—1919, 1925, 1934, and 1938 (the two hundredth anniversary of Wesley's Aldersgate conversion).

Gradually the two episcopal churches, sometimes in conversation with the Methodist Protestants as well, aspired to more than *federation* and explored *unification*. Consistently from the start, the MECS was emphatic that unification be a white affair (Sources 1918a). Southern Methodists entertained and suggested several ways in which African Americans could be separated off. In conversations[99] that extended over half a century, the MECS held out for some way of ordering the conference structure of Methodism that would (1) accord the southern white minority within a united church "the power to control its own affairs"[100] and (2) place another minority, namely, the African American members of the MEC, into a separate ecclesial structure, preferably one as distinct as the Colored Methodist Episcopal Church.[101] An early formulation—initially termed quadrennial conferences and providing a single quadrennial conference of African Americans—surfaced as the unification scheme from a 1911 Joint Commission on Federation comprising of representatives of the MEC, MPC, and MECS and held at Chattanooga. This Chattanooga "unity" proposal also provided, as would subsequent schemes, for fuller lay representation in annual conferences, a concession to the MPC and to advocates of lay rights within the MEC and the MECS.[102]

On this proposal the MPC General Conference deferred action pending resolution of issues between the two episcopal bodies. The MECS in 1914 recognized the agreement as containing the "basic principles of a genuine unification . . . by the method of reorganization" but insisted that African American Methodists be "formed into an independent organization holding fraternal relations with the reorganized and united church." Southern leaders soon added another condition, namely, the establishment of a supreme court or judiciary for the church so that no conference would have the authority to pass upon and determine the constitutionality of its own acts (a resolution of polity and authority differences that went back to 1844).[103] The MEC, meeting in 1916, also embraced the plan "as containing the basic principles of a genuine unification," conceding at that point that its "colored membership" should be reorganized "into one or more Quadrennial or Jurisdictional Conferences."[104]

These actions led to the constitution of an (all-male) Joint Commission on Unification representing the two episcopal bodies, which met from 1916 to 1920 and left on record three volumes and more than fifteen hundred pages of debates and speeches.[105] The central drama in these negotiations concerned the racial composition in any "unified" Methodism. The southern editor and commissioner A. J. Lamar made that clear:

> We all know and we have known from the beginning that the crux of the situation is the Status of the Colored Membership in the Methodist Episcopal Church. We can

arrange everything else, and yet when we come to that, if we can't arrange that, if we come to a deadlock on that, it renders null and void everything that we have done before.

Toward the end of the discussions, he affirmed,

A great many things are not vital. But three things are vital. One is the relation of the colored membership of the Methodist Church in the reorganized Church. A second is the organization, the powers and rights, of the Regional Conferences. The third is your Judicial Council. Those are the three big things we have got to consider.[106]

On such notes, the southern commissioners remained consistent and insistent. Early in the proceedings Bishop Horace DuBose proposed the creation "alongside the white membership of the reorganized Church a connection to bear the same name, perhaps to have some distinguishing description, an adjunct or subjunctive title to indicate that it is a colored connection." This, he thought, would house both the CME, to which the MECS still related, and the African American members of the MEC. It would enjoy something like the fraternal relations that pertained between the MECS and the CME. Bishop John M. Moore glossed the proposal by hoping that two unifications would occur, that between and among white Methodists and another among the MEC and the three "negro" churches (AME and AMEZ as well as CME). Bishop Edwin D. Mouzon added, "The Methodist Episcopal Church, South, in General Conference assembled, recommended that the colored membership of the Methodist Churches be erected into an independent denomination." Then speaking for the southern commissioners, he affirmed,

We are sure that race consciousness, the race consciousness of the colored people and the race consciousness of the white people, the race consciousness of all peoples, must be taken into consideration. We believe that this is better for the colored people. We believe that that is necessary to us.

Northern commissioners, particularly Bishop John W. Hamilton, resisted the notion that race consciousness should govern unification schemes:

You have all been talking as though these colored brethren were as clay, capable of being molded into a desired form, plastic in the hands of white people, as if we could handle them at our pleasure and do with them as we chose. There are difficulties in this matter that you brethren ought to see. In the first place, we have a body of colored brethren in our Church.... We have treated them as men and brothers. We have made no distinction in the rights they sustain of relationship to our membership, just as is the case with you in your foreign mission fields.... We have nearly 350,000 colored members within our borders, each of whom has the rights of every white member....

Now, are we going to stand up and take each one of these members individually and say to him: "You go off?" But go off where?... I have no more right to tell him to go out of our Church than he has to tell me to do the same.[107]

Such high moral ground proved difficult to hold, particularly since—as the southern commissioners were ever ready to point out—the MEC had largely segregated African Americans into separate annual conferences and congregations (see maps, Sources, pp. 26–27). Bishop E. E. Hoss responded,

If you are going to magnify the impropriety of drawing the color line, you must take it out of your Discipline; you must abolish the colored Conferences. What more wrong is there in a colored General Conference than in a colored Annual Conference? Show me a single white Church that has a colored pastor in your denomination or a single colored Church that has a white pastor in your denomination.

Registering Black acceptance of the status quo, one of the two African American commissioners, I. G. (Garland) Penn, replied,

The concession in the matter of the negro and his status cannot come from the Methodist Episcopal Church. These people are members of the Church like anybody else.... The white people have not drawn the color line in the Methodist Episcopal Church without our consent.... I have even written certain pages of the Discipline myself which drew the color line.... The colored people have colored Annual Conferences because they preferred such. All that there is in the colored line in the Church is with their consent.... The colored people are ready to be a jurisdiction of the united Church, with their own bishops and representation in the General Conference.[108]

Hamilton proved a lonely voice in resisting a race-conscious plan. One of the few other moral witnesses against racism and a racial division of the church came from an unnamed southern woman who wrote the commission a long letter of protest, calling for a vision "of the truth of God's word to teach us the right relation to our fellow man"; it was read into the record by R. E. Blackwell.[109] The jurisdictional scheme gradually emerged through the discussions as a structure (1) that would provide regional configurations among white Methodists, thus protecting the southern (white) minority from domination by the northern majority, and (2) that would establish a "compromise" between the southern desire for a CME-like solution and the northern resistance to a unification that would further divide the church and expel its Black members. Supporting such a compromise were the two African American (MEC) commissioners, I. Garland Penn and Robert E. Jones, who viewed jurisdictions as much preferable to excision, who did not aspire to union with the other Black Methodist bodies, and who welcomed a plan that would, at last, provide for Black episcopal leadership. They resisted what became another southern stratagem in the discussions, namely, a conference embracing both Africa and the U.S.[110] Jones, editor of the *Southwestern Christian Advocate* and future bishop, affirmed (Sources 1918a, p. 495; 1921) interracial cooperation and willingness to live with a (jurisdictional) conference within the U.S. and to so limit the jurisdiction of African American bishops. But, he insisted, "first of all, we do not want any caste written in the Constitution. That is fundamental. Second, we do not want any offensive name in whatever arrangement you make.... And it is fundamental that we should ask for representation in the General Conference." He sought to allay "any fear that any of our bishops shall ever preside over a white Conference."[111]

The Joint Commission reached just such an agreement, indeed guarantee, after five years of discussions,[112] a scheme for six white regional conferences, one for the "colored people in the United States," and four for membership in overseas conferences.[113] African American Methodists would be represented in General Conference, though not in the same proportions as would the white regional conferences (jurisdictions), and the foreign representation was even more reduced. To these regional conferences were conferred the rights of episcopal election, plans that a few commissioners recognized as divisive and constitutionally problematic. Bishop R. J. Cooke affirmed,

> We were sent here to unify the Church, not to divide it; but with these Regional Conferences with such regional powers we are dividing the Church again. We may deny it, and keep on denying it; but you do not do away with the thing. Where is your episcopacy? Were we sent here to destroy the itinerant general superintendency?

E. C. Reeves concurred, "That is what we are doing." Bishop Cooke continued, "Of course, and we know it, no matter what we say to the contrary. You know very well you have not got itinerant general superintendency in regional superintendency as localized in your regions. We all know that. And we were not sent here to do that."[114] In addition, provision was made for a judicial council and for a brake on General Conference action by vote of two regional delegations.[115]

The MEC General Conference met first (in 1920), and in putting forward the "unification" plan, the MEC bishops asked,

> 1. Does the movement make for a real brotherhood of Christian people? 2. Does the movement make for the real unity of all sections, races, nations, and classes within Christ's Church? 3. Does the movement make for unity of life, unity of sacrificial, atoning purpose toward men, unity in the holiness and passion of the church's life, like the unity between Christ and the Father? 4. Does the movement make for evangelistic efficiency and the triumph of the cross among all peoples, all classes, all races, and on all continents?

They went on to say,

> For the Church of Christ is not a racial church. The Church of Christ is not a national, sectional, or class church. Plans of union that sectionalize, that nationalize, that racialize the church are not plans for Christian union.[116]

The conference found other aspects of the plan troubling and, while reaffirming its commitment to unity, continued its commission and called for the convening of a Joint General Convention (of the MEC and the MECS) to iron out problems.[117] This General Conference recognized the service on behalf of unity of Robert E. Jones and his forceful advocacy, as editor, of the necessity for Black bishops (Sources 1912a) by electing him to the episcopacy, providing him yet another platform to pursue interracial cooperation (Sources 1921). Elected along with him as the first and long-desired African American itinerant general superintendents for service in the U.S. was Matthew W. Clair Sr., then presiding elder in the Washington Conference.

Where the MEC saw problems, the MECS experienced crisis. Virtual warfare broke out in the South over unification, warfare that badly divided the College of Bishops, roiled annual conferences, inflamed passions in MECS *Advocates*, and politicized the entire church. Progressives supported the commission's plan. To oppose it, conservatives formed organizations like the League for the Preservation of Southern Methodism. The party lines reinforced and were reinforced, as we note elsewhere in this chapter, by several other controversies of the 1920s and 1930s—reorganization, the Klan (Sources 1922), Prohibition (Sources 1916), fundamentalism, evolution, and Al Smith's presidential campaign.[118] Each issue entailed the others. Unification came to emblematize conservative fears of African Americans, the North, change, modernism, and secularism.

By its temporizing action of 1920, the MEC took the MECS General Conference of 1922 off the hook. The MECS rejected the notion of such a Joint General Convention but continued a commission and authorized the calling of a special session of its General Conference if the commissioners were able to work out a viable plan.

This new Joint Commission met in early 1923 and adopted a new plan, which continued some features of the 1916–20 proposal. It addressed southern racial and regional concerns by establishing just two white jurisdictions, one embracing the MEC, the other the MECS. The MEC General Conference adopted it with little fanfare, as did its annual and lay conferences (for its action on world peace, see Sources 1924a). By contrast, the MECS experienced a very tense special session General Conference, marked by prolonged debate over a procedural amendment proposed by A. J. Lamar and supported by four bishops. The Lamar motion challenged the legality of the special session and called for a year's delay.[119] The southern church eventually defeated the Lamar Resolution and passed the plan but not before the opposition to unification had scored its points, many of them detailed in a twenty-five-page Minority Report. The minority insisted that the issues of 1844 were not dead, that the plan surrendered the liberty and independence of the church, that it "practically strips the Annual Conferences of all power in the government of the Church" and confers it on "the Super-General Conference," and that "it established a relation with the negro race not best for him, not possible for us."[120]

Such sentiments carried the day when the plan was submitted, as such fundamental constitutional changes required, to the MECS annual conferences. New organizations emerged, the Friends of Unification and the Association to Preserve The Methodist Episcopal Church, South, by Defeating the Pending Plan of Unification. Each enjoyed backing within the church press and patronage on the College of Bishops. The southern *Advocates*, twenty for unification, six against, hoisted the battle banners. The bishops voiced their sentiments, employed their appointive power for their side of the cause, and used and abused their presiding role to sway annual conference votes. As leaned the presiding bishop, so voted the conference, with one exception.[121] The plan went down to defeat, 4,528 for and 4,108 against, far short of the required 75 percent and indicative of how badly divided the southern church found itself. Convening again two years later in regular session, the MECS accepted the recommendation of its Committee on Church Relations "That there be no agitation, discussion, or negotiation concerning unification during the ensuing quadrennium."[122]

As if to supply the controversy that the southern church had determined to avoid, the 1928 MEC General Conference seemed to concern itself throughout with the "color" of Methodism. It debated the powers and prerogatives of the central conferences, many of them in Africa and Asia. It elected bishops for such conferences, including E. Stanley Jones (who resigned his election). It brought to the podium by resolution and heard a speech from Dr. I. Garland Penn, senior member of the General Conference and one of the two African American representatives on the Joint Commission of 1916–20. It was presided over by the other African American representative, Bishop Robert E. Jones. And subsequently, it passed a resolution recognizing his precedent-setting presidency "as welcome evidence of a new and better day." It paid tribute to Bishop William A. Quayle as friend to "the Negro race" and effective mediator during the East St. Louis race riot. It recognized Mrs. M. A. Camphor, delegate from Delaware and widow of African missionary Bishop Camphor. It passed a resolution calling for equal educational opportunity in the South. It recognized the service of Joseph C. Hartzell "to the African race both in the United States and in Africa." It passed a motion against U.S. policy restricting "immigration and the rights of citizenship on grounds of race and color." It passed a resolution recognizing Melville Cox and the centenary of Liberian missions. It celebrated Mary McLeod Bethune, especially for her presidency of the National Federated Clubs of Colored Women.[123]

In response, Bishop Edwin D. Mouzon (MECS) proclaimed that these actions "postponed the union of the Church South and the Church North indefinitely."[124] Was a bishop like Mouzon merely a lone voice crying in the wilderness? Or was there a large residue of like opinion in the northern church? A partial answer was contained in the results of a poll conducted by the Evanston-based MEC newspaper, the *Northwestern Christian Advocate,* in February 1932. One of the questions the pollsters asked was: "Are you satisfied with the church's present attitude and action on the following subjects?" Race was one. Five thousand ministers and laypersons responded. They approved the church's policy of racial segregation by a five-to-one margin![125]

The MEC and the MPC continued conversations in the late 1920s and early 1930s, and the MECS rejoined in 1934, the resumption preceded by national youth gatherings, informal meetings of interested leaders, and exploratory sessions of standing commissions on union. The three churches formally authorized negotiations in General Conferences of 1932 and 1934. Yet another Joint Commission met in 1934 and 1935, accepted the principles of jurisdictional governance and full lay representation, and appointed a drafting subcommittee.

The new committee's plan reverted to the 1916–20 conception of multiple (white) regional jurisdictions and one central (black) jurisdiction. It provided for equal representation of laity and clergy in annual, jurisdictional, and general conferences; the retention of bishops and establishment of a Council of Bishops; a Judicial Council related to General Conference and the Council of Bishops; and a new name, The Methodist Church.

The plan was criticized by key denominational leaders, especially by Methodist women, including the southern women who for a decade and a half had labored through the Commission on Interracial Co-operation for better race relations (see separate discussion in this chapter and Sources 1936b). In the 1936 MEC General Conference many progressive leaders opposed the plan (Sources 1936a; map, p. 27). Mary McLeod Bethune (1875–1955), daughter of former slaves, speaking for Black conferences, pointedly urged delegates to reject the plan. Bethune, a four-time delegate to Methodist General Conferences, had been recognized two quadrennia earlier for her leadership. She had founded the Daytona Educational and Industrial Training School for Negro Girls in Daytona Beach, Florida, in 1904 (merged in 1923 with Cookman Institute to become coeducational Bethune-Cookman College)[126] and the Mary McLeod Hospital and Training School for Nurses in 1911, the only such school for African Americans on the East Coast. When the nation mobilized its resources for the First and Second World Wars, she pressed for the integration of the American Red Cross and Women's Army Auxiliary Corps. By the 1930's Bethune had become a powerful leader in civil rights and higher education. She worked tirelessly with the National Association of Colored Women's Clubs, then in 1935 founded the National Council of Negro Women, and became a valued member of Eleanor Roosevelt's "kitchen cabinet," advising the Roosevelt administration on minority affairs. Bethune indicated her unwillingness "to have the history of this General Conference written, and the Negro youths of fifty or a hundred years from today read and find that Mary McLeod Bethune acquiesced to anything that looked like segregation to black people." Methodists, however, decided that her advice should not stop progress toward unification.

In the end the MEC General Conference voted 470 for and 83 against the plan of union. The plan passed in General Conferences of the other two churches and in annual conferences of all three, again eliciting opposition in the South[127] and this time producing considerable anguish in African American conferences and among others committed to more genuine Methodist fraternity. African Americans contributed 36 of the 83 "no" votes in the 1936 MEC General Conference, 11 others abstaining (Sources 1936a). They sat in silence while the conference sang "We're Marching to Zion." Seven of the nineteen Black conferences defeated the proposal, a few others refusing to vote, the remainder resigning themselves to the inevitable.[128] Just as the nation was becoming more sensitive to its racial inequalities and to segregation as a blight on democracy, Methodism had made more visible and constitutional the color line it had long drawn within its fraternity, a step backward that southern white Methodist women clearly recognized (Sources 1936b). A united Methodism would be jurisdictioned, divided by race and region—all the African American conferences and most of its congregations gathered into one Central Jurisdiction, and white Methodism united by regions. Within the jurisdictions, the plan lodged the really critical "connectional" powers—namely, the election and deployment of bishops and the election of the governing board members of the national agencies. Unity? Or federalism in a new guise?

CHAPTER XIII

WARRING FOR WORLD ORDER AND AGAINST WORLDLINESS WITHIN: 1939–68

Christians seek unity that the world might believe. Pursuing that vision, Methodists united in 1939, the Evangelical and United Brethren churches in 1946, and EUBs and Methodists in 1968. Methodists and EUBs played important roles, moreover, in the multilateral and bilateral projects of the period—world, national, and state councils of churches; the Consultation on Church Union; and Vatican II–inspired Protestant-Catholic conversations. But a Methodist union predicated on racism and connection-ally structured segregation rendered a strange witness for the oneness of Christ's body. So Methodists plunged into a protracted war within, EUBs holding out for dissolution of the Central Jurisdiction as key to the 1968 union. Both churches also found them-selves embroiled in the wars without—WWII, Korea police-keeping, cold war, and Viet-nam. Initially it looked as though Methodism, led by its bishops, would play a huge role in bringing peace, order, and justice to the world. A house or a church divided against itself stands with difficulty, however, and The Methodist Church in particular—its poli-cies, practices, and governance accommodated to southern white preconditions for unity—found itself struggling for the whole period with internal structural stresses. Among its unfinished business were what to do about ordination and full conference membership for women and how to redefine the relation between General Conference and the U.S.-based mission boards and the churches that missions had spread across the globe.

Methodism and a New World Order

As the world's military powers marched toward another world war, the three Methodist and the Evangelical and United Brethren churches deepened their pacifist witness.[1] And on the very eve of war, the newly united Methodist Church urged Presi-dent Roosevelt to "avoid entanglement" in the unfolding world war and called on pastors to "train our children . . . in the arts of peace."[2] Such pacifist sentiments, under-girded by the prophetic critique of WWI, were widely held. Sixty-two percent of Methodist respondents to a 1931 national opinion poll of Protestant ministers had insisted that churches should refuse to support or sanction war. A 1936 MEC poll conducted by Bishop James C. Baker yielded 12,854 responses, over half of whom indicated that they would not sanction war.[3] Pacifism reigned in seminaries and annual conferences. Youth and young adult ministries and publications emphasized peace programming. The 1935 National Council of Methodist Youth proposed and requested general agency support for a national student strike against war.[4] The latter demurred, but mid-decade General Conferences of three converging members of the Methodist family of churches went on record favoring peace over war.[5] The MEC Commission on World Peace began in 1936 to register conscientious objectors (COs) with the government. Two years later, a full-page ad in the church's leading magazine called war "futile," "stupid," and "unholy."[6] In 1939, a national Methodist Peace Fellowship formed.

Theologians like Georgia Harkness (Garrett Biblical Institute, see Sources 1947b) and pacifist pastors like Ernest Tittle (First MEC, Evanston) continued to make their witness.[7] Tittle, for instance, added his anti-intervention witness to that of fellow Methodist Albert E. Day in the *Christian Century* series "If America enters the war— what should *I* do?" Bishop Francis J. McConnell, one of ten prominent religious leaders, including Reinhold Niebuhr and Harry Emerson Fosdick, approved a U.S. defensive entry. The 1940 Methodist General Conference passed and lodged in the *Discipline* a series of resolutions pertaining to war: a "Declaration of Patriotic Principles," a long "Statement on Peace and War," one titled "Peace," and a final one, "Aggressor Nations."[8] While pledging its patriotic loyalty and recognizing that Christians, including Methodists, differ on "what a Christian should do when his nation becomes involved in war," General Conference exhorted its leaders "to devise ways and means to keep the will to peace intelligence vocal and determined to help keep the United States out of war" and urged that every church and conference establish a peace commission. Bob Shuler, by 1941 already one of Methodism's best-known preachers, commended the "conscientious soldier" in a February 1941 article in the church's monthly magazine.[9] The spring of 1941 brought the nation and the churches one step closer to war, but the UBC General Conference continued to press for peace. Although making no attempt to bind the consciences of individual members, the conference pledged itself not to officially endorse, support, or participate in war. It promised conscientious objectors the support of the church.

Within months after the conference adjourned, the nation was at war, testing the peace resolve of the three denominations (MC, EC, and UBC). The December 1941 attack on Pearl Harbor further split opinion in the churches, some for collective security, others for nonintervention. MC conferences, heavily pacifist prewar, shifted toward support for the war.[10] Less than a year after Pearl Harbor, the Evangelical Church gathered for its General Conference. The 1942 conference affirmed the long-standing position of the church that "war and bloodshed are not agreeable to the Gospel of Jesus Christ," recognized the status of conscientious objectors, and approved the office and ministry of military chaplains, but added that such action was "not to be construed as implying the endorsement of war by our church."[11]

The second General Conference of The Methodist Church met two and a half years after the nation was officially at war. By that point Protestants had begun to grasp the enormity of the evil with which the Allies contended, a more serious crisis, insisted *Zion's Herald* editor, L. O. Hartman, than the civilized world had ever faced.[12] Would the Methodists in 1944 maintain their prewar pacifist stand as the Evangelicals had done? Two reports, "The Church in Time of War," were presented, a majority report reaffirming the position of 1939–40, along with a minority report that blessed the war, prayed for victory, and called for an all-out war effort. Pacifist Ernest Tittle introduced the majority report for the Committee on the State of the Church seeking reaffirmation of the 1940 resolution on peace and war. The majority report proudly applauded conscientious objectors, but offered no prayers for Allied victory. The dean of Drew Theological Seminary, Lynn Harold Hough, offered the minority report as a substitute resolution on behalf of seventeen of the sixty-four active committee members. "Must the Christian church condemn all use of military force?" it asked. Civilization was attacked by the forces of aggression. "God himself has a stake in the struggle." Intolerable wrongs had been committed. The state and the Christian are duty bound to fight to correct them. Use of military force is a necessity. U.S. citizens are already serving in the armed forces, and we "are sending over a million young men from Methodist homes to participate in the conflict."[13] After heated floor debate, the minority resolution prevailed by a 55 percent majority. The troubled conscience of Methodism on matters of war and peace was shared by the UBC, which met for its last General Conference during the closing year of the war. Delegates and bishops declared themselves "heartily in favor of the cessation of hostilities at the earliest possible hour, and of peace terms aimed to preserve peace and not avenge wrongs."[14]

Attitudes toward the war and the Allied cause evolved as Methodism threw itself into various war-related ministries—provision and support of chaplains, alternative service by conscientious objectors, relief efforts, and efforts to envision a postwar world. To alert individuals and churches to their responsibility for the victims of world war, Bishop Herbert Welch called on the 1940 Atlantic City General Conference to "constitute an agency to respond to the vast needs of human suffering around the world." Bishop Welch envisioned a relief body that would be a "voice of conscience among Methodists to act in the relief of human suffering without distinction of race, color or creed." General Conference responded with a Methodist Committee for Overseas Relief (MCOR).

Between 1940 and 1945, MCOR responded to the plight of thirty million refugees suffering in the midst of world war in China, as well as North Africa and Europe—providing assistance to those who had left everything behind and were living in camps or relocating in other countries and helping thousands of refugees resettle in the U.S. Later MCOR (after merger, UMCOR) moved beyond relief to training programs to instill skills that would make communities self-supporting and self-reliant and eventually to a third emphasis: to work for the renewal of life through the alleviation of the root causes of hunger.[15] Relief continued after the war, thanks to the Advance Program, a major churchwide "second-mile" giving program of the Board of Missions. Inaugurated in 1948, Advance giving enabled the church to cope with disasters, heal the sick, shelter the homeless, feed the hungry, and share the faith in the postwar world. While local churches were called to support the denomination first through World Service and other apportioned funds, the Advance offered individuals, church groups, congregations, districts, and conferences a way to voluntarily select and support specific ministries. The Advance became one of the great success stories of modern Methodism and has changed the lives of persons all over the globe for the better.[16]

The draft legislation for WWII (1940) provided for clergy deferment and for some rights for COs. The latter differed from those of WWI in recognizing the classification for personal religious convictions rather than on membership in a pacifist church. The legislation also provided for work of national importance as an alternative to military service. During the war, more than 15,000 registered as COs, two-thirds from "peace churches" (Mennonites, Quakers, and Brethren) but including a considerable number of Methodists and other mainline church members. Many served without remuneration in Civilian Public Service camps. About 5,000 others were sent to prison, either because they refused to register or because their objection was based on political grounds inadmissible under the law. Methodist seminarian George Houser, studying at Union Theological Seminary in New York, unrepentant after serving a year and a day in Danbury prison for refusing to register for the draft, publicized his dissent in *Motive*, Methodism's magazine for college students.[17] Concurring, the first convocation of the Methodist Youth Fellowship, in various statements, expressed concern for COs and conscientious soldiers, for alternative service opportunities, and for ways of participating in peace making (Sources 1942b).

In spite of the splendid work done by chaplains in World War I and the continuing ministry of those who became regulars, the church gave little recognition and practically no support to the ministry of chaplains in the interwar years. In 1941, realizing the critical conditions facing the world, the Council of Bishops (COB) of The Methodist Church created a Methodist Emergency Committee. The COB charged the committee with exploring the need for rendering special aid to communities adjacent to military bases. It also bore responsibility for recruiting, endorsing, and assisting chaplains ordered to active duty. In the latter part of 1942, as the church's ministry to the military grew, the bishops established a permanent Commission on Chaplains. Its function now clearly defined, the commission's top priorities were the recruitment and careful screening of chaplains. Methodist chaplains ministered to military personnel throughout the world. A devotional booklet for servicemen, *Strength for Service to God and Country*, reached a circulation of 720,000 in its first year (1942–43) and set an all-time record for a single year's sales in the entire 144 years of Methodist publishing. A million copies were distributed by war's end. The booklet has been twice revised and reprinted, in 1969 for use by the military in Vietnam and again in 2003 for use in the second Iraq War, this time sponsored by the Commission on United Methodist Men. Local churches close to military facilities provided spiritual, moral, and social services to training staff and trainees.[18]

Methodists, Evangelicals, and United Brethren alike developed a sustaining conviction about the need for a responsible world political organization to promote peace with justice. Methodist agency on this cause was spearheaded by Bishop G. Bromley Oxnam, COB secretary, member of the Commission on a Just and Durable Peace of the Federal Council of Churches, and close colleague in that initiative with John Foster Dulles, active Presbyterian layperson, foreign policy counselor and to be Secretary of State under President Dwight Eisenhower. With Oxnam's prodding, the COB mounted a parallel campaign on behalf of organized peace, of an international organization to safeguard peace, and of American participation therein—the "Bishops' Crusade for a New World Order." As his biographer explains, "It might with justice be named 'Oxnam's Crusade.' The idea originated with him, was given its initial impetus by him, was largely planned by him, and more than by another single individual, was implemented by him." Oxnam lobbied Washington personally; he wrote ferociously; he spoke everywhere; he ordered literature—2,000,000 copies of one leaflet, 600,000 of another, and 75,000 of a leaders' guide. The boards and agencies threw themselves vigorously into the effort. Women went house to house passing out the first pamphlet, "*Your Part*." Educational efforts did not stop with church members. The Methodist Commission on Public Information worked with nationwide broadcast networks. Three worldwide broadcasts took place with the help of the U.S. Office of War Information. Mass rallies for January 1944 drew some 200,000 Methodists in seventy-six cities. And all Methodists, young and old, Oxnam charged with writing the president, the Senate, and the House of Representatives on behalf of world peace, justice, brotherhood, and order. The letter-writing slogan? "The Peace May Be Won with a Three-Cent Stamp." Methodism's new conversion culminated in a day of consecration, March 26, 1944. The 1944 General Conference came around on this cause in seeing the war as instrumental to a new world order. Oxnam would later tell President Roosevelt that Methodists had contributed a million letters on behalf of the United Nations.[19] Earlier President Roosevelt publicly commended the Methodists for undertaking the "Crusade"[20] (Sources 1943).

Four years of study, worship, and action built support for the founding of the United Nations and committed the church to postwar reconstruction and church growth. When American Protestantism in 1945 rallied behind the United Nations, the moral and political voice of the U.S., in part at least, had been shaped by Methodism's brilliant crusade. A second four-year Crusade for Christ (1944–48) challenged the church to raise $25 million for world rehabilitation and relief. In addition to rebuilding efforts across the globe, the Crusade launched a Crusade Scholars program that supported study in the U.S. for international and minority students. The war had destroyed many Methodist educational institutions in Europe, China, Japan, and the South Pacific. The scholarship committee preferred younger candidates, not more than thirty years of age, so as to develop new leadership in war-devastated countries. By 1948, three hundred students had been brought to the U.S. as Crusade Scholars. By its half-century mark it could claim among its recipients Bishops Ole Borgen, Emilio Carvalho, Joseph Humper, Arthur Kulah, Dinesh Agarwal, José Gamboa, Emerito Nacpil, Paul Mattos, Frederico Pagura, Joel Martinez, and Melvin Talbert. Other scholars included Makarios III, Greek Orthodox archbishop and later president of Cypress; Graca Machal, first lady of Mozambique; Brazilian Lucia Panicett, president of its women's organization; Carmel de Dias, a Peruvian educator; José Bonino, a theologian; Emilio Castro, WCC general secretary; Homer Noley, a Native American scholar-pastor-mission executive; and Thomas Roughface, Native American district superintendent. The seeds of money and support that were put into the program by the church yielded harvests beyond all expectations. The program continues to provide quality education for international students in diverse contexts. The church actually raised $27 million—in addition to oversubscribing a $24 million World Service (mission) budget. The membership of the church was about 8 million then, but the dollar's buying power was far greater. In 1948, General Conference "re-upped" with a "Quadrennial Plan for Christ and His Church," and an important feature, Advance Specials, invited congregations and conferences to over-and-above giving targeted to particular missional projects.[21]

The Holocaust, Japanese Internment, Hiroshima, and Nagasaki

Although Methodist leaders expressed horror at Nazi attitudes and countered domestic anti-Semitism, they remained mostly blind to the limitations of their own "Waspish" perspectives. Some considered the possibility of a Jewish massacre in Germany, but tended to dismiss it. The Methodist press published only occasional stories about what later came to be called the Holocaust. Deceived by Allied propaganda during WWI, Methodists tended not to believe the worst stories about German behavior in this war. Instead they relied on the State Department for information, which was less than forthcoming about what it knew. Only later, after gazing into the pit of hell with the rest of the world, did Methodists learn the truth about the Nazi extermination campaign. On the fiftieth anniversary of Kristallnacht, the beginning of the Holocaust, in 1988, United Methodist bishops in East and West Germany issued a pastoral letter.

Despite intelligence reports that deemed the overwhelming majority of Japanese Americans loyal to the U.S., President Roosevelt's 1942 Executive Order 9066 authorized the military to remove 120,000 Japanese Americans from their West Coast homes to hastily built relocation camps in remote areas of several western states—Idaho, Oregon, and Washington. Internment produced great hardships: loss of jobs, property, and businesses; separation of fathers from families; barracks-style living; long lines for meals and showers; and loss of privacy and other threats to family integrity, in short, concentration camp conditions.[22] Popular (and racist) support for the internment on the West Coast was replicated in Chicago and other urban areas as Japanese Americans were resettled, producing tensions and conflict between and among Asian, black, and white communities. Some Methodists spoke decisively against such racism and against the policies of internment and relocation, notably the newly constituted Woman's Division (Sources 1942a).[23] Ecumenist-evangelist E. Stanley Jones detailed the life of "Barbed-Wire Christians" in the *Christian Century*.[24] And the Methodist Youth Fellowship, gathered for convocation in 1942, after receiving a greeting from an internment camp, responded with an offering (Sources 1942b, p. 562).[25] The COB in that year called attention to the plight of Japanese Americans and promoted Methodist involvement in resettlement. The 1944 MC General Conference, however, took little notice of Japanese internment.

The church received the August 1945 news that atomic bombs had been dropped on Hiroshima and Nagasaki and that Japan had sued for peace with simultaneous expressions of joy and fear. North American Methodists became aware that Methodist churches in Hiroshima and Nagasaki had been destroyed,[26] and all U.S. citizens become aware that one bomb can kill hundreds of thousands of persons instantly, fatally injure another hundred thousand, and reduce whole cities to rubble. One of the first contributions to the ethical debate about the use of nuclear weapons came from the Federal Council of Churches (FCC) on August 9, 1945, after the bombing of Hiroshima but before the bombing of Nagasaki. Bishop G. Bromley Oxnam, then president of the council, issued a statement (after conferring with FCC colleagues Dulles and others) requesting that no more bombs be dropped and fearing that continued use of nuclear weapons by a Christian nation would make them an acceptable part of warfare. Prominent clergy sent a letter to President Truman expressing the same sentiments, and a critical mass of Methodists began to condemn nuclear weapons. The Methodist Federation for Social Action was among the first Methodist organizations to comment on the bomb. And *Christian Advocate* editor Roy Smith pondered the morality of such superweapons. "We have sinned," editorialized *Motive*, and later (1949) invited the father of the atomic bomb, Albert Einstein, to comment on his progeny.[27]

Resolutely pacifist prewar, Methodism emerged from the traumas of WWII as chastened, realistic about the perilousness of peace, increasingly aware that wartime ally Communist Russia was no longer a partner and troubled by the future that atomic warfare opened. The General Conferences of 1948 and 1952 passed strong resolutions on peace, world relief, and support for the United Nations. The Methodist Peace Fellowship pushed pledge cards. Shortly afterward, in 1948, the FCC appointed a commission of Christian scholars to prepare a report to the churches on the use of nuclear weapons. The report, "The Christian Conscience and Weapons of Mass Destruction," issued in 1950, gave qualified approval as a deterrent to war. Georgia Harkness, the only Methodist theologian on the commission, publicly dissented.[28]

Council of Bishops, Judicial Council, Conferences, Agencies[29]

Bishop Nolan Harmon had very little to say about the Council of Bishops in *The Organization of The Methodist Church*, even when in 1962 he revised this authoritative survey of Methodist polity. Indeed, acknowledging the prominent spokesperson roles played earlier by the MECS College of Bishops and the salience, postunification, of comparable prophetic pronouncements by the church's boards and agencies, he urged the bishops not to give up such authority, which after all, they had exercised during WWII (see above).[30] The *Discipline* charged the COB to meet at least once a year and "plan for the general oversight and promotion of the temporal and spiritual interests of the entire Church."[31] And as we have already seen, under the guidance of Secretary Oxnam, the COB indeed lived into such a charge with the New World Order mobilization for relief and peacemaking. As his biographer indicates, Oxnam functioned as the COB's executive, setting agenda for meetings, ordering the proceedings, taking elaborate minutes, overseeing follow-up, arranging meetings with political figures, and in various ways energizing the COB. Fearing that the bishops would, as they subsequently did, reorient their horizons to the jurisdictions within which their primary duties were set, Oxnam arranged for a Plan of Visitation that would send each American bishop abroad once a quadrennium.[32] Had Oxnam continued to focus his energies on and pursue his interests through the COB even for the duration of his term as secretary (retiring in 1955), the COB might well have sustained its connectional wartime prophetic and teaching office roles. But Oxnam threw himself into the public roles that his assignments to New York and then Washington offered, oversaw the church's mission enterprise, carried the torch for mainline Protestantism, labored for the Federal and National Councils of Churches, shaped denominational ministerial educational policy, presided over the Council on World Service and Finance, fought McCarthyism (see below), and tended to the requisite episcopal appointment-making duties.

The COB would eventually reclaim the public role that Oxnam envisioned for it (or at least for himself as its effective head), as we shall see in the last chapter. For the period covered by this chapter, both the COB and the jurisdictional Colleges carried on their prescribed nominating and deploying duties but devoted much of their life together to becoming family for one another, letting their gatherings function as their "conference," adjusting to jurisdictional life, and building the old-boy relationships that the 1970s would work to upend.[33] And gradually the regional jurisdictions adjusted their notions of what constitutes episcopal timber, recalibrated what experience and exposure counted, passed over agency executives and others with connectional experience, and increasingly elected bishops from tall steeple churches, the district superintendency, and regional institutional leadership.[34]

Judicial Council

The case for a judicial council and provision for judicial review had long and different histories in the three churches.[35] The Methodist Protestants claimed the shortest, perhaps, with their creation in 1920 of a connectional Executive Committee, the last recourse for rulings of conference presidents or appeals against appointments. For the two episcopal churches, the foundation lay in the 1840 General Conference decision to entrust to the bishop decisions on "all questions of law in an annual conference, subject to an appeal to the General Conference; but in all cases the application of law shall be with the conference."[36] The 1844 division and quite different construals of the relative and relational powers of bishops and General Conference produced distinctive ways of dealing with rulings and decisions. The southern church in 1854 empowered the bishops, acting collectively and in writing, with the prerogative of challenging a rule or regulation and thereby obliging General Conference to muster a two-thirds majority on the question. This action, consonant with its understanding of conference and episcopacy, the MECS confirmed and clarified in 1874.[37] Consonant with its understanding of conference and episcopacy, the northern church proceeded in a different fashion, namely, by generating from out of General Conference itself and out of conference procedure a body with judicial authority. General Conference had served as the supreme court to which appeal was made from annual conference judicial decisions and rulings on the law by presiding bishops. From 1860 to 1872 the General Conference had established a Committee of Appeals and referred such matters to it. In 1876, the MEC established a Judiciary Committee, a body of twelve ("one from each General Conference District") "to consider and report their decision on all questions of law coming up to us from Judicial Conferences."[38] And in 1884, the body's authority was extended to include "all records of Judicial Conference, appeals on points of law, and all proposed changes in the Ecclesiastical Code."[39]

Both the MEC committee and the southern College of Bishops would thereafter render "court" decisions, thereby leaving a body of *connectional* law.[40] The MECS actually proceeded in formal fashion to direct its compilation, voting in its 1866 General

Conference to request the bishops "to prepare for publication a Commentary on the Discipline, embracing Episcopal decisions, with a view to produce a harmonious administration thereof."[41] That produced Holland N. McTyeire's *Manual of the Discipline of The Methodist Episcopal Church, South, including the Decisions of the College of Bishops,* a volume regularly updated.[42] The northern church proceeded somewhat later and in less formal fashion to compile a comparable manual. In 1903 Bishop Richard J. Cooke produced *The Judicial Decisions of the General Conference of The Methodist Episcopal Church.*[43] Another major compilation was undertaken in 1924 at the behest of General Conference.[44]

A separate body entrusted with the power of judicial review—not General Conference ruling on its own legislation or the bishops collectively confirming their individual rulings—became one of the MECS's several nonnegotiables, essentially from the beginning of the discussions. So insisted Bishop Warren Candler in 1916 in stating his understanding of powers and duties conferred by the MECS upon the southern commissioners.[45] In 1934, the southern General Conference created a Judicial Council, the one feature of a proposed new constitution to pass, and thus removed that prerogative from its College of Bishops. The Uniting Conference created an interim Judicial Council, and the 1940 MC General Conference, the statutes for the permanent body. And of course, the 1968 EUBC-MC union continued the Judicial Council.

Elected by General Conference from slates proposed by the bishops or nominated from the floor and staggered by quadrennia so as to provide continuity,[46] the Judicial Council, a body of nine (five clergy and four laity), succeeded in functioning as prescribed. It rules on the constitutionality of General Conference legislation, on the legality of actions taken by any connectional entity, and on decisions by bishops in annual conferences. In 1944, General Conference entrusted the Judicial Council also with declaratory decisions on the meaning of provisions of the *Discipline* or of proposed changes. The Judicial Council elects its president, vice president, and secretary, established its own Rules of Practice and Procedure, hears oral arguments on cases before it, and renders and publishes its decisions, concurrences, and dissents.[47]

The church has constituted the Judicial Council with an eye to its critical role, for instance, regularly including lawyers in the lay contingent. All four laypersons initially elected were attorneys, including the secretary, Henry R. Van Deusen. In 1948, another lawyer and the first African American, J. Earnest Wilkins, was elected. He was made secretary in 1953, and the following year appointed Undersecretary of Labor for International Labor Affairs by President Dwight Eisenhower. In 1968 the first woman and additional African Americans were elected: Kathryn Mowrey Grove, president of the EUBC Women's Society of World Service, and Dr. Charles B. Copher (clergy) and Theodore M. Berry (lay). The first clergywoman to serve is its post-2008 president, Susan T. Henry-Crowe, elected in 1992 (Susan Morrison had been elected in 1988 but was also elected to the episcopacy that summer). In 2000 the first Central Conference member, Rodolfo C. Beltran, was elected. That year also saw the politicization of the election process by Good News.

Annual Conferences

Unification changed the experience of annual conference for much of Methodism, especially for clergy of the former MEC, for Methodist Protestants generally, and for clergy and laity where the three churches overlapped—that is, across the Bible Belt from the Delmarva Peninsula to California. Bishop Harmon seized on two of the changes in dedicating *The Organization of The Methodist Church* to his MECS comrades of the Old Baltimore Conference who, for the sake of union, were dispersed into four different MC conferences and in noting that the addition of laity doubled the size of MEC conferences. Not many conferences could claim, as Harmon posited for Baltimore, 155 "years of unbroken Conference life," but radical disruption was a common experience, except perhaps in the Deep South.[48] Even there, white Methodists from former MEC or MPC conferences experienced dispersal. In Texas, clergy members of the MEC Southern Conference, which earlier had brought together the Southern German, Gulf (northern transplants), and Swedish Mission conferences, were transferred into six MC conferences.[49] (We treat African American conferences in the next section of this chapter.)

Northern all-clergy, all-male MEC conferences, even where left largely intact geographically, doubled in size with the addition of laity (men and women) as these statistics for Baltimore and Philadelphia indicate:[50]

| | Baltimore[51] | | | Philadelphia | |
Year	Clergy	Laity		Clergy	Laity
1860	73	0			
1870	115	"		118	0
1880	146	"		155	"
1890	144	"		156	"
1900	160	"		240	"
1910	178	"		215	"
1920	217	"		254	"
1930	202	"		217	"
1940	294	233		258	232

Former members of small MPC conferences were thrown into these aggregations of strangers.[52]

The Virginia Conference of the new church illustrates the change in scale for MPC members, indeed even for its primary predecessor body, that of the MECS. In 1939, it had convened with 269 ministers and 127 laity in attendance. The new (MC) conference meeting that same year experienced difficulty in opening, determining its new membership, and adjusting lists from the MEC, MPC, and MECS. The first General Conference ballot revealed its new size, 401 clergy and 276 laity. The next year (1940) the roll call was answered by 477 clergy and 179 laity.[53] In future years the laity would turn out in better proportions. The new West Virginia Conference of The Methodist Church grew even more dramatically. It brought together West Virginia conferences of the three churches and drew also from Baltimore and Holston. In its first meeting in 1939, the leadership also apparently despaired of straightening out membership and attempted no roll call. The first ballot for General Conference elections showed 353 clergy and 224 laity in session. The next year a roll call indicated 415 clergy and 286 laity. The predecessor conferences had simply not been of that scale. In the 1938 MEC Conference, 156 ministers (plus 23 supplies) had answered roll call. In the 1938 MECS Conference, 109 clergy and 44 laity answered. The MPC was of roughly the same size by equal numbers of laity and clergy (69 and 69).[54] Fraternities of 150 had become an institution of roughly 700.[55]

The change in conference size was but one of a series of adjustments for what had been, in both the MEC and the MECS, relatively stable, fraternal units into which clergy were "inducted" by ordination and from which they exited in death. Merged conferences found new clergy faces, strangers who would need to be made "brothers." Different styles of conference life and ways of doing business required harmonization. Former MPs had to adjust to new leadership (bishops). Former MEC clergy had to embrace the MPC practice of equal lay conference membership. Laity, of course, played their own role in redefining conference life as part of The Methodist Church and politically in relation to the new jurisdictional order. And these several adjustments came amidst the regimens and austerities of world war, a war that brought massive numbers of women into the workforce and made their presence in conference less remarkable.

Administrative Agencies

Among the adjustments for the new church were the realignment of the work and the integration of the organization of the agencies of predecessor denominations into new Methodist boards and commissions. That meant, for instance, putting under the Board of Missions and Church Extensions the home and foreign mission operations of the three churches, including pulling the several women's organizations into the board's Woman's Division of Christian Service (we treat the latter more fully below). Into The Methodist Publishing House went four corporations: the Methodist Book Concerns of New York and Ohio, the Board of Publication of The Methodist Protestant Church (Pennsylvania), and the book agents of The Methodist Episcopal Church, South (Tennessee). The new board was empowered to continue printing operations in New York,

Cincinnati, Chicago, Nashville, Pittsburgh, and Baltimore but to consolidate publication efforts as long as Nashville remained one of the principal plants.[56] The other agencies were Boards of Education, Temperance, Lay Activities, Hospitals and Homes, Evangelism, and Pensions; a Commission on World Peace; and a Department of Publicity. Into these large boards, scattered into seven cities, went various commissions and ongoing operations. The Board of Education, for instance, had responsibility for "Negro" education, Race Relations Sunday, the University Senate, education at all levels (including ministerial training and the Courses of Study), Wesley Foundations, Methodist Student Day, a World Comradeship Fund, its own editorial work, and promotion at all levels. To that end, protocols for the agencies, except for that of the publishing house, provided for counterpart bodies at jurisdictional, conference, and local levels, lacing the administrative and missional activities into giant corporate systems. A General Commission on World Service and Finance provided the new church financial oversight, centralized collection, and effective disbursement. A Council of Secretaries, formed in 1940, was intended to provide coordination on the program side.

Decentralization reigned. The bishops in 1939 requested a "department of Methodist Intelligence."[57] A committee led by Bishop Oxnam yielded in 1940 a Commission on Public Information, which he also chaired and which through the years featured prominent newspaper editors (initially William A. Bailey of the Kansas City *Kansan* and Josephus Daniels of the Raleigh *News and Observer*). The director, the Reverend Ralph Stoody, who had earned a doctorate in religious journalism, chose to locate staff in New York, Chicago, and Nashville. The commission and scattered staff understood their task to be placing news and features about the church's leaders, conferences, and agencies in secular newspapers. The same policy pertained to radio but involved working through the Federal, then the National, Council of Churches when it was Methodism's turn on the network *Protestant Hour*. In addition, the Reverend Walter Van Kirk, a member of the commission, had a regular program on *Religion and the News* and the Reverend Ralph Sockman on the *National Radio Pulpit*. Methodism created a Radio and Film Commission in 1948 (and added Television to the name in 1956, hence TRAFCO), initially giving it no money and no staff and expecting the agencies to fund it. The strategy of placing the church's news, stories, audio, or films into secular media worked well in a still Protestant and indeed mainstream Protestant America, whose editors and broadcasters remained committed to and interested in religious developments. But never well funded, Methodism's communication system and approach proved quite unequal to the challenges and opportunities that would emerge late in the twentieth century when the religious right, having built independent radio empires, grasped the significance of cable television. In addition, working for various masters, TRAFCO, the Commission on Public Information (later on Public Relations and Methodist Information), and the Commission on Promotion and Cultivation (established in 1952), were to train counterpart operatives in the agencies and conferences, attend to bishops and district superintendents, collaborate with and coordinate the production work done in the boards, and in general, try to make the church look like one thing. But one thing, it was not.

The Uniting Conference changed in a simple but fundamental way General Conference's power over its boards, stripping its authority to elect the general secretaries of the connectional agencies.[58] The proposal honored professionalism—election of agency staff by its own board was, as one proponent put it, in accordance with "the usual practice when you are seeking experts as these boards will require to perform an expert job." Speaking for the committee, Paul Quillian raised the specter of the great mass of General Conference acting moblike in selection and of the ephemeral character of General Conferences and contrasted that with the informed and careful selection possible in board election. He affirmed, "If you are a member of a general board at the present ask yourself this question: Would you desire to serve during the coming four years with your administrative officers chosen carefully by your General Board or chosen by the General Conference who did not understand your particular problems?" Would the nearly eight hundred members of the new General Conference have the competence, leisure, and judgment to choose as wisely?[59] A few thought that staff professionalism sacrificed important denominational values. J. M. M. Gray (Detroit) insisted, "[I]n some fashion we must combat effectively the disintegrating influence of Jurisdictional lines upon our general connectional influence. And when we elect all our secretaries by boards and elect all our boards by Jurisdictions we have flung away the last of the great influences that have bound us together as a connection." He continued, "I am in favor of the election of the Secretary by the General Conference." Agreeing, Harold Paul Sloan (New Jersey) spoke against the tendency to "ensmall" the church and of the divisive potential of elections by the boards of their staff.[60]

Sloan, earlier Methodism's preeminent fundamentalist (editor of *Call to Colors*, renamed *The Essentialist*), by 1939 the editor of the *Christian Advocate* (New York), grasped what 1939 achieved, though perhaps not with his neologism, "ensmall." Methodism would indeed fragment not into small groups but into centrifugal power centers:

boards and agencies located in different cities,
bishops settling into jurisdictional colleges and ever more diocesan presidential assignments,
annual conferences with a large agenda in understanding who and what they were,
a Judicial Council with significant authority,
so also jurisdictions, to which subject we turn below,
General Conferences, ostensibly the connective tissue in this new church, convening only briefly every quadrennium.

Where was the center? Who or what would connect, hold together, and coordinate the church's work and witness?

What might putting together three churches—each with such a distinctive ethos, understanding of authority, and history—have looked like had Oxnam been a real archbishop with a charge to keep the Methodist oxen pulling together? By 1952, The Methodist Church grasped that it had a problem, at least with the agencies, and put in place a Coordinating Council to work at relations between and among them, expecting the Council of Secretaries and the Council of Bishops somehow to add as well toward agency collaboration.

It's a wonder, in some ways, that the church responded as well as it did to the aftermath of the Depression and the world war; to the unraveling of colonialism and the transformation of mission; to the problems of race, including those it had created for itself; to the cold war, Korea, and Vietnam; and to poverty, civil rights, and feminism. In a world increasingly laced together by markets, communication, ideologies, conflicts, travel, and education, Methodism found a way of losing its traction, cohesion, or stature—of fragmenting and regionalizing itself. The MEC had wanted a unified Methodism to stand tall in American society and the world. It got instead a church slouching so as not to disturb the MECS's peculiar institution.

Jurisdictioned Church

The 1939 union entrusted the quadrennial jurisdictional gatherings with the decisive function of electing bishops. That polity and political regionalization gradually reshaped the episcopacy, the experience brought to the office, and the perspectives with which individual bishops and the council functioned. Elections elevated fewer individuals from churchwide office and more from the district superintendency, high steeple churches, and regional institutions. Annual conferences vied to put their own "man" in. Clergy and eventually lay power brokers instructed delegates whom to support. Conference delegations swapped commitments. The process favored larger annual conferences when they chose to cooperate.[61]

Three jurisdictions evolved in significant fashion into full-orbed conferences, developed an ongoing apparatus, sustained intrajurisdictional networks beyond those scripted by disciplinary mandates, evolved a distinctive regional or racial ethos, and played key roles politically in the church's struggle over racial justice.[62] By design the two southern jurisdictions, the Southeastern and South Central, effectively carried into their operations the all-white personnel, relationships, papers, schools, camps, style, and ethos of the southern church (MECS). The Southeastern, in particular—embracing the heart of the Confederacy and constituted overwhelmingly by former MECS conferences—owned Emory University and the Lake Junaluska Assembly ("the summer capital of Southern Methodism"),[63] developed a kind of axis between Junaluska and Atlanta, employed two executive secretaries, sponsored the Methodist portion of the *Protestant Hour*, established program committees covering the major areas of the church's life, and carried on promotional campaigns within the jurisdiction.[64] Even this level of white consolidation and defense did not reassure some segregationists. The year after union, a Laymen's Organization for the Preservation of The Methodist Episcopal Church, South, established the Southern Methodist Church. It would be an unabashed segregationist church, a safe haven for those who shrank from contagion with the "alarming infidelity and apostasy found in the M.E. Church, North."[65] The denomination reported 31 pastoral charges, 48 churches, and an active membership of 4,608 for 1960.

The Central Jurisdiction—as a de jure denominational policy of segregation, as a key polity structure, as a formalized practice of racial discrimination, and as a highly visible organizational self-display by a church seeking to exercise American public leadership— proved politically and symbolically problematic from the start, a sad chapter in the life of American Methodism. The church would spend the next quarter century debating this ecclesiastical apartheid and looking for a way to reorganize itself on a racially inclusive basis.

The Central Jurisdiction

For African American Methodists, the creation of a racially segregated Central Jurisdiction was an especially humiliating disappointment but also and ironically a new resource for networking (see maps, Sources, pp. 26–27).[66] An artifact of white racism and a vehicle for Black empowerment, an expression of ethical failure and an instrument of social witness, an emblem of a divided community and a structure for Black fraternity and sorority, the Central Jurisdiction lived a far more complex existence than the other jurisdictions. It began the campaign to end its own life, from within and virtually with its creation, and continued it as a quest for a fuller affirmation of Methodist inclusiveness throughout the 1950s and 1960s.[67] Black congregations from the five geographical jurisdictions, with few exceptions, were herded into the all-Black Central Jurisdiction. New England, California, Bronx (New York City), and Manhattan (New York City) churches were not included. Upstate New York and Brooklyn churches, however, went into Central Jurisdiction. The jurisdiction extended even to Liberia in Africa! The Central Jurisdiction dissociated Black Methodists from their crosstown white counterparts. It created large and unwieldy conferences and forced leaders to cover great distances. Never did it garner the resources or claim the denominational attention that its proponents had envisioned. Not surprisingly, the new segregated Central Jurisdiction did not grow. The 310,000 Black members of 1939 dwindled to 250,000 by 1952. From 1940 through 1960, the five white jurisdictions grew 12.9 percent while the Black Central Jurisdiction grew only 0.3 percent (three-tenths of 1 percent)!

The Central Jurisdiction did nevertheless connect African American Methodists across the entire church. It became a national enabling structure that provided for the identification, development, selection, and exercise of Black leaders.[68] The Central Jurisdiction guaranteed Black representation on national boards and committees (denominational and Woman's). It produced national leadership for the church. It sustained in the *Central Christian Advocate* a denominational paper with a significant Black readership. It gave national attention to the denomination's Black colleges and universities (Bennett, Bethune-Cookman, Claflin, Clark, Dillard, Meharry Medical, Morristown, Paine, Philander Smith, Rust, Samuel Huston, and Wiley), relied on Gammon Theological Seminary for ministerial supply, and supported an array of institutions, including Gulfside, an assembly ground in Waveland, Mississippi.

For Black women the Central Jurisdiction's Woman's Society of Christian Service (WSCS) proved an effective vehicle for sorority, for witness, for action, and for collaboration. The Woman's Society, working with its white counterparts and through the Board of Missions, played particularly important roles, from the early 1940s, in promoting interracial concord, campaigning for African American staffing and representation in denominational missions, and protesting segregation.[69] Prior to 1939, African American women in the Black annual conferences within The Methodist Episcopal Church[70] had contributed their energies to the work of the church from the local to the national levels, particularly through the Woman's Home Missionary Society. Black women like Mrs. Hester Williams (Baton Rouge, Louisiana) had pioneered in establishing schools for Black women and girls and the Friendship Homes that offered safe housing for young Black women moving to northern cities, as well as kindergartens, clinics, and community centers.[71]

In June 1940, women from the nineteen Black conferences (three delegates from each) met in St. Louis concurrent with the first meeting of the Central Jurisdiction. The women had two major concerns: "building fellowship among Central Jurisdiction women and electing black women to the Board of Missions and its Woman's Division of Christian Service." Elected for the 1940–44 quadrennium were Mrs. Hattie Hargis, Mrs. Irma Green Jackson (Shreveport, Louisiana), Mrs. Susie Jones (Greensboro, North Carolina), and Mrs. Ethel Clair, wife of Bishop Matthew W. Clair Sr. of the Baltimore (CJ) Area.[72] The charter meeting of the Central Jurisdiction WSCS was in December 1940 in Cincinnati, Ohio. Mrs. Margaret Bowen was elected the first president.[73] She had grown up in Cincinnati and was educated at the University of Cincinnati. At the time of her election, Mrs. Bowen was principal of Gilbert Academy (a Methodist high school for girls) in New Orleans. In 1948, her husband, J. W. E. Bowen, was elected a bishop. Thelma Stevens (see Sources 1972d) was speaker at that first meeting. A fellowship dinner was held that evening at Friendship House, where Mrs. W. H. C. Goode (the last national president of the WHMS) and Dr. Mary McLeod Bethune spoke. A member of The Methodist Episcopal Church since 1924, Dr. Bethune was president of

Bethune-Cookman College in Daytona Beach, Florida.[74] "Advisor to the White House, founder of the National Council of Negro Women and heroine to successive generations of black students, Dr. Bethune was one of the spiritual mothers of the Woman's Society of Christian Service."[75]

Many of the Black women who became leaders among Methodist women organized for mission were graduates of Gammon Theological Seminary, which opened a Woman's Department in 1934. There African American women trained to become "missionaries, deaconesses, directors of Christian education, local church workers, and pastors' wives." (Scarritt College for Christian Workers was not integrated until 1951.)[76] The Woman's Division held schools of Christian mission at both the conference and the jurisdictional levels. The Gulfside School (usually held at Waveland, Mississippi, in the 1940s and 1950s) became the school of mission for the Central Jurisdiction. There both black and white faculty offered "invaluable training experiences for black women assuming their proper leadership roles in the Methodist Church."

Two effective bishops, Robert Jones and Alexander Shaw, and one retired, Matthew Clair Sr., convened the 1940 session of the Central Jurisdiction. The delegates elected their own first two bishops, William Hughes and Lorenzo King. Hughes, son of a "slave preacher" who organized and built the first Methodist church for Black Methodists in Maryland, since 1917 had been secretary for "Negro Work" of the Board of Home Missions and Church Extension. Sadly Hughes died nineteen days after his consecration. King, born of slave parents in Mississippi, was in his tenth year as pastor of St. Mark's in Harlem, New York City. For the preceding ten years, King had edited the *Southwestern Christian Advocate*, one of two Black MEC *Advocates*. King was assigned to the Atlantic Coast Area conferences and died six years later, in 1946.

The *Central Christian Advocate*, especially, became the champion of the Black membership in The Methodist Church. Editor from 1944 to 1948, John Wesley Edward Bowen did his part to alert Black Methodists to the challenges and opportunities in the church. Almost no issue of the paper failed to have editorial comment on racism in church and society. Bowen's education at Wesleyan and Howard Universities and his years as a teacher and as a pastor gave him a steady determination to uphold Black rights, without bitterness, but also without fear. "There is no such thing as a Negro problem.... The real problem is the unwillingness of the white people of America to grant first class and complete citizenship to Negroes," he wrote on March 8, 1945. When southern editors and Black leaders met to discuss ways to eliminate voting restrictions he hailed the event as a new day of advancement and affirmed (August 9, 1945) that African Americans knew that "Southern white people are just as sensitive to matters of right and wrong...as any people in the world." Almost a year before the General and Jurisdictional Conferences of 1948, Bowen was calling attention (July 24, 1947) to the racial issues to be faced and urged "clear heads and sound reasoning.... Beware of depending too much on our feelings." His leadership on these issues caused the Central Jurisdiction to elect him bishop in 1948. Similarly, Prince Taylor, editor of the *Central Christian Advocate* in the 1950s who applauded the Supreme Court's Brown decision (Sources 1954) in a forceful editorial, was elected to the episcopacy in 1956. Other bishops who had edited the *Advocate* were Lorenzo King, Robert Brooks, and Scott Allen.[77]

In various ways and from the start, the Central Jurisdiction witnessed prophetically against the very racism that it emblemed and spoke out against the un-Christian and unjust character of the church's discrimination, segregation, and racial exclusivism.[78] It did so within its own arena, through its paper, as noted, and through addresses to jurisdictional gatherings. It did so, as well, in prophetic words to the denomination. For instance in 1951, on behalf of the Lexington Conference (the Central Jurisdiction's conference covering the midwestern states from Illinois to Colorado), Charles F. Golden petitioned General Conference for a study commission that would plan for integration, the elimination of racial discrimination, and "a racially inclusive policy at all organizational levels" (Sources 1951). Golden, the first African American staff member of the Board of Missions, would be a member of the 1956 General Conference Commission to Study the Jurisdictional System and was then elected to the episcopacy in 1960.[79] Another important Central Jurisdiction statement came in 1962 with the issuing by its leadership of a manifesto for integration, *The Central Jurisdiction Speaks* (discussed below).

Methodism vs. Its Own Segregation

From the start, other churchwide organizations witnessed against and lobbied aggressively to end segregation in the church—the unofficial Methodist Federation for Social Action (MFSA), the Methodist Student Movement (MSM), and the Woman's Division of the Board of Missions and its local affiliate, the Woman's Society of Christian Service (WSCS). The MFSA, under its new leader Charles Webber, tried to persuade the church's publishing house to sign a contract with the printing trades and attempted to desegregate the dining room at the Methodist Building in Washington, D.C. In 1948, the MFSA elected as president African American Bishop Robert Brooks. The MSM, from its beginning, had no racial barriers in its organization and program. Its first national student leadership training conference held at Berea, Kentucky, in the summer of 1939 adopted a set of "objectives" for the two-year-old Methodist campus ministry organization, including a commitment to racial understanding. A number of actions at the Berea conference of 1939 spoke to their convictions on racial issues: the inclusion of W. J. Faulkner, dean of the chapel of Fisk University, a prominent African American University in Nashville, as a leader of the conference; the decision at that conference to include student representatives from the all-Black Central Jurisdiction in the MSM's National Student Council; and a stated desire that all student leaders should be "eager to establish understanding, cooperation and fellowship on local, state and jurisdictional levels, working for the day when we can be truly unified [by the elimination of the Central Jurisdiction]."[80]

The Woman's Division led the church in its proactive struggle toward inclusiveness. It did so by its staffing policy, hiring its first Black secretary in the New York City office, Charlotte R. French, in 1941, and in 1948 electing its first Black senior staff person, Theressa Hoover (see Sources 1973, and see Women's Organizations section below for further discussion of staffing). Also in 1941 the division adopted a policy of holding its meetings only in places where all members of its group could be entertained without any form of racial discrimination. WSCS conference and jurisdictional leaders made plans to bring together leaders of the then racially segregated annual conferences in a series of meetings and retreats. When the division discovered that St. Louis hotels would deny African American women access, it moved its first national assembly (1942) to Columbus, Ohio, with guarantees of hotel access (only to find that hotels and restaurants in Columbus were less open than had been promised).[81]

The Department of Christian Social Relations and Local Church Activities (CSR/LCA) of the Woman's Division is credited for having "mobilized Methodist women of all ethnic identities into one of the most sustained campaigns against racism ever witnessed in America."[82] In 1940 the CSR/LCA department named an African American woman, Mrs. Susie (David D.) Jones of Greensboro, North Carolina, co-chairperson (with Mrs. Paul Arrington of Jackson, Mississippi) of its standing Committee on Minority Groups and Interracial Cooperation.[83] An early CSR/LCA slogan was "All Action Is Local," and much of the significant work under the third department depended on grassroots initiatives. Dorothy Rogers (Mrs. Milton E.) Tilly of Atlanta, Georgia, was an outstanding example of a Methodist woman who brought together black and white women throughout the South to work on issues of racial justice. She was secretary of the Southeastern Jurisdiction CSR/LCA and, from 1949, head of the interracial and ecumenical church women's organization called the Fellowship of the Concerned.[84]

The Woman's Division memorialized the 1944 General Conference asking for a policy that would forbid segregation at national meetings. The General Conference did not support the initiative and enacted legislation making Liberia a part of the Central Jurisdiction. The Liberia Conference remained in this segregated relationship for twenty years. In 1947 a Woman's Division National Seminar recommended drafting a charter of racial policies and gathering data on national, state, and local laws relating to race and color. The recommendations, adopted by the division and referred to a new committee for implementation—the Committee on Racial Practices—resulted in a 750-page book detailing state laws on race (1951). It was written by a Black lesbian feminist, Pauli Murray, whose lifetime activism began with an unsuccessful attempt to desegregate the

University of North Carolina, Chapel Hill, in 1939. Three years later (1954), Murray's Methodist-sponsored book, *States' Laws on Race and Color*, became a key source for research for the U.S. Supreme Court in its deliberations on the landmark desegregation decision *Brown v. Board of Education*. In 1952, the Woman's Division, continuing its commitment to eliminate institutional racism, at its annual meeting unanimously adopted a landmark "Charter of Racial Policies" (Sources 1952). Two years later, the Woman's Division asked annual conferences to ratify the charter and to commit to its implementation. The charter was revised in 1962 and 1978. The Woman's Division also began to desegregate its schools and institutes, hospitals and homes, and hired its first Black program staff.

The division led the church on public policy regarding the integration of public schools, housing, and the workplace. Seeking to change attitudes within their own organizations and in the communities of which Methodism was a part, the women affirmed theological foundations for racial equality, illuminated social problems inherent in desegregation, and encouraged personal moral influence in local and state affairs. For instance, the WSCS, black and white, gathered in Milwaukee in late May 1954 for its fourth quadrennial assembly, went on record on the *Brown* decision:

> We affirm anew our determination to work with greater urgency to eliminate segregation from every part of our community and national life and from the organization and practice of our own church and its agencies and programs. We rejoice that the highest tribunal in this land, the Supreme Court of the United States, proclaimed on May 17, 1954 that segregation in public education anywhere in this nation is an infringement of the Constitution and a violation of the Fourteenth Amendment.
>
> We accept our full Christian responsibility to work through church and community channels to speed the process of transition from segregated schools to a new pattern of justice and freedom.[85]

Similarly, the women of the new Evangelical United Brethren Church deplored segregation and applauded the Supreme Court's actions (Sources 1955).

Criticism of the church's institutionalized segregation came from various quarters and in various forums and on every level. Students and faculty at Methodist colleges, universities, and theological seminaries wrestled with the race issues (frequently, especially in the South, prodding reluctant administrations and trustees). A 1958 Candler School of Theology (Emory) student survey showed mixed feelings about desegregating the seminary. Two years later the Drew seminary faculty petitioned General Conference to abolish the Central Jurisdiction.[86]

Advocacy came also from the top. In November 1963, the Methodist Council of Bishops issued a pastoral statement in which they said,

The Methodist Church must build and demonstrate within its own organization and program a fellowship without racial barriers. The church must also seek to change those community patterns in which racial segregation appears, including education, housing, voting, employment and the use of public facilities. To insist that restaurants, schools, business establishments, and hotels provide equal accommodations for all peoples without regard to race or color, but to exempt the church from the same requirements is to be guilty of absurdity as well as sin.[87]

Methodists in the National Campaign against and for Segregation

Two Methodist University of Chicago graduate students committed to nonviolent resistance, African American James Farmer and white George Houser, founded in 1942 the Congress of Racial Equality (CORE), which conducted the first sit-ins, protesting discrimination in Chicago restaurants, and within five years launched the first Freedom Riders to test compliance with the 1946 Supreme Court declaration that segregation in interstate travel was illegal. In 1946, creating by executive order the President's Committee on Civil Rights, Harry Truman appointed to its ranks a white Methodist anti–lynching, anti–Ku Klux Klan, race relations activist from Georgia, Dorothy Tilly. In 1947, Branch Rickey, manager of the Brooklyn Dodgers, a Bible-loving Methodist who refused to attend games on Sunday, brought Methodist Sunday school–trained Jackie Robinson to his team, breaking the "color barrier" in major league baseball. (Rookie of the Year, Robinson became a longtime member of Scott UMC in Pasadena, California, when the Dodgers moved west.) The appellant in *Brown v. Board of Education* was Oliver Brown, father of third grader Linda and an AMEZ pastor, and one of the lawyers arguing the 1954 case before the Supreme Court was Charles S. Scott, a prominent Black Methodist layman.

The spark in the 1955 Montgomery bus boycott, Rosa Parks, was an AME deaconess, NAACP branch secretary, and seamstress at a department store. Out of the Montgomery movement came the Southern Christian Leadership Conference (SCLC), cofounded by Martin Luther King, Jr. and Joseph Lowery, then (1952–61) pastor of Warren Street Methodist Church in Mobile, Alabama. Also in the late 1950s, African American Methodist laywoman Dorothy Height (St. Mark's MC, New York City) began a forty-year presidency of the National Council of Negro Women, the nation's foremost advocacy group for Black women, effective in combating hunger, illiteracy, and inferior education and health services; and in collaborating with other civil rights leaders. (Height was one of the "Big Six" civil rights team, along with Dr. King, James Farmer, John Lewis, Roy Wilkins, and Andrew Young.)

Southern whites greeted the *Brown* decision with bitter hostility. Methodists from six southern states organized a "segregation forever" caucus in several annual conferences— Association of Methodist Ministers and Laymen to Preserve Established Racial Customs—a Klan-like structure to harass ministers who spoke out. The organization launched a concerted attack, using both legal and illegal means, on NAACP branches and "uppity" Black churches.[88] In November 1957, eighty Atlanta clergy, including some twenty Methodists, broke the white silence and issued a "Ministers' Manifesto" to the press. They condemned racial prejudice and segregation, supported integrated public schools, called for greater communication and cooperation between the races, and affirmed the freedom of the pulpit. Many pastors who spoke out were criticized, and their families were the object of cruelty as well. Some were ousted from their congregations. Methodist superintendents and bishops did little to support their clergy and their families.

James Lawson, an African American Methodist, was expelled from Vanderbilt Divinity School in 1960 for his part in organizing Nashville sit-ins, punitive action that prompted Dean Robert Nelson and eleven of its sixteen faculty members to sign a declaration of conscience and eventually to submit letters of resignation.[89] In 1961, Leontyne Price made her debut at the Metropolitan Opera House in New York. Price, who had two Methodist grandfathers, began her musical life at an early age in the Central Jurisdiction St. Paul Methodist Church in Laurel, Mississippi. In 1963, on the one hundredth anniversary of President Lincoln's Emancipation Proclamation, the Methodist governor of Alabama, George C. Wallace, master of the politics of rage, made an infamous stand in the schoolhouse door, shouting, "Segregation now, segregation tomorrow, segregation forever!"[90] Twelve people died in Alabama in civil rights slayings in Wallace's first term between 1963 and 1966. During at least one of the protests, Bishop Kenneth Goodson was in the governor's office with Wallace, seeking to be a moderating spirit. Bishops Nolan Harmon and Paul Hardin were among those addressed by Martin Luther King, Jr. in the *Letter from Birmingham Jail*. Also in 1963, some twenty-eight Mississippi Methodist pastors dared to speak out against racial discrimination (Sources 1963a). Reaction to their witness forced many to leave the conference. At that point, Methodist segregationists dominated annual conferences in the South, intimidating such prophetic acts, encouraging economic boycott of "Communist-inspired" local and national church integration efforts, resisting notions that the racially defined Central Jurisdiction should be ended, even forcefully removing interracial teams coming to integrate worship services.

One such incident occurred on Easter 1964 at the prominent Galloway Memorial Methodist Church in Jackson, Mississippi. Its official board dominated by members and supporters of the white Citizen's Council had, in 1961, adopted a formal resolution barring admission "of any persons, white or colored who, in the judgment of the greeters or ushers, seek admission for the purpose of creating an incident resulting in a breach of the peace." Two years later, the board reinforced its policy, indicating "we prefer to remain an all-white congregation. The practice of the separation of the races in Galloway

Memorial Methodist Church is a time-honored tradition." Testing of that policy by five African Americans in 1963 led to the resignation of the pastor and Associated Press coverage of his sermon protesting the exclusion. In 1964 there was continued testing by teams of white and Black ministers, some from Chicago. And on Easter Day 1964, two Methodist bishops, James Mathews (white) and Charles Golden (Black), and seven other ministers presented themselves for seating at Galloway and another white Jackson church. The seven ministers were arrested for trespassing and jailed, as had been the practice that spring. Thereafter the Galloway official board voted to repudiate its World Service apportionment because some of it supported the National Council of Churches (later reversed). Not content to get their Methodist dollars out of the NCC, a sizable contingent from Galloway led the way out of The Methodist Church to form a pure white Independent Methodist Church.[91]

Slow Transitions

Faced with such resistance, Methodism made slow progress toward a policy and practice of fuller Christian community, though each successive General Conference received increased numbers of petitions from individual churches and conferences on the race issue.[92] The church expressed a commitment to "the ultimate elimination of racial discrimination in The Methodist Church" in 1944. It redrew some western boundaries in 1948 to make easier the voluntary transfer of Black churches out. It eased such transfers in 1952, establishing a constitutional principle in 1956 (Amendment IX) of voluntary transfer of entire conferences or parts of conferences as well as congregations, embroiling itself in a major debate over elimination of the Central Jurisdiction, but failing to agree on a deadline.

The 1956 and 1960 General Conferences created committees to study ways of eliminating the Central Jurisdiction and in 1960 established a quadrennial program on race to create a climate for reconciliation. The Woman's Division published a manual for the quadrennial program, *We Can and We Will*. A white majority at the conference also drafted a plan to speed up the process of eliminating the Central Jurisdiction. Alarmed that African American churches would be dropped into segregated systems and contexts, Black leaders in 1960 created a broadly representative study process, involving some two hundred women, youth, pastors, district superintendents, educators, agency personnel, and other leaders, and overseen by a jurisdictional Committee of Five to frame Black expectations of merger.[93] The work from this hearing process was issued by the jurisdiction's College of Bishops as the 1962 manifesto *The Central Jurisdiction Speaks*. Demanding input, the manifesto insisted that dissolution of the Central Jurisdiction "must be sought by The Methodist Church as a whole within a framework of overall planning, procedures, programs and Christian understanding designed to promote in demonstrable and concrete ways ultimate achievement of an inclusive Methodist

Church." Central Jurisdiction churches and pastors should be transferred so as to empower, involve, and engage them in their new districts and conferences, not isolated, and certainly not dumped into contexts where colleges, homes, cabinets, and other institutions remained segregated. Inclusiveness meant real change on the part of white Methodism, sensitivity to Black interests, and efforts to deal with the disparities in salaries, facilities (parsonages), pensions, and training programs.[94]

White bishops in the South issued their own pastoral letter aimed at disarming fears of forced integration. "The principle of regional autonomy for which we from the first contended has been preserved," they reassured their constituents. When the 1964 General Conference convened in Pittsburgh, church and society had experienced a year of extraordinary turmoil—bishops having been just refused entrance to a Methodist church, the NCC and other civil rights organizations then gearing up for a southern civil disobedience summer, the nation coming to terms with a presidential assassination, a church in Birmingham having been bombed, M. L. King and others having challenged Americans at the March on Washington, and Mississippi Methodists having spoken out. The Methodist Student Movement and Methodists for Church Renewal brought crisis into the hall with demonstrations demanding that the church desegregate. Following lengthy debate, the conference adopted a "Charter of Racial Policies" promising equal access to church facilities and programs and a voluntary plan to transfer all Black conferences into regional white jurisdictions and then merge Black and white annual conferences.[95] Though rejecting a mandatory deadline to end the Central Jurisdiction, it resolved with respect to projected unity with the EUBC that "no racial structure[s] be carried over into the Constitution of the new United Church." (Sadly, the Joint Commission on Church Union with the EUBC evaded the spirit and intent of that action and merely deleted references to labels used historically by Methodists to denote race in their church. Thus the term *"Central Jurisdiction"* was not used, but the reality of racial separatism was incorporated in the plan of union.) Further, General Conference voted that clergy appointments should be made "without regard to race and color,"[96] and it passed and lodged in the *Discipline* a resolution supporting principled civil disobedience, then a flash point of controversy across the South.

Seventeen Black conferences remained and were realigned by the Central Jurisdiction in its June meeting into sixteen so that Black conference lines did not cross those of the five regional jurisdictions. That summer two Black conferences merged with their white or largely white counterparts—Delaware in Northeastern Jurisdiction and Lexington in South Central Jurisdiction. The previously all-white Philadelphia Conference received 18 churches; New Jersey Conference, 23; West Virginia Conference, 25; and Baltimore Conference, more than 200. That summer the first Black bishops—Prince Taylor in New Jersey and James Thomas in Iowa—were assigned to predominantly white episcopal areas. By year's end (1964) four Black conferences in the Northeastern and

North Central Jurisdictions had been welcomed into the white conferences in which they were situated, which left thirteen more to go, all in the South. The Central Jurisdiction met last in a special session in 1967, elected L. Scott Allen, implored the prospective United Methodist Church to make its cabinets, committees, and agencies inclusive, and adopted measures for dissolution of the remaining conferences. The final transfers and mergers were completed by 1973.[97] Some of the jurisdiction's energy and vision lives on in Black Methodists for Church Renewal, a caucus expression to jurisdictional life, as we shall see in the next chapter.[98]

Women's Organizations and the Pursuit of Clergy Rights for Women

Anticipating reunification and the formation of the Woman's Division of Christian Service of the Board of Missions, the six presidents of the three uniting denominations' home and foreign mission organizations called a series of planning meetings, including a retreat in Cincinnati in December 1938, attended by forty, and a larger gathering in Chicago.[99] The task? Preparing the members to take their separate histories into the future with a sense of common purpose and hope. The president of the MEC Woman's Foreign Missionary Society, Evelyn Riley Nicholson, wrote members of this oldest and largest of the uniting groups:

> It has had an extraordinary record, blessed of God. . . . Do not think of her as defunct. Her ideals and purposes live in the World Federation of Methodist Women and will be perpetuated in the W.S.C.S. She loses her life to find and enlarge it. In God's economy . . . there is change, but not loss. . . . [You] have come to the Kingdom for such a time as this.[100]

By the time the Uniting Conference of 1939 appointed a Joint Committee on Missions and Church Extension, the women who constituted the Woman's Section already "knew and respected and loved one another." The 1940 General Conference approved the proposed plans without a dissenting vote. Of the seventy-three women delegates to this General Conference, thirty had served on the Joint Committee on Missions.[101]

The Board of Missions and Church Extension of The Methodist Church organized in July 1940 with four divisions, one of which was the Woman's Division of Christian Service.[102] Its official (monthly) magazine, the *Methodist Woman*, united the heritages of at least four women's missionary magazines.[103] "Nearly two million women became charter members of the new organization and started down the road together, seeking to become one in spirit and in mission."[104] The model of Methodist women's missionary organization most closely resembled that of the Woman's Missionary Council (MECS) in several respects. The Woman's Division unified foreign and home missionary work in one organization. Although separately incorporated, the division functioned within and in a "coordinate administrative role" of the general board. And the division possessed a distinctive Department of Christian Social Relations and Local Church Activities, one of its three departments, along with Foreign and Home Missions. Each had an executive secretary who worked in a collegial relationship with the other two executive secretaries to recommend goals, initiate program ideals, draft resolutions, plan conferences, and then coordinate and implement the programs set by the approximately fifty elected officers. The position of chair of the Woman's Division rotated on an annual basis among the executive secretaries. Louise Oldshue became the first chairperson of the Christian Social Relations department and Thelma Stevens, its executive secretary. Stevens would give distinguished leadership to this department for the next twenty-eight years (Sources 1972d).[105]

The Wesleyan Service Guild became the only women's missionary organization to continue from the predecessor denominations (MEC) into the new church. An auxiliary to the Woman's Division for employed women, it sustained its threefold program division: Spiritual Life, Missionary Service, and Christian Social Relations (Christian Citizenship). Its secretary, Marion Lela Norris, became a full-time staff member of the Woman's Division and presided over the phenomenal expansion of the guild until retirement in 1951. Two significant additions to the earlier worship services developed for the guild came in the 1940s: a Guild Pledge Service in 1945 and the final form of the guild hymn, "This Is My Song" (to the tune of Jean Sibelius's "Finlandia"), with a third stanza written at Marion Lela Norris's request by Methodist theologian Dr. Georgia Harkness.

Nearly every local Methodist church had one or two women's missionary groups: a Woman's Society of Christian Service for full-time homemakers and a Wesleyan Service Guild (with evening meetings) for employed women. Local societies had close organizational ties with district, conference, jurisdictional, and national officers, including program officers who related to national staff. The Woman's Division staff required regular accountability from officers at every level, providing an effective connectional network and a strong sense of direction even in times of controversy. Most officers and many local Methodist women subscribed to the *Methodist Woman*, looking to it for information and guidance and for interpretation of the church's mission across the globe. The magazine and ample coverage also of the Woman's Division work in *World Outlook* acquainted members with politics, education and medical initiatives, and social-cultural issues and engaged Methodist women with decolonization efforts that would unfold across the world. Summer training schools equipped some ten thousand leaders to return to their churches to teach a half million members on the missional and biblical themes for the year.[106] Thus the Woman's Division was both a grassroots and a national organization.[107]

Critical from the start of the Central Jurisdiction and Methodism's national policy of segregation, the Woman's Division, as we noted above, participated actively in efforts to break down racial barriers; to model an inclusive church; to challenge segregation directly; to identify, equip, mentor, and deploy Black leaders; and to form networks and bonds between white and Black women. As early as 1941, the Department of Christian Social Relations and Local Church Activities hired an African American woman, Mrs. Charlotte R. French, as its office secretary. She would remain with the department until her retirement in 1959.

Black women first joined the professional staff of the Woman's Division as field workers assigned to the Central Jurisdiction. Four served during the 1940–68 period: Lillian Warrick (later Pope), 1941–43; Vivienne Newton (later Gray), 1945–46; Theressa Hoover, 1948–58; and Dorothy L. Barnette, 1958–64. "These workers itinerated, taught, interpreted, organized, trained, cultivated and, when called upon, handed out corsages. They were expected to be experts on everything related to Methodist women organized for mission, and they usually were." In her three years as field worker, Warrick visited all nineteen Black conferences at least once and was instrumental in developing an awareness of what needed to be done to encourage WSCS success at the grassroots level. Newton, a graduate of Gammon Theological Seminary, worked with the Woman's Division as a field worker for just a year. After her marriage to the Reverend Ulysses Gray, they would serve as missionaries in Liberia for twenty-five years. Born in Fayetteville, Arkansas, and a graduate of Philander Smith College in Little Rock and of New York University, Hoover served as a field worker for ten years. In 1958 she became a member of the staff of Christian Social Relations, and in 1965 she was named assistant general secretary for the newly created section of Program and Education for Christian Mission. In 1968 she was the natural choice for associate general secretary (chief executive officer) of the Women's Division of the General Board of Global Ministries of The United Methodist Church (see Sources 1973). Barnette, a social worker and assistant superintendent with the People's Community Center of New Orleans, before becoming field worker for the Woman's Division in 1958, moved to the Joint Commission on Education and Cultivation in 1964 and was tragically killed in an accident while in Nairobi, Kenya, in 1970. The first African American woman to be elected to a professional staff position other than field worker was Ethel Watkins (later Mrs. Harold Cost), who became an associate secretary for CSR/LCA in 1952.

In the unification of The Evangelical Church and the Church of the United Brethren in Christ in 1946 to become The Evangelical United Brethren Church, the model that prevailed was that of The Evangelical Church. The separate women's organizations of the two denominations became the Women's Society of World Service, which was governed at the national level by a twelve-member Women's Council. The United Brethren women's mission organization had been separately incorporated while the Evangelical women's missionary work had always been auxiliary to the general Missionary Society. By 1946, however, both United Brethren and Evangelical women had developed unified women's organizations for foreign and home missions, and both were within a general denominational board.

In 1964, the Methodist Board of Missions reorganized and transferred from the Woman's Division the work of its home and foreign mission departments to other divisions of the board.[108] In this restructuring, about which the women were not entirely happy, Mrs. Ann Porter Brown, the general secretary of the Woman's Division, became the first general secretary of the new unified board. This experience of integration was not, however, "as debilitating as that of women in other denominations" because organized Methodist women retained their "financial sovereignty—an essential ingredient of power and autonomy." The Woman's Division in 1964 was organized in three sections: Christian Social Relations, Program and Education for Christian Mission, and Finance. Members of the Woman's Division also sat on the boards of the World and National Divisions. Theressa Hoover commented on the significance of 1964: "In retrospect, 1964 can be seen as our year of inoculation. A painful dose of integration insufficient to kill our separate women's organization was injected. This has helped protect us against further attacks of the disease."

In 1968, The Evangelical United Brethren Church (EUBC) united with The Methodist Church to form The United Methodist Church. Methodist and EUBC women merged their work for mission "with no major upheavals." The name of the division became the Women's Division; auxiliaries at all levels were called the Women's Society of Christian Service and the Wesleyan Service Guild. When the Board of Missions became the Board of Global Ministries in 1972, women were able both to protect the independence of their work and to renew their grassroots organization of women for mission by creating United Methodist Women (UMW). This new structure ended the separation of women into two groups, one primarily for homemakers and the other for employed women. It was also an effort to encourage the active participation and leadership of women of color and of younger women. UMW would have three program areas: Christian Personhood, Christian Social Relations, and Christian Global Concerns. The new organization for women in mission was ratified by the General Conference of 1972 and implemented at the local level by the end of 1973.

In 1968, the Division successfully petitioned the Uniting Conference to create a Study Commission on the Participation of Women in The United Methodist Church. While the study commission proceeded with its work, the Women's Division created its own Ad Hoc Committee on Churchwomen's Liberation. In 1972, this committee "gave primary support" to the first conference held at the Grailville center in Ohio, "Women's Consciousness and Theology." It also played a significant role in working for the establishment of the Commission on the Status and Role of Women (COSROW) by the 1972 General Conference and in contributing to the creation of United Methodist Women.[109]

Full Clergy Rights for Women

Both the Methodist union of 1939 and the EUBC union of 1946 represented clergy-rights setbacks for women. The Methodists forced MPC clergywomen to yield their full clergy rights. And the EUBC made no provision to continue ordinations of women, a UBC practice and policy for a half century (since 1889). The Methodist Uniting Conference defeated full conference membership for female clergy by a narrow margin (384 to 371).[110] The campaign did not abate. Women continued to attend seminary. The UBC seminary had granted BD degrees to sixteen women in the decade before the 1946 union. And among Methodists, women not only attended but also occupied seminary faculty posts—Mildred Moody Eakin, assistant professor of Christian education, at Drew (1932–54) and Georgia Harkness, professor of systematic theology, at Garrett Biblical Institute (1939–50; now Garrett-Evangelical Theological Seminary) and later at Pacific School of Religion (1950–61). The AME authorized women as local deacons in 1948 and as local elders in 1956. The prior year, the General Assembly of the Presbyterian Church USA voted to approve the ordination of women to the office of Word and Sacrament. The amendment was approved by the presbyteries, and in 1956 the first woman was ordained.

For successive General Conferences—1944, 1948, and 1952—the Methodist Woman's Division of Christian Service petitioned conference delegates to grant full clergy rights to women, as had women in the MECS since 1926 and in the MEC since 1928. The MC General Conference, meeting in 1956 in Minneapolis, received more than two thousand petitions asking for full clergy rights for women. Many came from Woman's Societies in local churches across the country, stimulated by the Woman's Division of Christian Service through its section on the status of women. The Committee on the Ministry brought in a compromise recommendation (narrowly approved by a vote of 40–32 in the committee) granting full clergy rights to women but stipulating that "only unmarried women and widows may apply." A minority report signed by seven members of the committee would have retained the previous rules, granting women local ordination but not conference membership. The floor debate indicated the primary issue remained whether the appointment of a woman minister would be unacceptable to some churches. Two attempts were made to get around the issue: one permitting a woman to be located when she could not be placed, the other giving the annual conferences the right to decide the extent to which they would implement the legislation. Both went down to defeat.[111]

The minority report lost by a vote of 310 to 425, and by a vote of 389 to 297 the conference removed the majority report provision that married women could not apply. "Then by an overwhelming show of hands," the delegates passed the historic motion putting into the Methodist *Discipline* the following simple, but momentous words: "Women are included in all the provisions of the Discipline referring to the ministry."[112] Alluding to this action and a compromise worked out earlier to remove obstacles in the way of ending the Central Jurisdiction, Dr. Georgia Harkness commented, "I think maybe we've had a miracle twice this week."[113] That same evening, May 4, the General Conference saluted Harkness for the "valiant fight" she had waged for this cause throughout the years and recognized "the peculiar satisfaction" she must feel.[114]

Although Georgia Harkness had been ordained elder in the Troy (New York-Vermont) Annual Conference, she did not apply for annual conference membership in 1956. As the recognition by General Conference indicated and as we have seen by reference to her in this chapter, she had carved out a role as one of the important spokespersons for progressive Methodism. She exercised that prophetic leadership in talks and lectures, in ecumenical involvements, in Protestant papers and magazines, and especially in her books. Her *Understanding the Christian Faith* (Sources 1947b), which explained Christian doctrine in clear, concise, and understandable terms, enjoyed great popularity and represents well her ability to convey difficult theological points to the Christian reader. She would be the most visible woman theologian and let other women pursue the ordination that she had long advocated (Sources 1924b).

On May 18, 1956, Maud Keister Jensen was admitted on trial, in absentia, to the Central Pennsylvania Conference, becoming the first woman to receive full clergy rights in The Methodist Church (Sources 1956). A graduate of Drew Theological Seminary, who subsequently earned a PhD there, Jensen and her husband had been on missionary service in Korea. Kris Jensen had been captured during the Korean War and interned for three years and was not able to be with his wife when she received her elder's orders on May 25, 1952. After his release in 1953, they returned to Korea. Maud Jensen's ordination had been recognized fully by the Korean Methodist Church (which admitted women to full conference membership after 1930 when it became an autonomous church).[115] Among others received on trial that year were Grace E. Huck, Grace M. Weaver, Gertrude G. Harris, Alice T. Hart, Esther A. Haskard, Margaret K. Henrichsen, and Emma P. Hill, the latter the first African American woman.[116]

In The Evangelical United Brethren Church, as in the case of The Methodist Church, women's ordination was sacrificed for unity. Although the status of those already ordained was not impaired, no provision was made for the licensing and ordination of women in the new church.[117] A number of annual conferences did ordain women between the years 1946 and 1968, despite preunion agreements not to do so, "at least twenty-three" to elder's orders. Some served rural churches; others collaborated as part of a clergy couple.[118] In terms of official church policy, however, the ordination of women would have to wait until the 1968 union that formed The United Methodist Church.

The Methodist Youth Fellowship and the Methodist Student Movement

In 1941, following unification, the old Epworth League became the Methodist Youth Fellowship (MYF). No longer were youth from teens to thirties in the same organization. MYF planners targeted younger youth only, of high school age. The local church program centered on Christian nurture and outreach through morning Sunday school classes and Sunday evening social meetings.[119] Scout troops and other clubs sponsored by the church were also a part of the MYF. Paper drives, car washes, slave days (when youth performed services for church members), and rock-a-thons helped raise funds for the Methodist Youth Fund for missions. Organization and program extended beyond the local church to subdistricts, districts, annual conferences, and jurisdictions, including workshops, camps, conferences, and special events. A national conference of the fellowship brought together annually presidents of conference MYF organizations to discuss the youth program, its place in the church, and current issues of vital importance to MYF, the first of which was held on the campus of Baker University in Baldwin, Kansas, in September 1941. Participants included persons who went on to serve God and the church in many ways. Teachers and pastors, civil rights leaders and peace activists, missionaries and committed laity, and even a future bishop were among those who took part. Janet Metzger detailed a personal story of the 1942 national MYF conference in the church's youth magazine, *Highroad* (Sources 1942b). In the 1940s and 1950s when interracial meetings were virtually unknown, especially in the South, MYFers often met together across racial lines. A similar program in the EUBC was known as Christian Endeavor.[120]

Anticipating union of the separate Methodisms by two years, college and university students of each church met in a National Methodist Youth Conference (1937) in St. Louis, Missouri, and created a single student confederation to provide for student program needs—the Methodist Student Movement (MSM). With elected student leadership and sustained by campus ministry staff from the three churches, the innovative organization launched a new era in Methodist campus ministry. Upon unification in 1939, the new Board of Education established a Department of Student Work whose staff cooperatively helped direct and expand the work of the MSM. When local churches serving students were included along with the Wesley Foundations and college chaplaincies, some four hundred "preaching centers" served state, independent, and church-related campuses. In addition to worship and study, local MSM units carried out numerous social service projects and mission programs. An MSM publication for university students, *Motive* magazine, had been launched in the fall of 1940, promoting theological engagement with the academy; stimulating awareness of national and international concerns for world peace and nuclear disarmament, for racial, social, gender, and sexual justice; and advocating the arts to empower the imagination in the life of the church.[121] Dr. Martin Luther King, Jr. headed the list of speakers for the eighth quadrennial conference of the MSM in the tumultuous year of 1964. By 1966 the MSM included 198 accredited Wesley Foundations and 646 other campus ministry programs at Methodist-related colleges and universities. Aggressive advocacy of antiwar positions, civil rights, and rights for homosexuals led to loss of confidence in the campus ministry by many within the church during the student revolution of the 1960s and 1970s. The result was reduced dependence on the campus ministry for nurture of the church's youth and recruitment of church leaders and pastors.

Students demanded freedom from a conservative church hierarchy, and campus ministers and national staff sought new patterns of ministry. A central goal was an ecumenically based campus ministry. United Ministries in Higher Education (UMHE) emerged in the mid-1960s, including students and staff from seven mainline churches. On the eve of the MC's union with the EUBC, the Methodist Board of Education and the Methodist Association of College and University Ministers closed down the thirty-year ministry of the MSM and joined this ecumenical body in 1966. Leaders of several denominational student organizations formed the University Christian Movement (UCM) that same year, creating an independent, student-led Christian movement. But the high hopes that had surrounded the creation of the UCM were dissipated by the assassinations of Martin Luther King, Jr., and Robert Kennedy in 1968, the escalation of the Vietnam War, and the use of police and military force against student protesters. By 1969 the UCM council opted to dissolve the movement. "The necessary creative balance between the prophetic and the pastoral had by the close of the decade been lost," concluded the movement's most recent interpreter, Robert Monk.[122] The popular image of much campus ministry remained under a cloud through the 1970s and beyond. A slow process of renewal began in the mid-1980s. The General Board of Higher Education and Ministry (GBHEM) began to recruit national campus ministry staff and refresh budget lines. The first national Methodist student conference since 1964 convened in 1987, providing once again opportunities for denominational fellowship and programming on a national scale. The 1992 General Conference established "Mission at the Center: A Campus Ministry Special Program" to provide grants for distinctive ministries among students. By 1997 there were 699 campus ministers and chaplains related in some way to the UMC.[123]

A turning point in the new denomination's youth ministry program took place at the tumultuous 1970 General Conference. The renewal coalition that won gains for African Americans and women included a large delegation of the church's young people who draped the convention hall with enormous signs proclaiming "YOUTH NOW." At the end of the conference young people won ten seats as nonvoting delegates, succeeded in getting the United Methodist Council on Youth Ministries out from under the Board of Education, gained self-determination in the administration of their substantial Youth

Service Fund, and most important of all, won rights for youth representation in annual conferences. Two young people under the age of twenty-five from each district would be named members of annual conferences.[124]

The Evangelical United Brethren Church

Evangelicals and United Brethren had, like their Methodist cousins, traveled a long road to the 1946 union, or perhaps we should say several roads.[125] The United Brethren created a Commission on Church Union in 1901 and began unity explorations with kindred churches. In 1903, the UBC entered into conversations with the Methodist Protestant and Congregational churches. The negotiations produced a "Church Union Syllabus" and "Act of Union" but foundered in all three churches. The UBC and MPC then resumed unity explorations that yielded a constitution, "Declaration of Faith," and proposed name—the United Protestant Church. Methodist Protestants approved, but United Brethren opposition in annual conference balloting convinced UBC bishops to counsel against proceeding. The 1917 UBC General Conference, which concurred in that counsel, nevertheless committed "to fraternize with other Christian bodies and co-operate with them in the larger work of the Kingdom."[126] In the 1920s, the UBC responded to an overture from the Reformed Church in the United States, one extended as well to but declined by the Evangelicals. Also responding positively was another church with German and Pietist background, the Evangelical Synod of North America. By 1929, negotiations by commissioners for the three churches had drafted a "Plan of Union" and proposed a name, the United Church of America. The 1929 UBC General Conference responded favorably to proceeding, a stance not echoed by the very church that had concocted the plan, the Reformed Church.

By this point, the Evangelicals had healed an east-west division that went back to 1891. The western, Indianapolis-based Evangelical Association had favored the German language, greater authority for bishops, clergy-only governing conferences, and a conservative theological stance. The eastern, Philadelphia-based United Evangelical Church preferred a more collegial episcopacy, lay representation in governing conferences, and openness to biblical criticism and new theological developments. Both churches participated in early twentieth-century ecumenical ventures, including the Federal Council of Churches. By 1911, they had begun conversations to heal their own schism and achieved unity in 1922 under a new name, the Evangelical Church. A small group of dissidents withdrew and formed an independent denomination, the Evangelical Congregational Church, a continuing denomination with a theological seminary in Myerstown, Pennsylvania.

Shortly thereafter (1926), the reunited EC began union conversations with its historic partner, the United Brethren Church. The courtship between such nonidentical twins, so alike but so different, was predictably bumpy. The United Brethren, with roots in the free church heritage of the Mennonites and the mild Calvinism of western Germany, had responded to the democratic ethos of the young American republic and developed a highly participatory polity. Though the UBC continued work among German-speaking people, the use of English soon became the UBC norm. The EC, fueled by a steady influx of German immigrants, maintained a strong relationship with the fatherland and its ways. The EC was not impervious to democratic developments or Americanizing forces, yet the German language retained a strong, if not dominant, position among Evangelicals until the early decades of the twentieth century. Meanwhile, elements drawn from roots in Episcopal Methodism combined with similar principles from the fatherland to give the function and structure of the EC a hierarchical and authoritarian flavor. The Evangelical Church did not welcome women delegates into its governing conferences or open its seminaries or its pulpits to women throughout its whole life. And when the EC united in 1946 with the United Brethren, the new EUBC, as we noted, rejected full clergy rights for women at Evangelical insistence. United Brethren women clergy, who had won that right almost sixty years earlier (1889), were forced to give up that right, which was not fully restored until union with the Methodists in 1968.

Despite the differences, the two churches had not stopped "keeping company," a fact also true between each of them and various branches of Methodism. By 1934, the Evangelicals and United Brethren formed a joint commission on church union and readied a plan of union by 1941. The Plan of Union was favored by the Evangelical General Conference the following year (1942). But it was not until 1946, after the United Brethren General Conference approved the plan, that the two churches—250,000 Evangelicals and 450,000 United Brethren—now both clearly identified as "churches," consummated a long anticipated, but often despaired, union. Bishops of the uniting churches, John Stamm (Evangelical Church) and Arthur Clippinger (United Brethren), celebrated the new church as a "complete union," all conferences and congregations committing to "go forward together" (Sources 1947a).[127]

The formula for union, except perhaps with regard to women in ministry, was to conjoin names, practices, and institutions of the two churches.[128] So the denominational name. So also the *Evangelical Messenger* merged with the UBC's *Religious Telescope* to become the new church's *Telescope-Messenger*. Publishing enterprises continued initially in Harrisburg and Dayton, eventually to be focused in the latter. Three theological schools continued in Dayton (Bonebrake), Naperville (Evangelical), and Reading (the last affiliated with Albright College). Between 1952 and 1954, the Dayton and Reading schools merged, favored the UBC site, and took the name United. The latter would continue there after the EUBC-Methodist merger and become an important caretaker of the EUBC heritage. Evangelical, however, would merge with the Methodists' Garrett, and the two names would be conjoined.

In the first *Discipline* the two different conceptions of church membership coexisted in rituals for infant baptism and child dedication. The new church did the same with the UBC *Confession of Faith* and the EC *Articles of Faith,* publishing them side by side. As we have seen, both were originally German statements, the former reflecting Otterbein's Pietist Calvinism rooted in the Heidelberg Catechism, the latter echoing Albright's appreciation for Wesleyan discipline and holiness doctrine as captured by the creed written by George Miller (Sources, pp. 38–41).[129] In part, Miller had adapted the Methodist-Anglican Articles of Religion. But he had also annexed "The Doctrine of Entire Sanctification and Christian Perfection," his own six-page digest of Wesleyan theology, the gist of which would constitute a particularly important contribution to United Methodist "Doctrinal Standards," as Article XI of the *Confession of Faith of the Evangelical United Brethren Church.* This new confession the 1958 EUBC General Conference entrusted to the Board of Bishops and adopted in 1962. The bishops reduced what had been twelve paragraphs to three in Article XI—Sanctification and Christian Perfection. And as Steven O'Malley shows, the bishops brought over the Evangelical *Articles'* influence in the *Confession's* treatment of the Trinity, original sin, last judgment, the sacraments, property, and government. Much of the *Confession,* O'Malley argues, reflects the UBC's Reformed Pietism and the Otterbein conception of the *ordo* (or *via*) *salutis,* especially in articles on reconciliation, justification, regeneration, adoption, sanctification, and good works and in the conception of the work of Christ and the Holy Spirit.[130]

Worship: EUBC and Methodist

A "high church" or aesthetic or Romantic movement in worship developed in many American churches in the early and middle twentieth century. Methodist, Evangelical, and United Brethren worship spaces became more "catholic." Outside, lean and tall Gothic Revival churches replaced the fat, squat Romanesque Revival churches all the rage in the Victorian era. Inside, the churches featured the medieval two-room Gothic Revival plan, complete with narrow naves for the people and a raised narrower room up front (chancel) for choir and clergy. Pulpits were moved to one side and joined by a reading desk or lectern on the other side. Crosses and candlesticks showed up on "altars" placed against the wall at the "east" end of the chancel. Preaching gowns replaced frock coats, and pulpit, lectern, and eventually clergy began to be vested in liturgical colors. Such an environment for worship encouraged a more formal style of worship.

Theologically Methodists, Evangelicals, and United Brethren fled from generations of hellfire preaching. Emphases on confession weakened. Eucharistic theology and practice became more radically Protestant. Suspicion about "the holy mystery" of Communion led many to less frequent (at most quarterly) celebrations, now not out of necessity as in the founding era—most churches had a resident pastor—but out of choice. An attempt by Methodists to eliminate the word *wine* from the Communion ritual in 1936 was defeated.[131] Pentecostals, cast away by the Methodists early in the new century, were not embarrassed by the sense of Christ's presence in their assemblies. Indeed, they relished the immediacy of the Spirit's presence as evidenced by various gifts such as healing, interpretation, and speaking in tongues. But this immediacy with Christ was not expressed in mother Methodism. Modern Methodists got very nervous about words that had survived virtually intact since Wesley.

Methodist Liturgical Legacies

Southern Methodists remained ritually conservative and made only minor changes in the Communion rite after their split with the North in 1844, none of great theological consequence. Northern Methodists (MEC) were less reluctant to change and initiated the first major revisions of the ritual in the twentieth century, in 1932.[132] This revision of the MEC Communion ritual, for the first time since 1792, combined word and sacrament in a unified rite. Since Methodists abandoned Wesley's *Sunday Service* in 1792, the official ritual had not contained the so-called Ante-Communion but had begun with the offertory sentences. For more than a century the abbreviated Communion rite was appended to a preaching service. The instructions for the 1932 service explicitly assert that the new Communion order was "to take place of the regular order of morning worship." This was a plus. On the minus side, the Communion rite featured a radically *memorialist* rewriting of the inherited Prayer of Humble Access:

> Grant us therefore so to partake of these *memorials* of thy Son Jesus Christ, . . . [versus "eat the flesh of thy dear Son and drink his blood" in place since 1785].

and the Eucharistic Prayer:

> Grant that we, receiving this bread and wine . . . may be *partakers of the divine nature* through Him . . . [versus "may be *partakers of his most blessed body and blood*" in place since 1785].

Mainstreamed in the new common hymnal of 1935, this revised rite marks the low point of eucharistic realism in American Methodism after Wesley. And not a single eucharistic hymn remained in the new hymnal. With a few tweakings at reunion of the three Methodisms in 1939–40, this liturgy remained in place until 1964. The resultant liturgy may have been prettier, but was thinner on sacramental theology.

The MECS continued the old 1792 order through union in 1939 with these prayers unchanged, but with no service of the word appended. This 1939 rite was the last time the phrase "most blessed body and blood" appeared in Methodist worship after 150 years of use.[133]

With reunion in 1939, both the then current northern and southern services appeared in *The Methodist Hymnal*, though liturgically and theologically they had become distinct: the long northern service was more traditional liturgically, and the brief southern service more traditional theologically.

Modern Methodist liturgical scholarship was born with Nolan Harmon's *Rites and Ritual of Episcopal Methodism* published in 1926. Harmon studied the historical development of the rituals of the two Episcopal Methodisms, comparing the Ritual with Wesley's *Sunday Service* of 1784, the 1662 Book of Common Prayer still in use in Wesley's day, the late medieval Roman Catholic Mass books according to the use of Sarum (which Thomas Cranmer had used for the basis of his 1549 Book of Common Prayer), and a few other relevant sources. Other scholars and church leaders began to publish books on worship and the sacraments. Neo-Wesleyan in their worship concepts, their preference was for the fixed forms that Wesley provided in his *Sunday Service*. Scholarly support for Methodist restorationism came from English Methodists, especially John Bowmer, John Bishop, and Ernest Rattenbury.

Another impetus was given by the founding of two liturgical caucuses with mid-twentieth-century beginnings, which shaped many would-be liturgical reformers among the Methodists. The Methodist Sacramental Fellowship (MSF) was founded in 1935 by *British* Methodists who were influenced by the recovery of weekly Communion in the Church of England and the wider ecumenical movement. The Order of Saint Luke (OSL), a religious order dedicated to sacramental and liturgical renewal, was founded in 1946 by *American* Methodists. The stated aims of the MSF and the OSL from the beginning were to reaffirm the *catholic* faith based upon the apostolic testimony of Holy Scripture, witnessed to in the Nicene Creed, and professed by the church through the ages, and to restore to modern Methodism the sacramental worship of the universal church and in particular the centrality of the Eucharist, as set forth in the lifelong teaching and practice of the Wesleys. Both groups began publishing ministries designed to put into the hands of seminarians, pastors, and layfolk liturgical works that had theological, historical, ecumenical, and practical integrity.[134]

British Methodists published a new *Book of Services* in 1936. A decade later (1945) America Methodism published its first *Book of Worship* since 1792. In the American book, no new Communion liturgies appeared, but the Christian Year, with its many teaching and worship implications, was recovered. By 1960, seminary students were well aware of the Christian calendar, and more and more churches were celebrating Advent, keeping Lent, and observing Pentecost, appreciating the ties with historic Christianity. A few Methodist churches in the 1950s began to use Communion tablecloths and pulpit and lectern hangings of appropriate color for the various seasons of the Christian Year.

Two decades later, a second American *Book of Worship* was authorized and published in 1965. For the first time a woman's name appears on the Commission on Worship, Mrs. Floyd W. Rigg. By this time the worship agenda had become clearer. Methodists found the liberal sentiments of the early twentieth century too glib after a decade and more of Depression and war. Neo-orthodoxy now had a profound appeal and was reflected throughout the 1965 book. Many affirmations of the Reformation era rang true, especially the dependence on God's grace in the face of human rebellion and sin. For Methodists the recovery of liturgies of Wesley said it all very well. Penitential piety was back in fashion, the Psalter was recovered, and the Christian Year loomed large, begun with a one-year lectionary. The revised full Communion rite contained components that were very close to those of Wesley's *Sunday Service*, but with a somewhat altered pattern, and four Wesleyan eucharistic hymns found their way back into the new hymnal; however, a compromise on eucharistic theology was reached in the ambiguity of "so to partake of this *sacrament* of thy Son Jesus Christ" in the Prayer of Humble Access.[135] This was as far as most Methodists were willing to go as late as the mid-1960s. Most had a memorialist view of the sacrament then and probably do today. Three services from Wesley conclude the book. The new liturgies, mainstreamed in the new *Hymnal* published in 1966, were stronger theologically and sacramentally than the preceding ones.

United Brethren Worship

The first order of worship for the UBC—complete with organ prelude and postlude, responsive reading, Apostles' Creed, and Gloria Patri—appeared in the *Sanctuary Hymnal* of 1914. A minor revision of the presider's "outline liturgy" for Communion occurred in 1925, a short introduction added before each scripture passage. Inexplicably the invitation to the table was removed. The prayer at the table was now specifically called a "consecratory prayer," but no text was given. No Communion liturgies were printed in the UBC hymnals of the time.

Ten years later (1935) a new hymnal was published, which contained for the first time two Communion liturgies. The first order was a full and formal service "based in general on the Communion in the *Book of Common Prayer* [of the Episcopal Church], revised in accordance with the usage of non-liturgical churches and adapted to meet the need of our own Communion." The compilers believed that the Lord's Supper "constitutes the loftiest service in our common worship . . . [and] is truly a festival of thanksgiving and the occasion for penitential confession and consecration."[136] The liturgy is a curious mix of Methodist prayers, gospel hymns, evangelical poetry, and responsive readings. At the table the ministers prayed, "Hear us, O merciful Father, . . . grant that we, receiving this bread and wine in remembrance of his passion, may also be *partakers of the divine nature* through Jesus Christ our Lord, and so partake of these *memorials* of thy Son."[137] Here the UBC drafters almost certainly were following the Methodist lead, since the phrases "partakers of the divine nature" and "these memorials" were introduced in the revised Methodist Communion rite published in the *Discipline* of 1932 and in a trial-use booklet, although wide use of the new prayers awaited the publication of the new hymnal three years later. The order was novel at one point. The revisers omitted the sermon: "Nothing must be allowed to take the place of the supreme reality. It is believed that the Sacrament itself should be the central act of worship when we meet to remember him."[138]

Evangelical Church Worship

Among Evangelicals, the first ever scripted order of worship, patterned after the 1914 UBC order as described above, appeared in the hymnal copyrighted in 1921. The hymnal was adopted by the United Evangelical Church in 1922, when the two groups merged. The Methodist-based full-text Communion liturgy was slightly revised (for example, the confession) in 1923 and regularly included in the denomination's official hymnals as well as the *Book of Discipline*. This rite served the church until union with the UBC in 1946.

Worship in The Evangelical United Brethren Church, 1946–68

The Evangelical and United Brethren liturgies and hymnals continued to be used in the united church from 1946 until 1957, when a new hymnal with Communion liturgies and a new presider's *Book of Ritual* (1959) were published. The orders of worship for non-Communion Sundays followed the more or less common Evangelical and United Brethren pattern with the fullest order "enriched" with processional and recessional hymns and choral responses throughout the service. The liturgy for Communion, though more liturgical in style, was decidedly memorialist in content. Communicants approached the table with this prayer: "Grant, therefore, gracious Lord, that we may come with confidence to the Throne of Grace; that Christ may dwell in our hearts through faith, . . . that we may be filled unto all the fullness of God." Bread and "wine" were consecrated with these words: "Bless and sanctify with thy Word and Holy Spirit these thy gifts of bread and wine; that we receive them according to thy Son our Savior, Jesus Christ's holy institution, in remembrance of his death and passion may be partakers of his most blessed body and blood."[139]

A 1952 article on the importance of Communion published in the EUBC magazine *Telescope-Messenger* put it bluntly:

> [The Holy Communion] is a sacrament, an outward and visible ceremony that symbolizes inward and spiritual experience, a means through which divine grace is imparted to the believer. This means that the essence of the Lord's Supper is to be found not in its physical elements but in the mind and heart of those who participate.[140]

For most Methodists, Evangelicals, and United Brethren, Holy Communion functioned more as a memorial of Christ's past works than as a *present* encounter with him. More altar tables bore the words "In Remembrance of Me" than "Holy, Holy, Holy."

Environments for Worship

With the resumption of a peacetime economy in the late 1940s, congregations in cities as well as small towns, but most often in postwar suburbs throughout the country, launched building programs long postponed, first by the Depression, then by war. The new churches were not replicas of those of earlier periods. Instead the large plants were planned as "seven-day-a-week-churches" with large parking lots. In their sanctuaries the center pulpit of yore was replaced with a pulpit and lectern and a modest altar table placed against the back wall as dictated by Conover's favored divided chancel. Generous space was provided for Christian education, staff offices, and a fellowship hall as well. These types of churches were, and still are, being built in great numbers in a variety of exterior costume. Two widely different styles dominated through the 1960s—red brick, white-pillared, tall-spired Colonial Revival, and clean-lined, natural-finished, A-frame Modern.[141]

The Building and Care of Methodist Church Property, a church plan book written by Bonneau P. Murphy and first published by the National Division of the Board of Missions in 1951, favored Colonial Revival plans.[142] But by 1957, A-frame Modern designs joined Colonial designs in Murphy's updated plan book, which even featured an A-frame church on its cover. The plan book went through four revisions through 1969.[143] Through later editions and its companion, *Sanctuary Planning,* published in 1962, 1963, 1964, and 1967, the department encouraged congregations to explore new *exterior* designs but was more cautious about changing interior arrangements of the liturgical furniture (that is, moving altar tables away from the back wall, abandoning lecterns in favor of a single podium for reading and preaching, and seating the choir in a single, rather than a divided, area).

The pacesetter A-frame pattern of the late 1950s and 1960s sported a high and dramatic roofline. This gave the emotive power of great height. Frequently the interior was still the dominant divided chancel, although in a wider chancel. The details were not Gothic, yet something of its feeling was preserved. Three of the earliest of these were featured in a photo essay in the denomination's *Together* magazine in 1958—Gretna MC in Gretna, Louisiana; Northside MC in Greenville, South Carolina; and Linwood MC in Linwood, Pennsylvania—and their numbers multiplied throughout the 1960s.[144] Frequently these dramatic roofs combined with skylights or clerestory windows to create dramatic interior light effects, often focused on some spot, the altar or the pulpit. Another favored form for new churches became a fan-shaped plan with the congregation spread in 180 degrees around table and pulpit. It was obvious that Gothic would not work for a fan-shaped church, so modern architecture won an easy victory.

These years saw a few timid experiments in liturgical architecture, the most popular of which involved the simple act of moving the altar away from the "east" wall and celebrating Communion from behind it. The Episcopal Church published a booklet dealing with this practice as early as 1956.[145] The obvious advantage was that it gave the congregation a better view of the actions of the altar. It also recovered some of the dramatic aspects of the sacrament as a reenactment of the Last Supper, with some features of the intimacy of that meal. A second modest experiment was that of returning the Communion rail so as to enclose the table on three sides or even on four. Most experiments continued a fairly well-defined raised chancel area, but the basic floor plan was still the neo-medieval double rectangle of nave and chancel. The prophet of reformed worship space in late twentieth-century America among Methodists was liturgical historian James F. White. His 1966 essay, "Church Architecture and Church Renewal," was the first of many essays and books that contributed mightily to the field of modern church architecture.[146]

Articles in popular Methodist publications in the 1960s highlighted new developments. In *World Outlook*, Norman Byar, director of the Department of Architecture of the Section of Church Extension of the Board of Missions' National Division, noted trends in church architecture: toward the altar-centered worship space, toward a "unified room for worship that allows for no architectural division between the nave and the chancel," and toward wider worship rooms and away from balconies and basements, among others.[147]

Noted church architect Walter Wagoner of Philadelphia was asked to detail the struggle for new church forms within Protestantism in a "New Directions" series in the denomination's *Together* magazine, and editors highlighted five examples. First, Manhattan Avenue Methodist Church, Tampa, Florida, designed by Wagoner and opened in 1963. The boat-shaped church featured a free-standing altar in a slightly elevated, divided chancel. The chancel, with pulpit and lectern on either side, is surrounded by a chancel rail, but the rail is open at the center. A baptismal font holds a place of honor in the front of the church just outside the chancel rail. It is in full view of the assembly and suggests an understanding of baptism as the entryway into the sacramental life of the church. Second, St. Stephen Methodist Church, Mesquite, Texas, designed by James Pratt and John Box, opened in 1962. This free-form plaster-coated concrete block church broke new ground architecturally, though the semicircular worship space is reminiscent of the old auditorium churches with pulpit and oval table sharing front and center. Third, Good Shepherd Methodist Church, Park Ridge, Illinois, built in 1963, was at one and the same time a space of traditional and contemporary design. The sanctuary is circular, and the V-shaped Communion table is central. There is no chancel rail. Fourth, Bloomfield Methodist Church, Bloomfield, Connecticut, designed by Galliher & Schoenhardt in 1964, features octagonal worship space with seating in a three-quarter circle arrangement. A square white marble table is centered opposite the main entrance. An adjoining fan-shaped educational unit completes the building. The pulpit is placed close to one side of the space, with the Communion table in front. The font is in front of the table at the head of the center aisle; the choir sits among the assembly. Fifth, First Methodist Church, Palo Alto, California, designed by Carlton A. Steiner, opened in 1963. In footprint it is a long rectangle, with a circular apse containing the free-standing table, but pulpit, lectern, and choir seats are arranged in traditional divided chancel fashion. It is more innovative on the outside than on the inside.[148]

Four of these five experiments have a number of features in common. First of all, the altar (more often called the table and looking like one) was placed in the center of the congregation. Instead of the table being isolated from the congregation by the length of the chancel, it is placed in the midst of worshipers. The second common feature is the reduction in the number of liturgical centers. Instead of having pulpit, lecture, altar, and font at the extremities of a chancel, an effort was made to group these centers together and to simplify them as much as possible, as congregations gather around three centers: a book, a meal, and a bath. By the 1980s and 1990s, a new interest in the process of Christian initiation had reached many churches. This led to a preference for baptism by immersion or at least bigger bowls, fonts, or wading pools. The sign value of baptism is greatly increased by immersion.[149] Few of the churches detailed above are spectacular, structurally or aesthetically. Yet these congregations took the risk of conducting experiments to find more adequate settings for the liturgy. None was perfect but each was certainly more adequate than a divided chancel or concert stage arrangement. These largely A-frame or fan-shaped churches bridged the way to more adventuresome modern buildings.

At the same time a growing ecumenical-inspired liturgical movement made its impact felt on some pastors and congregations. A quick look at the new hymnals and service books shows a clear trajectory: stress on the sacraments as communion with God, the lectionary as a guide to the full gospel, the church year as a way to make time meaningful, and scriptural preaching as God's word made present. A growing appreciation of symbolic representations of interaction with the divine led to new arrangements of liturgical spaces and liturgical centers. It was a period of liturgical euphoria as accepted conventions came crashing down. In all this confusion, clear leadership was given in a 1988 book by James and Susan White, *Church Architecture: Building and Renovating for Christian Worship*: give primacy to the worshiping assembly and its functions, create one-room churches and move tables into the midst of the congregation, presume the celebrant will face the people, eliminate chancel/nave plans, reduce the number of liturgical centers, and minimize distinctions between clergy and laity.

In all these architectural reforms, the key word was *participation*. This latter principle had been introduced by the Second Vatican Council (1963) and reinforced by guidelines adopted by the U.S. Roman Catholic Bishops' Committee on the Liturgy in 1978, *Environment and Art in Catholic Worship*. Written largely by the late Robert Hovda, a former Methodist who became a Catholic priest, it is a classic statement that insists that "among the symbols with which the liturgy deals, none is more important than this, [the baptized] assembly of believers itself."

Architect Edward Sövik of Northfield, Minnesota, made an important contribution. The son of missionaries and a trained theologian, Sövik by his involvement with more than three hundred congregations and frequent articles and one book, *Architecture for Worship* (1973), reached a wide audience. It is not difficult, as James White has done, to hail him as the leading Protestant form-maker of the 1980s and 1990s, although his work began earlier. Sövik stressed building the best space available but leaving it flexible for a variety of uses in worship. Only his fonts and pipe organs were immovable (though keyboard/consoles were often movable). Frequently a cross appeared as a processional cross in the middle of the congregation. Arrangements of liturgical centers and liturgical spaces could be changed for different worship occasions. Worshipers convened in a "concourse" or gathering space. Typically his buildings were brick with flat roofs and did not flaunt their religious function. But they did welcome new forms of worship as they evolved. Sövik's work had and still has an enormous impact on other church architects.[150]

Trinity United Methodist Church, Charles City, Iowa, Edward Sövik's first design with his preferred concourse/centrum arrangement, opened in 1972. The exterior is composed of concrete bands with brick in-fill. A driveway entrance with clear glass doors serves as the primary entrance, the concourse of the facility. Concrete columns, resembling a simple scaffold, hold four bells and a small Greek cross at a minimal height above the flat roof. Trinity's worship space is square in shape with a platform area located on one side with seating on each of the other three sides. A concourse containing tables and chairs is located immediately outside the main worship space. The concourse is spacious enough to accommodate small gatherings of people and has a wall of glass opening on to an open court, allowing for ample light.

The interior of the worship space has a flat floor of paving brick. The walls of the space are brick and with some panels of wood. Areas of stained glass are placed in three of the four walls. The stained glass is abstract, angular geometric shapes in various hues. The stained glass was designed by the well-known firm Rambusch, Inc., of New York City. The baptismal font is placed near the entrance to the space, against the wall. The font is made of gray granite, three feet square by thirty-two inches high. Water is introduced to the font through a pipe. A drain has been placed in the bottom of the basin of the font. The capacity is significant enough to be able to baptize an infant by immersion.

A platform made up of several segments is usually placed along one longer wall of the space, providing a slight elevation for the altar/table, pulpit, and chairs for those presiding at liturgical celebrations. The platform area can be organized in any number of ways and can be readily removed. The altar/table is rectangular, made of oak with a clear finish. Four oak candle stands are positioned on the floor at each corner of the altar/table.

A simple oak pulpit and lectern are of the same general design. Congregational seating consists of chairs, designed by Sövik, placed on three sides of the platform area. The choir is located to the left side of the platform area, near the pipe organ, a tracker design built for Trinity in Austria. The console and ranks of pipes are located in a large, but simple case, designed by Sövik, minimally inhibiting the overall flexibility of the space. Sövik received a merit award for the design from the Guild of Religious Architecture in 1973.[151]

The latest development, especially in the 1990s, moved in a quite different direction, namely, the megachurches of the church growth movement. In the early 2000s the UMC tallied the second largest percentage of denominational megachurches (9 percent) after the Southern Baptists (20 percent) in a survey conducted by the Hartford Institute for Religious Research for the UMC.[152] Adam Hamilton's UMC of the Resurrection in Leawood, Kansas, is one of the best known. Liturgy is seen as a barrier to seekers and largely eliminated. At Willow Creek Community Church near Chicago, mother church of the megachurch movement, an altar is totally absent. The message is the opposite of Conover. Buildings are meant to look as unchurchly as possible in order to remove any barriers to evangelism. Willow Creek, and countless Methodist clones, could be mistaken for a nearby corporate headquarters. Participation is not a goal as the congregation relaxes in theater seating. All entertainment evangelism needs is a small portable lectern on the platform and room for the musicians backed up by multiple projection screens.[153]

Such extreme modernism was too much for most congregations. In the wake of 9/11 and the Persian Gulf wars, Americans simultaneously experienced a sense of foreboding and uncertainty. Postmodern eclecticism set in. When building new churches, many congregations sought comfort, a sense of rootedness, and continuity with the past. The dichotomy between a need for tradition and its reassurance and a demand for a new conception of religion befitting the modern era characterized the religious climate of the postwar years. The tension forced thoughtful church designers and architects to reconcile in physical form the demand for heritage and the expression of a fresh vision. There is every reason to believe that the variety of possibilities will increase, new spatial needs and resolutions will be forthcoming, and new cycles of dominant architectural trends will rise, mature, and fade from popularity.[154]

Cold and Korean Wars

In the post–World War II era the new threat of Soviet Russia as a world power and the fears engendered by Russian domination of neighboring states, especially Korea, magnified old fears of communism and gave rise to new ones. To the United Nations and the "free" world, the Korean conflict was a "police" action designed to contain Communist aggression at the thirty-eighth parallel, the line that divides present-day South Korea from North Korea. To Korea, it was and still is a civil war. To America, it is a war remembered in reruns of *MASH*, but a war that many veterans cannot forget. When truce was reached (after three years of carnage), 1.5 million men, women, and children were left dead. More than 250,000 Allies had been killed; 100,000 Americans were wounded, 7,000 were taken prisoner, and 8,000 were missing in action. Official records still cannot account for 3,200 MIAs and 390 POWs. Many Methodists, strongly committed to the UN and international means of dealing with conflict, viewed the war with ambivalence. In November 1950, the Methodist Commission on World Peace urged restraint. Later that month, the Council of Bishops promised prayer for leaders of the U.S. and the nation's armed forces. A year later, 1951, the bishops expressed support for a negotiated settlement and urged that "every honorable concession shall be made to achieve the desired goals." Their statement continued, "We further urge that the ultimate goal of our peace-making and the stated policy of the United Nations be to secure the economic rehabilitation of an independent and united Korea."

Dissent grew as the war became protracted and indecisive. The draft presented a problem for some young Methodists like James Lawson, an African American preministerial student who learned of Gandhi while in college and became a strong supporter of the principles of nonviolence. In 1951 Lawson was sentenced to three years in a federal prison for refusing the draft. After serving only thirteen months, he was released on the condition that he would do church work in India. The draft law changed in 1951 to provide for individual COs to volunteer for work with designated agencies with the approval of their draft boards and to receive pay for the work performed.

The Episcopal Address to the 1952 General Conference went further toward an endorsement of the war: "The issue of peace or war rests largely upon the people of the U.S. who have chosen to defend the Republic of Korea through the United Nations, from the aggression of a Communist invasion." The bishops paid high tribute to persons who "in mortal combat have given their all that freedom might not perish from the earth." By 1952, widespread sentiment surfaced in The Methodist Church, fostered in part by the Commission on World Peace, for a new quadrennial emphasis on peace. Interest in such an endeavor throughout the church was tremendous. More memorials to that year's General Conference concerned the crusade than any other issue. This interest was probably sparked by memories of the success of the original Crusade for a New World Order and by Methodist concern over the growing disillusionment with the UN. General Conference responded in those terms, producing no endorsement of the war, but instead exhorted the COB to lead the church in peacemaking and in a new Crusade for World Order that would strengthen the UN's effectiveness as an "instrument of peace."[155]

The U.S.-UN action in Korea never received clear official support from The Methodist Church as it had from both the World Council of Churches and the National Council of Churches. Instead, the church granted a tacit approval. Its strong support, as came also from the churches generally, went for effective U.S. participation in the humanitarian programs of the UN. Evangelical, United Brethren, and Methodist agencies joined with many other groups in asking Congress to increase appropriations to UNICEF, the United Nations Children's Fund. Thousands of churches across the country organized their children to engage in door-to-door trick or treat for UNICEF collections, thus raising many millions of dollars to aid children and mothers in other lands. UN officials often commented that the churches were the largest group engaged in these supportive activities.

Social Activism and "Red Scare"

During the 1950s, as the cold war intensified and the U.S. threw its soldiers into the proxy front in Korea, the Red scare and civil liberties situation worsened. The Korean conflict, Chinese participation, fears over Russian nuclear threats, and disclosure of Communist spying intensified hysteria over collusion and fellow traveling. The FBI added quite a few Methodists to a long list of Americans it considered disloyal. A document declassified in 2007 showed that J. Edgar Hoover of the FBI had a plan in 1950 to suspend habeas corpus and imprison some twelve thousand Americans he suspected of disloyalty. President Truman wisely demurred implementing Hoover's plan. In 1948 a congressional Committee on Un-American Activities issued the report *100 Things You Ought to Know about Communism and Religion*. It informed church folk what would happen to them and their churches if communism ever took over. The FBI labeled two Methodist groups—the MFSS (after 1948, the Methodist Federation for Social *Action*, MFSA) and the Methodist Epworth League—as "tools" of the Communist Party. Not quite up to date on its conspiracies with regard to the latter, the FBI had discovered infiltration and suspect leaders, programs, and publications in a group that had not existed since 1939, having been replaced in 1941 by the Methodist Youth Fellowship. The U.S. House Committee on Un-American Activities (HUAC) collected and republished attacks on the MFSA and MYF in 1952. In the Senate, Joseph McCarthy conducted similar denunciatory exposures. Clergy who rallied to the defense of Methodist social witness or questioned McCarthyism or evidenced any softening of cold war rhetoric faced charges of being tainted with communism.[156]

Because the social gospel and the social reforms of recent years were based on considerations of human welfare that were also professed by Soviet communism, it became the basic strategy of Methodist conservatives to identify them with each other. Thereafter, the war against liberalism in The Methodist Church was to be waged in the name of the battle against communism. As the oldest and most articulate organized group of social liberals in The Methodist Church, the MFSS/A was in the most vulnerable position to receive the assault that was launched by conservatives within the church. Particularly strong attacks were made against certain bishops and other church leaders affiliated with the federation, against the use of the term *Methodist* in its title, against federation pronouncements that could be construed to represent the whole church, and also against the influence of the federation on the educational and publication program of the church. Furthermore, the conservatives began to organize and to try to push The Methodist Church officially back to positions that they favored with respect to social issues.

The segregated jurisdictional system gave Methodism's social prophets, the MFSS included, another sin against God's covenant to denounce but a cause as well that conservatives would deem Communist. In 1940, Mary McLeod Bethune joined Bishop Edgar Love and others on the MFSS executive committee to continue MFSS's emphasis on combating racism in the new denomination's churches and agencies. Eight years later, Bishop Robert Brooks of the Central (all-Black) Jurisdiction was elected MFSS's president. Also in 1940 Harry Ward was hauled before the House Un-American Activities Committee. Although defended by Union Theological Seminary president Henry Sloane Coffin and Professor Reinhold Niebuhr, Ward was forced to resign his faculty post at Union Theological Seminary the following year. The retirement of Ward and of Bishop McConnell in 1944 triggered both internal dissension and external criticisms of Methodism's social justice caucus. MFSS chose the Reverend Jack McMichael, even more radical in ideas and methods than Ward and McConnell, as MFSS executive secretary. McMichael led the federation's period of greatest expansion, with some forty conference chapters and five thousand members by the end of the decade. In response, the FBI compiled thousands of pages of files on the MFSA and its executive McMichael, and the House Un-American Activities Committee published an eighty-eight-page government publication purporting to document the federation's subversive nature. In 1953 McMichael appeared before the HUAC and challenged its accusations of Communist subversion with such telling references to the ministry of Jesus that an aggravated committee member shouted, "Can't we leave Jesus out." McMichael replied that he absolutely could not, adding that "in a situation like this, where guilt by association seems to be the principle on which you are operating... I am sure [Jesus] himself would have long ago been hauled before this committee!"

Further fuel had been added to the fire of controversy by sinister innuendos in Rembert Gilman Smith's book *Moscow over Methodism* (1950)[157] and Stanley High's "Methodism's Pink Fringe," which appeared in the ever popular *Reader's Digest*, February 1950, charging several Methodist groups and leaders with having ties to international communism.[158] Walter Muelder, social ethics professor at the denomination's Boston University School of Theology and the MFSA's vice president, issued a public protest (Sources 1950). So did Bishop G. Bromley Oxnam, whose reply *Reader's Digest* refused to publish.[159] Other critics within The Methodist Church, especially the Texas-based Circuit Riders, Inc., capitalized on the prevailing McCarthyite hysteria to secure General Conference repudiation of the MFSA. Formed in 1948 with the single purpose of driving the federation out of Methodism, the group later attacked the federation for its support of racial integration.[160]

A storm of vilification was directed against the MFSA at the 1952 General Conference in San Francisco. Pressured from folks back home, conference delegates demanded that the MFSA stop using the name "Methodist" (though that matter was not legally within the jurisdiction of the conference) and vacate its offices in the Methodist building in New York City.[161] The MFSA was prohibited from appearing to speak for Methodists, a function rightly reserved for the General Conference itself, and certain statements made in the name of the MFSA were officially disclaimed by the denomination. Moreover, the General Conference brought the consideration of social issues more directly under its own guidance by creating a "safer," less "radical," Board of Social and Economic Relations.[162]

The federation did move out of the church's office building, but defiantly did not change its name. Declassified FBI files obtained by the MFSA in the 1980s under the Freedom of Information Act detail how thoroughly the government had been involved in getting The Methodist Church to repudiate the MFSA. Several prominent Methodist church leaders were put under suspicion and surveillance, including Bishop G. Bromley Oxnam, MFSA executive Harry Ward, and theological school professor Georgia Harkness, among others, accused of being members of the Communist Party. Professional informant Louis Budenz reported:

> Advised that Dr. Georgia Elma Harkness . . . was clearly associated with the CP [Communist Party] and subsequently agreed to join. Informant stated that from 1943 to 1945 Dr. Harkness was a member of CP fronts; it was publicly known that she was a member of perhaps 10 such fronts and that she was influenced by Dr. Harry F. Ward to become associated with the front groups.[163]

The HUAC summoned MFSA executive Jack McMichael, as already noted, to testify before it in 1953 and charged him with being second-in-command of a Communist cell in New York (when he had been a sixteen-year-old high school student in Georgia). Still, the FBI effectively blacklisted him. Harassment continued for a long time after he returned to pastoring congregations in the California-Nevada Conference.

The HUAC made Bishop Oxnam (1891–1963), a highly respected and highly visible church leader, president of the Federal Council of Churches in the U.S. (1944–46), and president of the World Council of Churches (1948–54), a favorite target.[164] The committee repeatedly released "unevaluated" reports implying that Oxnam was a member of several "subversive" organizations and either sympathized with the Communist Party or allowed himself to be used by it. The committee offered him the hard choice extended in those days to many Americans inside the churches and out: confess either to treason or to treasonable stupidity. To clear the record, Bishop Oxnam demanded a hearing before the congressional committee a year before broadcast journalist Edward R. Murrow famously took HUAC to task and at the peak of McCarthy's popularity and power. The hearing itself, a fatiguing session lasting from midafternoon till midnight on July 21, 1953, was televised across the nation. *U.S. News & World Report* reprinted the transcript of the hearing in full. The bishop, mountains of files at hand, exposed the sloppy research, unreliable reports, and deliberate falsehoods in committee records and statements, indirectly unmasking the committee's self-aggrandizing motivations in suggesting he was a Communist dupe (Sources 1953).

Bishop Oxnam publicly protested against "procedures that are in effect the rule of men and not of law; procedures subject to the prejudices, passions and political ambitions of Committeemen; procedures designed less to elicit information than to entrap; procedures that cease to be investigation and become inquisition and intimidation" (Sources 1953). *The Christian Advocate* for August 6, 1953, carried a summary of public reaction to the hearing, which it evaluated to be favorable to Oxnam, though it reported the negative responses as well, quoting one Methodist, "Still, with all those organizations mentioned, he must be a pinko." The summary noted that many daily papers, such as the *Louisville Courier-Journal*, the *Boston Herald*, the *Arkansas Gazette*, and the *New York Times*, editorially commended Oxnam.

The thinness of the evidence and the unfairness of the inquisitorial tactics resulted in broad public support for the bishop. The "trial" helped diminish public respect for HUAC. A brilliant defense of the rights of the individual citizen to security from unsubstantiated accusations and trial by gossip was subsequently set forth in Oxnam's book, *I Protest*, published the following year. That summer (June 28, 1953) *Parade* magazine, which accompanied countless Sunday newspapers across the country, carried a two-page article by Oxnam enticingly titled "How to Uncover Communists . . . without Throwing Mud on Innocent People."[165]

Bishop Oxnam exonerated himself, but the MFSA lived under a cloud for a decade. Between 1953 and 1960, the MFSA operated without an executive secretary. Pastor Lloyd Worley served as its president and chief executive officer. Throughout the 1950s, the MFSA cooperated with the religious Freedom Committee, which had been organized to protect radical clergy from conservative attacks and legal prosecution. It also demanded the repeal of the harsh internal security/anti-alien Smith and McCarran Acts as well as the abolition of HUAC. A dedicated remnant, including such leaders as Worley, Mark Chamberlain, and Lee and Mae Ball, saw the importance of an *independent* advocate for social justice and kept the federation alive until it blossomed again in the civil rights and antiwar movements of the 1960s. In the midst of the whirlwind, in 1951, the Board of Missions quietly launched the US-2 Program, recruiting young adults to serve as missionaries working for justice, freedom, and peace in U.S. communities. In fifty years the program trained about thirteen thousand young adults between the ages of twenty and thirty to serve in U.S.-based ministries—a breakthrough of social justice concern in this period.

The 1968 Union and Other Ecumenical Projects

The 1939 Methodist and 1946 EUB family unions represented key parts but just parts of the investment the churches made toward Christian unity. And the larger quest to reunite Christ's body informed the 1968 Methodist-EUB union. Methodists and EUBs worked ecumenically on various fronts—on their own global unity, in bilateral and multilateral dialogues, in faith and order discussions—the several explorations sometimes reinforcing, sometimes competing with efforts to put the Methodist family back together. The year 1939 saw also the formation of the World Federation of Methodist Women, and two years later the creation of Church Women United brought together missionary and cooperative organizations representing some seventy American denominations. Methodists and EUBs did not take prominent roles initially, as did their holiness counterparts, in the National Association of Evangelicals (1943) but certainly did five years later in the formation of the World Council of Churches (WCC). Lay leaders John R. Mott and Charles Parlin, together with Bishop G. Bromley Oxnam, helped found the WCC. Oxnam served as its first president. Parlin headed the finance committee (1948–68) and was a member of the Central Committee (1954–58) and of the Presidium (1961–68).

Through the years, others from Methodism's global family have served as presidents, including Sante Uberto Barbiere, Iglesia Evangelica Metodista in Argentina (1954–61); D. T. Niles, Methodist Church in Sri Lanka (1968–75); Jose Miguez Bonino, Iglesia Evangelica Metodista in Argentina (1975–83); Dame R. Nita Barrow of Barbados, Methodist Church in the Caribbean and the Americas (1989–91); and Bishop Vinton R. Anderson, African Methodist Episcopal Church in the U.S. (1991–98). D. T. Niles (MC, Sri Lanka), famed as preacher and spokesperson for the emerging "younger churches" of Asia, delivered the keynote address at the founding assembly (1948) of the WCC in Amsterdam and chaired the Youth Department and later the Evangelism Department of the WCC. Since its beginnings, three of the WCC's six chief executives have been Methodist—Philip Potter (1972–84), Emilio Castro (1985–92), and Samuel Kobia (2003–9). More recently Dr. Jan Love (UMC, USA) has held several leadership roles in the WCC, beginning in 1975 when she was elected to the WCC's Central Committee. Love remained a UMC representative on the 158-member Central Committee until 1998, filling a number of important posts. From 1983 to 1991, she was part of the WCC's 325-member Executive Committee. She served as moderator of the Commission of the Churches on International Affairs (1992–98) and was part of the Special Commission on Orthodox Participation in the WCC (1999–2002).

Methodist deaconesses contributed to the 1947 formation of the World Federation of

Diaconal Associations, a body that has met every three years. Methodists from several countries became charter members; UMC deaconess Betsy Ewing served as president from 1971 to 1975. In 1948, Bishop Oxnam delivered a strong affirmation of "The Reunion of the Churches" in the Episcopal Address to General Conference (MC, USA). General Conference responded by forming a standing Commission on Church Union to engage in dialogue with separated churches in the U.S. and a Commission on the Structure of Methodism Overseas (COSMOS) to rethink links between the MC (USA) and its overseas dependent churches. Lay leader Charles Parlin played major roles in both commissions through 1964. The same year intercommunion and union talks with the Episcopal Church began but stalled a decade later over issues of reordination and closed Communion. In 1949, representatives of eight mainline U.S. denominations, at a conference in Greenwich, Connecticut, unveiled the Greenwich Plan for church union. Bishop Ivan Lee Hold (MC) was elected the first president. Although the several denominations recognized the validity of each other's ordinations and appeared to have consensus on doctrine and sacramental practice, the plan foundered on polity matters.

In 1950, a successor organization to the Federal Council, the National Council of Churches (USA), representing thirty denominations from Quakers to Eastern Orthodox, organized in an assembly in Cleveland. It brought together twelve existing ecumenical and missionary agencies. Methodists played prominent leadership roles in governing body and executive staff in the council from the earliest years. During the 1950s, Professor Albert Outler (SMU faculty) and Bishop William Cannon emerged as leading Methodist voices of the ecumenical movement. In this cause Outler authored one of his most significant books, *The Christian Tradition and the Unity We Seek* (1957). Both Outler and Cannon played leading roles in the Faith and Order movement beginning at Lund, Sweden, in 1952; at the WCC third assembly (New Delhi, 1961) and fourth assembly (Uppsala, 1968); in the Consultation on Church Union in the United States beginning in 1962; and in the World Methodist Council–sponsored bilateral conversations with Roman Catholics beginning in 1966.

In 1951, the World Methodist Council (WMC), successor to the Ecumenical Methodist Conferences, was formed and decided to hold WMC Conferences at five-year intervals rather than ten-year intervals as previously. Elmer T. Clark (MC, USA) assumed the general secretaryship. Headquartered at Lake Junaluska, North Carolina, since 1953, the WMC within sixteen years linked sixty-four member churches in 108 nations, eight of which are united churches with Methodist roots. In 1952, The Methodist Church (USA) established the Interdenominational Cooperation Fund apportionment to support ecumenical efforts around the world, witness to the Christian faith, and foster renewal of Christian unity and understanding.

In 1958, the Methodist Commission on Church Union and the EUB Commission on Church Federation and Union held its first joint meeting in Cincinnati. It would take a decade for its work to consummate. In the interim, Methodists and EUBs joined the nine-communion project (including three Black Methodist denominations) in the Consultation on Church Union (COCU). Begun in 1962, the COCU produced by 1970 a plan of union, envisioning a new ecclesial body, including institutional merger. By 1963, Charles Parlin was backtracking, arguing for family-style ecumenism as the place to begin. Methodists of the world should unite first, then negotiate out of strength with Anglicans, Catholics, Lutherans, and Reformed. He saw union with the EUBC as the first step. In 1964, the Methodist delegation to the COCU plenary led by Parlin declared "Four Principles of Distinctive Methodist Witness": (1) bishops as itinerant general superintendents versus any notion of diocesan episcopacy, (2) a connectional system, (3) infant baptism, and (4) total abstinence as the sole interpretation of Christian temperance.

Another and less threatening multidenominational but Methodist family project began in 1959, the Oxford Institutes on Methodist Theological Studies. A sort of Methodist Faith and Order movement, bringing together scholars and church leaders from across the Wesleyan world, the Institute has met in Oxford University, roughly at five-year intervals, focused on key doctrinal or ethical concerns, and published its plenary addresses on the selected themes (biblical theology, ecclesiology, Christology, the doctrines of God and Holy Spirit, sanctification and liberation, the future of Methodist theological traditions, theological diversity, good news to the poor, the Trinity, and new creation).

When the Second Vatican Council convened (1962–65), Bishop Fred Corson (MC, USA), Harold Roberts (MC, GBr), and Professors Franz Hildebrandt (Drew), Albert Outler (SMU), and Jose Miguez Bonino (Facultad Evangelica de Teologia, Buenos Aires) represented the World Methodist Council.[166] In total, sixteen Methodists from the U.S. and the United Kingdom served as observers at the several sessions of the council in Rome through 1965. In the new spirit inspired by Vatican II, the Montreal Conference of Faith and Order, which met in 1963, revisited the issue that had divided Protestants and Catholics since the sixteenth century, the interrelationship between Scripture and tradition. Understanding the church's proclamation to be rooted in the gospel, tradition, and works of the Spirit, the gathering looked toward new relations between and among Protestant, Catholic, Orthodox, Anglican, and free churches.

In 1964, the Methodist General Conference established a Commission on Ecumenical Affairs. Continued in the UMC (1968–72), it became the Ecumenical and Interreligious Concerns Division of the General Board of Global Ministries (1972–80) and later a separate commission. In 1965, Robert W. Huston was named the first full-time executive of the Methodist Church's Commission on Ecumenical Affairs. By 1967, under Huston's guidance, Commissions on Ecumenical Affairs had been formed in sixty out of ninety conferences in the U.S.

In 1966, a World Methodist Structure Consultation (Green Lake, Wisconsin) considered three possible postcolonial futures for a Methodism with central conferences around the world. The church could make minor adjustments to the status quo, with Central Conferences overseas remaining accountable to U.S. General Conference. It could urge Methodists of American provenance in other countries to become autonomous or form united churches linked by a World Methodist Council of churches. Or it could create a World Methodist Church with regional General Conferences.

In 1966, Methodism began bilateral dialogues with "separated" sisters and brothers on national and international levels: Roman Catholic (USA) 1966, Roman Catholic (international) 1967, Lutheran (USA) 1977, Lutheran (international) 1979, Anglican (international) 1988, Anglican (USA) 1988, Reformed (international) 1992, Orthodox (international) 1992.

Conversation between Methodists and EUBs, which might be said to actually antedate the formation of the MEC, UBC, and EA denominations, could also be said to coincide with the formation of the EUBC in 1946. At that first EUBC General Conference, Bishop Oxnam relayed a unity overture from the MC Council of Bishops. By the late 1950s, the EUBC began conversation with several churches, among them the Methodists, stressing a union-promising, common heritage, doctrine, worship, and polity. Explorations continued between EUBs and Methodists in the early 1960s and by 1966 had yielded a plan of union.[167] The EUBC's Paul Washburn served as executive secretary of the joint commission, toured the church in interpreting what unity would mean, and summarized his counsel in question-and-answer format in the church's major paper (Sources 1966b). He reassured EUBs that they would not simply be swallowed up and that the projected new church would enhance, not undercut, their spiritual, ecumenical, ethical, strategic, and missional commitments, including the explorations represented by COCU, in which he was an active participant.

Sounding a similar concern, also in 1966, Professor Albert Outler urged Methodists to "fish or cut bait" in ecumenical waters at a second conference, Methodism in an Ecumenical Age, at Lake Junaluska, North Carolina. He warned of the dangers of world confessionalism—choose COCU or COSMOS! Outler also published that year a widely used study book for the denomination: *That the World May Believe: A Study of Christian Unity*. The next year, the Boards of Education, Mission, Lay Activities, and Commission on Ecumenical Affairs of MC (USA) convened a national conference, Educating for Ecumenism. The keynoter, seminary president Norman Trott, told the assembly Methodists they would feel at home in the new COCU church.

In some parts of the U.S., Methodists had little firsthand knowledge of the EUBs because the denomination was not represented in many communities where Methodists lived. That was especially true in the southern states, New England, and parts of the far West. By contrast, EUB membership was concentrated in a few northern and midwestern states.

Pennsylvania, a state where many German immigrants settled on their arrival from Europe, was the birthplace of the denomination and still home to more than one-fourth of all EUBs. To help Methodists become better acquainted with their proposed partners in denominational marriage, union negotiator-in-chief Charles Parlin wrote a study book for church schools in 1965, and the October 1966 issue of Methodism's *Together* magazine presented fourteen pages of texts and pictures introducing the EUBC and its history, organization, and examples of its ministries in the U.S. and other parts of the world.[168]

Both Methodists and EUBs had connectional systems in which local congregations were related to the general church through annual conferences under administration of bishops. Both churches were governed by General Conferences made up of equal numbers of lay and ministerial delegates elected by annual conferences, and both provided order for their organizational life through rules set forth in their books of *Discipline*. Both denominations operated administratively through general boards, commissions, and other agencies that oversaw work in missions, education, publishing, pensions, evangelism, and social concerns.

Yet differences there were—mostly of size and degree. Because the EUBC was a body of about three quarters of a million members, compared to the Methodist 10.3 million, the EUBC organization was smaller and less complex. The 4,300 EUB congregations in the U.S and Canada were grouped into 32 annual conferences; Methodism's 38,800 churches in the U.S. alone were in 90 conferences. Methodism had 46 episcopal areas, and the bishops who supervised them were elected by 6 jurisdictional conferences. EUBs had only 7 episcopal areas, and the bishops who served them were elected by the General Conference; there were no jurisdictional conferences. EUB district superintendents (DSs) were elected by annual conferences; Methodist DSs were appointed by the bishops. Administration of all EUB general agencies was centered in Dayton, Ohio; Methodist agencies were scattered in New York, Philadelphia, Cincinnati, Nashville, Washington, D.C., and Evanston.

Missionary activity among Evangelicals and United Brethren began in the mid-nineteenth century when each group sent missionaries to Europe. By the mid-1960s, EUBs had 156 full-time and 12 short-term workers in Asia, Africa, and Latin America. The largest contingent served in the West African nation of Sierra Leone, where work began in 1855 and which then had annual conference status. In other countries—Brazil, Ecuador, the Dominican Republic, Puerto Rico, Japan, the Philippines, Indonesia, Hong Kong, and Nigeria—EUBC missionaries worked in *unified Protestant* ministries. Similarly 165 EUBC home missionaries served both in their church's missions and in interdenominational projects.[169] This was not the Methodist pattern, which preferred to operate its own mission enterprise at all levels.

With their roots in the rural American past, both EUBs and Methodists had a major stake in the nation's small cities and towns. Times were changing, however. As people continued to move from rural areas to urban and suburban centers, both Methodists and EUBs faced the problem of having too many small, struggling congregations with too few trained pastors to serve them.

There were similarities in local church practices, but there were also differences. Most obvious was the EUB use of a body called the Program Council, a gift to Methodists at union. Locally the council's function was to adapt and supplement ideas from annual conference and general agencies in developing a comprehensive and unified program for the congregation. The council was required in all EUB congregations regardless of size, while the five commissions familiar to Methodists were optional and generally organized only in larger churches. In addition, EUB churches could organize three age-level councils (children, youth, and adults), which put the Program Council's plans into action in cooperation with the church school, Women's Society of World Service, EUB Men, and the Youth Fellowship.[170]

In late 1966, EUBs in their regular General Conference and Methodists in a special session approved the Plan and Basis of Union. In 1968, EUBs and Methodists united to form The United Methodist Church (USA). Paul Washburn was among those elected bishop. The Uniting Conference adopted a major resolution, "The UMC & the Cause of Christian Unity," proclaiming a vigorous commitment to open versus closed (or family-style) ecumenism. In a 1968 symposium, "Methodism's Destiny in an Ecumenical Age," Methodist ecumenists from around the world gathered at Methodist School of Theology in Delaware, Ohio. In his plenary address Professor Outler made it clear that for him the future of theology lay in its ecumenical intention and outreach.

Mission Churches Request Autonomy

Methodist and EUB mission churches across the world drew on ecumenical language and aspiration for rationale and self-understanding as they charted new directions in relation to the parent denominations.[171] Some elected to remain under the authority of General Conference as central conferences, others chose to become part of national or regional uniting churches, and still others elected autonomy and an affiliated relation.[172] And these decisions would yield ecumenical and ecclesial quandaries for the twenty-first-century church. Shorn of many Methodist-EUB-planted mission churches and indeed of whole regions (all of Latin America and much of Asia), how should the UMC General Conference understand the church's global nature? As the UMC itself a global denomination? As united with all its offspring, domestic and foreign, with its own British parent, with British mission churches, and with united churches of which Methodists became part through the World Methodist Council? As joined with the larger family of Christians in the WCC? As guided by the WCC maxim "all in each place" toward ecumenical self-expression on national-regional levels and toward encouraging independence of each mission or central conference as it reached self-sufficiency? Absent an

Outler to pronounce an ecclesial self-understanding, twenty-first-century United Methodism would be left to ponder how to make theological and organizational sense of the long legacy of missions and colonialism.

More determinative, initially, than ecumenical vision, particularly in demands for independence, were political-societal dynamics—nationalism, effects of WWII, cold war pressures, and efforts to throw off colonial yokes. By 1930, Brazilian, Mexican, and Korean Methodists had achieved autonomy, the first so as to elect its own bishops, the second to adjust to Mexican church-state legal constraints, and the third to unite Korean branches of the MEC and the MECS.[173] In 1937, Methodist missions in China merged, and in 1949 the Methodist Church of the Republic of China fled with the Nationalists to Formosa. In 1939 much of French Methodism went into a united church. In Italy, American and British Methodism united, initially (in 1946) aligning with the British conference. Japanese Methodism became part of the Kyodan during WWII.

Recognizing the anticolonial temper that followed the war and guiding the church in this new climate, the 1948 Methodist General Conference established the Commission on the Structure of Methodism Overseas (COSMOS). With more liberalized conditions under which central conferences could elect their own bishops,[174] mission churches took different directions. The Philippines elected to remain in, while Burma (now Myanmar), Pakistan, and Liberia chose independence. The Liberians (Sources 1963b), recognizing their historic status as the "first overseas African field," affirming their Methodist "faith, doctrine, practice and kinship," and celebrating the current leadership of Bishop Prince Taylor, deemed that African nationalism in general and their own "national pride and self respect" had brought them to maturity as a church. Some other West African conferences chose independence while a few East African missions elected to remain central conferences. An EUBC mission in Sierra Leone chose autonomy at first but became part of the West Africa Central Conference in 1972. All of Latin America opted for autonomy (Puerto Rico only in 1992), as did most of the Asian missions (save the Philippines). EUBC missions in Latin America became part of uniting churches. European Methodists found in cold war pressures and/or their minority status reason to cling to the American church.

The Board of Missions and COSMOS guided and counseled leaders from central conferences as they wrestled with the options that the church and local circumstance presented. For instance, as overtures concerning autonomy increased and at the 1964 MC General Conference's request for guidance, COSMOS convened some 150 representatives from churches in Asia, Africa, Latin America, and Europe in a 1966 consultation at Green Lake, Wisconsin. That important gathering influenced parent denominational policy and the directions of churches still sorting through directions.[175] The year 1969 saw the formation of the Council of Evangelical Methodist Churches in Latin America and the Caribbean (CIEMAL), a body that would successfully guide the autonomous churches in their local mission and in relation to The United Methodist Church.[176] Tracey Jones, general secretary of the new denomination's board of missions, risked a few predictions for the future of missionary strategy in a 1969 address. In his view Methodism's errand to the world was more important than it had ever been, but both the missionary and the work of missions were radically changing (Sources 1969).[177]

METHODISM IN 1968: DENVER

In June of 1968, the year that the Evangelical United Brethren and Methodist churches united, Warren United Methodist Church in Denver, Colorado, experienced its own significant transition, a change of pastors. Dr. Harley W. Farnham retired after a four-year stint at this inner-city church. The Reverend Edward P. Beck, the new minister, came to the church from outside the Rocky Mountain Conference. Just prior to this appointment in Colorado, he had served The Methodist Church on a national level as a member of the staff of the General Board of Evangelism in Nashville. The Denver newspaper article announcing his coming to Warren, with its own sense of what really mattered, headlined the pastoral change: "Ex-Basketball Star Pastor at Warren." In his senior year at the University of Kentucky, in 1958, Beck had captained his basketball team to its NCAA title. Beck went on to earn a BD (equivalent to the MDiv) degree at Candler School of Theology, graduating with honors in 1962 and being named the outstanding preacher in the senior class. Rocky Mountain Conference Bishop R. Marvin Stuart and District Superintendent William O. Byrd had gone outside the conference to recruit leadership that, as the newspaper article put it, would help Warren Church "move into its role as an effective institution in dealing with the needs of a changing parish in the core city."[1] The conference had replaced maturity with youth and done so in unusual fashion, moving a recent seminary graduate across conference lines into a significant pulpit.

A Legacy in Its Name and Architecture

Warren Methodist Episcopal Church was the result of a merger in 1913 of two churches serving Capitol Hill, the area directly east of the state capitol building and of downtown Denver. Many of the finest homes in Denver had been constructed in that area around the turn of the century. The Capitol Hill Methodist Episcopal Church was organized as a mission in 1899. A site was secured at East Fourteenth and Gilpin, and a chapel was completed. Dedication Sunday was January 20, 1901, with Chancellor

Buchtel of the University of Denver preaching. A larger sanctuary was begun in 1907 and first used on Easter Day 1909. Later that year the membership was listed as more than 300. The smaller church known as Warren Chapel was organized in 1906 near the corner of East Eighth Avenue and Ogden. By 1913 it seemed wise to merge the two churches located so close together. The new church took the property of Capitol Hill ME Church and the name Warren, in honor of Bishop Henry White Warren, who had died the year before (July 1912). The reported membership of the new church was more than 400, and it grew in its first decade to about 650.

In an anniversary service for Warren UMC, Pastor Eun-sang Lee described the "Birthday of a Church" in this way:

> The merger of Capitol Hill Methodist and Warren Methodist happened in the summer of 1913. The proximity and limited membership of the two churches prompted this merger. Folks here, the Capitol Hill Methodists, hosted the merger. They dropped their name and adopted the new name. One member of Capitol Hill Methodist proudly described the merger this way: "Capitol Hill played the role of bride at the ceremony by dropping her own name and taking that of Warren." This occasion bespeaks the spirit of hospitality of this body of Christ from the beginning.

The church's name promised a bright future. Under Bishop Warren, the first MEC bishop to be resident in the Denver Area, Methodism had experienced explosive growth. Denver had but ten MEC churches and the whole conference but fifty-one when Warren arrived in 1884. When he retired in 1912, Denver boasted fifty and the conference two hundred charges. A Phi Beta Kappa graduate of Wesleyan University, Warren had been ordained by Bishop Matthew Simpson in 1855 into the New England Conference along with his brother William Fairfield Warren, the latter eventually to be the first president of Boston University. Henry White Warren served as chaplain in the Civil War, had a brief political career (Massachusetts House of Representatives), and held important pastorates in the New England, New York, and Philadelphia Conferences. When elected to the episcopacy in 1880 from the prominent Philadelphia Arch Street Church, Warren had established a churchwide reputation. Methodists knew him from hearing him preach, through his articles in the *Advocates,* from his published sermons and lectures, and through popular books on a range of topics, the latter including astronomy.

Under his episcopal leadership, the church established institutions that continue to sustain Colorado Methodism, including Iliff School of Theology, founded initially as a department of Denver University with money from his wife, Elizabeth Iliff Warren, and named after her deceased first husband, John Wesley Iliff. The cornerstone of Iliff Hall was laid June 8, 1892, and the building formally opened the following year. On that occasion Bishop Warren spoke the words still repeated in all of the school's official ceremonies: "The Iliff School of Theology has been established to promote progress in doctrine and experience. In doctrine it fears no criticism, courts always an advance." It was an apt expression of the bishop's progressive views.[2]

Warren ME Church made an auspicious statement about itself with its architecture as well as with its name. By the beginning of the twentieth century, Methodists strove to build churches exhibiting beauty not only for its own end but also as a statement of their church's status in the community. By 1932 The Methodist Episcopal Church had replaced a long-standing disciplinary directive that Methodist churches be built "plain and decent" with instructions that they "be designed in keeping with the lofty purpose of providing for divine worship, for the administration of the Holy Sacraments and be suited to the ministries of preaching, religious education, and Christian fellowship and service."[3]

For the new building in 1909 Capitol Hill (later Warren) ME Church followed the path of upscale, progressive, Protestant congregations of the era and chose the neo-Gothic style, which Boston architect Ralph Adams Cram and Methodist church planner Elbert M. Conover and others were promoting at the time as the "most Christian" form of architecture (see discussion in chapter 12).[4] The congregation described its new sanctuary as "designed after an English style chapel." The modern interpretation of a Gothic exterior is evident in Warren ME Church's dark granite walls, broad-shouldered façade, and oversized arched windows flanked by hefty buttresses.

Initially its interior worship space retained a pulpit-centered theater style, which had been in fashion for the previous forty years. In 1952, when the education wing of Warren Church was added, the worship space was reconfigured following the divided chancel plan that Conover had been promoting and that many Methodist church buildings in the 1950s were adopting. A large raised platform was erected up front (liturgically named "the chancel"), demarcated by a low railing and cushions for kneeling on each side of the center aisle, with the pulpit on one side and the lectern on the other, the altar at the far end fitted out with cross and candles, and seats for the choir and worship leaders on either side of the chancel. The arrangement did little to encourage more frequent celebrations of Holy Communions at first. Four Communions a year remained the norm for thoroughly modern Methodists of the 1950s. As in Conover's ideal church, it was easy to feel alone with God rather than among God's celebrating people. Focusing people's attention on an altar against the far wall and opening the service with "Holy, Holy, Holy!" (as had many congregations for the several decades in which that hymn stood number 1 in the *Methodist Hymnal*)[5] suggested that God was "out there" somewhere rather than in the midst of God's people gathered around a bath and meal as well as a book. Warren dedicated the new 1964 hymnals on March 5, 1967, in time for use on Easter, and a year before Beck arrived and would begin rethinking worship and worship space (discussed below). Typical of Warren, a further note in Official Board minutes from January 10, 1968, states that the old hymnals were given to the church at Boys Ranch near LaJunta, Colorado, and dedicated before some three hundred people.

Renewal through Social Ministries

By the end of World War I, Warren Church's growth spurt had ended and its prospects changed, a consequence of the changing nature of Capitol Hill as a residential area. Older residents died, families moved out, investors moved in, and the new owners converted the grand homes into multiple-family dwellings. This trend would have a significant impact on the ministry of Warren Church. The membership of Warren reflected this change, gradually declining to just over three hundred by 1928.

However, under the distinguished leadership of two men, Dr. Frederick Cox, who served Warren from 1928 until his death in 1947, and Dr. Lowell Swan, from 1947 until he became president of the Iliff School of Theology in 1962, Warren Church rebounded to its membership peak and became one of the most influential Methodist churches in the Denver Area. On December 14, 1952, the new educational building, the Frederick J. Cox Memorial Building, was completed and consecrated. It contained a chapel, fellowship hall, lounge, classrooms, restrooms, kitchen, nursery, and pastor's study, the latter by then a typical feature of church architecture and certainly requisite for Swan, who had received the doctorate from Iliff a year earlier. The Reverend Lester Sperberg was appointed to replace Dr. Swan in 1962. On Sperberg's appointment to a position in California in 1964, Dr. Harley W. Farnham, near retirement, was moved from the church he was serving in Lakewood, a western suburb of Denver, to provide leadership for Warren Church.

New leaders would have to contend with the continued erosion of center city commerce, infrastructure, and church membership. Methodists along with other mainline Protestants moved out, spurring membership growth of suburban churches and the further decline of churches in the center cities. By 1941, Superintendent of City Work Channing Richardson, writing in the Board of Mission's chief magazine, *World Outlook*, sounded the alarm about out-migration to the suburbs, encouraged the church to plan for new congregations in the auto-produced periphery communities, and noted the challenges that the losses would pose for urban churches (Sources 1941).[6]

Denver's Metro Mission was the subject of a featured article in the March 1969 issue of *Together* magazine, "the Magazine for United Methodist Families."[7] A headline conveyed the significance and urgency of its content: "Sparked by United Methodist leadership, an innovative ecumenical team of pastors and laymen in Colorado's capital is building bridges—between denominations, between city and suburb, between church and society. But they're in a hurry to act, while Denver's problems are still manageable."

The article summarized Denver's demographics by noting (1) that the Denver metropolitan area's population had grown to almost 1,110,000, with 510,000 in the city itself, and (2) that as the city's outer limits had expanded and its suburbs grown, the old core city had changed dramatically. Among the pressing challenges of the 1960s were Denver's discovery of its racial problems, with new demands from the growing Hispanic population of about 80,000 and an "increasingly vocal" African American population of about 48,000 expanding eastward from the enclave of Five Points, near downtown Denver, into fashionable Park Hill. As one observer put it, "We have every major problem of urban America, but it's in microcosm. The problems here haven't multiplied the way they have in other places."

The article went on to say, "Fortunately, Denver's 'progressive' elements include some visionary leadership, not the least of which is found among its churchmen [sic]. United Methodists, both clergy and lay, play key roles." Bishop R. Marvin Stuart, of United Methodism's Denver Area provided important encouragement. On his assignment to Denver in 1964, Bishop Stuart told Denver Methodists: "We have the opportunity to make the church relevant to the total city, but it must be soon. If you try it, I'll back you in any creative or experimental ministry possible. We are not afraid of failure. We may fail and fall on our faces—but if we do, we'll fall forward."[8]

Bishop Stuart fostered support for metropolitan church strategy in his 1966 choice of "ebullient, gregarious" William O. "Bill" Byrd to be superintendent of the Denver District. A native of Louisiana, Byrd came to Colorado in 1962. His favorite metaphor to describe his work was "building bridges," and his enthusiasm for the Metro Mission strategy was contagious. Among DS Byrd's earliest promotions was a 1966 district consultation to ponder denominational programs for the metropolitan area. This consultation drew up five basic guidelines:

> 1) The church must serve the total city with no false separation of inner city and suburbia; 2) Resources for service must come from the area itself without depending on national mission agencies for all of our funds; 3) Problems of the city must be attacked on an ecumenical basis; it is poor stewardship and vain to try to "go it alone"; 4) The church must serve people, not institutions. Explore every possible co-operation with secular agencies to serve wherever there is need; 5) Freedom to experiment is essential.[9]

Conveying a sense of both urgency and hope, the article highlighted the prominence of United Methodists among Colorado's Protestant churches and pointed to the important resource for Denverites that their city was home of the Iliff School of Theology. This United Methodist seminary that trained pastors for churches throughout the Rocky Mountain region, it said, "uses the city itself as a laboratory for its students and plays a major 'bridging' role with other church and secular agencies in experimental efforts to find new strategies." Particular reference was made to the school's revised curriculum, which included a three-week orientation period for first-year students, immersing them in the life of the city, and a requirement for more advanced students of forty hours of field work a week in church and social agencies.

Other innovative ministries featured in the article were the Capitol Hill Ministry, including Warren Church and three other UMC congregations (St. Paul, Trinity, and Christ), all serving the transitional area east of the Colorado capitol, but each church having its own specialized ministry; Park Hill United Methodist Church under the pastoral leadership of the Reverend J. Carlton Babbs, for its role in founding the Interracial Park Hill Action Committee, seeking especially to create a balanced community by peaceful school integration; and Core City Ministries (CCM), five cooperating parishes located in inner-city poverty areas and offering social and religious services like Head Start classes, emergency food and clothing distribution, health care, Scouting, recreational facilities, worship, and educational efforts. Beyond the immediate work of the five parishes, CCM was also bringing together "an even more ecumenical cadre" to plan long-range strategies for "joint action in mission" and developing an extensive educational program to involve suburbanites as well as city residents in its metropolitan strategizing. "Denver church people are convinced," the article concluded, "that to be faithful to its calling the church must make its presence felt, as catalyst, innovator, and reconciler."[10]

What's ahead for Old First Church? queried then–General Board of Global Ministries executive Ezra Earl Jones and Duke researcher Robert L. Wilson in the early 1970s. It was the question for the era.[11] Warren clearly was posing the question for itself and doing its own reimagining. In 1967, with Warren as the "geographic hub," Methodist and other churches on Capitol Hill embarked on a new cooperative ministry in the area. The Reverend Robert Hunter was appointed to the Warren Church staff as apartment minister, after ten years of work in campus ministry. The Reverend George Loveland came to the staff that same year as minister of youth. Both ministers, along with others in the cooperative ministry, were prepared to venture "into new approaches to needs no longer adequately served by old methods." Financial support for this experimental ministry came from participating congregations and also from other churches not on Capitol Hill that were convinced of the importance of this ministry.

Other events at Warren Methodist Church in 1967 contribute further to a sense of the commitments of this congregation as well as its larger cultural context. In February there were a panel presentation and a discussion, "Next Steps in Viet Nam?" A Head Start program was begun at the church. In October, a series of community forums was held on the subject "Denver's Social Tensions—Threat or Promise?" Sponsored by the Committee on Social Concerns, these forums brought to the church prominent community leaders like Denver's African American state Senator George Brown. In December, Sister Simone Inkley, supervisor of education for the Roman Catholic Archdiocese of Denver, a Sister of Loretto, spoke at Warren Church on Catholic-Protestant dialogue. Also that month space was set aside at the church for a study hall–community center for youth.

Bishop R. Marvin Stuart set the tone for Methodist social activism in the Rocky Mountain Conference and especially in Denver. He was one of the twelve religious leaders, four of them Methodists, to address a letter of concern about Vietnam to General William C. Westmoreland, May 2, 1967.[12] He took an active part in the demonstrations against the Vietnam War and in the spring of 1970 would visit with the students who had pitched their tents on the campus of the University of Denver in protest against the invasion of Cambodia. He also participated in a number of marches in 1968 following the April assassination of Dr. Martin Luther King Jr. and the Vietnam protest on the state capitol steps. Some within the conference threatened to withdraw their financial and membership support from the church as a result.

The Weekly Program

During the first half of 1968, when Dr. Harley W. Farnham was the pastor, the principal Sunday morning worship service was held in the sanctuary at 11:00 a.m. There was also a smaller service held in the chapel at 8:00 a.m., followed by a coffee hour in the fellowship hall, and church school at 9:30. The Order of Worship was divided into several major sections: "Recognizing Who God Is," "Recognizing Who We Are," "Hearing the Possibilities of Life," and "Dedicating Ourselves to the Possibilities of Life." Holy Communion was celebrated quarterly at the eleven o'clock service and monthly at the eight o'clock service in the chapel.

In the 1960s, Warren Church prided itself on having activities for individuals of all ages and conditions. The Woman's Society of Christian Service was the most consistently active organization in the church. It met on the second Friday of each month for lunch and a program, with five circles holding monthly meetings during the day in the homes of members and a sixth circle meeting in the evening. Employed women were encouraged to become members of the Warren Evening Guild, which met for dinner and a program on the third Wednesday of each month.

The Men of Warren (Methodist Men) met bimonthly at 7:30 a.m. Saturday for breakfast at Heart O'Denver restaurant. Young Adults met once a month for dinner at Luby's restaurant or for an international potluck supper in the church fellowship hall, followed by a variety of programs, including entertainment, "serious study," and worship. There were weekly meetings for Jr. Hi MYF every Friday at 6:30 p.m. and for Sr. Hi MYF every Sunday from 5:30 to 7:30 p.m. The Official Board met in January, April, and May on Wednesday at 6:30 p.m., beginning with a potluck supper. An organization called "XYZ" for "our fine older folk" met monthly at the church for a potluck lunch.

Although there was some variation in the schedule from year to year and depending on the pastor, there were Sunday school classes for nursery, kindergarten, six elementary levels (from six-year-olds to eleven-year-olds), junior high, senior high, and adults. All met at the same hour, between the two worship services (that is, 9:30 a.m.).

A Calendar of Outreach and Mission

For a week in January (7–15) 1968, the General Board of Missions of The Methodist Church met in Denver at the Hilton Hotel. Members of Warren Church along with other Methodists in Denver were especially invited to two open meetings. Friday at 7:30 p.m. was a public meeting on the theme "Mission Issues in Urban America." The principal speaker was Sargent Shriver, director of the Office of Economic Opportunity since 1964 and former director of the Peace Corps. His address was followed by a panel, including Ted Velez, executive director of East Harlem Tenants Council; Cecil Howard, pastor of Denver's Shorter African Methodist Episcopal Church; and Leo D. Nieto, director of Migrant Ministry and Mission of the Texas Council of Churches.

On Sunday, January 7, there was a reception given by the Women's Division at Methodist Headquarters and the Iliff School of Theology, offering the opportunity to meet church leaders who were in Denver for the Board of Missions meeting.[13] This reception and other meetings were listed in the Warren Church bulletin. Speaking at Warren on Sunday morning, January 14, was the Reverend A. Finley Schaef, minister of New York City's Washington Square Methodist Church. The bulletin said he was conversant with the challenges and problems of a parish such as Warren's in Capitol Hill.

January 28 was Youth Sunday. Five youth helped conduct the service; an announcement in the bulletin requested money and donations for an experimental ecumenical ministry with the youth of Capitol Hill, including a community center that would provide study and recreational facilities for youth in the area. February 11 was Race Relations Sunday and Boy Scout Sunday. On Sunday, February 18, members of the congregation were to sit for a picture directory of church members. March 10 was Girl Scout Sunday.

March and April were busy and important months for the members of Warren Church. During the week of March 10, Warren held its quarterly conference, which unanimously approved the purchase of four properties on East Thirteenth Avenue and Gilpin Street, completing the ownership by Warren of the block of property bounded by East Fourteenth and East Thirteenth avenues, on the west side of Gilpin Street to the alley. On March 27 at 6:30 p.m. a congregational meeting was held to discuss financing of the property approved by the quarterly conference. All members of Warren Church eighteen years of age and older were urged to attend. By a unanimous vote, the membership affirmed the intent to build Warren Village, an eight-story apartment building comprising apartments for single-parent families, with a Learning Center for child care for working mothers. The project was the dream of Dr. Myron Waddell, a Denver obstetrician and member of Warren Church, who with his wife, Margaret, had become increasingly concerned about the growing number of single women in his care who were not supported financially or emotionally as they became new mothers. The Waddells had begun to wonder what their church could do to help these women and many more like them to receive job training so they could support themselves and their children. On Sunday May 12, Bishop Stuart recognized and installed the trustees for the new building project inaugurating Warren Village. DS Bill Byrd preached on the theme, "Where Is Warren Church?" Under the vigorous leadership of the new pastor of Warren Church, Ed Beck, this dream became a reality.[14]

Ground was broken in early 1972; an eight-story apartment complex was erected to accommodate 120 single-parent families with an additional thirty units for older couples or single persons who would come to live in the complex and work with the children and parents on a volunteer basis; Warren Village Learning Center was established; and the first residents moved in February 1974. The people of Warren Church, having decided that their ministry was to remain in the inner city, built Warren Village, a unique family community for "awakening the potential" in single-parent families and helping them move "from public assistance to personal and economic self-sufficiency." Warren Church has continued to provide members of the board of trustees, volunteers, and financial contributions, although it has relinquished ownership, making Warren Village, Inc., the sole owner.[15]

On Sunday, April 21, 1968, an announcement in the bulletin told Warren Church members that on Tuesday morning in Dallas, Texas, The United Methodist Church would come into being as the result of a union of The Methodist Church and The Evangelical United Brethren Church (Sources 1968b). The article went on to explain the new church. On Tuesday evening, May 7, the Denver District of the Woman's Society of Christian Service held a special meeting to install officers and discuss the new United Methodist Church.

Other notices in the bulletin reveal additional dimensions of the church's ministry. During March, there was a meeting for parents at Temple Emmanuel, First and Grape streets, to deal with the current problem of drugs and drug abuse. A note on May 12 reminded church members of the four men of Warren Church serving in Vietnam. The son of the church pastor and his wife had just returned to the U.S. that week, after completing a year of service in Saigon. On April 25, 1968, Mrs. Rachel B. Noel, Denver educator and the first African American to be elected to the Denver Public School Board (in 1965), presented to the board what became known simply as the Noel Resolution, asking the superintendent to develop a plan to integrate the Denver public schools (DPS). It would be 1970 before this courageous resolution was finally passed by the DPS Board. Notices in the Warren Church bulletin urged the support of church members for this plan being devised to integrate the public schools in Denver (copies of the Noel Resolution were in the church library). On May 13, the Denver East Central Human Relations Council would meet in Warren's fellowship hall (compare Sources 1969).

Calendaring Change

The Rocky Mountain Annual Conference met at Iliff, the University of Denver, United Methodist Headquarters, and University Park Church, June 1–14, 1968. With the guidance of its Board of Social Concerns, the conference passed resolutions favoring "a strong federal gun control law," the proscription of mail order gun sales, "strict registration and/or licensing of the sale of guns to qualified persons," collective bargaining rights for farm workers, conscientious objection to war, and such status as no barrier to ministerial orders. The board's preconference report highlighted the effect of the prior year's conference studies on Vietnam, China, and the UN, economic justice and order in the cities, tax exemption for religious organizations, and drug addiction. The board also highlighted its historic concern with alcoholism, its worries over nuclear holocaust, global issues of human rights, and the domestic challenge of (white) racism.[16] The Board of Hospitals and Homes pled for greater conference concern for older people, unwed mothers, single parents, low-income families, and shut-ins.[17] The conference also dealt with enabling resolutions that effected the union of the Rocky Mountain conferences of the EUB and Methodist churches.[18] Among the new members of conference who would be summoned to these challenges were those listed in answer to Disciplinary Question 38, "Who have been received by transfer?" The second named, transferring from Holston Conference, was Edward P. Beck.[19]

On Sunday, June 16, the new pastor, the Reverend Ed Beck, began his ministry at Warren United Methodist Church. On June 23, there was a survey in the Sunday bulletin about a proposed new format for Sunday morning. On Sunday, June 30, the old bulletin cover (representative of the window of the sanctuary through which opportunities could be seen, with a cross in the center, with stylized initials standing for W[arren] M[ethodist] C[hurch], representing the worshiper reaching up to God, reaching out in mission, and standing at the foot of the cross) had been replaced. In the first of his new bulletin covers, Ed Beck displayed very simply three suggestive and programmatic quotations:

> What White Americans have never fully understood—but what the Negro can never forget—is that White Society is deeply implicated in the ghetto. White institutions have created it, White institutions maintain it, and White Society condones it.
> (Report of the National Advisory Commission on Civil Disorders)

> He who takes a position exposes himself.
> (H. Thielicke)

> You shall know the truth and the truth shall set you free.
> (Bible)

Warren United Methodist Church
1630 East 14th Avenue
Denver, Colorado
388-4186

On Sunday, October 6, the bulletin announced changed worship times and a changed order of worship. The new headings were "We Recognize God," "We Recognize Who We Are," "We Are Involved in the Word," and "We Respond to the Word of Life." In August the choir had been moved from the front of the church to the balcony in the back of the church. On September 1, the project "Get with It" was announced. On Wednesdays, people could come to the church and help work on more than one hundred small and large projects on the church building. On Sunday, September 8, Sunday school teachers were to meet with the youth pastor to discuss the experimental education program that was to begin October 6. On Reformation Sunday (October 27, 1968), Pastor Beck nailed to the front door of Warren Church his "I Protest," specifically patterned on Martin Luther's Ninety-five Theses and addressed "to the United Methodists of Warren Church, Denver" (in case anyone hadn't yet seen that he intended nothing less than a reformation at Warren Church!). Among the grounds for his protest were these:

> I protest the deadly silence that grips the Christian witness of too many members. I
> protest the careless and indifferent attitude of the average member of Warren toward at-
> tending the services of public worship. I protest against the disuse the Holy Bible has
> fallen into in the life of the average Warren member. I protest the lack of prayer of any
> form in the life of the average member of Warren. I protest the lack of sponsorship by
> Warren's members and their unwillingness to give time and talent to community action
> projects.

At least their new pastor kept seeking feedback from his flock. On Sunday, November 10, there was another survey in the bulletin, and it asked these questions: Which areas should have priority at Warren Church for 1969? How would church members like to see the Sunday worship services improved? Did the congregation like the new schedule on Sunday mornings? What topics would people suggest for the pastor's sermons? What special features should be included in the church's program for the following year? What other ideas did people have to improve Warren Church? After the new pastor's arrival, the bulletins began to include the membership of Warren, attendance on the previous Sunday, total budget needs, and budget deficit. Membership at the end of November was 444; the total budget was $48,392, with a deficit of $2,083.

Perhaps most telling was the five-page report submitted to "Warrenites" as an accounting of his first year as their pastor. Two items are particularly revealing. One was his asking of this key question for the 1960s:

> The basic question we are just beginning to ask is "The Future of the Local Church or the Local Church of the Future?" It is a terrifying question for some to ask concerning Warren because of personal involvement and the mental image of the history of this great church. But to be honest we must ask what does Warren do now in this geographical area that no other institutional church is doing? If all we are doing is the same thing that all other Churches are doing we then must ask—Are we really necessary?

The second was his fascinating comment on the worship and sacramental life of the Warren Church community:

> The baptismal font and Lord's table have been moved in the Sanctuary to bring into harmony the two most powerful symbols of the Christian Faith. They are situated in their respective places in order to constantly remind the worshiper, as he or she enters or leaves corporate worship, of the death and resurrection of the Christ and therefore the agape love of God for you.

Also mentioned were the choir's move to the balcony, among other reasons, so that the voices of the small number of volunteers would project better, and the hope for new liturgical banners to fill the great many empty spaces of the sanctuary's neo-Gothic walls.

Only 33 (out of 450) responded to the pastor's questionnaire, but their views were also suggestive of not-so-uncommon church struggles, especially in the 1960s: "Have two services only. More lay participation. Change times of services. Sermons too negative; you preach too much Old Testament. Do not undertake anything else. And, put the altar back against the wall and the baptismal font in the corner!" Basically Pastor Ed Beck had told his congregation that "Imagineers" (his word) were needed as Warren attempted to pioneer and blaze new faith pilgrimages.

Coda: U.S. United Methodism and Mainline Denominationalism[20]

Denver Methodism struggled to reshape itself for a new day because like its Protestant congregational counterparts and like the predecessor churches of the new United Methodism generally, it had built and built into an urban America that was coming apart.[21] In witness to the city, early nineteenth-century Methodism had developed station churches and begun to think about the infrastructure for nurture and communication, as we noted for Baltimore in 1816. In the late nineteenth and early twentieth centuries, Methodism had erected towers, like the Chicago Temple, boasting the highest cross in the world, or the fourteen-story Wesley Building in Philadelphia to accommodate bookstore, conference societies, bishop's office, general church agencies, and a hotel. Like successive parson owners of the "Wonderful One-Hoss Shay," Methodism, for a century and more, had united in tending, laboring through, and adding to its machinery—hospitals and homes, camps and orphanages, colleges and assemblies. As we noted for Wilkes-Barre in 1884, it had institutionalized itself especially in center-city Gothic churches, deployed its men's Bible classes on Mondays into downtown offices and department stores, positioned its ministers with its laity in Rotary and Kiwanis, addressed the community through Sunday radio pulpits, trained up future civic leaders in vacation Bible and Sunday schools, enjoyed friendly coverage from morning and evening papers, and depended on its mayors and council "men" to govern in its interest.[22]

Throughout the late 1960s and the 1970s, Methodism ministered through and out of its properties only to witness, as the Trinity study indicated, white flight scatter and other churches follow what had been its primary constituency into the suburbia of guarded cul-de-sacs and gated communities. A few Trinitys, Warrens, and Chicago Temples held on only to watch—in cities large and small—American industries fly to the global south, department stores relocate to the suburbs, corporations build their own outlying campuses, de-institutionalization fill parks with the homeless, blight and petty crime spread over the once vibrant business districts, transportation networks disappear as highways plowed through, urban renewal break apart neighborhoods, and remaining racial-ethnic communities struggle to reach retreating jobs and grocery stores. What's ahead for Old First Church? asked Methodist sociologist Wilson and denominational executives Jones, but absent the capacity to envision, much less implement, an overall, coherent, compelling denominational strategy, United Methodism left it to congregations and conferences to experiment with ways to minister in racially changing urban contexts. In many places, as Warren's congregation indicates, courageous members continued to commute to the downtown church to launch congregational or support conference initiatives—pantries, shelters, addiction clinics, training centers, AIDS ministries, tutoring programs, Meals on Wheels, day care, and advocacy efforts.[23] In some cases, multiethnic or African American United Methodism succeeded to and sustained the Gothic facility, its maintenance often burdening ministry. Elsewhere, Methodism made Philadelphia's agonizing strategic decision to sell its aging, only partially occupied office building and relocate to the Valley Forge Corporate Center.[24] All too often, however, the urban church dwindled, aged, hunkered down, just died, and left the conference a distressed sale.

The annual conference would struggle as well—apportionments plateauing as memberships plummeted—but typically succeed in sustaining its incredible apparatus: retreat and camp grounds, conference centers, nursing and geriatric facilities, lay and clergy training ventures, children's homes, short-term missions, plus all the ministries undertaken collaboratively with other denominations and its urban churches. Rocky Mountain's Conference journal attests its impressive complex of ministries, institutions, facilities, and programs and the extraordinary ongoing commitments required to sustain the apparatus.[25] Its hands quite full, the conference nevertheless continued to add or augment ministries for older, infirm, and indigent people, undertook capital campaigns on its institutions' behalf, and faced similar challenges in closing funding gaps for pension and insurance programs. Health-care costs and regulations forced agonizing decisions, for instance, to spin off, sell, or partner Methodism's hospitals. And similar regulatory, funding, and societal pressures affected conference relations to its colleges. Nevertheless, more impressive were the programs, ministries, and institutions that annual conferences sustained. Maintenance perhaps—as pop sociologists and organizational gurus charged—but church leaders thought the alternatives would have constituted dereliction of duty and poor stewardship of ministry investment. Nevertheless, keeping programs and ministries going and staying the course in the cities as long and as much as it did cost United Methodism in the scramble for suburban religious loyalties.

As Warren and its new youthful pastor searched for the social ministry and the worship for a new day, so did the new denomination of which it was a part (Sources 1968b). The Rocky Mountain Conference sent Asian and African American clergy and lay delegates to the 1968 Jurisdictional Conference, an inclusiveness that reflected both the new church's history and its future. Into Denver's United Methodism came, of course, the congregations with German background out of Evangelical and United Brethren communions but also their Spanish missions. And the MEC contributed former German-speaking churches as well as those whose languages had been Swedish, Italian, Japanese, and Spanish. African American congregations and those from the formerly segregated MECS now belonged together.[26] This new unity, however, would not be undifferentiated. Indeed, "belonging" almost immediately elicited the formation of caucuses around identity, concern, and ideology, one of the first of which was Black Methodists for Church Renewal, formed just a couple of months before the Uniting Conference and with a clear sense that real unity required more than a few days of speeches and hymns (Sources 1968a). Pastor Beck had fittingly begun his new ministry headlining the bulletin with prophecies on race and the urban crisis.

A later Warren successor of Beck, Pastor Eun-sang Lee, caught the watershed import of the 1968 ministry in a sermonic retrospective:[27]

> In the 1930s and 40s, Dr. Cox called the people of Warren to a God-centered life. During that age of fascism and war he asked the people of Warren to light a candle for "there isn't enough darkness in all the world to put out the light of one small candle."
>
> In the 1960s during the age of white exodus to suburbia, the people of Warren decided that the place of their ministry was in the inner city, stayed in this location and built Warren Village.
>
> Throughout the urban decline and mainline Protestant denominations' membership decline in the 70s, 80s, and 90s, the people of Warren refused to dwell in the survival mode, but kept searching and seeking to expand their horizon and respond to the changing neighborhood. "A Community of Reconciliation serving Capitol Hill" became their

motto. They opened up the church building to diverse community groups such as Men's Coming Out Group, International Folk Dancers, Young at Heart, Narcotics Anonymous, and Warren Village. They decided to join the Reconciling Ministry of the United Methodist Church [in November 1999].

Now the neighborhood is changing once again. The majority of the Capitol Hill population are in their 20s and 30s. They are definitely urban, most of them live in "nontraditional family settings," are fiercely independent and very suspicious of traditional institutional religions. They respond to different styles of music and speak different spiritual languages. We have to become spiritually multi-lingual if we are to respond faithfully to God's call to ministry with our changing neighbors.

Since 1985, the church has been an active participant in Capitol Hill United Ministries, an interfaith coalition of eighteen churches. In November 1999, Warren UMC voted to become a member of the Reconciling Congregation movement, which welcomes all people to become members of the church and especially invites gay, lesbian, bisexual, and transgendered persons because of their being singled out as "incompatible with Christian teaching." In 2002, the Denver New Church (a Korean church) and Amazing Grace Mongolian Church began meeting at Warren. On Christmas Eve, in a joint service, the three congregations worshiped in four languages: Korean, Mongolian, English, and American Sign Language! Later in 2003, Denver New Church moved to a more convenient location for its members. Open Door Community Church, a "bridge-building place where gay, lesbian, bisexual, transgender, and non-gay people could worship together," began meeting in the Warren building.

Figure 1
Warren Statistics

Year	Church Members	Sunday School	SS Average Attendance[28]
1913	417	250	
1923	547	532	180[29]
1933	392	318	
1943	502	312	152
1953	836	476	
1963	864	531	160
1973	351	46	
1983	186	132	50
1993	147	58	30
2003	133	45	

CHAPTER XIV

MERGING AND REAPPRAISING: 1968–84

Lord of the Church
We are united in Thee
in Thy Church
And now in The United Methodist Church

With these words EUBC Bishop Reuben H. Mueller and Methodist Bishop Lloyd C. Wicke clasped hands over a table laden with symbolic documents—the Bible, hymnals, books of *Discipline* and *Worship* and the 307-page Plan of Union—and, together with 1,300 delegates and upwards of 10,000 visitors and guests in Dallas on April 23, 1968, proclaimed the formation of The United Methodist Church. The 10.3 million-member Methodist Church and the 750,000-member Evangelical United Brethren Church had become the second-largest and most truly national Protestant denomination in distribution of members throughout the country. Flags of fifty-three countries represented the reach of United Methodist work. The principal speaker, Professor Albert C. Outler from Perkins School of Theology, displayed his usual salty wit by likening the uniting of two churches to Pentecost and apologizing for the absence of fire and glossolalia (Sources 1968b).

General Conferences of the two churches separately had approved the Plan of Union in 1966, leaving tidying up to a joint union committee headed by Methodist layman-attorney Charles Parlin of New York and EUBC clergyman Paul Washburn, who became a bishop. The gathering morphed from being the Uniting Conference to constituting the new denomination's first General Conference. Delegates realized the work of actual uniting could not be completed in 1968 and authorized a special session of General Conference for 1970 to last only five days in St. Louis and to have as a major concern the merger and structure of the new denomination's boards and agencies. To guide efforts toward full unity, it created quadrennial study commissions on structure, social principles, and theology and doctrine; established a Program Council; authorized a

Book of Resolutions to exhibit the church's pronouncements; and created a Commission on Religion and Race to assist in the dismantling of the Central Jurisdiction. Bishop Eugene Frank delivered the final sermon, and Bishop William Martin pronounced the benediction. The new church was off and running.

That beginning, inspiring as it was, appears in retrospect more a grand pageant marking the merger of two similar bodies than the creation of something distinctively new. As Professor Outler noted, "No part of our venture in unity is really finished as yet!" Indeed, from the vantage of this writing, 1968 seemed to begin various ventures in disunity. The high moment of spiritual exultation at the Uniting Conference was to be followed by three quadrennia of difficult and divisive issues, which the drafters of the Plan of Union either could not have anticipated or preferred to postpone. No small part of Methodism's dilemmas, broadly shared across American society, concerned major national and international matters—the civil rights revolution, the women's movement, heightened ethnic consciousness, challenges of affirmative action and inclusion, the Vietnam War and its enduring social traumas, poverty and urban decay, the deindustrialization of American society, a new coalition of political conservatives and evangelicals, and continued cold war and nuclear holocaust tensions. Also to be divisive during this period were internal church developments, including a commitment to pluralism and diversity, structural change, affirmation of the "quadrilateral" as a doctrinal hermeneutic, the liberalization of UMC teaching about divorce and remarriage, abortion and homosexuality, inclusive language, and the emergence of a conservative Methodism with the latter two issues among its expressed concerns but with energies derived as well from matters of war, race, gender, doctrine, and scriptural authority. Some commitments made in this liberating atmosphere—for instance, the reorientation of mission theology and policy toward social, political, and economic redevelopment— would be questioned more vigorously as Methodism celebrated its bicentennial.

How truly unified would the new United Methodism be? The earlier merger on the Methodist side—that of 1939—had bought unity at the price of racial segregation and regional jurisdictions. The latter would continue into the new church, indeed, solidify further. Principled segregation in the form of the all-Black Central Jurisdiction would finally go. But how would a United Methodism honor the particular witness of the minority Evangelical United Brethren? And what would unity mean with respect to its various distinctive populations, within the U.S. and beyond? Diversity and pluralism would be the new church's first big challenge. Agenda item one: race!

From Jurisdiction to Caucus and Commission

Despite the passage of federal legislation guaranteeing basic political rights to Black southerners, most African Americans in 1968, North and South, had not achieved even a measure of social and economic equality with whites—a fact starkly demonstrated by devastating rioting in several major American cities in the late 1960s. As a denomination relatively strong in urban areas, long vexed with its own racial dilemmas, and facing full dismantling of the Central Jurisdiction to fulfill commitments made as part of the merger, a uniting Methodism could not afford to ignore this growing unrest.

Alarmed by the disastrous riots during the summer of 1967 in Detroit and Newark, Black Methodist leaders gathered in Cincinnati in February 1968 to form Black Methodists for Church Renewal (BMCR). James Lawson, veteran of the civil rights campaign, friend and confidant of Martin Luther King, Jr. and pastor of the all-Black Centenary UMC in Memphis, Tennessee, sounded the alarm in a lead article in the church's clergy journal. Suspecting Methodists were "playing a 'mickey-mouse' game" on race, he expressed the fear that after unification, the deadening game of racism would persist in less visible guise. Speaking for BMCR, he said bluntly, "[W]e reject tokenism. We refuse to tolerate a cheap, meaningless fellowship not rooted in Christian acceptance, dialogue and mission. We will settle for nothing less than a church where the love of Christ rules and where a man is a man not by race, or blood, but by the will and power of God." Lawson went on to challenge the upcoming Uniting Conference "to authorize genuine urban priorities and to get the Methodist household in order" (Sources 1968a). General Conference responded by establishing a Commission on Religion and Race. African American Methodists countered by constituting Black Methodists for Church Renewal.

These two organizational initiatives—an advocacy/monitoring agency and a caucus (or struggle society), the one establishing a toe-hold within the denomination's power structure, the other providing a belonging and commitment network—would, in various combinations and permutations, dominate United Methodist life for the next four decades. With the formation of Good News (Sources 1966a) in 1967 and of other racial-ethnic, gender, and sexual orientation caucuses soon after BMCR's founding (see Sources 1970, 1972a, 1972d, 1973, 1976, 1978, 1985, 1988a), United Methodism found itself both united around and divided by the several caucuses. That other mainline denominations, indeed American society, united and divided along similar lines would provide little comfort as local churches, annual conferences, and General Conferences roiled with the controversial proposals and demands that highly interested advocacy produced.

The agency-caucus axis yielded other ironies than unity in diversity and diversity in unity. Caucus advocacy aspired to ambitious transformations in society, politics, business, and religion, but in agitating conferences with resolutions and proposals, such advocacy had the effect of focusing United Methodism on itself. The caucuses pledged themselves to the renewal of United Methodism but in many instances found common interest and sometimes collaborative effort with counterparts across denominational lines. Perhaps most ironically, a Methodism that since World War I had sought to purge itself of "foreign" language conferences and in uniting would end the scandal of a racial juris-diction, increasingly needed non-English and racial-ethnic-sensitive ministries. And as United Methodism recognized its global character, translation and particularity re-entered connectional life. In anticipation of the 1968 merger, the Rio Grande Confer-ence voted (in 1967) to remain a separate entity. With the ending of the Central Jurisdiction, Black Methodism faced the loss of what had been an enabling structure (as well as an accommodation to white racism). Would BMCR serve in place of Black conferences and jurisdiction? With the creation of caucus (BMCR) and commission (on Religion and Race), United Methodism implicitly recognized that identity, partic-ularity, and commitment required their own space and structure. Making that implicit recognition into explicit and affirmed denominational practice would prove a big chal-lenge. In the course of the next three quadrennia, a newly united Methodism would find itself experiencing structural-ideological initiatives that would change the church as radically as had the innovations of the 1870s.

African Americans in United Methodism

In many respects BMCR functioned to sustain the more positive roles of the old Cen-tral Jurisdiction, convening African Americans for joyous worship and thoughtful strate-gizing, identifying and cultivating new leadership, and celebrating Black pride and Black culture in a predominantly white church. BMCR vigorously pressed the church to elim-inate racism, to implement inclusiveness, to care for underrepresentation, and to deal with economic disparities. An early test of intention came when the church began to provide basic justice for African American clergy by subsidizing their salaries as they came into previously all-white conferences. This alone cost a minimum of $2.4 million per year in the beginning.[1]

Although formed by activists in the civil rights movement and at the point that Black Power separatism shaped African American agendas, BMCR avoided the call of militant leaders inside the church and out to separate from the white church and early an-nounced its intention to work for change from within. Indeed, as its name suggests, it looked to the renewal of Methodism as the church ended the Central Jurisdiction and brought together the ten remaining Black conferences with their white counterparts. By 1970, all the jurisdictions and many annual conferences established chapters, and BMCR's monthly tabloid, NOW, enjoyed wide circulation. Over the next few years BMCR chalked up an impressive record of achievements. It lobbied successfully for the Commission on Religion and Race, urged church agencies to upgrade the level of Black leadership, and secured a General Conference commitment to raise substantial funds for the church's Black colleges and their students (the continuing Black College Fund). By the early 1970s, however, BMCR had to share the minority spotlight with other groups.[2]

BMCR shared agenda and leadership with the Commission on Religion and Race, whose mandate, staff, and budget were dedicated to actively and vigorously promoting the church's goal of developing a racially inclusive church.[3] Under the leadership of its executive secretary, the Reverend (later Bishop) Woodie White, the commission oversaw the merger of the remaining racially structured conferences of the Central Jurisdiction into the five geographically organized jurisdictional conferences. That would prove most challenging in South Carolina where Black and white conferences of comparable size shared the same boundaries.[4] Nor was merger everywhere a success. Some nine thousand members in ten states refused to enter the new church, joining instead the segregationist Southern Methodist Church, formed in 1939 by members who refused to enter the reunited Methodist Church. More positively, the 1968 Northeastern Jurisdiction elected Roy Nichols to the episcopacy, the first African American elected by a regional white majority jurisdiction. The same year, African American Theressa Hoover became associate general secretary in the Board of Global Ministries and chief executive officer of its Women's Division, a post she held until retirement in 1990. The following year, African American staff at the Board of Global Ministries formed their own Black Staff Network.

Under a program theme for the new quadrennium of "A New Church for a New World," the church pledged itself in 1968 to mobilize the energies and resources of the church around efforts at reconciliation, witness, and renewal. It urged members to study the Sermon on the Mount for learnings about how "to correct the long-standing attitudes which have brought about the present crisis in the nation and around the world, especially as this crisis is prompted by racial injustice." A Fund for Reconciliation was established, with a goal of $20 million to be raised during the 1969–72 quadrennium through voluntary contributions over and above regular giving. The fund would underwrite new programs, such as the United Methodist Voluntary Service Corps to enlist young adults in local projects of reconciliation and reconstruction, and it would support other mission ventures proposed by UMC boards and agencies.[5] In 1969 the Council of Bishops (COB) added its own voice to the theme, sending a "Message to the Church on Reconciliation."[6]

Renewal and reconciliation, however, produced conflicts over policy and money. The denomination's Nashville-based antiunion publishing house was ordered to integrate its workforce at all levels. A hard-hitting April 1968 investigative report "Practice What You Print" by New York City pastor James McGraw in *Christianity and Crisis* outed the problem. BMCR called all churches, especially Black churches, to boycott purchasing publishing house products until the house joined Project Equality.[7] Similar strategy informed United Methodism's international outlook. The Board of Missions withdrew a $10 million investment portfolio from New York's First National City Bank as a protest against the bank's involvement in a credit arrangement with the government of South Africa. The board's action drew protests by lay delegates John C. Satterfield of Mississippi, a former president of the American Bar Association, and Charles Parlin of New

Jersey, a president of the World Council of Churches and a former director of the New York bank. Despite the protests, the board had oriented United Methodism toward what would be an important stewardship venture in American capitalism, social investing.[8]

The following year a more costly demand came from the April 1969 Black Economic Development Conference (BEDC), headed by civil rights activist James Forman, in what came to be termed the "Black Manifesto." Calling for reparations to African Americans from institutions that benefited from the slave labor of their ancestors, Forman turned first to the churches and in a dramatic confrontation at historic Riverside Church (New York City) the following month demanded $5 million for investment in various African American–controlled enterprises, from banks to media and publishing concerns. The BEDC did not receive significant funding as a result, indeed prompted explicit repudiation by the COB in its "Message to the Church on Reconciliation," but the confrontation led denominations to allocate substantial amounts of money to minority programs and community organizations, and it helped build support within the churches for this type of funding. Later that year Black Methodists for Church Renewal organized a sit-in by African Americans at the Board of Missions offices in New York City. The board responded promptly and positively. In the following months the programs of the National Committee of Black Churchmen, BMCR, and other minority caucuses, the World Council of Churches Program to Combat Racism, and Black colleges related to the denomination received sizable grants, totaling $1.3 million, from sources determined by the National, World, and Women's divisions. Many conferences, on their own, adopted the Black church as a missional priority. Staffed through the conference budget, such programs focused on strengthening struggling congregations, ministerial training, and recruitment.[9]

Over the decade of the 1970s United Methodism dealt with problems related to racism in church life. To mainstream white leaders, at least, that problem seemed more immediately approachable than the problem of racism in society as a whole. At the 1970 special session General Conference in St. Louis, BMCR pressed the need for funding for education and economic development. Several hundred African Americans quietly encircled the delegates sitting in the arena. General Conference embraced some of BMCR's recommendations: a $2 million Minority Group Economic Empowerment Fund to be administered by the Commission on Religion and Race, a $1 million scholarship fund for minority students, and $4 million a year (to be raised) to support of the church's Black colleges.

The Commission on Religion and Race, in its first report to a General Conference, reported organized opposition to the merger of Black and white conferences in Mississippi and Alabama and commended the Women's Division and Women's Society of Christian Service (United Methodist Women after 1971) for leading the church by meeting together interracially.

Individual courageous acts continued Methodism's several decades of prophetic witness against racist violence. Among many such was that of the Reverend Vernon Tyson, who sought to get Oxford, North Carolina, to face a 1970 lynching—a stance that forced the family to leave town. Decades later (2007) Tyson's son Timothy won the prestigious Louisville Grawemeyer Award in Religion for *Blood Done Sign My Name*,[10] his revisiting of the lynching, accounting of both Black and white violence, and portraying his father's prophetic role. The year 1970 also saw the publication by Methodist James Cone of *A Black Theology of Liberation*, which with his *Black Theology and Black Power* of the prior year, launched the Black theology movement. Cone called Christians, Methodists included, in a constructive and mature voice to affirm the distinctive theological contribution of the Black understanding of the gospel. Black United Methodist laity also stepped into leadership. Doris Davis, for instance, a member of Wesley Methodist Church in Los Angeles, was elected mayor of Compton, California. She was the first African American woman elected as a mayor of a metropolitan city. Davis had grown up in Chicago's Bishop Hartzell Methodist Church.

The 1972 General Conference adopted a new Social Principles statement forthrightly condemning racism in all its forms and calling for justice for all racial-ethnic and oppressed peoples. It also made the General Commission on Religion and Race (GCORR) a permanent commission with an expanded mandate. Later that year, the General Board of Global Ministries took an important step toward healing the rift between Black and white in the church by electing the Reverend Randolph Nugent—the first director of its New York–based Metropolitan Urban Service Training (MUST) program and head of the Division of Overseas Ministries of the National Council of Churches—to the post of associate general secretary for the National Division. African Americans had finally penetrated the racial barrier of the denomination's powerful, strategic mission board. Melvin G. Talbert, a district superintendent from Long Beach, California, became the first Black general secretary in the denomination's history, leading the General Board of Discipleship until his election to episcopacy in 1980. The Reverend George Outen became the second Black general secretary upon his election to the General Board of Church and Society in 1976.

In November 1972, the last Black conferences, those in Mississippi and South Carolina, merged with the overlapping white conferences, albeit doing so by constituting Black districts, an evasion struck down by the Judicial Council two years later. By 1974, eighteen years after the Methodist General Conference had approved ecclesial integration, passing Amendment IX to the Constitution, and a decade after it had mandated integration, the scandal of Methodism's official policy of segregation finally ended. The prior year (1973) and ten years after guarding the University of Alabama against the "evil" of desegregation, United Methodist Governor George Wallace crowned the university's first Black homecoming queen. In a television interview in 1991, Wallace expressed remorse for his former stance on segregation.

In 1974, the Women's Division of GBGM held two leadership development workshops for women of color in dialogue with white women. From this event came the creation of a talent bank for nominations and training for committees on nominations, which led to a large presence of women of color in leadership among the church's women and the election in 1976 of the Women's Division's first Black woman president, Mai H. Gray. Also in 1974 there were two major publications about African American Methodists. *Dark Salvation: The Story of Methodism as It Developed among Blacks in America* was by Harry V. Richardson, president of Gammon Theological Seminary and later president of the Atlanta consortium into which Gammon entered, the Interdenominational Theological Seminary. James P. Brawley, one of Methodism's most respected Black scholars and educators, wrote *Two Centuries of Methodist Concern: Bondage, Freedom, and Education of Black People*. In 1974, following an unprecedented Africa-U.S. UMC Bishops Consultation in Salisbury, Rhodesia, the six bishops in Africa issued a statement calling for more self-determination and a larger decision-making role in missionary sending programs by the denomination in the U.S.[11] The following year, on a visit to missionary headquarters in New York, Bishop Abel Muzorewa of Zimbabwe (then colonial Rhodesia), the second indigenous United Methodist bishop in Africa elected in 1968, made the case for African-indigenized practice and leadership, citing white missionary mistakes in Africa (Sources 1975). Bishop Muzorewa's twenty-four-year term, which extended into the country's independence from Great Britain in 1980, would be marked by controversies surrounding his government involvement, including a stint as prime minister of the transitional Zimbabwe-Rhodesia government in 1979. After he criticized his successor, Robert Mugabe, in 1989, Muzorewa was detained by the government for almost a year. He became one of the UMC's best-known international figures in the late twentieth century.[12]

Viewing ethnic churches as an important potential for church growth or loss, the 1976 and 1980 General Conferences named the Ethnic Minority Local Church as one of the church's highest missional priorities. The 1976 General Conference also adopted a fresh resolution, "The United Methodist Church and Race."[13] By 1980 the effort to be more inclusive could be seen and felt in the presence of African American delegates and leaders at General Conference in Indianapolis. The delegates adopted the Women's Division's "Charter for Racial Justice" as churchwide policy. And Randolph Nugent, an African American pastor from the New York Conference, became the general secretary of the denomination's largest and most powerful board: the General Board of Global Ministries. White resentment of or opposition to such racial-ethnic empowerment—no longer tolerated in explicit form—would find alternative expression on matters of social policy, doctrine, and bureaucracy.

The New Church and War

An important initiative of the new United Methodist Church was to publish its statements on matters of policy, concern, and commitment as a separate book, *The Book of*

Resolutions of The United Methodist Church: 1968.[14] Three of the first five resolutions dealt with war and peace (the other two with race and Project Equality). The very first, "U.S. Policy in Vietnam," commended the president for a recent effort at negotiations. Another itemized various initiatives toward ceasefire, negotiations, and reconstruction. The third updated for cold (and hot) war conflict earlier Methodist and EUB commitments to peacemaking through international (including UN) accords. These cautious statements reflected the church. The UMC was born at a time when Americans were more divided than they had been for generations.[15] The Vietnam War brought an end to the domestic consensus that had sustained U.S. cold war politics since World War II. The nation was in the midst of its longest and most troubling war. President Johnson's dramatic escalation of the war in 1965 sparked fierce debate. Pacifism gradually became fashionable again as cold war in a nuclear age sowed doubt and fear. Conferences roiled in debate over resolutions on the war, disarmament, the military-industrial complex, ROTC, and conscientious objection. United Methodists took their place along the whole spectrum of and at both ends of the Vietnam debate—hawk to dove.

The UMC's initial official social principles statements retained both the old Methodist Social Creed, with its embrace within the church's fellowship of "those who sincerely differ as to the Christian's duty in regard to military service," and the former EUBC statement, which was more strongly pacifist in tone.[16] Similarly, just prior to union, in 1967, the Council of Bishops issued a statement on the Vietnam War calling on the governments of South Vietnam and the U.S. to initiate a ceasefire and begin negotiations to secure "the right of self-determination for the people of South Vietnam" and "phased withdrawal of all foreign troops and bases with arrangements for asylum for those who may require it."

Unlike these balanced statements, which catered to a church as divided as the nation, Methodist students, subject to the draft, were and had been less willing to pull their punches. The magazine of the Methodist Student Movement, *Motive*, openly opposed the war, supported "draft dodgers," and devoted substantial critical attention to the war. Writers contributed articles about it; poets agonized over it; artists painted it. B. J. Stiles's 1967 editorial was especially challenging: "In the name of God, *this* war, in *this* place, at *this* time, against *this* people, must stop" (Sources 1967). Stiles voiced the moral outrage and anti-administration sentiment of campus leaders, male and female, whose demonstrations and concerts moved American society gradually to join in opposition to the war. The Methodist Federation for Social Action and ecumenical Clergy and Laymen Concerned about Vietnam launched educational and lobbying efforts on behalf of conscientious objectors and urged the government to grant clemency to the 700-plus young men imprisoned for resistance and the 5,000-plus who had gone abroad rather than fight.

Many other leaders in the UMC boards and agencies joined the chorus—a liberal prophetic orientation that pundits later would view as the occasion of the ideological split within the church and even of its numerical decline. Important in the perspective of United Methodist leaders was the social-geographical location of key agencies— particularly the General Board of Church and Society and the General Board of Global Ministries—in New York and Washington, D.C. Earlier these two agencies—Board of Christian Social Concerns and the Woman's Division of the Board of Missions— had planned, financed, and built the Church Center for the United Nations in New York City, which as an interdenominational enterprise would become especially important in developing and expressing Methodism's and United Methodism's international perspective. Tellingly, the consecration of the $2 million interdenominational Church Center at 77 United Nations Plaza in 1963 had drawn Secretary of State Dean Rusk, U.S. Ambassador to the UN Adlai Stevenson, and UN Secretary General U Thant. Ambassador Stevenson foresaw its vocation:

> The Church Center for the United Nations, thanks to this location, will provide new and sharpened perspective for church leaders and laymen who come here. They will return to their congregations, wiser for their experience and better equipped to increase understanding and build up support for the bold, vigorous and unique experiment in security and social and economic progress by collective action.[17]

Methodist women who played a crucial role in the vision for and completion of the project had also foreseen its prophetic office as Theressa Hoover, associate general secretary and head of the Women's Division, explained to board members:

> Some may wonder how the Women's Division would have made such entangled commitments initially and compounded them with each successive loan or grant. The fact is their usual sound approach to finances was overcome by their commitment to an international program, and their belief in the values of an ecumenical Christian witness within the international sphere.

Hoover ended her remarks with these words: "So walk tall, speak clearly, act boldly. We are the church."[18]

Financed and owned jointly by the Board of Christian Social Concerns (later General Board of Church and Society) and the Women's Division but soon home as well to Baptist, Seventh-day Adventist, Lutheran, Presbyterian, Quaker, Unitarian, and African Methodist groups, the center enabled all the churches to expand their commitment to peace education and action and to speak forcefully on Vietnam.

By 1972, with casualties continuing to mount and President Nixon stepping up bombing of North Vietnam, United Methodism caught up with its prophetic leadership. Following a long debate, that year's General Conference, by a 5 to 4 majority, adopted a statement condemning the immorality of America's involvement in the war and calling on President Nixon to halt the bombing and withdraw all forces by the end of the year. The statement further urged Congress to withhold funding and appealed to the leaders in Hanoi and Washington to release all prisoners of war. In marked contrast to the Vietnam statement adopted by the church at its 1968 conference, which did little more than express growing concern, the 1972 statement contained a confession of guilt for the nation's war policy (Sources 1972b). The resolution on Vietnam reworked the paragraph on peace in the new statement of Social Principles adopted in 1972. The UMC position on peace changed boldly from acquiescence to rejection of war:

> We believe war is incompatible with the teachings and example of Christ. We therefore reject war as an instrument of national foreign policy and insist that the first moral duty of all nations is to resolve by peaceful means every dispute that arises between or among them; that human values must outweigh military claims as governments determine their priorities; that the militarization of society must be challenged and stopped; and that the manufacture, sale and deployment of armaments must be reduced and controlled. [A final clause—"and that the production, possession or use of nuclear weapons be condemned"—was added in 1980.][19]

And the first four statements in *The Book of Resolutions of The United Methodist Church, 1972*,[20] dealt with war, peace, and Indochina.

Such official acts elicited both applause and boos from the church members whose sons and daughters both served and protested, Vietnam constituting one of several sources of division. Among those serving and tying United Methodism to government and the military were chaplains and the Commission on Chaplains and its successor, the Division of Chaplains within the newly formed Board of Higher Education and Ministry. For more than half a century—covering World War II, the Korean War, the Berlin buildup, the Cuban crisis, and the war in Vietnam—more than 2,600 clergy, for varying lengths of time, held special appointment by their bishops to serve as full-time chaplains. By the 1980s, more than 600 chaplains functioned in full-time ministry with more than 100 serving part-time with various institutions and the Civil Air Patrol, and about 300 in the reserve components.

Union Homework: Ethical, Organizational, and Doctrinal

The ruling principle of the commission that worked out the 1968 Methodist-EUB merger was unite now, settle the differences later. Left for resolution were such issues as ministry and episcopacy, doctrinal standards and social principles, the number of seminaries, and an unbelievably complicated cluster of national program boards and agencies. (Note: Worship developments from 1968 to 1984 consummate thereafter and are treated in the next chapter.) The 1968 General Conference delegates realized the work of actual uniting could not be completed in Dallas. The Uniting Conference established a pattern of churchwide quadrennial study commissions. It called a special session of General Conference for 1970 to hear interim reports.

The Methodist and Evangelical United Brethren churches came to union in 1968 with strong statements on social principles that guided their life and witness. The new church ended up with not one but two statements of social principles—an aging Methodist Social Creed, originally adopted in 1908, and the EUB "Basic Beliefs Regarding Social Issues and Moral Standards." Similar at some points, they were sufficiently different at others to raise penetrating questions about their theological and ethical foundations. Furthermore, the new church faced a new world situation: old problems were becoming more complex, and difficult new ones had arisen. A quadrennial study commission was appointed by the Uniting Conference to resolve the matter. In the end a fresh statement of social principles and a new social creed for use in services of worship were drafted and adopted.

The new statement began with a call to responsible use of this world's natural resources. It gave vigorous support for control and limitation of population growth as well as cautious approval to abortion and remarriage of divorced persons. It recognized the right of responsible civil disobedience and extended support for conscientious objectors to include opposition to particular wars. More explicit approval was given to the struggle for racial and social justice. The statement on human sexuality was the most difficult of all to resolve, as we note below.

The Structure Study Commission attracted most attention during the first quadrennium and at the 1972 General Conference. Many hoped that the century-old trend of "one board after another" might be reversed and the church's bureaucracy pared. In the end, the program agencies were merely grouped into four superboards—Church and Society, Discipleship, Global Ministries, and Higher Education and Ministry—in a word, advocacy, nurture, outreach, and vocation. A quota system for board membership created space and opportunity for youth, women, and ethnic ministry representatives. The former members of the EUBC were guaranteed slots as well.

To oversee the agency structure on its program side, the church adopted the EUBC model of a Council of Ministries (preferring that to what had been the less effective Methodist Coordinating Council) and designed it initially to function between General Conferences in interim capacity. Although the Judicial Council ruled unconstitutional its role as an interim General Conference, GCOM nevertheless retained considerable power, including the prerogatives of electing general secretaries annually, nominating the respective program board, reviewing and evaluating all programs and plans, making recommendations on budget, and coordinating the work of and minimizing the competition between the several agencies. Following what had been Methodism's practice for well over a century, General Conference mandated for annual conference and local church what it prescribed for the connection as a whole. So congregations found themselves with new Councils of Ministry, which were to "consider, initiate, develop, and coordinate proposals for the church's strategy for mission" and to "elect teachers, counselors, and officers for the church school other than those subject to election by the Charge Conference." Mandating age-level and family coordinators and councils and work area chairs and commissions, General Conference, in effect, made it possible for every local church to experience on a day-to-day, month-to-month basis the reality that United Methodism had not pared and simplified but greatly complicated its order and procedure. Gradually over the next several quadrennia, successive General Conferences would make more and more of the structure and order permissive. However, the damage had been done. GCOM became and remained symbolic of excessively centralized (and distant) bureaucracy.[21]

The church initially embraced the report and recommendations of the Theological Study Commission on Doctrine and Doctrinal Standards but would experience its work, undertaken amidst doctrinal turmoil, as eventually both important and divisive. The doctrinal consensus and ties to the churches' theological moorings that Methodists, Evangelicals, and United Brethren enjoyed in the nineteenth century had been badly eroded by an explosion of twentieth-century theological ventures (for some but fads), each of which had found a niche within the church(es). The social gospel had institutionalized itself in the deaconess movement and the Methodist Federation for Social Service and become policy with the Social Creed. Boston personalism held sway among clergy across the northern church. Methodists invested less in fundamentalism than did other denominations but found other expressions for theological and social-cultural conservatism (prohibition, opposition to unification, the Klan). Against the successive tragedies of two world wars, the Great Depression in between, the rise of communism, fascism, and Nazism, neo-orthodoxy with its reemphasis of transcendence, human sin, revelation through Christ, and salvation by faith found favor, especially with faculty and in campus ministries. In the 1950s Christian existentialism, which stressed faith as a vivid personal experience and made effective use of the arts, appealed to leadership in the Methodist Student Movement and to evangelicals who wanted to be modern. At the same time, a small cadre of Methodists was rediscovering Wesley, and the ecumenical movement was leading others to reconsider the basic doctrines of church, ministry, and the sacraments. The flare of hope aroused by the election of President John F. Kennedy in 1960 called forth more radical theological options. The "death of God" hurrah and the flurry of excitement about the "Secular City" emerged and found their share of followers. A new interest in Asian faiths led others to become devotees of Zen Buddhism and followers of itinerant Hindu gurus. By the 1970s, while evangelicals were reawakening and charismatics were feeling the Spirit, liberation theologies began to take center stage—Black theology, feminist theology, and third-world theology.

The 1968–72 Theological Study Commission undertook its work mindful of the theological confusion, as its chair, Albert Outler, explained, "Somewhere in The United Methodist Church there is somebody urging every kind of theology still alive and not a few that are dead." Outler then went on to affirm doctrinal pluralism "as a positive theological virtue." He stated,

> [Y]our commission came to realize that this apparent bedlam is, at least in part, the perversion of an older, profounder principle of positive importance, that is to say, of doctrinal pluralism, doctrinal diversity-in-Christological-unity. Far from being a license to doctrinal recklessness of indifferentism, the Wesleyan principle of pluralism holds in dynamic balance both the biblical focus of all Christian doctrine and also the responsible freedom that all Christians must have in their theological reflections and public teaching.[22]

Outler's commission and General Conference enshrined this "new/old" doctrine of theological pluralism in what has become arguably the most important doctrinal guideline for United Methodism, a new, extended section in the *Discipline*, in 1972 titled, "Our Theological Task." This section also functioned, per the charge to Outler and company, to indicate how the separate theological trajectories of the EUB and Methodist churches converged in United Methodism, a convergence needing attention.

The Constitution of The United Methodist Church, following the Methodist pattern, explicitly prohibited any alteration in "our present, existing and established standards of doctrine." The 1968 *Book of Discipline* was full of procedures by which clergy and laity could be censured for teachings contrary to these doctrines. Yet nowhere were "our doctrines" defined and scarcely anywhere were they understood. The joint commission on church union simply printed back to back in the new *Discipline* the Methodist Articles of Religion dating from 1784 and the recently updated Evangelical United Brethren Confession of Faith of 1962, and the Judicial Council deemed them "congruent, if not identical in their doctrinal perspective and not in conflict." Yet they were not identical, and explicit references to the traditional Wesleyan foundations (Wesley's "standard" *Sermons*, and *Explanatory Notes upon the New Testament*, for instance) were absent from the Plan of Union.

To address this need for doctrinal development and clarification, the Uniting Conference empowered the Theological Study Commission if it deemed it advisable to "undertake the preparation of a contemporary formulation of doctrine and belief, in supplementation to all antecedent formulations."[23] Sensing such a course doomed to fail, the commission formulated a new "Part II Doctrine and Doctrinal Statements and the General Rules" for the *Discipline*. Into Part II it placed the new section "Our Theological Task" and an equally long "Historical Background," which reviewed doctrinal development in the predecessor churches. It sandwiched between these two United

Methodism's several "Landmark Documents." The latter included Methodist "Articles" and "General Rules," the EUB "Confession," and prefatory comment referencing Wesley's *Sermons* and *Explanatory Notes*. In its 1970 report and acknowledging the bitterly polemical character of the sixteenth-century Reformation-formulated Articles of Religion, the commission urged the church henceforth to interpret the historic standards "in consonance with our best ecumenical insights and judgment."[24] "Our Theological Task" and the "Historical Background" sustained that emphasis, enumerating basic Christian beliefs shared with other communions and reaffirming distinctive Wesleyan emphases as found in John Wesley's sermons as catholic in character. In particular and as noted, theological pluralism among United Methodists was acknowledged and affirmed as a modern reaffirmation of what Wesley called "the catholic spirit."

A hopeful, open, ecumenical, constructive, future-oriented spirit ran through Part II, culminating in a several-page subsection, "Theological Frontiers and New Directions." Here the church, with Outler's guidance, welcomed "all serious theological opinions developed within the framework of our doctrinal heritage and guidelines so long as they are not intolerant or exclusive toward other equally loyal opinions." "Of crucial current importance," it went on to affirm, "is the surfacing of new theological emphases focusing on the great struggles for human liberation and fulfillment. Notable among them are black theology, female liberation theology, political and ethnic theologies, third-world theology, and theologies of human rights."[25] To keep the ongoing theological enterprise faithful to the "'marrow' of Christian truth," Outler's commission formulated what was deemed a Wesleyan theological method, the testing of claims against a fourfold norm of Scripture, tradition, experience, and reason. Introduced in the first paragraphs of the "Historical Background" and developed in "Our Theological Task" the quadrilateral was viewed as orienting United Methodism to the living core of the gospel, which it had received through the witness of the Wesleys, Albright, Otterbein, and Boehm. "This living core, as they believed, stands revealed in Scripture, illumined by tradition, vivified in personal experience, and confirmed by reason."[26]

Adopted by General Conference 925 to 17, without amendment and with little discussion (barely seventeen minutes!), the quadrilateral, theological pluralism, affirmation of diversity, and the commission's work generally met with similar approbation by many Methodists back home. But the church's newly organized evangelical caucus, Good News, responded negatively. Fearing that the statement's blessing of theological pluralism would lead to doctrinal confusion, the by then not-so-silent minority soon drafted their own version of United Methodist fundamentals, which included the inspiration of Scripture, virgin birth of Christ, substitutionary atonement, and physical resurrection and return of Christ.[27] This "Junaluska Affirmation," adopted at a 1975 Good News convocation, however, failed to stir up significant comment from the larger church. In the following years, the Good News leaders continued to press the issue of theological integrity, focusing on the role of Scripture in the quadrilateral, the matter of pluralism, the definition of core beliefs, and the place of Wesley.[28] The UMC has ever since been wrestling with how best to understand, interpret, and apply the concept of the quadrilateral. Pressure for change continued to build so that by 1984, the General Conference, in response to a flood of petitions, established a commission to review the 1972 theological statement, a development we take up in the next chapter. (Worship developments in the 1968–84 period come to fruition thereafter and are treated in the next chapter.)

The 1972 General Conference continued to postpone other union homework by establishing three study commissions of its own—one to study the seminaries, another to study ministry and ordination, and a third to study episcopacy and superintendency. Four years later the reports came in. The general church accepted major responsibility for funding ministerial education and reduced the number of seminaries by one. A new statement, "The Ministry of All Christians," the creation of a new office of diaconal minister for full-time lay professionals, and an improved candidacy plan for ordinands resulted. The perennial question about whether district superintendents should be elected (EUB style) or appointed (Methodist style) was resolved in favor of the appointive pattern. Life tenure for bishops was reviewed. Some argued that term episcopacy, which was the EUBC pattern, would encourage the election of bishops who would be relatively young or female or of ethnic ministry background. Life tenure for bishops won, but their service as episcopal leaders in one geographical area was cut to a maximum of eight years.

New Organizations to Empower Women

Nineteen seventy-two saw the formation of a United Methodist Women's Caucus convened initially the prior year (Sources 1972d), the creation by General Conference of the General Commission on the Status and Role of Women (COSROW), and the merger of the several women's organizations in the UMC to form United Methodist Women (UMW), the latter to be administered by the Women's Division of General Board of Global Ministries. The former was "charged with the responsibility of fostering an awareness of problems and issues related to status and role of women with special reference to full participation in the total life of the Church at least commensurate with its total membership in The United Methodist Church."[29] It would be a shared and highly successful endeavor.

COSROW, UMW, the Caucus, and the Women's Division had advocacy, monitoring, inclusion, and empowerment issues with which to deal and about which they were painfully clear (Sources 1972d, p. 632). Having exercised for a century and a half in various organizations their self-appointed office as the conscience of Methodism and the prophetic voice of the church, Methodist women aspired to place, position, and prerogative that would provide the church needed leadership on pressing issues: "abortion, homosexuality, funding minority development programs, Black colleges, the Vietnam War, South Africa, amnesty, and many other deep concerns" (Sources 1972d, p. 633). Despite their preponderance in the church's membership, the proportion of women in Methodist General Conference lay delegations had hovered only in the 10 percent range. The number of deaconesses had steadily declined from nearly 1,000 in 1939 to 366 in 1963 and would continue downward to 185 in 1976 and to 70 by 1997, as the opportunities for these religiously trained women waned and social workers and secular nurses assumed their places.[30] The number of women missionaries had atrophied as the church had adjusted to decolonization and shifted leadership to foreign nations (see treatment below). Moreover, the overwhelmingly male delegates at the 1964 Methodist General Conference, in the name of efficiency, determined that the Woman's Division could no longer engage in direct service ministries. Ending a program of mission outreach for women by women begun in 1869, the church transferred the administration of programs to reorganized national and world divisions headed by a mostly male board and staff. While demand for religious educators had remained relatively constant, the percentage of women clergy (ordained as elders and full members of conference) remained small, under 1 percent.[31] On neither the professional nor the representational fronts did Methodist women seem to be making real progress, indeed, in places losing ground, at a time when a veritable social revolution for women was occurring, a revolution symbolized by activist-writer Betty Friedan's *The Feminine Mystique*. Friedan's debunking of the myth of the postwar docile soul who tended home and hearth forgoing her own ambitions and interests had been required reading for the 175 national leaders of Methodist women whose 1963 meeting was devoted to "Women in a New Age" and whose appreciation of the book, shared with the 1.2 million members of United Methodist Women, doubtless contributed materially to the 3 million copies sold.[32] Effective in conveying the Women's Division's several concerns was its magazine, *Response*, which in 1969 superseded the serials of the predecessor denominations, *World Evangel* and *Methodist Woman*.

Sensitive to the heightened aspirations of women generally and the minimal progress for women within the church in matters of program and policy making, the Women's Division had petitioned the 1968 General Conference to establish a study to "see how [the church's] woman power is used in this time of growing recognition of basic equality of men and women."[33] The Women's Division rejected a subsequent request that it fund the study (viewing it as a churchwide undertaking and obligation) but made its own material contribution to critique of current practice. For instance, Marian Derby, director of planning of the World Division (1969–71), examined the employment of single women missionaries, EUB and Methodist, documenting a drop in half, from 578 to 274. The Women's Division then pursued the issue with a consultation, "Single

Women in Church and Society." The consultation discovered problems for women clergy as well as missionaries, problems in bishops' adhering "to the mandate of the *Discipline* for guaranteed appointments for all ordained ministers." Finding single women to be most vulnerable and expressing concerns about discriminatory practices, the consultation called on the church "to affirm the validity and wholeness of singleness as a choice of life-style for clergy and laity, both women and men."[34]

The Study Commission on the Participation of Women in the Decision-Making Channels of the Church was not actually funded until the 1970 special session of General Conference. That year, in celebration of the fiftieth anniversary of American women's right to vote, a crowd of ten thousand people, mostly women of all ages, occupations, and viewpoints, marched down New York City's Fifth Avenue, August 26, 1970, to an enthusiastic rally in Bryant Park. The rally, the high point of a day of demonstrations in New York and around the country, Betty Friedan, by then originator of a notion of the "Women's Strike for Equality" and founder of the National Organization for Women, called "beyond our wildest dreams." "This is not a bedroom war, this is a political movement," Friedan said. Another speaker, Kate Millett, the author of the bestseller *Sexual Politics,* first published in 1970, told the crowd: "Today is the beginning of a new movement. Today is the end of millenniums of oppression."[35] At the city's Interchurch Center an ad hoc women's group sponsored a noon meeting attended by about 150 persons, mostly women. Theressa Hoover, associate general secretary of the Board of Missions of the UMC, said that the winning of equal rights for women would be a "bulldozing process that will have to go on for the rest of our lives."

Under her leadership, the Women's Division addressed power and decision-making issues with the board as well as problems inhibiting women's fuller participation in the life of the church. The division constituted an Ad Hoc Committee on Churchwomen's Liberation, which worked in parallel with the General Conference–authorized body. It sent to the 1972 General Conference proposals that formulae be established to guarantee women's, minority, and youth membership on general church agencies. It also expressed concerns about how minority-group women would fare in annual conferences and local churches as the final phases of Central Jurisdiction phaseout occurred, and it proposed other goals.[36] Hoover voiced these concerns forcefully in a hard-hitting article in 1973 in *Response* (Sources 1973), documenting the exclusion of Black women even from the liberation causes—feminist and Black.

The Women's Caucus (Sources 1972d) represented a grassroots initiative by women eager to discuss issues that concerned them and to have a say on any reform efforts that the Study Commission or Women's Division might formulate for the 1972 General Conference. Judy Leaming-Elmer and a group of Chicago-area women issued a call for a meeting on Thanksgiving (1971) weekend at Wheadon UMC, Evanston, Illinois. Approximately twelve hundred people showed up. Teenagers to elders, they came from all over the country, paid their own way, slept on the floor of the church, and formed a National Women's Caucus of the UMC. Meeting again the next year in anticipation of General Conference, the caucus functioned to add urgency and pressure to goals being formulated in other channels. For instance, mindful of the recommendation that all boards and agencies be constituted with one-third laymen, one-third laywomen, and one-third clergy, the caucus decided to ask that committee to reconsider its formula to ensure that half of the membership of these boards and agencies be women. A newsletter to broadcast the caucus's concerns, *Yellow Ribbon,* named in honor of badges of Victorian-era Methodist feminists, began publication in 1972.

The several efforts by caucus, Women's Division, and Study Commission and by United Methodist Women across the connection led the 1972 General Conference to establish the Commission on the Status and Role of Women (COSROW). The prior year, it should be noted, the U.S. Supreme Court ruled that hiring policies must be the same for women and men; the same year, both houses of Congress passed the (never ratified) Equal Rights Amendment; and the following year, the Supreme Court rendered its decision in *Roe v. Wade,* legalizing abortion, United Methodist layperson and Justice Harry Blackmun drafting the decision. In late 1974 Good News leader Charles Keysor warned of influence by "pagan women's libbers" on church policy and alleged that "top church leaders" (unidentified) shared his concern. Addressing a meeting of the Good News Fellowship of the New York Conference, Keysor also claimed that the denomination was the victim of a quota system in which women were given leadership positions solely because they were women. Two bishops, W. Ralph Ward of the New York Area and Jack Tuell of the Portland, Oregon, Area, publicly dissociated themselves from Keysor's claim.[37] The 1976 General Conference—apprised by the commission with a careful study of women's (minimal) participation in church governance and leadership—also sided with the feminists and made COSROW a *standing* (that is, permanent) commission and required COSROWs at annual conference level "to challenge the UMC at all levels to work for full and equal participation of women in the total life of the denomination."

Among COSROW's several tasks was ridding the denomination of the policy and practice of male-exclusive language, over time a highly successful campaign. More visible and more controversial was a second feminist enterprise, the elimination of sexism from religious language. COSROW and the UM women's caucus joined other feminists in protesting the use of male-exclusive language in worship and discussion. Evangelical feminist Virginia Mollenkott spoke for many devout UM women alienated by the traditional language of worship that made them feel "linguistically and structurally excluded.... If God is always man-like, and never womanlike," she protested, "then men are God-like and women are not."[38] On this cause, the church moved more cautiously, though the 1976 General Conference did approve inclusive language that appeared in official liturgies, specifically the 1976 revision of the 1972 trial-use service of Holy

Communion. In 1978 COSROW adopted its own official creedal affirmation, written by Barbara Troxell (see COSROW website),[39] and in 1980 called the UMC to develop a statement on inclusive language and images. And in 1981, COSROW called on UM agencies to adopt sexual harassment policies, another cause that would eventually succeed. The COSROWs joined with feminists in the Women's Division and United Methodist Women to encourage church endorsement of feminist concerns, especially ERA and abortion (on the latter, see discussion below). They succeeded in convincing the Council of Bishops in 1982 to express its support for the Equal Rights Amendment.

The campaign for full inclusion proceeded on the clergy front as well. In 1975 the first national UM clergywomen's consultation was held in Nashville (others followed in 1979, 1983, 1987, 1991, 1995, and 2002). In 1976 annual conferences sent ten clergywomen to General Conference, the first women *clergy* delegates to General Conference but only ten out of the five hundred clergy delegates. This General Conference moved on several issues about which women clergy were especially concerned, dealing with the matter of inclusive language in worship, authorizing a study of maternity and paternity leave and clergy/gender salary, passing resolutions on full personhood and on solidarity with women's rights as articulated by the International Women's Decade,[40] and of course, making COSROW a standing commission. By 1979, the number of ordained women reached 1,000 according to a GBHEM survey, of which about 886 were under episcopal appointment to local churches. By 1980, women represented more than 3 percent of the total professional ministry, an increase of 75 percent over 1975, and 29 percent of the United Methodists in Master of Divinity programs were women (736).[41] Increasingly women seeking full-time Christian service opted for elder's orders, the numbers in religious education waned, and several seminaries terminated master of religious education programs. While some local churches resisted the idea of a woman pastor, the appointment systems assured women of employment in ministry. Gradually bishops began appointing women to the district superintendency, beginning with Margaret Henrichsen in Maine in 1967; the number grew to seven by 1980. A major breakthrough occurred that year when the North Central Jurisdiction elected the Reverend Marjorie Swank Matthews the first woman bishop in the UMC and assigned her to the Wisconsin Area. Matthews retired four years later (1984) and died in 1986. In 1984, jurisdictions elected two women to the episcopacy, Judith Craig and Leontine T. Kelly, the latter bishop, an African American, the first woman of color.

The empowerment of women drew, as noted, on the larger feminist enterprise, and not surprisingly, women representing the spectrum of feminist views came into various positions of prominence, an ascendancy to which the growing conservative impulse took exception (as we shall discuss below). In the mid-1970s two women associated with the Good News caucus, Diane Knippers of the Goods News staff and Helen Coppedge of the Good News board, gathered interested "evangelical" women and formed the Task Force on Women in the Church (WTF). The group functioned as a subcommittee within Good News and took on as one task the editing of a newsletter, *Candle*, which was first published in 1977. By September 1983, the circulation of *Candle* had reached twenty-one thousand.[42] The newsletter critiqued the "liberal and often radical left wing bias" of United Methodist Women resources produced by the Women's Division, shared inspirational faith stories of women in mission, and disseminated alternative Bible and mission study books.[43] Good News and WTF would have cause for concern over the emergence of yet another caucus.

Homosexuality: Cause and Caucus

Before the 1968 union, Methodists and mainline Protestants had given homosexuality little sustained attention and not caught sight of early gay rights developments. The denomination's journal of opinion, *Religion in Life*, did not publish an article on homosexuality until 1966, then in an article by Baptist theological educator Carlyle Marney.[44] A summer 1970 issue carried six articles, "Ethical Concerns for the 1970s," none of which dealt with sexuality or homosexuality. Attitudes, perceptions, and "doctrine" soon changed, bifurcated, hardened.

World War II had aided the emergence of gay and lesbian identities and social movements, bringing previously isolated gay men and lesbians into discovery of one another. Some had same-sex experiences for the first time and, through these experiences, came to realize their homosexuality. The World War II generation "stretched their closet to its limit, neither proclaiming nor parading their homosexuality in public, but not willing to live lonely, isolated lives."[45] The first modern gay rights organization, the Mattachine Society, formed in Los Angeles in 1951. Four years later, lesbians organized the Daughters of Bilitis in San Francisco. The organizing indicated and facilitated consciousness of being a legitimate minority living within a hostile mainstream culture. Leaders adopted an assimilationist rather than a confrontational approach to social change. They began to work with psychiatrists and other mental health professionals to remove homosexuality as a medical pathology,[46] an effort aided by Alfred Kinsey's best-selling books, *Sexual Behavior in the Human Male* (1948) and *Sexual Behavior in the Human Female* (1953), and William Masters and Virginia Johnson's *Human Sexual Response* (1966). Such studies confronted Americans with scientific evidence of the diversity of human sexual expression. In between these two landmark scientific studies (1961) the American Bar Association recommended that laws dealing with private sexual relations between consenting adults be dropped. A wave of legal reform in the 1960s and 1970s wiped sodomy laws from the books of most northern, midwestern, and western states.[47] One by one, health-care professionals removed homosexuality from the list of mental disorders—the American Psychiatric Association in 1973 and the American Psychological Association in 1975.[48]

Early Methodist gay advocacy also centered in California, specifically Glide Memorial Methodist Church in San Francisco. Its African American minister, the Reverend Cecil Williams, had long led the church in the struggle for racial and economic justice. Situated in the heart of the Tenderloin district, Glide daily confronted the castoffs of American society—poor and older people, alcoholics and drug addicts, petty criminals and male hustlers. Besides traditional pastoral activities, Glide operated a number of special programs, including a Young Adult Project to cater to the needs of a growing population of teenage runaways living on Tenderloin streets. Williams brought the Reverend Ted McIlvenna, a young minister-social worker, from Kansas City to head the project in 1962. McIlvenna's work quickly brought him face-to-face with homosexuality. Many male runaways, he discovered, were gay, driven to street hustling by the hostility and ostracism of their parents and their peers. With the backing of other Glide staff and the Glide Foundation, McIlvenna provided meeting spaces at Glide for gay organizations, reached out to other area ministers prepared to work for social justice for gays and lesbians, and garnered the support of the Reverend Clifford Crummey, Bay Area district superintendent, who defended Glide's radical activities at the national level of Methodism.[49]

Under the sponsorship of the Glide Urban Center, McIlvenna organized a four-day consultation at the end of May 1964 between gay activists and the ministers, including a few from other cities, among them, Methodists B. J. Stiles, editor of *Motive,* and C. Dale White, future bishop. After a tour of the city that included visits to bars, drag shows, private parties, and gay activist meetings, the sixteen ministers met for two days with a group of gay women and men. For many it was the first time they had ever knowingly talked with a gay man or a lesbian. The ministers acknowledged the role that religion played in the persecution of gays and promised to initiate dialogue in their denominations on the churches' stand toward same-gender sexuality. The San Francisco contingent continued to meet for several months until December 1964, when the ministers and the city's gay and lesbian leaders formed the Council on Religion and the Homosexual, a groundbreaking coalition of clergy and lesbian and gay activists.

To kick off the new venture and to raise funds for the organization, the ministers planned a New Year's Eve dance for the gay community and so notified the police (against the advice of gay activists). The police then used mere touching by members of the same sex as grounds for arrest or the revocation of a liquor license, brought a large contingent to the scene, without a search warrant arrested a ticket taker and three lawyers who tried to block their entry, and broke up the party. In blatant intimidation, police photographers flashed pictures of each of the six hundred guests as they left the hall. On January 2 the ministers held a press conference at Glide, in which they accused the police department of bad faith, harassment, intimidation, and obvious hostility. Ministerial charges of police harassment earned press sympathy. And by arresting lawyers, the police provoked the wrath of the ACLU. When the four came to trial in February, the city's gay population felt vindicated. The judge directed the jury to return a not-guilty verdict before the defense had even presented its case. Gay activists in San Francisco, both then and retrospectively, perceived the New Year's Eve ball as a turn-ing point for the movement locally[50] (as the 1969 police raid on the New York City Stonewall drag bar and several days of gay riot thereafter inaugurated the movement nationally). In 1967, Glide Church and the Glide Foundation of San Francisco launched one of the first economic boycotts on behalf of gay rights, stating that they would not buy goods and services from companies that discriminated against gays and encourag-ing others to follow their lead.

The Social Principles Study Commission's drafting committee, headed by Bishop James Thomas (Iowa Area), labored in this increasingly charged atmosphere. The para-graphs dealing with homosexuality were among the most difficult for the commission to agree upon. Up to that time no predecessor body of the newly formed denomination had ever made any official statement about homosexuality or homosexual practice. How-ever, Bishop Thomas and a majority of his committee were convinced that the proposed Social Principles had to include some kind of statement on this topic.[51] The thirty-two-member committee's final report, drafted by the Reverend Alan Geyer, editor of the *Christian Century* and clergy member of the Northern New Jersey Conference,[52] was published in the March 1972 *Engage*, the denomination's social concerns magazine, and was widely circulated in pamphlet form prior to the General Conference. This pastoral statement neither condemned nor condoned homosexual practice, but said only: "We declare our acceptance of homosexuals as persons of sacred worth, and we welcome them into the fellowship of the church. Further, we insist that society ensure their human and civil rights."[53]

A handful of openly gay men traveled to Atlanta and offered General Conference delegates and visitors the opportunity for conversation about homosexuality. Few dele-gates or observers responded positively. But the legislative committee dealing with the church's proposed Social Principles invited one of the gay men, Gene Leggett, a former clergy member of the East Texas Conference, to speak to them about homosexuality. A year earlier (1971) Leggett told his peers that he was gay and was summarily discontin-ued as a clergyman.[54] Inspired to some extent by Leggett's testimony, the committee ap-proved this sentence: "Homosexuals no less than heterosexuals are persons of sacred worth, who need the ministry and guidance of the church in their struggles for human fulfillment. Further, we insist that all persons are entitled to have their human and civil rights ensured."

These words proved too strong for the General Conference Legislative Committee on Christian Social Concerns, which dealt with the proposed text. Although the delegates retained the affirmation that homosexuals are "persons of sacred worth," they could not bring themselves to say outright that homosexuals are *welcome* in the church.[55] Thus the committee changed the wording to read:

> Homosexuals, no less than heterosexuals, are persons of sacred worth, who need the ministry and guidance of the church in their struggles for human fulfillment, as well as the spiritual and emotional care of a fellowship which enables reconciling relationships with God, with others, and with self. Further, we insist that all persons are entitled to have their human and civil rights ensured.[56]

The committee recognized that homosexuals needed the ministry of the church, but refused to assure them that the guidance would be forthcoming.

When these two sentences reached the floor of General Conference on April 16, an extended, often emotional debate ensued, with lurid stories of kidnapping murders of young boys by homosexuals. "If we indicate by the last statement," one delegate declared,

> after having brought these people into the church and claimed them for Jesus Christ, if this in any way gives them a license to continue in their activities of preying upon the young men of our community and of our schools, I want it eliminated. Furthermore, if this gives these men a license to take a 14-year old boy, as happened, kidnapped him as he was delivering his papers. Two days later they found his body in an isolated place, murdered. I want it stricken out of here.

Such arguments were countered by other delegates, including one who noted, "There is a long list of crimes one could list to be carried out by heterosexuals. By the same token, in spite of the fact that heterosexuals may be involved in crime, we go to great lengths to see that their civil rights are protected."[57] In the end the final sentence remained substantially without alteration.

A turning point came when a lay delegate from the Southwest Texas Conference, Don J. Hand, an attorney from San Antonio, moved to add this clause after *civil rights ensured*: "though we do not condone the practice of homosexuality and consider this practice incompatible with Christian teaching."[58] Hand defended his motion as showing that "we stand by our Christian doctrine as it is given to us in our basic beliefs shown in the Bible." A medical doctor and Southern New Jersey Conference lay delegate, Hammell Shipps, asked in a substitute motion that the General Conference explicitly condemn the practice of homosexuality. He mentioned the promiscuous nature of gays and their contribution to the spread of venereal disease. The substitute motion failed.[59] Opposition to the Hand amendment was subdued. Walter Muelder, a professor of Christian ethics at Boston University School of Theology, asked that the statement on compassion and justice be allowed to stand alone and "not to make...final issues or judgments on any one aspect of [homosexuality] which would prejudge all future thinking and reflection in our church on our Social Principles." The church, he said, "as a whole has not yet matured its thought on this very complex question." The addition was approved by a General Conference eager to take a sterner view of homosexuality than the study committee that brought the report.[60] So the declaration that the practice of homosexuality is "incompatible with Christian teaching" entered United Methodist history in 1972.[61]

The debate on homosexuality seemed to be over when the section on human sexuality was approved, but then a delegate from the Philippines rose to amend the section on marriage. His amendment met with the favor of the body. It read: "We do not recommend marriage between two persons of the same sex." The statement is inserted with no other reference to homosexuality in a paragraph that spoke of the "sanctity of the marriage covenant."[62] It was only later that delegates and others noted that the provision did not *prohibit* same-gender marriages. Hostile attitudes solidified, led by *Good News* (see below). In a seven-page editorial published in the summer 1973 issue, editor Charles Keysor warned "Bible-believing" Methodists that "homosexuals, by their noisy and crude pressure tactics, are [invading] the church." Applauding the defrocking of Leggett in 1971 and forced retirement of Boston preacher William Alberts for conducting a gay marriage in Boston in 1973, Keysor urged readers to take "stronger disciplinary measures" more quickly to prevent the moral degeneration of American society. The editorial was reprinted and widely circulated by the Good News headquarters for six cents a copy or three cents for 250 or more to one address.[63]

In early 1972, the UMC college-student magazine *Motive* devoted successive issues in their entirety to gay and lesbian rights, each headed by forthright lead editorials (Sources 1972a). The advocacy prompted denominational officials to pull the plug on what had been perhaps Methodism's most creative publishing effort. Youth leaders, however, did not abandon the cause, recalling Methodism's championing of child labor reform, antislavery, and women's rights. In December 1973, the denomination's thirty-two-member national Council on Youth Ministries (UMCYM) got in hot water by announcing its intention to petition the 1976 General Conference to affirm that homosexuality "not be a bar to the ordained ministry" and that "homosexuality in itself not be in any way synonymous with immorality." The council adopted a policy not to discriminate in regard to sexual orientation when hiring UMCYM staff, urged other church agencies to follow suit, and publicly stated its intention to invite representatives of a newly formed gay caucus to the council's August meeting to help plan General Conference legislation.[64] The UMCYM coordinating committee voted in February 1974 to allocate four hundred dollars to the National Task Force on Gay People in the Church, an agency recognized by the governing board of the National Council of Churches.[65] A second grant to the task force came later that spring when the Office of Urban Ministries of the National Division of the Board of Global Ministries contributed five hundred dollars.[66]

In August 1974, the UMCYM confirmed its intention with respect to legislation for the 1976 General Conference,[67] a commitment reinforced by invited presentations and counsel from members of an unofficial "gay caucus"; from an openly gay UMC layman; from a professed lesbian who had been expelled from Brigham Young University, disfellowshiped by the Mormon Church, disowned by her family, and discharged dishonorably from military service; and from the Reverend William R. Johnson, San Francisco, one of the first openly gay men ordained in the Christian ministry by a mainline denomination, the United Church of Christ, then a staff member of the Methodist-birthed Council on Religion and the Homosexual.

The December 1974 council called for a churchwide study of human sexuality.[68] On January 1, 1975, welcoming further dialogue and debate in a spirit of "mutual respect," it requested the General Council on Ministries (GCOM) to "immediately face 'head on' the seriousness of dealing with human sexuality concepts and issues within the life of the church and society." Its resolution, adopted unanimously by the thirty present (two-thirds of them youth), called on GCOM to seek General Conference mandate to engage "all United Methodist persons, groups, boards and agencies" in a quadrennial human sexuality study "in the finest Wesleyan manner of education," drawing on Scripture, tradition, experience, and reason.[69] Under fire from across the church, the August council abandoned its legislative campaign but reaffirmed the call for a churchwide study. In a seven-hundred-word position paper on human sexuality the council said negative references to homosexuality then in the Social Principles should be removed to facilitate and provide "an objective atmosphere" for the churchwide study. The UMCYM reaffirmed its determination not to discriminate in its staff hiring policies against persons on the basis of sexual orientation and its insistence that "a particular sexual orientation not be included in criteria for ordination to the ministry of the church." The UMCYM also stated its intention as a council and as individual members to become better informed on matters of human sexuality, mentioning a seminar on the subject held at the present meeting as a starting point.[70]

More sympathetic clergy and laity in San Francisco, Kansas City, and Dallas began organizing to educate the denomination about lesbians and gay men in the church and to lobby for full inclusion. In July 1975 pastor William Krick (Chicago), seminarian Keith Spare (Kansas City), and lay members Richard Cash (Evanston), Peggy Harmon (Dallas), Ernest Reaugh (Rochester, New York), and Steven Webster (Madison, Wisconsin) joined Leggett and others at Wheadon UMC in Evanston to organize a United Methodist Gay Caucus. Renamed Gay United Methodists the next year, the caucus by 1977 took the name Affirmation after its primary goal.[71] The caucus made plans to be present and active at the 1976 General Conference.

Spokesperson Keith Spare, of Kansas East Conference, the first openly gay man to address a General Conference, affirmed:

> We come before this body breaking a history of silence and invisibility which has surrounded this issue. This silence has been a perpetuation of untold suffering not only of our gay brothers and sisters and their families, but the entire Christian community. As we move toward a new horizon of what we hope to be a grace-filled dialogue we cannot ignore the inevitability of residual fears and misunderstandings.[72]

Instead, delegates voted to retain the 1972 incompatibilist stance and banned church funding of pro-gay groups or programs favoring acceptance of homosexuality. The funding ban led in 1978 to the dismissal of two openly gay students by Garrett-Evangelical Theological Seminary, the school fearing the students' presence would threaten its receipts from the denomination's Ministerial Education Fund. A year later Saint Paul School of Theology placed five students on probation for distributing a pamphlet potentially read as the school's endorsement of homosexuality.[73] In 1979, a staff member of the Women's Division of the General Board of Global Ministries, Joan Clark, "came out" as a lesbian and was fired.[74]

In other contexts, the church behaved more sympathetically. In 1977, New York City pastor Paul Abels acknowledged his homosexuality and having conducted holy unions for lesbian and gay couples in his Greenwich Village church, affirmations broadcast in the Sunday *New York Times*.[75] The New York Conference, nevertheless, declared him "appointable," and Bishop W. Ralph Ward reappointed Abels to Washington Square UMC. The following November, Affirmation leaders invited some one hundred persons, gay and straight, to meet in that church for an "Education Conference on Homosexuality and The United Methodist Church." Speakers applauded diversity as one of the strengths of The United Methodist Church and declared that the church knew no outcasts. Encouraged by the prospect of tolerance, gay and lesbian Methodists envisioned full inclusion in the church, ordination, and official ceremonies to bless same-sex couples living in committed, monogamous relationships. Pastor Julian Rush (Denver) joined Leggett, Huskey, and Abels in publicly "coming out." A council of regional representatives began to meet twice yearly to map strategy, launched a newsletter to link widely scattered members and friends, encouraged regional chapters, and hired two staff persons, Peggy Harmon and Michael Collins, to become Affirmation's roving ambassadors and organizers. In the following years Affirmation itself became more inclusive, adding lesbian, bisexual, and transgendered concerns to the group's mission statement.

To assist United Methodists in dealing with the confusion, fear, and anger on homosexuality, the Board of Church and Society devoted its March 1980 *Engage/Social Action* to a forum on the subject of homosexuality. The articles, by pastors and laity, graduate students, and university and seminary professors, tilted heavily toward "reexamining and questioning" traditional condemnation of homosexual practices.[76] The forum offered a petition for the upcoming 1980 General Conference to replace the "incompatibility" statement with the following:

> While over the centuries Christian tradition and teaching have condemned homosexual practice, today some biblical scholars, theologians, and ethicists are critically reexamining and questioning this teaching. In faithfulness to Jesus Christ we are seeking the truth as we take seriously both the witness of our heritage and of the Spirit who is leading us.[77]

Readers looking for dogmatic claims about a "traditional Judeo-Christian viewpoint" found an extended, but less than favorable, review of Charles Keysor's *What You Should Know about Homosexuality*.[78] Throughout its chapters, Keysor's book held firmly to "the main fountainhead of belief that homosexuality constitutes a perversion of the divinely appointed relationship between the two sexes." In short, practicing homosexuals are sinners who need to repent and be saved. (Keysor's resolve on biblical orthodoxy led him soon thereafter to resign his post as *Good News* editor and to transfer his ordination in June 1982 to the Evangelical Covenant Church of America.)[79]

Contentiousness marked the 1980 General Conference. Bishop W. McFerrin Stowe denounced homosexuality in the opening Episcopal Address, and Hazel Decker's portion of the Laity Address condemned it under cover of phrases such as "family will prevail." Both statements elicited considerable applause from the assembly. Every effort was made to suppress dissent. Nevertheless, Bishop Melvin Wheatley, the only bishop to openly dissent to the anti-gay section of the Episcopal Address, caused a stir when he publicly stated that he did not consider homosexuality a sin. The father of a gay son, he had been a strong supporter of Affirmation. Days later a motion from the floor to ban the ordination and appointment of self-avowed, practicing homosexuals was narrowly defeated. On the conference's last day, delegates approved a churchwide study of human sexuality to be carried out during the coming four years.[80] Good News incompatibilist David Seamands asked for the Judicial Council to rule on whether such a study, with its inevitable consideration of homosexuality, would be out of order because the church had already defined its position on homosexuality.[81] The council declared in October 1980 that it lacked jurisdiction to rule on the matter.[82] So the study on human sexuality went forward and was published in 1983.[83]

The early 1980s witnessed several test cases on the ordination and appointment of gay pastors. In 1982, when Bishop Wheatley refused to remove Julian Rush, an "out" gay pastor from a Denver Church,[84] and proceeded to ordain a self-avowed lesbian, Joanne Carlson Brown, three churches in faraway Georgia filed charges that Wheatley's statements, appointments, and ordination had undermined "the authority of holy Scripture." The committee that investigated the charges found no "reasonable grounds" for accusing the bishop, and the charges were dropped.[85] A year later a 3,500-member church in Colorado Springs publicly censured Wheatley, their bishop, for his active support of homosexual persons as ministers, and ten other congregations in Colorado withheld funds to their annual conferences to show their disapproval.[86] In the meantime the Judicial Council ruled in October 1982 that nothing in UMC law prohibited the ordination of homosexual persons and that the final decision on ministerial candidates rested with the conferences.[87]

To make its own case to a church with a divided mind and to anticipate action at the 1984 General Conference, Affirmation created in September 1983 an antidote to homophobia. Terming it the Reconciling Congregation Program, Affirmation announced its purposes as threefold:

> 1) to identify local churches where we are welcome to participate in the full life of the congregation; 2) to provide a vehicle for ongoing education and ministries involving lesbians and gay men at the local level; and 3) to empower local churches to advocate lesbian and gay concerns in their communities and to work as a network for such advocacy on the national level.[88]

The first Reconciling Congregation was Washington Square UMC in New York with a rich tradition of hospitality to gay men and lesbians, led by the Reverend Paul Abels. Other pioneer Reconciling Congregations included Wesley UMC in Fresno, California, and Saint Paul UMC in Denver, Colorado. Two volunteer coordinators, Mark Bowman and Beth Richardson, gave exceptional leadership in the movement's founding years and helped establish a permanent office in Chicago.

Asian Americans and the Quest for Place

In March 1971 in Santa Monica, California, 170 concerned leaders of Asian American churches from various conferences met, with aid from the annual conferences, the National Division of the Board of Missions, and the Commission on Religion and Race. Virtually a plenary of Asian United Methodism, the convocation included thirty youth, eleven district superintendents, the Western Jurisdiction bishops, and pastors and laypersons from practically all of the then existing thirty-eight churches in the Western Jurisdiction. This first large-scale Asian American event—representing churches from Chinese, Korean, Filipino, and Japanese American congregations and extending over five conferences and the entire Western Jurisdiction—organized the Asian American Caucus of the Western Jurisdiction. The Reverend Peter Chen, chairman of the Advisory Committee on Asian American Ministries of BOM, reported that "the most significant result was the uplifting of morale."[89]

The organization of this caucus represented yet another indication that the integrative ideal with which United Methodism had come into being—the ideal expressed ethically in the commitment to end racism and the racist-inspired Central Jurisdiction, expressed structurally in ongoing board and agency consolidation, and expressed programmatically in the denomination's serial for families, *Together*—made insufficient allowance for the church's diversity and for the needs of particularity. Here, too, the tension would only increase. The Immigration Act of 1965 had opened America's western door and would over the next decades bring new diversity from Asia. Indians and Koreans, the fastest growing subgroups, came first; Cambodians, Formosans, Hmong, Laotians, and Vietnamese followed in the 1980s and 1990s. The 1960 census counted 1 million Asians; the 2000 census counted 10.8 million, 43 percent growth over the 1990 census, whereas the nation's white population grew only 7 percent. Methodism, however, had for half a century been moving away from structuring itself for language and culture-specific indigenized ministries and, after several years of discussion and spirited debate, had moved to dissolve the Asian conferences and integrate their churches into the various white annual conferences. The Oriental Provisional Conference, which administered Chinese, Korean, and Filipino churches, dissolved in 1952, and the Pacific Japanese Provisional Conference reluctantly followed suit in 1964.

The integration of Asian conferences in 1952 and 1964 into their Anglo counterparts proved to be a disappointing experience. The special concerns and needs of the local indigenous church were soon lost amid the agenda of the wider demands of the general church. The results were the loss of self-determination and the general demoralization of its leadership and membership. One Nisei layman wrote of the situation: "Unfortunately, what started out as a great step forward in 1964, by 1966–67 was mired in disillusionment by the insensitivity of the majority of the peculiar needs of our people."[90] Integration also weakened the church's commitment to new church development and recruitment, training, and deployment of ministers among Asian Americans.

Soon after merger, the widely scattered Asian American churches felt isolated and disconnected. Insensitivity of the white majority in the 1950s and 1960s led to despair among Asian church leaders, leaving Methodists unprepared for this second wave of immigration from Asia, which began in the late 1960s. Japanese American UMs took the first step in November 1967 when their leaders gathered in Denver, Colorado, to search for a means of strengthening their widely scattered local churches. From the meeting emerged a feeling of powerlessness and a desire to unite with the other Asian churches, concerns then conveyed to the Council of Bishops and the Board of Missions. In response the Board of Missions of the newly united church held consultations in three West Coast cities in October 1968.

By the end of the hearings, several needs became apparent: (1) the need to underline Asian American ministries with a theological base, (2) the need for freedom to make interconference clergy appointments, and (3) the need for a closer relationship with indigenous churches in Asia. An Advisory Committee on Asian American Ministries in BOM was set up the following year. Paul Hagiya, Japanese American pastor of Simpson UMC in Arvada, Colorado, expressed concern to the 1970 General Conference, telling delegates that the integration of 1964 had been "a swallowing up process" that resulted in a "loss of zeal and strength and passion to win the Asian-American communities to Christ."[91] Representatives of the Asian American churches participated in an ethnic consultation arranged by the new Commission on Religion and Race in Chicago in October 1970. The commission also funded an office of Research and Development for Asian American ministries with the Reverend George Nishikawa, a Japanese American, as director. Asian American statistics, the church discovered, represented little change from the late 1940s when the California Oriental Mission Conference numbered 1,200 members in eight Chinese churches, six Filipino churches, and four Korean churches, and the Pacific Japanese Provisional Conference, which had survived the terrible years of "relocation" during World War II, numbered 3,500 members in thirty-four churches.[92] The early 1970s numbers showed ethnic persistence but little growth:

Community	Congregations	Members[93]
Japanese	20	5,139
Chinese	6	925
Korean	6	786
Filipino	5	548
Totals	37	7,398

To address its several concerns, the 1971 Western Jurisdiction consultation constituted itself a caucus and drafted a manifesto that was presented to delegates the following year at General Conference:

We, the Asian-American caucus of The United Methodist Church, which includes at the present time Chinese, Japanese, Filipino, and many other groups who have similar ethnic roots, acknowledge the heritage that is peculiarly ours as Asians who have been a part of The United Methodist Church. While acknowledging the values of this heritage, we recognize that our participation within The United Methodist Church has been only partial and limited, and that our identity as Asians has been in terms of Euro-American values and culture.

We affirm that the Asian-American Caucus is at present the most viable means to achieve:

1. Self-determination to develop relevant Christian mission strategies on the local, annual conference, and national levels.

2. Openness to explore and to appreciate the values of our ethnic cultural and religious heritages that make the Gospel relevant and meaningful to Asian-Americans.

3. Liberation from the elements of racism with The United Methodist Church and society.

We recognize the need to understand and to cooperate with other ethnic caucus groups within The United Methodist Church.[94]

One of the first follow-up actions was negotiating with the Kyodan, the United Church of Christ in Japan, to provide two ministers to supply unfilled Japanese-language pulpits. With travel funds provided by the World Division of the Board of Missions, two families were brought to the U.S. The Reverend Akio Tsukamoto and his family went to Simpson UMC in Arvada, Colorado, and the Reverend Jun Ehara and his family to West Los Angeles UMC.[95]

In 1972 Asian American UMC leaders, including Roy Sano, Kathleen Thomas-Sano, and Lloyd Wake, founded and assumed leadership in the Pacific Asian American Center for Theology and Strategies (PACTS), one of the earliest Pan-Asian organizations to pursue the development of Asian American theology and build support for church involvement in civil and human rights struggles. Affiliated with the Graduate Theological Union in Berkeley, California, PACTS took the form of a community-based nonprofit organization that relied on individual and organizational support for its mission and ministry.[96]

The new caucus achieved early success when the first Asian bishop, Wilbur Choy, a Chinese American, was elected and consecrated in 1972. When Dr. Choy's candidacy and voting for him seemed to lag, Asian American delegates presented their cause to the Western Jurisdictional Conference, garnered help from other caucuses, marched down the center aisle in a demonstration, and prompted the withdrawal of the other two candidates. The caucus's struggles succeeded. Dr. Choy was elected and assigned to the Seattle Episcopal Area. Son of immigrant parents, while at college (College of the Pacific) and at seminary (Pacific School of Religion), Choy served as assistant pastor of the Chinese Methodist church in Stockton, California. Ordained in 1949, Choy joined the California-Oriental Provisional Conference, serving pastorates in Woodland and Sacramento. In 1969 he became one of the first Asian district superintendents in the denomination. Choy served the Seattle Episcopal Area for eight years and another four in the San Francisco Episcopal Area before retirement in 1984. Two additional Asian bishops followed: Roy Sano (the first Japanese American) in 1984 and Hae Jong Kim (the first Korean American) in 1992.

The Western Jurisdictional movement gave impetus three years later to the formation of regional caucuses and a national caucus to address their distinct needs for self-empowerment across the church. To aid in that endeavor, the caucus had already begun publication of a newsletter, *Asian American News*, in 1973. In 1974 the third regional convocation convened in Oakland, California, welcomed Asian American leaders from outside the Western Jurisdiction, and took the name National Federation of Asian American United Methodists (NFAAUM). The same year Asian American United Methodist Women gathered for the first of several consultations in Honolulu, Hawaii.

The first meeting of the board of directors of the now national NFAAUM was held in April 1975 in Chicago. Lloyd Wake, a Japanese American pastor from San Francisco and president of the Glide Foundation, was elected chairperson. The Reverend Jonah Chang, a native of Taiwan and head of the office of Asian-American Ministries in Oakland, California, was elected executive director, a position he held for ten years. A Center for Asian-American Ministry opened at Claremont School of Theology in 1977.[97] These initiatives soon had effects, and a resurgence of church growth ensued. One marked sign was the upsurge in clergy and lay leadership after a dearth of nearly a decade in new clergy candidates.[98] The denomination had an estimated 13,500 Asian American members in a national constituency of 10 million.[99]

A 1975 convocation of NFAAUM stated the following goals:

> To articulate the concerns, interests and needs of Asian American constituencies in all jurisdictions of the church, to advocate the causes of Asian-Americans before boards and agencies of the church, to coordinate the activities of the jurisdictional Asian-American caucuses in relationship with boards and agencies, to promote relevant and meaningful Asian-American ministries at all levels of the church, to encourage the full participation of Asian-American United Methodists in all aspects of the life of the church.[100]

In December 1978 the first national convocation of the caucus held in San Francisco at Glide Memorial Church drew five hundred Asian Americans from across the nation. NFAAUM reorganized itself into seven subgroups. Workshops trained leaders to communicate better in their communities.[101] A comprehensive Asian "Vision" statement, *Ripe for Harvest,* was issued in 1980, supplementing the denomination's 1981–84 missional priority "Developing and Strengthening the Ethnic Minority Local Churches." Asian American church leaders identified top priorities as enlistment, training, and deployment of clergy, along with the need for new strategies for leadership deployment, resources to build new facilities, and the publication of Asian-specific resources that would promote their mission and ministry.[102]

Almost simultaneously with the formation of the NFAAUM, Koreans—the fastest-growing Asian subgroup—began their own effort at caucus formation. (The 1980 census reported that the Korean population in the U.S. had increased 412 percent over the previous decade and had come to number more than a half million.) Korean American Methodists formed a caucus of their own in 1973—the National Association of Korean American United Methodist Churches (NAKAUMC). At that point the Korean

American congregations in the UMC numbered only twenty. By the mid-1970s, Korean Americans had established thirty congregations, and by 1977, with the blessing of the Asian American Caucus, they had persuaded United Methodist Communications to issue Korean-language editions of selected promotional resources, beginning with World Service leaflets. The same year, the Korean caucus took what seemed to be the next obvious step and asked the Council of Bishops to consider the formation of a Korean American language "missionary/provisional" conference. NFAAUM backed the recommendation at its spring meeting just before General Conference 1984, although the conference deferred.[103]

The melting pot of United Methodism was not boiling away language, identity, particularity, and culture. Indeed, some new commitments both put a premium on diversity and recognized how far the church had yet to go—among them, affirmative action appointments, hires, and elections; monitoring of such progress by GCORR and GCOSROW; indeed, the necessity for such commissions; and programmatic emphases (Ethnic Minority Local Church). One year before retirement, the denomination's first Asian American bishop, Wilbur Choy, preached the opening worship service of the 1983 national convocation of the Asian American Caucus he helped found. "It is an occasion to shout as we have shouted," the bishop preached, "for we are not really like the stereotype of the quiet Oriental. We have to shout to be heard. We have to shout to let others know how glad we are to be here."[104] It was also an occasion to rejoice and to sing from the new Asian American hymnal for which the caucus had longed from its beginning. Sponsored by the Section on Worship of the Board of Discipleship, the collection of Asian American hymns titled *Hymns from the Four Winds*, published a few months earlier, supplemented the twenty-year-old *Methodist Hymnal*, which contained only four Asian hymns.[105] The new hymnal was the first attempt of any major denomination to bring together the hymn repertory that had developed mostly outside the U.S. among mostly Chinese and Japanese, but few Korean, Christians over the previous three decades and to make it available to serve the emerging needs of Asian American Christian communities. Several hymns from the collection would find their way into the new *United Methodist Hymnal*, which was published at the end of the decade, including "God Created Heaven and Earth" and "Here, O Lord, Your Servants Gather."[106]

Asian Americans had found their voice, and the publishing enterprises knew how to deal with languages. Whether the rest of the denomination could hear Choy's shouts or Asian singing was quite another matter. At best the church's hearing was selective. Bishops appointed Koreans and other Asians to new or existing ethnic churches. But boards of ministry showed very little give, expecting Koreans and others to function in English as though the church were fully committed to open itinerary and crossracial appointments. Meanwhile Asian particularity blossomed, eventuating in a plethora of caucuses: National Chinese Caucus of the UMC, National Association of Filipino-American

United Methodists, Formosan Caucus of the UMC, Indochinese Caucus of the UMC, The Cambodian National Caucus of the UMC, Association of Hmong UM Churches, Laos National Caucus of the UMC, Vietnamese National Caucus of the UMC, National Japanese-American UM Caucus, National Association of Korean-American UM Churches, Southern Asian National Caucus of the UMC. The flowering of caucuses signaled that United Methodism would unite itself and divide itself by its several languages, cultures, and identities. Others joined Asian Americans in the flourishing of ethnicity.

Latino Self-Determination: Familia and Fiesta

As United Methodism formed, various Latino and Hispanic conferences clarified their ecclesial political status. In 1967 the Board of Missions gave the Rio Grande Conference the option of merging with Anglo conferences or continuing as a separate conference. On this occasion, as on a previous overture in 1955, the conference overwhelmingly opted for its own integrity. Latino American Methodism in the Southwest as well as in large cities of both coasts would continue to run counter to the tendency of other European ethnic ministries to merge with predominantly English-speaking conferences. Treated for decades as a stepchild of home missions activity, the Latino churches in Texas had achieved status as a separate Rio Grande Annual Conference with the formation of The Methodist Church in 1939. Spread over the lower Rio Grande Valley with headquarters in the heavily Spanish-flavored city of San Antonio, the conference was not granted full autonomy by the Board of Missions until 1967. For the first time in their history Mexican American Methodists had significant decision-making authority, a degree of self-determination, and the attendant opportunity for self-respect within a structure they had chosen.[107]

Elsewhere full independence seemed to be the route to self-determination. Nineteen sixty-seven also saw the establishment of the Puerto Rico Conference and the formation of the Methodist Church of the Caribbean and the Americas. The latter brought together the Methodist churches of Antigua, Costa Rica, Guyana, Haiti, Honduras, Jamaica, the Leeward Islands, and the South Caribbean (and soon thereafter the Bahamas). In 1968 the Methodist Church of Cuba opted for autonomy, as did the United Evangelical Church of Ecuador and the Methodist churches of Chile and Argentina. Cuban Methodist autonomy reflected the hostile political situation it faced under the revolutionary Communist government of Fidel Castro and the necessity of putting distance from the U.S. missionary heritage and ending episcopal supervision from the Florida Episcopal Area. Lost as well during the Cuban revolution were the Methodist missionaries who returned to the U.S., as did many Cuban pastors. Only when Cuba relaxed its antireligious policies in the 1990s would the number of churches and pastors begin to grow and then genuinely to prosper under indigenous and locally trained leadership. In

1969 the Methodist Churches of Latin America formed a regional council, the Council of Evangelical Methodist Churches in Latin America (CIEMAL), to provide for unity under their own auspices and to labor for common ends. Through CIEMAL and a Latin American Council of Churches (organized in 1982) and to some extent in relation to GBGM and through the World Methodist Council, Latin American Methodism voiced its own concerns, often in a progressive spirit, sometimes prophetically critical of U.S. policies in the region (notably in Nicaragua during its Sandinista phase).[108]

In the U.S. the Hispanic population tripled during the decade of the 1960s, pulled by economic opportunity and driven by repression and conflict, and began its own advocacy for civil rights. In 1965 Congress closed the last open immigration frontier, imposing qualitative and quantitative restrictions on immigrants from Mexico and Central and South America. The same year César Chavez organized the Mexican American farm workers into a union (United Farm Workers [UFW]), and the UFW struck California grape producers. Frustrated with the futility of picketing miles of fields and facing the local power of corporate agriculture, the UFW resorted to civil rights–era tactics to draw national attention to its plight. The protest marches, civil disobedience, consumer boycotts, and hunger strikes combined civil rights activism with appeals to unity based on Mexican Catholicism, liberation theology, and a sense of cultural pride. By 1970, the charismatic Chavez won contracts with grape growers. That year José Gutierrez established the first national Hispanic political caucus: La Raza Unida. Also LULAC (League of United Latin American Citizens), a forty-year-old Latino political action group, filed *Cisneros v. Corpus Christi Independent School District*, a lawsuit that defined Hispanic Americans as a minority for the first time. With the onset of a recession and the Nixon administration's 1971 bill imposing a penalty on employers hiring persons not authorized to work, an intensive anti-alien drive developed in which Latin Americans became the main targets.

United Methodism lacked structure and strategy for dealing with the explosive growth of Latino communities,[109] now coming from economically and politically troubled parts of Central America as well as Mexico and Puerto Rico and spreading across American society. Its Spanish-language ministries were now geographically rather than connectionally defined (along the Rio Grande, in Puerto Rico, and in Florida). Missionary or central conferences within the U.S.—the nineteenth-century scheme for attending to linguistic or cultural particularity—seemed unthinkable when the church was under self-imposed mandate to close just such down (the Central Jurisdiction). Scattered Anglo UMC congregations mounted Spanish ministries or opened their doors to a Latino congregation just organizing. But how could United Methodism supply trained Spanish-speaking pastors? And appoint one with a Guatemalan background to a largely Guatemalan ministry? And address needs in the urban areas of the North without bleeding the small cadre of trained leaders in the Rio Grande?[110]

In this context of missional opportunity and of self-consciousness, growth, and advocacy, Latino leaders within the UMC began to organize transregionally. In so doing they openly rejected the marginalization of segregated congregations, missions, and conferences; of unequal compensation; of minimal participation in policy decisions affecting their institutions; and of exclusion from leadership positions and leadership development (seminary education). While abhorring patterns of dependency and subordination of Latino Americans to Anglo American church leaders and mission structures, they covenanted to work within the church to move from dependence toward equality and mutuality with Anglo American and Euro American Methodists. Spokespersons made appeals for recognition and resources to boards and agencies of the church and within the Spanish-speaking community through a program journal, *El Interpreté* (launched in 1958 as *Acción Metodista*, retitled in 1968). Latino Methodists in California formed LAMAG, Latin American Action Group, led by future bishop Elias Galvan, to lobby for their interests in the West Coast area. In a report to the 1968 session of the Southern California-Arizona Conference (June 1968), LAMAG presented a position paper rejecting integration: "Integration seen as Angloization is an outmoded concept among Mexican Americans and can no longer be tolerated by our Latin churches." Instead LAMAG proposed that the church do the following:

1. Discard the concept of integration as Angloization and develop a partnership model.
2. Consult with Hispanic constituency in all decisions which affect Hispanic ministries.
3. Ensure Hispanic representation at all conference levels.
4. Raise minimum salaries of Hispanic pastors.
5. Make open accounting for all monies acquired through sale or acquisition of Hispanic property.
6. Create a well-defined educational program for clergy and ministerial candidates.
7. Use different criteria other than Anglo for measuring the success/failure of Hispanic churches.
8. Improve Hispanic church facilities as a means for a more effective ministry.
9. Enact and abide by an open pulpit policy.
10. Train Anglo ministers for Hispanic work.[111]

The 1970s continued the pattern of expanding horizons for and widening contacts across the larger Latino church community. Lamenting the tardy transition from Anglo to Hispanic leadership in the UMC, Latino UMC leaders organized into a national caucus in 1970, Metodistas Associados Representando la Causa de Hispano-Americanos (MARCHA; in English: Methodists Associated Representing the Cause of Hispanic Americans). At the 1970 special session General Conference, Dr. Elias Galvan, clergy visitor from Southern California Conference and pastor of Los Angeles's UM Church

of All Nations, was given an opportunity to present a brief statement on behalf of MAR-
CHA (Sources 1970).[112] Dr. Galvan told the delegates that the UMC was neglecting
growing Latino populations, locking them into patterns of discrimination based on language and culture. Successes in community organizing were presenting new opportunities for Latinos in the areas of education, housing, job training, and economic
development. Rejecting tokenism, Dr. Galvan called the new denomination "to accept
the ministry to Spanish-Americans as a top priority" and to instruct the boards and
agencies to appropriate funds, provide Spanish-language resources, and increase Latino
representation on the denomination's national staff. As Dr. Galvan left the podium,
many of the dreams and frustrations of Latino UMs were expressed in the cry "Viva
MARCHA!" Since that time MARCHA has played an important role in the struggle
of Latino UMs to find the necessary support and room for their mission, to empower
Latino leadership (high on MARCHA's agenda initially was the election of a Latino
bishop), to gain representation on connectional levels and within the agencies (GBGM
especially), but to maintain visible distinction from the Anglo churches. Early engagement with the National Division of GBGM led the agency to recognize the necessity for
a Latino missional strategy and especially for staffing (then consisting of only one full-
time administrator for the Rio Grande Conference).[113]

Anticipating action from the 1972 General Conference, two MARCHA leaders
spoke publicly to the church. In a March 1972 article in the church's principal clergy
magazine, *Christian Advocate*, Roberto Escamilla, director of bilingual ministries, Board
of Evangelism, reported that the Latino American church could no longer afford to dis-
regard the call to become an ally in the struggle for social justice. The Hispanic American church needed to identify more completely with the "barrio" (Spanish ghetto) and
needed the backing and support of the denomination to expand ministries to the burgeoning Latino population. Specifically, he urged the UMC to recognize its responsibility
to minister to migrant workers in California, Texas, Michigan, and other parts of the
U.S., be aware of its mission among thousands of Puerto Ricans in the nation's metropolitan centers and Cuban exiles in Florida, identify with the people of Puerto Rico in
the midst of their struggle for progress and identity, make a "supreme effort" to have a
wider representation of Hispanic Americans in key positions in the boards and agencies
of the denomination as well as in the Council of Bishops, develop a program that is adequate to the needs of youth, recruit and train Latino pastors and lay leaders for their
role in these new ministries, produce printed resources "written within the context of
our culture," find ways to cooperate with other denominations and community groups
that are struggling for justice, and proclaim the gospel with power and truth. "There is
not another mission field so fertile and responsive to the gospel," he insisted, "as that
which is present among Hispanic Americans."[114] At General Conference 1972 the Reverend Josofat Curti, MARCHA chairman and pastor of Messiah UMC in Pueblo, Col-

orado, presented demands for Hispanic representation on the church's boards and agencies and Council of Bishops:

> There is not one Hispanic-American superintendent outside the Rio Grande and Puerto Rico conferences. There are thousands of United Methodist Hispanic-Americans in the continental United States and in Puerto Rico, and still there is not a Hispanic bishop. A good number of you have said to us privately that these requests are honest and right. But, brethren, the time of sympathy and promises is past. Do something about it.[115]

Among the church's responses was the 1973 publication of a Spanish hymnal, *Himnario Metodista*. Latinos had earlier expressed dissatisfaction when the 1964 Methodist General Conference had approved revision of the *Methodist Hymnal* without a single hymn in Spanish. Addressing the neglect, the Rio Grande Conference began work on publishing a new hymnal, building on its own of 1955. Although *Himnario Metodista* in the end was published by the denomination's publishing house, the conference bore project costs, including cost of copyrighted material. The new "Latino" hymnbook contained only a few Latino hymns and songs; it was still largely a translation of the denomination's English hymnal; British and Euro American hymns continued to predominate. At that juncture it appeared that the time had arrived for the production of a songbook or supplement to *Himnario Metodista* for Latino Methodists with a broad ecumenical and global content and appeal. The project was assigned to the Section on Worship of the General Board of Discipleship. Publication began in 1979: *Celebremos: Primera Parte, Colección de Coritos*, a collection of familiar choruses. *Celebremos: Segunda Parte, Colección de Himnos, Salmos Y Canticos* followed in 1983 with a more global and ecumenical content, with selections from the global Latino community (Latin America, Spain, Puerto Rico, and the United States), a harvest of Hispanic music and of more current musical theology. Eighteen hymns and songs from the later collection were included in the denomination's principal hymnbook of 1989. Its companion, a revised *UM Book of Worship* (1992), included a Mexican Christmas Eve service, *Las Posada*. The first truly Latino UM hymnal and worship book, *Mil Voces Para Celebrar*, under the editorship of Raquel Mora Martinez, was finally ready in 1996.[116]

The late 1960s and early 1970s tested the church's resolve on a local level as well. For instance, a mid-1960s fire gutted the First Spanish UMC in Harlem, New York City. Although much of its congregation had moved up the class ladder and out to the suburbs, the members commuted back to their old neighborhood for church services and gatherings. After rebuilding, the church was ravaged by the Young Lords, a militant Puerto Rican liberation group, who occupied the church, claimed the building for the community, and held out until evicted by the police and the courts. The commuter church learned a lesson. It responded to the needs of the Spanish Harlem neighborhood and established a day care center and other community services.[117] During the 1970s, Latinos formed additional Latino congregations in the New York metropolitan area, Long Island, Connecticut, and New Jersey. The New York Conference appointed its first coordinator of Latino ministry, Pedro Piron, in 1983.

In 1974, the Mexican American Ministry Training Program was established at Perkins School of Theology, Southern Methodist University. Headed in its early years by Dr. Roy Barton, the program nurtured generations of lay and clergy leaders. With The United Methodist Publishing House support, the training program launched a journal of theology from a Latino perspective, *Apuntes,* in 1981. For the first time in the history of the UMC, in 1976 a Latino was elected as an associate general secretary—Roberto Escamilla—to head the Board of Discipleship.[118]

In 1976, a Latino women's consultation with Latin American Methodist women was held in Cuernavaca, Mexico. A similar consultation occurred in Puerto Rico the following year (1977). Such events prompted Latino women to give their own signal to the church that the melting pot was a myth (Sources 1978). So insisted Celsa Garrastegui, a Puerto Rican, global concerns coordinator for the Miami, Florida, district of United Methodist Women and a member of the World Division of the Board of Global Ministries. The persistent struggles of African Americans, Latinos, Native Americans, and others demonstrate, she argued, that the concept is only a "myth in the imagination of the Anglo majority" who did not want to hear the claims of the nations' and church's ethnic people. She also exposed a fallacy of the recently launched ethnic-minority local church quadrennial priority—paternalism. While acknowledging the program as an important step toward reconciliation, she derided the way it sustained the paternalistic status of ethnic congregations as objects of mission rather than fully part of the national church: "We want the right to maintain our cultural heritage: language, customs, ways of doing things." We "must have materials in Spanish at all levels, not only translations but resources written by Hispanics out of the Hispanic experience."

Along with MARCHA, a series of national meetings fostered Latino unity. An early consultation meeting in Los Angeles in 1979 gave Latinos for the first time a sense of the power and enthusiasm of United Methodism's Latino constituency.[119] In 1980 with MARCHA support, the first Hispanic bishop, Elias Galvan, was elected. A second Latino bishop, Joel Martinez, was elected in 1992.

The Voices of Native Americans

Self-determination, always a concern for indigenous people, received new impetus in the sociopolitical ferment of the 1960s, from the civil rights movement and from revived cultural self-consciousness among Native Americans. The restiveness expressed itself in the American Indian Movement (AIM), organized in 1968; the 1970s celebrations of Earth Day; the 1972 Trail of Broken Treaties March on Washington, D.C.; and

Vine Deloria's *God Is Red* (1973), launching Native American liberation theology.[120]

Native American missions within Methodism historically focused on the reservation populations of the southwestern U.S. with few follow-up ministries for Native Americans who took up residence off their reservations. And though the church's mission with Native Americans included education and medical services, it had not typically extended to dealing with the more profound systemic and oppressive conditions that America's indigenous people faced, to enlisting Native American leaders beyond their own congregations to the church as a whole, to recognizing the inherent values in Indian life, culture, and religion, and to empowering ministries of evangelism and nurture that fit Indian needs as they themselves assessed these needs. Vine Deloria put the issue squarely in 1969: "The determination of white churches to keep Indian congregations in a mission status is their greatest sin."[121]

Complaints about this state of affairs and perceived neglect from the Board of Missions prompted the BOM to call a consultation just a few months before union (January 1968) to consider means of empowering the denomination's Native American ministries. The outcome of the consultation was the formation of an advisory committee that included for the first time Native people from the Oklahoma Indian Missionary Conference (OIMC) and local churches scattered throughout the country. However, only three of the dozen members were Native Americans.

Thomas Roughface, a Ponca Nation pastor, spoke for the OIMC at the October 1970 meeting of the BOM: "The call for self-determination is the call to be involved in the total ministry of the Church. We [Native Americans] can no longer sit in the balconies of the Church or appear as mere observers while decisions that ultimately affect us are being made by the Church and its boards and agencies."[122]

Robert Pinezaddleby of the OIMC and the Kiowa Nation spoke for the emerging caucus at the interim General Conference, 1970, applauding first steps taken by the denomination. Native Americans feel, he said, quoting Winston Churchill, "that they are in the end of the beginning" of a new era.[123] Explaining what ought to follow the "beginning" to his own conference and speaking as president of the OIMC cabinet in 1971, Pinezaddleby affirmed:

> What the Indian [Methodist] wants now is a demonstration of the principles that have been articulated by the church at large and the Indian leaders. They want no more rhetoric, they want no more promises, they want no more philosophizing...they want action...but more importantly, they want a demonstration of good faith that they are going to get to participate in the process of making decisions involving or affecting them, and to do this through Indian leadership and participation....I feel that we have a "Red Power" that must be channeled to "Right Power."...We can now make a great jump in the direction of revitalizing the church's relationship with the Indian.[124]

In 1970, the National American Indian Committee, by this time mostly a Native body, became the core leaders of what was about to become a caucus. From that point Native American United Methodists began a drive for self-determination. Early in 1972 the committee met in Cherokee, North Carolina, and reorganized itself into an all-Native body, the Native American International Caucus (NAIC) with thirteen Native voting members, two Native staff (nonvoting), and five jurisdictional consultants. The word *international* signaled solidarity of America's Native people with sovereignty for Indian nations, a galvanizing cause across the Native American peoples. That translated within United Methodism to what would be NAIC's continuing concerns: voting rights at jurisdictional conferences and General Conferences; qualified Native Americans on all boards, agencies, and commissions of the UMC; the support for and strengthening of Native American ministries and local churches; sensitivity across the UMC to the customs and religious expressions of Native Americans; denominational advocacy for sovereign rights of Native peoples of North, Central, and South America; concerted efforts to raise education standards and salaries of pastors; and better communication among the fifty widely scattered churches outside the Oklahoma area.[125] Financial support for the new caucus came from the newly formed General Commission on Religion and Race, which reported on the status and role of the church's Native American constituency to the 1972 General Conference. Two representatives of the OIMC, the largest concentration of Indian Methodists with about twelve thousand church members, were seated at the opening day of the conference but without vote. Of the sixty-one ministers, only one was then a seminary graduate. The Women's Division also lent its support, and in 1975 the Native American Women's Caucus was birthed at a Native American United Methodist Women Consultation in Kansas City, Missouri. The caucus raised visibility of Native American issues in general agencies and General Conferences in the years that followed.

The new caucuses urged the creation of a new department for Native American ministries within the Board of Missions. Although the department was never established, a new Native American staff portfolio was created, which Homer Noley, director of Native American ministries in the Nebraska Conference and a member of the Choctaw Nation, ably filled (1971–75).[126] Raymond Baines of the Tlingit Nation was also appointed as ombudsman for Native American ministries. Noley laid bare the church's persistent pattern of "racism and paternalism" and drew conclusions about directions that Native American ministries should take in a 1975 article in the denomination's popular program magazine.[127] In a mid-1970s paper Homer Noley and Raymond Baines wrote concerning the meaning of empowerment:

> It means developing Indian leaders who understand the powerful events and trends of our troubled times and are willing and courageous enough to deal with those issues rather than shrink from them. . . . Structurally, Indian empowerment [now in the UMC]

is almost completely at the discretion of non-Indians.... Whatever gain we make will be made by a combination of two factors.... First... our own deliberative efforts. Second... the discriminatory assistance of those who care about us as people and who care about the things which concern us.[128]

United Methodist concern for a witness among Native Americans was not limited to the structures and constituents of the denomination. When organizers of AIM protested the injustices at the Wounded Knee Reservation in South Dakota, Noley, then with the Board of Global Ministries, and John Adams, executive staff member of the General Board of Church and Society, served as go-betweens in the negotiations of the armed and impatient Native Americans and the federal officials. The UMC Women's Division was part of an ecumenical support network for the standoff. The division sent observers, medical personnel, equipment, food, and supplies. Had it not been for the direct involvement of UMC leaders, especially Noley and Adams, in negotiations to end the crisis, there may very well have been a repeat of the 1890 Wounded Knee massacre.[129] In 1975 the Indian Self-Determination and Education Assistance Act was signed into law. In 1978 the American Indian Religious Freedom Act and Indian Child Welfare Act were signed.

In 1972, the Oklahoma Indian Mission became a "missionary" conference, permitting it the enabling licensing and ordaining of its own ministers but not the full representational prerogatives of an annual conference. Moves toward self-determination in Native American ministries caused an ideological rift between national church agencies and Native American leaders in the field that is not yet totally healed. The national board staff and the white church interpreted the mission in terms of self-support. Mission interpreted this way is not a spiritual mandate but a temporary and practical act of institutional benevolence—a welfare program. A devastating aspect of the church's definition of mission is related directly to the issue of self-determination. In a 1975 letter Betty Henderson, assistant general secretary of the National Division, attempted to explain why the National Division was not supporting the Indian Missionary Conference in the right to vote in the General Conference: "The Missionary Conference [is] defined (and there was consensus among the three conferences on this point) as being 'unique,' having limited membership, ministry, financial strength and property. Therefore, a conference so defined is not capable of the responsibility inherent in voting."[130] Only in 1988, when General Conference also adopted the missional plan "The Sacred Circle of Life: A Native American Vision," did the missionary conference finally gain the right to vote at General Conference.

In 1976 NAIC asked General Conference, the first General Conference to take major notice of the plight of the denomination's Native American membership, to authorize the formation of a Native American Study Committee to do a comprehensive on-site study of Native American missions and make recommendations to the 1980 General

Conference. NAIC also sought the formation of a General Commission on Native American ministries. Making the case was Thomas Roughface of the Ponca Nation, a nonvoting clergy delegate from OIMC (Sources 1976). He said,

> Throughout our history we have been the most studied species. . . . Now we call on General Conference to give us the right to set up the machinery by which we will be able to effectively conduct our own study. We believe we have the structure and the dynamic leadership within the ranks of Native Americans to do just such a study, and deal with the real issues now confronting Native Americans.

After listening to Native American demands among other ethnic groups, the 1976 General Conference delegates approved the formation of a study committee and voted to establish an Ethnic Minority Local Church (EMLC, later renamed "Racial Ethnic" and abbreviated RELC) priority with considerable fanfare and funding. They did not support the recommended commission.

The new quadrennial missional priority, EMLC, spread program development, staffing, and funding sources into four general agencies and across the array of annual conferences. For Native Americans, as for the other ethnic populations, it created new conference, jurisdictional, and general employment opportunities. It sensitized the denomination to its diversity. How well EMLC achieved its stated aims of strengthening congregations, enlarging the church's mission among Native Americans, and increasing lay and clergy leadership is harder to measure. To some extent the new employment opportunities in the upper echelons drained leadership, especially clergy leadership, which otherwise would have been deployed on a congregational level. And the funding and program opportunities set up new tensions between and among general agencies, conferences (Oklahoma for Native Americans), and caucuses (NAIC, which embraced nonreservation as well as reservation peoples).[131]

Those tensions surfaced in the General Conference–authorized study committee and in reaction to its 1979 draft report. The study document outlined the history and needs of ministries to and with the denomination's Native American pastors and people and proposed the establishment of a General Commission on Native American Self-Development with national staff and a considerable budget. The proposal drew fire not only from Oklahoma, but also from other ethnic groups who saw the commission as a threat to cooperative efforts among the several ethnic groups. The proposal failed to gain the endorsement of the UMC's Commission on Religion and Race.

By the time the opposing camps arrived in Indianapolis for General Conference, a storm of major proportions was brewing. To add to the conflict, representatives of AIM—an organization not affiliated with the UMC—arrived to try to influence the conference to take up such causes as American Indian treaty rights. Setting up a "teepee church" on the lawn of the Indianapolis Convention Center, the AIM representatives soon made contact with NAIC and took up the cause of the proposed commission. The legislative committee affirmed sections of the original proposal, which referred to the needs among Native Americans, but not a new commission.

During the presentation, a debate emerged on the floor between the delegates from the OIMC—who opposed the proposal—and the Reverend Marvin Abrams, a Native American member of NAIC and the study committee and a conference delegate from the Pacific and Southwest Conference—who supported the plan. General Conference embraced the legislative committee's direction, did not create a new commission, but called for existing boards and agencies to address the needs through current structure with an executive staff member in each board to be assigned the task of "advocacy, development and implementation of Native American ministries."

Despite their internal disagreements, Native Americans voiced their unhappiness with the perceived restrictions of comity agreements that governed tribal affairs. They appealed to General Conference to renounce these agreements as a form of denominational and governmental collusion. The 1980 General Conference approved a resolution objecting to the comity agreements:

> That The United Methodist Church states, as a matter of policy, that it is not a party to any international agreement that limits the ability of any Annual Conference in any jurisdiction to develop and resource programs of ministry of any kind among Native Americans, including the organization of local churches where necessary.[132]

General Conference also repented for cultural and religious genocide and adopted a major resolution, "The United Methodist Church and America's Native People," calling church and nation to "become more sharply aware and keenly conscious of the destructive impact of the unjust and injurious policies of the United States government upon the lives and culture of U.S. American Indians, Alaskan, and Hawaiian natives" and calling its congregations to "support the needs and aspirations of America's native peoples as they struggle for their survival and the maintenance of the integrity of their culture in a world intent upon their assimilation, westernization, and absorption of their lands and the termination of their traditional ways of life."[133]

By the late 1970s NAIC leaders concluded that widely scattered members in 158 churches, many of them isolated, needed a newspaper to communicate with one another. Such a paper could also be a voice for Native American concerns in the denomination. A grant from United Methodist Communications paid for a pilot issue edited by Lee Lonetree Mrotek. *Echo of the Four Winds* began regular publication in 1981 as a bimonthly tabloid.[134] The paper met a need, though again not without a struggle for acceptance among all of the disparate groups. The OIMC contained half of all Native American United Methodists, and it had its own conference paper published by United Methodist Reporter Communications in Dallas. *Echo* was readily accepted by the dispersed congregations and gradually won acceptance in Oklahoma as well. The modest newsletter has been a factor, along with the work of the caucus, in building unity within the Native American UM community and voicing deeply felt concerns.

A National United Methodist Native American Center (NUMNAC) opened in Oklahoma City in 1983. It relocated in 1992 to Claremont School of Theology in California. This center, like those for the other racial-ethnic communities and like the Multi-Ethnic Center at Drew University, helped the church focus resources for ministerial formation. Implicitly its creation recognized the church's past inadequacy to meet this basic need. It also symbolized an ongoing, institutionalized commitment to pluralism.

Care and Liability in an Age of Medicare and Medicaid

Three years before formation of the UMC, the U.S. Congress passed the Medicare and Medicaid legislation, enacting policy and program toward which official Methodist and EUB policy had been trending. The 1960 Methodist General Conference had created a new Division of Temperance and General Welfare as part of its General Board of Christian Social Concerns and assigned the division a new task—to develop programs of research, study, and action in a number of new areas of concern, among them, the field of medical care. To prepare for an adequate understanding of the problems of medical care, the division instituted a research and idea exchange program in 1961. Under the direction of Dr. Haskell M. Miller, a special research seminar was held at Wesley Theological Seminary, Washington, D.C. Top representatives of government, business, industry, labor, the medical profession, and the church came together to advise members of the division and its staff. The question for discussion was, *What contribution should Methodism make in the field of medical care?* Participants agreed that adequate health care constituted a problem but disagreed sharply on the role of government in solving it. The division issued a comprehensive report of the seminar in *The Methodist Church and Problems of Medical Care* and devoted a special issue of the board's magazine, *Concern*, as well (in 1962).[135] A policy committee chaired by Dr. Lester L. Keyser, director of Health Services of Southern Methodist University, drafted a new policy statement for the denomination adopted by the 1964 General Conference and added to the church's Social Creed:

> We stand for the provision of adequate medical care for all people with special attention being given the aging, the young and minority and low income groups. We strongly favor the healing ministries of the Church and other private groups. We support our government, individuals, and foundations in required research in public health; and we support legislation to meet these needs.[136]

Opposition by the medical profession and private insurance interests had kept health insurance out of the Social Security Act of 1935 and its various amendments of the 1940s and 1950s, and Methodists divided on supporting or opposing such reforms, which the industry successfully construed as "socialized" medicine. Despite the adverse lobbying, public support for the concept grew during these years, leading to the Kerr-Mills Act of 1960, which provided federal support for state medical programs serving aged poor people. By 1965, there was a growing consensus that a broader program was needed, with a stronger federal role and wider eligibility.

Two pieces of federal legislation in 1965—Medicare and Medicaid—changed American health care. Most Methodists celebrated.[137] Medicare provided federal money for most health needs of people over sixty-five; Medicaid paid the bills of poor people. The new programs funded a wide range of social services—home care; transportation; help with errands, chores, and emergencies; a nutrition program like Meals on Wheels; and employment services for part-time work. These programs brought a revolution in the health-care industry. Bitterly opposed by conservatives as a form of socialized medicine, the single-payer scheme encouraged physicians and hospitals to become medical entrepreneurs. Many hospitals and nursing homes, even church-related ones, became for-profit business corporations. Managers of Wesley Woods reported to the North Georgia Conference in 1966 that the impact of Medicare on their institution would be substantial:

> It is likely to create a demand for Health Center beds after January 1, 1967 at which time the part of Medicare applicable to extended care facilities will begin.... Medicare will point up the shortage of quality nursing home care throughout Georgia, eventually Wesley Homes may be able to offer such care in several areas throughout Georgia.[138]

A Supplemental Security Income system (SSI), enacted in 1972, established a national system of means-tested assistance for older and disabled poor people.

The effects of the new programs were far reaching. Most important, millions of poor people gained access to regular health care, though the programs proved to be far more expensive than their framers anticipated. Among the factors involved were the expanded market for health services that Medicare created, the growing number of older people in the population, and the increasing use of expensive medical technology. The rising cost of all health care during the 1970s and 1980s, dramatically reflected in growing Medicare budgets, provoked widespread debate.

Besides providing older people with means of support and altering their economic circumstances, the expansion and extension of old-age assistance and insurance programs changed the roles and relative importance of institutions caring for older people. Social Security had already accelerated the decline of the old people's home and the rise of the personal care and nursing homes, a trend to which Medicare and Medicaid gave further impetus. The promise of good return on investments, rather than altruism, created a nursing home boom, even among church-related institutions. While most church-related and some for-profit institutions offered high-quality care, many simply warehoused older people and provided waiting rooms for death. Outcry against such exploitation increased through the 1970s. Most of United Methodism's retirement communities, however, concentrated on residential and personal care rather than nursing care, continuing the service ideals of the denomination's earlier old people's homes.

By the late 1970s and early 1980s, financial insolvency threatened thousands of older people in the church's growing network of retirement homes with loss of hospitality and prompted litigation that twice reached the U.S. Supreme Court. Operating from their founding on the basis of prepaid contracts, which promised residents lifetime care for an initial fee, many institutions found themselves unable to cover mounting costs. Prepaid charges had been set without allowing for the effects of spiraling health-care inflation or the longevity of residents. Ironically, the excellent care received by residents may have contributed to their outliving the projections of the mortality tables! The matter came to a public focus in 1977 when Pacific Homes, a network of fourteen retirement homes and convalescent hospitals in California, Arizona, and Hawaii related to UMC's Pacific and Southwest Conference, filed for bankruptcy. In the late 1960s and the 1970s Pacific Homes's board of directors had converted from the prepaid system to a monthly fee system and worked out a plan to renegotiate new contracts with the life-care residents that would reflect actual costs and for the conference to set up a fund to pay the extra costs for needy residents. Nevertheless, 109 residents went to court with a class-action suit (*Barr v. United Methodist Church*) seeking $250,000 in damages and fulfillment of the original life-care contracts and suing for monetary damages against a number of defendants, including the conference, two general agencies, and the denomination as a whole. Five related cases were subsequently filed by various parties.

Was the UMC or any other denomination suable as an "unincorporated association" because its thousands of units and millions of members have a common name and a common purpose? UMC officials argued that the denomination had no central headquarters, no mailing address, no CEO, and no central management. The Pacific and Southwest Conference contended that although it was related to Pacific Homes and although it responded positively to every request for help from the board of directors of the homes, it had no legal responsibility for the corporation. The General Board of Global Ministries agreed that its Health and Welfare Division provided advisory services for the homes, but these activities in no way conferred legal responsibility for the homes. At question was whether the denominational process of consulting and accrediting institutions in order to encourage higher standards of performance established legal responsibility. One court contended that the General Council on Finance and Administration (GCFA) and the denomination were "one and the same" and as such had to answer for any liability imposed on the denomination. GCFA denied this. Church leaders breathed a sigh of relief when on November 26, 1979, the U.S. Supreme Court declined to consider whether the UMC could be sued for alleged wrongdoing of one of its units, the Pacific Homes retirement network. Several other denominations and the National Council of Churches had filed amicus briefs with the Court.[139]

For the United Methodist agencies involved, the case was a costly and time-consuming headache, and for the denomination, an "image problem." News reports accented the plaintiffs' sensational charges of "fraud" perpetrated on unsuspecting older people, giving inadequate balance to the news of the defense. Most egregiously a 1978 CBS television *60 Minutes* report made the whole church appear heartless toward the plight of older people and a November 9, 1979, front-page *Wall Street Journal* piece declared "Predators Find Elderly Are Often Easy Prey for Array of Rip-Offs." Inflation and unanticipated longevity were the real culprits, countered the church.[140]

A churchwide outpouring of financial sharing by individuals, conferences, and general agencies enabled the beleaguered network of homes to reorganize on a fiscally sound and humane basis of operation. Throughout the prolonged litigation, the homes remained in operation, made physical improvements, and attracted a waiting list of applicants. In the end no one lost his or her home, and Pacific Homes continued to serve the housing needs of those "contract residents" and other residents who entered the home after reorganization. In 1981, through a reorganization settlement agreement, a $19.5 million loan was given to Pacific Homes. Funds were obtained from local churches in the former Pacific Southwest (later divided into California-Pacific and Desert Southwest Conferences) and other conferences along with the denomination's finance and mission boards. The settlement followed the merger of Pacific Homes, California Lutheran Homes, and FACT Retirement Services. The loan was again restructured in 1993 with a resulting $7.5 million payment to the two conferences. The funds were used to repay all other conferences that had provided funds to complete the bankruptcy reorganization as well as GCFA. A final payment of $16.4 million in March 1999 retired the full loan amount provided to Pacific Homes by the California-Pacific and Desert Southwest Conferences and GCFA, thus ending a twenty-year saga. In light of this litigation, many of the church's institutions restructured their finances and renegotiated their covenants with the church's conferences and agencies.[141]

Despite and through the adversity around nursing facilities, the UMC continued exploration of principle and policy for older Americans, its own members included. Viewing the aging process as part of God's plan of creation and of the good news of Christ's redemption giving hope and purpose to life, the UMC called members to help translate this message through words and deeds in church and in society. A 1976 resolution defined the "Rights of the Elderly" as adequate income, quality housing, comprehensive health insurance, long-term nursing care, and equal access to social, cultural, educational, recreational, and religious activities.[142] A resolution, "Aging in the United States," adopted in 1988 General Conference exhorted the UMC to be "an advocate for the elderly, for their sense of personal identity and dignity, for utilization of experience, wisdom, and skills, for health maintenance, adequate income, educational opportunities, and vocational and avocational experiences in cooperation with the public and private sectors of society."[143] Further statements followed: "Mission and Aging of Global Population" adopted in 1992,[144] and "Care of the Elderly" adopted in 1996. The latter committed the church to explore new approaches in health care that provide quality health care and fullness of life at affordable cost for older people, their families and friends, and society as a whole.[145]

Divorce and Abortion

United Methodism's social policies on divorce and abortion evolved as they came to terms with long-term societal developments on the former and more contemporaneous transformations on the latter. Post–World War II America witnessed a liberalization of divorce laws and an increasing acceptance of divorce. During the first half of the twentieth century, adultery had been the only acceptable ground, and ministers could remarry only the innocent party of a divorce. By 1940 the grounds for divorce were extended to include physical cruelty or peril. By 1960 the legalistic provisions had been removed, and the emphasis was placed on counseling, self-understanding, and Christian intention in marriage. A cult of expressive divorce, as mediated by therapists, self-help books, and other vehicles of popular culture, changed attitudes toward marriage, becoming a major factor behind the doubling of divorce rates between 1950 and the 1980s. The normative image of marriage shifted from that of an enduring covenant to that of a limited contract—and later, under no-fault divorce laws, to a contract that could be dissolved by either partner for any (or even no) reason whatever. Expressive divorce also recast divorce in a positive light as a growth experience for everyone involved.

Divorce

As divorce laws became more liberal, as divorce became more acceptable, and as marital expectations expanded to include happiness and compatibility, the number of divorces grew steadily, especially after the enactment of no-fault divorce laws in the 1960s. Methodists and EUBs brought their most recent statements of social engagement into their union in 1968—the "Methodist Social Creed" and the "Basic Beliefs Regarding Social Issues and Moral Standards" of the EUBC. The Social Creed recommended "improved divorce laws," but said nothing about grounds of divorce; the Moral Standards condoned divorce only "on the ground of adultery."[146]

By 1972 when the Social Principles were redrafted, state no-fault divorce laws were being enacted. "We assert the sanctity of the marriage covenant. Marriage between a man and a woman has long been blessed by God and recognized by society." A few sentences later, the paragraph qualifies that statement: "In marriages where the partners are . . . estranged beyond reconciliation, we recognize divorce and the right of divorced persons to remarry."[147] From an American society talking openly about the goings-on inside marriages, Methodists learned a new theological lesson: marriages may not be forever. The lesson was also self-taught. Divorces had been occurring in Methodist, Evangelical, and United Brethren families for many years. United Methodists concluded officially, then, that divorce might be the most loving way to deal with marriages filled with silent indifference, verbal and physical abuse, and spousal rape. No-fault divorce, they reasoned, was better than forcing people to coexist in a loveless marriage, even though the institution of marriage needed to be upheld as a personal and social good.

Marital breakdown had become a major phenomenon in modern society taking a toll on clergy as well as members. Earlier, congregations seldom accepted the leadership of a divorced pastor. Divorce usually led to lifting of ordination credentials, early retirement, or some other altered status that brought the ministry to an end. By the 1970s the health of the UMC appointive system was challenged by the growing number of divorces among pastors who endeavored to stay in the ministry. A superintendent from New England, soon to be bishop, C. Dale White asked, "We Protestants have held for a long time that divorce may be a caring and redemptive way to end a marriage that is doomed to remain a sickly and distorted parody of a Christian family. How can we judge clergy families any differently?"[148]

Some pastors were permitted to remain in their charges after separation and divorce. More often, a move seemed to be a partial answer to the knotty problems that divorce involved. Some conferences recommended a leave of absence with salary and housing allowance. Most developed some support structure for clergy couples experiencing separation or divorce—counseling services, leaves of absence, and transitional funds.[149]

Churches could be reluctant to accept pastors who were single after being divorced. A remarried pastor seemed to have less trouble establishing good relationships in a new charge.[150] A 1976 UMC survey showed clergy divorce still a sensitive issue in the church, but more and more divorced clergy were staying in the ministry.[151] Could the church exercise the grace and forgiveness of God while not condoning or sanctioning divorce? As late as 1979, a pair of articles in *Circuit Rider* begged bishops and conferences to deal with divorce in a *pastoral* rather than a *punitive* fashion.[152]

By 1976, when more than a million marriages ended in divorce in the U.S., the church's Section on Worship invited controversy when it brought out a book of experimental liturgies, *Ritual in a New Day: An Invitation.* Among the new worship resources was "Rituals for Divorce," and Hoyt Hickman, who coordinated the staff work for the resource, told *UM Newscope* the intent was "to bring Christ into every decision and

experience of our lives, including the trauma of divorce." Calling divorce "bereave-
ment," Hickman insisted that people should not be forced to undergo this suffering
alone and faithless: "The book makes no argument as to when divorce is appropriate, but
faces divorce when it is a fact."[153] Produced by an interagency task force on the cultural
context of ritual, this new resource was the first of any denomination to offer religious
services for divorcing people. A greater tolerance toward divorce and remarriage had
been expressed in the 1976 *Discipline*: "In marriages where the partners are, even after
thoughtful consideration and counsel, estranged beyond reconciliation, we recognize
divorce and the right of divorced persons to remarry."[154]

While intended not to affirm divorce but to affirm divorcing persons in their trouble
and while proposed for optional and trial use in local churches, the resources exposed
the lack of unanimity among UMs on the changing protocols on divorce. The four brief
rituals for use with the divorced, one of which accentuated the new freedom of the couple rather than the need for repentance to healing, were too much for some to bear.
When word got out, William Willimon called the experimental UMC liturgy for the divorced (in *Ritual in a New Day*) "cheap grace" that speaks "more of our irresponsibility
and unfaithfulness than our love."[155] With debate fired by the attention of the secular
press, volume editor H. Grady Hardin and the UMC weeklies received numerous letters
of complaint. The rituals died a quiet death. The UMC *Book of Worship*, 1992, contained no "divorce ritual," only a prayer and suggested Scripture readings for "ministry
with persons going through divorce" in the section "Healing Services and Prayer." By
1980 the UMC recognized in its *Book of Discipline* that married couples were being "estranged beyond reconciliation" and gave divorce its own heading and section. The legal
fact of divorce did not, it continued, dissolve other covenantal relationships resulting
from the marriage, such as "the care and nurture of the children of divorced and/or remarried persons."[156] The new standards applied to clergy as well as laity. Increasingly
the UMC found itself with divorced and remarried pastors, district superintendents, and
bishops—something unthinkable as recently as 1950.

In 1979 the Council of Bishops adopted a *Handbook on Clergy Divorce* to guide the
leadership of their areas in strengthening parsonage families and dealing responsibly
with clergy divorce when it occurred. The bishops agreed that they could not justify a
double standard, one for lay and another for clergy, and that at times divorce was best.
If pastors behaved responsibly throughout the crisis, did everything possible to avoid divorce, including reaching out for the best counseling help available, and remained effective in ministry and emotionally capable of continuing in full service, their ministries
should continue without interruption. Whether a move to another church was desirable
depended, they judged, upon the circumstances unique to that situation. The bishops
further agreed that "exemplary conduct" was required of ordained persons, and their
covenant must be faithfully kept.[157] With gradual acceptance that this episcopal guid-

ance both provided and reflected, the UMC gradually gave up deeming divorce to disqualify candidates for ordination or appointment for deacons, elders, and bishops.

Abortion

Until the early 1970s, most U.S. states prohibited abortion, except to save the mother's life. The sexual liberation and feminist movements of the 1960s advanced the argument that a woman has the right to decide what happens in and to her body.

Even before the Supreme Court's historic *Roe v. Wade* decision, the UMC had concluded that abortion should be decriminalized and become a matter for the women involved to decide, and some of its clergy and members were risking arrest to make it safe for women seeking an abortion. The 1972 General Conference expressed support in the denomination's Social Principles for "removal of abortion from the criminal code, placing it instead under the laws relating to other procedures of standard medical practice." A resolution on responsible parenthood, passed in 1972, reflected major changes from that of 1968, warning of the consequences of bringing unloved and unwanted children into the world and rejecting "simplistic" arguments for and against abortion. In contrast to the earlier statement that favored abortion approved by a panel of physicians in case of rape, incest, or other extreme circumstances, the 1972 resolution called for women to be "free to make their own responsible decisions concerning the personal and moral questions surrounding the issue of abortion."

The 1972 Social Principles, in affirming the woman's responsibility for such a crucial decision, sought middle ground: "Our belief in the sanctity of unborn human life makes us reluctant to approve abortion," but we also recognize that "devastating damage" to the mother may be caused by "an unacceptable pregnancy"; therefore, "in continuity with past Christian teaching, we recognize tragic conflicts of life with life that may justify abortion," and "we support the legal option of abortion under proper medical procedures. Therefore, a decision concerning abortion should be made only after thoughtful and prayerful consideration by the parties involved, with medical, pastoral, and other appropriate counsel." The statement continued, "Good social policy calls for the removal of abortion from the criminal code, so that women in counsel with husbands, doctors, and pastors, are free to make their own responsible decisions concerning the personal and moral questions surrounding the issue of abortion."[158] Wouldn't it be better, the UMC suggested, to make abortion legal and medically safe rather than keep it illegal and force women, who have sought abortions since the earliest human days, to resort to back-alley abortionists?

Two UMC agencies, the Board of Christian Social Concerns and the Women's Division of the Board of Missions, had already banded together to give women information about abortion providers and to lobby for the repeal of anti-abortion laws. A 1971 Board of Christian Social Concerns study book, *Abortion: A Human Choice*, containing essays from three UMC seminary faculty, Allen J. Moore, Tilda Norberg, and John Swomley, was an early example of the board's abortion rights program.[159]

In 1973, the U.S. Supreme Court ruled (*Roe v. Wade*) that because the Fourteenth Amendment to the Constitution protects privacy, a woman had a right to terminate during the first three months of pregnancy. Seven of the nine justices had agreed, striking down the laws under which women and their doctors were forbidden this procedure, a decision widely interpreted by abortion opponents as a functional equivalent of abortion-on-demand. Justice Harry Blackmun, the only United Methodist on the court, wrote the Court's majority opinion. The Court did not view the matter lightly. Blackmun acknowledged "the sensitive and emotional nature of the abortion controversy" and worked to trace the history of attitudes and regulations extending back to ancient times. He noted that "the restrictive criminal abortion laws" then in effect in a majority of states were "of relatively recent vintage"—mostly from the latter half of the nineteenth century. Blackmun wrote that while the Constitution does not mention a right to privacy, "the court has recognized that a right of personal privacy does exist under the Constitution.... This right of privacy... is broad enough to encompass a woman's decision whether or not to terminate her pregnancy." However, it was not an unqualified right, the justice reasoned. He concluded that in the interests of maternal health, states could regulate abortion procedures and facilities from the end of the first trimester:

> We need not resolve the difficult question of when life begins. When those trained in the respective disciplines of medicine, philosophy, and theology are unable to arrive at any consensus, the judiciary, at this point in the development of man's knowledge, is not in a position to speculate as to the answer.... It should be sufficient to note briefly the wide divergence of thinking on this most sensitive and difficult question. There has always been strong support for the view that life does not begin until live birth. It appears to be the predominant, though not the unanimous, attitude of the Jewish faith. It may be taken to represent also the position of a large segment of the Protestant community, insofar as that can be ascertained; organized groups that have taken a formal position on the abortion issue have generally regarded abortion as a matter for the conscience of the individual and her family.[160]

He called the decision "a step that had to be taken as we go down the road toward full emancipation of women."

This ruling polarized American opinion, then and now, with proponents of legal abortion being styled pro-choice and opponents taking the label pro-life. In the months following the Court's decision, the Religious Coalition for Abortion Rights (RCAR) was formed by several Protestant denominations and Jewish groups to protect the ruling, and pro-life Roman Catholic and conservative Protestant forces also began to mobilize to overturn the decision. Initially much opposition to the ruling came from the Roman

Catholic Church, but some United Methodists also believed that abortion should be prohibited. The church's Board of Church and Society partnered with RCAR from the beginning and held a number of workshops on the abortion issue around the country.

The Women's Division of the UMC and women's groups in other mainline churches were a driving force in creating an effective pro-choice lobby. In December 1973, sixteen Jewish and Christian religious groups met at the United Methodist building in Washington, D.C., to discuss the Roman Catholic Church's pledge to overturn the Supreme Court decision of *Roe v. Wade*. This meeting, called by the UMC Board of Church and Society, led to the formation of the Religious Coalition for Abortion Rights (after 1993 known as the Religious Coalition for Reproductive Choice), a national organization that works to defend a woman's right to choose a legal abortion. In 1974 RCAR adopted a policy position on "conscience clauses," stating publicly funded health-care institutions—unlike individuals—have no legal right to refuse to provide abortion services. RCAR rented space in the Washington, D.C., headquarters of the UMC's Board of Church and Society, remaining there until 1993. In 1975 the Council of Bishops unanimously adopted a resolution in opposition to amending the U.S. Constitution in order to prohibit abortion.[161] The work of the Women's Division and the Board of Church and Society on the controversial issues such as the protection of women's reproductive rights and the passage of the Equal Rights Amendment to the U.S. Constitution required deft defenses of their position and choice of allies in the struggles.

Other United Methodists, however, believed that abortion should be prohibited. Antifeminist campaigns that had been in process for some time reached a new peak in 1977, winning victories that startled a liberal movement long used to victory. One area of setback was abortion. In 1976, Representative Henry Hyde introduced an amendment to the appropriation for the Department of Health, Education, and Welfare, forbidding the use of Medicaid funds for abortion except where the mother's life was at stake. The Hyde Amendment was the subject of impassioned hearings in the opening months of 1977, and not only did it pass, but it was upheld by the U.S. Supreme Court. In 1978, the principle of banning federal funds was extended to other appropriation bills, including medical provision for military personnel. In addition to encouraging conservatives, the success of the Hyde Amendment damaged the Democratic coalition. Feminists were incensed by President Carter's pallid response to the Supreme Court decision.

In 1977, after Congress had begun to restrict funds for abortions, the Women's Division and UMW challenged the denial of Medicaid reimbursements for abortions. The inclusive position of Methodist feminists on reproductive freedom embraced abortion rights for poor women and stood against sterilization abuse. Abortion continued to be a touchstone issue in the 1980s. The Moral Majority and President Reagan spoke repeatedly against abortion. In 1981 Congress considered the proposed Hatch

Amendment, which would have declared that a right to abortion is not secured by the Constitution. The Hatch Amendment met heavy public opposition, running at over 75 percent in one 1982 poll. The amendment eventually passed the Senate by a vote of 50-49 the following year, far short of the two-thirds majority required to change the Constitution. It was a token of frustration that beginning in the mid-1980s, the pro-life movement developed its strategy of direct action against abortion clinics, including physical attacks by extremists. Anti-abortion violence escalated sharply in 1984–85, including dozens of arson and bomb attacks, and the militant Operation Rescue emerged in 1986. The movement justified its existence by effecting the kinds of "rescues" that the government refused to do.

Pro-abortion activism on the part of official United Methodism spurred UMC pro-lifers to action, a development that we follow in the next chapter. The issues of divorce and abortion posed a conundrum for Good News and other Methodist conservatives: how to maneuver around the repeated New Testament denunciations of divorce (in part to avoid alienating the growing number of divorced evangelicals) and focus attention instead on what they characterized as other sexual "sins," particularly abortion and homosexuality. As evangelicals professing fidelity to the Scripture as inspired, inerrant, and immutable on matters of teaching and ethics, how could Good News come to terms with the biblical speck that could be construed as bearing on abortion (and homosexuality) when the beam of teaching on divorce loomed so large? As progressives discerned a canon within the canon or key hermeneutical touchstones, so conservatives resorted to selective literalism, which tended to ignore or explain away Jesus' admonitions about divorce and focus instead on politically charged issues: abortion and homosexuality. To the institutionalization of the concern with abortion into Lifewatch we turn in the next chapter. Here we take note of the larger conservative-evangelical network within which it emerged.

Good News: The Formation of a Shadow Connection or Church?

Highly visible and institutionally successful among the caucuses is Good News, which identifies itself as "a forum for Scriptural Christianity within the United Methodist Church." We might well have chosen to treat Good News toward the beginning rather than the end of the chapter, for it came into being as United Methodism was in the process of formation, its platform enunciated by Charles Keysor in a 1966 *Christian Advocate* article (Sources 1966a). And we have taken notice of Good News at several points in our discussion. We delayed fuller treatment until chapter's end because—unlike many of the other caucuses that found a niche within and advocacy for their causes by a general agency—Good News found itself battling connectional authority and gradually elaborating a set of alternative, parachurch, loyal opposition, or shadow connectional structures. Also unlike other caucuses—racial-ethnic ones especially—whose creation launched careers within UMC commissions or boards for caucus leaders, Good News leadership tended to come from persons who had already enjoyed prestigious and powerful posts within the denomination and recoiled to Good News–related endeavors when United Methodism refused to heed their counsel.

Keysor typified this pattern. He sounded the alarm for orthodoxy as pastor of Grace Methodist in Elgin, Illinois. Keysor had been a journalist; his second career followed conversion by Billy Graham and theological education within the Methodist seminary orbit at Garrett. He then helped launch and became the managing editor of Methodism's slick, wide-distribution family magazine, *Together*, which began with 700,000 subscribers and topped at 1.25 million. After that stint within the connectional structure (the publishing house), Keysor signed on as editor at the evangelical Sunday school powerhouse, David C. Cook Publishing Company.[162] Later capitalizing on the Graham and Cook publishing connections with the exploding conservative-evangelical, political-religious movement and his own journalistic experience, Keysor, then a pastor, determined that Methodism's "silent minority" would be voiceless no more. The first issue of *Good News* appeared in the spring of 1967. The magazine, produced by Keysor in the midst of pastoral duties, dreamed "that evangelical Methodists might be united in fellowship across the Church" and "that our voices may be heard as we seek to articulate historic Methodism."[163] Three years later this "virtual" fellowship gathered in Dallas—1,600 registered, some 3,000 for evenings—to hear invited speakers: Asbury College president Dennis Kinlaw; Bishop Gerald K. Kennedy; Ira Gallaway from the Board of Evangelism; lay evangelist Harry Denman; such evangelical notables as E. Stanley Jones, Oral Roberts, and Howard Ball (Campus Crusade); a couple of seminary faculty; and Asbury Seminary president Frank Stanger. Soon thereafter President Kinlaw invited Keysor to join the faculty and to bring *Good News* to Asbury. The Asbury institutional base connected the Good News caucus with an extended Wilmore conservative-evangelical family and with the family history of holiness grievance, of come-outer politics, and of true-believer conviction. Case notes that the relocation benefited Keysor and the magazine immensely: "Maintaining an office was inexpensive in Wilmore. There was a ready supply of talented students and student spouses to serve as support staff. And, perhaps most important, Keysor was able to recruit some of the brightest and best from his journalism classes to write for the magazine."[164]

Through the pages of *Good News*, with the support of an energetic and outspoken board, through connections with the burgeoning political-religious, conservative-evangelical movement, with the benefit of the larger Asbury networks, and from the insular world of Wilmore, the Good News caucus began what would become a several-decade campaign of parachurch institution building and of prophetic critique of United Methodism. To illustrate, an early 1970 editorial, "Cyanide in the Church School," complained, "Why should viewpoints contrary to United Methodist doctrine be forced upon large numbers of people who want only to be 100 percent Methodists in the church school?"[165] The editorial followed and would be followed by meetings between Good News and the church school editors in efforts to get evangelical perspectives, stronger Bible content, and David C. Cook–style pedagogy into United Methodist Sunday school curricula. Several years of jockeying against the "modernist" religious education establishment produced some "give" by church school editor Ewart Watts, notably the creation of a new children's series "Exploring the Bible." Demanding and being refused more, including a separate evangelical curricular track, Keysor, Riley Case, and Diane Knippers produced in 1975 on their own a confirmation curriculum, *We Believe*. After a decade of such production in-house, Good News spun off Bristol Books to be an Arminian voice in the Calvinist-dominated world of conservative-evangelical-fundamentalist publishing.[166]

Good News succeeded in its aspiration to become a forum for evangelical causes. The pattern with curriculum was to be repeated on other concerns that would also be championed in the magazine's articles or editorials. The journalistic campaign would lead to a convocation, a wider coalition, a petition-campaign aimed at the following General Conference, and an enlarged network. And in a number of instances, convocation(s) and coalitions would birth a closely related but independent institution offering evangelical services parallel to and competitive with the denomination's. The causes—doctrine, missions, seminaries, church funding, feminism, abortion, and homosexuality—would eventually generate an evangelical coalition: Good News, the Confessing Movement, the Mission Society for United Methodists, Aldersgate Renewal Ministries, the Foundation for Theological Education, Lifewatch, RENEW, Transforming Congregations, the Association for Church Renewal, and United Methodist Action (the latter, the United Methodist wing of the Institute of Religion and Democracy, or IRD).

The formation of several of these organizations and their efforts to work as a political coalition within the church lie beyond the purview of this chapter. However, the political caucus direction had been set early, really in anticipation of the 1972 General Conference when Good News prevailed upon board member, director of development at Asbury Seminary, and former general secretary of the Board of Lay Activities, Robert Mayfield, to flood General Conference with some 15,000 petitions (three-quarters of the total received). The strategy, with *Good News* publishing model petitions, would be followed in the upcoming quadrennial. In the next chapter we turn to one of its greatest successes and overriding concerns, the revision of the church's doctrinal statement, and particularly revision of the commitment to theological pluralism. As we noted above, Good News built a coalition around that cause at its 1975 convocation, out of which came an alternative statement of United Methodist belief, known by the meeting's locale, the Junaluska Affirmation. At the same convocation that approved the Junaluska Affirmation, the Reverend Ed Robb, pastor of St. Luke's UMC in Lubbock,

Texas, and vice chairman of the Good News board of directors, delivered a diatribe against the thirteen UMC seminaries, which drew the ire of SMU's Professor Albert Outler.[167]

Two of the collaborative action agencies, the IRD and the Mission Society, emerged before 1984. The IRD, like Focus on the Family and the American Family Association (the latter founded in 1977 by UMC pastor Donald Wildmon), linked United Methodists with conservatives in other communions concerned about financial support, programmatic assistance, and open advocacy for various progressive and revolutionary movements on the part of denominational and interdenominational bodies (particularly the National and World Councils of Churches). Making the case against the general boards of Global Ministries and Church and Society was David Jessup, who with his spouse, Virginia, had become involved with Good News after a stint in the Peace Corps. In the twenty-seven-page 1979 "Jessup Report," David Jessup, whose day job was to investigate the radical fringe of the labor movement, employed those skills in documenting similar connections by UMC agencies. With others levying similar charges against the interdenominational bodies and against other mainline denominations, Jessup raised the issue of denominational accountability. With Good News blessing and assistance, Jessup and Ed Robb brought together or gained the endorsement of a number of persons so agitated, including a number from within the Good News connection like Diane Knippers and Paul Stallsworth, but also evangelical spokespersons like Carl F. H. Henry and Catholics Michael Novak, George Weigel, and Richard John Neuhaus. Out of this 1981 Washington, D.C., meeting came the Institute of Religion and Democracy. It purposed "to illuminate the relationship between Christian faith and democratic governance . . . to oppose policies and programs in the churches which ignore or deny that relationship."[168] Supported then and thereafter by the Sarah Schaife Foundation and the Smith Richardson Foundation, the IRD quickly took its place within the emerging neoconservative, militantly free enterprise constellation of political action groups. The IRD succeeded in feeding its findings about denominational left-leanings to *Reader's Digest* and to CBS's *60 Minutes* for late 1982 and early 1983 exposés, the article in the former titled "Do You Know Where Your Church Offerings Go?" Thus began IRD's three-front neoconservative campaign, seemingly aimed at splitting the United Methodist, Presbyterian, and Episcopal churches.

The concerns that generated the Mission Society included perceptions that GBGM had committed itself to social and political transformation, to mission rather than the sending of missionaries, and to feminism. Especially agitated over the place of the Women's Division and its new head, Peggy Billings, in GBGM decision making, Ira Gallaway, then pastor of First UMC Peoria, Illinois, at the time the largest in the North Central Jurisdiction, and previously head of the Board of Evangelism, spelled out his concerns in a 1983 book, *Drifted Away*.[169] The same year he joined others in founding what Gerald Anderson of the Overseas Ministry Study Center and the *International Bulletin of Missionary Research* advocated, a second mission agency that would be in the business of actually sending missionaries.[170] The 1984 General Conference directed that mediation efforts be made between the new Mission Society and GBGM, but those proved unproductive and were soon halted.

More loosely knit into the conservative-evangelical political affairs were new groups committed to spiritual transformation and evangelization, among them, Aldersgate Renewal Ministries, an organization reflective of a broader charismatic-Pentecostal resurgence. Beginning in the 1960s, growing numbers of evangelical Methodists reported that they had experienced the "baptism of the Holy Spirit," manifested in glossolalia (speaking in tongues) and spiritual healing. Episcopalians, Roman Catholics, and other mainline Protestants who received these gifts usually referred to themselves as "charismatics" in order to differentiate their movement from established Pentecostal denominations such as the Assemblies of God. When mainline churches proved critical or inhospitable, "Spirit-filled" believers formed support networks within and across denominational lines. A high point for organized charismatic activities was in 1977 when 50,000 believers from dozens of denominations displayed their ecumenical enthusiasm at a gathering in Kansas City, Missouri. By that point, a leading interpreter, Vinson Synan, estimated there were 50 million Pentecostals and charismatics worldwide. In a decade the estimate ballooned to 200 million.

The charismatic phenomenon in the UMC first gained public attention in 1974 when a group of UMs organized a national conference on the Holy Spirit, which was highlighted by lively praise and worship. At their fourth annual conference on charismatic renewal in Kansas City, July 1977, the assembly formed a network, initially termed the United Methodist Renewal Services Fellowship (later Aldersgate Renewal Ministries, or ARM), to pray and work together for the renewal of the church by the power of the Holy Spirit. ARM held annual national conferences, formed regional chapters, planned "Life in the Spirit" seminars, published a newsletter (*Aldersgate Journal*, later *ARM Update*), and became a self-supporting affiliate of the UMC General Board of Discipleship (GBOD). By 2007 some 1,500 to 2,000 people would attend ARM annual meetings, and 3,000 were on its support list.

Since its beginning, ARM has worked with and within the UMC as a self-advertised "non-adversarial" group that is more concerned about "lighting candles than cursing the darkness."[171] Executive director Gary Moore of Goodlettsville, Tennessee, in a 2006 interview, said that "being within our denomination opens some doors and acceptance it would not otherwise have, and it also gives us a line of accountability that maintains equilibrium." He added, "We've not gotten involved in internal politics. Groups like Good News are flagbearers for political [change]; we choose to focus on bringing personal and church renewal."[172] However, ARM's website in August 2007 included a link to

Transforming Congregations network, a politically active caucus on a hot-button issue in the denomination, and charismatics tend to share with evangelicals a conservative political-moral outlook.

Spiritual Resources, Liturgical Norms, and Inclusive Language

In various ways, the bishops, the agencies, and the connectional leaders labored to honor the church's first name and to keep the several caucuses and causes from disintegrating and effectively reterming it *Untied*. The efforts just mentioned by GBOD to support Aldersgate Renewal Ministries represented just such an effort. So also its programs like Covenant Discipleship and the Academy for Spiritual Formation. Notable as well was its influential "Walk to Emmaus," an adaptation of a Roman Catholic retreat called Cursillo, which originated in Spain in 1949. The Upper Room adapted the program in 1978 for a primarily Protestant audience and later renamed it "Walk to Emmaus." The name recalls the story in the Gospel of Luke (24:13-35) when the risen Christ appeared to two disciples walking together along the road from Jerusalem to Emmaus on the first Easter afternoon. At first the disciples did not recognize Jesus, but after breaking bread with him, their eyes were opened. Just so, modern-day Walk to Emmaus pilgrims find their own spiritual awareness has grown significantly after participating in the events. By 2007 about three hundred Emmaus communities had sprung up around the U.S.; they organize weekend retreats as well as monthly gatherings for those who have completed the program. Another eighty-nine communities are active outside the U.S., and plans were laid to start an Emmaus community in Russia. Emmaus also organizes similar programs for high school youth (called Chrysalis Flights) and for college-age young people (Chrysalis Journeys).[173]

If such programmatic gestures looked out to United Methodism's evangelical wing, other initiatives, especially in worship and hymnody, catered to the racial-ethnic caucuses and to the churchly side of the denomination. In the decade prior to unification the EUBC and the Methodists undertook major revisions of worship. In both cases— the EUBC *Hymnal* of 1957 and *Book of Ritual* of 1959 and the Methodist *Book of Worship* of 1964 and *Hymnal* of 1966—the churches retained the inherited, premodern, Reformation-era words and phrases that set the dominant liturgical tone and pattern. Publishing these resources on the eve of a decade-long movement of liturgical renewal, the churches brought into union norms and practices that did not and could not take full advantage of the new insights that soon brought forth fresh liturgies from sister churches, Catholic and Protestant alike, or cater to the experimental mood of mid-1960s worship leaders (casual communions, chummy prayers, balloons and banners, guitars and folk songs), or honor hopes and expectations that the church's prayer and praise reflect its diversity.

Well into the 1980s the denomination's publishing house maintained a cautious and conservative attitude toward supplements to the church's two official hymnals. Its first attempt was the songbook *Ventures in Song,* 1972, compiled by the Section on Worship, a part of the new General Board of Discipleship. While the songbook's content reflected alternative religious song, its cluttered format and poor marketing made little impact. A second *Supplement to the Book of Hymns* was issued in 1982. By the mid-1970s the concern for ethnic churches informed the case for alternative religious songs. When the 1976 General Conference made ethnic local churches a missional priority for 1977–80, money became available to enable the Section on Worship to work with ethnic caucuses and to fund the task forces, consultations, and editors needed to produce ethnic hymns and songbooks and supplements to the authorized hymnals in due course. *Songs of Zion* (1981) gathered together hymnody of the Black tradition; *Hymns from the Four Winds* (1983), Asian hymns; *Celebremos* 1 and 2 (1979 and 1983), Latino offerings; and *Voices: Native American Hymns and Worship Resources* (1992). Developed and distributed by Discipleship Resources, the supplements found greatest use among the respective ethnic communities. The UMs more generally, through the mid-1980s, remained ill at ease with multiethnic and multilanguage hymns. Of the four supplements, *Songs of Zion* with its generous fare of teachable and singable spirituals, standard evangelical hymns, and gospel songs proved to be the most popular. *Celebremos* fared well in the Hispanic community, as did *Hymns from the Four Winds* in the Native American community, but elsewhere had little use.

To bring order out of liturgical chaos, the newly united church in 1970 authorized an Alternate Liturgies Project, the larger ecumenical and liturgical context for which its key leader, James F. White, detailed (Sources 1972c). The proposed twenty-one-volume Supplemental Worship Resources Series was to be the most ambitious worship project in the denomination's history. The new liturgies and worship resources were issued initially not to replace the services books of 1959 and 1966 but to give United Methodists more options. The first in the series, a reformed, new Lord's Supper service, appeared in English in 1972 and in Spanish in 1978. Fresh services of baptism, with provision for confirmation and renewal, followed in 1976 and new wedding and burial rites in 1979. (We revisit these new services in the next chapter when they are adopted.) Here we note their use of contemporary language, adherence to classical patterns reflecting the new ecumenical and liturgical consensus, adoption of a eucharistic and eschatological tone, and provision for experimentation and wider participation. In abandoning the Wesleyan texts derived from the Book of Common Prayer, United Methodism drifted somewhat from Pan-Methodism (AME, AMEZ, CME), which retained the Cranmerian liturgies. Instead, the UMC became part of a new liturgical consensus, sharing worship patterns with the rest of mainstream Protestantism, indeed of English-speaking, ecumenical Christianity. Along the way, United Methodists traded the literary preaching of the early decades of the twentieth century for preaching based on a set of Scripture readings for each Sunday. Freestanding Communion tables replaced altars attached to the chancel wall. Communicants stood to receive the bread and drank from or practiced intinction in a common cup. White robes and colorful stoles replaced the long-standing ministerial black. United Methodism, it appeared to one theologian, by tradition a preaching movement, had become a liturgical church.

The imagery and phrasing for worship increasingly reflected heated but fruitful debates about inclusive language, focused initially on references to humanity, but eventually raised in relation to language for God and for the divine nature. By 1974 several other mainline churches, including the United Church of Christ, the Presbyterian Church, and the Lutheran Church, and the National Council of Churches had examined language in religious materials and published guides to more inclusive speech. An *Inclusive Language Lectionary,* the first formal effort to eliminate exclusively male metaphors for God in the Scriptures, was released by the National Council of Churches in 1982. Although the inclusive language initiative was controversial across the church, the 1976 General Conference authorized GCOM to establish a task force to draw up "guidelines for eliminating sexism, racism and ageism in language content, theology, and imagery from all church resource materials and mandate that such guidelines shall be adhered to." Two years later the council approved the task force report and recommended the guidelines to the general boards and agencies and to annual conferences for their immediate use.[174] The 1980 General Conference approved the guidelines and asked GCOM to add a section on "handicappism." GCOM complied, approved the new section in 1983, and referred the revised guidelines to the 1984 General Conference, which gave approval and recommended them for immediate use.[175]

The 1984 United Methodist General Conference responded to a report from the Task Force on Language Guidelines and adopted *Words that Hurt and Words that Heal.* This statement on inclusive language counseled church members to use fewer male pronouns in reference to God, look for alternatives to words such as *Lord, King,* and *Father,* and develop more expansive and inclusive language and imagery to address and describe God, the people of God, and God's presence and divine action in the world. On connectional levels, in seminaries, and in some locales, United Methodists reshaped worship accordingly. On more local levels, the guidelines and their counsel were either not known or ignored. Indeed, efforts to address concerns of caucuses on the progressive side fueled agitation on the conservative-evangelical side. And vice versa. United? Untied?

CHAPTER XV

HOLDING FAST/PRESSING ON: 1984–2000

Nineteen hundred eighty-four marked two hundred years since Thomas Coke and Francis Asbury convened preachers to accept John Wesley's transmissions and to found The Methodist Episcopal Church. United Methodists commemorated the bicentennial by holding scholarly consultations, by taking stock in articles and books, and by having celebrations at annual conferences. General Conference returned home to Baltimore, "Proclaiming Grace and Freedom." While that theme, various speeches, and gala events looked back to polity and preaching foundations, the politics and rhetoric of the prior two decades framed the conference's and the year's work. And structural dislocations in Methodist life might well have focused the church's attention on centennial, not bicentennial, on 1884 rather than 1784. In anticipation of and to facilitate both assessment and celebration, the General Council of Ministries commissioned seventeen inquiries into the state of the connection, each a readable one hundred pages or so. This *Into Our Third Century Series* took a hard look at the changing world within and beyond the church.

Strategies and politics of diversity continued to be salient. Jurisdictional conferences in 1984 elected to the episcopacy the church's first woman of color, Leontine Kelly; its first Hispanic, Elias Galvan; another Asian American, Roy Sano; another woman, Judith Craig; and several other African Americans—Felton May, Forrest Stith, Woodie White, and Ernest Newman, the latter the first by the Southeastern Jurisdiction. The quadrennium saw important vision statements from Hispanic and Native American leaders seeking to continue the unfinished task of developing and strengthening churches and ministries in their communities (Sources 1985, 1988a). GBGM in 1986 decided to establish Korean American mission districts in each jurisdiction. The 1988 General Conference created a National Hispanic Ministries Committee to stimulate congregational development, clergy recruitment, lay missioners, and new connective mission structures and approved the plan to build a Methodist-related university for all of Africa (opened in 1992). Also in 1992 appeared a Native American hymn and worship book titled *Voices,* the first ever for the denomination, containing folk parables, prayers, and gospel songs indigenous to the more than twenty-five Native American tribes. That year as well, the South Carolina Conference celebrated the assignment of a new episcopal leader, Joseph Bethea, the first Black bishop assigned to South Carolina since the dissolution of the former Central (all-Black) Jurisdiction, and his appointment of the conference's first cross-racial appointments to local churches. Two Black clergymen were appointed senior pastors of predominantly white churches and three white ministers likewise were appointed to predominantly Black churches. South Carolina's first steps were mirrored in actions in other conferences that summer. In 1996, General Conference adopted the resolution "Racialism: The Church's Unfinished Agenda,"[1] and the church launched two related programs, "Strengthening the Black Church for the 21st Century" and "Holy Boldness—A National Plan for Urban Ministry."

Caucus ambitions on the right also prospered. On the eve of 1984 General Conference, Good News birthed the Mission Society for United Methodists, rejecting the service-oriented, ecumenical, liberationist mission policy that Tracey Jones had enunciated for GBGM (Sources 1969) and reverting to the pattern of sending evangelists. With its various political action committee (PAC) offspring, Good News succeeded in pressing its agenda in the 1984 General Conference. Posturing by Methodism's progressive and conservative wings—on matters of doctrine and hot-button social issues construed doctrinally—continued over the next several decades, sometimes concerning, sometimes obscuring important changes in the church's governance and makeup, its place in American society, the evolution of its institutions, and its dealing with challenges of employee health care and pensions.

A grassroots initiative declaration designed to lift up the need to preach and practice an evangelistic ministry, both biblically oriented and holistic, developed during the bicentennial celebration of the UMC. Framing a declaration, the activists circulated it across the denomination prior to the 1984 General Conference. Hundreds of local church persons from the five jurisdictions endorsed the declaration for presentation to and approval by the General Conference. The declaration appealed to the church and individuals

- to strengthen their efforts in Christian mission;
- to reaffirm their commitment to work toward racial justice and inclusiveness;
- to address the grim reality of hunger in America and the world;
- to call for renewed efforts toward achieving a nuclear freeze and arms limitation;
- to confront the ever widening gap between rich and poor nations;
- to accentuate basic education and work among young people.

Presented to the General Conference from the floor as a matter of personal privilege, this Baltimore Declaration was approved by the body and referred to the Council of Bishops and the General Council on Ministries for study and implementation.[2]

Increasingly in this period, United Methodism claimed its global nature. A signature gesture was the building of Africa University in Zimbabwe, endorsed by the General Conference of 1988 and opened in 1992. Ninety hundred ninety-two also saw the creation of Communities of Shalom, a response of the church to "third world" conditions within the U.S. and specifically to devastation and destruction that followed the video-taped beating in LA of motorist Rodney King. A National Shalom Committee, overseen by the GBGM, offered initial training, start-up funding, technical assistance, a newsletter, brochures and videos, and biennial Shalom Summits. In Communities of Shalom, where poverty, neglect, despair, and crime ruled, churches collaborated with local organizations, businesses, institutions, and residents to transform the conditions that affect people's lives—to change negative forces within the community to positive actions for shalom (Hebrew word for peace). The UMC met its objective of organizing three hundred Shalom sites by the year 2000. The church became more aware of the well-being of the globe as well. California-Pacific Conference successfully lobbied the 1992 General Conference to encourage UMC congregations "to defend creation and live as an ecologically-responsible community."[3]

United Methodism became increasingly aware that it was growing outside the U.S. and, with mainline denominations generally, declining within the country.[4] As we have noted (see 1968 "Snapshot"), keeping programs and ministries going and staying the course in the cities as long and as much as it did cost United Methodism in the scramble for suburban religious loyalties. Fragmented by cause and caucus, Methodism muted the voice of its once dominant middle and veered toward the precipice of schism, in part, because like its Protestant counterparts, it had built and built into an urban America that was coming apart.[5] By 1984, United Methodism's membership, less than 11 million at merger, had dropped to near 9. Average worship attendance, hovering around 4 million in 1968, stood at 3.5. And the church school decreased from 6.2 million to 4, an indicator of more bad news to come.[6] Meanwhile, Pentecostal, conservative, and evangelical denominations and congregations built in the suburbs as the mainline had in the cities and experimented with televangelism as Methodism had with print ministries. Of course, blame for all of United Methodism's decline and woes lay at the feet of the liberal elite at the helm of boards and agencies, just as Washington insiders could be charged with causing American industrial flight, economic woes, foreign policy debacles, or energy problems. So Good News and the IRD knew.[7]

Doctrine Defined and Tested

Over several quadrennia, the Good News coalition had perfected a campaign strategy of blitzing General Conference with petitions on focused concerns. Sustain the incompatibilist language on homosexuality! Clarify that policy with a prohibition against ordaining any self-avowed and practicing homosexual! Increase conservative clout by allowing associate conference members and local pastors to be elected to General Conference! Strengthen the judgments against abortion! Permit designated giving! Increase the number of evangelical hymns if hymnal revision is undertaken! And fix doctrine, scrap pluralism, and reshape the doctrinal statement in the *Discipline*! Good News registered its convictions for the 1984 General Conference with a deluge of petitions, swelling the total received to thirteen thousand. On its key concerns it could claim some measure of success. In particular, it applauded General Conference's decision to entrust hymnal revision to the publishing house, which it deemed customer-oriented. And it took special pride in the establishment of a Committee on Our Theological Task, the delegation of its staffing to the bishops, their selection of conservative Bishop Earl Hunt as chair, and the presence thereon of Asbury Seminary historical theologian Kenneth Kinghorn.[8]

General Conference indeed charged the Council of Bishops (COB) with creating a committee "on our theological task," one "representative of the whole church," and directed the committee to prepare for the *Discipline* "a new statement which will reflect the needs of the church" and "define the scope of our Wesleyan tradition in the context of our contemporary world."[9] The Committee on Our Theological Task construed its mandate broadly: (1) elucidate United Methodist doctrinal standards and guidelines, their nature, scope, and use; (2) clarify an appropriate understanding of pluralism and the catholic spirit in The United Methodist Church; (3) address the significance and proper use of the "Wesleyan quadrilateral"; (4) illuminate the relationship between The United Methodist Church's theological heritage and its mission, life, and polity; (5) strengthen United Methodist participation in ecumenical conversations within the global context; (6) reflect our global nature; (7) strive for inclusiveness in concept and language; and (8) employ a literary style that allows the statement to be readily understood.[10]

The COB appointed the twenty-four-member committee in December 1984: five bishops, five seminary faculty, five clergy, five laity, and four at-large members, attending to race, gender, age, and geography (with European and Pacific members). After three years of study and consultation, the study committee, with Bishop Hunt as chair and Richard Heitzenrater as writer, tested a draft of its statement in the broadly circulated *Circuit Rider*.[11] The committee largely achieved its ambitious aims. The proposed statement reimagined the quadrilateral as the rule of Scripture within a trilateral hermeneutic of tradition, reason, and experience. It asserted the primacy of Scripture, but argued that the Bible cannot function with a negation of tradition, reason, and experience or be read or interpreted accurately without their mediation. At the same time the revised doctrinal statement expanded the discussion of the sources and criteria of theology in a number of striking ways. It acknowledged the importance for the continuing theological task of neglected traditions, particularly traditions arising out of the sufferings and victories of the downtrodden. By emphasizing the place of experiences of oppression and liberation in theological reflection, the new statement made direct contact with recent discussion of liberation theology. From the latter, it lifted up key themes: regard for poor, disabled, imprisoned, oppressed, and outcast people; the equality of all persons in Jesus Christ; and the openness of the gospel to human diversity. The report also claimed the authority of Wesley's sermons resided not in an article in the church's constitution but in the church's continuing reference to them over three centuries as model expositions of Methodism's common heritage as Christians.

The preliminary report ignited serious discussion in both progressive and conservative camps that increased as the 1988 General Conference approached. Widespread hostility became evident with the appearance of the "Houston Declaration" just weeks before General Conference. Produced by an invited assemblage of lay and clergy evangelicals, tall-steeple pastors, bishops-to-be William Morris and Cornelius Henderson, and theologian Geoffrey Wainwright, and hosted by William "Bill" Hinson of First Church, the declaration applauded the report's stress on primacy of Scripture but assailed the continuance of the quadrilateral. Backers disseminated the "Houston Declaration" to fifty-five thousand clergy and laity.[12] The committee's draft drew critique from the left as well. In "Perfect Love Casts Out Fear," progressives, including many feminist and racial-ethnic leaders, indicated that they saw "no compelling reason" to change the 1972 doctrinal statement, fearing the revised statement "would move the church into a narrow sectarian and repressive stance."[13]

Individuals and groups began to align with one or the other of these two positions. Conspicuously, the Good News caucus supported the former. And the Methodist Federation for Social Action, the Women's Division of the Board of Global Ministries, and the Commission on the Status and Role of Women supported the latter. Professor Thomas Oden of Drew Theological School stirred additional controversy, claiming that the new statement had "abandoned" Wesley's *Sermons* as doctrinal standards and "had eliminated every standard reference to them." Professor John Cobb of Claremont School of Theology contributed an incendiary article, "Is Theological Pluralism Dead in the UMC?" Albert Outler, apparently piqued that his successor and protégé, Richard Heitzenrater, would so totally rewrite his (Outler's) prior effort with the 1972 statement, weighed in with various criticisms.[14]

Debate on the doctrine report at the 1988 General Conference proved strident, often more political than doctrinal, theologizing by catchword, slogan, and innuendo. However, the General Conference legislative committee, chaired by Thomas Langford, dean of Duke Divinity School, negotiated the turbulent, negative waters through a careful consideration of the document and a deliberative process, which became for committee members an adventure in growing unity. Substantive changes in the text were few. Much of the discussion focused on refinements of terminology to address concerns of the whole committee: restore traditional trinitarian language, clarify the relationship between Scripture and the other three elements of the so-called Wesley quadrilateral, reaffirm Wesley's *Sermons* as standards, and strengthen the section on ecumenism. The process and result garnered an overwhelmingly positive approval (94 percent majority) by lay and clergy delegates. Two changes proposed from the floor of the conference drew little discussion and did not pass.[15]

The 1988 version of "Doctrinal Standards and Our Theological Task," enduring into the twenty-first century, functioned in relation to the "Doctrinal Standards," as had the predecessor statement. And as with the 1972 disciplinary statement, the hermeneutic in "Our Doctrinal Heritage" and "Our Theological Task" became far more usable and used than the standards—Articles of Religion, Confession of Faith, Wesley's *Sermons*, *Explanatory Notes*, and General Rules—to which it pointed. (See discussion in chapter 14.) The hermeneutic and its treatment of our "traditional evangelical doctrines" upstaged Wesley's *Sermons*. It did so particularly within the population of persons preparing for leadership under the *Discipline*'s strictures (as local pastors, elders, lay speakers, deacons), within the district and conference boards charged with their oversight, and of course, among the faculties of training programs, Courses of Study, and seminaries. In this restricted but important subset of United Methodist leadership, the theological consensus and balance achieved by the Hunt, Heitzenrater, and Langford effort have had great value. Beyond those cadres, the theological and social concerns of United Methodism's conservative and progressive wings have continued to test the church's unity.

Of particular force in roiling debate has been the Good News insistence that the church- and society-dividing issues of abortion and homosexuality have as much to do with doctrine as with ethics, as we will note below. However, the decades after 1984 also saw the bishops, and particularly the COB, assume a role in the articulation and dissemination of the church's doctrine, one not effectively exercised, perhaps, since the days of Wesley, Coke, and Asbury.[16]

The Teaching Office

The bishops indeed reclaimed national theological, missional, and ethical leadership. Their initiative has been a long time in developing. Ambiguous incentives derived from the 1939 union. In some ways the polity that emerged in 1939 actually accelerated the momentum toward a diocesan episcopacy. Considerable blame could be allocated to the jurisdictional structure and patterns of residence that followed. By electing and deploying bishops on that regional basis, the church effectively imaged the bishops as sectional leaders. The bishops' efforts to reduce their assignments to single conferences and to lengthen tenure therein made them more diocesan than itinerant general superintendents.

On the other hand, as we have seen, the 1939 union provided a foundation for collective episcopal leadership. The southern church brought into union the principle of an effective College of Bishops. Its successor, the Council of Bishops, gave the episcopacy a structural cohesion, a vehicle through which to act collectively on behalf of the whole church. The COB did not immediately reclaim such connectional leadership. It took some time for the COB to overcome two centuries of centrifugal, parochial, and regional inertias. One hurdle, perhaps a fairly high one, was the essential social character of their unity. The bishops made themselves into a great fraternity. They dedicated their gatherings to social and peer-support functions. They treated one another with codes of "southern" deference and courtesy. They became an extended family of regional superintendents gathered for dinner on the grounds. Nevertheless, from 1940 when G. Bromley Oxnam assumed the secretary's office and essentially ran the operation, the COB set agenda, recorded minutes, gained the capacity to act as a body, and possessed a designated (or self-designated) spokesperson.[17]

In reclaiming the teaching office, the bishops had to build on such foundations to develop the will to work together, to set patterns of work that would give them a united voice, and to discipline themselves to labor as a magisterium. Various stimuli encouraged concerted and representative action. The 1968 union and the sense of a fresh start may have had a role. The growing sense of crisis in the church over faltering programs and declining membership demanded initiatives of a connectional nature. The faltering of other leadership, particularly that of the boards and agencies, left space for agency and advocacy. The U.S. National Conference of Catholic Bishops modeled what might be achieved by collective action. And from time to time, the Methodist bishops had enjoyed some measure of similar success with various initiatives, including pastoral letters.[18] Internal structuring, particularly the formation of a Committee on Episcopal Initiatives for Ministry and Mission, focused the council's growing resolve to act collectively. And ecumenical wisdom pointed to the crucial dimension of *episkopé* in the church's exercise of its basic functions. That was concisely summarized in the 1982 Faith and Order publication *Baptism, Eucharist and Ministry*:[19]

> **M29.** Bishops preach the Word, preside at the sacraments, and administer discipline in such a way as to be representative pastoral ministers of oversight, continuity and unity in the Church. They have pastoral oversight of the area to which they are called. They serve the apostolicity and unity of the Church's teaching, worship and sacramental life. They have responsibility for leadership in the Church's mission. They relate the Christian community in their area to the wider Church, and the universal Church to their community. They, in communion with the presbyters and deacons and the whole community, are responsible for the orderly transfer of ministerial authority in the Church.

Into such understandings the bishops lived publicly in the 1980s and so reclaimed something of the teaching mantle of Wesley, Coke, and Asbury. Some of the recovery derived from efforts of individual bishops, exercising a representative teaching authority and gaining the ear or eye of the church. Bishop Richard Wilke, for instance, sounded the alarm on United Methodism's hemorrhaging membership in 1986 with his best-selling *And Are We Yet Alive?*[20] Of the making of bishop-books—to explain polity, to guide and cajole, to interpret Methodist history, to tell their own life stories—there had been and would be no end. Bishop Wilke, however, acted on his book's diagnosis and prescription, persuading the General Board of Discipleship and The United Methodist Publishing House (UMPH) that church renewal could come through an intensive long-term Bible study program geared to train Christian disciples. In March 1986, Wilke gathered a small group of pastors, theologians, laypeople, Christian educators, Bible scholars, publishers, editors, and marketers. Together they developed his idea into DISCIPLE Bible Study and produced a resource combining video instruction from the denomination's leading Scripture scholars with personal reading and discussion. It aimed, as Wilke foresaw, to transform, not merely inform—to develop closer followers of Christ. In DISCIPLE I: *Becoming Disciples through Bible Study,* for instance, participants read more than 70 percent of the Bible in thirty-four weeks, spending an equal number of weeks studying the Old and New Testaments. A study manual guides the daily reading of Scripture and provides expert commentary. A leader and twelve participants meet for two and a half hours each week to watch a ten-minute video, then discuss what they have read. The thought-provoking discussion questions in the leader's guide promote both learning and life application.

UMPH conducted the first training event for leaders for the Bible study in 1987. Over the next fifteen years, it put more than 400,000 people, some beyond the United Methodist family, through training to lead DISCIPLE in their own congregations. The series became one of the publishing house's most successful ventures. And it prospered beyond the English-speaking world. UMPH commissioned translation of the study into French, Cantonese, Mandarin, German, Korean, Spanish, and Russian. In the course of twenty years, three additional long-term studies (DBS-IV) along with four short-term Bible studies were added. By 2006 more than 1.2 million people from 34 denominations had participated in DISCIPLE.[21] To follow up on its success and its agenda, UMPH released *Christian Believer,* a study of core Christian beliefs by J. Ellsworth Kalas and Justo Gonzales. Published in 1999, this adult study explored core Christian beliefs in the DISCIPLE Bible Study family of resources in a thirty-session format examining Scripture in relation to aspects of Christian doctrine.[22]

In 1986, the church also experienced the bishops' capacity for corporate leadership. What really signaled the new day in episcopal teaching—and did so dramatically—was *In Defense of Creation: The Nuclear Crisis and a Just Peace.*[23] The bishops delivered this biblical-theological prophecy against the nuclear arms race, call of the church to peace-making, and critique of the U.S. and Soviet policies of deterrence to all United

Methodist congregations and pastors in a Duke Chapel kickoff service, in a pastoral letter to be read from the pulpit (Sources 1986b), in a forty-page *Guide for Study and Action,* and in a roughly hundred-page foundation document. An Episcopal Initiatives Committee, Dale White, chair, and C. P. Minnick, project coordinator, had employed as drafter Alan Geyer, executive director of the Churches' Center for Theology and Public Policy, and brought an array of other experts to testify in COB sessions. The entire two-year process—from the bishops' study of Scripture, of traditional postures on war and peace, and of commissioned background studies, to hearings and gathering of opinion in draft preparation, to first release, to formal presentation, to the mandated reading in its pastoral letter form, to the study of the larger statement in the congregations—represented an incredibly important experiment in episcopal exercise of the teaching office. Their efforts to motivate church members to face their responsibilities as citizens and Christians for the continuing nuclear arms race earned them both commendation and criticism, but it brought the bishops into a new relationship with the faithful. Here, really for the first time in almost two hundred years, the bishops in united fashion gave theological leadership to the church. Something of the same process of sustained study, research, consulting, reflection, delegated writing, and pastoral exhortation informed the 1990 statement *Vital Congregations, Faithful Disciples: Vision for the Church.*[24] In the interim, the bishops, continuing what had been an established practice of pastoral letters, issued a pastoral on immigration and the plight in American society of legally undocumented people (Sources 1988b).

Other initiatives indicated a greater sense of episcopal agency. To add a collective word on membership attrition to that from Wilke, the COB, supported by the General Board of Discipleship, sponsored a church growth and evangelism event in the fall of 1990 for three thousand lay and clergy persons. The Fort Worth, Texas, "Gathering" combined training, inspirational worship, and addresses by bishops in an effort to encourage and undergird church growth efforts across the denomination. In a pastoral letter for the event, the bishops called individual members and congregations to be "more intentional" in responding to the command of Jesus to teach, baptize, and make disciples. Earlier in 1990, having addressed the urban crisis in a statement the prior year,[25] the bishops named one of their own, Bishop Felton May, to an unprecedented year-long special assignment in Washington, D.C., to provide concentrated leadership in the war on drugs and violence. At year's end, Bishop May returned to his regular post, but continued to serve as a resource person for the COB and as a liaison with the UMC and ecumenical agencies to establish an advocacy campaign to generate more realistic governmental response to the national crisis. May's experience prepared the bishops and the church to launch the Shalom Project after the 1992 Rodney King riots. Several Methodist bishops took the lead in pressuring governments to impose economic sanctions against South Africa as a way to end that country's policy of racial discrimination.

Thereafter followed other initiatives replicating the engagement procedures for teaching the church—on urban ministries, children and poverty, and the children of Africa. The COB addressed pastorals or released position papers on the Middle East, the ERA, racism, terrorism, AIDS, ethnic cleansing, biblical authority, ministry, and evangelism. In 1998, the COB weighed in on homosexuality and homosexual unions and the issues of discipline, order, and unity posed thereby (Sources 1998b), to which we will return below. Increasingly, then, the bishops have used their gatherings to bring in scholars and resource persons, to produce and work over their own position papers, to help them shape pastoral letters and position papers, and to educate them individually and corporately for the exercise of theological leadership for the church.[26] The COB enjoys ongoing staffing from the General Commission on Christian Unity and Interreligious Concerns (GCCUIC), which has helped the bishops guide the denomination's ecumenical investments (COCU/CUIC, bilaterals, WCC, NCC, interreligious—see below). And the COB offers its own knowledge and views to the ecumenical enterprise. In particular, it designates one of its members to be the church's chief ecumenical officer, its spokesperson on matters of doctrine, policy, and practice as they bear on Christian unity and its realization. So the bishops bid to reclaim Asbury's and Wesley's mantle and exercise the teaching office. They now have the resolve, the leadership, and the internal structures[27] to act with something of the unity that the episcopacy could when it was, in effect, one person.

Ministries to/for/by the Oldest and Newest Americans

Native Americans

By 1984, the UMC claimed some 20,000 Native American members in 160 congregations and missions served by about 80 pastors. Of that total, the Oklahoma Indian Missionary Conference (OIMC) reported 8,245 members in 110 congregations, served by 55 pastors and 4 superintendents among 30 tribes in Oklahoma, Texas, and Kansas. The executive committee of the Native American International Caucus (NAIC), meeting in Oklahoma City in 1985, criticized UMC general agencies for not taking seriously Native American leadership and ministry. Reporting on a recent missional priority coordinating committee meeting, Thomas Roughface, an OIMC DS, complained that there were "stacks and stacks of reports and studies by boards and agencies about what they have done for Native Americans, but we see very little actual evidence." Marvin Abram, caucus chairperson, pastor of the Native American UMC in Norwalk, California, and member of the Seneca Nation, expressed frustration that the board staff said, " 'Tell us your needs,' but have taken little action to further Native American ministries and leadership. 'We want self-determination,' " he insisted.[28]

The next quadrennium saw important steps toward that end. In 1987, 140 women in ministry from 40 tribes and 43 annual conferences gathered for the first national meeting in Albuquerque, New Mexico. This Native American Women's Consultation was sponsored by the General Commission on the Status and Role of Women. In 1988, the OIMC gained full conference rights. The General Board of Church and Society (GBCS) elected its first Native American general secretary, Thom White Wolf Fassett (Seneca Nation, New York). NAIC appointed its first (part-time) executive director, Sam Wynn (Lumbee Nation, North Carolina), and presented a vision document—"The Sacred Circle of Life"—to General Conference (Sources 1988a). The statement invited the church to (1) *confess* failures, past and present, (2) *develop* partner relationships and ministries of mutual trust and accountability, and (3) *implement and fund* a plan for congregational and leadership development. General Conference "received" but did not fund or staff the plan. GBGM did, however, adopt a Native American Urban Ministries Initiative targeting three cities: Denver, Seattle, and Los Angeles.[29]

To remind the church of the gifts and contributions made by Native Americans to our society, General Conference added to the church's calendar a Native American Awareness Sunday (after 1992, Native American Ministries Sunday).[30] It urged congregations to undertake planning for the programming and dedicated offering on the third Sunday of Easter in consultation with representatives of the Native American community in their region. The worship, it indicated, should respect the traditions of the Native peoples and may involve repentance and reconciliation between indigenous and immigrant peoples. Resources for such services had been slow in coming. The 1966 *Methodist Hymnal* was the first of any major hymnal to include a Native American hymn, the traditional Dakota "Many and Great, O God" (#148). The 1989 *United Methodist Hymnal* added another, a traditional Kiowa prayer, "Great Spirit, Now I Pray" (#330), plus a Cherokee rendering of the first stanza of "Jesus Loves Me" (#191). A long-sought NAIC and OIMC project finally came to fruition in 1992 when the Board of Discipleship aided in the publication of *Voices*, a collection of Native American hymns and prayers.[31] And the 1992 *Book of Worship* provided hymns and liturgical resources for NAM Sunday. By the twenty-first century, NAM Sunday raised more than $350,000, half of which annual conferences retained to develop and strengthen local Native ministries and the rest of which went to scholarships for Native American students attending UMC-related seminaries and to new and existing urban missions.

By 1989, a year after the ministry initiative launched in Denver, similar ministries were burgeoning in Los Angeles and Seattle, and conversations had started in four other states. By then more than half of the nation's Native Americans lived in major metropolitan areas. Additional exploratory consultations followed in Minneapolis, Chicago, the western part of New York State, and Alaska. Delegates to the NAIC annual meeting celebrated the organization's twenty years of advocacy. "We have never been so visible and such a part of the life of the church as we are today," reported the Reverend Sam

Wynn, the caucus's executive. Wynn went on to pledge that the caucus would rally its forces for passage of a proposed comprehensive plan for Native American ministries mandated by the 1988 General Conference. He also reported that forty UMC annual conferences had developed or were strengthening Native American ministries in their areas. In 1990, when the one hundred members of the General Council on Ministries voted to affirm the global nature of the church by meeting outside the U.S., Native Americans objected. At GCOM's annual meeting a year later (1991), Sam Wynn expressed frustration that the church that declared itself "global" had little knowledge or awareness of indigenous cultures within the U.S.

In response to a NAIC request, the 1992 General Conference opened with a Service of Reconciliation and Healing to observe the five hundredth anniversary of Columbus's arrival in North America, elaborated protocols for a race-and-ethnic-sensitive retelling of that half millennium of history ("Toward a New Beginning Beyond 1992"), as noted added a Native American observance to the church's calendar, and adopted a "Confession to Native Americans."[32] General Conference also adopted and funded a Native American Comprehensive Plan (NACP). By contrast to past missions developed *to* and *for* Native Americans, this plan sought to honor Native American culture, values, traditions, and spirituality. The church pledged to work *alongside* Native Americans in mission and ministry. The plan sought (1) to acknowledge failures, past and present, (2) to develop partner relationships, and (3) to develop ministries of mutual trust and accountability. Ann Saunkeah, Cherokee schoolteacher from Tulsa, became director of the UMC program in 1997.

Among other steps toward self-determination, the Reverend Thomas Roughface of the Ponca Nation became, in 1990, the OIMC superintendent, the first Native American in recent times to hold the quasi-episcopal office and perhaps the first ever. In 1992, an Oklahoma City clergywoman, the Reverend Lois G. Neal, became the first Native American woman superintendent in the UMC. A member of the Cherokee Nation and former pastor of Angie Smith Memorial UMC in Oklahoma City, she began her duties with the forty-two churches in the OIMC Southeast District. One month later, Neal was named dean of the conference cabinet.

In 1994, OIMC celebrated its 150th anniversary. Two years later it adopted a capital fund campaign to plant new churches and to establish volunteers-in-mission "to continue the journey from a mission *of* the church to a mission *with* the church" (that is, to become autonomous and self-supporting). That year OIMC was one of only eleven conferences to pay 100 percent or more of their World Service apportionment. Also in 1996, NAIC appointed a full-time director, Alvin Deer (Kiowa-Creek Nation, Oklahoma), and *Eagle Flights: Native Americans and the Christian Faith*,[33] a congregational study resource (student's book plus leader's guide), became available from Cokesbury. The 1996 General Conference offered a formal apology for the Sand Creek, Colorado, massacre led by Colonel John Chivington, a Methodist pastor, in 1864 and adopted a resolution "Concerning Demeaning Names to Native Americans." The latter critiqued team names and mascots that stereotyped Native peoples as "violent and aggressive." In 2000, NAIC successfully petitioned General Conference to affirm the "Human Rights of Native People of the Americas." General Conference also adopted the resolution "Ecumenical Dialogues on the Native Community." For the next four years the church's Native American Comprehensive Plan focused on spirituality, the common thread that Native Americans share regardless of tribe or nation.[34]

Hispanics

In 1985, the Latina/Latino caucus, MARCHA, issued a vision document, "Hispanic Vision for Century III" (Sources 1985). Taking as signs for the church's future the election of its first Hispanic, Japanese American, and Black woman bishops, the vision statement lamented little progress among Hispanics through the Ethnic Minority Local Church missional priority, identified a variety of chronically enervating conditions, and summoned "the whole denomination" to engage in seven transformative goals.[35] For the first time MARCHA's executive director, Dalila Cruz, and president were both laywomen, and the first national Latino Women's Consultation was held. MARCHA leaders also signaled its determination to support the Sanctuary Movement and work for autonomy for the Methodist Church of Puerto Rico.

In 1986, the first Latina district superintendent was appointed, the Reverend Minerva Carcaño in the Rio Grande Conference. By the end of the year, three Hispanic superintendents had also been appointed outside the predominantly Hispanic Rio Grande and Puerto Rico Conferences. MARCHA had other good news to report that year: fifty-seven new Hispanic congregations had been formed since 1980; representation on boards and agencies increased (twenty-two Hispanic executive staff and fifty-two members of boards and agencies); and publication of Spanish-language resources by the Board of Publications and the Board of Discipleship had increased. The caucus held an important strategy consultation the following May in Denver (1987).

The 1988 General Conference authorized development of a comprehensive national plan for Hispanic ministries. A National Hispanic Ministries Committee, chaired by Bishop Elias Galvan of Phoenix, for the next four years gathered information, assessed demographic trends, surveyed 320 Hispanic congregations about needs and ministries, and in the end drafted a plan for 1992 General Conference.[36] The 1988 General Conference also authorized a Spanish-language translation of the full *Book of Discipline* and adopted a resolution against establishing English as the official language of the U.S., supporting a MARCHA-backed "English-plus" alternative to the "English-only" movement. In a related action, MARCHA vigorously supported the Sanctuary Movement. To the same end, the Council of Bishops issued and General Conference endorsed an important pastoral letter "Undocumented Migration: To Love the Sojourner" (Sources 1988b), urging church members to join them in an effort "to correct the injustices that may be perpetuated" by the 1986 U.S. Immigration and Control Act, to recognize God's preferential option for the "sojourner" (or stranger), and with respect to immigrants "to know them, their circumstances and needs, to love them, to embrace them and their struggle, [and] to bid them welcome to our communities, religious and civil."[37] The 1988 pastoral letter breathed a different spirit than California's 1994 Proposition 187, which cut health, social, and educational services to undocumented immigrants and their children or the similarly adverse 1996 federal Illegal Immigration Reform and Immigrant Responsibility Act.

Over the next quadrennium, the church produced several resources supportive of MARCHA's goals. In 1989, UMC pastor and theological educator Harold Recinos addressed the church in a personal and social book, *Hear the Cry: A Latino Pastor Challenges the Church. The United Methodist Hymnal* (1989) featured eighteen hymns of Latino origin, including one of the most widely sung bilingual hymns, Carlos Rosas's "Cantemos al Señor" ("Let's Sing unto the Lord," #149). The hymn captures the spirit of Psalm 19:1: "The heavens are telling the glory of God; and the firmament proclaims God's handiwork," demonstrates the strong relationship of Latino cultures with nature, and brings the spirit of post–Vatican II Catholicism into engagement with the rich Protestant tradition of great congregational singing. *The United Methodist Book of Worship* (1992) included Mexican Advent and Christmas Eve liturgies, *Las Posadas,* services of preparation for the birth of the Savior and shelter for the newborn babe and the Holy Family.

The 1992 General Conference approved a National Hispanic Ministries Plan, the first coordinated, comprehensive denominational effort to focus on the development and strengthening of Latino ministries in the U.S. Finally a strategy for Latino ministry, one conceived and shaped by Latinos for Latinos, the plan by 2000 had encouraged 61 of the 66 U.S. conferences to develop some sort of ministry to Hispanics. By contrast, when MARCHA organized and began its initiatives in the early 1970s, only 38 conferences had some type of Hispanic ministry. In further actions to reorient its global mission toward the South as well as to the East and West, the General Conference granted autonomy to the Church in Puerto Rico; began a Cuban initiative; and established a permanent church fund, "Encounter with Christ," to provide long-term support and development in Latin America and the Caribbean in areas such as evangelization and new church development; work with women, children, and youth; and community-based health care. In the jurisdictional episcopal elections that summer, the UMC elected a second Latino bishop, Joel Martinez, and assigned him to the Nebraska Area. The previous year, the Reverend Pedro Piron, a pastor in Manhattan, had been named the first Hispanic DS in New York City and assigned to the Long Island West District of the New York Conference. In 1993, the National Ecumenical Council of Hispanic Ministries, an NCC affiliate, organized with a UMC chair, Eli Rivera.

State and federal initiatives on immigration drew further UMC response. In 1994, MARCHA, at its annual meeting, went on record denouncing the passage of California's Proposition 187. In 1996, General Conference concurred on 187 and adopted a fresh resolution on immigration policy, "Immigration and Refugees: To Love the Sojourner."[38] And United Methodist Committee on Relief (UMCOR) launched a new program called "Justice for Our Neighbors." Modeled after a local immigration project in Virginia, it led to the establishment of church-related legal clinics for immigrants at fourteen sites and became an ongoing program.

The same year, MARCHA celebrated its twenty-fifth anniversary in El Paso, Texas, the largest gathering in the organization's history, and for the first time in its history elected a female majority to its executive committee. MARCHA joined efforts to end the Cuban embargo. Two important resources appeared that year, *Obras de Wesley*, a fourteen-volume scholarly translation of the modern critical edition of John Wesley's *Works* and *Mil Voces Para Celebrar*, the first truly Hispanic hymnal and worship book under editorship of Raquel Mora Martinez. In 1997, the UMC and the Methodist Church of Mexico established the Mexico Border Bilateral Mission Committee. And Florida United Methodists renewed their relationship with Cuban Methodists, establishing a covenant to strengthen both ministries. The Florida Conference, for instance, sent work teams to Cuba to rebuild churches and parsonages and to help build Canaan Camp Assembly, a retreat area for Cuban Methodists. That year also saw the new collection of hymns for Hispanic churches: *Cantos Del Pueblo*. In 1999, Jo Harris and Russ Harris published a manual for non-Hispanic churches in ministry with Hispanics, *Partners in the Mighty Works of God*.

By 1999 the National Plan had trained 796 lay missioners and 100 pastor-mentors representing 46 conferences. National and regional facilitators were trained to assist with the training of lay missioners and pastor-mentor teams. Sixty-one of the 66 U.S. conferences had some sort of ministry to Hispanics. A group of Hispanic young people, meeting in Nashville, created a Young Hispanic Methodist Movement. Leaders from MARCHA, the National Plan for Hispanic Ministry, the General Board of Discipleship, the General Board of Global Ministries, and the National Youth Ministry Organization also attended.

In 2000, MARCHA proposed the creation of a Portuguese-language ministry. It endorsed Minerva Carcaño as candidate for bishop in the Western Jurisdiction (elected in 2004 as the first Latina bishop). David Maldonado became the first Latino UMC theological seminary president/dean (Iliff, Denver). General Conference went on record opposing the 1996 immigration act. GBGM launched a $25 million fund-raising initiative dubbed "Encounter with Christ" to help UM churches partner with Methodist churches in nineteen countries throughout Mexico, Central America, South America, and the Caribbean.[39]

Korean Americans

The 1984 General Conference charged GBGM to "consider appropriate missionary structures to strengthen Korean language ministries and new church development."[40] The next year, Korean American Women Clergy (KAWC) gathered at its first national consultation under leadership of the Reverend Heisik Oh, and the National Committee on Korean-American Ministries (NCKAM) was formed under GBGM. By 1987, Korean Mission superintendents had been appointed in each jurisdiction. The first Korean American Mission (KAM), the Eastern Seaboard KAM, covered the region from Maine to Maryland. KAMs followed in the South Central and Western Jurisdictions (1988), the North Central Jurisdiction (1993), and the Southeastern Jurisdiction (1995).The number of Korean American churches more than doubled, from 105 in 1982 to 212 in 1986, according to unofficial figures assembled by general agencies of the UMC. The Northeastern Jurisdiction had the largest number. The Western Jurisdiction had the second largest number.[41] By 1987, Korean-language congregations accounted for more than half of the UMC churches formed in the U.S. since 1980.[42] By the turn of the twenty-first century, the 6 congregations from 1970 had increased to about 360, in addition to which there were 260 Korean Methodist Church (KMC) congregations. By 2000, the KMC had contributed 41 percent of the UMC's approximately 500 Korean American pastors, perhaps not surprising since 95 percent were born in Korea. Only 20 of the 360 Korean American congregations were English speaking. Of the 90 Korean American clergywomen, fewer than 21 percent served Korean-language churches.[43]

The church took its time in launching enabling initiatives for Korean Americans. Trial worship materials were created as early as 1984, but it took until 2002 for the publication of *Come, Let Us Worship,* the first Korean-English hymnal with liturgies, and then jointly produced with the Presbyterians. In the late 1980s and early 1990s, Koreans struggled on a number of fronts:

- With UMC officialdom, church organizational procedures, and cumbersome English-only ministerial education and credentialing processes;
- With a constituency of professionals, managers, health workers, and others well educated and with children who expected bilingual ministerial services;
- With non-Korean pastors and congregations when church facilities were shared;
- With other Asian American and ethnic groups competing for ecclesial, economic, and societal space and prerogative.

In 1990, the Council of Bishops named seven bishops to meet with leaders of the Methodist Church in Korea early in 1991 to "regularize the relationship between the two churches." Also in 1990, a Korean-language program journal, *United Methodist Family,* began publication. The Reverend Jungrea Chung was chosen as the first editor. By 1992, the National Association of Korean American United Methodist Churches (NAKAUMC) began to advocate and lobby for a nongeographical Korean-language conference that would unite some three hundred Korean congregations across the U.S., would compete more effectively with the Seoul-based Korean Methodist Church and its missionary activities in the U.S., and would provide something of the latter's supportive cultural and linguistic services. The caucus modeled its plan after the Spanish-speaking Rio Grande Conference. General Conference said no in 1992 and again in 1996 (Sources 1996a).

The 1992 General Conference did authorize the formation of a committee to explore ways in which the general church could assist development of Asian American ministries in a comprehensive manner. That summer the Northeastern Jurisdiction elected a Korean American to the episcopacy, Hae Jong Kim, and NAKAUMC began a more serious drive for nongeographical conferences for Korean American churches. In 1994, GBGM published A Manual on Shared Facilities[44] to ease tensions between congregations sharing the same building, offering suggestions on leadership responsibilities, property, and budgets. The General Commission on Religion and Race also began offering resources for facility sharing at the same time. NAKAUMC laid out a more formal proposal for Korean American missionary conferences in an open letter to delegates to the 1996 General Conference (Sources 1996a). Some Korean American clergywomen and GBGM lobbied against the plan, and General Conference again rejected it. General Conference did approve the proposed comprehensive plan for Asian American ministries that had been formulated over the quadrennium. Funded at $900,000, it addressed congregational development, leadership training, community outreach ministry, and language resources development. This Asian American Language Ministry (AALM) study program has served as an important resource for developing new ministries as well as strengthening existing ones in the Asian American community. General Conferences 2000, 2004, and 2008 continued substantial appropriations for the program. By 2004 ten different Asian American ethnic groups with fifteen languages were being supported by AALM.

In 1997, Korean American caucus leader Dal Joon Woon repeated the call for a nongeographical Korean American Conference. The UMC's national Task Force on Korean American Ministries organized for 1997–2000, chose officers, and began work toward recommendations to the 2000 General Conference. In April 1998, the GBGM commissioned the first group of Korean American "mission pastors," part of a plan to help developing congregations become chartered as official Korean United Methodist churches. The next month, the first national Korean-American United Methodist Mission Convocation met in Los Angeles. It offered sessions on sensitivity training, ministry with second-generation Korean Americans, and development of leadership roles for the growing number of Korean American clergywomen. Most of the seventy-plus ordained UMC Korean American clergywomen serve non-Korean or multicultural ministries. Also in 1998, United Methodist Communications launched a bimonthly magazine for Korean UMC pastors and lay leaders: *United Methodists in Service.* The 2000 General Conference responded to and approved several Korean and Asian Caucus proposals: (1) a fund to expand ministries for more than fifteen Asian-language groups, including Cambodian, Chinese, Filipino, Formosan, Hmong, Japanese, Korean, Laotian, South Asian, and Vietnamese; (2) a Council on Korean American Ministries with program funding; and (3) adoption of a bilingual Korean-English hymnal as an official church resource.

Abortion: Protecting Life, but Whose?

Earlier phases of the church's concern with abortion we treated in the last chapter. Bowing to pressure, the 1984 General Conference altered the 1972 Social Principles statement to more clearly imply that the UMC considers "abortion on demand" morally wrong. As amended, the Social Principles continued to acknowledge "tragic conflicts of life with life that may justify abortion" and stated support of the "legal option of abortion under proper medical procedures." In 1987, nine United Methodists led by North Carolina pastor Paul Stallsworth formed "a national organization to help United Methodists deal with our church's inability to minister to the problems of our pro-abortion society," as he later explained.[45] The organization, which named itself the Taskforce on United Methodists on Abortion and Sexuality, functions as an unofficial anti-abortion caucus of the denomination, contests UMC involvement in the Religious Coalition for Abortion Rights (RCAR), and presses to circumscribe or eliminate the church's sanction of abortion. Under such guidance, the 1988 General Conference added to the "Abortion" section of the Social Principles the proviso, "We cannot affirm abortion as an acceptable measure of birth control, and we unconditionally reject it as a means of gender selection."[46]

In 1990, Stallsworth and colleagues launched a newsletter, *Lifewatch,* and the same year convened thirty UMC leaders, primarily from the Southeast. They issued the Durham Declaration (Sources 1990), calling on the church to address abortion theologically, and offered a first attempt to do just that. By invitation, affirmation of faith, and proclamation (by pledges) of the message of salvation in Jesus Christ, they summoned United Methodists to "let the children come to me" and to rely on God's sufficient grace "to meet the massive test" of abortion. Viewing the test as akin to that of slavery, it accused the denomination of treating in political terms what has fundamentally to do with God's creation and ought to be constitutive of the church's mission. Among the nine pledges or "promises" that the declaration made and invited other United Methodists to make was this:

We pledge, with God's help, to teach our churches that the unborn child is created in the image of God and is one for whom the Son of God died.... So the life of this child is not ours to take. Therefore, it is sin to take this child's life for reasons whether of birth control, gender selection, convenience, or avoidance of embarrassment.

The document also urged United Methodists "to become a church that hospitably provides a safe refuge for the so-called 'unwanted child' and mother." Although the document pledged "to offer the hope of God's mercy and forgiveness" to women who obtain elective abortions, it contrasted with the church's existing teaching on abortion by giving no indication that abortion is ever a justifiable option for Christians. Signers of the declaration included retired UMC bishops Ole Borgen, William Cannon, Ralph Dodge, and Lance Webb; Duke Divinity School professors Stanley Hauerwas, William Willimon (later elected to the episcopacy), and Geoffrey Wainwright; Drew Theological School professor Thomas Oden; and the Reverend Donald Wildmon, president of the conservative American Family Association.[47]

Two years later, United Methodist participation in the Religious Coalition for Abortion Rights was warmly debated at the 1992 General Conference but affirmed by an 84 percent majority vote. Delegates were assured that neither the Board of Global Ministries nor the Board of Church and Society had given financial support to the RCAR since 1986, although both boards had seats on the RCAR board. At the end of 1993, RCAR moved to larger quarters in Washington, D.C., thus leaving space it rented in the United Methodist Building.[48] That same year, abortion terrorists wreaked deadly violence at birth control clinics across the country. In the wake of the murders and with a renewed sense of urgency, some UMC clergy set to work across the country to reestablish the old tradition of public clergy support for Planned Parenthood and the entire pro-choice movement. Despite efforts by pro-life voices in the church, the 1996 General Conference defeated a "rights of the unborn" addendum to its pro-choice-with-stipulations stance on abortion. Delegates also voted to continue support for the Religious Coalition for Reproductive Choice (RCRC, previously RCAR).

Anti-abortion strategy, in church as in state, continued to chip away at language protective of choice. The 2000 General Conference, for instance, voted to add a sentence to the church's statement on abortion: "We oppose the use of late-term abortion known as dilation and extraction (partial-birth abortion) and call for an end of this practice except when the physical life of the mother is in danger and no other medical procedure is available, or in the case of severe fetal anomalies incompatible with life."[49] Less conciliatory than Stallsworth and *Lifewatch*, the Institute on Religion and Democracy (IRD) and its UM*Action* continued to vilify the church's Women's Division, the General Board of Church and Society, and progressive church leaders generally on abortion and other culture war issues.

Homosexuality: Reconciliation, Transformation, or Schism?

Wide diversity and confusion continued to trouble church and society over the issue of human sexuality, especially homosexuality, in the last decades of the twentieth century. An official prohibition in the *Discipline* against ordination of gay men and lesbians became a key Good News agenda item for and the central "gay issue" at the 1984 General Conference. The delegates approved "fidelity in marriage and celibacy in singleness" as a standard for all ordained clergy. However, when the Judicial Council was consulted and declared that the "seven last words," as the statement became commonly known, did not forbid gay and lesbian clergy, General Conference adopted a stronger prohibition. This statement explicitly spelled out eligibility: "Since the practice of homosexuality is incompatible with Christian teaching, self-avowed practicing homosexuals are not to be accepted as candidates, ordained as ministers, or appointed to serve in The United Methodist Church."[50]

While General Conference creates church law, it falls to annual conferences and their bishops to interpret the law. What did "self-avowed practicing homosexuals" mean? Several conferences and bishops sought to define it. Many, noting the absence of a comma separating "self-avowed" and "practicing," thought orientation alone no bar to ordination. In an April 1987 statement the Council of Bishops complained that "unless 'self-avowed' homosexuals admit that they are 'practicing' that lifestyle, the decision to ordain them rests with the clergy members of each annual conference, not a bishop or the Council of Bishops."[51] Confusion reigned.

Affirmation (see chapter 14) continued its efforts to end confusion by making the church more welcoming to gays and lesbians and by removing restrictions such as that just passed. Through its Reconciling Congregation Program (RCP), formed on the eve of the 1984 General Conference, it made covenant with congregations, as well as annual conferences, general commissions, and campus ministry units. As this networking expanded and advocacy grew, RCP and Affirmation moved ahead to develop a unifying theology for the cause and resources through which to transmit it. It commissioned position papers. And in 1985 RCP launched a quarterly magazine to further educate the church about homosexuality and reconciling ministries, *Manna for the Journey*, later renamed *Open Hands*. At successive General Conferences, beginning with that of 1988, RCP has coordinated a public reconciling witness by constituents of the RCP movement. By the early 1990s, fifty congregations, four annual conferences, and one general agency (GCCUIC) had committed themselves to hospitality, healing, and hope. In 1996 a Reconciling Parents Network, MoSAIC (Methodist Students for an All-Inclusive Church), and United Methodists of Color for a Fully Inclusive Church formed. These groups organized with the support of the national RCP office but were independently led. Following a survey of constituents across the denomination in the fall of 2000, the RCP board decided to change the name of the movement to more accurately reflect the movement and better coordinate the efforts of the several reconciling groups. RCP became the Reconciling Ministries Network.[52]

To clarify the church's mind in quite a different direction and in anticipation of the 1988 General Conference, as we have already noted, a carefully selected number of theologically and politically conservative pastors and seminary professors gathered in Houston to strategize and adopt an agenda for the upcoming conference. Conferees endorsed a three-part Houston Declaration bemoaning a "crisis of faith." The declaration commented in turn on "the Primacy of Scriptures," "The Trinity," and "The Ordained Ministry." The third section, devoted entirely to the matter of homosexuality, labeled homosexual practice as sinful, urged support of ministries that helped gay men and lesbians change their lifestyle, even if their orientation was immutable, and called it "unacceptable in the context of the Christian faith" for gay and lesbians to "be ordained to ministry or continue in representative positions within the Church."[53] Host church pastor Bill Hinson and Professor Geoffrey Wainwright of Duke Divinity School led in drafting the document. The Houston group sent the statement to all UMC clergy and all local church lay leaders, a mailing of more than 55,000. A laity statement, "A Call to Action," which supported the Houston Declaration, was released to the church in early March.[54]

A rebuttal by progressives, "Perfect Love Casts Out Fear," issued in December by fifty pastors and seminary professors and signed by more than one hundred other church leaders, charged that the Houston statement presented "truths as Wesleyan which are anathema to the spirit of Wesley and Methodism." Noting that the "diversity of our people is the glory of this UMC," the declaration maintained, "They do not speak for us. They do not speak for us as women. They do not speak for persons of color. They do not speak for Wesley. We pray that they do not speak for the General Conference." As to the Houston Declaration's emphatic rejection of gays and lesbians, the dissenters charged:

> The Bible does not have a great deal to say about homosexuality. In the original language, the term is not used. Whatever homosexual acts are mentioned, the acts are always committed in a very negative context, such as adultery, promiscuity, violence or idolatrous worship. We ignore contextual exegesis at our peril. The Bible knows nothing of sexual orientation and leaves open many questions which are not best served by saying "persons may not be able to change their sexual orientation; persons can change their life-style."[55]

Responding to efforts by other groups to "liberalize" the UMC's stance against homosexuality, the denomination's bishops issued a "statement of concern" during their November 1987 meeting. It called upon all United Methodists to "join with us in being faithful to the standards, 'fidelity in marriage and celibacy in singleness,' which have been adopted through the struggles of our covenant community of faith over the years." Their statement was prepared in response to a blunt presidential address given early in the body's week-long meeting by Bishop Earl Hunt of Florida. Raising the specter of schism, Hunt urged colleagues to lead the church in "warfare against evil," beginning with racism and sexual immorality, especially homosexuality. On the latter issue Bishop Hunt said, "I believe the intercession of episcopal leadership on this issue is warranted because of the involvement of basic principles of historic Christian teaching." The bishop also cautioned against compromise:

> Our collegiality with friends and coworkers who favor a more liberal perspective has often made us reluctant to voice convictions which might offend them; and so we have risked becoming *unintentional accomplices in the perpetration of a monstrous and fatal compromise*.[56]

Ironically, as the writers of the Houston Declaration were organizing support for their anti-gay agenda and as Bishop Hunt was firing up his episcopal colleagues, one of their number, retired Bishop Finis Crutchfield of Houston, died allegedly of AIDS. When the Crutchfield family implied that the virus had been acquired through Crutchfield's acts of pastoral care to persons with AIDS, the Texas gay community broke its silence and outed Crutchfield as a gay man who lived a double life—a heterosexual bishop and a sexually active gay men with multiple sex partners.[57]

The 1988 General Conference reaffirmed the UMC's negative legislation on gay and lesbian issues by a wide margin. Concerning homosexuality, a statement that "compassionate evangelicals" could support was added to the incompatible statement: "Although we do not condone the practice of homosexuality, and consider this practice to be incompatible with Christian teaching, *we affirm that God's grace is available to all. We commit ourselves to be in ministry for and with all persons*." The italicized portion of this sentence was new.[58] By a narrow margin, the conference approved an official four-year study of homosexuality. Fourteen years earlier (1974), as we noted in the last chapter, the church's national youth organization had been first to call for a churchwide study of the subject, a plea rejected at every General Conference up to 1988.[59] An addition to the Social Principles statement called the UMC "to take the leadership role in bringing together the medical, theological, and social science disciplines to address this most complex issue"—human sexuality.[60]

Although roiled by intense debate on homosexuality, the 1988 General Conference proved able to separate the issue of AIDS from that debate and made only oblique allusions to it in the denomination's first comprehensive treatment: "AIDS and the Healing Ministry of the Church." The statement proposed broad programmatic recommendations in the best tradition of Methodist activism. It directed church agencies and congregations to develop a plan for ministry to persons with AIDS and to act to change public policy, especially in the area of civil rights for persons with AIDS. In a second resolution, "Resources for AIDS Education," the UMC mandated an education program to be implemented through the entire church by the several general boards most directly concerned with the AIDS issue.[61] Affirmation served as a key resource behind the scenes in developing the UMC's response to the AIDS epidemic.[62]

To counter the highly successful Reconciling Congregation Program of progressives, a group of conservatives in the California-Nevada Conference gathered in October 1988 and, led by the Reverend Robert Kuyper, formed the Transforming Congregation Program (TCP). The January-February 1989 *Good News* introduced the TCP to caucus readership. Kuyper later described the ministry of TCP for *Good News* readers as a theological and medical concern. Homosexuality is a sin that can be forgiven and a sickness that can be cured:

> The Transforming Congregation Program is based on the passage in Romans 12:2, "And do not be conformed to this world, but be transformed by the renewing of your mind. . . ." The TCP is a program for United Methodist churches. Its premise is there's hope for the homosexual; transformation is possible. Our churches should be better informed about homosexuality. They should support ex-gay ministries both prayerfully and financially.[63]

Good News adopted the movement as a task force and supported its development of the TCP by providing a $10,000 start-up grant that enabled the organization to pay a small stipend to Kuyper, pastor of Trinity UMC, Bakersfield, as national coordinator and to provide a part-time secretary. TCP became a separate ministry in 1996, and in 1998, the organization hired layman Jim Gentile as full-time executive director.[64]

The study committee created by the 1988 General Conference worked over the next quadrennium, gathering testimony from experts in biblical studies, theology, ethics, and the sciences; hearing grassroots United Methodists share their experiences; and mulling over and debating materials and contributions. Interim reports showed the community hopelessly divided on whether to lift or reinforce the church's ban on ordained practicing homosexuals. After its four years of information gathering, the study committee on homosexuality agreed to disagree about what the church can and cannot affirm with regard to homosexuality. And so it reported to General Conference eight "Things the Church Can Responsibly Teach" and ten "Things the Church Cannot Responsibly Teach" on the subject of homosexuality (Sources 1992).[65] Nevertheless, at the close of the substantial report, the overwhelming majority of the committee concluded certain assertions to be true:

> a) the seven biblical references and allusions cannot be taken as definitive for Christian teaching about homosexual practices because they represent cultural patterns of ancient society and not the will of God;

b) the scientific evidence is sufficient to support the contention that homosexuality is not pathological or otherwise an inversion, developmental failure, or deviant form of life as such, but is rather a human variant, one that can be healthy and whole;

c) the emerging scholarly views in biblical studies, ethics, and theology support a view that affirms homosexual relationships that are covenantal, committed and monogamous;

d) the witness to God's grace of lesbian and gay Christians in the life of the Church supports these conclusions.[66]

The 1992 General Conference "received" the report, rejected the recommendations of the study committee on homosexuality, but directed that the report be made available for study in congregations throughout the denomination. The report, therefore, did not represent the official position of the UMC. The Social Principles statements remained policy. By 1994 the report was in print and being used for study in local UMC congregations.

The study committee report captured the church's indecision. Affirmation had led a coalition of progressive UMC groups at the 1992 General Conference to press for full inclusion, but to no avail. Conference delegates did vote to include two sections in the Social Principles that supported the human and civil rights of gay men and lesbians. Later in 1992, charges against the Reverend Jeanne Knepper, a lesbian, became one of the first cases to go to the Judicial Council. The council ruled that she continue to be appointed by a bishop to ministry in the denomination. Early in the 1996 General Conference, fifteen bishops broke ranks and spoke out against church policies, highlighting the depth of division among United Methodists. The bishops' statement, which was released to the press, read in part:

We, the undersigned bishops... believe it is time to break the silence and state where we are on this issue that is hurting and silencing countless faithful Christians. We will continue our responsibility to order and discipline of the church but urge our United Methodist churches to open the doors in gracious hospitality to all our brothers and sisters in the faith.[67]

In spite of this admonition, other lobbying efforts, and statements in favor of change, the 1996 General Conference not only reaffirmed the UMC's exclusionary rules but also included a new prohibition in the Social Principles regarding gay unions: "Ceremonies that celebrate homosexual union shall not be conducted by our ministers and shall not be conducted in our churches."[68]

The 1996 prohibition against holy unions had not been UMC's first word about same-sex unions. The 1972 Social Principles had been permissive, declaring "we do not recommend marriage between two persons of the same sex."[69] Since this legislation did not specifically prohibit holy *unions*, such services had been celebrated, usually quietly, by UMC clergy from the early 1970s. The Reverends Cecil Williams in San Francisco (1965), William Alberts in Boston (1973), and Paul Abels in New York (1977) conducted some of the earliest documented UMC holy unions, with considerable notice by the press.[70] As word spread about these ceremonies, some United Methodists rejoiced; others were deeply troubled. Banning such unions began around 1990 when Bishop Joseph Yeakel forbade a Washington, D.C., congregation from holding such a service, stating it would violate church law.[71] Several other bishops imposed similar bans. Holy unions suddenly became a flash point for heightened conflict between conservatives and progressives. Attempts by two conferences, Minnesota and Troy (upstate New York and Vermont), to allow congregations or pastors discretion on such unions were appealed to the Judicial Council. In a decision in October 1993, the Judicial Council ruled that only the General Conference had the authority to establish the church's rites and rituals. This ruling set the stage for decisive action by the 1996 General Conference. During the same year, the church's stance echoed politically as the U.S. Congress passed and President Clinton signed the Defense of Marriage Act, which defined marriage as being "between a man and a woman."

Holy unions heightened conflict between conservatives and progressives within the UMC over the new quadrennium. Groups lined up to attack or defend the ban on same-sex unions. Progressives issued a "Statement of Conscience," dated January 1, 1997, along with the document "In All Things Charity," drafted by fifteen clergy and signed by thirteen hundred UMC clergy across the nation who vowed to continue to celebrate holy unions.[72] Later that year signers and their Affirmation friends across the church formed a Web-based Covenant Relationship Network (CORNET) to support the right of UMC clergy to perform holy unions.[73] Conservatives countered with "The More Excellent Way: God's Plan Reaffirmed" manifesto, urging those who seek acceptance of homosexuality in all its forms to find other venues than "UM pulpits, boards, agencies, educational institutions and other affiliated entities" to express their views.[74]

A request in 1997 for a union service at Emory University elicited permission, denunciation by trustee Bishop Lindsey Davis and others, controversy within the school's alumni, faculty, and student communities, and finally a policy permitting such celebrations for Emory-related persons by chaplains whose denominations permit them. The same year, the Reverend Jimmy Creech, pastor of First UMC, Omaha, Nebraska, performed a covenant service for two women after his bishop requested that he refrain from doing so. Charges were successfully brought against him, and after his second holy union and church trial in North Carolina, Creech's ministerial credentials were revoked. In (Sources 1998a) Jimmy Creech defends his disobedience at his trial. As a layperson, Creech continued to proclaim that "the church, not gays had sinned" and to campaign for gay unions.[75] Later that spring the Council of Bishops issued a pained pastoral statement on holy unions in hopes of healing the rift (Sources 1998b).[76] In August, the Judicial Council determined the disciplinary prohibition against gay unions to be enforceable, notwithstanding the law's curious placement in the Social Principles, a matter that the decision examines (Sources 1998c).[77]

Several congregations and their pastors continued to defy the ban. In October 1998 the Reverend Gregory Dell celebrated a holy union of two men in his Chicago church, which resulted in a one-year suspension from ministry without pay.[78] In a major act of ecclesiastical disobedience more than one hundred clergy co-officiated at a holy union in California in January 1999. Organized by the Reverend Donald Fado, pastor of St. Mark's UMC of Sacramento, the holy union celebrated the relationship of life partners Jeanne Barnett and Ellie Charlton, active laywomen within the California-Nevada Conference (Barnett was the conference lay leader; Charlton was a member of the conference board of trustees) and long-term Affirmation members. Complaints were filed against sixty-eighty of the California-Nevada Conference clergy, dubbed the "Sacramento 68," who co-officiated at the "holy union." The bishop responsible for the California-Nevada Conference, Melvin Talbert, announced that he was handling the charges in the way mandated by the *Book of Discipline*, but called the charges an "act of injustice," adding, "I will not be silenced. I will continue . . . working to change the position of our church to be more in keeping with the teachings and compassion of Jesus." A hearing in February 2000 by the conference Committee on Investigation found insufficient cause to order a church trial.[79] Almost immediately, complaints were filed against Bishop Talbert for allowing the committee to reach a conclusion that seemed to ignore the facts of the case and the laws of the denomination. The complaints against Bishop Talbert were dismissed in August.

The Methodist Federation for Social Action long supported same-sex unions and ordination for gays and lesbians and was active around the church trials of the Reverends Jimmy Creech, Greg Dell, and the Sacramento 68. Following the murder of Matthew Shepard in 1998, the UMC's two gay caucuses, Affirmation and Reconciling Congregation Program, joined the Human Rights Campaign and others in a national movement supporting hate-violence legislation to protect lesbian, gay, bisexual, and transgender Americans.

Theologizing Left and Right

Much of the church's theological formulation takes place in the quiet of clergy and faculty offices. But as we have seen, contest and controversy stimulate research and reflection as well. The Re-Imagining Conference of November 1993 (treated in the final section below) both expressed and occasioned theologizing. This national coming-out party for theological feminism caused a stir in the churches. Women bishops, feminist leaders, and other progressives applauded the conference. However, almost immediately,

Good News and especially its women's affiliate, RENEW, charged heresy and sexual perversion. In a retrospective, Riley Case affirmed, "Every Christian truth at the core of the faith—the Trinity, the Incarnation, the Atonement, the primacy of Scripture, the supremacy of Christ—was either denied outright or at least undercut by one or more of the speakers at the Conference."[80] A number of progressive women and two key UMC agencies, COSROW and the Women's Division, immediately announced their support for embattled church leaders who attended the Minneapolis conference (Sources 1994a).[81] The event came to symbolize, for Good News, embedded liberalism.

Conservatives in the church, certainly since the emergence of Good News, had complained of theological drift, liberal hold on bureaucratic reins, the leftward tilt on seminary faculties, the bishops' inattention to doctrine and doctrinal discipline, and until 1988, the sanction of such by the *Discipline*. Increasingly, evangelicals and conservatives framed concerns about abortion and homosexuality in theological and biblical terms. In Houston (1988), Durham (Sources 1990), DuPage (1990), Louisville (1990), and Memphis (1992) declarations, Good News and company interlaced social and theological concerns and, with each, added campaigners to the coalition. United Methodism's problems went deeper than faulty communication, flagging connectionalism, and indifferent leadership to apostasy. United Methodists must confess the uniqueness of Jesus Christ as the only Savior and renew their dedication to holy living and world evangelization. Over successive strategy sessions, Good News etched bold prescriptions for Methodist reform: (1) enact membership requirements; (2) abolish guaranteed clergy appointments; (3) begin automatic four-year clergy appointments; (4) add laypeople to boards of ordained ministry; (5) give laity a voice in the executive session of the annual conference; (6) bring back local preachers; (7) enhance consultation in the process of appointing pastors; (8) make apportionments voluntary; (9) highlight preaching and worship services versus business at annual conference meetings; (10) make youth ministry a missional priority; (11) put the ministerial Education Fund on a voucher system and funds directly in student hands, not seminary coffers; (12) remove the trust clause, which prevents splinter groups from taking church property away from the denomination; (13) split the Board of Global Ministries; (14) retire the quota system; and (15) make bishops lead.

In the spring before the Re-Imagining Conference, leadership from the Good News board held two successive meetings, which included Thomas Oden of Drew, Maxie Dunnam, then in Memphis, later to be president of Asbury Seminary, Bill Hinson from Houston, John Ed Mathison of Frazer Memorial, Montgomery, and Bishop William Cannon, to plan a Consultation on the Future of the Church for the following year. Invitations went to a hundred church leaders for an April 1994 meeting in Atlanta, from which came the prophetic judgment that United Methodism faces an either/or of "abandoning the Christian faith" or leading a new awakening (Sources 1994b). Among signers of this "Invitation" were Bishops William Cannon, Earl Hunt Jr., Richard Looney, Mack Stokes, and William Morris. From this meeting came another a year later, also in Atlanta, with some nine hundred attendees, consternation courtesy of the Women's Division, to found the Confessing Movement. Doubtless with an eye to too much feminist re-imagining, they declared that the UMC had abandoned classical Christianity and "lost its immune system with regard to false teaching."[82] Pledging to contend for the ancient classical ecumenical faith within United Methodism and to affirm Jesus Christ as Son, Savior, and Lord, the new movement claimed that the UMC *was a confessional church* in principle, if not in practice, because of constitutional established doctrinal standards. So the Confessing Movement dedicated itself to "repudiate teachings and practices that misuse principles of inclusiveness and tolerance to distort the doctrine and discipline of the church" and to "contend for the apostolic faith."[83]

Progressive Methodists responded in a widely circulated February 1996 open letter, "A Critical Challenge to the Confessing Movement," signed by thirteen clergy, including five pastors and five faculty members at UMC seminaries. It charged that the movement aimed to make bishops, clergy, and church members "confess" a specific interpretation of Scripture and core beliefs and claim that other world religions were not means of salvation. These statements, they argued, contradicted a tradition extending back to Wesley that not only affirmed a variety of theologies within the denomination, but also respected and celebrated the diversity of world religions through which God continues to speak.[84]

The continued controversy over homosexuality, the authority of the Bible, and interpretation or applicability of specific parts of Scripture posed the possibility of schism, indeed, rumblings of just that. In an effort at peacemaking over these issues, GCCUIC General Secretary Bruce Robbins held diversity dialogues in Nashville (1997) and Dallas (1998). Could theological liberals and conservatives live in the same United Methodist house? Some of the twenty-two participants in the first of these extraordinary meetings were not so sure. They had difficulty even being in the presence of people with highly different worldviews and theological perspectives. On the other hand, one person expressed the hope that they might at least coexist under the same roof, even if in separate rooms, and that they might have an occasional meeting together. That metaphor was but one that surfaced in the meeting and was captured by GCCUIC. Many attendees were affiliated with unofficial caucuses and renewal movements on the right and the left that have for decades castigated one another. That name-calling and stereotyping must stop, insisted several members at the outset. The most significant breakthrough came well into the second day when members pushed for identifying and dealing with issues that threatened the unity of the church. The theological Diversity Dialogue Team continued its discussion at a second meeting in Dallas in February 1998 and reported its findings to the church. One of the most fruitful outcomes was a set of

"Guidelines for Civility in The United Methodist Church." Those along with efforts to map areas of agreement and disagreement appear in GCCUIC's published report (Sources 1998d) on these conversations, *In Search of Unity: A Conversation with Recommendations for the Unity of The United Methodist Church*.[85] The Diversity Dialogue Team named the polarization, noting the increasingly hardened stances of "compatibilists" and "incompatibilists" within the church:

> Compatibilists believe that both sides on the issue of the morality of homosexual behavior and the nature and status of divine revelation can be held together within the same denomination.... Incompatibilists do not believe that these divergent judgments can be housed indefinitely within the same denomination.

Then the Dialogue Team identified ways by which compatibilists and incompatibilists could receive and create the unity that Christ wills, outlining eight action steps and recommending the reading of John Wesley's sermonic injunctions to unity: "On Schism," "A Caution against Bigotry," and "Catholic Spirit." GCCUIC has led United Methodism in more conventional ecumenical endeavors as well.

United Methodism's "Other" Ecumenical Fronts

At its birth, the UMC took a giant step toward Christian unity, adopting a major new commitment, one open rather than closed (or family style—Methodists-of-the-world-unite style). The resolution, at a point ironically at which family-style marriage had been consummated, acknowledged the gospel imperatives toward unity and pledged United Methodist continued participation in the ecumenical movement at all levels. Acknowledging the anti-Catholic bias of our eighteenth-century Articles of Religion, the 1970 General Conference adopted a "Resolution of Intent—with a View to Unity," reaffirmed in 2000, "henceforth to interpret all our Articles, Confession and other standards of doctrine in consonance with our best ecumenical insights and judgment." In the revised doctrinal statement of 1988, "Our Theological Task," the church committed itself to "the theological, biblical and practical mandates for Christian unity."[86] And successive General Conferences have embedded affirmations of Christian unity as the official policy and earnest hope of the denomination and statements on its several ecumenical endeavors throughout the *Discipline* and *The Book of Resolutions of The United Methodist Church*.[87]

This transformation in Methodism's ecumenical project had been a long time coming. United Methodism and its predecessor churches participated strongly and actively in the several initiatives that have fed the ecumenical movement. In the founding of the Evangelical Alliance in London in 1846, Stephen Olin, president of Wesleyan University, Connectictut, pledged the MEC's cordial cooperation. And Methodists participated in the dozen meetings in the nineteenth century of this transatlantic Protestant gathering, as also in the several meetings of its American branch, constituted in 1867. Of the dialogues and conversations between and among the several Methodist churches and the United Brethren and Evangelical Churches that eventuated in the Methodist (1939), EUB (1946), and United Methodist (1968) unions, we have already taken note, as also of American Methodist participation from 1881 onward in the Ecumenical Methodist Conferences (now World Methodist Council).

In the late-nineteenth- and twentieth-century efforts at missionary cooperation and at unity in life and work, faith and order, Methodists provided key leadership. John R. Mott, a Methodist layperson, participant in the Student Volunteer Movement and staff for the YMCA, helped found (1895) and then led till 1930 the World Student Christian Federation, which in turn helped launch both the International Missionary Council (1921) and the World Council of Churches (1948).[88] Mott, an active figure in cooperative relief in WWI and in both Faith and Order and Life and Work conferences, fittingly preached for the WCC's inaugural assembly and was elected its honorary president. MEC mission executive Frank Mason North and UM Bishop William Bell played major roles in the 1908 founding of the Federal Council of Churches, a Protestant body of thirty-three churches, committed to securing "a larger combined influence for the churches of Christ in all matters affecting the moral and social condition of the people, so as to promote the application of the law of Christ in every relation of human life."[89] Among other Methodists contributing to ecumenical endeavor—leadership in the National Council of Churches, observers at Vatican II, participation in the Consultation on Church Union, multilateral, bilateral, and interreligious dialogues—were Bishops G. Bromley Oxnam[90] and William R. Cannon; theologians Albert C. Outler, J. Robert Nelson, John Deschner, and Geoffrey Wainwright; GCCUIC staff Jeanne Audrey Powers and Bruce Robbins; COCU executive Gerald F. Moede; and Harvard champion of interreligious studies and dialogue Diana Eck.

In COCU's first decade, the nine U.S. communions, including Methodists, the EUBC, and the three Black Methodist denominations, reached sufficient agreement on ministry and sacraments to formulate in 1970 a plan for merger and the creation of a new ecclesial body. The plan for a megadenomination failed, and COCU began exploration of nonstructural forms of unity. In 1974, Moede, a major interpreter of COCU's vision, became general secretary, an office he held until 1988. By 1984, under his leadership, COCU negotiators and its plenary reached agreement on a Doctrinal Consensus. The 1988 UMC General Conference found the COCU consensus a "faithful expression of the apostolic faith, order, worship and witness of the church." That same year, the seventeenth COCU plenary approved a definitive Statement of Covenanting. Its eight elements are "claiming unity in faith, commitment to seek unity with wholeness, mutual recognition of members in one baptism, mutual recognition of each other as churches, mutual recognition and reconciliation of ordained ministry, celebrating the Eucharist together, engaging together in Christ's mission and formation of covenant councils."[91] In 1996 the General Conferences of AME, AMEZ, and UMC adopted the COCU Covenant Proposal "Churches in Covenant Communion." Known briefly then as CICC, the multilateral soon thereafter metamorphosed into Churches Uniting in Christ.[92]

Among COCU's commitments was that of combating racism. On that campaign United Methodism opened another front directly with the AME, AMEZ, and CME churches (and as of 2000, with the Union American Methodist Episcopal Church). In 1985, the four Methodisms established a Commission on Pan-Methodist Cooperation (USA). Constructive talks led the commission in 1991 to request the churches to authorize a study commission to explore merger. By 1996, the General Conferences of the AME, AMEZ, and UM churches authorized a Commission on Pan-Methodist Union to proceed to develop a plan of union. As a gesture of reconciliation, members of the 2000 UMC General Conference and leaders from the Pan-Methodist churches participated in a service of repentance and reconciliation. General Conference also authorized voting representatives from Pan-Methodist denominations on its agencies.

United Methodism continues active participation in, monetary support of, and leadership for such multilateral ecumenical endeavors, including the WCC, the NCC, and state and local councils of churches. That investment and its yield were symbolized in 1982 with British-Methodist-but-American-theologian Geoffrey Wainwright playing a major role in drafting the landmark WCC Lima text, *Baptism, Eucharist and Ministry*.[93] The Faith and Order Commission of the WCC transmitted this statement to member churches and sought formal responses. The Council of Bishops acted on behalf of United Methodism, its affirmation included in the ten volumes of *Churches Respond to BEM*. Such ecclesiological investment continues, but the UMC's most serious ecumenical efforts in the last two decades of the twentieth century were directed toward the bilateral dialogues and, to a lesser extent, interreligious dialogue (see declarations on relations with Jews [1972] and on interreligious dialogues generally). Facilitating agents have included the General Commission on Christian Unity and Interreligious Dialogue, given independent commission status by the 1980 General Conference; a chief ecumenical officer elected by the COB; and the dialogue-creating apparatus of the World Methodist Council. In 1992, for instance, GCCUIC began interreligious dialogues with Muslims, and General Conference adopted the resolution "Our Muslim Neighbors."[94]

Dialogues have been one of the very few places where United Methodism and the World Methodist Council have called on their professional theologians.[95] Conversations with the Roman Catholic Church began in 1967, and after the rather general reports of Denver (1971) and Dublin (1976), participants fixed their focus on pneumatology ("Towards an Agreed Statement on the Holy Spirit," Honolulu, 1981) and ecclesiology ("Towards an Agreed Statement on the Church," Nairobi, 1986). "The

Apostolic Tradition" followed in Singapore (1991). Conversations with the Orthodox, begun in 1992 under the sponsorship of the Ecumenical Patriarchate, also focused on pneumatology and ecclesiology. Dialogues with the Lutheran World Federation and the World Alliance of Reformed Churches produced, respectively, "The Church: Community of Grace" (1984) and "Together in God's Grace" (1987). The 1988 Lambeth Conference of Anglican bishops invited Methodists to begin formal dialogue. The conversations, influenced by several phases of conversations between British Methodists and the Church of England, yielded in 1996 "Sharing in the Apostolic Communion," an exploration of issues that separate the two churches.

International conversations with Anglicans and Lutherans led to sustained dialogues in the U.S. with the Episcopal Church and the Evangelical Lutheran Church of America (ELCA). Unity explorations on a national basis and beyond the family had occurred sporadically with the UBC and EA and the several Methodists. In the period 1928–32, there were talks between Methodists and Presbyterians. And Methodists launched explorations of intercommunion and union with Episcopalians in the 1930s and again from 1948 to 1958, stalling over the historic episcopate and sacramental issues (reordination and closed Communion). In the 1990s, chastened by the spectacular failure of organic union with COCU, the UMC began new dialogues with the ELCA and Episcopalians seeking eucharistic fellowship and mutual recognition of ministries. At this writing, full eucharistic unity with the ELCA and interim eucharistic unity with the Episcopalians have been approved by the respective churches. In 1999, having started these serious initiatives toward embrace of Asbury's and Albright's home churches (Anglican and Lutheran), United Methodism gestured toward its own daughter denominations and held the first consultation with churches within the Wesleyan holiness tradition. Meeting in Dallas, representatives of the Church of the Nazarene, the Church of Christ Holiness, Church of God (Anderson), Free Methodist Church, Korean Holiness Church, and Wesleyan Church and UMC discussed history and tradition, sanctification and perfection, women's issues, racial concerns, ecumenism, and next steps.

A Sacramental Church?

Holy Communion

Among the most significant transformations effected within Methodist, EUB, and United Methodist churches by their ecumenical involvement came in sacramental understanding and practice. Greater appreciation of the Eucharist and of baptism derived also from the interconfessional liturgical movement and from the twentieth-century reappraisal of the Wesleys and rediscovery of their sacramentalism. J. Ernest Rattenbury contributed to the recovery in a groundbreaking 1948 *theological* study—and reprinting—of all 166 eucharistic hymns.[96] John C. Bowmer in an equally illuminating 1951 study, *The Sacrament of the Lord's Supper in Early Methodism,* detailed for the first time the devout, devoted, and frequent *practice* of Holy Communion in Methodism's founding era.[97] British and American liturgical caucuses, the Methodist Sacramental Fellowship (1935) and the Order of Saint Luke (1946), stimulated interest in liturgical theology and reform, especially among younger clergy. The stated aims of MSF and OSL from the beginning were to reaffirm the *catholic* faith based on the apostolic testimony of Holy Scripture, witnessed to in the historic creeds, and professed by the church through the ages and to restore to modern Methodism the sacramental worship of the universal church and in particular the centrality of the Eucharist, as set forth in the life-long teaching and practice of the Wesleys.

As these statements indicate, Methodism's sacramental recovery oriented it to the early church and to ecumenical dialogues, which also found common ground in early Christian texts, so reminding Methodists of the Wesleys' appreciation of tradition. The Methodist and Roman Catholic International Dialogue, begun in 1967, focused on Eucharist in the first two published reports, 1971 and 1976. The 1971 report noted that Roman Catholics may "speak warmly of Charles Wesley's eucharistic hymns," and yet it had regretfully to be admitted that "the eucharistic devotion of the Wesleys and the hymns of Charles Wesley are no index at all to the place of Holy Communion in the life and thought and devotion of modern Methodists." The Methodist and Roman Catholic Dialogue in the U.S., also begun in 1967, issued a shared statement on the Eucharist in 1981 detailing "converging theology" and divergent practice.[98]

Parallel to and informing such ecumenical conversations, the twentieth-century liturgical movement also stimulated Methodist worship renewal. Scholars and reformers from various churches, including especially the Roman Catholic, provided a better understanding of worship in the Bible, in the early church, and in later centuries. Methodist scholars contributed, as indicated above, a fuller understanding of the Wesleys and early American practice, plus an understanding of how much of the heritage was gradually lost and forgotten during the nineteenth and twentieth centuries. Vatican II brought a century's liturgical developments to focus—as it did in various dogmatic, policy, and polity matters—in its "Constitution on the Sacred Liturgy." That 1963 document revolutionized Roman Catholic worship. An English-language and much reformed Mass was introduced in the U.S. in 1969. Protestants still worshiping with sixteenth-century liturgies, Methodists essentially with that crafted by Archbishop Thomas Cranmer, discovered themselves outreformed. The Episcopal Church in 1966 and the Lutheran Church in 1970 responded by introducing new eucharistic rites.

The Consultation on Church Union (USA), launched on the eve of Vatican II, explored Protestant unity across the several communions' sacramental practice. As early as 1968, COCU published a common eucharistic rite, *An Order of Worship for the Proclamation of the Word and of God and the Celebration of the Lord's Supper, with Commentary.*

COCU issued revised rites in 1978—*Word, Bread and Cup*—and in 1984—*The Sacrament of the Lord's Supper: A New Text*. In 1973 COCU's Commission on Worship published *An Order for the Celebration of Holy Baptism with Commentary*, and in 1980 *An Order for an Affirmation of the Baptismal Covenant (also called Confirmation)*, resources commended to Methodist and participant churches for trial use and comment.

Similar and perhaps even more transformative effect came from Methodist participation in and harvest from the WCC's Faith and Order Commission and its production of its 1982 consensus statement, *Baptism, Eucharist and Ministry (BEM)*, and ecumenical eucharistic rite, the *Lima Liturgy* (1982). The theology-changing and rite-shaping ecumenical document, seventy-five years in the making, provided authoritative warrant for reformation of sacramental theology and practice. And the *Lima Liturgy*, a Communion service, dramatized the ecclesiological convergence on the Eucharist reached in *BEM*.[99] In its 1986 formal written response, the UMC (USA) welcomed *BEM*'s appropriation of the scriptural and traditional understanding with regard to Christ's presence in the Eucharist, recovered by twentieth-century liturgical scholarship and focused in the Greek terms *anamnesis* (dynamic conjoining of Christ, past, present, and future) and *epiclesis* (the effective invocation of the Holy Spirit) to "realize the sign" as the Wesleys said in their *Hymns on the Lord's Supper*, no. 72. It notes: "All this we find explicitly taught by John and Charles Wesley, who knew and respected the apostolic, patristic and reformed faith of the Church." With regard to the sacrificial aspect of the Eucharist, the UMC response argued that "as Wesleyans, we are accustomed to the language of sacrifice, and we find *BEM*'s statements to be in accord with the Church's tradition and with ours."[100] The response made similar affirmative comment on *BEM*'s rich baptismal teaching.

Through these several international, interdenominational sacramental conversations, United Methodism came to the perception that it needed a theology of baptism, an understanding of Communion as more than memorial, and liturgical practices so informed. In 1968 the newly formed United Methodist Church found itself facing a rapidly changing world that challenged old assumptions about Sunday worship. The first regular General Conference of the newly united church adopted a resolution to "encourage regular and frequent (perhaps monthly) celebrations of Holy Communion within each congregation."[101] Reception of its two authorized Communion rites, the former Methodist rite of 1966 and the EUBC rite of 1957, was mixed from the start, some relishing the familiar King James phrasing. Others, who were stimulated by the sacramental revolution under way, experimented with new forms—casual Communions, chummy prayers, guitars and folk songs, balloons and banners. To bring order out of chaos, the 1970 special session General Conference began a process of rethinking and development that led to a new *Hymnal* in 1989 and a new *Book of Worship* in 1992 (treated in the section below, "Hymnal and Worship Books").

The development of new liturgical texts for Communion became a churchwide process. The study commission set to work with four goals, a fifth added in the middle 1970s at the urging of the newly formed UMC Women's Caucus and the Commission on the Status and Role of Women: (1) use modern English in place of sixteenth-century Tudor, "thee and thou" English; (2) restore the classical and ecumenical shape of Communion, uniting Word and Table with a fourfold action (taking, blessing, breaking, and giving), a form documented by Hippolytus (ca. 217) via Gregory Dix (1945) in place of the late medieval pattern mediated through Cranmer's Reformation-era rites (Book of Common Prayer, 1549 and 1552) and Wesley's eighteenth-century reiteration of those sixteenth-century forms; (3) express a contemporary theology of Eucharist with focus on Easter (resurrection) in place of the Good Friday–centered rites derived from medieval piety; (4) provide maximum pastoral flexibility; and (5) use inclusive language.

The Commission on Worship produced *The Sacrament of the Lord's Supper: An Alternate Text* in 1971 and the next year circulated widely a trial-use leaflet version with directions for ministers. The 1972 General Conference opened with this service. Liturgical scholar James White, principal drafter, introduced the new rite to the church's clergy in their journal, *Circuit Rider*, four months later (Sources 1972c).

He explained that the new rite constituted an entire service and was no mere appendage to a preaching service. It gave opportunity to accent the value of communal acts, each of which needed to be explained to the congregation. Ministers were to stand *behind* the table, facing the congregation, many wearing white albs with colorful stoles as a modern/ancient alternative to black robes. The "passing the peace," the offering of bread and wine from and by the congregation, and the breaking of the loaf were ancient sign-acts. The great prayer at the table followed the classical Christian pattern of giving thanks, yet allowed variety for the great festivals of the Christian Year, weddings, and ordinations. Congregations gradually abandoned kneeling at the Communion rail and swallowing precut tidbits of bread and sipping grape juice from tiny glasses and began receiving the elements standing and dipping the bread into a common chalice, sometimes filled with wine. More radically, reformers like White strongly suggested that weekly celebrations are rooted in Scripture and tradition, including Wesleyan.

The theology of the rite also needed to be rethought and taught. Methodists through the years, at their best, have always believed that Jesus Christ is *truly present* in this sacrament. Although the term *real presence* had not been used in historic Methodist doctrinal sources, it captures what is said in John Wesley's sermons and Charles Wesley's hymns dealing with the Lord's Supper. But most Methodists after Wesley had a *memorialistic* view of the sacraments. They were nervous with Cranmer's "Prayer of Humble Access" ("so to eat the flesh of thy Son Jesus Christ, and to drink his blood") and "Prayer of Consecration" ("may be *partakers of his most blessed Body and Blood*"), which Wesley retained in the Communion rite he sent to Methodists in America. Reformers under

Asbury as early as 1792 (one year after Wesley's death!) changed the prayer to read—"so to partake of *this sacrament*"—which remained through 1939 when reformers further diluted the concept of sacramental presence—"so to partake of *these memorials* of thy son Jesus Christ." In 1964 Methodist liturgy reformers returned to an earlier phraseology—"so to partake of *this sacrament* of thy Son Jesus Christ." That was as far as mid-twentieth-century Methodists were willing to go, which did not commit Methodists to any particular view of Christ's presence. A significant shift occurred in the denomination's theological understanding when the 1972 rite shed its embarrassment about the real presence of Christ in the "gifts of bread and wine." By 1982 the new eucharistic prayer boldly invoked the Holy Spirit:

> Pour out your Holy Spirit on us gathered here,
> and on these gifts of bread and wine.
> *Make them be for us the body and blood of Christ,*
> *that we may be for the world the body of Christ,*
> *redeemed by his blood.*

A deliberate return to language that John Wesley would have loved,[102] the revised "Great Thanksgiving" again permitted modern Methodists to speak of Christ as giving himself as bread and wine in the sacred meal. God-in-Christ is truly, though spiritually, present and active in the celebration.[103]

In 1975, 1976, and 1979, the commission produced revised texts incorporating inclusive language. The 1980 General Conference commended the 1979 revised text to local churches for trial use with other new rites with the title *We Gather Together: Services of Public Worship.* The 1980 text, revised again beginning in 1981, was officially adopted by the 1984 General Conference and published in 1985 in *The Book of Services, Containing the General Services of the Church,* "A Service of Word and Table (Complete Text)." The BOS (1985) included also a "Basic Pattern for Sunday Worship," an "Outline of Sunday Worship," and a "Brief Text" and a "Minimum Text" for the Lord's Supper. These texts were not fully mainstreamed across the church until they appeared in *The United Methodist Hymnal* (1989).

Abstemious Methodists had specified in the 1966 hymnal that only "the pure unfermented juice of the grape shall be used." Methodism's liturgical reformers had in the 1971 alternative eucharistic text deliberately dropped the century-old rubric, a deletion that the 1972 General Conference did not reverse. Teetotalers attending the 1984 General Conference tried but failed to get that clause inscribed into church law, and the new hymnal omitted the rule, allowing congregations to use wine if they wish. In 1996, Methodism's temperance "Communion police" did succeed. A motion from the floor of the General Conference passed, mandating usage of "the pure, unfermented juice of the grape."

Baptism

Development of a new baptismal rite followed a similar trajectory. Neither the Methodists nor the EUBs brought a highly developed baptismal theology into union.[104] Indeed, both churches were conflicted about the meaning and practice of baptism.[105] In 1972, the new church took action and appointed a Baptism Study Commission. Its mandate was to strengthen United Methodism's "sacramental" understanding of baptism and design a unified rite for (1) baptism of infants and children, (2) baptism of youth and adults, (3) confirmation, and (4) renewals and any combination of the above. As with eucharistic theology and practice, so also on baptism, United Methodism found itself returning to Wesleyan origins, to liturgical developments across the Christian world, to growing ecumenical consensus, and back through the life of the church to the apostolic age. Important developments included the groundbreaking *Order for Holy Baptism* by the uniting Church of South India in 1955 (revised 1962). Similarly, COCU's Commission on Worship produced *An Order for the Celebration of Holy Baptism with Commentary* in 1973. COCU followed in 1980 with *An Order for an Affirmation of the Baptismal Covenant (also called Confirmation)* commended to member denominations. Revisions by individual communions, following the ancient, ecumenical pattern, also proved influential, including Roman Catholic reformed rites for baptism of infants in 1969 and for adults in 1972. The Lutheran Church followed in 1974, the Episcopal Church in 1977, and the Presbyterian Church in 1985. A reformed baptismal rite of the British *Methodist Service Book* of 1975 also served as a model. Dialogue between the UMC and the Lutheran Church in the U.S. (1977–79) helped clarify understandings of baptism in both churches.[106]

The growing ecumenical convergence on the meaning of baptism took most dramatic expression in the widely acclaimed 1982 Faith and Order document, *Baptism, Eucharist and Ministry*, as we have already noted.[107] Its treatment of infant and believer's baptisms reflects the persistent tension in Wesley—which he himself never clearly thematized theologically—between a baptismal regeneration in infants and the necessity of a subsequent spiritual rebirth. An ecumenical baptismal liturgy based on the Lima convergence statement, published in 1983, contained a liturgy-shaping Great Thanksgiving over the water, termed at the Reformation and in the Wesleys' days the "flood prayer" because of its evocation of the saving of and covenant with Noah.[108] Of particular interest and critical in United Methodist reform was the identification of norms and necessary elements for baptism named in *BEM*: the proclamation of the Scriptures referring to baptism, a renunciation of evil, profession of faith in Christ and the holy Trinity, generous use of water, a Great Thanksgiving over the water with an invocation of the Holy Spirit, a declaration that the persons baptized have acquired a new identity as sons and daughters of God, and as members of the church, and are called to be witnesses of the gospel.[109]

A further step in the late-twentieth-century liturgical and theological convergence regarding baptism was the publication in 1988 of an ecumenical celebration of baptism by the Consultation on Common Texts (CCT).[110] The CCT originated in the mid-1960s as a forum for consultation on worship renewal among many of the major Christian churches in the U.S. and Canada, including the UMC, and it is best known for bringing us the Common Lectionary (1983) and Revised Common Lectionary (1992). These several documents and rites encouraged a reunderstanding of baptism that moved away from a narrow focus on cleansing from original sin to emphasize ecclesial initiation and the paschal motif of identification with Christ's death and resurrection.

In 1976, United Methodism produced a rite so shaped and presented an official alternative, *A Service of Baptism, Confirmation, and Renewal,* for trial use.[111] A theological introduction and commentary accompanied the text. Lawrence Stookey,[112] a professor at Wesley Theological Seminary, was principal drafter for the committee. Hoyt Hickman, chair of the drafting committee, introduced the new rite that year in *Circuit Rider.* The reshaped service attempted to recover the early church's *unified* initiation process and used the same ritual sequence for infants and adults. A new development, confirmation, was seen as the first of many "reaffirmations" of baptism that may take place in the life of an individual or congregation, or when a person joins The United Methodist Church from another denomination.

Trial use ended in 1984 when the new rites became official. Although the rites were published in leaflet form for use in churches, widespread use awaited their publication in a new hymnal in 1989. Five closely related services were gathered in the new hymnal under the heading "The Baptismal Covenant." Understood as sacrament and mystery, the rites dramatize baptism as primarily God's act—God's pledge. In baptism, a person enters into God's covenant, a covenanting that involves promises and responsibilities of both parties. The essential response of faith is made by the whole assembly. Within this recommitment, individual candidates and their sponsors make their responses. The baptism of infants and the baptism of adults are essentially the same, and so there is essentially only one baptismal liturgy. Both an infant candidate and an adult candidate are "babes in Christ." Neither has earned the right to be baptized by a faith that is adequate in itself. In both cases what the candidates are able to do, limited by their stages of development, is incorporated into the larger faith commitment of the church. The new rite, three times longer than the older, was intended to be a *major focus of worship*, not something slipped in as an incidental item.

The rite's novelty, length, and theology took some getting used to, more so than to the new hymnal (see below) or to the eucharistic rites, with their alternatives, a shorter form and the older Cranmerian-Wesleyan version. To address such concerns—including whether the new rite teaches baptismal regeneration and, if so, whether it should—the 1988 General Conference established a churchwide study commission of bishops, pastors, laity, and seminary professors to prepare an official theological and functional "understanding" of baptism embedded in the new liturgies. The study committee presented a preliminary report to the 1992 General Conference, which approved it for study in local churches (1993–96). Dwight Vogel, faculty member at Garrett-Evangelical Theological Seminary, prepared a study guide.[113] Eight years of study and comment on successive drafts honed the document. *By Water and the Spirit: A United Methodist Understanding of Baptism* was adopted overwhelmingly by the 1996 General Conference.[114] Gayle Felton followed with a study guide, *By Water and the Spirit: Making Connections for Identity and Ministry*,[115] first published in 1997, with revised editions in 1998, 1999, and 2002.[116] Her article on baptism in the November-December 1999 issue of *Circuit Rider* also explained the new "understanding." "Baptism is the source of our Christian identity and mission," she concludes. "It marks us as the people of God and impels us into ministry."[117]

Hymnal and Worship Books

Methodism has had its differences over worship at least since the 1780s when, as Jesse Lee reported, congregations in "the large towns, and in some country places" used Wesley's Sunday service and morning prayers, but after a few years, the preachers generally laid the prayer book aside "fully satisfied that they could pray better, and with more devotion with their eyes shut, than they could with their eyes open."[118] Over the years, camp meetings, Sunday schools, holiness and prayer meetings, temperance campaigns, and other social reforms added styles and practices to Methodism's worship repertoire. From its founding in 1939, The Methodist Church accommodated such divergence by providing both an upstairs formal and a downstairs *Cokesbury* hymnal. United Methodism featured its ethnic, linguistic, and liturgical diversity with multiple resources, especially from the Section on Worship of the General Board of Discipleship that, as we noted in the last chapter, produced, beginning in 1972, a variety of alternatives or supplements to the two official hymnals brought into the 1968 union. And from 1984 to 2000, many congregations experimented with "contemporary" musical worship practices, introduced digital and media resources, and accordingly abandoned hymnals, prescribed liturgies, and bulletins.[119]

Recognizing the need for a hymnal to feature the new liturgies and be more generous in its recognition of the church's diversity, the 1984 General Conference established a Hymnal Revision Committee. It committed oversight to The United Methodist Publishing House, rather than to Discipleship, a delegation much to the pleasure of *Good News*. A twenty-five-member committee, aided by a large number of readers and consultants, worked from 1984 until 1988 to prepare a new hymnal.

Controversy swirled around using expansive and inclusive language and imagery, by the 1980s expanded from describing the people of God to addressing and describing

God and God's presence and divine action in the world. Hymns with militaristic metaphors also raised hackles. The committee entertained dropping "Am I a Soldier of the Cross" in its first round of deletions, October 1985. After protests, the committee restored that hymn in its May meeting. In the same session, the hymnal revision committee by a split vote of 11-10 deleted "Onward, Christian Soldiers" from the approved list and modified the text of "The Battle Hymn of the Republic." The story made print and TV media, and the rumor circulated that the committee would use only gender-inclusive language. By July 1986, the committee had received more than eleven thousand pieces of mail, only forty-four of which supported the action of the committee. Bowing to public outcry, the committee moderated its commitment to publish a fully sensitive hymnal (Sources 1996a). It restored "Onward, Christian Soldiers" and dropped "Strong Mother God," which stretched God imagery. Masculine imagery was restored to the proposed gender-inclusive Psalter. The revisers managed to take greater liberties with texts that used masculine terms for humanity. In Charles Wesley's "Hark! the Herald Angels Sing," "pleased as man with men to dwell" became "pleased with us in flesh to dwell." In his "Christ the Lord Is Risen Today," "earth and heaven" replaced "sons of men." "God of Our Fathers" became "God of the Ages"; "Good Christian Men, Rejoice" metamorphosed into "Good Christian Friends, Rejoice"; and the angels in "O Little Town of Bethlehem" promise peace to "all on earth," not "men on earth." Revampers also bent over backward to avoid offending other constituencies. In "Have Thine Own Way, Lord," sinners no longer ask Jesus to wash them "whiter than snow" because of objections from Black Methodists. In Wesley's "O for a Thousand Tongues to Sing," editors originally dropped a stanza proclaiming the spiritual uplifting of the "dumb" and the "lame," lest disabled persons take umbrage. They later restored the words, but suggested in a footnote that the stanza may be omitted.

The 1988 General Conference overwhelmingly approved *The United Methodist Hymnal: Book of United Methodist Worship*. Published in 1989, it met similar reception across the church, more than half of the congregations ordering the new book in the first year. While honoring traditional hymns, the hymnal shed the elitism of past hymnals, making generous space for gospel song, verse from a wide range of ethnic groups, and contemporary hymns. The editors downplayed King James verbiage and included songs that highbrows scorn but the people love, such as the treacly "In the Garden." The wide-ranging collection features such songs as the civil rights anthem "We Shall Overcome," Duke Ellington's "Come Sunday," gospel singer Bill Gaither's "He Touched Me," and Brian Wren's "God of Many Names." The hymnal contained more than a hundred pages of worship services and resources, not counting the Psalter, and brought the basic pattern, baptism, and Lord's Supper up front for emphasis. New liturgies for weddings and funerals, in trial use since 1972 and adopted by the 1984 General Conference, saw first general usage. In the new wedding rite the father no longer giveth away the bride.

These resources and many more went into *The United Methodist Book of Worship*, designed for worship leaders, not for pews. Prepared for presentation to the 1992 General Conference, it was published the same year. Replacing that of 1964 and reflecting the harvest of United Methodism's liturgical and ecumenical engagement, it featured the Revised Common Lectionary, services for and fourteen alternative Great Thanksgivings for seasons of the Christian Year, a huge array of devotional and worship materials, and rituals for every thinkable church officer or building.

Women Get the Last Word

In the closing decades of the twentieth century, women continued to experience firsts. Leontine Kelly in 1984 became the first African American woman to be elected bishop in any mainline Protestant denomination. The next year Barbara Thompson took the reins of the General Commission on Religion and Race, the first woman general secretary of a general board or agency other than COSROW. An African American church leader from Washington, D.C., Thompson headed the agency from 1985 until her retirement in 1998. In 1986, the Reverend Minerva Carcaño was appointed district superintendent in the Rio Grande Conference, the first Hispanic woman in that office, and would be elected bishop in 2004, another first. Bishop Sharon Zimmerman Rader assumed the prestigious position of secretary of the Council of Bishops, serving from 1996 until her retirement in 2004. Nineteen ninety saw the first three African American women elected district superintendents (of fifty women DSs that year): the Reverend Charlotte Ann Nichols, Peninsula Conference; the Reverend Mary Brown Oliver, Baltimore Conference; and the Reverend J. Jeannette Cooper, West Ohio Conference. In 1985 and 1987, respectively, Hispanic and Native American women gathered for consultations. Another initiative to develop women's leadership, GBHEM's Women of Color Scholars Program, began in 1989, providing scholarships up to $10,000 a year for doctoral studies and with the mission of placing faculty women of color in all thirteen UMC seminaries.[120]

It was not all "Kum ba yah." As women continued to strive for equality in society, churches confronted and sometimes differed radically on a vast array of issues—often tagged glass ceiling or "family issues"—related to advancement, gender roles, affirmative action, human sexuality, abortion, child care, sexual harassment, the trauma of divorce, single-parent/income families headed by women, often impoverished, and other matters of justice or equity. Research on sexual harassment in the UMC by the General Council on Ministries in 1990 revealed that 77 percent of women clergy had experienced sexual harassment. In 1992 and 1995, GCOSROW developed recommendations on sexual harassment and issued a policy statement regarding abuse within ministerial relationships. Pro-life advocates, as we noted, continued to challenge United Methodists' moderate position on abortion. Delegates to the 1988 General Conference narrowly defeated a petition to abolish the General Commission on the Status and Role of Women. The commission had been dogged by critics who charged that it had outlived its usefulness and had "expanded" its scope beyond the intent of its creators. One of the most controversial actions was its support for a study of the effects of homophobia.

That year the Women's Task Force of Good News reorganized under the name Evangelical Coalition for United Methodist Women (ECUMW), a joint effort among women from Good News, the Mission Society for United Methodists, and the Institute on Religion and Democracy. Renamed "Renew" in 1989, it dedicated itself to renewing the Women's Division. Key leaders included Diane Knippers (who later joined the staff of IRD), Faye Short and Helen Coppedge of Good News, and Julia Williams of the Mission Society. By 1991, it claimed 11,100 members or UMW member affiliates. Bolstered and resourced by the interlocking network of conservative caucus groups (Good News, IRD, Mission Society, Confessing Movement, Lifewatch, Association for Church Renewal, Foundation for Theological Education, Transforming Congregations, and as of 2000, the Coalition for United Methodist Accountability), Renew kept up constant attack on the Women's Division. Its several "Financial Files," for instance, offered exposés of Women's Division funding of faith "subversive" programs.[121]

Renew and its collaborators took special umbrage at the November 1993 Re-Imagining Conference (as already noted in "Theologizing Left and Right"). Sponsored by local and state ecumenical councils to mark the midpoint of the World Council of Churches' "Decade in Solidarity with Women," the conference met in Minneapolis. Major funding for the conference came from the American Baptist Church, the Evangelical Lutheran Church, the Presbyterian Church (USA), and the UMC. More than twenty thousand participants from forty-nine states and twenty-seven countries attended. The preface to the conference program justified the need for radical theological reform from a feminist perspective. The conference celebrated the feminine attributes of God, the gift of lesbianism, and the spiritual experiences of persons who found God within themselves. Sexism, racism, and classism took center place in theological reflection.

The *Christian Century* identified the Re-Imagining Conference as one of the top ten religious stories of the year.[122] However, the gathering attracted little Methodist notice until Good News charged that it had been rife with heresy—among other things, participants celebrated homosexuality, worshiped the goddess Sophia, and rejected Christ's atonement. The church's mood gradually shifted—glowing evaluations yielding to horror stories, charges of heresy, hate mail, job losses, and even death threats. By January, the silence unbearable, Beryl Ingram-Ward, United Methodist pastor, complained, "Wasn't some agency or official group within the United Methodist Church going to step forward to refute the charges of heresy and goddess-worship related to the Re-Imagining Conference?"[123]

In February, in response to continued public attacks on the leadership, theology, and funding of the international ecumenical conference, and in an effort to counter charges of heresy, eight hundred UMC women, including bishops, pastors, deaconesses, lay-women, church agency staff, and college and theological school faculty, signed a statement supporting the aims of the conference and challenging critics of the event. "We decided it was time to break the silence and be proactive," said the Reverend Jean Audrey Powers, a veteran UMC national executive and one of the drafters of the statement, at a news conference March 8, 1994—International Women's Day—at the Interchurch Center in New York City. She was joined by five presenters who addressed various themes relating to the event: Bishop Susan Morrison of the Philadelphia Area, Bishop Forrest Stith of the New York Area, Professors Catherine Keller and Heather Murray Elkins of Drew University Theological School, and Beryl Ingram-Ward, graduate student at Union Theological Seminary in New York. The open letter, "A Time of Hope—Time of Threat" (Sources 1994a), released in the March press conference, drew endorsements from five additional women bishops and 830 other UMC women. "We printed them in big, bold type, two columns to a page, page after glorious page."[124] Heated exchanges nevertheless continued, some online, and stimulated the formation of a supportive online network of people—men and women across the church. A council was formed to organize small groups, plan gatherings, and network across denominational lines.[125]

The next year, the Reverend Jean Audrey Powers, associate general secretary of GCCUIC, became the highest-ranking United Methodist official to "come out" as a gay person. Powers described her action as "a political act" committed "as an act of resistance to false teachings that have contributed to heresy and homophobia within the church." In a statement Powers declared, "I have been a lesbian all my life. I've never known my identity as otherwise." While expressing dismay over "some of the actions of the United Methodist conferences on a variety of matters, especially those affecting gay and lesbian persons," Powers said she believes that "the Holy Spirit continues to nudge the church into faithfulness and self-correction."[126]

Methodist First Lady Hillary Rodham Clinton addressed her church at the 1996 General Conference (1996b). For a moment, it seemed as though rebuttal would be needed. After General Conference had been alerted that she would speak, Charles Appleby, a delegate from Florence, South Carolina, asked that the conference also invite Elizabeth Dole, wife of Senator Bob Dole, the presumed Republican presidential nominee "to avoid sending confusing signals during an election year." But the motion was defeated after Ronald Bretsch of Norwood, New York, describing himself as an "enrolled Republican," said that the nation had "one President at one time, and we have one First Lady at a time." Later another delegate expressed concern that not inviting Mrs. Dole could be seen as political, and the conference agreed to send her a letter expressing "deep appreciation" for her work as president of the American Red Cross.[127]

So with no formal rejoinder, we give Clinton the last word. Methodist residents of the White House had been a rarity in the twentieth century. Ulysses Grant was a Methodist, as was his successor, Rutherford B. Hayes. William McKinley and his wife, Ida, more than ninety years earlier, were the last Methodist occupants of the executive mansion until Hillary Rodham Clinton became First Lady in 1993. So for the nearly one thousand United Methodists gathered at the Denver Convention Center for their church's quadrennial General Conference in 1996, Mrs. Clinton's talk to them was something of a historic event.

In a thirty-minute speech, interrupted by no fewer than five standing ovations, Mrs. Clinton blended her familiar message of society's obligation to help its children with recollections of growing up Methodist (Sources 1996b).[128] She applauded her church's bishops for their recent call to make the welfare of children the denomination's top priority.[129] At one point she said that corporations could help children by giving employees time off to attend parent-teacher meetings and that churches could open their doors to offer after-school havens to youth. At another point she recited lyrics from the child's hymn "Jesus loves me! This I know," which tells of Christ's love for children of all colors. She said it had given her an "early lesson" in positive race relations. Mrs. Clinton cited other religious sources, too, quoting once from the Gospel of Mark, and she frequently invoked the name of Methodism's founder, John Wesley. Noting that people "who did not want to hear him" pelted Wesley with whiskey bottles, she said, "We know acting on our faith is never easy."

ABBREVIATIONS

For Denominations

AME	The African Methodist Episcopal Church (1816–)
AMEZ	The African Methodist Episcopal Church Zion (1820–)
CME	The (Colored) Christian Methodist Episcopal Church (1870–)
CN	The Church of the Nazarene (1907–)
EA/EC	The Evangelical Association/Church (1803–1946)
EUBC	The Evangelical United Brethren Church (1946–68)
FMC	The Free Methodist Church (1860–)
MC	The Methodist Church, USA (1939–68)
MC (GBr)	The Methodist Church, Great Britain (1932–)
MCC	The Methodist Church, Canada (1874–1925)
MEC	The Methodist Episcopal Church (1784–1939)
MECS	The Methodist Episcopal Church, South (1844–1939)
MPC	The Methodist Protestant Church (1830–1939)
PHC	The Pilgrim Holiness Church (1897–1968)
SA	The Salvation Army (1865–)
UBC	The United Brethren in Christ/Church of the United Brethren (1800–1946) ("United Brethren in Christ" is used on Disciplines and in self-identification through the nineteenth century. The denomination begins to refer to itself formally as "church" in the 1860s and 1870s. With the 1917 *Discipline*, the UBs begin the formal "Church of the United Brethren in Christ.")
UEC	The United Evangelical Church (1894–1922)
UMC	The United Methodist Church, USA (1968–)
WC	The Wesleyan Church (1968–)
WMC	The Wesleyan Methodist Church, USA (1843–1968)
WMC (GBr)	The Wesleyan Methodist Church, Great Britain (1791–1932)

For Denominational Periodicals and Journals

AMECR	A.M.E. *Church Review*
AMEZQR	A.M.E. *Zion Quarterly Review*

CA	*Christian Advocate*, New York (MEC)
CAp	*Christliche Apologete* (MEC)
CBot	*Christliche Botschäfter* (EA)
CCA	*Central Christian Advocate* (MEC, African American edition)
CI	*Christian Index* (CME)
CR	*Christian Recorder* (AME)
EpRe	*The Epworth Review* (MC [GBr])
EM	*Evangelical Messenger* (EA)
Ev	*The Evangelical* (EA)
LQHR	*London Quarterly and Holborn Review* (WMC [GBr], MC [GBr])
MPR	Refers to quarterly journal of MPC under its fluctuating names (*Methodist Recorder, Methodist Protestant, Methodist Protestant-Recorder*)
MQR	Refers to quarterly theological journal of the MEC under its fluctuating names (*Methodist Magazine, Methodist Review, Methodist Quarterly Review*)
MQRS	Refers to *Methodist Quarterly Review* of the MECS
MR	*Methodist Recorder* (MC [GBr])
NCA	*Nashville Christian Advocate* (MECS)
NWCA	*Northwestern Christian Advocate* (MEC)
QR	*Quarterly Review* (UMC)
RelLife	*Religion in Life* (MC, UMC)
RT	*Religious Telescope* (UBC)
SZ	*Star of Zion* (AMEZ)
UBQR	*United Brethren Quarterly Review* (UBC)
UMR	*United Methodist Reporter*
WA	*Wesleyan Advocate* (WC)
WCA	*Western Christian Advocate* (MEC)
WMM	*Wesleyan Methodist Magazine* (WMC [GBr])
ZH	*Zion's Herald* (MEC)

For Scholarly Journals

AsbSem	*The Asbury Seminarian*
AsbTJ	*The Asbury Theological Journal*
BJRL	*Bulletin of the John Rylands Library*
DDSB	*The Duke Divinity School Bulletin*
DDSR	*The Duke Divinity School Review*
DGW	*The Drew Gateway*
EvJo	*Evangelical Journal*
MethH	*Methodist History*

PCWS	*Proceedings of the Charles Wesley Society*
PSTJ	*The Perkins School of Theology Journal*
PWHS	*Proceedings of the Wesley Historical Society*
TFor	*Teologisk Forum*
WQR	*Wesleyan Quarterly Review*
WTJ	*Wesleyan Theological Journal*

For United Methodism and American Culture (UMAC) Volumes

CEMI	*Connectionalism: Ecclesiology, Mission, and Identity*, Russell E. Richey, Dennis M. Campbell, and William B. Lawrence, eds. UMAC, vol. 1 (Nashville: Abingdon, 1997).
PCM	*The People(s) Called Methodist: Forms and Reforms of Their Life*, William B. Lawrence, Dennis M. Campbell, and Russell E. Richey, eds. UMAC, vol. 2 (Nashville: Abingdon, 1998).
DD	*Doctrines and Discipline*, Dennis M. Campbell, William B. Lawrence, and Russell E. Richey, eds. UMAC, vol. 3 (Nashville: Abingdon, 1999).
QTCC	*Questions for the Twenty-First Century Church*, Russell E. Richey, Dennis M. Campbell, and William B. Lawrence, eds. UMAC, vol. 4 (Nashville: Abingdon, 1999).
MARKS	*Marks of Methodism: Practices of Ecclesiology*, Russell E. Richey with Dennis M. Campbell and William B. Lawrence, UMAC, vol. 5 (Nashville: Abingdon Press, 2005).

For Other Publications

ACJ/church/name/year	Annual Conference Journal/Minutes/Proceedings/Register for conference named.
Annual Report/board or institution/church/year	Annual reports, however titled.
Asbury/Coke/*Discipline*	*The Doctrines and Discipline of The Methodist Episcopal Church in America, with Explanatory Notes by Thomas Coke and Francis Asbury* (Philadelphia: Henry Tuckniss, 1798; reprint, Rutland, Vt.: Academy Books, 1979).
Baker, *Incredible Methodists*	Gordon Pratt Baker, ed., *Those Incredible Methodists: A History of the Baltimore Conference of The United Methodist Church* (Baltimore: Commission on Archives and History, Baltimore Conference, 1972).
Bangs, *History*	Nathan Bangs, *A History of the Methodist Episcopal Church*, 12th ed., 4 vols. (New York: Carlton & Porter, 1860).

Barclay, *Missions*	Wade Crawford Barclay, *History of Methodist Missions*, 3 vols. (New York: Board of Missions of The Methodist Church, 1949–57). Barclay's three volumes carry separate titles. Later contributions to the ME-UMC History of Missions series are referenced by author and title.
Behney/Eller, *History*	J. Bruce Behney and Paul H. Eller, *The History of The Evangelical United Brethren Church*, ed. Kenneth W. Krueger (Nashville: Abingdon Press, 1979).
Bradley, *AMEZ History*	David H. Bradley, *A History of the A.M.E. Zion Church*, 2 vols. (Nashville: AMEZ Publishing House, 1956–60).
Buckley, *History*	James M. Buckley, *Constitutional and Parliamentary History of The Methodist Episcopal Church* (New York: Methodist Book Concern, 1912).
Catechism/church/year	Official catechisms for the denomination named with their year of first publication.
Curts, *General Conferences*	*The General Conferences of The Methodist Episcopal Church from 1792–1896*, ed. Lewis Curts (Cincinnati: Curts & Jennings, 1900).
Davies/Rupp, *History*	Rupert Davies and Gordon Rupp, eds., *A History of the Methodist Church in Great Britain*, 4 vols. (London: Epworth Press, 1975–87).
DCA/church/year	*Daily Christian Advocate* for denomination named (publishes daily proceedings for General Conferences).
Debates/MEC/1844	Robert A. West, reporter, *Report of Debates in the General Conference of The Methodist Episcopal Church . . . 1844* (New York: G. Lane & C. B. Tippett, 1844).
Discipline/church/year	The book of discipline (under slightly varying names) for the denomination cited, e.g., *Discipline*/UMC/1996.
Emory, *Discipline*	Robert Emory, *History of the Discipline of The Methodist Episcopal Church*, rev. W. P. Strickland (New York: Carlton & Porter [1857]).
EWM	Nolan B. Harmon et al., *The Encyclopedia of World Methodism*, 2 vols., sponsored by the World Methodist Council and the Commission on Archives and History, UMC (Nashville: The United Methodist Publishing House, 1974).
Gregg, *AME History*	Howard D. Gregg, *History of the African Methodist Episcopal Church: The Black Church in Action* (Nashville: AME Church Sunday School Union, 1980).

HAM	*The History of American Methodism*, ed. Emory S. Bucke, 3 vols. (New York and Nashville: Abingdon Press, 1964).
Hymnal/church/year	Official hymnals for the denomination named with their year of first publication.
JGC/MEC	Refers to the *Journal of the General Conference of The Methodist Episcopal Church* for the year indicated. Includes citations from *Journals of the General Conference of The Methodist Episcopal Church, 1796–1856*, 3 vols. (New York: Carlton & Phillips, 1856). Vol. 1, 1796–1836; vol. 2, 1840–44; vol. 3, 1848–56.
JGC/MECS	Refers to the *Journal of the General Conference of The Methodist Episcopal Church, South*, for the year indicated. Includes citations from *Journals of the General Conference of The Methodist Episcopal Church, South, held 1846 and 1850* (Richmond: Published by John Early for the MECS).
JGC/MPC	*Journal of the . . . General Conference of The Methodist Protestant Church.*
JLFA	*The Journal and Letters of Francis Asbury*, ed. Elmer T. Clark, 3 vols. (London: Epworth Press; Nashville: Abingdon Press, 1958).
Lakey, *CME History*	Othal L. Lakey, *The History of the C.M.E. Church*, rev. ed. (Memphis: CME Publishing House, 1996).
Lee, *Short History*	Jesse Lee, *A Short History of the Methodists* (Baltimore, 1810; reprint, Rutland, Vt.: Academy Books, 1974).
McTyeire, *History*	Holland N. McTyeire, *A History of Methodism* (Nashville: Publishing House of the MECS, 1904).
Mathews, *Slavery*	Donald G. Mathews, *Slavery and Methodism* (Princeton: Princeton University Press, 1965).
Minutes (British)	*Minutes of the Methodist Conferences, from the First, held in London, by the Late Rev. John Wesley, A.M., in the Year 1744* (London: Thomas Cordeaux, Agent, 1791–1836; London: John Mason, 1862).
Minutes/church/year	Annual or General Minutes however titled and aggregated. Reference for the early years of the MEC is to *Minutes of the Annual Conferences of The Methodist Episcopal Church for the Years 1773–1828* (New York: T. Mason & G. Lane, 1840) unless alternative edition indicated, e.g., reference for 1784 in *Minutes of the Methodist Conferences,*

Neely, *Bishops*

Neely, *Conference*

Neely, *Missions*

Organization MECS

Perspectives

Peterson, *Revisions*

Pilkington/Vernon,
Methodist Publishing House

Redford, *History* MECS

Resolutions/UMC/year

Richey, *Conference*

Schmidt, *Grace Sufficient*

Semple, *Dominion*

Annually Held in America; From 1773 to 1813, Inclusive (New York: Published by Daniel Hitt & Thomas Ware for the Methodist Connexion in the United States, 1813) as *Minutes*/MEC/1784 (1813), page.

Thomas B. Neely, *The Bishops and the Supervisional System of The Methodist Episcopal Church* (New York: Eaton & Mains, 1912).

Thomas B. Neely, *A History of the Origin and Development of the Governing Conference in Methodism, and Especially of the General Conference of The Methodist Episcopal Church* (Cincinnati: Curts & Jennings, 1892).

Thomas B. Neely, *The Methodist Episcopal Church and Its Foreign Missions* (New York: Methodist Book Concern, 1923).

History of the Organization of The Methodist Episcopal Church, South, with the Journal of Its First General Conference (Nashville: Publishing House of the MECS, 1925).

Perspectives on American Methodism, ed. Russell E. Richey, Kenneth E. Rowe, and Jean Miller Schmidt (Nashville: Kingswood Books, 1993).

P. A. Peterson, *History of the Revisions of the Discipline of The Methodist Episcopal Church, South* (Nashville: Publishing House of the MECS, 1889).

James Penn Pilkington and Walter Newton Vernon Jr., *The Methodist Publishing House*, 2 vols. (Nashville: Abingdon Press, 1968, 1969).

A. H. Redford, *History of the Organization of The Methodist Episcopal Church, South* (Nashville: A. H. Redford, for the MECS, 1871).

The Book of Resolutions of The United Methodist Church for the year named.

Russell E. Richey, *The Methodist Conference in America* (Nashville: Kingswood Books, 1996).

Jean Miller Schmidt, *Grace Sufficient: A History of Women in American Methodism, 1760–1939* (Nashville: Abingdon Press, 1999).

Neil Semple, *The Lord's Dominion: The History of Canadian Methodism* (Montreal: McGill-Queen's University Press, 1996).

Sherman, *Revisions*	David Sherman, *History of the Revisions of the Discipline of The Methodist Episcopal Church* (New York: Nelson & Phillips, 1874).
Simpson, *Cyclopaedia*	Matthew Simpson, *Cyclopaedia of Methodism: Embracing Sketches of Its Rise, Progress, and Present Condition with Biographical Notices and Numerous Illustrations*, 4th rev. ed. (Philadelphia: Louis H. Everts, 1881).
Sweet, *Methodists*	William Warren Sweet, ed., *Religion on the American Frontier, 1783–1840*, vol. 4, *The Methodists: A Collection of Source Materials* (New York: Cooper Square, 1964; reprint of 1946 ed.).
Tigert, *History*	Jno. J. Tigert, *A Constitutional History of American Episcopal Methodism*, 3rd ed., rev. and enlarged (Nashville: Publishing House of the MECS, 1908).
Tigert, *Methodism*	Jno. J. Tigert, *The Making of Methodism: Studies in the Genesis of Institutions* (Nashville: Publishing House of the MECS, 1898).
Unification	*Joint Commission on Unification of The Methodist Episcopal Church, South, and The Methodist Episcopal Church*, 3 vols. (Nashville: Publishing House of the MECS; and New York: Methodist Book Concern, 1918–20).
Walls, *AMEZ*	William J. Walls, *The African Methodist Episcopal Zion Church* (Charlotte, N.C.: AMEZ Publishing House, 1974).
Wesley, *Journal* (Curnock)	*The Journal of the Rev. John Wesley, A.M.*, ed. Nehemiah Curnock, 8 vols. (London: Epworth Press, 1909–16).
Wesley, *Letters* (Telford)	*The Letters of the Rev. John Wesley, A.M.*, ed. John Telford, 8 vols. (London: Epworth Press, 1931).
Wesley, *Works*	*The Works of John Wesley*; begun as the Oxford Edition of *The Works of John Wesley* (Oxford: Clarendon Press, 1975–83); continued as the Bicentennial Edition of *The Works of John Wesley* (Nashville: Abingdon Press, 1984–); 15 of 35 vols. published to date.
Wesley, *Works* (Jackson)	*The Works of John Wesley*, ed. Thomas Jackson, 14 vols. (London, 1872; Grand Rapids: Zondervan, 1958).

For Denominational-related Agencies and Groups

AALM	Asian American Language Ministry
BMCR	Black Methodists for Church Renewal

BOM	Board of Missions
CIEMAL	Council of Evangelical Methodist Churches in Latin America
CJ	Central Jurisdiction
COB	Council of Bishops
COCU	Consultation on Church Union
COSMOS	Commission on the Structure of Methodism Overseas
COSROW	General Commission on the Status and Role of Women
CSR/LCA	Christian Social Relations and Local Church Activities
ECUMW	Evangelical Coalition for United Methodist Women
EMLC	Ethnic Minority Local Church
GBCS	General Board of Church and Society
GBGM	General Board of Global Ministries
GBHEM	General Board of Higher Education and Ministry
GBOD	General Board of Discipleship
GCAH	General Commission on Archives and History
GCCUIC	General Commission on Christian Unity and Inter-religious Concerns
GCFA	General Council on Finance and Administration
GCOM	General Council on Ministries
GCORR	General Commission on Religion and Race
GCOSROW	General Commission on the Status and Role of Women
KAM	Korean American Missions
KMC	Korean Methodist Church
LPCU	Ladies' and Pastors' Christian Union
MARCHA	Methodists Associated Representing the Cause of Hispanic Americans
MCOR	Methodist Committee for Overseas Relief
MFSA	Methodist Federation for Social Action
MFSS	Methodist Federation for Social Service
MoSAIC	Methodist Students for an All-Inclusive Church
MSF	Methodist Sacramental Fellowship
MSM	Methodist Student Movement
MYF	Methodist Youth Fellowship
NAKAUMC	National Association of Korean American United Methodist Churches
NFAAUM	National Federation of Asian American United Methodists
OIMC	Oklahoma Indian Missionary Conference

RCP	Reconciling Congregation Program
SSU	Sunday School Union (MEC)
SVM	Student Volunteer Movement
TCP	Transforming Congregation Program
UMCOR	United Methodist Committee on Relief
UMCYM	United Methodist Council on Youth Ministries
UMPH	United Methodist Publishing House
UMW	United Methodist Women
WFMS	Woman's Foreign Missionary Society
WHMS	Woman's Home Missionary Society
WMC	World Methodist Council
WMUSS	Wesleyan Methodist Union for Social Service
WSCS	Woman's Society of Christian Service (Central Jurisdiction)
WSG	Wesleyan Service Guild

For Other Agencies and Groups

ASWPL	Association of Southern Women for the Prevention of Lynching
BEDC	Black Economic Development Conference
CIC	Commission on Interracial Cooperation
CORE	Congress of Racial Equality
CORNET	Covenant Relationship Network
CTS	Chicago Training School for City, Home, and Foreign Missions
FCC	Federal Council of Churches
HUAC	House Un-American Activities Committee
IAWM	International Association of Women Ministers
IAWP	International Association of Women Preachers
IRD	Institute on Religion and Democracy
LAMAG	Latin American Action Group
NAIC	Native American International Caucus
NCC	National Council of Churches
NCKAM	National Committee on Korean-American Ministries
OSL	Order of Saint Luke
RCAR	Religious Coalition for Abortion Rights
RCRC	Religious Coalition for Reproductive Choice
SCLC	Southern Christian Leadership Conference
USSC	United States Sanitary Commission

WCC	World Council of Churches
WCRA	Woman's Central Relief Association
WCTU	Woman's Christian Temperance Union
WSCS	Woman's Society of Christian Service
YMCA	Young Men's Christian Association
YWCA	Young Women's Christian Association

NOTES

Preface

1. Abel Stevens, *The Centenary of American Methodism: A Sketch of Its History, Theology, Practical System, and Success*, with a statement of the plan of the Centenary Celebration of 1866 by John M'Clintock, D.D. (New York: Carlton & Porter, 1865), 180, 185–87. Stevens prefaced his statement about American Methodist missions with the insistence that Methodism was, from the beginning, intrinsically missionary: "Methodism was essentially a missionary movement, domestic and foreign. It initiated not only the spirit, but the practical plans of modern English missions." Stevens, indeed the whole church, then endeavored to make and keep missions central.

2. *Discipline*/UMC/1996, 114.

3. See David Hempton, *Methodism: Empire of the Spirit* (New Haven and London: Yale University Press, 2005).

4. (New York: Cambridge University Press, 2005), vii.

5. See www.drew.edu/uploadedFiles/depts/Library/methodist/resources/UM_Biblio_5th_ed.pdf.

6. Richard P. Heitzenrater, *Wesley and the People Called Methodists* (Nashville: Abingdon Press, 1995); Thomas Edward Frank, *Polity, Practice, and the Mission of The United Methodist Church* (Nashville: Abingdon Press, 2006); Rex Matthews, *Timetables of History for Students of Methodism* (Nashville: Abingdon Press, 2007); Theodore Runyon, *The New Creation: John Wesley's Theology Today* (Nashville: Abingdon Press, 1998); Thomas A. Langford, *Practical Divinity*, 2 vols. (Nashville: Abingdon Press, 1998, 1999); Scott J. Jones, *United Methodist Doctrine: The Extreme Center* (Nashville: Abingdon Press, 2002); Ted A. Campbell, *Methodist Doctrine: The Essentials* (Nashville: Abingdon Press, 1999); Walter Klaiber and Manfred Marquardt, *Living Grace: An Outline of United Methodist Theology*, translated and adapted by J. Steven O'Malley and Ulrike R. M. Guthrie (Nashville: Abingdon Press, 2001); and Karen B. Westerfield Tucker, *American Methodist Worship* (Oxford and New York: Oxford University Press, 2001); W. Harrison Daniel, *Historical Atlas of the Methodist Movement* (Nashville: Abingdon Press, 2009); and Russell E. Richey, Kenneth E. Rowe, and Jean Miller Schmidt, *Perspectives on American Methodism: Interpretive Essays* (Nashville: Kingswood Books, 1993).

I. Launching the Methodist Movements: 1760–68

1. The German rendering of the name, Philip Wilhelm Otterbein, may also be encountered, but evidence suggests Otterbein went by and signed his name William. The following analysis

depends on J. Steven O'Malley, *Pilgrimage of Faith: The Legacy of the Otterbeins*, ATLA Monograph Series, no. 4 (Metuchen, N.J.: Scarecrow Press, 1973), and *Early German-American Evangelicalism: Pietist Sources on Discipleship and Sanctification* (Lanham, Md.: Scarecrow Press, 1994); Harry Yeide Jr., *Studies in Classical Pietism* (New York: Peter Lang, 1997); K. James Stein, *Philipp Jakob Spener: Pietist Patriarch* (Chicago: Covenant Press, 1986); Arthur Wilford Nagler, *Pietism and Methodism* (Nashville: Publishing House of the MECS, 1918); Scott Kisker, "Radical Pietism and Early German Methodism: John Seybert and the Evangelical Association," *MHist* 37 (April 1999): 175–88; Peter C. Erb, ed., *Pietists: Selected Writings* (New York, Ramsey, Toronto: Paulist Press, 1983); the several writings by F. Ernest Stoeffler, *The Rise of Evangelical Pietism* (Leiden: Brill, 1965), *German Pietism during the Eighteenth Century* (Leiden: Brill, 1973), and *Continental Pietism and Early American Christianity* (Grand Rapids: Eerdmans, 1976). On John Wesley's relation to Pietism see Martin Schmidt, *John Wesley*, 2 vols. (Zurich, 1953–66), and *John Wesley: A Theological Biography*, trans. Norman P. Goldhawk (London: Epworth Press, 1962–71).

2. In *The Religion of the Heart: A Study of European Religious Life in the Seventeenth and Eighteenth Centuries* (Columbia: University of South Carolina Press, 1991), Ted A. Campbell establishes the coherence of the Pietist world and treats major characteristics discussed below. A very different approach, that by W. Reginald Ward, in *The Protestant Evangelical Awakening* (Cambridge: Cambridge University Press, 1992) and in *Early Evangelicalism: A Global Intellectual History, 1670–1789* (Cambridge, UK; New York: Cambridge University Press, 2006), also traces the interconnections between and among the international Pietist movements and the several awakenings.

3. Edwards will not concern us here. He becomes important to nineteenth-century Methodism as its foremost intellectual antagonist, the American who gave the most compelling statement of Calvinist theology. On Whitefield's activities and their relation to the Wesleyan and other Pietist movements, see Stuart C. Henry, *George Whitefield: Wayfaring Witness* (New York and Nashville: Abingdon Press, 1957); Harry S. Stout, *The Divine Dramatist: George Whitefield and the Rise of Modern Evangelicalism* (Grand Rapids: Eerdmans, 1991), and "Religion, Communications, and the Career of George Whitefield," in *Communication and Change in American Religious History*, ed. Leonard I. Sweet (Grand Rapids: Eerdmans, 1993), 108–25; Frank Lambert, *"Pedlar in Divinity": George Whitefield and the Transatlantic Revivals, 1737–1770* (Princeton: Princeton University Press, 1994); Dee E. Andrews, *The Methodists and Revolutionary America, 1760–1800: The Shaping of an Evangelical Culture* (Princeton: Princeton University Press, 2000), 19–31; and Frank Baker, *From Wesley to Asbury: Studies in Early American Methodism* (Durham: Duke University Press, 1976), 23–27.

4. On the Georgia experience, see Richard P. Heitzenrater, *Wesley and the People Called Methodists* (Nashville: Abingdon Press, 1995), 56–73. For a more positive assessment of the Georgia experience and its connection with later American Methodism, see Baker, *From Wesley to Asbury*, 3–13.

5. O'Malley, *Pilgrimage of Faith*, 94–188; J. Bruce Behney and Paul H. Eller, *The History of The Evangelical United Brethren Church* (Nashville: Abingdon Press, 1979), 31–38; Arthur C. Core, *Philip William Otterbein: Pastor–Ecumenist* (Dayton: Board of Publication, The Evangelical United Brethren Church, 1968).

6. O'Malley, *Pilgrimage of Faith*, 166.

7. For further commentary on and the full version of Otterbein's sermon, see O'Malley, *Early German-American Evangelicalism: Pietist Sources on Discipleship and Sanctification* (Lanham, Md.: Scarecrow Press, 1994), 19–41.

8. Behney/Eller, *History*, 38–45.

9. Long's Barn, the meeting place of Boehm and Otterbein, was dedicated as a UMC Heritage Landmark on May 31, 2009.

10. *Discipline/UBC-1819*, 7–17. Note that this text in the gray box, taken from the first UBC *Discipline*, will be paralleled by similar official historical statements from the first or an early *Discipline* of other important Methodist movements. We have positioned the historical statements in gray boxes at the point each denomination takes up its story. The historical statement belongs as well to the organizational saga of the movement and its writing of its *Discipline*, and so exhibits the remarkable historical orientation of Methodism. Methodists constituted themselves in classes and societies, on the ground as it were, by telling and hearing one another's experience. Methodists constituted themselves in denominations, nationally as it were, by telling and hearing of their collective experience.

11. Andrews, *The Methodists*, 31.

12. Baker, *From Wesley to Asbury*, 28–50.

13. *Discipline/MEC-1787*, 3–7. See the note above concerning the UBC historical preface.

14. On women's role in the creation of Methodism, see Schmidt, *Grace Sufficient*; Paul Wesley Chilcote, *John Wesley and the Women Preachers of Early Methodism* (Metuchen, N.J.: Scarecrow Press, 1991); Earl Kent Brown, *Women of Mr. Wesley's Methodism* (New York: Edwin Mellen Press, 1983); Andrews, *The Methodists*, 31–38; Cynthia Lynn Lyerly, *Methodism and the Southern Mind, 1770–1810* (New York and Oxford: Oxford University Press, 1998), 94–118; Christine Leigh Heyrman, *Southern Cross: The Beginnings of the Bible Belt* (New York: Knopf, 1997), 161–205; John H. Wigger, *Taking Heaven by Storm: Methodism and the Rise of Popular Christianity in America* (New York and Oxford: Oxford University Press, 1998), 151–72.

15. Robert Strawbridge's log house, near New Windsor, Maryland, was placed on the national register of UMC Heritage Landmarks in 1968.

16. Baker, *From Wesley to Asbury*, 55–59; Andrews, *The Methodists*, 35–45. For Webb's preaching, see John Pritchard, *Sermon Occasioned by the Death of the Late Capt. Webb and Preached at Portland Chapel, Bristol, December 24, 1796, at the Time of HIs Interment* (Bristol: R. Edwards, 1797), 21–23.

17. On the role of Heck and the emergence of Canadian Methodism see the superb recent history thereof, Semple, *Dominion*, esp. 42, 58.

18. Andrews, *The Methodists*, 32.

II. Structuring the Immigrant Initiatives: 1769–78

1. Frederick E. Maser and Howard T. Maag, eds., *The Journal of Joseph Pilmore for the Years August 1, 1769, to January 2, 1774*, with a Biographical Sketch of Joseph Pilmore by Frank B. Stanger (Philadelphia: Message Publishing Co. for the Historical Society of the Philadelphia Annual Conference, UMC, 1969), 20.

2. For the New York version of the Wesleyan system and its divergences from the British

template, see Philip F. Hardt, *The Soul of Methodism: The Class Meeting in Early New York Methodism* (Lanham, Md.: University Press of America, 2000).

3. *Journal of Joseph Pilmore*, 25–29. *Discipline/UMC/1996*, 582–84. For "Large Minutes," Wesley, *Works* (Jackson), 8:299–338, the 1791 version, and for "Model Deed," 329–31. See Richard Heitzenrater, *Wesley and the People Called Methodists* (Nashville: Abingdon Press, 1995), 212–14.

4. *Journal of Joseph Pilmore*, 43, 29, 25–26.

5. *JLFA*, 1:4, for Sept. 12, 1771; 1:6, for Oct. 27, 1771; 1:9, for Nov. 12, 1771; 1:10, for Nov. 19, 21, 1771.

6. Jesse Lee, *A Short History of the Methodists* (Baltimore: Magill & Clime, 1810; facsimile ed., Rutland, Vt.: Academy Books, 1974), 43.

7. *JLFA*, 1:25, for April 2. *Journal of Joseph Pilmore*, 134–205. See 137, 139, for June 8, 16 in Maryland; 140, for June 21 in Baltimore Forrest; 141, for June 28, 29; 148, for July 26; 154, for Sept. 15, 16.

8. *Journal of Joseph Pilmore*, 163, for Nov. 23–26, 1772.

9. See Fred Hood, "Community and Rhetoric of 'Freedom': Early American Methodist Worship," *MethH* 9 (Oct. 1970): 13–25; Donald G. Mathews, "Evangelical America—The Methodist Ideology," in *Perspectives*, 17–30, and "United Methodism and American Culture: Testimony, Voice, and the Public Sphere," in *PCM*, 279–304.

10. *JLFA*, 1:43, for Sept. 11, 14, 1772; 1:41, for Sept. 5, 1772; 1:46, for Oct. 10, 11, 1772; emphases in citations ours.

11. *JLFA*, 1:51–52, for Nov. 8, 1772.

12. *The Life of the Reverend Devereux Jarratt*, foreword by David L. Holmes (Cleveland: Pilgrim Press, 1995; first published 1806), 62; emphases in the original. *JLFA*, 3:28, letter dated Pennsylvania, Aug. 1783.

13. *JLFA*, 1:59–60, for Dec. 22, 1772.

14. Lee, *Short History*, 54. *JLFA*, 1:59–60, for Dec. 22, 1772; 1:74–75, for March 30, 1773.

15. *JLFA*, 1:80, for June 3, 1773.

16. Wesley, *Letters* (Telford), 6:57, dated Dec. 4, 1773.

17. Francis Holsclaw, "The Demise of Disciplined Christian Fellowship: The Methodist Class Meeting in Nineteenth-Century America" (PhD diss., University of California, 1979), 39–40; Hardt, *The Soul of Methodism*, 27–33, 61–62.

18. "The Life of Mr. Thomas Rankin. Written by Himself," in *The Lives of Early Methodist Preachers, Chiefly Written by Themselves*, ed. Thomas Jackson, 4th ed., 6 vols. (London: Wesleyan Conference Office, 1873), 5:135–217, esp. 193. Compare the accounts in *Journal of Joseph Pilmore*, 210, for July 13, 1773; *JLFA*, 1:85, for July 14, 1773.

19. Gordon Pratt Baker, ed., *Those Incredible Methodists: A History of the Baltimore Conference of The United Methodist Church* (Baltimore: Commission on Archives and History, Baltimore Conference, 1972), 26.

20. "Journal of Thomas Rankin, 1773–1778," 15, for Saturday, July 30, 1774, transcribed by Francis H. Tees, United Methodist Archives and History Center, Drew University, Madison, New Jersey. For the argument, based on a recently surfaced letter of Rankin, that greater numbers of African Americans attended than were counted as members, see Robert Glen, "Methodism and the American Revolution: Insights from a Neglected Thomas Rankin Letter," *Proceedings of the Wesley Historical Society* 52 (May 1999): 34–38.

21. Arthur C. Core reproduces those *Minutes* in *Philip William Otterbein: Pastor–Ecumenist* (Dayton: Board of Publication, the EUBC, 1968), 115–19. *JLFA*, 1:114, for May 3, 1774.

22. "A Short Account of Mr. Thomas Rankin: In a Letter to the Rev. Mr. John Wesley," *Arminian Magazine* 2 (1779), 182–98, 196.

23. "The Life of Mr. Thomas Rankin," 135–217, 202. "Journal of Thomas Rankin, 1773–1778," United Methodist Archives and History Center, Drew University, Madison, New Jersey, 21, 30. These first interesting reflections for Dec. 25, 1774, and Jan. 1, 1775, Rankin made along with new year's resolutions and comment on Asbury's sickness. The latter entry was for Sept. 1776.

24. John Wesley, *Thoughts upon Slavery* (Philadelphia: Reprinted with notes and sold by Joseph Crukshank, 1774), 56–57, emphasis in original.

25. Wesley, *Letters* (Telford), 6:142–43, March 1, 1775.

26. "The Life of Mr. Thomas Rankin," 204.

27. *Minutes/MEC/1784* (1813), for 1775, 10.

28. Heitzenrater, *Wesley and the People Called Methodists*, 262.

29. Dee E. Andrews, *The Methodists and Revolutionary America, 1760–1800: The Shaping of an Evangelical Culture* (Princeton: Princeton University Press, 2000), 51–55.

30. Lee, *Short History*, 60. Shadford declaration cited by Andrews, *The Methodists*, 51–52. Jackson, *The Lives of Early Methodist Preachers, Chiefly Written by Themselves*, 6:171–72.

31. Semple, *Dominion*, 42.

32. *Journal of Joseph Pilmore*, 133n11. Jackson, *The Lives of Early Methodist Preachers*, 6:173. Lee, *Short History*, 64. On Rankin's sufferings, see also Glen, "Methodism and the American Revolution."

33. Baker, *Incredible Methodists*, 47. *JLFA*, 1:263–64, for March 13, 1778.

34. Baker, *Incredible Methodists*, 47–50.

35. For his persecutions see Garrettson's *The Experience and Travels* and ample selections from the manuscripts that underlie his account in Robert D. Simpson, *American Methodist Pioneer: The Life and Journals of the Rev. Freeborn Garrettson, 1752–1827* (Rutland, Vt.: Academy Books for the Drew University Library, 1984).

36. Lee, *Short History*, 64–65. These points are developed fully by Christine Leigh Heyrman, *Southern Cross: The Beginnings of the Bible Belt* (New York: Knopf, 1997).

37. *Sketches of the Life and Travels of Rev. Thomas Ware . . . Written by Himself* (New York: Lane & Sandford for The Methodist Episcopal Church, 1842; reprint, Holston Conference), 24–79.

38. R. Yeakel, *Jacob Albright and His Co-Laborers*, trans. from the German (Cleveland: Publishing House of the EA, 1883). *EWM*, 1:79–80.

39. Baker, *Incredible Methodists*, 47–52. Minton Thrift, *Memoir of the Rev. Jesse Lee, with Extracts from His Journals* (New York: N. Bangs & T. Mason for The Methodist Episcopal Church, 1823), 26–33.

40. Frederick E. Maser, "Discovery," *MethH* 9 (Jan. 1971): 34–43. Maser reproduces statements and phrases from *An Extract from the Journal of Francis Asbury, One of the Bishops of the Methodist Episcopal Church: From January 1st, 1779, to September 3d., 1780* (Philadelphia: Ezekiel Cooper, 1802). Compare *JLFA*, 1:296. For other forceful statements by Asbury against slavery or efforts he made to convince slaveholders to free their slaves, see further entries in the Maser article for March 27 and April 23, 1779, and May 22, 23, 1780.

41. *Minutes*/MEC/1773–84 (1813), 6–48. Figures for 1778 derive from the Philip Gatch version of the "Minutes of the Early Methodist Conferences in America" distributed by the Baltimore Conference Methodist Historical Society. A figure of 6,881 is given in another set of the minutes, apparently kept by John Cooper and Thomas Haskins. It lacks a return for the Carolina Circuit, which Gatch lists as 300. See "The Leesburg Minutes of the Methodist Connection, 1775–1783," *Virginia United Methodist Heritage* 5 (Fall 1977): 5–43. For New York compare Samuel A. Seaman, *Annals of New York Methodism: Being a History of The Methodist Episcopal Church in the City of New York* (New York: Hunt & Eaton; Cincinnati: Cranston & Stowe, 1892), 496–97.

III. Making Church: 1777–84

1. *JLFA*, 1:239, for May 12, 1777.

2. For the published collected versions see *Minutes*/MEC/1777 (1813), 13–15, or the first published collection, *Minutes of the Methodist Conferences Annually Held in America, from 1773 to 1794, Inclusive* (Philadelphia, 1795; reprint, Strawbridge Shrine Assn.), or the standard *Minutes*/MEC/1777. The question number was 7. See n. 40 in chap. 2 of this book; also "The Leesburg Minutes of the Methodist Connection, 1775–1783," *Virginia United Methodist Heritage* 5 (Fall 1977), 15. Philip Gatch, "Minutes of the Early Methodist Conferences in America," "Minutes of a Conference Held in Baltimore, May, 1777," 6. This is a version kept by Philip Gatch and originally printed in the *WCA*, May 19, 26, 1837. It is also reproduced in *Sourcebook of American Methodism*, ed. Frederick A. Norwood (Nashville: Abingdon Press, 1982), 56. For the procedures by which the *Minutes* were expurgated, see Tigert, *History*, 130. The 1782 *Minutes* stipulated (Quest. 18) the erasure of items dealing with the ordinances, *Minutes*/MEC/1782 (1813), 37.

3. During Rankin's tenure, Asbury's name came second. See the *Minutes* of 1774, 1775, 1776, and 1777, *Minutes*/MEC/1774–1777 (1813), 7, 9, 11, 13. On Asbury's activity during confinement, see *JLFA*, 1:269n, 269–313.

4. "The Leesburg Minutes," 15–17; Gatch, "Minutes of the Early Methodist Conferences in America," 6–8; Tigert, *History*, 94.

5. "The Leesburg Minutes," 20–22.

6. *JLFA*, 1:300, for April 28, May 3, 1779.

7. *Minutes*/MEC/1779 (1813), 19–20; "The Leesburg Minutes," 19–20. The latter provided "What provision shall be made in case of Br. Asburys Death or absence Ans. Let Br. Ruff, B. Garrettson and Br. McClure act as general Assistants for the Northrin Stations."

8. *Minutes*/MEC/1780 (1813), 23–27. *JLFA*, 1:347, for April 25, 1780; see 347–49 for Asbury's lobbying.

9. "The Leesburg Minutes," 28. *JLFA*, 1:349–50, for May 9, 10, 1780. See Garrettson's published and MS account in Robert D. Simpson, *American Methodist Pioneer: The Life and Journals of the Rev. Freeborn Garrettson, 1752–1827* (Rutland, Vt.: Academy Books for the Drew University Library, 1984), 104, 176.

10. Simpson, *American Methodist Pioneer*, 104.

11. Lee, *Short History*, 72.

12. *JLFA*, 1:403, for May 13, 21, 1781; 1:413, for Oct. 27, 1781; J. Gordon Melton, *A Will to Choose: The Origins of African American Methodism* (Lanham, Md.: Rowman & Littlefield, 2007), 35–51.

13. *Minutes/MEC/*1780 (1813), 26; "The Leesburg Minutes," 28. Simpson, *American Methodist Pioneer*, 182, a MS portion of Garrettson's journal for Nov. 11, 1780. *JLFA*, 1:386–87, for Nov. 3, 6, 1780.

14. Lee, *Short History*, 74, 77. *Minutes/MEC/*1777–1783 (1813), 13–42. For the middle years, because of the war, New York could not report.

15. *JLFA*, 1:346, for April 24, 1780. Lee, *Short History*, 75. *Minutes/MEC/*1781 (1813), 28–32. The "Baltimore system" is a formulation of and chapter by Jno. J. Tigert in *The Making of Methodism: Studies in the Genesis of Institutions* (Nashville: Publishing House of the MECS, 1898). See also Tigert, *History*, 122–24, 523–31.

16. Tigert, *History*, 123–24.

17. Still the title language of the American *Minutes*: "Minutes of Some Conversations between the Preachers in Connection with the Reverend Mr. John Wesley"; *Minutes/MEC/*1781 (1813), 28. The Leesburg title for this session was "Minutes of Conference Held April 16 1781 at Choptank Delaware State and Adjourned to Baltimore"; "The Leesburg Minutes," 30.

18. *Minutes/MEC/*1781 (1813), 28–32. "The Leesburg Minutes," 30–31. Richey, *Conference*, 37–39. *JLFA*, 1:411, for Sept. 11, 1781; 1:413, for Oct. 27, 1781; 1:414, for Dec. 6, 19, 1781.

19. *Minutes/MEC/*1782 (1813), 33–37.

20. *JLFA*, 1:44n, 442n, 451n for notices on priests and their support of the Methodists; 1:450–51 for Asbury's staying with Pettigrew; and 3:24–34 for letters to Wesley. Asbury spoke of four clergy—Jarratt (Virginia), Pettigrew (North Carolina), Magaw (Philadelphia), and "Mogden," actually Ogden (East Jersey)—"who behaved themselves friendly in attending Quarterly Meetings." *JLFA*, 3:28, letter to George Shadford of Aug. 1783.

21. "The Leesburg Minutes," 1783, 42–43. Compare *Minutes/MEC/*1783 (1813), 41–42. Wesley, *Letters* (Telford), 7:191; Lee, *Short History*, 85–86; and Tigert, *History*, 134–35 reproduce Wesley's letter, dated Oct. 3, 1783, which was addressed "To the Preachers in America." *JLFA*, 1:450, for Dec. 24, 1783.

22. "The Leesburg Minutes," 1783, 42–43. Compare *Minutes/MEC/*1783 (1813), 41–42. Lee, *Short History*, 82–86. For earlier legislation on support for spouses, without specification of names or apportionments, see 1780, Quest. 4, *Minutes/MEC/*1780 (1813), 25.

23. See Richard Heitzenrater, *Wesley and the People Called Methodists* (Nashville: Abingdon Press, 1995), 281–92; John Vickers, *Thomas Coke: Apostle of Methodism* (London: Epworth Press; Nashville and New York: Abingdon Press, 1969). For the Benson and Fletcher plans for reform see Wesley, *Journal* (Curnock), 8:328–34.

24. L. Tyerman, *The Life and Times of the Rev. John Wesley*, 3 vols. (New York: Harper & Brothers, 1872), 3:428, 429, and Vickers, *Thomas Coke*, 75–76, 77–78, for letters of April 17, 1784, and Aug. 9, 1784.

25. For Coke's "Certificate of Ordination," see Vickers, *Thomas Coke*, 367.

26. Heitzenrater, *Wesley and the People Called Methodists*, 288–90. See the reprinted *Sunday Service, John Wesley's Sunday Service of the Methodists in North America*, with an introduction by James F. White (Nashville: Quarterly Review, 1984), and Karen Westerfield Tucker, *American Methodist Worship* (New York and Oxford: Oxford University Press, 2001).

27. *The Journals of Dr. Thomas Coke*, ed. John A. Vickers (Nashville: Kingswood Books, 2005), 34–35.

28. "Adam Fonerden to Stephen Donaldson, Baltimore, November 28th, 1784," Baltimore Conference United Methodist Historical Society.

29. In addition to the account by Coke (Sources 1784b), see those easily accessible ones by Garrettson and Asbury: Simpson, *American Methodist Pioneer*, 243, a manuscript portion of Garrettson's journal, and 122, the published version; and *JLFA*, 1:471–72, for Sunday, Nov. 14. For the titles of the early *Disciplines*, see Tigert, *History*, 463–76.

30. P. P. Sandford, *Memoirs of Mr. Wesley's Missionaries to America* (New York: G. Lane & P. P. Sandford for the MEC, 1843), 365–66.

IV. Constituting Methodisms: 1784–92

1. *JLFA*, 1:474, for Dec. 24, 1784. The subheading is intended to evoke that classic parody of symbolic dates, *1066 and All That: A Memorable History of England Comprising All the Parts You Can Remember including One Hundred and Three Good Things, Five Bad Kings, and Two Genuine Dates* by Walter C. Sellar and Robert J. Yeatman, 5th ed. (London: Methuen, 1930).

2. Otterbein offered the use of his German Reformed congregation's warm new church to the Methodists for several sessions during their wintry conference. Restored buildings still house the Old Otterbein UMC congregation in the historic inner harbor area, since 1978 a designated UMC Heritage Landmark.

3. *Minutes/MEC/1785* (1813), 49–55. *Sketches of the Life and Travels of Rev. Thomas Ware . . . written by Himself* (New York: G. Lane & P. P. Sandford for the MEC, 1842), 106. John Vickers, *Thomas Coke: Apostle of Methodism* (London: Epworth Press; Nashville and New York: Abingdon Press, 1969), 86–91.

4. Lee, *Short History*, 94; Tigert, *History*, 180–94.

5. Tigert, *History*, 188–94.

6. The relation of *Discipline* to "Large Minutes" is best viewed in the parallel columns provided by Tigert, *History*, 532–602. *JLFA*, 1:476.

7. The legislation included (Sources 1785, Q. 46) permission for rebaptism, a provision rescinded in 1787. See the discussion on this point by Karen B. Westerfield Tucker, *American Methodist Worship* (Oxford and New York: Oxford University Press, 2001).

8. Compare the itemization of accomplishments by Lee, *Short History*, 94–111.

9. The sermon was subsequently published as Thomas Coke, *The Substance of a Sermon Preached at Baltimore, in the State of Maryland, before the General Conference of The Methodist Episcopal Church, . . . at the ordination of the Reverend Francis Asbury, to the office of a superintendent*, published at the desire of the conference (Baltimore, 1785; reprint, New York: T. Mason & G. Lane, 1840). For the "grand characteristics of a Christian bishop," see 10–15. They were humility, meekness, gentleness, patience, fortitude, impartiality, zeal, wisdom, communion with God and confidence in God, and seriousness. For the ordination certificate, see *JLFA*, 1:474, for Dec. 24, 1784, and Vickers, *Thomas Coke*, 369.

10. This section's discussion follows Behney/Eller, *History*, 45–57, and Arthur C. Core, *Philip William Otterbein: Pastor, Ecumenist* (Dayton: Board of Publication, EUBC, 1968). For the Pipe Creek minutes, see the latter, 115–19.

11. Behney/Eller, *History*, 56–66.

12. Robert D. Simpson, *American Methodist Pioneer: The Life and Journals of the Rev. Freeborn Garrettson, 1752–1827* (Rutland, Vt.: Academy Books for the Drew University Library, 1984), 243, a MS portion of Garrettson's journal; compare 122, the published version; Lee, *Short History*, 107.

13. See the accounts of Livingston (Garrettson) by Diane H. Lobody, "'That Language Might Be Given Me': Women's Experience in Early Methodism," in *Perspectives*, 127–44, and "'A Wren Just Bursting Its Shell': Catherine Livingston Garrettson's Ministry of Public Domesticity," in *Spirituality and Social Responsibility*, ed. Rosemary Skinner Keller (Nashville: Abingdon Press, 1993), 19–38. On Rogers, see Schmidt, *Grace Sufficient*. The first American edition (New York, 1804) is available in Early American Imprints, second series, no. 7207.

14. On Methodist counterpoint to gentility, see Cynthia Lynn Lyerly, *Methodism and the Southern Mind, 1770–1810* (New York and Oxford: Oxford University Press, 1998); Williams, *The Garden of American Methodism*; Christine Leigh Heyrman, *Southern Cross: The Beginnings of the Bible Belt* (New York: Knopf, 1997); and Russell E. Richey, *Early American Methodism* (Bloomington and Indianapolis: Indiana University Press, November 1991).

15. *A Journal of the Travels of William Colbert, Methodist Preacher: thro' parts of Maryland, Pennsylvania, New York, Delaware and Virginia in 1790 to 1838*, 10 vols., typescript copy, Drew University, 1:6.

16. See Garrettson's "Substance of the Semi-Centennial Sermon . . . ," in Simpson, *American Methodist Pioneer*, 48–50, 390–91, 404–5, 158.

17. "A Journal and Travel of James Meacham, Part II, 1789–1797," *Historical Papers*, Series X, 1914, published by the Trinity College Historical Society, 92–93, 97. Excerpt from the James Meacham Journals, 1788–1797, located in the Rare Book, Manuscript, and Special Collection Library, Duke University.

18. "A Journal and Travel of James Meacham, Part I, May 19 to August 31, 1789," *Historical Papers*, 9:66–95, 88.

19. *A Journal of the Travels of William Colbert*, 1:157 for Saturday, February 15, 1794; 2:58, for Aug. 27, 1794. Tuesday, March 22, 1796: "I preached at William Conwells. . . . My feelings have been hurt in this place, when I was informed, I was to be spoken to, for calling the Black people *Brethren*, and sisters, here and in Milford." He then enters into his journal a long defense of the practice on theological grounds with an appeal to Philemon, 2:84.

20. "Tuesday 27th. I preached at Brother Wm. Warren's and my Soul was grieved . . . professors of Religion so careless and trifling." "William Spencer's Diary on the Surry Circuit, June-July, 1790," *Virginia United Methodist Heritage* 3 (Fall 1975): 9–27, 24–25.

21. "Addicted to social pleasures and dissipations. . . . 4. Showily dressed." *The Oxford Universal Dictionary on Historical Principles*. Prepared by William Little, H. W. Fowler, and J. Coulson, rev. and edited by C. T. Onions, 3d ed. Rev (Oxford: Clarendon Press, 1955), 780.

22. Stith Mead, *A Short Account of the Experience and Labors of the Rev. Stith Mead* (Lynchburg, 1829), 47–48. For treatment of the genteel foil for early Methodism, see A. Gregory Schneider, *The Way of the Cross Leads Home: The Domestication of American Methodism* (Bloomington and Indianapolis: Indiana University Press, 1993); Lyerly, *Methodism and the Southern Mind*; Williams, *The Garden of American Methodism*; Heyrman, *Southern Cross*; and Richey, *Early American Methodism*.

23. *JLFA*, 1:489, for May 22, 1785. Of the meeting with President Washington, Asbury noted, "We waited on General Washington, who received us very politely, and gave us his opinion against slavery," 2:41, for Feb. 5, 1795.

24. See Lyerly, *Methodism and the Southern Mind*, 47–72. On Methodist contribution to manumissions and consequent appeal to African Americans, see Christopher Phillips, *Freedom's Port: The African American Community of Baltimore, 1790–1860* (Urbana and Chicago: University of Illinois Press, 1997), esp. 58–61, 117–44; and Charles G. Steffen, *The Mechanics of Baltimore: Workers and Politics in the Age of Revolution, 1763–1812* (Urbana and Chicago: University of Illinois Press, 1984), 255–73.

25. On Coke, see Vickers, *Thomas Coke*, 94–98. Apparently Coke's antislavery statements at the conference at Green Hill's caused Lee to object to the passage of Coke's character (*JLFA*, 1:487n). Letters of Francis Asbury to Freeborn Garrettson, Sept. 2, 1785, Sept. 1786, New York, Wesleyan University Library, Special Collections & Archives. In both letters, Asbury worried over and counseled unity. He expressed special concern over Br. Pilmore, returned with Anglican orders, and over Br. Glendenning's continued stirring of unrest.

26. Lee, *Short History*, 102. On Methodism's steady retreat from its antislavery commitments and "compromise" of its principles, see Donald G. Mathews, *Slavery and Methodism* (Princeton: Princeton University Press, 1965).

27. Simpson, *American Methodist Pioneer*, 127, for Aug. 1785; 266–70, for June-July 1790, from the MS journal to be compared with the comparable period in the published version, 141–43.

28. *Minutes/MEC/1787* (1813), 67–68.

29. The misdating of the founding incident at St. George's seems to have originated in Richard Allen and Jacob Tapisco's introduction to the *Doctrines and Discipline of the AME Church*, published in 1817 after Allen had made final his split with the Methodists. The introduction—a "brief statement of our rise and progress"— dates the incident as Nov. 1787. The AME Church continues to date itself from 1787. Many early Methodist historians, and almost all historians writing since, have accepted this date. Milton Sernett, however, in 1975 provided convincing evidence that Allen, writing a quarter of a century after the fact, telescoped the two walkouts, 1787 and 1792. In his autobiography, published in 1833, Allen related that the incident occurred after the galleries and new flooring had been installed; but using the building records in the vault at St. George's Church, Sernett showed that the galleries were not finished until May 1792. Moreover, the initials of the elders and pastors that Allen recounted as connected with the incident cannot be associated with any St. George's officials in 1787 but correspond to those serving in 1791–92. Sernett, *Black Religion and American Evangelicalism: White Protestants, Plantation Missions, and the Flowering of Negro Christianity, 1787–1865* (Metuchen, N.J.: Scarecrow Press, 1975), 117–18, 219–20. See Dee E. Andrews, *The Methodists and Revolutionary America, 1760–1800: The Shaping of an Evangelical Culture* (Princeton: Princeton University Press, 2000); Carol V. R. George, *Segregated Sabbaths: Richard Allen and the Rise of Independent Black Churches, 1760–1840* (New York: Oxford University Press, 1973); *The Life Experience and Gospel Labors of the Rt. Rev. Richard Allen*, 2nd ed. (New York: Abingdon Press, 1960); Will B. Gravely, "African Methodisms and the Rise of Black Denominationalism," in *Rethinking Methodist History*, ed. Russell E. Richey and Kenneth E. Rowe (Nashville: Kingswood Books, 1985), 111–24, and in *Perspectives*, 108–26.

30. *The Doctrines and Discipline of the African Methodist Episcopal Church*, published by Richard

Allen and Jacob Tapisco for the African Methodist Connection in the United States (Philadelphia: John H. Cunningham, 1817), 11–14.

31. Edward J. Drinkhouse, *History of Methodist Reform*, 2 vols. (Baltimore and Pittsburgh: Board of Publications of the MPC, 1899), 1:267–68n; Vickers, *Thomas Coke*, 90–91, 176–91; Frederick V. Mills Sr., *Bishops by Ballot* (New York: Oxford University Press, 1978), 255–56.

32. *The Life of the Reverend Devereux Jarratt, Rector of Bath Parish, Virginia, written by himself in a series of letters addressed to the Rev. John Coleman* (Baltimore: Warner & Hanna, 1806); see David Holmes, ed., *The Life of the Reverend Devereux Jarratt* (Cleveland: Pilgrim Press, 1995). William H. Williams, "The Attraction of Methodism: The Delmarva Peninsula as a Case Study, 1769–1820," in *Perspectives*, 31–45, and *The Garden of American Methodism*, 89–120.

33. Vickers, *Thomas Coke*, 99n, 114; Wesley, *Letters* (Telford), 7:339; Lee, *Short History*, 124–27; Simpson, *American Methodist Pioneer*, 132, 133, 254–55; Wesley, *Journal* (Curnock), 7:300n. Though termed a "General Conference" by Wesley, this 1787 event was not properly a general conference in the sense that that of 1792 and those quadrennially called thereafter would be. For an exhaustive canvassing of this point, see Tigert, *History*, 237–39.

34. *JLFA*, 1:535–39. Note Asbury's account of his sermons on Isaiah 64:1-5 and Romans 10:14-15 (Sources 1789a).

35. See the letter of April 1787 from O'Kelly in *JLFA*, 3:49–54; *Minutes/MEC/1786* (1813), 61; 1787, 62–68; *Sketches of the Life and Travels of Rev. Thomas Ware*, 129–31; Lee, *Short History*, 125; Tigert, *History*, 225–40.

36. Simpson, *American Methodist Pioneer*, 132, 133, 254–55. Compare his later account in his "Semi-Centennial Sermon," *American Methodist Pioneer*, 392–93, where he disputed the reading by Lee. See Lee, *Short History*, 126–28. See also there 120, on the office of presiding elder. See Sherman, *Revisions*, 26, 68–69; Vickers, *Thomas Coke*, 117–20.

37. Lee, *Short History*, 127. Wesley's letter was dated Sept. 20, 1788. See Wesley, *Letters* (Telford), 8:91; *JLFA*, 3:64–65.

38. The Wesley letter was cited in *A Rejoindre: Being a Defence of the Truths Contained in an Appeal to Truth and Circumstances* [William Hammett] (Charleston, 1792), 25–26.

39. Lee, *Short History*, 134–37; *Minutes/MEC/1787*, 1788 (1813), 66–67, 74–76.

40. Lee, *Short History*, 149–50; *The Life and Travels of Rev. Thomas Ware*, 181–82.

41. Tigert, *History*, 244–45; Lee, *Short History*, 150–59; *The Proceedings of the Bishop and Presiding Elders of The Methodist-Episcopal Church, in Council Assembled, at Baltimore, on the First Day of December, 1789* (Baltimore: William Woodard & James Angell, 1789) and *Minutes Taken at a Council of the Bishop and Delegated Elders of The Methodist Episcopal Church: Held at Baltimore in the State of Maryland, December 1, 1790* (Baltimore: W. Goddard & J. Angell, 1790).

42. Lee, *Short History*, 151–55. Legislation so passed "shall be received by every member of each conference" (153). Neely, *Conference*, 304.

43. See Charles F. Kilgore, "The James O'Kelly Schism in the Methodist Episcopal Church" (PhD diss., Emory University, 1961).

44. *JLFA*, 1:620, for Tuesday, Jan. 12, 1790. Asbury registered his own sense of the constraints on his power and influence.

45. *JLFA*, 1:625, Feb. 14, 1790; 1:642, June 14, 1790; 3:87. Commentary on letter "To the Virginia Preachers," Autumn 1790, *JLFA*, 1:649. "Journals," 4, for Sept. 1, 5, 1790, in James

Meacham Papers, 1788–1797. Excerpt from the James Meacham Journals, 1788–1797, located in the Rare Book, Manuscript, and Special Collection Library, Duke University. Robert Paine, *Life and Times of William M'Kendree*, 2 vols. (Nashville: Publishing House of the MECS, 1874), 1:61, 113, 129. *A Journal of the Travels of William Colbert*, 1:130.

46. *Minutes Taken at a Council of the Bishop and Delegated Elders*, 3; Lee, *Short History*, 155.

47. Candy Gunther Brown, *Word in the World: Evangelical Writing, Publishing, and Reading in America, 1789–1880* (Chapel Hill and London: University of North Carolina Press, 2004), 46, 9–12. On the settling of the publishing enterprise, see Pilkington/Vernon, *Methodist Publishing House*, 1:80–116.

48. *Minutes Taken at a Council of the Bishop and Delegated Elders*, 3–8. *Proceedings of the Bishop and Presiding Elders of The Methodist-Episcopal Church*, 6–7. Methodist communication through publishing would be an important part of the evangelistic effort. The effect of a venture like the *Arminian Magazine* is harder to gauge. However, William Colbert noted for Dec. 30, 1790, "spent some time in reading in the Arminian Magazine" and entered similar comments for May 29, June 20, June 30, 1791. *A Journal of the Travels of William Colbert*, 1:26, 39, 40, 41.

49. JLFA, 1:667–68, for Feb. 23, 1791; 1:672, for Tuesday, April 19, 1791. Vickers, *Thomas Coke*, 192–93. Coke, *The Substance of a Sermon Preached in Baltimore and Philadelphia, on the First and Eighth of May, 1791, on the Death of the Rev. John Wesley* (London, 1791).

50. Lee, *Short History*, 149, 177; JLFA, 1:687, for July 1, 1791; Leroy Lee, *The Life and Times of The Rev. Jesse Lee* (Nashville: Southern Methodist Publishing House, 1860, c. 1848), 268–71, 282. *The Impartial Statement of the Known Inconsistencies of the Reverend Dr. Coke, in His Official Station as Superintendent of the Methodist Missions in the West-Indies: With a Brief Description of one of his Tours through the United States* (Charleston, 1792), 6–7.

51. Lee, *Short History*, 180; a reconstruction of the minutes, effected by Thomas B. Neely, can be found in Lewis Curts, ed., *The General Conferences of The Methodist Episcopal Church from 1792 to 1896* (Cincinnati: Curts & Jennings; New York; Eaton & Mains, 1892); Frederick A. Norwood, "A Crisis of Leadership: The General Conference of 1792," MethH 28 (April 1990): 129–201; Tigert, *Methodism*, 145; Buckley, *History*, 68–69; and Tigert, *History*, 263.

52. Lee, *Short History*, 181; Tigert, *History*, 263–64; Tigert, *Methodism*, 123.

53. Lee, *Short History*, 183; Tigert, *History*, 264–65. Note the exposition and defense given the office by the bishops in their 1798 annotation of the *Discipline* (Sources 1798, section V).

54. On O'Kelly see Charles Franklin Kilgore, *The James O'Kelly Schism in The Methodist Episcopal Church* (Mexico, D. F.: Casa Unida de Publicaciones, 1963); Lee, *Short History*, 178–79.

55. See a letter that December to a local preacher from James O'Kelly, JLFA, 3:114, "To Jesse Nicholson."

56. *The Life and Travels of Rev. Thomas Ware*, 220–21; Paine, *William M'Kendree*, 1:64.

57. JLFA, 1:734, for Thursday, Nov. 8, 1792.

58. "Journals," 6, for Nov. 6, 1792, excerpt from the James Meacham Journals, 1788–1797, located in the Rare Book, Manuscript, and Special Collection Library, Duke University.

59. *Causes* . . . (Philadelphia: Printed by Parry Hall and sold by John Dickins, 1792). Nicholas Snethen, *A Reply to an Apology for Protesting against the Methodist Episcopal Government: Compiled Principally from Original Manuscripts* (Philadelphia: Printed by Henry Tuckniss, 1800), see 28, 32, 51–53. Harlan L. Feeman, *Francis Asbury's Silver Trumpet* (Nashville: Parthenon Press, 1950).

60. *HAM*, 1:617–22; Lee, *Short History*, 206–9 (the "drawing off" image is Lee's); Vickers, *Thomas Coke*, 114, 146, 153, 158, 162–63, 171, 173–74. *A Rejoindre* [William Hammett].

61. For an analysis of the import of these developments in the longer process of independence, see Will B. Gravely, "African Methodisms and the Rise of Black Denominationalism," in *Rethinking Methodist History*, ed. Russell E. Richey and Kenneth E. Rowe (Nashville: Kingswood Books, 1985), 111–24, and *Perspectives*, 108–26.

62. Mother Zoar Methodist Church, Philadelphia, Pennsylvania, was placed on the national register of UMC Heritage Landmarks in 1984.

63. William Warren Sweet, *Methodism in American History*, rev. ed. (New York: Abingdon Press, 1953), 134. The Hammett movement, centered in Charleston and taking the name Primitive Methodists, made less of an impact on the movement. Buckley regarded the loss as only that shown in the *Minutes*, some 7,352, which he, too, spreads over various causes. *History*, 76.

V. Spreading Scriptural Holiness: 1792–1816

1. Mathews, "United Methodism and American Culture: Testimony, Voice, and the Public Sphere," in *PCM*, 279–304.

2. See chart in *MEA*, 2:22. John H. Wigger, *Taking Heaven by Storm: Methodism and the Rise of Popular Christianity in America* (New York and Oxford: Oxford University Press, 1998), 3, 197–200. On the latter pages he constructs Methodist membership as a percentage of total population, state by state, and compares growth rates as well. See Lee, *Short History*, 358–59, for his aggregate numbers, 1771 to 1809. On Methodist growth patterns, see Roger Finke and Rodney Stark, *The Churching of America* (New Brunswick: Rutgers University Press, 1992), 145–98 and the various charts therein. See also Dee E. Andrews, *The Methodists and Revolutionary America, 1760–1800: The Shaping of an Evangelical Culture* (Princeton: Princeton University Press, 2000), appendix A, 247–54, for analyses by gender, race, and class. For the official annual reports of numbers, see *Minutes of the Methodist Conferences, Annually Held in America; From 1773 to 1813, Inclusive*.

3. Wigger, *Taking Heaven by Storm*; Andrews, *The Methodists*; Hempton, *Methodism*; and Christine Leigh Heyrman, *Southern Cross: The Beginnings of the Bible Belt* (New York: Knopf, 1997).

4. See Philip F. Hardt, *The Soul of Methodism: The Class Meeting in Early New York Methodism* (Lanham, Md.: University Press of America, 2000), esp. 27–33, 61–62, for delineation of the class meeting's functions and the contrast between British and American usage. See also the invaluable appendices, 109–48, which identify class meeting leadership (gender, occupation, years of service) and chart class meeting composition, size, gender, race, and evolution.

5. Boehm's Chapel, Willow Street, near Lancaster, Pennsylvania, was placed on the register of UMC Heritage Landmarks in 1984.

6. Behney/Eller, *History*, 97–111; see 103 on ordinations.

7. Ibid., 106–11.

8. Later named Albright Memorial Chapel, the building was placed on the national register of UMC Heritage Landmarks in 1968.

9. Behney/Eller, *History*, 67–95.

10. *The Doctrine and Discipline of The Evangelical Association, Together with the Design of Their Union*, translated from the German (New Berlin: George Miller, 1832), iii–vi, 7–9.

11. The first Evangelical Association Church Building and Publishing House, New Berlin, Pennsylvania, was placed on the national register of UMC Heritage Landmarks in 1988.

12. The Bishop John Seybert/Flat Rock Cluster, Flat Rock and Bellevue, Ohio, was placed on the register of UMC Heritage Landmarks in 1992.

13. Richey's *The Methodist Conference in America* traces out the interrelations of camp meeting and conference development, summarized here.

14. JGC/MEC/1796, 1:11–12.

15. Ibid., 1:11.

16. These can be followed in the successive Journals, but may be most conveniently visualized in Robert Emory, *History of the Discipline of The Methodist Episcopal Church*, ed. W. P. Strickland (New York: Carlton & Porter [1857]). His section, "Of the Boundaries of the Annual Conferences," 246–94, details the changes in General Conference legislation, for each successive General Conference, including the specific wording of provisos.

17. The last included "an annual conference on the western coast of Africa, to be denominated The Liberian Mission Annual Conference." See Emory, *Discipline*, 246–60.

18. JGC/MEC/1796, 1:12.

19. Wallace Guy Smeltzer, *Methodism on the Headwaters of the Ohio: The History of the Pittsburgh Conference of The Methodist Church* (Nashville: Parthenon Press, 1951), 73.

20. JGC/MEC/1804, 1:48. This differs from the enumeration given by Lee, *Short History*, 297.

21. Buckley, *History*, 101–2. New England had "Voted that this Conf. judge it expedient to send delegates to the general Conf. Voted that seven be considered a sufficient number to represent this Conf. in the general Conf." *Minutes of the New England Conference of The Methodist Episcopal Church . . . 1766 to . . . 1845* (1808), 1:118.

22. HAM, 1:475–76; Tigert, *History*, 301.

23. See Thomas A. Langford, *Doctrine and Theology in The United Methodist Church* (Nashville: Kingswood Books/Abingdon Press, 1991), and particularly the articles by Thomas Oden and Richard Heitzenrater. See also Thomas Edward Frank, *Polity, Practice, and the Mission of The United Methodist Church* (Nashville: Abingdon Press, 2002), 144–48; Ted A. Campbell, *Methodist Doctrine: The Essentials* (Nashville: Abingdon Press, 1999); Scott J. Jones, *United Methodist Doctrine: The Extreme Center* (Nashville: Abingdon Press, 2002); and Walter Klaiber and Manfred Marquardt, *Living Grace: An Outline of United Methodist Theology*, trans. and adapted by J. Steven O'Malley and Ulrike R. M. Guthrie (Nashville: Abingdon Press, 2001).

24. James E. Kirby, *The Episcopacy in American Methodism* (Nashville: Kingswood Books/Abingdon Press, 2000), 69–75.

25. *A Journal of the Travels of William Colbert, Methodist Preacher: thro' parts of Maryland, Pennsylvania, New York, Delaware and Virginia in 1790 to 1838*, 10 vols., typescript copy, Drew University, 1:122–23. Colbert's entries are for June 30 to July 7, 1793. He met Bishop Asbury in Northumberland and traveled with him to Wilkes-Barre, where the bishop preached in the courthouse, one of four sermons preached there.

26. Kirby, *Episcopacy in American Methodism*, 59–62.

27. Robert Paine, *Life and Times of William M'Kendree*, 2 vols. (Nashville: Publishing House of the MECS, 1874), 2:265–70. McKendree had written Asbury in October of 1811, proposing that he collaborate with Asbury in appointments, taking Asbury's plans for stationing to "a council of

Presiding Elders, 2:260–61. The address, submitted in writing, was reproduced by Bangs, *History*, 2:308–12. See Kirby, *Episcopacy in American Methodism*, 77–80.

28. *Methodist Magazine* 25 (London, 1801): 217, letter dated Aug. 20, 1801; 25 (London, 1801): 262–63, letter dated Oct. 23, 1801; 25 (London, 1801): 422–23, 523. For discussion of literature on the nature and origins of camp meetings, see Richey, *Early American Methodism* (Durham: Duke University Press, 1976), and *Conference*, 59–60.

29. *Methodist Magazine* 25 (London, 1802): 424, letter dated Sept. 7, 1801.

30. *JLFA*, 3:255, dated Dec. 30, 1802. *Methodist Magazine* 26 (1803): 285, letter dated Jan. 11, 1803.

31. See Lester Ruth, *A Little Heaven Below: Worship at Early Methodist Quarterly Meetings* (Nashville: Kingswood Books/Abingdon Press, 2000).

32. Entries for a later period, July 28 to Sept. 15, 1836. Lanius was *effectively two months in camp meetings* and then began another on Oct. 7. *The Journal of The Reverend Jacob Lanius*, ed. Elmer T. Clark (1918), 270, 275, 277–80. He left conference "in company with Brother Waugh, in order to attend a camp meeting on my circuit at Mud Town the seat of our revival."

33. *Autobiography of Peter Cartwright*, ed. Charles L. Wallis (Nashville: Abingdon Press, 1956; first published 1856), 225–29; Peter Cartwright, *Fifty Years as a Presiding Elder*, ed. W. S. Hooper (Cincinnati: Hitchcock & Walden; New York: Nelson & Phillips, 1871).

34. Lee, *Short History*, 284–362.

35. For their character, see the standard treatments, Charles A. Johnson, *The Frontier Camp Meeting* (Dallas: Southern Methodist University Press, 1955); Dickson D. Bruce Jr., *And They All Sang Hallelujah: Plain-Folk Camp-Meeting Religion, 1800–1845* (Knoxville: University of Tennessee Press, 1974); John B. Boles, *The Great Revival, 1787–1805: The Origins of the Southern Evangelical Mind* (Lexington: University of Kentucky Press, 1972); Paul Conkin, *Cane Ridge, America's Pentecost* (Madison: University of Wisconsin Press, 1990); and Wigger, *Taking Heaven by Storm*. For illustrations of such religiosity see Lester Ruth, *Early Methodist Life and Spirituality* (Nashville: Kingswood Books/Abingdon Press, 2005), 135–87.

36. See Schmidt, *Grace Sufficient*, 63–65. For the dependence of American patterns on those encouraged by John Wesley in Britain, see the several works by Paul Wesley Chilcote, esp. *Her Own Story: Autobiographical Portraits of Early Methodist Women* (Nashville: Kingswood Books/Abingdon Press, 2001).

37. Schmidt, *Grace Sufficient*, 104–32. On class leadership and the waning thereof, 13, 27–35, 51–52.

38. See Hardt, *The Soul of Methodism*; A. Gregory Schneider, *The Way of the Cross Leads Home: The Domestication of American Methodism* (Bloomington: Indiana University Press, 1993).

39. Schmidt, *Grace Sufficient*, 51–75.

40. Ibid., 53.

41. See the discussion in the 1816 "Snapshot" and William R. Sutton, *Journeymen for Jesus: Evangelical Artisans Confront Capitalism in Jacksonian Baltimore* (University Park, Pa.: Pennsylvania State University Press, 1998).

42. B. T. Tanner, D.D., *An Outline of Our History and Government for African Methodist Churchmen* (Philadelphia: Grant, Faires & Rodgers, 1884), 145–49.

43. Lee, *Short History*, 270–71.

44. On this see Will B. Gravely, "African Methodisms and the Rise of Black Denominationalism," in *Perspectives*; Mathews, *Slavery*; H. Shelton Smith, *In His Image, But* . . . (Durham: Duke University Press, 1972); J. Gordon Melton, *A Will to Choose: The Origins of African American Methodism* (Lanham, Md.: Rowman & Littlefield, 2007); Carol V. R. George, *Segregated Sabbaths: Richard Allen and the Rise of Independent Black Churches, 1760–1840* (New York: Oxford University Press, 1973); William B. McClain, *Black People in The Methodist Church: Whither Thou Goest?* (Nashville: Abingdon Press, 1984); David H. Bradley, *A History of the A.M.E. Zion Church, 1796–1968*, 2 vols. (Nashville: AMEZ Publishing House, 1956, 1960); William J. Walls, *The African Methodist Zion Church: Reality of the Black Church* (Charlotte: AMEZ Publishing House, 1974); Howard D. Gregg, *History of the African Methodist Episcopal Church* (Nashville: AME Sunday School Union, 1980); Lewis V. Baldwin, *"Invisible" Strands in African Methodism: A History of the African Union Methodist Protestant and Union American Methodist Episcopal Churches, 1805–1980* (Metuchen, N.J.: Scarecrow Press, 1983).

45. Abel Stevens, *History of The Methodist Episcopal Church in the United States of America*, 4 vols. (New York: Carlton & Porter, 1867), 4:176.

46. The text was not included in the standard edition of the *Journals of the General Conference* published in 1855. Curiously neither Jesse Lee nor Nathan Bangs mentions the historic address in his account of the 1800 General Conference in either of their published histories in 1810 and 1839. A full text of the address was reprinted in Charles Elliott, *History of the Great Secession from The Methodist Episcopal Church in the year 1845* (Cincinnati: Swormstedt and Poe for the MEC, 1855), document 8, appendix 845–46. A more authoritative text copied from an original 1800 broadside in Lovely Lane UMC Museum in Baltimore appeared in *World Parish* 7, no. 2 (Aug. 1959): 58–60.

47. JLFA, 2:281.

48. JGC/MEC/1808, 1:93.

49. JGC/MEC/1816, 1:169–70.

50. For an effort to theologize out of Asbury's pattern, see *MARKS*.

51. See especially the published and longer version of Cooper's *The Substance of a Funeral Discourse . . . on the Death of the Rev. Francis Asbury*. Bishop Richard Whatcoat had died a decade earlier, in 1806.

Snapshot I. Methodism in 1816: Baltimore

1. For a portrayal of New York Methodism at this period, see Samuel A. Seaman, *Annals of New York Methodism: Being a History of The Methodist Episcopal Church in the City of New York* (New York: Hunt & Eaton; Cincinnati: Cranston & Stowe, 1892), esp. 468–73.

2. Terry D. Bilhartz, *Urban Religion and the Second Great Awakening: Church and Society in Early National Baltimore* (Rutherford: Fairleigh Dickinson University Press, 1986); William R. Sutton, *Journeymen for Jesus: Evangelical Artisans Confront Capitalism in Jacksonian Baltimore* (University Park: Pennsylvania State University Press, 1998).

3. On the tensions in Methodism, see Hempton, *Methodism: Empire of the Spirit* (New Haven and London: Yale University Press, 2005).

4. Robert J. Brugger, *Maryland: A Middle Temperament* (Baltimore: Johns Hopkins University

Press, 1988); Barbara Jeanne Fields, *Slavery and Freedom on the Middle Ground: Maryland during the Nineteenth Century* (New Haven and London: Yale University Press, 1985); J. Gordon Melton, *A Will to Choose: The Origins of African American Methodism* (Lanham, Md.: Rowman & Littlefield, 2007), 63–75.

5. Fields, *Slavery and Freedom on the Middle Ground*, xi–5.

6. Brugger, *Maryland*, 179–85. For a Methodist's perspective on Baltimore and the war, see George Brown, *Recollections of Itinerant Life: Including Early Reminiscences* (Cincinnati: R. W. Carroll & Co., 1866), 69–72.

7. Brugger, *Maryland*, 189–95.

8. Ibid., 187–89.

9. Ibid., 211; Fields, *Slavery and Freedom*, 1.

10. Bilhartz, *Urban Religion*, 32–33.

11. Ibid., 35–36.

12. Will B. Gravely, "African Methodisms and the Rise of Black Denominationalism," in *Perspectives*, 108–26, 119.

13. JGC/MEC/1816, 1:169–70.

14. Bilhartz, *Urban Religion*, 32–33; Melton, *A Will to Choose*, 63–75.

15. "City Station 3: Colored Classes, 1809–1822," Lovely Lane Museum, Baltimore, pp. 33–59.

16. Carol V. R. George, *Segregated Sabbaths: Richard Allen and the Rise of Independent Black Churches, 1760–1840* (New York: Oxford University Press, 1973); Gravely, "African Methodisms and the Rise of Black Denominationalism," 117–20.

17. See George, *Segregated Sabbaths*, 88–89, 111–12, 119–20, for discussion of the mysterious reasons for Coker's refusal of the election and involvement in missions and colonization.

18. The figures are from *Minutes*/MEC and the typescript minutes, Baltimore Conference, Lovely Lane Museum.

19. Bilhartz, *Urban Religion*, 23.

20. Baker, *Incredible Methodists*, 110–12; *Minutes of the Annual and General Conferences of the Church of the United Brethren in Christ, 1800–1818*, trans. and ed. A. W. Drury (Dayton: Published for the United Brethren Historical Society, United Brethren Publishing House, 1897); typescript minutes, Baltimore Conference, Lovely Lane Museum, 1809, 40–41; 1810, 46–47; 1811, 52–53; 1812, 59, 61; 1813, 68, 70; 1814, 74, 78.

21. Ibid., 1809, 40–41; 1814, 78.

22. See George Brown, *Recollections of Itinerant Life: Including Early Reminiscences* (Cincinnati: R. W. Carroll & Co., 1866), 72–73, for just such a Baltimore love feast.

23. See also *Christian Newcomer: His Life, Journal and Achievements*, ed. Samuel S. Hough (Dayton: Board of Administration, Church of the United Brethren in Christ, 1941), 182–90.

24. Typescript minutes, Baltimore Conference, Lovely Lane Museum, 1816, 85.

25. James Edward Armstrong, *History of the Old Baltimore Conference* (Baltimore: Printed for the Author, 1907), 175–76.

26. *Minutes*/MEC/1815–16, 1:262, 280.

27. Brown, *Recollections of Itinerant Life*, 74.

28. Isaac P. Cook Papers, Lovely Lane Museum.

29. Typescript minutes, Baltimore Conference, Lovely Lane Museum, 1817, 104–5, 95. Fechtige

and Stier were also made stewards along with Henry Smith, who had been recently on the Baltimore Circuit.

30. Ibid., 1816, 90.

31. *Autobiography of Peter Cartwright*, ed. Charles L. Wallis (Nashville: Abingdon Press, 1956, 1984; first published 1856), 110.

32. For reflections by a traveling companion on the passing of Asbury and an account of that service and funeral sermons preached the following Sunday, see J. B. Wakeley, *The Patriarch of One Hundred Years; Being Reminiscences, Historical and Biographical of Rev. Henry Boehm* (New York: Nelson & Phillips, 1875; reprint, Lancaster, Pa.: Abram W. Sangrey, 1982), 430–33.

33. Henry Boehm, presiding elder on Chesapeake District for that year, records the weekend pattern, either Saturday-Sunday or Friday-Sunday, a rhythm that clearly defined his work. See "The Journals of the Rev. Mr. Henry Boehm, 1800–1839," Journal from 8 May 1810 transcribed by Annie L. Winstead, microfilm copy of MS, Drew University Library, esp. 198–210.

34. Accounts of many early itinerants detail this pattern. See Samuel W. Williams, *Pictures of Early Methodism in Ohio* (Cincinnati: Jennings & Graham; New York: Eaton & Mains, 1909), 52–58.

35. Seaman, *Annals of New York Methodism*, 482–85.

36. George Peck, ed., *Sketches and Incidents; or a Budget from the Saddle-bags of a Superannuated Itinerant* (New York: G. Lane & P. P. Sandford for the MEC, 1844–45; reprint, Salem, Ohio: Schmul Publishing, 1988), attrib to Abel Stevens, 101.

37. Typescript minutes, Baltimore Conference, Lovely Lane Museum, 1814, 78–79.

38. Baker, *Incredible Methodists*, 119.

39. Manuscript Plan of Appointments for the Stationed Preachers in Baltimore, Lovely Lane Museum. See, for instance, 1813, which is particularly clear.

40. Edwin Schell of Lovely Lane Museum in conversation.

41. [Edward Lecompt Hubbard], *The Baltimore Century Plant: History of Eutaw Street Methodist Episcopal Church* (n.p., 1908?), 55, 58.

42. Typescript minutes, Baltimore Conference, Lovely Lane Museum, 1817, 95–97. General Conference had affirmed that "the manner of building houses of religious worship with pews is contrary to the rules of our economy, and inconsistent with the interests of our societies." JGC/MEC/1796–1836, 1:157. See the letter, 1:155–58.

43. Henry Smith, *Recollections and Reflections of an Old Itinerant: A Series of Letters Originally Published in the* Christian Advocate *and* Journal *and the* Western Christian Advocate, ed. George Peck (New York: Carlton & Phillips, 1854), 206–8.

44. Edwin Schell of Lovely Lane Museum in conversation.

45. "City Station 3: Colored Classes, 1809–1822," Lovely Lane Museum.

46. Bilhartz, *Urban Religion*, 35; Melton, *A Will to Choose*, 63–75.

47. Bilhartz, *Urban Religion*, 35, 56, 58. The term *sub-pastor* is Bilhartz's.

48. Baker, *Incredible Methodists*, 135–37.

49. [Isaac P. Cook], *Early History of Methodist Sabbath Schools, in Baltimore City and Vicinity* (Baltimore: Henry F. Cook, 1877), 7–22. East Baltimore apparently established a boys' Sunday school a year earlier, which met on Bond Street. See [Hubbard], *The Baltimore Century Plant*, 40.

50. Baker, *Incredible Methodists*, 123–26.

51. See William Warren Sweet, *Religion on the American Frontier, 1783–1840*, vol. 4, *The Methodists: A Collection of Source Materials* (New York: Cooper Square, 1964; reprint of 1946 ed.), 698–709, esp. 703, 705, 709. Profits from the sale of books could constitute a major source of income for the preachers. Sweet compares the quarterage received by Benjamin Lakin with the profits he made from the sale of books, suggesting that the two might be quite comparable sources of income.

52. See "Notes on Early Methodism," 1878, Isaac P. Cook Papers, Lovely Lane Museum.

53. Baker, *Incredible Methodists*, 135.

54. JGC/MEC/1816, 1:171.

55. Typescript minutes, Baltimore Conference, Lovely Lane Museum, 1817, 99–100. Compare Baker, *Incredible Methodists*, 132–33.

56. Baker, *Incredible Methodists*, 402.

57. "Notes on Early Methodism," 1878, Isaac P. Cook Papers, Lovely Lane Museum, 44.

58. Smith, *Recollections*, 204–5. See also "Notes on Early Methodism," 1878, Isaac P. Cook Papers, Lovely Lane Museum, 44.

59. Smith, *Recollections*, 208–9.

60. Cited in Baker, *Incredible Methodists*, 100.

61. Smith, *Recollections*, 203.

VI. Building for Ministry and Nurture: 1816–50s

1. John McClintock, "Rev. Nathan Bangs, D.D.," *Ladies' Repository* 19 (1859): 321–24, 321. McClintock, teacher, editor, pastor, first president of Drew Theological Seminary, is perhaps best remembered today as the joint author with James Strong of the twelve-volume *Cyclopaedia of Biblical, Theological and Ecclesiastical Literature* (1883–87).

2. Bangs, *History*, 2:390–418. Bangs covers the errors, 2:413–17.

3. For a very different take on Bangs's agenda, see Roger Finke and Rodney Stark, *The Churching of America* (New Brunswick: Rutgers University Press, 1992), 145–69; John H. Wigger, *Taking Heaven by Storm: Methodism and the Rise of Popular Christianity in America* (New York and Oxford: Oxford University Press, 1998), 189–90.

4. Beth Barton Schweiger, *The Gospel Working Up: Progress and the Pulpit in Nineteenth-Century Virginia* (New York and Oxford: Oxford University Press, 2000), 6–7, 35, 39–40, 42, 57, and E. Brooks Holifield, *The Gentlemen Theologians: American Theology in Southern Culture, 1795–1860* (Durham: Duke University Press, 1978).

5. On Bangs's life and work, see Richard Everett Hermann, "Nathan Bangs: Apologist for American Methodism" (PhD diss., Emory University, 1973).

6. Journals of the New York Annual Conference, 1800–1839, transcribed by William R. Phinney, 3 vols., Drew University Library. Notations refer to year with x/y denoting page numbers in manuscript (x) and typescript (y), in this instance, 1802: 12/42.

7. Journals of the New York Conference from 1821 to 1829, 1827: 98, 101, 102, 111, 112, 117.

8. For listing of MEC, MECS, and MC book agents and editors, see *EWM*, 2:2709–11.

9. Candy Gunther Brown, *Word in the World: Evangelical Writing, Publishing, and Reading in America, 1789–1880* (Chapel Hill and London: University of North Carolina Press, 2004), 9–13, 46.

10. Bangs played a role in the American observance of the 1839 Centenary. English Methodists appointed October 25, 1839, as a day of festive religious observance throughout their churches in all parts of the world in celebration of the centenary of the formation of Wesley's first societies in Bristol and London. It is interesting that nineteenth-century Methodists chose to commemorate *not John Wesley's conversion* (which would have been celebrated the previous year, 1838, and twentieth-century Methodists tended to use 1738 as the start date for global Methodism) but Wesley's *first societies*. Nathan Bangs was active in promoting the plans on this side of the Atlantic at district, conference, and local levels. Cash contributions "for certain great interests of the Church" were called for on Centenary Day, and the call was answered liberally: church members and friends raised $600,000 for clergy pensions, missions, and education. The bishops and delegates to the 1840 General Conference sent a pastoral letter to their flock thanking them for their generosity. See Abel Stevens, *Life and Times of Nathan Bangs* (New York: Carlton & Porter, 1863), 326–27; UK Methodists raised $1,080,000 in American dollars, according to Simpson's *Cyclopaedia*, 179. The 1840 "Pastoral Address" was immediately published in the CA, July 32, 1840, 181, and in the *MQR* 22, no. 3 (July 1840): 351–55, and later included in the *Journals of the General Conference of The Methodist Episcopal Church* (New York: Carlton & Phillips, 1855), 2:158–59. The centenary commemorative book was Thomas Jackson's *Centenary of Wesleyan Methodism: A Brief Sketch of the Rise, Progress, and Present State of the Wesleyan Methodist Societies throughout the World* (New York: T. Mason & G. Lane for the MEC, 1839).

11. *The Errors of Hopkinsianism Detected and Refuted (New York, 1815); The Reformer Reformed: or A Second Part of the Errors of Hopkinsianism Detected and Refuted* (New York, 1816); *An Examination of the Doctrine of Predestination* (New York, 1817); *A Vindication of Methodist Episcopacy* (New York, 1820).

12. See Thomas A. Langford, *Practical Divinity*, 2 vols. (Nashville: Abingdon Press, 1998), 1, 73–88.

13. Typescript journal, courtesy of Edwin Schell, Baltimore Conference Archives, Lovely Lane Museum, 1817, 99–100. Compare Baker, *Incredible Methodists*, 132–33.

14. On these works and their multiple British and American editions, see the relevant volumes of Kenneth E. Rowe, *Methodist Union Catalog: Pre-1976 Imprints* (Metuchen, N.J., and London: Scarecrow Press, 1975–).

15. For committee reports on Bangs's manuscript in 1815 and book in 1818, see Journals of the New York Conference from 1800 to 1820, 1815: 99–100/129–30; and 1818: 138/168.

16. JGC/MEC/1816, 1:155.

17. In relation to this whole discussion, see Pilkington/Vernon, *Methodist Publishing House*, 1:80–219.

18. *Minutes*/MEC/1804, 121; 1809, 174.

19. Pilkington-Vernon, *Methodist Publishing House*, 1:117–68.

20. See the preachers' accounts reproduced by Sweet, *Methodists*, "The Preacher as Book Agent in the West," 698–709.

21. Pilkington/Vernon, *Methodist Publishing House*, 1:151, 161.

22. Brown, *Word in the World*, 155.

23. Ibid., 147.

24. Ibid.

25. Pilkington/Vernon, *Methodist Publishing House*, 1:179, 192, 209–10.

26. Wigger, *Taking Heaven by Storm*, 180–95.

27. Behney/Eller, *History*, 120–21, 126–28, 85–91, 141–52.

28. Schweiger, *Gospel Working Up*, 67. See the whole chapter "Reading, Writing and Religion," 55–75.

29. Bangs, *History*, 3:279–80, 303–4.

30. Ibid., 2:293–96; 4:124–25, 152.

31. Minutes of the North Carolina Annual Conference, 1838–1885, 2 vols., photocopy of original handwritten minutes, 1840–41, 1:51b–54a-b. Rare Book, Manuscript, and Special Collection Library, Duke University.

32. Republished by Carolyn De Swarte Gifford, ed., *The Nineteenth-Century American Methodist Itinerant Preacher's Wife* (New York and London: Garland Publishing, 1987), in the thirty-six-volume series Women in American Protestant Religion, 1800–1930.

33. "An Editorial Paper: A Few Thoughts Suggested by Our Annual Minutes," *Ladies' Repository* 18 (1858): 124–26.

34. JGC/MEC/1832, 408. The third among eight resolutions. Bangs in his *History*, 3:101, reproduced these 1832 General Conference actions.

35. JGC/MEC/1844, 157.

36. Philip F. Hardt, *The Soul of Methodism: The Class Meeting in Early New York Methodism* (Lanham, Md.: University Press of America, 2000), 69–70, 186–87nn28–29.

37. Naomi L. Nelson, "She Considered Herself Called of God: White Women's Participation in the Southern Methodist Episcopal Church, 1820–1865" (PhD diss., Emory University, 2001), see chap. 2, "Surely There Is Nothing on Earth Worth Living for but This: The Methodist Preacher's Wife," 92–151, esp. 106–8, 111–18, 124.

38. Ibid., see chap. 2, 92–151, esp. 93–94, 126–28, 131–51. See also A. Gregory Schneider, *The Way of the Cross Leads Home: The Domestication of American Methodism* (Bloomington and Indianapolis: Indiana University Press, 1993), 130–32; Schmidt, *Grace Sufficient*, chap. 5, "Partners in Ministry: Itinerant Preachers' Wives," 113–32, and also 54, 86, 251–52, 294; and Leonard I. Sweet, *The Minister's Wife: Her Role in Nineteenth-Century American Evangelicalism* (Philadelphia: Temple University Press, 1983).

39. Hardt, *The Soul of Methodism*, and particularly the several pages of articles in the CA, often three or four each year, from 1827 to 1884. See also Francis Holsclaw, "The Demise of Disciplined Christian Fellowship: The Methodist Class Meeting in Nineteenth-Century America" (PhD diss., University of California, 1979); and the several studies by David L. Watson, *Accountable Discipleship: Handbook for Covenant Discipleship Groups in the Congregation* (Nashville: Discipleship Resources, 1984, 1985); *Class Leaders: Recovering a Tradition* (Nashville: Discipleship Resources, 1991); *Covenant Discipleship: Christian Formation through Mutual Accountability* (Nashville: Discipleship Resources, 1991); *The Early Methodist Class Meeting: Its Origins and Significance* (Nashville: Discipleship Resources, 1985); *Forming Christian Disciples: The Role of Covenant Discipleship and Class Leaders in the Congregation* (Nashville: Discipleship Resources, 1991).

40. Sweet, *Methodists*, 4:685–709.

41. See Carlton R. Young, *Companion to The United Methodist Hymnal* (Nashville: Abingdon Press, 1993), esp. 75–122.

42. Ibid., 76–77, 106–7.

43. On this transition, see Schneider, *The Way of the Cross Leads Home*, esp. 111–208.

44. Bangs, *History*, 3:133.

45. Ibid., 3:137. He reproduces the preface, 135–39.

46. Ibid., 3:139–40.

47. JGC/MEC/1824, 298; JGC/MEC/1828, 394; *Discipline*/MEC/1824, 72.

48. Cited from *A Collection of Hymns for the Use of The Methodist Episcopal Church, Principally from the Collection of the Rev. John Wesley, A.M.* (New York, 1845), 4–5. This MEC edition still carried the names of Joshua Soule and James O. Andrew.

49. Young, *Companion to The United Methodist Hymnal*, 110–12.

50. Peter Cartwright, *Autobiography* (Nashville: Abingdon Press, 1956), 96–97, emphasis in original.

51. See Gayle Felton, *This Gift of Water: The Practice and Theology of Baptism among Methodists in America* (Nashville: Abingdon Press, 1993); Karen Westerfield Tucker, *American Methodist Worship* (New York: Oxford University Press, 2001); Gayle Carlton Felton, *By Water and the Spirit: Making Connections for Identity and Ministry*, rev. ed. (Nashville: Discipleship Resources, 2002).

52. "Confession of Faith," Church of the United Brethren in Christ (New Constitution), *Origin, Doctrine, Constitution, and Discipline . . .* (Dayton, Ohio: United Brethren Publishing House, 1889).

53. Richard Watson, *Theological Institutes*, 12 vols. (London: John Mason, 1834–38).

54. *The Works of the Reverend John Wesley . . . , comprehending also numerous translations, notes and an original Preface, &c. by John Emory* (New York: Published by J. Emory & B. Waugh, for the MEC, 1831), 6:15.

55. In all Methodist churches prior to 1848, the two sexes occupied opposite sides of the sanctuary, and whom the church had separated, no one dared join together. From the first *Discipline* of 1784, patterned after Wesley's "Large Minutes" of the British Conference, until 1848 this question was put and answered:

> Question. "Is there any exception to the rule, Let the men and women sit apart?"
> Answer. "There is no exception. Let them sit apart in all our churches."

Methodism's first two bishops, in their notes on the *Discipline* published in 1798, simply asserted that such an arrangement was "the universal practice in the primitive church." They concluded, "A general mixture of the sexes in places of worship is obviously improper." American Methodists kept Wesley's laws faithfully until the middle of the nineteenth century when women and men looked longingly across church aisles and devoutedly preferred closer contact during worship services. Grimly old-guard conservatives vowed to suppress this vicious heterodoxy.

Interwoven with the battle over seating was the equally hallowed practice of banning pew rents and requiring all churches to offer "free seats." The founder's advice on pews, also incorporated in the *Discipline*, was equally emphatic: "Let all our churches be built plain and decent, and with free seats." However, during this period many congregations, especially in urban areas of the East, began to finance new church buildings by renting pews to families, a practice that suggested females and males could sit together in the family pew. An Ohio pastor, John S. Inskip, was removed from his church for advocating pew rentals in the 1840s. A test case at the denomination's

1852 General Conference settled the matters by offering local option. Congregations could choose to remain true to tradition or forge a new tradition for the future. The love for separate seats and the ban on pew rents died slowly, but the democratic way finally prevailed and churches gradually adopted "promiscuous" seating and welcomed pew rentals as a way to finance up-scale church buildings befitting the denomination's new social status as a Main Street denomination.

56. John P. Durbin, "Building Churches," CA, July 13, 1832, 183.

57. Samuel A. Seaman, *Annals of New York Methodism* (New York: Hunt & Eaton; Cincinnati: Cranston & Stowe, 1892), 469n.

58. JGC/MEC/1844, 158.

59. For the history of American Methodist Sunday schools see the Rowe chapters in James E. Kirby, Russell E. Richey, and Kenneth E. Rowe, *The Methodists* (Westport, Conn. and London: Greenwood Press, 1996), 177–244; John Q. Schisler, *Christian Education in Local Methodist Churches* (Nashville: Abingdon Press, 1969); Cawthon A. Bowen, *Child and Church: A History of Methodist Church School Curriculum* (Nashville: Abingdon Press, 1960). Pilkington and Vernon in their two-volume *Methodist Publishing House* document the development of Sunday school publications. An older work, but still useful, because of elaborate documentation, is Addie G. Wardle, *History of the Sunday School Movement in The Methodist Episcopal Church* (New York: Methodist Book Concern, 1918), upon whom Schisler and Bowen depend. For the larger context and interpretation see Anne M. Boylan, *Sunday School: The Formation of an American Institution, 1790–1880* (New Haven: Yale University Press, 1988); Robert W. Lynn and Elliott Wright, *The Big Little School: Sunday Child of American Protestantism*, 2d ed., rev. and enl. (Birmingham: Religious Education Press, 1980), and Marilyn Hilley Pettit, "Women, Sunday Schools, and Politics: Early National New York City, 1797–1827" (PhD diss., New York University, 1991).

60. "Sunday School Union of The Methodist Episcopal Church, Extract from the First Annual Report," MQR 11, no. 9 (Sept. 1828): 350. See also JLFA, 1:349n35.

61. Wardle, *History of the Sunday School Movement*, 46f.

62. For the parallels of *Discipline* and "Large Minutes," see Tigert, *History*, 565.

63. *Minutes of the Methodist Conferences, annually held in America from 1773 to 1794, inclusive* (Philadelphia: Henry Tuckniss for John Dickins, 1795), 147; JLFA, 1:625.

64. JLFA, 3:102–3. The earliest printing apparently appeared in the first collected minutes of the denomination: *Minutes of the Methodist Conferences, annually held in America from 1773 to 1794, inclusive*, 162–64, and *Minutes taken at the Several Conferences of The Methodist-Episcopal Church in America for the year 1792* (Philadelphia: Printed by Parry Hall and sold by John Dickins, 1792), 16–19.

65. Asbury/Coke-*Discipline*, 104–5.

66. The first Sunday school in New York was established at John Street Church in 1812 by Mary Mason. See G. S. Disosway, "First Methodist S. School in New York," CA, May 25, 1865, 162, and Elizabeth Mason North, *Consecrated Talents: or, the Life of Mrs. Mary W. Mason* (New York: Carlton & Lanahan, 1876; reprint, New York: Garland, 1987).

67. *Pioneering in Penn's Woods: Philadelphia Methodist Episcopal Annual Conference through One Hundred and Fifty Years* (Philadelphia: Philadelphia Conference Tract Society, 1937), 169f.

68. Baker, *Incredible Methodists*, 123-28.

69. John B. M'Ferrin, *History of Methodism in Tennessee*, 3 vols. (Nashville: Southern Methodist Publishing House, 1869–79), 3:20.

70. Boylan, *Sunday School*, 22–59, 144f.

71. "Constitution Adopted April 2, 1827, Sunday School Union of The Methodist Episcopal Church," *MQR* 10, no. 8 (Aug. 1827): 367.

72. JGC/MEC/1824, 295; *Discipline*/MEC/1824, 58; *Discipline*/MEC/1828, 58.

73. Bangs, *History*, 3:345.

74. See James C. Wilhoit, "An Examination of the Educational Principles of an Early Nineteenth Century Sunday School Curriculum: The Union Questions" (PhD diss., Northwestern University, 1983).

75. "Scripture Questions" were included in each monthly issue of the *Child's Magazine*. This example is taken from 3, no. 1 (July 1829): 14.

76. *MQR* 11, no. 9 (Sept. 1828): 351. The Union did not print its own literature, but bought at cost from the Methodist Book Concern.

77. See [Nathan Bangs], "Sunday School Library Books," *MQR* 13, no. 3 (July 1831): 352–53.

78. JGC/MEC/1840, 127f.; *Discipline*/MEC/1840, 65.

79. The *Sunday School Advocate* was published from 1841 until 1921.

80. For description of these series see Pilkington/Vernon, *Methodist Publishing House*, 1:282–85.

81. Wardle, *History of the Sunday School Movement*, 83.

82. Methodist Episcopal Church, Sunday School Union, *Annual Report*, 1848, 36–39; JGC/MEC/1848, 113.

83. See the reviews by John McClintock, *MQR* 34, no. 4 (Oct. 1852): 633, and 35, no. 3 (July 1853): 476, and his *Lectures on Theological Encyclopaedia and Methodology* (Cincinnati: Hitchcock & Walden, 1873), 136.

84. *Catechism of The Methodist Episcopal Church*, no. 1 (New York: Carlton & Phillips, Sunday-school Union, 1852), [3].

85. *Catechism*, no. 3 (1852), 5.

86. Pilkington/Vernon, *Methodist Publishing House*, 1:214.

87. Abel Stevens, *The Centenary of American Methodism: A Sketch of Its History, Theology, Practical System, and Success, with a statement of the plan of the Centenary Celebration of 1866 by John M'Clintock, D.D.* (New York: Carlton & Porter, 1865), 180, 185–87.

88. *History of The Methodist Episcopal Church in the United States of America*, 4 vols. (New York: Carlton & Porter, 1864–67); *The History of the Religious Movement of the Eighteenth Century Called Methodism* (New York: Carlton & Porter, 1858–61); *A Compendious History of American Methodism* (New York: Eaton & Mains; Cincinnati: Curts & Jennings, n.d. [but 1867–68]); *Supplementary History of American Methodism* (New York: Eaton & Mains, 1899); *Memorials of the Introduction of Methodism into the Eastern States* (Boston: Charles H. Pierce, 1848); *Memorials of the Early Progress of Methodism in the Eastern States* (Boston: C. H. Pierce, 1852); *An Essay on Church Polity* (New York: Carlton & Porter, 1847); *The Women of Methodism* (New York: Carlton & Porter, 1866). Many of these items went through several editions. He also produced a variety of other works.

89. J. M. Reid, *Missions and Missionary Society of The Methodist Episcopal Church*, 2 vols. (New York: Phillips & Hunt; Cincinnati: Cranston & Stowe, 1879), 1:14–25.

90. Barclay, *Missions*, 1:200–205. See also Dana L. Robert, *American Women in Mission: A Social History of Their Thought and Practice* (Macon: Mercer University Press, 1996).

91. *The Missionary Pioneer, or A Brief Memoir of the Life, Labours, and Death of John Stewart*,

(Man of Color): Founder under God of the Mission among the Wyandotts at Upper Sandusky, Ohio (New York: Printed by J. C. Totten, 1827); Thelma R. Marsh, Moccasin Trails to the Cross: A History of the Mission to the Wyandott Indians (Sandusky, Ohio: John Stewart United Methodist Church, 1974); Barclay, Missions, 2:113–285.

92. Bangs reproduced the society's "Constitution," the "Address of the Missionary and Bible Society of The Methodist Episcopal Church in America," and a "Circular," History, 3:83–92.

93. "Circular Address, and Constitution of the Missionary and Bible Society, of The Methodist Episcopal Church in America," MQR/MEC (June 1819): 277–79. Note: The name was subsequently simplified to Missionary Society.

94. Barclay, Missions, 1:280–358.

95. Bangs, History, 3:93.

96. North, Consecrated Talents, 84.

97. On the development and role of auxiliaries, see Barclay, Missions, 1:291–303.

98. Ibid., 45–46, 49.

99. Ibid., 36–37, 59–60, 67–74, 75–76. G. P. Disosway, "First Methodist S. School in New York," CA, May 25, 1865, 162.

100. See Elaine Magalis, Conduct Becoming to a Woman: Bolted Doors and Burgeoning Missions (Cincinnati: Women's Division, Board of Global Ministries, UMC, 1973), 15–16.

101. Louise McCoy North, The Story of the New York Branch of the Woman's Foreign Missionary Society of The Methodist Episcopal Church (New York Branch, 1926), 18–20.

102. Ibid., 20–21.

103. Barclay, Missions, 1:280.

104. William Warren Sweet, Circuit-Rider Days in Indiana (Indianapolis: W. K. Stewart Co., 1916), 97. The report was ordered to be sent to New York for publication in the Christian Advocate.

105. Minutes of the New England Conference of The Methodist Episcopal Church . . . 1845; Minutes of the Philadelphia Conference of The Methodist Episcopal Church, 1846–52 (1848), 10.

106. In American Notes the English novelist wrote, "Let us . . . plunge in the Five Points, a square of leprous houses which take their names from robbery and murder. . . . All that is loathsome, drooping and decayed is here. . . . From every corner, as you glance about you in these dark retreats, some figure crawls half-awakened, as if the Judgment-hour were near at hand, and every obscene grave were giving up its dead. Where dogs would howl to lie, women, and men, and boys slink off to sleep, forcing the dislodged rats to move away in quest of better lodgings." Charles Dickens, American Notes (New York: P. F. Collier, [1920]), 96–98. For Palmer's role see Charles E. White, The Beauty of Holiness: Phoebe Palmer as Theologian, Revivalist, Feminist and Humanitarian (Grand Rapids: Francis Asbury Press, 1986), 217–21.

107. The Old Brewery and the New Mission House at the Five Points, by Ladies of the Mission (New York: Stringer & Townsend, 1854). For the early program of the mission, see Henry J. Camman and Hugh N. Camp, The Charities of New York, Brooklyn and Staten Island (New York: Hurd & Houghton, 1868), 349–60, and White, Beauty of Holiness, 217–27.

108. Lewis M. Pease, "Five Points Mission," Monthly Record of the Five Points House of Industry 1 (Aug. 1857): 114–16.

109. For a contemporary description of this new ministry see "Five Points House of Industry,"

American Church Monthly 3, nos. 3–5 (March, April, May, 1858): 209–22, 289–97, 349–60. See also Carroll Smith-Rosenberg, *Religion and the Rise of the American City* (Ithaca, N.Y.: Cornell University Press, 1971), chap. 8.

110. "Five Points House Marks a Century," *New York Times*, Feb. 9, 1950.

111. "Letter from New York, Five Points Mission," *ZH* (Boston), Dec. 27, 1854, 2; *MQR* 36, no. 2 (April 1854): 315; "Chicago City Mission," *NWCA* (Evanston), Jan. 10, 1855, 6.

112. Harold E. Raser, *Phoebe Palmer: Her Life and Thought*, vol. 22, Studies in Women and Religion (Lewiston, N.Y.: Edwin Mellen Press, 1987), 45. See also Richard Wheatley, *The Life and Letters of Mrs. Phoebe Palmer* (New York: W. C. Palmer, 1876; reprint, Garland, 1984), and White, *Beauty of Holiness*.

113. Wheatley, *Life and Letters*, 30–32; White, *Beauty of Holiness*, 9. See also Thomas C. Oden, ed., *Phoebe Palmer: Selected Writings*, Sources of American Spirituality Series (New York: Paulist Press, 1988), 98–102.

114. Phoebe Palmer, *The Way of Holiness, with Notes by the Way: Being a Narrative of Religious Experience, Resulting from a Determination to Be a Bible Christian* (New York: Piercy and Reed, 1843); *The Devotional Writings of Phoebe Palmer*, Higher Christian Life Series (reprint, New York: Garland, 1985), 125–26. Compare Wheatley, *Life and Letters*, 36–44.

115. Jean Miller Schmidt, "Holiness and Perfection," in Charles H. Lippy and Peter W. Williams, eds., *Encyclopedia of the American Religious Experience*, vol. 2 (New York: Charles Scribner's Sons, 1988), 813–29.

116. Phoebe Palmer, *Promise of the Father; or, a Neglected Specialty of the Last Days* (New York: W. C. Palmer, 1859; reprint, New York: Garland, 1985), 228–34.

117. *Guide to Christian Perfection* 1, no. 1 (July 1839): 24.

118. Ibid., 1, no. 9 (March 1840): 213.

119. Ibid., 3, no. 1 (July 1841): 8–16. Also 2, no. 12 (June 1841): 274.

120. Raser, *Phoebe Palmer*, 58–59, 215; White, *Beauty of Holiness*, 217–27.

121. Kathryn Teresa Long, *The Revival of 1857–58* (New York and Oxford: Oxford University Press, 1998).

122. On the class meeting's decline and reasons assigned for it, see Hardt, *The Soul of Methodism*, 45–47, 55–58, 74–87, and see the highly useful appendices covering leadership, class size, and attendance, 110–48; see also Holsclaw, "The Demise of Disciplined Christian Fellowship," 57–82.

123. Cited by Holsclaw, "The Demise of Disciplined Christian Fellowship," 62–63.

124. Hardt, *The Soul of Methodism*, 128.

125. (Boston: H. V. Degen, 1854).

126. *Essays on the Preaching Required by the Times*, 1855; "Our Public Worship—Its Form and Matter," *CA*, April 23, 1857, 66; "The Music Question," June 11, 1857, 94.

127. Francis I. Moats, "The Educational Policy of The Methodist Episcopal Church prior to 1860" (PhD thesis, Graduate College of the State University of Iowa, 1926), 38–56.

128. Bangs, *History*, 3:105–7.

129. On Methodist efforts in higher education and the distribution, purposes, curricula, finances, and prospects of the early colleges and academies, in addition to Moats and a contemporary statement in *CA*, June 13, 1828, 162–63, see Robert H. Conn with Michael Nickerson, *United Methodists and*

Their Colleges, foreword by F. Thomas Trotter (Nashville: United Methodist Board of Higher Education and Ministry, 1989); A. W. Cummings, *The Early Schools of Methodism* (New York: Phillips & Hunt, 1886); Merrimon Cuninggim, *Uneasy Partners: The College and the Church* (Nashville: Abingdon Press, 1994); Sylvanus M. Duvall, *The Methodist Episcopal Church and Education up to 1869* (New York: Bureau of Publications, Teachers College, 1928); T. Michael Elliott, ed., *A College-Related Church: United Methodist Perspectives* (Nashville: National Commission on United Methodist Higher Education, 1976); T. Michael Elliott et al., *To Give the Key of Knowledge: United Methodists and Education, 1784–1976* (Nashville: National Commission on United Methodist Higher Education, 1976); John O. Gross, *Methodist Beginnings in Higher Education* (Nashville: Division of Educational Institutions, Board of Education, MEC, 1959); *Handbook of United Methodist–Related Schools, Colleges, Universities and Theological Schools* (Nashville: GBHEM, UMC, updated regularly); Quentin Charles Lansman, *Higher Education in The Evangelical United Brethren Church: 1800–1954* (Nashville: Division of Higher Education, UMC, 1972); James Henry Morgan, *Dickinson College: The History of One Hundred Fifty Years, 1783–1933* (Carlisle, Penn.: Dickinson College, 1933); Samuel Plantz, *The History of Education in The Methodist Episcopal Church, 1892 to 1917* (New York: Board of Education of MEC, 1918); David B. Potts, *Wesleyan University, 1831–1910: Collegiate Enterprise in New England* (New Haven and London: Yale University Press, 1992); James E. Scanlon, *Randolph-Macon College: A Southern History, 1826–1967* (Charlottesville: University Press of Virginia, 1983); Charles Coleman Sellers, *Dickinson College: A History* (Middletown, Conn.: Wesleyan University Press, 1973).

130. On the American efforts within the larger Wesleyan educational impulse, consult Sharon J. Hels, ed., *Methodism and Education: From Roots to Fulfillment* (Nashville: GBHEM, UMC, 2000). The following discussion is informed by the ongoing conversation about the church and higher education. See especially Douglas Sloan, *Faith and Knowledge: Mainline Protestantism and American Higher Education* (Louisville: Westminster John Knox, 1994); James T. Burtchaell, *The Dying of the Light: The Disengagement of Colleges and Universities from Their Christian Churches* (Grand Rapids: Eerdmans, 1998); Edward LeRoy Long Jr., *Higher Education as a Moral Enterprise* (Washington, D.C.: Georgetown University Press, 1992); George M. Marsden, *The Soul of the American University: From Protestant Establishment to Established Nonbelief* (New York and Oxford: Oxford University Press, 1994); George M. Marsden and Bradley J. Longfield, eds., *The Secularization of the Academy* (New York and Oxford: Oxford University Press, 1992); Donald G. Tewksbury, *The Founding of American Colleges and Universities before the Civil War* (New York: Arno Press & New York Times, 1969); and Glenn T. Miller, *Piety and Intellect: The Aims and Purposes of Ante-Bellum Theological Education* (Atlanta: Scholars Press, 1990).

131. *The Works of Stephen Olin, D.D., LL.D., Late President of the Wesleyan University* (New York: Harper & Brothers, 1852), 2:240–53, esp. 242–45, 249, 251.

132. Samuel Luttrell Akers, *The First Hundred Years of Wesleyan College, 1836–1936* (Macon: Wesleyan College, 1976). "Greensboro College . . . was chartered by the Methodist Church in 1838 as a women's college." *Handbook of United Methodist–Related Schools, Colleges, Universities and Theological Schools* (Nashville: GBHEM, UMC, 1996), 89.

133. Duvall, *The Methodist Episcopal Church and Education*, 39–40. For comparable figures for southern Methodism (MECS), see Scanlon, *Randolph-Macon College.*

134. For commentary and Virginia statistics on first career and father's vocation, see Schweiger, *Gospel Working Up*, 20, 21, 24, 199–200, 205–7.

135. JGC/MEC/1856, 150; JGC/MEC/1860, 313–14, 457.

136. On Durbin's epitomizing the connectional role of the college presidents, see Russell E. Richey, *Extension Ministers: Mr. Wesley's True Heirs* (Nashville: GBHEM, UMC, 2008), 53–62.

137. *Autobiography of Peter Cartwright*, with introduction, bibliography, and index by Charles L. Wallis (Nashville: Abingdon Press, 1986; originally published in 1857), 266–67. See also 11, 12, 63–66, 164, 264–68, 314–17, 327–28.

138. On croaking and croakers, see especially Wigger, *Taking Heaven by Storm*, 181–88.

VII. Dividing by Mission, Ethnicity, Gender, and Vision: 1816–50s

1. The proposal, in part and in amended form, read: "The bishop . . . shall nominate an elder for each district, and the Conference shall, without debate, either confirm or reject such nomination." JGC/MEC/1816, 140.

2. On these matters see Edward J. Drinkhouse, *History of Methodist Reform: Synoptical of General Methodism 1703 to 1898 with special . . . reference to the History of the Methodist Protestant Church*, 2 vols. (Baltimore: Board of Publication of the MPC, 1899), 1:525. Drinkhouse provides a distinctively "reform" perspective on the whole issue before us.

3. JGC/MEC/1796, 1:11.

4. See Emory, *Discipline*. His section "Of the Boundaries of the Annual Conferences," 246–94, details the changes in General Conference legislation for each successive General Conference, including the specific wording of provisos. See also *EWM*, 2:2656–85.

5. The last included "an annual conference on the western coast of Africa, to be denominated The Liberian Mission Annual Conference." See Emory, *Discipline*, 246–60.

6. See on the latter, Neil Semple, *The Lord's Dominion: The History of Canadian Methodism* (Montreal: McGill-Queen's University Press, 1996).

7. See J. Gordon Melton, *A Will to Choose: The Origins of African American Methodism* (Lanham, Md.: Rowman & Littlefield, 2007); Will B. Gravely, "African Methodisms and the Rise of Black Denominationalism," in *Rethinking Methodist History*, ed. Russell E. Richey and Kenneth E. Rowe (Nashville: Kingswood Books, 1985), 111–24, or in *Perspectives*, 108–26; Carol V. R. George, *Segregated Sabbaths: Richard Allen and the Rise of Independent Black Churches, 1760–1840* (New York: Oxford University Press, 1973); *The Life Experience and Gospel Labors of the Rt. Rev. Richard Allen*, 2d ed. (New York: Abingdon Press, 1960); William B. McClain, *Black People in The Methodist Church* (Nashville: Abingdon Press, 1984).

8. For a firsthand treatment, see Jesse Lee, *Short History*, 178–80. The standard is Charles F. Kilgore, "The James O'Kelly Schism in The Methodist Episcopal Church" (PhD diss., Emory University, 1961).

9. Gravely, "African Methodisms and the Rise of Black Denominationalism," in *Rethinking Methodist History*, 111–24, and *Perspectives*, 122–26; HAM, 1:609–14.

10. Journals of the New York Conference from 1821 to 1829, typescript, Drew University, 2:11–12.

11. JGC/MEC/1864, 485–86.

12. Journals of the New York Conference from 1821 to 1829, 4; Samuel Stilwell, *Historical Sketches of the Rise and Progress of the Methodist Society in the City of New York* (New York, 1821), includes the *Discipline* adopted in 1821.

13. Behney/Eller, *History*, 97–111.

14. Another phrase used was *Die sogenannten Albrechts.* Ibid., 91.

15. R. Yeakel, *Jacob Albright and His Co-Laborers*, trans. from the German (Cleveland: Publishing House of the EA, 1883); see "Life and Labors of John Dreisbach, Evangelical Minister and the First Presiding Elder in the Evangelical Association," 294–96.

16. W. W. Orwig, *History of the Evangelical Association* (Cleveland: Published by Charles Hammer for the EA, 1858), 1:56–57.

17. The Evangelicals, like the Methodists, wanted only itinerants to be members. Behney/Eller, *History*, 94.

18. See Schmidt, *Grace Sufficient*, chaps. 4 and 5, and Catherine A. Brekus, *Strangers and Pilgrims: Female Preaching in America, 1740–1845* (Chapel Hill: University of North Carolina Press, 1998), and *The Religious History of American Women: Reimagining the Past* (Chapel Hill: University of North Carolina Press, 2007).

19. Herrick M. Eaton, *The Itinerant's Wife: Her Qualifications, Duties, Trials, and Rewards* (New York: Lane & Scott, 1851). It is reprinted by Carolyn De Swarte Gifford, ed., *The Nineteenth-Century American Methodist Itinerant Preacher's Wife* (New York: Garland, 1987). Gifford's volume includes Mary Orne Tucker's *Itinerant Preaching in the Early Days of Methodism, by a Pioneer Preacher's Wife*, ed. her son, Thomas W. Tucker (Boston: B. B. Russell, 1872), from which we excerpt (Sources 1838). See also Leonard I. Sweet, *The Minister's Wife: Her Role in Nineteenth-Century American Evangelicalism* (Philadelphia: Temple University Press, 1983), esp. 79–86, 117–20, 127–43, 177–80.

20. Eaton, *The Itinerant's Wife*, 7–28.

21. Thompson's *Trial and Defence* was first printed in West Troy, New York, in 1837 (Sources 1830a) and two years later (1839) reprinted in Lowell, Massachusetts, for her Boston fans.

22. A full transcript of the quarterly conference trial was published nine years later, following Sally Thompson's own account of the whole affair published after she joined another church in 1837: Matteson Baker, ed., *A Brief Statement of the Administration of Westford Circuit, in relation to Mrs. Sally Thompson, Arraigned, Tried and Expelled from The Methodist Episcopal Church, According to the Order and Discipline of Said Church; Designed also, as a Corrective in view of Certain Remarks and Reports, as have appeared in a pamphlet published by herself, entitled "Trial & Defense," &c.* (Lowell, Mass.: Printed by A. B. F. Hildreth, 1839).

23. This storyline follows Brekus, *Strangers and Pilgrims*, chap. 7, "Suffer Not a Woman to Teach," 267–71, 305–6.

24. *Diary of Fanny Newell; with a sketch of Her Life, and an Introduction by a Member of the New England Conference of The Methodist Episcopal Church*, 4th ed. (Boston: Charles H. Peirce, 1848), 99.

25. Ibid., 176.

26. Ibid., 134.

27. The shorter version was published in *Sisters of the Spirit: Three Black Women's Autobiographies of the Nineteenth Century*, ed. William L. Andrews (Bloomington: Indiana University Press, 1986). The longer and later version, *Religious Experience and Journal of Mrs. Jarena Lee*, appears in *Spiritual Narratives*, ed. Sue E. Houchins, Schomburg Library of Nineteenth Century Black Women Writers (New York: Oxford University Press, 1988).

28. Nellie Y. McKay, "Nineteenth-Century Black Women's Spiritual Autobiographies: Religious Faith and Self-Empowerment," in *Perspectives*, 178–91. See also Jean M. Humez, "'My Spirit Eye': Some Functions of Spiritual Visionary Experience in the Lives of Five Black Women Preachers, 1810–1880," in *Women and the Structure of Society*, 5th Berkshire Conference (Durham: Duke University Press, 1984), 129–43.

29. See Jualynne Dodson, "Nineteenth-Century A.M.E. Preaching Women," in Rosemary Skinner Keller and Hilah Thomas, eds., *Women in New Worlds* (Nashville: Abingdon Press, 1981), 2:276–89. The spiritual autobiographies of two other African American women preachers, Mrs. Zilpha Elaw (1846) and Mrs. Julia A. J. Foote (1879), are also included in Andrews, *Sisters of the Spirit*.

30. George Brown, *The Lady Preacher: or the Life and Labors of Mrs. Hannah Reeves* . . . (Philadelphia: Daughaday & Becker, 1870; reprint, Garland, 1987), 100.

31. *Mount Vernon Gazette*, Ohio, Oct. 1831, and reprinted in the *Methodist Protestant*. Quoted in Brown, *The Lady Preacher*, 116–17.

32. Brown, *The Lady Preacher*, 137–38.

33. *Autobiography of Lydia Sexton* (Dayton, Ohio: United Brethren Publishing House, 1882; reprint, Garland, 1987), 200–202.

34. Ibid., 209.

35. Ibid., 240.

36. Bruce David Forbes, "'And Obey God, Etc.': Methodism and American Indians," in *Perspectives*, 209–27; Homer Noley, *First White Frost: Native Americans and United Methodism* (Nashville: Abingdon Press, 1991). For a wider interpretation of Native American identity, see Richard A. Grounds, George E. Tinker, and David E. Wilkins, eds., *Native Voices: American Indian Identity and Resistance* (Lawrence: University Press of Kansas, 2003).

37. Barclay, *Missions*, 3:509–35. Compare Robert W. Sledge, *"Five Dollars and Myself": The History of Mission of The Methodist Episcopal Church, South, 1845–1939*, United Methodist Church History of Missions Series, 2 (New York: GBGM, 2005), 12–13.

38. James B. Finley, *Life among the Indians* (Cincinnati: Methodist Book Concern, 1857). The Wyandotte Indian Mission, Upper Sandusky, Ohio, was placed on the national register of UMC Heritage Landmarks in 1968.

39. Barclay, *Missions*, 2:117–26. See esp. notes on 124–25 identifying the succession of non–Native American appointments to the Wyandotte Mission (1823–44).

40. For an account of Ross's Methodist churchmanship, see Gary E. Moulton, *John Ross, Cherokee Chief* (Athens: University of Georgia Press, 1978). Ross Cemetery, an 1842 Cherokee burial ground in Park Hill, Oklahoma, including Trail of Tears medallions and a granite memorial to Chief John Ross, is listed on the National Register of Historic Places.

41. Barclay, *Missions*, 2:128–29 for citation and statistics, and 126–34 for narrative.

42. William G. McLoughlin, *Cherokees and Missionaries: 1789–1839* (New Haven: Yale University Press, 1984), 291–92.

43. Barclay, *Missions*, 2:130–34.

44. Asbury Manual Labor School and Mission, Fort Mitchell, Alabama, was placed on the national register of UMC Heritage Landmarks in 1984.

45. Barclay, *Missions*, 2:139–43. Also Walter N. Vernon, "Indian Methodists in South Central

States," in *One in the Lord: A History of Ethnic Minorities in the South Central Jurisdiction of The United Methodist Church*, ed. Walter N. Vernon (Bethany, Okla.: Cowan Printing and Litho., 1977), 3–5.

46. Barclay, *Missions*, 2:134–38.

47. Noley, *First White Frost*, 149; Forbes, "'And Obey God, Etc.,'" 214.

48. Noley, *First White Frost*, 109; Barclay, *Missions*, 2:146–51.

49. Noley, *First White Frost*, 106.

50. Forbes, "'And Obey God, Etc.,'" 216.

51. Barclay, *Missions*, 2:200, 204–5, 212.

52. Willamette Mission, near Salem, Oregon, has been a national UMC Heritage Landmark since 1992.

53. Noley, *First White Frost*, 141; Barclay, *Missions*, 2:210–17.

54. Noley, *First White Frost*, 151–53; Barclay, *Missions*, 2:262–85.

55. Sledge, *"Five Dollars and Myself,"* 22, 39–53, 70–74.

56. Barclay, *Missions*, 2:262–85.

57. See William Apess, *A Son of the Forest, and Other Writings*, ed. with an introduction by Barry O'Connell (Amherst: University of Massachusetts Press, 1997), and *On Our Ground: The Complete Writings of William Apess, a Pequot*, ed. with an introduction by Barry O'Connell (Amherst: University of Massachusetts Press, 1992).

58. On Methodism's slave missions see Mathews, *Slavery*, "The Southern Compromise of Conscience: The Mission to the Slaves, 1824–1844," 62–88; and Albert J. Raboteau, *Slave Religion: The "Invisible Institution" in the Antebellum South* (New York: Oxford University Press, 1978), chap. 4.

59. JGC/MEC/1816, 1:169–70.

60. Mathews, *Slavery*, 109, 47–49, 88–110; Raboteau, *Slave Religion;* Curts, *General Conferences*, 271–309.

61. *Minutes*/MEC/1828, 572; also 538, "Indians."

62. George G. Smith, *The Life and Letters of James Osgood Andrew* (Nashville: Southern Methodist Publishing House, 1882), 180–82; Mathews, *Slavery*, 62–87; Sledge, *"Five Dollars and Myself,"* 55–59.

63. *First Annual Report of the Missionary Society of The Methodist Episcopal Church, South* (Louisville, 1846), 13–14, 49–52.

64. Raboteau, *Slave Religion*, 95–288. Sylvia R. Frey and Betty Wood, *Come Shouting to Zion: African American Protestantism in the American South and British Caribbean to 1830* (Chapel Hill and London: University of North Carolina Press, 1998).

65. Joseph C. Hartzell, "Methodism and the Negro in the United States," *Journal of Negro History* 8 (July 1923): 304.

66. W. P. Harrison, letter, CA, May 29, 1835, 40.

67. (Charleston, S.C.: Printed by J. S. Burges, 1833), 16 pages.

68. Thomas Summers revised and reissued Capers's two-part catechism in 1860. As late as 1874, the General Conference of the MECS ordered the continued use of Capers's catechisms (JGC/MECS/1874, 431–32). The latest documented printings by the Publishing House of the MECS: for Part 1, 1918; for Part 2, 1900.

69. Cited by William M. Wightman in *Life of William Capers, D.D. One of the Bishops of The Methodist Episcopal Church, South, Including an Autobiography* (Nashville: Southern Methodist Publishing House, 1858), 296.

70. Holland N. McTyeire, *Duties of Christian Masters* (Nashville: Southern Methodist Publishing House, 1859), a prize-winning essay first published by the Southern Baptists in 1851, as *Duties of Masters to Servants: Three Premium Essays* (Charleston, S.C.: Southern Baptist Publication Society, 1851). James O. Andrews, "Four Letters on the Religious Instruction of Negroes," *New Orleans Christian Advocate* (1856), republished in McTyeire's 1859 *Duties of Christian Masters*, 219–266. William A. Smith, *Lectures on the Philosophy and Practice of Slavery* (Nashville: Stevenson & Evans, 1856). Richard H. Rivers, *Elements of Moral Philosophy* (Nashville: Southern Methodist Publishing House, 1859). For the larger context see H. Shelton Smith, *In His Image but . . . Racism in Southern Religion, 1780–1919* (Durham, N.C.: Duke University Press, 1972), esp. 129–65.

71. William Capers, *Catechism for the Use of the Methodist Missions, First Part* (Louisville: Published by John Early for the MECS, 1847). Preface designated "third edition." Part 2 was published the next year: *Catechism for the Use of the Methodist Missions, Second Part, Comprehending a Brief Outline of the History of Redemption* (Richmond, Va.: Published by John Early for the MECS, 1848).

72. Barclay, *Missions*, 1:272–73; 3:262–64.

73. James E. Kirby, Russell E. Richey, and Kenneth E. Rowe, *The Methodists* (Westport, Conn. and London: Greenwood Press, 1996), 329–31; Barclay, *Missions*, 1:274–79; 2:455–56; 3:265; Paul Douglass, *The Story of German Methodism: Biography of an Immigrant Soul* (New York: Methodist Book Concern, 1939).

74. Justo L. González, ed., *Each in Our Own Tongue: A History of Hispanic United Methodism* (Nashville: Abingdon Press, 1991), 19–30. Alfredo Nañez, "Methodism among the Spanish-Speaking People in Texas and New Mexico," in *One in the Lord: A History of Ethnic Minorities in the South Central Jurisdiction of The United Methodist Church*, ed. Walter N. Vernon (Bethany, Okla.: Cowan Printing and Litho., 1977), 50–94.

75. Joel N. Martínez, "The South Central Jurisdiction," in *Each in Our Own Tongue*, 41.

76. Justo L. González, gen. ed., *Each in Our Own Tongue: A History of Hispanic United Methodism*, 51–42.

77. Sledge, *"Five Dollars and Myself,"* 68–70.

78. Stephen Olin, *The Works of Stephen Olin*, 2 vols. (New York: Harper Brothers, 1852), 2:434.

79. J. M. Reid, *Missions and Missionary Society of The Methodist Episcopal Church*, 2 vols. (New York: Phillips & Hunt; Cincinnati: Cranston & Stowe, 1879), 1:79.

80. Barclay, *Missions*, 3:194–299.

81. Cox Memorial UMC, Hallowell, Maine, was placed on the national register of UMC Heritage Landmarks in 1992.

82. Sledge, *"Five Dollars and Myself,"* 80–83. Her dedicatory donation provides Sledge with his title and motif.

83. *Discipline*/MEC/1860, 91, 43; *Discipline*/MEC/1856, 43.

84. James E. Kirby, *The Episcopacy in American Methodism* (Nashville: Kingswood Books/Abingdon Press, 2000), 177–87; Barclay, *Missions*, 3:176–80, 176n, 876–83.

85. Tigert, *Methodism*, 34–35; Lee, *Short History*, 119–20. The second *Discipline* was titled *The General Minutes of the Conferences of The Methodist Episcopal Church in America, forming the Constitution of the Said Church* (London, 1786), 11. See also Emory, *Discipline*, 137.

86. Tigert, *Methodism*, 37.

87. *Discipline/MEC/1792*, 18.

88. Robert Paine, *Life and Times of William M'Kendree*, 2 vols. (Nashville: Publishing House of the MECS, 1874), 1:397–404.

89. For a narrative of the conference, see Bangs, *History*, 3:100–157; HAM, 1:642ff.; Tigert, *History*, chap. 18; Buckley, *History*, chaps. 41 and 42; and Drinkhouse, *History of Methodist Reform*, vol. 2, chap. 1.

90. Tigert, *History*, 339.

91. Paine, *Life and Times of William M'Kendree*, 1:420–21.

92. Ibid., 1:419.

93. Ibid., 1:444–58.

94. For the text of two of these quite varying interpretations of the Constitution, namely, those of Philadelphia and South Carolina, see Tigert, *History*, 370–71.

95. Created as a vehicle for the Baltimore Union Society, it is considered a continuation of the *Wesleyan Repository and Religious Intelligencer*. On the Methodist Protestant movement see William R. Sutton, *Journeymen for Jesus: Evangelical Artisans Confront Capitalism in Jacksonian Baltimore* (University Park: Pennsylvania State University Press, 1998).

96. "Remarks and Observations Addressed to Travelling Preachers," *Wesleyan Repository* 2 (Aug. 1822). Initially printed in Dec. 1820 and circulated among traveling preachers. Reprinted by Nicholas Snethen in *Snethen on Lay Representation* (Baltimore: John J. Harrod, 1835), 37–58.

97. "On Church Freedom," *Wesleyan Repository* 1 (Dec. 20, 1821), in *Snethen on Lay Representation*, 75–78.

98. Emory, *Discipline*, 191–202. Lee, *Short History*, 255, 359, 362. McKendree gave the proportions for 1812: 2,000 to 700. James Mudge, *History of the New England Conference of The Methodist Episcopal Church, 1796–1910*, 239–40.

99. See Lee, *Short History*, 354, or the year-end tally for any prior year. Bangs took a similar "body" count. See Bangs, *History*, 3:183 for the 1820 accounting.

100. JGC/MEC/1816, 148–52. That concern made the conference no more receptive to petitions by local preachers for representation (1816), 166–69.

101. Emory, *Discipline*, 193–96.

102. "Matters Worthy of the Serious Reflection of Travelling Preachers," *Mutual Rights* 2 (April 1826), in Nicholas Snethen, *Snethen on Lay Representation*, 316–20.

103. For discussion of the complex intertwinings of these two ideological constellations see J. G. A. Pocock, ed., *Three British Revolutions: 1641, 1688, 1776* (Princeton: Princeton University Press, 1980), and particularly the essay therein by John A. Murrin.

104. Bangs, *History*, 2:342–43.

105. JGC/MEC/1824, 278–79.

106. Not included in JGC/MEC but reproduced by Curts, *General Conferences*, 95–97.

107. Drinkhouse, *History of Methodist Reform*, 2:62–63; HAM, 1:650–51.

108. Journal of the Baltimore Conference, April 20, 1827, 203, typescript, courtesy of Edwin

Schell. For the Methodist Protestant take on the case, see Drinkhouse, *History of Methodist Reform*, 2:105–8.

109. Alexander McCaine, *History and Mystery of Methodist Episcopacy* (Baltimore, 1827), 74.

110. Both appeared in 1827. Emory's bore the full title *A Defence of "Our Fathers," and of the Original Organization of The Methodist Episcopal Church, Against the Rev. Alexander McCaine, and Others* (New York: N. Bangs & J. Emory, for the MEC, 1827). Bond's was reprinted in Thomas E. Bond, *The Economy of Methodism Illustrated and Defended* (New York: Lane & Scott, 1852), 9–56.

111. "An Appeal to the Methodists, in Opposition to the Changes Proposed in Their Church Government," in Bond, *The Economy of Methodism Illustrated and Defended*, 20.

112. Ibid., 48.

113. Cited by Drinkhouse, *History of Methodist Reform*, 2:128. See also "A Narrative and Defence of the Proceedings of The Methodist Episcopal Church in Baltimore City Station, Against Certain Local Preachers and Lay Members of Said Church," in Bond, *The Economy of Methodism Illustrated and Defended*, 57–136.

114. Attendees were listed by Drinkhouse, *History of Methodist Reform*, 2:137–39.

115. Bangs reproduced the committee report on the Reformers' memorial and the resolutions on trials in *History*, 3:413–30. See Sutton, *Journeymen for Jesus*.

116. JGC/MEC/1828, 346, 355–56. See Tigert, *History*, 400–403, for analysis and interpretation.

117. See Drinkhouse, *History of Methodist Reform*, 2:211–12, for a summary of the seventeen articles.

118. On the leadership provided by and centrality of Baltimore, see Baker, *Incredible Methodists*, 165.

119. For the text see Drinkhouse, *History of Methodist Reform*, 2:257–67.

120. It bore the name *The Mutual Rights and Methodist Protestant* from 1831 to 1834 and then continued only the latter designation.

121. *Constitution and Discipline of The Methodist Protestant Church*, published by John M. Harrod (Baltimore: W. Woody, 1830), iii–ix.

122. *Constitution and Discipline of the Methodist Protestant Church* (Baltimore: Published for the Book Committee of the Methodist Protestant Church, 1830), 21. This had been the posture of the MEC from 1808 until 1820, when rescinded by General Conference at the prompting of the bishops and in the face of continued antislavery activity in northern and western conferences. For the MEC's "Missouri Compromise," see Mathews, *Slavery*, 46–52; for the successive legislation on slavery, see the appendix in Mathews, 293–303, and/or Emory, *History of the Discipline*, 17, 20, 372–79.

123. *Constitution and Discipline of the Methodist Protestant Church*, Articles VII and XII, 21–22, 29. See also Drinkhouse, *History of Methodist Reform*, 2:261, 265.

124. See Mathews, *Slavery*, and *Religion in the Old South* (Chicago: University of Chicago Press, 1977), and for the North, A. Gregory Schneider, *The Way of the Cross Leads Home: The Domestication of American Methodism* (Bloomington and Indianapolis: Indiana University Press, 1993). For transformations in evangelicalism as a whole, see Leonard I. Sweet, ed., *The Evangelical Tradition in America* (Macon: Mercer University Press, 1984).

125. On Methodist relation to society see John H. Wigger, *Taking Heaven by Storm: Methodism and the Rise of Popular Christianity in America* (New York and Oxford: Oxford University Press,

1998); Hempton, *Methodism*; Christine Leigh Heyrman, *Southern Cross: The Beginnings of the Bible Belt* (New York: Knopf, 1997); Cynthia Lynn Lyerly, *Methodism and the Southern Mind, 1770–1810* (New York and Oxford: Oxford University Press, 1998); Schneider, *The Way of the Cross Leads Home*; and the older item, Richard M. Cameron, *Methodism and Society in Historical Perspective*, vol. 1 of *Methodism and Society* undertaken by the Board of Social and Economic Relations and the Boston University School of Theology (New York: Abingdon Press, 1961).

VIII. Dividing over Slavery, Region, Authority, and Race: 1830–60s

1. On the disciplinary retreat, see the appendix in Mathews, *Slavery*, 293–303.

2. On the increasing commitment to slavery and the movement from acquiescence in, to defense of, to sanctifying slavery, see Mitchell Snay, *Gospel of Disunion: Religion and Separatism in the Antebellum South* (Cambridge: Cambridge University Press, 1993; Chapel Hill and London: University of North Carolina Press, 1997); on the spirituality of the church, see Christopher H. Owen, *The Sacred Flame of Love: Methodism and Society in Nineteenth-Century Georgia* (Athens and London: University of Georgia Press, 1998), 38, 53, 63–65, 69, 88.

3. See Pilkington/Vernon, *Methodist Publishing House*, vol. 1, chap. 5.

4. JGC/MEC/1836, 428.

5. JGC/MEC/1840, 11–14. A committee on slavery had been established at the prior General Conference.

6. Tigert, *History*, 386–409, quotation from 392–93; see also James E. Kirby, *The Episcopacy in American Methodism* (Nashville: Kingswood Books/Abingdon Press, 2000), 87–111, quotation from 106.

7. C. C. Goen, *Broken Churches, Broken Nation: Denominational Schisms and the Coming of the American Civil War* (Macon: Mercer University Press, 1985). Snay in *Gospel of Disunion*, 141–42, points out that some southern editors saw the church divisions as helping to preserve the Union by curtailing abolitionism.

8. See Behney/Eller, *History*, 123–25, 165–67, 198–99.

9. For a thorough assessment of the impact of the church splits on the nation, see Goen, *Broken Churches, Broken Nation*.

10. The former is vigorously represented by Tigert, *History*, and Holland N. McTyeire, *A History of Methodism* (Nashville: Publishing House of the MECS, 1904). The latter is represented in various MEC histories, but especially in the "external" perspectives of Mathews, *Slavery*, and H. Shelton Smith, *In His Image but . . . Racism in Southern Religion, 1780–1919* (Durham, N.C.: Duke University Press, 1972). See Mathews, 250n, for an especially telling rebuttal to the constitutional readings.

11. James Mudge, *History of the New England Conference of the Methodist Episcopal Church, 1796–1910* (Boston: Published by the Conference, 1910), 278–97.

12. Shipley W. Willson et al., *An Appeal on the Subject of Slavery; Addressed to the Members of the New England and New Hampshire Conferences* (Boston: D. H. Ela, 1835), see 3–23. See also Mathews, *Slavery*, 122–28.

13. The *Zion's Herald . . . Extra* follows the May 13, 1835, issue in the APS (American Periodical Series) II microfilm series (reel 1574). Both D. D. Whedon, professor, and Wilbur Fisk,

president of Wesleyan University, figured prominently in criticism of the "Appeal" and the anti-slavery advocates.

14. Mathews, *Slavery*, 133; Mudge, *History of the New England Conference*, 281. See also the discussion of such conference activity under "Episcopacy."

15. Mathews, *Slavery*, 139–47.

16. Bangs, *History*, 4:259–60, 261. He reproduced the entire address, 250–64.

17. Cited by Mathews, *Slavery*, 138.

18. Mathews, *Slavery*, 148–57; Mudge, *History of the New England Conference*, 283–86.

19. On the evolution of southern evangelicalism and its "conscience," see Donald G. Mathews, *Religion in the Old South* (Chicago: University of Chicago Press, 1977), 136–84; on the doctrine of the spirituality of the church, see Owen, *The Sacred Flame of Love*, 38, 53, 63–65, 69, 88.

20. *Southern Christian Advocate*, June 21, 1837, 1.

21. Reported in *Southern Christian Advocate*, Jan. 5, 1838, 114; cited by Mathews, *Slavery*, 181.

22. See Homer L. Calkin's chapter in Baker, *Incredible Methodists*, 192–228.

23. JGC/MEC/1840, 134–37. Bangs reproduced the entire Episcopal Address, *History*, 4:336–71.

24. JGC/MEC/1840, 139. Bangs, *History*, 4:350.

25. JGC/MEC/1840, 60, 61, 87, 88, 109. See Tigert, *History*, 429–33; Mathews, *Slavery*, 201–4, 213–16. Mathews says, "The Few resolution became the 'scarlet letter' that signified the shame of the Methodist Episcopal Church" (213).

26. Baker, *Incredible Methodists*. The petition is reproduced by Frederick A. Norwood in *Sourcebook of American Methodism* (Nashville: Abingdon Press, 1982), 252–53.

27. On these developments and their implications, see Mathews, *Slavery*, 225–28. They declared their intention to be antislavery, but not radical.

28. Norwood, *Sourcebook*, 255–58, and *HAM*, 2:39–47.

29. "Pastoral Address" reproduced by Norwood, *Sourcebook*, 258–61.

30. *ZH*, Dec. 7, 1842, 190, cited by Mathews, *Slavery*, 233.

31. See *HAM*, 2:33; Mathews, *Slavery*, 235–40.

32. The limits placed on women and laity would be issues at later conferences.

33. JGC/MEC/1844, 20. See also 18–22, 25–27, 35–37, 39–41, 42–43, 44, 47–48, 54. For examples, see Charles Elliott, *History of the Great Secession from The Methodist Episcopal Church* (Cincinnati: Swormstedt & Poe, 1855), 971–73. Mathews observes, "Almost every Northern annual conference petitioned the General Conference to take more decisive action against slavery." *Slavery*, 240.

34. JGC/MEC/1844, 20–21, 41.

35. Curts, *General Conferences*, 121, 128. Robert A. West, reporter, *Report of Debates in the General Conference of The Methodist Episcopal Church . . . 1844* (New York: G. Lane & C. B. Tippett, 1844), hereafter *Debates/MEC/1844*.

36. *HAM*, 2:56–57; Baker, *Incredible Methodists*, 207.

37. *Debates/MEC/1844*, 5.

38. JGC/MEC/1844, 13.

39. Ibid., 29. For the narrative, see Baker, *Incredible Methodists*, 207–10; Mathews, *Slavery*, 251–54; *HAM*, 2:51–54. For the text of the arguments, see *Debates/MEC/1844*, 18–52.

40. JGC/MEC/1844, 156.

41. *The Life and Letters of Stephen Olin*, 2 vols. (New York: Harper & Brothers, 1853), 2:158. See also *Debates/MEC/1844*, 54–55.

42. *The Life and Letters of Stephen Olin*, 2:181.

43. George G. Smith, *The Life and Letters of James Osgood Andrew* (Nashville: Southern Methodist Publishing House, 1882), 342–43.

44. JGC/MEC/1844, 64. *Debates/MEC/1844*, 73, 82.

45. JGC/MEC/1844, 65–66.

46. *Debates/MEC/1844*, 150, or Elliott, *History of the Great Secession*, 987.

47. *Debates/MEC/1844*, 128–31, 134.

48. Ibid., 154–55.

49. Ibid., 168–69. See also *Organization MECS* 67–84 for Soule's remarks.

50. *Debates/MEC/1844*, 174.

51. JGC/MEC/1844, 75; the letter extends to 76. Also in *Debates/MEC/1844*, 184–85.

52. See James Porter, "General Conference of 1844," *MQR* 53 (April 1871): 234–50, 246.

53. JGC/MEC/1844, 81; *Debates/MEC/1844*, 188–89.

54. Tigert, *History*, 445.

55. JGC/MEC/1844, 86. Four more enabling resolutions followed (86–87). See also *Debates/MEC/1844*, 192, or Elliott, *History of the Great Secession*, 1008–9.

56. JGC/MEC/1844, 109. Referred to the select committee of nine.

57. "The Protest of the Minority in the Case of Bishop Andrew," *Debates/MEC/1844*, 203–12; Elliott, *History of the Great Secession*, 1017–29; or *Organization MECS*, 102–23.

58. *Debates/MEC/1844*, 209.

59. JGC/MEC/1844, 112. Conference took action, passing the first item.

60. *Debates/MEC/1844*, 229–37, 235. See also Elliott, *History of the Great Secession*, 1030–41.

61. *Debates/MEC/1844*, 220.

62. Ibid., 223–24.

63. On the propriety and legality of this gathering, see Tigert, *History*, 450–51.

64. *Organization MECS*, 147–52, or Elliott, *History of the Great Secession*, 1045–48.

65. Address "To the Ministers and Members of The Methodist Episcopal Church, in the Slaveholding States and Territories," in *Organization MECS*, 150. This was, of course, the southern construction of the division.

66. See *Organization MECS*, 153–75, and Redford, *History MECS*, appendix B, 594–628.

67. Minutes of the North Carolina Annual Conference, 1838–1885, 2 vols., photocopy of original handwritten minutes (1844), 2:15b. They subsequently "Ordered that Conference sit with closed doors during the examination of Character," 2:17b, 29b.

68. Soule's Address to the convention in *Organization MECS*, 246.

69. See, for instance, the Kentucky "Address. To the Members of The Methodist Episcopal Church within the bounds of the Kentucky Annual Conference," in *Organization MECS*, 156–75.

70. The easiest access to this warfare, albeit from an MEC perspective, is through Elliott, *History of the Great Secession*. Himself editor of the *WCA*, Elliott collected clippings from these MEC (northern) papers and from their southern (MECS) counterparts, the *Southern Christian Advocate* (Charleston), the *Richmond Christian Advocate*, and the *Southwestern Christian Advocate*

(Nashville). From what came to eight volumes and a total of 6,727 fourteen-inch columns, he produced his *History*, which cites liberally from these papers, includes full statements of various conference actions, and represents a companion to the southern *Organization MECS*. Reading the two together puts one into the fray.

71. Elliott, *History of the Great Secession*, 404.

72. Ibid., 405.

73. *Organization MECS*, 338.

74. Ibid., 262.

75. These are the words of Messrs. Wesley themselves.

76. *The Doctrine and Discipline of The Methodist Episcopal Church, South* (Richmond: Published by John Early for the MECS, 1846).

77. *Organization MECS*, 264–65. The language was that of the Plan of Separation. Of importance here is simply the fact of its implementation and the evocation of what would amount to warfare to establish a border.

78. Frederick A. Norwood, *The Story of American Methodism* (Nashville: Abingdon Press, 1974), 207–9; Baker, *Incredible Methodists*, 214–15; HAM, 2:127–28, 159–67.

79. Elliott, *History of the Great Secession*, 585–90, 1083–85.

80. Ibid., 590–91, 1086–92.

81. Ibid., 591–93.

82. Charles Elliott, *South-Western Methodism: A History of the M.E. Church in the South-West, from 1844 to 1864*, ed. and rev. Leroy M. Vernon (Cincinnati: Poe & Hitchcock, 1868).

83. JGC/MEC/1848, 16, 21–22. Redford, *History MECS*, 533–38.

84. JGC/MEC/1848, 80–85, 154–64.

85. JGC/MECS/1850, 130–43, 141.

86. Laura L. Mitchell, " 'Matters of Justice between Man and Man': Northern Divines, the Bible, and the Fugitive Slave Act of 1850," in *Religion and the Antebellum Debate over Slavery*, ed. John R. McKivigan and Mitchell Snay (Athens and London: University of Georgia Press, 1998), 134–65.

87. HAM, 2:339–60.

88. Howard A. Snyder, *Populist Saints: B. T. and Ellen Roberts and the First Free Methodists* (Grand Rapids, Mich., and Cambridge, U.K.: Eerdmans, 2006).

89. JGC/MEC/1860, 260.

90. *Minutes of the Philadelphia Conference of The Methodist Episcopal Church*, 1861, 12.

91. For treatment of this and the following see Baker, *Incredible Methodists*, 218–28.

92. *Register of the Baltimore Annual Conference of The Methodist Episcopal Church*, 1862, 22–23. The action did provide for consideration of that withdrawal as null and void, if such members presented themselves and cooperated at next conference.

93. An easy access to this political character, albeit only on the northern side, is through Rumsey Smithson's *Political Status of The Methodist Episcopal Church*, 2nd ed. (Canton, Ill.: H. S. Hill, 1868). Smithson excerpted the "political" resolutions passed by MEC annual conferences from 1861 to 1866 (pp. 11–54). He argued that since the 1844 division, "the Methodist Episcopal Church, has maintained a non-secular character, while the M.E. Church (north) has boldly entered the arena of political agitation" (3).

IX. Embracing the War Cause(s): 1860–65

1. See the various graphs in Roger Finke and Rodney Stark, *The Churching of America: Winners and Losers in Our Religious Economy* (New Brunswick: Rutgers University Press, 1992), esp. 55, 113, 147.

2. James W. May, "The War Years," in *HAM*, 2:206–56; William Warren Sweet, *The Methodist Episcopal Church and the Civil War* (Cincinnati: Methodist Book Concern Press, 1912).

3. For the citation, the episcopal counsel, and the complexities of attitudes toward slavery and secession see Christopher H. Owen, *The Sacred Flame of Love: Methodism and Society in Nineteenth-Century Georgia* (Athens and London: University of Georgia Press, 1998), esp. 104–6, 93–95; also Beth Barton Schweiger, *The Gospel Working Up: Progress and the Pulpit in Nineteenth-Century Virginia* (New York and Oxford: Oxford University Press, 2000), 93–95; Mitchell Snay, *Gospel of Disunion: Religion and Separatism in the Antebellum South* (Cambridge: Cambridge University Press, 1993; Chapel Hill and London: University of North Carolina Press, 1997), 151–80.

4. John W. Brinsfield, "The Chaplains of the Confederacy," in *Faith in the Fight: Civil War Chaplains*, ed. John W. Brinsfield et al. (Mechanicsburg, Pa.: Stackpole Books, 2003), 51–92, 62.

5. John Wesley Brinsfield Jr., comp. and ed., *The Spirit Divided: Memoirs of Civil War Chaplains: The Confederacy* (Macon: Mercer University Press, 2005), 7, 10. From the full members of conference, the MECS bishops appointed 318 of the Methodist chaplains and permitted 109 to serve in other capacities (96). Brinsfield, "The Chaplains of the Confederacy," 61. Gardiner H. Shattuck, *A Shield and Hiding Place: The Religious Life of the Civil War Armies* (Macon: Mercer University Press, 1987), 51–72.

6. Robert W. Sledge, *"Five Dollars and Myself": The History of Mission of The Methodist Episcopal Church, South, 1845–1939*, United Methodist Church History of Missions Series, 2 (New York: GBGM, 2005), 85–109; Brinsfield, *The Spirit Divided*, 183–93, 140–42; Steven E. Woodworth, *While God Is Marching On: The Religious World of Civil War Soldiers* (Lawrence: University Press of Kansas, 2001), 160–63.

7. Brinsfield, "The Chaplains of the Confederacy," 55–58, 71–72.

8. Schweiger, *Gospel Working Up*, 107, 99–100; Brinsfield, "The Chaplains of the Confederacy," 81–82, 84–85.

9. William W. Bennett, *A Narrative of the Great Revival in the Southern Armies During the Late Civil War between the States of the Federal Union* (Philadelphia, 1877).

10. Schweiger, *Gospel Working Up*, 101–2.

11. Brinsfield, *The Spirit Divided*, 185–86.

12. Ibid., 191.

13. Drew Gilpin Faust, *Mothers of Invention: Women of the Slaveholding South in the American Civil War* (Chapel Hill: University of North Carolina Press, 1996), xi–52.

14. Ibid., 179–95.

15. Owen, *The Sacred Flame of Love*, 96–99.

16. "Address of the 'Confederate' Clergy, 1863," in Edward McPherson, *The Political History of the United States of America, during the Great Rebellion*, 2nd ed. (Washington, D.C.: Philip & Solomons, 1865), 517–21, citation from 519, emphasis in the original.

17. Sweet, *The Methodist Episcopal Church and the Civil War*, 98–99.

18. On his importance in Tennessee consult Herman A. Norton, *Religion in Tennessee, 1777–1945* (Knoxville: University of Tennessee Press; published in cooperation with the Tennessee Historical Commission, 1981), 61–73, and David B. Chesebrough, *Clergy Dissent in the Old South, 1830–1865* (Carbondale and Edwardsville: Southern Illinois University Press, 1996), 52–56.

19. Owen, *The Sacred Flame of Love*, 99–100, 104, and "'To Keep the Way Open for Methodism': Georgia Wesleyan Neutrality toward Slavery, 1844–1861," in *Religion and the Antebellum Debate over Slavery*, ed. John R. McKivigan and Mitchell Snay (Athens and London: University of Georgia Press, 1998), 109–33.

20. Rumsey Smithson, *Political Status of The Methodist Episcopal Church*, 2nd ed. (Canton, Ill.: H. S. Hill, 1868). Section 3 extracted 97 political platforms from 46 annual conferences covering the years 1861–67, followed a given conference through that period, for example, New England, and provided then a very handy summation of the political statements for that and other conferences. Smithson gathered thirty-two "teachings and principles" from these platforms, among them those listed, 12–14, 52–53.

21. *Minutes of the Mississippi Annual Conference*, MECS, 1865, 25–29. Cited in HAM, 2:269.

22. Owen, *The Sacred Flame of Love*, 101–3.

23. See A *Collection of Hymns for Public, Social, and Domestic Worship* (Charleston: John Early for the MECS, 1847).

24. Sweet, *The Methodist Episcopal Church and the Civil War*; May, "The War Years"; Donald G. Jones, *The Sectional Crisis and Northern Methodism: A Study in Piety, Political Ethics and Civil Religion* (Metuchen and London: Scarecrow Press, 1979); William Gravely, *Gilbert Haven, Methodist Abolitionist: A Study in Race, Religion, and Reform, 1850–1880* (Nashville and New York: Abingdon Press, 1973); Shattuck, *A Shield and Hiding Place*; James H. Moorhead, *American Apocalypse: Yankee Protestants and the Civil War, 1860–1869* (New Haven and London: Yale University Press, 1978).

25. May, "The War Years," 211–14.

26. Kenneth Brown and P. Lewis Brevard, *History of the Churches of Christ in Christian Union* (Circleville, Ohio: Circle Press, 1980), 28.

27. George R. Crooks, *The Life of Bishop Matthew Simpson of the Methodist Episcopal Church* (New York: Harper & Brothers, 1891), 366–406.

28. *Minutes of the . . . Philadelphia Conference of the Methodist Episcopal Church*, 1862, 7, 45–46.

29. Ibid., 1864, 15, 44–45, 48, 49.

30. *Minutes of the Sixth Session of the Newark Conference*, 1863, 16–20, 32–33.

31. *Proceedings of the Sixth Annual Meeting of the National Association of Local Preachers of The Methodist Episcopal Church . . . Union M. E. Church, Philadelphia . . . October 10–12, 1863. Together with an Appendix, Containing the Annual Sermon and the Constitution of the Association* (Pittsburgh, 1863), 14.

32. JGC/MEC/1864, 281–91.

33. JGC/MEC/1864, 380–83. "Report No. III of the Committee on the State of the Country"; Moorhead, *American Apocalypse*, 141–42.

34. A. W. Drury, *History of the Church of the United Brethren in Christ*, rev. ed. (Dayton: Otterbein Press, 1953), 456.

35. Edward J. Drinkhouse, *History of Methodist Reform: Synoptical of General Methodism 1703 to 1898 with special . . . reference to the History of the Methodist Protestant Church*, 2 vols. (Baltimore: Board of Publication of the MPC, 1899), 2:452–55.

36. Sweet, *The Methodist Episcopal Church and the Civil War*, 93–95.

37. Woodworth, *While God Is Marching On*, 94.

38. May, "The War Years," 226–28.

39. Benedict Maryniak, "Union Military Chaplains," in *Faith in the Fight: Civil War Chaplains*, 3–49, 45.

40. Ibid., 9–12, quotation from 12; Brinsfield, "The Chaplains of the Confederacy," 55; Shattuck, *A Shield and Hiding Place*, 51–72.

41. Kathryn Teresa Long, *The Revival of 1857–58* (New York and Oxford: Oxford University Press, 1998), 119, 87–91, 117–20; Maryniak, "Union Military Chaplains," 20–21, 28–31; Woodworth, *While God Is Marching On*, 167–74; Shattuck, *A Shield and Hiding Place*, 24–33, 81–92.

42. Lemuel Moss, *Annals of the United States Christian Commission* (Philadelphia: J. B. Lippincott, 1868), 106–8, 110–13, 131; May, "The War Years," 222–25.

43. Shattuck, *A Shield and Hiding Place*, 89–92, quotation from 89.

44. Nina Silber, *Daughters of the Union: Northern Women Fight the Civil War* (Cambridge and London: Harvard University Press, 2005), 162–93.

45. Ibid., 194–221.

46. Paul F. Douglass, *The Story of German Methodism* (New York: Methodist Book Concern, 1939), 176–80. For a mid-twentieth-century account of the Berea home, see Clarence D. Marston, *The World I Lost* (Berea, Ohio: Methodist Children's Home, 1946).

47. Paul H. Eller, *These Evangelical United Brethren* (Dayton: Otterbein Press, 1950), 106–7.

48. For early descriptions of the orphanage, see Freedmen's Aid Society of the MEC, *Fourth Annual Report*, 1871, 11–12, and *Fifth Annual Report*, 1872, 26–27. See also annual reports in the journal of Louisiana Conference: 1871, 15–16; 1873, 44–45.

49. Ruth Esther Meeker, *Six Decades of Service, 1880–1940: A History of the Woman's Missionary Society of The Methodist Episcopal Church* (New York: Woman's Division, Board of Missions, UMC, 1969), 196–98.

50. Jesse Boring, "Church Orphans' Home I," *Southern Christian Advocate*, Nov. 5, 1869, 178; "Church Orphans' Home II," *Southern Christian Advocate*, Dec. 3, 1869, 194.

51. "Report of Special Committee on Orphans' Homes," JGC/MECS/1870, 225–27, 344.

52. Boring, "Church Orphans' Home," *Southern Christian Advocate*, Nov. 5, 1869, 178, and Dec. 3, 1869, 194; JGC/MECS/1870, 161, 171, 173, 185, 222–26, 344.

53. Artemio R. Guillermo, *Churches Aflame: Asian Americans and United Methodism* (Nashville: Abingdon Press, 1991), 72. For an early report on Gum Moon Home in San Francisco, see Mrs. E. C. Gibson, "The Pacific Coast," *Woman's Home Missions* 1, no. 4 (April 1884): 25–26.

54. John Wesley addressed the health-care crisis in his time, when the rich had good medical care and the poor had none. His 1740s Foundery Chapel clinic, stocked with medicines and staffed by Wesley himself and a few volunteer doctors and druggists, is sometimes called the first free public medical dispensary in London. He later opened similar health-care clinics at Newcastle and Bristol. Sadly, all were closed within a decade for lack of donations to keep up with the demand. A more important contribution to England's health and welfare was his publication of an inexpensive

family medical manual, first published in 1745, recommending cures for sixty-three illnesses. Two years later he released a more comprehensive self-help book of diagnoses and remedies, containing remedies for more than 250 maladies. *Primitive Physic, or, An Easy Method of Curing Most Diseases* quickly became one of the most popular family medical manuals in eighteenth-century England. The manual was also among the earliest publications of the Methodists in North America. In the same decade Wesley also opened the "Poorhouse," two small leased houses near the Foundery Chapel in which Wesley provided clean and warm accommodations for a dozen or so "feeble, aged widows" with whom he and the preachers occasionally visited and dined. When he opened a large preaching house in Newcastle in 1742, it included a home and school for orphaned children in addition to an infirmary. The most authoritative reprint is *Primitive Physic, with an Introduction by A. Wesley Hill* (London: Epworth Press, 1960), from the 1791 edition, the last in Wesley's lifetime. In the late 1990s Wesley's manual was still in print: *Primitive Remedies* (Santa Barbara, Calif.: Woodbridge Press, 1973), an unannotated reprint of the 1755 edition. For details and context, see index (medicine) in Richard P. Heitzenrater, *Wesley and the People Called Methodists* (Nashville: Abingdon Press, 1995); E. Brooks Holifield, *Health and Medicine in the Methodist Tradition* (New York: Crossroad, 1986); and Harold V. Vanderpool, "The Wesleyan-Methodist Tradition," in *Caring and Curing: Health and Medicine in the Western Religious Traditions*, ed. Ronald L. Numbers and Darrel W. Amundsen (Baltimore: Johns Hopkins University Press, 1986), 317–53.

55. Joanna B. Gillespie, "The Emerging Voice of the Methodist Woman: *The Ladies' Repository*, 1841–1861," in *Rethinking Methodist History*, ed. Russell E. Richey, Jean Miller Schmidt, and Kenneth E. Rowe (Nashville: Kingswood Books, 1993), 248–58.

56. Philadelphia Conference, MEC, *Journal*: 1873, 56; 1874, 43–44; 1874, 47. For a historical sketch, see Harold C. Koch, *The Origin and Development of the Methodist Home for Children in Philadelphia* (Philadelphia: The Home, 1978).

57. *Constitution of the Orphanage Society of The Methodist Episcopal Church*, Philadelphia (Philadelphia: The Society, 1873), 1.

58. For a description of the 1889 building and campus, see reports in ACJ/Philadelphia/1889, 98; 1898, 155–56; 1899, 128.

59. Meeker, *Six Decades of Service*, 186–88.

60. Grant S. Shockley, *Heritage and Hope: The African American Presence in United Methodism* (Nashville: Abingdon Press, 1991), 65–66.

61. Peter C. Holloran, *Boston's Wayward Children: Social Services for Homeless Children 1830–1930* (Rutherford, N.J.: Fairleigh Dickinson University Press, 1989).

62. John Patrick McDowell, *The Social Gospel in the South: The Woman's Home Mission Movement in The Methodist Episcopal Church, South, 1886–1939* (Baton Rouge: Louisiana State University Press, 1982), 38.

63. Sara Joyce Myers, "Southern Methodist Women Leaders and Church Missions, 1878–1910" (PhD diss., Emory University, 1990), 138–39.

64. Douglass, *German Methodism*, 176–80. "Committee on Orphans' Home," *Methodist Protestant North Carolina Annual Conference Journal*, 1910, 34–35. For a history, see Mabel W. Russell, *History of the Methodist Protestant Children's Home, 1910–1935* (High Point, N.C.: The Home, 1935); see also Ethel W. Born, *By My Spirit: The Story of Methodist Protestant Women in Mission 1879–1939* (New York: Women's Division, GBGM, UMC, 1990), 121–22.

65. For the larger context see Timothy A. Hacsi, *Second Home: Orphan Asylums and Poor Families in America* (Cambridge: Harvard University Press, 1998); Kenneth Cmiel, *A Home of Another Kind: One Chicago Orphanage and the Tangle of Child Welfare* (Chicago: University of Chicago Press, 1995).

66. For context see W. Andrew Achenbaum, *Old Age in the New Land: The American Experience Since 1790* (Baltimore: Johns Hopkins University Press, 1978); David H. Fischer, *Growing Old in America* (New York: Oxford University Press, 1977); Carole Haber and Brian Gratton, *Old Age and the Search for Security: An American Social History* (Bloomington: Indiana University Press, 1994); and Thomas R. Cole, *The Journey of Life: A Cultural History of Aging in America* (Cambridge, U.K.: Cambridge University Press, 1992).

67. "Methodist Home for Aged and Infirm," *Ladies' Repository* 31, no. 1 (Jan. 1871): 48.

68. Methodist Episcopal Church Home for the Aged, Philadelphia, *Twenty-fifth Annual Report for the Year 1891*, 14.

69. For the architect's drawing, see ACJ/Philadelphia/1898, 150–51; for an account of the 1899 dedication by three bishops of the church, see ACJ/Philadelphia/1900, 123–24. For a compact history, see David R. Adam, " 'Rays of Light and Comfort': A History of Simpson House," *Annals of Eastern Pennsylvania, Journal of the Historical Society and the Commission on Archives and History of the Eastern Pennsylvania Conference of the UMC*, no. 3, 2006, 3–14.

70. Following Haber and Gratton, *Old Age and the Search for Security*, 131–32.

71. Grant Shockley, "The A.M.E. and A.M.E. Zion Church," in HAM, 2:551.

72. Washington Conference, MEC, *Journal*: 1872, 11; 1886, 81–82; 1894, 69–70; 1895, 62–63.

73. ACJ/Louisiana/1887, 348, 365; 1888, 426.

74. Methodist Episcopal Church Home for the Aged, Philadelphia, *Annual Report*, 1891, 14, emphasis in original.

75. Methodist Episcopal Church Home, Philadelphia, *Twenty-fifth Annual Report*, 1891, 15; *Twenty-sixth Annual Report*, 1892, 15.

76. Methodist Episcopal Church Home for the Aged, Philadelphia, *Annual Report*, 1876, 13.

77. Gravely, *Gilbert Haven*, 129–42.

78. JGC/MEC/1864, 485–86.

79. "Philadelphia Correspondence," CA, Aug. 11, 1864.

80. Henry B. Ridgaway, *The Life of Edmund S. Janes* (New York: Phillips & Hunt; Cincinnati: Walden & Stowe, 1882), 277. The official history of this conference is William C. Jason Jr., "The Delaware Annual Conference of the Methodist Church, 1864–1965," *MethH* 4 (July 1966): 26–41.

81. See Edward N. Wilson, "Washington Conference, 1864–1965," and Edward G. Carroll, "The Washington Annual Conference: Early Period, 1864–1915," in Baker, *Incredible Methodists*, 245–49 and 284–313, respectively.

82. See Gravely, *Gilbert Haven*.

83. JGC/MEC/1868, 127, 128, 130.

84. David B. Chesebrough, *"No Sorrow Like Our Sorrow": Northern Protestant Ministers and the Assassination of Lincoln* (Kent, Ohio, and London: Kent State University Press, 1994), 126–38; Crooks, *Bishop Matthew Simpson*, 397–403.

85. Chesebrough, *"No Sorrow Like Our Sorrow,"* 138, 136; Crooks, *Bishop Matthew Simpson*, 402–3.

86. Jones, *The Sectional Crisis and Northern Methodism*; Paul E. Grosjean, "The Concept of American Nationhood: Theological Interpretation as Reflected by the Northern Mainline Protestant Preachers in the Late Civil War Period" (PhD diss., Drew University, 1978); Mark A. Noll, *The Civil War as a Theological Crisis* (Chapel Hill: University of North Carolina Press, 2006).

87. The Episcopal effort, on Mount St. Albans in Washington, D.C., began construction in 1907. First services were conducted in 1912, and the building was completed in 1990.

88. Fund-raising dragged on until 1884. "Episcopal Address," JGC/MEC/1884, 39.

89. Lillian B. Brown, *A Living Centennial: Commemorating the 100th Anniversary of Metropolitan Memorial United Methodist Church* (Washington, D.C.: The Church, 1969). By the 1920s the expansion of government buildings in central Washington altered residential patterns. Old Metropolitan Church was abandoned in 1930 and demolished in 1935. In the meantime the congregation relocated and built an even larger Gothic church at Nebraska Avenue and Newark Street (near Methodist-related American University) in 1932.

90. JGC/MECS/1858, 385, 416–18.

91. JGC/MECS/1906, 194–95; see also Harvey Marinus King, *The Board of Church Extension, a History: Semi-Centennial 1882–1932* (Louisville, Ky.: Board of Church Extension of the MECS, [1932]), 106–8. Fund-raising dragged on until 1932.

92. *25th Session of the Church Erection Society of the United Brethren in Christ held in Dayton, Ohio, May 10, 1893* (Dayton, Ohio: United Brethren Publishing House, 1893), 4–5; "Our Work in Washington City," *Religious Telescope*, Feb. 1, 1893, 7; Feb. 8, 1893, 83. A much larger stone church in the required Gothic style was completed and dedicated debt free in 1905.

93. *Annual Report of the Pennsylvania Conference: Minutes of the 116th Annual Session of the Pennsylvania Conference of the United Brethren in Christ held in the First Memorial U.B. Church, Washington, D.C., Oct. 17–23, 1905* (Dayton, Ohio: United Brethren Publishing House, 1905), 18–19.

94. "[Our] Church at Washington, D.C.," *Religious Telescope*, Jan. 16, 1907, 21. The 1893 building was refitted for Sunday school and social meetings.

95. "Proposed Albright Memorial Evangelical Church," *Evangelical Messenger* 81, no. 3 (Jan. 15, 1927): 6–9; *Proceedings of the General Conference of the Evangelical Church, 1926*, 113–14.

X. Reconstructing Methodism(s): 1866–84

1. *The Centenary of American Methodism*, with a Statement of the Plan of the Centenary Celebration of 1866 by John McClintock, D. D. (New York: Carlton & Porter, 1865), and *The Methodist Centennial Year-Book for 1884* (New York: Phillips & Hunt; Cincinnati: Walter & Stowe, 1883). For the preparatory and 1884 activities of the two episcopal churches and other members of the Methodist family, see esp. 305–19.

2. See Melvin E. Dieter, *The Holiness Revival of the Nineteenth Century* (Metuchen: Scarecrow Press, 1980); Timothy L. Smith, *Called unto Holiness*, vol. 1, *The Story of the Nazarenes: The Formative Years* (Kansas City: Nazarene Publishing House, 1962); Howard A. Snyder, *Populist Saints: B. T. and Ellen Roberts and the First Free Methodists* (Grand Rapids, Mich., and Cambridge, U.K.: Eerdmans, 2006).

3. Simpson, *Cyclopaedia*, 176–82; Abel Stevens, *A Compendious History of American Methodism* (New York: Carlton & Porter, 1868), 574–84; J. M. Buckley, *A History of Methodists in the United States*, 4th ed. (New York: Charles Scribner's Sons, 1900), 518–20.

4. JGC/MECS/1850, 215.

5. JGC/MECS/1866, 108–9; HAM, 2:270–75.

6. For a fuller account and references see Kenneth E. Rowe, "Power to the People: George Richard Crooks, *The Methodist,* and Lay Representation in The Methodist Episcopal Church," *MethH* 13, no. 3 (April 1975): 145–76.

7. CA, Dec. 25, 1851, 206.

8. Thomas E. Bond, Sr., *To the General Conference of the Methodist Episcopal Church, Now in Session in the City of Boston* (Philadelphia, 1852), 5.

9. JGC/MEC/1860, 319.

10. See William McGuire King, "The Role of Auxiliary Ministries in Late Nineteenth-Century Methodism," in *Rethinking Methodist History,* ed. Russell R. Richey and Kenneth E. Rowe (Nashville: Kingswood Books, 1983), 167–72, and his "Denominational Modernization and Religious Identity: The Case of the Methodist Episcopal Church," *Perspectives,* 343–55.

11. Alpha J. Kynett, "Church Extension," *MQR* 54, no. 2 (April 1872): 268–94.

12. Quoted in CA, May 1872, 171.

13. Francis H. Tees et al., *Pioneering in Penn's Woods: Philadelphia Methodist Episcopal Annual Conference through One Hundred Fifty Years* (n. p.: Philadelphia Conference Tract Society of the MEC, 1937), 117–19.

14. *Minutes of the Troy Conference,* 1851, 21–22.

15. "Minutes of the Erie Conference for the Year 1850," in *Minutes of the First Twenty Sessions of the Erie Annual Conference* (Published by Order of the Conference, 1907), 257.

16. *Annual Report*/Missionary Society/MEC/ 1854, 9, 33.

17. *Minutes of the Philadelphia Conference*/MEC/1856, 14, 1.

18. The monthly publication, *The Manual of The Methodist Episcopal Church,* began publication in 1880.

19. *Minutes*/MEC/1859, 1.

20. Ibid., 603.

21. See Peterson, *Revisions,* 38, and Nolan B. Harmon, *The Organization of The Methodist Church,* 2nd rev. ed. (Nashville: Methodist Publishing House, 1962), 189–213.

22. JGC/MEC/1876, 134.

23. JGC/MEC/1884, 74.

24. JGC/MECS/1866, 42.

25. (Nashville: Southern Methodist Publishing House, 1870).

26. In 1903 Bishop Richard J. Cooke produced *The Judicial Decisions of the General Conference of The Methodist Episcopal Church.* See, for instance, the third edition, which was "published under a resolution adopted unanimously by the General Conference of 1916" (New York and Cincinnati: Methodist Book Concern, 1918), xiii. See *Reports of the Committee on Judiciary of the General Conference of The Methodist Episcopal Church with Rulings by the Board of Bishops,* compiled under the authority of the General Conference by Arthur Benton Sanford (New York: Methodist Book Concern, 1924).

27. *Discipline*/MEC/1868, 331. George R. Crooks, "Origin of Children's Day," CA, June 4, 1884; reprinted in *Manual of the MEC,* July 1885, 223–55. The first Ecumenical Methodist Conference (London, 1881) recommended that one Sunday of the year be observed as Children's Day throughout global Methodism.

28. Stephen Perry, "The Revival of Stewardship and the Creation of the World Service Commission in the Methodist Episcopal Church, 1912–1924," in *Perspectives*, 400–414, and *MethH* 23, no. 1 (July 1985): 223–39.

29. This section depends on Schmidt, *Grace Sufficient*, chap. 7.

30. Dana L. Robert, *American Women in Mission: A Social History of Their Thought and Practice* (Macon: Mercer University Press, 1996), 131.

31. [Mrs. Susanna M. D. Fry], *Ladies' Repository* 32 (Feb. 1872): 109–12, and 32 (Oct. 1872): 242–45.

32. Ladies' and Pastors' Christian Union, *First Annual Report, 1869* (Philadelphia: Methodist Episcopal Book Rooms, 1869), 23, 8.

33. Ibid., 33. Appeals for the LPCU regularly noted that more than two-thirds of the church's members were women.

34. Ibid., 38, emphasis added.

35. Mrs. Annie Wittenmyer, *Women's Work for Jesus* (New York: Nelson & Phillips, 1873), 41, 45–47, emphasis in the original. Although she did not name the Ladies' and Pastors' Christian Union, her description perfectly fit the new organization.

36. Ibid., 99.

37. The Reverend I. W. Wiley, "Adaptation of Woman to Home Missionary Work," included by Wittenmyer as a chapter in ibid., 81, 87.

38. JGC/MEC/1872, 392–93.

39. Mary L. Griffith, *Women's Christian Work* (New York: Tract Dept., Phillips & Hunt, [between 1879 and 1889]), 3, 5, 7. "Measured by the standard of years her life was brief; but gauged by the standards of usefulness and activity, it was well filled." Obituary notice, *Minutes*/Philadelphia Annual Conference/1885, 72–73.

40. JGC/MEC/1872, 392.

41. We tried in every case to discover and use a woman's full given name. Where we use the titles *Miss* and *Mrs.*, it is usually in order to emphasize the distinctiveness of their roles. For example, in discussions of women in missions, we wanted to distinguish between the single women, being sent out in their own right as foreign missionaries in the latter part of the nineteenth century, and the leaders of women's missionary organizations, often women married to prominent clergy, even bishops. Sometimes we use the *Mrs.* or *Miss* designations where it is important to reflect the usage in primary materials, which routinely identify women in terms of their marital status.

42. The Woman's Foreign Missionary Society founding site in Boston, Massachusetts, was placed on the register of UMC Heritage Landmarks in 2004.

43. Clementina Butler, *Mrs. William Butler: Two Empires and a Kingdom* (New York: Methodist Book Concern, 1929), 107–8; Louise McCoy North, *The Story of the New York Branch of the Woman's Foreign Missionary Society of The Methodist Episcopal Church* (New York: New York Branch, WFMS, MEC, 1926), 39; Frances J. Baker, *The Story of the Woman's Foreign Missionary Society of The Methodist Episcopal Church, 1869–1895* (Cincinnati: Curts & Jennings, 1898), 22–24.

44. Robert, *American Women in Mission*, 125–88.

45. Mary Isham, *Valorous Ventures: A Record of Sixty and Six Years of the Woman's Foreign Missionary Society, Methodist Episcopal Church* (Boston: WFMS, MEC, 1936), 15–17.

46. Robert, *American Women in Mission*, 137.

47. Robert W. Sledge, *"Five Dollars and Myself": The History of Mission of The Methodist Episcopal Church, South, 1845–1939*, United Methodist Church History of Missions Series, 2 (New York: GBGM, 2005), 257–71; Schmidt, *Grace Sufficient*, 168–72; Mrs. F[rank] A. [Sarah Frances Stringfield] Butler, *Mrs. D. H. M'Gavock: Life-Sketch and Thoughts* (Nashville: Publishing House of the MECS, 1896), 9, 16, 190–91; Sara Joyce Myers, "Southern Methodist Women Leaders and Church Missions, 1878–1910" (PhD diss., Emory University, 1990).

48. Behney/Eller, *History*, 173–74, 212–17; Schmidt, *Grace Sufficient*, 173–74; Donald K. Gorrell, "'A New Impulse': Progress in Lay Leadership and Service by Women of the United Brethren in Christ and the Evangelical Association," in *Women in New Worlds* (Nashville: Abingdon Press, 1982), 1:233–45; *Woman's Evangel* 1, no. 1 (Jan. 1882): 20–21.

49. Ethel W. Born, *By My Spirit: The Story of Methodist Protestant Women in Mission 1879–1939* (New York: Women's Division, GBGM, UMC, 1990); Schmidt, *Grace Sufficient*, 172–73.

50. Many leaders of the temperance movement that began in England and America in the 1820s by the late 1830s espoused total abstinence from all alcoholic beverages. Methodists, however, in both England and America, bolstered by medical and scientific opinion, opposed this radical stand—by appealing to the Bible and Christian tradition, including Wesley. As liquor, beer, and wine became identified with numerous social problems and as national prohibition became equated with social reform, however, this moderate stance declined among Methodists in the 1870s and 1880s. See "The Temperance Movement," CA, April 23, 1874, 132; Ivan B. Burnett, "Methodist Origins: John Wesley and Alcohol," *MethH* 13, no. 4 (1974): 3–12. See also Burnett's "Methodism and Alcohol: Recommendations for a Beverage Alcohol Policy Based on the Ever-changing Historic Disciplinal Positions of American Methodism" (PhD diss., School of Theology at Claremont, 1973).

51. That Willard's Methodist faith was at the very core of her identity and life's work is persuasively demonstrated in Carolyn De Swarte Gifford, ed., *Writing Out My Heart: Selections from the Journal of Frances E. Willard, 1855–96* (Urbana: University of Illinois Press, 1995), quotation from 81. See Gifford, "Home Protection: The WCTU's Conversion to Woman Suffrage," in Janet Sharistanian, ed., *Gender, Ideology, and Action: Historical Perspectives on Women's Public Lives* (New York: Greenwood Press, 1986), 95–120. See also Gifford, ed., *The Ideal of "The New Woman" according to the Woman's Christian Temperance Union* (New York: Garland, 1987). For studies of Willard and the WCTU, see Ruth Bordin, *Frances Willard: A Biography* (Chapel Hill: University of North Carolina Press, 1986); Mary Earhart (Dillon), *Frances Willard: From Prayers to Politics* (Chicago: University of Chicago Press, 1944); and Barbara Leslie Epstein, *The Politics of Domesticity: Women, Evangelism, and Temperance in Nineteenth-Century America* (Middletown, Conn.: Wesleyan University Press, 1981). The definitive interpreter of Frances Willard is now Carolyn De Swarte Gifford. In addition to "Home Protection," see two other foundational articles: "'For God and Home and Native Land': The WCTU's Image of Woman in the Late Nineteenth Century," in *Perspectives*, 309–21; and "'My Own Methodist Hive': Frances Willard's Faith as Disclosed in Her Journal, 1855–1870," in Rosemary Skinner Keller, ed., *Spirituality and Social Responsibility* (Nashville: Abingdon Press, 1993), 81–97.

52. Frances E. Willard, *Do Everything: A Handbook for the World's White Ribboners* (Chicago: Woman's Temperance Publishing Association, 1895), 91, 171, 173.

53. The title of an 1889 Frances Willard book. See Carolyn De Swarte Gifford, ed., *The Defense of Women's Rights to Ordination in The Methodist Episcopal Church* (New York: Garland, 1987), reprinting Frances E. Willard, *Woman in the Pulpit* (Chicago: Woman's Temperance Publication Association, 1889), following quotation from 56–57.

54. Schmidt, *Grace Sufficient*, 185, 331n27.

55. John O. Foster, *Life and Labors of Mrs. Maggie Newton Van Cott, the First Lady Licensed to Preach in The Methodist Episcopal Church in the United States* (Cincinnati: Hitchcock & Walden, 1872), republished in 1876 under a different title, *The Harvest and the Reaper: Reminiscences of Revival Work of Mrs. Maggie N. Van Cott, the First Lady Licensed to Preach in The Methodist Episcopal Church in the United States* (New York: N. Tibbals & Sons, 1876). Both editions included an introduction by Gilbert Haven and an essay, "Woman's Place in the Gospel," by David Sherman. See esp. Foster, *Life and Labors*, 67, 152–53, 168. See also Janet S. Everhart, "Maggie Newton Van Cott: The Methodist Episcopal Church Considers the Question of Women Clergy," in *Women in New Worlds* (Nashville: Abingdon Press, 1982), 2:300–317; *Autobiography of A[lonzo] C[hurch] Morehouse* (New York: Tibbals Book Company, 1895), 120, in a chapter titled "Mrs. Van Cott's Call."

56. Everhart, "Maggie Newton Van Cott," 303–4.

57. ZH, April 7, 1870, 167.

58. CA, April 7, 1870, 106, 108.

59. See Kenneth E. Rowe, "Evangelism and Social Reform in the Pastoral Ministry of Anna Oliver, 1868–1886," in *Spirituality and Social Responsibility*, ed. Keller (Nashville: Abingdon Press, 1993), 117–36, and "The Ordination of Women: Round One; Anna Oliver and the General Conference of 1880," in *Perspectives*, 298–308.

60. Rowe, "Evangelism and Social Reform," 128–29.

61. See Rowe's treatment in James E. Kirby, Russell E. Richey, and Kenneth E. Rowe, eds., *The Methodists* (Westport, Conn., and London: Greenwood Press, 1996), 177–220.

62. Rowe, "The Ordination of Women," 302.

63. See in addition to Sources 1880c, Anna Howard Shaw, *The Story of a Pioneer* (New York: Harper & Brothers, 1915); *Anna Howard Shaw: The Story of a Pioneer*, foreword by Leontine T. C. Kelly (Cleveland: Pilgrim Press, 1994); Beverly Ann Zink-Sawyer, *From Preachers to Suffragists: Woman's Rights and Religious Conviction in the Lives of Three Nineteenth-Century American Clergywomen* (Louisville: Westminster John Knox Press, 2003); Wil A. Linkugel, *Anna Howard Shaw: Suffrage Orator and Social Reformer* (New York: Greenwood Press, 1991); and Mary D. Pellauer, *Towards a Tradition of Feminist Theology: The Religious Social Thought of Elizabeth Cady Stanton, Susan B. Anthony, and Anna Howard Shaw* (Brooklyn: Carlson, 1991).

64. JGC/MEC/1880, 353, 316; *Daily Christian Advocate*, May 22, 1880, 79, col. 6; May 26, 1880, 90.

65. E. E. Griswold, CA, Feb. 23, 1854, 29.

66. James R. Joy, *The Teachers of Drew, 1867–1942* (Madison: Drew University, 1942), 10–11; on Strong, see 77–81. On McClintock, see Michael D. Ryan, "John M'Clintock," in *Something More than Human*, ed. Charles E. Cole (Nashville: United Methodist Board of Higher Education and Ministry, 1986), 141–57. See also John T. Cunningham, *University in the Forest: The Story of Drew University*, rev. ed. (n.p.: Afton Publishing, 1990). On the development of theological education see Glenn T. Miller, *Piety and Intellect: The Aims and Purposes of Ante-Bellum Theological*

Education (Atlanta: Scholars Press, 1990), and *Piety and Profession: American Protestant Theological Education, 1870–1970* (Grand Rapids: Eerdmans, 2007).

67. See Richard M. Cameron, *Boston University School of Theology, 1839–1968* (Boston: BUST, 1968); Frederick A. Norwood, *From Dawn to Midday at Garrett* (Evanston: Garrett-Evangelical Theological Seminary, 1978); Gerald O. McCulloh, *Ministerial Education in the American Methodist Movement* (Nashville: United Methodist Board of Higher Education and Ministry, 1980).

68. Thomas A. Langford, *Practical Divinity*, 2 vols. (Nashville: Abingdon Press, 1998, 1999), 1, 88–115.

69. See Melvin E. Dieter, *The Holiness Revival of the Nineteenth Century* (Metuchen and London: Scarecrow Press, 1980), 103–55.

70. This was already noted in Simpson, *Cyclopaedia*, 162. See Troy Messenger, *Holy Leisure: Recreation and Religion in God's Square Mile* (Minneapolis and London: University of Minnesota Press, 1999); Kenneth O. Brown, *Holy Ground, Too: The Camp Meeting Family Tree* (Hazleton, Pa.: Published by Holiness Archives, 1997).

71. Christopher H. Owen, *The Sacred Flame of Love: Methodism and Society in Nineteenth-Century Georgia* (Athens and London: University of Georgia Press, 1998), 149–87; Briane K. Turley, *A Wheel within a Wheel: Southern Methodism and the Georgia Holiness Association* (Macon: Mercer University Press, 1999), 89–148.

72. On the various dimensions of nurture, see Rowe's discussion in Kirby, Richey, and Rowe, *The Methodists*, 163–230.

73. In 1872 the whole section in the *Discipline* was rewritten as the question-and-answer style was abandoned. The "Design of the Origin of Classes and the Appointment of Leaders" now ran: "I. To establish a system of pastoral oversight that shall effectively reach every member of the Church. II. To establish and keep up a meeting for social and religious worship, for instruction, encouragement, and admonition, that shall be a profitable means of grace to our people. III. To carry out, unless other measures be adopted, a financial plan for the raising of money."

74. *Discipline/MECS/1866*, 95, 93–99. The specific section on classes, however, was retained until 1934.

75. "Reception of Members: Form for Receiving Persons into the Church after Probation," *Discipline/MEC/1864*, 145–49. The 1866 MECS "Form of Receiving Members into the Church" was included in a special appendix of *Discipline/MECS/1866*, 328–31.

76. James E. Gilbert, *Preparation for Church Membership: Methodist Probationers Trained* (New York: Eaton & Mains; Cincinnati: Jennings & Pye, 1903), 156, 164.

77. Daniel P. Kidder, *The Christian Pastorate* (Cincinnati: Hitchcock & Walden; New York: Carlton & Lanahan, 1871), 283f.

78. *Origin, Articles, General Rules and Ritual of The Methodist Episcopal Church* (New York: Nelson & Phillips; Cincinnati: Hitchcock & Walden, 1872), 27, 238–336.

79. Edward Cary Bass, *The Probationer's Manual* (Cincinnati: Hitchcock & Walden; New York: Nelson & Phillips, 1875), 4.

80. James Porter, *Helps to Official Members of The Methodist Episcopal Church, indicating their Powers, Duties and Privileges, suggesting Sundry Mistakes, Methods and Possibilities with regard to their Respective Departments of Service; designed to Render them more Efficient and Useful* (New York: Nelson & Phillips; Cincinnati: Hitchcock & Walden, 1878).

81. Stephen Olin Garrison, *Probationer's Catechism and Compendium: Religious, Historical, Doctrinal, Disciplinary and Practical* (New York: Phillips & Hunt, 1883). Revised editions were published in 1885, 1887, 1896, 1904, and 1909. The title changed to *Probationer's Hand-Book* in 1885. The title page of the 1909 edition included the publisher's note "500th thousand" printing.

82. Jonathan T. Crane, *First Words for a Probationer* (New York: Phillips & Hunt; Cincinnati: Hitchcock & Walden, Tract Department, [between 1879 and 1880]).

83. John Heyl Vincent, *The Revival and After the Revival* (New York: Eaton & Mains; Cincinnati: Jennings & Pye, 1882), 63–65.

84. John H. Vincent, "Our Own Church" series (New York: Phillips & Hunt; Cincinnati: Cranston & Stowe, [between 1884 and 1889]). In 1890 Vincent's series of tracts was published in book form as *Our Own Church* (New York: Hunt & Eaton, 1890).

85. *Discipline*/MEC/1860, 205. Sherman, *Revisions*, 214. The MECS *Discipline* changed "children" to "persons" in 1878.

86. The best modern study is Edward A. Trimmer, "John Heyl Vincent: An Evangelist for Education" (PhD diss., Columbia University, 1986); the vintage biography is Leon H. Vincent's *John Heyl Vincent: A Biographical Sketch* (New York: Macmillan, 1925); see also "Autobiography of Bishop Vincent," *NWCA*, April 13; June 1, 22, 29; July 13, 20; Aug. 3, 24, 1910. For Vincent's role in Methodist Sunday school publishing, see Pilkington/Vernon, *Methodist Publishing House*, 2:70–77.

87. Ellwood Hendrick, *Lewis Miller* (New York: G. P. Putnam's Sons, 1925). The best study of the Akron Plan Sunday school is A. Robert Jaeger, "The Auditorium and Akron Plans" (master's thesis, Cornell University, 1984), chap. 4, 139–80. See also Lewis Miller's essay, "The Akron Plan," in *Seven Graded Sunday Schools*, ed. Jesse L. Hurlbut (New York: Hunt & Eaton, 1893), 11–32. An older and briefer study is Marion Lawrence's "The Akron Plan: Its Genesis, History and Development," in his *Housing the Sunday School; or, A Practical Study of Sunday School Buildings* (New York: Eaton & Mains, 1911), 83–92. An abbreviated version of Lawrence's chapter on the Akron Plan was reprinted by the MECS Board of Church Extension in its *Thirty-second Annual Report, 1913–1914*, 268–71.

88. Vincent's oft-quoted maxim became almost as famous as the architecture it inspired. Cited from Marion Lawrence's *Housing the Sunday School* (New York: Eaton & Mains, 1911), 84.

89. Hendrick, *Lewis Miller*, 144–47.

90. For early description and floor plan see "The Model Sunday-School Room," *Sunday School Journal*, new series 2, no. 1 (Oct. 1869): 11. Jaeger's detailed description is based on a description of the building in the *Akron Daily Beacon* at the time of the dedication, 1870, Jaeger, "Auditorium," 150–54.

91. "The Model Sunday-School Room," 11; John H. Vincent, *The Modern Sunday-School* (New York: Hunt & Eaton; Cincinnati: Cranston & Curts, 1887), 160–61.

92. Architect Oscar S. Teale was also secretary of the Sunday school. See "A Model Sunday School Room" in *Seven Graded Sunday Schools*, ed. Jesse L. Hurlbut (New York: Hunt & Eaton, 1893), 113–20, and "Building of Vincent Chapel," First Methodist Episcopal Church, Plainfield, New Jersey, in *Program of the 100th Anniversary Exercises October 16–23, 1932, and Historical Sketch* (Plainfield, N.J.: The Church, 1932), [8–9]. For description and floor plan, see Lawrence, *Housing the Sunday School*, 59–63.

93. Thomson was born in Scotland in 1843 and came to Buenos Aires with his parents as a young boy in 1851, and there they joined the English-speaking MEC. Fluent in Spanish and feeling called to the ordained ministry, he was sent by his pastor to Ohio Wesleyan University to be trained for the ministry. He returned to Argentina as an ordained minister in 1866, beginning Spanish work first with a Sunday school, which soon grew into a Spanish-speaking ME church. Thomson later expanded Spanish-speaking Methodist work throughout Argentina and neighboring Uruguay. He is said to have excelled in polemics and debate with the Roman Catholic clergy. He died in Buenos Aires in 1933. For biography see Juan C. Varetto, *El Apostol del Plata, Juan F. Thomson* (Buenos Aires: n.p., 1943).

94. Sledge, *"Five Dollars and Myself,"* 194–200; Schmidt, *Grace Sufficient*, 248–52.

95. Otis Gibson, *The Chinese in America* (Cincinnati: Hitchcock & Walden, 1877), 176.

96. Schmidt, *Grace Sufficient*, 257–63.

97. Homer Noley, *First White Frost: Native Americans and United Methodism* (Nashville: Abingdon, 1991), 198.

98. Leland D. Case, *Preacher Smith, Martyr* (Mitchell, S.D.: Friends of the Middle Border, 1961). The Deadwood Cluster, Deadwood, South Dakota, was placed on the national register of UMC Heritage Landmarks in 1984.

99. Frederick A. Norwood, ed., *Sourcebook of American Methodism* (Nashville: Abingdon, 1982), 485–86.

100. "The Sand Creek Apology," *Resolutions/UMC/1996*, 395–97.

101. Sledge, *"Five Dollars and Myself,"* 145–60.

102. JGC/MEC/1872, 387–88.

103. Ibid., 402–3.

104. JGC/MECS/1874, 560.

105. *Formal Fraternity: Proceedings of the General Conferences of the Methodist Episcopal Church and of the Methodist Episcopal Church, South, in 1872, 1874, and 1876 and of the Joint Commission of the Two Churches on Fraternal Relations* (New York: Nelson & Phillips; Nashville: A. H. Redford, 1876), 60–61, 67.

106. *Journal of the Proceedings of the Board of Commissioners of The Methodist Episcopal Church, South, 1876*, 112.

107. HAM, 2:667.

108. *Formal Fraternity*, 69–70.

109. HAM, 3:407–78; James H. Straughn, *Inside Methodist Union* (Nashville: Methodist Publishing House, 1958), 52–55.

110. *Proceedings of the Oecumenical Methodist Conference . . . 1881* (London: Wesleyan Conference Office, 1881). See HAM, 2:696–701.

111. See H. K. Carroll et al., eds., *Proceedings, Sermons, Essays, and Addresses of the Centennial Methodist Conference . . . 1884* (New York: Phillips & Hunt, 1885), and W. H. DePuy, ed., *The Methodist Centennial Year-Book for 1884* (New York: Phillips & Hunt; Cincinnati: Walden & Stowe, 1883).

112. Carroll, *Proceedings, Sermons, Essays*, "Historical Statement," ix–xi. Also not apparently included were the small delegations (two persons) of Methodist Protestants, Independent Methodists, Primitive Methodists, Canadian Methodists, and the Bible Christian (one). For the delegations see 7–18.

113. *HAM*, 2:391–419 on the MPC; Behney/Eller, *History*, 167–69, 217–19.

114. See Reginald F. Hildebrand, *The Times Were Strange and Stirring: Methodist Preachers and the Crisis of Emancipation* (Durham and London: Duke University Press, 1995); Paul Harvey, *Freedom's Coming: Religious Culture and the Shaping of the South from the Civil War through the Civil Rights Era* (Chapel Hill and London: University of North Carolina Press, 2005); William E. Montgomery, *Under Their Own Vine and Fig Tree: The African-American Church in the South, 1865–1900* (Baton Rouge: Louisiana State University Press, 1993); Katharine Dvorak, *An African-American Exodus: The Segregation of the Southern Churches* (Brooklyn: Carlson, 1991); Clarence Walker, *A Rock in a Weary Land: The African Methodist Episcopal Church during the Civil War and Reconstruction* (Baton Rouge and London: Louisiana State University Press, 1982); *HAM*, 2:279–87, 360–80; William Gravely, *Gilbert Haven, Methodist Abolitionist: A Study in Race, Religion, and Reform, 1850–1880* (Nashville and New York: Abingdon Press, 1973).

115. Again see Dvorak, *An African-American Exodus*, for exploration of the Black agency in this separation. On 1866, see 134–37.

116. This discussion follows Hildebrand, *The Times Were Strange and Stirring*.

117. This latter question the General Conference of 1872 resolved in the negative, JGC/MEC/1872, 253; Gravely, *Gilbert Haven*.

118. For MEC permissive legislation see Report No. II of the Committee on the State of the Church, JGC/MEC/1876, 329–31.

119. JGC/MEC/1892, "Report of the Freedmen's Aid and Southern Education Society," 692–704, and "On Freedmen's Aid and Southern Education Society," 479–81. The statements, including the heading, are from 696–97.

120. (n.p.: Atlanta, 1909).

121. JGC/MEC/1892, "Report of the Freedmen's Aid and Southern Education Society," 692–704.

122. Osmon C. Baker, *A Guide-Book in the Administration of the Discipline of The Methodist Episcopal Church*, rev. ed. (New York: Carlton & Porter, 1855), 58–59.

123. JGC/MEC/1852, 116.

124. JGC/MEC/1864, 261, 404–5.

125. JGC/MEC/1884, 337.

Snapshot II. Methodism in 1884: Wilkes-Barre, Pennsylvania

1. Sam H. Schurr and Bruce C. Netschert, *Energy in the American Economy, 1850–1975* (Baltimore: Johns Hopkins University Press, 1960), 67.

2. By the 1880s Wilkes-Barre had become one of the nation's fifty largest cities with populations in excess of 20,000.

3. Three recent studies of Wilkes-Barre stand out: Edward J. Davies, *The Anthracite Aristocracy: Leadership and Social Change in the Hard Coal Regions of Northeastern Pennsylvania, 1800–1930* (DeKalb: Northern Illinois University Press, 1985); Sally T. Lottick, *Bridging Change: A Wyoming Valley Sketchbook* (Wilkes-Barre, Pa.: Wyoming Historical and Geological Society, 1992); and Donald L. Miller and Richard E. Sharpless, *The Kingdom of Coal: Work, Enterprise and Ethnic Communities in the Mine Fields* (Philadelphia: University of Pennsylvania Press, 1985).

4. Gilbert Schappert, *The First United Methodist Church of Wilkes-Barre, a 150th Anniversary History* (Wilkes-Barre, Pa.: The Church, 1980); see also *Historical Addresses Delivered at the Eighty-fifth Anniversary of the First Methodist Episcopal Church of Wilkes-Barre, Pa, October 10th, 1915* (Wilkes-Barre, Pa.: Published by order of the Official Board of the First Methodist Episcopal Church, 1917).

5. "Churches in Wilkes-Barre," *The Wilkes-Barre Record Almanac*, 1886, 42. The three MEC churches accounted for 800 members alone. See "A Note from Wilkes-Barre, Pa," CA, Nov. 12, 1885, 738, col. 5. Other houses of worship listed: 6 Presbyterian, 2 Episcopal, 2 Baptist, 3 Lutheran, 1 Reformed, 2 Roman Catholic, and 2 Jewish synagogues.

6. See the chart at end of this chapter.

7. Davies, *Anthracite Aristocracy*, 43, Table 3–1. Social Characteristics of Members of Wilkes-Barre's Upper Class, 1848–1856 and 1870–1885, Religion:

Denomination	1848–1856	1870–1885
Episcopalian	62%	49%
Presbyterian	20%	29%
Methodist	11%	14%

8. Rowland Berthoff, "The Social Order of the Anthracite Region, 1825–1902," *Pennsylvania Magazine of History and Biography* 89, no. 3 (July 1965): 261. See also Paul Boyer, *Urban Masses and Moral Order in America, 1820–1920* (Cambridge: Harvard University Press, 1978).

9. See Vincent J. Scully, *The Shingle Style and the Stick Style: Architectural Theory and Design from Richardson to the Origins of Wright* (New Haven: Yale University Press, 1955), 77–79, 126–29; Russell Sturgis, *A Critique of the Works of Bruce Price* (New York: Architectural Record Co., 1899), the June 1899 issue of the *Architectural Record*. See also the restoration proposal *Cherishing the Past, Charting Our Future: The First UMC of Wilkes-Barre* (Wilkes-Barre, Pa.: First UMC, [1989]), 1.

10. "The First M.E. Church, Wilkes-Barre, Penn., Mr. Bruce Price, Architect," *American Architect and Building News* 1 (Sept. 23, 1876): 308.

11. *Annual Minutes of the Wyoming Conference*, 1884, 15.

12. George S. Bennett, *A Paper on the Organization, Management and Grading of the Sunday School of the First Methodist Episcopal Church of Wilkes-Barre, Penn'a* (Wilkes-Barre: Wilkes-Barre Record, 1889), 4–5. See also an account of the dedication: "The New M.E. Sunday School," *Daily Record of the Times* (Wilkes-Barre), Monday, Feb. 12, 1877, 2, cols. 2–4. The dedication was briefly noticed in the *Sunday School Times* (Philadelphia) 19, no. 9 (March 8, 1877): 139, col. 2.

13. A second, grander organ with 64 stops and 2,273 pipes built by the Votey Company was given by Mrs. Bennett in 1897 at a cost of $10,000. It was rebuilt by the Austin Company in 1915 at a cost of $4,500, and a harp stop and antiphonal organ in the balcony were added in 1925. In 1942 the organ was completely rebuilt and enlarged by the famed organ builder Ernest M. Skinner.

14. See Rowe, "Redesigning Methodist Churches: Auditorium-Style Sanctuaries and Akron-Plan Sunday Schools in Romanesque Costume, 1875–1925," *CEMI*, 117–34; Jeanne Halgren Kilde, *When Church Became Theatre: The Transformation of Evangelical Architecture and Worship in Nineteenth-Century America* (New York: Oxford University Press, 2002); and Anne C. Loveland

and Otis B. Wheeler, *From Meetinghouse to Megachurch: A Material and Cultural History* (Columbia: University of Missouri Press, 2003), esp. chap. 3, "The Auditorium Church."

15. "Description of a Handsome and Ornamental Structure, the New Church Edifice Erected by the Franklin St. M.E. Congregation," *Evening Leader* (Wilkes-Barre), Saturday, Oct. 3, 1885; "The New Methodist Church," *Record of the Times* (Wilkes-Barre), Sunday, Oct. 4, 1885; "Dedication, Interesting Services at the New M.E. Church Yesterday, Bishop Foster's Sermon, an Eloquent, Thoughtful and Powerful Discourse, Afternoon and Evening Exercises, a Large Attendance and a Glorious Season," *Evening Leader* (Wilkes-Barre), Monday, Oct. 5, 1885. *Historical Addresses delivered at the Eighty-fifth Anniversary*, 1915, 33. The denomination's national newspaper carried two accounts of the dedication: "The New Church in Wilkes-Barre," CA, Oct. 15, 1885, 668, cols. 3–4; and "A Note from Wilkes-Barre, Pa," CA, Nov. 12, 1885, 738, col. 5.

16. "The Methodists and Their New Church," editorial, *Evening Leader* (Wilkes-Barre), Monday, Oct. 5, 1885.

17. The 300-member congregation completed the first phase of a building restoration project in 1992.

18. *Annual Minutes of the Wyoming Conference*, 1884, statistics following p. 77.

19. *Discipline*/MEC/1884, ¶548, "Negotiations between Preachers and People," 336.

20. The Reverend James O. Woodruff, pastor from 1883 to 1886, received a DD degree from Wesleyan University in Middletown, Connecticut, in 1894 and held various conference-level posts. See his obituary in *Wyoming Conference Journal*, 1896, 98–100; see also the brief sketch in A. H. Chaffee, *History of the Wyoming Conference of The Methodist Episcopal Church* (New York: Eaton & Mains, 1904), 266–67.

21. For discussion of social congregations in the Victorian era see E. Brooks Holifield, "Toward a History of American Congregations," in *American Congregations*, ed. James P. Wind and James W. Lewis (Chicago: University of Chicago Press, 1994), 38–43.

22. *Report of the First M.E. Church of Wilkes-Barre, Pa, for the Conference Year of 1882–1883* (Wilkes-Barre: First MEC, 1883). Includes officers of the church for 1883–84.

23. A hundred additional hymnals were ordered in April 1884. See *Record of the Meetings of the Official Board of the First Methodist Episcopal Church, Wilkes-Barre, Pa.* [Book 2, 1880–93], April 7, 1884, 60; April 21, 1884, 62f., Archives, First M.E. Church, Wilkes-Barre, Pennsylvania.

24. Karen B. Westerfield Tucker, *American Methodist Worship* (Oxford and New York: Oxford University Press, 2001), 14–15, 49–51.

25. *Scribner's Monthly*, May-Oct. 1875, 243.

26. For a vivid description of the 1878 camp meeting, see J. K. Peck, *Luther Peck and His Five Sons* (New York: Eaton & Mains, 1897), appendix B, 233–36. See also Leroy E. Bugbee, *He Holds the Stars in His Hands: The Centennial History of the Wyoming Conference of The Methodist Church* ([Scranton]: Wyoming Conference, 1952), 64–74.

27. D. Sturdevant, Treasurer, Board of Stewards, and George A. Wells, Secretary of the Envelope System, *To the Members and Congregation of the First M.E. Church, Wilkes-Barre, PA* (Wilkes-Barre: First MEC, 1883). Includes church budget and pledge sheet: "I, _____ , have this day promised to pay to the First M.E. Church of Wilkes-Barre, Pa, the sum of __ ___ Dollars, _ ___ cents weekly, from April 5th, 1883 to April 5th, 1884, to meet the expenses of the Church and Benevolent Collections (except Missions)."

28. *Report of the First M.E. Church of Wilkes-Barre, Pa.* (Wilkes-Barre: First MEC, 1885); *Report of the First Methodist Episcopal Church of Wilkes-Barre, Pa for the Conference Year ending April 1887* (Wilkes-Barre: First MEC, 1887).

29. Wyoming Conference *Journal*/MEC/1884, 45.

30. Wyoming Conference *Minutes*/MEC/1885, statistical tables, 89.

31. *Discipline*/MEC/1884, ¶294, 162. "The funds of the [Women's Foreign and Home Missionary Societies] shall not be raised by collections or subscriptions taken during any of our church services, nor in any promiscuous public meeting, nor in any Sunday-school, but shall be raised by such methods as the Constitution of the Society shall provide, none of which shall interfere with the contributions of our people and Sunday-schools to the treasury of the Missionary Society." In 1884 women of First Church raised $102 for the Woman's Foreign Missionary Society and an even larger amount for the Woman's Home Missionary Society, $213. Wyoming Conference *Minutes*/MEC/1885, [89].

XI. Reshaping the Church for Mission: 1884–1939

1. *Proceedings, Sermons, Essays and Addresses of the Centennial Methodist Conference held in Mt. Vernon Place Methodist Episcopal Church, Baltimore, MD, December 9-17, 1884*, ed. Henry K. Carroll et al. (Cincinnati: Cranston & Stowe; New York: Phillips & Hunt, 1885), 317–23. The delegates hailed "the dawn of the better day," rejoiced "in the rising spirit of fraternity, which promises much for the future success of the cause we love," and congratulated Canadian Methodists for their recent uniting of the two churches that had derived from U.S. and British missions there.

2. The scope and consequence of these missions can be seen in the four volumes required to cover MEC efforts in the History of Methodist Missions series and in the seven-volume sequel that gave comparable attention to MECS, MPC, UBC, EA, and UMC missions.

3. See Harry Westcott Worley, *The Central Conference of The Methodist Episcopal Church: A Study in Ecclesiastical Adaptation, or a Contribution of the Mission Field to the Development of Church Organization* (Foochow, China: Christian Herald Mission Press, 1940), on the topic of his title and on the international delegates, see 129.

4. "Declaration of Principles of the First General Holiness Assembly," *Guide to Holiness* 76, no. 1 (July 1885): 27–28.

5. Jean Miller Schmidt, *Souls or the Social Order: The Two-Party System in American Protestantism*, preface by Martin E. Marty (Brooklyn: Carlson Publishing, 1991).

6. On these developments, see chap. 10 of Schmidt's *Grace Sufficient*, on which this account depends. For narrative and documents, see also Carolyn De Swarte Gifford, ed., *The Debate in The Methodist Episcopal Church over Laity Rights for Women* (New York: Garland, 1987).

7. Gifford, *Debate over Laity Rights for Women*, introduction.

8. "Address of the Bishops," JGC/MEC/1888, 51.

9. Frances E. Willard, *Glimpses of Fifty Years* (Chicago: WCTU, 1889), 465.

10. The report as adopted asserted that the church in amending the second Restrictive Rule "contemplated the admission of men only as lay representatives" and therefore "That under the Constitution and laws of the Church as they now are women are not eligible as lay delegates in the General Conference." JGC/MEC/1888, 463.

11. When the report was considered, T. B. Neely proposed the submission to the annual conferences of an amendment of the second Restrictive Rule "by adding the words, 'and said delegates may be men or women,'" *JGC/MEC/1888*, 95; Buckley, *History*, 307–9.

12. [James M. Buckley,] *"Because They are Women" and Other Editorials from "The Christian Advocate" on the Admission of Women to the General Conference* (New York: Hunt & Eaton, 1891), and Reverend G[eorge] W. Hughey, *The Admission of Women to the General Conference* (Chicago: Press of WTPA, 1891), both works reprinted in Gifford, *Debate over Laity Rights for Women*.

13. Gifford, *Debate over Laity Rights for Women*, introduction.

14. Karen Heetderks Strong, "Ecclesiastical Suffrage: The First Women Participants at General Conference in the Antecedents of The United Methodist Church," 29–30; Darryl W. Stephens, "Can a Woman Be a 'Layman'? Does 'all mean all'?" *The Flyer* (GCOSROW, UMC) 40, no. 4 (Oct.-Dec. 2009): 1, 3–4.

15. *RT* 59, no. 20 (May 17, 1893): 308.

16. Ibid.

17. Virginia Shadron, "The Laity Rights Movement, 1906–1918: Woman's Suffrage in the Methodist Episcopal Church, South," in *Women in New Worlds*, ed. Hilah F. Thomas and Rosemary Skinner Keller, 2 vols. (Nashville: Abingdon Press, 1981–82), 1:261–75.

18. Robert W. Sledge, *Hands on the Ark: The Struggle for Change in The Methodist Episcopal Church, 1914–1939* (Lake Junaluska, N.C.: Commission on Archives and History, 1975), 55–72, 70; and *"Five Dollars and Myself": The History of Mission of The Methodist Episcopal Church, South, 1845–1939*, United Methodist Church History of Missions Series, 2 (New York: GBGM, 2005), 257–302.

19. Methodist Brotherhood, *The Constitution, By-Laws and Ritual of the Methodist Brotherhood* (St. Joseph, Mo.: A. E. Hagle, 1911); the Brotherhood's monthly magazine, *Methodist Men*, 1908–11, resumed 1927–?; "The Methodist Brotherhood," in *The Methodist Year Book*, 1911, 136–38; *Militant Methodism: The Story of the First National Convention of Methodist Men, Indianapolis, 1913*, ed. David G. Downey et al. (Cincinnati: Methodist Book Concern, 1913), see esp. W. S. Bovard, "The Methodist Brotherhood," 247–48; Frederick DeLand Leete, *Christian Brotherhoods* (New York: Eaton & Mains, 1912); "Brotherhood, Historical Statement," WCA, Nov. 22, 1928, 1171–74; George L. Morelock, *A Steward in the Methodist Church* (Nashville: Cokesbury Press, 1936), 47–48. For context and interpretation see Mark C. Carnes, *Secret Ritual and Manhood in Victorian America* (New Haven: Yale University Press, 1989); David D. Gilmore, *Manhood in the Making: Cultural Concepts of Masculinity* (New Haven: Yale University Press, 1990); Clifford Putney, *Muscular Christianity: Manhood and Sports in Protestant America, 1880–1920* (Cambridge, Mass.: Harvard University Press, 2001); Ralph LaRossa, *The Modernization of Fatherhood: A Social and Political History* (Chicago: University of Chicago Press, 1996); E. Anthony Rotundo, *American Manhood: Transformation in Masculinity from the Revolution to the Modern Era* (New York: Basic Books, 1993). The popular hymn "Rise Up, O Men of God" (*UM Hymnal*, 1989, #576) was written by William P. Merrill in 1911 at the time when the Brotherhood Movement was emerging among Protestant churches and quickly became the theme song of the Methodist men's movement.

20. "For Brotherhood Unity," editorial, CA, March 5, 1908, 366; "One Brotherhood for Methodism," CA, March 19, 1908, 445–56.

21. The Brotherhood of The Evangelical United Brethren Church, *Manual, 1947–1951* (Har-

risburg, Pa.; Dayton, Ohio: The Evangelical United Brethren Bookstores, [1947]), includes historical sketch. See also Behney/Eller, *History*, index.

22. Dan B. Brummitt, *The Epworth League's History and Pledge* (Chicago: Central Office of the Epworth League, 1918); Paul Hutchinson, *The Story of the Epworth League* (Cincinnati: Methodist Book Concern, 1927); Emanuel L. Blount, "The History of the Epworth League: A Concept of Youth in the Nineteenth Century" (PhD diss., State University of New York at Buffalo, 1996).

23. *Epworth League Handbook* (Nashville: Publishing House of the MECS, 1915), 10.

24. JGC/MEC/1864, 199; Barclay, *Missions*, 3:167.

25. JGC/MEC/1868, 283, 497; Barclay, *Missions*, 3:167.

26. Quoted by Barclay, *Missions*, 3:168–69, from CA, Aug. 18, Dec. 15, 1870; and MQR 65 (July 1883).

27. On the relation of the two actions, see Worley, *Central Conference*, 95–154, and Barclay, *Missions*, 3:171–80.

28. Barclay, *Missions*, 3:509–32.

29. Worley, *Central Conference*, 103–4; see 99–112 for the larger context.

30. Ibid., 150; *Discipline*/MEC/1884, 163–65, ¶296.

31. Barclay, *Missions*, 3:170–71; Worley, *Central Conference*, 151.

32. JGC/MEC/1884, 162–63, ¶295.

33. John Patrick McDowell, *The Social Gospel in the South: The Woman's Home Mission Movement in The Methodist Episcopal Church, South, 1886–1939* (Baton Rouge: Louisiana State University Press, 1982).

34. See Hartzell's long report to the 1900 MEC General Conference on African missions and on his succession to Taylor, JGC/MEC/1900, 349–66.

35. Mrs. T. L. Tomkinson, *Twenty Years' History of the Woman's Home Missionary Society of The Methodist Episcopal Church, 1880–1900*, 2nd ed. (Cincinnati: Woman's Home Missionary Society, MEC, 1908), 9, 22, 27.

36. At the third annual meeting of the society in Cleveland in October 1884 (after its official recognition by the MEC General Conference in May), Lucy Webb Hayes insisted that "the claims upon us for Christian civilization" in the home missions field were no less pressing than those of "the heathen of foreign lands." Her major theme could be summed up in one sentence: "We believe that the character of a people depends mainly on its homes." "Addresses by Mrs. Hayes," in *Lucy Webb Hayes: A Memorial Sketch* (Cincinnati: Woman's Home Missionary Society, 1890), 81–84.

37. Ruth Esther Meeker, *Six Decades of Service, 1880–1940: A History of the Woman's Home Missionary Society of The Methodist Episcopal Church* (Cincinnati: Continuing Corporation of the Woman's Home Missionary Society, MEC, 1969), 19, 29. The report of the WHMS to the 1896 MEC General Conference detailed no fewer than eighteen divisions of the work, including bureaus for immigrants, "Orientals," industrial homes and schools in the South, Alaska, city missions, and a deaconess bureau. "Report of the Woman's Home Missionary Society," JGC/MEC/1896, 675–86.

38. See Sara Joyce Myers, "Southern Methodist Women Leaders and Church Missions, 1878–1910" (PhD diss., Emory University, 1990). Myers's dissertation examines the five leaders who established these societies in terms of the categories of "True Womanhood."

39. McDowell, *The Social Gospel in the South*.

40. Ibid., 6–35; Sledge, *"Five Dollars and Myself,"* 257–302.

41. Ruth A. Daugherty, *The Missionary Spirit: The History of Mission of the Methodist Protestant Church, 1830–1939*, United Methodist History of Mission Series (New York: GBGM, 2004), 20–28, 150–56, and chart on 132–33; Ethel W. Born, *By My Spirit: The Story of Methodist Protestant Women in Mission, 1879–1939* (New York: Women's Division, GBGM, UMC, 1990); Donald K. Gorrell, "'A New Impulse': Progress in Lay Leadership and Service by Women of the United Brethren in Christ and the Evangelical Association," in *Women in New Worlds*, 1:233–45.

42. Ann Fagan, *This Is Our Song: Employed Women in the United Methodist Tradition* (New York: Women's Division, GBGM, UMC, 1986), 34, 36, 43.

43. Ibid., 45–47, 67–72, quoting the *Forty-second Annual Report of the Woman's Home Missionary Society of The Methodist Episcopal Church for the Year 1922–23*, 267.

44. C. Howard Hopkins, *John R. Mott, 1865–1955: A Biography* (Grand Rapids: Eerdmans, 1979), and on SVM founding, 60–62.

45. See four volumes (Barclay three and Copplestone one) that cover the MEC, the History of Methodist Missions Series, and the seven-volume United Methodist Church History of Mission Series that attends to MECS, MPC, UBC, EA, and UMC missions.

46. Daniel M. Davies, *The Life and Thought of Henry Gerhard Appenzeller (1858–1902)* (Lewiston, Lampeter, Queenston: Edwin Mellen Press, 1988).

47. Barclay, *Missions*, 3:741–57.

48. Gunshik Shim, "Methodist Medical Mission in Korea," *MethH* 46, no. 1 (Oct. 2007): 34–46.

49. This section draws on *Churches Aflame: Asian Americans and United Methodism*, ed. Artemio R. Guillermo (Nashville: Abingdon Press, 1991).

50. See S. Raynor Smith, "The Attitudes and Practices of the Methodist Church in California with Reference to Certain Significant Social Crises, 1847 through 1949" (PhD diss., University of Southern California, Los Angeles, 1955), 139ff.

51. "Woman's Missionary Society of the Pacific Coast," *Methodist Centennial Year-Book for 1884* (New York: Phillips & Hunt, 1883), 138–39. In 1893 the society became part of the Woman's Home Missionary Society.

52. Ronald Takaki, *Strangers from a Different Shore: A History of Asian Americans* (New York: Penguin, 1990); and David Palumbo-Liu, *Asian/American: Historical Crossings of a Racial Frontier* (Stanford, Calif.: Stanford University Press, 1999).

53. Otis Gibson, "California Anti-Chinese Legislation," *CA*, March 11, 1880, 161; Jean Pfaelzer, *Driven Out: The Forgotten War against Chinese Americans* (New York: Random House, 2007); Stuart C. Miller, *The Unwelcome Immigrant: The American Image of the Chinese, 1785–1882* (Berkeley: University of California Press, 1969); and S. Raynor Smith, "Attitudes and Practices of the Methodist Church in California."

54. JGC/MEC/1880, 357.

55. NWCA (Chicago), Jan. 5, 1928, 30.

56. Homer Stuntz, *The Philippines and the Far East* (New York: Eaton & Mains, [1904]), 454.

57. See Ronald C. White Jr., *Liberty and Justice for All: Racial Reform and the Social Gospel (1877–1925)* (San Francisco: Harper & Row, 1990).

58. Sledge, *"Five Dollars and Myself,"* 405–8; Daniel H. Bays and Grant Wacker, eds., *The Foreign Missionary Enterprise at Home* (Tuscaloosa and London: University of Alabama Press, 2003); Dana L. Robert, *American Women in Mission: A Social History of Their Thought and Practice* (Macon: Mercer University Press, 1996), 255–316.

59. *Re-thinking Missions: A Laymen's Inquiry after One Hundred Years,* by the Commission of Appraisal, William Ernest Hocking, chairman (New York and London: Harper & Brothers, 1939).

60. William R. Hutchison, *Errand to the World: American Protestant Thought and Foreign Missions* (Chicago: University of Chicago Press, 1987).

61. But see Jean Miller Schmidt, "Reexamining the Public/Private Split: Reforming the Continent and Spreading Scriptural Holiness," in *Perspectives,* 228–47, a nuancing of her argument in Schmidt, *Souls or the Social Order: The Two-Party System in American Protestantism.*

62. William R. Hutchison, *The Modernist Impulse in American Protestantism* (Cambridge and London: Harvard University Press, 1976).

63. Tarbell, an active Methodist laywoman, set the standard for investigative reporting by revealing how John D. Rockefeller monopolized the early oil industry in her 1904 *History of Standard Oil Company.* Her book began a national discourse that led to the 1911 Supreme Court decision to break up the Standard Oil monopoly. President Theodore Roosevelt urged Congress to take the antitrust action but neglected to credit Tarbell and her pioneering work. Her exposé of the ruthlessness of big business and other national ills made her a leader in the early muckraking movement. A postage stamp bearing her image was released by the U.S. Postal Service, Sept. 2002.

64. See Grant Wacker, *Heaven Below: Early Pentecostals and American Culture* (Cambridge and London: Harvard University Press, 2001).

65. On the relation of the social gospel to reconstruction efforts, see Ronald C. White Jr., *Liberty and Justice for All.*

66. See JGC/MEC/1920, chap. 8, 591–641. On BU and personalism, see Richard Morgan Cameron, *Boston University School of Theology, 1839–1968* (Boston: Boston University School of Theology, 1968), and Paul Deats and Carol Robb, eds., *The Boston Personalist Tradition in Philosophy, Social Ethics, and Theology* (Macon: Mercer University Press, 1986).

67. Thomas A. Langford, *Practical Divinity,* 2 vols. (Nashville: Abingdon Press, 1998, 1999).

68. See George H. Shriver, ed., *American Religious Heretics: Formal and Informal Trials* (Nashville: Abingdon Press, 1966), and Shriver, ed., *Dictionary of Heresy Trials in American Christianity* (Westport, Conn.: Greenwood Press, 1997).

69. Norman W. Spellmann, *Growing a Soul: The Story of A. Frank Smith* (Dallas: Southern Methodist University Press, 1979), 49–54.

70. Kenneth E. Rowe, "Pastorals for the People: Pastoral Letters in the Methodist Tradition," in *Scholarship, Sacraments and Service: Historical Studies in the Protestant Tradition,* ed. Daniel B. Clendenin and W. David Buschart (Lewiston: Edwin Mellen Press, 1990), 123–46.

71. See Creighton Lacy, *Frank Mason North: His Social and Ecumenical Mission* (Nashville and New York: Abingdon Press, 1967), and "Frank Mason North: Ecumenical Statesman," *Duke Divinity School Review* 31 (Winter 1966): 56–70.

72. *UM Hymnal,* 1989, #427.

73. The first American organization dedicated to labor and religion was the Christian Labor

Union. It was founded in 1872 by a Methodist minister, Jesse Jones, and a lay preacher and ship carpenter, Edward Rogers. Jones's fame came from his song-poem, "Eight Hours," which became a labor union anthem. For a full study see Robert James Henning, "Methodist Response to Labor Unrest in Late Nineteenth Century America: A Cultural Theory" (PhD diss., Michigan State University, 1994).

74. William H. Carwardine, *The Pullman Strike* (1894; reprint, Chicago: Published by C. H. Kerr for the Illinois Labor History Society, 1973); Stephen G. Cobb, *Reverend William Carwardine and the Pullman Strike of 1894: The Christian Gospel and Social Justice* (Lewiston: Edwin Mellen Press, 1992); Matthew C. Lee, "Onward Christian Soldiers: The Social Gospel and the Pullman Strike," *Chicago History* 20 (1991): 4–21; "W. H. Carwardine," *Rock River Conference Journal/MEC/1929*, 99–100.

75. In the effort at full disclosure, we should indicate that one of our parents, namely, McMurry Richey, father of one author, experienced such a punitive appointment away from a textile company church in Concord, North Carolina, after preaching a Labor Day sermon.

76. Jeanne Gayle Knepper, *Thy Kingdom Come: The Methodist Federation for Social Service and Human Rights: 1907–1948* (Staten Island, N.Y.: Methodist Federation for Social Action, 1996); *Encyclopedia of Chicago* at www.encyclopedia.chicagohistory.org, 2410. See Women throughout History at www.sistersinthebuildingtrades.org/Docs/history/mmcdowell.pdf.

77. See Kenneth E. Rowe, "Trans-Atlantic Social Gospel: British Influences on American Methodist Social Thought and Practice, 1890–1910" (paper, 9th Oxford Institute on Methodist Theological Studies, 1992). The best study of the central hall movement is George W. Sails, *At the Centre: The Story of Methodism's Central Missions*, Home Mission occasional papers, no. 15 (London: Methodist Church Home Mission Department, 1970). See also Kenneth S. Inglis, *Churches and the Working Classes in Victorian England* (London: Routledge & Kegan Paul, 1963). For the context of these developments within English Methodism, see J. Munsey Turner's chapter in *History of the Methodist Church in Great Britain*, ed. Rupert Davies et al., 3 vols. (London: Epworth Press, 1983), 3:351–61. For a fuller treatment see D. W. Bebbington, *The Nonconformist Conscience: Chapel and Politics, 1870–1914* (London: Allen & Unwin, 1982).

78. The designation *institutional church* was used by William Jewett Tucker in referring to the social activities of Berkeley Temple, a Congregational Church in Boston; he was probably the first to use the term. The church began its widened social ministry in 1888. Barclay, *Missions*, 3:66.

79. For studies of the movement see Robert D. Cross, ed., *The Church and the City 1865–1910* (Indianapolis: Bobbs-Merrill, 1967); Charles H. Hopkins, *The Rise of the Social Gospel in American Protestantism* (New Haven: Yale University Press, 1940), and J. H. Dorn, "Religion and the City," in *Urban Experience: Themes in American History*, ed. Raymond A. Mohl and James F. Richardson (Belmont, Calif.: Wadsworth Publishing, 1973).

80. Fred Hamlin, *S. Parkes Cadman, Pioneer Radio Minister* (New York: Harper & Brothers, 1930), esp. chap. 8, "New York," 88–97. In 1901 Cadman was called to Central Congregational Church, Brooklyn, where he remained as pastor for thirty-six years. One of the first radio preachers, he broadcast regularly from 1923 on, in later years to a nationwide audience. Cadman was president of the Federal Council of Churches (1924–28) and chaired the American section of the Ecumenical Conference on Life and Work at Stockholm (1925). For additional biographical de-

tails see the Hamlin biography cited above, and Frederick E. Fagley, "Cadman, Samuel Parkes," in *Dictionary of American Biography*, 2nd supplement, 1958, 85–86; [Harold P. Sloan], "Dr. S. Parkes Cadman Attains the Eternal Presence," CA, July 23, 1936, 699; *Religion in Life* 5 (1936): 483–93; and the *New York Times*, July 13, 1936.

81. The Open and Institutional Church League, founded in 1894, openly opposed pew rental as a means of church finance.

82. The program of the church was detailed in *New York Tribune*, Dec. 1, 1897. Fuller accounts are Cadman's "The Advance Movement of the Church in Great Cities," *Christian City* 9, no. 12 (Dec. 1897): 278–82; and Stephen J. Herben, *Report of the Forward Movement, Metropolitan Temple Parish, New York City: Seventh Anniversary 1892–1899* (New York: Press of Walter Logan, 1899).

83. Isabelle Horton, *The Burden of the City* (New York: Revell, 1904). See also Horton's "Institutional Work," *Christian City* 18, no. 10 (Dec. 1906): 309–12.

84. Barclay, *Missions*, 3:67.

85. Horace Clarence Boyer, "Charles Albert Tindley: Progenitor of Black-American Gospel Music," *Black Perspective in Music* 11 (Autumn 1983): 103–32, accessed online via JSTOR; http://www.jstor.org/; Carlton R. Young, *Companion to The United Methodist Hymnal* (Nashville: Abingdon Press, 1993), 843; *Beams of Heaven: Hymns of Charles Albert Tindley*, ed. S. T. Kimbrough Jr., music editor Carlton R. Young, with an introduction by James Abbington (New York: GBGM, UMC, 2006).

86. Charles Albert Tindley, *New Songs of Paradise: A Collection of Popular and Religious Songs for Sundays Schools, Prayer-Meetings, Epworth League Meetings and Social Gatherings*, 6 vols. (Philadelphia: J. C. Tindley, 1934).

87. Ed. J. Jefferson Cleveland and Verolga Nix (Nashville: Abingdon Press, 1981).

88. Birdie Wilson Johnson, *Succeed, My People! The Story of Charles Albert Tindley, African-American Pastor, Theologian, Hymn-Writer* (Newark, N.J.: Preston Publications, 1992); Ralph H. Jones, *Charles Albert Tindley: Prince of Preachers* (Nashville: Abingdon Press, 1982); E. T. Tindley, *The Prince of Preachers: The Remarkable Story of Charles Albert Tindley of Philadelphia, Pennsylvania* (Philadelphia: the author, 1942); and William C. Jason Jr., "The Delaware Annual Conference of the Methodist Church, 1864–1965," *MethH* 4 (July 1966): 26–41.

89. Edgar J. Helms and Melvin Pelesare, *The Goodwill, Not Charity, but a Chance* (Boston: Morgan Memorial Press, 1920–1929?); Edgar J. Helms, *The Goodwill Industries, a Manual, a History of the Movement, Departmental Methods of Work, Cultural Activities, Administration and Organization* (Boston: Morgan Memorial Goodwill Press, 1935), and *Pioneering in Modern City Missions* (Boston: Morgan Memorial Printing Department, 1927).

90. See Edgar James Helms, "The Relation of the Church to Industrial Evangelism," in his *Pioneering in Modern City Missions*.

91. For a detailed history of this movement, see John Fulton Lewis, *Goodwill: For the Love of People* (Washington, D.C.: Goodwill Industries of America, 1977).

92. *The Social Message of Our Lord* (Dayton, Ohio: Otterbein Press, 1909), 9, 126f., 7–8, 16.

93. JGC/UBC/1909, 21–24.

94. Lucy Rider Meyer, *Deaconesses, Biblical, Early Church, European, American, with the Story of How the Work Began in the Chicago Training School, for City, Home, and Foreign Missions, and the Chicago Deaconess Home*, 3rd ed., rev. and enl. (Cincinnati: Cranston & Stowe, 1889), 94, 100.

95. JGC/MEC/1888, 95, 100.

96. Jane M. Bancroft, *Deaconesses in Europe and Their Lessons for America* (New York: Hunt & Eaton, 1889). The motherhouse of the German Lutheran deaconess movement was at Kaiserswerth. Established in 1836 by Lutheran pastor Theodor Fliedner, it became a model for the deaconess movement in a number of American Protestant denominations.

97. Paul F. Douglass, *The Story of German Methodism* (New York: Methodist Book Concern, 1939), 131–38.

98. Dorothy Graham, *Saved to Serve: The Story of the Wesley Deaconess Order, 1890–1978* (Peterborough, Eng.: Methodist Publishing House, 2002). Philip S. Bagwell, *Outcast London: A Christian Response, The West London Mission of the Methodist Church, 1887–1987* (London: Epworth Press, 1987), 29. Through 1901 deaconesses were "recognized"; between 1902 and 1936 they were "consecrated"; and from 1937 on they were "ordained." Ordination was to lifelong service, but until 1965 they were required to resign on marriage. The order was closed to recruitment from 1978 to 1987 and renamed the Methodist Diaconal Order when it was opened to both women and men in 1988.

99. James M. Thoburn, *My Missionary Apprenticeship* (New York: Philips & Hunt, 1884), 246, 255. Chapter 18 is titled "Woman's Work." See also James Thoburn, *Life of Isabella Thoburn* (Cincinnati: Jennings & Pye, 1903), 218.

100. Christian Golder, *History of the Deaconess Movement* (Cincinnati: Jennings & Pye, 1903), 309.

101. John F. Hurst, "Charitable Institutions in Europe," *Ladies' Repository* 26 (1866): 452–55. A brief flurry of articles in Methodism's Boston-area newspaper, *Zion's Herald*, in the spring of 1852, a decade earlier, had launched discussion of reviving a diaconate for women.

102. Charles H. Fowler, "A Noble Field for Women," CA, July 14, 1870, 220. Fowler published a similar plea in an 1871 article in his paper by Pastor Lewis R. Dunn: "Deaconesses," CA, Nov. 8, 1871, 353.

103. Susanna M. D. Fry, "Ancient and Modern Deaconesses," *Ladies' Repository* 32 (Feb. 1872): 109–12; and "Ancient and Modern Sisterhoods," *Ladies' Repository* 33 (Oct. 1872): 242–45.

104. Susanna Fry, "The Deaconess Institutions at Kaiserswerth," *Ladies' Repository* 34 (Aug. 1874): 123–27. See also Emma Winner Rogers, *Deaconesses in the Early Church, Deaconesses in the Modern Church*, Deaconess Bureau Publications of the Woman's Home Missionary Society, first series, no. 2, (Evanston, Ill.: Index Company, 1891).

105. Isabelle Horton, *High Adventure: [The] Life of Lucy Rider Meyer* (New York: Methodist Book Concern, 1928), 24–25; Mary Agnes Theresa Dougherty, "The Methodist Deaconess, 1885–1918: A Study in Religious Feminism" (PhD diss., University of California, Davis, 1979), 34. On the history of the deaconess movement in the broader United Methodist tradition, see also her book *My Calling to Fulfill: Deaconesses in the United Methodist Tradition* (New York: Women's Division, GBGM, UMC, 1997), and article "The Social Gospel according to Phoebe: Methodist Deaconesses in the Metropolis, 1885–1918," in *Perspectives*, 356–70.

106. Horton, *High Adventure*, 58–63, 73.

107. Ibid., 78.

108. Dougherty, "Methodist Deaconess," 41–44. Raised among Pennsylvania Quakers, Josiah Shelly Meyer had been dedicated to both religion and business. In addition to his work with the YMCA, he attended McCormick Theological Seminary in 1884 and served as student pastor of

a mission church. See Horton, *High Adventure*, 88–90; Rider Meyer, *Deaconesses*, 100–108. *The Message* displayed the slogan of CTS: "Lo, I have set before thee an open door," and declared the threefold purpose of the school: to give instruction in the Bible, to provide training for "lady missionaries," and to encourage and develop the work of city missions (Horton, *High Adventure*, 120). The title of this publication changed over the years to *The Message and Deaconess World* in 1893, *The Message and Deaconess Advocate* in 1894, and finally *The Deaconess Advocate* in 1903.

109. Rider Meyer, *Deaconesses*, 115–18; Horton, *High Adventure*, 117.

110. Horton, *High Adventure*, 141–44. (At the time she wrote this announcement Rider Meyer was still in bed after giving birth to a son, Shelly.) Isabella Thoburn was the sister of the Reverend James M. Thoburn, a Methodist Episcopal minister and member of the Pittsburgh Conference, who had served as a missionary to India since 1859. At the 1888 MEC General Conference he was elected missionary bishop for southern Asia; he would be an important advocate for the deaconess office in the MEC.

111. Lucy Rider Meyer, "Deaconesses and Their Work," in *Woman in Missions: Papers and Addresses presented at the Woman's Congress of Missions, October 2–4, 1893, in the Hall of Columbus, Chicago* (American Tract Society, 1894), 182–97. See also Catherine M. Prelinger and Rosemary S. Keller, "The Function of Female Bonding: The Restored Diaconessate of the Nineteenth Century," in Hilah F. Thomas and Rosemary Skinner Keller, eds., *Women in New Worlds*, 2 vols. (Nashville: Abingdon Press, 1981, 1982), 2:318–37. See also Keller et al., *Called to Serve: The United Methodist Diaconate* (Nashville: GBHEM, UMC, 1987); Elizabeth M. Lee, *As Among the Methodists: Deaconesses Yesterday, Today and Tomorrow* (New York: Woman's Division of Christian Service, Board of Missions, The Methodist Church, 1963); Betty Letzig, *"The Deaconess in The United Methodist Church": A Presentation to the Committee to Study the Ministry of the Council of Bishops*, Dec. 1993; and Letzig, "Deaconesses Past and Future," *New World Outlook*, May-June 1992, 29–31.

112. Dougherty, "Methodist Deaconess," 46, 147. See also Horton, *High Adventure*, 154–57.

113. Rider Meyer, *Deaconesses*, 210. Bishop Ninde went on to affirm the urgency of "parity" for women—in the churches, schools, and learned professions.

114. Lucy Rider Meyer, "The Mother in the Church," *Message and Deaconess Advocate* 17, no. 10 (Oct. 1901): 5–6, 11–12.

115. Bancroft, *Deaconesses in Europe and Their Lessons for America*.

116. Ruth Esther Meeker, *Six Decades of Service, 1880–1940: A History of the Woman's Home Missionary Society of The Methodist Episcopal Church* (Cincinnati: Woman's Home Missionary Society, 1969), 91.

117. "Jane Marie Bancroft Robinson," in *Notable American Women: A Biographical Dictionary*, ed. Edward T. James et al. (Cambridge: Belknap Press, 1971), 3:183–84.

118. Horton, *High Adventure*, 190; Dougherty, "Methodist Deaconess," 52, 57–60. Dougherty saw this disagreement over strategy as similar to that in the woman suffrage movement, which split in 1869 into the National and the American Woman Suffrage Associations.

119. Ibid., 62; "The Early History of Deaconess Work and Training Schools for Women in American Methodism, 1883–1885" (Detroit: Hines Press for the Woman's Home Missionary Society, MEC, 1912), reprinted in Carolyn De Swarte Gifford, ed., *The American Deaconess Movement in the Early Twentieth Century* (New York: Garland Pub., 1987), 10; Horton, *High Adventure*, 230–31, 197.

120. Dougherty, "Methodist Deaconess," 67.

121. Virginia Lieson Brereton, "Preparing Women for the Lord's Work," in *Women in New Worlds*, 1:178–99.

122. Mabel K. Howell, "The Service Motive," manuscript, Scarritt College, n.d., 35; quoted in Brereton, "Preparing Women for the Lord's Work," 186.

123. Noreen Dunn Tatum, *A Crown of Service: A Story of Woman's Work in The Methodist Episcopal Church, South, from 1878–1940* (Nashville: Parthenon Press, 1960), 325.

124. Ibid., 326.

125. Ibid., 326–31.

126. See *Discipline/MEC/1920*, ¶665, 639–41.

127. Harry F. Ward and Richard Henry Edwards, *Christianizing Community Life* (New York: Association Press, 1917).

128. MEC General Deaconess Board, Wallace MacMullen et al., *Directions and Helps: Course of Study for Deaconesses* (New York and Cincinnati: Methodist Book Concern, 1922).

129. *Deaconess Advocate*, April 1914, 3.

130. For a fuller study, see Kenneth E. Rowe, "Temples of Healing: The Founding Era of Methodist Hospitals, 1880–1900," *MethH* 46, no. 1 (Oct. 2007): 47–57.

131. David Rosner, *A Once Charitable Enterprise: Hospitals and Health Care in Brooklyn and New York, 1885–1915* (Princeton: Princeton University Press, 1982); Ecumenical Methodist Conference, 1st London, *Proceedings of the Ecumenical Methodist Conference Held in City Road Chapel, London, September 1881* (New York: Phillips & Hunt, 1882), 462.

132. For a contemporary description by the hospital's first (clergy) superintendent, see John S. Breckinridge, "Hospitals, Ancient and Modern," *Methodist Review* 73, no. 1 (Jan. 1891): 80–87.

133. *JLFA*, 3:500; Barclay, *Missions*, 3:12–13.

134. "The Medical Profession," *MQR* 47 (1865): 100–115; "Small Pox," *CA*, Jan. 25, 1872, 31; B. A. Brooks, "Anesthesia," *CA*, June 19, 1873, 193; "Blood Transfusion," *CA*, March 23, 1876, 89; "Saving Human Life," *CA*, April 21, 1873, 271.

135. For the larger context see Charles E. Rosenberg, *The Care of Strangers: The Rise of America's Hospital System* (Baltimore: Johns Hopkins University Press, 1987); Rosemary Stevens, *In Sickness and in Wealth: American Hospitals in the Twentieth Century* (New York: Basic Books, 1989); and Paul Starr, *The Social Transformation of American Medicine: The Rise of a Sovereign Profession and the Making of a Vast Industry* (New York: Basic Books, 1982). For the Methodist context through 1950, see David C. Crummey, "Factors in the Rise of Methodist Hospitals and Homes" (PhD diss., University of Chicago, 1963). See also Harold V. Vanderpool, "The Wesleyan-Methodist Tradition," in *Caring and Curing: Health and Medicine in the Western Religious Traditions*, ed. Ronald L. Numbers and Darrel W. Amundsen (Baltimore: Johns Hopkins University Press, 1986), 317–53.

136. Dougherty, *My Calling to Fulfill*, 107–12; John M. Versteeg, ed., *Methodism: Ohio Area (1812–1962)* ([Cincinnati?]: Ohio Area Sesquicentennial Committee, 1962), 268–70. From its inception, the hospital sought to adhere to the purpose of its founders in making no distinction as to race, color, creed, or economic status. One hundred and fifteen years after its founding, Christ Hospital, Cincinnati, has grown to become a leader in medical excellence by continuing to plan and innovate for the future. The now 555-bed hospital is consistently recognized as one

of the best hospitals in the U.S. For the past eleven years Christ Hospital has been awarded Cincinnati's "Most Preferred Hospital." In 2006 it was listed in *U.S. News & World Report*'s top hundred hospitals in four key medical specialties. See www.christhospitalcincinnati.com.

137. The six German nurses performed at heroic levels. Nursing often for eighteen hours a day for the pittance of $5 or $10 a week, and more often with no remuneration at all, they paid a monthly rent of $40 out of a combined income that rarely exceeded $100. Deaconesses also were promised a room and monthly allowance for life, free care in sickness and old age, and a modest pension. See Douglass, *The Story of German Methodism*, 145–46; *Fiftieth Anniversary of the Bethesda Institutions* (Cincinnati: Bethesda Institutions, 1948); Versteeg, *Methodism: Ohio Area (1812–1962)*, 266–74. In 1995 Cincinnati's Bethesda Hospital partnered with Good Samaritan Hospital, founded in 1852 by Roman Catholic Sisters of Charity, to form Tri-Health, a modern integrated network of hospitals, physician groups, hospice, and community outreach programs serving the greater Cincinnati area. See www.trihealth.com.

138. Douglass, *Story of German Methodism*, 145–46.

139. Vanessa Northington Gamble, "Roots of the Black Hospital Reform Movement," in *Sickness & Health in America: Readings in the History of Medicine and Public Health*, ed. Judith Walzer Leavitt and Ronald L. Numbers, 3rd ed., rev. (Madison: University of Wisconsin Press, 1997), 369–91.

140. For a full history, see James Summerville, *Educating Black Doctors: A History of Meharry Medical College* (University: University of Alabama Press, 1983). For a 1920s snapshot of the school, see Jay S. Stowell, *Methodist Adventures in Negro Education* (New York: Methodist Book Concern, 1922), chap. 3, 50–66. By the late 1990s, the college included the schools of Medicine, Dentistry, Graduate Studies and Research, and Allied Health Professions, housed the Lloyd C. Elam Community Mental Health Center, and was the nation's first Institute on Health Care for the Poor and Under-Served. In 1999 the college established a five-year alliance with Vanderbilt University to improve physician education, research, and patient care.

141. The Jacksonville medical institution was closed temporarily in 1966, renamed Methodist Hospital, and reopened as a racially integrated hospital in new twin ten-story tower facilities financed through a consortium of banks, insurance companies, and the Women's Division of the UMC in 1967.

142. Ralph Diffendorfer, ed., *The World Service of the MEC* (Chicago: Methodist Episcopal Church Council of Benevolences, 1923), 602–3; Walter G. Muelder, *Methodism and Society in the Twentieth Century* (New York: Abingdon Press, 1961), 308–11; Richard C. Cameron, *Methodism and Society in Historical Perspective* (New York: Abingdon Press, 1961), 299–325.

143. Although the American Hospital Association was formed in 1899, not till 1913 did the AHA agree to inspection, classification, and standardization of hospitals. Stevens, *In Sickness and in Wealth*, 69.

144. By 1920 only four of the MEC's fifty-six hospitals had been accredited by the American College of Surgeons as meeting the standards for diagnosis, surgery, and medical service. By 1928 the new board could report that almost all of the related MEC hospitals met minimum standards. MEC Board of Hospitals and Homes, *Annual Report*, 1928, 15. Early publications of the board included *Practical Suggestions on Building, Equipment, and Co-operative Buying for Hospitals* by Clarence W. Williams; *The Correlation and Co-operation of Protestant Denominational Hospitals and*

Homes by Frank C. English; *Standardization of Nurses' Training Schools* by Blanche M. Fuller; *Putting Hospitals and Homes in the Hearts and Minds of the People* by Ralph W. Keeler; and literature on the White Cross movement and recruitment of nurses.

145. An article by the association's secretary made a compelling case for the new board: W. H. Jordan, "The Call of the Hospital," CA, Feb. 5, 1920, 199. Associations of Catholic, Lutheran, and Jewish hospitals had already been formed in response to the standardization movement. Later that spring the NMHHA, representing 156 hospitals and homes, sent a memorial to the MEC General Conference pleading for the creation of a board. By the late 1990s the UMC Association of Health and Welfare Ministries, acknowledged in the *Book of Discipline* and incorporated in 1983 as a separate, not-for-profit charitable membership organization, served more than 400 UMC-related retirement and long-term-care communities, hospitals, child and family service organizations, community centers, organizations serving persons with physically and mentally challenging conditions, and individual health-care and human-service professionals.

146. The MEC board was formed in 1920, the MECS board in 1922, and the EUB Commission on Health and Welfare in 1962. Hospitals and homes in missions outside the U.S. remained under the respective mission boards. Since 1972 in the UMC, oversight of the church's hospitals and homes has been lodged with the Division of Health and Welfare Ministries of the General Board of Global Ministries. By 1944 a full-time executive secretary, Dr. Karl P. Meister, was appointed, and the offices moved from Columbus to Chicago. For early history of the MEC board, see the founding general secretary's unpublished study: Newton E. Davis, "A History of the Organization of the Board of Hospitals and Homes," 1942, UMC Archives. For an early snapshot of the work of the board, see Diffendorfer, *World Service*, 601–14.

147. Diffendorfer, *World Service*, 607.

148. During the 1920–24 quadrennium the White Cross Society in the MEC raised more than $1 million! Following the Depression of 1929, White Cross giving fell drastically, and appropriations to the board were cut. The plans never again achieved great success until after reunion in 1939 when the Golden Cross program was established in the united church. For a time the UBC Otterbein Home in Lebanon, Ohio, met its entire budget from red stocking offerings received during the Christmas season. In the late 1990s the first Sunday of May was the traditional time for the Golden Cross offering—on Gold Cross Sunday. In accordance with the EUB tradition some UM churches take the Golden Cross offering on the Sunday before Christmas. Conferences are free to use the offerings in whatever way they choose, as long as it is related to health and welfare ministries.

149. As early as 1890, Methodist Hospital, Brooklyn, recognized the importance of the paying patient when its superintendent declared that the "completion of the Central Building would...furnish us with far more suitable apartments" for private patients. "It would also add some thousands of dollars to our income," he noted, "by rendering available a dozen or more private rooms for which invalids having means would gladly pay handsome prices." Methodist Episcopal Hospital, Brooklyn, *3rd Annual Report*, 1890, 16.

150. Stevens, *In Sickness and in Wealth*, 22; JGC/MEC/1920, 681.

151. The standard, though unpublished, histories of MFSA's founding and early years are Milton J. Huber, "A History of the Methodist Federation for Social Action" (PhD diss., Boston University, 1949), and William McGuire King, "The Emergence of Social Gospel Radicalism in

American Methodism" (PhD diss., Harvard University, 1977). More accessible are George D. McClain, "Pioneering Social Gospel Radicalism: An Overview of the Methodist Federation for Social Action," in *Perspectives*, 371–85; William Maguire King, "The Emergence of Social Gospel Radicalism," *Church History* 50 (Dec. 1981): 436–49; Jeanne Gayle Knepper, *Thy Kingdom Come: The Methodist Federation for Social Service and Human Rights: 1907–1948* (Staten Island, N.Y.: MFSA, 1996); Alice G. Knotts, *Lifting Up Hope: Living Out Justice* (San Diego: Frontrowliving Press, 2007); and *Pioneers in the Faith: The Methodist Federation for Social Action at 100 Years, 1907–2007* (Washington, D.C.: MFSA, 2007). For a brief history see MFSA's website, www.mfsaweb.org. The best contextual studies are Muelder, *Methodism and Society in the Twentieth Century*, and Donald K. Gorrell, *The Age of Social Responsibility: The Social Gospel in the Progressive Era, 1900–1920* (Macon: Mercer University Press, 1988).

152. Herbert Welch, "The Church and the Social Need," in *The Socialized Church: Addresses before the First National Conference of Social Workers of Methodism, St. Louis, November 17–19, 1908*, ed. Worth M. Tippy (New York: Eaton & Mains; Cincinnati: Jennings & Graham, 1909), 21, 30–31. See also Welch's autobiography, *As I Recall My Last Century* (New York: Abingdon Press, 1962).

153. Elbert Robb Zaring was born in Rockport, Indiana, graduated from DePauw University in 1891, and was a clergy member of the Indiana Conference until his death in 1954. Active in community service work, he was also assistant, later editor of the MEC's WCA based in Cincinnati for many years. He was a cosigner of the letter inviting leaders to the 1907 conference that founded MFSS.

154. Tippy was born in Larwill, Indiana, one year after the Civil War ended (1866) and educated at DePauw and Cornell universities. He served two of Methodism's most prestigious city churches—Epworth Memorial Church in Cleveland and Madison Avenue Church (later Christ Church) in New York City. From 1917 to 1937 he was executive secretary of the Church and Social Service Commission of the Federal Council of Churches, now the National Council of Churches. Dr. Tippy returned to DePauw in 1951 to organize and develop the archives both of the university and of Indiana Methodism and served as director of both for six years; then he retired to Laurel, Mississippi, where he lived with his daughter until his death in 1961.

155. Huber, "History of MFSA," 58f.

156. Welch, *As I Recall My Last Century*, 51–52.

157. Worth M. Tippy, "Autobiography," Worth M. Tippy Papers, Archives of Depauw University and Indiana Methodism, Greencastle, Indiana, Box DC627, "Europe 1908"; Gorrell, *The Age of Social Responsibility*, 91–92.

158. Worth M. Tippy, *The Church, a Community Force: A Story of the Development of the Community Relations of Epworth Memorial Church, Cleveland, Ohio* (New York: Missionary Education Movement of the United States and Canada, 1914).

159. The two best studies of Keeble are Maldwyn Edwards, *S. E. Keeble: Pioneer and Prophet* (London: Epworth Press, 1949), and Michael S. Edwards, *S. E. Keeble: The Rejected Prophet* (Broxton: Wesley Historical Society, 1977).

160. *The Social Outlook: Papers on Social Problems Read at the Second Oxford Conference of the Wesleyan Methodist Union for Social Service*, 1910, iii.

161. Maldwyn Edwards, *S. E. Keeble*, 65.

162. *MR*, June 11, 1905.

163. Published 1906–17 with a single editor, Henry Carter.

164. *The Social Outlook*, 1910, 210.

165. Lacy, *Frank Mason North*, 129–45.

166. Quoted in Huber, "History of MFSA," 62–63.

167. Ward was reared in a revivalist Methodist family on the outskirts of London and immigrated to the U.S. in 1891. He began college at the young University of Southern California, transferred to Northwestern University, and earned a master's degree at Harvard. He studied under George Coe at Northwestern and solidified a nascent social gospel; his first position following Harvard was as the director at the Northwestern University Settlement House in the "back-of-the-stock yards" district of Chicago, where he was later appointed to an ME church.

168. The "sweating system" was a method of exploiting labor by supplying materials to workers and paying by the piece for work done on those materials in the workers' homes or in small workshops (sweatshops).

169. *Discipline*/MEC/1908, 479–81.

170. "The Battle of Columbus," *Christian Century* 53, no. 14 (April 1, 1936): 486–87.

171. Donald K. Gorrell, "The Social Creed and Methodism through Eighty Years," *MethH* 26, no. 4 (July 1988): 213–28; and *Perspectives*, 371–85.

XII. Taking On the World? 1884–1939

1. William Maguire King, "The Emergence of Social Gospel Radicalism," *Church History* 50 (Dec. 1981): 436–49; Donald K. Gorrell, *The Age of Social Responsibility: The Social Gospel in the Progressive Era, 1900–1920* (Macon: Mercer University Press, 1988).

2. David Moberg, *The Great Reversal: Evangelicalism Versus Social Concern* (Philadelphia: J. B. Lippincott, 1972); Timothy L. Smith, *Revivalism and Social Reform in Mid-Nineteenth Century America* (New York: Abingdon Press, 1957), rev. ed. (Baltimore: Johns Hopkins University Press, 1980).

3. JGC/MEC/1908, 479–81, ¶59.

4. Pilkington/Vernon, *Methodist Publishing House*, 2:227–30, 309–12.

5. *Called unto Holiness: The Story of the Nazarenes*, 1:50, 103–10. This is a two-volume work, vol. 1, *The Formative Years*, by Timothy L. Smith; vol. 2, *The Second Twenty-five Years*, by W. T. Purkiser (Kansas City: Nazarene Publishing House, 1962, 1983). See also Vinson Synan, *The Holiness-Pentecostal Movement in the United States* (Grand Rapids: Eerdmans, 1971). Donald W. Dayton, *Theological Roots of Pentecostalism* (Grand Rapids: Francis Asbury Press, 1987); Melvin E. Dieter, *The Holiness Revival of the Nineteenth Century*, Studies in Evangelicalism, 1, ed. Kenneth E. Rowe and Donald W. Dayton (Metuchen, N.J.: Scarecrow Press, 1980). For a Methodist rejoinder, see John L. Peters, *Christian Perfection and American Methodism* (New York and Nashville: Abingdon Press, 1956).

6. Charles Edwin Jones, "The Holiness Complaint with Late-Victorian Methodism," in *Rethinking Methodist History*, ed. Russell E. Richey and Kenneth E. Rowe (Nashville: Kingswood Books/UMPH, 1985), 59–64.

7. Ibid., 59.

8. See Thomas A. Langford, *Practical Divinity*, 2 vols. (Nashville: Abingdon Press, 1998, 1999).

9. George Marsden, *Fundamentalism and American Culture: The Shaping of Twentieth Century Evangelicalism, 1870–1925* (New York: Oxford University Press, 1980).

10. Smith, *Called unto Holiness*, 1:26–30, 29.

11. JGC/MECS/1894, 25–26. Wesley had issued a similar warning in his 1762 essay "Cautions and Directions to the Greatest Professors in the Methodist Societies," in *John Wesley: Representative Collection of His Writings*, ed. Albert C. Outler (New York: Oxford University Press, 1964), 298–305.

12. Peters, *Christian Perfection*, 148–49; Charles Edwin Jones, *Perfectionist Persuasion: The Holiness Movement and American Methodism, 1867–1936* (Lanham, Md.: Scarecrow Press, 1974; reprint, 2002), and his *Wesleyan-Holiness Movement: A Comprehensive Guide* (Lanham, Md.: Scarecrow Press, 2005).

13. See treatment in chapter 11.

14. *The Socialized Church: Addresses before the First National Conference of the Social Workers of Methodism, St. Louis, November 17–19, 1908*, ed. Worth M. Tippy for the Methodist Federation for Social Service (New York: Eaton & Mains, 1909).

15. J. W. Magruder, *The Methodist Church in Organized Charity* ([Dover, N.H.]: Methodist Federation for Social Service, 1909), 32 pp. Excerpts were published in the New York–based Charity Organization Society's journal, *Survey* 22 (April 1909–Oct. 1909): 131–32. Another popular early pamphlet, *Suggestions for Individual Service*, published in 1910, urged members, pastors, and district superintendents to perform community service.

16. Excerpted in Magruder, *The Methodist Church in Organized Charity*.

17. See King, "The Emergence of Social Gospel Radicalism," and Gorrell, *Age of Social Responsibility*.

18. Paul B. Maves and J. Lennart Cedarleaf, *Older People and the Church* (New York: Abingdon-Cokesbury, 1949), 223–43. No general church action on clergy or lay church employee eligibility for Social Security was taken, but data gathered from annual conference journals beginning in the early 1950s indicate pastors and perhaps lay employees in several annual conferences began to enroll in the nation's Social Security program.

19. Alice G. Knotts, *Lifting Up Hope, Living Out Justice* (San Diego: Frontrowliving Press, 2007).

20. Walter G. Muelder, *Methodism and Society in the Twentieth Century*, Methodism and Society, 2 (New York and Nashville: Abingdon Press, 1961), 45.

21. Behney/Eller, *History*, 246, 271.

22. Before World War II, only Methodists and Roman Catholics had established permanent lobbies in the nation's capital. Quakers followed in 1943, Presbyterians in 1946, and Baptists in 1948. A 1951 study found fifteen church lobbies in the capital. For the full story see Allen D. Hertzke, *Representing God in Washington: The Role of Religious Lobbies* (Knoxville: University of Tennessee Press, 1988), 28.

23. See the caustic study by Virginius Dabney, *Dry Messiah: The Life of Bishop Cannon* (New York: Knopf, 1949), and *Bishop Cannon's Own Story: Life as I Have Seen It*, ed. Richard L. Watson (Durham: Duke University Press, 1955).

24. Dabney, *Dry Messiah*, 99–100.

25. Ibid., 180. Cannon's views were shared by Bishop John M. Moore, who wrote to A. Frank Smith: "I will never vote for Al Smith. If he is nominated I shall do everything within my power

to bring about his defeat in November. His nomination would be an open affront to the moral and religious leadership of the South if not to the nation." Norman W. Spellmann, *Growing a Soul: The Story of A. Frank Smith* (Dallas: Southern Methodist University Press, 1979), 152.

26. Lawrence Oliver Kline, "H. L. Mencken's Controversy with the Methodists, with Special Reference to the Issue of Prohibition" (PhD diss., Duke University, 1975).

27. See David Nelson Duke, *In the Trenches with Jesus and Marx: Harry F. Ward and the Struggle for Social Justice* (Tuscaloosa: University of Alabama Press, 2003), and Eugene P. Link, *Labor-Religion Prophet: The Times and Life of Harry F. Ward* (Boulder, Colo.: Westview Press, 1984).

28. Quoted by Mueder, *Methodism and Society in the Twentieth Century*, 159.

29. JGC/MEC/1932, Report No. 14, "A Christian Appraisal of the Acquisitive Society," 654–55; compare 452, 656–57.

30. See Duke, *In the Trenches with Jesus and Marx*; Link, *Labor-Religion Prophet*; and Mueder, *Methodism and Society in the Twentieth Century*, 159–69.

31. "The Battle of Columbus," *Christian Century* 53, no. 14 (April 1, 1936): 486–87.

32. On Lewis and Faulkner, see Langford, *Practical Divinity*, 1:189–91, 173–75.

33. CA, March 15, 1923, 336. The issue also carried a letter of response by Lewis.

34. Edwin Lewis Papers, Drew University Archives, Madison, New Jersey; *Call to the Colors* (June 1926); see also William J. McCutcheon and William Neill, "United Methodist Evangelicals in Two Generations, the 1920s and the 1930s," *Explor* 2, no. 2 (Fall 1976): 59–72.

35. *The Essentialist* 3 (Nov. 1927): 166.

36. HAM, 3:272.

37. Edwin Lewis Papers, 1934 file, Drew University Archives.

38. Harold Paul Sloan, "A *Christian Manifesto* Appreciated," *Christian Faith and Life* 41 (Jan. 1935): 76–78.

39. Walter Newton Vernon Jr., *The United Methodist Publishing House*, 2:358–62, 368, quotation on 358.

40. Robert Watson Sledge, *Hands on the Ark: The Struggle for Change in The Methodist Episcopal Church, South, 1914–1939* (Lake Junaluska, N.C.: Commission on Archives and History, UMC, 1975), 107–8. The following discussion depends on Sledge's analysis of southern Methodism.

41. W. J. Cash, *The Mind of the South* (Garden City, N.Y.: Doubleday Anchor Books, 1954), 27, 336–37.

42. Spellmann, *Growing a Soul*, 109–11; Walter N. Vernon et al., *The Methodist Excitement in Texas: A History* (Dallas: Texas United Methodist Historical Society, 1984), 263–65.

43. Alice G. Knotts, *Fellowship of Love: Methodist Women Changing American Racial Attitudes, 1920–1968* (Nashville: Kingswood Books, 1996), 42–43; John Patrick McDowell, *The Social Gospel in the South: The Woman's Home Mission Movement in The Methodist Episcopal Church, South, 1886–1939* (Baton Rouge: Louisiana State University Press, 1982), 84–87.

44. Wilma Dykeman and James Stokely, *Seeds of Southern Change: The Life of Will Alexander* (Chicago: University of Chicago Press, 1962), 85. The CIC itself neither advocated racial equality nor challenged segregation. It was an attempt to bring together whites and middle-class blacks to work on solutions to some of the South's most pressing racial problems. It actually took more than a year before the CIC had African American members!

45. Quoted by Jacquelyn Dowd Hall, *Revolt against Chivalry: Jessie Daniel Ames and the Women's Campaign against Lynching* (New York: Columbia University Press, 1979), 89.

46. Dykeman and Stokely, *Seeds of Southern Change*, 92.

47. Quoted by Hall, *Revolt against Chivalry*, 93–94.

48. Dykeman and Stokely, *Seeds of Southern Change*, 85.

49. McDowell, *The Social Gospel in the South*, 91–92.

50. Hall, *Revolt against Chivalry*, 96; Paula Giddings, *When and Where I Enter: The Impact of Black Women on Race and Sex in America* (New York: Bantam, 1984), 175–76.

51. Knotts, *Fellowship of Love*, 55, 81.

52. *The Interracial Front* (Atlanta: CIC, 1933), pamphlet, 10–11. Quoted in Arnold M. Shankman, "Civil Rights, 1920–1970: Three Southern Methodist Women," in *Women in New Worlds*, ed. Hilah F. Thomas and Rosemary Skinner Keller, 2 vols. (Nashville: Abingdon Press, 1981, 1982), 2:222–23.

53. William T. Noll, "A Welcome in the Ministry: The 1920 and 1924 General Conferences Debate Clergy Rights for Women," *MethH* 30, no. 2 (Jan. 1992): 91–99.

54. "How the Licensing of Women to Preach Came to Pass," *CA*, Oct. 28, 1920, 1436–37; JGC/MEC/1920, 167n, ¶219; 539–40, ¶577.

55. Kendra Weddle Irons, "From Kansas to the World: M. Madeline Southard, Activist and Pastor," *MethH* 43, no. 1 (2004): 33–44. See also Irons's *Preaching on the Plains: Methodist Women Preachers in Kansas, 1920–1956* (Lanham, Md.: University Press of America, 2007).

56. Noll, "A Welcome in the Ministry," 98–99; *Daily Christian Advocate*, May 9, 1924, 208; and May 10, 1924, 233 (summary of proceedings on May 8–9); JGC/MEC/1924, 1697–98 (commission report). See Elizabeth Wilson, ed., *The Relative Place of Women in the Church in the United States* (New York: n.p., 1927), 56–57.

57. *Woman's Pulpit*, Sept. 1922, 1. For full study see Mark Chaves, "The Women That Publish the Tidings: The International Association of Women Ministers," in *Women and Twentieth-Century Protestantism*, ed. Margaret L. Bendroth et al. (Chicago: University of Illinois Press, 2002), 257–75.

58. Oscar Penn Fitzgerald, *The Class Meeting in Twenty Short Chapters* (Nashville: Southern Methodist Publishing House, 1880), 48, emphasis ours.

59. Daniel Curry, "Ritual for the Pews," *CA*, Dec. 8, 1864, 388.

60. For a full study see Karen Westerfield Tucker, *American Methodist Worship* (New York: Oxford University Press, 2001); for a compact study see James F. White, "Methodist Worship," in his *Protestant Worship Traditions in Transition* (Louisville: Westminster/John Knox Press, 1989), 150–70.

61. Simpson, *Cyclopaedia*, 546.

62. See Daniel Benedict, "Changing Wine into Grape Juice: Thomas and Charles Welch and the Transition to Unfermented Fruit of the Vine," www.gbod.org/worship/articles/wine.html. For the full story, see Jennifer Lynn Woodruff, "Purifying the Poisoned Chalice: Grape Juice and Common Sense Realism in The Methodist Episcopal Church, 1860–1900" (PhD diss., Duke University, 2005).

63. By 1895 the WCA, published in Cincinnati, Ohio, and other Methodist newspapers carried advertisements for "Individual Communion Cups" available from the Sanitary Communion Outfit Company of Rochester, New York; J. G. Thomas & Co., Lima, Ohio; and other entrepreneurs who rushed Communion sets to market. That same year a liberal bishop, John H. Vincent,

praised their use at a Communion service at the annual meeting of the Ohio Conference and a conservative bishop, Edward G. Andrews, *refused to use* the new cups at the Communion service of the Baltimore Conference.

64. Betty A. O'Brien, "The Lord's Supper: Traditional Cup of Unity or Innovative Cups of Individuality," *MethH* 32, no. 2 (Jan. 1994): 79–98; and Tucker, *American Methodist Worship*, 152–54.

65. Erastus Wentworth, "Methodists and Music," *MQR* 47 (July 1865): 375–78.

66. Thomas O. Summers, "The Organ," Nashville *MQR* (April 1882): 358–67.

67. Anne Bagnell Yardley, "Choirs in The Methodist Episcopal Church, 1800–1860," *American Music* 17, no. 1 (Spring 1999): 40–64.

68. *The Centenary Singer: A Collection of Hymns and Tunes Popular during the last One Hundred Years, compiled as directed by the Music Committee of the Gen. Conference & Assoc. M.E. Choirs* (New York: Carlton & Porter, 1867).

69. JGC/MEC/1884, 202, ¶381; JGC/MEC/1920, 239, ¶357.

70. Abel Stevens, *The Centenary of American Methodism* (New York: Carlton & Porter, 1865), 233–34.

71. Resources of the homeless congregation were so large and the congregation so scattered throughout the city that the congregation divided the proceeds equally between members living in the east end of Pittsburgh and in Allegheny, a western suburb. The western portion of the congregation built an equally grand new church, Calvary Church, though in Gothic style. Cornerstones of the twin churches were laid on the same day, May 18, 1893. Other notable auditorium and Akron Plan churches clothed in Gothic costume are Trinity Methodist Episcopal Church, Denver, designed by Robert S. Roeschlaub, completed in 1888, and First MEC, Germantown, Philadelphia, designed by Rankin and Kellogg, completed in 1898.

72. See Kenneth E. Rowe, "Redesigning Methodist Churches: Auditorium-Style Sanctuaries and Akron-Plan Sunday Schools in Romanesque Costume, 1875–1925," in *CEMI*, 117–34; Tucker, *American Methodist Worship*, 247–54; see also Jeanne Halgren Kilde, *When the Church Became Theatre: The Transformation of Evangelical Architecture and Worship in Nineteenth-Century America* (New York: Oxford University Press, 2002); and James F. White, "Nineteenth Century American Liturgical Architecture," in his *Christian Worship in North America* (Collegeville, Minn.: Liturgical Press, 1997), 243–63, and his pioneering *Protestant Worship and Church Architecture: Theological and Historical Considerations* (New York: Oxford University Press, 1964).

73. "Our Architectural Plans," *Manual of The Methodist Episcopal Church* 5, no. 3 (July 1885): 210–11; see also Paul Neff Garber, *Methodist Meeting House* (New York: Board of Home Missions and Church Extension, The Methodist Church, 1941), 76. For the larger context see Brian C. Zugay, "Towards a New Era in Church Building: Architectural Reform in American Protestantism in the Nineteenth and Early Twentieth Centuries" (PhD diss., Brown University, 2004), which focuses on the development and operations of church extension agencies within Congregational, Presbyterian, Baptist, and Methodist churches.

74. The Methodist Episcopal Church, Board of Church Extension, *Catalogue of Architectural Plans for Churches and Parsonages* (Philadelphia: Board of Church Extension, MEC, 1885). This new plan, which cost $10,000 to $16,000 to build, was featured in the *Manual of The Methodist Episcopal Church* 5, no. 3 (July 1885): 208–9. The same plan appeared as no. 35 in The Methodist Episcopal Church, South, Board of Church Extension, *Catalogue of Architectural Plans for Churches, Parsonages and Dwellings* (Louisville: Board of Church Extension, MECS, 1885), 48.

75. The Methodist Episcopal Church, Board of Church Extension, *Catalogue of Architectural Plans for Churches and Parsonages* (Philadelphia: Board of Church Extension, MEC, 1889), 35, 72, 74. The plans were first featured in the *Manual of the Methodist Episcopal Church* a year earlier, 1888. Plan 54 was also featured in the *Catalogue of Architectural Designs for Churches and Parsonages Furnished by the Church-Erection Society of the United Brethren in Christ for the year 1889–90* (Dayton, Ohio: Church Erection Office, UBC, 1889), 17.

76. Elbert M. Conover, "A Hundred Years and More of Methodist Church Building," CA, Sept. 9, 1926 (Centennial number), 56.

77. *The Restoration of the Lovely Lane Church, Part 1, Conception to Realization: A Historic Building Statement*, by David G. Wright; Part 2, *Perpetuation: A Restoration Feasibility Study*, by Calvin Corell (Baltimore: Architectory, 1980).

78. First United Methodist Church, Birmingham, *Cornerstone & Spire, Celebrating the First Century of the Sanctuary of First United Methodist Church* (Birmingham: The Church, 1991).

79. Other notable Methodist churches in Romanesque style are Cleveland's Epworth Memorial ME Church (Sydney R. Badgley, 1893), Denver's Asbury ME Church (Kidder & Humphreys, 1890), Detroit's Cass Avenue ME Church (Malcomson and Higgenbotham, 1891), Hartford's St. Paul's ME Church (Kramer, 1900), Johnstown, Pennsylvania's First United Brethren Church (Kramer, 1912), Minneapolis's Wesley ME Church (Warren H. Hayes, 1891), Nashville's West End ME Church, South (1889), New York's Park Avenue ME Church (Kramer, 1883), Philadelphia's Union ME Church (Hazlehurst and Huckel, 1889); Reading, Pennsylvania's Holy Cross ME Church (1893), Scranton, Pennsylvania's Elm Park ME Church (Weary and Kramer, 1893), and Washington's Union ME Church (Kramer, 1895).

80. David Ralph Bains, "The Liturgical Impulse in Mid-twentieth Century American Mainline Protestantism" (PhD diss., Harvard University, 1999), chaps. 2–3, 41–130; James F. White, "Theology and Architecture in America: A Study of Three Leaders [includes Cram and Vogt]," in his *Christian Worship in North America* (Collegeville, Minn.: Liturgical Press, 1997), 265–91, and "Methodist Worship," in *Perspectives*, 474–79.

81. Conover, "A Hundred Years and More of Methodist Church Building," 57. Halford E. Luccock, contributing editor of the *Advocate* and soon (1928) to become professor of preaching at Yale Divinity School, made the same point in his "Seven Deadly Sins of Church Architecture," CA, April 3, 1924, 417–18.

82. Elbert M. Conover, *Building the House of God* (New York: The Methodist Book Concern, 1928), 36.

83. Benjamin Guy Childs, *Centennial History of Trinity Methodist Church* (Durham, N.C.: Trinity Church, 1961), 57–66.

84. Conover, *Building the House of God*, 15, 16, 19.

85. Ibid., 111; interpretation follows Bains.

86. Edward G. Schutz, "The Setting for Public Worship," NWCA, March 25, 1926, 269. Fred Winslow Adams, "The Altar of Worship," *Methodist Review* 109 (May 1926): 384–87. Two years later, in a textbook for seminarians titled *The Technique of Public Worship* (New York: Methodist Book Concern, 1928), 60–61, Schutz and J. Hastie Odgers pushed new medieval divided chancels. Two additional printings of their textbook through 1937 were marketed.

87. *Congressional Record*, Senate, 56th Congress, 1st sess., vol. 30 (1899–1900), Jan. 1900, 704–12, emphasis added.

88. J. Tremayne Copplestone, *History of Methodist Missions: Twentieth Century Perspectives, 1896–1939*, IV; 204–39 of Barclay, *Missions*.

89. JGC/UBC/1901, 153.

90. John F. Piper Jr., *The American Churches in World War I* (Athens, Ohio, and London: Ohio University Press, 1985); Creighton Lacy, *Frank Mason North: His Social and Ecumenical Mission* (Nashville and New York: Abingdon Press, 1967); C. Howard Hopkins, *John R. Mott, 1865–1955: A Biography* (Grand Rapids: Eerdmans, 1979).

91. *Methodism and the Flag*, Reports of Committees, Bishop L. B. Wilson's Address and Poem (New York: New York Conference, MEC, 1917). Compliments of the Methodist Book Concern.

92. "Bombshell: Dr. Ryland Ousted from High Office on Pacifism Charges," *Los Angeles Times*, Dec. 11, 1917, section 2, p. 1.

93. Nolan B. Harmon, *Ninety Years and Counting: Autobiography of Nolan B. Harmon* (Nashville: The Upper Room, 1983), 53.

94. Hopkins, *John R. Mott*, 428–597. He shared the prize with Emily Greene Balch, Wellesley College Professor, peace activist, counselor to governments and international organizations. See http://nobelprize.org/nobel_prizes/peace/laureates/1946/press.html.

95. Clarence True Wilson, "Methodism and the Temperance Reform," *Quadrennial Handbook of the General Conference of The Methodist Episcopal Church* (New York and Cincinnati: The Methodist Book Concern, 1920), 333–43.

96. JGC/MEC/1920, ¶590, 551–58.

97. "The Korean Situation: A Statement by the Board of Bishops," *CA*, July 24, 1919, 948.

98. John M. Moore, *The Long Road to Methodist Union* (Nashville: The Methodist Publishing House, 1948), 67–72. Resolutions favoring a uniform order of worship and a common hymnal in all Methodist bodies were proposed by Bishop Randolph Foster of the MEC at the Pan-Methodist Centennial Conference held in Baltimore, Dec. 1884. *Proceedings, Sermons, Essays, and Addresses of the Centennial Methodist Conference*, ed. H. K. Carroll, W. P. Harrison, and J. H. Bayliss (New York: Phillips & Hunt, 1885), 47, 50.

99. See Morris L. Davis, *The Methodist Unification: Christianity and the Politics in the Jim Crow Era* (New York and London: New York University Press, 2008); Peter C. Murray, *Methodists and the Crucible of Race, 1930–1975* (Columbia and London: University of Missouri Press, 2004); *A Record of All Agreements Concerning Fraternity and Federation between The Methodist Episcopal Church and The Methodist Episcopal Church, South . . .* (Nashville: Publishing House of the MECS, 1914); Thomas B. Neely, *American Methodism: Its Divisions and Unification* (New York: Revell, 1915); *A Working Conference on the Union of American Methodism, Northwestern University* (New York: Methodist Book Concern, 1916); Paul N. Garber, *The Methodists Are One People* (Nashville: Cokesbury Press, 1939); John M. Moore, *The Long Road to Methodist Union* (Nashville: The Methodist Publishing House, 1948); James H. Straughn, *Inside Methodist Union* (Nashville: The Methodist Publishing House, 1958); Frederick E. Maser, "The Story of Unification, 1874–1939," in *HAM*, 3:407–78; Walter G. Muelder, *Methodism and Society in the Twentieth Century*, Methodism and Society, 2 (New York and Nashville: Abingdon Press, 1961), 251–71; Nolan B. Harmon, *The Organization of The Methodist Church*, 2nd rev. ed. (Nashville: The Methodist Publishing

House, 1962), 167–82; Sledge, *Hands on the Ark*, 90–123; Grant S. Shockley, ed., *Heritage and Hope: The African-American Presence in United Methodism* (Nashville: Abingdon Press, 1991); William B. McClain, *Black People in the Methodist Church* (Cambridge: Schenkman Publishing, 1984); James S. Thomas, *Methodism's Racial Dilemma: The Story of the Central Jurisdiction* (Nashville: Abingdon Press, 1992).

100. The language is that of A. J. Lamar, one of the southern commissioners, in the *Joint Commission on Unification of The Methodist Episcopal Church, South, and The Methodist Episcopal Church*. Its proceedings appeared in a work of that title in 3 vols. (Nashville: Publishing House of the MECS; New York: Methodist Book Concern, 1918–20), 1:274.

101. *Unification*, 1:46.

102. See *A Record of All Agreements Concerning Fraternity and Federation*, 38–39, 43–44. HAM, 3:415–23. This Joint Commission and round of discussions had been stimulated by a conference of MPC and MEC laity in Baltimore and out of that lay conference by a spirited address to the 1908 MEC General Conference presented by the MPC college president, Thomas H. Lewis of Western Maryland.

103. *Unification*, 1:42–43; JGC/MECS/1914, 263–64.

104. JGC/MEC/1916, 710–15, 711, 712.

105. For a probing reflection on these debates and on the racial/racist drama of which they played the central part, see Davis, *Methodist Unification*.

106. *Unification*, 2:24; 3:368.

107. Ibid., 1:131, 133, 134–35, 137–38.

108. Ibid., 1:144, 148.

109. Ibid., 2:228–31.

110. One early version of the jurisdictional plan, proposed as "preferred" by the Committee on the Status of the Negro in the Reorganized Church, put Africans and African Americans in one "Associate Regional Conference," parallel to four others, missionary in their character, embracing Latin America, Europe, Eastern Asia, and Southern Asia. A minority report held out for an "Associate General Conference" for Black members, with all the episcopal, conference, judicial, and board structure of the white church and tied to the latter only by a Constitutional Council. See *Unification*, 2:100–103. A perfected version of this scheme, worked out by a Joint Committee of Eight, retained its African American and African definition and provided for an overture to the CME to join (2:438–40).

111. Note this important statement by future bishop R. E. Jones (Sources 1918a, pp. 492–95). For the kind of sentiments that concerned Jones, see excerpts of the prepared statement by H. H. White (Sources 1918a, pp. 490–92) and the full account in *Unification*, 2:136–39.

112. For a summation thereof, see HAM, 3:423–34.

113. "Report Submitted by the Ad Interim Committee, Richmond, VA., November 7, 1919," *Unification*, 3:561–67.

114. *Unification*, 3:41.

115. "Report," 3:565–67.

116. JGC/MEC/1920, 181–82.

117. Ibid., 701–4.

118. Sledge, *Hands on the Ark*, 90–123.

119. *Journal of the Special Session of the General Conference of The Methodist Episcopal Church, South,* 1924, 20, 22, 52–54.

120. Ibid., 114–17; the entire Minority Report, 96–120.

121. Sledge, *Hands on the Ark*, 104–7.

122. JGC/MECS/1926, 161–63. It did constitute a Committee of Research and Investigation and order it "to make a careful and scientific study of the whole question in its historic, economic, social, legal, and other respects, and report their findings in detail to our next General Conference in 1930."

123. JGC/MEC/1928, 257, 259–60, 262, 271, 276, 296, 399.

124. Moore, *Long Road to Methodist Union*, 183.

125. "The Mind of Methodism," NWCA, Feb. 11, 1932, 139.

126. Bethune-Cookman College was placed on the register of UMC Heritage Landmarks in 1984.

127. After the College of Bishops, MECS, declared the plan's adoption, Bishop John M. Moore, president of the college, submitted a written request for a declaratory opinion about the adoption and its legality to the southern Judicial Council, a maneuver calculated to stave off a future legal challenge to unification. See Moore, *Long Road to Methodist Union*, 200–207.

128. Shockley, *Heritage and Hope*, 115; HAM, 3:456–57.

XIII. Warring for World Order and against Worldliness Within: 1939–68

1. On the contrast between Methodist attitudes toward the two world wars see Gerald L. Sittser, *A Cautious Patriotism: The American Churches and the Second World War* (Chapel Hill and London: University of North Carolina Press, 1997), and John F. Piper Jr., *The American Churches in World War I* (Athens, Ohio, and London: Ohio University Press, 1985).

2. *Discipline/MC/1939*, ¶1697.

3. Sittser, *A Cautious Patriotism*, 24–25. The percentage on the MEC poll was 56 percent.

4. *Proceedings of the Board of Education of The Methodist Episcopal Church* (Chicago: Board of Education, 1936), 35–37, 64–65.

5. *Discipline/MEC/1936*, ¶1464; *Discipline/MECS/1938*, ¶¶169, 594; *Discipline/UBC/1937*, ¶171.

6. CA (Chicago), May 19, 1938, 496.

7. Georgia Harkness, "A Spiritual Pilgrimage," *Christian Century* 56, no. 11 (March 11, 1939): 348–51.

8. *Discipline/MC/1940*, 773–80, ¶¶1715–17. The first resolution was carried over from the 1939 General Conference: *Discipline/MC/1939*, 697–98, which followed with a very short "Statement on Peace and War," 698–99.

9. On the very different Protestant attitudes toward the two world wars, see Sittser, *A Cautious Patriotism*. See also Ray Hamilton Abrams, *Preachers Present Arms: The Role of the American Churches and Clergy in the World Wars I and II, with Some Observations on the War in Vietnam* (Scottdale, Pa.: Herald Press, 1969), and Walter G. Muelder, *Methodism and Society in the Twentieth Century*, Methodism and Society series, vol. 2 (New York and Nashville: Abingdon Press,

1961). Two biographies by Robert Moats Miller provide interesting studies in the church's leadership on matters of war and peace: *Bishop G. Bromley Oxnam: Paladin of Liberal Protestantism* (Nashville: Abingdon Press, 1990), 216–96, and *How Shall They Hear without a Preacher? The Life of Ernest Fremont Tittle* (Chapel Hill: University of North Carolina Press, 1971), 434–76.

10. Muelder, *Methodism and Society in the Twentieth Century*, 183–84. Five thousand seven hundred Methodist students in eighty colleges and universities from UCLA to Emory and from Texas Tech to Albion spoke their minds about war in *Motive* magazine's first nationwide poll, published in the April 1941 issue. Nine out of ten students in the country were opposed to the U.S. entering World War II, yet close to half of those voting believed it was more important to help England, even at the risk of war, than to concentrate on staying out of war. Nearly six out of ten were convinced the draft was a good thing. "Peace, the Draft, and Aiding England, Motive Poll No. 1," *Motive* 1, no. 3 (April 1941): 35.

11. "Peace War," Evangelical Church, *General Conference Proceedings*, 1942, 170–72.

12. L. O. Hartman, "While It Is Day," *ZH*, March 18, 1942, 248, cited by Sittser, *A Cautious Patriotism*, 4–5.

13. JGC/MC/1944, 733–34.

14. "Report of Committee on Social Justice and International Relations," United Brethren Church, *General Conference Journal*, 1945, 619.

15. Norma Kehrberg, *Love in Action: UMCOR: 50 Years of Service* (Nashville: Abingdon Press, 1989); Robert J. Harman, *From Missions to Mission: The History of Mission of The United Methodist Church, 1968–2000*, United Methodist Church History of Mission Series, vol. 5 (New York: GBGM, 2005), 155, 249–52.

16. The sixtieth anniversary of the Advance Program was celebrated in 2008. During the sixty years, Methodists gave more than 4 million Advance gifts, totaling more than $750 million for thousands of ministries in more than 100 countries. In a typical year, the Advance receives between $30 and $35 million for missions, with a number going much higher when catastrophic human-made or natural disasters occur.

17. George Houser, "A Year and a Day: Thoughts of an Unrepentant Non-registrant," *Motive* 2, no. 3 (Nov. 1941): 23–24. For a full study of Methodist nonviolent activists in this period, see David Scott Cooney, "A Consistent Witness of Conscience: Methodist Nonviolent Activists, 1940–1970," (PhD diss., Iliff School of Theology and the University of Denver, 2000).

18. Walter N. Vernon et al., *The Methodist Excitement in Texas: A History* (Dallas/Bridwell Library, SMU: Texas United Methodist Historical Society, 1984), 286–88.

19. See Miller, *Bishop G. Bromley Oxnam*, 216–96, 280–85; Sittser, *A Cautious Patriotism*, 234–40.

20. Elmer T. Clark and Dorothy McConnell, eds., *World Outlook* 34, no. 1 (Jan. 1944): 6.

21. Linda Gesling, *Mirror and Beacon: The History of Mission of The Methodist Church, 1939–1968*, United Methodist Church History of Mission Series, vol. 3 (New York: GBGM, 2005), 415n40, 138–39; Sittser, *A Cautious Patriotism*, 246–47.

22. See Lester E. Suzuki, "Persecution, Alienation, and Resurrection: History of Japanese Methodist Churches," in *Churches Aflame: Asian Americans and United Methodism*, ed. Artemio R. Guillermo (Nashville: Abingdon Press, 1991), 113–34, esp. 128–29. For the full story see also Suzuki's *Ministry in the Assembly and Relocation Centers of World War II* (Berkeley, Calif.: Yardbird

Publishing, 1979), and Daisuki Kitagawa, *Isei and Nisei: The Internment Years* (New York: Seabury Press, 1967).

23. Gesling, *Mirror and Beacon*, 79–81.

24. E. Stanley Jones, "Barbed-Wire Christians," *Christian Century* 40, no. 47 (Nov. 24, 1943): 1364–65. See also Kazuyoshi Kawata, "Japanese Americans in World War II—A Nisei Remembers," *New World Outlook* 42, no. 5 (Jan. 1982): 19–21.

25. For the Methodist Youth Fellowship, see J. Warren Smith, "Youth Ministry in American Methodism's Mission," *MethH* 19, no. 4 (July 1981): 224–30. For the larger context, see Jon Pahl, *Youth Ministry in Modern America, 1930 to the Present* (Peabody, Mass.: Hendrickson Publishers, 2000).

26. Gesling, *Mirror and Beacon*, 132–37.

27. "Statement on Atomic Power Authorized by Executive Committee, Methodist Federation for Social Service," Sept. 18, 1945, MFSA Papers, 1945, United Methodist Archives, Drew University, Madison, New Jersey; Roy L. Smith, "Military Mathematics Must Be Revised: An Editorial," CA (Chicago), Nov. 27, 1945, 3; "We Have Sinned: The Use of the Atomic Bomb," *Motive* 6 (Oct. 1945); 10, no. 2 (Nov. 1949): 36.

28. "The Christian Conscience and Weapons of Mass Destruction: Report of a Commission Appointed by the Federal Council of Churches of Christ in America," *Christian Century* 67, no. 50 (Dec. 13, 1950): 1489–91.

29. These are discussed as created or re-created by the 1940 Uniting Conference.

30. Nolan B. Harmon, *The Organization of The Methodist Church*, 2nd rev. ed. (Nashville: Methodist Publishing House, 1962), 74–75, 91. Roy Hunter Short, writing a decade and a half later, provided little more on the COB. See his *Chosen to Be Consecrated: The Bishops of The Methodist Church, 1784–1968* (Lake Junaluska: Commission on Archives and History for the Council of Bishops, 1976).

31. *Discipline/MC/1940*, 96, ¶325.

32. Miller, *Bishop G. Bromley Oxnam*, 206–15.

33. James K. Mathews and William B. Oden, eds., *Vision and Supervision: A Sourcebook of Significant Documents of the Council of Bishops of The United Methodist Church* (Nashville: Abingdon Press, 2003); Gerald F. Moede, "Bishops in the Methodist Tradition: Historical Perspectives," in *Episcopacy: Lutheran-United Methodist Dialogue* II, ed. Jack M. Tuell and Roger W. Fjeld (Minneapolis: Augsburg, 1991), 52–69; Gerald F. Moede, *The Office of Bishop in Methodism: Its History and Development* (Zurich, New York, and Nashville: Abingdon Press, 1964); James E. Kirby, *The Episcopacy in American Methodism* (Nashville: Abingdon Press/Kingswood Books, 2000); Thomas Edward Frank, *Polity, Practice, and the Mission of The United Methodist Church* (Nashville: Abingdon Press, 2006), 229–53; James K. Mathews, *Set Apart to Serve: The Meaning and Role of Episcopacy in the Wesleyan Tradition* (Nashville: Abingdon Press, 1985); Short, *Chosen to Be Consecrated*; Roy H. Short, *The Episcopal Leadership Role in United Methodism* (Nashville: Abingdon Press, 1985); Norman Woods Spellman, "The General Superintendency in American Methodism, 1784–1870" (PhD diss., Yale University, April 1961); and Part 4 of the study authorized by the 1960 General Conference and the Co-ordinating Council, authored by Murray H. Leiffer, *The Episcopacy in the Present Day* (Evanston: Bureau of Social and Religious Research, 1963).

34. On election of bishops from other connectional leadership positions, see Short, *Chosen to Be Consecrated*, 17–22.

35. See Frank, *Polity, Practice, and the Mission of The United Methodist Church*; Jack M. Tuell, *The Organization of The United Methodist Church* (Nashville: Abingdon Press, 2005); Harmon, *The Organization of The Methodist Church*, 45–49, 189–213. Short, *Chosen to Be Consecrated*. The discussion is also informed by historical notes, analyses of rulings, commentary on bishops' decisions, and records of recusals made by longtime Judicial Council member Sally Curtis AsKew.

36. *Discipline*/MEC/1840, 27.

37. The 1854 measure had been passed with a majority vote and was judged in 1870 to be of constitutional significance, therefore requiring both a two-thirds majority and concurrence of the annual conferences. The constitutional corrective action conveying such judicial review on the College of Bishops was achieved in 1874. See Peterson, *Revisions*, 38; and Harmon, *The Organization of The Methodist Church*, 189–213.

38. JGC/MEC/1876, 134.

39. JGC/MEC/1884, 74. The MEC body did not have the power of judicial review that the southern bishops possessed, the ability to "arrest" or challenge legislation as unconstitutional.

40. Bishops also contributed to the genre of commentaries on the *Discipline*, a literature that had a quasi-judicial character as the *Discipline* itself functioned as canon law. On the evolution of the *Discipline* from a guide to Christian living into canon law, see Charles W. Brockwell Jr., "Methodist Discipline: From Rule of Life to Canon Law," *Drew Gateway* 54 (Winter-Spring 1984): 1–24.

41. JGC/MECS/1866, 42.

42. (Nashville: Southern Methodist Publishing House, 1870). For one of its updatings, see, for instance, under the same title the nineteenth edition: "Originally prepared by Holland N. McTyeire, revised and enlarged by Collins Denny, 19th ed." (Nashville: Publishing House of the MECS, 1931). An older but different genre was the episcopal commentary on the *Discipline*. See Bishop Stephen M. Merrill's *A Digest of Methodist Law* (Cincinnati: Cranston & Stowe; New York: Phillips & Hunt, 1885; rev. ed., Cincinnati: Jennings & Graham; New York: Eaton & Mains, 1904). Despite its title, this volume did not embrace episcopal rulings or judicial committee decisions but was really a commentary on the *Discipline*.

43. See, for instance, the third edition, which was "published under a resolution adopted unanimously by the General Conference of 1916," 3rd ed. (New York and Cincinnati: Methodist Book Concern, 1918), xiii.

44. See *Reports of the Committee on Judiciary of the General Conference of The Methodist Episcopal Church with Rulings by the Board of Bishops compiled under the authority of the General Conference* by Arthur Benton Sanford (New York: Methodist Book Concern, 1924). In an "Introduction," Henry Wade Rogers, chair of the Committee on Judiciary (1908, 1912, 1916, 1920), complained: "The Committee on Judiciary has heretofore been seriously embarrassed in the discharge of its duties by not having ready access to the reports of the action of the Judiciary Committees of former years and of the action of General Conference relating thereto" (v).

45. "The Commission does feel bound, however, by certain essential and specific basal principles from which we do not feel free to depart.... The first of these principles is that we consider ourselves bound, with reference to the powers of the General Conference and Quadrennial Conferences, that no one of these Conferences shall be authorized to pass upon and determine the

constitutionality of its own acts. In the second place, we feel bound, as to the Jurisdictional Conferences, that they shall have their autonomy, legislating upon matters involved in their own jurisdictions. And in the third place, that the colored membership of the Methodist Episcopal Church, and of such Colored Churches as may elect to enter into the reorganization of American Methodism, are to be dealt with in such manner as shall make full recognition of race consciousness and at the same time offer them the most fraternal cooperation and brotherly assistance." *Unification*, 1:46.

46. The following discussion benefits immensely from and the authors express appreciation for access to various historical notes, analyses of rulings, commentary on bishops' decisions, and records of recusals made by longtime Judicial Council member Sally Curtis AsKew.

47. Five large volumes cover 1940 to 2000. The numbered decisions can also now be found on the UMC website, http://archives.umc.org/interior_judicial.asp?mid=263, and in each year's *General Minutes*.

48. Harmon, *Organization of The Methodist Church*, 5, 137. "The unwieldiness of present Annual Conferences in The Methodist Church has been much complained of. This is, of course, due to the doubling of conference membership in those conferences largely made up of former Methodist Episcopal or/and Methodist Episcopal Church, South units. The admission of one layman for every charge had the effect of doubling such bodies, and at once presented conference entertainment committees, and those in charge of conference program with a problem in housing, feeding, and organizing such largely increased bodies. The expense of entertaining each Annual Conference leaped accordingly, and as a consequence there has been a tendency to cut to a minimum the actual time of holding such conferences."

49. Vernon et al., *The Methodist Excitement in Texas*, 283–85.

50. For these figures we have used the first roll call vote rather than the opening call of the roll.

51. The Baltimore Conference had been split in 1857 into Baltimore and East Baltimore in consequence of having grown to 363 traveling preachers, the largest conference in Methodism, too large. Hence the division, but only one of many that Baltimore had experienced over the years.

52. Note, for instance, the size of the MPC conferences of Indiana and Ohio:

		Indiana	
Year	Clergy	Probationers	Laity
1937	51	5	36
1938	48	8	36
1939	56	12	50
		Ohio	
Year	Clergy	Probationers	Laity
1937	53	7	48
1938	58	7	50

Official Minutes, Indiana Annual Conference, MPC, 1937, 12; 1938, 13; 1939, 14. *Official Minutes*, Ohio Annual Conference, MPC, 1937, 8; 1938, 22.

53. The pattern in the Virginia (MECS) Conference was the following:

Year	Ministers	Laity
1936	251	115
1937	275	115
1938	247	94
1939	269	127

Virginia Conference Annual, MECS, 1936, 31; 1937, 28; 1938, 21; 1939, 23. *Virginia Conference Annual*, MC, 1939, 39–41; 1940, 32.

54. The 1939 MEC Conference had included laity (in anticipation of unification), and the numbers had been 170 clergy, 33 supply, and 41 laity. *Official Record and Year Book*, West Virginia Annual Conference, MEC, 1938, 17; 1939, 31. *Journal*, West Virginia Conference, MPC, 1936, 9–12. *Journal*, Western Virginia Conference, MECS, 1938, 25–26. *Official Record and Year Book*, West Virginia Annual Conference, MC, 1939, 368–69; 1940, 15.

55. West Virginia's experience did not typify that of conferences more remote from the swath across the country where the MEC and the MECS competed or where episcopal Methodism overlapped with MPC strongholds. Some conferences remained small. In the Northeastern Jurisdiction, in fact, only West Virginia and Baltimore were of this scale. New York East, Newark, Philadelphia, New Jersey, Central Pennsylvania, and Pittsburgh had ministerial membership of 200 or so. And two New England conferences, New Hampshire and Vermont, were under 100. In the Western Jurisdiction, Southern California had 285 ministers in effective relation, and California had 225, with other conferences, including the Japanese, Hawaiian, and Latin American being quite small. Still for all the prior MEC conferences, unification doubled their numbers and did so including people (the laity) whose membership was good only one year at a time. The East German, Eastern Swedish, and Puerto Rico Conferences were even smaller, each having about 20 effective ministers.

56. *Discipline/MC/1940*, 275–76, ¶865.

57. The following discussion draws upon Edwin H. Maynard, *Keeping Up with a Revolution: The Story of United Methodist Communications, 1940–1990* (Nashville: United Methodist Communications, 1990).

58. See *Discipline/MC/1940*, 350–51, for stipulations for staffing of the Board of Education and elsewhere for other boards.

59. Judge Nathan Newby (Pacific), *Daily Christian Advocate* (1939), May 4th: 181, 183–84.

60. "1) I feel there is grave danger of breaking our great American Methodism up into a lot of small groups, each Board will be a group, each Jurisdiction will be a group, and the large interests of the Church instead of coming into focus in the great United General Conference, will never come to focus at all, but will be in expression in these small groups.

"2) [T]he responsibility in most instances with these executive leaders is a responsibility in which they can commend themselves to the Church as a whole. A man who has not made an impression upon the Church as a whole as an effective leader for a Board ought not to be elected to that place.

"3) [W]e masses do elect the President of the United States . . . we ought to be able to pick out a man big enough to run a Methodist board. . . . [T]he Methodist Church, if it moves from election in its General Conference back to election in its board, is going in exactly the opposite direction from that in which political life in America is going.

"4) [Y]ou will open the door to the influence of smaller values upon the creating of these great offices." *Daily Christian Advocate* (1939), May 4th: 179, 181, 182.

61. See the seven volumes by Joseph Mitchell, *There Is an Election! Episcopal Elections in the Southeastern Jurisdiction of The United Methodist Church*, esp. the second (Troy, Ala.: Leader Press, 1980) and seventh (Privately published, 2004). The seventh, which offers a summary from 1944 to 2001, carries the subtitle: "1996, 2000 and 2001."

62. See *EWM*, 1:1290–1303, "Jurisdictional Organization" and "Jurisdictions."

63. Cited by Maynard, *Keeping Up with a Revolution*, 9.

64. *HAM*, 3:482–83.

65. Lynn Corbett, *What, Why, How: History, Organization, and Doctrines of the Southern Methodist Church* (Greenville, S.C.: Foundry Press, 1956), 3.

66. Grant S. Shockley, ed., *Heritage and Hope: The African American Presence in United Methodism* (Nashville: Abingdon Press, 1991); Donald E. Collins, *When the Church Bell Rang Racist: The Methodist Church and the Civil Rights Movement in Alabama* (Macon: Mercer University Press, 1998); Alice G. Knotts, *Fellowship of Love: Methodist Women Changing American Racial Attitudes, 1920–1968* (Nashville: Kingswood Books, 1996); James Thomas, *Methodism's Racial Dilemma: The Story of the Central Jurisdiction* (Nashville: Abingdon Press, 1992); Woodie W. White, *Our Time Under God Is Now: Reflections on Black Methodists for Church Renewal* (Nashville: Abingdon Press, 1993).

67. See Peter C. Murray, *Methodists and the Crucible of Race, 1930–1975* (Columbia and London: University of Missouri Press, 2004), and W. Astor Kirk, *Desegregation of the Methodist Church Polity: Reform Movements that Ended Radical Segregation* (Pittsburgh: Rose Dog Books, 2005).

68. Dona L. Irvin's *Unsung Heart of Black America: A Middle-Class Church at Midcentury* (Columbia: University of Missouri Press, 1992) gives voice to an uncelebrated multitude with biographical glimpses into the lives of forty members of the Downs Memorial UMC in the post–World War II San Francisco Bay area.

69. Shockley, *Heritage and Hope*, 131–37; Task Group on the History of the Central Jurisdiction Women's Organization, *To a Higher Glory: The Growth and Development of Black Women Organized for Mission in The Methodist Church, 1940–1968* (Cincinnati: Women's Division, Board of Global Ministries, UMC, 1978).

70. Between 1864 and 1939, twenty-five Black annual conferences were organized in The Methodist Episcopal Church. They were Delaware, Washington, Mississippi Mission, South Carolina, Tennessee, Texas, Central Alabama, Mississippi, Louisiana, North Carolina, Lexington, Florida, West Texas, Savannah, Little Rock, East Tennessee, Central Missouri, Upper Mississippi, Atlanta, Mobile, Okaneb, Lincoln, South Florida, Southwest, and Central West. From Albea Godbold, "Table of Methodist Annual Conferences (USA)," *MethH* 8 (Jan. 1969): 25–64, quoted in Shockley, *Heritage and Hope*, 310–11.

71. Task Group, *To a Higher Glory*, 14–18.

72. Ibid., 23–24.

73. There would be four presidents of the Central Jurisdiction WSCS: Margaret Bowen (New Orleans), 1940–48; Ruth Carter (New Orleans), 1948–60; Anita Fields (Kentucky), 1960–64; and Mary Drake (Tennessee), 1964–68. Ibid., 57.

74. Bethune-Cookman College, Daytona Beach, Florida, has been a UMC Heritage Landmark site since 1984.

75. Task Group, *To a Higher Glory* (Cincinnati:Women's Division of the Board of Global Ministries, UMC, [1980?]), 27.

76. Ibid., 27, 31–33, 42, 73. See also Clarence G. Newsome, "Mary McLeod Bethune and the Methodist Episcopal Church North: In but Out," in *This Far by Faith: Readings in African–American Women's Religious Biography*, ed. Judith Weisenfeld and Richard Newman (New York: Routledge, 1995), 124–39.

77. Short, *Chosen to Be Consecrated*, 17. Short notes that "almost all the editors of the *Southwestern Christian Advocate*, and its successor, the *Central Christian Advocate* . . . have been elected bishops."

78. Shockley, *Heritage and Hope*, 117–72. This really is the motif of *Methodism's Racial Dilemma* by Bishop Thomas.

79. Gesling, *Mirror and Beacon*, 150.

80. *Report of the First National Methodist Student Leadership Training Conference, Berea, KY, 1939*, 99–100. GBHEM records, UMC Archives, Madison, New Jersey.

81. Task Group, *To a Higher Glory*, 80, 86.

82. Ibid., 73.

83. Ibid., 74. See also Knotts, *Fellowship of Love*, 111. Peggy Billings, one of five leaders of CSR/LCA profiled by Knotts, noted the courageous public stands in race relations taken by Mrs. Arrington, whose husband was lieutenant governor of Mississippi.

84. Helena Huntington Smith, "Mrs. Tilly's Crusade," *Collier's*, Dec. 30, 1950, 29, 66–67 (reprinted in the *Negro Digest* [July 1951]: 3–11); Dorothy Tilly, "The Fellowship of the Concerned," *Woman's Press*, Feb. 1950, 8–9, 19; Ruth H. Collins, "We Are the Inheritors," *Response*, July-Aug. 1971, 30–32.

85. *Methodist Woman* 14, nos. 1–12 (July-Aug. 1954): 43.

86. For the full story see Thomas J. Sugrue, *Sweet Land of Liberty: The Forgotten Struggle for Civil Rights in the North* (New York: Random House, 2008).

87. "Statement on Equal Rights [of racial, cultural, and religious groups] Adopted by the Council of Bishops, The Methodist Church, November 13, 1963, Detroit, Michigan," in *Messages of the Council of Bishops of The Methodist Church [and] The United Methodist Church During its First Forty years 1939-1979* (Washington, D.C.: Office of the Secretary of the Council of Bishops of the United Methodist Church, [1979]), 36–37.

88. Glenda Gilmore's indictment of the bankruptcy of moderate organizations, white clerics, and academics is powerful and profound in her book *Defying Dixie: The Radical Roots of Civil Rights* (New York: W. W. Norton, 2007).

89. "The Lawson Affair, 1960," in *Vanderbilt Divinity School: Education, Contest, Change*, ed. Dale A. Johnson (Nashville: Vanderbilt University Press, 2001), 131–77.

90. In press coverage "the school house door" was a tag line. The "door" was the entrance to the University of Alabama's Foster Auditorium in June 1963. Wallace first used the "Segregation now..." line in his inaugural address in Montgomery earlier that year, January 4, 1963.

91. W. J. Cunningham, *Agony at Galloway: One Church's Struggle with Social Change* (Jackson: University Press of Mississippi, 1980), 3, 5–6, 58–59, 61–62, 62–67.

92. Shockley, *Heritage and Hope*; Knotts, *Fellowship of Love*; Thomas, *Methodism's Racial Dilemma*; White, *Our Time Under God Is Now*.

93. See Murray, *Methodists and the Crucible of Race,* 116–38; and esp. Kirk, *Desegregation of the Methodist Church Polity,* 67–177. Kirk was secretary of the Committee of Five, and its work is the central concern of his narrative. He reproduces in text, notes, and appendices a huge array of documents or excerpts pertinent to the church's desegregation.

94. *Central Jurisdiction Speaks* (Washington, D.C.: Central Jurisdiction Study Committee, 1962), 4–5, 7, 11–14. James S. Thomas, clergy member of the South Carolina Conference (CJ) and chair of the Central Jurisdiction's Committee of Five created by the CJ in 1961 to make recommendations concerning integration, made many of the same points in his essay for the denomination's young people: "The Central Jurisdiction: Dilemma and Opportunity," *Motive* 24, no. 6 (March 1964): 17–21.

95. *Discipline*/MC/1964, ¶¶1813, 1824.

96. Ibid., ¶432.1.

97. Charles H. Lippy, "Towards an Inclusive Church: South Carolina Methodism and Race, 1972–1982," in *Rethinking Methodist History,* ed. Russell E. Richey and Kenneth E. Rowe (Nashville: Kingswood Books/Abingdon Press, 1985), 220–27.

98. Major J. Jones, "The Central Jurisdiction: Passive Resistance," in Shockley, *Heritage and Hope,* 189–207; Thomas, *Methodism's Racial Dilemma,* 84–147.

99. Noreen Dunn Tatum, *A Crown of Service* (Nashville: Parthenon Press, 1960), 396–97. See also Ruth Esther Meeker, *Six Decades of Service, 1880–1940, A History of the Woman's Home Missionary Society of the Methodist Episcopal Church* (Cincinnati: Steinhauser, 1969), 87.

100. Evelyn Riley Nicholson Papers, Garrett-Evangelical Theological Seminary Archives, Evanston, Illinois, reproduced and cited in Schmidt, *Grace Sufficient,* 285, 346.

101. Tatum, *Crown of Service,* 397; Meeker, *Six Decades,* 88.

102. The others were the Division of Foreign Missions, Division of Home Missions and Church Extension, and a joint Division on Education and Cultivation. See Thelma Stevens, *Legacy for the Future* (Cincinnati: Women's Division, Board of Global Ministry, UMC, 1978), 18–23.

103. *Woman's Missionary Friend* and *Woman's Home Missions* (MEC), *Missionary Record* (MPC), and *The Bulletin* (local church and community); also *Woman's Missionary Advocate* and *Our Homes* (former magazines of MECS; merged with *World Outlook* in 1910).

104. Stevens, *Legacy for the Future,* 18.

105. Gesling, *Mirror and Beacon,* 11–14.

106. Ibid., 111–22.

107. Knotts, *Fellowship of Love,* 18, 22–23.

108. Gesling, *Mirror and Beacon,* 284–88.

109. Theressa Hoover, *With Unveiled Face: Centennial Reflections on Women and Men in the Community of the Church* (New York: Women's Division, GBGM, UMC, 1983), 28–29, 26, 27, 30–31, 33, 40–44, 36–39.

110. *Journal of the Uniting Conference of the Methodist Episcopal Church, the Methodist Episcopal Church, South and the Methodist Protestant Church, Kansas City, Missouri, April 26-May 10, 1939* (Nashville and Chicago: Methodist Publishing House, 1939), May 10th: 382. See also Alice Knotts, "The Debates over Race and Women's Ordination in the 1939 Methodist Merger," *MethH* 29, no. 1 (Oct. 1990): 42–43.

111. "News of the World Parish," CA, May 24, 1956, 663.

112. *Discipline*/MC/1956, ¶303, 115.

113. *CA*, May 24, 1956, 663. The next issue (May 31, 1956) explained that the new legislation would open the way for "many of the church's 300 or so women ministers" to become members of annual conferences (694).

114. *Daily Christian Advocate*, May 7, 1956, 534.

115. Maud Keister Jensen, interview by Naomi Kooker, 1984, United Methodist Women's Oral History Project, General Commission on Archives and History, UMC. On the Korean Methodist Church, see J. S. Ryang, "How Two Methodisms Unite," *Missionary Voice*, Oct. 1931, 13–15, 50.

116. *Daily Christian Advocate*, June 14, 1956, 762.

117. James E. Will, "The Ordination of Women: The Development in the Church of the United Brethren in Christ," in *"Women's Rightful Place": Women in United Methodist History*, ed. Donald K. Gorrell (Dayton, Ohio: United Theological Seminary, 1980), 33; Behney/Eller, *History*, 360–61. Behney and Eller noted that there had been several "isolated instances" where women were ordained in the EUBC, but that they "neither provoked any recorded objections nor inspired any generally accepted practice."

118. Jonathan Cooney, "Maintaining the Tradition: Women Elders and the Ordination of Women in The Evangelical United Brethren Church," *MethH* 27:4 (Oct. 1988): 25–35. (In the EUBC there was just one order of ordained ministry, that of elder, in contrast with the two-step deacon-elder process of the Methodist tradition.)

119. *The Methodist Youth Fellowship: A Brief Description of the Youth Program of The Methodist Church* (Nashville: Youth Department, Division of the Local Church, Board of Education, MC, 1941). See also Hoover Rupert, *I Belong* (Nashville: Youth Department, Division of the Local Church, General Board of Education, MC, 1955).

120. J. Warren Smith, "Youth Ministry in American Methodism's Mission," *MethH* 19, no. 4 (July 1981): 224–30; *Celebrating 50 Years of Youth Ministry, 1941–1991: Commemorating the First National Conference of the Methodist Youth Fellowship, August 29–September 2, 1941* (n.p., 1991); Edgar Huffstutler, *The Youth Caravan Movement* (Dallas: Mission Communications, 1996). For larger context see Jon Pahl, *Youth Ministry in Modern America: 1930 to the Present* (Peabody, Mass.: Hendrickson, 2000). (Sources 1942b) mislabels the Metzger account as for the first national MYF conference.

121. See Frank Lloyd Dent, "*Motive* Magazine: Advocating the Arts and Empowering the Imagination in the Life of the Church" (PhD diss., Columbia University, 1989).

122. Robert C. Monk, "United Methodist Campus Ministry and the Methodist Student Movement," in *CEMI*, 179–202, 192.

123. The basic histories of the movement are Monk, "United Methodist Campus Ministry," and Raymond Norman Fedje, "The Wesley Foundation: A Selective History" (PhD diss., Boston University, 1964).

124. See Dent, "*Motive* Magazine."

125. This section draws extensively on Behney/Eller, *History*, 221–23, 277–81, 353–55, 357–92.

126. UBGC *Official Report*, 1917, 658, cited in Behney/Eller, *History*, 254.

127. Behney/Eller, *History*, 357.

128. Ibid., 357–92.

129. J. Steven O'Malley, "The Distinctive Witness of the Evangelical United Brethren Confession of Faith in Comparison with the Methodist Articles of Religion," in *DD*, 55–76.

130. O'Malley, "The Distinctive Witness of the Evangelical United Brethren Confession of Faith," 74–75.

131. "Methodists Retain Policy on Divorce … Attempt to Eliminate Word 'Wine' from Communion Ritual Is Defeated," *New York Times*, May 8, 1936, 24.

132. Methodist Episcopal Church, *The Book of Service, Orders of Worship: The Ritual of the Methodist Episcopal Church and Responsive Readings* (New York: Methodist Book Concern, 1932), 21.

133. *The Methodist Hymnal* (Nashville: The Methodist Publishing House, 1939), 530.

134. See www.saint-luke.org.

135. *The Methodist Hymnal* (Nashville: The Methodist Publishing House, 1966), 830.

136. *The Church Hymnal: The Official Hymnal of the Church of the United Brethren in Christ*, ed. Edmund S. Lorenz (Dayton, Ohio: United Brethren Publishing House, 1935), 418.

137. Ibid., 419, emphasis added.

138. Ibid., 418.

139. *The Hymnal of The Evangelical United Brethren Church* (Dayton, Ohio: Board of Publication of the EUBC, 1957), 16.

140. "Communion Is Important," *Telescope-Messenger*, Oct. 4, 1952, 3.

141. For a survey of developments from 1964 through 1976, see James F. White, "Church Architecture of Change," in his *Christian Worship in Transition* (Nashville: Abingdon Press, 1976), chap. 8, 143–55. See also White's "Church Architecture of the 1970s," *Liturgy* 20 (May 1975): 151–57, reprinted in *Faith and Form* 9 (Spring 1976): 8–11, 25–27, and "Disappearing Building Types," *Country Journal* 6 (Jan. 1979): 70–77.

142. For a full study, see Dale Woolston Dowling, "For God, For Family, For Country: Colonial Revival Church Buildings in the Cold War Era" (PhD diss., George Washington University, 2004).

143. Bonneau P. Murphy, *The Building and Care of United Methodist Churches*, rev. and enlarged (New York: National Division, Board of Missions, UMC, 1969). Murphy (1909–86) was a pioneer in the location, organization, and financing of new congregations, first for The Methodist Church and for the first few years of the UMC, during which time he helped found the United Methodist Development Fund. Officed in Philadelphia, he was a member of the Church Extension Section of the National Council of Churches and the Guild of Church Architecture and the author of several books and pamphlets.

144. "8 'Modern' Methodist Churches," *Together* 2, no. 2 (Feb. 1958): 35–42.

145. Massey H. Shepherd Jr., *Before the Holy Table: A Guide to the Celebration of the Holy Eucharist, Facing the People* (Greenwich, Conn.: Seabury Press, 1956).

146. "Church Architecture and Church Renewal," *CA*, Dec. 29, 1966, 7–9.

147. Norman G. Byar, "Trends in Methodist Church Architecture," *World Outlook*, Sept. 1961, 473–75.

148. Walter E. Wagoner, "Church Architecture: Five Distinctive Churches," *Together* 8, no. 10 (Nov. 1964): 30–42. See also Paige Carlin, "Bright New Church Architecture," *Together* 13, no. 5 (May 1969): 34–43.

149. James F. White and Susan J. White, *Church Architecture: Building and Renovating for Chris-*

tian Worship (Nashville: Abingdon Press, 1988). The Whites discuss the "needed space" for various liturgical celebrations written from an ecumenical perspective. See also his "Liturgy and the Language of Space," *Worship* 52 (Jan. 1978): 57–66; "Church Architecture as if People Mattered," *Christian Ministry* 9 (Nov. 1978): 23–25; "The Environment of Worship," in *New Forms of Worship* (Nashville: Abingdon Press, 1971), chap. 4, 80–99; "Why You Should Change Your Worship Setting," *Circuit Rider* 9 (July-Aug. 1985): 5–7; "Liturgical Space Forms Worship," *Reformed Liturgy and Music* 22 (Spring 1988): 59–60; "Know Your Needs before You Build," *Your Church* 35 (July-Aug. 1989): 12–14; and Susan J. White, "Creating Space for Holy Communion," in *Worship Matters*, vol. 2 (Nashville: Discipleship Resources, 1999), 85–92.

150. Mark Allen Torgerson, "Edward Anders Sövik and His Return to the 'Non-Church' " (PhD diss., University of Notre Dame, 1996).

151. Description based on detailed analysis by Torgerson.

152. Scott Thumma et al., *Megachurches Today* (Hartford, Conn.: Hartford Seminary, 2005), 4.

153. The basic work is Anne C. Loveland and Otis B. Wheeler, *From Meetinghouse to Megachurch: A Material and Cultural History* (Columbia: University of Missouri Press, 2003). Interviews with the congregational leaders of sixty-three U.S. megachurches and material gleaned from congregational newsletters shine new light on the meanings that congregations attach to these buildings and on the buildings' role in shaping contemporary evangelicalism. See also their summary in "Gimme That Big Box Religion," *Faith & Form* 38, no. 2 (2005), a special issue titled "God's McMansions" critiquing megachurches; Jeanne H. Kilde, "Reading Megachurches: Investigating the Religious and Cultural Work of Church Architecture," in *American Sanctuary*, ed. Louis P. Nelson (Bloomington: Indiana University Press, 2006), 225–49; Paul Goldberger, "The Gospel of Church Architecture," *New York Times*, April 20, 1995; and Gustav Niebuhr, "Where Religion Gets a Big Dose of Shopping-Mall Culture," *New York Times*, April 16, 1995.

154. Leonard Sweet offered ten commandments of architecture for the postmodern church in his "Church Architecture for the 21st Century," *Your Church*, March-April 1999.

155. JGC/MC/1952, 1408–9.

156. During the 1940s and 1950s, FBI surveillance of the MFSA is recorded in 5,000 pages of FBI files, now open to researchers in MFSA Archives, Drew University Library, Madison, New Jersey.

157. (St. Louis: John S. Swift Co. for the Methodist League against Communism, Fascism, and Unpatriotic Pacifism, 1936; reprint, Houston: University Press, 1950). Smith, a former Emory College faculty member, was pastor of several MECS, later Methodist, churches in Oklahoma.

158. *Reader's Digest*, Feb. 1950, 134–38. High was a Presbyterian layman who had graduated from Boston University School of Theology and who had been active in identifying Communists and persons with Communist leanings in mainline churches.

159. G. Bromley Oxnam, *The Reply the* Reader's Digest *Refused to Publish* (New York: Bishop's Office, [1950]).

160. Other conservative groups to find expression in the 1950s were the Committee for the Preservation of Methodism, One Methodist Voice, Volunteer Committee of Christian Laymen, Committee of Loyal American Methodists, The Protest Committee of Lay Methodists, Unofficial Methodist Opposition, and Bible Protestant Press, Inc.

161. The federation office was based in Oregon for eight years before returning to the New

York area, first for thirteen years in Lee and Mae Ball's home in Ardsley, New York, and then for twenty-five years out of George McClain's Staten Island home. Since 2000, the office has been two blocks from the U.S. Capitol in Washington.

162. *Discipline/MC/1952*, 391.

163. *Social Questions Bulletin*, March-April 1983, 1–2. The citation is from the FBI file on Harry F. Ward and the professional informant Louis Budenz. Harkness biographer Rosemary Skinner Keller surmises that it was because of her pacifism and opposition to World War II that Harkness was placed under surveillance by the FBI and accused of being a member of the Communist Party. Rosemary Skinner Keller, *Georgia Harkness: For Such a Time as This* (Nashville: Abingdon Press, 1992), 282–84.

164. Miller, *Bishop G. Bromley Oxnam*, 519–601.

165. Ibid.

166. Two of the observers published reflections: Franz Hildebrandt, *Rome Diary* (London: Epworth Press, 1965), and Albert Outler, *Methodist Observer in Rome* (Westminster, Md.: Newman Press, 1967).

167. Behney/Eller, *History*, 388–92.

168. Charles C. Parlin, *The Evangelical United Brethren and Methodism: Their Heritage and History*, an Elective Unit for Adults, with a Leader's Guide by Curtis Chambers (Nashville: Graded Press, 1965); Paige Carlin, "These Are the EUBs," *Together* 10, no. 10 (Oct. 1966): 31–45.

169. For a full history of EUBC missions, see J. Steven O'Malley, *On the Journey Home: The History of Missions of the Evangelical United Brethren 1946–1968* (New York: GBGM, UMC, 2003). For EUBC women in mission, see Audrie E. Reber, *Women United for Missions: A History of the Women's Society of World Service of The Evangelical United Brethren Church, 1946–1968* (Dayton, Ohio: Otterbein Press, 1969).

170. For EUBC, the primary text is Behney/Eller, *History*. See also Paul H. Eller, *These Evangelical United Brethren* (Dayton, Ohio: Otterbein Press, 1950).

171. On the autonomy movements, see Robert J. Harman, *From Missions to Mission: The History of Mission of The United Methodist Church, 1968–2000*, United Methodist Church History of Mission Series, vol. 5 (New York: GBGM, 2005), 21–24, 443–52, 459–65.

172. *Discipline/MC/1940*, ¶¶399–423, 432.

173. The progress of churches toward autonomy or into united churches can be followed in the H column, "British & World Methodism," in Rex Matthews, *Timetables of History for Students of Methodism* (Nashville: Abingdon Press, 2007).

174. *Discipline/MC/1940*, ¶¶424–30.

175. Harman, *From Missions to Mission*, 445–49.

176. Gesling, *Mirror and Beacon*, 270–77.

177. For context, see William R. Hutchison, *Errand to the World: American Protestant Thought and Foreign Missions* (Chicago: University of Chicago Press, 1987).

Snapshot III. Methodism in 1968: Denver

1. On Denver and Rocky Mountain Methodism see *The Methodist, Evangelical and United Brethren Churches in the Rockies, 1850–1976*, ed. J. Alton Templin, Allen D. Breck, and Martin Rist (n.p.: Rocky Mountain Conference, UMC, 1977).

2. Ibid., 90–95, 98–99, 116–19.

3. *Discipline*/MEC/1932, 311, ¶363.

4. See Norman G. Byar, "Trends in Methodist Church Architecture," *World Outlook*, Sept. 1961, 17–19.

5. See Sources, p. 29, for the schema of authorized Methodist hymnals.

6. By 1968, Warren's crosstown rival, Trinity, had seen a membership drop from 3,800 in the late 1950s to 1,637, some 750 of the membership loss coming after a drastic fire. Other downtown churches could put a less dramatic narrative around their losses. "All of the old downtown Methodist churches suffered as population shifted," noted Trinity's historian. Clearly worried about its prospects in the city, Trinity commissioned a study by consultants from Saint Paul School of Theology. Their sunny conclusion? "It is quite improbable that the downtown churches will ever re-establish themselves as great congregationally based preaching centers." More than 50 percent of the congregation, the consultants discovered, lived more than six miles from the church and close to 75 percent over four miles. A quarter of the membership was age sixty-five or over. "Half of the membership," they noted, "had moved their place of residence within the last five years." How long would Trinity members, how long would Warren members, continue to commute in, bypassing other churches on a Sunday morning, and how vigorous a program could the churches mount as congregations aged? The consultants for Trinity recommended that the church transmute itself into a social service center, a route taken by a sister Methodist congregation, Grace. See Church-Community Relations and Research, Saint Paul School of Theology Methodist, "Summary of Consultation Findings and Recommendations Prepared for Trinity Methodist Church" (1966–67), cited by Linda K. Kirby in *Heritage of Heroes: Trinity United Methodist Church, 1859–1988* (Denver: Trinity United Methodist Church, 1988), 239, 254. See also 242, 248, 253–54 on membership matters.

7. "Target: Denver," text by Paige Carlin, pictures by George P. Miller, *Together*, March 1969, 18–24. Used by permission of The United Methodist Publishing House.

8. Ibid., 19.

9. Ibid., 20.

10. Ibid., 20, 24.

11. Ezra Earl Jones and Robert L. Wilson, *What's Ahead for Old First Church* (New York: Harper & Row, 1974).

12. *Concern*, May 15, 1967, 25.

13. *1968 Year Book and Official Minutes*, Rocky Mountain Methodist Annual Conference, UMC, 108.

14. See the *Together* article, "Target: Denver," for a picture of Pastor Ed Beck of Warren Church showing DS Bill Byrd about the church's plans for Warren Village.

15. See the church's website; also *The Methodist, Evangelical and United Brethren Churches in the Rockies, 1850–1976*, 580–81.

16. *1968 Year Book and Official Minutes*, 52–53, 75–78.

17. Ibid., 89–91.

18. Ibid., 117–36.

19. Ibid., 40, 60.

20. This section appears, with minor adjustments, in "The United Methodist Church at 40:

Where Have We Come From?" *Methodist Review* 1 (2009): 27–56, and is used with permission. See http://www.methodistreview.org/index.php/mr.

21. See James W. Lewis, *The Protestant Experience in Gary, Indiana, 1906–1975: At Home in the City* (Knoxville: University of Tennessee Press, 1992). On mainline denominationalism, see Richey's article in the *Encyclopedia of Religion in America* (Washington, D.C.: CQ Press, 2010). and the "Bibliography of Scholarly Writing about Denominations," Hartford Institute for Religion Research website, http://fact.hartsem.edu/resources/index.html.

22. For pictures of such churches and particularly of one such Methodist church, see the 1950 *Christian Century* series "Great Churches of America," and specifically of First Methodist Church, Orlando, Florida, the fifth in a series of twelve, *Christian Century*, May 17, 1950, 608–14.

23. See, for instance, Mildred Morse McEwen, *First United Methodist Church, Charlotte, North Carolina* (Published by the church, 1983), and Herchel H. Sheets, *Methodism in North Georgia: A History of the North Georgia Conference* (Milledgeville, Ga.: Boyd Publishing Company for the Commission on Archives and History and the Bishop and Cabinet of the North Georgia Annual Conference, 2005), 322–38. For parallels in an urban Presbyterian congregation see James K. Wellman Jr., *The Gold Coast Church and the Ghetto: Christ and Culture in Mainline Protestantism* (Champaign: University of Illinois Press, 1999). For perspective on congregations, see James P. Wind and James W. Lewis, *American Congregations*, 2 vols. (Chicago: University of Chicago Press, 1994).

24. Joseph F. DiPaolo, "From Methodist Bookstore to Valley Forge Conference Office," *Annals of Eastern Pennsylvania*, 2007, 4:57–76.

25. *1968 Year Book and Official Minutes.* Compare Sheets, *Methodism in North Georgia.*

26. *The Methodist, Evangelical and United Brethren Churches in the Rockies, 1850–1976*, 596–600.

27. Excerpts from "Responding to God's Call for Faithful Living," a sermon by Pastor Eun-sang Lee, preached Jan. 26, 2003, Warren UMC's anniversary. Eun-sang Lee had earlier been a student pastor at Warren under the Reverend Paul Kottke and was appointed to Warren in 1997.

28. When given, statistics taken from the Colorado and Rocky Mountain conference journals for the year indicated.

29. The statistics for the following year were more in line with prior and following decade numbers, church membership 407, Sunday school membership 174.

XIV. Merging and Reappraising: 1968–84

1. "What Issues and Priorities Face Our New Church?" *Together* 12, no. 5 (May 1968): 30.

2. Woodie White, gen. ed., *Our Time under God Is Now: Reflections on Black Methodists for Church Renewal* (Nashville: Abingdon Press, 1993); *Findings of Black Methodists for Church Renewal* (BMCR, 1968).

3. Roy Nichols, "Address" to General Conference, *Daily Christian Advocate*, April 20, 1968, 197–99.

4. See Charles H. Lippy, "Towards an Inclusive Church: South Carolina Methodism and Race, 1972–1982," in *Rethinking Methodist History*, ed. Russell E. Richey and Kenneth E. Rowe (Nashville: Kingswood Books, 1985), 220–27.

5. "A Union . . . and Much More," *Together* 12, no. 7 (July 1968): 6.

6. James K. Mathews and William B. Oden, eds., *Vision and Supervision: A Sourcebook of Significant Documents of the Council of Bishops of The United Methodist Church, 1968–2002* (Nashville: Abingdon Press, 2003), 245–47.

7. James M. McGraw, "Practice What You Print," *Christianity and Crisis* 28, no. 7 (April 29, 1968): 87–92.

8. See *Progressive Christian* 181, no. 6 (Nov.-Dec. 2007) and its feature article, "Faith & Money."

9. Robert J. Harman, *From Missions to Mission: The History of Mission of The United Methodist Church, 1968–2000*, United Methodist Church History of Mission Series, vol. 5 (New York: GBGM, 2005), 10–11.

10. Timothy B. Tyson, *Blood Done Sign My Name* (New York: Three Rivers Press/Random House, 2004).

11. United Methodist Communications news release, March 6, 1974, UMC Archives.

12. Abel Tendekayi Muzorewa, *Rise Up and Walk: The Autobiography of Bishop Abel Muzorewa*, ed. Norman E. Thomas (Nashville: Abingdon Press, 1978); Dickson A. Mungazi, *In the Footsteps of the Masters: Desmond Tutu and Abel T. Muzorewa* (Westport, Conn.: Praeger, 2000).

13. *Resolutions/UMC/1976*, 59–60.

14. Edited by the Program Council (Nashville: The Methodist Publishing House, 1969).

15. Robert S. Ellwood, *The Sixties Spiritual Awakening: American Religion Moving from Modern to Postmodern* (New Brunswick, N.J.: Rutgers University Press, 1999), 175–76; Paul A. Crow Jr., "Still on Pilgrimage," *Christian Century* 116 (1999): 380–82; Michael Kinnamon, "Ecumenical Rebirth," *Christian Century* 117 (2000): 526–27; Jean Caffey Lyles, "Dealing with Rebels," *Christian Century* 117 (2000): 781.

16. *Discipline/UMC/1968*, ¶¶96, 97.

17. Robert McClean, "The Church Center for the United Nations," *Christian Social Action* 8, no. 9 (Oct. 1995): 31.

18. Ibid., 32.

19. *Discipline/UMC/1972*, ¶76; 1980, ¶75.

20. *Resolutions/UMC/1972*. After 1976, the church alphabetized the statements, giving up on prioritizing them.

21. *Discipline/UMC/1972*, ¶¶ 809, 818, 824–29, 148-62.

22. Albert C. Outler, "Introduction to the Report of the 1968–72 Theological Study Commission," in *Doctrine and Theology in The United Methodist Church*, ed. Thomas A. Langford (Nashville: Kingswood Books/Abingdon Press, 1991), 20–25. Reprinted from the *Daily Christian Advocate*, April 19, 1972, 218–22. The Langford volume provides extensive commentary on both the 1972 and the 1988 disciplinary statements and provides an entrée to the controversy that the first elicited and to which the second responded.

23. Outler, "Introduction," 20.

24. "Resolution of Intent—With a View to Unity," *Resolutions/UMC/2004*, 271–73 (adopted 1970, reaffirmed 2000).

25. *Discipline/UMC/1972*, 79, ¶70.

26. Ibid., 40, ¶68.

27. "The Junaluska Affirmation of Scriptural Christianity for United Methodists," *Good News*

9, no. 1 (Fall 1975): 22–28. The *UMR*, Aug. 1, 1975, printed the Affirmation in full (3). See also Sharon Mielke, "Evangelicals State Faith Position," in the same issue. The Affirmation is presented and interpreted by one of its framers, Paul A. Mickey, in a commentary, *Essentials of Wesleyan Theology* (Grand Rapids: Eerdmans, 1980).

28. James Heidinger, "The Problem of Pluralism," *Good News* 15, no. 6 (May-June 1982): 35–43; Robert G. Tuttle, "The Wesleyan Quadrilateral—Not an Equilateral," *Good News* 16, no. 6 (May-June 1983): 58–62; Jerry L. Walls, *The Problem of Pluralism: Recovering United Methodist Identity* (Wilmore, Ky.: Good News Books, 1986). For the full story see Riley Case, *Evangelical and Methodist: A Popular History* (Nashville: Abingdon Press, 2004).

29. *Discipline*/UMC/1972, 478, ¶1282.

30. Sarah Sloan Kreutziger, "Wesley's Legacy of Social Holiness: The Methodist Settlement Movement and American Social Reform," in *CEMI*, 137–75.

31. Jackson W. Carroll, Barbara Hargrove, and Adair T. Lummis, *Women of the Cloth* (San Francisco: Harper & Row, 1981), 6. See also Catherine Wessinger, ed., *Religious Institutions and Women's Leadership* (Columbia: University of South Carolina Press, 1996).

32. Anne Braude, ed., *Transforming the Faiths of Our Fathers* (New York: Palgrave Macmillan, 2004), 2.

33. "Report of Women's Division Highlights," *Journal of the First Annual Meeting of the Board of Missions of The United Methodist Church, January 2–13, 1969, including the Organizational Meeting, September 5–9, 1968* (New York: BOM, UMC, 1969), appendix D, 166.

34. Harman, *From Missions to Mission*, 17–20.

35. Linda Charton, *New York Times*, Aug. 27, 1970, 1.

36. UMC, Study Commission on the Participation of Women, *The Status and Role of Women in Program and Policy Making Channels of the UMC* (Dayton, Ohio: Study Commission, 1972), 21–24; Harman, *From Missions to Mission*, 18.

37. *UM Newscope*, Nov. 22, 1974, 2, and Dec. 6, 1974, 4.

38. Letty M. Russell, ed., *The Liberating Word: A Guide to Nonsexist Interpretation of the Bible* (Philadelphia: Westminster Press, 1976), 89, 120. For other examples of the passion that Christian women felt about sexism in the Bible, see the book by a longtime educator at United Methodist Drew Theological School, Nelle Morton's *The Journey Is Home* (Boston: Beacon Press, 1985).

39. See http://www.gcsrw.org/.

40. *Resolutions*/UMC/1976, 36, 125–26.

41. Carroll, Hargrove, and Lummis, *Women of the Cloth*, 7.

42. By the 1990s, *Candle* had become an ongoing column in *Good News* magazine.

43. Case, *Evangelical and Methodist*.

44. Carlyle Marney, "The Christian Community and the Homosexual," *Religion in Life* 35, no. 5 (Winter 1966): 760–73.

45. Allan Berube, *Coming Out under Fire: The History of Gay Men and Women in World War II* (New York: Free Press, 1990), 271; John D'Emilio, *Sexual Politics, Sexual Communities: The Making of a Homosexual Minority in the United States, 1940–1970*, 2nd ed. (Chicago: University of Chicago Press, 1998); Nicholas C. Edsall, *Toward Stonewall: Homosexuality and Society in the Modern Western World* (Charlottesville: University of Virginia Press, 2003); Jonathan Katz, *Gay Amer-*

ican History: Lesbians and Gay Men in the U.S.A.: A Documentary History, rev. ed. (New York: Meridian, 1992); Urvashi Vaid, *Virtual Equality: The Mainstreaming of Gay and Lesbian Liberation* (New York: Anchor Books, 1995).

46. Henry L. Minton, *Departing from Deviance: A History of Homosexual Rights and Emancipatory Science in America* (Chicago: University of Chicago Press, 2002); Jennifer Terry, *An American Obsession: Science, Medicine, and Homosexuality in Modern Society* (Chicago: University of Chicago Press, 1999).

47. D'Emilio, *Sexual Politics*; Edsall, *Toward Stonewall*; Katz, *Gay American History*; Vaid, *Virtual Equality*.

48. Heather Rachelle White, "From Sin to Sickness: Pastoral Counseling and the Sex Variant, 1946–1977," in her "Homosexuality, Gay Communities, and American Churches: A History of a Changing Religious Ethic, 1947–1977" (PhD diss., Princeton University, 2007).

49. See Williams's account in *I Am Alive! An Autobiography* (San Francisco: Harper & Row, 1980), and *No Hiding Place: Empowerment and Recovery for Our Troubled Communities* (San Francisco: Harper Collins, 1992).

50. Elizabeth A. Armstrong, *Forging Gay Identities: Organizing Sexuality in San Francisco, 1950–1994* (Chicago: University of Chicago Press, 2002); D'Emilio, *Sexual Politics*.

51. *UMR*, March 3, 1972.

52. Geyer is identified as principal drafter in *Methodists Make News*, Feb. 5, 1971, and CA, Feb. 18, 1971, 19.

53. "Report of the Social Principles Study Commission," *Engage* 4, no. 6 (March 1972): 18.

54. Affirmation, Leggett Collection, UMC Archives.

55. Allan R. Brockway, "A Struggle for the Faith of the Church," *Engage* 4 (June 1972): 37.

56. *Daily Christian Advocate*, April 25, 1972, 484; April 28, 1972, 707–9.

57. Ibid., April 28, 1972, 709.

58. *Discipline/UMC/1972*, ¶72, 86. For full debate on the committee report and the Hand amendment on April 26, 1972, see *Daily Christian Advocate*, April 28, 1972, 712–13.

59. *Daily Christian Advocate*, April 28, 1972, 712–13.

60. Ibid., 710.

61. Since 1972, official UMC statements about various matters of social justice and responsibility, including human sexuality, are contained in a statement of Social Principles that is published every four years following a General Conference. According to a preface that introduces these Social Principles, these are "intended to be instructive and persuasive" and to summon "all members of the United Methodist Church to a prayerful, studied dialogue of faith and practice." Only the General Conference, at present constituted of almost a thousand delegates—an equal number of lay and clergy—can speak officially for the denomination. This body determines the contents of the Social Principles and establishes policies and standards for the governance of the whole church.

62. *Daily Christian Advocate*, April 28, 1972, 710–11; Eleanor Blau, "Homosexual Marriages Opposed by Methodists: Conference Adopts Statement as Part of New Doctrine on Social Principles," *New York Times*, April 27, 1972; *Discipline/UMC/*, 1972, 85.

63. Charles Keysor, "He Sets the Prisoner Free," *Good News* 6, no. 4 (Summer 1973), 9. Alberts had recently performed one of the first documented Methodist "holy unions" of a same-sex

couple. " 'Gay Rites' Clergyman Called 'Ill,' " *UMR*, May 25, 1973, 1, and "Minister Ousted for 'Marrying' Two Men," *UMR*, June 29, 1973, 3.

64. "UMCYM Reaffirms Priorities," *Share* 5, no. 1 (Feb. 1974): 1. (*Share* was the official publication of the UMCYM at the time.) United Methodist News Service, Jan. 4, 1974; reprinted in full in *Good News* 7, no. 2 (Winter 1974): 79–80 under title "U.M. Youth Promote Homosexuality"; "Youth Agency Responds to 'Gay Caucus,' " *UMR*, Jan. 18, 1974, 2.

65. "Youth Council Approves Grants," *Methodists Make News*, March 8, 1974, 2; *Christian Century*, April 17, 1974, 416.

66. "Briefly Noted," *Christian Century*, April 17, 1974, 416.

67. "U.M. Council on Youth Ministry Meets and . . . ," *Share* 6, no. 1 (June [i.e., Jan.] 1975): 1–2; "Youth Focus on Homosexuality, Third World," *UMR*, Aug. 30, 1974, 3; "Youth Consider Wide Range of Issues," *Methodists Make News*, Aug. 30, 1974, 1.

68. "Youth Desire Dialogue," *Texas Methodist*, June 10, 1975.

69. "Youth Urge Human Sexuality Study," *Methodists Make News*, Jan. 10, 1975, 1.

70. "UMCYM Issues 'Sexuality Paper,' No Legislation on Homosexual Issue Now Planned by Council," *UMR*, Aug. 22, 1975, 1; "Call for Sexuality Study Reaffirmed," *Methodists Make News*, Aug. 29, 1975, 2; "Sexuality Study Call Reaffirmed," *United Methodist Highlights*, Sept. 1, 1975, 3.

71. "Gay Caucus Formed: Homosexual Ordination One Goal for 1976," *UM Newscope* 3, no. 4 (Jan. 24, 1975): 2; "Gay Church Meetings," *Christian Century* 92 (Sept. 17, 1975): 784. Gay caucuses had already been formed in several other U.S. mainline churches: Roman Catholic Church (Dignity) in 1969; Unitarian/Universalist in 1970; United Church of Christ in 1972; American Baptists in 1972; and Presbyterian Church USA (More Light) and the Episcopal Church (Integrity) in 1974. The National Association of Evangelicals formed a gay-friendly caucus (Evangelicals Concerned) in 1975.

72. *Daily Christian Advocate*, May 7, 1976, 783.

73. *UMR*, May 25, 1979.

74. *Affirmation Newsletter*, July 1979, 1.

75. George Vecsey, "Minister Sponsors Homosexual Rituals," *New York Times*, Nov. 27, 1977, 53. See also United Methodist News Service, June 26, 1978. Abels continued to bless same-gender unions until he took early retirement from the pastorate in June 1984. In 1982 Abels entered into a holy union with his life partner, Thom Hunt. Abels earlier served two churches in New Jersey and was director of the arts for the National Council of Churches. He was also an accomplished organist, pianist, and hymn composer.

76. "Homosexuality: A Re-examination" (E/SA Forum 60), *Engage/Social Action* 8, no. 3 (March 1980), a 56-page insert, also circulated separately for study groups.

77. Ibid., 27.

78. Charles Keysor, *What You Should Know about Homosexuality* (Grand Rapids: Zondervan, 1979).

79. "Charles Keysor Leaves UM Church," *Good News* 16, no. 1 (July-Aug. 1982): 46.

80. For a transcript of the debate see *Daily Christian Advocate* 5, 1980, part 2: *Daily Reports*, April 26, 1005–7, covering the Friday afternoon, April 25 session.

81. Ibid., 1007.

82. Decision No. 490, Oct. 31, 1980, in "Request of General Conference for a Ruling on the Constitutionality of a Study Document on Human Sexuality," *Digests of Decisions of the Judicial Council of The United Methodist Church, 1940–1999* (Nashville: UMPH, 1999), 209; *Decisions of the Judicial Council of The United Methodist Church, Nos. 301–609, 1968–1988* (Nashville: UMPH, 1988), 525–26.

83. George E. Koehler, *Guide to the Study Document on Human Sexuality* (Nashville: Discipleship Resources, 1983).

84. Julian Rush, *Julian Rush—Facing the Music: A Gay Methodist Minister's Story* (San Jose: Writers Club Press, 2001).

85. *UM Newscope*, May 28, 1982, 1; United Methodist News Service, May 28, 1982, 1; "Bishop Exonerated," *Christian Century*, June 23–30, 1982, 720.

86. "Colorado Congregation Raps Bishop; Wheatley Rejects Call to Step Down," *UMR*, Jan. 28, 1983, 1; "Denver Area Churches Threaten Withholding over Bishop's Stances," *UMR*, Jan. 12, 1983, 1.

87. *UM Newscope*, Nov. 5, 1982, 1.

88. "Reconciling Congregation Program," *Affirmation Newsletter*, Feb. 1984, 1; "Update: The Reconciling Congregation Program," *Affirmation Newsletter*, Oct. 1983, 5; Mary Gaddis, "Reconciling Program Flourishes," *Affirmation Newsletter*, June 1985, 6.

89. Commission on Religion and Race Report, JGC/UMC/1972, 1860–65.

90. Ibid., 1860.

91. Paul H. Hagiya, "Address to General Conference, April 20, 1970," *Daily Christian Advocate*, April 22, 1970, 101; Toge Fujihira, "Oriental Inclusion Act," *Interpreter* 17, no. 1 (Jan. 1973): 20.

92. *Oriental Methodists in America* (New York: Editorial Department, Joint Division of Education and Cultivation, Board of Missions and Church Extension, MC, [1947]).

93. "Report: Asian American United Methodists," JGC/UMC/1972, 1860–65.

94. Commission on Religion and Race Report, JGC/UMC/1972, 1863.

95. Fujihara, "Oriental Inclusion Act," 20.

96. See www.pactsnetwork.org.

97. Jonah Chang, "Movement of Self-Empowerment," in *Churches Aflame: Asian Americans and United Methodism*, ed. Artemio R. Guillermo (Nashville: Abingdon Press, 1991), 135–53.

98. Guillermo, *Churches Aflame*, 129–34.

99. *UM Newscope*, April 18, 1975, 3; *Engage/Social Action* 3, no. 6 (June 1975): 51–52.

100. Maxine M. Langston, "The National Federation of Asian-American United Methodists Are Beginning a National Venture," *Engage/Social Action* 23, no. 6 (June 1975): 49–53.

101. "A Golden People" (E/SA Forum 49), *Engage/Social Action* 7, no. 3 (March 1979): 9–56.

102. "A Golden People," *Ripe for Harvest: A Comprehensive Plan for Asian American Ministries* (San Francisco: National Federation of Asian American United Methodists, [1980]). For a snapshot of mid-1980s Asian American concerns, see also "Pacific and Asian Ministries" (E/SA Forum 92), *Engage/Social Action* 11, no. 4 (April 1983).

103. *Asian American News*, April 1984.

104. Wilbur W. Y. Choy, "Sermon for Opening Worship Service, Transcribed from Spoken Sermon," in Asian-American United Methodists, *Report of the 1983 National Convention of Asian-American United Methodists, April 5–9, 1983, Chevy Chase, Maryland*, ed. Peter Sun and Heran Choi (Bethesda, Md.: 1983 National Convocation Office, 1983), 54–57.

105. *Hymns from the Four Winds: A Collection of Asian American Hymns*, Supplemental Worship Resources 13 (Nashville: Abingdon Press, 1983).

106. *UM Hymnal*, 1989, #151, #552.

107. Justo L. Gonzales, ed., *Each in Our Own Tongue: A History of Hispanic United Methodism* (Nashville: Abingdon Press, 1991), 58–60; Alfredo Nanez, *History of the Rio Grande Conference* (Dallas: Bridwell Library, Southern Methodist University, 1980); *Apuntes commemorativos de 150 años de ministerio de la Conferencia del Rio Grande, 1853–2003* (Chihuahua, Mexico: Imprenta LEGZA, 2003).

108. Harman, *From Missions to Mission*, 53–57.

109. Gonzales, *Each in Our Own Tongue*, 34.

110. Harman, *From Missions to Mission*, 254.

111. "Report of Latin American Ethnic Committee," UMC, *Southern California-Arizona Conference Journal*, June 1968, 179–84. For the full story of LAMAG's organization, see José Moreno Fernandez, "The History and Prospects of Hispanic Methodism in the Southern California-Arizona Conference of the United Methodist Church" (PhD diss., School of Theology, Claremont, Calif., 1973), 143–48.

112. Hector Navas, a Florida Conference pastor, had cited a similar set of demands on behalf of Hispanic American Methodists during the presentation of the Commission on Religion and Race report a few days earlier: *Daily Christian Advocate*, April 22, 1970, 100–101.

113. Harman, *From Missions to Mission*, 12–13.

114. Roberto Escamilla, "Hispanic-American Churchmen Find Identity amidst Pluralism," CA 16, no. 6 (March 6, 1972): 11–12.

115. Josafat Curti, "Methodists Associated Representing Concerns of Hispanic Americans," JGC/UMC/1972, 363–65.

116. Gonzales, *Each in Our Own Tongue*, 152–59.

117. Robert L. Wilson, *The First Spanish United Methodist Church and the Young Lords* (New York: Department of Research and Survey, National Division of the Board of Missions, UMC, 1970); Dean M. Kelley, "The Young Lords and the Spanish Congregation: A Contest Between Revolution and Religious Liberty," *Christian Century*, Feb. 18, 1970, 208–11.

118. Roberto Escamilla was educated in a Methodist missionary school in Monterrey, Mexico, and came to the United States, where he continued his education in religion and philosophy at Iowa Wesleyan College and Perkins School of Theology at Southern Methodist University, from which he received the BD degree in 1955. Ordained the following year, he joined the Rio Grande Conference and served pastorates in Sherman, Dallas, San Antonio, and Austin, Texas, until 1964 when he joined the National Division of the Board of Missions in New York City.

119. For other mid-1970s snapshots of Hispanic concerns, see Michael Germinal Rivas, "The Church and Hispanic Americans," *New World Outlook* 68, no. 2 (Feb. 1978): 79–81; Finees Flores, "What Is Needed from the Denomination?" *Engage/Social Action* 6 (June 1978); Joel Martinez, "A Challenge for the Future," *Engage/Social Action* 6 (June 1978): 37–40.

120. Deloria's book remains a seminal work on Native American religious views, detailing a religious life that is independent from Christianity and that reveres the interconnectedness of all living things.

121. Vine Deloria, *Custer Died for Your Sins* (New York: Macmillan, 1969), 115.

122. Comments of Thomas Roughface, a presentation to the BOM, *Journal of the Third Annual Meeting of the Board of Missions of the UMC, October 21–30, 1970* (New York: BOM, UMC, 1970), appendix J, p. 91.

123. *Daily Christian Advocate*, April 22, 1970, 101.

124. *Oklahoma Indian Mission Conference Journal*, UMC, 1971, 42–54.

125. Homer Noley, *First White Frost: Native Americans and United Methodism* (Nashville: Abingdon Press, 1991), 225–26.

126. Harman, *From Missions to Mission*, 14.

127. Homer Noley, "Indian Missions: A Perspective," *Interpreter* 19, no. 2 (Feb. 1975): 8–10.

128. Homer Noley and Raymond Baines, "The American Indian within The United Methodist Church," quoted in *One in the Lord: A History of Ethnic Minorities in the South Central Jurisdiction of the United Methodist Church*, by Walter Vernon, Alfredo Nanez, and John H. Graham (Oklahoma City: Commission on Archives and History, South Central Jurisdiction, UMC, 1977), 41. See also Noley, "Indian Missions: A Perspective."

129. "Church Role Said Vital at Wounded Knee," *UMR*, May 25, 1973, 1. For a full account see John P. Adams, *At the Heart of the Whirlwind* (New York: Harper & Row, 1976), chap. 11, 100–113.

130. Quoted in Noley, *First White Frost*, 225.

131. Harman, *From Missions to Mission*, 252–58.

132. "Comity Agreements Affecting Development of Native American Ministries by The United Methodist Church," *Resolutions/UMC/1980*, 69–70. In 1984 this statement was made as a part of the responsibilities of GBGM. *Discipline/UMC/1984*, ¶1403.

133. The resolution was revised and expanded by General Conference of 2000. Compare *Resolutions/UMC/1980*, 206–10; and 2004, 375–79.

134. Edwin H. Maynard, *Keeping Up with a Revolution: The Story of United Methodist Communications 1940–1990* (Nashville: United Methodist Communications, 1990), 129.

135. Lee Ranck, *The Methodist Church and Problems of Medical Care* (Washington, D.C.: General Board of Christian Social Concerns, 1962); special issue on medical care, *Concern*, Jan. 15, 1962, 1–20.

136. *Discipline/MC/1964*, ¶1820, 661–62.

137. Robert Hermann, "The Age of Medicare Ahead," *Concern*, Jan. 1–15, 1965, 4–8.

138. *Journal*, North Georgia Conference, MC, 1966, 124.

139. "Update on Pacific Homes Trial," *UM Newscope*, July 18, 1980, 2.

140. A paid advertisement in the Nov. 23, 1979, *Wall Street Journal* carrying the names of 35 church women and men took issue with the reporter's unwarranted association of the UMC with con-man schemes, physical crimes, rip-offs, and criminally fraudulent practices. UMC news release, Nov. 26, 1979.

141. By century's end Pacific Homes was maintaining five homes in California. Five members of its board of directors are elected by the California-Pacific Conference of the UMC. Under terms of the final settlement, the Desert Southwest Conference received $2.6 million, the California-Pacific Conference nearly $9.1 million, and GCFA $4.7 million.

142. *Resolutions/UMC/1976*, 56–57.

143. *Resolutions/UMC/1988*, 138-51; *Resolutions/UMC/1996*, 165–76.

144. *Resolutions*/UMC/1992, 641–44.

145. *Resolutions*/UMC/1996, 199–200.

146. *Discipline*/UMC/1968, 54, 63.

147. *Discipline*/UMC/1971, 85–86.

148. C. Dale White, "If Your Pastor Gets a Divorce," *United Methodists Today*, April 1975, 25, and M. Lawrence Snow, "Grace for Divorce," *United Methodists Today*, March 1975, 76–80.

149. The Minnesota Conference was among the first; see "Clergy Divorce Guidelines Adopted," *UMR*, June 24, 1966.

150. William C. Henzlik, "Divorce and the Appointive System," Today's Ministry Section, *United Methodists Today*, March 1975, 72–75.

151. "U.M. Survey Shows Clergy Divorce Still Sensitive Issue with Church" and "Divorced Clergy Staying in Ministry," *UMR*, Aug. 13, 1976, 1.

152. Douglass W. Gilbert, "A Broken Vessel and God's Grace," and Paul D. Lowder, "The Forgivable Sin: Clergy Divorce," *Circuit Rider*, Feb. 1979, 6–9.

153. "Divorce Rituals Proposed in New Church Resource," *UM Newscope*, Oct. 8, 1976, 4. The Reverend Jeanne Audrey Powers chaired the task force and wrote the chapter on divorce.

154. *Discipline*/UMC/1976, 89, ¶71.

155. William H. Willimon, "The Risk of Divorce," *Christian Century*, June 20–27, 1979, 669.

156. *Discipline*/UMC/1980, 89–90, ¶71.

157. C. Dale White, "The Bishops Address Clergy Divorce," *Circuit Rider*, June 1979, 19–20.

158. *Discipline*/UMC/1972, ¶ 72, 86–87.

159. *Abortion: A Human Choice* (Washington, D.C.: Division of Welfare and Department of Population Problems, Board of Christian Social Concerns, UMC, 1971).

160. See www.tourolaw.edu/patch/roe.

161. *Options* (Religious Coalition for Abortion Rights newsletter), May 1975, 5.

162. Case, *Evangelical and Methodist*, 25–29; Pilkington/Vernon, *Methodist Publishing House*, 2:431–35, 483–84.

163. Quoted by Case, *Evangelical and Methodist*, 30.

164. Case, *Evangelical and Methodist*, 42.

165. *Good News*, Jan.-March 1970, 32.

166. Case, *Evangelical and Methodist*, 45–49.

167. Ed Robb, "The Crisis of Theological Education in The United Methodist Church," *Good News* 9, no. 1 (Fall 1975): 32–40; Albert C. Outler, "Attack on Seminaries Answered," *UMR*, Aug. 15, 1975, 2. The *UMR* staff headlined their article "Seminaries: Proposals for Reform Given," *UMR*, Aug. 1, 1975, 3.

168. *Case, Evangelical and Methodist*, 109–33; quotation from 115. For a very different take on these developments see Leon Howell, *United Methodism @ Risk: A Wake-Up Call*, with a study guide by Bishop C. Dale White and the Reverend Scott Campbell (Kingston, N.Y.: Information Project for United Methodists, 2003). See also Steve Tipton, *Public Pulpits* (Chicago: University of Chicago Press, 2007).

169. (Nashville: Abingdon Press, 1983).

170. Case, *Evangelical and Methodist*, 95–108, 121–25.

171. See www.aldersgaterenewal.org/background/aboutus.

172. John Dart, "Charismatic and Mainline," *Christian Century*, March 7, 2006, 24.

173. Mary Jacobs, "A Spiritual Walk," *UMR*, Nov. 30, 2007, 1, 3A.

174. UMC, General Council on Ministries, *Guidelines for Eliminating Racism, Ageism, and Sexism from United Methodist Resource Materials* (Dayton, Ohio: GCOM, 1979).

175. *Guidelines for Eliminating Racism, Ageism, Handicappism and Sexism from United Methodist Resource Materials* (Dayton, Ohio: GCOM, 1983).

XV. Holding Fast/Pressing On: 1984–2000

1. *Resolutions/UMC/1996*, 374.

2. *The Baltimore Declaration: A Call to Commitment and Action as United Methodists Move into Their Third Century* (Dayton, Ohio: GCOM, UMC, 1984).

3. *Discipline/UMC/1992*, ¶ 202.

4. A portion of this paragraph appears, with minor adjustments, in "The United Methodist Church at 40: Where Have We Come From?" *Methodist Review* 1 (2009): 27–56, and is used with permission; http://www.methodistreview.org/index.php/mr.

5. See James W. Lewis, *The Protestant Experience in Gary, Indiana, 1906–1975: At Home in the City* (Knoxville: University of Tennessee Press, 1992). On mainline denominationalism, see Richey's article in the *Encyclopedia of Religion in America* (Washington, D.C.: CQ Press, 2010), and the "Bibliography of Scholarly Writing about Denominations," Hartford Institute for Religion Research website, http://fact.hartsem.edu/resources/index.html.

6. Charles Yrigoyen Jr., John G. McEllhenney, and Kenneth E. Rowe, *United Methodism at Forty* (Nashville: Abingdon Press, 2008), 40, statistics derived from the General Minutes.

7. "The denomination needs a new social action agency to speak out against 'moral evils' currently not addressed by the UM's General Board of Church and Society." That proposal was made by some six hundred participants attending the July 1984 Good News convocation in Granville, Ohio. "Scriptural holiness no longer includes moral social issues," said Donald Wildmon, head of a television monitoring group based in Tupelo, Mississippi. He criticized GBCS, the Council of Bishops, and other general agencies for their "silence on moral issues" such as gambling, pornography, child abuse, drug and alcohol abuse, and antireligious sentiments. He suggested an alternate social action agency to address those ills. GBCS head Haviland C. Houston told *Newscope* editors those issues had been discussed in special issues of the board's magazine, *Engage/Social Action*, and said he would be happy to meet with Wildmon and other Good News leaders "to bring them up to date in those areas." *UM Newscope*, July 20, 1984, 2. For that perspective, historically rendered, see James V. Heidinger II and Steve Beard, eds., *Streams of Renewal: Welcoming New Life into United Methodism* (Wilmore, Ky.: Living Streams Publications, 2004), and Riley Case, *Evangelical and Methodist: A Popular History* (Nashville: Abingdon Press, 2004).

8. Case, *Evangelical and Methodist*, 225–30, 239–43.

9. *DCA/UMC/1984*, 412, 613–14. On the import of the committee's work, see Thomas A. Langford, ed., *Doctrine and Theology in The United Methodist Church* (Nashville: Kingswood Books/Abingdon Press, 1991), and esp. Richard P. Heitzenrater's chapter, "In Search of Continuity and Consensus: The Road to the 1988 Doctrinal Statement," 93–108.

10. Heitzenrater, "In Search of Continuity and Consensus," 95.

11. "The New Doctrinal Statement: A First Draft Proposal," *Circuit Rider* 11, no. 2 (Feb. 1987): 9–15.

12. Case, *Evangelical and Methodist*, 239–47.

13. "Perfect Love Casts Out Fear," unpaid advertisement, *Circuit Rider* 12, no. 3 (April 1988): 18.

14. Case, *Evangelical and Methodist*, 249–50.

15. For the full story, see Heitzenrater, "In Search of Continuity and Consensus," 93–108.

16. See chapters "Itinerant General Superintendency" and "Episcopacy" in *Doctrine Out of Methodist History: Theologizing about Church and Ministry* (Nashville: Kingswood Books/Abingdon Press, 2009).

17. See Robert Moats Miller, *Bishop G. Bromley Oxnam: Paladin of Liberal Protestantism* (Nashville: Abingdon Press, 1990), 206–15. For a short history of the COB and its exercise of authority, see Bishop William B. Oden's presidential address in the collection of COB documents edited by James K. Mathews and William B. Oden, *Vision and Supervision: A Sourcebook of Significant Documents of the Council of Bishops of The United Methodist Church, 1968–2002* (Nashville: Abingdon Press, 2003), 557–69.

18. See the collection thereof edited by Mathews and Oden, *Vision and Supervision*.

19. *Baptism, Eucharist and Ministry*, Faith and Order Paper no. 111 (Geneva: WCC, 1982), abbreviated BEM. Copyright 1982 World Council of Churches, ISBN 2-8254-0709-7, thirtieth printing, 1996; www.wcc-coe.org/wcc/what/faith/bem5.html. Not to be reproduced mechanically or electronically for commercial purposes or with changes in the text without prior permission. The reference is to the paragraph number of the section, Baptism #, Eucharist #, or Ministry #, which should guide the reader to the appropriate place whether in the printed or electronic version.

20. (Nashville: Abingdon Press, 1986).

21. *UMR*, Feb. 3, 2006, 4A.

22. J. Ellsworth Kalas and Justo Gonzales, *Christian Believer: Knowing God with Heart and Mind* (Nashville: Abingdon Press, 1999). Kit includes 2 videodisks and leaders' and participants' books.

23. UMC, Council of Bishops, *In Defense of Creation: The Nuclear Crisis and a Just Peace* (Nashville: Graded Press, 1986).

24. UMC, Council of Bishops, *Vital Congregations, Faithful Disciples: Vision for the Church* (Nashville: Graded Press, 1990).

25. Mathews and Oden, *Vision and Supervision*, 78–81.

26. Portions of the many initiatives, along with various internal and public statements expressive of the Council of Bishops' teaching office, are gathered in Mathews and Oden, *Vision and Supervision*.

27. In addition to several committees that now guide the council, the bishops draw on the theological expertise of one general agency, the General Commission on Christian Unity and Interreligious Concerns. For illustration of how the bishops have used that expertise, see John Deschner, "United Methodism's Basic Ecumenical Policy," in *Perspectives*, 448–59, and in *Ecumenical and Interreligious Perspectives: Globalization in Theological Education* (Nashville: QR Books, 1992), 45–57.

28. Marvin Abram, "Chairperson's Report, NAIC Annual Meeting, Oklahoma City, 1985,"

United Methodist Archives; see also Abrams's "Native Americans Seek Self-Determination in the Church," *Response* 17, no. 5 (June 1985): 24–27.

29. *Resolutions/UMC/1988*, 176–77.

30. *Resolutions/UMC/1992*, 349–50.

31. *Voices: Native American Hymns and Worship Resources* (Nashville: Discipleship Resources, 1992).

32. *Resolutions/UMC/1992*, 386–92, 210–11, 349–50.

33. (Nashville: Graded Press, 1996).

34. *Resolutions/UMC/1996*, 395–97, 207–18; *Resolutions/UMC/2000*, 331–32, 333–34; *Resolutions/UMC/2004*, 359–60; readopted 2004.

35. A resolution adopted by the 2004 General Conference recommended replacing the term *ethnic minority* with *ethnic person* in all future UMC *Disciplines* and discourse as a nomenclature for ethnic people or groups. *Resolutions/UMC/2004*, 213.

36. *Resolutions/UMC/1988*, 176–77.

37. Ibid., 136–38, 184–90, 322–23.

38. *Resolutions/UMC/1996*, 568–69, 542–49, 549–51.

39. *Resolutions/UMC/2000*, 300–301; *Resolutions/UMC/2004*, 340–41.

40. *UMR*, Aug. 15, 1986, 1.

41. UM News Service, Dec. 18, 1986.

42. *UMR*, Sept. 4, 1987.

43. The historical development of Asian American Methodism is based in part on Artemio R. Guillermo, ed., *Churches Aflame: Asian Americans and United Methodism* (Nashville: Abingdon Press, 1991).

44. UMC General Board of Global Ministries, *Manual on Shared Facilities*, ed. James A. Craig (New York: The Board, 1996).

45. "UMs Offer Opposing Views of Abortion," *UM Newscope*, Jan. 27, 1989, 1.

46. *Discipline/UMC/1988*, 96, ¶71g.

47. For proceedings that led to the the the Durham Declaration and further theological reflections by Ruth Brown, Michael J. Gorman, Stanley Hauerwas, and William Willimon, see *The Church & Abortion: In Search of New Ground for Response*, ed. Paul T. Stallsworth (Nashville: Abingdon Press, 1993).

48. Much of this material was gleaned from a UM News Service release, "United Methodists Agreed More on Abortion Issue 25 Years Ago," by Jorette Purdue, Jan. 21, 1998.

49. *Discipline/UMC/2000*, 102, ¶161j.

50. *Discipline/UMC/1984*, 189, ¶402.2.

51. "Conferences Said to Control 'Gay' Clergy," *UMR*, April 3, 1987.

52. "Reconciling Congregation Program Changes Name," press release, Oct. 30, 2000. For a full study of the Reconciling Congregation Program/Reconciling Ministries Network, see Karen P. Oliveto, "Movements of Reform and Movements of Resistance: Homosexuality and The United Methodist Church, a Case Study" (PhD diss., Drew University, 2002), chap. 4, 104–30. In 2008 RMN reported 243 congregations, 30 campus ministries, 62 reconciling communities, and more than 18,000 individuals.

53. "Houston Declaration," six-panel folder, 1987, United Methodist Archives; "*Discipline's*

Principles Upheld in Houston," *Good News* 21, no. 4 (Jan.-Feb. 1988): 39–40; Bruce Buursma, "Methodist Group Stands by Tradition," *Chicago Tribune*, Jan. 8, 1988; Case, *Evangelical and Methodist*, 246–48, 253–54.

54. Glen Larum, "Houston Declaration Gets 'Booster Rocket,' " *UMR*, March 4, 1988, 3. "The Houston Declaration Impact Felt," *Good News* 21, no. 6 (May–June 1988): 20.

55. "Perfect Love Casts Out Fear," unpaid advertisement, *Circuit Rider* 12, no. 3 (April 1988): 18; "Houston Declaration Draws Stinging Rebuttal," *UMR*, March 19, 1988, 1; "Pastors Oppose Houston Declaration," *UM Newscope* 16, no. 10 (March 4, 1988): 1–2; Theodore W. Jennings Jr., "The Houston Declaration Is Heretical," *Christian Century*, April 20, 1988, 399–401.

56. Earl G. Hunt, "[Presidential Address], November 17, 1987," in Mathews and Oden, *Vision and Supervision*, 526–31, emphasis added; "Bishops Back UMC Moral Standards," *Good News* 21, no. 4 (Jan.-Feb. 1988): 41–42. Mathews and Oden do not include that particular collective bishops' statement.

57. Emily Yoffe, "The Double Life of Finis Crutchfield," *Texas Monthly* 15, no. 10 (Oct. 1987): 102–6, 188–90, 192–200; "Story Chronicles Bishop's Lifestyle, 'Secret Existence' " *UMR*, Oct. 9, 1987; James Heidinger, "Bishop Crutchfield, AIDS and Methodism: The Bishop's Tragic Death Shows Why the Church Must Stand Firm," *Good News* 21, no. 1 (July-Aug. 1987): 5–6; "Obituary of Retired United Methodist Church Bishop," *Houston Chronicle*, May 30, 1987.

58. *Discipline*/UMC/1988, 96.

59. *Blair Blurbs* (newsletter of UM Gay Caucus) 1, no. 2 (Winter 1976): 7.

60. *Discipline*/UMC/1988, 95.

61. *Resolutions*/UMC/1988, 101–6, 108–9. General Conference added further resolutions on AIDS in 1996, 2000, and 2004.

62. Bishop Fritz Mutti and his wife, Etta, would later write a book about how their family faced living with HIV/AIDS. Fritz Mutti and Etta Mae Mutti, *Dancing in a Wheelchair: One Family Faces HIV/AIDS* (Nashville: Abingdon Press, 2001).

63. Frank York, "Is Homosexuality a Curable Illness?" *Good News*, Sept.-Oct. 1989, 32.

64. Case, *Evangelical and Methodist*, 224, 235, 261. For a full study of the Transforming Congregation Program, see Oliveto, "Movements of Reform and Movements of Resistance," chap. 5, 131–57.

65. For the full report as delivered to General Conference, see *Daily Christian Advocate*, 1992 (Advance Edition), 1:265–86.

66. Dorothy L. Williams, ed., *The Church Studies Homosexuality* (Nashville: Cokesbury, 1994), 35. Includes the full text of the Report of the Committee to Study Homosexuality.

67. "Fifteen Bishops Express 'Pain' Over Church Polity on Gay, Lesbian Issues," *UMNS* April 18, 1996, and *United Methodist Daily News*, Release 010, April 18, 1996, on http://archives.gcah.org/GC96/NEWS/tbishops.html. For the COB's rejoinder to the statement by fifteen of its members, see the *Daily Christian Advocate*, April 23, 1996, or the UMDN release #034 for that day at http://archives.gcah.org/GC96/NEWS/tbishop.html.

68. *Discipline*/UMC/1996, 87, ¶65g. For a full study of the mind of Methodism on homosexuality at the 1996 General Conference, see James Rutland Wood, *Where the Spirit Leads: The Evolving Views of United Methodists on Homosexuality* (Nashville: Abingdon Press, 2000).

69. "Social Principles," *Discipline*/UMC/1972, 85, ¶72, section IIB. In 1976, this statement was amended to read: "We do not recognize a relationship or agreement between two persons of the same sex as constituting marriage." "Social Principles," *Discipline*/UMC/1976, 87, ¶65g.

70. Kay Longcope, "Minister [William Alberts] Marries Gays Over Bishop's Objection," *Boston Sunday Globe* (April 8, 1973), 5, with photo. Assisting in the wedding were the Rev. and Mrs. Dennis Hett, the congregation's resident ministerial interns. "Minister, Bishop Disagree on Wedding for Homosexual Men," *United Methodist Newscope*, April 27, 1973, 1; "Boston Pastor Reprimanded," *Christian Century*, May 9, 1973, 528. For Abels, see chapter 14.

71. "An Understanding of Lesbian/Gay Holy Unions," *Mid-Atlantic Affirmation News*, May 1990, 203; *Christian Century*, June 27–July 4, 1990, 626–27.

72. "Statement of Conscience" and "In All Things Charity," Jan. 1, 1997, mailing, Affirmation Archives, UMC Archives; "Group of UM Clergy Call for Statement of Conscience," UM News Service, Jan. 6, 1996.

73. See www.umaffirm.org/cornet.

74. "The More Excellent Way: God's Plan Reaffirmed," *Good News*, May-June 1997, 34.

75. "Creech Says the Church, Not Gays, Has Sinned," *Omaha World Herald*, Oct. 17, 1998.

76. "A Pastoral Statement Adopted by the Council of Bishops, May 1, 1988." See Mathews and Oden, *Vision and Supervision*, 263–66, and "UM Bishops See Pastoral Letter as Healing Tool," UM News Service, May 1, 1998.

77. "Prohibition against Performing Homosexual Unions Ruled Enforceable," UM News Service, Aug. 11, 1998; Joretta Purdue, "Reactions Mixed to Ruling on Same-Sex Unions," UM News Service, Aug. 14, 1998.

78. Louis Westberg, "Honoring Vows, Local Pastor Defies Methodists' Marriage Ban," *Windy City Times*, Oct. 20, 1998; "Complaint Filed against Chicago Pastor for Same-Sex Service," UM News Service, Oct. 21, 1998.

79. UM News Service, Feb. 11, 2000. Richey reproduces Talbert's statement and treats it at some length in *MARKS*, 67–90.

80. Case, *Evangelical and Methodist*, 255. See his chapter "The Struggle for Doctrinal Integrity," 239–67.

81. Patricia Lefevre, "Women Church Leaders Issue Reply to 'Re-Imagining' Critics," *UMR*, March 18, 1994, 3; Beryl Ingram-Ward, "The Nine of Us," in *Re-Membering and Re-Imagining*, ed. Nancy J. Berneking and Pamela Carter Joern (Cleveland: Pilgrim Press, 1995), 162–65.

82. *"What Is the Confessing Movement Within The United Methodist Church?* [s.l.: The Confessing Movement, 1995] (Unpaged announcement flyer); Alice M. Smith, "Traditionalists Address Liberal Trend in UM Church," and "Atlanta Consultation Forms Steering Committee, Sends Letter of Information," *Good News*, July-Aug. 1994, 35–36, 42.

83. For the full text of the "Confessional Statement of the Confessing Movement within The United Methodist Church," see UM News Service, May 3, 1995; www.gcah.org/UM News/1995/stories/242cnfess.txt.

84. "A Critical Challenge to the Confessing Movement," March 1996 (Kansas City, Mo.: n.p., 1996). See also UM News Service, Feb. 26, 1996; www.gcah.org/UMNews/1996/stories/ 111confess.txt. Copies were mailed to all delegates to the 1996 General Conference meeting later that spring.

85. (New York: GCCUIC, 1998).

86. *Discipline*/UMC/2004, 84. For further discussion of the UMC's ecclesial location and commitment to ecumenical dialogue, see Geoffrey Wainwright, *The Ecumenical Moment: Crisis and*

Opportunity for the Church (Grand Rapids: Eerdmans, 1983), chap. 11, and *Methodists in Dialogue* (Nashville: Kingswood Books, 1995); and John Deschner, "United Methodism's Basic Ecumenical Policy," in *Perspectives*, 448–59.

87. See the chapter "Catholic" in MARKS.

88. C. Howard Hopkins, *John R. Mott, 1865–1955: A Biography* (Grand Rapids: Eerdmans, 1979).

89. "Plan of Federation," cited in Charles S. Macfarland, *Christian Unity in Practice and Prophecy* (New York: The Macmillan Company, 1933), 56.

90. See esp. Miller, *Bishop G. Bromley Oxnam.*

91. *Churches in Covenant Communion: The Church of Christ Uniting,* approved and recommended to the churches by the Seventeenth Plenary of the Consultation on Church Union (New Orleans: COCU, 1988), 15.

92. Churches Uniting in Christ, see www.cuicinfo.org.

93. *BEM.*

94. *Resolutions/UMC/1992,* 606–12. See also "Dialogue Between Jews and Christians," *Resolutions/UMC/1972,* 25–29; "Guidelines for Interreligious Relationships 'Called to Be Neighbors and Witnesses,'" *Resolutions/UMC/1980,* 114–25. See also in the 1992 volume "Prejudice against Muslims and Arabs in the U.S.A.," 245–46 (adopted 1988), and "Guidelines for Interreligious Relationships 'Called to Be Neighbors and Witnesses,'" 263–73 (adopted 1980).

95. On these dialogues, their status, and the agreements issuing therefrom, see Wainwright, *Methodists in Dialogue,* and Nicholas Lossky et al., eds., *Dictionary of the Ecumenical Movement* (Geneva: WCC Publications; Grand Rapids: Eerdmans, 1991).

96. John Ernest Rattenbury, *The Eucharistic Hymns of John and Charles Wesley, to which is appended Wesley's Preface extracted from Brevint's Christian Sacrament and Sacrifice, together with Hymns on the Lord's Supper* (London: Epworth Press, 1948); reprinted by the Order of Saint Luke in 1990 and still available at www.saint-luke.org.

97. John C. Bowmer, *The Sacrament of the Lord's Supper in Early Methodism* (London: Dacre Press, 1951).

98. "Eucharistic Celebration: Converging Theology—Divergent Practice," in *Building Unity: Ecumenical Dialogues with Roman Catholic Participation in the United States,* ed. Joseph A. Burgess and Jeffrey Gros (New York: Paulist Press, 1989), 307–22.

99. So named because it was first used in Lima, Peru, in 1982. For full text with commentary, see www.wcc-coe.org/wcc/what/faith/lima-e.

100. *Churches Respond to BEM: Official Responses to the "Baptism, Eucharist and Ministry" Text,* ed. Max Thurian (Geneva: WCC, 1986), 2:177–99. See also Geoffrey Wainwright, "Methodism through the Lens of Lima [BEM]," in *"The Sunday Service of the Methodists": Twentieth-Century Worship in Worldwide Methodism,* ed. Karen B. Westerfield Tucker (Nashville: Kingswood Books, 1996), 305–22.

101. *Resolutions/UMC/1972,* 90.

102. Cranmer's strong statement of eucharistic presence in the first (1549) Book of Common Prayer (BCP), "that they may be unto us the body and blood of Thy most dearly beloved Son Jesus Christ," was changed in the second (1552) BCP to "that we may be partakers of his most blessed body & blood." This latter text was retained in the standard 1662 BCP and in Wesley's

1784 revision. For full texts of the 1549 and 1552 eucharistic prayers, see Bard Thompson, *Liturgies of the Western Church* (New York: World Publishing Co., 1961), 257–58, 280.

103. In the following years, these new understandings—historical, theological, and ecumenical—led to the first-ever official Methodist doctrinal statement on Holy Communion, "This Holy Mystery: A United Methodist Understanding of Holy Communion," approved in 2004.

104. For the historical development of the theology and practice of baptism, see Karen Westerfield Tucker, *American Methodist Worship* (New York: Oxford University Press, 2000), 82–117, and Gayle Carlton Felton, *This Gift of Water: The Practice and Theology of Baptism among Methodists in America* (Nashville: Abingdon Press, 1993). For the historical development of confirmation and church membership, see James Kirby, Russell Richey, and Kenneth Rowe, *The Methodists* (Westport, Conn.: Greenwood Press, 1996), Part 3, "Members," 163–254.

105. For debate on baptism in the UMC (1969–72), see Felton, *This Gift of Water*, 163–71.

106. See "A Lutheran-United Methodist Statement on Baptism," *Perkins Journal* 34, no. 2 (1981): 1–56.

107. *Resolutions/UMC/2004*, 860; also in Gayle Carlton Felton, *By Water and the Spirit: Making Connections for Identity and Ministry*, a study guide and text, rev. ed. (Nashville: Discipleship Resources, 2002), 5.

108. "Ecumenical Baptismal Liturgy," in *Baptism and Eucharist: Ecumenical Convergence in Celebration*, ed. Max Thurian and Geoffrey Wainwright (Geneva: WCC, 1983), 94–96.

109. *BEM*, section 5, 20, p. 6.

110. Consultation on Common Texts, *A Celebration of Baptism* (Nashville: Abingdon Press, 1988).

111. *A Service of Baptism, Confirmation, and Renewal: The United Methodist Church, an Alternative Text* (Nashville: UMPH, 1976), included introduction, text, commentary, and notes.

112. Professor Stookey later detailed a rationale for the liturgy in his book *Baptism: Christ's Act in the Church* (Nashville: Abingdon Press, 1982).

113. Dwight Vogel, *By Water and the Spirit: A Study of Baptism for United Methodists* (Nashville: Cokesbury, 1993).

114. For the full text see *Resolutions/UMC/2004*, Resolution 343, "By Water and the Spirit," 857–76.

115. Gayle Felton has long been associated with the study of baptism in United Methodism. She wrote her doctoral dissertation on the theology of the sacrament in 1987. She was a member of the Baptism Study Commission (1988–96) and served as principal drafter.

116. Felton, *By Water and the Spirit*, 2002.

117. Gayle Felton, "The Sacrament of Baptism," *Circuit Rider*, Nov.-Dec. 1999, 14.

118. Lee, *Short History*, 107.

119. See Yrigoyen, McEllhenney, and Rowe, *United Methodism at Forty*, 76–79.

120. A DVD, *Following the Path: The Women of Color Scholars Program*, shares the experiences and candid observations of courageous women who dared to dream and who, through the support of the program, are now changing how universities, seminaries, and pulpits of the UMC look. Produced by GBGM in 2006, available from EcuFilm, DVD #6202, ecufilm.org; 1-888-346-3862.

121. Case, *Evangelical and Methodist*, 129–30; Leon Howell, *United Methodism @ Risk: A Wake-Up Call*, with a study guide by Bishop C. Dale White and the Reverend Scott Campbell (Kingston, N.Y.: Information Project for United Methodists, 2003), 21–24.

122. "The Year's Top Stories," *Christian Century*, Dec. 21–28, 1994, 1211.

123. Beryl Ingram-Ward, "The Nine of Us," 162–65.

124. Ingram-Ward, "The Nine of Us," 165.

125. See www.reimagining.org/history.

126. Jean A. Powers, "The Journey, A Sermon" in *The Loyal Opposition: Struggling with the Church on Homosexuality*, edited by Tex Sample and Amy E. Delong (Nashville: Abingdon Press, 2000), 109, 117–18.

127. JGC/UMC/1996, 391–92, 398, 655–58, 677–88.

128. She did not reference there, as she had elsewhere, our late Drew colleague Donald Jones's tutelage of her as a youth.

129. A reference to the Council of Bishops' Episcopal Initiative on Children and Poverty proposed at their April 1995 meeting and adopted at their fall 1996 meeting. See Mathews and Oden, *Vision and Supervision*, 82–90.

Asbury College, 99, 330

Asian American Language Ministry (AALM), 527

Asian American Methodists, 293–97, 475–81

Association of Health and Welfare Ministries, UMC, 630n145, 630n146

Association of Methodist Ministers and Laymen to Preserve Established Racial Customs, 395

Association of Southern Women for the Prevention of Lynching (ASWPL), 346

Association to Preserve The Methodist Episcopal Church, South, by Defeating the Pending Plan of Unification, 369

ASWPL. *See* Association of Southern Women for the Prevention of Lynching

Atlantic City GC, 375

"The Attitude of Jesus toward Women" (Southard), 346

authority: of bishop, 74, 381–82, 664n27; division over, 175–96; GC check on, 232

Autobiography of Peter Cartwright and Fifty Years as a Presiding Elder (Cartwright), 84, 139

Baker, Osmon C., 134, 164, 237, 261

Baltimore, 25; African American Methodists, 181; Annual Conference (1862), 196; GC (1792) in, 50, 67–68; Methodism in 1816, 91–101; Museum and Gallery, 91; system of governance, 41

Baltimore Church. *See* Evangelical Reformed Church of Baltimore

Baltimore Conference, 62, 75, 80, 81, 83–84, 93, 145, 146, 163, 169–70, 170, 182–83, 193, 218, 581n29, 644n51; Course of Study authorization by, 107; finances and, 95; laity and, 196

Bangs, Nathan, 120–21, 130, 138, 140, 141, 158, 178, 179, 182, 580n46, 584n10; Asbury eulogy of, 103–4; as book agent, 105, 106–7; itinerancy of, 105; publishing house of, 108–9

baptism, 117, 408, 547–49

"Barbed-Wire Christians" (Jones), 379

Barnett, Jeanne, 536

Barr v. United Methodist Church, 494

Barratt's Chapel, 40, 46–47, 50

"The Barren Fig Tree" (Hosier), 39

Bascom, Henry, 158, 247

Baxter, Richard, 42, 161

BCP. *See* Book of Common Prayer

Beck, Edward P., 431, 439, 440–42

BEDC. *See* Black Economic Development Conference

Bell, William, 302, 307–8, 540

benevolent institutions conference (1872), 231–32

Bennett, Belle Harris, 282–83, 289, 314–15

Bennett, George, 264, 266–67

Benson, Joseph, 44, 107

Bethel Church, 1, 50, 87, 143

Bethlehem Centers, social settlements of, 343–44

Bethune, Mary McLeod, 369–71, 390, 420

biblical doctrine, Pietism emphasis on, 2, 5

bishop, 519; authority of, 74, 381–82, 664n27; corporate leadership of, 519; *Discipline* on, 63; election of, 387; unity of, 519. *See also* Council of Bishops

Black Economic Development Conference (BEDC), 452

"Black Harry." *See* Hosier, Harry

Black MEC Mississippi Mission Conference, 209

Black Methodisms, competing, 257–61; educational rules for, 260; local choice, of official policy, 259; MECS conference (1866) alienation of, 257

Black Methodists. *See* African American Methodists

Black Methodists for Church Renewal (BMCR), 449–52

Black Theology and Black Power (Cone), 453

A Black Theology of Liberation (Cone), 453

Blood Done Sign My Name (Tyson, Timothy), 453

CPSIA information can be obtained at www.ICGtesting.com
Printed in the USA
BVOW071539060112

279909BV00002B/2/P